Group Insurance Handbook

THE IRWIN SERIES IN RISK AND INSURANCE

EDITORS

EDISON L. BOWERS   DAVIS W. GREGG
The Ohio State University   *The American College of Life Underwriters*

GROUP INSURANCE
HANDBOOK

Planned and Edited by

ROBERT D. EILERS, Ph.D., C.L.U.

Associate Professor of Insurance,
Wharton School of Finance and Commerce, University of Pennsylvania
and Executive Director, S. S. Huebner Foundation for Insurance Education

AND

ROBERT M. CROWE, Ph.D., C.L.U.

Associate Professor of Insurance
and holder of the W. Frank Hipp Chair of Insurance
School of Business Administration, University of South Carolina

WITH THE COOPERATION OF
SEVENTY-SEVEN OUTSTANDING
AMERICAN INSURANCE AUTHORITIES

1965
RICHARD D. IRWIN, INC.
HOMEWOOD, ILLINOIS

To

two big girls,
two little girls
and two little boys—
who have been a more important
force in the preparation of
this volume than they possibly
imagine.

PREFACE

The expansion of group insurance coverages in recent years has often been described as dramatic, if not phenomenal. Total group life insurance, including creditor group life coverage, exceeds $295 billion, with approximately half of this amount having been placed in force in the last seven years. The bulk of the medical expense coverage in the United States has always been group protection, which currently accounts for about 70 per cent of the total coverage in the nation. A slightly smaller proportion of the disability income protection is also group coverage. In addition, the group insurance concept has been extended in a number of directions, including liberalized benefits, new types of coverage and new types of acceptable groups.

In spite of this growth in group coverages, up to this point no text has covered the entire field of group life and health coverages. The void was acknowledged particularly by insurance professors and insurance company executives who were concerned with various types of educational courses involving group insurance. The Editors were among this group, but both recognized their incompetence to author a volume that covered such a broad area. The solution was to structure a group insurance book and ask experts (an overworked, but entirely applicable, term in this case) to author individual chapters.

After the two Editors had decided upon a tentative outline for the book, the counsel of a number of professors of insurance and executives of insurance companies and other organizations was sought regarding possible changes. After the final outline had been drawn, invitations to author chapters were extended to forty-three men who were acknowledged for their competence in the subjects to be discussed in the various chapters. The breadth of knowledge of most of these individuals would be sufficient for each to author a group insurance text, if time only permitted. The initial outline for each chapter was reviewed by the Editors before a chapter was written in order to reduce overlapping discussions, insure completeness and give continuity to the volume. In addition to the Contributing Authors, a group of Consulting Editors, representing virtually every major party interested in group coverages, was selected to review the first drafts of chapters for the volume. Each chapter was reviewed by the two Editors and by at least four Consulting Editors; in some instances chapters were reviewed by as many as eight Consulting Editors. The suggestions of the Editors and Consulting Editors were then transmitted to the Contributing Author for consideration in completing the final draft of his chapter.

Thus, the monumental task of preparing this volume was shared by approximately eighty individuals, each of whom devoted untold hours to this educational endeavor. The unstinting personal sacrifice of these persons was a constant source of gratification for the Editors, who wish they could do more in acknowledgment than merely include a list naming these individuals.

The Editors divided primary editorial responsibility for the various chapters in the following manner:

Dr. Eilers—Chapters 5, 13 through 24, 27 through 30, 33, and 36 through 38.

Dr. Crowe—Chapters 1 through 4, 6 through 12, 25, 26, 31, 32, 34, 35, and 39 through 41.

A number of subjects discussed in the *Handbook* are highly controversial. Yet, it was felt by the two Editors and most of the others who had a part in the preparation of the volume that such matters needed to be removed from the emotional settings in which some problems are often viewed and should, instead, be discussed on conceptual and analytical bases. In some instances proponents of particular points of view were selected as Contributing Authors, since contra-positions were being shown in one or more other chapters. This approach has provided, it is believed, a representative, yet objective, portrayal of the institutions and issues associated with group insurance.

The preparation of the *Handbook* took place over a period of more than two years. It was inevitable that, in a volume involving a fast-moving business in an equally fast-moving society, parts of certain chapters would require extensive alteration to keep abreast of new developments arising while the volume was in the incubation state. The two chapters dealing with medical expense coverage for the elderly posed a particular problem, inasmuch as all methods of providing this coverage in the private sector undoubtedly will be affected profoundly by the passage— in the "twelfth hour" in the preparation of this volume—of a federal program to provide medical care protection to the elderly on a social insurance basis. In spite of this development, the discussion of private coverage for the aged in Chapters 36 and 37 has considerable value for the student of group insurance, in part because at least some of the current private approaches will undoubtedly continue to be used—for instance, to provide catastrophic medical expense protection. Moreover, these chapters document the imaginative and many-faceted approaches used by insuring organizations in attempting to solve significant risk problems. Quite possibly some of these same approaches may be adapted in the future as means of resolving other coverage problems.

As would be expected, the style of writing differs somewhat among

the Contributing Authors, and, although the Editors exercised considerable discretion in assuring a consistency in the organization of material
within chapters, every attempt was made to retain the eloquence of
expression of individual Contributing Authors. Terminology presented a
particular problem, however. Throughout the book a conscious effort
was made to bring consistency in the use of technical terms. For this
reason, the terminological decisions of the various committees of the
Commission on Insurance Terminology of the American Risk and Insurance Association were adopted in all applicable chapters. Since the work
of the terminology committees is not yet finished it was necessary for the
Editors to make many decisions regarding the use of particular words.
The Contributing Authors were very cooperative in accepting most of
the suggested terminology for the sake of consistency throughout the
book, even when a particular term had not been used previously in a
particular company or organization. Health insurance terminology presented particular difficulties. "Medical expense coverage," for instance,
has been used in the insurance field to refer to the coverage of nonsurgical physicians' visits, X-rays, physical therapy and other related procedures in some cases, while in other instances the same term has applied to
the entire range of hospital-surgical benefits as well as nonsurgical physicians' visits, etc. In this volume, the unqualified term "medical expense
coverage" refers to protection against all forms of health care expenses,
while "medical coverage" refers to the nonsurgical services mentioned
above. In addition, "percentage participation" is used rather than "coinsurance," in keeping with the apparent trend away from the use of the
latter term. Then, too, "insurers" is used in place of "carriers." Numerous
other decisions on terminology are noted in footnotes throughout the
volume.

In addition to the Contributing Authors and Consulting Editors, special
attention should be directed to the contributions of several other individuals in the preparation of this *Handbook*. Foremost among these is Dr.
Davis W. Gregg, President of the American College of Life Underwriters
and a close friend of both Editors, whose counsel was sought in connection with many aspects of the preparation of this *Handbook*. He also
authored a chapter for the volume and read all of the galley proofs.
Dr. Gregg is a recognized expert in the field of group insurance, having
authored three widely accepted editions of *Group Life Insurance*. In
addition, he is the editor of *The Life and Health Insurance Handbook*
and a co-editor of *The Property and Liability Insurance Handbook*. His
sound and extensive assistance, in spite of an extremely demanding personal schedule, was of inestimable value to the Editors as a result of his
knowledge of the group insurance field, his experience in the preparation
of Handbooks and his broad interests and wisdom.

Mention should also be made of the vast secretarial and record-keeping functions that were performed by Mrs. Patricia Crowe and Mrs. Louise Morrison. It is probably well that neither of these extremely competent assistants realized the enormity of the task that lay before them when they agreed to work on the *Handbook,* inasmuch as the Editors would have been hard-pressed to obtain replacements who would have worked as efficiently and as cheerfully on this project.

Finally, we acknowledge the fine assistance of our publisher, Richard D. Irwin, Inc., whose staff displayed patience and competence in handling every stage of a volume that had many complications for the publisher as well as for those involved in its preparation.

In spite of the help of all these fine folks, some errors have undoubtedly been successful in eluding our eyes. For these we take our whip lashes in advance with the hope that the errors will be far outshone by other aspects of this first edition.

ROBERT D. EILERS
ROBERT M. CROWE

July, 1965

CONTRIBUTING AUTHORS AND CONSULTING EDITORS

DR. JOHN F. ADAMS, Assistant Vice President in charge of Research and Specialized Services and Professor of Economics, Temple University, Philadelphia, Pennsylvania

J. C. ARCHIBALD, Senior Vice President, Bankers Life Company, Des Moines, Iowa

CARL R. ASHMAN, F.S.A., Second Vice President and Actuary, The Lincoln National Life Insurance Company, Fort Wayne, Indiana

RICHARD W. BAKER, C.L.U., Senior Consultant, Ostheimer & Co., and President, Benefit Administrators, Inc., Philadelphia, Pennsylvania

ALLISON S. BEEBE, Vice President and Manager, Group Department, The Paul Revere Life Insurance Company, Worcester, Massachusetts

L. M. BRANSON, Manager, Health Insurance Claims, Liberty Mutual Insurance Companies, Boston, Massachusetts

ARTHUR M. BROWNING, Vice President, New York Life Insurance Company, New York, New York

STEWART H. CARR, Administrative Assistant—Group Division, North American Life and Casualty Company, Minneapolis, Minnesota

LAWRENCE M. CATHLES, JR., Vice President, Group Division, Aetna Life Insurance Company, Hartford, Connecticut

BROOKS CHANDLER, Vice President and Secretary, Provident Life and Accident Insurance Company, Chattanooga, Tennessee

DR. JAMES J. CHASTAIN, C.L.U., C.P.C.U., Assistant Dean, American Institute for Property and Liability Underwriters, Bryn Mawr, Pennsylvania

MILTON F. CHAUNER, F.S.A., Senior Vice President, Milliman & Robertson, Inc., Philadelphia, Pennsylvania

DR. ALBERT H. CLARK, Chairman, Department of Finance, Georgia State College, Atlanta, Georgia

DONALD D. CODY, F.S.A., Vice President, New York Life Insurance Company, New York, New York

DR. HERBERT S. DENENBERG, C.P.C.U., Associate Professor of Insurance, University of Pennsylvania, Philadelphia, Pennsylvania

DR. O. D. DICKERSON, C.L.U., C.P.C.U., F.C.A.S., Associate Professor of Risk and Insurance, Florida State University, Tallahassee, Florida

C. Manton Eddy, F.S.A., Senior Vice President and Director, Connecticut General Life Insurance Company and Director, Aetna Life Insurance Company, Hartford, Connecticut

Edwin M. Erickson, C.L.U., Vice President—Life & Health, Nationwide Insurance Companies, Columbus, Ohio

Gordon N. Farquhar, Assistant Vice President, Group Division, Aetna Life Insurance Company, Hartford, Connecticut

E. J. Faulkner, President, Woodmen Accident and Life Company, Lincoln, Nebraska

Thomas B. Fitzpatrick, Director of Research and Consulting, Blue Cross of Western Pennsylvania, Pittsburgh, Pennsylvania

J. F. Follmann, Jr., Director of Information and Research, Health Insurance Association of America, New York, New York

Kenneth C. Foster, C.L.U., Senior Vice President, The Prudential Insurance Company of America, Newark, New Jersey

Loring P. Gillespie, Assistant Vice President, Disability/Group Life Division, Fireman's Fund—American Insurance Companies, Chicago, Illinois

Stanley W. Gingery, F.S.A., A.C.A.S., Vice President and Associate Actuary, The Prudential Insurance Company of America, Newark, New Jersey

Dr. Robert C. Goshay, Assistant Professor, School of Business Administration, University of California, Berkeley, California

Edward A. Green, F.S.A., Vice President and Group Actuary, John Hancock Mutual Life Insurance Company, Boston, Massachusetts

Dr. Davis W. Gregg, C.L.U., President, American College of Life Underwriters, Bryn Mawr, Pennsylvania

Dr. Charles P. Hall, Jr., C.P.C.U., Assistant Director, Department of Medical Finance and Economic Research, American Medical Association, Chicago, Illinois

A. B. Halverson, Vice President, Occidental Life Insurance Company of California, Los Angeles, California

William A. Halvorson, F.S.A., Consulting Actuary, Milliman & Robertson, Inc., Milwaukee, Wisconsin

Dr. J. D. Hammond, C.L.U., Associate Professor of Insurance, The Pennsylvania State University, University Park, Pennsylvania

Lyman R. Hanson, Senior Consultant, Ostheimer & Co., Philadelphia, Pennsylvania

James C. Higgins, Vice President, Marsh & McLennan, Inc., New York, New York

Charles G. Hill, A.S.A., Vice President, Massachusetts Mutual Life Insurance Company, Springfield, Massachusetts

JOHN HILL, C.L.U., Senior Vice President, New England Mutual Life Insurance Company, Boston, Massachusetts

JOHN M. HILL, II, Group Counsel, John Hancock Mutual Life Insurance Company, Boston, Massachusetts

PETER A. HINRICHS, F.S.A., Assistant Group Actuary, Home Life Insurance Company, New York, New York

E. MARCUS HOUSE, Vice President, Great Southern Life Insurance Company, Houston, Texas

PAUL H. JACKSON, F.S.A., Actuary, The Wyatt Company, Washington, D.C.

DR. HARRY M. JOHNSON, Associate Professor of Finance and Insurance and Assistant Dean of the School of Business Administration, University of Connecticut, Storrs, Connecticut

WILLIAM W. KEFFER, F.S.A., Vice President, Group Operations, Connecticut General Life Insurance Company, Hartford, Connecticut

HERBERT C. LASSITER, Secretary, Council on Insurance, American Dental Association, Chicago, Illinois

R. J. LEARSON, A.S.A., Vice President for Group Insurance, Mutual Life Insurance Company of New York, New York, New York

GEORGE E. LIGHT, Secretary (retired), The Travelers Insurance Company, Hartford, Connecticut

DR. CHE LIN, C.L.U., M.A.S.P. (Member, Actuarial Society of the Philippines), Vice President and Actuary, The Insular Life Assurance Company, Limited, Makati, Rizal, Philippines and Filipinas Life Assurance Company, Manila, Philippines

EDWARD E. MACK, JR., C.L.U., C.P.C.U., President, Mack and Parker, Inc., and President, Mass Insurance Consultants and Administrators, Inc., Chicago, Illinois

THOMAS F. MANLEY, President, Blue Cross of Greater Philadelphia, Philadelphia, Pennsylvania

CARROLL J. McBRIDE, J.D., Second Vice President, The Travelers Insurance Company, Hartford, Connecticut

MURRAY M. McCULLOCH, Vice President and Counsel, Fidelity Bankers Life Insurance Company, Richmond, Virginia

RAYMOND G. McCULLOUGH, Assistant Vice President, Claims Department, The Equitable Life Assurance Society of the United States, New York, New York

WILLIAM S. McNARY, President, Michigan Hospital Service, Detroit, Michigan

DR. JOSEPH J. MELONE, C.L.U., C.P.C.U., Associate Professor of Insurance, University of Pennsylvania, Philadelphia, Pennsylvania

MORTON D. MILLER, F.S.A., Vice President and Associate Actuary, The

Equitable Life Assurance Society of the United States, New York, New York

WENDELL MILLIMAN, F.S.A., Milliman & Robertson, Inc., Seattle, Washington

DANIEL W. PETTENGILL, F.S.A., Vice President, Group Division, Aetna Life Insurance Company, Hartford, Connecticut

DR. JESSE F. PICKRELL, C.L.U., C.P.C.U., Chairman, Division of Finance and Insurance, North Texas State University, Denton, Texas

H. LADD PLUMLEY, Chairman of the Board and President, State Mutual Life Assurance Company of America, Worcester, Massachusetts

ALBERT W. RANDALL, Executive Vice President, United Benefit Life Insurance Company and Executive Vice President, Group Insurance, Mutual of Omaha, Omaha, Nebraska

PAUL H. RINKER, Vice President in charge of Group Insurance, Continental Assurance Company, Chicago, Illinois

JAMES W. ROSE, Secretary, Life Department, The Travelers Insurance Company, Hartford, Connecticut

GERALD K. RUGGER, F.S.A., Vice President—Group Insurance, Home Life Insurance Company, New York, New York

DR. STUART SCHWARZSCHILD, C.L.U., C.P.C.U., Associate Professor of Insurance, Georgia State College, Atlanta, Georgia

WILLIAM N. SEERY, Vice President, The Travelers Insurance Company, Hartford, Connecticut

J. HENRY SMITH, F.S.A., Vice President and Actuary, The Equitable Life Assurance Society of the United States, New York, New York

ROBERT N. STABLER, F.S.A., Vice President, General American Life Insurance Company, St. Louis, Missouri

PHILIP STARR, Manager, Life & Health Department, R. B. Jones & Sons, Inc., Kansas City, Missouri

CLARENCE H. TOOKEY, F.S.A., Consulting Actuary, Pasadena, California

ROBERT C. TOOKEY, F.S.A., Vice President, Milliman & Robertson, Inc., Pasadena, California

GEOFFREY TYSON, Manager, Group Insurance Department, Pacific Mutual Life Insurance Company, Los Angeles, California

LARUE S. WAGENSELLER, F.S.A., Second Vice President—Group Insurance, Metropolitan Life Insurance Company, New York, New York

W. RAY WEBB, Senior Vice President, Provident Life and Accident Insurance Company, Chattanooga, Tennessee

T. ROBERT WILCOX, Vice President, The Hartford Life Insurance Company, Hartford, Connecticut

Dr. C. Arthur Williams, Jr., Professor of Economics and Insurance, University of Minnesota, Minneapolis, Minnesota

William G. Williams, Director of Group Sales Research, Provident Mutual Life Insurance Company of Philadelphia, Philadelphia, Pennsylvania

Horace H. Wilson, Senior Vice President, The Equitable Life Assurance Society of the United States, New York, New York

Avram Yedidia, Consultant, Organization of Prepaid Health Care Services; Kaiser Foundation Health Plan, Oakland, California; Community Health Foundation, Cleveland, Ohio; Orinda, California

TABLE OF CONTENTS

APPENDIXES

CONTENTS

INDEXES

LIST OF ILLUSTRATIONS

FIGURES

TABLES

PART I

Employee Benefit Plans

Chapter 1

COMPONENTS OF EMPLOYEE BENEFIT PLANS

BY C. ARTHUR WILLIAMS, JR.

DEFINITION OF EMPLOYEE BENEFIT PLANS

Most group life and health insurance is part of an employee benefit plan, but these plans provide many benefits in addition to payments in case of death or poor health. Employee benefit plans have been defined in many ways. Two definitions have been selected for discussion here because of their importance and because one represents a broad approach to the definition while the other represents a narrow approach.

A broad definition of employee benefit plans equates them with any arrangement for compensation other than direct wages. Initially, employee benefits other than compensation were relatively unimportant, and these benefits were labeled fringe benefits. The term still persists despite the fact that these benefits now comprise a significant part of the compensation package for most employees. The scope of the employee benefit plans defined in this way is indicated by the list of fringe benefits included in the biennial surveys by the Chamber of Commerce of the United States of fringe payments made to wage earners.

The Chamber divides fringe payments into five major classes.[1] First are the legally required payments for employee security—Old-Age, Survivors and Disability Insurance, unemployment compensation, compulsory temporary disability insurance (in four states) and the special retirement, disability and unemployment benefits for railroad workers.

Pensions and other agreed upon payments constitute the next class of fringe payments. In addition to pensions, this class includes life insurance and other death benefits, medical expense insurance including service benefits provided by nonprofit medical expense associations and other medical expense payments, disability income insurance and other pay-

---

[1] Chamber of Commerce of the United States, *Fringe Benefits 1961* (Washington, D.C., 1962), p. 9.

ments in the event of disability other than paid sick leave (which is included in the fourth category), private unemployment benefits and separation or termination pay allowances. It also includes a host of other agreed upon payments, such as discounts on goods and services purchased by employees, free meals, workmen's compensation payments in excess of legal requirements, payments to needy employees, tuition refunds and stock purchase plans.

The third and fourth categories include payments for time during which the worker is not producing, the distinction between the two categories being that the worker is on the job when he receives the benefits listed under the third category and off the job under the fourth category. Thus, the third category includes payments for rest periods, lunch periods, wash-up time, travel time, clothes-change time, get-ready time and similar breaks in the work period. Payments under the fourth category include paid vacations and bonuses in lieu of vacations, payments for holidays not worked, paid sick leave (which is closely related to the benefits in the second category), payments for State or National Guard duty, jury, witness and voting pay allowances, payments for time lost because of personal reasons such as a death in the family and similar payments.

The fifth and final category includes all those payments other than salary which have not been included in the other four categories. Illustrative of the items included under this category are the following: profit sharing payments, Christmas or other special bonuses, service awards, suggestion awards, payments to union stewards or officials for time spent in settling grievances or in negotiating agreements and special wage payments ordered by courts or wage adjustment boards.

As broad as this definition may be, it is not the broadest in use.[2] For example, this definition does not include deferred compensation for executives because it does not include any benefits paid to this group of employees. Some other examples covered under other definitions, but not included in the Chamber survey, are periodic medical examinations, most services rendered by company physicians and nurses and recreation facilities.

A more narrow definition is employed by the Social Security Administration in its annual review of employee benefit plans. According to this definition, an employee benefit plan is

any type of plan sponsored or initiated unilaterally or jointly by employers and employees and providing benefits that stem from the employment relationship and that are not underwritten or paid directly by government (Federal, State,

---

[2] For one example of a broader list, see Dale Yoder and H. G. Heneman, Jr., *Labor Economics and Industrial Relations* (Cincinnati: South-Western Publishing Co., 1959), p. 139.

or local). In general, the intent is to include plans that provide in an orderly, predetermined fashion for (1) income maintenance during periods when regular earnings are cut off because of death, accident, sickness, retirement, or unemployment and (2) benefits to meet specified expenses usually associated with illness or injury. The series thus excludes such fringe benefits as paid vacations, holidays, and rest periods; leave with pay (except formal sick leave); savings and stock-purchase plans; discount privileges; and free meals.[3]

Under this definition, then, employee benefit plans are limited to those providing private protection against five major threats to the worker's economic security. Workmen's compensation benefits are excluded because they are determined by statute, but private plans written in conjunction with the compulsory temporary disability legislation found in four states are included because the benefits provided under these plans are permitted to and often do deviate from the statutory pattern. Unlike the Chamber definition, the Social Security Administration definition does include some benefits paid to executives, but, like the Chamber definition, it excludes services provided by company physicians and nurses and special arrangements for executives such as split-dollar life insurance plans and deferred compensation arrangements.

IMPORTANCE AND RECENT GROWTH

Under either definition, the importance and recent growth of employee benefit plans is impressive. Table 1–1 shows how employee benefit payments by employers, expressed as a per cent of payroll, increased from 1951 to 1961 according to the surveys by the United States Chamber of Commerce. These survey results must be used with care because of the definitional problem mentioned above, because the surveys were limited to larger firms and because not all those contacted responded to the request for information. Furthermore, some of the firms responding in 1951 did not respond in 1961 and vice versa. Despite these limitations, however, the data do provide some useful indications concerning the importance and recent growth of fringe benefits.

The Social Security Administration surveys provide additional information concerning the importance and growth of the private economic security type employee benefit plans included within its definition. In addition to showing the number of persons covered, the S.S.A. survey indicates the contributions, the benefits and, in the case of pension plans, the assets. The S.S.A. data, for the most part, are not based upon samples and apply to firms of all sizes. Consequently, they provide a fairly accurate indication of the importance and growth of the plans included in these surveys. Some of the S.S.A survey results for 1954, 1958 and 1962 are

---

[3] Alfred M. Skolnik, "Growth of Employee Benefit Plans," *Social Security Bulletin*, Vol. XXVI, No. 4 (April, 1963), p. 4.

TABLE 1–1

EMPLOYEE BENEFIT PAYMENTS BY EMPLOYERS, AS PER CENT OF PAYROLL,
BY TYPE OF PAYMENT, 1951 AND 1961

| | Per Cent of Payroll | |
Item	1951	1961
Legally required payments:		
Old-Age, Survivors and Disability Insurance	1.4	2.7
Unemployment compensation	1.4	1.5
Workmen's compensation	.6	.8
Compulsory temporary disability insurance and special plans for railroad workers	.1	.1
Total	3.5	5.1
Pension and other agreed upon payments:		
Pensions	3.6	4.2
Payments in case of death or poor health	1.4	2.7
Separation or termination pay allowances	*	.1
Contributions to private unemployment benefit funds	*	.1
Others	.4	.8
Total	5.4	7.9
Payments for nonproduction time while on the job	1.9	2.6
Payments for time not worked:		
Paid sick leave	.6	.7
Other	5.4	6.9
Total	6.0	7.6
Other items	1.9	1.7
Total Payments†	18.7	24.9

* Less than .05 per cent.
† For 91 identical firms responding in the 1951 and 1961 surveys, the total payments increased from 18.8 per cent to 26.4 per cent. Legally required payments increased from 2.9 per cent to 4.5 per cent and pension and other agreed upon payments from 5.7 per cent to 8.7 per cent.
Source: Derived from Chamber of Commerce of the United States, *Fringe Benefits 1951* and *Fringe Benefits 1961* (Washington, D.C., 1952 and 1962).

summarized in Table 1–2. The assets of retirement plans increased from $23.1 billion in 1954, to $39.5 billion in 1958 and $60.7 billion in 1962. Under both surveys, group life and health insurance and related plans emerge as important parts of the total employee benefit picture and as one of the most rapidly growing components.

ECONOMIC SECURITY AFFORDED BY EMPLOYEE BENEFIT PLANS

Employee benefit plans designed to combat economic insecurity among employees deserve closer investigation because group life and group health insurance, which are the major concern of this volume, fall into this category. A bird's-eye view of all the economic security employee benefit plans will provide the reader with some valuable perspectives. In the discussion which follows, these employee benefits will be classified first according to the peril with which they deal—death, poor health, unemployment or retirement—and then subclassified according to whether they are public or private plans.

Plans Providing Death Benefits

Public Programs. Most workers today are covered under Old-Age, Survivors and Disability Insurance. Although the old-age benefits are more generally understood and appreciated, OASDI does, subject to some fairly liberal requirements, furnish some important death benefits in the form of a lump-sum benefit designed to defray funeral expenses, a monthly income for a widowed mother with children under age eighteen and a lifetime income for a widow aged sixty-two or over. These benefits

TABLE 1-2

SELECTED MEASURES OF EMPLOYEE BENEFIT PLANS, BY TYPE OF PLAN, 1954, 1958 AND 1962

Type	Number of Wage and Salary Workers and Their Dependents (in Millions)			Contributions by Employers and Employees (in $ Billions)			Benefits (in $ Billions)		
	1954	1958	1962	1954	1958	1962	1954	1958	1962
Pensions...........................	14.2	18.8	23.1	$3.4	$4.7	$5.6	$ .7	$1.3	$2.2
Life insurance and death benefits.......	30.9	41.8	52.1	.7	1.2	1.8	.5	.9	1.3
Disability income insurance and payments including paid sick leave.......	22.9	24.9	27.0	.8	1.1	1.6	.6	.9	1.3
Hospitalization insurance and benefits...	75.3	95.0	110.7	1.2	1.9	3.1	1.1	1.9	3.0
Surgical expense insurance and benefits...	66.2	89.5	105.8	} .7	1.1	1.6	.6	.9	1.4
Nonsurgical physician's care insurance and benefits........................	38.1	63.6	82.8						
Major medical expense insurance.......	1.9	16.2	35.1	*	.3	.8	*	.2	.7
Supplemental unemployment benefits...	†	1.7	1.8	†	.1	.2	†	.1	.1

* Less than $.1.
† Supplemental unemployment benefits were not introduced until 1955.
Source: Joseph Krislov, "Employee Benefit Plans, 1954–62," *Social Security Bulletin*, Vol. XXVII, No. 4 (April, 1964), pp. 6–9.

are expressed as a percentage of the deceased worker's "primary insurance amount." This amount, in turn, depends upon the worker's average monthly earnings subject to OASDI taxes. For example, for average monthly earnings of $200 and $400 (the maximum earnings taxed), the primary insurance amounts are $84 and $127, respectively. The lump-sum death benefit is three times the primary insurance amount but no more than $255; the benefit for the widowed mother with children under age eighteen is 75 per cent of the primary insurance amount plus 75 per cent for the mother, subject to a family maximum; and the benefit for the widow aged sixty-two or over is 82.5 per cent.

Workers qualify for all of these survivorship benefits except the last if they are either "fully insured" or "currently insured." The worker is fully insured if he has quarters of coverage (calendar quarters during which he earned at least $50 in covered employment) equal to the number of years which have elapsed since 1950 or, if later, the year in which he was twenty-one years of age. The required number of quarters of coverage, however, never exceeds forty. The worker is currently insured if at least six of the last thirteen calendar quarters were quarters of coverage. The benefit for the widow aged sixty-two or over is payable only if the deceased worker was fully insured. Benefits are also available for dependent parents. The purpose of these survivorship benefits is to provide a "floor of protection" upon which private employee benefit plans and individuals can build a protection program. OASDI benefits are financed through a tax on employers and employees which is scheduled to reach a maximum of 4⅝ per cent each or a total of 9¼ per cent on the first $4800 of the worker's earnings by 1968.

Other public programs providing dollar benefits in case of death, regardless of the cause, are limited to certain types of workers. The most important of these special programs is the Railroad Retirement System which provides important benefits for survivors. Other examples are the Civil Service Retirement System and plans covering state and local government employees.

Death benefits are also provided under the workmen's compensation acts which have been enacted by all states and for certain employees by the federal government. These acts obligate employers to pay prescribed benefits to disabled workers or to the beneficiaries of deceased workers if the worker was disabled or died as a result of a work accident or, in most states, an occupational disease. The employee or his dependents need not prove fault in order to collect. Employees do not contribute to the cost of this protection, which is usually secured by the purchase of a workmen's compensation insurance policy from a private insurer. In seven states, however, only monopolistic state funds write this insurance, and in eleven others, state funds compete with private insurers. One of the most controversial issues of the day is whether (as is now the case) a person should be able to receive concurrently full OASDI benefits and workmen's compensation benefits.

Private Plans.   The most important private employee benefit plans providing death benefits are group life insurance plans. Usually these plans cover the employees of a single employer or group of employers and the protection is yearly renewable term insurance. Group life insurance differs from individual life insurance in several ways. Instead of underwriting each person in the group, the group is investigated and if the group is acceptable to the underwriter, every member of the group is eligible for insurance. Instead of tailor-making the protection to the needs of each individual in the group, it is necessary for underwriting reasons to base the amount of protection automatically on some factor such as salary, position, service or some combination of these factors. Finally, because of the marketing methods employed and the assumption by the employer of some administrative costs, the premium for group life insurance is less than for equivalent individual insurance.

If the protection for the individual employee is group term life insurance, the employee is not entitled to any cash value if he should terminate his employment. He can, however, convert his group insurance to some form of individual insurance without proving insurability. Group life insurance can be written on some basis other than term insurance, the most popular alternative being group paid-up insurance. In its most common form, this program provides for the purchase of paid-up insurance with the employee's contributions and enough term insurance to bring the protection up to the plan limits with the employer's contributions.

Group life insurance is usually limited to groups of ten or more, although several states permit issuance of group insurance to groups smaller than this. For the most part, however, small groups and in many cases groups with between ten and twenty-five members are insured under wholesale insurance instead of group insurance. Under this insurance, each individual is underwritten separately although there is usually no physical examination, and individual contracts are issued.

Individual life insurance is sometimes used to provide death benefits for employees under arrangements known as split-dollar plans. Under these plans, the employer pays that part of the annual premium corresponding to the increase in the cash value in return for an assignment of the cash value. The effect is an interest-free loan for the employee.

In recent years, there has been some interest and activity in self-insured plans providing essentially the same benefits as group life insurance plans for employees. Under these plans, the employer (or a group of employers under a multi-employer plan) retains the risks which under an insured plan would be transferred to an insurer.

Plans Providing Benefits in Case of Poor Health

Plans providing benefits in case of poor health may involve two types of benefits: (1) income replacement if a person is disabled, and (2) medical expense reimbursement or medical services.

Public Programs. OASDI provides disability income benefits if a person, in addition to meeting some other requirements, is totally and permanently disabled. The disabled worker receives an income to age sixty-five equal to his primary insurance amount, the amount being increased if the disabled person has certain eligible dependents. He also retains the death and retirement benefits to which he was entitled when he became disabled. Although not strictly an income replacement in this instance, this second benefit does in effect, and subject to some qualifications, excuse the worker and his employer from the taxes they would have paid during his disability.

The Railroad Retirement System provides a lifetime income if an eligible worker is totally and permanently disabled, while the Railroad Temporary Disability Insurance System provides income for a short period to totally disabled persons.

The principal benefits provided under state and federal workmen's compensation programs are disability income and medical expense benefits. The laws are notable for their heterogeneity, but the objective of most laws is to provide the worker who is disabled due to occupational causes with a specified fraction, such as one half or two thirds, of his weekly wage at the time he was disabled subject to certain limitations on the weekly dollar amounts and, in most instances, the number of weekly payments. Medical expenses are reimbursed in part or completely.

Four states—Rhode Island, California, New Jersey and New York—have enacted compulsory temporary disability insurance legislation. Under this legislation, most employers are required to provide certain cash payments for employees who are disabled because of nonoccupational sicknesses and injuries. The California act also provides for the reimbursement of hospital bills up to a specified amount per day for a short period. All plans in Rhode Island must be insured by a monopolistic state fund; in the other three states private insurers are permitted to compete with a state fund if they provide at least as liberal (except in California, where the private plan must be more liberal) a plan as the public plan. Employee contributions finance the Rhode Island plan completely, but in the other states employers may pay part or all of the cost. Similar legislation has been and is still being introduced in many state legislatures, but no state has passed an act of this type since 1949 when the New York act was passed. The most persuasive argument against passage of this legislation in the other states has been the rapid expansion of voluntary plans, to be described below, providing similar benefits. It is interesting to note that this expansion in the other states has been aided by the compulsory programs in these four states because interstate employers often extended the same protection to all their employees voluntarily or in response to demands by labor unions.

Private Plans. With the exceptions noted above, current public employee benefit plans providing benefits in case of poor health are chiefly limited to disability income protection. Private plans provide important protection against medical expenses as well as loss of income.

The two most important types of private disability income plans are short-term disability income insurance plans, underwritten by commercial insurers, and paid sick leave plans which, although they may supplement a short-term disability insurance plan, are usually self-insured by the employer. Short-term disability insurance plans most commonly provide thirteen or twenty-six weeks of income for totally disabled workers, the benefit starting on the first day when the disability is caused by an accident and on the eighth day when it is caused by sickness. The disability income is generally a stated per cent of the worker's wage at the time he was disabled, subject to some specified maximum amount. Occupational injuries and diseases are excluded under most contracts; some plans cover work-connected disabilities but deduct any workmen's compensation payments.

Paid sick leave plans usually continue the disabled worker's income in full for a specified time which may increase with the length of service. Most firms make sick leave payments out of current operating income.

Other private employee benefit plans providing disability income protection worthy of notice at this point include (1) supplementary workmen's compensation plans, which are usually self-insured and which usually bring the disabled worker's income up to the level of any nonoccupational disability income benefit or even to his full wage at the time he was disabled; (2) group long-term disability income insurance, which is a relatively new product developed by commercial insurers, providing income for an extended period of years or until some advanced age such as sixty-five; and (3) disability income provisions in group life insurance and pension plans.

Plans providing benefits against medical expenses can be divided for exposition purposes into three categories: (1) commercial insurance plans, (2) Blue Cross and Blue Shield plans and (3) the so-called "independent" plans. Commercial insurance plans can be divided in turn into basic medical expense plans, major medical plans and comprehensive medical plans. Basic medical expense plans are designed to provide fairly complete protection against the expenses associated with the relatively less costly illnesses. The plan usually provides one or more of the following types of benefits: (1) hospital expense benefits covering room and board and other hospital expenses, (2) surgical expense benefits covering the cost of operations and (3) benefits for physicians' visits. The latter benefits may cover only nonsurgical care by a physician when the employee is confined in a hospital or they may also cover home and office visits. Diagnostic X-ray and laboratory expenses not covered under the hospital expense benefits may also be covered. Major medical plans are designed to provide protection against the medical expenses associated with the more costly illnesses. These plans usually obligate the insurer to pay a specified proportion of the medical expenses of almost any type in excess of some deductible amount, such as the benefits provided under a base plan or some stated dollar figure. Comprehensive medical expense plans combine elements of basic and major medical insurance protection under one program. For example, the plan may cover hospital expenses up to $500 and 80 per cent of the excess hospital expenses and other medical expenses in excess of $100.

Blue Cross association plans offer protection against hospital expenses, while Blue Shield association plans offer protection against surgical fees and other types of doctors' bills. One of the most distinctive features of many of these association plans is a "service" approach to providing benefits. Many Blue Cross subscribers are eligible for ward or semiprivate accommodations, plus many other hospital services, for a specified period of stay in a member hospital, regardless of the specific dollar charges for these services. Under many Blue Shield plans, participating physicians agree to accept the Blue Shield payment as their fee if the subscriber's income is below a stated level.

The "independent" plans include a variety of approaches, such as plans self-insured by employers or unions and private group clinics. Many of these plans cover most types of medical expenses including such items as the cost of physical examinations. Many also provide service benefits through salaried personnel or through contractual arrangements with hospitals and group practice clinics.

Company physicians and nurses may also provide medical care for employees on the premises. Such care usually includes physical examinations, first aid and treatment of minor conditions.

Plans Providing Benefits in Case of Unemployment

Public Programs. As indicated in Table 1–2, unemployment is the one peril covered under employee benefit plans for which most employees can turn only to public programs. Under the Social Security Act of 1935, the federal government levied a tax on employers employing most of the labor force which was to be used to pay the administrative costs of state unemployment compensation programs. Employers, however, were permitted to offset up to 90 per cent of this tax with contributions to state unemployment compensation programs. Thus, because employers in a state without an unemployment compensation program would have to pay federal taxes to support programs in other states, each state had good reason to enact its own unemployment compensation insurance program, and today all fifty states have programs of this sort. The programs provide weekly cash benefits (usually $\frac{1}{25}$ or $\frac{1}{26}$ of the unemployed worker's wage during his quarter of highest earnings in his "base" period, subject to some maximum dollar amount) for workers willing and able to work. The benefits continue during his unemployment for a period which varies with his wage credits or weeks of employment during the base period and is usually limited to twenty-six weeks. Benefit durations in many states were increased by 50 per cent up to thirty-nine weeks under two temporary federal unemployment compensation programs in the late 1950's and early 1960's. The Railroad Unemployment Insurance System is a federal program providing similar benefits for a special class of workers.

Private Plans. The major private programs providing benefits in case of unemployment are designed to supplement the public programs described above. These supplemental unemployment benefit plans, which are usually administered jointly by the employer and a union, provide a combined weekly benefit equal to some percentage, such as 65 per cent, of the employee's take-home pay. The payments, which are usually made out of trust funds financed through employer contributions, continue for a period which depends largely upon the employee's length of service. The principal plans are those in the steel, automobile and glass industries.

A different and much less common approach is the "conventional guarantee" plan under which eligible workers are assured that they will either be employed a specified number of weeks each year or receive a stated minimum income. A third approach, which is not contingent upon the employee's remaining unemployed, is a dismissal compensation plan or severance pay plan which provides benefits for persons leaving the firm permanently. The benefit is usually a lump-sum payment which varies with the employee's length of service and his wage or salary. Plans which continue group life and group health insurance for certain periods of unemployment provide, in essence, peripheral private unemployment benefits.

Plans Providing Retirement Benefits

Public Programs. The death and disability benefits provided under OASDI have already been mentioned, but it is the old-age benefits for which this program is best known. Subject to certain eligibility requirements, a fully insured worker can receive as early as age sixty-two a monthly income equal to his primary insurance amount for the remainder of his life. This income is increased if the worker has at the time of his retirement certain dependents. For example, if the retired worker has a wife aged sixty-five or over, the benefit is increased 50 per cent. The wife can elect to receive a reduced benefit as early as age sixty-two. Other public retirement programs include the Railroad Retirement System, the Civil Service Retirement System, and the numerous retirement plans covering state and local government employees.

Private Plans. Pension and deferred profit sharing plans are the private vehicles for providing old-age benefits. As indicated by Tables 1–1 and 1–2, these plans require more financial support from employers than any of the other private economic security plans despite the fact that the number of employees covered is relatively small.

Profit sharing plans permit employees to participate in the profits of an employer. Deferred profit sharing plans, which comprise a special class of profit sharing plans, distribute the funds credited to a particular employee only upon the occurrence of certain events such as retirement or termination of employment. Although profit sharing plans have many advantages as a pension vehicle, such as the direct incentive they provide for employees to increase profits, a major disadvantage is that the retirement income credits earned by employees each year are subject to considerable variation because of the possible fluctuation in profits. Although deferred profit sharing plans are gaining increasing acceptance, many more persons are covered under pension plans than deferred profit sharing plans at the present time.

The principal benefit under a pension plan is a lifetime income for the employee after he retires. Decisions must be made and incorporated in the plan documents with respect to the normal retirement age, whether retirement is to be voluntary or compulsory, and under what conditions, if any, early retirement is to be permitted. The more common benefit formulas are a defined contribution formula under which the annual contributions are specified, such as 10 per cent of salary, and the benefit is whatever amount can be purchased with these contributions; a defined benefit formula under which the benefit is specified, such as 1 per cent of final salary for each year of service; or a flat percentage or amount formula, such as 50 per cent of final salary or $100 a month.

Although optional forms are available, the normal benefit is a straight life annuity if the employee does not contribute to the cost of the plan. If he does contribute, provision is made under a modified refund annuity for the return in cash or in installments of the excess of the employee's contributions, with or without interest, over the retirement income received prior to his death. Although most plans do not make any adjustments for changes in the cost of living before and after retirement, an increasing number are beginning to include some provision for these changes.

Death and disability benefits are provided under many pension plans. Otherwise the rights of an employee who terminates his relationship with the plan for reasons other than retirement depend upon the plan's vesting provisions. These may range all the way from no vesting to complete vesting of the employer's contributions.

The benefits may be financed on a pay-as-you-go basis or funded in advance. The degree of advance funding varies greatly. For example, under one method the annual contribution is that required to provide a lifetime income for the employees retiring that year. Under another method, enough money is contributed each year to make it possible in case the plan terminates to continue benefits to retired persons and to provide some "fair" return to active employees.

Most pension plans are insured, but most employees are covered under self-administered trusteed plans. Under the latter type of plan, the employer typically engages the services of a consulting actuary for actuarial advice and a bank or trust company to perform the investing function. Self-insured plans give the employer considerable flexibility in designing benefit formulas, budgeting costs and investing, but the employer retains the mortality, investment and expense risks.

The principal types of insured plans are group deferred annuity plans, individual policy pension trusts and deposit administration plans. Under a group deferred annuity plan, the employer usually purchases each year enough paid-up deferred annuities to provide the retirement benefits earned during that year of service. Under an individual policy pension trust, a trustee typically purchases individual level premium life insurance policies or annuity contracts in an amount sufficient to provide the estimated retirement benefit to which the individual will be entitled. Under a deposit administration plan, contributions are accumulated in an undivided fund with the monies in the fund being used to purchase annuities for retiring employees. Deposit administration plans can be almost as flexible as self-insured plans, particularly in those states which permit the investment of the deposits in equities. On the other hand, the insurer makes fewer guarantees than under the other insured plans.

Another type of employee old-age benefit is deferred compensation. Under a deferred compensation plan, key employees who meet certain conditions, such as not entering into any competing employment, are promised an annual income after they retire in exchange for a reduced salary during their earning career. Large firms may elect to fund these plans on their own, but many firms, particularly the smaller ones, purchase insurance of some sort. Although all the tax advantages of a qualified pension plan are not available under this type of arrangement, it is possible to select the individual employees to be covered.

PARTIES INVOLVED IN ECONOMIC SECURITY PROGRAMS

The preceding discussion has emphasized the wide variety of benefits included under economic security employee benefit plans and the different ways in which these benefits can be provided. Another measure of the widespread scope of these plans is the diversified talents which must be employed in organizing, servicing and supervising them.

The direct interest of the employer and his employees in these programs is clear, but even a partial listing of the other parties is impressive. The employer usually relies heavily upon his officers in charge of personnel and finance and, in many cases, the risk manager, in making decisions concerning the development and operation of the program. The employees are commonly represented by a union which may not only bargain with the employer concerning changes but which may also participate in the joint administration of the plan. The employee's dependents are interested in the plan as potential beneficiaries or as active participants.

Banks, trust companies, consulting actuaries, lawyers, investment counsel, loss prevention and claims adjustment agencies, insurance personnel, Blue Cross and Blue Shield representatives and others compete with one another for the right to organize and service employee benefit plans. Among the insurance personnel involved are agents or brokers, group representatives who provide technical information at the time of the sale and service the plan after it is accepted, actuaries, underwriters, loss adjusters and members of the legal and investment departments.

The success of a plan providing benefits in case of poor health depends to a large extent upon the actions of physicians, dentists, nurses and hospitals, although these may not be direct parties to the contract. These parties not only render the medical care provided under medical expense plans, but they also serve as experts in determining the degree of a claimant's disability. The quality of their services under different arrangements influences employer and employee attitudes toward public programs versus private programs, indemnity programs versus service programs and programs relying upon individual practice by doctors versus group practice plans. The charges these practitioners make for their services not only affect attitudes toward the different approaches, but also determine the level and types of benefits which it is feasible to provide and, in some cases, the ability of a program to survive.

Public officials are also deeply involved. Public programs are established through legislation and usually involve some government agency directly in daily operations. Under some public programs, such as workmen's compensation and compulsory temporary disability, the government may not be the underwriting agency but it supervises rather closely the operation of private underwriters. Even when the operation, such as a pension plan or group insurance, is ostensibly private, the government exercises considerable supervision, most often through state insurance departments and more recently through state and federal legislation requiring disclosure of certain aspects of employee benefit plans. The government also bears indirectly a significant portion of the cost of employee benefit plans by allowing various tax deductions.

Even the rare citizen who is not directly involved in these employee security plans is indirectly affected. The increased economic security they afford reduces the need for charity and public assistance following a loss and the economic costs of uncertainty itself. These plans have also affected hiring and retention practices which, in turn, have far-reaching economic and social implications. The local business community is influenced since these plans continue employee purchasing power despite unemployment, disability, death and retirement. Finally, these plans, particularly the pension plans, have become one of the principal sources of funds for the capital market, and what they choose to do with these funds should concern every citizen.

SELECTED REFERENCES

AMERICAN MANAGEMENT ASSOCIATION. *The Growing Job of Risk Management.* Management Report No. 70. New York: American Management Association, 1962.

BELCHER, DAVID W. *Wage and Salary Administration,* chaps. 15, 16, and 18. 2d ed. Englewood Cliffs, N.J.: Prentice-Hall, Inc., 1962.

CHAMBER OF COMMERCE OF THE UNITED STATES. *Fringe Benefits 1961.* Washington, D.C., 1962.

GREGG, DAVIS W. *Group Life Insurance.* 3d ed. Homewood, Ill.: Richard D. Irwin, Inc., 1962.

HABER, W., AND COHEN, W. J. *Social Security: Programs, Problems, and Policies.* Homewood, Ill.: Richard D. Irwin, Inc., 1961.

KRISLOV, JOSEPH. "Employee Benefit Plans, 1954–62," *Social Security Bulletin,* Vol. XXVII, No. 4 (April, 1964), pp. 4–21.

McGILL, DAN M. *Fundamentals of Private Pensions.* 2d ed. Homewood, Ill.: Richard D. Irwin, Inc., 1964.

PICKRELL, JESSE F. *Group Health Insurance.* Rev. ed. Homewood, Ill.: Richard D. Irwin, Inc., 1961.

SOMERS, H. M., AND SOMERS, A. R. *Workmen's Compensation.* New York: John Wiley & Sons, Inc., 1954.

TURNBULL, J. G.; WILLIAMS, C. A., JR.; AND CHEIT, E. F. *Economic and Social Security.* 2d ed. New York: The Ronald Press Co., 1962.

YODER, D., AND HENEMAN, H. G., JR. *Labor Economics and Industrial Relations,* chap. 18. Cincinnati: South-Western Publishing Co., 1959.

Chapter 2

RATIONALE OF EMPLOYEE BENEFIT PLANS

BY WENDELL MILLIMAN

As was indicated in Chapter 1, the components of employee benefit plans have now become one of the more important approaches to the problem of reducing personal economic insecurity. The present chapter will examine the purposes which these plans are intended to serve and the influences and forces which have caused their growth. In addition, the fundamental principles which should underlie the development and operation of an employee benefit plan if it is to accomplish these purposes will be discussed.

OBJECTIVES OF EMPLOYEE BENEFIT PLANS

Basic Purpose

The fundamental purpose served by employee benefit plans is that of providing some degree of protection against the loss of, or reduction in, the earning power of the employee. His earning power is subject to loss or reduction as a result of premature death, disability, unemployment or superannuation. Thus the major components of employee benefit plans generally attempt to offset part or all of the financial loss that would be occasioned by several, if not all, of these events. Benefit plans provided through the medium of the employee group have been found to possess certain advantages over other means of accomplishing this fundamental purpose.

Ancillary Purposes

In addition to the primary purpose of an employee benefit plan, certain of the typical components of such plans serve ancillary purposes. For example, benefits provided under workmen's compensation laws, while dealing only with limited perils, those where death or disability is a direct result of the job, are concerned with expenses of medical care and rehabilitation of the injured workmen, as well as the replacement of lost income.

Moreover, the cost of workmen's compensation benefits is borne by employers, and the premium structures for such benefits usually contain a large element of experience rating. Stimulated by their financial self-interest, both employers and insurance companies engage in accident prevention and rehabilitation programs. As a consequence, the reduction of occupational disabilities and the minimization of the accompanying interruption or loss of earning power have become ancillary purposes of workmen's compensation plans.

Unemployment compensation legislation has a secondary purpose also. The basic purpose of unemployment compensation plans is to provide protection against loss of earning power due to unemployment. The cost of such benefit plans is borne by the employers, and unemployment compensation taxes usually are dependent in part upon the rate of unemployment experienced by the employees of the employer. Again, the reduction in the hazard of unemployment may be regarded as an ancillary purpose of unemployment compensation plans.

When originally introduced, hospital, surgical and medical expense insurance was intended to serve the basic purpose of protecting the employee's paycheck. An employee becoming entitled to hospital and surgical benefits usually will be disabled and, consequently, without current income. In the absence of insurance to cover the expenses of hospital care, such expenses would compound the problem of income lost due to disability. Insurance to meet part or all of the substantial and unpredictable expenses of hospital and surgical care is, therefore, viewed as a form of protection of income. Although an employee's ability to continue work and earn an income normally is not affected by the need for hospital and surgical care for his dependents, insurance of expenses incurred for such care for dependents can likewise be viewed as a method of protecting an employee's paycheck, since these expenses would otherwise have to be met from it.

The extension of employee benefit plans into other areas of medical expense insurance, with coverage of expenses for the early treatment of illness, has introduced the ancillary purpose for such plans of improving the quality of medical care by encouraging use of preventive and early therapeutic care. The quality of medical care and the health of the population both will be improved, it is argued, if the financial barriers to periodic health examinations and to early visits to a physician in the event of an illness are removed, or substantially lowered, through medical expense insurance. The administration of benefit plans designed to serve this ancillary purpose, by removing financial barriers to medical care, involves unique problems which sometimes conflict with other objectives of such plans. This has led to controversy between the proponents of medical expense insurance plans which emphasize protection against catastrophic medical costs on the one hand, and proponents of medical expense insurance plans which emphasize the elimination of financial barriers to early medical care, on the other hand.

The design of some dental care benefit plans involves great emphasis on the objective of increasing the quality of dental care by encouragement of early treatment. As a result, there is some question as to whether this is not the major purpose of such dental care benefits, with the protection of the employee's earning power the ancillary purpose.

REASONS FOR GROWTH OF EMPLOYEE BENEFIT PLANS

Employee benefit plans have developed out of the employee-employer relationship, and, obviously, the attitudes and actions of both employers and employees have influenced their growth. In addition, legislation, both actual and proposed, as well as court decisions, has influenced the development and growth of these plans. The same is true of insurance companies, financial institutions and providers of medical care.

Advantages of Employee Benefit Plan Mechanisms

Obviously, employee benefit plans do not constitute the only available vehicle for serving the purposes described above. They do, however, provide an efficient and economical basis for doing so. This is so for several reasons. First, the inclusion of all, or a large proportion, of the employees of an employer in an insured employee benefit plan substantially reduces the underwriting risks involved. Second, the expenses required to sell and administer an insured employee benefit plan normally are lower than they would be if the same benefits were obtained through individual insurance contracts, thereby making it possible to provide these benefits at a minimum cost. Third, the insurance of an employee is more likely to remain in force during the period the employee remains with the employer than would an individual contract, both because the employer pays part or all of the cost and because the employee's share in the cost, if any, is paid by payroll deduction. Finally, in most situations the employer's share of the cost is a tax deductible business expense and is not currently taxable as income to the employee. Therefore by channeling a portion of what might otherwise be paid to the employees in cash wages to pay costs of an employee benefit plan, fewer dollars are required than would be the case if the costs were paid by the employees with after-tax dollars.

Employee Motivations for Employee Benefit Plans

The forerunners of modern employee benefit plans probably were the early mutual benefit associations established by the collective action of employees. Typically, these plans were limited to provision of death benefits or short-term disability income benefits and were created because individual insurance for employees in such hazardous occupations as mining and railroading was either unattainable or priced at a level beyond the reach of most of the employees. These plans arose from the desire of employees to achieve security, and they utilized the common bond of employment by a single employer as a vehicle for doing so. Following the demonstration of the feasiblity of such plans and the introduction, in the form of group insurance, of a mechanism adapted to handling the problems of employee insurance, the desire and demand on the part of employees for employee benefit plans extended into nonhazardous as well as hazardous occupations.

The growth in size and strength of labor unions provided a voice and mechanism for effectively expressing this desire. Conversely, to obtain the protection provided by employee benefit plans is one of the justifications for labor unions. The negotiation of a plan, or the improvement of a plan, is evidence that the union leadership has effectively represented the employees.

The interest of the employees or their representatives in having benefits provided through an employee benefit plan rather than through individual action has been further influenced by the general absence of individual underwriting in such plans. By means of the employee benefit plan mechanism, many employees are enabled to obtain insurance protection who, for one reason or another, might be unable to obtain it on an individual basis.

Employer Motivations for Employee Benefit Plans

Both paternalism and self-interest have played a part in motivating employers to adopt employee benefit plans. It is difficult, however, to assess the relative importance of each as reasons for action in individual cases. The interplay between paternalism and self-interest is evident from the following motives, which often are suggested as reasons for an employer adopting an employee benefit plan. The adoption of an employee benefit plan will (1) eliminate "passing the hat" among a worker's fellow employees in case of illness or death; (2) place the assistance or charity given by the employer in such cases on an organized, nondiscriminatory basis; (3) improve the efficiency of employees by relieving them, to some extent, of concern over what might happen to their families in the event of the employee's illness or death; and (4) help in attracting and holding capable employees in a competitive labor market.

Representatives of insurance companies and others interested in promoting the adoption of employee benefit plans have used variations of these reasons as arguments for employers to adopt plans. The steady growth in popularity of group insurance is evidence that this line of reasoning has been persuasive. It should be noted that this growth in the popularity of group insurance has increased the importance to an employer of having an attractive employee benefit plan as an instrument for attracting and holding employees.

Another area involving an interplay of motivations has resulted from the increasing power of labor unions and their interest in employee benefits. Many employers have adopted group insurance plans only as a result of the collective bargaining process following union demands for such benefits. However, some employers of employees who were not unionized have adopted group insurance plans in an attempt to ward off or discourage unionization. In still other situations, employers with both union and nonunion employees have adopted employee benefit plans for their nonunion employees in order to match benefits which they have agreed to provide, as a result of collective bargaining, for their unionized employees.

The employer's portion of the cost of employee benefit plans is a part of his total payroll expense. In those industries where payroll costs are a large proportion of total costs, particularly where basic wages are controlled by union contracts, an employer is reluctant to increase his payroll by the adoption—or increase in liberality—of an employee benefit plan before his competitors. In such situations, even though an employer may be attracted by other reasons for adopting a plan, labor's demand may be the immediate motivation for doing so.

In the case of corporate employers, the officers who make recommendations or decisions for the adoption or liberalization of employee benefit plans usually are included themselves under the plans. The judgment of these officers may well be influenced by their self-interest, particularly where the size of benefits is substantial. This tendency has been intensified by the favorable federal income tax treatment given to employer contributions to provide such benefits. It is further intensified in those situations where one or more of the officers or key personnel who would be covered under the plan is an impaired risk. These considerations may be found in groups of any size, but they are often of controlling importance in the case of smaller groups of employees.

Governmental Influences

A variety of governmental actions and proposed actions, such as wage controls, tax policy, court decisions and proposals for extension of social insurance legislation, have contributed to the growth in popularity of employee benefit plans. Perhaps the burden of income taxes and the favorable tax treatment given to various forms of employee benefits have had the greatest effect.

Qualified pension and profit sharing plans have been stimulated by the combination of the tax shelter given to these forms of thrift and the high rate of income tax on personal and corporate income. Employer contributions to qualified plans constitute tax deductible business expenses but are not taxable as income to the employee until received in the form of benefits from the plan. Taxation of the investment earnings of such plans is similarly deferred. It is possible, consequently, not only to assure the employees of retirement income by means of such plans, but also to accumulate the funds to pay such benefits with a minimum amount of loss due to federal income taxes.

Similarly, employer payments toward the cost of most other forms of employee benefits are tax deductible business expenses to the employer without being taxable income to the employees. (Group life insurance in excess of $50,000 is a notable exception to this general rule.)[1] In addition, benefit payments provided at employer expense, subject to some limitations as to period and amount in the case of disability income benefits, are not construed to be taxable income to the employee.

This combination of circumstances has been used by employees and their representatives as a persuasive argument to adopt employee benefit plans. As indicated above, because of the greater impact of income taxes on higher paid employees and the general pattern of providing death benefits and income replacement benefits which are more or less proportionate to income, this argument has great appeal to the officers and key employees of an employer.

The possibility of compulsory health insurance provided by government has been proposed from time to time throughout most of the period of development of group medical expense insurance. The efforts of insurers to popularize voluntary plans have been stimulated by this possibility, and the atmosphere for cooperation between the insurers and the providers of medical care to make such plans more effective has likewise been improved. One can only speculate whether the possibility of compulsory health insurance has affected the receptivity of employers to proposals to extend employee benefit plans to include such coverage and whether, on balance, it has made labor more or less receptive to voluntary plans.

Two additional governmental actions have influenced significantly the adoption of employee benefit plans. First, the wage freeze imposed by the federal government during World War II and the Korean war which applied to cash wages but not to employee benefits, and second, the decision by the National Labor Relations Board and the courts that employee benefits are within the area of collective bargaining.[2]

Mention should be made of the fact that the statutory definitions of group insurance have been liberalized many times (e.g., by reduction in the minimum number of covered employees that must be included under

---

[1] For a complete discussion of the federal income tax treatment of group life insurance, see Chapter 8.

[2] More detailed information concerning these governmental actions is presented in Chapter 4.

a group policy) over the period of growth of employee benefit plans. In many circumstances these extensions in the statutory definitions of group insurance have made it possible for an employer to adopt an employee benefit plan.

Influence of Other Interests

Insurance companies, Blue Cross and Blue Shield plans and banks, as well as the providers of medical care, i.e., hospitals, physicans and dentists, also have had an influence on the growth of employee benefit plans. The efforts of the sales representatives of insurance companies and others in popularizing these plans is obvious. These efforts have been supported by the development of facilities for the design, effective communication, administration and funding of such plans, and by experimentation with new forms of coverage and extension of older forms of coverage. Competition among different insurance companies and among the insurance industry, nonprofit plans and self-insured plans has stimulated lower pricing, more imaginative design and more aggressive salesmanship. Regardless of the other results of such competition, it has contributed to both the growth in number of plans and the extension of coverage provided by such plans.

Through the medium of Blue Cross and Blue Shield plans, hospitals and physicians have contributed to pioneering in the development of practical mechanisms to provide insurance of the expense of medical care. The Blue Cross and Blue Shield associations have played a prominent part in the popularization and aggressive sale of these services, and the competition between them and insurance companies, by intensifying the competition for medical expense insurance, has contributed to the growth of voluntary insurance of such benefits.

Influence of Social and Economic Factors

The growth of employee benefit plans has occurred during a period in which, as a result of industrialization of the economy, the vast majority of workers have become dependent upon wages and salaries. The security of the average worker has, as a result, become closely identified with his employment. Certain economic and social factors have intensified this dependence of employees upon the continuance of their earnings and have, accordingly, encouraged the development of employee benefit plans.

For instance, increased urbanization has reduced the ability of the average worker to live off the land in case of loss of his regular employment. Ready availability of credit has made it easy for the wage earner to mortgage his future income to meet current needs or satisfy current desires. Inflationary forces have diminished the ability of the average individual to provide for his retirement or for unexpected termination of his earning power through individual savings. All of these factors have helped create a favorable climate for the development of employee benefit plans.

Productivity and, consequently, living standards have been rising during this era of growth of employee benefit plans. This, in turn, has tended to encourage liberalization of benefits under such plans.

REQUIREMENTS OF SOUND EMPLOYEE BENEFIT PLANS

In broad terms, a sound employee benefit plan might be described as one which provides an acceptable level of benefits at a price which those involved are willing to pay and which has been effectively communicated to the employees involved. Since the plan, once adopted, is not apt to be discontinued, both the level of benefits and the cost should be looked at from a long-term point of view. At the same time, it should be recognized that an employee benefit plan is a dynamic thing and can be expected to be changed from time to time if it is to continue to serve its purpose satisfactorily.

Acceptable Cost

The cost of an employee benefit plan may be borne entirely by the employer or shared by the employer and employees. If the employees are to share in the cost, their contributions should be at a level which is attractive at all ages in comparison with alternative forms of individually purchased benefits, and at an absolute level which a majority of the eligible employees will be willing to pay. The willingness of employees to contribute to the cost of a plan will be influenced by the level of benefits provided, the manner in which they are explained or sold to the eligible employees and, of course, the income brackets of the employees.

The employer's share of the cost constitutes an additional wage cost. It should be reasonable in the light of his operating margins and competitive situation.

Costs of employee benefit plans may vary from year to year, but, in general, they tend to increase with the passage of time. The more important factors which cause this tendency are, first, the fact that the average age in a group of covered employees tends to increase with the passage of time; second, the trend in the costs of health care services generally has been upward; and third, the rate of utilization of such services has been increasing.

It is awkward and difficult to abandon or curtail an employee benefit plan once it is adopted. However, increasing costs may cause a plan which was considered to have an acceptable level of cost when it was adopted later to become burdensome or even unacceptable. Some of the factors which will cause variations may be built into the plan. For example, continuation of coverage of life or health insurance benefits after retirement will cause continuous increases in costs. Other factors may be independent of the plan but still act to cause increases. For example, the increasing utilization of hospital facilities and increasing hospital costs will tend to cause steady and continuing increases in the cost of hospital insurance benefits. If the cost of a plan is to remain acceptable, both the probable future course of the cost, as well as the initial cost, should be known to the parties involved at the time the plan is adopted.

Acceptable Benefits

No employee benefit plan gives complete protection against all risks. Most plans when first established are quite limited and are extended and liberalized with the passage of time. Some liberalizations occur because new benefits become available or because they come to the attention of the parties involved. Some plans are liberalized to meet competition from other plans, some because the employer is prepared to incur higher costs, others because of employee demands.

Adequacy of benefits provided by an employee benefit plan—and therefore to some extent its acceptability to the covered employees—must be viewed in relationship to other benefits provided by either governmental plans or by individual action. Opinions may differ as to the relative role which should be filled by each of these forms of protection—individual insurance and savings, employer-employee plans and governmental plans. For certain types of benefits, by virtue of the nature of the risks involved, the provision of benefits by a governmental agency, or through the employer, may substantially eliminate the need for other protection. Unemployment insurance is an example of protection which is normally provided only at the governmental level, while hospital expense insurance is an example of a type of protection which in many cases may be covered adequately through an employee benefit plan without need for supplemental individual insurance.

In the areas of retirement benefits, death benefits and disability benefits, as a general rule, employee benefit plans should, on the one hand, take into consideration whatever benefits are provided for the employees by federal OASDI or other governmental plans and, on the other, should not eliminate the need for the employee to provide additional protection for himself. For instance, retirement plans generally provide a somewhat smaller benefit with respect to those earnings upon which OASDI benefits are based in order to integrate the two sources of retirement income. In addition, the average employee will need to supplement the income from these sources by individual savings if he is to avoid a substantial reduction in his standard of living following retirement.

Insurance company underwriting rules require that the classes of employees eligible for insurance be determined by conditions pertaining to the employment and that amounts of insurance be determined on a basis precluding individual selection. Even if the plan is not insured, these conditions probably will be necessary if the plan is to be acceptable to the employees as a whole. Within these broad limits, the range of sound and acceptable plans is almost limitless.

Communication

A sound employee benefit plan not only should give protection against perils but also should give the employees a sense of security because of the protection it provides. Consequently, an employee benefit plan is of limited value unless it is understood by the eligible employees. It is necessary, if a plan is to be fully effective, that it be well communicated. This may be by booklet or other written instrument, by meetings, by discussion with the supervisor or by a combination of these methods. Normally, a written description of the plan is provided at the time an employee first becomes eligible. At that time or shortly thereafter, he usually is given a printed description of the plan in the form of a plan booklet, insurance certificate or both. The development of effective tools of communication, therefore, becomes one of the ingredients of a sound plan.

Payment of Benefits

The purpose of an employee benefit plan is fulfilled when benefits are paid. There are many different procedures for handling payment of benefits. In the case of health care benefits, for instance, benefits may be paid directly by the insurance company, by the employer by means of drafts drawn on the insurer and in accordance with rules established by the insurer, by an administrator appointed by a labor-management committee or by an organization established by the providers of medical care. Whatever procedures are used, it is important that there be prompt and equitable adjustment of claims for a plan to perform satisfactorily.

Periodic Review

An employee benefit plan, if it is to continue to meet the purposes for which it was originally established, should be reviewed from time to time with the counsel of some knowledgeable advisor, such as the insurance broker, the administrator or a consultant. Such a review will serve a number of purposes. Among others, the cost of providing the benefits can be evaluated and compared with available alternatives. The emerging trends can be examined and the probable future level of costs projected. All aspects of the administration of the plan, including in the case of health benefits the payment of claims, can be reviewed and evaluated. The adequacy of the level of benefits can be appraised, and the feasibility and advisability of extending the plan of benefits to include different types of protection, or of modifying the plan to change the emphasis between coverages, can be considered in the light of current conditions. Also, the effectiveness of communication of the plan to the employees can be reviewed and revitalized if necessary.

SELECTED REFERENCES

GARDNER, COLIN, III. "Getting the Most from Employee Benefits," *General Management Series*, No. 170. New York: American Management Association, 1954.

STRONG, JAY V. *Employee Benefit Plans in Operation*. Washington, D.C.: Bureau of National Affairs, Inc., 1951.

WERMEL, MICHAEL T., AND BEIDEMAN, GERALDINE M. *Employee Benefit Programs: An Outline*. Benefits and Insurance Research Center Publication No. 6. Rev. ed. Pasadena, Calif.: California Institute of Technology, 1958.

ZISMAN, JOSEPH. "Private Employee Benefit Plans Today," *Social Security Bulletin*, Vol. XX, No. 1 (January, 1957).

PART II

*Group Coverages
Their Nature, Development and
Significance*

Chapter 3

FUNDAMENTAL CHARACTERISTICS OF
THE GROUP TECHNIQUE

BY DAVIS W. GREGG

Group insurance, a major component of employee benefit plans, provides an insurance technique of considerable economic, social and political significance. A substantial part of the labor force has protection under group insurance, and an increasing proportion of all persons in the United States is insured by some form of dependents' coverage, senior citizen coverage and the like. Extensions of the technique over the years suggest that ultimately the number of persons insured might be almost as great as under social insurance.

Group insurance is not simple to define. It can be viewed as an arrangement whereby a group of persons is covered by a single contract with an insurer. It can be thought of as a plan for insuring groups of persons without individual risk selection. It can be looked upon as a method of mass marketing and mass servicing of insurance.

In its broadest context, group insurance would include a considerable list of insurance coverages, including group life insurance, group health insurance, group annuities, group property insurance of various types and others. In this book, however, group insurance is considered to include primarily the various forms of group life insurance and group health insurance, with certain forms of group life insurance and group annuities commonly associated with funding pension plans being excluded.

Group insurance usually is distinguished from other forms of personal insurance (as contrasted with property insurance) in two ways. It customarily is differentiated as a separate field from *individual* insurance and *social* insurance, the distinctions being based primarily upon the social philosophy and methodology underlying each of the three types.[1] Then,

---

[1] Social insurance is generally considered to have several basic characteristics that distinguish it from private insurance. One authoritative textbook (John G. Turnbull, C. Arthur Williams, Jr., and Earl F. Cheit, *Economic and Social Security* [2d ed.; New York: The Ronald Press Co., 1962]) indicates that social insurance differs from the most

too, on the basis of state regulation and the operational practices of private insurance, group insurance is always distinguished from *ordinary* insurance and *industrial* insurance.[2] Group life insurance may be further divided into group *term* life insurance and group *permanent* life insurance. The group technique was initiated in the former context, and this type of group life insurance still represents by far the largest segment.

Group health insurance includes a variety of forms that can be broadly classified under group *disability income* insurance, providing both long-term and short-term benefits to replace income lost due to disability, and group *medical expense* insurance, including such widely used coverages as hospital expense, surgical expense, major medical and the like. A number of forms of group insurance, such as group accidental death and dismemberment insurance and group travel accident insurance, contain aspects of both life and health coverages.

BROAD CHARACTERISTICS OF GROUP INSURANCE

When group life and health insurance are contrasted with individual forms of life and health insurance, a number of unique features are evident. First, and probably foremost, is the group selection of risks as contrasted to individual selection of risks. With few exceptions, group

---

common forms of private insurance in four important respects:

"(1) Participation is compulsory (with a few exceptions) for all eligible persons. Otherwise some individuals would elect not to be covered and the policy objective of a floor of protection for all members of a defined group would be thwarted.

"(2) The benefits are prescribed by law. There are no contracts, and it is possible (but highly improbable) that Congress will rescind the benefits in the future. Periodic changes in the benefit structure are very likely through changes in the law.

"(3) The system redistributes income in addition to providing protection through a pooling arrangement. The lower-income groups, the insureds with many dependents, and the participants who were elderly when the system was inaugurated receive more benefits for their contributions than most other participants. If this were not true, it would be impossible to achieve the public policy objective of a floor of protection for all participants, since some insureds would be unable to afford adequate protection. The benefits are not equitable in the private insurance sense, but they are not meant to be. Other standards of performance have been deemed more important.

"The contribution rates are scheduled, but Congress may and has revised the schedule periodically. Consequently, bankruptcy is impossible as long as the government has an effective taxing power, although it is conceivable that the taxes may become unbearable. An individual's contribution may vary yearly even though the tax rate remains fixed, for the base (annual income) upon which the tax is levied may fluctuate from year to year. These fluctuations may have little or no effect on the benefits.

"(4) The government system is a monopolistic system. However, public pressure forces a continual reassessment of benefits and contribution rates."

[2] Increasingly, ordinary and industrial tend to be grouped together as individual insurance, thus making the logical distinction between group and individual. See Davis W. Gregg, "Is Life Insurance Really Ordinary?" *The Journal of the American Society of Chartered Life Underwriters,* Vol. XVII, No. 3 (Summer, 1963), pp. 197–202.

insurance is issued without medical examination or other evidence of individual insurability.

Another feature characteristic of group insurance is the coverage of a number of persons under a single contract. Interestingly enough, the persons insured are not actually parties to the contract, since legally the contract is between the insurer and the group policyholder, usually an employer.[3]

A third feature of group insurance is that it is essentially low-cost, mass protection. A number of economies of large volume operation are attained through mass distribution and mass administration methods.

Another special feature of group insurance lies in the fact that premiums usually are subject to experience rating. The actual experience of an individual group may figure heavily in the determination of dividends or premium rate adjustments. Generally speaking, the larger the group, the greater the weight attached to its own claims and expenses in any single year.

Group insurance contracts, as a rule, are of a continuing nature, in that the contract and the plan may last long beyond the lifetime, or membership in the plan, of any one individual. New persons are added to the group from time to time, and others terminate their coverage. However, it is relatively rare for group coverage to be discontinued by an employer, since normally it is part of his over-all employee welfare plan.

BASIC FEATURES

Group insurance appears quite complex when one considers the variety and types of groups, sizes of groups, underwriting rules, premium plans and funding methods. Actually, however, there are certain features of group insurance which have a high degree of universality and which may be looked upon as embodying the fundamentals of this insurance technique.

Eligible Groups

State insurance laws and company underwriting practices are the two major forces determining the types of groups eligible for group insurance. The laws, variable in considerable degree among the states, describe the kinds of groups eligible. Insurer underwriting practices vary among the group writing companies and may be more restrictive than any applicable statutory rules. Within the existing legal and underwriting framework, risks eligible for group insurance may be classified as individual employer groups, multiple-employer groups, labor union groups, creditor-debtor groups and miscellaneous groups.

---

[3] The legal relationships among the insured, insurer and policyholder are discussed in depth in Chapter 25.

Individual Employer Groups. By far the most important type of eligible group, from the standpoint of number of group contracts, number of persons insured and amount of insurance in force, is the individual employer group. The employer may be a sole proprietorship, a partnership or a corporation. The interpretation of "employees" is quite broad and includes, in addition to those normally thought of as employees of a firm, additional persons such as (1) proprietors and partners under group policies covering their employees; (2) employees of subsidiaries, affiliates and associated firms; (3) retired employees; and (4) and perhaps most interesting, independent contractors whose businesses are controlled by the master policyholder through contract or otherwise.

Multiple-Employer Groups. An increasing number of persons are covered by group insurance under labor-management negotiated plans. A large proportion of this insurance is provided through multiple-employer trust plans, wherein the employees of two or more employers are covered under one master contract. The most important types of multiple-employer groups are trade associations covering more than one employer in the same industry and union members who are employees of more than one employer. Typically, the latter type of group contract is a result of a collective bargaining agreement between a union and the employers of union members, and the group contract is issued to the trustees of the welfare fund.

Labor Union Groups. In labor union groups the coverage is provided union members under a contract issued directly to the union. The premium may come directly from the union's funds or jointly from those funds and member insurance contributions.

Creditor-Debtor Groups. A creditor-debtor arrangement provides group life and health insurance for debtors through a group contract issued to the creditor. Typically, the group insurance is provided through commercial banks, finance companies, small-loan companies, credit unions and retailers, with reference to debts such as time payment purchases, charge accounts, personal loans and other forms of consumer debt. If the borrower dies (or is disabled), benefits are paid to the lender to cancel the insured part of the debt (or to relieve the debtor of the need to make his periodic payments while disabled).

Miscellaneous Groups. A great variety of groups beyond the foregoing classifications are covered by group insurance where permitted by state insurance laws and by group insurer underwriting practices. Among such miscellaneous groups are associations of public and private employees; associations of teachers, lawyers, physicians and dentists; fraternal society members; college alumni groups; savings account depositors; veterans organizations; trade associations; and many others. A significant group insurance plan that might fall in this category, even though logically it is an employer-employee group, is the group plan covering United States federal employees. This is by far the largest single group insurance plan in the world.

Size Specifications

A fundamental issue in group insurance pertains to the number of persons needed to constitute a "group." Again, the issue is resolved by state insurance laws and company underwriting practices. There are rather well-defined—although changing—size specifications relating to the minimum number of persons and the minimum proportion of the entire group covered. These size and participation requirements also vary by type of coverage, that is, by the various forms of group life insurance and group health insurance.

Minimum Number. Group life insurance was the first form of group insurance written and, at the outset, the generally accepted minimum was 100 lives. Accumulated experience in group underwriting has resulted in the progressive reduction of the number considered to constitute a group until today, depending upon the state, the insurer, the type of group and the type of group insurance, it might be as small as two or three persons. The most common requirement in group life and health insurance (by law and by underwriting practice) is ten persons.

There are two basic reasons for requiring a minimum number of persons under group insurance; namely, (1) to reduce individual selection against the insurer, and (2) to spread the expense, thus lowering the rate of expense per insured person. A minimum of, say, ten or twenty-five persons gives the insurer some protection against the insurance being taken primarily for the purpose of covering one or more individuals with incipient losses and claims. The larger the group, the less likely it is that the decision to insure the group will be determined by the impaired health of one or more lives, and also the less likely it is to contain an undue proportion of impaired lives. Any theoretical exactness in determining a safe minimum number is not possible. In any case, it should be recognized that no magic inheres in the number selected as the minimum, such as ten or twenty-five.

From a practical standpoint, however, the very important element in determining minimum group size is that of expenses. One of the cost advantages of group insurance lies in the substantial risk-handling economies attained through the group method. Since there are certain initial and continuing "per case" expenses which must be met regardless of the size of the group, it is obvious that the smaller the case the greater the rate of expense on a per-person or per-unit-of-insurance basis.

Minimum Proportion of Group. The extent to which the members within a given group participate in the group insurance plan is significant for the same reasons as is the minimum size of the group, namely, the avoidance of adverse selection against the insurer and the reduction of expenses per unit. As a result, every effort is made to secure a high percentage of participation initially and to keep the participation high in subsequent years.

In noncontributory plans, that is, where the participants make no payment toward the cost of the group insurance, it is typically required that all eligible persons must be insured. In the case of contributory plans, that is, where the premium is paid at least in part by the plan participants, it is typically required that at least 75 per cent of the eligible persons must elect to take the insurance. The very practical reason for permitting somewhat less than 100 per cent participation in the case of contributory plans is that some eligible participants may refuse to contribute.

The minimum participation requirement is important also from an industrial relations viewpoint. A group insurance plan with only a small proportion of all eligible employees enrolled, even if sound from an insurance standpoint, obviously would not be performing its proper function as an employee welfare plan. Keeping at least three fourths of the employees under the plan assures its value to the employer from this standpoint.

Benefit Schedules

Group insurance benefit schedules are based upon some plan designed to preclude individual selection either by the insured persons (usually employees) or by the party arranging the plan (usually the employer). Some sort of predetermined schedule or plan of benefits is required in every group insurance situation.

Important factors usually considered in the selection of a benefit schedule are the needs of the employees, the employees' ability to pay if the plan is contributory, and the over-all cost of the plan. The interrelationship of these factors has, over the years, resulted in the development of benefit schedules related essentially to earnings, to position or occupational classifications, or to the simple plan of a flat benefit amount for everyone covered. There are instances where group life insurance plans relate the amount of benefit to length of service and, of course, benefit schedules may be a combination of two or more of any of these basic types.

The most widely used benefit schedule is that which bases the amount of insurance (except for group medical expense insurance) on an employee's earnings. An illustration of a simple scale of group life and disability income insurance benefits is as follows:

	Life Insurance	Disability Income Insurance
Weekly earnings less than $60	$3,000	$40 per week
Weekly earnings $60 but less than $80	4,000	45 per week
Weekly earnings $80 and over	5,000	50 per week

The plan may be based on any common earnings unit, e.g., annual, monthly, weekly or hourly rates of pay, the governing factor usually being the payroll setup of the employer. As a rule, only the base pay is considered in determining an employee's earnings classification for insurance, and bonuses and overtime pay are excluded.

The position schedule provides varying amounts of insurance for employees depending upon their employment positions. For example, the employees might be classified as factory, clerical, supervisory and executive. Or, there might be some division such as officers and department heads, salesmen and foremen, and all other employees. In any event, a uniform amount of insurance is provided within each classification, and different amounts are provided as between each classification. A typical position schedule, again for group life and disability income insurance, might appear as follows:

| | | Disability |
| | Life | Income |
Position	Insurance	Insurance
Officers and department heads	$7,500	$60 per week
Salesmen and foremen	5,000	50 per week
All other employees	2,500	30 per week

In group health insurance, disability income benefits are almost always related directly to earnings and, in order to avoid moral hazard (the tendency of the insured to prefer to receive insurance benefits rather than his wages), the benefit amount normally does not exceed about two thirds of average wages. Benefits under group medical expense insurance typically are uniform for all persons covered.

Financing

A group insurance plan may be financed on either a noncontributory basis with the employer paying the entire cost, or on a contributory basis with the employees sharing the cost with the employer. In some few cases, where not prohibited by law, participants may pay the entire cost.

In the history of group insurance there have been several trends and countertrends in financing. When group insurance began a half-century ago, the noncontributory plan was the most popular. Within a period of about five years after World War I there developed a trend away from employer-pay-all plans. Not only was most new group insurance written on the contributory basis, but many of the old plans were switched to this basis. Several factors underlay this shift, including the popularization of the payroll deduction idea in World War I, the business recession of the early 1920's, and the subsequent development of group health insurance benefits in the 1930's with a consequent need for employee contributions to share the cost of additional benefits.

During World War II a reverse trend became evident, and a majority of the new plans and many old ones were put on a noncontributory basis.

Probably the most important reasons for the change was the wage stabilization policy of the federal government that froze money wages but permitted group insurance as an extra employment benefit. Too, the fact that group insurance premiums paid by the employer usually are deductible as a business expense under the federal income tax law, and are not treated thereunder as income to the employee, no doubt encouraged many companies to absorb all the costs of group insurance and make these benefits available on a nontaxable basis to their employees. Still another factor of special importance since World War II has been the inclusion of group insurance as a negotiated welfare benefit under collective bargaining agreements. Under these arrangements, management often pays the entire cost through a trustee arrangement.

A number of advantages are claimed for the noncontributory, employer-pay-all basis for premium financing, including the following:

1. Simplicity of administration. The insurance records of individual employees under a noncontributory plan are somewhat simpler and, since no payroll deduction procedures are necessary, the employer obviously has fewer accounting operations to perform.
2. Economy of installation and administration. Since all employees are covered, it is not necessary for the insurance company and the employer to go to the expense of soliciting plan membership among individual employees. The continuing expense of soliciting new employees and getting waiver forms from nonsubscribing employees is avoided as well as certain other routine administration costs.
3. Tax advantages. Employer premium costs normally are deductible as an ordinary business expense for federal income tax purposes, whereas employee contributions are not deductible for personal income tax purposes. Furthermore, the employer's contributions usually are not taxable to the employees for federal income tax purposes.
4. All employees insured. All eligible employees who have completed the probationary period and are actively at work have the full amount of insurance. This gives the plan maximum participation and minimizes adverse selection. It avoids problems for the employer which might occur under a contributory plan when an eligible employee did not elect to take the insurance or dropped out of a plan without his dependents' knowledge. Also, there is less likelihood of clerical errors affecting the coverage of an individual.
5. More control of plan. Under a noncontributory plan the employer has more control over changes in coverage and benefits. In the absence of collective bargaining, unilateral action is justified and feasible where employees are not sharing the cost of the plan.

The principal advantages claimed for the contributory plan of financing group insurance benefits are the following:

1. Makes possible larger benefits. For a given money outlay by the employer, a more liberal group plan is available if the employees also contribute. The employer may not be able to afford the entire cost of a plan, and unless the employees contribute, no plan can be installed. In other cases,

employee contributions may permit additional types of insurance coverages or higher amounts of existing coverages.

2. Greater employee interest and appreciation. It is believed that employees generally have more interest in group insurance plans to which they are making some direct contribution. Also, because of their greater awareness of the plan, they probably are more appreciative of its values.

3. More effective use of employer's contributions. It is argued that a contributory plan permits the employer to channel his insurance funds to the more needful and more important employees. In other words, the employees who refuse to participate in a contributory plan are most often the younger single females, who have few insurance needs, and among whom employee turnover is greatest. Therefore, the employer's funds are used more effectively in sharing the cost of benefits for the employees who have greater needs and also who are most likely to make a career of their jobs.

4. Employees have more control. From the standpoint of the employees, the contributory plan affords them a greater voice in the benefits provided. The employer is more likely to respect the opinions of the employees and is less likely to discontinue the plan altogether.

Available evidence indicates that well over 50 per cent of all group life insurance in force is on a contributory basis. An even higher proportion of group health insurance benefits is on the contributory plan. There is some evidence that there is a trend toward providing group insurance benefits on a noncontributory basis, but most of this force seems to come through collectively bargained plans.

GROUP SELECTION

As mentioned earlier, perhaps the most important of the fundamental characteristics of the group technique is that of group selection, the effect of which is to provide life and health insurance coverage on an individual without any inquiry as to the quality of the individual risk and the likelihood of an early loss and claim. This unique element has permitted a rapid extension of group life and health insurance to a majority of our population.

Group insurance companies usually adopt selection standards or underwriting rules which are broad enough to allow acceptance of a large majority of insurable groups at standard premium rates. For certain types of groups, such as those engaged in particularly hazardous industries, the mortality and morbidity rates are consistently higher than for standard groups, and they are classified, therefore, as substandard risks and charged a higher premium rate. In rare situations, a risk may be rejected entirely because the mortality and/or morbidity risk is so great, or unpredictable, that insurance is not practicable.

Within each classification of insurable risks, that is, within the standard class and within each of the several substandard classes, the chance of loss is never exactly the same for all risks or groups. In other words, within each class there are relatively "good" risks and relatively "poor" risks.

Every insurance company is anxious to establish underwriting rules which will result in its getting at least an average proportion of good risks. If such a goal is attained, the average mortality and morbidity cost will be lower, and the company may be able to offer insurance at a lower net cost.[4]

The underwriting rules of any group insurance company, then, may be considered to rest logically on three basic objectives: (1) to obtain the proper balance between mass and homogeneity of risks to afford predictability of future results; (2) to establish standards which will permit acceptance of the large majority of groups at standard premium rates; and (3) to secure the largest possible proportion of the average and better than average risks within each classification. The rules which the various companies adopt to reach these objectives are based on experience, research, intuition and judgment. It is doubtful that the underwriting rules of any two companies are exactly the same.

Theory of Group Selection

Group selection is not concerned with the conditions of health, morals or habits of any particular individual in the group.[5] Instead, group selection is aimed at obtaining a group of persons or, what is even more important, an aggregation of such groups of persons, that will yield a certain predictable rate of mortality or morbidity. If a sufficient mass of risk units (groups of persons in this case) is obtained, and if these risk units are reasonably homogeneous in nature, then advantage can be taken of the predictability of the death and disability perils. There is no conceivable reason why the adoption of the group as the unit of selection is not theoretically sound so long as a proper degree of *mass* and *homogeneity* of risk units is obtained. To assure that the risk units (groups) obtained will be satisfactorily homogeneous, the insurer must determine that certain essential features are either inherent in the nature of the group itself or may be successfully applied in a positive way to avoid adverse selection by entire groups or a large proportion of the individuals within a given group. In the following paragraphs the more important theoretical underwriting principles of group insurance are described.

Insurance Incidental to Group. One of the first elements looked for in the underwriting of group insurance pertains to the inherent nature of the group of persons seeking insurance. If the group is based upon some

---

[4] From a practical standpoint, the concept of experience rating in group insurance affords the larger risks the full benefit of their better than average mortality, and hence their experience does not contribute to the lowering of the average net cost at which the insurer can provide insurance to other risks. See Chapters 12 and 22 for a complete discussion of this subject.

[5] As reflected elsewhere in this *Handbook,* individual risk selection is used at times in group insurance cases, but this does not detract from the theoretical premises of the group concept.

natural, pre-existing relationship, and if it represents a group of individuals bound together by some strong community of interest other than the opportunity to obtain low cost insurance, then a group selection plan may be feasible.

Should the group be organized mainly for the purpose of obtaining group insurance, there is a possibility of selection against the insurer. With no common interest other than life and health insurance, the poorer risks presumably would tend to seek and retain membership in the group, and the healthier persons presumably would tend to be indifferent to joining the group or continuing their membership. Thus, for a plan to be workable, it is desirable that the insurance be only a secondary or unessential feature motivating the formation and existence of the group.

Flow of Persons through the Group. A steady flow of persons through the group is another feature generally essential to sound group underwriting. If there is a stream of new entrants into the group representing the addition of young, healthy lives, and a flow out of the group by the aged and impaired lives, the obvious result is to keep the insurability of the group constantly "sweetened" and the rates of mortality and morbidity more or less stable. This is especially important in those groups where the employer may be unwilling to assume the full burden of any increases in cost resulting from increasing ages of employees in the group, because in this situation the younger employees would tend to drop out of the plan.

Automatic Determination of Benefits. The amount of benefits on individual persons should be determined in some automatic manner which precludes individual selection by either the employer or employees. Should employees have the option to take various amounts of insurance on their own volition, the unhealthy persons probably would tend to insure heavily and the healthy ones would not. If the employer had complete control in determining the amount of insurance on individual persons, there would be considerable chance for him to select against the insurer for the benefit of individual employees. Selection by either the employer or employee would serve to increase greatly the cost of the plan and probably would result in failure of the group insurance program.

Minimum Proportion of Group. Another essential element in sound group underwriting is the requirement that all or substantially all eligible persons in a given group be covered by insurance. In a noncontributory plan, all employees, or all employees in a given class, must be insured. Where employees contribute toward the premium, it usually is required that at least 75 per cent of the eligible employees must be enrolled in the plan, both at issue and thereafter. It is only by covering a large proportion of a given group that an insurer gains a positive safeguard against an undue proportion of substandard lives. Of course, it is likely that permitting less than 100 per cent coverage in contributory groups introduces some degree of adverse selection. Counteracting this, however, is the fact that an insurer's over-all spread of risk is increased, since many employers buy insurance on the contributory plan who would not do so if they had to bear the entire cost. Also, a powerful force at work is the reduction of expenses per individual and per unit of insurance where a high proportion of the group is insured.

Sharing of Cost. Except in unusual circumstances, a group insurance plan on a member-pay-all basis, especially in group life insurance where mortality rates climb sharply with age, possesses the seeds of its own destruction. Some plan of averaging individual premiums is desirable to avoid the increasing premiums for older persons for both life insurance and health insurance. Under member-pay-all coverage, the younger members help to pay for the older members. As they become aware of this, the younger members may tend to leave the group to purchase insurance at less cost elsewhere, thus aggravating the situation by raising average premiums still further. Eventually, if the aged and impaired lives should become the predominating members of the group, the scheme is almost inevitably doomed to failure because of the necessarily large premium charges.

Simplicity and Efficiency of Administration. If members contribute to the cost of group insurance, it is highly desirable that there be some simple, automatic method for them to pay their share, such as, for example, a payroll deduction plan. If the members' contributions are collected in this fashion, it is easier to keep participation at a high level than if each person must take the initiative to remit his contribution. There are many other details in the administration of a group insurance plan which, if left entirely to the employees to handle with the insurer, would be unwieldy and expensive and probably have serious effects on participation. Where administration is handled by an employer (or some other central administrative unit), it often is possible to integrate the activities into other administrative functions to the extent that simplicity and efficiency are attained.

Departures from Group Selection Theory

The foregoing analysis of group selection emphasizes theoretical guideposts. From the very beginning of group insurance, there have been variations from these theoretical requirements where permitted by law and where an insurer has been willing to experiment. Examples include providing insurance coverage for retired persons and writing group insurance on associations established essentially for insurance purposes. Some experiments have been highly successful and others less successful.

In the last decade, particularly, there have been many extensions of the group insurance principle, both "vertically" and "horizontally." Vertical extension has been characterized by increasing amounts of insurance on the lives of individual persons, whereas horizontal extension has been characterized by an ever widening variety of groups (sometimes to the extent of what might be called "fictitious groups" to which the group underwriting principle is applied). Part VI of this *Handbook* analyzes these extensions and the ways in which certain of the above "requirements" of sound underwriting have been circumvented. In addition, it delineates the forces that make some of them successful and others less successful.

SIGNIFICANCE OF THE BASIC CHARACTERISTICS

The characteristics of the group technique analyzed in this chapter are of significance from an economic, social and political standpoint. They are of significance within the insurance institution and to groups that have used this insurance technique to widen the security of their members.

The remarkable expansion in the kinds of group insurance and in the magnitude of benefits provided under group insurance has greatly broadened the ability of private insurance to provide security against premature death, disability and old age. Further, the group mechanism has permitted very efficient expansion of private insurance. It should be recognized, of course, that group insurance, like social insurance, provides security on a mass basis and cannot consider individual needs and desires to the extent that is possible where life and health insurance is provided on an individual basis. From a political standpoint, it seems obvious that the group technique has permitted the expansion of life and health insurance benefits to most members of our society, and this, in turn, has helped the private insurance institution to provide insurance service that might otherwise have been provided within the framework of social insurance.

Within the institution of insurance, the characteristics of the group technique have had an impact on company organization and operation. The organization of the home office of the insurer and the distribution of responsibility among its various departments are determined partly by the definition of group coverages as contrasted to individual coverages.

Certainly the group technique has implications from the standpoint of the self-insurance technique. The modification of the traditional characteristics and qualities of insurable groups seems to strengthen the ability of private insurers to save some of the business that might otherwise switch over to self-insurance. Whether this modification will have unfavorable results from the standpoint of group experience is yet to be seen.

SELECTED REFERENCES

BLACK, KENNETH, JR. *Group Annuities.* Homewood, Ill.: Richard D. Irwin, Inc., 1955.

FITZHUGH, G. W. "Group Life and Disability Insurance on the One-Year Term Premium Basis," *Transactions of the Actuarial Society of America*, Vol. XLVI (1945), p. 238. Discussion, Vol. XLVII (1946), p. 52, by W. A. Milliman, J. M. Woolery, and W. R. Williamson.

GREGG, DAVIS W. *Group Life Insurance.* 3d ed. Homewood, Ill.: Richard D. Irwin, Inc., 1962.

GUERTIN, ALFRED N., AND PIKE, ALBERT, JR. "Memorandum for the Joint ALC–LIAA Committee on Reexamination of Group Policy." New York: Life Insurance Association of America, November 2, 1957, revised to August 23, 1960.

ILSE, LOUISE W. *Group Insurance and Employee Retirement Plans.* Englewood Cliffs, N.J.: Prentice-Hall, Inc., 1953.

PICKRELL, J. F. *Group Health Insurance.* Rev. ed. Homewood, Ill.: Richard D. Irwin, Inc., 1961.

Chapter 4

DEVELOPMENT AND SIGNIFICANCE OF GROUP LIFE INSURANCE

BY C. MANTON EDDY

Group insurance as we now know it is a relatively new invention, having its origins only fifty or sixty years ago. Yet in its brief lifetime it has grown to the point where it now represents a major building block in the economic security program of most American families.

This volume is concerned primarily with the present-day operations of the group insurance mechanism and with the probable patterns of its future development. However, it seems appropriate to consider the background of group insurance in order to understand more fully how group insurance came to be what it is and to estimate more accurately what it is likely to be in the future.

There are two basic branches of group insurance, group life and group health insurance. In this volume the background of each one will be described separately. The present chapter deals only with group life insurance and includes a consideration of the major milestones in its development as well as its present significance.

DEVELOPMENT OF GROUP LIFE INSURANCE IN THE UNITED STATES

Early Development

The development of group life insurance in the United States presents an interesting picture of response to evolving economic and social patterns. At the turn of the century, the industrialization of the country was gaining momentum and creating recognition of the economic security needs of wage earners. In 1907, Professor Henry R. Seager, of Columbia University, suggested a program of social legislation which would bring an application of the principles of insurance to the solution of social problems. He identified industrial accidents, illness, invalidity and old age, premature death and unemployment as contingencies which would threaten the family's standard of living and against which wage earners

45

did not or could not make adequate provision themselves. "In consequence the losses they entail, in the absence of any social provision against them, fall with crushing force on the families which suffer from them, and only too often reduce such families from a position of independence and self-respect to one of humiliating and efficiency-destroying social dependency."[1] Recognition had been growing that existing employers' liability laws were failing to compensate workmen who were injured because of industrial accidents. Workmen's compensation laws were coming into being in many states and were providing improved insurance protection as to one of Professor Seager's contingencies. The growing development of social consciousness of the needs of wage earners and the desire of some employers to do more than "pass the hat" on the untimely death of an employee were factors creating a climate that was favorable for the birth of group life insurance as we know it today.

Montgomery Ward and Company is generally conceded to deserve credit for sparking the development of the concept and structure of group life insurance. The company wished to provide its employees with a definite death benefit at no cost to the individual. It rejected the idea of paying death benefits directly out of company funds and sought to achieve its objective through the use of life insurance. Negotiations for the purchase of life insurance on the employees as a group extended from 1910 to 1912 and resulted in a group contract written by the Equitable Life Assurance Society of the United States dated July 1, 1912. These negotiations interested a director of the Equitable who was also connected with the Pantasote Leather Company of New Jersey. Events there moved more rapidly, and in 1911 the New Jersey company received the first group contract actually written as such, although a few scattered plans covering groups of people had been in existence in the past. Some of the earliest contracts, in fact, had been issued years before covering the lives of coolies as indemnification to the shippers who were transporting them.

The Montgomery Ward group life insurance plan[2] provided a burial fund of $100 upon the death of a covered employee. In addition, a lump-sum death benefit equal to one year's salary, not to exceed $3,000, was paid if the deceased employee did not leave a dependent spouse or child. If, on the other hand, he left a widow, the death benefit was in the form of a weekly income payable for life and guaranteed for four years certain. This benefit, which was equal to 25 per cent of wages, continued for as long as the widow remained unmarried. If she remarried, the weekly

---

[1] John Dewey and James H. Tufts, *Ethics* (New York: Henry Holt & Co., 1908), p. 566.

[2] Louise Wolters Ilse, *Group Insurance and Employee Retirement Plans* (Englewood Cliffs, N.J.: Prentice-Hall, Inc., 1953), pp. 36–45.

income ceased, at which time she received a lump-sum benefit equal to two years' annuity payments.[3]

During the months and years immediately following the announcement of the Montgomery Ward plan, a substantial amount of opposition to group life insurance developed in several sectors of the insurance business. Charges were made that group life insurance constituted discrimination against policyholders who underwent regular medical examinations and that it represented a danger to the solvency of the companies writing this form of insurance. Bitter opposition to group life insurance was voiced by many of the fraternal societies, who regarded the new technique as a threat to their own insurance operations.[4]

Despite this opposition, many other group life insurance plans came into being shortly after the Montgomery Ward plan. In these early plans the maximum amounts usually were limited to $5,000 or $10,000, and these were reached in a comparatively small number of cases.

Only in exceptional instances of very large risks did the amount reach a figure of $20,000. Schedules of fixed amounts also were frequently used and at times were graded by years of service, starting as low as $250 initially. The benefits almost always were provided without cost to the individual. The rapid growth of group life insurance during these early years is evidenced by the fact that by the end of 1917 about 1,500 employers had plans in existence covering 450,000 employees for almost $350 million of insurance.[5]

The National Convention of Insurance Commissioners (NCIC) took early recognition of this new development. At the annual meeting in July, 1912, in Spokane, Washington, the Hon. Burton Mansfield, Insurance Commissioner of Connecticut, presented a paper "Life Insurance in Groups." After an introduction which reviewed progression in social philosophy, he identified some of the basic characteristics of group life insurance, commented on the question of discrimination and concluded with some very favorable observations:

As for the demand, there is perhaps nothing to show that it is spontaneous or born of necessity rather than nurtured by the insurance companies. It does exist, however, and by whatever cause produced it should be respectfully received and considered. . . . We may safely assume therefore that it is here to stay. . . .
Life insurance in groups is a progressive step, in consonance with acts regulating workmen's compensation in case of accident, sickness and death; old

---

[3] It is interesting to note that many of the same concepts underlying the original Montgomery Ward benefit structure are part of the present federal OASDI program.

[4] For an excellent discussion of some of the details of the controversy, see Ilse, *op. cit.*, pp. 48–54.

[5] Institute of Life Insurance, *Life Insurance Fact Book, 1960* (New York, 1960), p. 25.

age pensions and the like all striving for the better protection of those who are employed in mechanical, business or other pursuits. Any plan for its development cannot be perfect at the start. Many obstructions, real or imaginary, may block its progress, but they are only of a temporary nature and it seems to me that as public servants we should welcome such a measure and join with both employer and employed, with both the insurer and the insured in all reasonable efforts for its promotion.[6]

Somewhat later, a paper presented in April, 1917, to the Casualty Actuarial and Statistical Society of America, entitled "Group Life Insurance and Its Possible Development," referred to the first appeal of group insurance as a philanthropic measure but concluded also that ". . . group insurance produces a decided commercial advantage and it is upon this that its popularity in a large measure rests to-day."[7]

Activity in the group life insurance field gained such momentum that definition and control seemed desirable to many of the insurance commissioners. In December, 1917, the NCIC adopted a model bill of definition and standard provisions and, in 1918, this became law in New York, a state of considerable importance in insurance regulation. This definition, which has been important in the development of group life insurance, provided:

Group life insurance is that form of life insurance covering not less than fifty employees with or without medical examination, written under a policy issued to the employer, the premium on which is to be paid by the employer or by the employer and employees jointly, and insuring only all of his employees, or all of any class or classes thereof determined by conditions pertaining to the employment, for amounts of insurance based upon some plan which will preclude individual selection, for the benefit of persons other than the employer: provided, however, that when the premium is to be paid by the employer and employee jointly and the benefits of the policy are offered to all eligible employees not less than seventy-five per cent of such employees may be so insured.[8]

The group life insurance definition made possible a sharing of cost by the employer and employee, but, in fact, on most of the business written prior to 1921 the employer paid all the cost. During World War I, the payroll plan for war bonds promoted the concept of payroll deductions. The general depression in industry in 1921 created a temporary setback in the writing of group life insurance and brought into being greater emphasis on the contributory principle. By 1923, a large proportion of all the group life insurance business then being written was on the contributory

---

[6] *Proceedings of the National Convention of Insurance Commissioners,* 1912, pp. 235–43.

[7] Edward B. Morris, "Group Life Insurance and Its Possible Development," *Proceedings of the Casualty Actuarial and Statistical Society of America,* Vol. III (1916–17), p. 149.

[8] *Proceedings of the National Convention of Insurance Commissioners,* 1918, p. 28.

plan. The U.S. Government Life Insurance program of World War I had helped popularize life insurance ownership, and employers found employees willing to contribute to the group program. Larger amounts of insurance could be provided the individual by that means with the same or even lesser contributions by the employer. For the next two decades, the majority of programs were on the contributory basis.

Later Milestones

Depression Years. By the end of 1930, the group life insurance volume had reached a figure of $9.8 billion. Under the impact of the depression, it dropped to $8.7 billion by the end of 1933. By 1935, however, it had made a rapid recovery to a new high of $10.2 billion. The resiliency of group life insurance and the value in which it was held by employer and employee alike are apparent in the drop of barely 10 per cent despite the severe depression and in the quick recovery it demonstrated as business turned upward.

In 1938, the 75th Congress authorized and directed a select committee to make a full and complete study and investigation with respect to the concentration of economic power in, and financial control over, production and distribution of goods and services. This committee was named the Temporary National Economic Committee. By direction of this committee, the Securities and Exchange Commission was requested to conduct a study of legal reserve life insurance. In the course of this study, lengthy hearings were held with respect to many facets of the life insurance business. Among these were intercompany agreements and understandings which the investigators asserted were anti-competitive. The Group Association was one of the industry associations that was studied. It had been formed in 1926 with the knowledge of state supervisory authorities, and its constitution set forth its purposes as follows:

1. To promote the welfare of holders of group policies;
2. To advance the interests of group insurance;
3. To promote economy and reduce expense in the matter of general administration by an interchange of views on practice among insurance companies which issue contracts of group insurance;
4. To represent the members of the Association in matters pertaining to or which may affect group insurance before the insurance departments and other public and quasi-public bodies; and
5. To collect and analyze the group experience of the members of the Association, but nothing in this constitution, or in any rule adopted subordinate thereto shall be held to authorize the making or promulgation of premium rates.

The investigators contended that competition in the group insurance business had been unduly restricted by means of the Group Association. The member companies denied this strongly. However, the tenor of the investigation and the strong criticism directed at intercompany activities naturally led many to question whether such activities should be continued. The Group Association disbanded shortly thereafter.

World War II. The advent of World War II brought with it price and wage controls. However, the National War Labor Board did not prohibit increased employer contributions to employee benefit plans, including group life insurance. As a result, group life insurance became a popular wage supplement which was quickly evident in labor-management discussions. These wage freezes undoubtedly contributed importantly to the fact that the volume of group life insurance in force increased nearly 50 per cent during the period 1940 to 1945.

Postwar Years. On June 5, 1944, the Supreme Court of the United States handed down its decision in the South-Eastern Underwriters Association case.[9] The decision stated, in part, that the business of insurance was commerce. This reversed the historic decision to the contrary by the Court in 1869 in *Paul* v. *Virginia*.[10] As commerce, the business of insurance conducted across state lines was subject suddenly to certain federal statutes, importantly among them being the Sherman Act, the Clayton Act and the Robinson-Patman Act. Until then, the business of insurance had been subject only to state regulation. Congress quickly established its wish to have this continue, provided state regulation was effective. It did so through the passage of Public Law 15 of 1945, often referred to as the McCarran Act. This federal statute provided for a moratorium during which certain federal statutes, such as the Robinson-Patman Act, would not apply to the insurance business. It provided further that after the expiration of the moratorium, federal regulation would apply to interstate aspects of the business of insurance to the extent that it was not adequately regulated at the state level. While Public Law 15 accomplished its purpose of continued state regulation of insurance, it did not remove the consequences of challenge to industry agreements on practices under the Sherman and Clayton Acts.

Thereafter, insurance regulatory officials made concentrated efforts to strengthen state insurance regulation. One outgrowth of this activity was the adoption by the National Association of Insurance Commissioners of a new group life insurance model bill for possible inclusion in state insurance codes. More up-to-date, uniform regulation had become necessary because of the many changes that had taken place in the group life insurance business during the thirty years since the 1917 model bill had been adopted. Laws had been amended in individual states from time to time to extend eligibility to a wide variety of groups not contemplated in the original model bill—debtor groups, dependents of insured group

---

[9] 322 U.S. Reports 534.
[10] 8 Wall. 168.

members, multiple-employer groups, groups of less than fifty members and a host of miscellaneous groups. Moreover, most of the states had failed to enact any comprehensive group life insurance statutes by the mid-1940's. As a result, in 1946 the NAIC adopted a new model bill relating to group life insurance. Although it has since been revised a number of times in certain respects, the 1946 model bill has remained the foundation for the current regulation of group life insurance in most states.[11]

In 1949, the Supreme Court handed down a decision of major importance to the development of group life insurance. This decision, which constituted a reaffirmation of a ruling by the National Labor Relations Board in the Inland Steel Company case, established beyond question the fact that the right of labor to bargain collectively over wages, hours or other conditions of employment included bargaining over retirement and insurance plans.[12] This removed any doubt that group life insurance and other benefits were within the scope of collective bargaining.

Another important stimulus to the growth of group life insurance came in the early 1950's. At that time the Korean war brought about a reintroduction of wage and price controls and renewed emphasis on employee benefits as against wage increases.

A further significant impetus was provided group life insurance in 1954 when the federal government decided to insure death benefits for its more than two and one-half million employees. At the end of 1963, the volume in force was $16.6 billion, making it the largest group life insurance case in the world. More than 200 life insurance companies are participating as reinsurers of the plan which is administered by the Metropolitan Life Insurance Company.[13]

During the years since the Korean war, the volume of group life insurance has increased threefold. In the process of collective bargaining, unions and management regularly review employee benefits as well as wages. Bargaining frequently has been extended industry-wide, and it is common practice to issue group policies to trustees of a fund established by two or more employers and one or more labor unions. By 1956, the definition of group life insurance again was expanded by the National Association of Insurance Commissioners to include the foregoing in its model bill. Another change of substance has been the lowering of the minimum number of lives to ten in most states, and this has opened the field of coverage more effectively to the small employer.

Another important statutory development brought about changes in

---

[11] Chapter 6 contains a complete discussion of the current regulatory environment of group life insurance.

[12] 339 U.S. Reports 382.

[13] For a detailed discussion of the Federal Employees Group Life Insurance plan, see Chapter 9.

amounts of insurance per life. Previous limits on maximum amounts were removed, and amounts of insurance of $100,000 or even more were, at times, made possible in large cases. Benefit schedules of one year's earnings frequently were expanded to two or three times annual earnings. Concern has been expressed by the National Association of Life Underwriters that, through these larger amounts, group insurance is expanding outside of its proper sphere. Some states, by statute, have limited amounts of insurance to a maximum of $40,000 provided further that the amount of insurance in excess of $20,000 may not exceed 150 per cent of the employee's annual salary. Other states have provided for higher amounts up to $100,000, and a great number of states, including such important ones as New York, Michigan and California, have no statutory limit.[14]

The fact that the purchase of group term life insurance by an employer created no taxable income to the individual employee had been an important factor in the pressure for large amounts on the lives of executives. The income tax act of 1964 has limited such tax-free status to a maximum amount of $50,000, and in the future it is possible that pressures for large individual amounts may diminish. The fact remains, however, that the low acquisition and administrative expenses associated with group insurance continue to make the cost of such coverage attractive despite the taxability of part of the employer's contribution to certain employees.

GROWTH OF GROUP LIFE INSURANCE

In the course of slightly over fifty years, group life insurance has experienced a prodigious growth. As indicated in Table 4–1, the aggregate amount in force in the United States has increased in every year with the exception of a few years during the depression and one year at the end of World War II.

The current total amount of group life insurance, somewhat in excess of $228 billion, includes $3 billion on the lives of dependents and represents an average amount per certificate of approximately $4,500. The average amount of individual life insurance per policy is only about $4,100. Since group life insurance now constitutes almost one third of the total life insurance in force in the United States, it obviously has become a factor of major importance.

DEVELOPMENT OF GROUP LIFE INSURANCE IN OTHER COUNTRIES

With the exception of Canada, group life insurance did not have the early start nor has it had the phenomenal growth in many other countries throughout the world that has been the case in the United States. In part, this may be due to the lesser emphasis on life insurance in many of these countries. There have been only a few countries where in recent years

---

[14] Chapter 31 is devoted to a detailed discussion of this topic.

TABLE 4–1

GROUP LIFE INSURANCE IN FORCE IN THE UNITED STATES
(000 Omitted)

Year	No. of Master Policies	No. of Certificates	Amount	Year	No. of Master Policies	No. of Certificates	Amount
1912......	*	12	$ 13,000	1943......	28	12,700	$ 22,413,000
1915......	.3	120	100,000	1944......	29	12,800	23,922,000
1920......	6	1,600	1,570,000	1945......	31	11,500	22,172,000
1925......	12	3,200	4,247,000	1946......	34	13,200	27,206,000
1926......	13	3,800	5,362,000	1947......	40	15,600	32,026,000
1927......	15	4,400	6,333,000	1948......	46	16,300	37,068,000
1928......	17	5,000	7,889,000	1949......	52	17,258	40,207,000
1929......	19	5,700	8,994,000	1950......	56	19,288	47,793,000
1930......	19	5,800	9,801,000	1951......	61	21,458	54,398,000
1931......	19	5,600	9,736,000	1952......	68	23,590	62,913,000
1932......	18	4,800	8,923,000	1953......	75	26,463	72,913,000
1933......	16	4,900	8,681,000	1954......	81	28,624	86,395,000
1934......	17	5,500	9,472,000	1955......	89	31,640	101,300,000
1935......	18	6,400	10,208,000	1956......	106	34,918	117,324,000
1936......	18	6,800	11,291,000	1957......	120	37,378	133,794,000
1937......	19	7,400	12,638,000	1958......	134	38,716	144,607,000
1938......	20	6,600	12,503,000	1959......	154	41,260	159,807,000
1939......	20	7,600	13,641,000	1960......	169	43,507	175,434,000
1940......	23	8,800	14,938,000	1961......	180	46,154	192,202,000
1941......	24	10,200	17,359,000	1962......	193	48,434	209,178,000
1942......	25	11,100	19,316,000	1963......	203	50,908	228,540,000

* Fewer than fifty policies.
Source: Institute of Life Insurance.

total life insurance ownership equaled at least half of the national income. In the United States, the second ranking country, the ratio is about 150 per cent. In Canada, which has ranked first for many years, the ratio now is approximately 180 per cent. A country's economic development obviously influences the extent of life insurance protection. This is particularly true in the case of group life insurance which is so closely tied to employment and wage levels. The social system of a nation is also a factor, and the government security systems of many countries are much older and more extensive than in the United States and have appeared to preempt the field of protection for the individual. To a great degree, the United States has preferred systems of voluntary, private protection to compulsory government systems wherever possible.

In Great Britain and in the British Commonwealth countries, with the exception of Canada, insurance has tended more toward the savings forms than the term forms. In addition to the state social benefits, death benefits have tended more in the direction of widows' pensions and have made the growth of group term insurance very limited.

In the Latin American countries, there is generally the social philosophy which places more emphasis on benefits for the living and on endowment forms of insurance. There are in existence compulsory benefit programs, and there has been an absence of union pressures on employers. There has been, up to now, very little evidence of group life insurance.

In Japan, group life insurance came into being first in 1934, but it had very little early growth. In the last decade, however, with the development of the economy, a number of additional life insurance companies entered the group insurance field. Between 1959 and 1963, group life insurance increased two and one-half times to a total of approximately $5.5 billion of insurance, which represented approximately 15 per cent of the total life insurance in force in the country.

On the European continent, there has been some substantial evidence that the group life insurance business has been developing into an important factor in a number of countries. Trends in welfare benefits are in evidence, and there are pressures from the trade unions. In Belgium, France and the Federal Republic of Germany a large part of the insurance has been on permanent forms, rather than term.

DEVELOPMENT OF GROUP LIFE INSURANCE IN CANADA

Canada and the United States are closely related by geography and language. Canadian life insurance companies are welcome to do business in the United States and United States companies in Canada, provided, of course, the applicable regulatory requirements are met. The development of group life insurance in Canada parallels very closely that in the United States. In Canada, group life insurance was first permitted under the Insurance Act of 1917, and its pattern of growth is very similar to growth in the United States. The major difference between the two countries lies in the extent of group insurance regulation. In the United States legislation has tended to define and restrict the forms of group life insurance, whereas in Canada there is, in effect, freedom from such detailed legislation. Table 4–2 shows the growth of group life insurance in Canada and its relation to the growth of individual life insurance.

SIGNIFICANCE OF GROUP LIFE INSURANCE

Group life insurance now has developed to a point of such magnitude that it possesses great significance for all of society, but particularly for life insurance companies, employers and employees and their dependents. First, from the standpoint of the group writing insurers, obviously group life insurance has been a significant source of premium revenue, and for the most part a profitable source. In addition, its growth has significant implications for the field of individual life insurance. Whether these implications will promote or hinder individual life insurance sales, however, is a question concerning which considerable difference of opinion remains.

Some observers regard group life insurance as an important means of

TABLE 4–2

LIFE INSURANCE IN FORCE IN CANADA
Federally Registered Companies
(000,000 Omitted)

End of Year	Ordinary	Industrial	Group	Total
1890	$ 246	$ 2	———	$ 248
1900	415	16	———	431
1910	774	82	———	856
1920	2,275	305	$ 77	2,657
1925	3,465	553	141	4,159
1930	5,156	854	482	6,492
1935	4,926	824	509	6,259
1940	5,318	928	729	6,975
1945	7,374	1,313	1,064	9,751
1950	11,625	1,538	2,583	15,746
1951	12,563	1,582	3,090	17,235
1952	13,617	1,625	3,849	19,091
1953	14,835	1,667	4,725	21,227
1954	16,090	1,705	5,339	23,134
1955	17,634	1,694	6,123	25,451
1956	19,857	1,668	7,562	29,087
1957	22,324	1,599	9,164	33,087
1958	24,549	1,543	10,404	36,496
1959	26,781	1,503	12,590	40,874
1960	29,293	953	14,403	44,649
1961	31,304	908	16,072	48,284
1962	33,317	867	18,049	52,233
1963	35,579	823	20,402	56,804

Source: The Canadian Life Insurance Officers Association, *Canadian Life Insurance Facts 1964.*

increasing individual life insurance sales. They argue that it helps make individuals more aware of the functions and advantages of adequate life insurance protection and can be an important source of prospects for individual life underwriters. Others contend, however, that group insurance places undue emphasis on term insurance and insufficient emphasis on the values of permanent insurance tailor-made to fit the particular needs of the insured. Further, they fear that the growth of group life insurance reduces the market for individual life insurance.

Perhaps the next fifty years of group life insurance's development will provide the answer to this question. At least for the immediate future, however, each group writing insurance company must continue to wrestle with the problem of the proper role of group versus individual life insurance.

A second aspect of the significance of group life insurance is its importance to employers. In addition to the sizable cost it entails, group life insurance is significant because of the financial advantages it brings to employers. Certainly not the least of these advantages is the fact that it provides a means whereby the employer is enabled to meet, at least in part, whatever responsibility he may have to assist his employees in hedging against the monetary loss arising out of premature death.

Probably the greatest significance of group life insurance lies in the services it performs for the insured employees and their dependents. For many of these it is their major form of private life insurance protection; for some, it is their only form. The group technique has made life insurance available to large numbers who, by reason of inertia, inadequate income or uninsurability, would otherwise have little or no life insurance. At least to this extent there can be no question of its value.

Finally, group life insurance has significance to society as a whole in that it has helped promote certain social goals which in the United States generally are held to be desirable. It has aided greatly in reducing the burden placed upon society when a deceased employee's dependents are left without adequate income. In the absence of group life insurance many would be forced to rely on charity for their support.

In addition, it probably has helped reduce the need for further intervention by government into the business of life insurance. Group life insurance has provided an outstanding example of how the social problem of financial loss to dependents due to premature death of the breadwinner can be met within the framework of the private enterprise system.

SELECTED REFERENCES

"Group Life Thrives in Japan; Tax Break Spur to Funded Pension Plans," *Employee Benefit Plan Review*, April, 1964, p. 54.

ILSE, LOUISE WOLTERS. *Group Insurance and Employee Retirement Plans.* Englewood Cliffs, N.J.: Prentice-Hall, Inc., 1953.

MANSFIELD, BURTON. "Life Insurance in Groups." *Proceedings of The National Convention of Insurance Commissioners* (1912), p. 235. Discussion, p. 71.

MORRIS, EDWARD B. "Group Life Insurance and Its Possible Development," *Proceedings of the Casualty Actuarial and Statistical Society of America*, Vol. III (1916–17), p. 149.

Sweden: Its Private Insurance and Social Security, A Short Survey. Compiled by the Association of Swedish Insurance Companies, Stockholm, 1963.

Chapter 5

DEVELOPMENT AND SIGNIFICANCE
OF GROUP HEALTH INSURANCE

BY J. F. FOLLMANN, JR.

One of the most prominent developments in the insurance business in the United States during the past thirty years has been the growth of group health insurance. Concerned initially with providing coverage against the loss of income as a result of nonoccupational illnesses and injuries, and then extending to provide protection against the costs of medical care, group health insurance has become an institution of significance to the economy of the nation and to millions of individuals and families.

In many respects the development of the system of group health insurance found in the United States is unique. The high proportion of the population in the United States covered on a voluntary basis today has been possible only as a result of the resilience, dynamism and flexibility which have become characteristic of the group health insurance business.

EARLY DEVELOPMENT OF GROUP HEALTH INSURANCE

Development in Other Nations

The concept of spreading the personal economic risks inherent in injuries and illnesses on a mutual aid or insurance principle is not new. Examples include the artisans of imperial Rome, the craft guilds in medieval England, and subsequently the mutual aid systems which developed in Great Britain in the nineteenth century and which came to be known as Friendly Societies and Saturday Funds. As industrialization spread throughout much of the European continent, systems of mutual aid or insurance developed in Germany, Denmark, Sweden, Norway, Switzerland and the Netherlands. In the main, these systems were in the nature of sick clubs, mutual benefit funds, cooperatives, or societies developed variously by local groups or unions of craftsmen or other workers, by individual employers for the benefit of their employees, by physicians or medical societies, by religious groups, by rural groups or by private individuals or insurance companies. In most instances these plans appear to have been small and confined to a particular community or to certain people within a community, such as those employed in a certain plant or belonging to a particular trade union. The benefits provided appear, generally, to have been low, limited and lacking in diversity.

The provision of medical care benefits through governmental compulsion dates from 1883 in Bismarck Germany. By 1962, fifty-three nations had some form of compulsory governmental program to provide benefits for the costs of medical care, and fifty-four nations had a compulsory governmental program to supplement income lost as a result of nonoccupational illness or injury. The details of the programs differ markedly with respect to such major variants as the segments and proportions of the population covered, the types and degree of medical expenses covered, the methods of administration and financing and the employment or nonemployment of private insurance by such programs. There also are marked differences in the degree to which private insurance programs provide, or are not permitted to provide, coverages which supplement the benefits provided by the compulsory government program. While the various types of nongovernmental health insurance plans developed in other nations were concerned, in effect, with specific or localized groups of people, it is doubtful that they made any direct or significant contribution to the system of group health insurance developed by the insurance companies in the United States.

Development in the United States

Protection against the personal economic hazards inherent in illness and injury is made available in the United States in many forms and by several types of insurers. These include insurance companies, Blue Cross and other hospital prepayment plans, Blue Shield and other medical society approved plans, dental service corporations, group medical practice plans operating on a prepayment basis, community plans, vision care plans, industrial plans, plans self-administered by employers or labor unions, prepaid prescription drug plans, fraternal societies' plans, college health plans and rural or consumer health cooperatives. Each type of insurer has its own approach. Each serves a distinct purpose.

The following discussion outlines the milestones in the development of the private health insurance system found in the United States today.

Developments Prior to World War I. In 1847 the first insurer to issue sickness insurance was organized: the Massachusetts Health Insurance Company of Boston. In 1850 the first accident insurance company, the Franklin Health Assurance Company of Massachusetts, was formed. Neither of these companies is actively functioning today. The Travelers Insurance Company entered the accident insurance field in 1863 and contributed greatly to that form of insurance as it is known today. Other insurance companies formed for similar purposes prior to 1895 offered

coverage on an individual policy basis and were concerned with accidental death, dismemberment and loss of income resulting from accident or
sickness. Shortly after the turn of the century the first attempts by insurance companies to insure the costs of medical care (surgery, 1903; hospital, 1905; medical treatment, 1910; nursing care in the home, 1916)
became evident. These coverages were, however, incidental to the previously established pattern of coverage.

During the 1880's, establishment funds developed on a group basis
in the United States to provide small cash payments to workers in the
event of illness or injury. In the following decade workmen's collective
insurance, as an adjunct to employers' liability insurance, developed as
a forerunner to workmen's compensation insurance. About 1880 another
development occurred which eventually assumed significant proportions.
Prepayment arrangements for hospital care were developed by a few
separate hospitals in northern Minnesota to provide for the payment
of hospital services to lumberjacks. These plans subsequently failed financially.

Group health insurance initially developed in the United States in the
early part of the twentieth century as a response to the growing industrialization in the nation, the increasing degree to which people worked
together in large groups, and to the employers' and labor unions' realiza-
tion that employed persons needed economic protection against the unfore-
seeable losses which result from premature death and disability. The first
evidence of group insurance by insurance companies in the United States
appears to be a contract written by the Travelers Insurance Company in
1890 covering the members of the fire-fighting force in Baltimore. It is
probable, however, that this early effort is more analogous to what is
known today as blanket insurance than it is to group insurance. Generally,
it is recognized that a disability income contract written by the London
Guarantee and Accident Company on the employees of Montgomery
Ward and Company in 1911 represents the inception of group health
insurance in America.[1] The first noticeable impetus to the development of
group health insurance occurred as a result of increased business activity
during World War I. This paralleled organized labor's early interest in
workmen's compensation insurance at a time when employers had commenced to recognize a responsibility for the health and welfare of their
employees.

Birth and Expansion of Blue Cross–Blue Shield Plans. In 1921, a
hospital in Grinnell, Iowa, offered care on a prepaid basis. This was

---

[1] Among the other early writers of group health insurance were the Equitable
Life Assurance Society of the United States, the Continental Casualty Company,
the Great Eastern Casualty Company, the Connecticut General Life Insurance Company, the Metropolitan Life Insurance Company and the Aetna Life Insurance
Company. Several of these companies were already writing group life insurance
coverages, and several were well established in the individual disability income policy
field.

followed in 1929 by the formation of a prepaid hospital arrangement at Baylor University Hospital in Dallas, Texas, for the faculty at the University. This development is generally considered the forerunner of the Blue Cross plans. With the economically depressed years of the 1930's, the financing of hospitals became precarious, and other hospital prepayment programs were developed. In 1932, the first city-wide plan was offered by the hospitals in Sacramento, California, and by 1935 the shift to community-wide programs became general. The Blue Cross symbol for such plans was used first in St. Paul, Minnesota, in 1933. In 1939, this symbol, with the seal of the American Hospital Association superimposed, was adopted by the American Hospital Association to identify all non-profit plans which had met AHA standards and received its approval. Most of these programs functioned on a group administrative and underwriting basis.

During the same period prepayment plans for medical care services also began in the Northwest where contracts were made with physicians and hospitals for the care of employees in the mining, lumbering and railroading industries. It was not until 1939, however, that the first state-wide, prepaid, medical society sponsored plan was developed in California. Plans in Michigan and Western New York followed closely. Also, in 1939, the medical society sponsored plan of Buffalo, New York, was the first to adopt the Blue Shield symbol. This symbol, which signifies the plans are approved, nonprofit, medical society sponsored organizations, gradually came to be used by similar plans, although not all medical society sponsored plans are Blue Shield plans. In 1943, the American Medical Association created a Council on Medical Service to provide a source of information on medical service plans and to establish standards for such plans. As with the hospital prepayment plans, the medical service plans functioned principally on an employer group basis; however, family coverage and conversion privileges were provided by many plans from the onset.

Development of Other Health Care Plans.   Other approaches to financing the costs of medical care had also developed by the late 1930's. It is not possible to fully categorize or document these here. Most were sponsored by employers, employee associations, employers and employees jointly, or labor unions. Many were related to the spread of the network of railroads across the nation in the latter part of the nineteenth century and to the development of industries in the West and in areas where hospital and medical care were not readily available. The larger of the labor union sponsored plans developed somewhat later, however; the ILGWU program which began in 1913 was one of the earliest.

Still other approaches were community-wide programs that frequently, although not always, functioned on a prepayment basis with the care provided by physicians practicing in groups. These programs were initiated in the late 1930's, although their fuller development came in the period following World War II. Private medical group practice clinics functioning on a prepayment basis came into being in California in 1929. More details with respect to these various approaches appear later in this chapter and in Chapter 15. In addition, many cooperative organizations, particularly in rural areas, developed forms of cooperative payment for medical care services, although the largest, the Group Health Cooperative of Puget Sound, was not formed until 1947. In general, these programs functioned predominantly on a group basis.

Expansion of Health Insurance Companies. Following the development of the Blue Cross and Blue Shield plans, insurance companies gradually came to offer coverages specifically designed to provide protection against the costs of hospital care, surgery and other forms of medical care. Their reasons included a desire to serve their insureds more fully, a desire for expansion, and eventually a need to meet the competition of other insurance companies which had already entered the field. By 1938 hospital insurance for dependents of covered persons was developed, and surgical insurance for employees and their dependents emerged. By the end of the 1940's, the insurance companies were unquestionably established in the field of medical care coverages, and their position was further enhanced in 1949 by the introduction of major medical expense insurance by the Liberty Mutual Insurance Company.

GROWTH OF GROUP HEALTH INSURANCE

The importance which group health insurance has achieved in the national economy becomes evident from an examination of its growth in recent years. This growth is demonstrable in several ways, including (1) the number and variety of health insurers; (2) the number of persons with protection against the costs of medical care, and loss of income resulting from illness or injury; (3) the premium volume of health insurers; and (4) the amounts of benefits paid by health insurers.

Number of Insuring Organizations

One important measurement of economic growth is the number of producing, servicing and outlet agencies available to the public. All of these have a direct effect upon growth by increasing the availability of the product or service to the consumer, by heightening the effects of competition and by increasing the degree of diversity offered the consumer. They also are indicative of the degree of vitality in an economic enterprise. In the field of insurance, this growth is represented by the number of insuring organizations and, implicitly, by the number of marketing and servicing outlets which represent them.

In 1963, there were some 1,800 private health-insuring organizations in the United States. Of these, 903 were insurance companies, seventy-seven were Blue Cross plans, seventy-two were Blue Shield or medical society approved plans and some 800 were other types of plans. This latter category includes 668 industrial plans, seventy-five community plans, thirty-two private group clinics, twenty-two medical society plans, ten dental service corporations and an unknown number of college health plans.[2]

Not all the 903 companies writing health insurance in 1963 wrote group health insurance. Some offered individual insurance policies only, some offered group insurance coverage only, and some offered both. In 1963, 588 of the 903 insurance companies made coverages available on a group basis. This number has increased phenomenally from the thirty-seven companies which offered such coverages in 1942. This growth in the insurance company field for selected years between 1942 and 1963 is shown in Table 5–1.

TABLE 5–1

NUMBER OF INSURANCE COMPANIES WRITING GROUP HEALTH
INSURANCE IN THE UNITED STATES,
1942, 1951, 1960 AND 1963

Year	Number Writing Group Insurance
1942	37
1951	212
1960	474
1963	588

SOURCE: *Spectator Health Insurance Index, Argus Chart, Health Insurance Review* and Health Insurance Association of America.

All Blue Cross plans predominantly employ group enrollment techniques. Here, again, considerable growth is in evidence, although this growth was most rapid in the late 1930's and early 1940's. This is demonstrated by the fact that while nineteen such plans had developed by 1935, this number had grown to eighty-one by 1947. Since that time there has been a leveling off, however. In 1963, there were seventy-seven such plans in existence in the United States, the slight decrease from the 1947 total resulting principally from mergers among existing plans.

Blue Shield and medical society approved plans also utilize group enrollment techniques primarily. The first plan was established in 1939, seven others were organized by 1942, thirteen more by 1945, and twelve more in 1946. By 1963 eighty-two such plans were in existence.

The vast majority of the so-called other types of insuring organizations function primarily through group enrollment. The 668 so-called industrial plans operative in 1963 were employer, employee, employer-employee or labor union sponsored.[3] Inherently, then, these plans function on a group enrollment basis.

---

[2] The various types of insuring organizations, the methods by which they function and the nature of their benefits are described in detail in Chapters 13 through 15.

[3] Such as the programs established by the Endicott-Johnson Corporation, the Consolidated Edison Company, the International Ladies' Garment Workers Union and the United Mine Workers Union.

The seventy-five plans classified as community plans function entirely or principally on a group enrollment basis. Perhaps the best known of the community plans are the Kaiser Foundation Health Plan; the Health Insurance Plan of Greater New York; the Group Health Association of Washington, D.C.; the Community Health Association of Detroit; and Group Health Insurance, Inc., of New York. The Kaiser Health Foundation Plan is somewhat exceptional, with 20 per cent of its members having subscribed on an individual basis.

The thirty-two private group clinics functioning on a prepayment basis (such as the Ross-Loos Medical Group, the Palo Alto Clinic and the Rip Van Winkle Clinic) also generally enroll on a group basis, as do the ten dental service corporations. Then, too, the unknown number of college health plans in effect constitute an operation functioning on either a group or a blanket basis. Many of the larger universities make no attempt to identify those covered by their health plan. One needs only to be a student at such universities at the time of disability to be entitled to coverage, and this approach thus constitutes blanket coverage.

Because of the difficulty in documenting the development of these various other types of plans, it is not possible to indicate categorically their growth in numbers. Many unquestionably have been in existence for a long time. The probability is that the growth, in terms of numbers of plans, has not been great in recent years, although several important plans have developed since World War II. The following list indicates the dates on which specific plans were established. Since all have a large or reasonably large enrollment, this listing presents some crude indication of a growth pattern.

    1913—International Ladies' Garment Workers Union, New York
    1929—Ross-Loos Medical Group, California
    1937—Group Health Association, Washington, D.C.
    1938—Kaiser Foundation Health Plan, West Coast
    1938—Group Health Insurance, Inc., New York
    1946—United Mine Workers of America Welfare and Retirement Fund
    1946—Health Insurance Plan of Greater New York
    1947—Group Health Cooperative of Puget Sound, Washington
    1950—Group Health Dental Insurance, Inc., New York
    1955—California Dental Service Corporation
    1960—Community Health Association of Detroit

From the foregoing it is evident that a tremendous growth has occurred in the United States over the past thirty years with respect to the number of agencies which underwrite various health risks on a group enrollment basis.

Number of Persons Covered

Number with Medical Expense Coverage.   Another important indication of the growth of group health insurance is found in the rapid

TABLE 5–2

Number of People with Hospital Expense Protection in the United States,
by Type of Insurer, 1940–63
(000 Omitted)

End of Year	Grand Total*	Type of Insurer			Blue Cross, Blue Shield and Medi- cal Society Plans	Independ- ent Plans
		Insurance Companies				
		Total†	Group Policies	Individual and Family Policies		
1940..........	12,312	3,700	2,500	1,200	6,012	2,600
1945..........	32,068	10,504	7,804	2,700	18,899	2,665
1950..........	76,639	36,955	22,305	17,296	38,822	3,619
1955..........	107,662	59,654	39,029	26,706	50,726	4,530
1960..........	131,962	78,885	55,218	32,902	58,050	5,542
1962..........	141,437	85,174	59,153	36,061	60,566	6,993
1963..........	145,329	88,127	60,547	38,065	61,659	7,221

* Net total of people protected—eliminates duplication among persons protected by more than one kind of insuring organization or more than one insurance company policy providing the same type of coverage.

† Net total of people with insurance company protection.

Source: Health Insurance Council.

extension of its coverages for medical expenses in terms of the number of persons covered. Tables 5–2, 5–3, 5–4 and 5–5 display this growth pattern

TABLE 5–3

Number of People with Surgical Expense Protection in the United States,
by Type of Insurer, 1940–63
(000 Omitted)

End of Year	Grand Total*	Type of Insurer			Blue Cross, Blue Shield and Medi- cal Society Plans	Independ- ent Plans
		Insurance Companies				
		Total†	Group Policies	Individual and Family Policies		
1940..........	5,350	2,280	1,430	850	370	2,700
1945..........	12,890	7,337	5,537	1,800	2,845	2,708
1950..........	54,156	33,428	21,219	13,718	19,690	2,919
1955..........	91,927	56,645	39,725	22,445	39,165	4,340
1960..........	121,045	75,305	55,504	28,209	50,281	6,573
1962..........	131,185	81,983	59,787	31,443	51,769	8,241
1963..........	134,908	84,958	60,944	33,745	52,474	8,562

* Net total of people protected—eliminates duplication among persons protected by more than one kind of insuring organization or more than one insurance company policy providing the same type of coverage.

† Net total of people with insurance company protection.

Source: Health Insurance Council.

TABLE 5–4

NUMBER OF PEOPLE WITH REGULAR MEDICAL PROTECTION* IN THE
UNITED STATES, BY TYPE OF INSURER, 1940–63
(000 Omitted)

| | | Type of Insurer | | | | |
| | | Insurance Companies | | | Blue Cross, Blue Shield and Medi- | |
End of Year	Grand Total†	Total‡	Group Policies	Individual and Family Policies	cal Society Plans	Independ- ent Plans
1940............ 3,000		—	—	—	200	2,800
1945............ 4,713		535	335	200	1,300	2,878
1950............21,589		8,001	5,587	2,714	11,428	2,873
1955............55,506		25,031	20,678	6,264	29,451	4,639
1960............87,541		41,312	35,802	8,902	45,017	6,773
1962............98,204		47,010	40,012	10,974	48,093	8,343
1963...........102,177		49,708	42,066	11,884	49,302	8,647

*Coverage for physicians visits.
† Net total of people protected—eliminates duplication among persons protected by more than one kind of insuring organization or more than one insurance company policy providing the same type of coverage.
‡ Net total of people with insurance company protection.
SOURCE: Health Insurance Council.

separately by types of coverages and type of insuring organizations.

From these tables it may be observed that during the period from 1940 to 1963 most health insurance coverage provided by insurance companies was written on a group basis. The proportion of insurance companies'

TABLE 5–5

NUMBER OF PEOPLE WITH MAJOR MEDICAL AND COMPREHENSIVE MEDICAL
EXPENSE PROTECTION* IN THE UNITED STATES, 1951–63
(000 Omitted)

| | | Group Policies | | | Individual and Family Policies |
End of Year	Grand Total	Total	Supple- mentary	Compre- hensive	
1952.......... 689		533	533	—	156
1954.......... 2,198		1,892	1,841	51	306
1956.......... 8,876		8,294	6,881	1,413	582
1958..........17,375		16,229	11,072	5,157	1,146
1960..........27,448		25,608	17,285	8,323	1,840
1962..........38,250		35,053	25,301	9,752	3,197
1963..........42,010		38,268	28,248	10,020	3,742

* Represents people covered by insurance companies only.
SOURCE: Health Insurance Council.

hospital expense coverage that is written on a group basis has varied, however, as follows:

```
1940...........................67%
1945...........................74
1950...........................60
1955...........................65
1960...........................70
1963...........................61
```

In that period, insurance company group insurance coverage for hospital expenses increased from 2.5 million people to 60.5 million.

Another observation is that after 1951 insurance companies covered more persons for hospital insurance than did Blue Cross plans. By the end of 1963, 56 per cent of all persons protected against hospital expenses were covered by insurance companies, 39 per cent by Blue Cross–Blue Shield and 5 per cent by other types of plans. By 1963, the insurance company group coverages protected almost as many people as did the Blue Cross–Blue Shield plans.

In the decade 1953–63 hospital insurance issued by insurance companies on a group basis increased 80 per cent in terms of the number of people covered, while the growth rate was 62 per cent for insurance company individual and family policies, 35 per cent for Blue Cross–Blue Shield plans[4] and 49 per cent for other types of plans. In that same period the growth rate for surgical insurance in terms of numbers of persons covered was as follows: insurance company group coverage, 72 per cent; insurance company individual coverage, 67 per cent; Blue Cross, Blue Shield, and medical society approved plans, 67 per cent;[5] and other plans, 71 per cent.

The growth rate for physician nonsurgical care coverage was: insurance company group coverage, 205 per cent; insurance company individual coverage, 104 per cent; Blue Cross, Blue Shield, and medical society approved plans,[6] 127 per cent; and other plans, 64 per cent. A similar comparison cannot be made with respect to major medical expense insurance since data for insurers other than insurance companies are not available. The growth of group major medical insurance between 1953 and 1963 is noteworthy, however, as the number covered increased from 1 million persons to over 38 million persons.[7]

Number with Disability Income Coverage. The growth of group medical expense coverage has been paralleled to a considerable extent by

---

[4] Includes individual and group members.

[5] *Ibid.*

[6] *Ibid.*

[7] This growth can be compared with the growth in individual and family major medical expense policies in the same period from 156,000 persons to 3.7 million persons.

the development of group protection against loss of income. At the end of 1963, 47 million persons in the work force had some type of disability income protection. Of these, 34.9 million were covered by insurance companies, 10.9 million through formal (noninsured) paid sick leave plans in private industry and all levels of government employment, and 1.1 million through other arrangements. Of the insurance company coverages, 23 million were covered by group plans and 15 million under individual policies. The growth rate for disability income protection by types of plans for the period 1946–63 is shown in Table 5–6.

TABLE 5–6

NUMBER OF PEOPLE WITH LOSS OF INCOME PROTECTION IN THE
UNITED STATES, BY TYPE OF PROGRAM, 1946–63
(000 Omitted)

| End of Year | Grand Total | Insurance Companies | | | Formal Paid Sick Leave Plans† | Other‡ |
		Total*	Group Policies	Individual Policies		
1946 26,229		14,369	7,135	8,684	8,400	3,460
1950 37,793		25,993	15,104	13,067	8,900	2,900
1955 39,513		29,813	19,171	13,642	8,500	1,200
1960 42,436		31,836	20,970	14,298	9,500	1,100
1962 44,902		33,602	22,313	14,854	10,200	1,100
1963 46,956		34,956	23,418	15,182	10,900	1,100

* Net total of people with insurance company protection.
† People with formal paid sick leave plans but without insurance company coverage.
‡ Includes union-administered plans and employee mutual benefit associations.
SOURCE: Health Insurance Council.

From this table it can be seen that from 1950 onward the number of persons covered under group disability insurance plans written by insurance companies exceeded the number covered by individual policies. In 1963, 66 per cent of those with disability income insurance had group coverage.

Premium Volume

A further indication of the growth of group health insurance can be observed from the increase in the volume of premiums for such coverage. Naturally, this increase is not entirely reflective of an expansion in the use of the group insurance concept, since some of this increase would have been brought about, of itself, by economic inflation which has had its impact on both the costs of providing medical care and the level of wages, and consequently on the level of insurance benefits. Nonetheless, much of the increase in premium volume is indicative of actual growth, in terms of the numbers of persons covered and an increasing adequacy of coverage.

The total premium income of all health insurance organizations in 1963 for medical expense coverages was $8.4 billion. The growth in the health insurance premium volume for insurance companies is shown in Table 5–7, where it can be observed that the premium volume for group insurance has grown more rapidly than that for individual insurance. In 1951, for the first time, the premium volume for group insurance exceeded that for individual insurance. Each year since 1951 the gap has widened, the proportion of the total health insurance premiums represented by group premiums being 57 per cent in 1953 and 63 per cent in 1963. In 1935 group insurance accounted for only 15 per cent of insurance companies' health insurance premiums.

TABLE 5–7

HEALTH INSURANCE PREMIUMS* OF INSURANCE COMPANIES
UNITED STATES BUSINESS, 1919–63
(Millions of Dollars)

Year	Total	Group Policies	Individual and Family Policies	Year	Total	Group Policies	Individual and Family Policies
1920	85	†	†	1945	550	215	335
1925	144	†	†	1950	1,266	629	637
1930	221	†	†	1955	2,743	1,573	1,170
1935	175	26	149	1960	4,671	2,895	1,776
1940	286	65	221	1962	5,595	3,512	2,083
				1963	6,145	3,843	2,302

* Written premiums (for group policies, includes minor adjustments to reflect premiums of the particular year).
† Not available.
SOURCE: Health Insurance Association of America.

A comparison of insurance company group health insurance premium volume with the premium volume of other types of group coverages written by insurance companies in 1963 is also of interest. It reveals the following:

	1963 Premium Volume
Group health insurance	$3,843,000,000
Group life, creditor group and wholesale life insurance	2,427,000,000
Group annuities	1,380,000,000

It can be seen that in 1963, group health insurance premium volume exceeded the premium volume for all other types of group insurances and annuities. This situation occurred for the first time in 1961. In 1946 group health insurance premiums represented 25 per cent of all group insurance and group annuity premiums. This rose to 33 per cent in 1950, 42 per cent in 1955, 49 per cent in 1960 and 50 per cent in 1963. The

TABLE 5–8

Subscription Income* of Blue Cross, Blue Shield, and Other
Hospital-Medical Plans† in the United States, 1940–63
(Millions of Dollars)

Year	Subscriptions	Year	Subscriptions
1940	32	1955	1,523
1945	154	1960	2,814
1950	687	1962	3,674
		1963	3,921

* Earned income.
† Independent and Medical Society–approved or –sponsored plans.
Source: United States Department of Health, Education and Welfare, and *Argus Chart.*

growth in premium volume for other types of health insurers is shown in Table 5–8.

Benefits Paid

A final indication of the growth of group health insurance is observable in the increase in benefits paid yearly. Again, as in the case of the growth in premium volume, a certain amount of the rise in benefit payments would have been brought about even though no growth had occurred in the number of persons or contingencies covered. As medical care prices and expenditures rose, and as wages increased, benefit structures, of necessity, had to be adjusted upward in order to accomplish the original objectives of the group insurance. Regardless of this, much of the increase in benefit payments is representative of pure growth in terms of greater numbers of persons covered, more contingencies insured against and generally more adequate coverage. Health insurance benefits paid in the United States for all types of private health insurance coverages have increased from $772 million in 1948 to $7.8 billion in 1963.

Medical expense and disability income benefit payments by insurance companies have increased from $278 million in 1945 to $4.2 billion in 1963. The proportion of the total of insurance company benefits paid by group insurance has been increasing steadily. Whereas the amount of benefits was shared equally between group and individual policies in 1945, in 1963 group was 77 per cent of the total. The details of this growth are shown in Table 5–9.

For other types of health insurers the growth in benefits paid—generally limited to medical expense benefits—was as follows:

1948	$ 330 million
1950	550
1955	1,340
1960	2,619
1962	3,314
1963	3,649

TABLE 5–9

HEALTH INSURANCE BENEFIT PAYMENTS OF INSURANCE COMPANIES*
UNITED STATES BUSINESS, BY TYPE OF POLICY, 1945–63
(Millions of Dollars)

Year	Total	Group Policies	Individual and Family Policies
1945	278	139	139
1950	755	438	317
1955	1,785	1,252	533
1960	3,069	2,350	719
1962	3,763	2,911	852
1963	4,152	3,203	949

* Includes loss of income and excludes accidental death and dismemberment benefits.
SOURCE: *Accident and Sickness Review, Spectator Health Insurance Index*, Health Insurance
Council and Health Insurance Association of America.

FACTORS INFLUENCING THE GROWTH OF GROUP HEALTH INSURANCE

Factors outside the Insurance Field

A great many factors are responsible for the rapid and extensive growth of group health insurance. Several of these lie outside the insurance field itself, being inherent in changes which have taken place in the social and economic structure of the nation. Others, to be noted in the following section, emanate from within the insurance field. The notable growth factors from outside the insurance field are (1) population growth, (2) changes in the national economy, (3) the rising demand for and cost of medical care, (4) the influence of collective bargaining, (5) the effect of wage and tax laws and (6) the effect of statutory disability benefit programs.

Population Growth. The numerical increase in the United States' population from 76 million in 1900 to over 190 million in 1964 is accountable for some of the growth in group health insurance. The combination of a high birth rate and a declining mortality rate, a reduction in the incidence of communicable diseases and a control of diseases which at one time had a high incidence of fatalities in the early years of life have resulted in an increase in both the number and the proportion of the population in the higher age brackets. As a consequence, there is a greater number of persons with chronic, mental and long-term illnesses.

Simultaneously, the population has become increasingly mobile, moving from rural-farm living to large urban centers of population or their environs. Greater numbers of people work together in large groups. More people have ready access to hospital and medical care services and facilities. People tend to live in smaller dwelling units. A higher proportion of wives are employed outside the home or off the farm. There is a rising rate of broken marriages. The degree of education or skill attainment continues to rise. Immigration from other nations has been diminishing.

In general, demographic changes have increased the demand, and consequently the expenditures, for medical care, with growing emphasis on the use of institutionalized care. This, in turn, has had a direct effect upon the demand for additional health insurance protection, both in terms of numbers of people and scope of benefits. Similarly, as the labor force working in groups has grown in size, there has been a greater demand for health insurance protection against loss of income.

Changes in the National Economy. For the past quarter-century the economy of the United States has been identified with expanding industrialization and increasing gross national product, a rising national income, a more equitable distribution of wealth, a substantial increase in the average family income in terms of real dollars, a generally higher standard of living, a high though not full level of employment and an inflationary trend in both prices and wages, including the price of medical care. There has been a rising degree of personal and corporate taxation. Installment purchasing and mortgage indebtedness have increased. Pensions for retirees from the labor force, through private programs or other arrangements such as the OASDI program, or both, have become general.

Changes in the economy of the United States have influenced the growth of group insurance, and group health insurance is no exception. With expanded national wealth and a broader spread of this wealth, there has been a general increase in the proportion of dollars available in the family budget for products and services other than basic necessities. This has stimulated the demand for many products and services, including medical care. However, as yesterday's luxuries become today's demands, conflicting demands are made upon personal income. The growing use of credit and other budgeting means, combined with a high level of personal taxation, produced their effect upon spending patterns and the attitude of people toward paying "out of pocket" for the more expensive or emergency items, including sizable medical bills. A need developed for a method of financing medical care on a more systematic basis. As a consequence, the risk-transfer technique increased in popularity as a means of meeting portions of the health risk.

The Rising Demand for and Cost of Medical Care. In addition to the foregoing demographic and economic developments, other factors have served to stimulate the demand for medical care. The increasing effectiveness of medical care, the introduction and wide use of the many highly effective drugs, advances made in diagnostic services and new life-saving surgical procedures have increased the public acceptance and use of medical care services and facilities. So, too, have such factors as the greater availability and diversity of medical care services and facilities, the revolutionary change in the public image of the hospital, and the more frequent use of the hospital for diagnostic, nonsurgical and maternity purposes. A broader degree of health education, through the means of mass communication, the school system, medical societies, employers, labor unions, health insurers, voluntary agencies of many types and all levels of government, has also served to expand public awareness of health matters, and consequently an increased demand for medical care.

Meanwhile, medical care has become much more technical in nature and more highly specialized. The result has been an unavoidable increase in the price of care. The combination of greater demand and rising cost has produced a steady advance in medical care expenditures, as well as a growing interest in and need for health insurance protection.

The Influence of Collective Bargaining. The first collectively bargained agreement to provide medical benefits is reported to have been negotiated in 1926. Prior to that time, however, and paralleling somewhat the advancement of workmen's compensation legislation, organized labor had developed an interest in insurance protection against loss of income resulting from nonoccupational injuries and illnesses. In more recent years, the emphasis has been on insurance protection against the costs of medical care.

Of the persons protected under employee benefit plans in 1959, about 40 per cent, or 36 million, were covered through collectively bargained plans. This number constituted 86 per cent of all union members and their dependents. Of the persons covered under collectively bargained programs, 46 per cent were covered by insurance companies, 43 per cent by Blue Cross–Blue Shield plans, 7 per cent by union-operated plans and 4 per cent by other types of plans. In 1959, $943 million was paid in premiums by employers and $492 million was paid by workers for collectively bargained health insurance programs.

The Effect of Wage and Tax Laws. Four specific legislative and regulatory steps taken by the federal government are closely related to the role played by collective bargaining in the growth of group health insurance: (1) amendments to the federal Internal Revenue Code; (2) the wage stabilization policies of the War Labor Board, 1944–45; (3) the decision of the National Labor Relations Board, 1948–49; and (4) the rulings of the Wage Stabilization Board, 1951. Each of these factors was considered in Chapter 4 and therefore need not be expanded upon further.

In general, these developments encouraged employer contribution to the cost of the health insurance by providing for a tax offset. They also established the processes of collective bargaining in the field of health insurance and other employee benefits. In combination, they influenced the growth of group health insurance during and since that period.

The Effect of Statutory Disability Benefit Programs. Another factor which has had an effect on the growth of group health insurance has been the enactment of statutory disability benefit legislation. In this case, however, the effect in some instances has been to retard growth rather than to advance it. Essentially two types of legislation are involved: (1) nonoccupational temporary disability benefits legislation in four states, and (2) total disability benefit legislation at the federal level.

A. *Nonoccupational Temporary Disability Benefit Legislation.* In four states (Rhode Island, 1942; California, 1946; New Jersey, 1948; New York, 1949) laws have been enacted which place compulsory responsibilities upon specified categories of employers for certain economic losses to employees (and to a certain extent the temporarily unemployed) resulting from nonoccupational temporary disability. The nature and influence of these laws are discussed in detail in Chapter 20. Benefits under such laws are intended as corollary benefits to the disability income benefits provided under workmen's compensation and/or unemployment compensation laws. In addition, essentially similar benefits are provided by federal law for railroad employees. Over eleven million workers were covered by these five types of programs in 1960. In addition to the disability income benefits, California's statutory benefits since 1950 have included payments for certain costs of hospital care required as a result of nonoccupational temporary disability.

To the extent, if any, that these laws brought about health insurance coverages written by insurance companies on employees not previously covered, there was a positive effect on the growth of group health insurance. However, in instances such as the federally provided benefits for railroad employees, the monopolistic state fund in Rhode Island, and the situation in California and New Jersey, whereby insurance companies find it difficult to compete with the state fund, there has been a distinctly negative effect. Large numbers of employees, who formerly had been or who might eventually have come to be insured by insurance companies, were transferred to the government-established agency.

B. *Total Disability Benefit Legislation.* In 1956 the federal Social Security Act was amended to provide OASI income benefits for totally and presumably permanently disabled persons age fifty and over who were covered by the OASI program. Subsequently, in 1960, the age fifty limitation was removed, making such benefits available to all OASDI covered persons who become totally and permanently disabled. Since these benefits are part of the compulsory OASDI coverage administered by the federal government and financed by specially designated taxes on employers, employees and the self-employed, it is not possible for insurance companies to participate in the provision of this coverage. While the effect of these benefits upon the growth and development of group health insurance has never been measured, it seems that the effect would be negative, since to some degree the OASDI program provides benefits to persons or groups who might otherwise be covered by insurance companies or who might otherwise purchase greater benefits under a group insurance program than they consider necessary in light of the existence of the OASDI program.

Factors within the Health Insurance Field

Many other factors affecting the growth of group health insurance emanate from within the private risk-bearing field itself. These are discussed here under five headings: (1) broadened benefit pattern, (2) added forms of covered health care, (3) the further extension to specific population groups, (4) refinement of the group insurance technique and (5) the role of national associations of insurers.

Broadened Benefit Pattern. One of the primary functions of health insurance is to provide protection against loss of income resulting from illness or injury. The size of the disability income benefit is normally related to the level of income of the covered individuals. The majority of group disability income contracts provide protection for a thirteen-week period, although an increasing number provide coverage for twenty-six weeks and some for fifty-two weeks. Moreover, by 1964 there was considerable interest in providing group long-term disability income protection. A growing number of insurance companies offer this coverage, with benefit payments generally available for periods of one, two, five, or ten years, or to age sixty-five. Many will pay lifetime benefits for disability resulting from accident. The proportion of employees having such coverage has been increasing since 1960.

In connection with group medical expense coverage there also has been a trend toward a broader benefit pattern by all types of group health insurers. Insurance companies have been offering larger amounts of benefits for per diem hospital care (in part to remain abreast of the rising cost of hospital care). Daily room-and-board benefits rose from $5 or $10 a day to $15 to $25 a day or higher by 1965. Some covered the full cost of semiprivate accommodations. Commensurately, the amounts of the benefits for ancillary hospital services have grown from as little as $30 in the 1930's to $300 or more. At the same time, the number of covered hospitalized days per illness has increased sharply from thirty-one to seventy days, or even to 120 or 365 days. Blue Cross plans have followed an essentially similar pattern with respect to the number of days of hospitalization covered. Insurance company coverages for surgical care also have increased from $100 maxima to $200 or $300 maxima or higher.

Another indication of the broadening of the benefit pattern is found in the expansion of major medical expense insurance since its development by insurance companies in 1949. This coverage was developed to furnish protection against practically all types of personal health care expenditures provided in or out of the hospital, with emphasis on the more serious of such expenditures. Benefits are payable to a maximum amount of many thousands of dollars.

Major medical coverage gives protection not only against expenses incurred as a result of hospital care and surgery, but also covers such expenses as physician home and office visits, private duty nursing, prescribed drugs, treatment of mental illness in or out of hospital, and to some extent the services of dentists for accidental injury, visiting nurse service, care provided by organized home care programs and nursing home care. As will be discussed in Chapter 18, more budgetable expenses, or expenses covered by basic hospital-surgical coverages, are eliminated by the use of a stipulated deductible amount. In order to avoid abuse of the insurance benefits, participation in the expenses by the covered person is generally required through an established percentage, or coinsurance.

Public acceptance of major medical expense insurance was immediate. By 1963 over forty-two million people in the United States were protected under major medical expense contracts issued by insurance companies. The vast majority of these were covered under group programs. Under employer-employee benefit plans alone, the number of wage and salary workers and their dependents protected by major medical insurance increased from 1.9 million in 1954 to 3.5 million in 1961. These numbers represented an increase of from 2 per cent of all wage and salary workers to 20 per cent. By 1964 major medical expense insurance represented about one third of all insurance company coverages for medical expenses in terms of the number of people covered. Following this rapid public acceptance of major medical insurance, Blue Cross plans commenced offering optional additional coverages, called variously "major medical," "master medical," "extended benefits," "comprehensive benefit rider," "prolonged illness certificate" or "catastrophic illness contract."

Added Forms of Covered Health Care. A further factor in the growth of group health insurance has been the extension of protection to additional forms of health care. The first and predominant movement in this direction was brought about by the liberal provisions in major medical insurance. More recently, however, coverages for additional forms of health care, not always covered under major medical expense insurance, have been developed. These newer coverages have indicated possibilities of having a wide acceptance. Such coverages include (1) dental care, (2) nursing home care and (3) vision care.

A. Dental Care. Programs to provide protection against the expense of comprehensive dental care have been developed by insurance companies, state dental societies, groups of dentists and certain other organizations primarily on a group insurance basis, although a few insurance companies also issue individual policies.

The first dental care program was developed by the St. Louis Labor Health Institute in 1946. In 1954, the ILWU–PMA program on the West Coast established a dental care program for the children of maritime workers. The program had two parallel approaches: (1) an open-panel group indemnity plan with the Continental Casualty Company acting as a fiduciary agent and (2) a closed-panel program for the actual provision of care. In 1954, the Washington State Dental Service Corporation was formed to function as a part of the ILWU–PMA program. In 1954, also, Group Health Dental Insurance, Inc., commenced functioning in New York City under sponsorship of Group Health Insurance, Inc. The California Dental Service Corporation, currently the largest of the dental society sponsored plans, was organized in 1955. In 1956, a group dental program was developed by the Group Health Association in Washington, D.C., and the Dental Insurance Plan in New York commenced operation. The Group Health Dental Cooperative of Seattle, Washington, was formed in 1958. In 1959, the Continental Casualty Company was the first insurance company to develop a comprehensive dental insurance plan on a group basis. Since that time many major writers of group insurance have offered comprehensive dental insurance programs. In 1963, one Blue Cross plan offered dental care coverage, and in that same year one Blue Cross plan established an administrative arrangement with a dental service corporation. By 1965, dental service corporations, sponsored by state dental societies, were operative in nine states (California, Colorado, Connecticut, Hawaii, Michigan, New York, Ohio, Oregon and Washington).

According to the U.S. Public Health Service the number of persons covered under dental insurance and prepayment plans increased from 550,000 in 1960 to 1,145,000 in 1962. While these data are probably underreported, they give an indication of the rapid growth which has been taking place in this relatively new form of group health insurance coverage. According to the same source, the number of available dental plans increased in that same period from 128 to 296. The nature of the various forms of group dental coverage is discussed in detail in Chapter 38.

B. *Nursing Home Care.* Coverages designed specifically to provide protection against the costs of nursing home care (other than those provided by major medical and hospital insurance) are offered by certain insurance companies and some Blue Cross plans. The first Blue Cross plan to make such benefits available was the Massachusetts plan in 1954. By 1963, the number of such plans had increased to forty-one. Usually the nursing home benefit is provided under contracts specifically designed for persons age sixty-five and over (thirty-nine plans), or under the "major medical" or "extended benefit" types of contract (eight plans) and not under the "standard" or "regular" contract. As in the case of insurance company coverages, the benefits vary considerably among plans. According to the Social Security Administration, an estimated 2,686,000 persons were protected by this coverage under Blue Cross plans in 1961.

Nursing home benefits were first developed by insurance companies on a group insurance basis in 1959 when the Continental Casualty Company and the Guardian Life Insurance Company entered this new area. By 1963, twelve insurance companies made this coverage available on a group basis. At the end of 1962, 673,632 persons were specifically covered for the costs of nursing home care by nine companies which wrote such coverages on a group basis and which could furnish such data.

Other types of group health insurance mechanisms do not appear to provide nursing home care benefits to any appreciable extent. The Social Security Administration has reported twenty-two plans covering an estimated 526,000 persons in 1961. However, the majority were covered under one employee plan. None of the community-wide or group practice prepayment plans are known to have provided benefits for nursing home care in 1963.

C. Vision Care. Group health insurance coverages are also being extended with respect to the costs of vision care. In this instance, however, growth has been inconsequential. Several employer-employee and labor union groups make some provision for the costs of vision care, usually by the direct use of funds for such purposes or the actual provision of such care rather than through insuring organizations.[8] Other approaches include the organization of prepaid vision care plans by optometrists, such as the California Vision Service established in 1956 (which also has an indemnity program coordinated with insurance company coverages). By 1962, essentially similar plans had been organized in twenty-five states. Yet other approaches are indicated by the formation in 1957 of the Optometric Care Program, Inc., by the New York State Optometric Association, Inc., a closed-panel group prepayment plan. Another approach is that of including refractions in group medical community-wide or prepaid group practice plans as is done by the Group Health Association in Washington, D.C., Group Health Cooperative in Seattle, Health Insurance Plan of Greater New York, Kaiser Foundation Health Plan and the Ross-Loos Medical Group in Los Angeles.

While insurance companies provide considerable coverage for eye care under their group medical expense coverages, only a relatively few groups have been written to cover the expenses of vision care. The first such plan was written by the Occidental Life Insurance Company of California about 1957.

Further Extension to Specific Population Groups. Group health insurance has also experienced considerable growth as a result of its further

---

[8] Included are such programs as those of the Consolidated Edison Company, Endicott-Johnson Corporation, St. Louis Labor Health Institute, ILGWU and the Sidney Hillman Medical Center.

extension to specific population groups. More liberal statutory and underwriting requirements are responsible for these developments.

A. *Dependents of Covered Persons.* In the early years of group health insurance, coverage frequently pertained to an employed person alone and not to his dependents. This followed the pattern of workmen's compensation insurance and other governmental programs. It also arose from the fact that earlier coverages were related to loss of income and, hence, applied only to the wage earner.

Simultaneously with the development of medical expense insurance, a pronounced trend occurred toward including in the coverage the spouse and dependent children of the employed person. Today, dependents are normally included in the coverage. It is readily apparent how such an expansion of concept would have a strong influence upon the growth of group health insurance. Without this development, it is doubtful that private health insurance could have satisfied a broad public need for health insurance protection.

B. *Persons over Age Sixty-five.* A relatively recent extension of group health insurance, and one of considerable importance, concerns persons age sixty-five and over. This development has paralleled advances by insurance companies and Blue Cross–Blue Shield plans in the individual policy field. By the end of 1962, 10.3 million, or 60 per cent, of the aged population, had some form of health insurance protection, 6.1 million being covered by insurance companies and 5.3 million by Blue Cross–Blue Shield plans. Ten years earlier only 3 million of those age sixty-five and over had any health insurance protection.

Almost half of those age sixty-five and over with insurance company coverage obtained their protection as a result of group insurance. This has been brought about through five different approaches: (1) continuation of group insurance on older active workers and their dependents under group insurance plans; (2) continuation of group insurance on retired workers and their dependents (generally with part or all of the premium paid by the employer); (3) conversion of an employee's group coverage to an individual policy;[9] (4) issuance of group insurance to groups of retired persons such as teachers, retired civil servants and the American Association of Retired Persons; and (5) issuance of group-type guaranteed renewable coverage to aged persons through individual companies or State-65 plans in which several insurers cooperate.[10] In 1963 the

---

[9] Details concerning the first three approaches are set forth in Chapter 36.

[10] In October, 1961, residents of Connecticut aged sixty-five and over (and spouse, if fifty-five or older) became eligible for enrollment in the Connecticut-65 Extended Health Insurance Program written by several insurance companies through a voluntary association. Essentially similar programs became operative in Massachusetts and New York in 1962, in Texas in 1963 and in California, North Carolina, Ohio, and Virginia in 1964. Permissive legislation had been enacted by 1965 in several other states so that similar programs are possible in those states. The operation of these plans is discussed in Chapter 37.

Health Insurance Institute reported that four out of five employees covered under group coverages issued by insurance companies in 1962 could retain their protection into retirement.

Blue Cross and Blue Shield coverage is available at advanced ages on a group enrollment basis in the following ways: (1) continuation of regular group benefits at regular group rates to those over age 65 who are currently employed in enrolled groups; (2) retention of retirees under group programs, at regular rates and benefits, with the employer making deductions from pension payments, if any, and with or without employee contribution; (3) issuance of direct-pay coverage to members originally enrolled under group programs who have become sixty-five years of age; and (4) issuance of special "senior citizen" contracts on a group basis to persons age sixty-five and over who have not been previously enrolled in Blue Cross–Blue Shield.

C. *Those Employed in Small Groups.* For many years statutory and underwriting requirements (which followed group life insurance practices) did not allow group health coverage for persons employed in small groups. Gradually, the statutory and underwriting requirements were modified to permit the writing of smaller groups, ranging from groups of ten or more lives down to as few as two lives in some states. An important broadening of the extent of group health insurance resulted.

D. *The Temporarily Unemployed.* Group health insurance written by insurance companies, Blue Cross–Blue Shield plans and other types of health insurers tend increasingly to make available the means for the continuation of the coverage into periods of unemployment through several different methods. Many plans provide that, in the event of termination of membership in the group for whatever reason, the coverage may be converted to individual insurance coverage. Naturally, the exercise of this privilege is dependent upon the ability and willingness of the individual to continue premium payments.

A more effective means of continuing the group coverage is accomplished by various extended benefit provisions which allow a continuation of the group insurance coverage during a specified period of layoff or unemployment. Such continuation might be to the end of the policy month following the date of layoff, or for a period of three, six, or nine months thereafter, or longer. Continuation of coverage during the period of a strike is also available, by virtue of premium payment by the employer or by the labor union.

The continuation of group health insurance coverages into periods of unemployment is an important development to employed persons. While it has not contributed greatly to the growth of health insurance, it has enhanced the value of this form of insurance to many of the insured public.

E. *Association Groups.* Originally group health insurance was limited, both by statutory law and the underwriting practices of insurance companies, to groups of persons employed by a common employer. Gradually, this concept was broadened to include members of labor unions, trustees of a fund established by one or more employers or labor unions, two or more employers in the same industry or the employer members of a trade association (thereby making possible the coverage for certain small groups of persons). In some states, lack of legislative restrictions has resulted in a further broadening to include coverage on a group basis for members of various types of associations. These might include professional or self-employed people, or people employed singly or in very small groups, such as associations of small businesses, physicians, druggists, policemen and many others. It is obvious that as this concept of group health insurance expanded, greater growth was made possible.

F. Creditor Insurance. As consumer debt based on installment loans or purchases became an important aspect of the American economy, the need was recognized for insurance protection against the loss of income as a result of illness or injury, which in turn would jeopardize repayment of such loans. Banks, finance companies, credit unions, small-loan companies, department stores, furniture and appliance dealers and motor vehicle agencies rapidly sought such protection. It is doubtful if this type of financing could have grown so rapidly without the development and availability of insurance against health (and life) risks. Credit health insurance is written on either an individual policy basis or a group basis.

G. Rural Residents. Group health insurance has not been extended readily to rural-farm population groups. Although there are several reasons for this, the basic problem is one of marketing and relates to the nature of rural-farm employment. As a consequence, Blue Cross–Blue Shield plans have not been notably successful in covering the rural-farm population (although there are some exceptions, such as in Michigan)—nor have the community-wide or prepaid group practice plans which in the main are centered in large population areas or in industrial groups of various types. Rural health cooperatives have met with many problems. Insurance companies' group health insurance approaches have met with varying degrees of success and failure. However, where rural organizations exist with an active interest in group health insurance, workable plans have been established. These, in turn, indicate the possibilities of further development. Such organizations include farm bureaus, granges, cooperatives, creameries, farmers' unions, poultry producers' associations, elevator associations, oil associations, credit unions, local banks, church groups and educational organizations. Community-wide enrollment has also been employed with some success.

Refinement of the Group Insurance Technique. The refinement of group insurance processes and techniques has been a strong contributing factor in the growth of group health insurance. Sales and marketing approaches have been improved and expanded, so that group insurance coverages have reached large numbers of people. At the same time, as more experience has been gathered, underwriting concepts have been refined and broadened. Claim payment procedures also have been refined, thus allowing a more rapid payment of claims and improving the relationship between the patient, the provider of medical care and the insurer. Meanwhile, the development of automation and streamlined procedures has reduced operating costs for group health insurers.

These aspects of group health insurance will be considered in more detail in subsequent chapters. It is necessary here only to recognize that the refinement of processes in the marketing and administration of group health insurance has played an important role in the development and growth of group health insurance in the United States.

The Role of Insurers' Organizations. A final factor which should be noted in the growth of group health insurance is the role played by the various national associations of insurers. One of the characteristics of modern endeavor in the United States is the formation of institutional organizations by individuals, corporations or others having a common purpose or pursuit. In this manner, ideas are disseminated and shared, standards are established, common problems are approached, information is gathered, research is conducted and improved methods are explored.

Insurers, their agents and their professional staffs have established a great many organizations at the national, state and local level. While none exists solely as a result of group health insurance, several operate exclusively for health insurance, including group health insurance.

The Bureau of Personal Accident and Health Underwriters, formed in 1891, and the Health and Accident Underwriters Conference, formed in 1901, merged in 1956 to become the Health Insurance Association of America, thereby consolidating their respective standing and special committees, including their group insurance committees. The new Association also continued the practice of its predecessors in annually conducting a group insurance forum. The services of the new organization also were expanded to include research activities and educational courses for company personnel. At the same time the Health Insurance Institute was formed as a central source of public information. These developments all served importantly to advance the development, growth and progress of group health insurance.

Other national organizations which also provide important services in the field of group health insurance are the American Mutual Alliance, the Association of Casualty and Surety Companies, the International Health Underwriters Association, the International Claim Association, the Life Insurance Advertisers Association, the Life Insurance Agency Management Association, the Life Insurers Conference, the Life Office Management Association, the Life Insurance Medical Directors Association, the National Association of Insurance Agents and the Society of Actuaries.[11]

A federation of eight national insurance associations known as the Health Insurance Council (originally the Conference Committee on Health Insurance) provides a central source of information and technical and practical counsel regarding health insurance coverages for groups concerned with health services, including hospitals, physicians and the allied health services. Since its formation in 1946, the Council has contributed greatly to the relationship between group health insurers and the providers of medical care. It has brought about a better understanding of problems and improvement in techniques and processes, and it has served an important role in making a free system of health insurance and a free system of medicine a cooperative, workable endeavor.

The Blue Cross plans, as they developed, rapidly recognized the need for a national organization which would provide a common approach to their problems. In 1937 the Committee on Hospital Service was authorized by the American Hospital Association, and in 1941 this committee became the Hospital Service Plan Commission. In 1946 this Commission became the Blue Cross Commission, which under a reorganization in 1960 gave way to the Council on Blue Cross Financing and Prepayment Plans of the AHA. Meanwhile, in 1948 the Blue Cross Association was formed. With the reorganization in 1960, the Blue Cross Commission was merged with this Association, and the latter assumed greater responsibilities. Through these organizations Blue Cross plans have been provided a means for servicing national or multi-state accounts, servicing subscribers who require hospitalization in areas in which their particular plan does not function, conducting research, disseminating information and considering common problems.

The Blue Shield plans followed a pattern similar to Blue Cross in establishing a national coordinating agency. The first national Blue Shield organization was established by the American Medical Association in 1946 and was called the Associated Medical Care Plans, Inc. The name of the organization was changed to Blue Shield Medical Care Plans, Inc., in 1950, and to the National Association of Blue Shield Plans in 1959.

Many of the other plans, formerly constituted as the Group Health Federation of America (organized in 1936) and the American Labor Health Association (organized in 1954), formed the Group Health Association of America in 1959. At group health institutes conducted annually by this association, as by its forerunners, there is a free exchange of ideas and a discussion of common problems. By 1963 this association had embarked upon a program to collect statistics and was in process of establishing a set of standards for prepaid group practice plans. In 1964 it had

---

[11] From 1946 to 1949 a Joint Committee on Employee Disability Plans represented several insurance associations.

in process the formation of a national Service Agency for Group Practice Prepayment to contact and service national or multi-state accounts on behalf of prepaid group practice plans.

SIGNIFICANCE OF GROUP HEALTH INSURANCE

The development and growth of group health insurance has been significant to insurers, to management-labor relations, to the providers of medical care, to the field of health economics and to the broad segment of the public which has health insurance protection. It has revolutionized the field of medical economics in terms of how medical care in the United States is to be organized and financed. It is a uniquely American enterprise. Through many different mechanisms it fills a personal and social need for protection against the economic risk of illness and injury. Special approaches satisfy the needs of particular groups of people, and the group mechanism is recognized as being flexible, diversified and responsive to changing needs and demands. Group health insurance has become one of the predominant aspects of the nation's insurance structure. In fact, it has become the financial cornerstone of the system of medical care in the United States.

SELECTED REFERENCES

ANDERSON, ODIN W. *Voluntary Health Insurance in Two Cities.* Cambridge, Mass.: Harvard University Press, 1957.

APPLEBAUM, LEON. "The Development of Voluntary Health Insurance in the United States," *Journal of Insurance,* September, 1961.

BEERS, HENRY S. *Outlook and Social Significance.* Washington, D.C.: Chamber of Commerce of the United States, 1957.

CHAMBER OF COMMERCE OF THE UNITED STATES. *Health Insurance Programs in Industry.* Undated.

EILERS, ROBERT D. *Regulation of Blue Cross and Blue Shield Plans.* Homewood, Ill.: Richard D. Irwin, Inc., 1963.

FOLLMANN, J. F., JR. *Medical Care and Health Insurance.* Homewood, Ill.: Richard D. Irwin, Inc., 1963.

———. *Nursing Home Care and Health Insurance.* New York: Health Insurance Association of America, 1963.

———. "Trends in Health Insurance," *Best's Life News,* November, 1963.

———. "Dental Coverage in Insurance Plans," paper presented before the American Society of Oral Surgeons, April 26, 1963, Chicago, Ill.

HAY, DONALD G. "Independent Health Insurance Plans, 1961 Survey," *Social Security Bulletin,* February, 1963.

HEALTH INSURANCE INSTITUTE. *Source Book* annual.

———. *Group Health Insurance Policies Issued in 1962,* 1963.

REED, LOUIS S., AND RICE, DOROTHY P. "Private Consumer Expenditures for Medical Care and Voluntary Health Insurance, 1948–62," *Social Security Bulletin,* December, 1963.

SERBEIN, OSCAR N., JR. *Paying for Medical Care in the United States.* New York: Columbia University Press, 1953.

SIEGFRIED, CHARLES A. *Major Medical Expense Insurance.* New York: Health Insurance Association of America, 1957.

SKOLNIK, ALFRED M. "Growth of Employee-Benefit Plans, 1954–1961," *Social Security Bulletin,* April, 1963.

SLAVICK, FRED. *Distribution of Medical Costs and Benefits under Four Collectively Bargained Insurance Plans.* Ithaca, N.Y.: Cornell University, 1956.

SMITH, J. HENRY. "Group Insurance against Illness and Accidents," *American Economic Security.* Washington, D.C.: Chamber of Commerce of the United States, June–July, 1950.

UNITED STEELWORKERS OF AMERICA, *Medical Care Program for Steelworkers and Their Families.* Pittsburgh, Penn.: United Steelworkers of America, September, 1960.

WHITTAKER, EDMUND B. *A Dynamic Group Coverage.* Washington, D.C.: Chamber of Commerce of the United States, 1957.

WILSON, A. M. *Origin and Development of Major Medical Expense Insurance.* Washington, D.C.: Chamber of Commerce of the United States, 1957.

Chapter 6

LEGAL ENVIRONMENT OF GROUP INSURANCE

BY ARTHUR M. BROWNING

From its inception with the writing of the Montgomery Ward case in 1912, group insurance with its principle of insuring persons by groups has been opposed by various interests. Opposition has been voiced by actuaries,[1] by life insurance company trade organizations,[2] by fraternal orders,[3] by supervising officials[4] and by agent organizations.[5]

While originally the principal argument used by the opponents was the one of discrimination—selling at rates different from those for individual policies and not requiring medical evidence—the early adoption of statutes by various states[6] put an end to this attack. Later, new arguments against group insurance arose, particularly the issue of "unsound underwriting" and the fear that the agency system, the underpinning of individual insurance, would be destroyed.

---

[1] See, for example, Discussions by E. V. Dunlap and H. L. Rietz, *Record of the American Institute of Actuaries*, Vol. III (1914), pp. 276–77; also see comments by J. D. Craig, *Transactions of the Actuarial Society of America*, Vol. XXIII, No. 57 (1922), p. 132.

[2] *Proceedings of the Eighth Annual Meeting of the American Life Convention* (1913), p. 77.

[3] *Fraternal Monitor*, Vol. XXIV, No. 7 (February 1, 1914), p. 21.

[4] *Fraternal Monitor*, Vol. XXIV, No. 2 (September 1, 1913), pp. 18–19; also Discussions by B. S. Beecher, *Record of the American Institute of Actuaries*, Vol. III (1914), p. 282.

[5] The opposition of the National Association of Life Underwriters has been a continuing thing, the most recent manifestation occurring at the June meeting, 1964, of the National Association of Insurance Commissioners, when the Commissioners were asked to take all necessary steps to prevent group insurance contracts from crossing state lines if a particular contract did not conform with the particular state's statutes.

[6] Lower rates permitted, Florida, Acts of 1915, Chap. 6849; Maine, Laws of 1913, Chap. 84; Minnesota, General Statutes, 1913, Sec. 3617; Nebraska Insurance Pamphlet 1913, p. 85; New Jersey Insurance Pamphlet 1916, p. 84. No medical examination required, Arizona, Session Laws 1913, Chap. 94; Idaho, Laws 1913, Chap 185, Chap. 97; Massachusetts Insurance Laws 1913, Sec. 123.

As a result of these attacks on group insurance, many states have adopted strict statutory controls which define what group insurance is and the circumstances under which it may be issued. And yet, at the same time, the failure of several states[7] to enact any statutory restraints on group insurance causes many people to say that group insurance is anything anyone wants it to be.

LEGAL DEFINITION OF GROUP LIFE INSURANCE AND RELATED PROVISIONS

1917 Model Bill

In 1917 a definition of group life insurance was adopted by the National Convention of Insurance Commissioners, now known as the National Association of Insurance Commissioners, and was embodied in a model bill drafted by a committee of the NAIC in collaboration with a committee of the Actuarial Society of America. This model bill, which undoubtedly reflected the prevailing underwriting practices of the day, contained both underwriting restrictions and standard provisions. The model bill limited group life insurance to the employees of a single employer, stipulated that eligibility for coverage must extend to all employees of the employer or to all of a class or classes determined according to conditions pertaining to their employment, and required that each insured group contain at least fifty individuals. Other requirements were that the employers must pay some part of the cost, that if the employees were to bear part of the cost, at least 75 per cent of those eligible must be insured, and that the persons insured could not select the amount of insurance. Perhaps the most important of the standard provisions prescribed was the one requiring that the group insurance master contract grant a right of conversion to an individual policy of insurance in the event of termination of employment by an insured employee.

Although the National Association of Insurance Commissioners recommended the model group life insurance legislation, it had no staff facilities for follow-up. Neither of the two life insurance trade associations charged generally with the presentation of institutional viewpoints on matters of legislation, the American Life Convention and the Association of Life Insurance Presidents—the latter is now known as the Life Insurance Association of America—had or made plans for the promotion of group insurance laws. As a result, passage of state laws controlling group life insurance was not frequent. During the twenty-five years following the 1917 action of the National Association of Insurance Commissioners, only

---

[7] Even today, eleven states have not adopted statutes defining group life insurance. These are: Alabama, Alaska, Delaware, Minnesota (except for certificate requirements), Mississippi, Missouri, North Dakota, Rhode Island, South Dakota, Tennessee (except that it requires group life policies to contain a conversion period and imposes $25,000/$50,000 group term limits) and Wyoming.

sixteen states[8] and the district of Columbia adopted laws patterned more or less after the model bill. Most of these, however, were not as restrictive as the model bill. By 1945 eight of the seventeen jurisdictions had reduced the fifty-life minimum requirement in one way or another, eleven had specifically authorized extension of group coverage to the employees of subsidiaries and affiliates of the master policyholder, fifteen had authorized coverage on members of labor unions, nine on members of the National Guard, fifteen on borrowers from a financial institution, and various additional states of the total had permitted member-pay-all coverage on such groups as state police, teachers and other associations to which the usual employer subsidy was thought to be unavailable. The remaining thirty-two states without laws did not restrict the writing of group life insurance in any way.

The Group Association

In recognition of the continual opposition of some elements of the insurance industry to group insurance and the need for restraints to keep such opposition contained, and in the light of the slow development of state legislation, some of the group writing companies in 1926 formed a loose association of the group insurance divisions of their companies. The organization, called the Group Association, pursued the following goals, as set forth in its Constitution: (1) to promote the welfare of holders of group policies; (2) to advance the interests of group insurance; (3) to promote economy and reduce expense in the matter of general administration by an interchange of views on practices among insurance companies which issue contracts of insurance; (4) to represent the members of the Association in matters pertaining to or which may affect group insurance before the Insurance Departments and other public and quasi-public bodies; and (5) to collect and analyze the group experience of the members of the Association, but nothing in this Constitution, or in any rule adopted subordinate thereto shall be held to authorize the making or promulgation of premium rates.

Although reprimands and expulsion from the Association were its only means of disciplining members who departed from practices deemed wise in the preservation of group insurance, the Group Association nevertheless was effective. Its advocacy and policing of New York minimum group life premium rates, its promulgation of a table of extra hazardous occupations, its establishment of rules controlling transfers of business from one insurer to another and its representation before insurance departments and legis-

---

[8] California, Colorado, Illinois, Indiana, Iowa, Massachusetts, Michigan, New Jersey, New York, North Carolina, Ohio, Pennsylvania, Texas, Virginia, Washington and Wisconsin. Of these, six still have statutes predicated on the 1917 model bill. These are California, Illinois, Massachusetts, Michigan, New York and Ohio. Utah also has adopted a law based on the 1917 model bill.

latures did much to keep the progress of group insurance orderly and contained. However, on June 16, 1938, Congress created the Temporary National Economic Committee, generally referred to as the TNEC. This Committee's investigations included an attempt to determine whether intercompany associations had resulted in anti-competitive practices in the business. The Group Association naturally came within the investigation, and the TNEC representatives who conducted the hearings took the position that the Group Association was a vehicle for agreeing on rates and practices and thereby eliminating competition. Although the charges were strongly denied by the insurance companies, several of the larger companies withdrew from membership, and the effectiveness of the Group Association began to dwindle.

The final report of the TNEC, dated March 31, 1941, did not specifically refer to group insurance. However, certain of its recommendations for consideration by the states were broad enough to have immediate bearing on group insurance and the Group Association. Not long after that, in 1942, the Group Association was disbanded. Had it not, its demise probably would have occurred in 1944 with the decision of the Supreme Court of the United States in the South-Eastern Underwriters Association case[9] that insurance was commerce and that the Sherman Anti-Trust Act[10] was applicable to the insurance business.

South-Eastern Underwriters Association Case

For a period of seventy-five years, 1869–1944, the United States Supreme Court held that contracts of insurance were not commerce and therefore were not subject to the Commerce Clause of the Constitution which makes all matters of interstate commerce subject to federal control. In 1944, the Court reversed its own findings. This came about when 200 private stock fire insurance companies and twenty-seven individuals were indicted for alleged violations of the Sherman Anti-Trust Act. The indictment charged conspiracies in fixing premium rates and agents' commissions and boycotts, together with other types of coercion and intimidation, to force nonmember companies into the conspiracies and to compel persons who needed insurance to buy only from South-Eastern Underwriters Association members on SEUA terms. The District Court, following all

---

[9] 322 U.S. Reports 534.

[10] Passed July 2, 1890, 26 Stat. 209. The pertinent provisions appear in the Act as amended, 15 U.S.C. Secs. 1 and 2, and are:

"Sec. 1. Every contract combination in the form of trust or otherwise, or conspiracy, in restraint of trade or commerce among the several states, or with foreign nations, is hereby declared to be illegal. . . . Every person who shall make any contract or engage in any combination or conspiracy declared by sections 1–7 of this title to be illegal shall be deemed guilty of a misdemeanor. . . .

"Sec. 2. Every person who shall monopolize, or attempt to monopolize, or combine, or conspire with any other person or persons to monopolize any part of the trade or commerce among the several states, or with foreign nations, shall be deemed guilty of a misdemeanor. . . ."

precedents, held that ". . . the business of insurance is not commerce, either intrastate or interstate. . . ." The Supreme Court found that all previous cases had been brought to strike down state statutes in areas where Congress had taken no action, but that since the case before it was an attack on an Act of Congress, a reconsideration of whether insurance was commerce was in order. In a four to three decision, with two justices not participating, the Court held that, notwithstanding its previous opinions in cases involving insurance, its opinion in other cases where insurance was not involved but where findings were made as to what constituted commerce were so broad that an exception of the business of insurance could not be made.[11]

The decision of the South-Eastern Underwriters Association case made applicable to the business of insurance federal laws which in many instances were in direct conflict with the provisions of state laws. The rights of the states to regulate and tax insurance were placed in jeopardy. Accordingly, the National Association of Insurance Commissioners was instrumental in having introduced and passed what became known as Public Law No. 15, which became effective on March 9, 1945. Although it did not, as had been hoped by the Commissioners, grant an exemption from the Federal Trade Commission, the Robinson-Patman, and the Sherman and Clayton Acts, it did grant a moratorium as to those Acts until January 1, 1948, and provided for their effectiveness thereafter only ". . . to the extent that such business is not regulated by state law." Subsequently the moratorium was extended until July 1, 1948, to give the several states additional time to adopt the NAIC's recommended model regulatory legislation.

1946 Model Bill

With the dissolution of the Group Association in 1942, both the American Life Convention and the Life Insurance Association of America took real interest in group insurance legislation. As a result, the Commissioners, shortly after taking up for consideration the idea of a new model group law, including both a definition and standard provisions, in 1943 asked the Life Insurance Association to submit a memorandum on group insurance underwriting principles. Since the laws which had been enacted to that time had departed markedly from the 1917 model law, the memorandum recommended that the actual emerging pattern of laws be more closely followed. Accordingly, some of the more important suggestions were recognition of labor union coverage; reduction in the minimum number of lives from fifty to twenty-five; authorization to insure employees of subsidiaries and affiliates; authorization to insure partners and proprietors under group insurance policies covering their employees; authorization to insure persons who, while not employees, have their business under the

---

[11] 322 U.S. Reports 533.

financial control of the master policyholder through contract or otherwise; authorization to cover retired employees; recognition of group permanent life insurance (only term life insurance had theretofore been accepted); recognition of the right of the insurer to demand evidence of individual insurability; and authorization of multiple-employer coverage where the employers are not necessarily related financially. This last suggestion was made in the light of the impact of industry-wide collective bargaining which was just then emerging. An additional proposal was put forward at this time by the National Association of Life Underwriters to the effect that group life insurance amounts on individuals be limited to $20,000.

In 1946, the National Association of Insurance Commissioners adopted all the suggestions with only minor modifications. However, neither the American Life Convention nor the Life Insurance Association of America formally endorsed this new model bill. Instead it was accepted as a guide by which to test any legislation introduced by other sources. Legislation was not sponsored, but any which deviated too radically from "the guide" was opposed. The 1946 model bill was enacted in a number of states at the insistence of the insurance commissioner and is today the basis of the legislation in eight states,[12] although some variation from the model bill exists in each case.

Subsequent Revisions to the Model Bill

The 1946 revised model definition and standard provisions lasted for only two years. The $20,000 limitation was unpalatable to those companies desiring to develop group permanent life insurance to compete with the unrestricted amounts being written under individual policies held by pension trusts. Some of the insurance commissioners objected to the multiple-employer provision on the ground that it would permit the coverage of employees of employers who were members of a trade association, which they considered unsound underwriting. Consequently another model bill was adopted in 1948 which dealt with both the stated objections and made other minor changes. This model bill is the basis for the laws in twenty-four jurisdictions,[13] although again each has adopted its own variations.

An additional change was made in the model bill in 1953, when the so-called $20,000/$40,000 limit was introduced in place of the $20,000 limit, which still applied to term life insurance after the 1948 change. The new

---

[12] Colorado, Connecticut (by Insurance Commission Rulings, pursuant to statute), Iowa, Louisiana, New Hampshire, North Carolina, Vermont and Washington.

[13] Arizona, Arkansas, District of Columbia, Florida, Georgia, Hawaii, Idaho, Indiana, Kansas, Kentucky, Maine, Maryland, Montana, Nebraska, Nevada, New Jersey, New Mexico, Oklahoma, Pennsylvania, South Carolina, Texas, Virginia, West Virginia and Wisconsin. Oregon is in a class by itself. It has enacted a group life insurance law following the model bill standard provisions, but without underwriting restrictions other than a minimum of ten lives and 25 per cent participation.

rule permitted up to $20,000 of insurance irrespective of an employee's annual earnings and up to $40,000 if the amount of insurance did not exceed one and one-half times the employee's annual earnings from his employer. In 1954, the required minimum number of lives was reduced from twenty-five to ten. In 1956, changes were adopted affecting the maximum amount and types of loans which could be covered under creditor group life insurance. The current model bill[14] containing both a group life insurance definition and group life insurance standard provisions, was promulgated by the National Association of Insurance Commissioners in December, 1956.

From the foregoing it should be clear that much time and effort have been directed toward creating a uniform definition of group life insurance; however, the enactments in the various states have not produced a pattern of complete uniformity. Basically, all the statutes today provide for coverages of four types of groups: (1) employees of one employer; (2) members of a labor union; (3) debtors of a creditor; and (4) employees of two or more employers engaged in the same industry or in combination with members of one or more labor unions. The last always requires that the policy be issued to trustees. Beyond these four, the statutes bear little uniformity. Some states permit coverage of members of professional associations; dependents of insured employees; any association not formed or maintained for the purpose of providing insurance; public employee associations, with members paying the entire cost; credit unions; national guard; teachers; firemen; police; national veterans' associations; depositors of a bank; clergymen; fraternals; associations of students; agricultural or horticultural cooperatives; and agents under personal service contracts. The statutes also vary as to the number of lives necessary to constitute a group.[15] In those states which have not adopted a statute defining or controlling group life insurance, a group insurance contract may be issued

---

[14] The full text of the 1956 model bill may be found in Appendix 1.

[15] The minimum number of persons necessary for insurance of a single employer contract is ten in all jurisdictions having statutes except Georgia, Nebraska and Nevada, which states require five.

For issuance to a labor union, a minimum of twenty-five members is required in Arizona, Arkansas, California, Colorado, Connecticut, Georgia, Hawaii, Indiana, Kansas, Kentucky, Maine, Maryland, Montana, Nebraska, Nevada, New Hampshire, New Mexico, New York, North Carolina, Ohio, Pennsylvania, South Carolina, Utah, Vermont, Virginia, Washington, West Virginia and Wisconsin; a minimum of ten members is required in the District of Columbia, Florida, Idaho, Iowa, Louisiana, Michigan, New Jersey, Oklahoma, Oregon and Texas; a minimum of two is required in Massachusetts; and there is no minimum requirement in Illinois.

For issuance of a contract to a creditor the requirement is that of 100 new entrants yearly in all jurisdictions having statutes except that Michigan and Texas require only fifty; New York requires only twenty-five; and Georgia, Kentucky and Oregon have no requirement, while the statute in Utah is silent as to such a contract.

For issuance of a multi-employer trustee contract the minimum number of lives required is 100 in all jurisdictions having statutes, except that Michigan requires 250 lives; Arkansas, seventy-five lives; California, Ohio and Washington, fifty lives; Hawaii, Nevada and New York, twenty-five lives; and Illinois and Oregon, ten lives.

covering any of the aforementioned or any other group of individuals which an insurer might deem to be feasible in its underwriting judgment.

LEGAL DEFINITION OF GROUP HEALTH INSURANCE

Group health insurance has developed primarily without important statutory limitations. Although the first group health insurance policy predated the first group life insurance policy by a year, group health insurance was restricted to weekly indemnity or disability income insurance and accidental death and dismemberment insurance until the early 1930's, when the group writing companies ventured into the hospital expense insurance field. The number of companies concentrating on individual health insurance was not great, and the number of agents representing such companies was small. Thus the opposition which has always been raised against group life insurance did not arise. On the other hand, counterparts of the underwriting principles of the 1917 National Association of Insurance Commissioners group life insurance definition were opposed with success by one of the trade association predecessors to the Health Insurance Association of America, and to date the National Association of Insurance Commissioners has not adopted a model bill for group health insurance.

The reluctance to advance any statutory definition for group health insurance, insofar as the insurers are concerned, undoubtedly stems from the sincere belief that rigid restrictions applying to insurance companies would merely cause prospective group insurance business to be placed with Blue Cross and Blue Shield associations. Blue Cross and Blue Shield associations generally are established under special laws, and, while usually under the jurisdiction of the insurance departments, they are not subject to insurance laws. As a result, most of the statutes which govern group health insurance are merely a generalized description of virtually all types of group health insurance currently being underwritten, as in the model bill which has been prepared by the Health Insurance Association of America for use wherever a demand for such legislation arises.[16]

Despite the fact that the National Association of Insurance Commissioners, as well as the insurance industry generally, has shown little interest in developing a group health insurance definition, thirty-five states[17] have adopted laws defining what groups may be insured. Generally these laws follow the pattern of the Health Insurance Association of America's

---

[16] The full text of this bill may be found in Appendix 2.

[17] Arizona, Arkansas, California, Colorado, Florida, Georgia, Hawaii, Idaho, Illinois, Indiana, Iowa, Kansas, Kentucky, Louisiana, Maine, Maryland, Massachusetts, Michigan, Minnesota, Montana, Nebraska, Nevada, New Jersey, New Mexico, New York, North Carolina, Ohio, Oklahoma, Pennsylvania, South Carolina, Utah, Vermont, Washington, West Virginia and Wisconsin.

model bill, but a few states have added other underwriting features. In the remaining jurisdictions, any type of group health insurance deemed feasible by an insurer from an underwriting viewpoint may be written. This is possible because of an exemption for group health insurance from the Uniform Individual Accident and Sickness Policy Provisions Law in fifteen jurisdictions,[18] and by reason of no law at all in the remaining one.[19]

JURISDICTION OVER GROUP LIFE AND HEALTH INSURANCE

Although the various state statutes are not in complete agreement as to the types of groups that may be written for group life and health insurance, the doctrine of comity[20] and full faith and credit among the states has permitted a group insurance policy properly written in a given jurisdiction to cross over state lines and provide insurance for residents of a state who could not obtain such insurance under that state's own statutes. This is particularly true with respect to policies issued to cover members of a professional association, a veterans' organization, or a fraternal or religious organization. Certain states,[21] however, have provided in their statutes that no insurance shall be written to cover its residents by any admitted insurer unless its own laws specifically permit the issuance of such insurance. Even these statutes are not effective in the case of a nonadmitted insurer, since the state has no jurisdiction over such an insurer. [22]

The foregoing described state of the law gives to any insurer the ability to seek out a state for situs of a particular contract it may wish to issue. In

---

[18] Alabama, Connecticut, Delaware, District of Columbia, Mississippi, Missouri, New Hampshire, North Dakota, Oregon, South Dakota, Rhode Island, Tennessee, Texas, Virginia and Wyoming.

[19] Alaska.

[20] The courtesy by which states recognize and give effect within their own territory to the institutions or laws of another state.

[21] Ohio, Texas and Wisconsin. See Texas Insurance Law, Art. 3.50, Sec. 4, for an example of this type of law. Certain other states have statutes which, under given sets of circumstances, have been construed to have the same effect but are not generally so regarded. These are Florida, Massachusetts, Michigan, New Jersey and North Carolina. See New Jersey Insurance Commissioner's ruling of August 25, 1958.

[22] Some doubt on the conclusion drawn is raised in the case of *Ministers Life & Casualty Union* v. *Charles Manson, Commissioner of Insurance, and John Reynolds, Attorney General, State of Wisconsin*. This action was brought to test the constitutionality of Sec. 201.42 of the Wisconsin Insurance Laws. The law imposes a $5,000 penalty on an unauthorized insurer for effectuating insurance in Wisconsin. Service may be made on the Secretary of State. On October 9, 1964, Judge Norris Maloney of the Dane County, Wisconsin Circuit Court held the statutes constitutional. Appeal to the Supreme Court of Wisconsin is under consideration as of this writing. In this connection attention is drawn to a paper entitled "Unauthorized Insurance Law Trends," by Richard J. Francis, delivered before the Legal Section of the American Life Convention on October 9, 1962 and reported in *American Life Convention Proceedings of the Legal Section, 1962–1963*, pp. 257–69.

general, however, issuance of master contracts is restricted to (1) the state of incorporation of a corporation or settlement of articles of association of an association; (2) the state where the principal office of a business is located; (3) the state where the greatest number of those to be insured is employed; (4) the state where the trust under which a contract is to be made effective is created; or (5) any state in which is located any employer or any labor union which is a party to a trust. This latitude of choice has been the subject of much study by the companies engaged in writing group insurance, and has been and is under attack by the National Association of Life Underwriters. This organization is opposed to any extension of group insurance beyond the limits now set forth in the model bill and would like to see all states limit the group coverage permitted on its residents to that specifically permitted by its own statutes, regardless of where the master contract is issued.[23]

There is no clear-cut answer to the situs problem, and it is not probable that there will be in the near future. The majority of the companies writing group insurance do not want to see further restrictions introduced into the statutes, and some would like to see present restrictions removed. On the whole the companies are satisfied to seek situs of a contract in one of the jurisdictions outlined in the foregoing paragraph. The occasional exception does occur where a company seeks out a jurisdiction which has no law or a very lax one. However, the volume of group insurance written in this manner is so small as to provoke no comment except that which comes from those who would like to see group insurance drastically curtailed.[24]

MAXIMUM AMOUNTS OF GROUP LIFE INSURANCE[25]

As has been previously mentioned, the 1946 group life insurance model bill limited the amount of group life insurance permitted on any one life to $20,000. The 1953 model bill liberalized this maximum amount somewhat by substituting the $20,000/$40,000 limitation. However, the increasing federal income tax burden on persons of substantial income has encouraged higher and higher amounts of group life insurance because of the advantageous tax position enjoyed by such insurance. This advantage was gained in 1920 when a federal income tax ruling[26] declared that an employer's contributions for group term life insurance on his employees

---

[23] See report of statement made by Counsel of the National Association of Life Underwriters at the June, 1964 Meeting of the National Association of Insurance Commissioners; *Insurance,* Vol. XLV, No. 25, Part 1 (June 20, 1964) p. 3.

[24] See Chapter 25 for a more detailed discussion of the question of the proper situs of group insurance master contracts.

[25] The liberalization of maximum group insurance benefit amounts is the subject of Chapter 31.

[26] I.R.S.; Law Opinion 1014.

did not constitute taxable income to the employees. At the time the ruling was issued, group life insurance amounts were very small, with typical plans calling for a maximum of $1,000. Although many efforts were made to change this ruling, none were successful until 1964.

The increasing maxima have been opposed by the National Association of Life Underwriters, nongroup writing companies, and even some of the group writing companies which feel that the social aspects of group life insurance are no longer being served when top executives can use the group insurance approach to build estates. As a result, thirty[27] jurisdictions have adopted laws which provide for limitations on the maximum amount of group life insurance which may be issued on any one life. However, such important industrial states as California, Massachusetts, Michigan and New York have no maximum stipulated in their statutes. In fact, the legislature of New York, which had adopted a $20,000 maximum, saw fit, under pressure from industry generally, to repeal it just at the time that the $20,000/$40,000 type of law was gaining popularity. Georgia and Idaho also have repealed their laws establishing maxima.

As it became apparent that fixed dollar maxima were no longer gaining favor with state legislatures, and higher and higher maxima were being provided under contracts written in states having no limit, those opposed to unlimited amounts of group life insurance sought new ways to bring them under control. In addition, the American Life Convention and the Life Insurance Association of America appointed a "Joint Committee on Reexamination of Group Policy" in order ". . . that the entire question of statutory underwriting restrictions on group life insurance be reexamined." As is implied, the reexamination was to apply not only to amounts, but also to horizontal extensions of the group concept. In summary the Committee's report proposed the following:

1. Discontinuation of ALC–LIAA support of the $20,000/$40,000 limit on amounts of group life insurance permissible on individuals, in favor of a "nondiscrimination rule" based on the principle that higher salaried employees should not be insured for group life insurance in amounts appreciably greater in relation to their compensation than lower salaried employees in the same companies are insured for;

2. Relaxation of restrictions or prohibitions on certain special types of group

---

[27] The jurisdictions and limits are as follows: Arizona, Arkansas, Colorado, District of Columbia, Illinois, Indiana, Iowa, Kansas, Louisiana, Maine, Maryland, Montana, Nebraska, Nevada, New Jersey, Ohio, Oklahoma, Pennsylvania, South Carolina, Texas, Vermont, Washington, West Virginia and Wisconsin—$40,000, except that amounts over $20,000 (21,000 in Colorado) cannot exceed 150 per cent of annual salary; North Carolina—$40,000; Hawaii, Kentucky and Tennessee—$50,000, except that amounts over $25,000 ($30,000 in Hawaii) cannot exceed 150 per cent (200 per cent in Kentucky) of annual salary; New Hampshire—$60,000, except that amounts over $20,000 cannot exceed 150 per cent of annual salary; Florida—$100,000, except that amounts over $20,000 cannot exceed 200 per cent of annual salary.

Connecticut has a $100,000 maximum established by the Insurance Commissioner's ruling.

life insurance plans, notably those involving dependents of employees and mortgagors;

3. Tightening of restrictions or prohibitions on certain other special types of group life insurance underwriting, such as plans proposing to insure members of professional associations or to provide life insurance coverage on installment purchasers of shares in mutual funds; and

4. Direction of special attention to problems related to "wholesale" life insurance issued as an alternative to group coverage, and to those related to direct writing of group life insurance without commissions.

The report was rendered by the Committee and was adopted by the Associations in the fall of 1960. Committees to implement the report were immediately appointed. Though much effort has been expended to date no definitive action has taken place.

FEDERAL INCOME TAXATION OF GROUP LIFE INSURANCE[28]

In 1963, certain groups reopened the question of the tax-exempt status to the employee of employer contributions to a group life insurance program. This reopening coincided with the decision of the federal administration to seek a reduction in the federal income tax. The Treasury immediately saw this as an opportunity to eliminate or reduce the extent of the tax exemption enjoyed by those insured under employer-employee group life insurance plans.

As a result, the Revenue Act of 1964 provides that the cost of the first $50,000 of group life insurance paid by the employer will continue to be tax-exempt to the employee. The cost of amounts in excess of $50,000, reduced by the total amount of any employee contribution, will be taxed to the employee. A retired employee is not taxed for his group life insurance coverage no matter how much insurance is furnished him, provided his employment has terminated and he has reached retirement age or is disabled. The cost of the insurance to be included in the employee's income will be determined, not in accordance with the premium table set forth in the policy under which he is insured, but on the basis of a uniform premium table prepared by the Treasury Department on the basis of current group term life insurance rates averaged for five-year age brackets. Whether the change in income tax treatment for the employee of part of the premium paid by the employer will tend to put an end to so-called "jumbo" amounts of group life insurance remains to be seen.

UNION AND UNION-MANAGEMENT WELFARE FUNDS

While it will be remembered that Public Law No. 15 left the regulation of insurance in the hands of the states, certain other federal enactments, in

---

[28] Chapter 8 of this volume contains a detailed discussion of the federal income tax treatment of group term and permanent life insurance. See also Robert H. Bloom, "Life Insurance and the Revenue Act of 1964," *The Journal of the American Society of Chartered Life Underwriters*, Vol. XVIII, No. 3 (Summer, 1964), p. 233.

addition to the Internal Revenue Code, have had or are having a definite effect on the legal environment of group insurance. During World War II the National War Labor Board froze wages and salaries, but did not restrict employer contributions to employee benefit plans. As a result employers turned to group insurance and pension plans to supplement wages as a means of attracting and retaining workers. Union leaders, unable to obtain wage increases for members, began to stress demands for welfare plans. It was this circumstance which had much to do with the inclusion of the multiple-employer provision in the 1946 model bill, and which causes it to be frequently referred to as the "Taft-Hartley" provision or the collective bargaining provision. The Taft-Hartley Act requires that funds for employee welfare plans which are payable by the employer be paid into a trust fund rather than turned over to the union directly. It also requires that such trust have both management and labor trustees. With this state of the law, and given industry-wide collective bargaining, a form of group insurance which could be issued to the trustees of one or more employers and one or more labor unions became a must.[29]

While the Taft-Hartley Act does not prohibit an employer from buying a group insurance plan without the consent of the union or unions representing his employees, the United States Supreme Court has held that an employer must bargain collectively on employee benefit plans, if the employees request it. This was established as to pensions in 1949 in the Inland Steel Case[30] and as to insurance in the W. W. Cross and Company case.[31]

NAIC Code of Ethical Practices

The development of joint union-management welfare funds unfortunately was accompanied by abuses. These abuses led to scandals which came to light in the late 1940's and early 1950's. While there were few instances where insurance companies were involved, some of the practices of certain insurers—knowingly contracting with "dummy" agencies and granting agents contracts under which the commissions earned were in direct proportion to the claims incurred—were such that abuse was almost a natural outgrowth. Consequently, the National Association of Insurance Commissioners took cognizance of the situation and at its December, 1960, meeting adopted a "Code of Ethical Practices with respect to Insuring of the Benefits of Union or Union-Management Welfare and Pension Funds."

In the preamble to the Code it was pointed out that "in most instances fund trustees have scrupulously respected their fiduciary responsibilities, and insurance companies, agents and brokers dealing with them have

---

[29] The group insurance arrangements applicable to Taft-Hartley Welfare funds are the subject of Chapter 33.

[30] 77 NLRB 1; 170 Fed(2d) 247; 336 U.S. 960.

[31] 77 NLRB 1162; 174 Fed(2d) 875.

likewise generally conducted themselves in the best traditions of the insurance business in observing in both letter and spirit the laws of the several states. However, such has not been true in every case." The purposes which the Code is intended to serve were spelled out as follows:

The following Code of Ethical Practices, adopted by the National Association of Insurance Commissioners, is intended to serve as a declaration of applicable principles in the proper conduct of insuring welfare and pension funds, and will serve to complement such existing state insurance laws as require that insurance benefits be reasonable in relation to the premiums charged, and which prohibit unfair discrimination, rebates, misrepresentation, misleading or deceptive acts, and other unfair trade practices or unfair methods of competition, as being prejudicial to the interests of beneficiaries of insured welfare and pension funds.

The Code laid out practices to be followed in payment of benefits, commissions, fees and other allowances. In addition, it set forth principles governing the relationship between trustees and insurers, methods of acquiring new business and methods of handling business once it has been acquired. The Code was adopted by New York almost immediately and was promulgated to all companies doing business in New York on December 20, 1957.[32]

State and Federal Disclosure Laws

While this Code of Ethical Practices was well accepted by the group insurance industry and put into effect by almost all companies, there was no means of enforcing it except when acts such as those referred to in the preamble above ran afoul of existing statutes. Several states, feeling that a more effective weapon was needed, enacted what are known as disclosure laws. Such laws are currently in effect in Connecticut,[33] Massachusetts,[34] New York,[35] Washington[36] and Wisconsin.[37]

Since the laws enacted were not the same in their requirements, it soon became apparent that if every state adopted such laws the amount of administrative work which would fall on policyholders, funds and insurance companies would be almost prohibitive. Accordingly, when the federal government showed an interest in the subject, the insurance industry decided that this was an instance when federal law would best serve, and further backing of legislation at the state level ceased.

The United States Congress enacted the "Welfare and Pension Plan

---

[32] For the full text of the Code, see Appendix 3.

[33] Connecticut Insurance Law, Secs. 31–78 to 31–89.

[34] General Laws, Chap. 1510.

[35] New York Insurance Law, Sec. 37.

[36] R.C.W. Secs. 48:800–48:810.

[37] Wisconsin Statutes, Secs. 50:851–50:859. California permitted its disclosure law to expire in 1960.

Disclosure Act"[38] effective January 1, 1959. This law, as amended to date, requires that, subject to certain minor exceptions, every administrator of an employee welfare benefit plan covering twenty-six or more participants shall publish, as set forth in the Act, to each participant covered thereunder a description of the plan. In addition, if the plan has 100 or more participants, an annual financial report must be published. The financial report must include, among other things, (1) the unit rates being paid an insurer; (2) the total premium paid; (3) the total claims paid; (4) the dividend or refund, if any, paid; (5) the commissions and fees charged to the plan; and (6) to whom and for what such commission and fees were paid. All of this information must be furnished to the administrator by the insurer. Copies of both the plan description and the annual financial report must be filed with the Secretary of Labor, who must make them available for examination in the public document room of the Department of Labor. Teeth were given to the law by the enactment of criminal code provisions.[39]

While the five states mentioned above still have their disclosure laws on the books, the requirements are generally satisfied by the filing of a copy of the federal filings. However, the State of Washington still requires insurance companies to make filings directly with it on union-management welfare plans, and Massachusetts requires annual financial reports from plans having twenty-six to 100 participants.

POSSIBLE FUTURE DEVELOPMENTS

The treatment of the legal environment of group insurance in this chapter has not been exhaustive, nor was it so intended, since many other statutes, rulings and regulations are so interwoven with the subject matter of the other chapters that they are an integral part thereof. However, this chapter has pointed up the extent to which each step in the development of group insurance has been accompanied by new laws or changes in existing laws brought about either because of a desire within the insurance industry (1) to keep competition above the cutthroat level, (2) to keep group insurance from further encroachment on the field of individual insurance, or (3) to give greater protection to the third party beneficiaries of group insurance contracts, the insureds. In each of these areas the forces are still at work so that the future will see further developments. The American Life Convention and the Life Insurance Association of America have recently decided that, in view of the recent change in the federal tax law with reference to group life insurance, the two associations shall no longer give backing to amount limitations in the model group life law. Under consideration is a concentrated effort to have

---

[38] 29 USC et sequi, Title 29.
[39] 18 USC 1027, Title 18.

statutes defining group life insurance enacted in all states not currently having statutes on their books. On the other hand, the National Association of Life Underwriters is not certain that the federal tax law will be a sufficient deterrent to high group life insurance amounts and, while it would like to see a group life insurance law in every state, it is not willing yet to see the amount limitation dispensed with. New developments may be expected in this area.

The desire on the part of the National Association of Life Underwriters to see each state exercise its jurisdiction over a group insurance contract which covers persons residing within its borders regardless of the situs of the master group contract has not abated. The companies, on the other hand, are opposed to such a state of affairs, as it would make administration of group insurance contracts which extend across state lines almost impractical of administration unless completely uniform laws could be enacted in all states, which on past experience can be taken as an impossibility.

The further development and administration of federal laws in the fields of labor, minimum wages, disclosure, uniform employment practices and equal opportunities must all be watched with interest. Developments in all of these areas will have direct bearing on the future legal environment of group insurance.

SELECTED REFERENCES

BROOKE, DWIGHT E. "Some Phases of Group Life Insurance Law," *Proceedings of the American Life Convention*, Legal Section (October, 1948).

BROWNING, ARTHUR M. "The Status of Group Insurance for Public Employees," *Proceedings of the Association of Life Insurance Counsel*, Vol. XIII (1956).

GOSE, GEORGE B. "The Doing Business Rule and Group Insurance." Paper read before Association of Life Insurance Counsel, White Sulphur Springs, W. Va., May 15, 1950.

HALLETT, JAMES B. "Extra-Territorial Effect of State Regulatory Laws: Some 1955 Comments," *Proceedings of the Association of Life Insurance Counsel*, Vol. XII (1955).

KING, CECIL G. "Proper Situs of Multi-State Group Policies," *Proceedings of the Association of Life Insurance Counsel*, Vol. XV (1961).

MOSES, ALFRED S., JR. "The Conflict of Laws and Life Insurance," *Proceedings of the Association of Life Insurance Counsel*, Vol. XII (1954).

REEVES, GORDON C. "Recent Developments in the Field of Group Insurance," *Proceedings of the Association of Life Insurance Counsel*, Vol. XII (1955).

————. "Some Recent Legal Developments Resulting from Extension of Group Coverage to Union Members and Related Groups," *Proceedings of the American Life Convention*, Legal Section (October, 1951).

PART III

Group Life Coverages

Chapter 7

GROUP TERM LIFE INSURANCE

BY WILLIAM G. WILLIAMS

Group life insurance had its legal birth in June, 1911, when The Equitable Life Assurance Society of the United States issued a policy to insure the employees of the Pantasote Leather Company, Passaic, New Jersey, but the coverage was actually conceived during the 1910–12 negotiations between Montgomery Ward and The Equitable.[1] The policy form that was approved by the New York Insurance Department was known as a "Yearly Renewable Term Employees' Policy." It is interesting to note that such commonplace features as the insurance being issued on a nonmedical, one-year renewable term basis, the premiums being paid in advance, the right to participate in any year-end surplus, a thirty-day grace period, a one-year incontestable clause, a misstatement of age clause and a conversion privilege were included in the first group life insurance policy.

The tremendous growth and popularity of group term life insurance undoubtedly has been due to its ability to provide employers, unions, trustees, associations and certain creditors with needed low cost "death benefits" for the *protection* of their employees, members or debtors. This low-cost appeal has resulted from the use of one-year renewable term insurance, which by its very nature does not require the reserve element or cash or paid-up values found in level premium life insurance.

The term premium need only be adequate to provide *protection* during the current policy year (i.e., the costs of the currently expected level of claims and expenses plus a reasonable margin for profit and contingencies). At the end of each policy year the average premium rate is recalculated on the basis of one-year term premium rates and the distribution by age of the insurance then in force for the particular group. The actual renewal rate depends in part on the calculated rate and in part on the accumulated experience of the group. However, the very nature of the group tends to result in a continuing level premium cost because of the addition of young lives and the termination of old lives. Thus, turnover,

---

[1] See Chapter 4 for a more complete discussion of this subject.

experience credits and the tendency of an employer to assume any increasing costs offset the step-rate nature of group term life insurance premium rates.

Realisticallly, group term life insurance should be viewed by insureds as a type of insurance which has limited guarantees of permanence and few "living benefits," since it has no cash values, no savings features and provides no emergency funds upon which to draw. It is designed primarily for the purpose of providing low cost protection against economic loss in the event of death.

SCOPE OF GROUP TERM LIFE INSURANCE

By the end of 1963, 31 per cent of all life insurance in force in the United States was group life insurance, which represents a total volume of $228.5 billion of group insurance provided under 203,000 group master contracts for 50.9 million group life insurance certificate holders. Dependents group life insurance, which by law can be written in only about half of the states, represented about $3.0 billion of the $228.5 billion and was provided under 9,270 group master contracts.

Analysis of these figures shows that the average amount of *group* life insurance protection per individual certificate was $4,490, whereas the average size *individual* life insurance policy in force in the United States was $4,130.[2] Table 7–1 illustrates the fact that most group life insurance is issued on the one-year renewable term basis.

The two most important uses of group term life insurance are in con-

TABLE 7–1

GROUP LIFE INSURANCE IN FORCE IN THE UNITED STATES BY PLAN

	1950		1957		1962	
Plan of Insurance	Amount (000,000 Omitted)	Per Cent	Amount (000,000 Omitted)	Per Cent	Amount (000,000 Omitted)	Per Cent
Group:						
Regular term......	$47,300	99.0	$132,200	98.8	$203,300	97.2
Decreasing and extended term.....	——	——	——	——	400	.2
Whole Life.......	300	.6	700	.5	900	.4
Endowment and retirement income...........	200	.4	900	.7	900	.4
Combination policies:						
Permanent......	——	——	——	——	500	.3
Term..........	——	——	——	——	3,200	1.5
Total Group..	$47,800	100.0	$133,800	100.0	$209,200	100.0

SOURCE: Institute of Life Insurance.

---

[2] Institute of Life Insurance, *1964 Life Insurance Fact Book*, p. 15.

TABLE 7-2. GROUP LIFE INSURANCE IN FORCE BY TYPE AND BY SIZE OF GROUP—1963
(Excluding Dependent Coverage, Creditor Group Life, and Federal Employees Group Life)

	Number of Master Policies	Number of Members* (000 Omitted)	Amount of Insurance (000,000 Omitted)	Average Amount of Insurance per Member	Percentage Distribution of			
					Number of Master Policies		Amount of Insurance	
					1956†	1963	1956†	1963
I. Type of group								
A. Related to employment or occupation								
1. Employer-employee	174,300	26,685	$180,890	$6,780	82.9%	85.8%	89.5%	86.4%
2. Union and joint employer-union	4,770	4,718	10,078	2,140	2.8	2.3	6.9	4.8
3. Professional society	500	397	3,649	9,190		.2		1.7
4. Employee association	1,570	1,173	6,195	5,280	.9	.8	2.4	3.0
5a. Other—related to employee benefit program	1,010	470	1,849	3,930		.5		.9
b. Other—not related to employee benefit program	130	153	1,050	6,860		.1		.5
Total Type A	182,280	33,596*	$203,711	$6,060	86.6%	89.7%	98.8%	97.3%
B. Not related to employment or occupation								
1. Fraternal society	90	94	$ 285	$3,030	N.A.	.1%	N.A.	.1%
2. Savings or investment group	20,390	11,647	4,355	370	N.A.	10.0	N.A.	2.1
3. Other	380	324	953	2,940	N.A.	.2	N.A.	.5
Total Type B	20,860	12,065*	$ 5,593	$ 460	13.4%	10.3%	1.2%	2.7%
Total	203,140	45,661*	$209,304	$4,580	100.0%	100.0%	100.0%	100.0%
II. Size of group								
A. Fewer than 25 members	91,690	1,027	$ 5,090	$4,960	24.5%	45.1%	1.0%	2.4%
B. 25–99 members	60,280	2,601	11,140	4,280	42.3	29.7	5.2	5.3
C. 100–499 members	35,610	7,035	22,297	3,170	23.7	17.5	11.4	10.7
D. 500 or more members	15,560	34,998	170,777	4,880	9.5	7.7	82.4	81.6
Total	203,140	45,661*	$209,304	$4,580	100.0%	100.0%	100.0%	100.0%

NOTE: Total coverage in the United States at the end of 1963 by type of group is estimated on the basis of reports from life insurance companies having 78 per cent of the total master policies, 84 per cent of the total membership and 81 per cent of the total amount of group life insurance in force in the United States, excluding dependent coverage, creditor group life, and federal employees group life, on December 31, 1963.

Total coverage in the United States at the end of 1963 by size of group is estimated on the basis of reports from life insurance companies having 66 per cent of the total master policies, 77 per cent of the total membership and 70 per cent of the total amount of group life insurance in force in the United States, excluding dependent coverage, creditor group life, and federal employees group life, on December 31, 1963.

N.A. Not Available.

* Includes duplication where individuals are included as members of more than one group.

† 1956 percentages are adjusted to include a substantial number of savings or investment type groups which were originally omitted in the 1956 survey.

SOURCE: Institute of Life Insurance.

nection with the underwriting of employer-employee groups and creditor-debtor groups. An analysis of group life insurance in force in the United States by type and size of group, made by the Institute of Life Insurance in 1964, shows that employer-employee groups continued to account for the bulk of such insurance. For example, 85.8 per cent of the number of master contracts and 86.4 per cent of the amount of group life insurance in force in the United States in 1963 were attributable to employer-employee groups. The results of this analysis are shown in Table 7–2.

Creditor group life insurance, which is used to repay a debt in case the borrower should die, is the fastest growing of all forms of life insurance in force today. About 85 per cent of the creditor life insurance in force in the United States at the end of 1963 was group insurance. The total creditor group life insurance volume, amounting to $37.0 billion, was divided among 46.3 million certificates issued under 52,000 master contracts.[3]

Except for Canada, the growth of group life insurance throughout the rest of the world has been quite slow. The issuance of group life insurance in Canada was first permitted under the Insurance Act of 1917. At the end of 1963, there was $21 billion of group life insurance in force in Canada, as compared with $39 billion of individual life insurance.[4]

By the end of 1963, there was 730.6 billion of all forms of life insurance in force in the United States. Table 7–3 shows the growth since the turn of

TABLE 7–3

GROWTH OF LIFE INSURANCE IN FORCE IN THE UNITED STATES*
(000,000 Omitted)

Year	Ordinary	Group	Industrial	Credit	Total
1900	$ 6,124	$ ——	$ 1,449	$ ——	$ 7,573
1910	11,783	——	3,125	——	14,908
1915	16,650	100	4,279	——	21,029
1917	19,868	349	5,026	†	25,243
1920	32,018	1,570	6,948	4	40,540
1925	52,892	4,247	12,318	18	69,475
1930	78,576	9,801	17,963	73	106,413
1935	70,684	10,208	17,471	101	98,464
1940	79,346	14,938	20,866	380	115,530
1945	101,550	22,172	27,675	365	151,762
1950	149,071	47,793	33,415	3,889	234,168
1955	216,600	101,300	39,682	14,750	372,332
1960	340,268	175,434	39,563	31,183	586,448
1963	418,856	228,540	39,672	43,555	730,623

* Totals for "In the United States" represent all life insurance (excluding reinsurance acquired) on residents of the United States, whether issued by United States or alien companies. Beginning with 1959, United States totals include Alaska and Hawaii.
† Less than $500,000.
SOURCES: *Spectator Year Book* and Institute of Life Insurance.

[3] *Ibid.*, p. 32.
[4] *Ibid.*, p. 105.

the century for group and other principal types of life insurance.

It is important to remember that during the decade 1910 to 1920, and even as late as the early 1930's, group life insurance was the principal group coverage underwritten. Furthermore, although group life insurance master contracts may be issued to labor unions, associations and other groups, most of them are issued to employer-employee groups.

EMPLOYER-EMPLOYEE GROUP TERM LIFE INSURANCE

Group life insurance benefits are designed to replace an employee's earned income for a limited period of time in the event of his death. The basic death benefit is, however, only one of many types of benefits provided by an employer for the protection of his employees under a group life insurance master contract.

Type of Benefits Provided

The basic benefit provided under a group term life insurance policy is the payment of the face amount (death benefit) to the designated beneficiary upon the death of the insured at any time while the coverage is in effect and from any cause. In addition, supplemental features which benefit the insured or his beneficiary include the *continuation of insurance* provision, the *extension of the death benefit on termination of employment*, the *conversion privilege*, the provision of *disability benefits*, the *beneficiary* provisions and the availability of certain *settlement options*. Each of these will be discussed in the following sections.

Death Benefit. Under a group term life insurance plan, the death benefit, unlike most other group benefits, is payable even if the cause of death is due to an occupational accident or sickness. The amount of death benefit in force on any insured employee at the time of death is determined by the application of the formula included in the employer's group master contract. This contractual formula includes the eligibility provisions, the individual's effective date of insurance and the schedule of insurance stated in the group policy. For employer-employee groups, these formulas usually are based on conditions pertaining to employment, and the schedule of insurance amounts is keyed to earnings, occupation, length of service, a flat amount, dependency status or a combination of two or more of these types of classifications. Since the current objective of most employers is to provide an extension of the deceased worker's pay, the most common classification is by income, and the schedule of insurance is designed to replace the loss of one, one and one-half, two or three years earnings.

Continuation of Insurance. During temporary interruptions of continuous active full-time employment, such as when an employee is laid off or granted a leave of absence, the employer may elect to continue, on a basis which precludes individual selection, the employee's group term life insurance in force for a limited period (e.g., three months) by the payment of the premium due. This continuation of insurance benefit may be extended by mutual agreement between the employer and the insurance company.

Upon the expiration of the continuation period, premium payments are discontinued, and the employee's insurance is terminated. However, the terminated employee still has available to him an extension of the death benefit for thirty-one days after this termination of insurance as well as the right to exercise the conversion privilege within this same thirty-one-day period.

Extension of the Death Benefit upon Termination of Employment. A death benefit is payable as a claim against the group policy when an employee dies within thirty-one days after the termination of his employment with the group policyholder. This extension of the death benefit prevents any lapse in coverage while the employee is exercising his conversion privilege. The amount of this death benefit is equal to the maximum amount for which a converted policy may be issued to him. Thus a terminated employee has an additional thirty-one days of protection while debating the pros and cons of exercising his conversion privilege or while awaiting coverage under the group life insurance plan of a new employer.

Conversion Privilege. An insured employee has the right to convert his group term life insurance to an individual policy of permanent insurance if his insurance, or any part of it, ceases because of termination of employment or of membership in the classification or classifications eligible for coverage under the master contract. A more restricted conversion privilege is provided for an insured employee if the master contract is terminated or is amended so as to terminate the insurance in force on his particular classification. Needless to say, this privilege is very valuable to the terminating employee who is in poor health or uninsurable. (It is for this reason that insurers assess a conversion charge against employers in the experience rating formula, as will be explained in Chapter 12.)

A. Termination of Employment or Membership. In the event of termination of insurance because of termination of employment or of membership in an eligible classification, the insured employee, subject to limitations described below, is entitled to convert, without evidence of insurability, his group term life insurance to an individual policy of life insurance. Many insurance companies will extend this conversion privilege to an insured employee if the amount of the employee's insurance is reduced by reason of a change in classification, retirement or the attainment of an age (e.g., age sixty-five or seventy) at which a reduction is specified in the master contract.

The conversion privilege is subject to the following conditions:

(1) The employee must apply for conversion within thirty-one days after the termination of his employment or membership in an eligible classification. He must prepay the premium required for the form of policy selected when completing the conversion application. The individual conversion policy is effective at the end of the thirty-one-day period after termination of his group term life insurance because the terminating employee is automatically covered during this period under the extended death benefit clause in the master contract, and overlapping coverage is, thus, avoided. A conversion application may be back-dated if the employee wishes to avoid the effect of an age change on the required premium.

(2) The individual policy may, at the option of the applicant, be any form, except term insurance,[5] then customarily issued by the insurer at the age and for the amount applied for, provided that such policy shall not contain disability benefits nor other supplementary benefits.

(3) The face amount of the individual policy may not exceed the amount of the group term life insurance which terminated. Special amount limits may restrict the available minimum and maximum amount of a particular form of individual policy applied for, based on the insurer's then current practices.

(4) The premium payable on the individual policy shall be at the insurer's then current rate applicable to the form and amount applied for, the class of risk to which the applicant belongs and his age on his birthday nearest to the effective date of his individual policy. Ordinarily, the converted policy will be issued at standard rates. However, the insurer has the right, in some cases, to charge a nonmedical rating such as may be required for certain occupations, special hazards (e.g., military service or aviation activities), travel or foreign residence. Even though the converting employee may be an impaired risk or totally uninsurable, no extra premium may be charged for reasons of health.

B. Termination or Amendment of the Group Master Contract. Upon the termination of a group term life insurance master contract with respect to all of the insured employees or an amendment to the contract which terminates any classification or classifications eligible for employee life insurance thereunder, or upon the termination of the employee life insurance provisions under a combined master contract, any employees who have been insured under the life insurance provisions are entitled to a conversion privilege. This conversion privilege is subject to the same four conditions which have been discussed previously. However, the privilege is affected by certain additional statutory restrictions.

---

[5] Group term life insurance contracts issued in the states of New York and West Virginia must contain a provision which permits the issuance of one year, single premium, preliminary term insurance preceding the permanent insurance.

(1) The terminated employee must have been insured under the policy for a five-year period[6] immediately preceding the date of his termination to be eligible for this conversion right.

(2) The amount of insurance to be converted may in no event exceed the lesser of (*a*) the amount of the employee's life insurance under the policy at the date of termination, less any amount of life insurance for which the employee becomes eligible under any group policy issued by the present insurer, or by any other insurer, within thirty-one days after the date of termination of the employee's life insurance, or (*b*) $2,000.[7]

These restrictions protect the insurer against possible adverse selection of substantial proportions upon the termination or amendment of a master contract which has been in force only a few years. Moreover, they prevent the employer from buying a group contract for a short period of time and then lapsing it in order to obtain substantial new amounts of life insurance for known uninsurable employees.

C. Extent of Group Life Conversions. The extent of group term life insurance conversions is reflected in the annual statistics developed by an insurer's individual life insurance department, and experience indicates that the actual utilization of this important privilege is quite minimal. On the average, conversions are made by only about 1.25 per cent of the terminating employees who possess the conversion right.

Although the conversion privilege is an integral part of the employer's group master contract, is included in the individual employee's booklet and certificate of insurance and is explained both as to procedures and rules in the employer's group administration manual, it is apparent that many employers do not encourage terminating employees to convert, so that the conversion charges assessed against their claims experience will not be excessive. Many reasons have been advanced to explain the fact that terminating employees seldom avail themselves of this privilege. (1) An employee who is leaving his job has many other, apparently more important, things to think about than converting his group life insurance. (2) The employee often expects to enter new employment and be covered under the new employer's group life insurance plan. (3) The attained age cost of an individual policy of permanent life insurance may be beyond the present means of the terminating employee. (4) The employee does not always understand the nature or the value of this privilege. (5) The employer may fail to send a conversion notice to the employee. (6) The employee may be able to qualify on a medically examined basis and, thus, is not reported as a group conversion. The present extent of group life conversions probably is due to the fact that known impaired and uninsurable employees convert and those who are insurable do not.

---

[6] In West Virginia, the employee must have been insured for a three-year period, and the group contract must have been in force for at least five years.

[7] $3,000 in Nebraska.

TABLE 7–4

GROUP CONVERSIONS—SELECT MORTALITY RATIOS OF DEATHS BY THEORETICAL
TABLE TO TABULAR EXPECTED BY 1946–49 SELECT BASIC TABLES

	Age at Conversion			
Policy Years	25–34	35–44	45–54	55–64
1.	1,460%	1,359%	1,065%	1,278%
2.	835	718	624	659
3.	574	469	428	418
4.	480	379	352	333
5.	414	317	299	277
6.	375	285	272	250
7.	347	271	261	235
8.	312	244	234	209
9.	291	228	220	195
10.	270	214	205	183
11.	242	195	186	169
12.	226	185	174	161
13.	211	177	163	153
14.	196	166	152	146
15.	180	151	139	137
16.	176	140	123	115
17.	169	135	120	115
18.	165	132	118	113
19.	159	128	116	113
20.	154	125	115	110

D. Experience and Cost of Group Life Insurance Conversions. Few
persons question the need for, or the value of, having a conversion
privilege. This privilege has, however, created a problem in group insurance because it produces a high degree of selection against the insurer by
those who convert. The mortality experienced on group conversions is
very high, at all ages, in the period immediately following conversion.
Although it tapers off to some extent for the first few policy years, it again
takes an upward course and continues at a relatively high level for many
years. Louis Levinson, in his paper "The Cost of Recent Additional
Mortality under Group Conversions,"[8] discusses this matter as follows:

While there is a definite pattern in the shape of the curves in the four age
groups, there is a significant difference in the underlying mortality relative to a
fixed standard. What is meant may be perceived if the percentage ratios of
actual deaths to those expected by the 1946–1949 Select Basic Tables are
examined.

It will be observed immediately that there is almost a complete inverse
association of high mortality ratios with age at time of conversion—that is, the
younger the age, the greater the relative mortality. This might have been ex-

[8] Louis Levinson, "The Cost of Recent Additional Mortality under Group Conversions," *Transactions of the Society of Actuaries,* Vol. XIV, Part I (1962), pp.
450–61.

pected. The standard mortality at the younger ages is absolutely so low that only a few extra deaths per thousand may represent a large percentage of the basic rate. It may be, too, since turnover is proportionately much higher in the area of the young ages and in view of the irrepressible optimism of youth, that the conversions actually made, by and large, occur among poorer risks than those at the older ages.

The nature of the experience under group life conversions has long been known, and the means for offsetting the high mortality costs involved in this form of protection has been established by interdepartmental accounting. Consequently, a conversion charge is made by the group insurance department against the employer's claims experience for credit to the individual insurance department whenever group life insurance is converted. The need for this internal adjustment stems from the fact that, while the conversion privilege is a group life insurance benefit, the excess mortality cost under converted policies is included in the over-all experience of the insurer's individual life insurance business.

The amount charged at the time of conversion is in the nature of an extra single premium which represents the present value of the excess future mortality under converted policies over similar standard individual policies. When a group life insurer computes its conversion charge, lapse rates are taken into account, and the savings in expenses due to the absence of commission, medical examinations, inspection reports and underwriting reviews are used as an offset to the excess mortality. Typical conversion charges range from $55 to $75 per $1,000 of insurance converted. It is common practice for an insurer to use the same average conversion charge for all plans and ages at issue, and this charge is made regardless of insurability if the terminating employee converts under a group conversion application.

Disability Benefits in Case of Total and Permanent Disability. Throughout the history of group life insurance, employers have been permitted to continue insurance in force on disabled employees, at least for a limited period of time, by continuing to pay premiums, whether or not the employees were continued on the payroll. In addition, three basic types of separate disability benefit provisions, which are described below, have been used frequently in connection with group life insurance plans. Until about 1932, the first and most liberal of the three provisions, the so-called *maturity value benefit*, was commonly written. However, the stock market "crash" of 1929 and the tremendous influx of total and permanent disability claims which followed in the depression years of the early 1930's led to the discontinuance of this type of provision in all new contracts. From 1932 to 1938, insurers issued their group life insurance contracts without a disability benefit provision or offered the most restricted type of the three provisions, the so-called *extended death benefit* or *one-year extension* disability clause. Beginning about 1938, life insurance companies began to offer a more liberal disability provision, and the third type was called a *waiver of premium benefit*. The cycle is now complete, since the maturity value benefit has returned to popularity in recent years, especially in Canada. A summary of the relative amount of coverage in force under the three types of disability clauses from a recent study shows that the maturity value type accounts for about 38 per cent of the total, the one-year extended death benefit type accounts for 22 per cent, and the waiver of premium type accounts for 40 per cent.[9]

A. *Maturity Value Benefit.* The maturity value type of disability clause provides for the payment of the face amount of an employee's group term life insurance in a lump sum or, more often, in monthly installments when an employee becomes totally and permanently disabled prior to age sixty. Typical maturity value benefit wording is as follows:

Payment of Insurance—If a covered person who has been continuously insured hereunder for at least six months becomes totally and permanently disabled as defined herein while insured hereunder and prior to his sixtieth birthday and if within twelve months after the date the policyholder ceases premium payments on behalf of such covered person due proof is received by the Company at its Home Office that such disability has existed continuously for at least nine months, the Company, in full settlement of all obligations under this policy to such person, will pay the face amount of such covered person's Group Life Insurance in sixty monthly instalments at the rate of $17.70 per month per $1,000 of insurance payable. If the amount of each monthly instalment so computed shall be less than $50 the covered person may, at his option, elect to receive instalments for a number of months less than sixty, provided however that the amount of each instalment when computed so as to include interest on the unpaid balance of insurance at the rate of $2\frac{1}{2}$ per cent per annum compounded annually shall not exceed $51. The first monthly instalment shall be payable immediately upon receipt of due proof of total and permanent disability, but not earlier than nine months from the date of commencement of such disability. Benefits hereunder are not assignable nor may the covered person commute the instalments due him.

At the death of any covered person then receiving disability instalments hereunder, the Company, on receipt of due proof of such death, will pay, in a lump sum, the commuted value of the unpaid instalments, computed at the rate of $2\frac{1}{2}$ per cent per annum compounded annually, to the person or party entitled to the proceeds of the policy in accordance with Article VI—Beneficiary.

The Company shall have the right at any time during the first two years after benefits hereunder have become payable to require the covered person to furnish due proof of the continuance of his total and permanent disability and thereafter not more frequently than once a year. Failure to furnish such proof within ninety days of the date of request therefore shall immediately terminate all benefits hereunder. In addition, the Company shall have the right during the instalment paying period hereunder, to have a physician of its choice examine the covered person at reasonable intervals during the first two years of the instalment paying period and thereafter not more frequently than once a year.

If the covered person returns to work in a class of employees eligible for

---

[9] See Chapter 11 for the sources of these data.

insurance, he may, subject to payment of premiums by the policyholder, be insured in accordance with the Schedule of Insurance, provided however that the amount of insurance to which such person shall be entitled under said Schedule shall be reduced by the sum of all instalments paid to the covered person during all previous periods of total and permanent disability (exclusive of any portion of such instalments representing interest). Following the termination of monthly instalments for reasons other than receipt of all the monthly instalments, if the covered person does not return to work in a class of employees eligible for insurance, he shall have the right to convert to an individual policy of life insurance, the amount of which shall be equal to the then unpaid monthly instalments commuted on the basis of interest at the rate of 2½ per cent per annum, subject to the rights and limitations set forth under Article V-A, Conversion Privilege.

The term "total and permanent disability" as used herein shall mean the complete inability of the covered person to engage in any and every gainful occupation for the remainder of his lifetime as a result of accidental bodily injury, sickness or disease.

From the above, it can be seen that the principal characteristics of the maturity value type of disability benefit are as follows:

(1) The disability must commence before age sixty. Age sixty-five has been used, but the tendency to use this maturity value benefit as an early retirement benefit can lead to abuse.

(2) The disability must commence after the individual becomes insured. Most companies require six months of coverage prior to the commencement of disability, and some contracts state that the disability must have commenced prior to termination of employment.

(3) The total and permanent disability definition must be specific and presumptive. For example, the individual must be prevented from engaging in any occupation or employment for compensation, profit or gain, and the insurer must be reasonably certain that the disability will continue during the remaining lifetime of the individual.

(4) Payments generally are made on a monthly installment basis, although insurers have permitted such provisions as lump sum; balance in monthly installments; lump sum or option; entire amount paid in monthly installments over five, ten, fifteen, twenty, sixty or 120 months; a percentage of pay (e.g., 2 per cent of monthly salary per year of service, with a maximum of twenty-five years).

(5) The group life insurance coverage is continued in the event of recovery. The usual practice is to reinstate only the unpaid balance, and this is also true if the employee is in a position to exercise his conversion right.

(6) A facility of payment clause is used. Practically all contracts have a facility of payment clause which permits the insurer to meet contractual obligations and make payments to the designated beneficiary if the insured employee is mentally incompetent.

As to the future of this type of disability provision, it would seem that the increased development and integration of disability benefits under long-term disability income plans and pension plans should reduce the interest in providing a maturity value type disability benefit under a group term life insurance plan.

B. *Extended Death Benefit.* The extended death benefit type of disability clause provides for the payment of group life insurance death claims incurred within one year after termination of employment, providing the insured employee had been continuously and totally disabled from the date of termination of employment and death occurred before age sixty-five. Specimen contractual language for this type of clause is as follows:

In addition to death occurring while the covered person is insured under this policy, the death of such person occurring prior to his sixty-fifth birthday and within one year of the date of cessation of premium payments for such person by the policyholder will be deemed a death for the purpose of the life insurance benefit hereunder if such person shall have been totally disabled as of such date and shall have remained continuously so disabled until the date of his death and due proof of such disability is submitted to the Home Office of the Company within one year following the date of his death.

The term "totally disabled" as used herein shall mean the complete inability of the covered person to engage in any and every gainful occupation as a result of accidental bodily injury, sickness or disease originating after the date such covered person's insurance became effective.

If, at the time of such covered person's death, he holds an individual policy obtained through the exercise of the conversion right, the amount payable under this Article will be reduced by the amount of such individual policy unless such individual policy is surrendered to the Company without claim other than for return of the premiums paid thereon, less dividends and indebtedness, if any.

In 1938, most insurers began to issue a new, more liberal type of disability benefit, and the extended death benefit fell into relative disuse.

C. *Waiver of Premium Benefit.* Under the waiver of premium type of disability benefit, death claims occurring after termination of employment are payable regardless of the amount of time that has elapsed since such termination, providing the insured employee, prior to age sixty (or sixty-five), becomes totally disabled, and such disability continues from the date of his termination of employment to the date of his death. Initially, a totally disabled employee is provided a one-year extension of his group term life insurance. A typical contract provision applicable to this first year of disability appears below.

If a covered person while insured hereunder and prior to his sixtieth birthday becomes totally disabled as defined herein, his insurance will continue in force during the period he remains continuously and totally disabled but not to exceed a period of one year from the date the policyholder stops paying the premium for such insurance.

If, prior to a covered person's sixtieth birthday and within one year after the policyholder stops paying the premium for such person's insurance, due proof is submitted to the Home Office of the Company that total disability has existed continuously for a period of nine months as to such covered person, the insurance for such covered person will be continued in force, without further payment of premiums, during the continuance of such total disability.

The term "total disability" as used herein shall mean the complete inability of the covered person to engage in any and every gainful occupation as a result of accidental bodily injury, sickness or disease originating after the date such covered person's insurance became effective. The loss of both hands or of both feet or of one hand and one foot or of the sight of both eyes after a covered person's insurance becomes effective, shall be considered total disability even though such person may be able to pursue a gainful occupation, and no further proof of disability will be required. Loss of hands or feet means severance at or above the wrist or ankle joint. Loss of sight must be total and irrecoverable.

If death occurs during this initial period of twelve months, payment is made upon the insurer receiving due proof of such continued disability and death. Additional one-year extensions, without the payment of premiums, are provided to meet the continuing disability of the employee, as follows:

Subject to the yearly submission of due proof of the continuance of such total disability within three months preceding each anniversary of the receipt of the original proof of such disability, and submission to examination by a physician as herein provided.

The Company shall have the right during the continuance of insurance under any of the terms of this Section to have a physician of its choice examine the covered person, provided that no examination will be requested more often than once a year after the covered person's insurance has been in force under this Section for two full years.

The insurance afforded by this disability provision terminates under the following conditions:

Insurance of a covered person under this paragraph shall terminate upon the happening of any one of the following events: (a) cessation of total disability, (b) failure to submit required proof of the continuance of total disability, or (c) failure to submit to examination by a physician as herein provided.

If the disability coverage is terminated and the employee is then eligible for insurance under the group policy, he will again become insured on a premium-paying basis. If the disability terminates and the employee is not eligible for insurance under the group policy, he becomes entitled to the rights and benefits under the conversion privilege. For example:

In the event of termination of such insurance under paragraphs 1 or 2, the covered person shall be entitled to the rights set forth in Article V-A, Conversion Privilege, in the same manner as if employment had been then terminated, unless he returns to work and is again insured under this policy.

The experience under this provision has been generally favorable although major business recessions (e.g., the recession of 1958) have caused sharp increases in disability claims.

Designation of a Beneficiary. Group life insurance, like individual insurance, allows the insured employee to name and change his beneficiary as desired. The face amount of insurance must be for the benefit of persons other than the employer, and it is recommended that the payment be directed to a named beneficiary rather than to the employee's estate. The designation of a named beneficiary eliminates much delay and expense, as well as inheritance taxes (in some states), to the beneficiary by by-passing the probate and other legal expenses that are present when proceeds are paid to one's estate.

If at the death of the insured employee there is no named beneficiary, or if such named beneficiary does not survive the insured employee, the proceeds may be payable at the insurer's option to any one or more of the following surviving relatives of the employee: wife, husband, mother, father, child or children, or to the executor or administrator of the deceased covered person. If any beneficiary is a minor or is physically, mentally or otherwise incapable of giving a valid release for any payment due, the insurer is able to take positive action under a "facility of payment" clause. A typical facility of payment clause provides as follows:

The Company may, at its option, and until claim is made by the duly appointed guardian or committee for such beneficiary, make payment to any person or institution who appears to the Company to have assumed responsibility for the care, custody or support of such beneficiary. Such payments will be made in installments in the amount specified in any optional method of settlement previously elected or in the absence of such optional method of settlement in instalments not in excess of $100 monthly.

Payment in the manner and to the persons described above shall to the extent thereof release the Company of all further liability.

Historically, group life insurance policies also contain a nonassignability provision. The rationale behind the nonassignability provision lies in the generally held opinion that it is neither feasible nor possible to effect a valid assignment of all the incidents of ownership possessed by an insured employee with respect to group life insurance benefits.

Settlement Options. The insured employee or, if he is deceased, his beneficiary can elect that the face amount be paid on an installment certain basis, rather than in a lump sum. The installments are paid according to the procedures and table set forth in the master contract. For example:

Upon written election by the covered person during his lifetime, or in the absence of such election, on election by the beneficiary at such covered person's death, the Company in lieu of payment in one sum will pay the proceeds in such number of equal monthly installments certain, in accordance with the table below, as may be designated in the election of the option, the amount of each installment to be determined from the table and the first installment to be payable immediately:

Number of Monthly Installments Certain	Amounts of Each Installment Certain per $1,000 of Proceeds
12	$84.37
24	42.76
36	28.89
48	21.96
60	17.80
120	9.50
180	6.75
240	5.39

If any installment payment would amount to less than $10, this option shall not be available. Yearly, half-yearly or quarterly installments will be paid in lieu of monthly installments certain if so provided in the election of this option. Such installments may be computed by multiplying the monthly installment by 11.852, 5.966 or 2.993, respectively. Installments certain shall participate in such proportion of the divisible surplus as the Company may allot and set apart thereto. After the death of any payee, any remaining installments certain will be paid in such manner as may be directed in the election of the option with the consent of the Company.

Subject to stated option rules, an insurer generally offers other optional modes of settlement (e.g., amount certain, life contingencies), but the basis is seldom mentioned or guaranteed in the contract, and current practices will govern.

In the programing of life insurance, it usually is recommended that group life insurance proceeds be utilized as a "clean-up" fund (i.e., to meet immediate cash needs at the death of the employee), to pay outstanding bills and final funeral expenses and to create an emergency fund for unforeseen cash needs. Such use of group insurance proceeds thus frees the employee's individual life insurance for long-range needs under settlement options.

Effectiveness of Yearly Renewable Term Plan

The ever increasing cost of a step-rate term premium has had little appeal for buyers of individual insurance. However, this basis has worked well in group life insurance. It is important to understand the reasons why the yearly renewable term plan is so well adapted to group insurance.[10]

Generally the employer and the employees share the cost, and the employer's portion of the premium "fills the gap" between the fixed contributions by the employees and the total cost of the plan. The normal turnover of employees, experience refunds and the eventual attainment of a fairly constant average age tends to keep the employer's share fluctuating within narrow cost limits.

The administration of a step-rate term life insurance plan by the

---

[10] Material adapted from *Group Insurance Study Notes* (*Part 8*), 1963 Examination Edition, Society of Actuaries, p. 41.

employer and the insurer is both simple and economical. Since the plan contains no cash or paid-up values, there is no deferred liability such as is encountered in level premium insurance, and the insurer need not be concerned with the distribution and administration of individual equities when an employee's coverage terminates. If conditions so warrant, the plan can easily be changed or terminated by the employer or the insurer, as there are no vested interests to be disturbed.

Unlike the situation in individual life insurance, the insurer can adjust rates from one policy year to the next without being unduly concerned about the liability for benefits that are deferred far into the future. Equitable adjustments of the employees' contributions and the employer's subsidy can be made promptly, based on predictable future costs, without concern for long-range commitments.

Finally, a favorable federal income tax situation exists for both the employer and the employee, and this form of protection is spared the tax complications present in many forms of permanent life insurance. The following chapter of this volume considers this subject in detail.

Advantages of Group Term Life Insurance

Advantages to the Employer. While facts and figures relating to the extent of group term life insurance are impressive, the individual employer is more interested in the answer to the question, "What does group life insurance have to offer me?" The following are among the more important advantages that an employer may realize through the purchase of group term life insurance.

1. The benefits may represent the difference between the adequacy of individual and family resources and the necessity for turning to the employer and the community for financial help.

2. The employer is provided with a low cost, accepted, impartial and predetermined plan for furnishing death benefits to the dependents of deceased employees.

3. The protection is an aid to attaining good public and employer-employee relations, as it prevents an employee's family from being abruptly cut off the payroll without funds.

4. The coverage is competitively desirable, inasmuch as it helps the employer to hire and retain quality employees.

5. Under current tax laws and regulations, the employer's contributions are deductible as a business expense for corporate income tax purposes.

6. Employee morale and productivity is enhanced by offering this base of life insurance protection to them.

7. The employer is able to "weather" the effects of expected as well as catastrophic death losses at a relatively predictable, budgetable and stable cost.

8. Its presence has helped to delay further government intervention into areas of private industry.

Advantages to the Employee. It is readily apparent that group term life insurance fits into an employee's pattern of living when analyzing the following advantages to the employee.

1. It adds a layer of low-cost protection to personal savings, individual life insurance and OASDI benefits.

2. For many employees it is their only form of protection in case of death because they are unable to purchase individual life insurance due to conditions of health or hazardous occupation or because they simply do not bother to purchase individual life insurance.

3. It provides peace of mind by relieving the anxieties and consequences of a possible premature death or total and permanent disability.

4. If employees are contributing toward the cost, the premiums are automatically withheld from earnings, thus reducing the chance of lapse.

5. It can provide the greatest amount of protection for the lowest cost.

6. The death benefit usually is not considered taxable income to the designated beneficiary under the federal income tax laws, even though the employer's contributions toward the cost of the coverage usually are not taxable as income to the employee.

7. The conversion privilege enables a terminated employee to convert his life insurance to an individual policy without having to pass a medical examination.

Limitations of Group Term Life Insurance

Group term life insurance has satisfied a very real need by helping to alleviate the loss suffered by the average employee's family in the event of his untimely death. It was never intended to supplant the need for a well planned and systematically developed individual life insurance estate. It does have some limitations which are of concern to the employers and employees involved.

First, the employee does not have complete assurance that his employer will continue the master group policy in force from one year to the next, unless, of course, he happens to be a sole proprietor, partner or company officer who has a voice in the renewability of the contract. The employer and the insurer are the parties who control this all important renewability, and the lack of any permanent guarantees emphasizes the temporary nature of this coverage. In actual practice these plans are seldom discontinued, but business failures can and do occur, and the conversion privilege upon termination of a master group life policy, as previously discussed, is of limited value to the employees.

Another limitation is quite evident when individual employees move from employer to employer, as group term life insurance does not possess "portability." Nevertheless, only about one out of every hundred terminating employees exercises the conversion privilege. Of course, as group term life insurance has become more widespread the importance of this weakness has declined, since many transitory employees will be insured for the same or a higher face amount with their new employer.

Next, some employees forget that group term life insurance provides *protection only*. These employees have been lulled into a state of complacency by having this coverage during their working years and are disappointed when they find, after years of participation and contributions, no cash or paid-up values available to them. This temporary form of insurance can obscure the need for permanent individual life insurance and the valuable services of a professional life underwriter.

Finally, the employee is confronted with the fact that upon attaining a specified age (e.g., sixty-five) or retirement, his group term life insurance either will be reduced or eliminated, and that the high costs of conversion probably will be beyond his means. Fortunately for the employee, due to general business practices, collective bargaining and employer concern, more and more employers are continuing reduced amounts of group term life insurance in force on older or retired employees under various types of reduction formulas. However, as the group ages, employers become understandably concerned about the ever increasing costs and search for long-range solutions to their dilemma.

Terminal Funding with Group Term Life Insurance[11]

Most group life insurance after retirement is continued under the employer's group term life insurance plan on a "pay-as-you-go" basis because of the favorable income tax situation and the cost when compared with other funding methods. The deferred high cost of current funding, especially in a fairly static group, has interested some employers in finding ways to prefund their accruing liabilities.

One approach that has been developed involves the establishment by the employer of a separate fund out of which to meet this deferred cost. Such a fund usually is administered by an insurance company, and the deposits may consist of employer contributions, employee contributions, dividends or experience rating refunds from the basic group term insurance policy and credited interest earnings. Disbursements from this so-called "deposit fund" or "insurance continuation fund" may be made either to pay term insurance premiums as they fall due on retired employees or to fund fully death benefits of retired employees as deaths occur. The insurer does not guarantee the adequacy of the fund toward

---

[11] *Ibid.*, pp. 53–54.

meeting all obligations, but it will make periodic actuarial calculations, involving assumptions as to turnover, retirement, interest and other cost factors, to determine the deposits needed. While this method of advance funding helps the employer prepare to meet future liabilities, it still lacks the guarantees of permanence and equity that employees desire.

This type of insured terminal funding device contains elements which are open to considerable debate and conjecture, and in certain areas the tax status has not been ruled on by the Internal Revenue Service. For example, what is the status of the insurer and/or the employer relative to credited interest earnings? When can the employer deduct his contributions to the fund? What rights do the employees possess? What are the stated purposes of the fund, how does it operate, for whose benefit and what happens at termination? It is readily evident that the employer should seek competent legal counsel when considering the establishment of such a fund. In Chapter 8, the tax status of these deposits, the cost of continuing group term life insurance in force on retired lives and other possible terminal funding arrangements are discussed in depth.

CREDITOR GROUP LIFE INSURANCE

Creditor group life insurance is a specialized form of group term insurance issued to a creditor (policyholder) under which the lives of the borrowers (debtors) of money or purchasers of goods are insured in connection with specific loans or credit transactions, subject to statutory and underwriting maxima. This second important application of group term life insurance now represents a total of over $37 billion in force and covers over forty-six million debtors.[12]

Creditor Group Life Insurance versus Conventional Group Term Life Insurance

There are several basic differences between the nature of creditor group life insurance and conventional group term life insurance. First, in conventional group term life insurance situations, there usually is an employer-employee relationship, but creditor group life insurance is concerned only with a creditor-debtor relationship. For example, the group (debtors) may be the borrowers of a bank (creditor), with the master group policy issued to the creditor, or the group may have purchased goods under conditional sales contracts from a vendor, with the group policy issued to the vendor.

Under group term life insurance contracts involving an employer-employee relationship, each classification is insured for a level face amount of life insurance. However, under a creditor group life insurance contract each debtor usually is covered for an amount of life insurance

---

[12] Institute of Life Insurance, *1964 Life Insurance Fact Book*, p. 32.

equal to the amount of his indebtedness to the creditor. Thus, decreasing term insurance is used to secure his debt, and, as the debtor makes his installment repayments and reduces the amount of his indebtedness, the amount of insurance on his life reduces correspondingly. If the unpaid balance exceeds the maximum amount of life insurance provided under the group contract, the debtor may be insured for (1) the maximum permitted under the policy until his indebtedness is reduced to this amount, or (2) the proportion that the original amount of his indebtedness bears to the maximum amount of insurance, and, hence, the amount of his coverage is continually decreased.

Creditor group life insurance proceeds must be used for the specific purpose of extinguishing the debtor's indebtedness. When an insured debtor dies, the then outstanding amount of creditor life insurance is automatically payable to the creditor to be applied toward the discharge of the indebtedness. Unlike other group insurance situations, the creditor is in the unusual position of being both policyholder and beneficiary.

Eligible Creditors, Loans and Purchases

In its early development, this form of insurance was underwritten on unsecured personal loans made by banks. Today's eligible creditors, subject to statutory and underwriting considerations, may include commercial banks, savings and loan associations, trust companies, sales finance companies, dealers, retail vendors, small-loan companies, employee credit unions, colleges and universities, credit card companies, mutual funds, production credit associations, memorial parks and federal land banks. The eligible creditor may wish to insure types of indebtedness involving unsecured personal loans, certain types of secured personal loans, motor vehicles, farm equipment, appliances, mobile homes, home modernization, crops, seed and livestock, educational loan plans, revolving credit (including bank line of credit), furniture, burial plots, credit card charges, real estate mortgages, and the purchase of securities, or a combination of types.[13]

Creditor Modifications of Conventional Term Plan

Many modifications have been introduced in adapting the conventional group term plan to fit the creditor-debtor relationship.

Contract Provisions. The uniqueness of a creditor group life insurance contract is immediately apparent upon reading the contract's insuring clause, as the creditor is both the policyholder and the beneficiary. This clause also stipulates that the creditor must apply the death benefit toward the discharge of the debtor's indebtedness. Thus, it is obvious that such conventional group term life insurance provisions as a conversion

---

[13] Chapter 35 contains a discussion of the extensions of creditor insurance, including its application to several of these comparatively new types of indebtedness.

privilege, designation of a beneficiary, settlement options and facility of payment are not needed or appropriate.

Another unusual aspect is the fluctuation in the amount of insurance on the life of each insured debtor. These fluctuations generally occur on a monthly basis when the debtor reduces the amount of his indebtedness by making his installment repayment. A proper insurable interest is maintained at all times, since the amount of insurance at any time is usually the amount necessary to pay the debtor's indebtedness, subject to the maximum amount stated in the group policy. This aggregate amount of insurance which is in force on the life of the debtor may not exceed the policy maximum, regardless of the total amount of his debts.

Only one person may be insured with respect to any one indebtedness, but since co-signers often are involved in credit transactions the creditor is given the right to select which debtor shall be insured. For example:

> If more than one person signs the instrument evidencing the indebtedness, the person whose signature appears as debtor nearest the top of the instrument, or if more than one signature is on the same line, the person whose signature appears to the left, shall be the person covered hereunder with respect to such indebtedness.

The misstatement of age clause has little or no application to creditor group life insurance, since practically all insurers forego the calculation of rates based on actual age data in favor of the promulgated initial premium rate. Likewise, the incontestable clause has little applicability because the facts provided by the creditor are readily verifiable by the insurer, and seldom does the insurer require any evidence of insurability from the individual debtors. As a result of the length of the repayment period and the amount at risk, a suicide clause normally is found only in creditor group mortgage contracts.

The master contract may be terminated in any one of four ways, namely: at the request of the creditor, for nonpayment of premium, for failure to maintain a minimum volume of insurance or for failure to obtain a minimum number of new debtors each policy year (e.g., 100). An individual debtor's insurance is terminated if (1) the master policy is terminated, (2) the indebtedness is discharged, (3) the indebtedness is transferred to another creditor or (4) the debtor fails to make installment repayments when due. Depending upon the agreement between the creditor and insurer, loans in default may be covered for up to, e.g., six months.

Most insurers issue a certificate of insurance to the individual debtors, although usually this is done only in those states where it is required by law or regulation. Actually, this document is called a "statement of insurance," and it describes the nature of the insurance protection provided, the conditions under which the coverage terminates and the refund formula which must be used in case the indebtedness is repaid prior to its scheduled maturity date.

Premium Rates. Creditor group life insurance premium rates were originally intended to be based upon the ages of the lives insured, like conventional group term plans. However, due to the impracticality of obtaining age data and maintaining age records, an initial premium rate based upon the volume of indebtedness to be insured under the group policy is determined. For example, if the volume of insurance is less than $250,000, the rate might be $.75 per month per $1,000 of outstanding balance; if the volume is $500,000 or more, the rate might be $.60, and between $250,000 and $500,000 of volume the rate might be prorated between $.75 and $.60.

Various states have issued regulations to help insurers and state insurance authorities establish what may be considered a reasonable rate, and some states require that filed rates may not exceed the established maxima. These regulations have been issued because of the "reverse competition" that often characterizes creditor group life insurance. Lending institutions often receive a commission and/or experience rating refund in connection with this coverage. Since the cost of the protection often is borne entirely by the borrower, lenders are interested in the highest available insurance rates, rather than the lowest rates.

The most common premium payment method is to base the premium on the amount of insurance outstanding on each monthly premium due date. The popularity of the "outstanding balance method" of premium payment is almost equaled by the use of the "single premium method." Under the single premium method, the full premium, which is based on the initial amount of indebtedness and its anticipated decrease over the repayment period, is immediately turned over to the insurer by the creditor. Another method is the "equal payment method," which provides for a level amount of monthly premium, under each insured loan, over the duration of the loan.

Underwriting. Since the creditor underwrites the debtors, adverse selection is always a matter of serious concern to the insurer. Fierce competition among lenders can lead to the acceptance of installment accounts based more on past credit experience than on age, health and conditions of employment. Most creditor group life insurance plans are debtor-pay-all, and a proper spread of risk is endangered when the consumer credit department of the lending institution does not aggressively sell the insurance protection to all eligible debtors or require the purchase of insurance as a condition for the debtor obtaining the loan. This matter of low participation has become an especially acute problem under creditor group mortgage plans.

An additional opportunity for individual selection is present in many creditor insurance plans due to the fact that the borrower may elect to take a loan of any size up to the maximum permitted by the creditor. An insurer is definitely encouraging lax creditor underwriting practices and adverse selection when loans secured by marketable collateral are insured.

Administration. The administration of a creditor group life insurance plan is normally simple and economical, since the record keeping is performed by the creditor. For example, under the outstanding balance method of premium payment the creditor usually completes a brief premium statement by multiplying his premium rate by the average amount of insurance outstanding during the period. A statement is also made as to the number of new insured loans for the month, and this information is used at renewal time to determine the number of new entrants added during the policy year. On large cases the creditor may be given the right to pay the claims directly by means of an insurance company draft book.

Due to the usual growth of a creditor plan during the early policy years, it has become quite common to pay additional first-year commissions in the second policy year. This additional first-year commission is based on the excess of the second year premiums over those for the first year.

Unlike a conventional group term life insurance plan, the installation of a creditor group life insurance plan is relatively quite simple. The insurer's representatives contact only the creditor, and even in a debtor-pay-all case the individual debtors never are approached by these representatives.

Regulation. Creditor group term life insurance, unlike conventional group term life insurance, is influenced by indirect regulatory sources as well as by direct statutory regulation. Indirect regulatory sources would involve, at the federal level, the Comptroller of the Currency and the Federal Trade Commission; at the state level, it is subject to regulation through state banking departments, state interest and usury laws and conditional sales acts.

A model bill which placed group and individual creditor life insurance in the same category for regulatory purposes was drafted by the National Association of Insurance Commissioners in 1958 and revised in 1960.[14] Most states have adopted this model bill, sometimes with variations, or a law with similar objectives. The bill establishes a control on maximum rates and imposes requirements that charges for insurance made to the debtor may not exceed the premium, that complete disclosure of the charge must be made to the debtor, and that a descriptive policy, certificate or statement of insurance must be issued to the debtor in every case.

---

[14] The full text of this model bill is contained in Appendix 24.

It is interesting to note that the Comptroller of the Currency has authorized national banks to guarantee that the outstanding amount of any loan will be considered paid in full if the borrower should die. State insurance commissioners have resisted vigorously this development on the grounds that any such guarantees by banks would constitute an insurance transaction which should be subject to regulation by the insurance departments of the various states. In fact, banks have been notified by certain insurance departments that they will be subject to such regulation if they offer this death benefit.

SELECTED REFERENCES

CAMMACK, E. E. "Group Life Insurance—Recent Mortality, Insurance of Pensioners, and Cost of Conversions," *Transactions of the Society of Actuaries,* Vol. XLI (1940), p. 416. Discussion, Vol. XLII (1941), p. 88, by W. R. Williamson, E. B. Whittaker, and R. D. Baldwin.

GREGG, DAVIS W. *Group Life Insurance.* 3d ed. Homewood, Ill.: Richard D. Irwin, Inc., 1962.

HORELICK, N. E. "The Development of Group Life Insurance," *The Journal of the American Society of Chartered Life Underwriters,* Vol. VI, No. 4 (September, 1952), pp. 347–59.

INSTITUTE OF LIFE INSURANCE. *1964 Life Insurance Fact Book.* New York, 1964.

JACOBSON, JAMES B. *An Analysis of Group Creditors Insurance.* M.B.A. thesis at University of Southern California, published by Prudential Insurance Company of America, Newark, New Jersey, 1955.

LEVINSON, LOUIS. "The Cost of Recent Additional Mortality under Group Conversions," *Transactions of the Society of Actuaries,* Vol. XIV, Part I (1962), pp. 450–61. Discussion, pp. 462–86, by Milton J. Wood, Fred H. Holsten, George C. Campbell, Edward A. Lew, Julia Oldenkamp, Julius Vogel, Russell M. Collins, Jr., Guy W. Pickering, Garnett E. Cannon, Paul H. Jackson, Rea B. Hayes, W. Rulon Williamson, and Frederick S. Townsend.

MILLIMAN, WENDELL. *Is Group Insurance for You.* New York: North American Reassurance Co., 1958.

TROWBRIDGE, CHARLES L. "Funding of Group Life Insurance," *Transactions of the Society of Actuaries,* Vol. VII (1955), pp. 270–85. Discussion, pp. 482–88, by H. L. Feay, B. R. Thomas, and W. R. Williamson.

Chapter 8

FORMS OF GROUP PERMANENT LIFE INSURANCE

BY WILLIAM W. KEFFER

The financial problems of the aged have become a matter of great public concern, and widespread efforts are being directed toward possible solutions of these problems. One result has been growing attention on the part of employers, union groups and employees generally to the benefits available after retirement under group life insurance plans. A number of studies over the past fifteen years have shown that an increasing and substantial proportion of such plans provide for a continuation of some life insurance coverage after retirement. In one survey,[1] over 85 per cent of larger employers' plans provided such benefits, as against 65 to 70 per cent a decade ago. Among the more stable businesses, such as financial institutions and public utilities, some group life insurance after retirement appears to be available in more than nine out of ten cases. For smaller employers, such coverage is less frequently offered but is nevertheless available under a large proportion of plans.

When an employee retires, the amount of his group term life insurance generally is reduced from that provided just prior to retirement. Continuation of 50 per cent is very common, and over one half of the plans in two recent studies provided this level of benefits or more.[2] Average amounts of group life insurance per person after retirement have been increasing, following the trend toward larger amounts for active employees.

A number of factors have combined to contribute to these trends. The development of the social security system and the rapid growth of retirement pension plans have drawn attention to the value of continued group life insurance benefits after retirement. The proportion of older persons in

---

[1] National Industrial Conference Board, *Management Record*, Vol. XXV, No. 2 (February, 1963), p. 12.

[2] *Ibid.*, p. 13; also U.S. Department of Labor, *Life Insurance and Accidental Death and Dismemberment Benefits, Early Summer, 1960*, Bulletin No. 1296 (Washington, D. C.: U.S. Government Printing Office, June, 1961), Tables 10, 11, 13, pp. 18–20.

the population is increasing, and there is a maturing of the work force in some industries, the railroads and some utilities being notable examples. Then, too, union bargaining representatives have increasingly included benefits for retired employees in their proposals.

GROUP TERM LIFE INSURANCE FOR RETIRED EMPLOYEES

Extent of Use of Group Term Life Insurance

The vast majority of present plans providing life insurance for retired employees do so through extension of the group term insurance. In a 1961 study,[3] about 5 per cent of plans providing post-retirement life insurance benefits included permanent insurance, and examination of the group life insurance business of several major insurers reveals that 95 per cent of total master contracts in force provide term insurance only. Also, in a substantial majority of plans where benefits are provided retired employees, the full premium after retirement is paid by the employer, probably indicating recognition of the limited financial resources of most retired persons as well as the difficulty of establishing an efficient system for collecting employee contributions. This use of term insurance and employer payment for retired employees' benefits can create difficulties, and recognition of this fact leads in some cases to consideration of permanent forms of group life insurance.

Problems under Group Term Life Insurance

Group term life insurance is justifiably popular and effectively provides low-cost protection to millions of employees. As increasing numbers of employees approach and reach retirement under a given plan, however, problems can arise from the use of the term insurance approach. Among the factors which can contribute to such problems are the increasing cost of insurance to the employer as his employees grow older, the high cost of conversion to individual insurance on termination, the lack of cash values, the lack of guarantees of continued protection and accruing liabilities for the employer.

Increasing Costs at Older Ages. Group term life insurance rates increase rapidly with age. Under the rate scale presently established as standard for the state of New York, and followed by many companies, the gross monthly premium per $1,000 for group term life insurance, ignoring loadings and expense adjustments, is $.32 at age thirty-five, $3.78 at age sixty-five (a tenfold increase), and $8.56 at age seventy-five.

Continuation of term coverage after retirement can have a substantial impact upon the cost of a group life insurance plan. Yet this may not be apparent for many years after a plan is established, while the number of

[3] National Industrial Conference Board, *Corporate Retirement Policy and Practices,* Studies in Personnel Policy No. 190 (New York, 1964), p. 50.

TABLE 8–1

ILLUSTRATION OF EFFECT OF CONTINUING GROUP TERM LIFE INSURANCE ON
RETIRED EMPLOYEES

Features of Group Life Insurance Plan	Amount of Insurance	Average Monthly Premium	
		Per $1,000	Per $1,000 on Active Employees
Flat $1,000 per person:			
Coverage on 10,000 active			
employees....................$10,000,000		$ .73	$ .73
Coverage on 1,200 retired employees:			
100 per cent continued...........	1,200,000	8.48	1.02
50 per cent continued...........	600,000	8.48	.51
Combined (100 per cent continued)..	11,200,000	——	1.75
Combined (50 per cent continued)...	10,600,000	——	1.24
Graded salary schedule:			
Coverage on 10,000 active em-			
ployees......................	33,245,000	.82	.82
Coverage on 1,200 retired em-			
ployees:			
100 per cent continued...........	4,800,000	8.48	1.22
50 per cent continued...........	2,400,000	8.48	.61
Combined (100 per cent continued)..	38,045,000	——	2.04
Combined (50 per cent continued)...	35,645,000	——	1.43

persons covered after retirement gradually increases. Terminations and replacements of active employees tend to hold down average premiums; but when insurance becomes effective on a retired employee—without his contribution, as is usually the case—an eventual benefit payment is a certainty.

For a representative group, the ultimate proportion of retired employees to active employees may well reach 15 to 20 per cent, and 12 per cent can usually be considered a relatively low estimate of this ratio.[4] If the 12 per cent figure and a typical distribution of ages are assumed, it can be shown that the average monthly premium per $1,000 of insurance per *active* employee, using the New York rate table referred to, can increase to as much as two and one-half times its initial level, as coverage continued after retirement increases. Typical results might be somewhat as shown in Table 8–1.

Under the flat $1,000 program shown above, it can be seen that, if 100 per cent of coverage is continued after retirement, the total cost of the plan per $1,000 of insurance on active employees could increase from $.73 to $1.75. This amounts to 240 per cent of the original cost on active

[4] Society of Actuaries, *Group Insurance Study Notes* (Chicago, 1963), Sec. 82–2–63, pp. 50–52.

employees only, by the time the number retired has reached 12 per cent of those active. For the salary schedule illustrated, the eventual cost per $1,000 reaches 249 per cent of that for active employees only. Obviously, cutting back coverage at retirement, or soon thereafter, reduces these costs, and this is frequently done.

If employees contribute to the cost of the term plan, the effect of these increases on the employer's cost can be relatively greater. For example, in the first illustration above, if active employees pay $.60 per $1,000, the employer's average cost could rise from $.13 per $1,000 to $1.15 per $1,000. Increasing the amount employees contribute at higher ages, or requiring contributions from retired employees, is not a satisfactory answer, since this tends to discourage continued participation, on a selective basis. Also, some states limit the permissible employee contribution for group term life insurance.[5]

Problems in the Event of Termination of the Plan or of Individual Employment. The situation under group term life insurance plans when coverage is terminated can also cause difficulties or dissatisfaction. No cash or paid-up values are provided for individuals leaving employment, even after long service and participation. Although this is entirely proper and equitable under the term insurance concept, it may be misunderstood. The same is true if for any reason the insurance plan as a whole is discontinued.

The privilege of converting to individual insurance at attained age rates is required under most state laws and is universally offered. But at the higher ages these rates may be unattractive or even prohibitive for some employees, particularly when compared with contributions under the group plan. For one company, as an example, an individual permanent life insurance policy issued at age sixty-five would require an annual premium of $65.00 per $1,000, compared with $20.00 at age forty, and with $7.20, a common employee contribution rate for group term life insurance at all ages.

Other Problems. Under group term life insurance plans, there is no guarantee that the program will be continued since it is subject to cancellation by the policyholder, or by the insurer for nonpayment of premiums. As a practical matter, complete discontinuance of group term life insurance plans is unusual. However, business failures, particularly among smaller firms, are not so unusual. Older or retired employees may find this a matter for concern, especially if they have become uninsurable.

From the employer's point of view, even though there is often no formal guarantee of continuation, an employer may be effectively committed to providing benefits after retirement through past practice, gen-

---

[5] New York and Michigan have established such limits; $.60 per month per $1,000 or 75 per cent of total premiums being the maximum applicable to most standard groups.

eral understanding or bargaining agreements. In most cases, the cost of the protection can be considered a deferred liability, for which no provision is being made under term plans during an employee's active working lifetime. If the scope of operations of a firm is cut back at some future date, these higher costs could fall on an employer at exactly the time when he was least able to absorb them. In other words, 12 per cent retired employees, with their associated insurance costs, could become 24 per cent, if the active working force were cut in half. The practice of advance funding of retirement pensions has developed out of recognition of these circumstances, and the principle has similar applicability to group life insurance.

ALTERNATIVES TO GROUP TERM LIFE INSURANCE

A number of different modifications of the usual group term life insurance arrangement have been developed to meet some of the problems and needs described above. These modifications can be divided into three general categories: plans employing level premium life insurance forms; plans combining paid-up life insurance with term insurance; and plans using deposit funds.

Exact figures are not available, but probably no more than $10 billion of the more than $225 billion of group life insurance (excluding creditors) in force in the United States is written on forms involving level premium group permanent or group paid-up coverage (exclusive of pension plans). Two to three per cent of total new group life insurance issues is a reasonable estimate of current activity.

For companies encouraging the sale of these plans, however, particularly those writing group paid-up life insurance, the relative volume of such business can be significant. In at least one case, it has reached more than 15 per cent of total group life insurance issued by the company in a given year.

Level Premium Group Permanent Forms

Under level premium group permanent plans, level premiums for all or part of the group life insurance on each participant are determined, using such forms as life paid up at sixty-five or whole life insurance. Cash and paid-up values are available to the employee if he contributes to the cost.

Since 1950, employer contributions toward the cost of such plans, where the employee has a nonforfeitable right in the policy, have been considered taxable income to the employee, except under qualified pension plans. Their current use, therefore, has been largely restricted to providing insurance auxiliary to pension plans, a subject not considered here, and to modifications where the tax situation is taken into account. The volume of the latter currently being written is small compared with plans involving group paid-up life insurance, but there is a growing interest in them. The uses of the level premium group permanent plan will be discussed in detail later in this chapter.

Group Paid-up Life Insurance

Under the group paid-up plan, the group insurance available under the benefit schedule is made up of two parts. The first part is *paid-up insurance*, where employee contributions are applied to purchase units of paid-up insurance, the amount of which gradually accumulates over the years, reducing the balance of the total scheduled benefit which must be provided by term insurance. The second part consists of *term life insurance*, where employer contributions purchase an amount of term insurance which is always equal, for each individual, to the difference between the total benefit according to the group plan's schedule and the accumulated amount of paid-up insurance. Cash or paid-up values are available under the paid-up insurance portion only upon termination of employment. Since all employer contributions buy term insurance under this arrangement, the tax problem mentioned in connection with level premium group permanent insurance does not occur.

This plan was developed in 1941, and substantial amounts of coverage have been issued on this form, although they are still relatively small in comparison to the total volume of group life insurance being sold. Recent variations have included the introduction of a *deferred* paid-up arrangement under which all current insurance is provided on a term basis by employer contributions, and employee contributions buy units of post-retirement insurance. A later section of this chapter will examine the basic group paid-up life insurance plan and the variations of it in some depth.

Deposit Funds

Recognizing the eventual cost of providing group life insurance benefits for retired employees, insurers and employers have considered the establishment of special funds, usually held by the insurer, similar to deposit administration funds under pension plans. Dividends arising under the term plan or special employer deposits are held by the insurance company to average out the current cost of the plan and the higher costs expected in the future. Interest is credited, with the rate usually guaranteed for one or more years. Withdrawals from the fund are applied as term insurance premiums for retired employees or, in some cases, used directly to provide benefits.

The coverage on retired employees is usually term insurance, just as for active employees, without any guarantee that the protection will be continued, and without cash or loan values to the individual. Existence of the fund does not change the benefits available to active employees or the treatment of insurance when an individual terminates employment for reasons other than retirement.

The insurer assists in determining the necessary deposits, but the sufficiency of these deposits to cover future benefits is not guaranteed. Amounts in the fund are usually irrevocably committed to provide employee benefits. In the event of termination of the plan, term benefits are usually extended until the fund is exhausted. Since these deposit fund arrangements are not permanent insurance in the usual sense, they are not considered more fully in this chapter, but rather were treated in detail in Chapter 7.

FEDERAL TAXATION OF GROUP TERM AND GROUP PERMANENT LIFE INSURANCE

The development of group permanent life insurance has been greatly affected by the federal tax treatment involved, primarily the federal income tax, and to a lesser degree the federal estate tax. Of major importance are the deductibility of employer contributions as a business expense to the employer and the status of such contributions as income to the employee. The federal income tax on insurers is also a factor in some situations. Before consideration is given to the special tax rules applicable to the various forms of group permanent life insurance, it is desirable to review the general federal tax rules applying to group term life insurance.

Taxation of Group Term Life Insurance

For many years, it had been established that employer contributions for group term life insurance did not represent taxable income to the individual employee, provided certain conditions were met. The initial ruling dates back to 1920,[6] and it reflected the fact that benefits do not go to the employees personally, but only to their heirs after death. Moreover, payment of the death benefit is contingent upon continuance of employment and upon payment of premiums by the employer. Finally, the employee has no option to take the amount of the premiums instead of the insurance, and the policy has no cash or paid-up value either to the employer or to the employee.

In order to receive this favorable income tax treatment, it is necessary that the contract clearly be group insurance and that the beneficiary be someone other than the employer. This favorable treatment is not available to persons not actually "employees," such as partners or inactive owners of a firm.

Taxability of Employer Contributions. Under the 1964 Revenue Act,[7] employees must include in income the cost of group term life insurance provided directly or indirectly by an employer on insurance amounts in excess of $50,000. The cost is determined from a uniform premium table

---

[6] L.O. 1014, Cumulative Bulletin 1920–2, p. 88.

[7] Public Law 88–272, Sec. 204.

prescribed by the Treasury Department. Any contributions for current term insurance by the employee under the plan may be deducted from the cost in determining the amount of taxable income resulting from the employer's contributions. This new provision affects only the larger amounts and, hence, only a very small proportion of the total group life insurance in force.

The United States Senate Committee on Finance explained the purpose of this legislation as follows:

This tax-free status for employer-financed group term life insurance is inconsistent with the tax treatment of other types of life insurance protection furnished employees by their employers. While this complete exclusion might have been considered relatively insignificant when tax rates were low, the present relatively high rates as well as the growing volume of group term life insurance now provided makes it particularly inequitable to continue this complete exclusion. The employee in such case receives a substantial economic benefit from this insurance protection whether or not the policy for a specific year leads to a payment to his beneficiary. The provision of this insurance by the employer relieves the employee of substantial costs of providing his own insurance protection for his family which he would otherwise have to provide out of tax-paid dollars.

The House, despite recognizing that the entire cost of this insurance protection represents compensation to the employee, provided an exemption with respect to the premiums paid on the first $30,000 of such insurance because it believed, from the standpoint of the economy as a whole, that it is desirable to encourage employers to provide life insurance protection for their employees. Provision of such a basic amount of insurance does much to keep together family units where the principal breadwinner dies prematurely. Your committee is in accord with the reasoning of the House on this subject but believes that $70,000 represents a more appropriate exemption level.[8]

The House-Senate Conference Committee agreed on $50,000 as the exemption level in the final legislation.

It should be noted that an employee's contributions, if any, for the entire amount of insurance, rather than just the excess over $50,000, are deducted from the cost in determining taxable income. This can be clarified by an illustration. Assume an employee aged fifty-six is provided with $150,000 of group term life insurance by his employer. The employee contributes $.50 per month per $1,000 toward the cost.

Portion of insurance coverage taken into account ($150,000 less $50,000) $100,000
Annual "cost," using Treasury Department table below ($1.10 × 100 × 12) . . . .$ 1,320
Employee's total contribution ($.50 × 150 × 12) . . . .$ 900
Amount to be included in employee's income tax base ($1,320 less $900) . . . .$ 420

---

[8] Report of the Committee on Finance, United States Senate, *Revenue Act of 1964,* January, 1964, p. 46.

The complete table established by the Treasury Department for determining the cost of insurance in these calculations is shown in Table 8–2.

Deductibility of Employer Contributions. The deduction by the employer of group term life insurance premiums as a business expense is generally still permitted, even though the premiums do not represent income to the employee, this interpretation again going back to early rulings.[9]

TABLE 8–2

TREASURY DEPARTMENT TABLE FOR DETERMINING COST OF GROUP TERM LIFE INSURANCE

Five-Year Age Bracket	Cost per $1,000 for One-Month Period
20–24	$ .08
25–29	.08
30–34	.10
35–39	.14
40–44	.23
45–49	.40
50–54	.68
55–59	1.10
60–64	1.63

Taxation of Group Permanent Life Insurance

Just as for group term life insurance, the deductibility of employer contributions for group permanent life insurance from his taxable income and the effect on the taxable income of the employee must both be considered.

Taxability of Employer Contributions. The position of the Internal Revenue Service, as established in 1950, is that premiums paid by an employer for permanent life insurance on the lives of his employees may not be excluded from the employee's gross income but are taxable to the employee if he has nonforfeitable rights in the coverage. This 1950 ruling severely limited the development of permanent plans not qualified with pension programs, except where the permanent portion of the insurance could be clearly distinguished from the term portion and no employer contribution was involved with respect to the permanent portion. The pertinent portions of the ruling by the Internal Revenue Service are as follows:

All insurance provided on a typical level premium form is considered a permanent form, and all of each premium paid with respect to an employee under such a form, less any employee contributions on account of the premium, is required to be included in the income of the employee for the year in which the premium is paid.

---

[9] L.O. 1014, *op. cit.*; Revenue Ruling 56–400, Cumulative Bulletin 1956–2, p. 116.

Where a portion of the insurance is provided by units of paid-up insurance on a typical single premium form or is on a typical level premium form and the balance is provided on a typical current term form with separate premiums specified in the policy for each portion, only the paid-up or level premium insurance is considered a permanent form, and all of each premium paid for paid-up or level premium insurance with respect to an employee under such a plan, less any employee contributions on account of such premium, is required to be included in the income of the employee for the year in which the premium is paid. Thus, if each premium for paid-up or level premium insurance for an employee is provided from employee contributions on account of it, no premiums are considered paid by the employer for a permanent form of insurance under such a plan.[10]

It will be noted that this ruling makes clear that the group paid-up form of permanent coverage, where the employee contributes for the paid-up insurance and the employer purchases the balance of coverage as term insurance, does not involve taxable income to the employee (except for amounts over $50,000 which may involve taxable income under the 1964 Revenue Act).[11] This favorable status has contributed to the current predominance of group paid-up plans among the various approaches to group permanent life insurance.

Effect of Forfeitability. Where the right of the employee to permanent insurance is forfeitable in case of subsequent termination of employment, he does not incur taxable income from the employer's premium payments; however, it appears that generally a subsequent change to nonforfeitable status, through guaranteeing him future rights in the contract or through actual transfer of a cash value or permanent insurance to him on termination, would create taxable income at the time such an event occurs. This interpretation has limited the use of single premiums to purchase benefits at retirement, for example, or the making available to employees of cash or other values from deposit funds or level premium plans paid for by the employer.

It has also been held, however,[12] that the right of *conversion* to permanent insurance on termination of employment under a normal group term life insurance contract, where both employee and employer contribute, does not create taxable income to the employee. Such a conversion right is almost universally offered under group term life insurance contracts.

Deductibility of Employer Contributions. Internal Revenue Service regulations cover the status of employer contributions under pension plans but are not clear with respect to the tax deductibility of such

---

[10] Mimeograph 6477, Cumulative Bulletin 1950–1, p. 16.

[11] Where a plan is qualified under a pension program, the reverse situation is generally true: any employer payment toward the cost of current term insurance protection is considered taxable income to the employee; in these situations, it would be customary to apply employee contributions first toward the term insurance.

[12] Revenue Ruling 54–165, Cumulative Bulletin 1954–1, p. 17.

contributions for group permanent life insurance not qualified under pension plans. It is generally necessary for tax counsel to examine circumstances in the latter case individually for each plan, and there is a lack of rulings with respect to many of the situations arising.

Section 404 of the 1954 Internal Revenue Code covers the tax deductibility of contributions by an employer to an employees' trust or annuity plan and compensation under a deferred payment plan. It is indicated therein that for plans other than pension trusts, employee's annuities and stock bonus and profit sharing trusts, employer contributions which are otherwise ordinary and necessary business expenses may be deducted "if the employee's rights to, or derived from, such employer's contribution or such compensation are nonforfeitable at the time the contribution or compensation is paid."[13] Under a regulation[14] which has been subject to some challenge, nonforfeitability under pension plans is described with reference to the rights of *individual employees,* rather than their rights as a group.

Group term life insurance plans normally have not been considered as "deferred compensation," and Section 404 has not applied. For group permanent life insurance, consideration should be given to the possibility that these portions of the law and regulations may apply to the particular plan and, if they do, to whether or not the employees' rights are forfeitable and whether the employer's payments are irrevocably made.

Federal Income and Estate Taxation of Death Proceeds

Proceeds of group term and permanent life insurance are treated in the same manner as other life insurance benefits for federal income tax purposes. The general rule[15] is that, subject to certain conditions, the gross income of a beneficiary does not include amounts received as death benefits under a life insurance contract. Similarly, taxation of installment settlements follows the rules applicable to other life insurance benefits.

Group life insurance proceeds are treated for estate tax purposes generally in the same manner as other life insurance. The rule[16] is that such proceeds are part of the estate for taxation if at the time of death the insured possessed any of the incidents of ownership. Under most group contracts, the insured has the right to change the beneficiary, and this has been considered as representing an incident of ownership.

There has been some interest in assigning, through the use of an absolute assignment form, the rights of individual employees in their group insurance benefits. Some companies discourage the use of assignments under group insurance plans, but others will permit them, generally

---

[13] Internal Revenue Code, Sec. 404(a)(5).

[14] U.S. Treasury Regulation, Sec. 1.404(a)–12, September 24, 1956.

[15] Internal Revenue Code, Sec. 101(a).

[16] Internal Revenue Code, Sec. 2042.

without accepting responsibility for their validity. The consent of the employer may be necessary.

Where an absolute assignment can be effectively accomplished, it may eliminate the benefit proceeds from the employee's estate at death. Such assignments should be used only with careful consideration of the problems which may be created by the assignment, as well as of the advantage of any estate tax savings.

Tax Status of Deposit Fund Arrangements

Deposit fund arrangements for providing benefits after retirement have been referred to only briefly in this chapter. However, their tax status deserves special comment. The conditions under which they are held vary among insurance companies, and tax questions have arisen to which definite answers are not available.

Concerning the individual employee, the tax status is reasonably clear. The employee is generally given no vested rights in the benefits to be provided, either while active or subsequent to retirement, and amounts paid into the deposit fund are thus handled so as not to represent taxable income to him. Employer contributions, or amounts allocated from experience margins under the plan, may nonetheless be irrevocably committed to providing benefits under the plan, with extension of term insurance until the fund is exhausted in event of discontinuance of the program.

The tax effects on both the employer and the insurance company from establishment of these funds can be important. Frequently, additions will be made to a deposit fund from experience margins under the term insurance plan for active employees, amounts which might otherwise be available as dividends to the employer. Dividends received by the employer reduce the net premiums paid by him for insurance and, hence, reduce his business expense deduction from taxable income. It is, therefore, necessary to establish whether or not such fund additions are in effect paid to the employer, in the sense that the fund belongs to him and is under his control, or alternatively, is irrevocably committed to insurance purposes and is not under his control.

Similarly, employer payments for permanent insurance, rather than term insurance, may possibly not be considered a current deductible business expense. It is necessary to establish whether payments into the deposit fund can be considered a current expense.

Insurance companies are taxed on investment income and, on a different basis, on gains from operations other than investment income. The insurer's taxable investment income is reduced by interest on life insurance reserves and interest paid, as defined in the law.[17] The interest rate which an insurer allows on a deposit fund can thus be affected by whether

---

[17] Internal Revenue Code, Secs. 804(a), 805(a).

or not it expects to obtain this deduction, and this in turn can depend on the conditions under which the fund is established.

There are at least three approaches in determining the conditions which will apply to these funds, but it is not certain that the tax status expected will actually result in every similar case. The approaches are:

1. The fund is established so that it is not under the control of the employer at all; it does not represent money declared as a dividend or money which would otherwise have been declared as a dividend. The retention of experience margins for the fund is clearly described in the insurance contract. Interest credited to the fund is thus not received by the employer, but the insurer is required to allow such credits and deducts them from its investment income. The fund is of a nonforfeitable character.

2. The fund is established as the retention of monies which otherwise would have been paid as dividends under the insurance contract. Additions to the fund, whether from dividends or by special deposits, are comparable to the payment of premiums due under the plan. The fund is treated by the insurance company as a clear indebtedness on its part, but one which may be discharged only in certain specified ways; no cash return to the employer is available once monies have been committed to the fund. Interest credits are deducted from the insurer's taxable investment income as interest paid on indebtedness.

3. The fund is established by the insurance company as a liability meeting the requirements under the law for "life insurance reserves,"[18] which means that the reserves are "computed or estimated on the basis of recognized mortality or morbidity tables and assumed rates of interest" and "are set aside to mature or liquidate . . . future unaccrued claims arising from life insurance. . . ."

LEVEL PREMIUM GROUP PERMANENT INSURANCE

Because of the possibility of employer contributions being considered taxable income to employees, level premium group permanent plans are most commonly used with qualified pension plans to provide supplemental life insurance benefits under various arrangements where the value of the life insurance at retirement may be applied to provide annuity benefits. However, two illustrations can be provided of applications of the level premium group permanent approach to group plans in which pensions are not involved. These have been designed with the objective of avoiding tax problems.

In the first of these plans, employee contributions, on an individually optional basis, may be applied for the purchase of permanent insurance, with the employer paying the cost of term insurance for the balance of the coverage provided. In the second, a level premium form is used, but the employer's money is applied to purchase nonvested benefits, with no values accruing for employees.

---

[18] Internal Revenue Code, Sec. 801(b).

Optional Permanent Insurance, with Employee Contributions

The optional permanent insurance plan with employee contributions is designed to permit each individual eligible employee under a group life insurance plan to elect permanent insurance in specified amounts if he chooses to contribute. A minimum percentage participation in the permanent coverage is required. A plan such as whole life insurance or life paid up at age sixty-five is used as the basis for the permanent coverage.

If the employee elects to contribute on the permanent plan, his level contributions pay a portion of that cost sufficient to provide the accumulating paid-up and cash values of that plan. The employer pays the balance on a level premium term insurance basis approximating the cost of the current insurance coverage (amount at risk) on the permanent plan. For a given individual, this amount at risk decreases as employee contributions accumulate, but the cost of each dollar of insurance at risk increases with advancing age; the level employer payment is thus reasonably related to each year's cost, slightly more at the outset but less in the later years. This arrangement results in a cost to the employee which is significantly less than would be the case if he contributed the full premium for the permanent plan. In addition, the employer pays for all group term coverage for those employees who do not elect permanent coverage.

The permanent insurance accumulates cash and paid-up values. At retirement, the employee may continue the permanent plan or apply these values for paid-up insurance or retirement income, as he could under individual insurance. The employee is assured of cash values after a few years at least equal to his contributions. The plan requires a substantial employer contribution, exceeding that he would initially pay for the full cost of a conventional term plan; but the permanent or paid-up insurance available at retirement reduces his potential burden for continuing term coverage. In addition, the employer's cost is stabilized, as compared with the increases occurring in term insurance costs with increasing age. Once minimum participation requirements are met, flexibility is available, since employees electing only term insurance originally are permitted to convert to the permanent plan at any subsequent anniversary.

Results and costs under this approach are compared with conventional term life insurance and with group paid-up life insurance in Table 8–3, using as an example an employee eligible for $4,000 of insurance, entering at age forty.

These figures are illustrative and would vary among companies, but they illustrate the differences in incidence of cost and accumulated values under the various approaches. Under the conventional group term insurance plan, there is initially no employer cost since the employee contribution covers the full one-year term premium rate at age forty. The em-

TABLE 8–3

COMPARISON OF OPTIONAL PERMANENT PLAN WITH CONVENTIONAL GROUP
TERM AND GROUP PAID-UP PLAN

Employee Age 40 @ Entry $4,000 Total Insurance	Optional Permanent Plan (Whole Life)	Conventional Group Term Plan (Employee Contribution $.50 per Month per $1,000)	Group Paid-up Plan (Employee Contribution $4 per Month)
Initial monthly cost:			
Employee..................	$ 5.16	$ 2.00	$ 4.00
Employer..................	4.28	—	1.80
Monthly cost 15 years later:			
Employee..................	5.16	2.00	4.00
Employer..................	4.28	4.60	4.14
Monthly cost at age 65:			
Employee..................	5.16	2.00	4.00
Employer..................	4.28	13.12	6.61
Total employee contributions to Age 65....................	1,548	600	1,200
Cash value at age 65...........	2,016	0	1,500
Paid-up value at age 65.........	2,684	0	2,252

ployer's cost increases rapidly with the increasing age of the employee. Although employee contributions over the twenty-five-year period total $600, there are no cash or paid-up values available. On the optional permanent plan, both the employee and employer contributions are level throughout the individual's service. The employee has cash value available at age sixty-five substantially exceeding his total contributions, his excess cost over the conventional term plan of $948 yielding an equity at age sixty-five of $2,016. On the group paid-up life insurance plan, the employer's cost is not averaged over the years; also, since the optional feature is lacking, administrative expenses and the premium loading for them may be somewhat less under this plan than for the optional permanent plan.

Employer Contributions for Nonvested Benefits

An employer may be prepared to make substantial contributions toward the cost of group life insurance after retirement and may wish to pre-fund this cost during the working lifetime of the employees involved, at his own expense. An approach intended to permit this while avoiding tax problems has been designed.

Under this plan, premiums for the employer are set on a level premium, limited payment life basis, such as life paid up at age sixty-five. A relatively high age for initial eligibility is established to reduce the administrative and accounting work. From the employee's point of view, benefits are completely nonvested, with no values either before or after retirement. The description of the benefits for the employee is identical with that provided under a conventional group term life insurance plan. With no vesting, it is intended that taxable income to employees be avoided (except as applicable under the 1964 Revenue Act for amounts of group term life insurance in excess of $50,000).

Annual accountings are furnished the employer showing accumulated reserves under the permanent insurance. On cancellation of an employee's coverage, the reserve is applied as a credit against future premiums. In the event of termination of the entire plan, reserve credits from all employees would be used to extend term insurance until the reserve was exhausted. In this manner, employer contributions are irrevocably committed to the program, with the objective that they be deductible as a business expense from the employer's taxable income.

The advantages of this program are as follows:

1. The potential liability for insurance coverage after retirement is paid for during an employee's working lifetime.
2. The ultimate costs of the program are recognized and averaged out through the level premium approach.
3. Since, from the employee's point of view, the arrangement is identical to term insurance, adoption of the plan is relatively simple and flexible. The employee need not be involved in the arrangements worked out, and no changes in existing insurance certificates are necessary, for example.

Possible disadvantages of this plan are:

1. The tax effects must be carefully examined in each case, since there are no definite Internal Revenue Service rulings.
2. Administrative arrangements must permit determination of individual reserves for termination credits. Hence, valuation and record-keeping procedures are somewhat more complicated than for group term life insurance alone.
3. Initially, the cost to the employer is high compared with that of a group term life insurance plan.

Differences in Policy Provisions from Group Term Life Insurance

Level premium group permanent life insurance plans normally contain provisions identical with group term life insurance plans as respects beneficiary designations, use of settlement options, suicide, contestability, general rights under the contract and method of modification of the contract. The conversion privilege on termination of employment is modified to limit the amount which may be converted to that actually being discontinued, without duplication of any paid-up amounts continuing in force under the permanent plan. Where cash and paid-up values are available to the employee, appropriate nonforfeiture provisions are included in the contract. If the employer is paying for the permanent insurance, the contract may provide for application of surrender values on an employee's termination as a credit toward the payment of premiums.

With term insurance, the premium rate table is usually subject to change by the insurance company from year to year. For a permanent plan, the company usually reserves the right to change premium rates, but such changes would not affect premiums for units of permanent insurance already in force. The rate basis might be guaranteed at issue for a period, such as five years. Under one arrangement for the optional permanent plan, which has been described, neither the employer nor employee portions of the premium are guaranteed indefinitely; the contract specifies the total premium and the cash and paid-up values being provided by the employee's contribution. In the event of a change in rates, values already accrued would not be affected, but future accumulations could change.

GROUP PAID-UP LIFE INSURANCE

Basic Features

Group paid-up life insurance is by far the most popular form of group permanent life insurance. A primary factor in its popularity has been the clear distinction in application of employee and employer contributions and the avoidance of tax difficulties thereby.

Since this is the most widely used form of permanent group coverage, benefits and administration will be described in some detail. The usual group insurance underwriting rules apply, with some special considerations as discussed below.

A schedule of total group insurance is established, just as with group term life insurance plans. The insurance benefit is then divided into two parts: employee contributions applied exclusively to purchase units of paid-up life insurance; employer contributions applied exclusively to purchase term insurance in an amount equal to the balance of the scheduled benefit.

Employee Contributions. Employee contributions are normally set at a level which, for most employees, will produce reasonable amounts of accumulated paid-up insurance at retirement. A common rate of employee contributions is $1.30 per month per $1,000 of total insurance (term plus paid-up). Under rate tables currently in use, $1.30 per month will accumulate to $1,000 or more at age sixty-five for individuals entering the plan at ages up to thirty or thirty-five; even for an individual becoming insured at age forty-five, the paid-up benefit available at age sixty-five exceeds 50 per cent of the initial term insurance amount. Plans are also often written with a specified dollar contribution not directly related to the total amount of insurance, such as $2.00 or $4.00 per month per employee.

Under some plans, the employee contributes for term insurance under a conventional group term life insurance plan until he attains a specified age or length of service. The paid-up plan then becomes effective, and a relatively higher contribution rate may be specified. This approach reduces the proportion of employees and the periods of time for which the special paid-up insurance records must be maintained. The higher contribution also provides more insurance at retirement for those entering the plan at relatively high ages, such as fifty or fifty-five.

Amounts of Paid-up Insurance Purchased. Under typical programs currently offered, employee contributions are applied using the 1958 CSO table at 3 per cent interest. Contributions of $1.30 per month ($15.60 annually) provide amounts of accumulated paid-up insurance for representative ages at entry as shown in Table 8–4.

For the higher entry ages, it is evident that contributions do not accumulate to more than a nominal amount of paid-up insurance by age

TABLE 8–4

AMOUNTS OF PAID-UP INSURANCE ACCUMULATED
(Contribution of $1.30 per Month)

	Age at Entry			
Years Insured	25	35	45	55
5...................................	$ 263	$204	$160	$130
10..................................	495	385	304	248
20..................................	879	689	552	—
30..................................	1,092	936	—	—
At age 65...........................	1,431	936	552	248

sixty-five. To offset this, a higher level of contributions may be specified for the higher ages at entry, and some supplemental term insurance after retirement may be provided.

Employer Contributions. The employer pays the premium necessary to purchase term insurance in an amount equal to the difference between the total benefit and the accumulated amount of paid-up insurance on each individual. Normally, the rate table for term insurance is the same as that employed for regular group term life insurance plans. As amounts of paid-up insurance accumulate, the employer's total cost in the normal situation can be expected to decline; initially he must pay for term insurance on all his older employees, but eventually the older employees will have accumulated significant amounts of paid-up insurance under the plan.

The developing costs can be illustrated by taking as an example a typical group of 100 employees with total group life insurance in force of $412,000 initially and no one retired. The following assumptions are made:

Amounts of insurance: $2,000 to $5,500, reducing 50 per cent at retirement (amounts increase periodically during each employee's working lifetime).

Average term life insurance rate: $.95 per month per $1,000, initially.

Employee monthly contribution per $1,000, while active:

Term plan: $ .40
Paid-up plan: 1.00

About five new employees enter the plan at the younger ages each year, and a smaller number terminate employment.

Projected employer costs for this group could develop somewhat as follows:

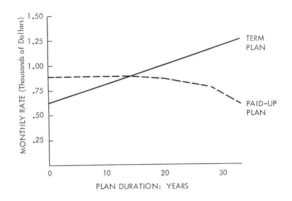

	Total Insurance		Paid-up Insurance Purchased	Employer Cost			
				Term Plan		Paid-up Plan	
	Active	Retired		Rate	Annual Premium	Rate	Annual Premium
Initially....$412,000	$ 0	$ 0	$ .55	$ 2,702	$.95	$4,680
10 years.... 492,400	31,800	115,100	.80	5,041	.93	5,844
20 years.... 571,500	50,700	228,700	1.06	7,937	.84	6,288
30 years.... 640,800	64,200	334,200	1.24	10,496	.59	4,968

FIG. 8–1. Projected employer costs under group term plan and group paid-up plan.

The employer's cost on the full term insurance plan would eventually level off at a relatively high rate as the full burden for retired employees is reached. On the paid-up insurance plan, his cost eventually reaches stability at a lower rate, as the younger employees initially, and as the first groups of new employees after plan installation, approach and enter retirement, with their full quotas of paid-up insurance accumulated. Other assumptions than those used could give somewhat different results, but this pattern is typical: increasing cost on a pure term insurance plan; and initially higher, but then decreasing, employer cost with installation of a paid-up insurance plan.

Cash or Paid-up Values on Termination of Employment. The employee is guaranteed paid-up insurance or a cash surrender value on termination of his employment. The surrender value is the larger of the cash value of the accumulated paid-up insurance or the sum of the employee's contributions. The latter may be greater during the first few years of his coverage. In order to maintain participation in the program, cash values are usually restricted or prohibited in connection with temporary layoffs or voluntary withdrawal from the plan, unless accompanied by termination of employment. For example, a delay of two years might be required before release of cash values in the latter case. Frequently, however, if the amount of paid-up insurance is less than some minimum, such as $250, the cash surrender value is automatically paid to avoid continued record keeping on small amounts.

Conversion Privilege. At termination of employment, the same conversion privileges are available for the term insurance portion of the coverage under a paid-up plan as are provided under a regular group term life insurance plan. If the amount of paid-up insurance is less than some minimum amount, such as $250, and surrender for the cash value is required, conversion of the full face amount (term plus paid-up insurance) may be permitted.

Death Benefit. The benefit payable upon death is the total face amount, including the term insurance and the paid-up insurance portions. In addition to payment in one sum, normal optional methods of settlement are available, similar to those offered under regular group term life insurance.

Other Details of Coverage. There are certain other customary features of group paid-up life insurance plans. First, a waiver of premium disability benefit is usually provided for the term insurance portion of coverage, in the event of total disability, under the same conditions applicable for regular group term insurance plans. Frequently, contributions for paid-up insurance cease also, with the amount already purchased remaining in effect, of course. Some companies permit continuation of paid-up contributions.

Second, continuation of term insurance coverage for a temporary period is usually permitted in connection with layoffs and leaves of absence, sixty days or one year being common. Continuation without limit in the event of sickness is generally permitted. In all instances, paid-up insurance remains in force, and contributions for it may be continued for the period during which term insurance continues in effect, or longer in some cases.

Third, both a term insurance premium rate table and a paid-up insurance purchase rate table are included in the contract. The term insurance premium rates usually are guaranteed for one year and subject to change annually thereafter; but the paid-up insurance purchase table would be guaranteed for a longer period, five years being common.

Deferred Paid-up Variation

A variation on the conventional group paid-up life insurance plan described above has been developed. In this case, employee contributions are applied to purchase a *deferred* benefit. The employer's contribution pays for all current insurance. The deferred post-retirement paid-up benefits have cash values, and in the event of termination of employment may also be converted to immediate paid-up insurance.

This plan requires continued employer contributions at a level sufficient to pay for 100 per cent of current term insurance costs, without the potential reductions which normally develop under the conventional paid-up approach. However, the employer is relieved of the increasing cost of benefits after retirement. Employee contributions are applied completely to post-retirement coverage, with no portion of this contribution required for *immediate* paid-up insurance, as is the case under the conventional paid-up insurance plan. Larger amounts of post-retirement protection thus develop from a given contribution rate than for conventional paid-up insurance. Of course, the total annual cost of the program is greater. To illustrate these differences, $10 per month from an employee joining at age forty-five would purchase $5,530 of paid-up insurance at age sixty-five on the deferred plan as against $4,240 on the conventional paid-up plan, using typical rate tables.

Underwriting and Administration of Group Paid-up Plan

Group paid-up life insurance plans are designed for stable groups with low turnover (5 per cent a year, or even less, is desirable), and company underwriting rules are designed accordingly. In addition, it is necessary that employee contributions sufficient to purchase reasonable amounts of paid-up insurance be available, and it is undesirable to include very short-term employees until their permanence is established.

For these reasons, probationary periods before employees become eligible to participate in the plan typically are longer than for regular group term life insurance plans, with three, six or twelve months being common. Classes of employees with low incomes or those subject to high turnover may be excluded completely, or longer probationary periods may be established.

Records of the amounts of paid-up insurance purchased for each individual employee must be maintained. Only larger employers with a definite interest and proper facilities can keep these records, and self-administration is, therefore, less common with smaller groups than under group term life insurance plans. Simplified methods have been developed for calculating term insurance premiums so that each individual change in paid-up insurance purchased will not require lengthy recomputation of the term coverage balance. These and similar problems have been reduced by companies specializing in this plan to efficient and streamlined procedures.

Advantages and Limitations of Group Paid-up Plan

In summary, the advantages of the group paid-up method of providing permanent group life insurance are as follows:

1. To the extent employee contributions so provide, the cost of insurance after retirement is paid for by the employee during his working lifetime.

2. The employer's cost under a typical arrangement will decrease as the accumulated total of paid-up benefits increases.

3. The employee has cash or paid-up values upon leaving employment, and guaranteed lifetime coverage increases with the accumulation of paid-up amounts.

4. The income tax status is clear, both as respects deductibility of the employer's contributions and as respects avoidance of additional taxable income to the employee.

On the other hand, there are certain limitations which must be carefully considered before establishing a group paid-up life insurance program:

1. The plan is usually not suitable for high turnover groups or those where substantial employee contributions are not available.

2. The initial cost to the employer will be higher than with group term life insurance, although normally decreasing after a few years.

3. Additional record keeping is involved.

4. It may be that the portion of premiums needed to pay cash surrender values might better be used to provide larger amounts of insurance without such surrender values.

5. Special arrangements may be needed for providing adequate benefits after retirement for employees who have already reached an advanced age when the plan is established or when they first become eligible to participate in it.

SELECTED REFERENCES

INSTITUTE OF LIFE INSURANCE. *1964 Life Insurance Fact Book.* New York, 1964.

INTERNAL REVENUE CODE, RULINGS AND REGULATIONS:
  Internal Revenue Code, Sec. 101(a).
  Internal Revenue Code, Sec. 404(a) (5).
  Internal Revenue Code, Secs. 801–811.
  Internal Revenue Code, Secs. 804(a), 805(a).
  Internal Revenue Code, Sec. 2042.

U.S. Treasury Regulation, Sec. 1.404(a)–12, September 24, 1956.

U.S. Treasury Mimeograph 6477 (Cumulative Bulletin 1950–1, p. 16).

Revenue Ruling 54–165 (Cumulative Bulletin 1954–1, p. 17).

Revenue Ruling 56–400 (Cumulative Bulletin 1956–2, p. 116).

L.O. 1014 (Cumulative Bulletin 1920–2, p. 88).

The Revenue Act of 1964, Sec. 204.

JACKSON, PAUL H. "Group Paid-up and Group Permanent Life Insurance," *Life and Health Insurance Handbook* (ed. DAVIS W. GREGG), ch. 30. 2d ed. Homewood, Ill.: Richard D. Irwin, Inc., 1964.

NATIONAL INDUSTRIAL CONFERENCE BOARD. *Corporate Retirement Policy and Practices.* Studies in Personnel Policy No. 190. New York, 1964.

————. "Life Insurance for Retired Employees," *Management Record*, Vol. XXV, No. 2 (February, 1963), pp. 12–19.

SOCIETY OF ACTUARIES. *Employee Retirement Plans Study Notes*, Sec. 83–0–57. Rev. ed. Chicago, 1962.

————. *Group Insurance Study Notes*, Secs. 82–2–63 and 9E1–3–63. Chicago, 1963.

U.S. DEPARTMENT OF HEALTH, EDUCATION AND WELFARE. "Population," *Health, Education and Welfare Indicators*, February, 1964.

U.S. DEPARTMENT OF LABOR. *Life Insurance and Accidental Death and Dismemberment Benefits, Early Summer 1960*, Bulletin No. 1296. Washington, D.C.: U.S. Government Printing Office, June, 1961.

Chapter 9

ACCIDENTAL DEATH AND DISMEMBERMENT, DEPENDENTS AND FEDERAL EMPLOYEES GROUP LIFE INSURANCE

BY CARL R. ASHMAN

As is true of all group coverages, certain fundamental, guiding principles underlie the underwriting, issuance and administration of group acciden-tal death and dismemberment insurance and dependents group life insurance. The interpretation and specific application of these principles, however, is, of course, a matter of individual company judgment and discretion. The following discussion of these coverages is intended only to outline these principles and their application in broad, general terms.

ACCIDENTAL DEATH AND DISMEMBERMENT INSURANCE

Nature of Accidental Death and Dismemberment Coverage

One of the earliest forms of group coverage to be developed was accidental death and dismemberment insurance. While, as is indicated later, the actual economic need for the coverage is debatable, it always has been, and continues to be, very popular.

Often accidental death and dismemberment insurance is considered to be a form of group health insurance. However, because the accidental death aspect of the coverage is much more significant than the dismem-berment aspect[1] (the "health insurance" portion of the risk) and because it is most commonly issued in conjunction with group life insurance, the explanation and discussion of this coverage is incorporated in the group life insurance section of this volume.

---

[1] It is roughly estimated that the dismemberment aspect represents not more than 10 per cent of the total risk.

As its name indicates, this coverage provides benefits for loss of life or certain body members as a consequence of accidental bodily injury. With respect to hands or feet, "loss" is usually defined as dismemberment by severance at or above the wrist or ankle joint. With respect to eyes, the usual definition of "loss" is the entire and irrecoverable loss of sight.

As indicated above, the coverage is most commonly issued in conjunction with and as a supplement to group life insurance. It may be, however, and frequently is, issued with one of the other group coverages, such as short-term disability income insurance. Because the incidence of loss, and, hence, the premium, is comparatively low, it is ordinarily uneconomical and, therefore, inadvisable to issue and administer this coverage by itself.

Nevertheless, there is a growing trend toward writing the coverage by itself for extremely high amounts either on a group or on a wholesale or franchise basis. In addition to employee groups, coverage is available for other groups of individuals such as members of professional societies or associations. In many instances the individual may select the amount of his coverage up to some established maximum such as $100,000 or $200,000 and, on occasion, the same privilege is extended to his dependents.

Benefit Structure and Amounts

Amount of Benefits. The full amount of insurance, usually called the "principal sum," is payable for loss of life or for loss of two or more members (usually defined as a hand, foot or eye but sometimes extended to include a thumb or index finger, speech or hearing). One half of the principal sum is payable for the loss of one member.

The maximum payment for all losses sustained as a result of any one accident is the principal sum. Aggregate payments may, however, exceed the principal sum in the event of more than one accident involving the same individual because benefits are payable for each accident without regard to or adjustment on account of previous accidents. Theoretically, it would be possible to pay benefits for losses sustained as a result of as many as seven accidents, and aggregate payments to or on behalf of one insured person might ultimately amount to as much as four times the principal sum.

On the other hand, benefits are not cumulative. To illustrate, should an insured person suffer the accidental loss of sight of one eye in one accident and then lose the sight of the other eye in a second accident, the benefit payable for the loss sustained in the second accident would be only one half of the principal sum. This would be true even though the person had not been insured at the time of the first loss and, consequently, had received no benefits.

Coordination with Group Life Insurance. When accidental death and dismemberment insurance is written in conjunction with group life insurance, the most common arrangement is to have the principal sum equal the amount of life insurance coverage. However, depending on the size of the case, the maximum permissible principal sum may be somewhat lower than the maximum amount of group life insurance available on a single life. For example, the schedule of benefits might provide for individual amounts of group life insurance up to a maximum of $40,000 and for equivalent individual amounts of accidental death and dismemberment insurance, but up to a maximum of only $20,000.

The maximum principal sum permissible is also usually less when the coverage is written with a form of group insurance other than life. It may be still further restricted if written on a twenty-four-hour coverage (occupational as well as nonoccupational) basis in a hazardous industry, the extent of the restriction varying with the degree of occupational hazard involved.

Conditions for Payment. Establishment of the insurer's liability for payment of benefits requires that the loss must be sustained as the direct result of accidental bodily injury and independently of all other causes. If some other factor, such as a chronic illness, is primarily responsible for or even contributes to the result, that circumstance alone constitutes sufficient grounds for denial of liability. To substantiate and support this requirement, it is further provided that the injury must be evidenced by a visible contusion or wound on the exterior of the body. (This provision is waived in the event of drowning or internal injuries revealed by an autopsy.)

The insuring clause also stipulates that the date of occurrence of the injury and the date the loss is sustained must not be separated by more than a specific interval of time, generally ninety days. This may appear, on the surface, to be a wholly arbitrary and unduly harsh requirement. It must be borne in mind, however, that the determination of whether a particular loss was solely the result of accident becomes more and more difficult with the passage of time between the date of the accident and the date of the actual loss. While there is nothing particularly significant about a period of ninety days, experience has demonstrated that it is reasonably adequate in the vast majority of instances. Certainly the establishment of such a requirement eliminates any room for argument and, thus, is of great assistance in the prompt settlement of claims.

Many insurers also require that the accidental bodily injury must have been sustained by reason of "accidental means." This "double-barreled" requirement, i.e., that both the cause of the injury and the injury itself be "accidental," while entirely legitimate, is a rather fine distinction which may be difficult for the layman to understand and appreciate. It is also one which the courts may be disposed to minimize or ignore. For these reasons, there is a division of opinion about its advisability and effectiveness.[2]

Limitations and Exclusions

In the preceding section, the conditions which must be satisfied in order to establish a claim for benefits have been cited and discussed. In addition there are a number of conditions and situations which may result in losses of the type for which benefits are ordinarily provided but which are specifically excluded from consideration by the terms of the group contract.

One large company's "exclusions" clause reads as follows:

No Accidental Death, Dismemberment and Loss of Sight Benefits will be paid for any loss which results directly or indirectly, wholly or partly, from: (1) self-destruction or attempted self-destruction or intentionally self-inflicted injury, while sane or insane (2) insurrection, or war, or any act attributable thereto (3) participating in a riot, committing an assault or felony (4) disease of the body or mental infirmity, or as a result of medical or surgical treatment or diagnosis therefor (5) ptomaines or bacterial infection (except only pyogenic infection occurring simultaneously with and in consequence of a visible accidental cut or wound) (6) taking of poison or asphyxiation from or inhaling of gas, whether voluntarily or involuntarily.

The purpose of the first and third exclusions is obvious. The insurer, it is felt, should have no obligation to pay benefits when the loss is occasioned, either wholly or in part, by the deliberate act of the insured, even though there may be occasions when the loss could not necessarily have been foreseen.

The effectiveness of the first exclusion is considerably weakened in the case of two states by their insistence upon a modification in the language. In Maryland the word "intentional" must precede the words "self-destruction" and "attempted self-destruction." In Missouri the words "or insane" must be deleted. Thus the burden of proof rests on the insurer to establish that the act was intentional in the one instance and that it was committed while the insured was sane in the other.

The war risk exclusion is necessary because, if the coverage were continued under the circumstances indicated, there would be a greatly increased exposure to accident largely immeasurable and not contemplated in the rate structure. In other words, the coverage is designed and priced to operate in a more or less normal peacetime economy. The exclusions relating to physical and mental disease and to medical and surgical treatment supplement and support the requirement that the loss must be the direct result of accidental bodily injury and must be independent of all other causes.

---

[2] *Association of Life Insurance Counsel Proceedings* (1925–1927, Vol. III). An extended discussion of this problem is contained in an address entitled "Accidental Means" delivered by Wm. Marshall Bullitt, of Louisville, Ky., before The Association of Life Insurance Counsel, New York, December 7, 1927.

The sixth exclusion is not in general use. It does, however, protect the insurer in those instances, involving the taking of poison or inhalation of gas, where there is a strong suspicion of suicide which cannot be completely substantiated. If there is no such suspicion, the exclusion is ordinarily ignored and the claim allowed if all other conditions for payment are satisfied.

The insertion of an "aviation exclusion" has fallen into general disuse and is now seldom utilized unless the group is characterized by unusual flight activity which substantially increases the hazard of accidental death or dismemberment. When this exclusion is used, it is common practice to waive any restrictions on flying as a fare-paying passenger on commercial airlines.

When the coverage is written on a nonoccupational basis only, there must also be an exclusion for losses arising out of occupational injury. This restriction is sometimes incorporated in the insuring clause rather than being cited as one of the exclusions.

Treatment of Retired Employees

Unlike group life insurance, which is frequently provided for retired personnel, accidental death and dismemberment benefits almost invariably terminate upon retirement. Among the reasons for this more restrictive requirement is the fact that not only are the consequences of an accident apt to be much more serious for older persons, but, also, as age increases and health impairments become more frequent, it becomes more and more difficult to establish that the loss was due solely to accidental bodily injury.

Although it would, of course, be possible to extend this coverage into retirement, such an extension would require a substantial increase in risk charges and, therefore, premium rates. It would also limit to some extent the possibilities for prompt and satisfactory claim settlement.

Recent Developments

Accidental death and dismemberment coverage has not been immune from the many changes and innovations which have characterized the dynamic growth and progress of the group insurance business. Reference has already been made to a growing trend toward writing the coverage by itself for extremely high amounts. Other innovations, some of which seem to be fast becoming an integral part of the picture, include:

1. Provision for payment of twice the principal sum in the event of loss of life because of accidental bodily injury resulting from travel in a "public conveyance";
2. Provision of additional amounts of accidental death and dismemberment insurance, sometimes equal to the basic amounts, for various forms of travel accident, i.e., payment for losses resulting from accidental bodily

injury sustained while in a common carrier, a private automobile or a company-owned or chartered airplane;

3. Provision for the form of travel accident coverage referred to in (2) but by means of a separate contract rather than in conjunction with other group coverages (very substantial amounts of insurance are usually made available under this arrangement);

4. Provision of amounts of basic coverage considerably larger than the normal maxima previously indicated, with the experience usually being pooled with that of other policyholders having similar abnormally large benefits;

5. Extension of relatively modest amounts of coverage to dependent spouses and children;

6. Provision of twenty-four-hour accidental death and dismemberment coverage for all employees on a voluntary basis, with the premiums paid entirely by the employee on a payroll deduction basis;

7. Provision of an additional principal sum benefit if dismemberment results in total and permanent disability.

These and similar developments indicate that in the area of group accidental death and dismemberment insurance, as in other areas of group coverage, the industry is sensitive and responsive to the apparent desires of the insuring public.

Critique

Accidental death and dismemberment insurance is, at least as far as benefits for loss of life are concerned, a valued rather than a reimbursement coverage, in the sense that there can be no accurate measurement of the extent of additional economic loss occasioned by the accidental death of the insured. Indeed it may be argued that in many instances the extent of that loss is actually reduced by reason of the accidental death of the insured, since unusually heavy hospital and other medical expenses or long periods of disability with little or no income which might have preceded death from natural causes are avoided. The actual need and consequent economic justification for the coverage is, therefore, a moot question.

Nevertheless the coverage seems to have great appeal, presumably because, although premium rates are commensurate with the risk, there is the superficially attractive possibility of a comparatively high rate of benefit return for a nominal premium outlay. That appeal is strengthened considerably by the increased exposure to accident which characterizes modern-day living.

DEPENDENTS GROUP LIFE INSURANCE

Nature of Dependents Group Life Insurance

Dependents group life insurance extends to dependents of insured employees the same general form of group term life insurance as is available to the employees themselves. This type of coverage may be written in most jurisdictions[3] and is offered by most companies writing group insurance.

Unlike employee group life insurance, where, for statutory or other reasons, the employer generally assumes at least a portion of the cost, it is usually not only permissible but also common for the employee to pay the entire cost of the coverage for his dependents. Undoubtedly one of the reasons that dependents group life insurance is ordinarily written on an employee-pay-all basis is that employer contributions for it would be considered as taxable income to the employee. This effectively limits its sale to groups where the total employee contribution at least equals the cost of the dependent coverage. Whatever the reason, there is no particular objection to this arrangement since the benefits are usually comparatively modest so that the cost involved is nominal and, under normal conditions, remains reasonably stable from year to year.

Ordinarily, only dependents of employees who are themselves insured for group life insurance are eligible for this coverage. Under certain conditions, however, it may be offered to dependents of employees insured for coverages other than group life insurance. Rarely, if ever, is it offered without some form of employee coverage.

The same definition of "dependents" as is used for other dependent coverages, such as hospital and surgical expense insurance, is applicable except where a more restrictive definition is required by the statutes of the state or states involved. For example, in California, group life insurance for dependent children is restricted to children under twenty-one years of age, whereas no such age restriction is applicable to group health insurance. Consequently, a plan written in that state which included both group life insurance and group health insurance for dependent children would have to contain the statutory age restriction for the group life insurance even though it provided for the continuance of the group health insurance until age twenty-five.

Benefit Amounts

The coverage is designed primarily to help defray the expenses attendant upon the last illness and burial of the dependent. For that reason,

---

[3] As of this writing, the following states do not permit the issuance of dependents group life insurance:

Arkansas	Maine	Ohio
Colorado	Maryland	Oklahoma
Connecticut	Massachusetts	Pennsylvania
Florida	New Hampshire	Texas
Indiana	New Jersey	Vermont
Kentucky	New York	Wisconsin

In Michigan, each case must be submitted to the Insurance Commissioner for his individual consideration under the section of the group life insurance law of that state relating to discretionary groups.

therefore, and also sometimes because of statutory limitations, benefit levels are, as has been indicated, usually comparatively modest.

A typical schedule might, for example, provide the dependent spouse with an amount of group life insurance equal to 50 per cent of the employee's coverage but not more than $1,000 or $2,000, with each dependent child being insured for $1,000[4] or possibly $500.

Waiver of premium or other disability benefits are rarely provided, and settlement options are not ordinarily made available. Benefits are normally payable in one sum to the employee or, in the event of the prior death of the employee, either to the employee's estate or, at the option of the insurer, to one of certain specified classes of "order of preference" beneficiaries. The usual order of preference is first the surviving spouse, then the surviving child or children, and finally the surviving parent or parents under a facility of payment provision.[5]

Termination of Coverage

Dependents coverage ordinarily terminates when the employee's own coverage terminates. Other reasons for termination include: (1) termination of contributions, if any, by the employee; (2) transfer of the employee to a class not eligible for dependent benefits; (3) termination by the insurer of all dependents life insurance for failure to fulfill renewal requirements.

The coverage also terminates when the individual concerned no longer meets the contractual definition of "eligible dependents," e.g., in the case of a spouse, upon the date of divorce or legal separation or, in the case of a child, upon the attainment of the specified limiting age, such as age eighteen or nineteen. It is also usually provided that the coverage terminates upon the employee's retirement, even though the employee's own

---

[4] The benefit for the first six months of life is usually limited to $100. Six states— Montana, North Carolina, South Carolina, Virginia, Washington and West Virginia— require that benefits be graded in accordance with the following schedule:

Age of Child	Maximum Benefit
Under 6 months	$ 100
6 months but less than 2 years	200
2 years but less than 3 years	400
3 years but less than 4 years	600
4 years but less than 5 years	800
5 years and over	1,000

[5] The facility of payment provision used by one large company is reproduced in the following paragraph:

"If the employee does not survive the dependent, payment shall be made to the duly qualified executors or administrators of the employee's estate, except that the Insurance Company may in such case, at its option, pay such insurance to the employee's widow or widower, if living; if not living, to the surviving children born to or legally adopted by the employee, if any, equally; if none, to the parents of the employee equally, if both survive and otherwise to the one that does survive, if either survives."

life insurance continues, or upon a reduction in the amount of the employee's insurance by reason of the attainment of a specified age, such as age sixty-five.

Continuance of Coverage in the Event of Employee's Death or Disability

The dependents' coverage sometimes may be continued after the employee's death for a short readjustment period, such as six months. Some companies also provide for its continuance without payment of premiums while the employee coverage is being continued during a period of disability under a disability premium waiver or extended death benefits provision.

The privilege of conversion to a permanent form of insurance is usually extended only to the dependent spouse and then only if the spouse's group coverage has been terminated because of the employee's death or termination of employment. There are some states, however, that require extension of the conversion privilege if the spouse's group coverage has terminated for other reasons. For example, if the spouse's group coverage is terminated on account of termination of the group policy, it is sometimes required that the conversion privilege be extended to the spouse, provided the spouse has been insured for dependent life coverage thereunder for at least five years, and also provided that the coverage is not replaced by the same or another insurer within thirty-one days after such termination. A few states also require that the conversion privilege be made available to insured dependent children.

Critique

Dependents group life insurance would seem to be a logical extension of the group insurance concept and a legitimate function of the group insurance mechanism, provided that, as has been the case, benefits are kept at reasonable levels. Nevertheless, its growth, in sharp contrast to the growth of employee coverage, has been relatively slow. This may be attributed to a number of reasons. When dependents coverage was first introduced there was some feeling that it was an unnecessary and unwarranted encroachment upon the market for individual insurance, particularly of the industrial variety. (The passage of time has, however, invalidated or at least mitigated that criticism with the consequence that, as previously indicated, it is now part of the portfolio of most group insurers.) Then again, those states in which it may not be written, although in the minority, include a number of the more heavily populated, industrial states. Also, requests for dependents group life insurance are not as yet usually contained in collective bargaining agreements, nor do insurers usually make the coverage available to small groups.

During 1963, sales of dependents group life coverage amounted to $399,000,000, and there was in force at the end of that year

$3,018,000,000.[6] While these figures represent only a relatively small percentage of the corresponding figures for employee coverage, they are much more substantial than they were only a few years ago. Sales of the coverage during 1958, for example, amounted to $172,000,000, and there was in force at the end of that year $1,441,000,000. They also indicate that there still remains an as yet untapped market of considerable proportions. This, in turn, suggests that an increasingly large volume of dependents group life insurance will be written in the years ahead.

FEDERAL EMPLOYEES GROUP LIFE INSURANCE

Background

An event of major importance in group insurance history, and one which has had a substantial and continuing impact upon the insurance industry, was the enactment in 1954 by the United States Congress of legislation establishing a plan of group life and accidental death and dismemberment insurance for civilian employees of the federal government. The Act,[7] entitled "Federal Employees Group Life Insurance Act of 1954," was the culmination of several years of intensive study by the United States Civil Service Commission and other government officials of the advisability and feasibility of such a program. An invaluable contribution to that study was made by an Industry Advisory Committee, composed of high-ranking officers of some of the leading group writing companies, and many of their suggestions were included in the Act.

Eligibility and Enrollment

Eligibility is extended under the Act to all civilian federal employees except noncitizens employed at locations outside the United States, and certain small groups of employees because of the nature or type of their employment, such as part-time, seasonal or intermittent employment. Provision is also made for coverage of retired employees who meet a certain minimum number of years of service and other requirements.

Unlike the usual contributory private plan, eligibility does not require the completion of a waiting period. Each eligible employee is automatically insured immediately upon becoming eligible, unless he has previously given written notice of his desire to "elect out" of the plan. Such an election may later be rescinded by an employee, but only prior to his fiftieth birthday and not less than one year after the effective date of his prior written notice. Furthermore, the employee will then be admitted to the plan only if he furnishes at his own expense satisfactory evidence of insurability. These features of the plan not only reduce administrative

---

[6] Data compiled by the Health Insurance Association of America and the Institute of Life Insurance.

[7] See Appendix 4 for the full text of the Act.

expense but also have proved conducive to a high percentage enrollment.

Another unique feature, which also simplifies the administrative procedure, is that although the employee has the right to designate his beneficiary, he is not required to do so. In the absence of a specific designation, prompt settlement is facilitated by provision for payment of the proceeds to certain named classes of beneficiaries, i.e., surviving spouse, children, parents, and so on, in order of precedence.

Benefit Structure and Amounts

Life insurance benefits for active employees are graded by salary brackets with amounts equaling one year's compensation rounded to the next higher $1,000, with a minimum benefit of $1,000 and a maximum of $20,000. At retirement or upon attainment of age sixty-five, whichever occurs later, benefits begin reducing at a monthly rate of 2 per cent to an ultimate minimum of 25 per cent of the amount of insurance in force immediately prior to retirement. Life insurance benefits are supplemented by identical amounts of accidental death and dismemberment coverage, except that no such coverage is provided for retired employees.

Cost

Since a complete census of participants by age and salary for the purpose of determining accurate premium rates would have been an extremely formidable and time-consuming task, the government and insurance industry conferees agreed that an empirical rate, based upon a study of large existing groups with similar characteristics, should be used. Accordingly, premiums are calculated at a biweekly rate of $.37 per $1,000 of coverage, which is equivalent to $.80 per month for each $1,000 of coverage—$.75 for life insurance and $.05 for accidental death and dismemberment insurance.

Active employees are contributing at a biweekly rate of $.25 for each $1,000 of coverage. No contributions are made by retired employees.

Insurers

Issuing and Administering Company. To qualify as an issuing and administering insurer under the Act, a company had to meet the two following requirements:

1. It should be licensed to transact life and accidental death and dismemberment insurance in each of the then forty-eight states and the District of Columbia.
2. On the most recent December 31 for which information was available, the amount of its employee group life insurance should have equaled at least 1 per cent of the total amount of such insurance in force in the United States in all life insurance companies.

There were eight companies which met these criteria. However, in the interests of efficiency and economy, it was the wish of the Civil Service

Commission to purchase a policy from one rather than several insurers. It was also the recommendation of the Commission that the selection of the one insurer be made solely on the arbitrary basis of size. On that basis, and with the consent of the other seven companies, the Metropolitan Life Insurance Company was selected as the issuing and administering vehicle.

The invitation to that company stipulated the terms under which the policy should be issued and administered, including, among other things, the rate basis to be used and the maximum expense and risk charges to be assessed for the first policy year. These terms being agreeable to the company, the invitation was accepted, and a policy was issued to the United States Civil Service Commission effective August 29, 1954.

All financial and other transactions with the policyholder are handled exclusively by the Metropolitan through an administrative office maintained by that company in New York. However, reinsurers are kept fully informed of all important developments and are supplied with copies of financial statements, statistical data and pertinent correspondence. Apart from its administrative responsibilities, the Metropolitan participates in the plan on the same basis as any reinsurer, except that it is reimbursed for the additional expense involved in the operation of the administrative office.

Reinsuring Companies. The Act also provides for participation in the plan by other qualified life insurance companies acting as reinsurers. The criteria for qualification by a company as a reinsurer are:

1. It must be licensed by a state or the District of Columbia to transact life and accidental death and dismemberment insurance.
2. On the December 31 next preceding its election to participate it must have had some group life insurance in force.

The formula for allocating reinsurance set forth in the Federal Employees Group Life Insurance Act gives proportionately more to the smaller companies by assigning sharply decreasing weight to the amount of a company's group life insurance in force as that amount increases. While 100 per cent weight is given to the first $100 million, only 75 per cent weight is given to the second $100 million, 50 per cent to the third, 25 per cent to the fourth, and finally only 5 per cent to any amount in excess of $400 million. There is also a stipulation that the amount retained by or ceded to any company must not exceed 25 per cent of the amount of that company's total life insurance in force in the United States. The Commission is authorized to redetermine the allocation each year on a basis consistent with the foregoing formula, and is required to make such a redetermination any time a reinsurer withdraws, and at least once every three years.

As of the effective date of the master contract on August 29, 1954, there were 161 reinsurers. That number has steadily grown until as of July 1, 1964, there were 253 companies reinsuring a portion of the risk. The combined effect of the increase in number of reinsurers and the operation of the weighted allocation formula has been to reduce substantially the original percentage shares of the larger companies.

Conversions

Nature of the Conversion Privilege. The usual privilege of conversion of the employee's group life insurance to an individual contract is available. The terminating employee is not, however, required to purchase his individual contract from the issuing company. He may, instead, purchase it either from the issuing company or from any other participating company acceptable to the Civil Service Commission.

Each company participating in the group insurance program as a reinsurer may apply to the Civil Service Commission for authority to issue individual life insurance contracts to terminating employees under the conversion privilege. The granting of such authority is, however, subject to agreement by the insurer to meet certain conditions promulgated by the Commission. For example, it must keep on file with the Commission a list of the jurisdictions in which it is licensed and must advise the Commission as to the steps it has taken to inform all its branch offices, agents and employees of the proper procedures to be employed in effecting conversions.

The Conversion Pool. In order that no "converting" company will be exposed to an unduly burdensome share of the excess mortality which might develop under converted policies, a so-called "Conversion Pool" has been established. A company authorized to issue converted policies must become a member of the Pool by signing a Conversion Pool Agreement, which recites the conditions under which the Pool is to be operated.

Each member is required to include in the Pool the life insurance coverage on all converted policies with the exception of (1) any contract issued to an applicant whom the member determines to be a standard risk on the basis of its normal underwriting standards; (2) any contract issued to an applicant who has entered, or been accepted for entry into, the armed forces of any country; and (3) any contract issued after the effective date of discontinuance of the member's right to include additional converted policies in the Conversion Pool.

A separate account is maintained in the Pool for each calendar year of issue beginning with the year 1955. Each converted contract is normally covered by the Pool for a period of ten years from its effective date. Any funds then remaining in the Pool account for a particular calendar year of issue are, after the discharge of all obligations, divided among the members on an equitable basis. Similarly, provision is made for the equitable assessment of any deficits.

The Pool is credited with all conversion charges for excess mortality assessed against the policyholder in accordance with the terms of the group master contract. Each member is also required to pay into the Pool certain Pool charges computed in accordance with a table of rates contained in the Conversion Pool Agreement. In addition each member pays into the Pool account the full amount of any extra premium received by it on a converted contract. In the event of the death of the insured under a converted contract while it is covered by the Pool, the particular company involved is reimbursed from the Pool to the extent of the net amount at risk under the individual contract.

The Pool is operated by the Metropolitan Life Insurance Company as Pool Agent, which is also the custodian of all Pool account funds. There are also five individuals, called Pool Managers, who have general authority to make rules and regulations pertaining to the Pool's operations. The Pool Managers are elected from time to time by the members, each member having one vote for each converted contract issued by it and covered by the Pool on the December 31 preceding the election. Each Pool Manager must be an officer of a member company. As of January 1, 1964, there were eighty-two Pool members, or about one third of the number of reinsurers.

Critique

As of December 31, 1954, it was estimated that there were outstanding under the contract 1,750,000 certificates for an aggregate volume of $7 billion. Early in 1955 the original issue figures were revised to 1,800,000 certificates and $9 billion. By July 1, 1964, the amount in force had grown to 2,565,000 certificates for $18,100,000,000. This very substantial growth may be attributed to several factors, including continuing increases in the number of federal employees, the growth of the insured retired group—which started at zero and now accounts for 275,000 lives and $1.2 billion of insurance—and liberalizations from time to time in the eligibility qualifications and upward adjustments in salary scales.

The program has been operated with a maximum of efficiency and a minimum of expense. Relations between the policyholder and the administering company and, in turn, between the company and the reinsuring companies have been excellent. It has been, and continues to be, an outstanding demonstration of the willingness and ability of the insurance industry to cooperate in providing benefits for this large and important segment of our population.

SELECTED REFERENCES

MacDonald, Donald J. "Federal Employees' Group Life Insurance Act of 1954." M.A. thesis submitted to faculty of the University of Pennsylvania, 1955.

Taft, Nathaniel B. "Dependents' Coverage," *The Journal of the American Society of Chartered Life Underwriters*, Vol. VII (March, 1953), pp. 183–89.

Chapter 10

UNDERWRITING GROUP LIFE INSURANCE

BY J. C. ARCHIBALD

Insurance statutes of the various states tend to incorporate few or no provisions that prescribe the basis for underwriting life insurance issued on individual policies. At one time there were laws governing the amount of insurance which could be written on a nonmedical basis under individual policies, but these have been eliminated.

Contrary to the situation found in the law governing individual policies, a number of underwriting restrictions are included in the laws pertaining to group life insurance. These include such items as a definition of the minimum size and characteristics of an eligible group, the minimum percentage of eligible persons who must participate if the group is to qualify for group life insurance and, in many cases, the maximum amount of group life insurance that may be provided any one life.

An important feature of underwriting group life insurance is to determine that the prospective policyholder meets the legal requirements for group life insurance in the state or states in which the coverage will apply. Earlier chapters of this volume covered in detail the legal environment of group insurance and the fundamental characteristics of the group technique. For this reason, these two important phases of group life insurance underwriting will not be stressed in this chapter.

This chapter will approach group life insurance underwriting from the standpoint of (1) underwriting the organization or business firm to be insured; (2) design of operational features of the plan; (3) design of benefits to be provided for the persons insured under the group contract; (4) renewal underwriting; (5) use of reinsurance in group life insurance.

The preponderance of group life insurance in force in this country is term insurance covering the employees of a single employer. This chapter deals primarily with insurance of this type. However, most of the same principles apply equally to forms of group permanent life insurance and to group life insurance which covers multiple employers through a trust arrangement or an employer association. In the latter case, additional underwriting factors need to be considered. These are discussed in Chapters 32 and 33.

UNDERWRITING THE GROUP POLICYHOLDER

Occupational Hazards

A fundamental part of underwriting is the need to evaluate the probable mortality experience of the particular group. An important factor in this evaluation is the occupation of the employees to be insured. Extra mortality due to occupation may arise from a special accident hazard or sickness hazard, or both. The occupational hazard arising from the work itself may vary widely from one firm to another even though both are engaged in the same industry. Further, in even the most hazardous industries, the proportion of life insurance on employees with high-mortality occupations to that on employees with standard mortality occupations will vary considerably. For these reasons, industry classification is necessarily made on a rather broad basis without a high degree of refinement.

For many employers, the occupational classification may be substandard for employees located at one plant, substandard to a different degree at another plant and standard at still other plants. This is particularly likely if the employer is widely diversified in the products which are produced and in the working conditions at the various plants. If the variation in the degree of extra mortality is considered significant, and if a large proportion of the total insurance on the group is subject to extra mortality, the underwriter should develop a composite occupational classification. This classification will be obtained by multiplying the amount of insurance at each location by the loading factor applicable to each location and dividing this product by the total amount of insurance for the entire case.

Typically, under current conditions, extra mortality may be assigned to such occupations as iron ore milling, blast furnace operation, metal or mineral mining, quarrying, flight personnel, manufacture of acids or gases, manufacture of explosives, breweries, police and fire departments and woodsmen and loggers. Industry classification with respect to occupational mortality is a continuing project, and rating changes are made periodically.

Fortunately, relatively few industries are considered sufficiently substandard to require an extra loading. In five states there are laws or regulations in regard to the minimum group life insurance premiums which may be charged a new policyholder.[1] This rate basis has been revised from time to time and is now designated as the J rate. This basis is such that only

---

[1] For a full discussion of group life insurance minimum premium laws, see Chapter 11.

the most hazardous occupations are rated for extra mortality due to occupation alone.[2] Over the years the loadings for occupation have become less common.

Other Hazards

The living conditions and economic and moral levels of the group to be insured should also be considered by the underwriter. While the author knows of no study which correlates such conditions and mortality, most underwriters believe that extra mortality definitely exists among those whose environment includes substandard living, economic and moral conditions.

Finally, the group should be evaluated from the standpoint of possible catastrophe hazards. The less the risk is concentrated geographically, the less is the risk that an explosion, storm or other catastrophe will cause such a loss of life that the insurer will become insolvent or at least seriously damaged economically. The possibility of a special type of reinsurance to cover such situations is discussed later in this chapter.

Administrative Facilities of Policyholder

The successful underwriting of group life insurance depends, to a large extent, on the ability and willingness of the group policyholder to assume definite responsibilities in the operation of the program provided under the contract. There are a number of administrative duties which the policyholder should expect to handle. These include making payroll deductions for employee contributions, if required, and remitting this amount, together with the policyholder's share of the premium, to the insurer promptly with each billing. In addition, the employer is responsible for reporting to the insurer new entrants into the plan, terminations from the plan and any change that may occur in an employee's benefit classification.

Other duties include determining eligibility dates, termination dates and benefits of employees according to the terms of the plan, notifying the insurer of beneficiary changes and name changes of employees and providing the insurer with accurate census data of the insured employees. In addition, the employer is responsible for submitting claims to the insurer and obtaining evidence of insurability for late entrants in the case of contributory plans.

Employer Cooperation

From an underwriting standpoint, it is important that the group policyholder enthusiastically endorses the program on a continuing basis. At the

---

[2] The underwriter may wish to examine the variation in mortality between a particular industry that is not usually rated by group companies and the average mortality of all industries not usually rated. Such a study is published periodically by the Society of Actuaries in its *Reports of Mortality and Morbidity Experience*. The most recent such comparison may be found in the 1960 Reports.

inception, he should be willing to aid the agent and the insurer in the enrollment of employees. Preferably, the enrollment meetings to explain the plan to employees should be conducted on company time. After the initial enrollment is complete, the policyholder must take the responsibility for explaining the plan to new employees before they become eligible to enroll and giving them strong encouragement to enroll. A high percentage of employee enrollment is necessary at the start, and it is equally important that at least as high a percentage of the future eligible employees enroll.

A group life insurance program relies on the willingness of the employer or policyholder to pay part of the premium required. In some states the statute requires that the policyholder pay part of the premium. In some states the maximum employee contribution is $.60 per month per $1,000 of group term insurance for groups written at standard rates.

If expected mortality is to be achieved, a high percentage of the eligible employees must be enrolled. This percentage, in turn, depends to a large extent on the level of employee contributions. Although the laws require only 75 per cent of the eligible employees to participate initially in a group life insurance plan written with an employer, a higher percentage is desirable from an underwriting standpoint. The more closely participation approaches 100 per cent, the greater are the odds that individual selection will be minimized. In order to make the plan more attractive to the younger employee, without introducing contributions that vary by age, some plans provide for a lower employee contribution rate for each of the first few thousand dollars of coverage on an employee and a higher rate (such as $.50 or $.60 per month per $1,000) on the excess coverage on the employee. This method is particularly effective if the employees scheduled for the lower amounts of insurance tend to be the younger employees.

If the group to be underwritten involves only a single employer covering his own employees and if the policyholder is of sufficient size that he has a regular accounting or clerical staff, the underwriter will seldom need to be concerned with the employer's ability and willingness to perform the duties required of him. For very small groups, the question of satisfactory policyholder performance of administrative functions, particularly, requires careful attention in the underwriting process.

If the plan is to cover an association of small employers, the underwriting of employer responsibility becomes very difficult. There probably will be a wide variation of administrative capability among the employer units. Other complicating factors include the fact that normal policyholder responsibilities may be split between the association and the employer units and the inherent lack of control by any one organization over employer support of the plan. The underwriter should satisfy himself that the necessary mechanics for proper administration exist. This has been accomplished by the development of special administrative systems with the insurer performing all of the administrative functions or by the office of the executive secretary of the association taking over some or all of these functions. Another common technique is the use of an outside administrator who specializes in this type of work. Whichever method is used, the total administrative costs are likely to be considerably higher than those observed in connection with a plan of similar size which insures only a single employer. These features of an association or grouping of small employers add so materially to the complexity of the underwriting function that some companies have developed a home office staff of specialists in the underwriting of such groups.

Transfer Business

For group life coverage which in the past has been insured with another company, generally it is not necessary to secure the actual mortality experience of the group. However, there are several items that must be closely examined. If there are disabled employees, it is important to find out whether or not the policy provisions under the previous insurer's contract provided for continuation of benefits in event of termination. If not, then provision in the rates should be made for disabled lives on which the risk will be assumed. If the person disabled is over age sixty, or if retired people are to be covered, inquiry has to be made in regard to continuance of coverage for these classes of individuals.

DESIGN OF OPERATIONAL FEATURES OF THE GROUP LIFE PLAN

Eligibility

Group life insurance plans usually establish eligibility requirements that will restrict the plan to full-time, permanent employees. In order to accomplish this, the plan may require that the employee be hired on a permanent basis and have been so employed continuously for at least a minimum period of time, such as one to six months, before he is eligible to participate. Sometimes the waiting period applies only to new employees hired after the effective date of the contract. The plan often will specify also that full-time employees include only those scheduled to work more than a minimum number of hours per week. This minimum may be, for example, twenty-five hours or thirty hours. Negotiated plans, particularly those established in industries where employment is seasonal, sometimes determine eligibility for coverage in a calendar quarter on the basis of the number of hours worked in the preceding calendar quarter.

The importance of the eligibility provision in group life insurance underwriting stems from two considerations. In the first place, it is necessary to avoid individual selection by the employer or administrator. Satisfactory mortality under group life insurance can be achieved only if a relatively high percentage of a typical cross section of actively working people can be insured. For this reason it is necessary to define clearly the classes of employees that are eligible and attempt to make sure that the definition is consistently followed. In the second place, it is important from the standpoint of administrative costs that high turnover, temporary employees be excluded. Otherwise, costs are increased unnecessarily by establishing the initial records for many employees who will be covered only a relatively short time. A less common reason for some waiting period is to avoid the possibility that a person in known bad health will be employed or seek employment purely for the insurance.

The length of the period of full-time employment required for a plan is likely to vary from industry to industry. If turnover is very low, some plans permit eligibility to date from the person's date of full-time employment. Under group term life insurance plans, it is probably the exception to utilize waiting periods in excess of six months, and one month waiting periods are not uncommon. If group term life and group health insurance are presented to the employees as one benefit package, the eligibility for both plans probably will be identical. Once the prospective policyholder understands the purpose of a waiting period, he is normally in the best position to establish the time that would best fit his own turnover situation and still leave him a plan that will be attractive to prospective employees, when compared to plans of other employers they are likely to be considering.

Group life plans on the permanent forms require greater administrative costs and, hence, typically provide for longer waiting periods than are provided for group term insurance. Where a combination of term and permanent insurance is jointly written, it is quite common to provide group term insurance prior to the date of eligibility for the permanent coverage.

With larger employers, whose personnel practices and employee classifications tend to be formalized, there is seldom a problem of enforcing uniform administration of the full-time, permanent employee classification. The occasional problem that does develop in these cases is likely to involve a director or other senior member of the organization who no longer is engaged in full-time employment. Group life insurance laws, for the most part, specify that directors of corporations are not eligible unless they otherwise qualify as active employees. This is another example of underwriting safeguards being included in the law. If this provision is not enforced, adverse selection by specific individuals will be encountered, which will adversely affect the claims cost of the entire program.

The smaller the group to be insured, the more difficult it becomes to enforce a clear definition of the full-time permanent employee. Particularly in the small units, the business may be primarily a family business with few or no employees other than those with some family relationship.

The bookkeeping may be handled by the wife of the owner on a part-time basis, but she may be reported as a full-time employee. The owner may be in semiretirement, having turned the management over to his son or a junior partner, and may not even spend a large portion of the year in the geographical area of the business. Yet, his eligibility for insurance may be a condition of the sale.

To the extent that the underwriter is unable to prevent individual choice as to eligibility, he is increasing the risk of unsatisfactory mortality. It should be recognized that this is a problem that may exist not only at the inception of the plan but also during its operation, as the employer, through loose handling of the administration, fails to report properly terminations and new entrants on a continuing basis.

Where the underwriter suspects that the group policyholder is not enforcing the eligibility in a manner consistent with the terms of the contract, he may investigate by requiring an inspection report or he may require a simple statement of health on all eligible employees—in both events, adding noticeably to the costs of the insurance. This problem of eligibility and loose administration has been a major factor in determining the minimum size group to which many insurance companies will offer group insurance.

Actively-at-Work Requirement

Group life insurance contracts require that an eligible employee be actively at work on the date his insurance is to become effective or on the last working day preceding such date if his eligibility date is a holiday. The purpose of this provision is to make sure that the plan is insuring a typical cross section of the able-bodied workers of a particular business organization.

It is not unusual, particularly among the larger groups, for the group policyholder to request that the actively-at-work provision be waived for those eligible to be insured on the effective date of the group contract. If the group is sufficiently large that the insurer's experience rating will charge all claims against the group involved, and if the underwriter believes the rates to be adequate to absorb the expected excess mortality, it is not uncommon to agree to such a waiver. The underwriter, before agreeing to the waiver, should satisfy himself either that the amounts of insurance to be made effective as a result of the waiver are small relative to the total insurance involved on the case or that the employees involved are not seriously ill.

The actively-at-work requirement is inapplicable to those who have previously retired from the group if they are eligible under the policy. The underwriter, under such conditions, must determine what protection, if any, the plan needs against the unhealthy and disabled among this group. Factors to consider are the proportion of retired coverage to total coverage, the ability of premium rates to absorb mortality and whether a substitute for the actively-at-work requirement may be needed. One form of a substitute requirement could be the test of whether the individual is currently engaging in all activities that are normal for his age or, alternatively, a statement of health might be required.

If an insured person's benefit is changed due to a change in his benefit classification or due to a revision in the benefit schedule, it is customary to require that the change will not become effective until he is actively at work on a full-time basis. Not only does this protect the insurer from the cost of additional benefits for a person known to be seriously disabled, but also it protects the disabled person from having his benefits reduced just when his need is greatest.

On some occasions, when the amounts of insurance on certain individuals are large relative to the size of the case, insurance companies impose a more stringent actively-at-work test. This may take the form of a certification by the employee involved that he is currently actively at work on a full-time basis and has been continuously for the last month (or such other period as may be used by the insurer).

Late Entrants

Group life insurance contracts issued on a contributory basis typically include a provision that permits the insurer to require evidence of insurability from any person who does not enroll in the plan within thirty-one days following the date he becomes eligible. The underwriting purpose of such a provision is obvious. Most insurers appear to feel that the late entrant to a group plan is attempting to second guess the plan's value to him. The underwriting standards for such an application are typically as stringent as those applied by the insurer in the underwriting of applications for individual policies of life insurance.

Termination of Coverage

Proper design and operation of the termination of coverage provisions are necessary features of group life underwriting. The underlying principle is that some basis be developed that can and will be followed uniformly so that adverse selection is minimized.

Complete termination of employment creates no problem. Attention should be directed to plan design as it applies to continuation of coverage due to temporary layoff, leave of absence, strike, illness or retirement. The specific provisions may vary widely from one group contract to another. Generally speaking, any reasonable provision needed by the group policyholder should present no underwriting concern so long as the basis for continuance of coverage is clearly described, precludes the possibility of individual selection and can be consistently administered.

DESIGN OF BENEFITS

Types of Benefit Schedules

There is a wide variety of benefit schedules in use today. In considering a benefit schedule, the underwriter should be concerned with two factors: first, that the schedule be so designed to preclude individual selection as to amount, and second, that the maximum benefit permitted on any one life be reasonable in relation to the total benefits under the plan. In addition, the underwriter should be alert to the benefit schedule's acceptability to all segments of the group to be insured, in order to improve the acceptance of the plan by the eligible group. Some classes of employees have less need or desire for coverage than do others. An example is the interest in life insurance on the part of the young female employee who has no family responsibilities as compared with the male employee with family responsibilities. If the plan is contributory, the schedule or contributions, or both, should reflect to some extent divergent interests such as these.

The most common type of benefit schedule relates the amount of insurance to earnings. It provides the greatest benefit to the highest paid employees who are, presumably, the key employees in the organization. The earnings base is relatively stable and is easily determined except for the owners or partners of an unincorporated firm.

It is likely that the second most common type of schedule relates benefits to the employee's position in the insured business organization. For example, owners and officers might have one benefit amount, supervisory employees and salesmen another benefit amount and all other employees a third benefit amount. Schedules of this type frequently have greater differences from one benefit class to the next than do salary schedules. They appear to be most common among smaller business units and are very common among unincorporated units where salary determination for the owners is likely to be difficult or arbitrary. One important disadvantage is the difficulty of employee classification, particularly if several benefit classes are desired. It has been observed that, under the position schedule, many more situations arise where an employee is apparently upgraded when his health fails or may even appear to have been retroactively upgraded following death. The employer may try to accomplish this by stating that he overlooked reporting the class change. As might be expected, such problems are more prevalent among the smaller business firms.

Schedules which base benefits on the employee's length of service provide the largest amounts for employees with long service. While these were once quite popular, few schedules of this type are written at the present time. There are also many other types of schedules in use; for example, schedules that provide a uniform benefit for all insured persons (found often in union negotiated plans), schedules that relate the amount of life insurance to the size of the employee's pension benefit, schedules that are a function of age and, finally, schedules that combine two or more of these factors.

Maximum Benefit Amounts

In some states the maximum amount of group term life insurance on one individual is limited by statute. These laws take various forms, but the most common is the so-called 20/40 law, which requires that amounts over $20,000 cannot exceed the lesser of one and one-half times the employee's annual pay, or $40,000. If the group life insurance plan is written in a state where the maximum benefit is restricted by law, this automatically imposes some restriction on the amount of benefit.

From the underwriting standpoint, it is desirable to have a reasonably balanced schedule. A balanced schedule tends to preclude individual selection of amounts and to prevent a disproportionate amount of the total coverage on the group on the lives of a very few individuals. If, within a broad category of employees, the ratio of benefits to salary does not increase materially as salary increases, the schedule usually can be considered well balanced. Certainly a schedule that provides a very modest amount of coverage for all employees except the head man and $100,000 or more for him cannot be considered balanced, whether or not the ratio of benefits to salary decreases with increased pay. If a reasonable number of employees is eligible within each benefit classification, one important test of a balanced schedule has been met.

Group insurers have set up tables of maximum amounts of insurance which will be issued on one life without evidence of insurability.[3] Although some attempts to develop a mathematical approach to the no-evidence maximum have been made, a practical approach, based on judgment and observation of the levels that appear to give satisfactory results, has been the basis used by most companies. The no-evidence maxima have been liberalized many times during the history of group life insurance.

The no-evidence limit under a group permanent type contract, whether level premium or group paid-up in form, can be justified at a somewhat higher level than is possible under group term insurance. This results from the fact that, under the permanent forms, there is a lower amount of death benefit at risk, per $1,000. Before becoming too enthusiastic in his liberalization of the no-evidence limit for the permanent forms, however, the

---

[3] For samples of no-evidence tables currently in use, which vary considerably from company to company and change periodically, the reader should refer to the group underwriting manuals of group writing companies.

underwriter should recognize that, during the early years of the insured's permanent coverage, there is only a negligible difference in the amount at risk between term and permanent insurance.

State law permitting, very large amounts of insurance may be scheduled for certain employee classes in a particular group. It is not the purpose of this chapter to discuss the pros and cons of jumbo insurance amounts and the criticisms leveled at the practice by some individual insurance agents. From the standpoint of group life insurance underwriting alone, experience has proven that there are circumstances under which these jumbo amounts can be safely scheduled. When the total volume of insurance on the group is large relative to the maximum amount on any one life, companies have successfully underwritten substantial schedule maxima. If the desired maximum benefit is higher than the no-evidence limit normally offered by the insurer, the excess of the maximum over the no-evidence limit may be offered subject to evidence of insurability. In such a situation, the insurer underwrites individually each person entitled to insurance in excess of the no-evidence limit. When individual underwriting is utilized, the insurer will apply the underwriting rules normally applicable to the underwriting of an individual policy of life insurance for an amount equal to the amount of insurance in excess of the no-evidence limit.

The use of individual underwriting may include substandard classification of specific lives with respect to the amount of insurance in excess of the no-evidence limit. This permits the insurer to charge the group policyholder the additional premium applicable to the amounts of insurance so classified, if the underwriter feels there is an inadequate margin in the rate structure to absorb the extra mortality.

Amounts of insurance in excess of the no-evidence limit are usually pooled for experience rating purposes. Thus, in the dividend or retrospective rate calculation, the portion of a death claim that is represented by insurance in excess of the no-evidence limit is not charged against the experience of the group policyholder. Instead, in each dividend or retrospective rate calculation, a cost of insurance or pooling charge is made against the group policyholder's experience. This charge is based on the normal mortality assumed applicable to each unit of scheduled benefit in excess of the no-evidence limit and reflects both the age of the person so insured and his classification of risk, as determined by individual underwriting.

When the maximum life insurance benefit permitted by a schedule is quite high under a group policy, a special reserve applicable to that policy may be accumulated. Such a reserve provides some financial stability for the group policyholders in years when death claims under the policy are unusually high. Usually pooling is not used on those group life insurance policies where special reserves are held.

As the scheduled maximum increases, the underwriter should consider the effect of the higher amounts on the disability provision in the contract. Although the disability income provision requires particular attention as the amounts of insurance become large, the waiver of premium provision also requires attention. It is possible to provide a modified disability benefit or no disability benefit with respect to amounts in excess of a specified limit. If the schedule is particularly high, the underwriter should consider these possibilities.

Retired Lives

With increasing frequency, group policyholders are arranging benefit schedules which cover employees after they have retired. Although there are exceptions, a plan installed or changed to include coverage on retired lives usually covers only those who retire in the future and who were covered under the active life group program.

Both because of the reduced need for life insurance among the retired and because of the very high cost of the benefits, it is customary to provide lower amounts of life insurance for retired employees than for the active employees. Benefits after an employee's retirement are frequently related to his benefit immediately preceding retirement. However, it is not unusual to find schedules which provide uniform benefits for all retirees.

The benefit reduction at retirement may be immediate or may be gradual over a period of years. The mechanics, as long as they apply to all, are not a serious underwriting consideration. From the standpoint of plan acceptance by the insured persons, a schedule providing some type of gradual reduction appears desirable.

If the group policyholder does not have a formal retirement program or if he does not require automatic retirement at a stated age, it is sometimes difficult to ascertain definitely whether or not a person is retired. This problem is especially noticeable among the smaller cases where one or two owners control the business even though they may be in semiretirement. A satisfactory solution can be found by making the benefit reductions depend on age rather than retirement. In this manner the difficult task of challenging the owner's status is avoided and all employees are treated alike, even though some may remain employed after their normal retirement date.

Superimposed Coverage

During most of the history of group life insurance, superimposed coverage has been considered an unsound practice unless the group eligible for the benefit schedule superimposed on the basic schedule was either a high percentage of the total eligible group or was itself a relatively large group. There is no doubt that many superimposed schedules have produced disastrous financial results.

In recent years it appears that there has been increased experimentation with the superimposed benefit schedule. A superimposed schedule may provide additional benefits to only a limited number of those insured under the original plan, or it may provide additional benefits to all members insured under the original plan. In this still experimental field the probability of satisfactory underwriting results will be enhanced if the following two tests are met: first, the total group life insurance program, including both the basic and superimposed schedules, meets the normal underwriting standards of the insurance company; and second, each portion of the program underwritten by the insurance company qualifies by itself according to the insurer's normal underwriting standards.

RENEWAL UNDERWRITING OF GROUP LIFE INSURANCE

The problems of renewal underwriting of a group life insurance plan are not as great as those of a group medical expense insurance program. Initial premium rates, particularly among companies that use the statutory minimum basis required by several states, contain larger margins of safety with respect to claims and expenses than do most initial premium rates under the medical expense coverages; the trend in claim costs under group life insurance is downward as opposed to upward under group medical expense insurance; and the low frequency rate applicable to group life insurance claims makes reliance on the actual claim experience of a particular group impossible unless the experience covers many thousands of life years of exposure.

A review of some of the same features that require attention at the time the case is initially underwritten will usually provide adequate renewal underwriting for group life insurance. The case should be checked to make sure satisfactory enrollment percentages are being maintained, to determine whether the group policyholder is properly reporting new entrants and terminations, to see to it that new employees are being enrolled promptly and to ascertain whether the benefit schedule needs revision. The basic purposes of this type of renewal underwriting are to determine whether the group policyholder understands the plan and is facing up to the responsibilities required of him under the plan and to determine whether the plan design is accomplishing the purpose for which it was intended. If so, probably no further action is needed. If some of these features are found to be unsatisfactory, the underwriter should take whatever steps appear to be needed.

The claim experience under any but the very large cases is seldom very credible. However, if claims are abnormally high the underwriter should review the claims to determine whether adverse selection appears to be involved and whether the proper enrollment, reporting and classifying procedures are being followed. He will not usually find a significant violation of the terms of the plan but, when he does, the underwriter must act quickly and decisively if further adverse financial results are to be avoided.

If employee participation in the plan has dropped significantly, the underwriter should try to determine the cause and the steps that should be taken to prevent such a decrease in the future. If he is satisfied that the necessary corrective action for future operations has been taken, he may also consider an open enrollment period for purposes of enrolling in the plan those eligible employees who have not previously joined the plan.

An open enrollment period is a limited period of time, such as one month, during which the evidence of insurability requirement for late entrants is waived. During this period an active solicitation is made of those who have previously failed to enroll in the plan. They are given another opportunity to join without furnishing individual evidence of insurability. In order to reduce the degree of selection against the plan, it is customary to require that some minimum percentage of such employees apply during the open enrollment period. This percentage might depend on the number of eligibles involved, such as 100 per cent if there are less than ten eligible employees, grading to 50 per cent if there are fifty eligible employees. Other restrictions which may also be employed are to require evidence of insurability from those over age sixty and from any who previously have been declined for life insurance because of health reasons.

REINSURANCE OF GROUP LIFE INSURANCE

Reinsuring the Catastrophe Hazard

By its very nature, group life insurance tends to result in a heavy concentration of risk in one location. A sudden disaster could cause many deaths in a very short period of time and develop a sufficiently great liability that the group insurer would have difficulty maintaining solvency or, at the very least, would experience a serious drain on its surplus.

Some companies, in order to protect against the financial impact of such a disaster, have obtained reinsurance against excess loss due to a single event. Such reinsurance could vary widely in detail, but would normally provide for the reinsurer to pay all or some agreed upon proportion of the excess of the insurer's death claims resulting from a single catastrophe over a deductible, subject to some stated maximum payment by the reinsurer for each catastrophe. The deductible is usually a substantial amount and would depend on the surplus strain the insurer felt it could conveniently stand, as well as the price it felt it could pay each year for such coverage. The reinsurance agreement might cover only the insurer's group life claims due to the event, or it could be expanded to cover all death losses (group and individual) for which the insurer is liable as a result of the event.[4]

Reinsuring the Individual Life

If the benefit schedule permits a large amount of coverage on an individual life, relative to the acceptable level of fluctuation in the surplus of the group department, it may be desirable to reinsure the scheduled death benefit on each life to the extent that it exceeds a stated amount. Reinsurance of this type is similar to that which is obtained by the individual departments of insurance companies when an application involves risk in excess of the level the insurer is willing to retain.

Normally the amount on each life for which the group department desires reinsurance is underwritten individually on a basis comparable to that used for underwriting individual policies. If this is the situation, the group department may obtain reinsurance for such amount through one of the reinsuring companies the insurer uses for individual insurance. If the scheduled benefit on a particular person is considered too large relative to the size of the group department but not too large relative to the over-all size of the insurer, the reinsurance may be provided by the insurer's own individual life insurance department. In either event the surplus of the group department receives some protection against unwanted mortality fluctuations by means of the reinsurance technique.

Reinsurance by Spreading the Risk among Group Insurers

Most group insurers appear to feel little need to share the risk of a group life insurance policy with other insurers. It is not unusual, however, for the group policyholder to request that more than one insurer participate in the underwriting of his group life insurance. In this situation, the goal is more likely that of improved public relations for the group policyholder, rather than any need for the insurers to share the risk. The most notable example of this type of reinsurance is the group life insurance policy which covers the employees of the federal government. The desire to place their business with more than one insurer has also led some public utilities and banks, among other business organizations, to the use of the reinsurance device.

In the typical reinsurance arrangement being discussed, one insurance company will be named the primary insurer. The primary company will in turn cede some fraction of the total risk to one or more reinsuring companies. Usually the primary company will handle all of the administrative duties connected with the group life insurance policy. Its decisions

---

[4] For an excellent discussion of catastrophe reinsurance, see Edward A. Green, "Concentration of Risk, and the Catastrophic Accident Hazard," *Transactions of the Society of Actuaries*, Vol. VI (1954), p. 506.

as to rates, contract changes, administrative questions and claim settlements are final. Each reinsuring company reserves the right to withdraw from the arrangement as of the date of any contract or rate change, if it disagrees with the primary company's decision.

There are many variations in the arrangements under which this device operates. Typically, the group life insurance policy is issued by the primary company to the group policyholder. The group policyholder deals only with the primary company, and all individual life insurance policies issued under the conversion privilege of the group policy are issued by the primary company. Each reinsuring company enters into an agreement with the primary company in which the reinsurer agrees to underwrite a stated percentage of the total group life risk. The primary company remits to each reinsurer the stated percentage of the total premium, reduced by the same percentage of total claims and by the same percentage of the primary company's direct expenses. Dividends or retroactive rate credits may then be computed by each insuring company on the portion of the group it insures or, in some arrangements, the reinsuring companies may be committed by the experience rating determined by the primary company.

SELECTED REFERENCES

BARBER, KENNETH S. "The Administration of Group Life Maximums," *Proceedings of the Insurance Accounting and Statistical Association* (1962), pp. 268–71.

GREEN, EDWARD A. "Concentration of Risk, and the Catastrophic Accident Hazard," *Transactions of the Society of Actuaries,* Vol. VI (1954), pp. 506–11.

GREGG, DAVIS W. *Group Life Insurance,* chap. 7, "Selection and Reinsurance," 3d ed. Homewood, Ill.: Richard D. Irwin, Inc., 1962.

HUDSON, W. J. "Administration of Group Life Maximums," *Proceedings of the Insurance Accounting and Statistical Association* (1962), pp. 271–73.

McQUEEN, ROBERT C. "Administration of Group Life Maximums," *Proceedings of the Insurance Accounting and Statistical Association* (1962), pp. 273–76.

PETTENGILL, DANIEL W. "Group Life Insurance—Current Practices and Techniques in the United States," *Transactions of the Fifteenth International Congress of Actuaries,* Vol. I (1957), pp. 289–300.

SMITH, J. HENRY. "Group Life Insurance in the United States and Canada," *Transactions of the Fifteenth International Congress of Actuaries,* Vol. I (1957), pp. 274–84.

Society of Actuaries, Transactions of the. "Considerations in Determining Group Life Insurance Maximum Limits," Vol. XII (1960), informal discussion by H. F. Harrigan, A. W. Brosseau, E. A. Rode and L. C. Cocheu, pp. 133–35.

———. "Underwriting Large Amounts of Group Life Insurance on Individual Lives in Small Groups," Vol. XII (1960), informal discussion by J. M. Bragg,

I. R. Taylor, H. V. Lyons, H. F. Cerwinske, J. W. Moran, M. D. Miller and J. F. Coleman, pp. 389–90.

————. "Methods Used to Provide for Exposure to Higher than Normal Limits under Group Life Insurance," Vol. XIV, Part II (1962), informal discussion by R. H. Hoffman, W. S. Thomas, J. M. Bragg, J. B. Walker, A. Ford, R. V. Young, J. F. MacLean, R. E. Galloway, R. D. Albright, D. E. Williams and G. J. Varga, pp. D77–D83.

————. "Underwriting Small Group Life Cases," Vol. XIV, Part II (1962), informal discussion by D. D. Cody, P. Briggs, I. R. Taylor, Anna M. Rappaport and Josephine W. Beers, pp. D373–D375.

————. "Committee on Group Insurance Mortality, Report of the," 1960 Reports Number, pp. 93–104.

TRABER, RALPH E. "High Maximum Amounts of Group Life Insurance," *Proceedings of the Insurance Accounting and Statistical Association* (1957), pp. 142–45.

Chapter 11

MANUAL RATE MAKING IN GROUP LIFE INSURANCE

BY MORTON D. MILLER

DISTINCTIVE CHARACTERISTICS OF GROUP INSURANCE PRICING

The price of an article or a service is its monetary value to the purchaser. For the seller, it represents the cost of materials, manufacture, distribution and a margin for profit. The price may be paid in a single sum or in installments. The price often will involve a reduction or discount for quantity purchasing.

Insurance is a service for which the price is called the premium.[1] While the pricing of insurance is fundamentally similar to that of goods and other services, it is in many respects considerably more complicated. The services provided under an insurance contract are complex in themselves and usually extend over a long period of time. Furthermore, their pricing involves an evaluation of events that will occur in the future, such as the likelihood of death or disability. In addition to the benefit cost, the premium must provide for sales and other initial expenses, for the continuing expenses, including taxes, associated with the maintenance of the contract, and for profit to the company's stockholders or a contribution to the company's surplus. The insurance purchase may be concluded by a single premium or may be paid for in installments as, for example, in the case of a twenty-payment life insurance policy or the monthly premiums for group life insurance.

In individual life insurance the quantity discount is a function of the face amount of the policy. The monthly or annual premium is the measure of the size of the contract for group insurance premium purposes.

The gross premium shown in the contract is the final price when a life insurance policy is issued on a nonparticipating basis. However, much life insurance, including almost all group life insurance, is sold on a mutual or

---

[1] The premium rate is the premium per unit of benefit, whereas the premium is the product of the rate times the amount of benefit; e.g., if $10 is the rate per $1,000 of insurance at a given age, then $50 is the premium for $5,000 of insurance at that age.

participating basis, and this is an aspect of insurance pricing not found in commerce and industry. Additional margins are included in the gross premium under a participating contract with the expectation that premium refunds[2] will be made to the policyholder annually during the life of the contract if experience shows the added margins are not needed by the company for its operations. Thus, the cost to the purchaser is not the gross premium, but rather it is the gross premium less any policy dividends declared subsequently by the company. This is sometimes referred to as the net cost or the net premium. Some confusion may be introduced thereby, because the term "net premium" also is used to describe the portion of the gross premium calculated to be the cost of the benefits before loading for expenses. Thus the term "net cost" is preferable to "net premium" when referring to gross premiums less dividends.

Individual insurance dividends are based upon the claims, expenses and investment history of a class of similar policies, such as all whole life insurance policies. In group insurance, the master contract with the employer, not the insurance on the individual employees, is the unit for dividend calculation purposes. Where a group contract insures a large enough number of persons so that its claims experience over a period of time takes on sufficient reliability from a statistical point of view, the policy may be looked upon as being in a class by itself for purposes of dividend participation. This is the practice of experience or merit rating, through which a dividend or retroactive rate credit for the policy may be based upon its own claims experience in whole or in part depending upon its size. The larger the group, the more weight may be attached to the group's experience in this determination. The procedures employed are discussed in the next chapter.

Lastly, group insurance pricing differs from individual insurance pricing in another important respect. The insurance company reserves the right to review the gross premium and to reestablish the rates prospectively at the beginning of each renewal year or at some other point during the year. This re-rating process is similar to the determination of dividends or retroactive rate credits, in that for the larger cases the rates for the new policy year are based on the group's actual claims and expense history.

In summary, group insurance pricing involves the initial gross premium arrived at in accordance with the manual rating procedure. For the larger policies, a dividend or retroactive rate credit may be then paid at the end of the first year, determined wholly or partly from the group's own claims and expense history. A premium rate for the forthcoming year is arrived at also in the light of the experience history, and this process is repeated from year to year as long as the contract continues.

---

[2] Premium refunds are called dividends in mutual company operations and retroactive rate credits by stock companies. See Chapter 12.

BASIC GOALS OF RATE MAKING

The process of manual rating involves first a system of risk classification and then a schedule of premium rates through which the premium for each group is established after it has been appropriately classified. In group life insurance, the manual rate becomes the gross premium rate for the first policy year except possibly on transferred business where the record of experience with the previous insurer might require a higher rate.

The classification of risks must depend upon factors that are known to differentiate one risk from another and should be objective as far as possible. Of necessity, the system of classification must be practical and relatively easy to apply. There is less need for refinement in risk classification for group insurance than for some other forms of insurance, because adjustments in the financial results for minor differences between risks will be achieved over a period of time through the experience rating process. The factors recognized in the classification of group insurance risks are some or all of the following, depending on the type of coverage: the industry in which the employer is engaged, the age and sex distribution of the employees, the proportion with families and their composition, the income level of the employees and their geographical location. Age distribution and type of industry are the two most important factors in group life insurance.

The broad objective of a manual rating system is to provide a consistent basis for determining adequate premiums for all classes of risk. Equity requires that, within the bounds of practicality, each group pay a premium which reflects its expectation of loss. Practical competitive selling generally leads to this result. These principles also are recognized in the state laws which regulate the companies in the conduct of their business, where it usually is provided that ". . . the benefits provided under a policy must be reasonable in relation to the premium charged." Most state laws also contain the injunction ". . . no insurer shall make or permit any unfair discrimination between individuals of the same class in the amount of . . . premiums or rates charged for any policy. . . ."[3]

The elements in the computation of manual premium rates are the estimated cost of the benefits to be provided, the effect of assumed interest earnings and the loading for expenses and contingencies. Group life insurance benefits include the value of the anticipated death claims, the additional worth of the disability provisions of the contract and the cost of permitting a terminating employee to convert his group insurance to an individual policy without evidence of health. Interest is a comparatively minor consideration for group term life insurance but assumes the same

---

[3] *New York Insurance Law,* Sec. 154, Subdivision 1; and Sec. 209, Subdivisions 1 and 2.

importance in connection with permanent forms as in individual life insurance. The loading formula must include provision for expenses of all kinds: agents' commissions, managerial compensation and other sales costs; the preparation of the master contract, employee certificates and announcement booklets, and the establishment of home office and policyholder records; state premium and other taxes; and the expenses of premium collection, claim settlement and the other continuing administrative functions. The loading must also be sufficient to allow for a contribution to the company's surplus or a profit in the case of a stock company.

As in individual insurance, the first year's premium usually is not sufficient to cover the high level of initial expenses. Except for the largest policies, it is recognized that these initial expenses must be amortized over several policy years. Although group life insurance is written on a one-year term basis, it is assumed that policies will remain in force for a sufficient time on the average so that money advanced by the insurance company in the first year will be repaid in time, usually in five years or less except for the smallest cases.

NET PREMIUMS FOR TERM COVERAGE

Characteristics of Group Mortality

Group mortality experience has been compiled and studied almost since the inception of group insurance in 1911. The early studies were carried out by the Group Association, which was formed among the relatively few companies then writing group insurance to consider underwriting and other common problems, and were reported in the *Transactions of the Actuarial Society of America* from time to time. The demise of the Group Association took place under the influence of the T.N.E.C. investigations in the late 1930's at which it was contended that the Association interfered with the free flow of competition. Experience analyses were resumed under the auspices of the Group Mortality Committee of the Society of Actuaries after the end of World War II.

One of the early group actuaries, Mr. E. B. Morris, observed: "That there has been a fundamental difference in the mortality curves of group and regular life insurance . . . has been evident since group experience was first tabulated."[4] This has continued to be the case, which should not be surprising in view of the way in which the two forms are underwritten. Applicants for individual insurance are examined one by one on the basis of a medical or other statement evaluating their health and other circumstances. Only the lives that fall within defined rating limits are accepted

---

[4] E. B. Morris, "A Comparison of Mortality Elements between Group and Regular Life Insurance," *Transactions of the Actuarial Society of America*, Volume XXIV (1923), p. 325.

on a standard basis. Group insurance underwriting, on the other hand, usually does not rely upon individual evidence of health to obtain satisfactory underwriting results. Instead the group is considered as a whole, and underwriting standards are established to insure the inclusion of a broad cross section of all eligible employees, whether standard or substandard, in each insured group.

Group life insurance usually includes a form of total and permanent disability coverage which serves to complicate direct comparisons with individual insurance mortality, as will be explained later. Also, the higher mortality under individual policies issued pursuant to the group conversion right should be considered as an addition to the group experience. While the mortality experience patterns of group and individual coverages have not been the same, it is nonetheless striking how favorable group mortality has been. Group insurance death rates are not much higher than ultimate mortality rates under individual policies,[5] i.e., those experienced after the lower-level mortality rates of the early policy years are omitted.

Mortality differences from industry to industry were among the first to be examined. Accident and other occupational hazards, the type of employees and the conditions of employment produced substantially higher mortality for some industries. With improved safety procedures, better plant methods and the advent of automation, the variation in mortality by industry has gradually narrowed, so that today only a very few industries are underwritten with an extra premium.

Group life insurance experience among female employees has not been studied separately. The data that would be required to determine group mortality rates for women have not been maintained. The recognition of lower female mortality in individual insurance operations naturally suggests a similar differentiation for group life insurance, but there are good practical reasons for not making one.

First, although the number of working women who become covered by group life insurance is substantial, the proportionate effect of the coverage on women is considerably reduced when amounts of insurance are taken into account, because they usually qualify for smaller amounts than men. Another consideration is the fact that the effect on the employer's cost of lower mortality among his insured women employees will be reflected, at least to some extent, in his experience rating refund. The cost to the individual insured is determined by his or her rate of contribution, which

---

[5] The use of a physical examination or other evidence of good health in individual insurance eliminates impaired lives and gives rise to lower mortality among insureds in the early policy years. The period for which this is so, usually five to ten years, is known as the select period and the mortality rates as select mortality rates. The mortality rates gradually rise and by the end of the select period approach those expected among a mixture of selected and impaired lives. They are then referred to as ultimate mortality rates.

may be varied by sex to permit women to contribute at a lesser rate if considerations of individual equity appear compelling. These factors, together with the desire to maintain the simplicity of the present procedures, make it unlikely that separate group life insurance premiums will be established for males and females.

The mortality levels under individual policies issued in accordance with the group conversion privilege are substantially higher than among individual policies underwritten in the usual course. This comes about because the persons most likely to convert their group life insurance on termination are those whose health is impaired and who would otherwise be unable to secure individual coverage. Indeed, the purpose of the conversion privilege is to protect an uninsurable group member against the loss of protection which he may have come to depend on.

Table 11–1 shows how the mortality rates under converted life insurance policies compare with the select and ultimate mortality rates of the 1946–1949 Basic Tables[6] which are representative of actual experience levels under regularly underwritten individual policies. The mortality ratio of 1138 per cent in the first policy year means that the mortality of the converted policies in the year after issue was more than eleven times that of comparable regularly issued policies. The substantially higher mortality of the converted policies is evidenced at the later policy durations as well and persists for twenty years or more.

TABLE 11–1
MORTALITY EXPERIENCE UNDER CONVERTED POLICIES FROM 1953
POLICY ANNIVERSARIES TO 1959 POLICY ANNIVERSARIES

Policy Year	Ratio of Actual Deaths to Deaths Expected by the 1946–49 Basic Tables
First	1138%
Second	571
Third	437
Fourth	353
Fifth	313
Sixth to tenth	238
Eleventh to fifteenth	168
Sixteenth to twentieth	118

SOURCE: *Transactions of the Society of Actuaries*, 1960 Reports of Mortality and Morbidity Experience; 1953–1959 Group Conversion Mortality and Withdrawal Experience, p. 105.

The regularly underwritten individual policyholders should not be expected to pay for these extra mortality losses which come from the group insurance line. Consequently, a compensatory transfer of funds is made between the two lines when group coverage is converted to individ-

---

[6] *Transactions of the Society of Actuaries*, Vol. II, pp. 505–12.

ual insurance. The amount transferred is an estimate of the higher mortality costs less any savings in commissions and underwriting expenses associated with the issuance of converted policies. In order to carry the cost back to the particular group policies whence the conversions originate, a charge is assessed against these policies as part of the experience rating formula. The amount may range from $65 to $80 per $1,000 of insurance converted.

Sources of Group Mortality Data

Mortality tables were developed from time to time from the various group experience studies for use in connection with cost projections for retired lives and similar purposes. Until the Commissioners 1960 Standard Group Mortality Table, however, no group table had been employed to compute group life insurance premiums or otherwise was recognized as an official table. Instead, first the American Experience Table and later the American Men Ultimate and the Commissioners 1941 Standard Ordinary Mortality Tables, all of which were developed from individual insurance experience, were applied to group life insurance.

In 1957, when the work leading up to the establishment of the Commissioners 1958 Standard Ordinary Mortality Table was being carried out, group insurance actuaries realized that, unless an official group mortality table were created, the 1958 CSO Table probably would come into use for group life insurance by default, as had the other individual insurance mortality tables. Since group mortality patterns and premium requirements differ from those of individual life insurance, it was felt that this would be undesirable. Furthermore, insurance companies not bound by the minimum premium laws of Maine, Michigan, New York, Pennsylvania and Ohio were using scales of rates for new business well below the prescribed minimum rates, based on the 1941 CSO Table, that were then in use.[7] This put the other companies, which were not in a position to reduce their rates for new cases, at a serious competitive disadvantage from which some immediate relief was desirable.

Effective July 1, 1958, a lower scale of group life insurance minimum premiums, which recognized in part the substantial improvement in group insurance mortality that had taken place along with the general improvement in mortality levels but still used the 1941 CSO Table as the standard for mortality, was promulgated by the insurance commissioners of the five minimum premium states as a temporary measure. Then, later in 1958, an Industry Advisory Committee consisting of company actuaries and a Technicians Committee composed of insurance department actuaries was appointed by the National Association of Insurance Commissioners to work together on the development of a group mortality table and a new

---

[7] The minimum premium laws and the several scales of minimum premiums are described later in this chapter.

scale of minimum gross premiums based on the table. The Commissioners 1960 Standard Group Mortality Table, which was formally adopted by the National Association of Insurance Commissioners in November, 1960, was the result of this joint effort.

The new table was to be based upon recent mortality experience. Furthermore, its principal use was to be in the computation of minimum statutory premiums, which meant sufficient margins would have to be included at all ages to allow for mortality fluctuations. In the process of constructing the table, the necessary margins would have to be built-in specifically because recent mortality data would contain little or nothing in the way of margins. This is a fundamentally different approach to the selection of a mortality standard for premium purposes, it should be observed, from that used in the development of other mortality tables. For example, the experience data upon which the American Experience and American Men Tables were constructed were drawn from a much earlier period and so automatically included margins over current mortality levels by reason of the substantial improvement in mortality that occurred before they were put into use. In other words, the margins provided by such tables are implicit in their construction, whereas in the case of the new group mortality table they were added explicitly.

Group insurance covers such a broad cross section of individuals that group mortality patterns tend to follow those of the population as a whole. Consequently, it would have been possible to turn to a current census table as the starting point for the group table. However, the ready availability of a large volume of experience under group policies argued strongly for its being the more appropriate to use.

Development of the 1960 CSG Table

Accumulation of Raw Mortality Data. The intercompany studies of the Group Mortality Committee of the Society of Actuaries are conducted on a continuous basis. For each calendar year the contributing companies submit data with respect to their group life insurance policies setting forth in quinquennial age brackets the number of lives insured and the number of claims. Accidental death claims, other death claims and disability claims are separately distinguished. Most of the companies with significant volumes of group life insurance in force participate, so that the studies are broadly representative of group mortality experience throughout the country.

Only the experience of employer-employee type groups with twenty-five employees or more is included. Special classes of groups, such as multiple-employer groups, union groups, and professional or other types of association groups are omitted from the analyses because their experience might not be homogeneous with that of the more widespread employer-employee cases.

The data submitted to the Committee are classified according to the industry of the employer and are tabulated separately for substandard or rated industries, i.e., those which are charged an extra premium, and for standard industries. Recent data were available for the nine calendar years 1950 through 1958. In the construction of the 1960 CSG Mortality Tables the experience of the relatively small number of rated industries was eliminated so that the table might be representative of standard experience. The remaining experience on standard industry groups comprised about 93 per cent of the total.

Treatment of Disability Claims. The experience for nonrated industries appears in Table 11–2 separately for each of the three disability provisions commonly found in group life insurance policies. Briefly, these are (1) the extended death benefit clause, which provides, in general, for payment of the full face amount at death within one year after termination of employment and prior to age sixty or sixty-five if the employee is disabled at the time of termination of employment and continues so until death; (2) the waiver of premium disability clause, which, in general, provides for continuous waiver of premium upon receipt of proof of total disability of at least nine months' duration and occurring before age sixty; and (3) the total and permanent disability clause, which provides upon disability prior to age sixty for the payment of the face amount of insurance in one sum or in installments over a relatively short period, such as sixty months.

It was necessary to find a way of handling the disability claims if the experience under the three clauses was to be combined and all of the data in Table 11–2 were to be used. There was no difficulty with respect to the extended death benefit clause. The one-year extended period is relatively short, and the claims occurring during this period were counted as if they were death claims occurring while the claimant's insurance was in force.

Under the waiver of premium clause, an approved disability claim may not actually be paid as a death claim for many years or indeed may not be paid at all if the claimant should recover from his disability. Other studies[8] showed that at the time of approval a waiver of premium claim was equal in value to about three quarters of a death claim, and hence these claims were counted in on this basis.

The total and permanent clause is the most valuable of the three disability clauses. In accordance with its provisions, the disability installments which reduce the face amount of insurance commence immediately upon satisfactory proof of disability. The payout of the face amount in this way before death occurs represents a substantial additional policy benefit,

---

[8] Sec. II—"Disability Claims under the Group Life Waiver of Premium Clause," *1949 Report of the Committee on Group Mortality and Morbidity,* Society of Actuaries, pp. 19–25.

TABLE 11–2
GROUP MORTALITY EXPERIENCE FOR CALENDAR YEARS 1950–58 FOR NONRATED INDUSTRIES BY TYPE OF DISABILITY BENEFIT
(Quinquennial Ages 18–98)

Central Age	Extended Death Benefit			Waiver of Premium				Total and Permanent Disability			
	Years Exposed	Total Claims	Accidental Deaths	Years Exposed	Total Claims*	Accidental Deaths	Disability Claims*	Years Exposed	Total Claims	Accidental Deaths	Disability Claims
18	401,645	397	262	707,716	758	494	28	794,947	751	445	64
23	1,225,556	1,209	680	2,104,444	2,416	1,323	160	2,342,349	2,358	1,155	311
28	1,692,030	1,786	789	2,931,588	3,254	1,317	318	2,999,104	3,375	1,282	497
33	1,774,278	2,143	676	3,161,130	4,363	1,336	399	3,026,988	4,139	1,107	688
38	1,784,888	3,375	676	3,110,908	6,290	1,205	521	2,934,662	5,991	1,047	930
43	1,689,622	5,434	680	2,898,544	9,956	1,175	749	2,724,529	9,566	993	1,404
48	1,492,881	7,923	613	2,487,354	14,419	1,085	1,033	2,363,484	14,056	891	2,093
53	1,238,143	10,649	554	1,986,634	18,453	907	1,483	1,898,618	19,348	837	3,402
58	983,675	13,702	519	1,543,296	22,908	837	2,558	1,472,081	25,822	682	6,747
18–58	12,282,718	46,618	5,449	20,931,614	82,817	9,679	7,249	20,556,762	85,406	8,439	16,136
63	689,220	14,590	449	1,099,261	22,109	715	—	1,049,444	21,833	656	—
68	366,362	11,751	297	566,690	16,693	436	—	586,158	19,383	446	—
73	158,996	7,782	193	236,796	10,761	254	—	285,567	14,756	288	—
78	60,851	4,748	116	84,426	5,986	131	—	122,496	10,168	179	—
83	18,248	2,319	59	24,057	2,712	61	—	44,037	5,634	112	—
88	3,580	768	25	5,015	869	16	—	11,134	2,161	45	—
93	449	140	5	643	153	6	—	1,743	509	13	—
98	21	13	0	59	23	3	—	159	52	2	—
63–98	1,297,727	42,111	1,144	2,016,947	59,306	1,622	—	2,100,738	74,496	1,741	—
Total	13,580,445	88,729	6,593	22,948,561	142,123	11,301	7,249	22,657,500	159,902	10,180	16,136

* 75 per cent of disability claims on waiver of premium.
SOURCE: Morton D. Miller, "The Commissioners 1960 Standard Group Mortality Table and 1961 Standard Group Life Insurance Premium Rates," *Transactions of the Society of Actuaries*, Vol. XIII (September, 1961), pp. 586–606.

for which an extra premium is charged.[9] More or less on the basis of judgment, it was decided to consider that the extra premium defrayed the cost of one half of the disability claims and that the remaining half should be combined with the death claims.

Mortality rates were derived separately for each of the three clauses, with the disability claims adjusted in the way described above in the case of the waiver of premium and total and permanent disability clauses. Inspection showed the three resulting sets of mortality rates to be very similar. Consequently, the risk exposure for the three clauses on the one hand, and the actual death claims and assumed value of the disability claims on the other, could properly be combined into one set of data.

The composite data, consisting of 59,000,000 life years[10] exposed to risk and nearly 400,000 claims, made up a tremendous body of experience and were equal in size to those used in the construction of the 1958 CSO Table. The mortality rates produced from the composite data are shown in Table 11–3, together with the corresponding accidental death rates. The composite mortality rates without margins constituted the underlying experience level for the 1960 CSG Table, on which the necessary mortality margins described below were superimposed.

Addition of Mortality Margins. The next step was to decide on the mortality margins to be included in the final table. Here cognizance was taken of a number of factors relating to the data and the day-to-day operations of group life insurance.

First of all, the inclusion of a margin was needed to cushion the fluctuations in claims that could be anticipated on individual groups from year to year. Data were available to show the degree of variation in claims experience that actually occurs among groups of different sizes. Second, it was felt that a margin should be added to permit the companies to continue writing all except the few highly hazardous industries on a standard premium basis. Third, it was observed that the data were on the basis of lives and not amounts insured; the experience by amounts of insurance would likely be at a somewhat higher level, especially in view of the larger amounts of insurance offered under today's more liberal underwriting practices. Fourth, at the younger ages, accidents are the major cause of claim and represent an extreme element of possible loss fluctuation. It was thought that this should be countered by a constant addition to the experience mortality rates. This would have the effect of increasing the experience rates at the younger ages proportionately more than those at the older ages. Lastly, the finished table would have to allow for the cost of conversions to individual policies. After a number of different formulas were tried, the total margin produced by a combination of 20 per

---

[9] The minimum extra premium requirement is discussed later in this chapter.
[10] A life year equals one life insured for a period of one year.

TABLE 11–3

COMPOSITE GROUP MORTALITY RATES FOR NONRATED INDUSTRIES BY LIVES 1950–58,
WITH AND WITHOUT MARGINS

(Quinquennial Ages 18–98)

				Mortality Rates per 1,000†	
				All Claims	
Central Age	Risk Exposure	Death and Disability Claims*	Accidental Deaths Only	Without Margins	With Margins Included
18	1,904,308	1,874	.63	.98	1.95
23	5,672,349	5,828	.56	1.03	2.21
28	7,622,722	8,166	.44	1.07	2.31
33	7,962,396	10,301	.39	1.29	2.55
38	7,830,458	15,191	.37	1.94	3.33
43	7,312,695	24,254	.39	3.32	4.98
48	6,343,719	35,352	.41	5.57	7.68
53	5,123,395	46,749	.45	9.12	11.94
58	3,999,052	59,058	.51	14.77	18.72
18–58	53,771,094	206,773	.44	3.85	5.61
63	2,837,925	58,532	.64	20.62	28.04
68	1,519,210	47,827	.78	31.48	42.95
73	681,359	33,299	1.08	48.87	66.00
78	267,773	20,902	1.59	78.06	98.15
83	86,342	10,665	2.69	123.52	151.31
88	19,729	3,798	4.36	192.51	223.24
93	2,835	802	8.47	282.89	340.56
98	239	88	20.92	368.20	850.69
63–98	5,415,412	175,913	.83	32.48	43.34
Total	59,186,506	382,686	.47	6.47	9.06

* The number of death and disability claims is equal to the number of death claims, including 100 per cent of the extended death benefit claims, plus 75 per cent of the waiver of premium and 50 per cent of the total and permanent disability claims.

† Because of the way in which the data are compiled, the mortality rates are actually for ages one-half year younger than the central ages shown.

SOURCE: Morton D. Miller, "The Commissioners 1960 Standard Group Mortality Table and 1961 Standard Group Life Insurance Premium Rates," *Transactions of the Society of Actuaries*, Vol. XIII (September, 1961), pp. 586–606.

cent of the composite mortality rate at each age and a constant of one additional death per thousand was found to provide reasonable margins at most of the working ages.

Other Adjustments in the Data. In order to complete the table down to age zero,[11] it was necessary to find a means of extending the data below age eighteen, where there was no group mortality experience. The mortality rate with margin at age eighteen was about 117.5 per cent of the corresponding rate from the 1958 CSO Table, and so it was decided to use

[11] Mortality rates for children might be useful for dependents group life insurance calculations, for example.

this percentage of the latter for the mortality rates below age eighteen. At the other end of the table, because the data were less voluminous and so less reliable it was decided to modify the mortality rates in such a way that the final table would have a consistent margin above the 1958 CSO Table throughout. This was done by substituting 105 per cent of the 1958 CSO mortality rates for the "with margin" mortality rates at the advanced ages.

The composite mortality rates, with the margins included and with these modifications, are shown for quinquennial ages eighteen to ninety-eight in the right-hand column of Table 11–3. Over this range of ages the rates are, on the average, 110 per cent of the corresponding 1958 CSO death rates.

Over the full range of ages the average death rate including margins is 9.06 per thousand and may be compared with 6.74 per thousand, the corresponding rate without margins. The basic rates, without margins, are therefore 71 per cent of the rates with margins on the average.

The last stage in the development of the 1960 CSG Table was to obtain individual age rates of mortality from these composite quinquennial rates with margin included. Appropriate interpolation techniques were used, and then minor modifications were made where necessary in order that the mortality rates should progress smoothly from age to age.[12] The full table of death rates, the number living, the number dying and the expectation of life from age zero to the terminal age ninety-nine appears in Table 11–4. The table is intended to apply to plans with the waiver of premium or extended death benefit disability clause; it is assumed that additional provision will be made for the extra benefit value where the total and permanent disability clause is included in the plan.

A complete mortality table was also derived from the composite rates without the margins added. This table, which corresponds to the experience level underlying the 1960 CSG Table, is known as the 1960 Basic Group Mortality Table.[13] This table is useful for retirement cost projections and similar purposes.

Net Premium Calculation

The net premium is that portion of the policyholder's charge which covers the value of the benefits, after allowing for the effect of interest earnings but before loading for expenses. An interest rate must be assumed (3 per cent has been used in the different scales of statutory group term life insurance minimum premiums) and a premium paying

---

[12] This process of interpolation and smoothing the progression of the rates is known as graduation.

[13] Morton D. Miller, "The Commissioners 1960 Standard Group Mortality Table and 1961 Standard Group Life Insurance Premium Rates," *Transactions of the Society of Actuaries,* Vol. XIII (September, 1961), pp. 586–606.

TABLE 11–4

COMMISSIONERS 1960 STANDARD GROUP MORTALITY TABLE

Age	Deaths per 1,000	Number Living	Number Dying	Expectation of Life— Years
0	8.32	10,000,000	83,200	66.86
1	2.07	9,916,800	20,528	66.41
2	1.79	9,896,272	17,714	65.55
3	1.72	9,878,558	16,991	64.67
4	1.65	9,861,567	16,272	63.78
5	1.59	9,845,295	15,654	62.88
6	1.53	9,829,641	15,039	61.98
7	1.48	9,814,602	14,526	61.08
8	1.45	9,800,076	14,210	60.17
9	1.42	9,785,866	13,896	59.25
10	1.42	9,771,970	13,876	58.34
11	1.45	9,758,094	14,149	57.42
12	1.48	9,743,945	14,421	56.50
13	1.55	9,729,524	15,081	55.58
14	1.63	9,714,443	15,835	54.67
15	1.72	9,698,608	16,682	53.76
16	1.81	9,681,926	17,524	52.85
17	1.90	9,664,402	18,362	51.95
18	1.99	9,646,040	19,196	51.04
19	2.03	9,626,844	19,542	50.14
20	2.09	9,607,302	20,079	49.25
21	2.14	9,587,223	20,517	48.35
22	2.18	9,566,706	20,855	47.45
23	2.21	9,545,851	21,096	46.55
24	2.24	9,524,755	21,335	45.65
25	2.26	9,503,420	21,478	44.76
26	2.28	9,481,942	21,619	43.86
27	2.30	9,460,323	21,759	42.96
28	2.33	9,438,564	21,992	42.05
29	2.36	9,416,572	22,223	41.15
30	2.40	9,394,349	22,546	40.25
31	2.45	9,371,803	22,961	39.34
32	2.51	9,348,842	23,466	38.44
33	2.60	9,325,376	24,246	37.53
34	2.71	9,301,130	25,206	36.63
35	2.85	9,275,924	26,436	35.73
36	3.02	9,249,488	27,933	34.83
37	3.21	9,221,555	29,601	33.93
38	3.45	9,191,954	31,712	33.04
39	3.72	9,160,242	34,076	32.15
40	4.02	9,126,166	36,687	31.27
41	4.37	9,089,479	39,721	30.39
42	4.75	9,049,758	42,986	29.53
43	5.18	9,006,772	46,655	28.66
44	5.64	8,960,117	50,535	27.81

TABLE 11–4 (*Continued*)

Age	Deaths per 1,000	Number Living	Number Dying	Expectation of Life— Years
45	6.15	8,909,582	54,794	26.97
46	6.70	8,854,788	59,327	26.13
47	7.31	8,795,461	64,295	25.30
48	7.98	8,731,166	69,675	24.49
49	8.72	8,661,491	75,528	23.68
50	9.52	8,585,963	81,738	22.88
51	10.40	8,504,225	88,444	22.10
52	11.37	8,415,781	95,687	21.32
53	12.44	8,320,094	103,502	20.56
54	13.61	8,216,592	111,828	19.82
55	14.88	8,104,764	120,599	19.08
56	16.24	7,984,165	129,663	18.36
57	17.70	7,854,502	139,025	17.66
58	19.24	7,715,477	148,446	16.97
59	20.87	7,567,031	157,924	16.29
60	22.62	7,409,107	167,594	15.63
61	24.51	7,241,513	177,489	14.98
62	26.60	7,064,024	187,903	14.34
63	28.86	6,876,121	198,445	13.72
64	31.31	6,677,676	209,078	13.11
65	34.00	6,468,598	219,932	12.52
66	37.00	6,248,666	231,201	11.94
67	40.32	6,017,465	242,624	11.38
68	44.01	5,774,841	254,151	10.84
69	48.03	5,520,690	265,159	10.32
70	52.33	5,255,531	275,022	9.81
71	56.86	4,980,509	283,192	9.33
72	61.58	4,697,317	289,261	8.86
73	66.42	4,408,056	292,783	8.41
74	71.53	4,115,273	294,365	7.97
75	77.04	3,820,908	294,363	7.54
76	83.14	3,526,545	293,197	7.13
77	89.98	3,233,348	290,937	6.73
78	97.71	2,942,411	287,503	6.35
79	106.25	2,654,908	282,084	5.98
80	115.48	2,372,824	274,014	5.63
81	125.32	2,098,810	263,023	5.30
82	135.63	1,835,787	248,988	4.99
83	146.35	1,586,799	232,228	4.70
84	157.51	1,354,571	213,358	4.42
85	169.20	1,141,213	193,093	4.15
86	181.46	948,120	172,046	3.89
87	194.39	776,074	150,861	3.65
88	208.16	625,213	130,144	3.41
89	223.08	495,069	110,440	3.17

TABLE 11–4 (*Continued*)

Age	Deaths per 1,000	Number Living	Number Dying	Expectation of Life— Years
90	239.55	384,629	92,138	2.94
91	258.06	292,491	75,480	2.70
92	279.23	217,011	60,596	2.47
93	303.76	156,415	47,513	2.23
94	332.49	108,902	36,209	1.99
95	368.80	72,693	26,809	1.73
96	420.59	45,884	19,298	1.45
97	512.84	26,586	13,634	1.13
98	701.56	12,952	9,087	.80
99	1,000.00	3,865	3,865	.50

period and the payment frequency must be specified. The present value of the benefits at a given age on the basis of the death rates in the mortality table chosen must then equal the present value of the net premiums.

The calculation of net premiums for group term life insurance is relatively simple since the policy period runs for only one year. The assumption is made that the premium is paid at the beginning of the year and that claims will occur and be paid uniformly throughout the year, or in the middle of the year on the average.[14] Thus, the net premium will earn interest for only a half-year before being required to pay the claims anticipated.

To illustrate, the death rate at age forty-five according to the 1960 CSG Table is 6.15 per thousand. If it is assumed that 100,000 persons are insured at age forty-five for $1,000 each, there will then be 615 claims expected and $615,000 in benefits to be paid out. The present value as of the beginning of the year at 3 per cent interest of the anticipated benefits which will, on the average, be disbursed a half-year later is $615,000 multiplied by .985329, the discount factor for a half-year, or $605,977. Dividing by the 100,000 persons insured gives $6.06 as the net annual premium per $1,000 for one-year term insurance at age forty-five. The calculation of net premiums at other ages follows in the same way. Net premiums payable more often than annually would be computed from the annual premiums by the application of the fractional factors discussed later in the chapter.

GROSS PREMIUMS FOR TERM COVERAGE

Loading

Immediately after the adoption of the 1960 CSG Table, the Industry Advisory and Technicians Committees turned their attention to adapting

---

[14] Since the death rates vary continuously with age, the assumption that claims occur uniformly during each year of age does not fit the facts precisely. When the death rate is increasing, more of the claims occur toward the end of the year of age. The assumption is a practical approximation made in the interests of simplicity of calculation.

it to a new scale of statutory minimum gross premiums. With the realistic margins in the table for experience fluctuations and the other mortality factors, the net premiums make adequate provision for the mortality element. Only the formula for loading the net premiums for expenses and contingencies remained to be determined.

This was complicated somewhat by the desire to have a single formula which would make reasonable provision for the expense needs for all sizes of groups from the smallest to the largest. At the lower end of the size scale and with heavier expenses, there were the ten-to-twenty-five-life "baby" groups that companies were writing in volume; at the other end were the jumbo groups, involving thousands of employees, for which the expense requirements as a percentage of premium were much smaller.

Certain expenses vary with the size of the premium. Examples of these are commissions, managerial compensation and state premium taxes. Other expenses are relatively constant such as the expenses of processing the application, setting up the necessary policy records and issuing the contract. Still other expenses, like the expenses of printing announcement booklets and certificates and of setting up and maintaining the records of lives insured, depend on the number of lives. Claims expenses tend to be a function of the number of claims. The task of the loading formula was to incorporate such a complex pattern of expense variation in a way that was reasonably in accord with the facts and at the same time would be practical to use for "baby" as well as jumbo groups.

To overcome this problem, a loading formula in three parts was decided upon. First, a basic loading percentage was applied to the net premiums age by age to obtain a set of tabular gross premiums. The percentage was equal to 33.3 per cent of the net premiums, or the equivalent of 25 per cent of the tabular gross premiums. The tabular premiums are shown in Table 11–5.

The second phase of the loading formula was to add a policy constant to take care of the extra expense needs of "baby" groups. This constant per $1,000 of insurance applied only to the first $40,000 of coverage in the group. The amount of the addition was $2.40 per thousand on an annual premium basis, $1.20 semiannually, $.60 quarterly and $.20 monthly. For a group with more than $40,000 of life insurance volume, the policy constant would thus be $96 per year, $48 semiannually, $24 per quarter or $8 per month.

Third, the formula called for the application of a scale of size discount factors, or advance expense adjustments, as a means of recognizing the lesser expense loading needed for a group as its size increases. In the application of the advance expense adjustment factors, a group's size is measured by the sum of its tabular gross premium and the policy constant. A similar practice for determining a group's size is used in connection with group health insurance premiums.

TABLE 11–5

TABULAR GROSS PREMIUM RATES PER $1,000 OF GROUP TERM INSURANCE
1960 CSG TABLE AT 3 PER CENT LOADED BY THE
BASIC LOADING PERCENTAGE
(Ages 15–95)

Age Nearest Birthday	Annual	Semiannual	Quarterly	Monthly	Age Nearest Birthday
15	$ 2.26	$ 1.14	$ .57	$ .19	15
16	2.38	1.20	.60	.20	16
17	2.50	1.26	.63	.21	17
18	2.61	1.31	.66	.22	18
19	2.67	1.35	.67	.23	19
20	2.75	1.39	.69	.23	20
21	2.81	1.42	.71	.24	21
22	2.86	1.44	.72	.24	22
23	2.90	1.46	.73	.25	23
24	2.94	1.48	.74	.25	24
25	2.97	1.50	.75	.25	25
26	3.00	1.51	.76	.25	26
27	3.02	1.52	.76	.26	27
28	3.06	1.54	.77	.26	28
29	3.10	1.56	.78	.26	29
30	3.15	1.59	.80	.27	30
31	3.22	1.62	.81	.27	31
32	3.30	1.66	.83	.28	32
33	3.42	1.72	.86	.29	33
34	3.56	1.79	.90	.30	34
35	3.74	1.88	.94	.32	35
36	3.97	2.00	1.00	.34	36
37	4.22	2.13	1.07	.36	37
38	4.53	2.28	1.14	.38	38
39	4.89	2.46	1.23	.41	39
40	5.28	2.66	1.33	.45	40
41	5.74	2.89	1.45	.49	41
42	6.24	3.14	1.58	.53	42
43	6.81	3.43	1.72	.58	43
44	7.41	3.73	1.87	.63	44
45	8.08	4.07	2.04	.68	45
46	8.80	4.43	2.22	.74	46
47	9.60	4.84	2.42	.81	47
48	10.48	5.28	2.65	.89	48
49	11.46	5.77	2.89	.97	49

NOTE: To the foregoing rates a constant should be added on the first $40,000 of insurance equal to $2.40 per M annually, $1.20 per M semiannually, $.60 per M quarterly and $.20 per M monthly. The foregoing rates are exclusive of any reduction on account of premium size.

TABLE 11–5 (*Continued*)

Age Nearest Birthday	Annual	Semiannual	Quarterly	Monthly	Age Nearest Birthday
50	$ 12.51	$ 6.30	$ 3.16	$ 1.06	50
51	13.66	6.88	3.45	1.16	51
52	14.94	7.53	3.77	1.26	52
53	16.34	8.23	4.13	1.38	53
54	17.88	9.01	4.51	1.51	54
55	19.55	9.85	4.94	1.65	55
56	21.34	10.75	5.39	1.80	56
57	23.25	11.71	5.87	1.97	57
58	25.28	12.73	6.38	2.14	58
59	27.42	13.81	6.92	2.32	59
60	29.72	14.97	7.50	2.51	60
61	32.20	16.22	8.13	2.72	61
62	34.95	17.61	8.82	2.96	62
63	37.92	19.10	9.57	3.21	63
64	41.13	20.72	10.39	3.48	64
65	44.67	22.50	11.28	3.78	65
66	48.61	24.49	12.27	4.11	66
67	52.97	26.68	13.37	4.48	67
68	57.82	29.13	14.60	4.89	68
69	63.10	31.79	15.93	5.34	69
70	68.75	34.63	17.36	5.81	70
71	74.70	37.63	18.86	6.32	71
72	80.90	40.75	20.43	6.84	72
73	87.26	43.96	22.03	7.38	73
74	93.97	47.34	23.73	7.95	74
75	101.21	50.98	25.56	8.56	75
76	109.23	55.02	27.58	9.24	76
77	118.21	59.55	29.85	10.00	77
78	128.37	64.67	32.41	10.86	78
79	139.59	70.32	35.25	11.81	79
80	151.71	76.42	38.31	12.83	80
81	164.64	82.94	41.57	13.93	81
82	178.19	89.76	44.99	15.07	82
83	192.27	96.86	48.55	16.26	83
84	206.93	104.24	52.25	17.50	84
85	222.29	111.98	56.13	18.80	85
86	238.40	120.09	60.20	20.16	86
87	255.38	128.65	64.48	21.60	87
88	273.47	137.76	69.05	23.13	88
89	293.08	147.64	74.00	24.79	89
90	314.71	158.54	79.46	26.62	90
91	339.03	170.79	85.61	28.68	91
92	366.84	184.80	92.63	31.03	92
93	399.07	201.03	100.77	33.75	93
94	436.82	220.05	110.30	36.95	94
95	484.52	244.08	122.34	40.98	95

NOTE: To the foregoing rates a constant should be added on the first $40,000 of insurance equal to $2.40 per M annually, $1.20 per M semiannually, $.60 per M quarterly and $.20 per M monthly. The foregoing rates are exclusive of any reduction on account of premium size.

To qualify for any reduction, the group's size must be such that its tabular annual premium plus the policy constant is more than $2,400. This effectively rules out "baby" groups. Groups with an annual premium size of $720,000 or more qualify for the maximum reduction of 20 per cent. If the minor effect of the policy constant for these large groups is ignored, the final gross premium becomes 80 per cent of the tabular gross premium, or 106.7 per cent of the net premium (i.e., the net premium plus the basic loading of 33.3 per cent of the net premium multiplied by 80 per cent). In other words, the minimum expense loading applicable to the jumbo groups is 6.7 per cent of the net premium, which may also be expressed as 6.3 per cent of the gross premium. Table 11–6 contains the complete scale of advance expense adjustment factors.

TABLE 11–6

ADVANCE EXPENSE ADJUSTMENT FACTORS FOR USE WITH COM-
MISSIONERS 1961 STANDARD GROUP LIFE INSURANCE PREMIUM
RATES

Net Premium Plus Basic Loading Percentage Plus Policy Constant (Annual Basis)	Net Premium Plus Basic Loading Percentage Plus Policy Constant (Monthly Basis)	Advance Expense Adjustment Factor
Under $ 2,400	Under $ 200	0%
$ 2,400– 2,999	$ 200– 249	1
3,000– 3,599	250– 299	2
3,600– 4,199	300– 349	3
4,200– 4,799	350– 399	4
4,800– 5,399	400– 449	5
5,400– 5,999	450– 499	6
6,000– 7,199	500– 599	7
7,200– 8,399	600– 699	8
8,400– 9,599	700– 799	9
9,600– 11,999	800– 999	10
12,000– 17,999	1,000– 1,499	11
18,000– 35,999	1,500– 2,999	12
36,000– 59,999	3,000– 4,999	13
60,000–119,999	5,000– 9,999	14
120,000–179,999	10,000–14,999	15
180,000–239,999	15,000–19,999	16
240,000–359,999	20,000–29,999	17
360,000–479,999	30,000–39,999	18
480,000–719,999	40,000–59,999	19
720,000 and over	60,000 and over	20

SOURCE: Morton D. Miller, "The Commissioners 1960 Standard Group Mortality Table and 1961 Standard Group Life Insurance Premium Rates," *Transactions of the Society of Actuaries*, Vol. XIII (September, 1961), pp. 586–606.

The tabular gross premiums, together with the policy constant and advance expense adjustment factors, constitute the 1961 Standard Group Life Insurance Premium Rates. The scale of rates was promulgated in 1961 by the insurance commissioners of Maine, Michigan, New York, Ohio and Pennsylvania to be applicable as the minimum initial rates for new groups written thereafter in those states. A minimum addition to the tabular gross premiums of $.96 per $1,000 of face amount on an annual basis, $.48 semiannually, $.24 quarterly and $.08 monthly was prescribed for plans with the installment total and permanent disability benefit clause. These regulations permit a company to charge a premium in excess of the 1961 scale on any case if, in its underwriting judgment, an extra premium is required.

Companies not subject to the minimum premium laws are in a position to use whatever scale of rates they choose and often charge 5 per cent to 15 per cent less, depending upon the size of the case. The companies governed by the minimum premium statutes are able to counter this sales advantage through their experience refunds which may be made at the end of the first year. The minimum premium laws do not apply to premiums for group permanent, dependents group life or creditor group life insurance which will be discussed later in this chapter.

Nonstandard Industries

While most industries are considered standard in relation to the 1961 scale, there are a few where special hazards still exist that are treated as substandard and to which an extra premium will apply. Where ratings are applicable, they usually are expressed as 1961 scale plus one, 1961 scale plus two, and so forth. Plus one means that the scale of premiums is increased by $.96 per $1,000 on an annual basis, or $.08 monthly. Where the scale is plus two, two times $.96 is added and so on. Each unit provides for a greater than normal number of expected claims to the extent of about one extra death per thousand persons insured. The underwriting rules of one large company call for ratings for the following industries, among others:

	Extra Premium Rating
Acids (manufacture) (heavy-carbolic, hydrochloric, hydrofluoric, nitric, prussic, sulphuric, sulphurous, etc.)	+2
Explosives and fireworks	+3
Fertilizer (manufacture)	+2
Mining (underground)	+3

A detailed description of the operations performed is required in connection with quarrying (rock, minerals, clay, sand, etc.); marble and stone yards and mills; lumbering, especially for insurance on woodsmen and loggers; railroads of all kinds; and stevedoring, lightering, tugs, barges and dredges and, based on the facts of the individual case, extra premiums are made applicable in at least some instances.

Other than Annual Premiums

Premiums for group insurance almost universally are paid on a monthly basis. This is distinctly different from the situation which prevails in individual insurance where the other modes of premium payment are of equal or greater importance.

The expense of handling monthly as against annual group insurance premiums is a minor consideration, because the same amount of record keeping by the insurance company is required in either situation. This comes about because new and terminating employees must be accounted for each month in any event. The loss of interest by reason of the deferment of part of the annual premium is the principal concern in the computation of fractional premiums. The factors in the 1961 scale which are used in calculating fractional premiums are as follows:

	Percentage of the
Mode of Payment	Annual Premium
Semiannual	50.375%
Quarterly	25.250
Monthly	8.458

Application of Gross Premiums

The calculation of gross premiums for a case begins with its solicitation. It is usual to request the employer to prepare schedules showing the year of birth, the date of employment, the sex and the earnings or occupation of each eligible employee. The amount of insurance to which each employee will be entitled under the proposed plan of insurance may then be determined.

The amounts must be summarized for each age for which there are eligible employees. A punched card may be prepared from the schedules for each employee to facilitate this summarization for larger cases; it may be done by hand for small cases. At each age, the aggregate amount of insurance is multiplied by the appropriate tabular gross monthly premium rate. For example, if as shown in the illustrative calculation the five employees at age forty-two, where the rate is $.53, are to have $32,000 of insurance, the tabular monthly cost is $16.96 ($.53 × $32,000). These products are summed for all ages to secure the total of the tabular gross premiums. The policy constant of $.20 per month on the first $40,000 of insurance, the extra premium for total and permanent disability benefits, if applicable, and any other extra premium, e.g., for industry, are added in, and the applicable size discount is deducted. Lastly, the average monthly premium rate per $1,000 of insurance is computed by dividing the total premium by the total amount of insurance. In the illustrative calculation, the monthly premium before discount is $467.06, which qualifies the group for an expense adjustment of 6 per cent and a premium reduction of $28.02. The reduced premium of $439.04, when divided by $666,000, the volume of insurance for the 102 employees, establishes the average monthly premium rate of $.66 per $1,000.

When a case actually is sold, the premium is recalculated using the age

ATTAINED AGE	NUMBER OF LIVES	INSURANCE		MONTHLY AGE RATE FACTOR		MONTHLY PREMIUM	
15					19		
16					20		
17					21		
18					22		
19					23		
20	1	6	000		23	1	38
21					24		
22					24		
23	2	12	000		25	3	00
24	3	16	000		25	4	00
25	5	24	000		25	6	00
26	2	12	000		25	3	00
27	4	24	000		26	6	24
28	6	40	000		26	10	40
29	5	34	000		26	8	84
30	6	36	000		27	9	72
31	2	12	000		27	3	24
32	2	12	000		28	3	36
33	3	16	000		29	4	64
34	4	28	000		30	8	40
35	6	36	000		32	11	52
36	1	6	000		34	2	04
37	5	34	000		36	12	24
38	3	18	000		38	6	84
39	4	24	000		41	9	84
40	1	6	000		45	2	70
41					49		
42	5	32	000		53	16	96
43	4	26	000		58	15	08
44	3	22	000		63	13	86
45	4	32	000		68	21	76
46					74		
47	3	24	000		81	19	44
48	1	8	000		89	7	12
49	4	26	000		97	25	22
50	2	18	000	1	06	19	08
51				1	16		
52				1	26		
53				1	38		
54	2	16	000	1	51	24	16
55	1	10	000	1	65	16	50
56				1	80		
57				1	97		
58	3	24	000	2	14	51	36
59	1	6	000	2	32	13	92
60				2	51		
61	1	6	000	2	72	16	32
62				2	96		
63				3	21		
64	2	12	000	3	48	41	76
65				3	78		
66				4	11		
67				4	48		
68	1	8	000	4	89	39	12
69				5	34		
70				5	81		
Total	102	$666	000	Sub Total (1)		$459 . 06	

Loading (.20/$1000 not to exceed $8.00)   (2)   8 . 00

T.&P. loading per $1000: .08 x T.&P. insurance in $1000's   (3)   −

Other extra premium per $1000:____x insurance in $1000's   (4)   −

Basic premium: Total = (1) + (2) + (3) + (4)   (5)   467 . 06

Expense adj. (E.A.) factor 6% x total (5)   (6)   − 28 . 02

E.A. 1961 scale premium total = (5) − (6)   (7)   439 . 04

E.A. 1961 scale average monthly premium rate per $1000 = (7) ÷ total insurance   (8) $.66

FIG. 11–1. Monthly premium rate calculation for group life insurance.

distribution of those employees who actually become insured on the effective date. This distribution, obviously, may differ from that for all eligible employees or that for the employees upon whom the quotation was based. The average monthly premium rate so determined is used throughout the first policy year and applied each month to the volume of insurance then in force to compute the monthly gross premium due. Adjustments of the monthly premium rate due to the ages and amounts of insurance of new employees becoming insured and of insured employees whose insurance ceases by death or termination of employment are not made until the beginning of the next policy year, when the rate per $1,000 is recomputed as part of the renewal process.

Ordinarily, a group's average premium rate does not change significantly from year to year. The new lives becoming insured tend to offset the terminations and to keep the age distribution relatively stable. This is not likely to be the case, however, if too high a contribution rate or unsatisfactory administrative procedures for securing participation as employees become eligible discourage the new employees from joining the plan. Also, the continuation of insurance for retired employees will cause the average rate to rise as the volume of insurance on pensioners grows.[15]

MANUAL RATE MAKING FOR SPECIAL FORMS OF GROUP LIFE INSURANCE

Group Paid-up Life Insurance[16]

The combination of term and paid-up insurance is the most widespread form of group permanent life insurance. As explained in Chapter 8, under the group paid-up plan the employee's contribution is applied as a single premium each year on an attained age basis to buy paid-up insurance. The employee's term life insurance benefit equals his scheduled amount of insurance less the sum of his paid-up purchases. The employer pays the entire cost of the term insurance, the premiums for which are computed in accordance with the 1961 scale in the usual manner.

The single premium rates used for the paid-up benefits currently are based on the 1958 CSO Table with interest at 3 per cent per annum and without loading for expenses. Some companies differentiate in their premiums between males and females, using a three-year setback in age for the latter. The expense loading is omitted in order to make the plan more attractive to the employees. This is necessary because they are called upon to contribute at a substantially higher rate than for regular term plans. It is

---

[15] This subject is dealt with more fully in Chapter 8.

[16] Robert G. Espie, "Group Life Insurance with Paid-up Values," *Transactions of the Society of Actuaries,* Vol. VII (June, 1955), p. 201.

expected that to the extent interest and mortality margins in the single premium rates are insufficient to cover the cost of administering the paid-up benefits, this cost will be borne by the premiums which the employer pays for the term insurance.

Level Premium Group Permanent[17]

Level premium group permanent plans are similar to level premium permanent insurance plans sold on an individual basis. The most common types of plans offered are the endowment at age sixty-five, life paid up at age sixty-five, whole life and, especially if used for pension programs, retirement income forms. The computation of premiums involves the usual consideration of mortality, interest and expense.

The mortality experience should be similar to that of group term insurance, which would normally suggest the choice of the 1960 CSG Table as the mortality standard. However, the 1958 CSO Table is used instead by reason of the fact that it is incorporated as a standard table in the state valuation laws, whereas the group table is not. An interest rate of 3 per cent usually is assumed. Level premium group permanent is more expensive to sell and to administer than group term and, except for small cases, less expensive than individual insurance. Accordingly, the expense loadings usually are between the two. For small cases, either a policy constant addition or a minimum size requirement often is imposed.

Dependents Group Life Insurance

A simple premium structure is desirable for the modest amounts of group life insurance underwritten on dependents of employees. To this end, a separate flat rate may be charged for the coverage of spouses and the coverage of children, since either may be provided without the other, or the spouse rate may be expressed as a function of the employee rate, with a flat rate applicable to the children. A rate of $.60 per $1,000 for spouse coverage and a rate of $.30 per family unit for the coverage of children, whether one or more, are typical.

The spouse rates are almost always lower than the average employee rate in recognition of the generally favorable experience with this coverage and the fact that wives are usually three to five years younger than their husbands. The family unit rate for children assumes an average number of children per family taken from population data. When the flat rate is used for spouses, an extra rating may apply to the spouse coverage if the age distribution of the employees is above average. Expenses for the plan are minimal because the benefit structure is so simple and the coverage is issued as a supplement to the employee's benefits.

---

[17] Dennis N. Warters, "Group Insurance on Level Premium Plans," *Transactions of the Actuarial Society of America*, Vol. XLVIII (May, 1947), p. 95.

Group Accidental Death and Dismemberment

Manual rates for group accidental death and dismemberment benefits depend on whether the coverage (1) is for nonoccupational accidents only, or (2) includes both nonoccupational and occupational accidents on a twenty-four-hour basis. For the rating of twenty-four-hour coverage, an occupational classification based on the industry in which the employees are engaged is used. There are four categories of risk, depending on the degree of accident hazard. Table 11–7 shows a portion of one company's classification of industries. The tabulations developed in the intercompany group life studies, which show the accidental deaths in each industry, are an important guide to rating classifications for these benefits. For nonoccupational coverage, the rate is ordinarily independent of industry.

The following manual premium rates for group accidental death and dismemberment coverage are typical:

	Tabular Monthly Premium per $1,000 of Principal Sum
Nonoccupational coverage................	$ .06
Twenty-four-hour coverage:	
Industry Class A.....................	.06
" " B.....................	.10
" " C.....................	.15
" " D.....................	Individually rated but not less than $.24

The premium rates for accidental death coverage without the dismemberment benefits usually are approximately 90 per cent of those shown. For the larger cases, a size discount applies.

Creditor Group Life Insurance

Creditor group life insurance is a special form of group term life insurance. As such, premium rates theoretically should depend upon the distribution of the ages of the debtors and be computed in much the same way as for employer-employee group term life insurance. However, in practice such a distribution is seldom available, so rates independent of age are established which are appropriate for an average age distribution.

The most common method of charging premiums is the outstanding balance method, wherein the rate per $1,000 of insurance is applied to the aggregate amount of the outstanding indebtedness each month. A new case may start out with no insured loans and gradually increase in the size of the outstanding balances as loans are made through the years. The

TABLE 11–7

CLASSIFICATION OF INDUSTRIES FOR GROUP ACCIDENTAL DEATH AND
DISMEMBERMENT PREMIUM RATING

Class

Agriculture:

Care of trees...C
Cotton compressing (no ginning)...............................B
Cotton ginning or cotton ginning and compressing..............D
Florists, market gardening and nurseries......................A
General farming and ranching..................................B

Chemical Industries:

Heavy acids...C
Light acids, paints, varnish and other chemicals..............A
Drugs and medicines...A
Explosives..D
Fertilizer manufacture (no quarrying or mining)...............B
Soap, tallow, candles, glue...................................A

Clay, Glass and Stone (No Quarrying or Mining):

Brick, tile, terra cotta—unglazed.............................C
Brick, tile, terra cotta—glazed...............................B
Cement or lime manufacture, cement products...................B
Glass (excluding polished plate glass)........................A
Glass (polished plate glass)..................................B
Grinding of minerals and manufacture of abrasives.............B
Pottery and earthen ware......................................A
Stone cutting and polishing...................................C

Clerical and Professional:

Actors, actresses, orchestras, opera companies................A
Banks, insurance companies and other office forces............A
Colleges (faculty and/or nonfaculty)..........................A
Medical nurses, sanitaria, hospitals, etc.....................A
Motion-picture production.....................................B
Radio stations..A
Theatres (including movies) ....A

Construction:

Bridges...D
Buildings...C
Plumbing..A
Road construction...D
Sewers, ditches and caissons..................................D
Shipbuilding..C

Food, Drink and Tobacco:

Breweries and distilleries....................................A
Cereals, prepared foods, bakeries and confectionary...........A
Cigars and tobacco..A
Dairy products..A
Grain mills and elevators.....................................B
Macaroni manufacture..B
Manufacture or bottling of nonalcoholic beverages.............A
Preserving, canning...A
Slaughter, and packing houses and stock yards:
    Less than ½ of the employees in slaughter houses and stock yards......B
    More than ½ of the employees in slaughter houses and stock yards.....C
Sugar factories and refineries................................B

initial manual rate depends on the average volume of outstanding balances during the first year. A typical manual rate schedule is as follows:

	Monthly Premium Rate Per $1,000 of Insurance
Average Amount of Outstanding Indebtedness	
Less than $285,334.	$.75
$285,334 but less than $341,667	.70
$341,667 but less than $425,000	.65
$425,000 or more	.60

Higher premiums may be charged for a group with an above-average age distribution or where experience or other underwriting factors require, subject to the requirement in many states that the higher rate be filed and approved by the superintendent of insurance.

Another method of computing creditor group insurance premiums is the single premium approach, under which a charge is made only once for each debtor at the time the loan is entered into. The amount is based on the initial amount of indebtedness and the duration of the loan. An allowance is made for the decreasing amount outstanding as repayment is made.

RATE REGULATION IN GROUP LIFE INSURANCE

Initial Rates

The statutory determination of minimum rates for group term life insurance is unique in the life insurance business. This was a development that first came about in 1926, when group insurance was still in its infancy, and had its origin in the somewhat chaotic competitive situation which prevailed at that time. The Superintendent of Insurance of the State of New York became concerned that the companies and their other classes of policyholders might be hurt financially by inadequate group insurance rates and that public confidence in the business and the future growth of group insurance might be impaired. Consequently, after discussion with the companies, he sought and received legislative authority to prescribe minimum rates for new group life insurance contracts issued in the state. Companies were permitted to charge more if they wished to do so generally or judged it to be necessary in underwriting a particular case. It should be noted that the law applied only to the initial policy year. Thereafter, premiums might be reduced in the judgment of the company as experience warranted.

Similar laws were passed by Michigan and Pennsylvania in 1929, Ohio in 1935 and Maine in 1957. New York's law was subsequently changed so as to apply not only to policies issued within the state but also to policies issued in all other states by an insurance company which is licensed to operate in New York. Thus a company doing business nationally is bound by the New York statute throughout the country. The justification of this broadening of New York's regulatory authority beyond its borders rests on the concept that only in this way can the interests of the New York policyholders of a company be protected fully. Since most of the large group insurers issue coverage in New York, the effect of these regulatory statutes extends far beyond the limits of the five states which have such enactments.

The 1961 scale of premiums was the fourth adopted under this legislation. The three earlier scales were as follows:

1. The 1926 scale was based upon the American Men Ultimate Table with interest at 3 per cent and a loading of $1.70 per $1,000, plus 6½ per cent of the gross premium.
2. The 1950 scale employed the 1941 CSO Table at 3 per cent interest, with a loading of 10 per cent of the net premium, plus a policy constant equal to $1.80 per annum per $1,000 on the first $75,000 of insurance.
3. The 1958 scale was similar to the 1950 scale, except that it graded the policy constant and the percentage loading commencing with an insurance volume of $250,000, so that for cases of over $500,000 in volume the premium rates became the 1941 CSO Table net premiums with interest at 3 per cent and no loading.

Employer and Employee Contributions[18]

Where employees share in the cost of the plan, a prime requisite is that their contribution rate be low enough for participation to be attractive to them. In addition to appearing reasonable in relation to their earnings and the benefits, the rate of contribution should be attractive in comparison with the cost of individual policy benefits.

A New York regulation of May 1, 1929, and similar rules in a number of other states, have had an important influence on maximum employee contributions. New York stipulated that employee contributions could not exceed the greater of (1) the maximum permitted by the following table, or (2) 75 per cent of the aggregate premium for the policy.

Applicable Rate Scale	*Maximum Employee Contribution per $1,000*
Standard....................................	$.60 per month or $.14 per week
Standard plus 1...........................	.70 " " " .16 " "
Standard plus 2...........................	.75 " " " .17 " "
Standard plus 3 or more..................	.80 " " " .18 " "

The concern of the regulatory officials was that, in the absence of some such limitation, group life insurance might suffer the same difficulties experienced by assessment insurance. They could see the specter of

---

[18] Chapter 8 deals with the tax aspects of employer contributions including the 1964 amendments to the Internal Revenue Code relating to amounts of group term life insurance in excess of $50,000.

Chapter 12

EXPERIENCE RATING IN GROUP LIFE INSURANCE

BY PAUL H. JACKSON

NATURE OF EXPERIENCE RATING

The insurance protection provided under a group life insurance policy can be identical to the insurance protection provided under a particular type of individual policy. Under a group contract, however, the group, and therefore the policyholder, continues to exist after a claim has occurred, whereas under an individual policy of life insurance a death claim will terminate the contract in its entirety. Since the group plan does continue after individual claims, claim statistics can be maintained on a policy-by-policy basis, and, to the extent that they are statistically significant, they can be taken into account by the insurance company in determining the premium it is going to charge thereafter for the insurance provided under that group plan.

Experience rating is the general process whereby the manual premium charged during the first policy year for each eligible group in a given rating class is adjusted upward or downward for subsequent policy years on the basis of the claim experience that has actually emerged for that group. The process of experience rating has two distinct purposes. Viewed prospectively, it should operate so as to increase or decrease the premium for the insurance on a particular group to a level that will exactly support the *probable future experience* of that particular group. Viewed retrospectively, after the group insurance plan has been in existence for a number of years, the experience rating process should operate so as to produce a total net cost (premium charges less experience refunds) which approaches, ever more closely, the *actual past experience* of the group.

In group life insurance the fundamental elements that make up the cost of a plan are mortality, expenses, including any risk charges, and, in some cases, interest. A soundly designed experience rating plan must take account of all of these factors.

Mortality

With respect to the mortality element, the experience rating process should give more and more weight to the effect of those employer practices or those particular characteristics of the group which, while not taken into account in setting the manual premium for the plan, will result in the group having better or poorer experience than the average group in the particular rating class.

For example, employers who require pre-employment physical examinations and practice careful screening of new employees will have a more healthy group on the average than will employers who simply accept applicants on the basis of job qualification without regard to physical condition. Similarly, those groups with high employee morale and pleasant working conditions frequently attract a better grade of applicant and can exhibit better than average claim experience. The social class of the employees who work for a company, their living conditions, community health and safety measures, all can exert an influence on claim costs. Physical working conditions and accident hazards in and around the plant clearly have their effect. Further, the employer's retirement practices and the manner in which employees are terminated can affect claim costs, because those practices may result in the elimination of the less healthy risks from the active working group. Clearly, not all of these factors can be foreseen, but their effect will emerge inevitably in the claim experience for each particular group. Thus each individual group will have a true expected claim cost of its own, in some cases better and in others worse than the over-all average for all groups combined.

When the experience of an individual group emerges, the number of employees and number of claims involved usually will not be large enough to assure that the actual claim cost will be exactly equal to the true expected claim cost for that particular group in each and every year. Statistical theory tells us that where only a small number of claims are expected in a year one must also expect a wide variation in the number of actual claims arising from one year to the next, due simply to chance fluctuation. One major problem in studying the actual experience results under a particular case is to eliminate those variations which are due only to chance fluctuation so as to take into account only those variations which are due to actual differences in risk characteristics of the group and its true underlying expected claim costs. Further, actual claim experience can be distorted by catastrophes, such as plant explosions, epidemics, plane crashes, or other accidents involving a number of simultaneous deaths. Such catastrophes occur so infrequently that their full effect should not be included in the experience of the individual case but rather spread out over all groups through some average risk charge.

Expenses

In addition to variations in mortality among groups, there is bound to be some variation in the expenses incurred by an insurance company in providing the various services necessary to maintain a group life insurance plan. Insurance company expenses are lower for a plan where all administration is carried on by the employer than where practically all administrative details are performed by the insurance company. In addition, there can be significant variations in the amount of commissions paid to the insurance agent or broker, due to the fact that group life insurance commission scales typically provide higher commissions in the first year than in renewal years and frequently provide for no commissions at all, or modest service fees, after the tenth policy year. The experience rating process provides the means whereby substantial expense variations from group to group can be reflected in the net cost of the insurance.

Risk Charges

A third element entering into the experience of a group life insurance plan is the risk charge imposed by the insurance company and usually combined with the expense charge into a single charge referred to as the insurer's "retention." The risk charge can be used to spread the cost of catastrophic and epidemic losses over all groups. The risk charge can provide funds from which the insurer can pay certain specific claims which may be "pooled" and not charged against the experience of the particular group, such as claim amounts on a single life in excess of some predetermined amount. Risk charges provide funds from which the insurer can pay the experience deficits arising on the poorer risks in a given class while still returning the experience surplus on the better risks in the form of cash refunds. Finally, in practice, the risk charges may also be designed to produce a contribution to the general surplus funds of the insurance company as protection against major catastrophes or epidemic losses affecting its entire group life insurance business.

Interest

Some group life insurance plans involve permanent insurance or substantial reserve accumulations to provide life insurance for retired employees. The initial cost of such plans must be based on assumptions as to the rate of interest which these funds will earn in future years. Clearly, there can be substantial variations between the interest actually earned and that initially assumed. The experience rating process provides the mechanism by which such variations can be reflected in the ultimate cost of the plan.

All insurance companies recognize these elements in their experience

rating formulas. Due to the different objectives and circumstances surrounding each company, however, there are wide variations in the details
of the experience rating plans currently in use and in the size of the
various factors used. Substantial judgment is required in determining the
factors and details that go into an experience rating plan. While there are
many theoretical discussions on the subject of experience rating and
collective risk theory, the real test of any experience rating plan lies in the
results it produces on each individual case and whether it enables the
insurance company to keep the better risks on the books and to obtain
realistic premiums from the poorer risks.

BASIC REASONS FOR THE USE OF EXPERIENCE RATING

Conservatism of Manual Rates

The minimum manual rate for group life insurance is prescribed by
statute in several states. These rates apply to the bulk of all group life
insurance written in the United States, due primarily to the extra-
territorial application of the New York law. The New York minimum rates
are generally recognized as relatively conservative and contain ample
margins relative to the risk characteristics of the average group. New
minimum premium tables are developed infrequently, so that the long-
range trend of improvement in mortality rates serves to compound their
conservatism. Hence experience rating is desirable as a means of adjusting
the initial manual rates to make them more sensitive to the current level of
mortality experienced by all groups.

Broad Rating Classes

Group life insurance manual rates are developed in such a way that a
single rate applies to a broad class of employers. Variations in the manual
rates are introduced only for those clear-cut conditions, such as a serious
industrial accident hazard, which can be determined impartially in all
cases. As a result, group life insurance manual rates fail to reflect many of
the basic differences in the risk characteristics of different insured groups.
Considerations of equity, therefore, require that modifications in the
manual rate be made, through experience rating, to take these differences
into account.

Competition with Self-insurance

Another reason for the necessity of experience rating is the fact that
group life insurance is not the only method by which employers may
provide death benefits for their employees. A large employer has the
option of paying death benefits directly to the families of his employees
without purchasing group coverage from an insurance company. If a
single average price is charged all group clients regardless of their actual

experience, those groups with more favorable experience will be encouraged to self-insure their plans. Those groups with the least favorable experience, on the other hand, will continue to purchase group life insurance, because the average price will be lower than the claim payments which they expect will emerge. The premium for a specific group must, therefore, be set as accurately and equitably as possible and must be adjusted through experience rating as soon as any additional information having a bearing on the risk becomes available.

Competition among Insurance Companies and Brokers

Closely related to the above factors making experience rating necessary is the fact that the group life insurance business is characterized by intense competition, both among insurance companies and among brokers. The insurance broker wants to make sure that his group client is reasonably happy with the net cost of his group life insurance plan. If the premium rate is not gradually decreased over a prolonged period in which claim experience has been generally favorable, dissatisfaction will arise, and the broker may lose his account. The insurance broker is also interested in obtaining new insurance accounts and can do so more easily when the insurance company can promise fair financial treatment. In fact, the selection of the insurance company to underwrite a group life insurance plan probably will depend on a comparison of the factors used in the experience rating plans of the quoting companies, since minimum premium statutes prevent direct competition in initial premium rates.

Similarly, the competitive environment within which insurance companies themselves operate makes experience rating necessary. Each insurance company is interested in keeping the good risks in force. In order to do so, it must provide coverage to such groups at a reasonable net cost, both prospective and retrospective. Failure to do so involves running the risk of losing the business to a competing insurer.

Part of the task of retaining the groups with favorable experience entails charging adequate rates for the groups with unfavorable experience. Naturally, the process of increasing rates for groups with poor experience makes it possible for the insurance company to reduce the rates for those groups with the best experience, thus maximizing the chance that the better risks will remain with the particular insurer.

STATISTICAL CONSIDERATIONS IN EXPERIENCE RATING

In the experience rating process, the insurance company normally maintains for each group a record of the manual premium and the claims that occur. The manual premium for a particular case can then be used as a statistical measure of the risk associated with that case, and a "manual loss ratio" can be determined by dividing the actual claims under a particular group life insurance plan by the total manual premium for that plan. Individual case statistics of this type can be developed on an accumulated-to-date basis as well as on a year-by-year basis. The policy year[1] is the usual period for which experience is maintained and reported to the policyholder.

The manual loss ratio for an entire class of groups can also be determined for each year and, after appropriate adjustment for trends and catastrophes, can be assumed to be the true expected loss ratio for the average case in that class. The manual loss ratios which actually emerge for individual cases, however, will vary about the over-all class loss ratio; first, because some of the groups are inherently poorer insurance risks than the over-all average, while other groups are inherently better, and second, because the manual loss ratio for any one case will be subject to chance fluctuation due to the limited size of the group.

Probable Loss Ratio

The "probable loss ratio" for a given case can be defined as that manual loss ratio with the highest probability of being the true expected loss ratio for the case, based on the actual manual loss ratio that has emerged for that case since its issue. It is thus the insurer's best estimate of the loss ratio which that individual case would have experienced if the period of exposure had been long enough to reduce the effect of chance fluctuation to a negligible level. The probable loss ratio for a new group will be simply the over-all class loss ratio, because of the absence of any actual experience data. After actual experience has developed under the case, the probable loss ratio will change. For example, with very favorable experience it becomes more likely that the particular group is a better than average risk, whereas if the experience has been far worse than average over a number of years, it becomes more and more likely that the group is inherently a poorer insurance risk than the average group.

In practice the probable loss ratio is determined as a weighted average of the manual loss ratio for a given case and the manual loss ratio for the combined class of groups. Thus $P = zM + (1 - z)C$, where P is the probable loss ratio for the particular group, M is the accumulated-to-date manual loss ratio for that group, C is the over-all class loss ratio, and z is some weight between zero and one. The weight, z, which is given to the actual loss ratio for the individual case is sometimes called the credibility, and it increases as the size of the case increases or as the number of years of experience under a particular case increases. In short, the credibility is

---

[1] The first policy year would commence on the date of issue of the plan and run for twelve months to the first anniversary of issue. Subsequent policy years would run from one anniversary of issue to the next. The policy year is usually spelled out in the contract of insurance and may be set so that it coincides with the employer's fiscal year, or it may be changed from time to time for other reasons. Thus "policy years" longer or shorter than twelve months are occasionally encountered.

proportionate to the statistical significance of the actual experience results under the case.

Large Groups

Some individual cases may be so large that any chance claim fluctuation would not have a significant influence on the actual manual loss ratio as it emerges from year to year. Such a policyholder is, in effect, insured only against the occurrence of catastrophic losses and, in general, will demand that any excess of billed premiums over incurred claims must bear some reasonable relationship to the insurance services provided. Thus, for such very large cases, 100 per cent credibility is granted to the actual experience each year, and the experience rating plan operates on a "cost plus" basis. The insurance company would credit the premium paid, subtract the incurred claims, the expense and risk charges and, if there is any balance remaining, return that balance to the employer as an experience refund. For such groups the probable loss ratio, P, equals M, where M is the manual loss ratio based on experience accumulated only in the most recent n policy years, n being chosen as the smallest integer for which the credibility, z, will remain 100 per cent.

Smaller Groups

In determining the probable loss ratio for smaller cases, the insurer must accumulate the experience from year to year in order to give greater statistical significance to the emerging experience. To the extent that a long-range trend may exist, the experience used should be adjusted to reflect this trend, and, further, experience beyond some reasonable period in the past should be eliminated from consideration entirely. For example, there are employers who have had group life insurance in effect with a single insurance company for as long as fifty years. Clearly, the experience fifty, forty, or even thirty years ago does not have any real bearing on the risks involved today, since the lives insured are all different today and the management practices, industrial hazards, morale and other miscellaneous factors affecting the risk do not remain constant over so long a period of time.

Treatment of Catastrophic Losses

From time to time there are bound to be large losses which result from plant accidents, epidemics and other similar occurrences. Even though they occur rarely, the effect on a particular plan can be disproportionate, and allowance must be made in the experience rating process for such losses which, at the individual case level, appear to be catastrophic. Abnormally large losses usually are eliminated entirely from the experience of the particular group, and an average charge, which is called a "contingency charge" and is sufficient in total to cover such catastrophic losses, is levied upon all groups as part of the expense charge. The usual statistical formulas cannot be used to predict the occurrence of catastrophes, nor can the average cost of such catastrophes be estimated by looking at the past few years' experience of the groups insured by a particular insurance company, or even of all groups insured by all insurance companies combined. Thus, the determination of the level of contingency charges appropriate for a particular insurer will depend heavily on judgment and on competitive considerations.

Large Amounts on Individual Employees

The experience rating of group life insurance poses a rather interesting inconsistency. If one individual with a large amount of insurance should die, the manual loss ratio under the group plan may be increased sharply, and thus the probable loss ratio for that case will be increased to the extent that the manual loss ratio is given credibility. At the same time, coverage in the future applies only to persons other than the claimant. Thus a group life insurance plan which initially covers a handful of uninsurable employees may be charged a higher than average rate after those uninsurable employees have died, and yet the group after their death may be a better than average risk.

In order to minimize the effect of a single large claim on the experience results, premiums and claims for the insurance amounts on any single employee which are in excess of some preset amount can be removed from the experience for the group and put in a company-wide pool. The effect of such individual life pooling is to break the group life plan into two component parts, one of which is given zero credibility and charged an over-all class average price, namely the cost of insurance in the company-wide pool. The remaining part of the group life insurance plan can then be given greater credibility than could have been given to the total plan, because of the smaller variation in experience rated claim amounts.

Experience Rating Deficits

If in the calculation of the experience rating refund for a particular group life insurance case, it is found that incurred claims plus expense charges exceed the premium, the deficit will have to be carried forward into the following accounting period, with the only source of repayment being any possible experience gain in that subsequent period. The amount of any deficit which is to be carried forward in this manner must be relatively small, or else the potential reduction in future experience refunds and the potential increase in future net costs will force the intelligent policyholder to cancel his insurance program and purchase it from another insurance company. Thus the experience rating plan should be modified so that incurred claims in excess of some specified per cent of manual premium are waived, i.e., not charged against the experience of the particular group. Any deficit that is waived for continuing policyholders or not recovered due to cancellation of such plans must be made up out of the risk charges which are levied against all similar groups.

By way of example, on a 1,000-life case an insurer might charge incurred claims only to the extent that they are less than 150 per cent of billed premium. Incurred claims in excess of 150 per cent of billed premium would then be waived so far as the individual case experience is concerned. In order to cover the excess incurred claims which have been waived, the insurance company might then include a risk charge of 2 per cent of billed premium with the expense charges for each 1,000-life case. For 500-life cases, the claims over 200 per cent of premium might be waived for a risk charge of 3 per cent of premium; for 2,000-life cases, claims over 130 per cent might be waived for a risk charge of 1.5 per cent; and so on. In this way the experience rating plan for the larger groups can be modified so that a true insurance element is introduced into the "cost plus" type of arrangement.[2]

Other Considerations

An experience rating plan must make allowance for the statistical characteristics of the claim experience for each of the various kinds of group coverage. For example, group life insurance experience is characterized by a fairly low claim frequency rate. Further, there can be a substantial variation in amount of benefit paid from claim to claim. Because of the low claim frequency rate and the wide variation in claim amounts, the credibility granted to the actual experience for group life insurance tends to be substantially less than for certain health insurance coverages, where the number of expected claims is relatively great and the amount of each individual claim is fairly small. Similarly, the life insurance claim frequency rate is higher for older persons than for younger employees, so that group life insurance plans with substantial coverage continued for pensioners (or, for that matter, with a fairly high average insurance age for any other reason) should be given greater credibility than younger groups.

A wide variety of statistical tables are available by which to estimate the expected variation in the number of claims because of chance fluctuation. For the largest cases, these variations can be assumed to occur in accordance with the normal curve of error. For the smaller cases, the Poisson or Pearson Class III distributions can be used.[3]

---

[2] An empirical method for determining the risk charges required at various loss levels is described in the author's article, "Experience Rating," *Transactions of the Society of Actuaries,* Vol. V (1953), p. 239.

[3] These statistical distributions are described in most standard college level statistics texts. Tables of values are readily available, for example see *Tables for Statisticians* by Arkin and Colton, College Outline Series. The classical method of using such tables is described in the articles by Jackson and Feay cited in the list of Selected References at the end of this chapter. A completely different statistical approach called "collective risk theory" is described in the articles by Kahn and Ammeter.

FACTORS USED IN EXPERIENCE RATING

Incurred Claims

The premium paid for a group life insurance plan in a particular policy year is intended to provide insurance coverage for all deaths arising in that policy year. Group life insurance plans which contain the standard premium waiver benefit provide an extension of coverage throughout any period of total disability which commences before age sixty. Under such plans the date on which the employee last worked, if before age sixty, usually is considered to be the date his death claim arose or was incurred under the group life insurance plan. Where the date last worked is beyond age sixty, the date of death would be considered as the date the claim was incurred.[4]

All death claims will not necessarily be paid or approved for payment prior to the end of the policy year, so that, in theory, the experience records should be held open until all late claims incurred in a particular policy year have been charged back against the experience of the case for that policy year. In actual practice, an insurance company cannot delay indefinitely the experience rating or annual accounting to clients. Accordingly, at the end of each policy year, claims approved during the year are charged to the experience of the group case, and an "incurred and unreported claim reserve" is set up to cover those death claims which already have been incurred but which have not yet been charged off to the case. The accounting practices obviously will vary from company to company, so that in one case an insurance company may charge a claim to the experience of the case only when the check has been cashed and returned to the home office, and the claim has subsequently been entered on the claim record for the particular group case. Many companies charge all of the claims which have been approved for payment. Still other companies require that the employer notify them at the end of a policy year if any death has occurred for which claim papers have not yet been submitted, and include the insurance amounts for such late claims with the approved claims for the policy year of death. Naturally, the more current the basis for approved claims, the smaller the number of incurred claims that have not yet been paid, and the smaller the reserve for incurred but unreported claims.

---

[4] Essentially the same treatment would apply to death claims arising under group life insurance plans providing for a lump-sum payment in case of disability occurring before age sixty. For group life insurance plans with the waiver of premium benefit applying to disabilities occurring before age sixty-five, the death claims would be considered as incurred on the date last worked, if before age sixty-five, otherwise on the date of death. Under those plans with the old "ex-disability" benefit (a one-year extension of coverage for disabilities occurrring before age sixty-five) the death claims would be considered as incurred on the date last worked, if before age sixty-five and not earlier than one year prior to the date of death.

In addition to the death claims arising under a group life insurance plan, some provision must be made for the charging of any disability or other claims to the experience of each case. When a claim for waiver of premium is approved, most companies charge the experience of the group with an average claim charge, usually $750 for each $1,000 of insurance. This average claim charge is based on the proportion of approved premium waiver claims that terminate in death, as opposed to those terminating in recovery. When an approved premium waiver claim does terminate in death, the excess of the face amount of insurance over the average claim charge made ($250 in the case of the $750 average claim charge) would be added to the approved claims for the particular group in the year death occurs. Similarly, a claim terminating in recovery would release a credit, equal to the charge previously made, to the experience of the case in the year of recovery.

Group life insurance plans occasionally provide for the payment of the face amount, in a lump sum or in installments, in the event of permanent and total disability. Lump-sum disability payments would be charged off in the year of claim approval. Some installment disability benefits do not require any further test of disability, and the present value of all installments due would be charged against the case in the year of claim approval. Some group life insurance policies which provide for installment disability benefits require continuing proof of disability, and thus the benefit payments will terminate in the case of subsequent recovery. Most companies would charge the experience of the group with the present value of the full benefits at the time the claim is approved, and in case recovery should subsequently occur the present value of the remaining installments would be credited to the experience of the case in the year of recovery.

The cost of issuing converted policies of life insurance without medical evidence of insurability to terminating employees may be considered as an added benefit provided under a group life insurance plan. For larger cases, a conversion charge ranging from $65 to $85 per $1,000 of insurance converted would be included with the approved claims for the group in the year of conversion. For smaller groups, an average charge such as 1 per cent or 2 per cent of premium would be included with the approved claims, or in some companies, with the expense charges, rather than charging the conversion costs on an individual basis.

In any case, the incurred claims used for financial accounting and experience rating will be the sum of the paid death claims for the particular policy year, the approved disability claims charged to that policy year, the charges for conversion, and the increase in the total required reserves over the policy year. This figure thus is the insurer's best estimate of the claims that actually were incurred during the policy year, regardless of how long it may be before all of them are paid.

Expense Charges

The expenses incurred by the insurance company in providing group life insurance will vary by the type of administrative service provided. Normally there will be higher expenses in the first policy year than in renewal years because of the costs of printing announcement booklets, soliciting employees and setting up home office records, and because of the unlevel commission scale often used. The actual expenses will vary also by type of coverage. In addition, the expenses per plan will be reduced if the employer has a number of insurance plans with the same insurance company, because of the broader premium base over which to spread the "per case" expenses, such as the cost of annual experience statements and service calls.

There are substantial variations in the actual expense incurred from case to case and from year to year on a given case. Visits by home office officials, long-distance telephone calls and certain other expenses which can be traced to particular groups normally are not charged back exactly to the cases on which they were incurred because of the inordinate expense of the record keeping that would be required. Each insurance company conducts various expense studies from time to time in order to determine a formula by which to charge the actual total expense of operations back to the individual cases. The expense formulas usually include a flat dollar charge "per policy," a flat dollar charge "per life," and a charge expressed as a percentage of premium. The per life and per policy charges are intended to produce, for all cases combined, the actual administrative expenses of the insurance company including home office and field salaries, rent, travel, printing, and other costs. Occasionally these charges vary by the number of lives insured or by the number of coverages in force in an employer's group package.

The percentage of premium charge would include any commissions, risk charges, contingency charges, charge for profit and a charge to cover state premium taxes and other assessments. First-year expenses can be charged off fully in the first year or, alternatively, the excess of the first-year expenses over a renewal year's expenses can be amortized over some period, such as five or ten years. Naturally, an insurance company in setting its expense charges must consider the competitive aspects, and a new company with fairly high actual expenses may choose expense charges which will not immediately recapture its actual incurred expenses in order to remain competitive. Such companies may well adopt the marginal theory of expenses, at least during the early years of their group business. Thus, in allocating internal company expenses, they may charge their group department with only those additional expenses which have been created by and can be attributed directly to the group insurance operations.

In contrast to the administrative expenses which for practical reasons must be charged by formula, the premium taxes and commissions paid are usually charged back to each case as they are incurred. The premium tax varies from state to state from a minimum of 1.75 per cent to a maximum of 4 per cent of paid premiums, net after dividends, and in some states domestic insurers pay no premium tax whatever. Some insurers include the exact tax in their expense formula, while other companies include a charge based on the company's over-all average tax rate. The commissions paid might vary between first year and renewal years, by the type of coverage, the type of broker and the size of the total premium paid for all group coverages by the employer. Any commission payment due on account of the premiums paid in a particular policy year usually will be charged as an expense to that plan for that policy year, although the excess of first-year commissions over renewal commissions may be amortized over five or ten years.

Claim Fluctuation Reserves

After charging off the incurred claims and formula expense charges, an experience rating plan may require that a part or all of the remaining funds be set aside in a special claim fluctuation reserve. For very small cases, experience surplus set aside in this fashion would serve to give the case greater financial stability and would enable the insurance company to make a lower risk charge thereafter. Also, an insurance company is interested in treating policyholders with similar experience in a similar fashion, and the buildup of such claim fluctuation funds tends to assure similar treatment between the group which has a year of unusually favorable experience followed by a year of very unfavorable experience and the group with the unfavorable year occurring first and the favorable year second. Clearly, the order in which the experience years emerge should not be a major factor in determining the current net cost of the plan to the policyholder.

Package Plans

Frequently employers will carry all of their group insurance coverages, including both life and health insurance, with a single insurance company. Expense savings clearly result and would be reflected in the experience rating expense charges. It is also common practice to apply any experience surplus developed under one coverage first to offset any deficits developed under any other coverage before paying an experience refund or dividend to the policyholder. To the extent that the expected surplus under one coverage is available as a margin for the other coverages in the package, the risk charge or the claim fluctuation reserve, or both, for a particular coverage can be decreased. Thus, the risk charge required for the package plan as a single entity will be somewhat less than the sum of the risk charges that would be required for each of the individual coverages separately.

Discounts

The simplest and most direct experience rating plan would operate with all cases paying the full manual premium for the insurance coverage and with any experience surplus refunded in cash at the end of each policy year. In some cases, however, the experience will be so much more favorable than the average that in practically every year an abnormally large experience refund would be returned to the policyholder. This quite naturally creates pressure from both the employer and broker to lower the advance premium rate for coverage. Thus most group writing companies will apply an advance experience discount to the manual premium in determining the required premium for the very good risks, rather than handling all reductions from manual premium through cash experience refunds.

From the insurance company's standpoint, an experience discount on the manual premium can help to avoid competition from other insurance companies who normally would be willing to write the particular risk at their own manual premium rate. Any discount that applies to the manual premium, however, serves to reduce the margin for claim fluctuation in the subsequent policy years, and this greater risk of loss must be reflected in a greater risk charge made against the plan. Normally the use of experience discounts would be restricted so that the increase in risk of loss is negligible, and no specific additional risk charge is needed. In addition to experience discounts, insurance companies frequently grant discounts from manual premiums to reflect expense savings. Such discounts are referred to as advance expense adjustments. A table of advance expense adjustments is included as a part of the current New York minimum rate basis for group life insurance.[5]

SELECTED REFERENCES

AMMETER, HANS. "A Rational Experience Rating Technique for Group Insurance on the Risk Premium Basis," *Transactions of the Fifteenth International Congress of Actuaries*, Vol. I (1957), pp. 507–17.

FEAY, HERBERT. "Introduction to Nonproportional Reinsurance," *Transactions of the Society of Actuaries*, Vol. XII (1960).

JACKSON, PAUL H. "Experience Rating," *Transactions of the Society of Actuaries*, Vol. V (1953), pp. 239–55.

KAHN, PAUL M. "An Introduction to Collective Risk Theory and Its Application to Stop Loss Reinsurance," *Transactions of the Society of Actuaries*, Vol. XIV (1962).

KEFFER, RALPH. "An Experience Rating Formula," *Transactions of the Actuarial Society of America*, Vol. XXX (1929), p. 130.

WHITNEY, ALBERT W. "The Theory of Experience Rating," *Proceedings of the Casualty Actuarial Society*, Vol. IV (1917–1918), p. 274.

---

[5] See Chapter 11.

PART IV

Group Health Coverages

Chapter 13

TYPES OF HEALTH RISK BEARERS: INSURANCE COMPANIES

BY WILLIAM N. SEERY

Health insurance is written by a wide variety of companies, including stock and mutual life, stock and mutual casualty and monoline health insurance companies. The coverage is offered in the United States by over 900 insurers, of which 588 provide health insurance through group, as well as individual, policies. The latter number reflects an increase of 199 companies during the five-year period commencing with 1959.[1] Some of the reasons for the expansion in the number of insurance companies issuing group health insurance will be explored subsequently.

TYPES OF INSURANCE COMPANIES WRITING GROUP HEALTH COVERAGE

Life Insurance Companies

Of the twenty-five largest writers of group health insurance in 1964, twenty were life insurance companies. Not only do such companies play a tremendous part in the health insurance business, and particularly in the group field, but life insurance itself (individual and group) serves a traditional and highly important function of providing funds to cover the economic loss caused by last illness, as well as death. In the early days of group life insurance, this function was strongly emphasized, and it contributed to the rapid spread of that form of coverage.

While life insurance has not provided hospital and medical benefits as such, many individual life insurance policies and nearly all group life insurance contracts contain disability benefit provisions. Generally, these are limited to waiver of premium in event of total disability, although a number of life insurance policies have provided regular income payments during a part or all of the remaining lifetime of the continuously disabled insured.

---

[1] Health Insurance Institute, *Source Book of Health Insurance Data 1964* (New York, 1964), pp. 54–55.

Life insurance companies, probably without exception, are authorized to write health insurance, since it is a normal complement of the death benefits themselves. An increasing number of life insurance companies exercise their right to sell health insurance. This trend involves a recognition of the fact that without the availability of insurance against temporary loss of income and against medical expenses, the life insurance company and its agents do not have a complete program to offer prospective clients.

Casualty Insurance Companies

Health insurance is a natural line for the casualty company and the casualty agent. The casualty insurance company generally has offered accident insurance with loss of time and medical expense coverage on a broad basis; it needs to have sickness insurance policies available in order to complete the protection packages. As with life companies, the number of casualty insurers offering group health policies has been increasing rapidly.

Monoline Companies

There are, in addition to life and casualty insurance companies, about forty monoline health insurance companies or associations, organized and operated for the purpose of providing health insurance only. The number of concerns in this category has shown a modest increase in recent years but their participation in group health insurance has been limited.

All-Lines Groups of Companies

All-lines groups of companies, *offering life and health insurance together with property and liability insurance,* as well as multiple line insurance,[2] have been on the increase in the last few years. Property and liability insurance companies have felt the necessity of being able to offer life insurance as well as casualty and health insurance. Life insurance companies, for their part, have seen opportunities to expand the size and utility of their field forces through property-liability affiliates which are in a position to offer well-rounded insurance programs. All-lines insurers include several of the leading group insurance companies. All-lines insurers are actually a fleet or group of insurance companies rather than being a single company.

NATURE OF INSURANCE COMPANY GROUP HEALTH COVERAGE

Indemnity Approach

Insurance contracts generally, with the exception of life insurance and certain property insurance policies, are "indemnity contracts"—which are

---

[2] "Multiple line" generally refers to property *and* liability coverages, while all-lines refers to life, health, property and liability coverages.

defined as contracts whereby, for a stipulated compensation, usually called a premium, one party undertakes to indemnify or guarantee another against loss by a certain contingency or peril.[3] In one sense, the usual definition of an indemnity contract fits most health insurance contracts. "However, in a pure sense, health insurance policies providing a benefit for loss of income are not contracts of indemnity,"[4] inasmuch as they generally pay a stipulated amount per week or month during the period of covered disability regardless of the actual loss sustained. "As a practical matter, health insurance companies exercise great care to see that the total benefits promised in all the insurance applicable to the risk do not exceed the value of the insured's time;"[5] the objective of such "great care" is, of course, to bring the protection closer to the pure indemnity approach. It should be noted, however, that "health insurance contracts that provide benefits which reimburse the insured for hospital, medical or other expenses . . . are true contracts of indemnity as to these benefits."[6]

The group health insurance contract is between two parties, the insurer and the group policyholder, for the benefit of others who are insured persons. It fits generally the definition of a contract of insurance and provides for the payment of a benefit to the person insured or his beneficiary based on a covered loss or expense incurred. The premium or consideration may be paid by the group policyholder, by the persons insured, or jointly by the group policyholder and the persons insured. Actually, group health insurance premiums are paid directly or indirectly by the persons insured, and the benefits are payable to or for the benefit of the insured. Benefits are not ordinarily payable where there would be no charge or expense to the insured in the absence of insurance coverage. In the case of medical expense coverage the insurance is not purchased for the sake of the person or institution rendering services to an insured individual, as a result of which services the insured may be indebted, although the purveyors of care generally benefit directly or indirectly by the presence of insurance.

A group health insurance contract may contain provisions under which payment may be made by the insurer to a party or parties providing the hospital or medical services; yet rarely, if ever, does the insurance company have a contract with the person or institution providing the services. Assignments of benefits by persons insured to hospitals or physicians providing services are frequently made, and the benefits as-

---

[3] See Buist M. Anderson (ed.), *Vance on Insurance* (3d ed.; St. Paul, Minn.: West Publishing Co., 1951), chap. 1, sec. 1, for a more detailed description of this concept.

[4] Edwin J. Faulkner, *Health Insurance* (New York: McGraw-Hill Book Co., Inc., 1960), p. 86. Faulkner observes: "Like life insurance, these covers [disability income contracts] are issued for a fixed amount, determined in advance of the loss."

[5] *Ibid.*

[6] *Ibid.*

signed are paid by the insurance company directly to the hospitals or physicians.[7]

Experience Rating

One of the primary aspects of virtually all group insurance, including group health insurance, is "experience rating." Specific features involved in experience rating for group life insurance were discussed in Chapter 12, and similar considerations regarding group health insurance will be discussed in Chapter 22. It is important at this point, however, to recognize both the concept underlying experience rating and the fact that this concept had its origin with insurance companies.[8] Although other types of insuring organizations, such as Blue Cross and Blue Shield plans and group practice prepayment plans, were generally opposed to the use of experience rating in earlier years, an increasing number of these organizations are utilizing experience rating techniques in some form. Thus, experience rating is no longer a unique characteristic of group coverage issued by insurance companies, but it nevertheless remains a vital aspect of insurance companies' contracts.

Lest the true nature of experience rating be confused, it should be observed that all forms of rate making take into account known experience. This includes directly related experience, such as a company's own loss and expense and statistical studies of past experience in connection with the specific benefits under consideration. It also includes published experience of other companies and actuarial studies published by the Society of Actuaries relating to such things as the frequency of disabling illness, the number of claims involving absence from work and the duration of absences for various causes. With regard to the surgical field, the rating process considers the frequency of particular operations. With regard to the hospital field, it concerns itself with the number and duration of confinements for specific causes. In fact, rate making involves experience pertaining to every known situation that may have a bearing on claim costs.

Experience rating, however, is not merely an approach that takes into consideration the broad types of loss experience mentioned above. Rather, experience rating is a technique in which the premium paid by a policyholder is affected by the actual loss and expense experience of the particular group being covered. Thus, experience rating modifies manual (or "class") rates, in which the experience of a given class of risks is used in the rate determination without regard to the experience of a particular

---

[7] See Chapters 16 and 29 for an elaboration of the procedure by which insureds may assign their insurance benefits to the purveyors of care.

[8] Giving reasonable effect to the experience of the individual group in the premiums and dividends applicable to the group was a feature of group life insurance and group disability insurance before other health insurance benefits, such as medical and surgical expense benefits, were incorporated into group health insurance contracts.

policyholder. As a matter of fact, experience rating is sometimes referred to as "individual risk rating" in order that the distinction between this approach and that limited to calculating manual rates might be more obvious.

Although experience rating might be viewed in one sense as a modification of the pooling or averaging concept upon which most forms of insurance are based, in reality experience rating is intended to foster greater equity among policyholders. It is true that if every policyholder—both individual and group—were to have his premium determined solely by his loss and expense experience, there would be no pooling or averaging, and there would be no insurance protection. On the other hand, it should be observed that all lines of insurance are subdivided into classes for rate making purposes. That is, risks with similar (or relatively "homogeneous") loss and expense characteristics are placed in separate classes. Experience rating is merely an extension of this procedure. "The theory underlying individual risk rates is that the number of exposure units of some insureds is large enough to conclude that losses which are (or are not) incurred are not necessarily [or wholly] due to chance but, rather, reflect to some extent the actual character of the risks of the particular policyholders."[9]

Thus, experience rating has the objective of dealing equitably with large policyholders. Such policyholders would generally object if they had to pay premiums based upon the experience of a class with considerably higher losses than their own over a substantial period of time. In this regard, employers, labor unions and trustees of union-management funds are sophisticated buyers and generally well informed as to insurers' practices and costs. It must be observed, however, that unfavorable experience on the part of a policyholder will increase his premiums under the experience rating approach. Customarily, buyers require experience rating for larger risks.

A medium-sized policyholder[10] has a portion of his premium determined by the loss experience of his employees or group, and the remainder is based upon the manual rate in recognition of the fact that the medium-sized policyholder is not sufficiently large to conclude that his loss experience is due solely to the characteristics of his group. Even with groups whose experience is given full credibility in the experience rating formula, some residual risk element is customarily retained by the insurance company through the use of maximum premiums or maximum loss ratios that the policyholder may have to bear. Often, for example,

---

[9] Herbert S. Denenberg, Robert D. Eilers, G. Wright Hoffman, Chester A. Kline, Joseph J. Melone, and H. Wayne Snider, *Risk and Insurance* (Englewood Cliffs, N.J.: Prentice-Hall, Inc., 1964), p. 387.

[10] See Chapter 22 for a discussion of the applicability of experience rating to groups of various sizes.

annual losses in excess of some stated amount or proportion of premiums may not be charged against the particular group, but will be spread over all groups.

The applicability of experience rating to groups of particular sizes varies considerably among insurance companies writing group health insurance, thus attesting to the fact that the actual degree of credibility of a particular group's experience is partially dependent upon judgment. This lack of unanimity among insurers in the rating treatment of some groups, particularly small groups, further testifies to the fact that "equity" in dealing with policyholders depends importantly upon one's view of equity. Indeed, it is on this point that insurance companies disagree with some other insuring organizations. Insurance companies feel that there is greater over-all equity through the use of experience rating designed to provide premiums for individual policyholders commensurate with the risk assumed; some Blue Cross and Blue Shield plans and group practice prepayment plans disagree. More will be said of this theoretical debate in the following chapter in the section dealing with "Community Rating."

National Coverage

Many, if not most, of the insurance companies that write the major part of group health insurance are authorized to issue coverage in the bulk of the states. That is, a group insurance company generally has authority to issue coverage on a policyholder's employees or members even when they are located in many different states. Thus, it is possible for the purchaser of group insurance to deal with one insurance company and at the same time to have uniform benefits for employees located throughout the United States. This aspect of insurance companies' operations has given them some advantage over insuring organizations that are local in operation, such as many group practice prepayment plans, when dealing with groups whose members are located in a number of states.

Premium Taxes

The premium tax has had a long, if not entirely distinguished, career. The device was first introduced over a century ago and, at the outset, was employed against foreign, i.e., out-of-state, companies[11] as a sort of protective tariff at the state level. From this rather humble beginning, the premium tax has grown to the point where today it is of paramount importance to the several states and to the insurance industry.

Premium taxes are essentially "gross" rather than "net" levies; that is, the tax is levied on premiums received without deductions for claims or expenses. This is true even though certain deductions are allowed in

---

[11] Technically, a "foreign" company is one that is domiciled in another state within the United States, while an "alien" company is one that is domiciled in another country.

arriving at taxable receipts in the various states. These deductions include such items as returned premiums and policyholder dividends. Where there is reinsurance, the direct insurer usually pays the premium tax and the reinsurance premium is not included in the premium base for taxation of the reinsurer. A gross premium tax is not a property tax. It is sometimes said to be in the nature of an excise levy,[12] and sometimes in the nature of a franchise tax which the insurer must pay for the privilege of doing business. It is interesting to note that only about 5 per cent of the funds collected through premium taxes are used to operate the insurance departments of the various states, with the remainder becoming a part of the general revenue of the states.

Premium taxes are not taxes to be paid out of profits, and their nature and effect is frequently misunderstood. Perhaps their nature can best be explained by a comparison with sales taxes. The latter are paid by the purchasers, collected by the sellers, and turned over to the government. The premium tax also is the first item to come out of the total price paid by the insurance purchasers, since government tax claims are a priority item against insurance company assets. The premiums, of course, are paid by the purchasers of the insurance, and the direct comparison between premium tax and sales tax is apparent.

The sales tax is paid and collected regardless of whether or not the seller is a nonprofit organization. In most states, however, the premium tax is not paid by some competitors of the insurance companies.

There is considerable variation among the premium tax laws of the several states. The various jurisdictions agree upon one thing, however; they generally tax out-of-state companies at a prevailing rate of 2 or 3 per cent upon premiums for business within their borders. The courts have upheld the right of a state to classify insurance companies and impose upon them different rates of tax, depending upon the type of insurance they write, for example, or where they are incorporated. Preferential rates for domestic companies are used in more than a dozen states,[13] while an additional number impose no premium tax whatever upon companies domiciled within their borders.[14] Health insurance premiums are taxed, with few exceptions, at the same rate as are life insurance premiums.

Combination Coverage

As has been indicated, many insurance companies that write group medical expense coverage and group disability income coverage also issue

---

[12] An excise levy is a tax imposed upon the manufacture, sale or consumption of a product or service.

[13] These states are Alabama, Alaska, Arizona, Colorado, Hawaii, Maine, Mississippi, Nebraska, North Carolina, South Carolina, South Dakota, Tennessee, Texas and Washington.

[14] They are Arkansas, Florida, Illinois, Indiana, Kansas, Kentucky, Michigan, North Dakota, Ohio, Oklahoma, Oregon and Wisconsin.

group life insurance. In addition, a number of these companies issue specialized types of group coverage, such as for dental expense benefits. On the other hand, Blue Cross–Blue Shield and group practice prepayment plans concentrate on benefits that pay for various types of medical expenses.

The fact that an insurance company can offer a combination package of employee benefits has some inherent advantages, one of the more obvious of which is simply that the purchaser of group insurance can deal with one insuring organization rather than several for most, if not all, of the insured employee benefits that are desired. In many instances combination coverage may afford cost savings through lower administrative expenses than would be involved if each major type of group insurance were to be insured with a different insurance company. The insurance companies and other types of insuring organizations that do not offer combination coverage feel that they can offer better and more complete services because they specialize. Regardless of the advantages or disadvantages of combination coverage, a sufficient number of insurance companies write a full line of group insurance to warrant considering combination coverage as a distinct characteristic of insurance companies.

Profit Factor

The basic principle of treating all policyholders equitably, as well as a consideration of the insurance statutes of the various states, suggests that each class of business written by an insurance company should be self-supporting over the long run. This implies, therefore, that the premiums and any investment income received in connection with the group health insurance written by an insurance company should be sufficient over the long run to pay the claims and expenses that arise in connection with this type of business. Moreover, in theory both the group medical expense insurance and the group disability income insurance should be generally self-supporting. This is not to imply that an insurance company entering the group health insurance business must have income from such business that exceeds expenditures in connection therewith during initial years of operation. Few, if any, insurers could ever meet such a standard. Neither is it realistic to suggest that a company once established in the group health business should never have a year in which claims and expenses exceed premiums and miscellaneous income. What is to be expected, however, is that each type of group health insurance will be self-supporting over a period of years and that such business will also contribute to the surplus of the insurance company, i.e., a profit will be realized from the business, regardless of whether it is a stock or a mutual insurance company. It is this surplus that contributes to a company's over-all financial stability and allows it to expand its business to additional insureds, broaden the coverages it offers and experiment generally with benefit structures in attempts to meet more adequately the needs of the public. (Major medical and long-term disability coverages are examples of somewhat recent experimentations in benefits.) Finally, it is to be expected that a stock insurance company will be able to pay a reasonable rate of return to the stockholders who provide the capital funds for the company, and that an appropriate portion of this stockholder dividend generally will be provided through the group health insurance business.

While both stock and mutual insurance companies have the aim of making a contribution to their surpluses through the operation of their group health business, such contributions have been difficult to obtain. In each year since 1957, approximately twelve of the twenty-five largest group health insurers have experienced underwriting losses on this business.[15]

Whether health insurance takes the form of temporary loss of time benefits, permanent total disability benefits or hospital and medical expense benefits, underwriting problems have been found difficult because of the impact of changing economic conditions, rising price levels and subjective factors such as morals and morale. Also in the picture are changing patterns in the use of hospitals, expanding medical knowledge and improvements in facilities and care.

COMPETITION AMONG GROUP HEALTH INSURANCE COMPANIES

In the group health insurance field, mutual companies—which are organized for the benefit of policyholders and must consider equity among classes of policyholders—and stock companies—which must have the interests of stockholders, as well as policyholders, continually in mind—compete directly on a cost basis. In addition, both types of companies compete with Blue Cross and Blue Shield plans and group practice prepayment plans in the area of medical expense coverage. The underwriting difficulties suggested in the preceding section increase the complexities of the competitive situation for all.

Competitive pressures work in a number of different directions. Large employers frequently have their own ideas as to the exact benefits to be incorporated in the group health insurance contract covering their employees. On the other hand, unions may have quite different views as to the benefits they would like for their members. Then, too, trustees of union-management funds are often charged with making decisions regarding the detailed benefits to be provided beneficiaries of the funds, and such trustees work out ideas which they would like to have incorporated in group policies purchased by them. The situation is often made more complex and more flexible by consultants and brokers, who sell their

---

[15] "Experience of the 25 Leaders in Group Health Insurance," *The Health Insurance Review* (August, 1964), p. 2.

services and their suggestions to prospective group policyholders. While the programs of an insurer may be subject to less variation for smaller groups, competition encourages as many permissible variations as an insurance company can administer with reasonable economy and efficiency.

Competition is magnified by the fact that each insurer drafts its own policy forms and develops its own premium rates, even though making use of Society of Actuaries' studies based on information furnished by a number of insurers. Rating organizations and joint determination of rates have not existed in the health insurance area which in this respect differs markedly from the property and liability insurance fields. Yet, it should be recognized that in the group health insurance field, policies and policy provisions are not always prepared by the insurance company alone. Officials and attorneys of group policyholders frequently take a significant part in the development and wording of the policy forms.

An insurer must make immediate decisions when employers and unions are engaged in collective bargaining, and these decisions often involve the willingness or capacity of the insurer to make and live up to agreements for a specified type of administration. Questions as to the appropriate rate for a new benefit, or for a new variation of a benefit, or for a new combination of benefits designed specifically for the particular group to be insured, may also be involved. Thus, the urgency of making decisions with far reaching financial consequences is, in itself, a type of competition.

In spite of the intensely competitive nature of the group health insurance business, 199 additional insurance companies commenced writing this type of coverage between 1959 and 1964. The reason many companies entered the field is simply to be able to offer a complete package of insured employee benefits. The lack of such a package could result in loss of group life insurance coverage to competitors, for example.

REGULATION OF GROUP HEALTH INSURANCE[16]

Rationale of Regulation

For more than a century the conduct of the insurance business has been closely regulated by the several states. The basic function of this regulation is the fair treatment of the insured public. Among the fundamental reasons that underlie the regulation of insurance is the fact that the insurer's promise to pay claims often is to be performed in the distant future. The insurer's capacity to fulfill its obligation when performance falls due was recognized early as a matter of vital public interest and concern.

---

[16] See Chapter 6 for a detailed discussion of the "Legal Environment of Group Insurance."

Moreover, the need for regulation is increased by the fact that insurance policies—including those for group health insurance—are technical in nature, and the purchasers of insurance may not be fully aware of what they are buying. Yet, the insurance contract must be specific in defining the risk that the insurer is willing to cover at the price charged. Every effort is made to describe the benefits, conditions and restrictions in language that can be readily understood by all parties concerned. The health insurance policy of today is necessarily so complex and deals with so many situations that an occasional misunderstanding arises from those unaccustomed to the use of accurate, but technical, language.

Regulation is also encouraged by the sheer number of persons whose lives and financial positions may be influenced to an important extent by their group insurance protection. Over three fourths of the population of the United States have health benefit coverage, and the majority of these have group protection. Thus, society as a whole, as well as individuals in particular, has a major interest in the operation of the group health insurance business.

Nature of Regulation of Group Health Insurance

General Supervision.   The group health insurance business of an insurance company is subject to the supervision of the state insurance department in each jurisdiction in which it operates. The only major exception to this rule is that of insurance purchased through the mails, in which case it is difficult for a state other than that where the insurer is domiciled to supervise the company effectively. Group health insurance is not sold to any extent through the mails, however, so mail-order business is not a regulatory problem in this type of coverage.

Financial Responsibility.   The fact that insurers will be called upon to make good their promises at future dates has led to elaborate requirements with respect to such aspects as capital and surplus requirements that a new insurance company must meet and the maintenance of detailed records. Then, too, information concerning the group health insurance operations must be submitted annually to the state insurance departments on forms known as "Convention Blanks." A copy of the appropriate sections of the Convention Blank is contained in Appendix 5. Generally, insurance companies' operations—including their group health insurance business—are examined every three years by a team of examiners from the insurance departments of several states in accordance with the Zone System for examinations established by the National Association of Insurance Commissioners.[17]

Group health insurance rates are an important determinant of an

---

[17] Under the Zone System, members of specific state insurance departments are designated as representatives of all states within a zone in order to minimize the number of examinations each insurance company must undergo.

insurance company's financial responsibility, but, as was noted in Chapter 11, there is little regulation of group insurance rates other than for group life insurance rates in the first year of coverage. Some states, however, require the filing of group health insurance rates.[18] New York Insurance Law[19] authorizes the Superintendent of Insurance, after taking appropriate steps, to establish minimum rates for group health benefits, but the practicability of implementing this Section of New York's Insurance Code has been questioned. Also at the time the Section was incorporated into the statutes the group health benefits provided by insurance companies were simple in comparison with those provided today. For instance, major medical coverage was yet to come, and it is now unlikely that the law could be implemented effectively with the complex benefit structures that are being included currently in group health insurance contracts.

The general lack of rate regulation in group health insurance is undoubtedly attributable to such factors as the intense competition in the group insurance business and the sophistication and knowledge of group insurance purchasers. These factors give considerable assurance that rates will not be excessive. Moreover, the concern about rate adequacy apparently has not been sufficient to foster rate supervision.

Finally, financial responsibility of insurance companies depends significantly upon the adequacy of reserves. The reserves of insurance companies are their primary liabilities, and if such liabilities are not valued properly there is a possibility that the company will incur financial difficulties. Although there is extensive regulation of reserves in connection with individual life insurance contracts and certain types of individual health insurance contracts, there is little regulation of group health insurance reserves. Of course, an insurance company must meet the general requirements with respect to reserves, and the adequacy of group health insurance reserves is tested in the periodic examinations of the companies. The reason for the lack of other supervision is somewhat analagous to the reason there is little rate regulation in connection with group health insurance. In addition, group health insurance contracts are normally noncancelable though in some cases the insurance company has reserved the right to cancel the arrangement if it wishes. As a consequence of the insurance company having the power to increase the rates or in some cases to terminate the contract, the financial stability of the insurance company cannot be imperiled to the same extent that would be possible if premium rates were guaranteed indefinitely.

---

[18] The following jurisdictions require the filing of health insurance rates for group policies generally: Alabama, Colorado, Connecticut, Florida, Indiana, Louisiana, Maine, Maryland, Michigan, Minnesota, Nebraska, New Mexico, New York, North Carolina, North Dakota, Ohio, Oklahoma, Oregon, Vermont, Washington, Wisconsin and Puerto Rico.

[19] Sec. 221.8.

Filing and Approval of Policy Forms. All states require the filing and approval of individual health insurance forms and the filing of rates for such insurance. Many also require the filing or approval of group health insurance forms.

The most extensive regulation exists in New York where Section 221.7 of the Insurance Law requires that each company's classification of risks and premium rates be filed with the Superintendent. These are reviewed by him under authority of Section 154, which provides that the Superintendent may disapprove any policy form dealing with health insurance if he finds that the benefits provided therein are unreasonable in relation to the premium charged, or if the form contains provisions which encourage misrepresentation or are unjust, unfair, inequitable, misleading, deceptive, or contrary to law or to the public policy of the state.

Critique of Group Health Insurance Regulation

Due in large part to the complexity of health insurance coverage, complaints to state insurance departments have been relatively numerous in this field. However, a relatively small proportion of these complaints has been in connection with group health insurance. This is explained in part because group policyholders (employers, labor unions, etc.) are more knowledgeable about their coverage than are individual policyholders. Where complaints have been justified, the state insurance departments have provided a ready and inexpensive instrument through which to resolve difficulties between policyholders or insured persons and their insurance company. This has been a particularly valuable function of state regulation.

In general, the intelligent forebearance by the various states with respect to the enactment of restrictive legislation, such as that defining the types of groups which may be covered, has provided a favorable regulatory climate for the development of group health insurance. The deterrent to the expansion of group health insurance coverage and benefits is to be found in underwriting difficulties, rather than in undue statutory or regulatory restraints.

THE PERFORMANCE OF GROUP HEALTH INSURANCE FUNCTIONS WITHIN AN INSURANCE COMPANY

Certain basic functions are necessary for satisfactory performance by any company in the group health insurance area, including actuarial, underwriting, accounting, marketing and claims. The location of these functions within a company depends, of course, both on the objectives of the company with regard to group health insurance and upon the size of the group health insurance operation. Some insurers are primarily group insurance companies with a substantial part of their business represented by group life and health insurance. Others aggressively try to sell group insurance and grow in the group area but do not desire group insurance as their predominant type of business; still others maintain group health insurance as an accommodation line. Thus, the size and objectives of a company determine whether some or all of the functions are handled by a separate group insurance department.

With the individual company, particularly one starting in the group health insurance business, there may be little choice. It may not be practical to set up a separate group division. On the other hand, with the large group underwriters, a separate group division may be a practical necessity. The question of how far a particular company should go in that direction, for example, whether it should have a separate group law division, group claims division, group actuarial division or group sales division, will be influenced by its particular organizational arrangement and the capacities of the personnel that may be available for the various functions.

SELECTED REFERENCES

AMERICAN LIFE CONVENTION—LIFE INSURANCE ASSOCIATION OF AMERICA. Premium Tax Manual Part I "Explanatory Remarks."

ANDERSON, BUIST M. (ed.). Vance on Insurance, "Statutory Regulation of Insurance Business," chap. 1, p. 36; "Taxation of Insurance," chap. 1, p. 75; "What Is a Contract of Insurance," chap. 2, p. 82. 3d ed. St. Paul, Minn.: West Publishing Co., 1951.

ANDERSON, RONALD A. Couch Cyclopedia of Insurance Law, "Regulation and Taxation of Insurers—Antitrust Legislation," chap. 21. 2d ed. Rochester, N.Y.: Lawyers Cooperative Publishing Co., 1959.

ANGELL, FRANK JOSEPH. Health Insurance, "Group Insurance Principles," chap. 18. New York: Ronald Press Co., 1963.

BLANCHARD, RALPH H. (ed.). Insurance—Its Theory and Practice in the United States, "Theory and Development of Governmental Supervision," chap. 30. 5th ed. New York: McGraw-Hill Book Co., Inc., 1961.

BLOYS, JOHN V. "Premium Taxation of Life Insurance," Journal of the American Society of Chartered Life Underwriters, June, 1950.

COMMERCE CLEARING HOUSE. State Tax Guide. 2d ed. Par. 88–100 "Insurance Gross Premiums Taxes."

DINEEN, ROBERT E.; PROCTER, CLIFFORD R.; AND GARDNER, H. DANIEL. Economics and Principles of Insurance Supervision, Symposium on Insurance and Government—School of Commerce, University of Wisconsin. Reprinted by Northwestern Mutual Life Insurance Company, Milwaukee, Wisconsin, 1960.

DIRIAM, JOEL B., AND STELZER, IRWIN M. "The Insurance Industry: A Case Study in the Workability of Regulated Competition," Insurance Counsel Journal, Vol. XXVI, No. 2 (April, 1959), pp. 208–17.

FAULKNER, EDWIN J. Health Insurance, "Regulation, Taxation and Investments," chap. 15. New York: McGraw-Hill Book Co., Inc., 1960.

FOLLMANN, J. F., JR. "Indemnity vs. Service Benefits," *Best's Insurance News —Life Edition* (June, 1962), pp. 53–55, 88–90.

GREENE, MARK R. *Risk and Insurance*, "Functions and Organization of Insurers," chap. vii; "Government Regulation of Insurance," chap. xxv. Cincinnati, Ohio: South-Western Publishing Co., 1962.

GREGG, DAVIS W. (ed.). *Life and Health Insurance Handbook*, chap. 71. 2d ed. Homewood, Ill.: Richard D. Irwin, Inc., 1964.

Insurance Law and Practice, Appleman, chap. 361, s. 10581 et seq. "State Taxes Upon Franchise or Revenue of Insurer."

LIFE INSURANCE ASSOCIATION OF AMERICA. Memorandum of November 2, 1962, "Preferential Tax Treatment for Domestic Insurance Companies in Relation to Out-of-State Insurance Companies."

PARKER, HON. T. NELSON. "Government, Insurance and the Practicing Attorney," Address before American Bar Association, San Francisco, Calif., August 6, 1962.

Chapter 14

TYPES OF HEALTH RISK BEARERS: BLUE CROSS AND BLUE SHIELD PLANS

BY THOMAS B. FITZPATRICK

Blue Cross and Blue Shield are the companion names of the pioneering prepayment plans in the health care field. Blue Cross plans have been organized for the prepayment of the expenses of hospital care, and Blue Shield plans have been organized for the prepayment of the expenses of physicians' care.

In the opinion of some observers, these plans are not insurance organizations. They are intimately associated with, and oriented toward, the health care system of the country. Their basic business is not dollars, nor financial loss, but rather the delivery of health services. Regardless of semantic differences concerning the relationship between Blue Cross–Blue Shield and insurance, an understanding of Blue Cross and Blue Shield is essential to persons studying the field of health insurance.

There are presently[1] seventy-seven Blue Cross plans operating in the United States and Puerto Rico (as well as four in Canada and one in Jamaica). Almost all are nonprofit,[2] voluntary organizations, authorized to operate under the name and emblem of Blue Cross by the American Hospital Association, which certifies the plans as having met certain minimum standards.

Most Blue Cross plans (in all but eleven states) operate under enabling legislation specifically enacted to cover nonprofit prepayment plans. The plans are regulated to some extent in forty-four states—in forty-one of these by the insurance department.[3]

Most of the plans are state-wide in operation, and two embrace more

---

[1] As of 1965.

[2] The few exceptions exist because of state laws. Even these, however, operate not-for-profit.

[3] See R. D. Eilers, *Regulation of Blue Cross and Blue Shield Plans* (Homewood, Ill.: Richard D. Irwin, Inc., 1963), for a detailed discussion of the development and distinguishing features of the plans as well as their regulatory status.

than one state or parts of states; in a number of cases, there are two or more plans in a given state. For example, New York has eight; Pennsylvania, five; Ohio, six; California, two. These variations reflect the actual history of the plans' development and also, to some extent, their community-sponsored nature. The existence of the various local and regional plans has enabled them to take into account area hospital costs and practices as well as other features of popular appeal, such as some benefit structure characteristics. Nationally, the combined Blue Cross plans have enrolled 32 per cent of the population of the United States (at latest report,[4] more than fifty-nine million people in the United States). About 78 per cent of this is group membership, the balance being individual and family nongroup members. Individual plans vary considerably in their enrollment—from a low of 10 per cent or less of the population in some plans in southern and western states to 60 per cent or more of the population in Delaware; New York City; Rochester, New York; Cincinnati, Ohio; Allentown, Pennsylvania; and Rhode Island. This variation also exists within states and within plans. These variations reflect, to some extent, population and industrial concentrations and result from the early efforts of Blue Cross with regard to enrollment of groups.

The seventy-two Blue Shield plans in the United States have an enrollment of over forty-nine million, of whom approximately 80 per cent are under group contracts.[5] These plans are nonprofit organizations, sponsored by state or local medical associations, and authorized to use the Blue Shield name and emblem by their own National Association of Blue Shield Plans, which certifies that the plans meet minimum standards set and maintained by the Association.

As with Blue Cross, Blue Shield plans have local autonomy and are established, for the most part (thirty-five states), under special legislation. In nine states, however, the statutes for nonprofit corporations govern them, and in two states, the regular insurance statutes apply.[6]

OBJECTIVES OF THE PLANS

Blue Cross

"Health" and "hospital support" might define generally the basic objectives of Blue Cross plans. These objectives are served by an intermediate objective, the removal of financial barriers to adequate health care for the maximum feasible proportion of the population within the voluntary

---

[4] Blue Cross Association and National Association of Blue Shield Plans, *Blue Cross and Blue Shield Fact Book—1964* (Chicago: The Associations, 1964), p. 7. There are about four million additional members in Canada.

[5] As of the end of 1964. The five plans in Canada and one in Jamaica have a total enrollment of over four million.

[6] Eilers, *op. cit.*, p. 104.

system. Achievement of this objective makes hospital care available and guarantees hospital support at one and the same time.

Most immediately relevant to the objectives stated are the enrollment objectives of the plans, which Professor Robert D. Eilers characterizes as the "one vital and all-important characteristic of Blue Cross and Blue Shield which sets these organizations definitely apart from most insurance companies."[7] As Eilers puts it, these objectives require the plans to attempt to provide protection "to those for whom coverage is not available at reasonable rates." This, of course, applies with special force to individuals and groups who are substandard from the risk standpoint, as well as in terms of income and other possible measures.

When Blue Cross plans were organized, coverage was available to almost no one in the nation, at reasonable or unreasonable rates.[8] The primary emphasis of the plans from the beginning has been group enrollment, but, also, all plans offer group conversion privileges to the laid-off, retired, unemployed and other individuals and families who have been compelled to cancel group membership. Most plans have offered this right from the beginning.

The enrollment objective can be stated as follows: to enroll as many groups as possible (in the interests of efficiency, economy and low rates), including the favorable risk groups as a matter of course, but including also, to the fullest extent possible, the disadvantaged, low-income and/or high loss ratio groups; to guarantee continued protection to those who leave groups; and finally, to extend this individual and family protection to those not associated with groups.[9]

In discussing the objectives of Blue Cross, it is important to remember that, during the passage of time, objectives, emphases and priorities can change. It is reasonable to conclude that concern for hospital support gave a powerful impetus to the formation and early enrollment success of Blue Cross. At that time, although many hospitals had empty beds and others were full, largely with nonpaying patients, the hospital system in the whole country was seriously underbuilt in terms of population needs. Thanks to private initiative and philanthropy, buttressed by local, state and federal governments (chiefly through the Hill-Burton Act), the bed supply picture has changed radically. Also, as a greater proportion of the

---

[7] R. D. Eilers, "The Fundamental Nature of Blue Cross and Blue Shield," *Journal of Insurance,* Vol. XXIX (September, 1962), pp. 400–401.

[8] W. J. McNerney *et al., Hospital and Medical Economics* (Chicago: Hospital Research and Educational Trust, American Hospital Association, 1962). See especially chaps. i–vi for historical perspective on the plans and a discussion of the current setting of prepayment problems and issues.

[9] In the United States, at the end of 1964, approximately 22 per cent of all Blue Cross members were in the nongroup category. This fact, together with the high proportion of members over age 65 (about the same as in the general population—9 per cent), has important consequences for Blue Cross policies and operations, as will be seen.

population enrolled, as insurance companies began to compete importantly with Blue Cross, and as the uncovered population shrank, the problems changed. For one thing, hospital support became substantially assured. For another, attention has shifted to the quality of hospital care, the impact of overbuilding on utilization, the significance of hospital cost control, hospital planning and a host of related issues.

"Hospital support," then, has become qualified considerably as an objective. Support of needed hospital facilities, rendering a good quality of service and in the presence of cost and utilization controls, is a better statement of the current objective. Another change has occurred in that the emphasis is being placed more strongly on the objective of extending protection to more of the population and especially to more of its disadvantaged members.

Blue Shield

The history of physician sponsored prepayment plans is different from the history of Blue Cross plans. Blue Shield plans developed later and were somewhat slower in building membership. However, in most cases they were quickly allied to Blue Cross plans in enrollment efforts, and Blue Cross plans often have served as the administrative agents of Blue Shield. In a number of cases, Blue Cross and Blue Shield organizations are operated by the same board and the same staff. In some others, the two organizations share the top executive officer.

Although different emphases may have prevailed at various times, removing financial barriers to adequate health care for the public while safeguarding the professional and financial interests of the physician within the voluntary system remains an appropriate general statement of Blue Shield objectives.

In the early days of Blue Shield, during the same general era as that of Blue Cross, the ability of the population as a whole to pay for physicians' services was limited severely. This was especially true for the unanticipated and large expense of catastrophic illness, including hospitalized illness. Again, insofar as Blue Shield has been successful, the picture has changed considerably. Blue Shield still has the problem, however, of making medical care available without financial barriers to as large a proportion of the population as possible within the voluntary system. Inasmuch as its coverage is offered to the same groups and individuals as is Blue Cross and the enrollment efforts of the two kinds of plans are usually combined or synchronized, the same considerations apply to the enrollment objectives of Blue Shield as Blue Cross. Blue Shield, too, must be concerned about low risk and high risk groups, group conversions and individual and family subscribers. As shall be seen, however, the differing conditions of financing hospitalization and physicians' expenses present special sets of practical problems.

BLUE CROSS OPERATIONS

Principles and Operational Aspects of Blue Cross

Nonprofit and Tax Status. Most Blue Cross plans are incorporated as not-for-profit organizations under special legislation; where state law requires them to register as insurance companies they are still operated not-for-profit.[10] This is an essential part of achieving community sponsorship and is also a necessary element in keeping rates as low as possible.

Blue Cross has been characterized by extremely low administrative expense. The plans have been conservative in such things as managerial compensation, advertising expenditures, research and development expenditures, marketing and market research activities and other activities. Probably they have been too conservative in these areas, to their own competitive detriment. However, the plans have been oriented strongly to a sense of trusteeship with regard to subscribers' funds and in terms of low rates for high risks.

In view of their nonprofit status and their enrollment objectives, Blue Cross plans have been accorded tax-free status by most states. This status has a dual value in emphasizing the community orientation of the plans and in further removing an element of expense from the ultimate rate for coverage. The exemption from taxation means, in effect, that the whole community bears a small share of the cost of health coverage of the Blue Cross members in return for the greater availability of coverage organized by Blue Cross for substandard groups and individuals.[11]

Marketing Methods. Most Blue Cross plans use a salaried enrollment force and follow a general policy of no commissions. Some plans have incentive payments for enrollment men, but this is usually tied to group effort or to merit in some way, not to the securing of specific accounts. This policy accounts for a considerable portion of the differences between Blue Cross and insurance company retention rates.

The problem of motivating enrollment representatives in the face of the very stiff competition in today's health coverage market and the problem of attracting and retaining the best personnel should lead to consideration of some form of incentive payment where this will help solve the problem. However, this would not have much effect on the nongroup enrollment since individuals and families are not usually solicited directly by Blue Cross representatives. Only about ten of the seventy-seven plans use individual solicitation. The nongroup subscribers typically are solicited through their groups at the time of leaving, in open enrollment campaigns and, to some extent, through advertising and continuous enrollment. The

---

[10] Indiana, Louisiana, Nebraska and Nevada.

[11] The tax status of plans in various states—which is by no means uniform—is reviewed in Eilers, *Regulation of Blue Cross and Blue Shield Plans,* chap. 13.

complete absence of individual contact canvassing in the majority of plans means a far smaller enrollment force than would otherwise be required—a fact that compounds the savings involved in the no-commission policy.

Service Benefits. In keeping with their general approach of offering subscribers an opportunity to prepay the bill for future hospital care, Blue Cross plans have, in the main, offered service benefits. That is to say, they have offered a certain number of *days* of a given type of hospital care, with all the hospital services entailed, rather than a dollar indemnity for each day of care received.

A service benefit implies that regardless of how the cost or price of the service varies during the term of the contract, the service will still be provided with no additional charge. Of course, this arrangement makes the plans' liability vary somewhat unpredictably, but the hospital's and the subscriber's security is increased considerably as a result.

Service benefits involve a prior commitment of hospitals to provide the services. In the early days of Blue Cross, this commitment had real value in promoting enrollment since there was some doubt about the financial success of the plans. The subscriber was, in effect, guaranteed hospital service independently of hospital reimbursement. This is still technically true in some Blue Cross hospital contracts; but it is obvious that, when Blue Cross accounts for a high proportion of a hospital's income, some extraordinary steps would have to be taken should a plan fail to meet its hospital commitments.

The concept of service benefits serves to stress the involvement of Blue Cross with needed health care rather than with indemnification of loss. In certain cases, this may seem like a minor distinction—as, for example, when the benefit structure is adequate and the indemnification high in a given insurance company policy. However, the intention of the Blue Cross plan is to enable more people to have adequate care; the intention of the insurance company is to reimburse an individual for a loss incurred in receiving care which, theoretically, he would have received anyhow. This apparently small divergence in intention often becomes a very wide divergence in practice, as will be mentioned later.

A few Blue Cross plans have followed a locally preferred indemnity pattern without loss of Blue Cross identity or motivation. This is possible because of a high percentage of payment of subscribers' hospital bills through comprehensive benefit structures. The American Hospital Association requires that a plan using the Blue Cross name and emblem cover no less than 75 per cent of the hospital bill for the usual services received under its most widely held coverage. Most plans exceed this requirement considerably—90 to 98 per cent of the hospital bill is a common average for the usual services (charges for blood are generally not covered, nor are charges for certain personal services, such as telephones and television sets). Because of these facts, there is a tendency to confuse "service benefits" with "first-dollar coverage;" both concepts are clung to by many Blue Cross people with equal fervor, but they actually are different, as will be seen.

Comprehensive Benefit Structure. The fact that Blue Cross hospitalization coverage is designed to provide as closely as possible for full payment of the hospital bill for most cases of hospitalization has meant coverage for all expenses incurred in a hospital for in-patient care for a specified number of days. Early formulas often provided twenty-one days of full coverage in a semiprivate room plus ninety days of half coverage; the half-coverage concept has tended to disappear while the full days of coverage have been lengthened—typically to thirty, seventy, ninety, 120 or 365 days. In addition to the daily service charge (for room, board and general nursing care), most ancillary services, such as operating room, delivery room, X-ray, laboratory, drugs and medical and surgical supplies have been covered in full.

In many plans, readmission to the hospital within ninety days has been charged to the same benefit period—that is, if ten days were used in the first admission on a seventy-day contract, only sixty days of eligibility would be left. Ninety days after the last discharge, full eligibility generally is restored. Some plans use the calendar or contract year as the benefit period.

Limits sometimes are placed on maternity benefits. Basically, the effort is always to have the most common form of contract as comprehensive and as free from restrictions, exclusions and underwriting as possible. Personal luxuries, such as telephones, are not covered and blood is excluded, while administration of blood is generally covered.[12]

Attempts to make hospital in-patient coverage more comprehensive generally have taken the form of extending the number of days of eligibility or of lifting previous restrictions on some categories of illness— chiefly tuberculosis and psychiatric conditions. Hospital out-patient benefits have been added in many contracts—chiefly accident treatment, but also out-patient diagnostic examinations and minor surgical procedures. Increasingly, plans are experimenting with or increasing the scope of other forms of coverage for care in lieu of in-patient care, e.g., home care, visiting nurse care and nursing home care.

Another aspect of comprehensiveness is the proportion of the bill covered. In line with their desire to provide "first-dollar coverage"—really total coverage—Blue Cross plans have generally been reluctant to resort to deductibles or percentage participation requirements. W. J. McNerney, President of the Blue Cross Association, characterizes the opposition to

---

[12] This is in keeping with the feeling of the American Red Cross, community blood banks and hospital blood banks that, unless blood is replaced with blood, rather than money, the total supply of blood to the community will shrink.

these provisions as resulting from the fact that small deductibles do not depress utilization, while large deductibles bar some people from receiving adequate care.[13] The saving from the lower premiums on deductible and percentage participation contracts is also felt to be largely illusory. The premium dollar and the benefit dollar must in some way balance, regardless of the point at which benefit payments begin. Thus, those who oppose deductible and percentage participation requirements feel that premium savings for some individuals will be at the expense of greater financial outlays for sick people and greater losses for hospitals.[14]

Nevertheless, in response to various pressures, many Blue Cross plans do offer contracts with deductible or percentage participation features. These have not sold well, nor has Blue Cross attempted to encourage their use. Approximately 89 per cent of all Blue Cross contracts do not have these features.[15]

Blue Cross plans traditionally have taken the paths of adding benefits to the basic contract, or offering extended benefits in riders, endorsements or special contracts. Blue Cross plans are not happy with the major medical approach. For one thing, it is based generally on both the deductible and percentage participation approach. For another, it is felt to redistribute dollars away from the basic need of covering adequately the *average* costs of all hospitalization.

Blue Cross and Blue Shield plans in many cases jointly offer major medical coverage, again, in order to provide flexibility, trying to acquiesce to the desires of particular accounts and meet competitive pressures. When major medical coverage is offered, the holding of the basic Blue Cross contract is essential to eligibility for the major medical coverage. As might be expected, benefit structures vary considerably among the many plans.[16]

Relations with Hospitals. Hospital financing is a basic consideration for Blue Cross, since the plans were organized by or in cooperation with

---

[13] W. J. McNerney, *The Past and Future of Blue Cross* (Chicago: The Blue Cross Association, 1962), p. 8. W. J. McNerney, "A New Era of Hospital Financing," Eighth D. Spencer Berger Lecture, New Haven, Connecticut, Yale-New Haven Medical Center, 1963. Also published in modified form in *The Modern Hospital*, Vol. CI, No. 3 (September, 1963), pp. 140–47.

[14] As W. H. Ford points out, contributing employers can lose in two additional ways (increased contributions to voluntary hospitals and increased taxes), while the contribution saved is probably disbursed in another portion of the labor contract. W. H. Ford, "A Look at the Logic of Hospital Care Financing," a paper published by Blue Cross of Western Pennsylvania, Pittsburgh, Pennsylvania, 1963.

[15] See W. J. McNerney, "Hospitals—the Need for Coordinated Action," address at the Annual Meeting of the American Hospital Association, Chicago, August 25, 1964.

[16] For a good summary of Blue Cross benefits, see chap. 15 of Herman M. Somers and Anne R. Somers, *Doctors, Patients and Health Insurance* (Washington, D.C.: The Brookings Institution, 1961).

hospitals. As has been noted, the American Hospital Association sets the standards for Blue Cross plans and controls the use of the Blue Cross name and emblem. Hospitals are represented on Blue Cross boards, often furnishing the majority representation. In short, hospitals consider Blue Cross to be their plan. In most plan areas Blue Cross is the major single source of hospital income, sometimes accounting for half or more of a hospital's total income from patients. Consequently, Blue Cross has developed unique relations with hospitals. These relations are beneficial to subscribers and plans alike and are a source of competitive strength for Blue Cross. Some of the more prominent features of Blue Cross arrangements with hospitals include the following.

A. *Subscriber Identification.*   The Blue Cross identification card means a great deal to hospital admitting and business offices because they usually see it more often than any other single identification. It is a signal to commence a series of well-known routines with which the hospital employee is familiar. The identification card is also recognized by the patient as an aid in obtaining admittance to a hospital.

B. *Eligibility Acceptance.*   Many plans immediately notify the hospital of a subscriber's eligibility, including the balance of benefits when some have been used, by telephone or within a day on some routine clearance basis. This gives the hospital an opportunity to investigate the patient's credit, seek other sources of guarantee of payment, or begin negotiations for a plan of payment with the patient if any of these are necessary.

C. *Claims Procedure and Payment.*   Blue Cross plans usually make every effort to simplify the claims procedure and to expedite payment of claims. The need to protect themselves against fraud and abuse requires detailed information from the hospitals, but this is, again, a uniform procedure applying in many instances to a large number of patients. Claims are filed by the hospital, and payments by a plan are made directly to the hospital. In addition to circumventing nonpayment or delayed payment on the part of some patients, this system results frequently in bulk payments by the plans (e.g., weekly or five times a month) to hospitals.

D. *Reimbursement Mechanisms.*   Blue Cross plans have traditionally used three different bases for paying hospitals. These are on the bases of billings, flat rates and reimbursable cost. In each case, the method of arriving at the figure to be paid and the presence or absence of cost controls are of paramount importance.

The payment of a flat, identical rate for each day of care to hospitals in a particular area has been the least used method and does not have a great deal to recommend it, either to hospitals or to Blue Cross.

Billings are the usual method of charging individuals or other third parties, and many Blue Cross plans pay the amount billed at the hospital's usual rates or a percentage of the amount billed. In these cases, the relation of rates to costs and the hospital's method of setting rates is extremely important. It is at the point of setting rates that plans exercise varying degrees of control, although in some cases a plan hardly enters into this picture at all but simply pays what is billed.

The most common arrangement is for Blue Cross to pay, according to a reimbursable cost formula, a stipulated per diem amount based on actual costs of the hospital. These are usually lower than billings. Because of the wide variation in the rate setting practices of hospitals, the average reimbursement by formula might vary from exact charges down to 80 per cent of average charges. As Table 14–1 indicates, only 11 per cent of the plans paid on a cost basis in 1946, while 68 per cent of the plans paid this way in 1963.

TABLE 14–1

DISTRIBUTION OF BLUE CROSS PLANS BY REIMBURSEMENT METHOD

	Per Cent of Plans, by Year			
Reimbursement Method	1946	1950	1957	1963
Cost-based............................11		28	48	68
Full charges or per cent of charges.......45		40	35	30
Other................................44		32	17	2 (one plan)

SOURCE: American Hospital Association, *Report of the Task Force on Principles of Payment for Hospital Care* (Chicago, 1963).

The plans paying on a cost basis have a higher proportion of the total Blue Cross membership than do plans paying by other methods. Table 14–2 indicates that 77 per cent of the membership is covered by plans using cost-reimbursement methods.

TABLE 14–2

BLUE CROSS ENROLLMENT AS OF 1962, BY REIMBURSEMENT METHOD

Reimbursement Method	Per Cent of Total Blue Cross Enrollment
Cost-based..77	
Charges-based:	
100% of charges................................18	
99% or less of charges........................... 5	
Other (negotiated rate).............................— (less than 1%)	

SOURCE: American Hospital Association, *Report of the Task Force on Principles of Payment for Hospital Care* (Chicago, 1963).

Hospitals and Blue Cross plans make cost-reimbursement arrangements for their mutual benefit as well as that of the subscriber and patient. The hospital, in effect, furnishes care at cost to a very large, bulk purchaser of care, who provides a continuing and stable income. Other considerations which have motivated cost-based reimbursement include the substantial amount of free care and bad debts which a large Blue Cross enrollment eliminates; the greater enrollment resulting from the larger benefits and lower Blue Cross rates that are made possible; and the savings made possible by the simplified arrangements for obtaining payment.

On the other hand, the payment of full cost for a large group of patients on a guaranteed in advance basis, particularly in a long period of continuously rising costs, can amount to underwriting the hospital's budget by a certain proportion regardless of what the hospital does. The hospital administrator who is sophisticated in his orientation to financing sees this readily and does not regard the cost-reimbursement arrangement as a discount. Consequently, cost controls become conspicuously necessary, although in reality they are just as important where billings are the basis of reimbursement.

Whatever the method of reimbursement, it is specified in a contract negotiated between the plan and the hospital. This contract is an important document and often is subject to approval by the regulatory authority in a particular state.

E. Services to Hospitals. The close relationship of Blue Cross to hospitals leads Blue Cross to render many services to hospitals even though a number of such services are only remotely related to claims as such. Most of these services are related to helping improve management, to reduce costs or utilization or to improve quality of care. Included are regular cost, statistical, diagnostic and utilization reports, accounting consultation, central data processing, assistance in research, hospital planning and other activities of mutual interest.

Community Rating. Rates based on community-wide experience have long been characteristic of Blue Cross, although the situation is changing. Most plans still use community rating for a major or substantial part of their subscribers, or have practiced a modified form of experience rating which contains some community factor.

Community rating has been the favored and traditional device of Blue Cross plans to subsidize the high risk, disadvantaged groups and individuals in order to make hospital protection available to all at a reasonable rate. Experience rating, developed by insurance companies, raises the rates for the high risk groups, lowers it for the low risk groups. This conflicts with the basic orientation of Blue Cross, which is to *lower* the premium for the low-income, high need groups. It is not experience rating per se, which is only a method of operation, but the concept of equity theoretically required by insurance principles that distinguishes Blue Cross plans from insurance companies.[17]

Community Sponsorship. Community sponsorship of Blue Cross plans is a varying and sometimes nebulous concept which is reflected in such things as nonprofit operation, enabling legislation, tax status, regulation, hospital relations and board composition. Hospitals are usually well represented on the boards of trustees of Blue Cross plans—sometimes their representatives constitute a majority. However, these representatives are often hospital trustees, who represent their corporations or professions and the general public as well as their hospitals. If hospital administrators are on the board, they constitute only a minor portion of its membership. Other than hospital representatives, board members represent a wide range of community interests. Industry, business, labor, education, law, the clergy and physicians are commonly represented. Regardless of special interests, however, board members are aware of the need to operate a plan in the interest of the whole community and at the same time to maintain a close alliance with the providers of health care—hospitals and doctors.[18]

There is some feeling that Blue Cross boards should represent subscribers as such, and of course, they do, but not exclusively. Because of the plans' objectives, the boards feel a great deal of responsibility toward hospitals. They also have a responsibility toward those sections of the community not enrolled in Blue Cross. This responsibility is partly discharged through support of hospitals and partly through policies designed to make health coverage available at reasonable rates to the whole community. Neither of these methods permits exclusive orientation to the present group of subscribers, although with achievement of total enrollment of a community the sets of interests would merge.

Over the past ten years, there has been a slow, but steady, shift toward larger public representation and smaller professional representation (particularly of hospital administrators and other hospital employees) on Blue Cross boards. In 1962, the public members, including hospital trustees, constituted 58 per cent of the board membership for all Blue Cross boards combined. However, even in 1952, the public members were a majority.

Table 14–3 shows the changing picture for 1952, 1959, 1960 and 1962.

It is important to note that the community of interest varies between plans. A multi-state or state-wide plan certainly has a different kind of community than a local or area-wide plan. Yet, even within the latter there

---

[17] Subsequent sections of this chapter will discuss the limitations of experience rating as a competitive method, the responses of Blue Cross plans to experience rated competition and the influence of this competition on the prospective role of government in health care expenses.

[18] Somers and Somers, *op. cit.*, chaps. 15 and 20, discuss thoroughly the conflicting demands of these relationships.

may be many different communities with varying problems. Each Blue Cross plan, however, is identified with a specific geographic area and reflects its health problems, economic character and interests.

TABLE 14–3

MEMBERSHIP ON BLUE CROSS BOARDS OF TRUSTEES

	Professional Members			Public Members		
	Per Cent Hospital Adminis- trators and Em- ployees	Per Cent MD's	Total Per Cent Profes- sional	Per Cent Hospital Trustees	Per Cent General Public	Per Cent Total Public
1952	29	16	45	23	32	55
1959	26	18	44	24	32	56
1960	24	19	43	21	36	57
1962	24	18	42	20	38	58

SOURCE: Blue Cross Association.

Controls on Cost and Care.[19]   The unique relationship between Blue Cross plans and hospitals and physicians enables the plans to influence the quality, quantity and cost of hospital care used by subscribers and others. Blue Cross Plans assume, whether they wish to or not, a responsibility for the character of the health care provided. This responsibility may be discharged simply by approval of a given hospital for participation in the plan. Standards for this approval can be state licensing, approval by the health or welfare departments, designation by the insurance commissioner, accreditation (by the Joint Commission on Accreditation of Hospitals) or simply approval by the plan itself. The latter can be based on a set of written specifications or can be a matter of individual decision each time a hospital applies. At least two major plans have established in the courts their right to refuse to contract with substandard hospitals.

It is not entirely clear how far the concern about hospital standards can go beyond the definition of eligible hospitals. This is an issue continually in the fore. While no plan is obligated to support inappropriate hospitalization and inadequate or harmful treatment, there is a question (in a legal and a professional sense) regarding the means a plan can reasonably be expected to use to assure that proper care is given.

The higher the cost of hospital care and the greater the use of hospitals,

[19] Controls exercised by purveyors of medical care are discussed in detail in Chapter 23 of this volume. For additional discussion of kinds of control in the health care field, particularly as they apply to Blue Cross and hospitals, see S. R. Gottlieb and P. W. Spaulding, "Controls Within and Upon the Voluntary Health System," in *Hospital and Medical Economics* (W. J. McNerney *et al.*) (Chicago: Hospital Research and Educational Trust, American Hospital Association, 1962), chaps. 80 and 87.

the more pressure Blue Cross plans will feel to assure themselves, the public and the regulatory authorities about the quality and cost of the care. When more comprehensive benefits are offered by a plan, it may mean that Blue Cross is promoting use of the hospital, whether appropriate or not, and is helping to inflate hospital costs, irrespective of the quality of the product.

Controls may be professional, financial or legal and, from another aspect, may be direct or indirect. Professional controls are exerted by members of the profession on themselves and each other and are direct controls, in the sense that any sanctions may be applied immediately. A county medical society, for example, may expel a member, to his social and economic detriment, for failing to meet certain standards of behavior. Blue Cross, of course, cannot attempt to exercise direct controls of this (professional) kind. It can, however, exercise indirect control by coming to an agreement with a county medical society or a regional hospital council and then monitoring the implementation of the agreement. Another way in which a plan can encourage the exercise of professional controls by the relevant profession is by encouraging a program of improvement and supporting it with money, staff, advice and educational and public relations activities.

Many kinds of financial controls also are open to Blue Cross in its relations with hospitals. Some are direct controls necessarily involved in effectuating the terms of contracts—claims processing, for example. Others are indirect financial controls, concerned with motivating hospitals, not with dictating details of management.

Some controls of utilization, for example, are possible only by establishing and policing contractual arrangements. A common variety is the exclusion of hospitalization for diagnostic purposes when diagnostic procedures are feasible on an out-patient basis. Removal of the financial motivation to hospitalize patients unnecessarily, however, can be and is being used as an indirect financial control. Although their effectiveness remains in doubt, out-patient diagnostic benefits are being offered increasingly to help solve this problem.

Controls on quality of hospital care by Blue Cross plans consist mainly of the approval of hospitals for membership or participating status. Plans are also involved in a wide variety of cooperative endeavors, chiefly with hospital associations, to improve standards. Most of these are educational programs, although some may involve benefit structure. Refusal to cover an experimental procedure and, conversely, expanding benefits to cover it when it has been established and accepted are two ways in which benefit structure may support quality concepts. Plans are becoming increasingly involved in provision of skilled nursing home care as an alternative to hospitalization. Nursing institutions must meet certain newly established standards of quality in order to participate.

Hospital utilization controls are being exerted increasingly. In addition to claims processing, many plans have medical review and recertification procedures, as is discussed in Chapter 23.

Cost controls also are exerted generally through some form of audit of hospital financial records to insure that only appropriate and agreed upon components enter into cost determination. Audits of cost are frequently combined with a reimbursement mechanism which sets ceilings on cost reimbursement (e.g., 10 per cent above the weighted average per diem cost of the group in which the hospital is classified). Where billings are the basis of reimbursement, changes in hospital charges are reviewed for approval in some cases. In at least one plan, prior approval of any change is required; the schedule must be supported by a budget about which a detailed hearing is held before a review committee with hospital and Blue Cross representation.

Marketing Considerations regarding Blue Cross

With respect to group enrollment, the Blue Cross plans have the problems of keeping present groups, upgrading the coverage of present groups, enrolling groups presently uncovered and enrolling groups currently covered by insurance companies. In each of these, competition of insurance companies is a factor. In competition with Blue Cross plans, insurance companies have some strengths, including some advantages which may be more apparent than real.

Nature of Competitive Pressures. An insurance company can sell insurance on a nation-wide basis, simplifying the sales problem in the case of corporations with many branches or divisions and making for uniform benefits and premiums. Also, an insurance company can sell a package program, including life and disability income, as well as medical expense insurance. This may help in one or both of two ways—it offers administrative simplicity to the buyer; the profit on the life insurance or other elements of the package may be used to subsidize the medical expense coverage. In the opinion of many large buyers, however, expertise in the various fields of insurance more than offsets the advantages of administrative simplicity. Also, a decidedly lower Blue Cross premium can offset pricing advantages that accrue through packaging several insurance coverages.

An insurance company can hold premiums level for longer periods of time by paying an indemnity in dollars—a relatively fixed liability in comparison with service benefits. Insurance companies also have great marketing flexibility in the ability to offer a great variety of coverages at a great variety of prices. In effect, they can tailor the coverage to suit the price needs of the selling situation, regardless of how low they may be.

Universal use of experience rating enables an insurance company to place low premiums on favorable risk groups. These may be low enough to outbid Blue Cross for new coverage, to retain presently insured groups against Blue Cross competition and, theoretically, to pull good risk groups out of Blue Cross. In actual practice, this has probably helped historically in selling coverage to uncovered groups, but Blue Cross generally has been able to hold presently enrolled groups against this kind of rate competition.

Insurance companies, setting premiums by formula, usually avoid the unfavorable publicity attendant on public hearings before insurance commissioners. Their premium increases are annual and staggered over the year and over the groups, rather than besetting all groups at one time.

Changes to Meet Competition. Blue Cross has met the competitive advantages of insurance companies in a number of ways—partly by using historical advantages and partly through adjusting to the changed situation by new methods. The plans have attempted to meet the nation-wide advantages of the single insurance company by a number of national and interplan arrangements which will be discussed later.

Blue Cross cannot sell a package program including life and disability income insurance, and the associated administrative advantages cannot be gained by Blue Cross plans. As a matter of fact, Blue Cross' own package—with Blue Shield—has some administrative complexities which do not trouble insurance companies, since the latter can sell both hospitalization and medical expense coverage as single companies.

Administrative simplicity alone, however, may not be attractive enough to offset the advantages of buying health coverage from specialists (and life insurance from specialists in this field). Some Blue Cross plans have experienced an increasing recognition of this factor, especially on the part of large employers.

Any price advantage the package may have, and many of the other price advantages of insurance companies referred to above, can be partially or wholly overcome by Blue Cross plans with certain price advantages of their own. These have all been mentioned previously—nonprofit, tax exemption, no commissions, simplified administration, volume business (there are 1,200 insurance companies writing health coverage, compared to seventy-seven Blue Cross plans) and, in many cases, cost reimbursement to hospitals. Community rating also provides a price advantage in many situations. There are other price advantages of Blue Cross, some so difficult to measure as to be considered intangibles, some accruing to the benefit of the whole community and thus not being *competitive* advantages.

Many employers are aware that, in taking care of "left-employs" through good group conversion practices, Blue Cross is saving the employer tax and philanthropic dollars; most of these employers are willing to take this into account in comparing prices. These same employers may also be conscious of the community advantages and be willing to pay something for these.

Blue Cross plans have made many advances in recent years to meet the challenge of flexibility. They offer a far wider variety of coverages than in the past. This generally has taken the form of developing better coverages and added features, while holding on to older, less adequate types of contracts. Thus, the price differential among Blue Cross coverages has increased.

The plans also have offered deductible and percentage participation contracts to maintain competitive, low price offerings. In general (except where they were long established as part of a local, preferred pattern), these features have not attracted many new groups. As has been previously indicated, no more than 11 per cent of Blue Cross contracts contain such features.

The use of experience rating by insurance companies has been a difficult challenge for Blue Cross. Experts both inside and outside of Blue Cross have been urging more experience rating for Blue Cross. Others have sharply criticized Blue Cross for engaging in experience rating as a means of adapting to the competitive situation. This last view generally takes the form of accusing Blue Cross of becoming too much like insurance companies.

While community rating is traditional in Blue Cross, it is not the rating *method* that is at issue, but, rather, the question of subsidy of high risk groups. The principle involved is making adequate coverage available to as many people as possible at a reasonable rate through some form of subsidization, especially of the most disadvantaged people. This is the principle that Blue Cross seeks to preserve, and its actual rating history is one of moving forward experimentally to new forms of rating that will solve particular account, area or interplan (including nation-wide) problems within the framework of this principle.

Some plans initially had a single community rate for group and nongroup subscribers. A rating accommodation had to be made very early from practical necessity. The development of individual, two-person and family rates (within a group) is a similar accommodation, since it is not possible to convince people that the same rate is equitable, in the broader sense of the term, for an individual and a family.[20]

---

[20] See Chapter 22 for a discussion of the technical aspects of experience rating. For the most thorough discussion of experience versus community rating in print, see Duncan M. MacIntyre, *Voluntary Health Insurance and Rate Making* (Ithaca, N.Y.: Cornell University Press, 1962). This is, in general, an excellent treatment of the subject and sheds light on many aspects of prepayment and health insurance, although some observers disagree with some of MacIntyre's observations and conclusions.

See "Voluntary Health Insurance and Rate Making," Duncan M. MacIntyre (a book review), *Hospitals*, Vol. XXXVII, No. 5 (March 1, 1963), pp. 136–37. An important aspect of the experience rating concept is referred to in another place by Duncan M. MacIntyre, "Pricing Health Insurance," *The Economics of Health and Medical Care*, Proceedings of the Conference on The Economics of Health and Medical Care (Ann Arbor: The University of Michigan, 1964), p. 167.

In the negotiation of national contracts, experience rating has become a competitive necessity for Blue Cross plans. These contracts encompass a number of plans which must agree to offer uniform benefits and, usually, uniform rates. Since some plans may lose money while others gain surpluses from such arrangements, an equalization formula is needed to even out the financial impact on the various plans.[21]

The formulas used in determining experience premiums allow some subsidy, at least for the additional expense of group conversion (including that of retirees) of the employees of the employer involved. Thus, the principle of subsidizing high loss contracts is maintained to some extent. The same is true of group contracts individually tailored to a particular company's or union's requirements. These are experience rated with a plus-factor for subsidization of group conversions. The master agreement also has the effect of allowing some accommodation for the especially low loss ratio group that would otherwise bear an inordinate share of the cost of supporting the community rate.

In one other type of situation Blue Cross plans have found that their basic objectives can be better served by experience rating. This is the case where a large, high-income group also happens to have a high loss ratio. On pure community rating, this type of group would actually be supported by many groups of low-income people in the community rate.

As Eilers, MacIntyre and Somers and Somers[22] all point out, experience rating has been growing rapidly as a practice of Blue Cross plans. Eilers cites Blue Cross Commission figures indicating that thirty-five of the plans, representing 36.2 per cent of the subscribers, were using only community rating in 1958. However, thirteen of these used experience rating for national accounts, so the "pure" remnant, as MacIntyre[23] points

---

"An analytical approach to much so-called community rating practice will show that only a handful of Plans (out of four or five hundred) still rely almost exclusively on rate averaging. When Blue Cross–Blue Shield divide the subscriber universe into three (group, original non-group and group conversion) contract segments, when rates differ for individual subscribers, two-person families, families with dependent children, one-parent families, when a variety of optional contracts are available, when Plans participate in national syndicates, underwrite national accounts, experience-rate large groups and segregate the experience on senior citizen contracts, they have moved a long way from average-theory, toward equity-based rate classification under a different name. Likewise, when independent plans refuse to enroll non-group subscribers over 60 years of age, load (increase) monthly rates for over-65 subscribers or, like some of the Blue Plans, enroll non-group subscribers only with a medical statement, the equity influence is obvious."

[21] Premiums on equalized accounts are generally paid to one Blue Cross plan. This plan then distributes the premiums among those Blue Cross and Blue Shield plans with local enrollment in each specific account underwritten on this basis according to an underwriting risk formula.

[22] R. D. Eilers, *Regulation of Blue Cross and Blue Shield Plans*, pp. 218–19; MacIntyre, *Voluntary Health Insurance and Rate Making*, p. 164; and Somers and Somers, *op. cit.*, p. 312.

[23] MacIntyre, *Voluntary Health Insurance and Rate Making*, p. 164.

out, numbered only twenty-two. The same report indicates that twenty-six plans had community rating with experience rating optional (37.5 per cent of the subscribers were in these plans), and seventeen of the plans (covering 26.3 per cent of the subscribers) require experience rating for groups above a minimum size.

Table 14–4 reveals that the number of plans with community rating only has dropped considerably since 1958. The number of plans with experience rating available has increased from twenty-six to thirty-one, while the number with experience rating only (for groups above a certain size) has doubled—from seventeen to thirty-four.

Blue Cross plans will probably have to go still further in the direction of developing new rating methods, including various forms of experience rating, while retaining, where feasible and applicable, community rating

TABLE 14–4

BASIC RATING METHODS OF BLUE CROSS PLANS, 1962

Type of Rating	Plans*		Group Membership†	
	Number	Per Cent	Number‡	Per Cent
Community rating only.........11		14.5	9,525,654	20.8
Community rating with group rating available...............31		40.8	14,677,882	32.0
Group rating or other form of experience rating§.............34		44.7	21,612,653	47.2
	76	100.0	45,816,189	100.0

    * Plans as of December 31, 1962.
    † All membership figures based on group membership as of December 31, 1962.
    ‡ Total group membership of the plans involved—the number of members actually on a group experience rating basis would be somewhat less.
    § Otherforms of experience rating include category rating based on size and/or loss ratios, county or other area rating, etc.
    SOURCE: Blue Cross Association.

for various segments of the membership. Yet, for some plans community rating may apply to the major part of their membership for a long time.

Community-rated plans have maintained and increased their membership in the face of extremely stiff competition from insurance companies utilizing experience rating. Experience rating may have been a necessity—and has been a competitive asset—in the wide exploitation of national account markets by Blue Cross. There seems to be no evidence, however, that experience rating is a cure-all for enrollment problems.

Plans need further association with experience rating to gauge its long-term effect, and some methods already adapted may have to be altered again to solve particular problems. For example, under group experience rating with a percentage added in the formula for subsidization of group conversion contracts, the percentage falls on high loss ratio groups and low loss ratio groups alike. Thus, a burden in addition to its own poor experience is added to the disadvantaged group, which no longer has the support of the favorable risk groups previously associated with it in the community rate.

National and Interplan Aspects of Blue Cross

The growth of national corporations, development of multiple plant locations, decentralization of production and company mergers over the past generation have increased the importance of national operations (versus local or state-wide operations) for Blue Cross. The more recent development of management preference for company-wide uniform benefits, uniform rates and central administration, has rendered national and interplan arrangements imperative.

The Blue Cross Association (BCA) was founded in 1948 primarily to facilitate the handling of national account enrollment by the plans. The Association, constituted by its member plans in the United States and Canada, has expanded its functions significantly since 1948. In 1960, it took over many of the functions of the American Hospital Association's Blue Cross Commission, with which it was merged. This action signalized the advance of Blue Cross "from agency to partnership status" with voluntary hospitals.[24] The American Hospital Association (in its Council on Blue Cross, Financing and Prepayment) retained the Blue Cross approval program and the protection of the name and insignia.

One of the Blue Cross Association's early activities was the establishment of a wholly owned insurance company, Health Service, Inc., (HSI) licensed in Illinois. This organization maintains a standard national contract, with riders, for employers operating in many plan areas. HSI sets up agreements and parcels out the collection of premiums and administration of claims among the plans involved so that it generally liquidates its own interest once the national contract has been sold. However, it supplements agreements when local plans are not able to match fully the benefits of a uniform national agreement. At the end of 1962, only about 110,000 Blue Cross members were covered directly by HSI.

BCA also helps plans to administer the Local Benefit Agreement for National Accounts. This is an arrangement whereby local benefit patterns can be given to a particular national account in each plan area. Thus, one national contract can be administered which gives a corporation's employees the full benefit of whatever local or regional benefits seem desirable in the area in which they live. The control plan, usually the plan in the company's home office area, administers the benefits for itself and for the other Blue Cross plans involved (which are called participating plans). The local benefit agreements are a relatively minor factor today, since there are so many uniform national accounts.

The most important and most effective interplan account mechanism is

---

[24] Address by Walter J. McNerney, "Hospitals—the Need for Coordinated Action," American Hospital Association Annual Meeting, Chicago, Ill., August 25, 1964.

the syndicate, which is, in effect, a federation of plans to cover a given national account or group of accounts in a given industry. Most large Blue Cross and Blue Shield national accounts are now of the syndicate type. Again, there is a control plan, which originally may have sold the agreement, possibly with the assistance of BCA personnel, and participating plans. The syndicate differs from HSI programs and from local benefit programs in that it provides uniform benefits nationally, but tailored to the needs and desires of the particular industry or company. Syndicates actually antedate BCA, the first having been established in 1946. Some of the larger syndicates provide benefits in the steel, telephone, food and paper industries.

It has always been a BCA function to take the lead where it can do so effectively in national enrollment efforts, whether of the syndicate or local benefit type. Its activities in this area have intensified, while the scope of its total activities has broadened considerably. These include broad scale educational efforts for plans' staffs, a large and active research and development division, and many plan service activities including a national wire service linking all plans through a central communications hub in Chicago.

Among the most useful of BCA's activities has been administration of the Inter-Plan Service Benefit Bank, which enables a subscriber to receive hospital services in any plan area and arranges payment with his home plan. Also of importance is the Inter-Plan Transfer Agreement, which enables a subscriber to transfer coverage from one plan to another when he moves, retaining certain waiting period standing and seniority rights with regard to eligibility for benefits. These various arrangements help to overcome inconveniences which accompany the autonomy and local practice of the plans when dealing with a nation-wide corporation or other employer.[25]

BLUE SHIELD OPERATIONS

Principles and Operational Aspects of Blue Shield

Blue Shield plans generally are younger than Blue Cross plans, although many physician-sponsored prepayment plans for medical care are actually older. In many ways Blue Shield plans consciously followed operational principles and patterns established by Blue Cross. As a result, many similarities exist between these allied forms of health coverage, and their differences appear more marked because of their general likeness.

---

[25] For a more detailed description of national and interplan aspects than is possible here, and of some of the problems and issues involved, see Eilers, *Regulation of Blue Cross and Blue Shield Plans*, pp. 55–69; MacIntyre, *Voluntary Health Insurance and Rate Making*, pp. 148–51, 169–72 and 190–92; and Somers and Somers, *op. cit.*, pp. 299–300.

Nonprofit and Tax Status. Blue Shield plans generally have been established in accordance with special enabling legislation or by the same enabling acts that apply to Blue Cross. Also, because of their nonprofit status and their objectives, they generally are tax-exempt.

Service Benefits. Most Blue Shield plans provide service benefits, but the concept and the applications are quite different from Blue Cross. Inasmuch as the physician customarily charges a fee for his service, depending upon the ability of the patient to pay, the question of guaranteeing or providing his services is a different matter than in the case of hospitals. The "cost" of his services, for example, is more elusive. The physician's sliding scale of fees has meant traditionally that the patient with comfortable means pays the full fee, possibly including an amount to help cover the patient who pays a part fee or none at all. This tradition is strong and ancient. Physicians generally regard their ability to set their own fees as a professional privilege of great value. Since freedom to set the fee also enables the physician to care for all patients without regard to ability to pay, the prerogative is guarded jealously.

Hence, the provision of service benefits to patients within certain income limits seems reasonable to many physicians because it reflects the ability-to-pay criterion. Service benefits to all subscribers, without reference to income, would not be so acceptable. Many Blue Shield plans provide contracts with two or three income limits below which service benefits are guaranteed, but above which the physician is entitled to charge the patient in addition to his Blue Shield reimbursement.

Earlier service benefit provisions were based on income limits, for example, of $2,500 and $4,000 per year. A different premium is paid and a different fee schedule is provided for physicians under contracts with different income limits. Income limits generally are different for a single individual and for a family. Customarily, total family income is specified, although this is difficult to determine. Changing times have elevated the limits, sometimes by the addition of a third income plan on top of the other two. Annual family income limits of $4,000, $6,000 and $8,000 often are used, and some proposals for a plan with an upper limit of $9,000 have been made. A rule of thumb provides that the top income limit of a service benefit plan should cover 75 to 80 per cent of the population.

The number of Blue Shield plans with service benefit programs has been increasing steadily, and there is great pressure from organized consumers, particularly labor, for further increase. The need to be able to offer national contracts with uniform benefits is a related factor. The service benefit is difficult to write, for instance, when a number of Blue Shield plans—whose participation is needed in national arrangements —do not have any service benefits.

In the absence of service benefits, or for over-income members, Blue Shield benefits are a straight indemnity of a given amount for a given service, toward the payment of the physician's full fee. Approximately 30 per cent of Blue Shield benefits are provided on this basis.

Benefit Structure. The desire to cover catastrophic illness led to coverage of physicians' fees for in-hospital treatment of patients. In fact, in-hospital *surgical* benefits were the earliest and most widespread form of coverage. Later, maternity and medical benefits, again for in-hospital care, were added. Total in-hospital benefits are now as common in Blue Shield as medical-surgical benefits, but some agreements still provide for surgical benefits only.

Home and office visits of the physician are rarely covered. Some plans are experimenting with this type of coverage, in which case it usually is offered only for the subscriber (not dependents) and after the first four visits or after the first week of treatment.

The chief form of Blue Shield extended coverage to date is major medical protection. Basic Blue Cross and Blue Shield coverages are a prerequisite for this protection, which is offered jointly with Blue Cross. Some of the benefits are additional physician services, such as the amount of the physician's fee over and above the fee schedule for those having higher incomes than the service benefit limit, or the amount over the fee schedule in straight indemnity contracts; out-patient diagnostic and treatment services rendered by physicians and not covered by Blue Cross (in the hospital) or Blue Shield; and home and office visits. Other coverage includes additional hospital benefits, e.g., the difference between the indemnification of Blue Cross and the full charge for a private room; and out-patient hospital services not covered by Blue Cross. A third group of additional benefits may also be covered in some Blue Cross basic agreements, such as visiting nurse services, home care or nursing home care. Major medical also covers some items, such as prescription drugs, not usually covered in any basic Blue Cross or Blue Shield contract.

Major medical coverage was developed and fostered initially by insurance companies. Blue Cross and Blue Shield offered it later and, in many cases, reluctantly. Some plans have sold major medical enthusiastically and have had reasonable success with it. Others have supplied it only when the sale of the basic contract hinged on this offering. Some still do not offer major medical. Since major medical contains both the deductible and percentage participation features, since it is based on the principle of indemnification of catastrophic loss exclusively (no service benefits) while ignoring first-dollar coverage, Blue Cross and Blue Shield plans generally do not view the coverage as being able to solve basic problems for the majority of people.[26]

Relations with Physicians. Blue Shield plans are the physicians' own plans. Therefore, it would be expected that the relationship between plans

---

[26] For a discussion of major medical coverage by a Blue Cross executive see W. H. Ford, "A Look at the Logic of Hospital Care Financing," paper published by Blue Cross of Western Pennsylvania, Pittsburgh, Pennsylvania, 1963.

and physicians would be close and cordial, although such is not always the case.

This relationship does facilitate the same kind of arrangements with regard to subscriber identification, eligibility acceptance and claims procedure and payment as is the case between Blue Cross plans and hospitals. With physician payments, the problem is of much greater complexity, however, since there are so many more of them and their office staffs are not in as good a position to process paper work. Delays in filing claims and difficulty in identifying subscribers from the claim forms are among the administrative problems. Blue Shield plans usually do not have extensive programs of services to physicians other than for claims payment.

A. *Physician Sponsorship.* The sponsorship of Blue Shield plans generally emanates from state and county medical societies. These societies continue to supervise closely or control Blue Shield plan activities.

Usually physicians have a majority membership on the board of trustees of a plan. Sometimes only token representation of nonphysicians is included and sometimes none at all. The laymen on the boards often are selected by the state or county medical society or at least by the physician majority.

Fee schedules adopted by Blue Shield plans often are subject to approval of the state medical society's House of Delegates. Sometimes every basic policy question is decided in this way. Even without such overt control, it is usually difficult or impossible for a Blue Shield board to resist medical society pressure.

Medical societies and Blue Shield plans feel that their subscriber orientation is self-evident through their objective of making prepayment for physicians' services available to people at a reasonable price. There has been too little awareness on the part of the plans and physicians that the consumer's interests require further consideration, and, therefore, lack of adequate representation for him is seen as no anomaly. There is positive evidence that this situation is changing for the better. On the other hand, protecting the physician's independence, his income and his professional goals has generally been considered of paramount importance.

Blue Shield boards and executives are being compelled by competition and the regulatory authorities to assume a broader view. Some of the issues involved will become more apparent in subsequent discussions.

B. *Physician Reimbursement.* The close ties between Blue Shield plans and physicians make it imperative that equity among physicians be a major consideration. This includes setting a uniform fee schedule for specified services. There may be more than one schedule for reimbursement under different income level service benefits, but in general, like services receive like reimbursement under each type of agreement.

Actually, one of the chief complaints of physicians is that a uniform fee schedule does not produce equity. One of the basic criticisms is that similarly named services are often not identical. For example, an "office visit" to a general practitioner may be a very brief service, including prescribing drugs or diet, for a condition already well known to the physician. This same service in an internist's office may involve a general physical examination and the taking of the patient's history—a service that may require an hour's time. More refined definitions of service have been attempted to overcome this problem.

Another aspect of equity is the relative worth of various kinds of physician's services, some of which may be provided by only one type of physician, e.g., a surgeon. Relative value schedules have been developed from studies on a state-wide basis by state medical societies which attempt to state all values in units. Such a schedule can be applied whether a monetary value of one dollar or ten dollars is attached to the unit. Thus, an office visit might be called one unit, an appendectomy thirty units. In such a system, if the area standard of reimbursement for an office visit were to be set at $4.00, the reimbursement for an appendectomy would be $120.

The relative value schedule is usually based on a study of existing fee practices and, therefore, reflects any existing inequities. Some physicians feel, for example, that surgical attention is often overvalued while other forms of medical attention are undervalued. Thus, this kind of inequity is a problem with or without a relative value schedule.[27]

Another reimbursement problem relates to services having the same definition, but provided in the one case by a general practitioner and in the other case by an individual especially trained to perform the particular service. Internists, pediatricians and anaesthesiologists, for example, frequently disagree strongly with reimbursement of general practitioners at the same rate for services nominally the same as the specialists perform. They assert, in effect, that their services are qualitatively superior. This same argument is used by individual physicians without regard to the definition of the service, traditional inequities or specialist training.

In the face of these problems, there is little wonder that many physicians are reluctant to provide service benefits under a participating contract with Blue Shield. It suits the physician much better to consider the fee schedule reimbursement as an indemnity toward whatever higher fee he might feel appropriate. Many physicians, however, have accepted and use the Blue Shield fee schedules for their total practices, in the interest of simplicity and also of equity among their patients.

C. *Participating Status.* Physicians may or may not elect to become Blue Shield participating physicians. This status has the most meaning where service benefits exist because the physician must agree to accept the Blue Shield fee schedule as full reimbursement for patients in the appropriate income classes.

---

[27] Chapter 17 discusses relative value schedules in detail.

When the physician does not elect to participate, the plan usually will make the benefit payment directly to the patient. Most plans provide payment directly to the nonparticipating physician if the patient signs an assignment of benefits to him. This almost eliminates the financial penalty of nonparticipation, while for the physician the privilege to charge any fee may be retained and for his patient the service benefit may be fully circumvented.

The physician's participation is important to the plan, not only to provide service benefits, but also so that it can maintain to the public that it really prepays physician's services. The National Association of Blue Shield Plans requires that at least 51 per cent of the physicians in a plan's area participate before the plan will be approved. Some enabling acts have similar requirements. In areas where Blue Shield has large enrollment, to have as low as 51 per cent of the physicians participating would probably be catastrophic. In fact, Blue Shield plans are accustomed to having 80 per cent or more of the physicians participate.

The threat of nonparticipation, therefore, is a powerful weapon in the hands of disgruntled physicians. Any massive use of this threat would tend to control plan decisions, regardless of the composition of the board of trustees or the relationship to the medical society.

Community Rating. Blue Shield plans have used community rating from the beginning and have remained with this method to a far larger extent than have Blue Cross plans. However, the same factors have been at work on Blue Shield as on Blue Cross, and there has been a substantial increase in experience rating. This has been especially true for national accounts.

Controls on Cost. Most of Blue Shield's control activities are related to its problem areas—reimbursement and claims processing. Unlike Blue Cross, it is not dealing with organizations, but with individuals. It is allied to the professional societies, which are very much concerned with quality control. Blue Shield has found that it can best deal with cost control through reimbursement methods and with utilization control through claims processing. In the latter endeavor, efforts may include administration of claims to prevent overpayment through error or fraud, handling of subscribers' complaints, and measurement of statistical variation for identification of possible areas of unwarranted use.

Marketing Considerations regarding Blue Shield

Nationally, about 80 per cent of Blue Cross members also carry Blue Shield coverage. Obviously, the marketing and associated problems of the two kinds of plans are closely linked.

Coordination between particular Blue Cross and Blue Shield plans is often difficult due to their autonomous nature. The problem is greater in areas where the territories of the plans are not the same. In Pennsylvania, for example, one Blue Shield plan covers the entire state, and must coordinate its offerings and its operations with five separate Blue Cross plans.

Competition with insurance companies and pricing difficulties in the face of this competition are the chief handicaps. Lack of service benefits, use of income limits that are too low, or lack of adequate enforcement of service benefit provisions are also important problems for Blue Shield. In addition, limitation of benefits (to in-hospital physician's care, for example) is a drawback. Extension of Blue Shield benefits to such care as out-patient diagnosis and treatment and home and office care of the physician carry with them the penalty of a higher price for coverage and an intensification of competition from insurance companies. In the recent development of coverage for the Federal Employees Plan and in the auto industry, Blue Shield has shown that it can cope with these problems.

National and Interplan Aspects of Blue Shield

Blue Shield plans have their own, autonomous national association, the National Association of Blue Shield Plans, which approves plans and controls the name and insignia of Blue Shield. The National Association, like the Blue Cross Association, renders many services to individual plans and also fosters the sale of national contracts.

A local benefit form of agreement has not been considered necessary for Blue Shield plans. No interplan bank is used; the subscriber in another plan area simply pays the doctor and forwards his claim to his home Blue Shield plan. Syndicates are used to some extent in Blue Shield for national accounts. Many syndicates include both Blue Cross and Blue Shield plans.

The National Association has also established a wholly owned stock insurance company, called Medical Indemnity of America, Inc. (MIA), to provide uniform benefits in a national contract to country-wide or multi-state employees. MIA, which was organized in Ohio, is operated jointly with the Blue Cross Association's Health Service, Inc., in marketing and servicing national accounts. It also places the coverage of the various groups of subscribers with the appropriate Blue Shield plan wherever possible. Those accounts which it retained or partially retained covered only 133,412 members as of the end of 1962. The National Association of Blue Shield Plans also has an interplan transfer arrangement similar to that of the Blue Cross plans.

SELECTED REFERENCES

American Medical Association. *Charts and Graphs: 1961 Statistical Data on Voluntary Prepayment Medical Benefit Plans.* Chicago: The Association, 1961.

————. *Report of the Commission on Medical Care Plans,* Parts 1 and II. Chicago: The Association, 1958.

————. *Voluntary Prepayment Medical Benefit Plans.* Chicago: The Association, 1961.

BREWSTER, A. W. "Financing Hospital Care Services," *Modern Concepts of Hospital Administration* (ed. J. K. OWEN), chap. 42. Philadelphia: W. B. Saunders Co., 1962.

CUNNINGHAM, R. M., JR. *The Story of Blue Shield.* Chicago: The Public Affairs Committee, 1954. Reprinted by the National Association of Blue Shield Plans, Chicago, 1954.

COLEMAN, J. D. "Providing for Illness in Times of Health: The Creation of the Blue Cross Plans," *Business Decisions That Changed Our Lives* (eds. S. FURST and M. SHERMAN). New York: Random House, Inc., 1964.

DICKERSON, O. D. "Group Medical Expense Insurance—Blue Cross and Blue Shield," *Life and Health Insurance Handbook* (ed. DAVIS W. GREGG), chap. 34. Rev. ed. Homewood, Ill.: Richard D. Irwin, Inc., 1964.

DIOKNO, A. W. *Hospital and Medical Economics* (W. J. MCNERNEY *et al.*), chaps. 58–71. Chicago: Hospital Research and Educational Trust, American Hospital Association, 1962.

EILERS, R. D. *Regulation of Blue Cross and Blue Shield Plans.* Homewood, Ill.: Richard D. Irwin, Inc., 1963.

FAULKNER, E. J. "Human Life Values—Role of Health Insurance," *Life and Health Insurance Handbook* (ed. DAVIS W. GREGG), chap. 3. Rev. ed. Homewood, Ill.: Richard D. Irwin, Inc., 1964.

FOLLMANN, J. F., JR. *Medical Care and Health Insurance,* chaps. 6 and 8. Homewood, Ill.: Richard D. Irwin, Inc., 1963.

GOLDMANN, F. *Voluntary Medical Care Insurance in the United States.* New York: Columbia University Press, 1948.

HARRIS, S. E. *The Economics of American Medicine,* chaps. 14 and 15. New York: The Macmillan Co., 1964.

MACEACHERN, M. T. *Hospital Organization and Management,* chap. 15. 3d ed. Chicago: Physicians Record Co., 1957.

MACINTYRE, DUNCAN M. *Voluntary Health Insurance and Rate Making.* Ithaca, N.Y.: Cornell University Press, 1962.

MCNERNEY, W. J. "Why the Blue Cross Is Changing Its Plans," *The Modern Hospital,* Vol. XCV, No. 4 (October, 1960), pp. 75–79, 147–55.

NEW YORK LABOR-MANAGEMENT COUNCIL OF HEALTH AND WELFARE PLANS, INC. *Blue Shield in New York City: A Report and Program.* New York, 1963.

REED, L. S. *Blue Cross and Medical Service Plans.* Washington, D.C.: Federal Security Agency, U.S. Public Health Service, 1947.

SINAI, N.; ANDERSON, O. W.; AND DOLLAR, M. L. *Health Insurance in the United States.* New York: The Commonwealth Fund, 1946.

SOMERS, HERMAN M., AND ANNE R. *Doctors, Patients and Health Insurance.* Washington, D.C.: The Brookings Institution, 1961.

WIRICK, G. C.; MORGAN, J. N.; AND BARLOW, R. "Population Survey: Health Care and Its Financing," *Hospital and Medical Economics* (W. J. MCNERNEY *et al.*), chaps. 7–19. Chicago: Hospital Research and Educational Trust, American Hospital Association, 1962.

~~~~~~~~~~~~~~~~~~~~~

Chapter 15

TYPES OF HEALTH RISK BEARERS: GROUP PRACTICE PREPAYMENT PLANS

BY AVRAM YEDIDIA

NATURE OF MEDICAL GROUP PRACTICE

Advances in medicine during the twentieth century, and particularly in the last few decades, have brought about profound changes in the organization of medical care. Some of these changes have been formalized into new patterns. However, the subtle changes which have been introduced into the structure and method of providing medical care outweigh the formalized changes. Because of scientific developments, interdependence among persons in the health care field has increased. Physicians have to depend on one another and on trained ancillary personnel, as well as upon persons in other related fields. The hospital today bears only superficial resemblance to its predecessor of thirty years ago. The same is true of a physician's office. It is in this setting of evolution and change that group practice has emerged as one pattern of rendering medical care.

In commenting on the history of group practice, Dr. J. E. McFarland states that the "origins of the group practice idea are not subject to specific analysis."[1] He points out, for example, that when the Mayo brothers were credited with the honor of originating the modern clinic, William J. Mayo said, "Well, if we did it, we didn't know it."[2] McFarland further indicates that even fixing the founding date of a clinic is difficult, i.e., while the term "Mayo Clinic" was used as early as 1909, the official clinic was not founded until 1914.

Since group practice is part of an evolving pattern of change in the organization of medical care, it understandably eludes precise definition. There are many forms of association among physicians in office practice and in hospitals. At what stage does an association among physicians

---

[1] J. E. McFarland, "Historical Comments on the Group Practice Movement," *The Physician and Group Practice* (Chicago: The Year Book Publishers, Inc., 1958), p. 15.

[2] *Ibid.*, p. 16.

become *group practice?* This is a question to which there is no uniform answer. One researcher in this field has suggested that "group practice is a process rather than a form of organization."[3]

In a study by the U.S. Public Health Service on medical groups in the United States in 1959, group practice was defined as follows: "Any group of three or more physicians (full-time or part-time) formally organized to provide medical services, with income from medical practice distributed according to some pre-arranged plan."[4] This study reported 1,623 medical groups involving 14,841 physicians. In 1959, 9 per cent of all practicing physicians in this country were involved in group practice arrangements as defined above.

Medical group practice evolved under the impetus of specialization and increased complexity of medical science. The economics of group practice differs from that of solo practice because, in addition to distributing professional income according to a pre-arranged formula, physicians in group practice also share common facilities, diagnostic equipment and ancillary personnel. Further, proponents of group practice assert that the physician gains distinct economic advantages in this form of practice, such as more effective use of professional time, income security during periods of disability or postgraduate education and travel, and opportunity to arrange an attractive retirement program. This change in economics does not directly affect the patient who requires medical care. The patient's economic relationship with the *group* is largely the same as that between a patient and a *solo* practitioner, i.e., he pays for each service received.

GROUP PRACTICE PREPAYMENT

Nature of Group Practice Prepayment

Group practice *prepayment* has evolved, in part, as a result of the increased complexity of medicine, the need for more effective cooperation among the several medical disciplines and the consumer's desire to budget his medical care costs. In this setting, the plan assumes responsibility for arranging the medical services for its dues-paying membership. It uses the prepaid funds for organizing staff and facilities to meet the anticipated needs of this membership. The members rely on the organized staff and facilities for their medical care services. The program is financed by revenue from the total membership, and the patient does not pay fees for each service he receives. In contrast, then, to the traditional form of health insurance, which is characterized by reimbursement of charges incurred

---

[3] C. Rufus Rorem, "Pattern and Problems of Group Medical Practice," *American Journal of Public Health,* December, 1950, p. 1521.

[4] U.S. Department of Health, Education, and Welfare, Public Health Service, *Medical Groups in the United States, 1959,* Public Health Service Publication No. 1063 (July, 1963), p. 4.

for medical services, group practice with prepayment is often described as a *direct service plan.*

Types and Extent of Group Practice Prepayment Plans

A 1961 study by the Division of Research and Statistics of the Social Security Administration (U.S. Department of Health, Education, and Welfare) dealt, in part, with group practice prepayment plans. The study defined a group practice prepayment plan as "any (prepayment) plan with all or a substantial part of the plan members served by a group practice unit."[5] According to this study, in 1961, 143 group practice prepayment plans satisfied this definition; they were served by 4,345 physicians, 1,197 of whom were full-time in their groups. The reported total persons covered by these groups was 3,842,400.[6]

The study identifies three types of group practice prepayment plans. *Community plans* generally extend enrollment to all organizations in the community meeting their eligibility requirements and are usually governed by a board representing civic leaders or local consumer groups. The Health Insurance Plan of Greater New York, the Kaiser Foundation Health Plan on the West Coast and Hawaii, Community Health Association of Detroit, Group Health Association of Washington, D.C. and the Group Health Cooperative of Puget Sound in Seattle are representative community plans. *Private group clinics* are plans sponsored and owned by physicians, such as the Ross-Loos Medical Group of Los Angeles. Enrollment in such plans is usually open to the community. *Employer-employee-union plans* are usually designed to serve a particular employee group, often including dependents. Such plans are operated by employers, joint labor-management boards or unions. Examples of these are the plans of the International Ladies' Garment Workers' Union, the St. Louis Labor Health Institute and the railroad industries.

Of the 3,842,400 total enrollees reported in group practice prepayment plans in 1961, 6 per cent were enrolled in private group clinic plans. The balance were divided almost evenly between community and employer-employee-union plans. Each plan has evolved in a different setting out of special needs; characteristics, similarities and differences among the six largest group practice prepayment plans are discussed later in the chapter.

The American Medical Association's Attitude toward Group Practice Prepayment Plans

The growth of group practice prepayment plans provoked lively debate and controversy within the medical profession and among interested

---

[5] U.S. Department of Health, Education, and Welfare, Social Security Administration, Division of Research and Statistics, *Independent Health Insurance Plans in the United States 1961*, Research Report No. 2 (Washington, D.C., 1963), p. 21. The study used a definition for group practice similar to that mentioned earlier.

[6] *Ibid.*, pp. 21–22.

segments of the public. Ideologically, the American Medical Association's objections to "closed-panel medicine" (as group practice prepayment is often labeled) centered around two major issues: (1) that the patient was deprived of free choice of doctor and (2) that the door was opened to lay domination of medical practice. On the local level, the opposition to group practice prepayment plans was expressed in a variety of ways. The most common manifestations of this opposition, according to physicians participating in group practice prepayment plans, were that they often were refused membership in local medical societies and frequently were denied staff privileges in hospitals.

In 1954, the Board of Trustees of the American Medical Association appointed a fifteen-member Commission on Medical Care Plans which was charged with determining "whether current medical care plans are effectively promoting (1) the highest quality of health services, (2) the welfare of the public and the medical profession, and (3) the ethical standards of the medical profession."[7] The Commission included thirteen physicians, a representative of the insurance industry and one from a Blue Shield program. Chairman of the Commission was Dr. Leonard W. Larson, who, when the Commission's report was issued in 1958, was also Chairman of the Board of Trustees of the AMA.

Group practice prepayment plans were included in the study under "Miscellaneous and Unclassified Plans," and considerable text was devoted to these plans, although they served only about 6 per cent of the population enrolled in all plans reviewed by the Commission. From its four-year study came a number of pertinent observations:

The benefits provided through various miscellaneous and unclassified plans are broader and more comprehensive than those provided through most other prepayment mechanisms.[8]

In the closed-panel, direct service, type of plan visited, the committee has uniformly observed care of good quality being made available to patients who do not have "free choice of physician" in the literal sense of the term.[9]

Medical care for many persons in the low income groups now covered by these plans has improved. Some of these people live under conditions which make it difficult for them to obtain adequate care through the usual available sources.

The committee believes that good medical care is being provided, within the scope of services offered, by the units (of the plans) visited.[10]

The committee has noted a trend toward offering the individual employee more than one plan for medical care so that he may exercise his choice. The committee believes that this development is commendable. It indicates that

---

[7] "Report of the Commission on Medical Care Plans, Findings, Conclusions and Recommendations," *The Journal of the American Medical Association*, Sp. Ed. (January 17, 1959), p. 2.

[8] *Ibid.*, p. 48, item 11.

[9] *Ibid.*, p. 44.

[10] *Ibid.*, p. 49, items 6 and 7.

proponents of some closed panel plans have come to recognize the desirability of a wider choice of physician by the patient.[11]

In addition to these observations, the report expressed some apprehension over the organization of these plans and their future development:

Although little evidence of lay domination was found in the plans visited, it is apparent that the threat of lay interference is ever-present and may exert itself in various ways and degrees. This could result in interference with the independent thinking and actions of physicians, result in decisions which reflect uninformed concepts held by lay boards, and thus affect adversely the quality and quantity of medical care.[12]

The majority of the plans do not have medical representation on their policy-making bodies. However, their governing boards seek the advice of physicians in various ways before making decisions which involve medical policy.[13]

There is a small but significant number of patient complaints in different plans. The outstanding reasons deal with undue waiting periods for examinations, the physician's attitude toward the patient, and the amount of time alloted during the patient's visit to the plan.[14]

In conclusion, the Commission observed that:

The medical profession should assume a judicious, tolerant, and progressive attitude toward developments in the medical care field. The need for continued experimentation is recognized, and the profession should undertake, and actively participate in, the study and development of various mechanisms for the provision of medical care of high quality.[15]

In 1959, upon review of the Commission's report, the House of Delegates of the AMA adopted a resolution which states, in part:

The American Medical Association believes that free choice of physician is the right of every individual and one which he should be free to exercise as he chooses.

Each individual should be accorded the privilege to select and change his physician at will or select his preferred system of medical care and the American Medical Association vigorously supports the right of the individual to choose between these alternatives.[16]

Thus, the American Medical Association reaffirmed its traditional stand on choice of physician, but at the same time recognized and supported the rights of individuals to choose among systems of medical care. The implications of the Commission's findings were more far-reaching, however. It recognized that group practice prepayment plans have stimulated other types of health insurers to broaden their coverage and increase their

---

[11] *Ibid.*, p. 44.

[12] *Ibid.*, p. 50, item 22.

[13] *Ibid.*, p. 49, item 20.

[14] *Ibid.*, p. 49, item 13.

[15] *Ibid.*, p. 53.

[16] John S. DeTar, American Medical Association House of Delegates, "Report of Special Reference Committee to Consider the Report of the Commission on Medical Care Plans," June 9, 1959.

benefits; that physicians practicing in such plans provide care of "good quality"; and that this form of health insurance has improved medical services for many persons.

CHOICE OF PLANS

Government Employee Programs

The post–World War II period has seen a rapid growth of employee health insurance programs in the private sector of our economy. These programs, paid for in part or in full by the employer, have become an increasingly important part of the employee's compensation. Government on all levels was slow in developing similar programs for its employees. Public employees argued that in order to compete with private industry and business for high-caliber employees, the government should also adopt employee benefit programs. Legislation to facilitate health insurance benefits for government employees was debated in many areas throughout the 1950's.

Federal Employees. In 1959, Congress approved the "Federal Employees Health Benefits Act of 1959," after extensive committee hearings in both the Senate and House. The transcript of the hearings, particularly those held before the Senate Subcommittee, suggests that initially the Civil Service Commission favored the adoption of a single plan to cover all federal employees and their dependents. For economic and administrative reasons, a single plan seemed advisable, yet the Act, when passed, provided for a choice among approved plans available in the employee's area of residence. Among the choices available to federal employees were:

Comprehensive Medical Plans—
Group Practice Prepayment Plans. Group practice prepayment plans which offer health benefits of the types referred to in section 5(4), in whole or in substantial part on a prepaid basis, with professional services thereunder provided by physicians practicing as a group in a common center or centers. Such a group shall include physicians representing at least three major medical specialties who receive all or a substantial part of their professional income from the prepaid funds.[17]

The Act was implemented July 1, 1960. The ten group practice plans[18] participating in the Federal Employees Health Benefits Program in 1963

---

[17] Public Law 86–382, approved September 28, 1959. (Appendix A. Federal Employees Health Benefits Act of 1959, as amended.)

[18] Bridge Clinic (Seattle, Washington), Community Health Association (Detroit, Michigan), Group Health Cooperative of Puget Sound (Seattle, Washington), Group Health Plan, Inc. (St. Paul, Minnesota), Health Insurance Plan of Greater New York, Kaiser Foundation Health Plan, Inc. (including four autonomous regions in California, Oregon and Hawaii, with rates and benefits varying in each region), Physicians and Surgeons Association Health Plan (California), Ross-Loos Medical Group (Los Angeles, California), Western Clinic (Tacoma, Washington) and Group Health Association, Inc. (Washington, D.C.).

had a combined enrollment of a quarter million federal employees and their dependents.[19] It is noteworthy that in the San Francisco Bay Area, where a direct service prepayment plan existed for some years prior to the enactment of the 1959 law, more than one third of the federal employees selected this plan. The plan was most popular among the choices available in the area. While this law was designed to provide health benefits only to a segment of the population (i.e., two million federal employees and their four million dependents), establishment of the precedent of choice was of historical significance in the evolution of prepaid medical care.

State Employees. The New York State Legislature passed enabling legislation in 1956 calling for development of a health benefits program for state employees. A temporary health insurance board, aided by consultation from Columbia University School of Public Health and Administrative Medicine,[20] developed a program which provided for alternative choices of plans where different types of systems of care were available. Included in the choice was the Health Insurance Plan of Greater New York (hereinafter referred to as HIP).

The 1961 California Legislature passed the Meyers-Geddes Medical and Hospital Care Act,[21] which resembles the federal act in that it provides for choice of plans. The program was implemented in January, 1962; during the last half of 1963, about 18 per cent of the 83,000 employees enrolled in the program were in group practice prepayment plans. There are many areas in California, including the state capital, where group practice prepayment plans are not available.

Other governmental employee groups, such as the University of California, counties, municipalities and school boards, have adopted health benefits programs with a comparable choice of plans. The City and County of San Francisco, for example, provided a choice of plans in its Health Service System as early as 1949.[22] Well over half of the population (employees and dependents) covered by this System belong to group practice prepayment plans.

The 1961 session of the Hawaii State Legislature passed an act establishing "The Hawaiian Public Employees Health Fund,"[23] which also provides a framework similar to the federal program for choice of plans. This act was implemented in January, 1962.

[19] United States Civil Service Commission Bureau of Retirement and Insurance, *Health Benefits Report Fiscal Year Ended June 30, 1963,* p. 31.

[20] Frank Van Dyke, statement published in *Hearings before Subcommittee on Insurance of the Committee on Post Office and Civil Service* (U.S. Senate, 86th Cong., 1st sess., on S.94) (Washington, D.C.: U.S. Government Printing Office, 1959), pp. 260–75.

[21] Sec. 22751 *et seq.,* California Government Code.

[22] Files of the Health Service System, City and County of San Francisco, 450 McAllister St., San Francisco, California.

[23] S.B. No. 17, S.D. 2, H.D. 1, enacted by Legislature of State of Hawaii, June 2, 1961.

Collective Bargaining Agreements

The first arrangement whereby a group practice prepayment plan became an alternate choice in a nationally negotiated contract was in the collective bargaining agreement between General Motors Corporation and the United Automobile Workers in 1952. This arrangement permitted employees of General Motors located in the San Francisco Bay Area to choose The Permanente Health Plan (now known as Kaiser Foundation Health Plan) as an alternate to the nationally negotiated Blue Cross–Blue Shield Plan. General Motors contributed the identical sum on behalf of the employees choosing Permanente as for those selecting Blue Cross–Blue Shield. Other regional and local agreements permitting choice of plans were developed early in the fifties in California and, later, in other parts of the country.[24]

NATURE AND ORGANIZATION OF SEVERAL GROUP PRACTICE PREPAYMENT PLANS

Each of the existing group practice plans evolved in a different setting out of special needs. The origin of each plan had an impact on its structure. The basic similarities and differences among the plans are suggested in the following brief descriptions of six plans, each of which has over 50,000 members. The descriptions which follow are an abstract of the data supplied by the plans.[25]

Kaiser Foundation Health Plan[26]

In the Mojave Desert, some 200 miles from the closest community, an aqueduct was being built in the early 1930's. At the contractors' request, a young surgeon, Dr. Sidney R. Garfield, organized a small team of physicians and built a fifteen-bed hospital to treat industrial injuries and illnesses. Soon it became apparent that the customary fee-for-service method of payment would not support the personnel and facility. In industrial cases, insurance companies used the local group for emergency and minor care only, sending seriously injured patients to company physi-

---

[24] Avram Yedidia, "Dual Choice Programs," *American Journal of Public Health*, Vol. XLIX, No. 11 (November, 1959), pp. 1475–79.

[25] The benefit schedules, exclusions, rates and supplemental charges of each plan are not discussed here. One source of such information is a "Summary of Benefits Offered by Comprehensive Prepaid Group Practice Plans in the United States" prepared by Research and Statistics Division of Group Health Association of America, Inc., Washington, D.C., July, 1964.

[26] Kaiser Foundation Medical Care Program Annual Reports 1960–63; C. C. Cutting, "Medical Care: Its Social and Organizational Aspects," *New England Journal of Medicine*, 269:729–736, October 3, 1963; Arthur Weissman, "Different Ways of Looking at Prepaid Medical Care," presented at Industrial Relations Section of Commonwealth Club, San Francisco, October 8, 1956, and published in *Hearings before Subcommittee on Insurance of the Committee on Post Office and Civil Service* (U.S. Senate, 86th Cong., on S.94) (Washington, D.C., 1959), pp. 223–27.

cians in Los Angeles. For nonindustrial care, workers sought service from the on-site physician. Those with disabling illness frequently had no resources with which to pay for their care. Faced with the prospect of losing the only medical services available, the contractors joined the physicians in persuading the insurance companies to pay $1.50 per month for each man covered for industrial medical care. Thus, fee-for-service was supplanted by prepayment.

The prepayment method was subsequently applied to cover nonindustrial illness by voluntary enrollment of employees at the rate of $1.50 per month. With the combined prepaid income for industrial and nonindustrial care, the group was able to increase its staff and facilities and improve its services.

In 1938, the Kaiser organization was in charge of constructing the Grand Coulee Dam, and Dr. Garfield was asked to establish a similar service there. In the early 1940's, the war emergency created new medical exigencies. Thousands of defense workers and their families requiring medical services competed for attention from a physician force depleted by military needs. Dr. Garfield was again asked to organize prepaid medical services for hundreds of thousands employed in the Kaiser Shipyards and later at the Kaiser Steel Mill in Fontana, California.

At war's end, the special needs which gave impetus to the development of this program no longer prevailed. In the summer months of 1945, Mr. Kaiser, Dr. Garfield and their associates addressed themselves to the following question: Could this form of medical care organization which was successful under special circumstances serve the needs of people in a normal community? Based on the three separate experiences spanning a decade and a half, the following principles emerged as the essential characteristics of their program:

1. *Group practice*—physicians representing the various specialties of medicine practicing together as a team, devoting full time to the group and pooling their professional income.

2. *Integrated facilities*—combined out-patient and in-patient facilities which lend themselves to the provision of total care to the patient.

3. *Prepayment*—financing to support staff and facilities derived from a subscribing membership making periodic payments.

4. *Voluntary enrollment*—a subscribing membership composed of persons who enroll in this type of program by individual choice and not by group decision.

5. *Preventive medical care*—safeguarding the health of the prepaid membership for whose care the program assumes responsibility by providing health maintenance and early disease detection services.

The leaders of the program believed that this structure of medical care could play an important role in a normal peacetime community, and in the fall of 1945, enrollment on a voluntary basis started among community groups and individuals. At the end of 1963, the Kaiser Foundation Health Plan, a California nonprofit corporation, served a membership of more than one million in four regions: Los Angeles, San Francisco, Portland and Honolulu. The Health Plan contracts with four independent medical groups (one in each region) for professional services and with Kaiser Foundation Hospitals—a California nonprofit, charitable corporation—for hospital care. The four medical groups, in December, 1963, included 953 full-time physicians, 564 of whom were partners. These physicians practice in forty-two medical offices and in thirteen Kaiser Foundation Hospitals with a total bed capacity of 2,421.

The Kaiser Foundation Health Plan's payments to each of the four medical partnerships are based primarily on the size of the Health Plan membership they serve and on the prepaid income from the subscribers. There is some variation in the exact formula of payment to each group; the prevalent method, however, is referred to as *capitation,* i.e., a specified monthly amount for each Health Plan member. In addition to the capitation, the contracts with the medical partnerships provide for incentive increments based on the operating results of the total program in their region. The medical group utilizes its income to finance the provision of medical care at home, in the doctors' offices and in the hospital. Each group is autonomous and is in sole charge of medical policy and the management of its affairs. The partners have an income related to their background, experience and contribution to the group. In addition, they share in any surplus. Newly recruited physicians are employees of the medical groups and are eligible for partnership after three years. The Boards of Directors of the Kaiser Foundation Health Plan and Kaiser Foundation Hospitals are comprised of business and industrial leaders.

The Kaiser Foundation Health Plan utilizes community rating in setting its subscription charges, i.e., subscribers in groups with similar benefits pay equal rates without relation to their utilization experience. The rate structure is based on a forecast of the budgetary requirements to sustain adequate staff and facilities for the care of the members.

Health Insurance Plan of Greater New York[27]

Mayor Fiorello LaGuardia appointed a study group in 1943 to devise a comprehensive medical care prepayment plan for employees of New York City and other residents. The Mayor's concern with this subject was prompted by a report of the Municipal Credit Union indicating that the family medical bills were the major source of indebtedness and financial

---

[27] HIP Annual and Statistical Reports; George Baehr, *A Report of the First Ten Years* (HIP publication, 1957); Louis L. Feldman, "Organization of a Medical Group Practice Prepayment Program in New York City," based on Master's Thesis accepted by the Graduate School of Business, New York University, September, 1953; Edwin F. Daily, "The Health Insurance Plan of Greater New York," *Ontario Medical Review,* June, 1961.

distress among city employees. The recommendations of the study group resulted in the formation of the Health Insurance Plan of Greater New York.

In 1944, this prepayment plan was established as a nonprofit membership corporation authorized to conduct a medical prepayment program subject to the statutory provision of Article IX–C of the Insurance Law, which applies to all nonprofit prepayment plans in New York. This Article permits the organization of membership corporations and consumers' cooperative stock corporations for the purpose of furnishing medical expense indemnity, or dental expense indemnity, or hospital service to subscribers of such corporations. HIP is under the supervision of the State Superintendent of Insurance.

The planners of the program, under the leadership of Dr. George Baehr, were faced with the task of developing organized medical services for group subscribers—city employees and others—who resided throughout the vast complex of the New York metropolitan area. They set out to form medical groups in the various parts of the city. The professional standards drafted by the planners required that a medical group include family physicians and specialists in twelve fields of medicine in order to qualify for a contract with HIP. These groups were to assume the responsibility for providing complete professional services to subscribers at home, in the doctors' offices and in the hospital. Payments to the medical groups were to be on a capitation basis.

By March, 1947, twenty-two medical groups located in various parts of the city were ready to serve HIP subscribers. Initially, services were provided in the private office of each physician. Each group agreed, however, to construct a medical center within a reasonable time at its own expense.

At the close of 1963, HIP served a membership of 680,000 through thirty-one medical groups. Services are provided in the medical group centers as well as in the private offices of group physicians. There are approximately 1,000 physicians associated with HIP medical groups, with about 170 of the physicians being full-time in the groups. HIP is governed by a thirty-member board, including at least ten physicians, three of whom represent the medical groups.

HIP has several divisions and functions in addition to those found in most insurance organizations: a Medical Control Board, composed of distinguished physicians, which promulgates standards, rules and regulations relating to the professional and technical services for enrollees; a Research and Statistics Division to collect and analyze data on services provided to the membership and to conduct studies on all phases of the program; a Health Education Division to provide technical staff for the preparation of educational material and to conduct meetings of members; and a staff of social workers available to physicians and subscribers for counseling on special problems.

HIP insures members for out-patient care and in-patient professional care. However, HIP requires members to be covered by Blue Cross or other hospital insurance. The HIP plan is community-rated.

Ross-Loos Medical Group[28]

The Ross-Loos Medical Group of Los Angeles is a partnership of physicians. Drs. Donald Ross and H. Clifford Loos in 1929 formed a partnership to provide prepaid medical care to employees of the Los Angeles Department of Water and Power. Other employee organizations, and subsequently individuals, were permitted to subscribe to Ross-Loos, which served 140,000 members at the end of 1963.

The guiding principles of this group, as enunciated by Dr. Ross, are: pooling the combined skills and knowledge of a physician group; rendering medical and hospital service to individuals through voluntary affiliation with a health group or committee; prepayment based on the estimated cost of providing services and on the utilization experience of each group, all individual subscribers being considered as a single group; physician ownership and management; upholding the traditional medical ethical standards of physicians and applying them to the group as a whole; and no active solicitation for membership.

At the end of 1963, the group included thirty-six partners who employed a salaried medical staff of 109. Annually, the partners elect an Executive Committee of eleven who appoint an Executive Partner to administer the organization. Ross-Loos physicians are located in group-maintained medical clinics and private offices throughout Los Angeles. They provide subscribers out-patient and in-patient care as well as hospitalization (underwritten by an insurance company) in semiprivate accommodations.

Subscribers are linked to the clinic organization through representation on Subscribers' Health Committees. Each group selects or elects a liaison committee working with the medical partnership in developing agreements for services, collection of dues and relaying complaints or suggestions to the physicians. The medical group feels that this technique provides effective communication between subscribers and providers of services.

Community Health Association, Detroit, Michigan (CHA)[29]

Among the six plans described herein, the Community Health Association of Detroit is the youngest. Impetus for its organization stemmed from the United Automobile Workers who provided loans for planning and

---

[28] The Ross-Loos Medical Group, *California Medicine*, 78:477–483, May, 1953; Information provided by M. W. Shearer, Ass't Administrator, The Ross-Loos Medical Group, 947 West 8th St., Los Angeles, California, April 10, 1964.

[29] Carlton Smith, "What's Walter Reuther Trying to Prove?" *Medical Economics*, December 2, 1963; Frederick D. Mott, "Community Health Association of Detroit," presented at 11th Annual Group Health Institute, Portland, Oregon, May 10, 1961.

acquisition of facilities. CHA is a nonprofit, unincorporated membership organization whose general aim is to promote and conserve good health. It operates as a consumer-sponsored prepaid plan in the five-county Detroit metropolitan area. The Board of Directors of CHA, headed by Walter Reuther, President of the United Automobile Workers, includes prominent individuals representing labor, management, finance, education and the clergy.

CHA services to members started in December, 1960; by the end of 1963, CHA served 60,000 members. The organization adheres to a voluntary enrollment policy, each family in this plan having had at least one alternative plan from which to choose. Subscribers are entitled to the full range of medical and hospital services and some additional special services such as consultation, diagnosis and short-term hospitalization for psychiatric conditions, and to home visiting nurse services. CHA is community-rated, and its rate structure is similar to Blue Cross–Blue Shield in the area.

CHA contracts with the Metropolitan Hospital and Clinics, a nonprofit community organization comprising a general hospital and a full-time medical group, to provide medical and hospital care to its members. The physicians, now numbering sixty, are full-time employees of the hospital. In addition to caring for CHA members, they are engaged in an active scientific and educational program. Physicians' income is comparable to the net income of their colleagues in solo practice. In addition, they have retirement and other fringe benefits.

Group Health Cooperative of Puget Sound, Seattle, Washington[30]

The Group Health Cooperative of Puget Sound was formed in 1947 as a result of the combined efforts of a group of laymen and several physicians who were associated with the Medical Security Clinic. Initially, enrollment was limited to families who elected to join the cooperative. An investment of $100 and a physical examination were prerequisites for membership. In recent years, the investment has been increased to $200, half of which can be deferred and paid at the rate of $1.00 per month over a period of ten years. The investment is used essentially for development of facilities and purchase of equipment. The operating budget of the organization is derived from monthly dues.

At the end of 1963, this program served a membership of 60,000, 70 per cent of whom were Cooperative members, the balance being members of contract groups, including government and industrial employees. The policy-making body is a board of trustees elected by the Cooperative membership. A director, who presently is a physician, is selected by the

---

[30] J. A. Kahl, "Group Health Cooperative of Puget Sound: General Information," Seattle, Washington, April 24, 1963; Annual Report, 1961; By-Laws of Group Health Cooperative of Puget Sound.

board and is responsible for the over-all direction of the organization's affairs. The medical staff contracts with the board to provide comprehensive medical care services to the members and also elects a chief of staff to direct their affairs. The contract between the board and the medical staff prevents lay interference in the practice of medicine. The medical staff of sixty physicians at the end of 1963 was composed of full-time general practitioners and specialists. They practice in a 155-bed, centrally located hospital, an adjoining out-patient center and several outlying clinics. The current hospital was built to replace an older structure and was financed largely through a $2.5 million bond issue purchased by the Cooperative membership. The Group Health Cooperative of Puget Sound is community-rated.

Group Health Association, Inc., of Washington, D.C. (GHA)[31]

GHA was first organized in February, 1937, by employees of the Home Owners Loan Corporation (a federal agency) as a voluntary mutual association to provide for the health needs of the members. While expressing sympathy to the notion of spreading the cost of illness over a large group of people, the District of Columbia Medical Society had reservations regarding the ethics of the contemplated clinic practice. After the clinic opened in November, 1937, the intensified opposition of the Medical Society led to a prolonged court battle. A U.S. Court of Appeals decision in 1939 held that GHA was not an insurance company and did not violate any insurance laws of the District of Columbia. The court declared that GHA was acting as a consumer cooperative. Subsequently, the Supreme Court found the American Medical Association and the Medical Society of the District of Columbia guilty of conspiracy in restraint of trade in connection with their activities regarding GHA. During the same period, battles were also waged to gain hospital privileges for physicians associated with GHA.

Membership grew and facilities were built and acquired. Today, GHA physicians have hospital privileges, many hold teaching assignments in medical schools, and some are active in the District's medical society.

At the end of 1963, GHA had a membership of 53,000, of whom 60 per cent were federal employees and their dependents who chose this plan under the Federal Employees' Health Benefits Program.

The affairs and property of GHA are managed by a board of nine trustees elected by the prepaid membership. GHA is a nonprofit, nonstock corporation under Sections 121–126, Title 5, of the District of Columbia Code (1929). GHA has two executives: a Medical Program Administrator who is in sole control of medical services and policy, and a nonphysician

---

[31] Frank C. Watters, "Group Health Association, Inc., of Washington, D.C.," *Group Practice,* Vol. X, No. 9 (September, 1961); information provided by T. M. Arnett, Medical Program Administrator, April 8, 1964.

Executive Director who administers the business affairs of the Association. The Medical Program Administrator serves as chief of the professional staff. The full-time staff represents the various specialties of medicine and provides the members services at home, in the doctor's office and in the hospital. The usual array of preventive and therapeutic health services is augmented by a visiting nurse service and family counseling. Hospital services are included under GHA prepayment and are arranged in community hospitals in semiprivate accommodations. In addition, a portion of the membership has enrolled in a prepaid dental care program. Physicians have an annual income which compares favorably with incomes of their colleagues in the community.

CHARACTERISTICS OF THE SIX GROUP PRACTICE PREPAYMENT PLANS

Common Features

Although group practice prepayment plans vary considerably in their organization, benefit structures, rating procedures and other operational aspects, the six plans described have the following basic features in common:

1. Prepayment funds are used primarily for the organization of adequate staff and facilities to provide a broad range of medical care services to the membership.

2. Physicians' services (medical and surgical) are provided in the home, doctor's office and hospital. Services are organized to meet the needs of the membership on a twenty-four-hour, 365-day basis. The groups of physicians providing services represent the various specialties of medicine.

3. Care is not limited to illnesses and accidents—physical examinations and pediatric care are also provided. Out-patient diagnostic services are included. Emphasis on preventive services varies among the plans. Where prepayment does not fully cover any service, an explicit statement is made to members regarding the extent of additional charges.

4. All plans have group centers where practically all out-patient services are provided. (In the case of HIP, some family physicians are still located in their private offices, but all specialists' care is provided in the group facilities.)

5. Enrollment is based on the voluntary choice of each family and not on group decision. Membership groups participating in these plans generally give the subscribers a choice between a group practice prepayment plan and a health insurance plan which permits the subscribers to secure their medical care in the traditional manner. Under such arrangements, each member of a group is required to make a choice among the available plans annually or at other set intervals.

6. Physicians are in sole control of medical policy in the plans.

Significant Variations among the Plans

Hospital Coverage.   Kaiser, GHA, Group Health of Puget Sound and CHA include hospital services in their prepayment programs. Ross-Loos covers hospital services through an affiliated insurance company. HIP requires its members to be covered by Blue Cross or other hospital insurance.

Hospital Facilities.   Kaiser, CHA and Group Health of Puget Sound have their own hospitals which are integrated with the out-patient facilities. HIP, Ross-Loos and GHA use community hospitals.

Boards of Directors.   The Kaiser board is composed of business and industrial leaders. The boards of HIP and CHA represent community leaders. Puget Sound and GHA boards are elected by the consumers, while Ross-Loos is governed by the physicians.

Method of Compensating Medical Groups.   Kaiser and HIP contract with medical groups which are independent partnerships. The medical groups are paid on a capitation basis. CHA contracts with a hospital which employs the physicians, and payments to the hospital are on a cost-reimbursement basis. In GHA and Puget Sound, medical services are provided by organized medical staffs which are paid on a cost-reimbursement basis. Ross-Loos is a physician-owned plan.

Basis for Rate Making.   With the exception of Ross-Loos, the plans described are community-rated, i.e., subscribers in groups with similar benefits pay equal rates without relation to their utilization experience. Ross-Loos experience rates its subscriber groups, i.e., the utilization experience of a subscriber group has a bearing on its rates.

ADVANTAGES AND DISADVANTAGES OF GROUP PRACTICE PREPAYMENT PLANS

Advantages to Consumers

The purchaser of voluntary health insurance who selects a group practice prepayment plan also chooses a relatively new and different system of medical care. In all other forms of health insurance, the insuring organizations are in no way involved in the process of care. Their insureds are responsible for securing their own care, while the insurer, as a fiscal agent, merely pays for services in accordance with pre-arranged rules. On the other hand, the subscriber to a group practice prepayment plan, by design, selects a pattern of care. He may have had a voice in developing this system of care; he may have a continuing role in molding certain of its elements through membership committees, health councils and other forms of communication between subscribers and providers of service; but in all cases, the subscriber himself makes the decision that this is the system of care he desires. This decision is usually made at a time when the subscriber is not in immediate need of medical services. In a sense, therefore, a person who enrolls in a group practice prepayment plan is not only purchasing health care coverage, but is also making arrangements for securing his future medical care.

The relationship between the plan and the membership is not confined to episodes of illness when the member becomes a patient—members use their plan for physical examinations and pediatric care as well. Studies[32] indicate that in a population covered by group practice prepayment, the proportion of persons using their plan during a given year is significantly higher than in populations covered by fee-for-service plans. The process of the member's identification with his group practice prepayment plan is enhanced by the fact that, in addition to having a family physician, the member becomes acquainted with his physician's colleagues and the ancillary personnel working at the group center. He is therefore not dependent upon a single practitioner for his health needs. He has access to a variety of specialists, ancillary personnel and equipment to serve his health requirements as the need arises. Plan members are therefore reliant upon an organization which makes its services available and accessible not only during regular office hours, but also at night and on weekends and holidays.

The importance of the member's identification with the staff, facilities and system of care needs to be stressed. Persons who do not belong to a prepaid group practice plan often find themselves at a loss when in need of medical care services. When their efforts to reach a physician fail, they frequently turn to the emergency room of the hospital. This accounts for the rapidly increasing number of nonemergency patients treated in emergency rooms of hospitals.[33]

Significant economies in the total cost of health care accrue to the consumer from his participation in a group practice prepayment plan, according to a number of studies.[34] The data indicate that the combined expenditure for prepayment and out-of-pocket charges for persons covered by such plans is substantially lower than for those covered by fee-for-service health insurance programs.

---

[32] United States Civil Service Commission Bureau of Retirement and Insurance, *Health Benefits Report Fiscal Year Ended June 30, 1963.*

[33] This fact has been reported in several studies and was summarized in a *Wall Street Journal* article, August 10, 1964, p. 1.

[34] Malcolm S. Watts *et al.*, "Special Report of the Medical and Hospital Advisory Council to the Board of Administration of State Employees Retirement System," Sacramento, California, June, 1964; United Steelworkers of America, *Medical Care Program for Steelworkers and Their Families,* 10th Constitutional Convention, United Steelworkers of America, Atlantic City, September, 1960; *Family Medical Care under Three Types of Health Insurance,* A Survey Conducted for the Foundation for Employee Health, Medical Care and Welfare, Inc. (477 Madison Avenue, New York), by the School of Public Health and Administrative Medicine, Columbia University, with the cooperation of the National Opinion Research Center, University of Chicago (New York, 1962).

Economies of operation of a group practice prepayment plan, which in turn benefit the member, can be attributed to (1) maximum utilization of the physician's time in the care of patients, without concern for the business aspects of his practice; (2) nonduplication of equipment and ancillary personnel; (3) maximum utilization of physical facilities and plant; and (4) the growing evidence that provision of the full spectrum of medical services accompanied by coordination of such services, the continuity of care and its supervision by the medical team are associated with lower hospital utilization rates than are found in other forms of practice.[35]

In the opinion of some leaders of group practice prepayment plans, further economies can be realized in such plans with an ever-increasing emphasis on preventive services and the early detection of disease.[36] If their assumptions with respect to the value of preventive services and the resulting economies in the cost of medical care are correct, then, they say that in a group practice prepayment setting, the basic economic relationship between the patient and the doctor is reversed. Whereas, in solo practice, or in group practice without prepayment, the major source of the physician's income is the sick patient, in a group practice with prepayment, the healthy subscriber is the greatest asset; it is therefore economically sound to invest a substantial portion of the resources of the program in preventive services. Studies attempting to measure the effectiveness of preventive services and their impact on the cost of medical care are now in progress.[37]

Disadvantages to Consumers

Areas in which group practice prepayment plans fall short of meeting the expectations of their membership are disclosed in several studies on patient attitude and satisfaction.[38] The most common trouble spots relate to failure of communication between plan and patient, to impersonal attitudes on the part of personnel and to long waiting periods for appointments. All of these, when they occur, hamper the provision of effective medical care.

---

[35] Paul M. Densen, Eve Balamuth, and Sam Shapiro, *Prepaid Medical Care and Hospital Utilization*, Hospital Monograph Series No. 3 (American Hospital Association, 1958); United Steelworkers of America, *op. cit.;* Agnes W. Brewster, "Group Health Association's Use of Community Hospitals," *Proceedings, Tenth Annual Group Health Institute of the Group Health Association of America* (Columbus, Ohio, May, 1960), pp. 117–21.

[36] "Pretenses, Practices and Patterns in Group Health Programs," *Proceedings, Twelfth Annual Group Health Institute of the Group Health Association of America, Inc.* (Washington, D.C., May, 1962), pp. 135–57.

[37] Morris F. Collen *et al.*, "Automated Multiphasic Screening and Diagnosis," *American Journal of Public Health*, Vol. LIV, No. 5 (May, 1964), pp. 741–50.

[38] E. Richard Weinerman, "Patients' Perceptions of Group Medical Care," *American Journal of Public Health*, Vol. LIV, No. 6 (June, 1964).

Group practice prepayment plans, by their very nature, are restricted to the geographic area in which they function. This is a product of the most fundamental characteristic of these plans, viz., they *organize* and *arrange* the medical care services for their members. It follows that members in need of medical care while temporarily away from home cannot utilize the regular services of the plan. To meet such situations, the plans usually include an out-of-area cash indemnity benefit. The amounts available for each illness or injury range from $250 to $2,000. Indications are that claims for out-of-area emergency services constitute less than 1 per cent of the total cost of the program.[39]

Families who move away from their home community, irrespective of the type of health insurance they carry, disrupt their medical care arrangements. It would appear, however, that members of a group practice prepayment plan are subjected to the added disadvantage of having to secure a new health insurance plan. In many instances, this is easily accomplished. For example, the federal employee who belongs to a group practice prepayment plan, when transferred to a new area, has the option of joining any of the federal employee plans available in his new community. Likewise, a transferred employee of private business or industry has a built-in alternate plan through the mechanism of choice discussed earlier. Finally, the prevalence of employer paid or contributory health insurance plans provides persons who move to new jobs in the same community, or in a different one, with continued coverage. However, members of a group practice prepayment plan who lose their group status and must rely on a conversion plan for continued health coverage are at a distinct disadvantage when they find it necessary to move from the service area of the plan.

A person who joins a group practice prepayment plan restricts his choice of physician to the medical group associated with the plan. He cannot avail himself of the services of *any* physician in the community. Freedom of choice, its significance, its meaning, the advantages and disadvantages it affords the consumer of medical care, has long been a subject of lively debate. The selected references at the end of this chapter include material on this subject.

Advantages to Physicians

A physician who desires to devote his full working time to care of patients and other professional pursuits without the intrusion of the business aspects of practice can do so in a group practice prepayment setting. The business aspects of medical care in such an organization are carried on by personnel who are specifically trained for this purpose.

---

[39] Based on claim records of the Kaiser Foundation Health Plan, Northern California Region. Over a half-million members are covered by this plan and their out-of-area benefit amount is $500 or $1,000 for each illness or accidental injury.

Further, a physician in a group can lead an orderly personal life. Responsibility for his patients is shared by the group, and leisure time can be secured without neglect of patients.

A physician in such a group can have an income comparable to that of physicians in solo practice in his community and, at the same time, have the added advantage of certain benefits often unobtainable by a physician practicing alone, or even in partnership. These benefits include continuation of income during periods of illness, time off for continuing education and travel, adjustment of work schedule to meet special limitations occasioned by disability and, finally, an attractive retirement program. For the specialist who has just completed his training, group practice prepayment offers an opportunity of beginning a career without concern over starting-up costs.

A physician in a group practice prepayment setting has no economic pressures to perform beyond his competence in areas where other specialists can do a more adequate job. Referring his patients to a colleague represents neither a financial loss nor a loss of prestige. Instead, it enables the patient to receive the best care within the capacity of the total medical group and acts as a professional stimulus which is a by-product of exchange and communication among physicians in different specialties. The physician's satisfaction is enhanced by his ability to direct his patient's care in an environment in which specialization need not interfere with the treatment of the patient as a total human being. As a chapter in a publication regarding group practice concludes, "When a man becomes a part of an organization, he gives up a measure of independence, but he gains something too. Group practice is not for everyone. But for many it is a happy and satisfying way of life."[40]

Disadvantages to Physicians

Participation in a medical group associated with a group practice prepayment plan may not suit certain physicians. Any person who joins a group subordinates part of his individualism to it. He is subject to rules promulgated by the majority of his colleagues even though he may be part of a dissenting minority. Many physicians are temperamentally unsuited to a joint venture of this nature which requires a constant close relationship with others. Physicians in specialties which yield a particularly high income in solo practice may feel that a group arrangement which tends to equalize the income in the various specialties is to their economic detriment.

Other disadvantages to physicians have been expressed as follows:[41]

---

[40] *Group Practice: Guidelines to Forming or Joining a Medical Group,* a booklet published by the American Association of Medical Clinics, the American Medical Association and the National Association of Clinic Managers, 1962, chap. iii.

[41] *Ibid.,* p. 17.

Each group member shares in, and suffers to some degree by, the errors of his associates—and they from his. . . . Group practice sometimes leads to an undesirable degree of over-specialization in practice. . . . Group practice sometimes attracts men who are more interested (or become so) in professional and personal security than in excellence of practice, teaching and research. (It is said that the "organization man" sometimes finds his way into the practice of medicine, too.) . . . . There is increased possibility of disagreement over division of professional income.

ROLE OF GROUP PRACTICE PREPAYMENT PLANS

Group practice prepayment plans have emerged in widely separated areas of the country. Each plan is indigenous to its community and responsive to specific needs. Dialogue among the plans has developed in recent years, particularly under the auspices of the Group Health Association of America, Inc.[42]

In spite of the increased communication among group practice prepayment plans, their origin and growth to date can scarcely be looked upon as the product of a *movement*. As a matter of fact, the founders of the various plans came from vastly different backgrounds with widely divergent points of view. Yet, a review discloses similarities among the plans and suggests that group practice has developed in response to multiple medical and socioeconomic problems created by our complex society.

Specialization, a product of scientific advance and technological change, brings with it fragmentation. It is often felt that a physician practicing alone, or even in some association with others, cannot take care of the "whole man." Group practice without prepayment gives the physician an opportunity for collaboration with colleagues in various specialties of medicine. The patient under such an arrangement stands to gain from this association of specialists.

Increases in the cost of health services, the unpredictability of illness for the individual and the importance of medical care have all contributed to the phenomenal growth of health insurance in the United States. Group practice and health insurance each are important developments in themselves, but the fusion of the two is felt by many to offer new opportunities which are not present when they function independently of each other. Group practice with prepayment can bring about the integration of specialties not only for effective episodic treatment of disease which can be obtained from group practice without prepayment, but also for continuing comprehensive care. It provides an opportunity for organizing the total spectrum of health needs including preventive services,

---

[42] An association located in Washington, D.C., which includes approximately forty health plans and thirty other organizations (e.g., unions, insurance companies, etc.) as well as individual members. This association performs educational activities designed to advance group practice prepayment principles. It also conducts an annual institute which serves as a vehicle for exchange of information among plans and exploration of mutual problems.

health maintenance services, and continued care for chronic diseases, as well as care for acute disease. It enables development of facilities which permit maximum coordination of services for the convenience of physician and patient and for the most effective manner of providing care. Above all, it permits providers and consumers of care to join together voluntarily in a creative program. For the physician who joins in such a venture, it brings a new way of professional life, which provides for many needs that are difficult to satisfy in solo practice or even in group practice without prepayment. To the consumer it offers, in addition to medical economic security, a system of care of his own choosing.

The benefits of a group practice prepayment plan are not limited to the members and providers of service who participate in it; benefits also accrue to the general community in which the plan functions. It serves to stimulate other forms of health insurance programs to broaden their benefits. For employers and unions who are concerned with the cost of medical care, it brings into play a competitive system with demonstrated economies. To the researcher, the availability of a defined population which receives practically all of its medical care from one source offers a new and rich laboratory for studying morbidity, utilization patterns, effectiveness of specific therapy and other aspects of medical care. Among medical educators, there is increasing interest in finding ways of combining medical education with group practice prepayment. The process of providing comprehensive medical care to a prepaid population, in the opinion of some educators, offers the promise of expanding present methods of medical education which are primarily oriented to diagnosis and treatment of disease rather than to the health needs of the community.

Many observers feel that group practice prepayment has not yet realized its potential. As a social institution which applies prepaid funds to the organization of comprehensive services for its membership, it has many opportunities for enrichment of program and scope of service. Among the areas in which greater effort in organization of care is indicated are: mental illness, rehabilitation, out-patient drugs, home care and other special services for the aged and chronically sick. These are some of the missing or weak links in the chain of comprehensive care as it is now provided by most such plans. The vitality of group practice prepayment and its future growth and development depend on its ability to bridge the gaps in coverage and its capacity to be responsive and sensitive to the needs of the population it serves.

SELECTED REFERENCES

An expanded bibliography on this and related subjects is contained in *Administrative Aspects of Prepaid Group Practice* by LESLIE A. FALK, GRACE J. MUSHRUSH, and MIRIAM E. SKRIVANEK. Library of Congress Catalog Card No. 64–16014 (University of Pittsburgh Press).

CUTTING, C. C. "Medical Care: Its Social and Organizational Aspects," *New England Journal of Medicine,* 269:729–736, October 3, 1963.

DEARING, W. P. *Prepaid Group Practice Medical Care Plans,* Public Health Reports, Public Health Service, U.S. Department of Health, Education, and Welfare, Vol. LXXVII, No. 10 (October, 1962), pp. 855–58.

Family Medical Care under Three Types of Health Insurance, A Survey Conducted for the Foundation for Employee Health, Medical Care and Welfare, Inc., by the School of Public Health and Administrative Medicine, Columbia University, with the cooperation of the National Opinion Research Center, University of Chicago. New York, 1962.

GROUP HEALTH ASSOCIATION OF AMERICA, RESEARCH AND STATISTICS DIVISION. *Summary of Benefits Offered by Comprehensive Prepaid Group Practice Plans in the United States.* Washington, D.C., July, 1964.

Group Practice: Guidelines to Forming or Joining a Medical Group, a booklet published by the American Association of Medical Clinics, the American Medical Association and the National Association of Clinic Managers, 1962.

SOMERS, HERMAN M., AND ANNE R. *Doctors, Patients and Health Insurance.* Washington, D.C.: The Brookings Institution, 1961.

STEWART, WILLIAM H. "What Lies Ahead for Group Practice?" presented at 14th Annual Group Health Institute, Minneapolis, Minnesota, May, 1964, to be published in *Proceedings, 14th Annual Group Health Institute of the Group Health Association of America, Inc.*

UNITED STEELWORKERS OF AMERICA. *Medical Care Program for Steelworkers and Their Families,* 10th Constitutional Convention, United Steelworkers of America, Atlantic City, September, 1960.

WATTS, MALCOLM S., *et al.* "Special Report of the Medical and Hospital Advisory Council to the Board of Administration of State Employees Retirement System," Sacramento, California, June, 1964.

Chapter 16

GROUP HOSPITAL BENEFITS

BY GORDON N. FARQUHAR

At the end of 1964 nearly 149 million persons, about 78 per cent of the United States civilian population, were protected by some form of hospital insurance,[1] thereby making such protection the most widely held form of health insurance coverage. The popularity of hospital benefits is not surprising when one considers the fact that all but a few Americans begin their lives in a hospital and will return in all likelihood at some time for surgical or medical treatment of a restorative nature. For many, life will end in a hospital. While the fact of confinement is inescapable for most, the time of its occurrence is not readily predictable for any one person, and when necessary it can involve a significant expense.[2]

Hospitals have become the center of care for many types of illnesses and injuries ranging from the routine appendectomy to the long-range care of the psychiatrically disturbed. In 1963, personal consumption expenditures for all kinds of medical care totaled $23.7 billion. The largest single share of this expenditure, or thirty-one cents of every private medical care dollar, was spent for hospital services, totaling $7.6 billion.[3]

Hospital expense insurance, in a wide variety of benefit patterns and offered by many different types of insuring organizations, represents an orderly method of meeting hospital costs. In 1963, insuring organizations paid a total of $4.6 billion in hospital expense benefits, of which approximately three fourths was paid under group insurance plans.[4]

---

[1] *Health Insurance News* (December, 1964).

[2] The American Hospital Association reported an average cost per patient stay in nonfederal short-term hospitals of $298.05 in 1963: "Hospitals," *Journal of the American Hospital Association,* Vol. XXXVIII, Part 2 (August 1, 1964), p. 479.

[3] *Social Security Bulletin, December, 1964* (U.S. Department of Health, Education, and Welfare), "Private Consumers Expenditures for Medical Care and Voluntary Health Insurance," pp. 12–22.

[4] A significant portion of the difference between expenditures for hospital services, $7.6 billion, and the amount paid by insuring organizations, $4.6 billion, represents personal services, elective private room and other optional items generally not considered proper subjects of insurance.

About 70 per cent of the hospital expense coverage underwritten by insurance companies is provided under group policies. Similarly, a majority of the enrollments in Blue Cross and other noninsurance company hospital plans have been accomplished on the group, as opposed to the individual or family subscriber, basis.

NATURE OF GROUP HOSPITAL COVERAGE

The purpose of group hospital expense benefits is to pay or to help pay the cost of hospital services required in connection with the treatment of an illness or an injury. Since costs in connection with injuries that arise out of employment are usually covered under workmen's compensation laws, group hospital expense benefits are normally limited to illnesses and injuries that are nonoccupational in nature. While some group insurance plans pay virtually the entire costs of hospital services, most plans maintain an element of participation of the claimant in the cost of his hospital care. This is accomplished by scheduling benefits that are below the current level of costs, by excluding certain charges such as the excess of private room over ward or semiprivate charges, by limiting the number of days of confinement that will be covered, or by limiting the allowance for ancillary charges. Thus, the purpose of group hospital expense benefits is to minimize, but not to eliminate entirely, the financial impact of hospital costs when confinement is necessary.

In general the benefits payable for illness or injury under group hospital expense policies are divided into two major categories: a benefit for hospital room-and-board charges, including general nursing services and other routine daily items; and a benefit for charges by the hospital for special services and supplies, such as use of operating room, X-rays, laboratory tests and drugs. The benefit payable for maternity confinements is usually a stated amount payable for both room and board and special service charges combined.

Group hospital expense benefits are normally payable only for hospital charges incurred during a period of confinement as a bed patient and for hospital out-patient charges in connection with emergency treatment of an accident. Also, insurance company plans and an increasing number of Blue Cross plans pay hospital expense benefits for hospital out-patient charges when care is given in the out-patient department in connection with a surgical operation.

Most group hospital plans underwritten by insurance companies provide a cash indemnity or reimbursement for actual charges made by the hospital; thus, the risk insured is the hospital charge and not the confinement as such. This was not always true, since some earlier plans provided a fixed payment based on the number of days of confinement without regard to the cost involved. On the other hand, Blue Cross plans for the most part provide benefits on a service basis. The Blue Cross subscriber receives up to a stated number of days of hospital "service" in a hospital which has a contract with Blue Cross. The Blue Cross plan reimburses the hospital, according to the arrangements made in the contract. The hospital services covered are usually defined to include semiprivate room and board and most special services and supplies for the stated number of days.

CONDITIONS AND GENERAL PROVISIONS

A number of conditions must be met before an insured is eligible for group hospitalization benefits under a typical plan. For example, confinement normally must take place in a "hospital" as defined in the policy. While definitions vary, it is usually required that the hospital keep patients regularly overnight, have full diagnostic, surgical and therapeutic facilities under the supervision of a staff of doctors of medicine and provide twenty-four-hour nursing service by registered graduate nurses. Rest homes, nursing homes, homes for the aged and certain other specialized institutions are excluded from the definition of a hospital. Government hospitals are usually excluded unless they make a charge to all patients without regard to the existence of insurance.

Confinement must be recommended and approved by a physician. For this purpose a physician is usually defined so as to include doctors of medicine, doctors of osteopathy, dentists (sometimes) and, to some extent, other classes of practitioners. Also, confinement must commence while the insurance is in force, or if there is an extended insurance provision for persons totally disabled when the insurance was terminated, within a period thereafter such as three months. The payment of maternity benefits is usually contingent upon pregnancy commencing while insurance is in force.

The room-and-board benefit is usually defined to include routine or general nursing services provided by the hospital and any other charges which are made by the hospital on a regular daily or weekly basis or as a condition of occupancy. The benefit for special hospital services and supplies is normally payable on a "blanket" basis for necessary services and supplies other than room and board. In other words, the allowance is the total payable for use of the operating room, X-ray and laboratory examinations, drugs and dressings, or any combination of these services and supplies, without inside limits or scheduled amounts for each item.

Benefits generally are not payable for private duty nursing or for services furnished by physicians, interns or outside agencies. Exceptions have been made in many group insurance plans, however, to permit payment, under the benefit for special hospital services and supplies, for professional ambulance service to or from the hospital and for charges by a physician for the administration of anesthesia when not provided by the hospital.

Group insurance contracts usually require in-patient confinement with a charge by the hospital for board and room. However, the benefit for hospital services and supplies is payable for hospital out-patient care when the hospital provides services and supplies in connection with a surgical procedure performed in the out-patient department or emergency treatment of a nonoccupational injury within twenty-four (or forty-eight) hours of the injury.

The limits on the amounts payable apply to each continuous period of disability. Thus, most policies contain a provision under which successive periods of hospital confinement are considered as having occurred during one continuous period of disability unless separated by complete recovery or by return to active work or unless due to entirely unrelated causes. Blue Cross plans usually relate their benefits to a ninety-day out-of-hospital limitation, rather than to a "cause of illness" clause.

Few exclusions are used in group hospital coverage issued by insurance companies. Such policies rarely contain exclusions of or waiting periods for pre-existing conditions. Neither are conditions arising as a result of air travel or war excluded in most instances. Eligibility to become insured, as in other group coverages, merely requires that an employee be actively at work on the effective date and his dependents not currently confined in a hospital. Among the few exclusions are those for self-inflicted injuries or injuries which are the result of one's own improper acts.

BASIC COMPONENTS OF HOSPITAL EXPENSE BENEFITS

A description of the basic components of an illustrative group hospital expense plan, as underwritten by insurance companies and presuming a schedule of insurance calling for a basic daily room and board benefit of $20, is shown below.

Room and Board

The plan pays for the amount actually charged by the hospital for room and board but not more than [$20] (the amount of daily benefit shown in the Schedule of Insurance) for each day the employee or one of his insured dependents is confined in a hospital as a result of a nonoccupational disease or injury. The maximum amount so payable during any one continuous period of disability is [$1,400] (seventy times the rate of daily benefit shown in the Schedule of Insurance).

Special Hospital Services and Supplies

The plan also pays for the actual charges made by the hospital for necessary services and supplies other than board and room which are furnished by the hospital during the confinement but not more than [$400] (twenty times the rate of daily benefit shown in the Schedule of Insurance) during any one continuous period of disability. However, no benefits will be paid for services and supplies furnished after the first [seventy] days of confinement.

Maternity Benefits

If hospital confinement is due to pregnancy, or resulting childbirth or miscarriage, the plan pays for the actual charges made by the hospital for room and board and other necessary services and supplies, but not more than [$200] (ten times the rate of daily benefit shown in the Schedule of Insurance) is payable for all hospital confinements due to any one pregnancy.

AMOUNTS AND DURATION OF BENEFITS

While the above description of the basic components is representative of the design of group hospital expense plans, the amounts and durations of benefits are characterized by wide variations. This results from the fact that hospital charges differ substantially according to geographical area and particularly between urban and rural areas. Patterns in an industry or in collective bargaining, the cost which an employer and his employees are willing to pay and the emphasis placed on control of claim costs also affect benefit levels. In general, insurance companies have tended to tailor their offerings to meet the requirements of a particular group, whereas Blue Cross plans have tended historically toward a uniform plan or plans for all groups in a given community.

Room and Board

Room-and-board benefits range from about $6.00 or $7.00 per day to about $30 or more per day. Of employees covered under new group policies issued in 1964, 57 per cent have room and board benefits of $16 or more, and 34 per cent provided $20 or more per day.[5] It is generally believed that the amount selected for a given plan should be substantial enough to meet the needs of those insured, but not so high as to result in over-insurance. For example, while a $24 benefit might cover 80 to 100 per cent of the ward or semiprivate accommodations in hospitals on the West Coast, it would be excessive in parts of the South where the average charge might be $12 a day.

Alternatively, Blue Cross contracts customarily provide full reimbursement in ward or semiprivate accommodations. While this eliminates payment by the insured of a part of the charge, the cost of the insurance plan is more susceptible to rising hospital charges than a plan which contains a dollar limit. It should be recognized, however, that adequate coverage will require higher premiums under any benefit approach as hospital charges rise.

[5] *Survey of Group Health Insurance Policies Issued in 1964* (New York: Health Insurance Institute, 1964), p. 5.

The maximum period of coverage available ranges from twenty-one to as high as 365 days, but the most common durations are thirty-one, seventy or 120 days. A recent study showed that three out of five persons covered under new group contracts were protected for seventy or more days.[6] Such plans are considered adequate for most cases since only about one half of 1 per cent of hospital confinements extend beyond seventy days.[7]

In some group plans the specified benefits are payable for a stated number of days with one half the allowance payable during the next thirty-one, seventy or 120 days. One large Blue Cross plan provides, for example, semiprivate coverage for twenty-one days and one half the semiprivate charge for the next 180 days.

The Jesse Mayo Disability Insurance Hospital Benefits Law in California (Sections 2800–2804 of the California Unemployment Insurance Codes) currently requires employers in that state to provide benefits to covered employees of $12 per day for up to twenty days of hospital confinement. This benefit is in addition to the cash sickness benefits of the California Unemployment Compensation Code. Group hospital insurance plans usually provide a corresponding cutback in the amounts payable in California during the first twenty days, but some plans pay in addition to the benefit required under the Code.

Hospital Services and Supplies

The maximum allowance for hospital services and supplies ranges from five times the rate of daily benefit provided for room and board to full payment of substantially all such services and supplies. The most common plan provides benefits ranging from $200 to $400 of these charges, but plans providing full coverage during the period for which room-and-board benefits are payable are becoming more frequent under insurance company plans. Such full coverage is widespread among Blue Cross plans. A variation of the full coverage feature, found in about 15 per cent of new insurance company plans, provides for payment of up to twenty times the rate of daily benefit at 100 per cent reimbursement, plus payment of the next $1,000 (or the remainder of hospital charges for services and supplies) at 75 per cent.[8] Out-patient services, covered in the case of emergency accident treatment or in connection with a surgical operation, are usually subject to the same limits as apply for confinement, but in an occasional plan a separate limit, such as $10 or $25, is applied.

[6] *Ibid.*, p. 6.

[7] Stanley W. Gingery, "A Reinvestigation of Group Hospital Expense Insurance Experience," *Transactions of the Society of Actuaries,* Vol. XII (September, 1960), pp. 682–83.

[8] *Survey of Group Health Insurance Policies Issued in 1964, op. cit.,* Table 10, p. 18.

Maternity Benefits

As described above, maternity benefits are usually payable on the basis of a separate specified amount both for room and board and for hospital services and supplies. The most common allowance is ten times the rate of daily benefit regardless of the length of confinement. Alternatively, the maternity allowance might be a flat dollar amount, such as $200 for all hospital charges.

The limit is usually set somewhat below the average charge for maternity confinements, and, thus, the benefit becomes, in effect, a lump sum payable for childbirth. However, a large number of group insurance plans that result from collective bargaining provide the same benefits for maternity as are allowed for illness or injury.

It is not uncommon for insurers to consider the normal nursery charge of a newborn child as a part of the mother's maternity expense and payable thereunder to the extent of available maternity benefits. This occurs when the child is not eligible in its own right for insurance during the first few days of its life, usually seven or fourteen days.

There is a great variation in maternity hospital benefits among Blue Cross plans. Payments range from a $50 benefit in one plan to substantially full coverage in most plans.

Maternity coverage is sometimes excluded entirely by insurance company plans, and this was true for about one fourth of the employees and dependents covered under new group plans issued in 1964.[9] Where included, there usually is a requirement that pregnancy commence while insurance is in force, or alternatively, a requirement that insurance has been in force for at least nine (or ten) months when the pregnancy terminates in order to qualify for benefits. Also, insurance company plans customarily provide maternity benefits after insurance ceases provided pregnancy commenced prior to cessation of insurance. This generally has not been the case under Blue Cross plans when the master group policy is canceled. Blue Cross usually requires that a female be enrolled for "family coverage"; in other words, both she and her husband must be insured in order to receive maternity benefits.[10]

Deductible Provision

As hospital costs have risen in recent years, insurance companies and a few Blue Cross plans have offered a deductible provision under which the

---

[9] *Ibid.*, p. 5.

[10] A similar requirement, known as "switch maternity," has recently become prevalent under insurance company group plans. The cost of maternity coverage for a female employee is "switched" to the dependent premium, and she must enroll her husband.

hospital benefits are reduced by a deductible of $25 or $50 or by elimination of room-and-board benefits for the first one, two or three days in each period of confinement. The effect of this provision is to shift some of the cost to the insured employee for budgetable expenses, and the provision has been incorporated primarily as a control feature for those groups where the incidence of short-term confinements is high. It does not, however, influence the length of stay, since it serves only to eliminate from claims the first few dollars of payment and to reduce the incentive to be confined for minor treatment in order to be covered.

ELIGIBILITY FOR GROUP HOSPITAL INSURANCE

Many insurance companies, and the laws of thirty-seven states plus the District of Columbia, require that at least ten eligible employees be insured in order to issue a group health insurance policy to an employer. (The minimum number in three states is five employees, and ten states have no minimum.) When a group contract is issued, it is customary to require that the employee be actively at work in order for his group hospital insurance to become effective, and, if the plan is contributory, he must enroll and agree to pay the stated contributions.[11]

The policy may provide that new employees become eligible on the date that they are employed, or they may be required to serve a probationary period of one, two or three months, but rarely longer. Almost all group contracts include coverage for eligible dependents of an employee. If the employee under a contributory plan enrolls for coverage for himself and his dependents no later than thirty-one days following the date first eligible, insurance is made effective without a medical examination and without regard to prior health conditions. On the other hand, if enrollment is delayed beyond the prescribed period, evidence of insurability satisfactory to the insurance company is normally required.

Dependents' Coverage

It has been traditional under group hospital insurance contracts to define dependents as the wife of the employee and the employee's unmarried children between the ages of fourteen days and nineteen years. More recently, and as more wives have become employed, the definition has been expanded to include husbands of female employees. This can lead to over-insurance when both husband and wife are employed, and anti-duplication provisions have been developed partially in response to this problem. These new provisions are discussed in Chapter 24.

---

[11] According to the *Survey of Group Health Insurance Policies Issued in 1964* conducted by the Health Insurance Institute, 47.9 per cent of the employees surveyed had the entire cost of their coverage paid by the employer and 47.8 per cent shared the cost with the employer.

The definition of eligible children has also been expanded in recent years so that coverage often is provided from birth. This results in the payment of hospital nursery care charges for a newborn child. In addition, it is often provided that coverage may be continued for children beyond age nineteen if they are in school, dependent upon the employee for support and unmarried.

Sometimes the definition of dependents is expanded to include so-called collateral or sponsored dependents. These would include parents, grandparents, brothers, sisters or grandchildren of the employee or his wife who live with the employee and depend upon him for the major portion of their support. This feature is not common among insurance companies, and where it does occur, it is usually the result of collective bargaining. Blue Cross plans, on the other hand, often include a broad definition of dependents. Coverage for a dependent usually ceases when the employee's coverage terminates, when the employee fails to make the required contribution, when a child marries or reaches the maximum age or when a spouse ceases to be married to the employee.

In the early days of group hospital coverage, the amount of benefit for dependents was often at a level below that of the employee's coverage. For example, if the employee were insured for a $10 daily room-and-board benefit, his dependents might have been insured for $8 per day. Almost without exception, dependents' benefits currently are equal to employee benefits.

Retired Employees[12]

Continuation of Group Coverage. Precise figures are not available, but it is estimated that from one third to three fifths of employees actively at work currently will be able to continue hospital coverage for themselves and their dependents after retirement under the group plans of their employers.[13] These estimates do not include the substantial percentage of employees who will be eligible for hospital benefits after retirement by conversion from group coverage to individual policies. This conversion feature is described in the following section.

Because of the high frequency of hospital confinement and longer stays attributed to older persons and since group insurance was originally developed as a means of extending protection to those in the active work force, insurance companies and employers were initially slow to provide

---

[12] If the current (May, 1965) federal legislative proposal to provide medical care coverage for persons age sixty-five and over is enacted, such a program will have a significant influence on the types of coverage discussed in this section.

[13] The National Industrial Conference Board in a survey (Personnel Policy Study No. 190) of 862 employer health care plans in 1961 showed 62 per cent continuing basic hospital and related coverage after retirement. In over one third of the plans the employer paid the entire cost, and in another third, employers shared the cost with the retired employees.

group coverage beyond retirement. This is not surprising since very little experience information on which to base cost estimates was available until recently, and the challenge of covering the working population was first to be met.

Earlier group hospital plans for pensioners usually included a reduction in the amount of the benefit at retirement. For example, a $12 room-and-board allowance for active employees might have been reduced to $8 for pensioners with not more than thirty-one days available during the lifetime of the pensioner regardless of the number of separate confinements. These severely limited plans have been largely replaced, and it is not uncommon today to provide the same benefits after retirement as before.[14]

Conversion to Individual Coverage. Employees who leave the group have been permitted to convert their coverage from group to individual or family coverage on a direct premium payment basis almost from the inception of Blue Cross plans and since about 1951 in the case of insurance company and independent plans. Conversion is permitted without a medical examination or evidence of insurability, provided application is made and the first premium is paid within a specified period—usually thirty-one days—following termination under the group policy.

In addition to termination of employment, the conversion feature is also available for a dependent who ceases to qualify as a dependent under the group policy by reason of marriage or attaining the maximum age in the case of a child. It is also available to surviving dependents upon termination of their coverage following the death of the employee.

Conversion policies provide benefits similar in amounts but not necessarily identical with the benefits offered for direct sale to individuals and families by the individual underwriting departments of the companies. Surgical benefits are usually offered in conjunction with hospital benefits. In some instances only one plan for all those terminating from the group is offered. More frequently a choice of benefit levels is offered.

Of the new group policies surveyed in 1964, four fifths of the employees covered were eligible for the conversion right on termination of employment.[15] As previously indicated, virtually all persons covered under Blue Cross groups can become direct subscribers when they leave the group. The benefits are usually the same as those provided under group enrollment, but a higher individual subscriber rate applies. Details

---

[14] For example, the recently concluded collective bargaining agreement between the major auto companies and United Auto Workers provides for continuation of the full active employee and dependent hospital benefits for pensioners and their dependents following retirement with the entire cost paid by the companies. Full group benefits have been available to retirees from the auto industry since 1951, although there were no company contributions until 1961.

[15] *Survey of Group Health Insurance Policies Issued in 1964, op. cit.,* p. 7.

concerning the continuation of group coverage and the conversion right are discussed in Chapter 36.

HOSPITAL ADMISSION PLANS

In order to minimize collection problems, many hospitals have, over the years, required a cash deposit from their patients at the time of admission. As an alternative to the cash deposit, group hospital benefits could be assigned to the hospital. However, the wide variety of benefits available from insurance companies and the lack of a uniform claim form among the various companies, coupled with the rapid expansion of group hospital insurance during and immediately following World War II, created problems for hospital administrators and admissions clerks. On the other hand, Blue Cross plans offered essentially a single pattern of benefits within a particular area, and their contracts provided for payment directly to the hospital; thus, Blue Cross enrollees normally were admitted without a cash deposit. As a result, insurance companies working through the Health Insurance Council developed hospital admission plans designed to facilitate admission for their insureds and to assure the prompt payment of insurance benefits to hospitals. These plans are used to convert insurance benefits into credit against hospital bills. The essential elements consist of a standard procedure under which a hospital admissions department can determine that the patient is insured and for what benefits and a standard claim form to serve as an assignment of insurance benefits and to simplify hospitals' paper work.

The earliest type of hospital admission procedure was known as the *card index system*. This system is in use in several metropolitan areas, although it has been replaced by a *certification of benefits system* in most areas. Under the card index system, a card describing the benefits is filed by the insurer with the hospitals or with an agency acting on their behalf in a given area. The card lists the name of the group policyholder to be contacted by the hospital admissions department to determine if the patient seeking admission is currently insured. If coverage is in force, the patient is asked to sign a uniform claim form authorizing the hospital to release claim information to the insurer and assigning the insurance benefits to the hospital. The hospital credits the patient's bill with the amount payable by the insurance company.

The certification of benefits system eliminates the need for maintaining a card file. This system is based upon a standard hospital admissions form (known as "HAP-4" for Hospital Admissions Plan, fourth revision) and was developed by the Health Insurance Council. A copy of this form is contained in Appendix 19. The form has been accepted by the American Hospital Association for use by hospitals. Under this system the employer completes the top or certification section of the form in advance of admission and gives the form to the employee for presentation to the admissions department of the hospital. The certification section verifies that the employee is insured and summarizes the benefits available. On admission, the employee signs the form at the bottom authorizing the hospital to release information to the insurance company and assigning the benefits to the hospital. The hospital, upon discharge, completes a section of the form setting forth the charges, or it can attach a copy of an itemized bill. This is sent to the insurance company which pays its benefits directly to the hospital. Only the balance of the hospital bill is charged to the patient.

While the HAP-4 system has succeeded in simplifying admissions and collection problems, its effectiveness is dependent upon advance certification by the employer. This is not always possible in an emergency situation or where there is no authorized employer representative in the immediate area. Accordingly, insurance companies are experimenting with claim payment systems that do not involve the employer in certifying that the employee or his dependents are insured. For example, under the indemnity benefits plan for federal employees, the company administering the plan on behalf of the insurance industry maintains a current status record of the employees and dependents who are insured. The employee is issued an identification card which he presents to the hospital on admission and which guarantees payment by the insurance company of the benefits described provided the hospital promptly notifies the insurance company.

BENEFITS FOR MENTAL ILLNESS

In general, group hospital contracts written by insurance companies have made no distinction between mental illness and illnesses having objective physical manifestations, whereas many individual polices and a number of Blue Cross plans contain specific exclusions or limitations on confinement due to mental illness.[16] Most insurance company group major medical and comprehensive medical expense plans restrict benefits in the case of mental illness for treatment while the patient is not totally disabled or hospitalized, but these restrictions rarely reduce benefits otherwise payable for hospital charges.

Although group insurers normally do not exclude mental illness, the policy definition of a "hospital" may rule out confinement in certain specialized institutions that treat mental disorders and emotional problems. For example, homes for alcoholics, nursing homes or residential centers normally are not included in the definition of hospitals. As a rule,

---

[16] In 1958, fifty-seven of eighty-five Blue Cross plans provided hospital benefits for mental illness under their most common certificates. Some of these plans provided benefits only for a limited number of days in private mental hospitals with full benefits available in general hospitals. Coverage varies under individual plans.

however, the psychiatric wings of general hospitals, many private mental facilities and those state mental hospitals that make a charge to their patients are recognized under group contracts. Thus, the practical effect is broad coverage of hospital costs in connection with confinement for mental illness.

It is estimated that admissions for mental illness account for only 2 or 3 per cent of total hospital admissions.[17] On the other hand, it is estimated that about half of all the hospital beds in the United States are occupied by the mentally ill.[18] This suggests the long-term nature of psychiatric confinements and the fact that, historically, a great deal of care for mental illness is custodial or residential in nature, particularly the care rendered in state or publicly financed institutions. The difficulty in distinguishing between mental illness, requiring definitive psychiatric care and treatment, and personality disorders or mental deficiencies has created problems for insurers and undoubtedly has resulted in some extension of benefits beyond the original intent to cover only confinements necessary for treatment of illness or injury. Of those confined in publicly financed mental institutions, it has been estimated that about one half are over sixty-five years of age. Certainly, a significant portion of these are people with no other place to go. Despite the lack of clear definition in the psychiatric area, there is no apparent trend to restrict group hospital benefits. Rather, there is increased recognition that mental illness, like other illnesses, is not predictable and frequently can be cured with proper treatment.

There is, on the other hand, a trend toward noninstitutionalized care of mental illness with the advent of new treatment techniques, the increasing knowledge of the nature of mental illness, the growth of out-patient psychiatric clinics and the growing recognition that many mental patients will respond more effectively to treatment within their homes or communities. This has contributed to a marked reduction in the average length of stay in mental institutions.[19]

Major federal legislation was enacted in 1963 having as one of its primary purposes to encourage the construction and staffing of facilities within the community, so that mental patients can be cared for on an out-

---

[17] Lewis S. Reed, "Health Insurance Coverage of Hospital Care for Mental Illness," *American Journal of Public Health*, August, 1960, p. 1177.

[18] The American Hospital Association reported an average daily census in 1963 of 1,430,000 for all United States registered hospitals and 657,000 for nonfederal psychiatric hospitals. This latter figure does not include the census in federal hospitals for psychiatric care. "Hospitals," *Journal of the American Hospital Association*, Vol. XXXVIII, Part 2 (August 1, 1964), pp. 482–83.

[19] The number of resident patients in state and local governmental hospitals decreased from 551,390 in 1956 to 515,948 in 1962, despite a 46 per cent increase in the number of admissions during the same period. Robert H. Felix, "Breakthrough in Mental Illness," *Health, Education and Welfare Indicators*, U.S. Department of Health, Education and Welfare (November, 1963), pp. xxxv and xxxvii.

patient basis rather than in large public institutions.[20] These developments suggest that insurers should orient benefit programs toward nonconfining psychiatric care, but this is not likely to eliminate the need for coverage for hospital room and board and ancillary services in connection with mental illness.

NURSING HOME CARE

About 1955, one or two insurance companies included specific benefits in selected group contracts for room-and-board charges by nursing homes. This coverage is not yet widespread for a variety of reasons, but several group insurance companies and some Blue Cross plans are experimenting actively with extensions of group hospital benefits to pay for care in convalescent hospitals or skilled nursing homes. Aside from formal policy provisions, some group insurers as a matter of administrative practice pay benefits for confinement in a nursing home when it can be reasonably established that the patient requires confinement and continuing medical care.

Nursing homes and convalescent hospitals provide an important adjunct to hospital care for those who cannot be cared for adequately outside an institution, but who do not require all of the facilities, intensive care and treatment provided by the modern hospital. Accordingly, nursing homes fill a need in the spectrum of medical care. Since the cost of nursing home care is substantially less in most instances than is care in a general hospital, the use of nursing homes can result in more effective and economical care.

Nursing home standards are being upgraded, and public acceptance of this type of care is increasing. Also, insurance coverage specifically designed for people over age sixty-five is now widely available. These factors have led insurers and group policyholders to explore ways to finance this care on a prepayment basis.

It has been estimated that 90 per cent of the patients in nursing homes of all types are age sixty-five or over.[21] Thus, some of the leading illustrations of specific provision for nursing home care in group insurance plans are found in health insurance plans for retired employees. For example, the "uniform plan" for retired federal employees, adopted in 1961, provides up to $6.00 a day for thirty-one days of confinement in a convalescent hospital following a hospital confinement. Similar provisions are contained in the State-65 programs.[22]

---

[20] Mental Retardation Facilities and Mental Centers Construction Act of 1963 and Maternal and Child Health and Mental Planning Amendments of 1963.

[21] Subcommittee on the Aged and Aging, Committee on Labor and Public Welfare, U.S. Senate, *Condition of the American Nursing Home* (Washington, D.C.: U.S. Government Printing Office, 1960).

[22] In 1963, it was reported that forty-one Blue Cross plans made coverage for nursing home care available under some type of contract. Details of the coverage and experience information are not available.

Although data are not complete, a survey by the Health Insurance Association of America indicated that over 1.1 million persons were specifically insured for nursing home care at the end of 1962.[23] In some cases, nursing home benefits are made available as a part of a group hospital benefits plan and in other instances as a part of major medical or comprehensive medical benefits. Benefit amounts vary widely with daily limits of from $5 to $25 and maximum periods ranging from thirty to as many as 365 days. In some plans the maximum number of days is limited to the remaining number of hospital days available with two days of nursing home confinement counted as being equal to one day of hospital confinement.[24] In some instances, the daily allowance is limited to 50 per cent of the hospital room-and-board daily allowance or 50 per cent of the average semiprivate hospital rate in the area. When included in a major medical or comprehensive medical plan, the benefits usually are subject to the same deductible and percentage participation (or "coinsurance") requirements as other covered expenses. Sometimes an inside limit, such as $1,000, is placed on the amount payable for nursing home care within the over-all maximum of the plan.

Currently, most group plans that include nursing home coverage require prior confinement of at least three or five days in a recognized hospital with transfer to the nursing home immediately, or within a short period such as fourteen days, following discharge from the hospital. It is also required that the nursing home confinement result from the recommendation of a physician and that a physician continue to supervise the patient's care. Some plans require that the physician actually attend the patient at least once every fourteen days. This is to reduce the likelihood of the confinement being for residential rather than health purposes.

One of the major challenges facing group insurers is the problem of distinguishing among the many different types of institutions considered to be nursing homes. Under this generic heading are institutions which range from those providing intensive or skilled nursing care to those which provide essentially a housekeeping service. No single set of standards or classifications has been adopted as yet, although many have been given consideration. Licensing requirements furnish little help at this time, since they vary widely from state to state and frequently are more concerned with physical characteristics and fire hazards than with the nature of the care which the institution provides.

In view of the lack of uniform standards, insurance companies have attempted to develop definitions that will permit recognition of those

---

[23] J. F. Follmann, Jr., *Health Insurance and Nursing Home Care*, a monograph published by the Health Insurance Association of America, 1963, p. 74.

[24] The 1964 collective bargaining agreements between the major automobile companies and the UAW include a convalescent hospital feature (to become effective in 1966) on this basis, with up to 730 days of care in an "approved facility" after deducting each day of hospital stay as being equal to two days of convalescent hospital care.

nursing homes which provide intensive or skilled nursing care rather than purely residential or housekeeping care. According to the Health Insurance Association of America, at least thirty-six definitions are in use by insurers.[25] The following is an illustrative definition:

"Convalescent Hospital" or "Skilled Nursing Home" means only an institution which meets fully every one of the following tests: (1) it is duly licensed and operates in accordance with governing laws and regulations; (2) it is regularly engaged in providing, for compensation from its patients, skilled nursing care on an in-patient basis during the active or convalescent stage of an injury or illness; (3) it operates in accordance with medical policies supervised and established by a physician, other than the patient's own physician, who is a member of the medical staff of a general hospital; (4) it regularly maintains a complete daily medical record of each patient; (5) it provides continuous skilled nursing care, and there is a physician or a registered graduate nurse on duty at the institution twenty-four hours a day; and (6) it is not, other than incidentally, a place for the aged, a place for drug addicts or alcoholics, or a place for custodial care.

There are presently two separate national accreditation programs under way. The American Hospital Association has operated a program of registration of qualified nursing homes for two years. Beginning in 1965, it established an approval program based on higher standards than have been required for registration. In addition, the National Council for the Accreditation of Nursing Homes, under the sponsorship of the American Medical Association and the American Nursing Home Association, has developed accreditation standards for various types of nursing care. *Intensive nursing care* is defined as requiring that a registered professional nurse be on duty at all times. *Skilled nursing care* requires that a registered professional nurse be in charge of patient care for a minimum of five days and forty hours per week. *Intermediate care* requires the supervision of a licensed nurse on duty five days per week with a night attendant awake and fully dressed. In general, insurers are most likely to limit coverage to facilities of the first and second types.

In addition to the problem of uniform definitions and standards for nursing homes, insurers are also faced with a lack of relevant data on the utilization of nursing homes and the problem of distinguishing and paying benefits for care that is medically necessary or definitive as opposed to confinements that may be largely for the convenience of the family. No easy test to describe definitive care has yet been devised. This is the reason given for requiring hospital confinement prior to transfer to the nursing home and for limiting benefits to a specified daily amount and to a specified number of days of confinement. The fact that various studies record average lengths of stay in nursing homes (not differentiating as to type of home) from six months to two years or more[26] suggests clearly that much nursing home care, although involving intensive nursing at the

---

[25] Follmann, *op. cit.*, p. 84.

[26] *Ibid.*, pp. 50–54.

beginning, ultimately becomes residential or custodial and not necessarily essential for purely medical reasons.

Experience under group plans providing nursing home benefits is inconclusive. The cost varies depending upon definitions used, area characteristics, the availability of nursing home facilities, the age of the group to be insured, the limitations placed on benefits and many other factors which are difficult to predict, such as the development of progressive patient care, home care services, rehabilitation and public and professional attitudes.

RECENT DEVELOPMENTS

Hospital services are neither uniform nor static. The variety and change in the organization and provision of hospital care creates challenges for insurers in designing benefit plans. As an illustration of variety, most hospitals have their own X-ray equipment and charge for its use as a hospital special service, but some hospitals contract with an outside clinic for these services. Insurers have generally overcome this difference by recognizing charges for X-rays during confinement under group hospital expense plans, and, thus, insureds receive the same benefits regardless of the method employed by the particular hospital in which they receive treatment. On the other hand, not all changes in the organization of hospital care can be absorbed immediately within the framework of existing typical group hospital policies.

Intensive Care

One example of a change in the organization of hospital care is found in recently established intensive care units of some hospitals.[27] This has come about as a result of the shortage of available private duty nurses. Intensive care units make more extensive and effective use of available nursing services and contain special equipment needed for those acutely ill. The charge for confinement in an intensive care unit may be $40 or $50 a day in a hospital that otherwise charges $20 or $25 daily for room and board. While the intensive care unit may eliminate the need for more expensive round-the-clock private duty nursing, most group hospital policies do not contemplate payment for private duty nursing, nor do they normally provide a benefit related to a daily hospital charge of this magnitude.

There are at least three ways of handling an intensive care charge. One approach results in excluding the excess of the intensive care charge over the hospital's regular charge for room and board on the grounds that it represents private duty nursing. A second approach recognizes that intensive care involves the use of special equipment and facilities in addition to

---

[27] The Guide Issue of "Hospitals," *Journal of the American Hospital Association,* Vol. XXXVIII, Part 2 (August 1, 1964), p. 477, reports that 18 per cent of nonfederal short-term hospitals had intensive care units in 1963.

nursing, and, therefore, intensive care charges should be paid under the allowance for hospital services and supplies. A third approach is to consider the entire charge as room and board with payment limited to the daily room-and-board allowance of the plan. Since the part of the additional cost paid by hospital insurance will vary from no payment under the first approach to partial or complete payment under the second or third methods, and since the use of intensive care facilities is increasing, it may become necessary for insurers to include a specific benefit in group contracts which increases the regular room-and-board allowance of the plan for each day of confinement in an intensive care unit.

Progressive Care

A related development on the part of a few hospitals is known as progessive care, under which the hospital provides varying degrees of services ranging from full intensive care for the acutely ill to self-help for a patient who can be ambulatory or to home care for patients who return home for convalescence. A number of Blue Cross plans and some group hospital plans of insurance companies have established pilot programs designed to shorten hospital stays by paying for visiting nurse services and other forms of medical care provided under formalized home care programs. The effectiveness of these programs is not yet conclusive. Further study is necessary and desirable to determine how care can be related to patient needs in the most effective and economic manner.

SELECTED REFERENCES

American Hospital Association. *Daily Service Charges in Hospitals.* A report of a survey of charges by nonfederal, short-term hospitals in the United States. Chicago: American Hospital Association, 1964.

American Psychiatric Association. *Insurance Coverage of Mental Illness.* Joint Information Service of the American Psychiatric Association and the National Association for Mental Health, 1962.

Campbell, Rita R., and W. Glenn. *Voluntary Health Insurance in the United States.* New York: American Enterprise System, 1960.

Follmann, J. F., Jr. *Medical Care and Health Insurance,* chs. 10, 13, 14. Homewood, Ill.: Richard D. Irwin, Inc., 1963.

McNerney, Walter J. *Hospital and Medical Economics.* Chicago: Hospital Research and Educational Trust, 1962.

Somers, Herman M., and Anne R. *Doctors, Patients and Health Insurance.* Washington, D.C.: The Brookings Institution, 1961.

Chapter 17

GROUP SURGICAL AND
MEDICAL BENEFITS[1]

BY WILLIAM A. HALVORSON

NATURE AND SCOPE OF SURGICAL CARE AND PHYSICIANS' VISITS

Nature and Extent of Surgery

One person out of twenty-one in the United States is likely to undergo a surgical operation other than for pregnancy during an average year, but fortunately, most of these will be relatively minor in nature.[2] Less than 10 per cent of those who have surgery performed will incur surgical charges of more than $300 during the year.[3] More than half of the surgical operations will be performed in a hospital, while the patient is confined for at least one night, and, of course, the less complicated procedures will

---

[1] A substantial amount of confusion exists in connection with the terminology used to indicate benefits for physicians' services. Such services may be divided into those that entail surgery and those that are nonsurgical. The term "surgical benefits" generally involves no misunderstanding. Terminological problems have been fostered, however, by the use of the term "medical benefits" to describe physicians' nonsurgical services, i.e., services involving physicians' visits, X-rays, physical therapy and other procedures. In recent years, the term "major medical expense coverage" has been used to describe coverage that includes hospital, surgical and certain miscellaneous benefits *in addition* to coverage for nonsurgical services.

In this volume, the unqualified term "medical *expense* coverage" will refer, unless indicated otherwise, to all forms of health care expenses. The term "medical coverage" will refer to the nonsurgical services mentioned above, but wherever feasible the specific type of nonsurgical service will be mentioned, rather than using the general heading of "medical coverage."

[2] U.S. Department of Health, Education and Welfare, Public Health Service, "Medical Care Financing and Utilization," *Health Economic Series Number 1,* Table 164, p. 196. None of the statistics contained in this chapter are intended for use in determining actuarial costs, due to the widely divergent sources of information. They are included to indicate the distinguishing patterns of use of different medical services.

[3] Odin W. Anderson, Patricia Collete, Jacob J. Feldman, "Health Insurance Benefits for Personal Health Services, 1953 and 1958 Nationwide Surveys," *Health Information Foundation Research Series No. 15,* Table 11, p. 15.

be performed either in the out-patient department of a hospital or in a physician's office.

During the past fifteen years, the number of surgical operations performed outside of hospitals has apparently increased markedly. The Society of Actuaries' studies of intercompany experience showed an increase in out-patient and physician office surgery from 18 per cent of all procedures by number in 1947 to 43 per cent in 1957, although these procedures represented only 14 per cent of the total physicians' charges for all surgery in the 1957 study.[4] This increase in minor surgery may be surprising to many in view of the publicity often accorded to major surgical developments such as open-heart surgery, new brain surgery techniques and use of lasers in surgery.

Trends indicate that the frequency of surgery is increasing at a slower rate than the frequency of hospitalization, over-all, although there are indications that surgery is being performed more readily at older ages than in prior times. The general trend in frequency appears to be less than 2 per cent per year. Then, too, charges for surgery have been increasing at approximately 2 to 3 per cent per year, considerably less than the trend in hospital charges. Thus, total costs for surgery have been increasing by approximately 4 per cent annually for the average insured person.

Nature and Extent of Physicians' Visits

Physicians' visits for health care purposes other than surgery are more familiar to the average person than surgery, since in any year more than half of the people will visit a physician for medical attention. The average person who does visit his physician probably will see him seven or eight times during the year. Less than 8 per cent of all people who see their doctor at least once during a year are likely to find it necessary to visit him more than twenty times.[5] The bulk (77 per cent) of all visits are at a physician's office and 12 per cent in the patient's home, with the balance taking place while the patient is being treated in a hospital. (Telephone visits and visits in industrial health units are excluded.)[6]

Americans spend 23 per cent of their health care dollar on nonmaternity physician visits, as compared to 6 per cent on surgical procedures. Maternity visits and obstetrical procedures represent 3 per cent of all health care dollars spent.[7]

---

[4] Morton D. Miller, "1957 Study of Group Surgical Expense Insurance Claims," *Transactions of the Society of Actuaries*, Vol. X (1958), p. 377.

[5] Odin W. Anderson and Paul B. Sheatsley, "Comprehensive Medical Insurance—A Study of Costs, Use, and Attitudes under Two Plans," *Health Information Foundation Research Series No. 9*, Table 20, p. 37.

[6] U.S. Department of Health, Education and Welfare, Public Health Service, *op. cit.*, Table 178, p. 223.

[7] *Health Information Foundation Research Series No. 14*, Tables 8 and 14, pp. 11, 16.

The cost of a visit to a physician's office varies considerably by geographic location, ranging from as low as three to four dollars in many areas of the country to as high as $6.31 per visit average in 1962 in Los Angeles.[8] The frequency of physician visits seems to be increasing slightly, and the average cost per visit is also increasing. The average cost of physician visits appears to be increasing at approximately 5 per cent annually for groups of insured persons.

In summary, it can be stated that surgical costs are less when averaged among insured persons than are the average costs of physician visits, but that the financial impact per person having at least some charges is greater in the case of surgery. However, if we consider only charges in excess of $200 (in 1957–58) per family exposed in each area of service, the chance that a particular family will have physician visit charges higher than this amount is double (8 per cent as compared to 4 per cent) the chance that such family will have surgical charges at least this high.[9]

EXTENT OF COVERAGE

Since the probability of surgery is less predictable than that of physicians' visits, and since the average severity of surgery is considerably higher, it is not surprising that the number of persons currently having some kind of group surgical benefits is one and one-third times the number being insured for physician visits. In Table 17–1, the highlights of this development are shown.

The one type of physician coverage that has been developed extensively is that of physician visits while hospitalized. As in the case of surgery, the frequency of hospitalization is more limited than the frequency of visiting a physician's office, and the financial impact per claimant is greater. These facts, plus the obvious need for coverage of doctors' hospital visits and its limited cost, have contributed to its growth. If the physician visits coverage shown in Table 17–1 is divided into hospital visits versus home and office visits coverage, the extent of coverage for the latter is shown to be limited. Approximately 40 per cent of those covered for hospital visits have coverage for home and office visits.[10]

Since 1950, or the early days of major medical expense insurance, the picture has gradually changed. It can be assumed that major medical

---

[8] Health Insurance Institute, *Source Book of Health Insurance Data 1963*, p. 69.

[9] *Health Information Foundation Research Series No. 14*, Table 21, p. 24.

[10] A 1962 survey conducted by the Health Insurance Council showed that 41 per cent of those covered for hospital visits also had coverage for home and office visits. The April, 1964, issue of the *Social Security Bulletin* indicates that 35 per cent of the Blue Shield plans offered home and office visits benefits in 1962, as compared with only 9 per cent in 1957. The February, 1963, issue of the *Social Security Bulletin* indicates that 78 per cent of the enrollees in independent plans had coverage for home and office visits, only slightly less than the 82 per cent of enrollees of such plans that had in-hospital visits benefits.

plans insure both surgical and all types of physician visits due to treatment of an illness (as distinguished from health care checkups), although
in most cases the insured is required to pay the first charges incurred until
a deductible is satisfied.

In Chapter 5, where the development of group health insurance benefits
was traced, hospital insurance was seen to be the primary subject of early
experiments in group health insurance. Surgical benefits, costing less than
half of the typical hospital plans, were the next area of development and
were developed initially by the organizations offering group hospital
coverage. In-hospital physician visits coverage came next, typically cost-

TABLE 17–1

DEVELOPMENT OF SURGICAL AND PHYSICIAN VISIT COVERAGE IN NUMBERS
OF PERSONS COVERED, 1940 TO 1962

| | Numbers Covered | | As Per Cent of Population | |
Year	Surgical Benefits (000 Omitted)	Physician's Visit Benefits (000 Omitted)	Surgical	Physician's Visits
1940	5,350	3,000	4.0%	2.3%
1942	8,140	3,200	6.0	2.4
1944	11,713	3,840	8.4	2.8
1946	18,609	6,421	13.1	4.5
1948	34,060	12,895	23.1	8.8
1950	54,156	21,589	35.6	14.2
1952	72,459	35,670	46.0	22.6
1954	85,890	47,248	52.7	29.0
1956	101,325	64,891	60.0	38.4
1958	111,435	75,395	63.7	43.1
1960	121,045	87,541	67.0	48.5
1962	131,185	98,204	70.3	52.6

SOURCE: Health Insurance Institute, *Source Book of Health Insurance Data 1963*, pp. 15, 17 (except percentages of population).

ing the buyer less than one fifth the cost of surgical benefits. Home and
office visits coverage was next in the line of development.

Before major headway was made in this latter area, other areas of
medical care coverage were developed, including diagnostic X-ray and
laboratory expense insurance, supplementary accident coverage and polio
expense coverage. In each of these latter three areas of coverage, it was
possible for the insurer to provide benefits of significant value to persons
actually incurring these particular charges, while the average cost per
person exposed, or insured person, could be kept at a minimum. Thus, the
average premium for all three coverages, namely diagnostic X-ray and
laboratory expense insurance, supplementary accident insurance and polio expense insurance, would be less than the premium required for home
and office physician visits.

It would appear that because of the popularity and growth of the major medical forms, the specific types of coverage other than hospital, surgical and major medical will become less popular. This conclusion may be premature, however, due to another development in the health care financing field—namely, the so-called closed-panel or group practice prepayment plans. This will be reviewed in the next section, in which the types of organization providing surgical and medical benefits are discussed.

TYPES OF ORGANIZATIONS OFFERING PREPAYMENT

Group coverage of surgical and medical benefits is provided by three types of organizations, insurance companies, Blue Cross and Blue Shield

TABLE 17–2

Extent of Surgical and Physician's Visits Coverage by Type of Organization

		Numbers Covered by Type of Coverage (000 Omitted)		Ratio of No. with Physician to Surgical Coverage
	Year	Surgical	Physician's Visits	
Insurance Companies......	1940	2,280	.....	...
	1950	33,428	8,000	24%
	1960	75,305	41,312	55
	1963	84,958	49,709	59
Blue Cross and Blue Shield................	1940	370	200	54
	1950	19,690	11,428	58
	1960	50,281	45,017	90
	1963	52,474	49,302	94
Group practice medical service and independent plans................	1940	2,700	2,800	104
	1950	2,919	2,873	98
	1960	6,573	6,773	103
	1963	8,562	8,647	101

plans and group practice medical service plans (also called "closed-panel plans"). Their relative importance in terms of number of persons covered is shown in Table 17–2.

The Blue Cross plans offer surgical benefits either through a related Blue Shield organization, or independently. In the table above, these have been included in one category.

The typical Blue Shield plan usually has a greater percentage of its covered persons receiving benefits for physician visits than is true for insurance companies, and comprehensive medical service plans usually have an even higher percentage than Blue Shield. The reason for this is that the organizations offering prepayment of surgical and medical care benefits differ in their orientation to the insurance buying public.

Insurance Companies' Approach

Insurance companies entered the field of group hospital, surgical and medical benefits, initially, as a service to existing group life insurance policyholders. Whatever their hopes may have been for profits in offering this service, a historical review of their financial experience indicates that profits have been minimal in this area for many insurers. A related motive is that insurers wished to offer their sales forces the opportunity to serve new and existing policyholders. Their emphasis has been on sales and designing coverages to meet the needs of buyers. Thus, it is fair to typify the insurance companies' approach as being buyer oriented, or sales oriented. Their objectives might be typified as providing maximum protection for minimum premiums, with broad flexibility in coverage design and pricing and with experience rating practices to fit the needs of particular groups. Since the buyer of health insurance has been primarily the employer or group policyholder, insurers are policyholder oriented, and they attempt to sell protection which will be adequately priced while providing coverage where it is needed most.

Blue Shield Approach

As insurers began to sell surgical benefits, and then physicians' benefits, it became apparent to physicians that their practice of medicine and their finances were being affected by the presence of insurance benefits. The initial surgical benefits were quite limited in scope, and, according to many physicians, their design was not oriented to the needs of the physician and his patient. Therefore, Blue Shield organizations were formed by state medical societies to provide surgical and medical benefits that could be sold by Blue Cross plans. The objective of Blue Shield was to provide broader medical and surgical protection to insureds than typically offered by insurance companies at that time, and also to assure that such protection and its administration were controlled by physicians. The development of service benefits, as discussed in the next section, can be traced to this objective.

As Blue Cross and Blue Shield plans expanded and competed with insurance companies for new insureds during the post–World War II years, it became clear that the insurance companies were tending to become more like Blue Cross and Blue Shield in the extent of coverage they offered, and Blue Cross–Blue Shield were forced to operate more like insurance companies with respect to coverage and pricing techniques. Since hospital costs were rising faster than surgical or medical costs, an increasing proportion of the buyer's dollar was needed to reimburse hospitals, with less available to finance broad physician benefits.

Some of the Blue Shield organizations found that they were not meeting their original objectives of providing a better balance of broad surgical and medical benefits, but were instead being forced to keep their schedules of benefits limited, with primary emphasis on surgical care benefits. This has led to splits between some of the Blue Cross and Blue Shield plans which had formerly operated with joint management.[11] Where this has occurred, Blue Cross customarily offers an independent schedule of surgical benefits, in a manner similar to insurers, and the Blue Shield plan usually offers hospital insurance. The Blue Shield plans remain physician-patient oriented and the Blue Cross plans hospital-patient oriented, although in both cases they must compete with insurance companies who are buyer oriented. This generalization about the differences between orientation of the insurance companies and Blue Cross–Blue Shield might explain to some extent the different coverage emphasis with respect to surgical and medical benefits.

Group Practice Prepayment Approach

Group practice prepayment plans show a fuller development of benefits in the nonsurgical area of physicians' benefits than either the insurance companies or the Blue Shield plans. Under group practice prepayment plans, emphasis is placed on the total physician needs of the covered person, and care is taken to prevent either the physician or the patient from considering the benefits payable in either seeking or recommending treatment. Such groups often state that they are community oriented, since they believe that the health of the community can be greatly improved by encouraging all citizens to see their physician regularly for health examinations, without worry about cost, and to prevent illnesses rather than just treating them. Thus, they are largely patient oriented.

Experience shows that physician income is affected to a greater degree by the group practice prepayment plan than is true with Blue Shield or insurance company plans, since total physician care is financed by prepayment rather than just some of the surgical care and a small portion of the physician visits. This has resulted in many different methods of compensating physicians under group practice plans, including, but not limited to, per capita payment, salaries, fee-for-service and many other combinations.

Growth of group practice plans has been relatively slow for many reasons. Perhaps the policyholder orientation of both insurance companies and the Blues (in competition with insurance companies) and their concentration on the less frequent but more serious hospital, surgical and medical expenses than typically covered by comprehensive medical service plans explains the more rapid growth of the former organizations. As the public continues to prepay an ever-increasing proportion of their medical care needs through health insurance plans, it is probable that

[11] As of 1963, approximately ten Blue Shield plans were operating independently of Blue Cross, according to American Medical Association, Department of Medical Finance, *Voluntary Prepayment Medical Benefit Plans 1963* (Chicago, 1963).

such plans will cover more of the routine medical care expenses, and perhaps the group practice plans will then be able to attract a greater number of buyers.

Approach of Foundations for Medical Care

One of the more interesting developments in the field of medical care financing is a mechanism known as the Foundations for Medical Care, which had its beginning in San Joaquin County, California. Their orientation is similar to that of the Blue Shield plans, but they also attempt to meet competition with group practice plans head on, while utilizing the buyer orientation and sales force of the insurance companies. The Foundations are started by physicians in a county and sponsored by the county medical society. Minimum benefit standards are adopted by the Foundations. Insurance companies are invited to underwrite the risk involved in insuring groups using the mechanism, and the Foundations administer and pay all claims, for which they receive a specified percentage of the claims paid according to contract, or a specified percentage of the premium received by the insurance company (such as, 3 per cent of the first $50,000 of premiums on each group and 2 per cent on premiums above that figure). This fee is paid by the insurer out of the premium it receives. One of the keystones of the Foundation plan is to adopt specific maximum fee schedules, so that each buyer can know what percentage of total charges he is buying when he selects a particular benefit plan.

SURGICAL BENEFITS

Nature of Benefit Schedules

The typical insurance company surgical insurance contract provides that the company will reimburse the insured for expenses incurred due to surgery performed by a licensed physician, but in no case will payment for any one procedure exceed the benefit shown in the schedule of insurance for the particular procedure, nor will benefits for a series of surgical procedures due to the same or related causes during one period of disability exceed the maximum surgical benefit. A schedule of procedures and benefit allowances is incorporated into the contract; a portion of one such schedule is shown below:

Appendectomy	$150.00
Gastro-enterostomy	225.00
Amputation of thigh or leg	187.50
Removal of lung	300.00
Tonsillectomy, adenoidectomy	45.00
Tracheotomy	75.00
Operation for detached retina	300.00
Treatment of upper arm fracture	75.00
Hysterectomy	225.00
Single hernia	150.00
Benign tumors requiring hospital confinement	37.50

The above schedule would be known as a $300 schedule, the highest amount shown in the schedule. Different group buyers would be permitted to buy certain multiples or fractions of the schedule value, based upon their ability to pay the premium required and their need for higher (or lower) limits in their area.

Occasionally, only a highly abridged list of surgical procedures is included in the contract (as shown above). In all cases, the insurance contract would contain a statement that the insurance company retains the right to determine the benefit payable for unlisted procedures, consistent with the amounts shown for listed procedures.

An increasing number of surgical schedules include specific amounts for services of an anesthesiologist, for administration of anesthetics, where formerly such benefits were paid under the miscellaneous benefits of the hospital expense insurance plan. Also, it is common to pay specific benefits for obstetrical procedures where coverage for normal deliveries is elected by the group insurance buyer.

The contract usually provides that benefits will be paid to the insured, except that in many contracts the insured may assign benefits to the physician. In either case, the physician must seek payment of his total fee from the insured. The insurer does not enter into the discussion of what constitutes a fair fee for the particular procedure, but leaves this entirely to the patient and his doctor. The contract provides that the payments indemnify the insured for his loss, or a portion of his loss, up to specified limits. Thus, these insurance contracts are often referred to as *indemnity contracts*, and the benefits are called *indemnity benefits*.[12]

Although scheduled indemnity benefits constitute over half of all surgical coverage in existence, there has not been a great deal of standardization in the schedules themselves. Thus, it is not possible to know how much would be paid for any particular procedure without reference to the schedule itself. If a schedule has a maximum of $300 payable for the most expensive procedure, such as a detached retina procedure, it would generally be referred to as a $300 schedule; however, a different schedule with a $300 maximum might pay an amount that differs for all other procedures from the first schedule.

Development of Surgical Schedules

The complete historical development of surgical schedules is beyond the scope of this chapter, but certain aspects of this subject warrant brief discussion herein. It appears that the first schedules of indemnities for surgical procedures included in insurance plans were developed by insurance companies, most probably after consultation with qualified physi-

---

[12] The word "indemnity" does not appear to be used properly in this connection, since the degree of indemnity can be incomplete, but apparently it serves as a convenient distinction from *service benefits*, which will be discussed later.

cians. As different insurance companies became active in the field, they adopted the schedules of the earlier experimenters, sometimes weaving in additional procedures and often varying some limits in recognition of different patterns of surgical charges in their geographic areas. Changes were undoubtedly made in some instances to make a schedule appear more attractive to potential buyers.

In 1947, under the auspices of the Society of Actuaries, a broad study was made of actual charges under insured plans of surgical care. Based upon this study, a new surgical schedule was developed, commonly called the $200 schedule. Company variations of this basic schedule were many, especially in the individual health insurance field, where considerably less standardization is necessary than in group insurance. In the group field, competitive bidding requires more standardization of coverage specifications. Schedules of fees were also developed by governmental agencies, primarily in the area of state workmen's compensation laws, the Veterans Administration and the Public Assistance Program of the Social Security Administration, as an aid to administration of public laws providing for payments to physicians for eligible recipients.

After Blue Shield plans came into existence, beginning in 1939, physicians became familiar with the problem of developing surgical schedules, a problem accentuated by the fact that the participating physician was required to accept the schedule as full payment within the service income limits of the plan. In 1952, the California Medical Association sought to establish standards for use in developing medical fee schedules. Based upon a broad survey of actual charges of physicians in California, a relationship between fees for different procedures was developed. Before the survey was made, the CMA developed a nomenclature for all known procedures, based primarily on a pattern developed by Blue Shield–Blue Cross nationally and a coding of these procedures. The results were published early in 1956 in a publication entitled *Relative Value Schedule*. (Subsequent publications by the CMA have changed the title to *Relative Value Study*.)

The study was divided into four parts, namely: medical services, surgery, radiology and pathology. The following recommendations of the Committee on Fees states the objectives of this study:

The Committee on Fees recommends that the four schedules of relative values, relating medical services, surgical services, pathology and radiology be accepted at this time and that this study of relative values be furnished to the county medical societies, California Physicians Service and other interested groups or persons so that they may utilize this study to evaluate the various existing fee schedules in use in their respective areas of interest.

The Committee further recommends that any new schedules of fees or any changes in existing schedules be so arranged as to conform exactly to the format presented in this study.

The Committee also strongly urges that the same coding system be utilized

TABLE 17–3

ILLUSTRATIVE RELATIVE VALUES IN THE "MEDICAL SERVICES" SECTION OF
THE CALIFORNIA MEDICAL ASSOCIATION REPORT, 1956

Procedure No.	Procedure	Relative Value in Units
001	Office visit (first call—routine history and necessary examination)	2.0
002	Hospital visit	1.0
003	First home visit	2.0
004	Home visit (11 P.M. to 8 A.M.)	2.5
005	Home visit—each additional member, same household	.8
006	Follow-up office visit	1.0
007	Follow-up home visit	1.5
008	Mileage—per mile, one way, beyond radius of 10 miles, office or home	.2

SOURCE: *Relative Value Schedule*, 1956, prepared by the Committee on Fees of the Commission on Medical Services (California Medical Association), p. 9.

so that a uniform coding system and a uniform terminology can be developed for all existing schedules in California.

The Committee further recommends that this be a continuing study and that at periodic intervals it be critically analyzed and necessary adjustments made.

Tables 17–3, 17–4, 17–5, and 17–6 are from this initial report and illustrate the relative value system and the method physicians or insurers can use to convert the relative values into dollar schedules.

The California Medical Association revised their Relative Value Study (referred to as "CMA–RVS") in 1957 and again in 1960. Many insurance company plans have used the study in designing new plans of insurance and in administering major medical claims, by applying different "multipliers" (or "conversion factors" or "coefficients") to the unit values contained in the different segments of the study.

TABLE 17–4

ILLUSTRATIVE CONVERSION INTO DOLLARS OF RELATIVE VALUES IN THE
"SURGERY" SECTION OF THE CALIFORNIA MEDICAL ASSOCIATION
REPORT, 1956

Procedure No.	Procedure	Relative Value		Your Conversion Factor	Fee (Nearest Even $)
3261	Appendectomy	35	×	571%	$200.00
4801	Classic Caesarean section	50	×	571	285.00
4318	Prostatectomy retropubic	70	×	571	400.00
4613	Hysterectomy	50	×	571	285.00
2992	Tonsillectomy	15	×	571	86.00

SOURCE: *Relative Value Schedule*, 1956, prepared by the Committee on Fees of the Commission on Medical Services (California Medical Association), p. 9.

TABLE 17–5

ILLUSTRATIVE CONVERSION INTO DOLLARS OF RELATIVE VALUES IN THE
"MEDICAL SERVICES" SECTION OF THE CALIFORNIA MEDICAL
ASSOCIATION REPORT, 1956

Proce-dure No.	Procedure	Relative Value		Your Conversion Factor	Fee
001	Office visit (first call—routine history and necessary examination)...2.0		×	400%	$ 8.00
002	Hospital visit.....................1.0		×	400	4.00
003	Home visit.......................2.0		×	400	8.00
004	Home visit (11 P.M. to 8 A.M.)........2.5		×	400	10.00
005	Home visit—each additional member, same household..............8		×	400	3.20
006	Follow-up office visit..............1.0		×	400	4.00
027	Consultation requiring complete examination, office, hospital or home.........................7.0		×	400	28.00

SOURCE: *Relative Value Schedule*, 1956, prepared by the Committee on Fees of the Commission on Medical Services (California Medical Association), p. 9.

The California studies have been an aid in communication. However, both the 1957 and the 1960 studies are still in use, indicating that it is not easy to alter old benefit plans or to gain complete confidence in any new study. The introduction of the CMA–RVS spurred other states to adopt similar standards, most often based upon the California study, usually with some modification, until now there are many different state relative value studies in use. The American Medical Association has urged that state medical societies take the lead in developing relative value studies, based upon practice as it exists in their state but using the CMA nomenclature and coding if possible.

Reference was made earlier to the nomenclature developed by Blue

TABLE 17–6

ILLUSTRATIVE CONVERSION INTO DOLLARS OF RELATIVE VALUES IN THE
"PATHOLOGY" SECTION OF THE CALIFORNIA MEDICAL
ASSOCIATION REPORT, 1956

Procedure No.	Procedure	Relative Value		Your Conversion Factor	Fee
8628	Complete blood count............1.0		×	500%	$ 5.00
8636	Bone marrow, examination of material.....................3.0		×	500	15.00
8658	Coagulation time (Lea & White)......6		×	500	3.00
8710	Prothrombin utilization...........1.5		×	500	7.50
8930	Urine—routine chemical qualitative.........................2		×	500	1.00

SOURCE: *Relative Value Schedule*, 1956, prepared by the Committee on Fees of the Commission on Medical Services (California Medical Association), p. 9.

Shield–Blue Cross nationally which formed the basis for the California Medical Association's *Relative Value Study*. The National Association of Blue Shield Plans has continued its efforts to standardize the coding and nomenclature of medical and surgical procedures, and a guide known as the "Blue Shield Professional Service Index" was developed in 1961 for use by Blue Shield plans and other insurers and medical groups.

The Blue Shield Professional Service Index is a mathematical composite of the relationships between professional procedures, as they were found to exist in the schedules of the United States Blue Shield Plans, as of the year-end 1960. It has been called "a statistical concensus of the multiplicity of fee schedules for 47 million Blue Shield subscribers." It is not a surgical schedule, since it presents only a Professional Service Index and a Unit Value for each procedure. By applying a conversion factor, however, particular Blue Shield plans can develop schedules for their own use. A revised publication, released in late 1964, reflects changes that have occurred in schedules used by local plans.

The Health Insurance Council, an association of most major health insurance companies in United States and Canada, published in 1956 its own classification and nomenclature, having worked independently of the California Medical Association, but also in response to the general need for standardization. Since the introduction of the CMA–RVS, the Health Insurance Council has promoted better matching of benefits and surgical fees within each state, but has not attempted to influence physicians on their adoption of alternative schedules for their own use.

In 1957, the Society of Actuaries again studied the actual charges incurred for surgery under group insurance plans sold by insurance companies operating nationally. As a by-product of this study of a very large number of claims, a Society of Actuaries Relative Value Study was prepared.[13] This study, because of its national sources and statistical basis on actual charges, has been adopted for use by many group insurance companies. Currently, then, a group insurer will typically offer at least three different surgical schedules as standard products, and perhaps any other variation of the California Medical Association's *Relative Value Study* as may be adopted by different states in which they are concentrating their group insurance activities.

Nonscheduled Surgical Benefits

Nonscheduled surgical benefits are found most often as part of a major medical plan, where the benefit payable is defined as 75 or 80 per cent (sometimes 100 per cent) of the excess of reasonable and customary covered charges over the deductible amount. Since only reasonable and customary charges are covered, a standard schedule of charges in a

---

[13] Miller, *op. cit.*, p. 465.

geographic area, or for each income class, or for each physician is presumed to be present, or by necessity it will evolve through the administration of claims. Therefore, it can be argued that truly nonscheduled surgical benefits are rare. Nonscheduled contracts, however, do give the buyer coverage more closely related to the level of actual charges incurred for particular services. Also, where higher or lower charges than might have been included in a surgical schedule can be justified on the basis of complications of surgery, operating time, income of the patient, geographic location or trends in medical care costs, variations in benefits for the same procedure can be achieved through the same contract. Many nation-wide employers believe that nonscheduled benefits represent the best method for achieving equity in benefits between different geographic areas where charges vary considerably, and between employees with different incomes.

Historically there have been only a few known experiments with nonscheduled surgical benefits under plans other than major medical expense or comprehensive medical expense. Most often these have been found in employee benefit association sponsored plans, or benefits provided by some employers with the cooperation of some County Medical Bureaus in Washington and Oregon.

Service Benefits

Service Benefits from Blue Shield Plans. Blue Shield plans in most states offer *service benefits* to group subscribers whose income is less than a particular limit established by the Blue Shield plan. Service benefits exist only where the participating physicians agree on a schedule of fees that they will accept as full payment for any subscriber whose individual or family income (depending upon the type of coverage) is less than a particular limit. In some instances there may be several different schedules for different family income classifications.

A subscriber to a Blue Shield plan whose family income is less than the maximum income limit of the service plan pays no additional charge to the physician for covered procedures or services. This is referred to as the *service benefit approach,* which was discussed in detail in Chapter 15. For subscribers earning more than the Blue Shield's income limit for service benefits, the scheduled allowance for the procedure acts as a credit against the physician's regular fee, and, in essence, such subscribers receive indemnity benefits. Similarly, if services are provided by a nonparticipating physician (a physician who has not agreed to be bound by the income limits of a particular Blue Shield plan), a scheduled allowance is paid by the plan (to the physician or the patient), and the patient is liable to the physician for the balance of his fee.

Typical income limits range from $1,500 for a single subscriber for some plans, to as high as $7,500 to $9,000 for a subscriber with a covered family. A common family limit is $6,000. A few plans also have a net assets limit as well as an income limit, such as $20,000, and a subscriber having net assets greater than this limit would not qualify for service benefits regardless of the level of his current income.

Service benefits exist because of the physician's traditional practice of charging low-income persons less than what might be considered a reasonable charge for services performed. The argument given to convince physicians to agree to relatively modest surgical schedules as full payment for the lower-income families is that this merely formalizes what has been his traditional practice. And, because of the certainty of payment, in place of a large balance of uncollectibles, the physician's total income for services performed for subscribers in these income classes either will be improved, or at least it should not be adversely affected.

Thus, service benefits agreed to by the participating physicians in a Blue Shield plan give the Blue Shield plans a strong competitive argument in selling benefits and coverage to low-income groups, at least as compared to competitive insured plans, since the insurance company is not able to guarantee full payment under a scheduled plan of benefits. In actual practice, the surgical benefits are only one part of a package of benefits being purchased, and competition has maintained a balance in the manner in which the American public has chosen its group insurance for surgical care.

A typical Blue Shield plan provides not only benefits for the surgeon under their surgical benefits, but also includes benefits for an assistant surgeon, the anesthetist and consultants where their services are required. To this extent, they generally are broader in scope than some surgical schedules offered by insurance companies.

Service Benefits from Insurance Companies. Many physicians participating in Blue Shield plans also apply the same service benefit concept to insurance company plans, if such benefits are in line with their own Blue Shield service plan schedules. A formalization of this concept has occurred in the states of Illinois, Tennessee, Wisconsin, Maine, Georgia and Rhode Island. Under the Tennessee plan, for instance, the physicians of the State Medical Association establish certain principles and provisions which the insurance company or Blue Cross plan wishing to participate must include in its benefit plan and its administration in order to qualify to underwrite the plan. Under the plan, groups sold and administered by the insurance company can offer service benefits to their insureds, within the income limits established by the state medical association.

The Wisconsin and Illinois plans were organized in 1946, Rhode Island in 1947, Maine in 1948, Tennessee in 1949 and Georgia in 1950.[14] It is

---

[14] Although no service benefits were offered, the Community Surgical and Medical Care Plan of Toledo, Ohio, organized in 1944, was a forerunner in developing standards as a requirement for medical society endorsement of participating insurers.

interesting to note that all were organized prior to the development of major medical insurance, and that there has been little growth of these state plans since major medical. Part of the problem physicians encounter with service benefits is that of determining the family income of the patient's family, a burden which falls on his office and not on the plan's administrative office.

Service Benefits from Group Practice Medical Service Plans. A slowly growing method of financing medical care in America is the group practice prepayment or closed-panel plan. There is very little similarity between particular plans, and treating them all in one section might be misleading inasmuch as they differ in their sponsorship, services, compensation of doctors and relationship to the community. Chapter 16 reviewed these important differences, and this section will present only some of the common benefits provided by these plans.

The simplest type of closed-panel plan is one in which a physician or team of physicians is hired on a salaried basis to provide emergency and routine medical care to employees of a large corporation while they are at work. Care is provided according to the employees' needs and the physician's time and ability. The services may include only emergency care for illness, or if time permits, employees may be given periodic health check-ups.

When an employer moved into regions where adequate private medical facilities did not exist in earlier decades, for instance in lumbering or mining fields, the employer, or sponsor, sometimes would find it necessary to build hospital and medical facilities to take care adequately of the persons whom the company had encouraged to live in these locations. This historical fact accounts for the beginning of many of today's largest group practice prepayment plans.

In the case of one eastern plan, organized at the end of World War II, the incentive to organize a plan stemmed more from the lack of comprehensive medical care insurance at the time, rather than from a lack of adequate private hospital and medical facilities. Even in this case, however, it appears that there had been a serious shortage of physicians during the war period, and a large municipality wanted to attract returning physicians to the needs of its own employees through sponsorship of a group practice prepayment plan.[15]

Recent drives for more group practice prepayment plans come from some labor groups that have become dissatisfied with the rising cost of medical care and hope to find a way to provide more medical care for less employee out-of-pocket cost. Whether these efforts will materially influence the growth of group practice prepayment plans remains to be seen.

Approximately 6 per cent of the insured population in the United States

---

[15] The Health Insurance Plan of New York was given impetus by Major LaGuardia to furnish care to New York City employees.

TABLE 17–7

Benefits Provided by Selected Group Practice Prepayment Plans

Type of Medical Service	Plan A Clinic Group Practice Physicians	Plan B Private Physicians	Plan C Independent Medical Groups
Services offered:			
Surgery	Full care	Full care	Full care
Anesthesiologist	Payment up to 5 × Relative Value Study	Full care	Full care
In-hospital physician	Full care	Full care	Full care
Office calls	$2 charge	$1 charge	$2 charge
Home calls	$5 charge	$2 charge	$5 charge
X-ray and lab (in office)	Full care	Full care	Full care
Physical therapy (in office)	Full care	No mention	No mention
Eye examination (in office)	Full care	No mention	Full care
Injections	Reduced fees	Reduced fees	No mention
Drugs (out of hospital)	Reasonable rates	Reduced rates	Not covered
Nurses	Under Major Medical portion of plan	Full care where recommended (in hospital only)	Not covered
Obstetrical care:			
Normal	$50 charge	$75 benefit	No charge by M.D.
Caesarean	$75 charge	$150	No charge by M.D.
Miscarriage	$25 charge	$50	No charge by M.D.
Maternity hospital charges	$80 benefit	Included above	No benefit
Hospital expense	———	Various	———
Major medical	80% payment after corridor deductible of $100	No mention. Mostly covered above and polio benefit	None
Travel benefits	$1,000 full	$300 full	$500

are presently covered by group practice plans. Table 17–7 presents a recent comparison of the proposals of several different plans.

Group practice prepayment plans emphasize prevention of illness through periodic health examinations for all insureds or subscribers. There appears, however, to be some difference of opinion as to whether the health examinations offered to subscribers are utilized as fully in practice as they might be, although there is also some evidence that subscribers under such plans do see their physician more often than under conventional, or private, patient-physician relationships.

Because of the necessity for group practice prepayment plans to compete with insurance companies and Blue Cross–Blue Shield for particular groups, and to design plans geared to fit the purchaser's pocketbook, many plans have instituted a variety of surcharges to be made to subscribers for particular services. Thus, if a particularly low premium is needed, the service concept is retained, and the cost to the plan is reduced by charging the subscriber particular amounts for surgical procedures, such as $10 or $25 for a minor operation and $50 for a major procedure, with all charges above these amounts covered completely by the plan. Similarly, if there is a need for physician visits or X-rays, particular charges might be made for the services rendered, with the balance paid by the plan. From the covered person's point of view, this would be somewhat comparable to the deductible concept of major medical, only applied to particular surgical or medical services.

Only participating, or panel, physicians can provide the services contracted for under a closed-panel prepayment plan. Thus, convenience of location of the medical facilities is an important element in the evaluation of closed-panel plans by a potential group insurance buyer. In addition, the staffing of any particular medical office should be adequate to be able to diagnose and treat all patients adequately. Thus, the growth of group practice medical prepayment plans has been closely allied with the growth of medical specialists who practice together. Under this procedure, in some instances, the patient may not know which physician he will see when he visits the clinic or office. However, some medical prepayment plans operate with solo practitioners, rather than group practice, so one should be warned against over-simplication in studying the many types of plans covered under this section. In order to provide some coverage in areas other than that served by the medical offices of the prepayment plans, some plans have formed a business relationship with an insurance company to provide indemnity benefits (or the plan offers indemnity benefits directly) while subscribers are on vacation or when, in case of emergency, they are unable to reach one of the plan's medical offices.

As has been noted, group practice prepayment plans tend to emphasize complete medical care coverage for their subscribers, within the practical limitations of income available to the plan. Their concept is to provide complete physician care, rather than requiring the patient to pay a fee for services performed. And, where surcharges are levied to control the cost of the plan, such surcharges are usually limited also. Traditional insurance company coverage has concentrated on surgical care on a scheduled basis, and has left the question of reasonable charges to be resolved by the patient and his physician.

Service Benefits from Foundations for Medical Care. The San Joaquin Foundation for Medical Care, which is typical of foundations of this type, attempts to provide broad service benefits for all groups in its area while permitting the group to select its own insurer. Thus, the Foundation:

1. Sets minimum standards for medical care coverage;
2. Invites participation by physicians with the objective of achieving 100 per cent participation by physicians in the area and, thus, providing free choice of physician;
3. Permits any insurance company, or Blue Cross or Blue Shield plan to sell coverage to groups which meet the Foundation coverage standards;
4. Establishes fee schedules for particular groups, based on average income of the group, which will be accepted as full payment by participating physicians; and
5. Administers all claims under medical supervision, and receives an administrative allowance from the insurer for performing this service.

The insurer sets and collects its own premiums, maintains records on eligibility and applies its own experience rating methods to the group or class of insureds. Through this mechanism, insurance companies are able to offer the same kind of service benefits as offered by Blue Shield plans, as well as gaining the medical review of the plan's physician review panel.

Currently, fourteen foundations of this type are operative in California, serving twenty-eight counties under the auspices of the Western Conference of Foundations for Medical Care. Approximately 338,000 persons are now covered by these plans. It is reported that seven other states now have foundations in various stages of growth.

Benefits offered through the foundations are diverse. All plans provide benefits for surgeons and anesthetist services, as well as for in-hospital physician visits, X-ray costs and laboratory charges. Almost half of the groups also have coverage for home and office visits, usually with the first two visits for any one sickness excluded. The foundations also sponsor major medical coverages, in which case most types of medical care services are covered subject to a deductible and percentage participation.

The emphasis of the foundations has been on freedom of choice of physicians and acceptance of proven methods of selling and pricing medical care plans. The use of acceptable fee schedules has assured the cooperation of physicians and a certainty of coverage results.

MEDICAL BENEFITS

Medical benefits offered by insuring organizations include physician visits and consultations, diagnostic X-rays and laboratory charges, supplemental accident and polio and specified dread disease benefits. In addition, experiments in offering registered nurse benefits and prescription drug benefits have occurred.

In-Hospital Medical Benefits

A typical insurance company group plan with medical benefits reimburses the insured for medical fees charged in connection with a nonsurgical hospital confinement, but not more than $3.00, $4.00 or $5.00 times the number of days hospitalized during any confinement. The usual limit on the number of days confined will be the comparable number of days permitted under the basic hospital benefit plan covering the same group. Successive confinements are usually considered as one confinement, unless due to unrelated causes or separated either by a return to active work or by a three-month period.

Blue Shield contracts often provide higher benefits for night visits than for day visits and occasionally will provide benefits for prolonged detention of the physician at the hospital for critical illnesses. In addition, consultation charges often are covered under Blue Shield in-hospital benefits.

In the case of insurance companies and Blue Shield associations, operative visits are covered as part of the surgical procedure, and no separate allowance is payable. Some recent surgical schedules indicate the normal postoperative period for all common procedures as a guide in administration.

Home and Office Physician Visits Benefits

Insurance companies' benefits for home and office visits provide for reimbursement of expenses incurred because of an illness, but not in excess of a daily medical benefit or a maximum benefit for all visits during any six- or twelve-month period. In addition, benefits are generally restricted to one visit per day.

In an attempt to reduce premium expense, usually at least the first two visits are excluded for sickness, although benefits generally begin for the first visit in case of accident. The daily medical benefit for the group can be selected as $3.00 in the physician's office and $5.00 at home or elsewhere, or $4.00 office and $6.00 home, or any such combination. The maximum benefit is usually 50 to 100 times the maximum daily benefit provided.

The above benefits may be offered on one of two bases, either requiring total disability or not requiring total disability. Because of the difficulty in identifying total disability, usually only employees and not their dependents can be insured for benefits requiring total disability. As would be expected, the cost of covering dependents for home and office visits is very high, and such benefits are rarely sold.

Many Blue Shield plans offer benefits for physicians' home and office visits, and when offered such benefits are available on a service basis within the income limits. As reviewed elsewhere, most group practice prepayment plans also offer home and office visits, often making surcharges of $1.00 or $2.00 per office visit and $2.00 to $5.00 per home visit.

Diagnostic X-ray and Laboratory Benefits

As the science of symptom identification and diagnosis has advanced, X-rays and laboratory tests have become important tools in medical treatment. Most private physicians would not be able to maintain all the equipment, nor would they be able to achieve the degree of specialization necessary to keep abreast of the professional use of these tools. At one time, confinement in a hospital was necessary to diagnose many illnesses. Today, because of the growth of private laboratories and X-ray centers serving a community, identification and diagnosis of symptoms and signs of illness are more readily within every physician's reach.

Insurance company plans offer either scheduled or nonscheduled benefits for expenses incurred for diagnostic X-ray and laboratory examinations as a result of an illness. Under a scheduled contract, maximum allowances are set forth for each examination. Schedules for $25 and $50 are usually available, although greater maximum schedules are also written. Under a nonscheduled benefit, actual charges are reimbursed up to a particular maximum, such as $25 or $50. The maximum amount is applied to all illnesses during a six- or twelve-month period, although occasionally the maximum is applied to each disability.

Blue Shield plans offer diagnostic X-ray and laboratory benefits similar to those offered by insurers, since benefits, being payable to organizations or individuals who are not participating physicians, would be on an indemnity basis. Group practice plans also offer these benefits, either through contracts with independent organizations or by use of their own facilities.

Supplemental Accident Benefits

A common benefit offered under group health insurance contracts is a supplemental accident benefit. Such contracts reimburse the insured for expenses incurred as a result of an accident up to a maximum of $300 or $500. Any expenses paid for under the other parts of the group package are excluded, so that the supplemental accident benefits pick up where the other coverages leave off, at least with respect to expenses resulting from accidents. In fact, most indemnity contracts require the existence of basic benefit coverage before supplemental accident benefits can be included. Covered expenses usually include hospital, surgical, medical expenses, X-ray and laboratory, registered nurses and physical therapists. Usually, only expenses incurred within ninety days of an accident are covered. Blue Shield plans, and sometimes group practice plans, will offer these benefits on an indemnity basis, because of its popularity and relatively low cost.

Polio and Specified Disease Benefits

Polio coverage emerged in the mid-1940's as a popular and low-priced coverage because of the concern over the catastrophic economic consequences of polio. After the development of the Salk vaccine, the incidence of polio dropped dramatically, and new coverages were offered to cover other rare diseases. Such coverages are often called "Dread Disease

Benefits," and generally include protection against diphtheria, pulmonary tuberculosis, scarlet fever, typhoid, tularemia, rabies, leukemia, undulant fever, tetanus and others. Cancer, when included, requires special limits and additional costs, and its coverage in this form is rare.

Dread disease contracts provide for reimbursement of covered expenses incurred within two or three years after a disease is first contracted, subject to a maximum of between $1,500 and $10,000. Covered expenses usually are stated very broadly, including hospital, physician, registered nurses, X-ray and lab, drugs, physiotherapy, rental of equipment and ambulance service. Benefits payable under polio coverage are usually paid in lieu of benefits paid under other parts of the group package, in order to prevent duplication of benefits. The maximum thus payable is the maximum available under all parts of the group program for the specific disease. Under some contracts, benefits can be paid in addition to other benefits paid, in which case the maximum benefits payable for the disease under all parts of the program could exceed the maximum under the polio coverage alone. Blue Shield plans and group practice prepayment plans have seldom offered dread disease benefits as separate coverages.

Common Exclusions

All group health insurance plans contain exclusions and limitations. Usually these limitations fall into one of the following categories:

1. Exclusions designed to prevent duplication of benefits payable through other plans, such as workmen's compensation laws, or other group plans carried by the employer or other employers, or benefits provided by state or federal agencies;
2. Exclusions intended to prevent payment of expenses where there is no obligation for the insured, because of his status in the absence of insurance, to pay for the services rendered; for instance, services provided through governmental agencies such as the Veterans Administration;
3. Exclusions of benefits for services which are sought for cosmetic purposes, or which are not necessary for the treatment of an illness or injury, or which are for purely diagnostic purposes, or health checkup purposes;
4. Exclusion of liability if the illness is due to war or an act of war; and
5. Exclusions of intentionally self-inflicted injuries, or injuries sustained as a result of a criminal act of the insured.

Sometimes there are exclusions for services for nervous and mental conditions, tuberculosis, alcoholism or drug addiction. These exclusions historically have been more prevalent under service plans, probably because Blue Cross member hospitals have not been equipped to treat these illnesses, and transfer to a local county or state sanitarium was required after diagnosis. Under group practice prepayment plans, routine health examinations are covered, but service rendered outside of the service area is excluded, or modified to an indemnity basis.

SELECTED REFERENCES

AMERICAN MEDICAL ASSOCIATION, DEPARTMENT OF MEDICAL FINANCE. *Voluntary Prepayment Medical Benefit Plans, 1963.* Chicago, 1963.

ANDERSON, ODIN W.; COLLETTE, PATRICIA; AND FELDMAN, JACOB J. "Family Expenditure Patterns for Personal Health Services, 1953 and 1958: Nationwide Surveys," *Health Information Foundation Research Series* No. 14.

————, AND SHEATSLEY, PAUL B. "Comprehensive Medical Insurance—A Study of Costs, Use, and Attitudes under Two Plans," *Health Information Foundation Research Series No. 9.*

COMMISSION ON MEDICAL CARE PLANS, AMERICAN MEDICAL ASSOCIATION. "Report of the Commission on Medical Care Plans, Findings, Conclusions and Recommendations," *The Journal of the American Medical Association,* Special Edition (January 17, 1959).

HEALTH INSURANCE COUNCIL. *Surgical Procedures, Classification and Nomenclature for Use in Connection with Surgical Expense Insurance.* New York, 1956.

HEALTH INSURANCE INSTITUTE. *A Profile of the Health Insurance Public.* New York, 1959.

INSTITUTE OF LIFE INSURANCE. *Group Insurance Coverages in the United States.* New York. Published annually.

KRISLOV, JOSEPH. "Employee-Benefit Plans, 1954–62." *Social Security Bulletin* (April, 1964), pp. 4–21.

MILLER, MORTON D. "1957 Study of Group Surgical Expense Insurance Claims" and Discussion, *Transactions of the Society of Actuaries,* Vol. X (1958), pp. 359–504.

MILLIMAN, WENDELL A. "Insurance of the Expense of Medical Service," *Transactions of the Actuarial Society of America,* Vol. XLI (1940), p. 114.

PICKRELL, JESSE F. *Group Health Insurance.* Rev. ed. Ch. 2. Homewood, Ill.: Richard D. Irwin, Inc., 1961.

REED, LOWELL J. (AND OTHERS). *Health and Medical Care in New York City.* Prepared for The Commonwealth Fund. Cambridge, Mass.: Harvard University Press, 1957.

SHIPMAN, GEORGE A.; LAMPMAN, ROBERT J.; AND MIYAMOTO, S. FRANK. *Medical Service Corporations in the State of Washington: A Study of the Administration of Physician-Sponsored Prepaid Medical Care.* Cambridge, Mass.: Harvard University Press, 1962.

SOCIETY OF ACTUARIES, EDUCATION AND EXAMINATION COMMITTEE OF THE. *Part 8 Study Notes, Group Insurance* and *Study Notes for Part 9E.* Chicago.

Chapter 18

GROUP MAJOR MEDICAL BENEFITS

BY O. D. DICKERSON

GENERAL NATURE AND EXTENT OF MAJOR MEDICAL COVERAGE

Most criticisms of basic hospital, surgical and medical insurance have centered about the fact that such policies often fall far short of covering the total medical care bill. On the one hand, expenditures for drugs, appliances, prosthetics, blood and plasma, diagnostic services, physical examinations and preventive medicine, out-patient treatment, nursing services and many other costs are not provided for in most basic policies or combinations of policies. Frequently, the policies cover only treatment given in a licensed hospital.

On the other hand, basic medical expense contracts contain limits, express or implicit, on aggregate amounts payable and often specific internal limits on particular types of expense or procedure. Where full-service benefits are provided, they are available only for certain procedures and for limited time periods. Thus, these policies may prove grossly inadequate when it comes to meeting the costs of a really serious disability. Even the blanket accident type of policy, which imposes few restrictions on eligible types of expense, usually is written with so small a limit that it would not cover a really severe accident. Moreover, it is limited to accidental injuries only. This chapter is devoted to types of insurance that have developed in response to a growing recognition of the limitations of the basic forms.

Major medical insurance contracts protect against almost all types of medical care expenditure, with few, if any, internal limits and with a high over-all limit, from $5,000 to $25,000. Generally, such policies include deductible and/or percentage participation clauses.

Comprehensive medical contracts are similar to major medical, except that they provide lower deductibles and sometimes omit or limit the percentage participation feature. The original concept of the comprehensive contract involved most of the same features as major medical, viz., blanket coverage of all eligible expense, broadly defined, subject to percentage participation, and with almost no internal limits, but with a small deductible of $25 or $50 instead of a large deductible of $250 or more. Unlike most major medical coverage, this would be the only insurance carried by the group against the costs of medical care. This type of contract sometimes is referred to as a "pure" comprehensive policy.

However, many employees were loath to give up their first-dollar coverage of hospital and surgical expenses. In response to this feeling, insurers developed a contract referred to as "modified" comprehensive, which provides first-dollar coverage of hospital and/or surgical expenses up to certain limits and then covers the excess (perhaps after a small deductible) according to the percentage participation major medical approach.

Figure 18–1, in which type of expense is indicated on the horizontal axis, amount of expense plotted vertically and degree of reimbursement indicated by shading, illustrates graphically the extent of coverage provided by various plans. The basic plans cover initial hospital and surgical expense and a few other expenses at 100 per cent reimbursement, up to a moderate limit. The major medical policy is superimposed on this and covers, after a moderate deductible, all other medical expenses, at a 75, 80 or 85 per cent reimbursement level up to high limits. The pure comprehensive contract covers all expenses, after a small deductible, at the same reimbursement rate, up to the same high limit. The modified comprehensive plan is the same (in this illustration) except that 100 per cent of hospital expenses are covered, with no deductible, up to a moderate limit. Some authorities consider comprehensive contracts a variety of major medical and refer to major medical as "supplementary major medical," while others believe comprehensive is sufficiently different to warrant being considered as a separate classification.

Another variety of policy, comprehensive as to benefit but not as to peril, is the *dread disease* type of policy. This appeared first as a polio benefit contract but eventually was extended to cover a list of named serious diseases. It covers expenses incurred only in connection with the named diseases up to a medium-sized limit, e.g., $5,000, without a deductible or percentage participation clause.[1]

All major medical-type contracts are of comparatively recent origin. Polio policies appeared first in the late 1940's and were given great impetus by polio epidemics in the first years of the following decade. Major medical appeared as an experimental coverage about 1950, but soon gained widespread acceptance. By the end of 1963, about 42 million persons were covered by insurance company major medical and comprehensive contracts.[2] About 16.2 million were employed persons with pri-

---

[1] See Chapter 17 for a more extensive discussion of group dread disease coverage.

[2] Estimated enrollment figures for major medical and comprehensive indicated 43.5 million persons were covered at June 1, 1964. All figures are from publications of the Health Insurance Council or the Health Insurance Association of America.

mary coverage; the balance were dependents. For a considerable time, insurance companies were the only type of insurer to issue major medical in any quantity, but Blue Cross and Blue Shield plans recently have entered this field. Most of the coverage is on a group basis. In 1963, 28,248,000 persons were covered by 61,670 insurance company group supplementary major medical plans. In 1964 there were about 279 insurance companies offering major medical on an individual or group basis.

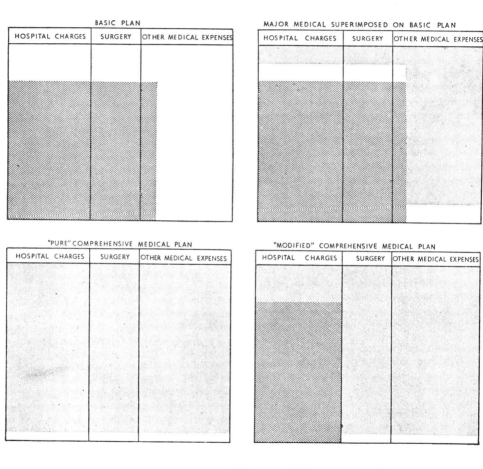

FIG. 18–1. Proportion of charges covered under various health insurance arrangements.

Source: Towers Perrin, Forster, and Crosby, Inc.

Insurance companies lead in the volume of comprehensive medical coverage, followed by "independent" plans and Blue Shield associations. At the end of 1963, 10,620,000 persons were covered by 28,160 insurance company group plans of this type.

Table 18–1 shows the rapid growth of major medical and comprehensive in detail and the division between individual and group.

In recent years, major medical has been growing more rapidly than comprehensive. In 1960, 63 per cent of new group plans issued by insurance companies were major medical and 37 per cent comprehensive. By 1963, 89 per cent of contracts of this type were major medical and 11 per

TABLE 18–1

NUMBER OF PEOPLE WITH MAJOR MEDICAL PROTECTION*
(In the United States, 1951–63; 000 Omitted)

| | | Group Policies | | | |
End of Year	Grand Total	Total	Supplementary Major Medical	Comprehensive	Individual and Family Policies†
1951	108	96	96	—	12
1952	689	533	533	—	156
1953	1,220	1,044	1,044	—	176
1954	2,198	1,892	1,841	51	306
1955	5,241	4,759	3,928	831	482
1956	8,876	8,294	6,881	1,413	582
1957	13,262	12,428	9,290	3,138	834
1958	17,375	16,229	11,072	5,157	1,146
1959	21,850	20,353	13,900	6,453	1,497
1960	27,448	25,608	17,285	8,323	1,840
1961	34,138	31,517	22,281	9,236	2,621
1962	38,250	35,053	25,301	9,752	3,197
1963	42,010	38,168	28,248	10,020	3,842

* Represents people covered by insurance companies only.
† Almost entirely "supplementary" coverage.
SOURCE: Health Insurance Council.

cent were comprehensive medical. In 1963, benefit payments by insurance companies under major medical and comprehensive plans equaled $812,750,000, an 18 per cent increase over 1962.

MAJOR MEDICAL BENEFIT PROVISIONS

Covered Expenses

Major medical policies cover almost all types of medical care expenditure without internal limits. However, use of limits on the daily hospital room-and-board benefit is becoming common. Such limits, usually $20 to $35 per day, serve as an added claims control. The covered expenditures include hospital charges for room and board and miscellaneous services and supplies, charges by physicians and surgeons for medical treatment and surgery, charges by a physician or anesthetist for administration of anesthesia, charges for professional radiology or physiotherapy, charges for nursing care, laboratory examinations, drugs, medicines, blood and plasma, casts, splints, braces, crutches, prosthetics, oxygen and rental of oxygen equipment, wheelchairs, hospital beds and iron lungs. Sometimes expenses of transportation to and from a hospital also are included.

Most plans cover these expenses wherever performed, as long as they are ordered or prescribed by a duly licensed physician. A few, however, require hospital admission at some time in the course of treatment in order to qualify. For example, a contract might cover expenses incurred in the hospital and nonhospital expenses for two months before admission and for six months thereafter. A few plans, with an "each cause" benefit period, require that the claimant be disabled.

A typical group major medical contract defines the covered types of expense as follows:

The term "covered expense" means only such of the following expenses as are incurred by an employee for the therapeutic treatment, while the employee is insured under this rider, of any disease or accidental bodily injury of the employee, and then only to the extent not hereinafter excluded.

(1) The charges made to the employee by a physician for professional medical or surgical services rendered to the employee by the physician; and

(2) the charges made to the employee by a registered graduate nurse other than one who ordinarily resides in the employee's home or who is a member of the immediate family (comprising the employee, the employee's wife or husband, and the children, brothers, sisters, and parents of either the employee or the employee's wife or husband) for, professional nursing services rendered to the employee by the nurse; and

(3) the charges made to the employee by a hospital, in its own behalf, for services and supplies required by and rendered to the employee during his hospital confinement in direct connection with the therapeutic treatment of the employee; except that for each day in which the employee occupies private room accommodations, the amount, if any, by which the hospital's charges for board and room for that day exceed _____ shall be excluded from covered expenses; and

(4) the charges made to the employee for any of the following services and supplies, to the extent such charges do not duplicate charges included under items (1), (2), and (3) above:
(a) drugs and medicines lawfully obtainable only upon the prescription of a physician;
(b) anesthesia and its administration;
(c) x-ray and laboratory examinations made for diagnostic purposes in connection with the therapeutic treatment of the employee;
(d) x-ray, radium, and radioactive isotopes therapy;
(e) oxygen and its administration;
(f) rental of wheelchair, hospital bed, iron lung, and other durable equipment for the therapeutic treatment of the employee;
(g) artificial limbs and artificial eyes;
(h) professional ambulance service when used to transport the employee directly from the place where he is injured by an accident or stricken by a disease to the first hospital where treatment is given.

Exclusions

As in any insurance policy, the complete description of major medical coverage requires a reading of the exclusions. Common major medical policy exclusions are expenses covered under other insurance, pregnancy, childbirth and miscarriage (sometimes covered for limited benefits only), dental expenses, cosmetic surgery,[3] alcoholism, narcotic addiction, nervous and mental disease,[4] health examinations, travel expenses (except as specifically covered), injuries or sickness covered by workman's compensation and treatment in government or other noncharge facilities. Convalescent home, nursing home or rest home care is sometimes excluded and sometimes subject to specific limits as to amount and duration. Often such care is not excluded specifically, but is not covered because the institution does not meet the definition of "hospital." Experimentation with benefits for nursing home care may result in an expansion of such coverage under major medical contracts, as it is viewed by many as a means of reducing the over-all cost of medical care.[5]

Common exclusions relating to peril are war and military service, self-inflicted injuries and attempted suicide, and sometimes aviation activities other than as a fare-paying passenger. Some policies exclude specifically expenses which are unreasonable in price or not reasonably necessary for treatment of the disability. Others implicitly exclude such expenses by inserting limiting adjectives, such as "reasonable and customary," in the definition of covered expenses. The enforcement of these provisions presents troublesome problems in claim administration.

The reasons for most of these exclusions are self-apparent. Since major medical policies define covered expenses so broadly in the insuring clause, more exclusions are needed to eliminate optional or elective treatment, such as cosmetic surgery, than in basic contracts.

Group contracts often do not exclude military service, since such service would result in termination of employment or dependency which would take the individual out of the group automatically. Similarly, most do not exclude pre-existing conditions because of the safeguards against individual selection inherent in group underwriting. However, in contracts issued to small groups and in some larger group coverage as well, pre-existing conditions frequently are not covered until an individual has been free of treatment for some period of time after joining the group.

Upper Limits

Upper limits of insurance companies' liability under major medical contracts vary from $5,000 to $25,000 or even higher in a few cases. The

---

[3] Dental surgery and cosmetic surgery are often covered if necessitated by an accident.

[4] Most group major medical contracts do cover mental and nervous diseases to some extent, sometimes with specific internal limits, especially on out-of-hospital care.

[5] See Chapter 16 for a discussion of basic nursing home benefits.

most popular choices are $5,000, $7,500, $10,000 and $15,000. In new group plans issued in 1963, the most common was $10,000 followed by $5,000.[6] A few had no dollar limit.

The limit may be stated in several different ways. Thus, it may apply to each injury or illness separately, which is called an "each cause" or "per disability" basis. On the other hand, the limit may apply to expenses for all illness and injuries combined (the "all cause" basis). In the latter case, a stipulation is made as to whether the maximum applies to covered expenses incurred during a policy year, a benefit year (defined below), a calendar year, or over a claimant's entire lifetime. "All cause" plans are the most common in group contracts.

It is not unusual to find a combination of an aggregate lifetime limit with a per disability or calendar year limit. Usually some limit is placed on the time within which expenses must be incurred, and this is referred to as the "benefit period."[7] This may run from one to three years or more, with one year being probably the most common. When the benefit period is exhausted, expenses for the same cause or all causes, as the case may be, are not covered until the deductible is again satisfied and then usually only for the remaining portion of the maximum benefit. Often the period is extended if the claimant is hospitalized when it expires. The use of the benefit year limit raises the possibility of mushrooming a claim to tremendous size. With this type of limit a prolonged illness could result in a company's paying the policy maximum limit year after year, subject only to an over-all limit of expense or duration, if any. Thus, most plans also have an aggregate or "each cause" limit in addition.

The use of an aggregate (lifetime) dollar limit is more common than the yearly limits or the per disability limit. When it is used, it is common to provide that after a certain amount of benefits, such as $1,000, has been paid, the original limit may be reinstated if the insured can produce acceptable evidence of insurability. In new group business in 1963, the "all cause" plan with a calendar year benefit period and a lifetime maximum was the most popular single plan.

Percentage Participation Provisions

Not all eligible medical expenses are reimbursed for the full amount in major medical contracts. Policies usually require that the insured bear 10 to 30 per cent of eligible expenses in excess of a specified deductible, with 20 per cent being used most commonly in group contracts. The purpose of the percentage participation is to encourage the insured to incur only

---

[6] Health Insurance Institute, *Group Health Insurance Policies Issued in 1963* (New York, 1964).

[7] The term "benefit period" is perhaps unfortunate, as it may lead to confusion with the benefit period in disability income policies where the claim settlement is directly proportionate to the elapsed time.

those expenses that are necessary. The extent to which such provisions are effective is difficult to measure, inasmuch as the impact varies with the living standard and resources of the claimant. However, the provision certainly has some beneficial effect, and most insurance company personnel seem firmly convinced that some such control on claims is absolutely necessary. Otherwise, it would be to every claimant's advantage to utilize as extensive and expensive health services as possible. Moreover, the lack of internal limits also invites higher charges by certain purveyors of medical care, unless it is recognized that the insured is paying part of the bill. The requirement is designed to make possible adequate payment for health necessities without encouraging the use of luxury services.

The benefit limit, it should be noted, applies to the company's maximum payment, not to the maximum covered expenses. Thus, in order to collect the maximum under a $7,500 policy with a $500 deductible and 80 per cent reimbursement, a claimant would have to incur eligible expenses of $9,875. He would have to bear over $2,000 of expenses himself, a substantial sum for most individuals.

It is interesting to note that percentage participation provisions are utilized by some Blue Cross and Blue Shield plans that issue major medical coverage. Such organizations traditionally opposed the requirement that insureds pay a portion of basic medical care expense, but the liberal nature of major medical contracts is often felt to necessitate a percentage participation as a type of claims control.

Deductible Provisions

Deductible provisions serve two purposes in group major medical contracts. One is to lower premium costs by insuring only substantial claims, eliminating small claims and the expense of handling them. The second is to minimize moral hazard by eliminating or reducing duplication with other health insurance policies and by making the insured bear the first portion of eligible loss. Deductibles may take a number of forms and may apply on a number of bases.

Forms of Deductibles. The *initial deductible* is the most common form. It applies to the first portion of medical care expense, so that the insured must bear expenses up to this amount before the policy begins to reimburse him. This is used almost always in individual and family policies and frequently in group contracts. Benefits collected (or paid on behalf of the insured) from basic policies are counted in meeting the deductible. The deductible may range from $50 up, on this basis; $500 probably is the most common amount.

In group insurance, a *corridor deductible* frequently is used to coordinate the plan with basic hospital, surgical and medical insurance contracts covering the same group. Here the deductible amount is applied to medical expenses which exceed the amounts covered in the basic contract or contracts. Basic benefits are not counted toward the deductible in this case. Corridor deductibles usually are lower than those which apply on an initial basis, with most of the former being in the $25 to $100 range. The most common figure in the new group business in 1963 was $100. The corridor deductible not only cuts premiums but, in effect, makes the claimant a coinsurer for a part of the basic plan benefits if he exceeds their limits.

Another approach used to coordinate group major medical insurance with underlying group contracts is the *integrated deductible*. This is essentially a combination of the two other approaches. This type of deductible is the greater of a specific dollar amount or the base plan benefits. Thus, the integrated deductible provides a varying corridor deductible which equals zero, in effect, when the base plan benefits equal or exceed the specified amount. This has the advantage of imposing no deductible on the insured when the claim is large and involves expenses covered under basic contracts.

The operation of these forms of deductible in combination with 80 per cent participation and a $15,000 limit may be clarified by the following illustration:

Amount of deductible	$500	$100	$500
Form of deductible	Initial	Corridor	Integrated
1. Small loss:			
a) Amount of loss	$ 300	$ 300	$ 300
b) Paid by basic contract	150	150	150
c) Paid by major medical	0	40	0
d) Borne by insured	150	60	150
2. Large loss:			
a) Amount of loss	3,000	3,000	3,000
b) Paid by basic contract	1,500	1,500	1,500
c) Paid by major medical	2,000	1,120	1,200
d) Borne by insured	(500 profit)	380	300
3. Very large loss:			
a) Amount of loss	20,000	20,000	20,000
b) Paid by basic contract	4,000	4,000	4,000
c) Paid by major medical	15,000	12,720	12,800
d) Borne by insured	1,000	3,280	3,200

Bases for Deductibles. Deductibles may apply to each cause or to all causes on a calendar year or a benefit year basis. Commonly, the deductible and upper limit apply on the same basis, but not always. In the calendar year or benefit year deductible, the deductible may apply to each individual separately or occasionally to the aggregate expenditures of the family. The deductible amount may be constant or may vary with employee class or income. About 21 per cent of the 1963 new group business had a per cause type deductible, while the balance applied the deductible to all causes during some eligibility period.

Where the deductible applies to *each disability* (or cause), it usually is required that the deductible expenses be accumulated within some time period, such as three or six months. The major objection to this plan is that an individual or, more frequently, a family may incur expenses for several different disabilities which aggregate large sums in a short period but which do not exceed the deductible for any one injury or disease.

Where the deductible applies to a *calendar year,* all covered medical expenses incurred by the individual in a calendar year are counted toward the deductible. The deductible must be met each year in the case of an extended disability.

The *benefit year* approach allows any twelve-month period to be used for accumulating expenses toward the deductible. The period is referred to as a benefit year because it customarily begins at the inception of a particular disability. Record keeping is complex for an insurer under this approach, as it may be to the insurer's advantage to carry the benefit year forward or back to cover periods beyond or before the major disability.

The use of the family as the unit for deductible purposes greatly complicates the administration of a plan, and few policies have been sold on this basis. A few insurance companies have used a variant called a *family budget* deductible, where the company simply reimburses a proportion of all medical care expenses incurred by the family in a given month in excess of a stated monthly deductible. This may range from $25 to $250, depending on income level and/or number of family members. Often such a deductible is waived entirely if total expenses exceed a specified (higher) amount. This approach is easily understood by the insured, as the aggregate family expenditure is held within predictable and budgetable limits. The family budget deductible is customarily used in connection with an aggregate lifetime limit per individual and the usual reinstatement privileges.

Where deductibles are on other than a family basis, it is common to provide that, in the event of accidental injury in a common disaster, the deductible shall be applied only once. In some contracts a similar provision applies to contagious diseases.

Benefit Provisions—An Example

The foregoing discussion suggests the heterogeneity of group major medical contracts. Although it would be pointless to quote provisions regarding all types of upper limit, percentage participation and deductible, the applicable provisions from one contract can be used for illustrative purposes. In this case, the contract utilizes an aggregate lifetime benefit for each insured individual (with the usual provision for reinstatement), along with a deductible imposed in each calendar year equal to the sum of a corridor deductible and benefits under the basic group contracts.

Employees' Major Medical Expense Benefits

The Insurance Company hereby agrees, subject to the terms of the group policy, including this rider, to pay benefits in an amount equal to 80 per cent of the amount, if any, by which the total covered expenses incurred by an employee in any calendar year exceed the deductible amount applicable for that calendar year; but the aggregate of the benefits payable under this section with respect to any one individual in such individual's entire lifetime (whether or not there has been any interruption in the continuity of the individual's insurance) shall not exceed the maximum benefit (except in accordance with the section entitled "Special Provisions For Establishing A New Maximum Benefit"). The terms "covered expenses," "deductible amount" and "maximum benefit" shall have the meanings assigned to them in the subsection of this section entitled "Definitions and Exclusions." An expense or charge shall be deemed to be incurred on the date on which the particular service or supply which gives rise to the expense or charge is rendered or obtained.

. . . .

The "deductible amount" is made up of two parts, one called the "basic benefits deductible" and the other called the "cash deductible." The "deductible amount" applies in respect of each calendar year.

The "basic benefits deductible," in respect of each calendar year, is an amount equal to the sum of

(1) the total cash value, computed on an equitable basis, of all services and supplies furnished during the calendar year through any "basic benefits" plan or plans under provisions thereof which provide for the furnishing of services or supplies rather than for payments in cash, and

(2) the total payments (whether such payments are contingent on expenses being incurred for services or supplies or whether such payments are contingent on the rendering of services or supplies) provided or available during the calendar year through any "basic benefits" plan or plans;

but only to the extent that such cash value or payments relate to any of the services or supplies which are recognized under this rider for the purpose of covered expenses.

The term "basic benefits" includes benefits, by whatever name called, under or on account of any one or more of the following items in respect of which any employer of the employee shall, directly or indirectly, have either contributed or made payroll deductions: the group policy (exclusive of this rider), any other insurance policy (whether issued by the Insurance Company or by any other insurer), any Blue Cross or Blue Shield plan or other hospital or medical benefit or service plan, any union welfare plan or other employee benefit organization plan, any federal or state or other governmental plan or law.

The "cash deductible," in respect of each calendar year, is $100.

If any part (or all) of an employee's "cash deductible" for a calendar year is applied against covered expenses incurred by the employee during the last three months of that calendar year, the employee's "cash deductible" for the next ensuing calendar year shall be reduced by the amount so applied.

The "maximum benefit" of an employee is $5,000; except that if an employee previously has been covered as a dependent under the rider providing for Dependents' Major Medical Expense Benefits, the "maximum benefit" as to that employee is limited to the amount, if any, by which $5,000 exceeds the amount of all benefits paid or accrued in respect of him under said rider, and if and while there is no such excess the employee shall not be insured for Major Medical Expense Benefits insurance in respect of himself under this rider.

The extension of benefits clause in the contract quoted above is typical of that found in other group medical expense contracts and provides that benefit payments will be continued during a claimant's total disability until a stated maximum time limit is reached. Unlike group hospital, surgical and medical contracts where the period of extension is usually ninety days, group major medical contracts often cover such expenditures until the end of the calendar year following the year in which contract coverage terminated.

Reinstatement of Benefits

The reinstatement of benefit clause is not quite as important in connection with a per disability upper limit, since subsequent disabilities are likely to result from a new and different cause. However, it is very important where the upper limit is on a lifetime aggregate basis. The reinstatement clause provides that if the insured individual is insurable, the limit will be reinstated to its original amount. In order to reduce administrative costs, usually a minimum benefit payment is required before this privilege can be exercised.

A typical reinstatement of benefit provision from a group policy with an aggregate lifetime limit reads as follows:

SPECIAL PROVISIONS FOR ESTABLISHING A NEW MAXIMUM BENEFIT

If an employee with respect to whom benefits of at least $1,000 have been paid under this rider submits, at no expense to the Insurance Company, evidence of insurability satisfactory to the Insurance Company, the Insurance Company will give its written consent to the ignoring of benefits paid for previous covered expenses in applying the maximum benefit provisions of this rider to benefits payable for covered expenses incurred with respect to the employee after the effective date of such written consent. If such written consent is granted after the employee's insurance under this rider has terminated for any reason, this rider shall, in all particulars, again apply as to the employee to the same extent that it would have applied if the employee had never been insured under this rider before the effective date of such written consent.

Some contracts provide for an automatic reinstatement of $1,000 per year regardless of insurability.

COMPREHENSIVE MEDICAL EXPENSE PLANS

Insurance Company Comprehensive Plans

Many names have been applied to coverage which was described earlier as comprehensive medical. In addition to comprehensive, it has been referred to as "minor-major medical," "basic and catastrophic," and "baby major medical." The term "comprehensive" is used here to refer to any plan which includes most types of health service in a single plan, provides coverage to very high limits and is designed to stand alone and provide basic benefits. While no plan can be comprehensive in the sense of being all-inclusive and free of limits, these plans qualify for the term at least as well as contracts in other lines of insurance to which the word has been applied and better than most.

Insurance company comprehensive plans are essentially of two types. The so-called pure comprehensive plan represents an extension of major medical down toward first-dollar coverage with the elimination of underlying coverage. Such a plan might provide for reimbursement of 80 per cent of covered medical care expenses in excess of a deductible of $25 or $50 per disability, up to a limit of $10,000 per disability. The coverage is not and should not be limited to cases requiring hospital confinement, as such a provision encourages unnecessary hospitalization.

The objectives of comprehensive coverage have been listed as: discouragement of unnecessary utilization, de-emphasis of small claims, more complete coverage of catastrophic expenditures, avoidance of duplicate coverage and of frequent plan revision, simple plan design and reasonable cost. The pure comprehensive plan accomplishes all these objectives well, but its acceptance in the market is limited by the tradition of first-dollar coverages. This tradition was originally established in hospital and surgical insurance by Blue Cross and Blue Shield plans.

The other type of comprehensive medical plan, referred to as "modified comprehensive," has been developed to meet some of the objection to the lack of first-dollar coverage for hospital and surgical expense. The modified approach represents a combination of basic hospital (and sometimes surgical coverage) with major medical in a single plan. Often no deductible is applied to hospital expenses and no percentage participation is used on the initial covered hospital expenses, such as the first $250. Surgeons' fees may be treated in a similar manner, subject to a surgical benefit schedule.

Figure 18–2 outlines the coverage of a plan of this type which imposes a deductible even on hospital expenses. Many different combinations are available. While a modified comprehensive plan is probably more salable in the face of employer and employee conditioning toward first-dollar benefits, it is considerably more expensive than a plan with a small deductible.

The variations in upper limit, benefit paid, percentage participation and deductible in comprehensive plans are similar to those in major medical plans. Table 18–2 shows some of this variation for major medical and comprehensive group business issued in 1963.

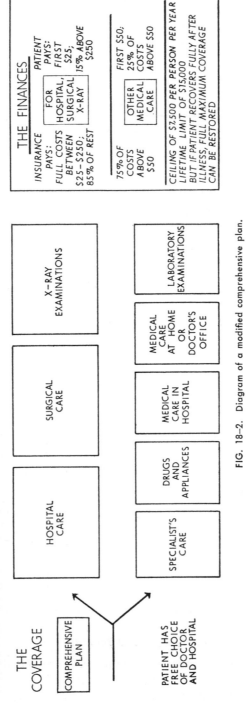

A MODIFIED COMPREHENSIVE PLAN MAY PROVIDE

THE COVERAGE

COMPREHENSIVE PLAN

PATIENT HAS FREE CHOICE OF DOCTOR AND HOSPITAL

HOSPITAL CARE

SURGICAL CARE

X-RAY EXAMINATIONS

SPECIALIST'S CARE

DRUGS AND APPLIANCES

MEDICAL CARE IN HOSPITAL

MEDICAL CARE AT HOME OR DOCTOR'S OFFICE

LABORATORY EXAMINATIONS

THE FINANCES

INSURANCE PAYS:

PATIENT PAYS:

FOR HOSPITAL, SURGICAL X-RAY

FULL COSTS BETWEEN $25–$250; 85% OF REST

FIRST $25; 15% ABOVE $250

OTHER MEDICAL CARE

75% OF COSTS ABOVE $50

FIRST $50; 25% OF COSTS ABOVE $50

CEILING OF $7,500 PER PERSON PER YEAR LIFETIME LIMIT OF $15,000 BUT IF PATIENT RECOVERS FULLY AFTER ILLNESS, FULL MAXIMUM COVERAGE CAN BE RESTORED

FIG. 18–2. Diagram of a modified comprehensive plan.

TABLE 18–2

DISTRIBUTION OF MAJOR MEDICAL AND COMPREHENSIVE INSURANCE
BY PLAN TYPE AND MAXIMUM BENEFIT, 1963

	Number of Employees			Per Cent of Total
	Major Medical	Compre- hensive	Total	
Total Employees................	195,686	23,086	218,772	100.0
All Cause Plans................	83,245	21,709	104,954	47.33
Calendar year benefit period— lifetime maximum...........	65,519	14,832	80,351	36.23
Calendar year benefit period— each cause maximum	11,987	2,381	14,368	6.48
Other than calendar year bene- fit period—lifetime maximum.	2,664	1,604	4,268	1.92
Other than calendar year bene- fit period—each cause maxi- mum.....................	3,075	2,892	5,967	2.69
Maximum Benefit Amount........	83,245	21,709	104,954	47.33
Under $5,000.................	26	—	26	—
$5,000......................	32,522	2,230	34,752	15.66
$7,500......................	1,959	374	2,333	1.12
$10,000.....................	48,003	16,208	61,211	28.95
$15,000.....................	698	1,964	2,662	1.2
All others...................	37	775	812	.37
Each Cause Plans...............	45,590	1,377	46,967	21.18
Disability required each cause benefit period—lifetime maxi- mum.....................	11,580	487	12,067	5.44
Disability required each cause benefit period—each cause maximum.................	248	0	248	.11
Disability not required each cause benefit period—lifetime maximum..................	30,526	778	31,304	14.12
Disability not required each cause benefit period—each cause maximum.............	3,236	112	3,348	1.51
Maximum Benefit Amount........	45,590	1,377	46,967	21.18
$5,000......................	12,263	54	12,317	5.56
$7,500......................	1,842	12	1,854	1.83
$10,000.....................	28,764	1,199	29,963	13.52
$15,000.....................	544	112	656	.29
Over $2,500 but less than $10,000...................	2,177	0	2,177	.98
All Others....................	66,851	0	66,851	30.14

SOURCE: Health Insurance Institute, *Group Health Insurance Policies Issued in 1963* (New York, 1964).

Blue Cross and Blue Shield Extended Benefits

Extended benefit arrangements in the Blue Cross and Blue Shield plans represent responses to the same need which led insurance companies to the development of major medical and comprehensive coverages. However, except for eleven plans offered by Blue Cross and Blue Shield in conjunction, benefits are limited to hospital or to medical-surgical expenses. Moreover, many of the combination plans do not cover such items as blood and plasma, expensive drugs or nursing services, which are included under insurance company group major medical and comprehensive contracts.

Forty-two Blue Cross plans offer extended benefit programs, either for hospital benefits only or in conjunction with Blue Shield to include medical-surgical benefits. Twenty of these resemble insurance company major medical contracts in that they include provisions for deductibles and percentage participation; twenty-two represent extensions of the basic hospital contract. Illustrative of the latter approach is the extended benefit program of the Colorado Hospital Service. It provides for an extension of the basic hospital coverage from 120 days to 240 or 610 days except in cases of pulmonary tuberculosis or nervous and mental diseases.

A somewhat typical Blue Cross–Blue Shield extended benefit program which follows the major medical approach is described below. The separate deductibles of $50 each for Blue Shield and Blue Cross are typical. A choice of upper limits is provided.

Blue Cross Master Medical Endorsement pays 80 per cent of the following charges after the basic contract benefits expire and the deductible is satisfied:
1. Hospital room and board up to $25 per day.
2. All hospital ancillary services.

Blue Cross Master Medical Endorsement pays 80 per cent of the following charges after the deductible has been satisfied:
3. In-hospital services for a Registered Nurse or Licensed Practical Nurse for private duty nursing care. (Not related to the subscriber by blood or marriage.)
4. Services of a Registered Nurse in the home for private duty nursing care. (Not related to the subscriber by blood or marriage.)
5. Physical therapy treatment other than as provided in the basic contract.
6. Rental of an iron lung or other durable equipment required for temporary therapeutic use.
7. Crutches, splints, casts and other such prosthetic appliances.
8. Drugs and medicines requiring a written prescription and dispensed by a licensed pharmacist, other than as provided in the basic contract.
9. Emergency ambulance service to the nearest hospital.

Blue Shield Master Medical Endorsement pays 80 per cent of the following charges after the basic contract benefits expire and the deductible is satisfied:
Services of physicians, including specialists, for surgical and for non-surgical care, for treatment of fractures and dislocations, including such care in a hospital, in the home and in the physician's office, except that for out-patient physicians care for mental and nervous disorders payments by Blue Shield will be limited to 50 per cent.

With a corridor deductible and percentage participation clause, contracts of this type resemble insurance company group major medical contracts closely, except that they do not cover certain types of expense. Approximately one third of the Blue Cross and Blue Shield plans offer benefits of this type, but not necessarily in conjunction with each other.

Eleven plans which depart from the insurance company approach are offered by Blue Cross and Blue Shield in conjunction. Benefits generally are extended without a corridor deductible, and the percentage participation usually is applied only to certain types of benefit which are subject to abuse, e.g., mental and nervous disease.

As of May, 1963, about two thirds of the Blue Shield plans offered some form of extended benefit or major medical coverage, and it is estimated that six million persons were covered under these programs. As of December 31, 1962, 4.7 million Blue Cross enrollees had major medical coverage, and 1.6 million had extended benefit coverage.

Independent Plans

Many of the so-called independent plans, including group practice prepayment plans, offer benefits which are comprehensive as to amount, type of service, or both. Many of them approach the broad coverage of insurance company comprehensive contracts. Some exceed it in certain respects, for example, in coverage of preventive services such as immunization and physical examinations.[8]

SELECTED REFERENCES

ASHMAN, CARL R. "Major Medical," *HIAA Group Insurance Forum*, 1958.

BLUE CROSS ASSOCIATION. *Blue Cross Guide*. Chicago, 1962.

CHAMBER OF COMMERCE OF THE UNITED STATES. *Major Medical Expense Insurance*. Washington, D.C., October, 1957.

COUNCIL ON MEDICAL SERVICES, AMA. *Voluntary Prepayment Medical Benefit Plans*. Chicago, 1963.

DICKERSON, O. D. *Health Insurance*. Rev. ed. Homewood, Ill.: Richard D. Irwin, Inc., 1963.

FARQUHAR, GORDON N. "Comprehensive Major Medical Expense Insurance," *HIAA Group Insurance Forum*, 1957.

————. "Major Medical," *HIAA Group Insurance Forum*, 1958.

HALVERSON, A. B. "Major Medical—Problems of Underwriting and Claims Handling," *HIAA Group Insurance Forum*, 1958.

————. "Major Medical—A Reappraisal," *HIAA Group Insurance Forum*, 1960.

McCULLOUGH, RAY. "Comprehensive Major Medical Expense," *HIAA Group Insurance Forum*, 1957.

MILLER, MORTON D. "Major Medical Expense," *Bests Insurance News*, Fire and Casualty Ed. (July, 1954), p. 41.

————. "Gross Premiums for Individual and Family Major Medical Expense Insurance," *Transactions of the Society of Actuaries*, Vol. III, p. 31.

---

[8] See Chapters 15 and 17 for a detailed discussion of comprehensive coverage under group practice prepayment plans.

SHERWOOD, HUGH C. "Fastest-Growing Health Insurance Today," *Medical Economics*, July, 1957.

SHINN, R. R. "Comprehensive Medical Care Plans," *Bests Insurance News, Fire and Casualty Ed.* (June, 1956), p. 6.

SIEGFRIED, CHARLES A. *Major Medical Expense Insurance*. HIAA, 1958.

THALER, ALAN M. "Group Major Medical Expense Insurance," *Transactions of the Society of Actuaries*, Vol. III, p. 429.

Chapter 19

UNDERWRITING GROUP MEDICAL EXPENSE COVERAGE

BY DONALD D. CODY

Group medical expense coverages provide benefits to protect against some or all of the expenses of hospitals, nursing homes, diagnostic laboratories, physicians, nurses, physiotherapists, podiatrists, psychologists, drugs, ambulances, prosthetic devices, radiological equipment and all other necessary medical and allied services. As was mentioned in Chapters 16 and 17, it is characteristic for these coverages to insure against losses that often are frequent, small and to some extent within the control of the insured. Moreover, the covered expenses are subject to inflationary trends and uncertainties regarding physicians' fees, as well as variations in the choice, extent and quality of medical care. This type of insurance is therefore very different from the ideal insurance design, such as life insurance, which involves losses which are infrequent, large, beyond the insured's control and definite in size. Thus, underwriting group medical expense insurance is generally more difficult than underwriting group life insurance.

Underwriting involves not only close examination of the general characteristics of the group case, but also, very importantly, the factors determining premium level. These factors include expected claims level; sales, installation and administrative expenses, commissions, taxes and risk charges; the experience rating system used in determination of renewal rates and dividends or retrospective premium credits; and the competitive posture of the market. Underwriting also involves a review of claims systems, including the practices and fees of physicians and hospitals, utilization of medical facilities by insureds and local medical cost trends. Similarly, a review of the policyholder's administration of the case must be made. All of these factors influence proper pricing.

It should be noted that experience rating does not allow careless underwriting. Competition generally narrows premium margins to an extent that, even on large cases with full experience rating, a sudden upward fluctuation in claims will encourage termination by the policy-holder to prevent the insurer from recovering the loss in subsequent years. Thus, experience rating tends to establish the pricing classification of a case, but it does not abolish the insurance risk by establishing a cost plus arrangement with the insurance company acting only as an administrator. Indeed, the larger the case, the more competent must be the underwriter, so that the premium properly reflects all characteristics of the case, consonant with the low risk charges applicable to large cases. On smaller cases with less experience rating, the underwriter has less indication from experience as to appropriate premium levels and must rely on manual premium rates to a greater extent. On the smallest cases, manual premium rates are used without any reference to experience on each case. However, risk charges are larger as a percentage of premium, the smaller the case, thereby reflecting the greater pricing uncertainty relative to claims to be realized. Even on the smallest cases, however, the underwriter must give close attention to the characteristics of the case to assure insurability under the pricing system of his company.

BASIS OF GROUP UNDERWRITING

Before treating the underwriting of group medical expense insurance for various types of groups, it is desirable to emphasize the general objectives and tests of group insurance underwriting.

Group Underwriting Objectives

For any group insurance plan to operate successfully, it is necessary that there be a spread of risk. In addition, no insurance company could be financially sound if it were careless enough to accept an unduly high percentage of bad risks. In connection with the issuance of individual life and health insurance, each individual risk is investigated as to state of health, medical history, habits, occupation and other insurance owned. In group insurance there is ordinarily no investigation of the individual.[1] Group insurance relies instead on the fact that if a sizable percentage of the employees of an employer are insured, a favorable cross section of risk can be obtained automatically. This follows since employers cannot afford to have a very large percentage of employees in poor health.

In selecting a sound group insurance risk, four underwriting objectives are pursued: (1) low expense through efficient administration; (2) predictable claim costs; (3) high persistency (that is, keeping groups "on the books"); and (4) compliance with state statutes and insurance department regulations.

---

[1] Exceptions are late entrants, small groups with less than ten or fifteen lives and older members of professional association groups.

Group Underwriting Standards

The first three underwriting objectives mentioned above are assured if the following tests, which were discussed in detail in Chapters 3 and 10, are met in all respects.

Permanency of Group. A cohesive group must exist involving a strong, mutual and continuing interest, and such interest must be other than for the purchase of insurance. Each member should have joined the group for a substantial economic reason in the form of wages, salary or other advantage and be able to leave the group only with a loss of such income or other advantage.

Stream of New Entrants. There must be a steady stream of young new entrants so that the average age and vitality of the group will be relatively stable as time passes.

Central Administrative Agency. Stable group coverage generally requires a permanent central agency, able and willing to assume responsibility for administration, which involves the enrollment of new lives, collection of contributions, remittance of premiums, record keeping and assistance with claims.

Automatic Collection Routine. In a contributory plan, there must be a simple routine method such as payroll deduction for collecting contributions of the members.

Reasonable Contributions. The cost to the insured members must be low both in relation to comparable forms of insurance available elsewhere and in keeping with the financial means of the insured member. Usually, this low cost can be realized only by means of a subsidy from the employer of at least 25 per cent of premiums.

Substantial Enrollment. The relationship of the policyholder to the individuals eligible for insurance must be such as to provide a ready means of obtaining and keeping up a substantial enrollment established at 75 per cent of the eligible group in cases of fifteen employees or more and sometimes higher in small cases.

No Individual Selection. The eligibility requirements must be formulated on the basis of conditions pertaining to employment, and benefits must be on some uniform plan (without excessive relative amounts as between classes of insured) precluding any individual selection of amounts.

Underwriting Standards—Conclusion. To the extent that any of the above tests are not met, the group insurance plan will tend to develop high administrative costs and high claim costs. Moreover, such high costs may increase over the years. Consequently, premiums in these instances are high originally and likely to become higher at each re-rating. Eventually the plan is likely to terminate, leaving the insurance company with a financial loss and the insured without coverage.

Professional association groups, written on either a franchise or group basis, do not fully satisfy a number of these tests but are usually underwritten successfully because of special administrative and enrollment procedures.

Statutory Group Underwriting Requirements

The statutes of the various states and the interpretative regulations of state insurance departments usually define the types of groups, types of coverages, eligibility of insureds, method of pricing and other procedural conditions so as to assure soundness of group insurance plans. Conformity with such statutes is the fourth underwriting objective previously noted. Although the tests listed help assure such soundness, the group underwriter must nevertheless consider the specific statutes and regulations of the state where the group insurance plan has its legal situs. Though there is some general conformity in statutes and regulation, variations must be noted. The insurance authorities of several states assert jurisdiction over a group contract delivered in another state but covering residents of their state.[2]

Single Employer Groups. In connection with employer-employee groups, many states have requirements or restrictions regarding the minimum number of insureds, participation percentage, contribution by the employer, minimum rates, eligibility of employees, nature of coverage, policy provisions and inclusion of affiliates or subsidiaries of the employer. In all jurisdictions, a group contract may be issued to an employer to provide benefits for the employees and their dependents. Organizations subsidiary to or affiliated with the employer, if under the control of the employer or under common control by reason of stock ownership or contract, usually may be included for coverage.

Various types of political entities may provide coverage for employees and their dependents. Although these groups bear a close resemblance to a single employer group, certain additional statutory factors must be taken into consideration. The charter of a municipal corporation must allow the corporation to provide the benefits. Enabling statutes otherwise are usually required. In addition, the inclusion of elected officials may be troublesome because of state constitutional provisions and, in any event, if the public entity is to contribute, there must be some affirmative grant of power for such contribution. Establishment of a proper legal framework thus can be quite time consuming.

Multiple Employer Groups. Statutes in most jurisdictions allow a number of employers to provide benefits for the employees and depend-

---

[2] Statutes vary from state to state, with notable differences between group life and group health statutes in many jurisdictions. In general, group life insurance statutes are more restrictive. No attempt is made here to show details of requirements, which must be ascertained by a study of each statute.

ents of employees under a single group contract. The usual procedure outlined in the statute requires the establishment of a trust, and normally the employers must be in the same industry. Labor unions may join with employers in the formation of the trust. In general, restrictions applicable to single employer groups also apply to multiple employer groups.

A. *Trust Organized by Two or More Employers in the Same Industry.* States differ in their rulings as to the meaning of the requirement that employers be in the same industry. Although the statutes of a few states may not expressly permit insurance for some groups of this type, in certain states the insurance commissioner has discretion to permit such groups.

B. *Trustees of Health and Welfare Funds.* Federal statutes require the establishment of a trust where employers and unions bargain regarding contributions by employers for employee welfare benefits. A few states do not expressly permit or place restrictions on groups in this area.

C. *Trade Association Groups.* The trade association group is in most cases merely a type of multiple employer group, where employers in the same industry are also members of an association. However, participation requirements usually are higher for trade association groups than for the normal multiple employer group.

Professional Association Groups. Some states provide that an association, including a labor union, may be the policyholder for health insurance for the benefit of its members. A common interest, such as a profession, is normally required, and the association must have been organized for purposes other than the purchase of insurance and usually must have been in existence for a period of time.

Groups Based on a Common Interest. In certain jurisdictions, the absence of a group insurance statute or the existence of a statute giving the insurance commissioner discretion to approve a group policy form have allowed the writing of group insurance for a policyholder even though the group does not fall within the normal statutory and regulatory provisions. Groups have been countenanced where a common interest is involved, such as alumni groups, veterans groups and fraternal groups.

UNDERWRITING PROBLEMS IN GROUP MEDICAL EXPENSE COVERAGE

In selecting risks the group medical expense underwriter is concerned primarily with type and design of benefits, the relationships of the various parties, and the costs and control of claims.

Medical Care Costs

The underwriter must give special attention to trends in the cost of medical care. The hospital has become a community facility accepted without fear by the public and freely used by doctors. Drugs are prescribed and purchased in expensive profusion. Medical care is primarily a personal service function, and its cost has increased with advances in the general price level and with increasing industrial productivity. Both of these factors, in turn, have caused increased salaries, wages and fees of medical personnel. Costs of items such as hospital buildings, therapeutic and diagnostic equipment needed for the new medical and surgical techniques, and teams of specialists have been increasing year by year. Some relief will develop in these costs with better regional planning of hospital locations and specialties and with improved hospital management. However, it must be recognized that increasing costs of medical care reflect better medical care by better trained personnel using better facilities for more and more people legitimately needing such care.

Between 1953 and 1963 national expenditures for medical care increased by about 8 per cent a year from about $11 billion to $24 billion and from 4.4 per cent of disposable personal income to 5.9 per cent.[3] In the same period, the price index for medical care items increased about 3.5 per cent a year, while the general price index moved up only 1.3 per cent. Physicians' fees advanced about 3 per cent a year, and drugs moved up about 1 per cent a year. The hospital cost index of average cost per patient day in nonfederal short-term general hospitals was the most volatile part of the medical care index, moving about 7 per cent a year. In New York City, for instance, semiprivate room and board charges increased from an average of about $12 a day in 1952 to $28 a day in 1962. In addition, utilization of medical facilities and personnel is increasing as Americans demand more and better care.

The effect of these spiraling costs and utilization on premium rates is about 8 per cent a year on major medical coverages, 5 per cent a year on hospital coverages with dollar maximums, and 2 to 3 per cent a year on physicians' fees coverage. The trend in claim cost is a fact of life in medical care underwriting and must be considered in premium determination at issue and at renewal.

Benefit Abuses and Overinsurance

In some cases physicians, for reasons of convenience for themselves or their patients, will confine patients unnecessarily for diagnostic reasons or for treatment of illness amenable to out-patient or home treatment. The introduction of a deductible of $25 or $50, or a percentage participation charge of 25 per cent in the benefits for special hospital charges, tends to discourage such practices by shifting costs back to the insured. Or the addition of a diagnostic X-ray and laboratory benefit to the policy may reduce unnecessary diagnostic confinements.

Sometimes, patients stay a day or more in the hospital beyond the date when home care would be indicated by medical considerations alone.

---

[3] Health Insurance Institute, *Source Book of Health Insurance Data 1964.* (New York, 1964), pp. 58–61.

This is more likely to occur when the insured is over-insured. In this connection insurance companies have developed an anti-duplication clause, which assigns claims by priority among the insurance companies so that aggregate payment is restricted to aggregate claims. This type of clause, which will be discussed in Chapter 24, is always included in major medical policies.

Use of Loss Control. When unnecessary utilization of facilities or improper fee levels exist, the underwriter may request the insurer's loss control specialists to visit with physicians, hospitals, personnel managers, union leaders and employees to explain the insurance plan and the effects of abuse on costs to the policyholder and his employees. Such loss control engineering sometimes shows quite startling results, with reductions in some instances of 5 to 10 per cent in claims, as will be seen in Chapter 23.

Effects of Deductibles, Percentage Participation and Schedules. Percentage participation and deductible clauses in major medical expense coverages tend to make the insured more interested in negotiating fees and reducing medical services to those necessary and, at the same time, shift the emphasis from coverage of frequent, minor medical treatment to infrequent major medical treatment. Where the major medical provision covering reasonable and customary fees for surgery, medical visits, radiological therapy and diagnostic procedures appears to be unworkable, schedules for maximum fees are sometimes introduced.

Uninsurable Groups

Some groups are uninsurable for medical care coverages except under unusual conditions. For instance, employees of hospitals may not be insurable because the hospital can recover in claim payments more than they pay in premiums simply by confining their employees freely and for excessive periods. Also, residents and nurses have no hotel facilities in their quarters and are therefore confined for simple ailments normally indicating home confinement.

Questionable Groups Requiring Higher Premium Rates

Certain types of groups present such significant underwriting problems that they can be covered only at an additional premium. Some groups have seasonal employment so that medical care peaks just before layoff, or dependents seek medical care just after hiring. Such industries include restaurants, hotels, laundries, contractors, canneries and vacation resorts. Other groups with abnormal proportions of older or female employees present similar problems because the employees' medical care needs are more frequent and lengthy. Department stores and street transportation firms often have a considerable number of such employees, as do companies in declining industries that are restricting their operations. Then, too, problems arise relative to groups whose employees have no facilities for home care of minor illnesses, such as staffs of private schools.

Groups transferring from another insurance company to escape premium increases need to be underwritten with special care. Where occupational coverage is included, certain high risk groups present particular problems because of on-the-job accidental injuries, such as mining and logging.

Underwriting concern is also present regarding groups with little or no employer contribution for either employee or dependent benefits. These groups are especially likely to seek another insurance company when cost trends require premium increases.

Thus, the underwriter of certain medical care coverages must continually be aware that the coverage provides for frequent and small losses as well as for infrequent catastrophic losses. Then, too, the underwriter must recognize that the utilization and costs of facilities and services are, to a considerable extent, within the control of the insured and the physicians.

UNDERWRITING OF REGULAR EMPLOYER-EMPLOYEE GROUPS

Basic Underwriting Procedure

A group insurance plan normally originates in the personnel department or the industrial relations department of an employer, or at the collective bargaining table. After a decision is reached as to the amount of money to be expended on a certain type of benefit, an insurance consultant (who may be a consulting actuary, a broker or an agent) works out detailed cost and design specifications with the officers of the employer or with representatives of labor and management. The consultant generally submits these specifications to various insurance companies, generally through group field men in the area.

Frequently, the local group field man can issue a proposal of insurance on his own authority, but within the limits established by his company. In complicated or large cases, however, the specifications usually come to the group underwriting division of the home office for consideration. The home office underwriters pass on the acceptability of the case, clarify benefit descriptions, agree to administrative procedures, establish premium rates and obtain retention[4] illustrations from the group actuaries.

The home office sales, or field sales, personnel then prepare a proposal or offer to insure. This combines specifications with cost estimates and various recommendations. Competing insurers' proposals are analyzed by the consultant and the employer. The insurance company is selected on the basis of ability to perform, financial strength, cost and possibly business relationships. Written notice of selection in the form of an application for insurance and a binding consideration are given to the insurance

---

[4] Retentions are the excess of premiums over claims and dividends (or retrospective rate credits), roughly reflecting the administrative expenses, taxes, commissions, risk charge and profit which the insurance company will charge.

company chosen. The local group field men then join immediately with the insurance consultant and the employer to install the plan, as will be discussed in Chapter 28.

After the plan is installed, there are the usual monthly billing procedures, claims payments and the service the group field man gives the employer in assuring smooth mechanics and conformance of benefits to needs. Each year the group underwriter gives consideration to adequacy of premium, and, if a premium increase or corrective changes in benefits are needed, the group field man will have to resell the case in a competitive atmosphere. It is also customary for benefits to be enlarged and modernized every few years, and group underwriters must pass on such changes.

Initial Underwriting

The acceptance of the group plan, whether by the salaried group field man (in smaller standard cases according to delegated authority) or by the home office group underwriter, is made in accordance with the principles and tests outlined earlier in the chapter. The rates used are determined as described in Chapter 22.

General Eligibility. The underwriter also must give careful attention to the definition of eligible employees and dependents. Only active, full-time, permanent employees should be eligible, with "full-time employees" being defined as those who work at least thirty hours a week. Employees not actively at work are insured only upon return to work. Dependents in the hospital are insured upon return to their home. Eligible dependents normally include wives and unmarried children from fourteen days to nineteen years of age.

Husbands of employed women preferably should not be eligible because men usually have group coverage with their own employers, and inclusion of husbands could cause duplication of coverage, adverse selection and difficulty in meeting the requirement of insuring at least 75 per cent of eligible dependents. Children also include step-children, adopted children and foster children if they are entirely dependent on the employee. For an extra premium, dependent children at college may be included. Also on major medical coverages, children in the first fourteen days of life are invariably covered for medical care of unusual illnesses. There is a requirement that 75 per cent of eligible employees and 75 per cent of eligible dependents become insured in contributory plans in order to assure spread of risk.

Inspection Reports. On smaller cases, it is desirable to obtain inspection reports regarding the financial condition of the employer, since this is important for persistency of the case. Also the legitimacy of employees' eligibility is often checked. This is pursued only on a sampling basis, such as one case in ten.

Transfer Cases. It should be recognized that initial underwriting of groups with more than twenty-five lives often entails consideration of cases transferred from another insurance company, inasmuch as the bulk of the large employer-employee groups in the United States have group medical expense protection of some type. Transfer cases require special attention because they are very likely to occur when the other insurance company requires a premium increase.

If the case involves more than 100 lives, most insurance companies will ask for a full two- or three-year history of annual premiums, incurred claims and premium rates. With such information, it is possible for the new insurance company to establish the level of expected claims during the next policy year with proper account taken of known trends in medical care costs in the geographical area. To this expected claim level the new insurance company adds provision for its expenses, taxes, commissions, risk charge and profit and usually a 5 per cent to 10 per cent margin for fluctuation in claims from the expected level. On large cases involving $100,000 or more of premium, special care is taken in this determination of premium.

On cases of under 100 lives, and especially those under fifty lives, more routine handling of transfer cases is usual. For instance, if the policy-holder has not been notified of an increase in rates and the present company's current rates are near the normal rates of the new company, the case could be accepted at normal rates by the new company. A further requirement may be that the coverage must have been with the previous company for at least three years. Special care must be taken to be sure that the motivation for transfer is not the reinstatement of a major medical maximum on a disabled dependent or on an employee with a nondisabling sickness like nonconfining psychiatric problems. Some companies, however, are more cautious than this even for the smallest cases and demand full claims and premium information and quote rates accordingly.

Those Blue Cross–Blue Shield plans that use community rating, rather than experience rating techniques, do not keep claims statistics for specific group cases. Thus, insurance companies tend to accept transfers from such organizations without special rate additions if the case has been with Blue Cross–Blue Shield for several years. This routine handling of Blue Cross–Blue Shield transfers may be restricted to cases of under 200 lives.

On transfer cases, it is sometimes necessary to accept liability for claims that have arisen. Special premium charges are usually made for the assumption of liability of such existing claims if such charges are expected to be more than 5 per cent of normal premium. For instance, Blue Cross–Blue Shield plans usually do not have any continued maternity coverage on subscribers after date of transfer, and the new company must assume this obligation. Instead of making an extra premium charge, the new company may remove the usual provision for continued maternity coverage on termination of the new policy as an offset to the assumption of claims that exist at issue.

Retired Employees. The underwriter on a new case also faces the problem of medical expense coverage for retired employees, if such persons are included in the group. Usually insurance companies charge higher rates for retired employees to reflect their more frequent and costly medical care expenses. It is usual also to reduce benefits on such retired employees. For instance, the deductible factor in major medical policies may be restricted to the accumulation of medical charges in a two- or three-month period, and the maximum amount payable may be reduced from the normal level. The various methods for providing coverage for retired employees are discussed in Chapters 36 and 37.

Renewal Underwriting

Group insurance premiums are guaranteed only for one year, and each case is reviewed on its anniversary for re-rating as part of the general underwriting review. The procedure used is similar to that described previously for transfer policies, except it is possible to underwrite renewal cases much more precisely because of the detailed information available.

One of the obvious considerations in renewal underwriting is to establish a satisfactory level of aggregate premiums in comparison with aggregate claims, expenses, taxes, commissions and dividends (retrospective rate credits) and, at the same time, to provide equity among policyholders and achieve maximum persistency of policyholders. The underwriter, therefore, is under obligation on the one hand to set adequate premiums on each case under the general system of re-rating and, on the other hand, to accomplish this with sufficient restraint so that it is not more attractive for the policyholder to transfer to another company.

On each renewal date the underwriter examines the experience of the group to see whether he should suggest appropriate benefit changes, request loss control activities or ask the field man to improve participation or alter the administrative system of the policyholder. Frequently, on renewal, either at the underwriter's request or at the policyholder's request, a resolicitation of eligible employees is made to improve participation. Special underwriting rules are needed for this procedure. The underwriter must consider the extent to which he is willing to waive the evidence of insurability required for employees joining the plan after their initial opportunity to join. The usual requirement for such waiver of evidence of insurability is the enrollment of a specified percentage of eligible uninsured employees. For instance, if there are five to twenty eligible uninsured employees, evidence is waived only if all agree to enroll. If there are between twenty and fifty eligible uninsured employees, evidence is waived if 75 per cent (but at least twenty) enroll. If there are more than fifty eligible insured employees, the required proportion is 50 per cent (but at least thirty-eight persons). A period of ten days or two weeks is usually set for this enrollment. Evidence is generally not waived for any employee who has previously been unable to provide satisfactory evidence of insurability, for employees not actively at full-time work or for employees over age sixty.

When benefits are increased, transitional problems must be faced regarding the handling of existing claims. For instance, the new benefits usually apply only to hospital confinements commencing after the date of change and to surgery occurring after such date. Additional premiums otherwise may be needed.

UNDERWRITING OF TRUSTEE GROUPS FORMED UNDER TAFT-HARTLEY ACT

Chapter 33 is devoted to group insurance plans issued to trustees of Taft-Hartley (United States Labor Management Relations Act of 1947) welfare funds. These funds are established for the employees of employers in such industries as construction, restaurants and retail stores to provide continuous group insurance coverage for employees who move among the various employers. The funds are always set up in accordance with labor-management agreements. The principles of underwriting are not substantially different from those for employer-employee groups but involve further considerations. For instance, the bargaining arrangement might provide for a credit of a month of coverage for each 100 hours of work in a month. If the union member works more than 100 hours in any particular month, he thereby earns credit, subject to maximums, toward an additional month's insurance coverage, the credit being applicable in a month when he works less than 100 hours. Other terms as to disability, termination of coverage with low work credits, initial eligibility and reinstatement are included. Various other credit systems, such as moving average systems, are used but do not vary in principle from this hour-credit system.

It is necessary for the underwriter to examine the hour crediting rules in relationship to the amounts of money being contributed to fund the plan. Such amounts might be, for example, $.15 to $.20 per hour of work by each employee and payable by each participating employer to the fund. Employer contributions for hours worked by ineligible employees enhance the funding in the plan. It is important that there be sufficient margins to enable a buildup of surplus in the fund (usually three to six months' premium) in anticipation of unusual layoffs and to permit the payment of increases in premium rates at renewal prior to the date when the employer's contributions can be renegotiated under the bargaining contract.

Because an administrator is needed to collect the employer's contributions and to keep records on the eligibility of insured union members, it is common in such plans for the administrator to settle claims using drafts on the insurance company. On renewal, the underwriter must review his claims handling to be sure that the insurance contract is being properly administered.

Adjustments in premium levels and modifications of benefits are especially difficult renewal problems in this type of case because the parties involved must deal with each other at the bargaining table. It is not unusual for these plans to be rebid among competing insurance companies nearly every year so that the parties can be assured they are getting the best available insurance arrangements as to price and quality.

UNDERWRITING GROUPS WHERE UNION IS POLICYHOLDER

Employer-employee groups, multiple-employer trusteed groups and Taft-Hartley trusteed groups are the proper vehicles for covering union members whose benefits are provided under labor-management bargaining agreements. Such groups, as previously described, can be successfully underwritten.

Under the Taft-Hartley Act, group coverage paid by employer contributions according to collective bargaining cannot be issued directly to unions. The Act also prohibits employers from volunteering contributions to union members without collective bargaining. Thus, group medical expense insurance policies issued to unions are almost invariably member-pay-all except for token union contributions. Lapse of such contracts at the time of renewal rate increases is likely, as on other insured-pay-all groups, because of pressures from the individual union members. Hence, it is difficult to underwrite a union group successfully where the union is the policyholder of the group medical expense coverage. There are, however, notable exceptions, such as group policies covering retired railroad employees previously covered during active employment under a labor-management sponsored plan.

UNDERWRITING TRADE ASSOCIATION GROUPS

Employers engaged in the same type of business often join together in trade associations to promote their mutual interests. Such associations, as explained in Chapter 32, frequently arrange for group insurance for the employees of their employer members. The policyholder is either the association or trustees of the association, depending on state laws.

For an insurance plan to be successful, the association must meet the requirements already outlined for a sound group. In addition, a large proportion of members must be small employers, its leaders must be competent and there must be enthusiasm for the insurance plan.[5] Premium rates must be low compared with those on group insurance plans available to members directly.

---

[5] Such enthusiasm is easily detected by the group field man and the group underwriter from the attitude of the association executive secretary as to plans for enrollment and administration.

Renewal underwriting of these groups is similar to that for employer-employee groups, except for special considerations regarding the effectiveness of the administration by the associations, continued promotion among old and new employer-members (especially new employees of enrolled employer-members), conservation of enrollment of eligible employees and strains caused by premium increases.

Medical expense coverage usually can be successfully written only on local employer associations whose membership is located in an area over which medical costs and practices are uniform. If costs vary, the members in high cost areas are subsidized by those in low cost areas, and this leads to a progressive lapse of the latter members with a resultant spiraling of premium rates at renewal. For similar reasons, the age of employees should not vary widely.

When underwriting group medical expense coverage for trade associations, it is typical to require that the plan contain group life insurance to add stability. In fact, life insurance is usually the basic coverage in such plans. It is important for the successful operation of medical expense coverage that life insurance premium rates be graded by age grouping, so that employer-members with high-average-age employees will not be subsidized by those with low-average-age employees.

In underwriting this coverage, it is also necessary to assure that the administrative office of the association be staffed to conduct initial and continuous solicitation of members, collect premiums, administer claims and service members at the association's expense. This office may be run by the broker acting as the administrator for the group. Regardless, the administrative office is the most important underwriting factor.

Insurers customarily require that minimum initial enrollment must be the larger of 100 employees or 10 per cent of total employees. Initial enrollment is rarely in excess of 200, but there must be a sure expectation of further growth. The average number of employees per employer-member must be at least five. Each employer-member must enroll at least 75 per cent of employees and 75 per cent of dependents. If the plan is noncontributory, all must be enrolled. New employees should be enrolled as part of the hiring procedure to obviate deterioration of enrollment. New employer-members should be ineligible for three months to reduce anti-selection. New employees of employer-members should be ineligible for at least one month to reduce effects of early employee turnover. Employer-members preferably should contribute 100 per cent of employee premiums or at least 50 per cent of employee and dependent premiums.

UNDERWRITING PUBLIC EMPLOYEE GROUPS

Special problems are involved in underwriting groups of persons employed by a government or subdivision of government or by a body which has been created by a governmental authority. State legislatures have been very active in recent years in passing laws enabling public employee units to contract for insurance, to finance contributions and to make payroll deductions. In order not to place his company in jeopardy of making an illegal contract, however, the underwriter must obtain reference to specific state or local statutes enabling the employer to contract for insurance, to pay part of the cost and to make salary deductions. This is sometimes very difficult to accomplish, especially in connection with local groups like towns or school boards, and frequently involves consultation with the employer's legal counsel and receipt of actual minutes of the meeting of the governing board or council at which authority is given. Attorneys general also are frequently asked for official opinions interpreting statutory authority.

Some companies limit their acceptance of public employee groups to those with at least fifty employees because of high underwriting and administrative expenses. Such expenses arise from the difficulties discussed above, and poor claims experience is caused by low participation, high ages and weak health requirements for new employees and appointees. These factors may require special premium determination. Then, too, elective or appointive officials should be excluded unless they devote at least thirty hours weekly to the employer.

Persistency of group medical expense contracts usually is poor on public employee groups because political favoritism encourages shifting among insurers and because routine premium increases lead to shopping for a new insurer as a result of fixed budgets. Hence 50 per cent of the premium should be required as a minimum employer contribution, and employee-pay-all plans should rarely be accepted. The maximum statutory contribution always should be required. Policy anniversaries should coincide with the ends of fiscal years so that budgets can be adjusted to meet premium increase requirements.

As was mentioned in connection with other types of groups, group life insurance also lends stability to a public employees' group medical expense plan. If another insurer already has the more stable group life coverage in force, medical expense coverage is declined by some companies, since the company writing the life insurance will inevitably inherit the medical care coverage.

UNDERWRITING SMALL GROUPS OF THREE TO TWENTY-FOUR LIVES

In the early 1950's, a few companies developed a successful extension of group insurance, first, to groups of ten lives or more and later to groups of three lives or more. These plans are standardized packages of life insurance, disability income insurance and medical expense insurance, and are sold directly by agents, usually without the assistance of salaried group field men. Commonly, life insurance is required in every package. Billing and other administrative tasks are streamlined. The insurance is usually written through a master group contract where statutes permit and with individual contracts elsewhere.

Regardless of the policy form used, the underwriting is the same. It is an extension of group underwriting with some elements of individual underwriting introduced to offset the effects of adverse selection known to exist in small groups. This type of underwriting may be called "quality control underwriting" and is aimed at developing among this type of case average mortality and morbidity typical of that in the working population. It is not intended to exclude substandard insureds as a prime objective.

Various companies use different mechanisms for determining acceptability of a group. One mechanism involves the use of ratings (as percentages of normal mortality and morbidity) for various medical histories and physical conditions similar to ratings used in underwriting individual risks. These ratings differ for life and medical expense insurance. On cases with less than ten lives, short form nonmedical questionnaires are requested from employees,[6] and in some instances attending physician's statements or medical examinations are required. From this information, it is possible to assign numerical ratings to each employee, and if these average below an acceptability index the group is accepted. Least acceptable lives may be excluded if those remaining do not have favorable enough ratings to permit all lives together to meet the acceptability index. Some lives may be accepted for life insurance, but not for health insurance. Substandard premiums usually are not used. Dependents usually are accepted without evidence of insurability if the employee is accepted.

On groups of ten to fourteen lives, evidence of insurability usually is asked only on lives over age fifty (or for higher life insurance amounts), in which case appropriate ratings are assigned. Other lives are assigned standard ratings, and the test as to the acceptability index proceeds as in smaller cases. On cases of at least fifteen lives full group underwriting without individual evidence of insurability is used in the expectation that individual adverse selection is less likely. This type of quality control underwriting gives more searching scrutiny to areas where adverse selection tends to appear.

Participation requirements usually are 85 to 100 per cent on the smallest cases, reducing to the traditional 75 per cent on cases with at least fifteen lives. Businesses (such as public employee groups, quarries, mines and explosive manufacturers) with poor persistency, accident hazards and other adverse features are declined. Special care must be taken to assure exclusion of fictitious employees, such as wives or relatives of proprietors in family businesses. Inspection reports are frequently used to assure the legitimacy of employment status.

Because the experience on each group is not statistically significant, no

---

[6] A typical questionnaire is contained in Appendix 6.

renewal underwriting is undertaken in small group cases, except to cancel cases with unacceptable participation. Premium rates for medical expense coverages are raised uniformly at one time on all cases over a year old to reflect the experience of the class as a whole. Premiums on cases still within the twelve-month premium guarantee period after issue are increased at the end of the period.

REINSURANCE OF GROUP MEDICAL EXPENSE COVERAGES

Two types of reinsurance are used in connection with group medical expense coverage: (1) automatic quota share reinsurance *treaties* designed to protect insurers against aggregate losses (on all group cases) in excess of amounts which companies can handle financially or which would cause undesirable variations in surplus, and (2) facultative quota share reinsurance *agreements* which transfer part of the risk on specific group cases. Since a group insurance policy usually provides both life insurance and health insurance coverages together, reinsurance arrangements usually provide for both coverages. Little, if any, nonproportional reinsurance is issued in connection with group medical expense coverage.

Automatic Quota Share Treaties

Reinsurance treaties for group medical expense insurance are handled by specialty reinsurance companies as an adjunct to similar reinsurance of individual lines of business. Such treaties usually apply automatically to all group policies and are used almost exclusively by small companies when they first enter the market with a new medical expense coverage and wish to expand their sales without a corresponding increase in risk of loss. Quota share treaties provide for the reinsurer to share a fixed percentage of each medical care claim and to receive the same percentage of premium, less an allowance for premium taxes, commissions and expenses.

Facultative Quota Share Agreements

Reinsurance of a particular group medical expense case usually arises from a request of the policyholder who wants to be insured with two or more insurance companies for business reasons, but desires the convenience and economy of dealing with only one company directly. Then, too, when two businesses merge, it is common for the insurer issuing the group insurance for one of the businesses to become the insurer for group coverage for the newly merged firm, while the other insurer becomes the reinsurer. In rare instances very large cases involving millions of dollars of annual premium may necessitate the use of reinsurance, but only a small proportion of reinsurance is purchased on this account. Thus, facultative quota share agreements are not a significant factor in the group insurance business as far as risk reduction and risk spread are concerned; rather, they are almost invariably requested by the policyholder himself. These agreements are quite common among the large group insurance companies.

At the time a group insurance case is awarded to the successful insurance company, the policyholder will specify the principal company and direct it to negotiate reinsurance agreements with one or more additional companies. The policyholder also generally specifies the percentages of risk to be undertaken by each company. For example, if only a principal company and one reinsurer are involved and each is to receive half of the business, the principal company cedes 50 per cent of the risk to the reinsurer, and the reinsurer accepts this 50 per cent.

The ceding company drafts a reinsurance agreement of a more or less standardized form, and submits it to the accepting company. After negotiation, the agreement is signed by both companies. The accepting company underwrites the case from the standpoint of the benefit design, administrative procedures, eligibility conditions and premium rates contained in the ceding principal company's group insurance contract. Occasionally, such underwriting may lead to a rejection of the reinsurance offer where the proposed reinsuring company finds the ceding company has accepted a poor risk or has stipulated an unacceptable premium.

The reinsurance agreement in the case being illustrated would provide for a monthly settlement of credits and charges. The reinsurer would be credited monthly with 50 per cent of the premiums and charged monthly with 50 per cent of the claims and 50 per cent of the insurer's expenses and taxes, other than federal income taxes. The reinsurer also is charged monthly during the first year for 50 per cent of the acquisition expense charges, other than commissions and sales overhead. Expense charges are provided for specifically in the reinsurance agreement on a preliminary basis and are determined finally at the year-end. They are based invariably on the charges used in the ceding company's dividend formula or retrospective premium credit formula.

Two methods of handling dividends (or retrospective premium adjustments) are used under group reinsurance agreements: the "New York Method" and the "Hartford Method." Under the New York Method, the reinsurer introduces administration and acquisition expense charges made by the ceding company into its own dividend formula in place of similar charges normally made and adds charges for commissions paid, sales overhead, federal income tax, risk and profit. These latter charges are not made by the ceding company for the reinsurer's share of the risk. The resulting dividend is then paid to the principal insurer, which adds it to its own dividend—similarly determined—and pays the combined dividend to the policyholder, noting the respective parts.

With the Hartford Method the reinsurer is charged for 50 per cent of the dividend determined by the ceding company as if there were no reinsurance. The Hartford Method binds the reinsurer to the risk and profit charges, sales overhead charges and federal income tax charges of the principal insurer, whereas the New York Method does not.

Certain other characteristics of reinsurance agreements should be noted. First, total commissions paid by the various insurers usually are approximately equal to those which would be paid if there were no reinsurance. Sometimes, all commissions are paid by the ceding company and charged proportionally to the reinsurer as are other expenses. In some instances, small additional charges are made by the insurers to reflect the accounting and communication expenses of the reinsurance agreement.

Reinsurance agreements and premium rates need not be filed with state insurance departments. The agreements may be terminated by the parties on short notice, are renegotiable from year to year, and are essentially "gentlemen's agreements" requiring good faith and fair dealing among the parties. The reinsurers are bound by renewal action and policy amendments of the ceding company as to rates, benefits and other conditions.

SELECTED REFERENCES

BRECHER, RUTH, AND EDWARD. *How to Get the Most Out of Medical Plans.* Englewood Cliffs, N. J.: Prentice-Hall, Inc., 1961.

HALVERSON, A. B. "The Force and Effect of Eligibility Rules on Health and Welfare Trusts," *Employee Benefit Plan Review Research Reports 434.* Chicago: Charles D. Spencer and Associates, Inc., 1964.

MacINTYRE, DUNCAN M. *Voluntary Health Insurance and Rate Making.* Ithaca: Cornell University Press, 1962.

TRABER, RALPH E. "Development of Reinsurance Agreements," *Eastern Underwriter* (June 8, 1956).

~~~~~~~~~~~~~~~~~~~~~~~~~~~~~~~~~

Chapter 20

GROUP DISABILITY INCOME BENEFITS

BY J. HENRY SMITH

The basic purpose of group disability income insurance is to reimburse the insured for a substantial part of loss of income resulting from disability caused by accident or sickness. Based on fundamental group insurance principles, the disability income contract provides a weekly or monthly payment in an amount related to the insured's normal rate of earnings. Payments start after a stipulated minimum period of absence from work and continue during disability up to a stipulated maximum time or age limit.

Most of the contracts now in force have a maximum benefit duration not greater than six months. These contracts are classed as "short-term" (or "temporary") disability income plans. A few contracts have maximum benefit periods between six months and one year, and they also are called "short-term" plans.

There is a separate, rather new, class of contracts called "long-term" disability benefit plans, which have somewhat different characteristics from short-term contracts. The principal difference is that the maximum benefit period is substantially greater than one year. Distinctions between short-term and long-term plans will be noted throughout this chapter.

DEVELOPMENT OF GROUP DISABILITY INCOME COVERAGE

Chapter 5 outlined the history of disability income coverage as a part of the general spectrum of group insurance benefits. Although short-term benefit plans, as we know them today, had their genesis in the second decade of this century, the great growth in this form of coverage occurred after 1930. Table 20–1 summarizes the growth since that time.

The importance which this form of insurance has achieved may be further measured in terms of benefits paid. It is estimated[1] that in 1963 the total of such payments in the United States amounted to over $600 million.

---

[1] By the Health Insurance Association of America.

As was mentioned in Chapter 5, the growth of group disability income plans, along with that of all group coverages, was influenced importantly by certain conditions that arose during World War II. In addition, spectacular increases occurred in disability benefits in connection with the adoption of compulsory disability benefit laws in California, New Jersey and New York during the period 1946 to 1950. In 1950 alone, the number of persons covered in the United States for group disability income insurance increased by nearly 50 per cent.

TABLE 20–1

GROUP DISABILITY INCOME INSURANCE IN THE UNITED STATES, 1935–63

Year	Number of Policies at Year-End	Number of Persons Covered	Premiums
1935	6,200	2,000,000	$ 26,000,000*
1940	13,300	3,840,000	48,000,000*
1945	23,059	5,928,000	125,000,000*
1950	175,780	15,104,000	272,300,000*
1955	226,920	19,171,000	510,000,000
1960	281,180	20,970,000	707,000,000
1963	364,900	23,418,000	779,000,000

* Includes an unknown amount of premium for accidental death and dismemberment protection.
SOURCE: Health Insurance Association of America.

The volume of this type of insurance has also been influenced importantly by the trend of wages and by inflation, because the amount of coverage is usually related to earnings. Further, the market for this as well as other forms of group insurance has been expanded from time to time as insurance companies have gradually reduced the minimum size of a group which they would consider for insurance.

Nearly all of the coverage tabulated in Table 20–1 is classified as short-term benefits. Since relatively few disabilities extend beyond a few weeks, the short-term form is adequate in most cases. There remains, however, a serious need for more extensive protection against the less frequent, but more severe, long-term disabilities. Past experience in attempting to provide protection against long disabilities has not been very successful under individual policies, and, therefore, insurance companies have been hesitant to underwrite this risk under group contracts. Nevertheless, in recent years they have been experimenting with new types of long-term disability income plans. These are now achieving widespread interest, and, while the actual coverage figures are not yet large and are not even separately tabulated, there is reason to believe that this form of insurance will expand rapidly.

ELIGIBILITY FOR COVERAGE

Most group disability income contracts are issued to employers covering their employees. Some are issued to trustees of employee welfare plans, usually under collective bargaining agreements encompassing a number of employers in an industry. A few are held by voluntary associations of employers in an industry or area for the benefit of their employees. In all these instances the basis of the insurance and of eligibility therefor is the employment relationship, and most of the discussion in this chapter will be oriented accordingly. In a few instances, relatively speaking, the members of an association of some sort, such as a professional association, may buy a group contract for their own benefit, although many insurers are skeptical about such coverage. Association coverage will be discussed in detail in Chapter 32.

Eligibility for Short-Term Coverage

Short-term benefit contracts usually have typical group insurance eligibility rules as discussed in Chapter 3. All classes of employees of the policyholder may be eligible, or certain classes may be excluded. For eligible classes there is usually a required probationary period of service with the employer, such as three months, six months or more, which the employee must complete to attain eligibility for coverage. Also, coverage is granted only to those who are actively at work. In the case of a noncontributory contract under which the employer pays the whole cost, the employee is automatically insured when he completes the probationary period and fulfills the actively-at-work requirement. Under the contributory form, in which the individual is called upon to pay all or a part of the cost, the insurance becomes effective when the employee agrees to make the contribution, usually through payroll deduction, and fulfills the tenure and actively-at-work requirements. Disability insurance has no special distinctions in these features as compared with other forms of insurance, except possibly there is some tendency to limit the disability forms to the more stable employment classes. Temporary employees usually are excluded from coverage, and in many instances employees who work less than a certain number of hours a week, such as twenty, are considered ineligible.

Eligibility for Long-Term Coverage

Theoretically, there is little reason for the eligibility provisions of long-term disability benefit contracts to differ in major respects from those of the short-term contracts. It happens, however, that because of the way in which long-term plans were developed, they have tended to restrict eligibility somewhat more closely. The early long-term plans were devised primarily for the protection of certain classes of higher salaried employees, such as those in the management and supervisory groups, the large class of wage earners already having relatively generous protection through OASDI provisions. For these reasons many of the long-term plans have eligibility provisions based on minimum salary requirements or on the rule that only salaried or supervisory employees will be included. It is probable, however, that long-term plans will gradually cover other classes of employees also.

It is often provided that the long-term benefits will be limited to employees who have substantial periods of service, such as five years. In essence, benefit eligibility is similar to that for the pension income granted in many retirement plans for employees who become disabled. The focus is on permanent disability, and it is often thought proper, as a matter of limiting costs, to restrict eligibility to those with substantial periods of employment; such persons are often felt to be more deserving and more in need. In other respects eligibility provisions under long-term plans resemble those of other group contracts.

CONTINGENCIES COVERED

Contingencies Covered under Short-Term Contracts

A typical group short-term disability income contract defines the contingencies against which coverage is provided in the following terms:

If the employee shall become wholly and continuously disabled as a result of nonoccupational accidental bodily injuries or nonoccupational sickness, and thereby be prevented from performing any and every duty pertaining to his employment, the company will pay. . . .

Different versions of this insuring clause are used by the various companies, but in general this quotation illustrates the nature of the protection commonly afforded.

As the quoted provision indicates, the test of disability lies in the phrase, " . . . and thereby be prevented from performing any and every duty pertaining to his employment. . . ." Two features stand out in this requirement. The first is that only complete disability, no partial disability, is recognized. The second point is that a disability is recognized if it prevents the individual from performing his usual duties. Some contracts use a more restricted definition of disability requiring that the individual be unable to engage in any employment for compensation. This seems to exclude a case where the individual cannot do his own usual work but can engage in some light occupation. In practice, however, most companies appear to administer this form of clause on the basis of whether the individual is prevented from engaging in his own usual work.

The determination of whether the individual is unable to work usually rests on certification by a physician. Contracts generally stipulate that benefits are not payable for a period of absence from work unless the employee is under the care of a physician during the absence. In practice a statement as to the nature and severity of disability is required from the physician. In an extended claim, continuation of benefits will require that the attending physician repeat the certification of disability periodically, sometimes weekly, depending on the nature of the disability.

Most group short-term disability income contracts limit protection to nonoccupational causes of disability. This results in coverage generally complementary to workmen's compensation; in fact, the determination of whether a disability had a nonoccupational or an occupational cause usually hinges in practice on whether compensation benefits are payable. In some instances, however, the group contract may be written to cover all causes, omitting the qualification "nonoccupational" from the insuring clause quoted above. This procedure is usually followed only where the workmen's compensation payments in the state in which the employee works are relatively low and it is felt that additional coverage is desirable. In such policies, the amount payable in the event of an occupational accident is a supplement to compensation benefits and is limited in amount and carefully controlled so that the combination of compensation and group insurance payments is consistent with the employee's income and the regular amount which would be payable for a nonoccupational accident.

The main insuring clause of the usual short-term disability contract rules out payments for absences from work because of pregnancy, miscarriage or childbirth. However, many contracts contain special provisions under which such absences are treated as if they were caused by sickness, subject to special provisions as to the amount or duration of payments, as later indicated in this chapter. Where the employer-policyholder desires, the policy may be written with a specific exclusion prohibiting all payments in the case of maternity.

Contingencies Covered under Long-Term Contracts

Long-term disability income benefits are still somewhat experimental, and there are many variations in the provisions of current contracts. In defining covered contingencies, a distinction is often made between a disability which prevents pursuit of the individual's usual occupation and disability which prevents any work for compensation. A frequent provision uses the so-called "his occupation" definition with respect to the initial period of disability and requires that after disability has continued for a substantial period of time, such as two years, further payments will be conditioned on disablement preventing any employment. The purpose of this dual clause is to provide a period of income to replace normal earnings where the individual cannot follow his usual occupation (as under short-term contracts) and to recognize that after a significant period of time the individual, if able, may be expected (and encouraged) to reorient himself and make a livelihood in any occupation which he can follow. If he is not able to engage in any occupation, the payments continue up to the specified limit provided by the contract.

Some other types of disability insurance provide payments when the insured is unable to follow "any occupation for which he is reasonably suited by education, training and experience." This (or even more liberal clauses) could be applied under long-term group contracts after the initial "his occupation" period, but so far companies seem to have felt it wise to use the more restricted definition so as to limit liability closely. Past history of seriously adverse experience in administering disability claims has made it clear that it is wise to limit the coverage to the minimum that will provide satisfactory protection.

Unlike short-term income contracts, the long-term forms often provide a limited amount of indemnity for partial disability, although the coverage may be restricted in duration as well as in amount. Also, unlike short-term contracts, most long-term contracts provide coverage of both nonoccupational and on-the-job accidents, supplementing workmen's compensation insurance in the latter case. One reason for this distinction is that, generally speaking, workmen's compensation laws are less adequate for the long-term disability and for the classes of persons generally covered under long-term plans than is true for the short-term disability coverage. As to maternity, however, long-term contracts usually do not provide benefits.

Limitations on Benefits

Limitations under group disability income contracts are remarkably few. Unlike many individual contracts, group contracts usually do not contain any exclusion of disabilities having a cause predating the insurance, except in some instances of very small groups and some classes of long-term contracts, such as those issued to associations covering their members. Furthermore, group contracts customarily do not exclude many of the causes (such as alcoholism or drug addiction) which are often excluded in other forms of health insurance, although there may be limitations on the period of benefits for mental diseases. It is customary, however, to exclude both self-inflicted injuries and sickness or injury sustained outside the continental limits of the United States and Canada or to provide that no payment will be made during disability while the insured is outside that area.

The broad coverage obtained in group disability income insurance and the lack of limitations constitute some of its most valuable aspects. Claims administration is greatly simplified thereby, and good policyholder relationships are much easier to maintain.

PERIOD OF BENEFITS

Contract provisions governing the period of time for which benefits will be payable with respect to a disabled employee are built on two principal features. The first of these is the "waiting period," which governs the date on which the disability benefit payment will begin in relationship to the date of disablement. The second feature is the maximum limitation on the period for which benefits will be payable. There are significant differences in both of these items between short-term and long-term disability income contracts.

Short-Term Benefit Periods

In the case of accidents, some short-term disability income contracts provide that payments will begin with the first day of absence from employment. Others call for a waiting period of three days of absence, and still others use seven days. For sickness, it is almost universal to require some waiting period. A three-day period is sometimes used, but the most common period is seven days.

The waiting period provisions of many contracts has been influenced by the provisions of the federal income tax law. Before 1954, all disability payments were excludable income. From 1954 to 1964, the tax law permitted employees to exclude from taxable income those benefits paid (not exceeding $100 a week where purchased by the employer) beginning with the first day for accident or seventh day for sickness or first day of hospitalization for any cause. For that reason many recent plans were set up calling for payments beginning immediately for accident and for sickness beginning on the eighth day or, if earlier, on the first day of hospitalization. The 1964 tax law has modified these provisions, however, restricting the deductibility in rather complicated ways.[2] It remains to be seen whether this change will result in some revision in the usual waiting period clause.

Except where the accident coverage starts on the first day, the two waiting periods for accident and sickness are often of the same length—either three days or seven days. In isolated cases some other period, such as five days or ten days, is used; and in a few instances, a relatively long period, such as fourteen or thirty days, is specified, particularly when salary continuance plans cover the initial part of the absence.

These waiting periods serve the primary function of reducing the cost of the insurance, because they eliminate payments in a great many trivial disabilities for which the individual has no great need for indemnity, and they eliminate payments for a few days in the longer disabilities. Obviously, there is a saving in both cases, and, perhaps of equal importance, there is a reduction in the administrative expenses because many small claims, with their disproportionate handling costs, are avoided.

---

[2] Under the 1964 tax law, amounts of disability income provided by an employer may be excluded from taxable income as follows: After the employee has been absent from work for thirty days he may exclude up to $100 a week. During the first thirty days he may be allowed an exclusion only providing the amount payable does not exceed 75 per cent of regular wages. In that event he may exclude up to $75 a week except that no exclusion may be taken during the first seven calendar days of absence from work unless and until the employee is hospitalized for at least one day. There is no distinction in taxation between sickness and accident.

Another important function of the waiting period, however, is to prevent the insurance from encouraging unwarranted absence from work. This function of the waiting period is discussed in Chapter 21.

There has been some experimentation in the past with waiting periods having retroactive features. For example, the formula might call for benefits starting with the first day of disability, provided the absence lasted longer than seven days. In general, this type of waiting period proved unsatisfactory because it encouraged malingering among those who could return to work before eight days. The bonus for the eighth day of absence was too attractive; statistics showed many more people out for eight days where such plans were used than elsewhere. Also, the retroactive feature was an unnecessary complication in claims handling.

Once payments begin they continue so long as the employee remains disabled until the end of the maximum benefit period specified in the contract. This period varies from group to group, but commonly runs either for thirteen or twenty-six weeks under short-term disability benefit contacts. Most early plans used a thirteen-week limit, but in recent times, particularly where the specifications are set by union bargaining, the twenty-six-week limit has become more frequent. In a few instances a short limit, such as ten weeks, is used, and on the other hand some rare plans permit payments as long as fifty-two weeks. Almost universally the limit is the same for both accidents and sicknesses.

In most contracts, the provision as to the maximum period of payments refers to each separate disability, and, therefore, a maximum period of payments may be followed later by further payments to the same person. In some instances, however, contracts are written with a cumulative payment limit. For example, it may be provided that no more than twenty-six weeks of benefit payments will be allowed during any one twelve-month period, regardless of the number or causes of absence. This type of limit appears in certain contracts written to conform to the minimum requirements of some of the state compulsory disability benefit laws discussed later in this chapter. Also, this form of limit was common some years ago as a special provision applicable to older employees whose disability rates are high, but it is not widely used for that purpose today.

Recurring disabilities create problems both as to the waiting period for benefits and the maximum benefit period. Does a recurring disability from the same cause as a previous disability require the individual to undergo the waiting period again or should his benefit start as soon as recurrence occurs? Also, in determining how long benefits may be paid for the second absence, is the period of payment for the first absence counted against the maximum benefit period for the second absence?

A typical solution is to provide that successive periods of disability will be considered as one period if separated by less than two weeks of active employment, unless the second disability can be shown to be due to unrelated causes. The result of this provision is that if the absences are separated by more than two weeks, they are treated as different and unrelated absences, regardless of cause. This is a practical solution which experience has shown is reasonably satisfactory in most situations.

Except in cases where the contract excludes coverage for maternity absences, there is a special limitation on the duration of benefits customarily used with respect to pregnancies and childbirth. This limitation generally provides that the period of payment will not exceed a fixed period, usually six weeks. In some policies it is provided that on cessation of work because of pregnancy, the total benefit computed for the specified period is payable in a lump sum.

Long-Term Benefit Periods

Waiting period and maximum duration provisions of long-term group disability income contracts take a variety of forms. This variety arises in part because such contracts usually are used as supplements to temporary disability income plans, uninsured wage or salary continuance plans, or sometimes in connection with disability annuities under pension plans.

In order to integrate the disability payments with such plans, the long-term contract usually has a long waiting period during which the individual must be disabled before payments start. A waiting period equal to the benefit period (often six months) under the short-term benefit plan or salary continuance plan is common. Even where the long-term plan is not a supplement to another plan but stands alone as the only disability benefit, it is likely to have a substantial waiting period, such as thirty or ninety days or even longer. Here again, the emphasis is placed on the permanent, or at least the very long, disability rather than on coverage of short-term illnesses.

Also there is wide variation in the maximum duration of benefits under long-term contracts. Some policies have a maximum as short as two years; some provide benefits until the individual reaches normal retirement age; and a few have a lifetime benefit, though usually for accidents only. Probably the most common provisions are for five years, ten years, and until the individual reaches age sixty-five. Some contracts may use different maximums for different classes of employees, such as those having different periods of service. The choice among these possibilities depends on the other provisions which the employer (sometimes acting under a bargained agreement) may make for disability protection and on what is deemed appropriate considering costs, the nature and duration of employment and on the philosophy governing the benefit structure.

The problem of recurring disabilities under long-term contracts may not be so troublesome as under the short-term benefit plans because the individual's disability is usually quite well established and less likely to be subject to periods of remission as under short-term plans. Nevertheless, provision usually is included in the long-term plans for resolving any problems which may arise. A typical provision is one which stipulates that if successive periods of disability arise from the same or related causes and are separated by less than three months of continuous, active work with the employer, they will be considered as one period of disability.

AMOUNTS OF BENEFIT

Consistent with the purposes of disability income insurance, the amounts of benefit generally are fixed so as to bear an appropriate relationship to the individual's normal earnings. There is wide variety as to the closeness of this relationship, but a cardinal principle is that the amount of benefit should always be sufficiently less than normal earnings to avoid having the insurance payment encourage absence from work. A number of different types of formulas are used to determine the amounts, and some distinctions have developed between short- and long-term plans, as will now be outlined.

Short-Term Disability Income Benefit Amounts

The most common type of formula for determining amounts of benefit under short-term contracts is one which provides that they will be graded according to wages or salaries. In some cases the amount is expressed as a fixed percentage of the employee's pay, subject to some maximum amount and possibly to some minimum amount. This percentage does not often exceed 66⅔ per cent and is seldom less than 50 per cent.

In many cases, the policy contains a schedule of salary groupings with an amount of insurance fixed for each group. For example, a schedule like the following might be used:

Normal Weekly Earnings	Weekly Benefit
Less than $50	$30
$50 but less than $70	40
$70 but less than $90	55
$90 but less than $110	65
$110 and over	75

In still other cases, the amount of insurance is determined according to the title or occupational classification of the employee. This type of schedule is not preferred by insurers because it does not necessarily maintain a satisfactory relationship between the amount of indemnity and the amount of compensation. Furthermore, it is often difficult to arrive at occupational groupings which are precise and properly differentiated.

In a number of cases, particularly where the specifications for insurance are set by union bargaining, the amount of benefit is the same for all persons covered under the contract. For example, it might be provided that the benefit is $60 a week for all. This type of formula is satisfactory where there is a fairly homogeneous group of wage earners covered, but it is usually underwritten carefully to be sure that the amount provided bears a satisfactory relationship to the lower extremes of pay in the group. In many instances, a clause is included requiring that the fixed amount will be modified if necessary, so that the benefit will not exceed some fixed percentage, such as 50 per cent or 66⅔ per cent, of the employee's normal earnings.

In their historical development, short-term weekly benefits generally have not been used to provide large amounts of indemnity for the higher-paid personnel of an employer. Insurers have tended to avoid high-amount risks, and furthermore the nature of the benefit has not made it a particularly attractive vehicle for providing the salary continuance arrangements usually applied to executive classes. For these reasons, short-term weekly benefits are not often written in excess of $100 a week.

Where the group contract provides for different amounts of insurance for different classes, or where it provides a fixed percentage of pay, it also calls for an automatic change in the amount of insurance when the employee's pay or insurance classification changes. This is subject, however, to the usual provision that if the employee is not actively at work, any increase may not be effective until he returns to work.

Inasmuch as simplicity of operation is desired and since the benefit periods are rather limited for short-term income policies, the benefit formulas usually are written without reference to other disability benefits to which the individual may be entitled. In some instances the result may be that the total benefit to which the individual is entitled from all sources exceeds what most underwriters would consider to be a satisfactory relationship to his normal pay. In most cases, however, there are not enough of these situations to cause any great concern in the establishment of the group contract. This matter will be considered further in the next chapter.

Long-Term Disability Income Benefit Amounts

In general, the amounts of benefit payable (usually payable monthly rather than weekly) under group long-term contracts are determined according to the same basic principles used for short-term contracts, but some additional considerations enter the picture. One factor is that this form of benefit has been used to a considerable extent for higher paid employees, and the maximum amount of insurance which is provided often runs to considerably higher figures than for short-term contracts. Many plans have a maximum benefit of as much as $1,000 a month, and a few are known to provide amounts as high as $2,000 a month in the large groups. As a limiting factor, however, considerable care is taken in underwriting long-term benefits to assure that the amount payable is significantly less than the individual would earn (net after taxes) if he were working.

In terms of gross pay, insurance companies generally do not want to provide a benefit much greater than 50 per cent of normal earnings, although a 60 per cent limit is sometimes used. This is a matter of added importance in long-term benefits because of the high amounts involved, their favored income tax position and the long duration over which payments may be made. The tax aspect of the matter is of considerable importance. Payments under insurance purchased wholly by the employee are not taxable at all; those paid for by the employer may be taxable at least in part during the first part of disability, but not for the longer durations except as to amounts exceeding $100 a week. This significant tax advantage, especially for the highly paid people whose income taxes are relatively high, causes insurers to focus attention on the employees' "take-home" pay, rather than their gross compensation, in determining benefit limits.

To a much greater extent than in short-term benefits, underwriters are concerned in the long-term field as to the possibility of providing over-insurance as a result of combining benefits from more than one source. There are many such sources to be considered, including workmen's compensation, disability benefits under federal OASDI, veterans' pensions, employers' pension plan disability benefits and even individually purchased disability income contracts. The large amounts and extensive durations of payment require integration of the different forms of benefit in order to avoid making the total of disability payments too attractive as compared with normal earnings. The sharply graded income tax again is an important consideration, for all forms of disability benefits have important tax advantages as compared with salary or wages. Therefore, the usual procedure is to provide that benefits from the other described sources will serve to reduce the benefits otherwise payable under the group long-term disability income contract.

Provision for such integration of benefits sometimes causes considerable difficulty in setting up a long-term benefit plan. Especially where the individual pays all or a substantial part of the cost of the insurance, there may be some misunderstanding or resentment induced by providing for a reduction of the long-term benefit in recognition of other payments which the individual receives. The resentment may be most pointed with respect to individual disability benefit contracts which the employee may have purchased on his own account. Many companies have found it necessary to make the integration (or "nonduplication" restriction) inapplicable to individual contracts; but generally speaking, the companies have insisted on adjusting the benefit to recognize amounts payable under governmental benefit plans and under those benefit systems which are a part of the employer's regular provisions for employees. An attempt is made in these situations, of course, to adjust the premium rate and employee contribution in as refined a way as is practical to take into account the adjustment of benefit as a result of this integration principle.

TERMINATION OF COVERAGE

As in other forms of group insurance, the existence and continuation of an individual's disability income coverage are closely related to the employment relationship. Termination of employment results in termination of the insurance. This simple principle becomes somewhat resilient, however, in those situations where there are temporary interruptions in work or where retirement for age occurs. The group insurance mechanism generally has developed considerable flexibility in meeting this problem, and various arrangements are used to permit continuance of group life and some forms of health insurance in these situations.

As for group disability income insurance, however, there is an overriding principle that permits little relaxation in linking termination of insurance to termination of active employment. This principle states that the purpose of disability income insurance is to substitute for earnings lost because of disability. If the individual is not in an active earning status (such as during layoff, leave of absence or retirement), the purpose of insurance no longer exists or is at least suspended. Furthermore, underwriting experience, which will be discussed in the next chapter, indicates that coverage during periods when the employee has no available work is very dangerous for the insurance company.

For these reasons, group disability income contracts call for termination of the individual's coverage upon, or closely following, cessation of active work for any reason, including lack of work, layoff, leave of absence or retirement. As a practical matter these provisions may be tempered somewhat in order to permit continuation of the insurance to the end of the contract month or for some other short period, such as two weeks, following the date of cessation of employment, but substantial periods of coverage during inactive employment are not often permitted. Reinstatement of insurance is allowed, of course, upon the employee's return to work.

Although in group life, and sometimes in other forms of group health insurance, conversion of the individual's coverage to an individual insurance contract is permitted upon termination of employment, conversion is not generally permitted as to group disability income insurance. This results from the principle that termination of employment brings about cessation of the purpose of disability income insurance—the employee no longer has an earning potential to protect. Of course, there are situations where the employee leaves one employer to find work with another, and it is possible that the employee will come into a new earnings relationship without significant interruption and without having disability income protection immediately available in his new relationship. This is not felt to be a responsibility of the first employer or of his insurance company, however, and the problem is left to be solved by the individual through the purchase of an individual contract in the usual way, or through the provision of group insurance in his new employment. In contrast, life and medical expense insurance covers risks which generally continue after a cessation of employment, thus justifying the common use of conversion privileges in such contracts.

As in all group insurance, the individual's group disability income coverage depends upon the continuance of the group insurance contract. Group disability income policies have no unusual characteristics in this matter. Under its terms the contract may be discontinued by the employer on any premium due date. Some contracts also give the insurance company the right to discontinue the contract on prescribed notice to the employer. Other contracts permit such cancellation only if certain conditions (such as a drop in number insured below a stated minimum) come about. Again, however, the insurance company will make every effort to avoid termination where it can reasonably do so. Terminations at the instance of the insurance company are rare. Nevertheless, no conversion to individual contracts is permitted when the group contract terminates.

STATE STATUTORY DISABILITY BENEFIT PLANS[3]

There was considerable movement in the United States for more than a decade after 1940 toward the establishment of state laws providing or requiring nonoccupational disability income benefits for workers in most businesses. Presumably, the theory of the proposals was that they would round out the workers' protection against major risks to continued employment. State and federal laws already covered unemployment, occupational injury and old-age retirement. The missing piece of armor was protection against nonoccupational accident and sickness. Before the movement ebbed, four states adopted laws. The first, Rhode Island, became effective in 1942; next came California in 1946, New Jersey in 1949 and New York in 1950. Legislatures in many other states considered the subject, but no laws have been passed since 1950. Currently, although bills still appear and sometimes become active in various states, the movement seems to have little remaining force. The spread of voluntary insurance, particularly as the minimum size for group contracts dropped, seems to have removed most of the motivation for legislation.

The laws of the four states as they stand in the spring of 1964 are

---

[3] A more comprehensive history and analysis of this subject is contained in the volume by Grant M. Osborn, *Compulsory Disability Insurance in the United States* (Homewood, Ill.: Richard D. Irwin, Inc., 1958).

summarized and compared in Appendix 7. The following discussion will highlight certain features of those laws and developments under them.

Form of Compulsory Disability Laws

The first law passed (Rhode Island) is the most drastic in form. It provides for a state monopoly in the provision and administration of certain prescribed short-term disability income payments. It is also the most comprehensive in that it covers employees of all employers having one or more employees (with certain types of employment excluded) on any day. No private plans are allowed in substitution for the statutory benefits. A tax payable by employees, now equal to 1 per cent of the first $4,800 of annual wages, supports the system, which is administered by the State Division of Employment Security. The state agency also handles unemployment insurance benefits, the provisions of the disability benefit law being closely related to the unemployment compensation law of the state.

The next state to adopt a law, California, also patterned its provisions after those of the unemployment compensation law of the state, and established a special state fund under the administration of the Division of Employment Security for financing the benefits. A tax on employees and related to wages has supported the benefits, and, in addition, an allotment was made of considerable funds previously accumulated under the unemployment insurance system to bolster the disability income benefit system.

California introduced an important provision under which the employer could provide private insurance under certain circumstances in substitution for the state-run system. However, for fear that private plans would be used mostly in the better classes of risk, leaving the state plan with a preponderance of the poorer classes, the law stipulated that the voluntary private plans must not result in "adverse selection" against the state fund. More will be said of this feature subsequently.

The New Jersey law was also modeled after the state's unemployment compensation system. It, too, is administered by the State Division of Employment Security. It permits employers to arrange alternative private plans under self-insurance or insurance, provided the benefits and employee contributions are as favorable as under the state fund and provided that no class of employees that would be covered by the state fund is excluded.

Another major feature of the New Jersey law differing from those of the two prior laws is the provision that a limited amount of experience rating is introduced into the financing of the state benefit system. The employer's share of the cost is adjusted between moderate limits from time to time, depending upon the experience of his employment group. Aside from the equity introduced by this experience rating, one of its purposes was to put the state fund and private insurers on a more equal footing in competition, so that stringent regulations dealing with anti-selection are not necessary as in California.

The New York law is significantly different in form. Instead of being modeled on unemployment compensation insurance, it is related to workmen's compensation insurance, and it is administered by the Workmen's Compensation Board of the state. Furthermore, instead of providing benefits under a state fund such as that used in the other three states, it requires employers to provide insurance (or self-insurance) under private auspices, or, if they wish, under a competing state fund established primarily to provide workmen's compensation insurance. The state fund is state operated, but it is quite similar to an insurance company in that it pays premium taxes and competes under reasonably equal conditions with private insurers.

Under the New York law, benefits must meet certain minimum standards, but there is an unusual provision permitting variations in benefit terms or even the substitution of other forms of health insurance, provided the benefits are actuarially equivalent (according to a formula established for the purpose) to those stipulated in the law.

Benefits under Compulsory Disability Laws

As indicated in Appendix 7, the details of coverage differ considerably from state to state, but in the main they follow a pattern consistent with that provided under short-term group disability income contracts. All have a seven-day waiting period for the commencement of benefits (first day of hospitalization in California), and all have a twenty-six week limit. The amounts of benefit range from one half to two thirds of the average wages, with maximum amounts running as high as $70 a week in California. The California law has an added benefit during hospitalization. Eligibility for coverage differs in some respects, usually following the provisions of the unemployment compensation or workmen's compensation law on which the statute is founded. Provision for maternity benefits differs substantially—New York and California laws provide none, whereas the other two states, New Jersey and Rhode Island, provide benefits of eight weeks' and fourteen weeks' duration, respectively.

Compulsory Disability Coverage during Unemployment

One of the significant features of the compulsory disability laws has to do with coverage during unemployment. While private disability income plans generally do not provide continued protection during unemployment, as explained earlier in this chapter, the fact that the three earliest laws were appended to unemployment compensation systems led to special provisions for disability benefits for the unemployed. The principle is that when an individual drawing unemployment compensation benefits becomes disabled, the unemployment benefit ceases, but a special benefit is payable under the disability benefit law. In California, a special account is set up for this purpose and funded with a portion of the tax on wages. In New Jersey the state plan makes the payments, but also makes a pro rata assessment on the private plans. In New York, a revolving fund is handled by the state for the payment of these benefits, with financing through an assessment on self-insurers and insurers.

Impact on Group Insurance Plans

The state monopoly created by the Rhode Island law resulted in the discontinuance of practically all group disability income contracts in Rhode Island. Some efforts were made to underwrite policies with benefits supplementing those provided by the law, but they were not very successful. The level and duration of benefits under the law leaves little room for supplementary plans except as the market for long-term disability income plans may become active.

At the other extreme, the New York disability benefit law results in the purchase of insurance from private insurers (or from the competing state fund) in most cases, the only alternative being self-insurance. The insurance companies have been quite successful in handling this business, and the New York type law is by far the most satisfactory of the four from the point of view of the insurance companies. From the standpoint of the public, it is also a very satisfactory law because it takes full advantage of competitive influences which tend to keep costs at a minimum and to keep services to clients at a high level. Furthermore, by utilizing a low minimum size group (originally four, now one) the law has encouraged the insurance companies to focus attention on very small size groups and has helped companies to learn how to deal with small units. The effect has been to increase the area which the insurance company can serve with group contracts not only in New York but throughout the country.

The impact of the California law on group insurance has been marked and varied over the years, the final result in 1963 being to force discontinuance of most of the private plans. At the outset, the conditions under which the private plans operated were reasonably satisfactory. Benefits could be provided for many groups at premium rates comparable to that charged by the state fund, and the provision of the law stipulating that private plans would not be permitted if they tended to result in adverse selection against the state fund was implemented in a reasonable manner. By 1951, voluntary plans (including self-insured) covered over 51 per cent[4] of the employees eligible under the law.

Gradually, however, the private plans began to lose their position in California. Minimum benefits required by the statute were increased from

---

[4] According to the Life Insurance Association of America.

time to time without increases in the tax rate for groups carried in the state fund, but the increases in benefits required the group insurers to raise their charges for groups they carried. Advantages enjoyed by the state fund in the form of absence of taxes and sales costs, and in certain expense charges, made it increasingly difficult for the insurance companies to compete. The disadvantage was exaggerated by the fact that the state fund had available over $100 million of the funds accumulated under the unemployment law some years before, which it could draw on for disability benefits without raising current tax rates. The cumulative effect of these factors caused a gradual decline in the proportion of employees covered by voluntary plans from the high point reached in 1951 to about 39 per cent in 1959, and a sharp decline thereafter, the 1963 figure being 7 per cent.[5]

The final *coup de grace* to most private plans in California occurred in 1963 when new, severe regulations were adopted implementing the adverse selection clause. Under those regulations every private plan had to meet three rather severe tests[6] based on the distribution of employees by sex, age and amount of wages received. If any one of these factors in a particular case did not meet the stipulated standard, the plan was discontinued and the coverage transferred to the state fund. After these regulations became effective, the bulk of the private group disability income business disappeared in California, and in effect the state has finally shifted, as was predicted long ago, to something approaching a state monopoly like that of Rhode Island.

The New Jersey law has somewhat more favorable characteristics from the point of view of private insurance. There is no specific adverse selection prohibition, the only requirement being that the majority of employees must accept the private plan and that its benefits must be as liberal in all respects as those provided by the state fund. Instead of the specific prohibition against adverse selection, the employer's contribution to the state fund, required when he does not have insurance under a private plan, is adjusted to some extent according to the experience of his group. This tends to put the state fund and private insurers on a more competitive footing than in California, as far as adverse selection is concerned.

Nevertheless, the future of private insurance under the New Jersey law is a little clouded. The private companies are at a cost disadvantage for the same reasons as in California, including the fact that New Jersey had a

---

[5] *Ibid.*

[6] The three tests pertain to (1) females, (2) employees age 50 or older and (3) employees with annual wages of less than $3,600. The Labor Department determines yearly for each category, a "standard risk" based on experience and "standards for approval" based on number covered by law. If an insurer's experience is less than the standard risk in any category, it can retain only such plans which combined meet all the "standards for approval."

substantial accumulated fund under unemployment compensation which was allocated to bolster the state disability fund. At the outset over two thirds of the eligible employees of New Jersey were covered by private plans. The latest estimate indicates, however, that in 1963 the figure had dropped to 47.4 per cent.[7] The inherent nature of the New Jersey plan creates very difficult competitive conditions for private insurers and tends to make for an uncertain future.

SELECTED REFERENCES

Bowers, Edison L. "The Nature of Accident and Sickness Insurance," *Accident and Sickness Insurance* (ed. David McCahan). Philadelphia: University of Pennsylvania Press, 1954.

Dickerson, O. D. *Health Insurance*, chap. 13. Homewood, Ill.: Richard D. Irwin, Inc., 1963.

Eddy, C. Manton. "Replacement of Income-Group Contracts," *Accident and Sickness Insurance* (ed. David McCahan). Philadelphia: University of Pennsylvania Press, 1954.

Ilse, Louise Wolters. *Group Insurance and Employee Retirement Plans,* pp. 1–45, 159–89. New York: Prentice-Hall, Inc., 1953.

"Long Term Disability," *Transactions of the Society of Actuaries,* Vol. XV, pp. D174–D179.

Nichols, Kenneth C. "Long Term Disability," paper presented at the Group Insurance Forum of the Health Insurance Association of America, Philadelphia, Pa., February 27, 1963.

Osborn, Grant M. *Compulsory Disability Insurance in the United States.* Homewood, Ill.: Richard D. Irwin, Inc., 1958.

Pickrell, Jesse F. *Group Health Insurance,* pp. 12–19, 71–75. Homewood, Ill.: Richard D. Irwin, Inc., 1961.

---

[7] Life Insurance Association of America.

Chapter 21

UNDERWRITING GROUP DISABILITY INCOME COVERAGE

BY BROOKS CHANDLER

The underwriting of group disability income insurance involves application of the same general concepts and principles used in the selection and classification of groups being considered for other forms of insurance, as discussed in Chapters 10 and 19. However, the existence of disability cannot be determined as readily on the basis of objective factors as can the death of an insured person or the incurral of expenses for medical care. Therefore, the plan of benefits to be provided and the possible influence of economic, employment and living conditions often may assume greater significance in underwriting disability income coverage than in underwriting other benefits.

On the other hand, disability rates have not shown the upward trend which has characterized medical care costs and the use of medical care services and facilities. Many of the improvements in medical care techniques and changes in medical care patterns which have increased the cost of medical expense insurance have served to reduce the frequency and duration of disability. Furthermore, the effects of inflation have not been reflected directly in disability benefit costs.

As explained in Chapter 20, group disability income plans usually are classified as short-term or long-term, and the distinction between the two is useful in considering underwriting characteristics because of the great difference in the insured contingencies. While losses covered by short-term plans are more frequent and often may be subject to an appreciable element of control by the insured person, no single claim will normally be expected to have a disastrous effect on the experience of the entire group. In the case of long-term plans, on the other hand, losses are less frequent but they may involve large sums, and the insured person may be influenced to withdraw completely from the labor market because of the existence of the insurance. Accordingly, certain factors are given far greater weight in underwriting long-term benefits than in underwriting

short-term benefits. These considerations, together with initial and renewal underwriting procedures and the relatively limited current use of
reinsurance, are discussed in this chapter.

GENERAL CONSIDERATIONS IN UNDERWRITING
GROUP DISABILITY INCOME COVERAGE[1]

The underwriter of group disability income insurance has the same
objectives as the underwriter of other group coverages: (1) legality under
statutory definitions of group health insurance and state insurance department regulations, (2) low expense through efficient administration,
(3) high probability of persistency and (4) predictable claim costs.
Virtually identical tests are applied in ascertaining whether a group
satisfies these objectives.

The considerations which are of concern to the underwriter of group
disability income insurance may be divided readily into two broad categories. The first comprises those factors which determine the acceptability of
the group as an insurance risk, since many insurers do not offer coverage
on a group underwriting basis to groups with certain characteristics.
These factors are discussed subsequently in detail. The second category
includes those characteristics of the group which affect the expected claim
cost and must necessarily influence the arrangement of the benefits to be
provided or be reflected in the calculation of the premium rates to be
charged.

Thus, if the first two objectives mentioned above—legality and low
expense of administration—are satisfied with reference to a particular
group, and if a satisfactory percentage of enrollment among the eligible
persons can be secured and maintained, the underwriter's remaining concern is with factors which are likely to affect the frequency and duration
of disability among the persons insured. As will be seen, certain of these
factors (such as the proportion of females in the group, the percentage of
persons at advanced ages and any special hazard resulting from the type
of employment or conditions in the area in which the insured persons
reside) are reflected in the premium rates charged. Others may indicate
that special attention should be given to eligibility requirements or that
the benefits should be arranged in an unusually conservative way. The
underwriter must ascertain not only that accurate information has been
secured in sufficient detail for rating purposes, but also that any special
circumstances which can be expected to result in an unusually high rate
of disability are disclosed.

The significance attached to any factor being considered in the underwriting process depends upon (1) the type of group, (2) the type of

---

[1] The principles underlying group medical expense insurance underwriting, as
described in Chapter 19, apply equally to the underwriting of group disability income
coverage and therefore provide the background for discussions in this chapter.

disability income coverage desired and (3) whether initial or renewal underwriting is involved. Consequently, later sections of this chapter will be concerned with specific types of groups, including single employer groups with more than twenty-five lives; single employer groups with less than twenty-five lives; employees of employers contributing to trust funds established under the provisions of the Taft-Hartley law; employees of members of trade associations and other groups of employers who have joined together voluntarily; and members of associations of individuals, including unions and professional groups. The differences in underwriting short-term and long-term disability income plans will be set forth in connection with each of the above types of groups.

UNDERWRITING PROCEDURE AND SOURCES OF INFORMATION

The procedures followed in plan negotiation, preparation of announcement material, formal home office processing including issuance of the group policy and certificates, and in the establishment of administrative procedures, are the same for group disability income coverage as for other group coverages.[2] The underwriter looks to the group fieldman as the primary source of information and data regarding groups being considered for disability income insurance, as well as other coverages. The credit standing of prospective policyholders is often investigated through the use of Dun & Bradstreet reports or the services of other credit reporting agencies. General information, such as location of plants or other establishments and the type of activity in which the employees are engaged, may be secured from business reference sources such as industry directories or the manuals published by Moody's Investors Service. Although responsibility for acceptance or rejection of applications for group policies is normally reserved to the home office, limited authority to bind risks is given to the field personnel of some insurance companies.

UNDERWRITING SINGLE EMPLOYER GROUPS OF TWENTY-FIVE OR MORE LIVES FOR SHORT-TERM DISABILITY INCOME COVERAGE

Under short-term disability income plans, benefit amounts are relatively small and periods during which they are payable seldom exceed six months to a year. The right to adjust premium rates at least annually furnishes substantial protection to insurers against serious loss.

Much group insurance experience has been gained in the underwriting and administration of short-term disability income plans for employees of single employers of twenty-five or more employees. As a result, underwriting practices with respect to these groups are quite firmly established. A

---

[2] See Chapters 26 and 28. In practice, disability benefits are often included in a package with life insurance or medical expense insurance, or both, and the premiums and claims are combined for experience rating purposes.

majority of all persons covered by group disability income plans are insured under policies issued to employers, and valuable intercompany statistical data are available from this class of business.

Initial Underwriting of Short-Term Disability Income Coverage

Certain basic requirements must be met by any group desiring disability income coverage. After these have been satisfied, the underwriter who is evaluating larger employer-employee groups for short-term disability income protection is concerned with unusual circumstances which might make a group unacceptable and with securing the information necessary for proper plan design and accurate rating.

Acceptability. Almost any group of employees of a single employer, or of a single employer and the employer's subsidiaries and affiliates, will constitute an acceptable short-term disability income risk if (1) the persons to be insured are actually engaged in compensated employment and are largely dependent upon their earnings from this employment; (2) the desired benefits are reasonable in relation to the employees' earnings, e.g., not more than 70 to 75 per cent; (3) temporary and part-time employees are excluded from eligibility; and (4) the employer does not insist that insurance be provided for semiretired owners and executives, part-time consultants and professional people or others who are not fully active in the employer's business. The exceptional situations with which the underwriter must deal are discussed below.

A. Part-Time or Seasonal Employment. Some employers are not able to make continuous full-time work available for all of their employees. Where a significant percentage of the employees will be working only a few hours each day or two or three days each week for extended periods, a group may not be a satisfactory insurance risk even though care is taken to exclude from eligibility those who are not *scheduled* to work full time.

If a substantial proportion of the employees work only a part of the year, as in the case of resort hotels or canneries, it may be impossible to provide group disability income insurance at reasonable cost. When the end of a period of employment approaches, there will be an incentive for employees to feign illness and look to insurance benefits as a source of income.

B. History of Frequent Change in Insurers. Some groups, because an abnormal percentage of the employees may be in bad health or for other reasons, develop benefit costs necessitating premiums higher than those normally used, and a particular policyholder may have made frequent changes from one insurance company to another to avoid paying adequate premium rates. Groups having a history of frequent changes of insurer may ultimately become unacceptable to any insurance company. This is encountered more frequently in medical expense insurance than in disability income insurance.

C. Substandard Living Conditions. In unusual circumstances, the members of an employee group may, by reason of economic or moral conditions in the environment in which they live, be uninsurable for group disability income coverage. The nature of the activities in which some employers are engaged exposes employees to these substandard conditions. Examples include taverns, parking lots and taxi companies. Employer-employee groups such as these are not acceptable to many insurance companies.

D. Superimposed Benefits. On occasion, an insurer may be asked to consider providing additional disability income benefits for all or a limited class of an employee group already insured. Interest in superimposed coverage is usually found where existing benefit levels are considered inadequate and cannot readily be increased, being limited either by the terms of union agreements or in accordance with statutory disability laws. The underwriter must exercise unusual care to be certain that the employees will not be over-insured in such cases. Furthermore, if the employees are to contribute toward the cost of insurance, there must be assurance that adequate participation can be secured and maintained.

E. Credit Standing of Employer. If the customary credit investigation discloses that an employer is in unsound financial condition or is a poor credit risk, the group may be unacceptable because of the possibility that premiums will be uncollectible.

Plan Design. After determining that a group is acceptable, the underwriter must analyze the available facts and data to determine whether the plan of benefits to be provided has been properly designed and can be accurately rated. For example, the underwriter must be assured that benefits will not be provided in amounts or under circumstances which will encourage employees to remain away from work in order to receive insurance payments as a substitute for earned income. The principal features involved are eligibility, participation, relation of benefits to earnings and continuation of coverage for inactive employees.

A. Eligibility. The provisions which determine eligibility for coverage should exclude part-time and temporary employees and, where indicated, those in classifications in which interruptions of employment are frequent or of long duration. In high turnover industries, the waiting (or probationary) period for eligibility should be of sufficient length to avoid insuring employees who cannot be assumed to be reasonably permanent. An adequate probationary period also will serve to discourage individuals in poor health from seeking employment with the group policyholder in order to become insured.

Because salaried employees may be more carefully selected and turnover among them is lower, an employer may wish to insure employees in this category immediately upon employment. In some cases, union contracts specify that immediate coverage is to be provided for new employees. If the usual requirement that an employee complete a period of employment before becoming insured is not included, the underwriter should exercise unusual care to assure that the plan will be administered in such a way that adverse selection is minimized.

B. *Participation.* Adequate spread of risk is necessary if group insurance premium rates and group underwriting techniques are to be justified, since no investigation is made of the condition of health of the individuals to be covered. Where the entire premium is paid by the employer-policyholder, all eligible employees are covered automatically. Where the employees are to make a contribution toward the cost, it is desirable to require that the employer also contribute some portion of the premium in order to make the coverage attractive to the employees. A 75 per cent participation requirement is virtually always applied in contributory plans.

C. *Benefits in Relation to Earnings.* As was discussed in Chapter 20, the most important consideration in designing disability income plans is to assure that a proper relationship is maintained between insurance benefits and the earnings of the insured persons. It is also desirable that disability benefits for rank-and-file employees not be too much larger than the unemployment compensation benefits for which they are eligible. Where the dollar amount of benefit is high and determined either on the basis of an employee's rate of hourly or weekly earnings (rather than actual earnings received), or by occupational classification without reference to earned income, contracts often specify that the amount payable cannot exceed a stated percentage of the employee's average earnings over a representative period immediately prior to the beginning of disability.

D. *Continuation of Coverage for Inactive Employees.* Although it is customary to permit continuation of group life insurance and medical expense coverage during temporary periods of inactivity due to layoff or leave of absence, continuation of disability income coverage during such periods is generally limited because insuring unemployed persons is hazardous, as well as inconsistent with the basic purpose of this form of insurance. That is, unemployed persons generally do not lose income because of disability, and, consequently, there is no risk to insure.

E. *Miscellaneous Considerations in Plan Design.* The excessive absenteeism reflected in high losses under a disability income insurance plan is expensive to the employer, as it is to the insurance company. Employers can exercise effective restraints on malingering by maintaining contact with disabled employees and requiring medical examinations upon return to work following extended periods of disability, and should be urged to do so. In the case of larger groups, where insurance costs directly reflect individual plan claim experience, the employer has a vital interest in working with the insurance company to control unnecessary utilization of plan benefits.

The history of short-term disability income insurance shows that high claim losses can be expected during periods of over-employment and under-employment. When work schedules include substantial overtime and jobs are plentiful, employees may be encouraged to remain away from work because they are not concerned with the effect on their relations with the employer. Experience in providing disability benefits for shipyard workers during wartime, for example, has been most unfavorable. Employers who are badly in need of workers do not select them with the care which would otherwise be exercised.

Similarly, experience in group disability income insurance generally has been unfavorable during periods of under-employment when short working schedules have prevailed. Under these circumstances, the employee may be influenced to rely on a regular insurance benefit rather than risk returning to a job which cannot be expected to continue indefinitely. Conditions such as these indicate the need for unusual conservatism in establishing benefit amounts and require control through close cooperation between the employer and the insurance company in prompt reporting of claims and early investigation of questionable claims.

Short-term plans usually insure against disability due to nonoccupational causes only, since virtually all employees in private employment are covered by workmen's compensation laws which provide periodic cash benefits during occupational disabilities. However, occupational coverage sometimes is desired by groups of employees not covered by workmen's compensation laws, such as employees of governmental units, or to supplement benefits provided under workmen's compensation. In the case of supplemental benefits, care must again be taken to assure an appropriate relationship between earnings and the combined benefit to which an employee will be entitled under both workmen's compensation and the group insurance plan.

Rating. Calculation of premium rates for group disability income coverage is discussed in Chapter 22, but it should be noted that as a part of the underwriting process it is the responsibility of the underwriter to assure that all the information which should be reflected in establishing rates is made available. The group characteristics normally reflected in calculating premium rates for short-term disability income plans include size of the group, age distribution, sex, race, location, type of industry and prior loss experience.

A. *Size of Group.* The number of lives is important since loss experience at the rate on which premium calculations are based becomes more likely as the number of persons insured increases. Furthermore, the insurance company's cost of administration will not increase in proportion to an increase in the total premium for the group.

B. *Age Distribution.* Both the frequency and duration of disability increase rapidly with advancing age. However, a loading normally is required on premiums for short-term plans only where employees over age sixty-five constitute more than 5 to 10 per cent of the total.

C. Sex. The cost of providing a specified monthly benefit during disability is considerably higher for females than for males even without regard to any benefits which may be provided for disability due to pregnancy and childbirth.

D. Race. Although it is no longer general practice to secure information as to the racial content of groups being considered for insurance, and discrimination between races in rating or other underwriting processes is illegal in some states, the known higher morbidity among non-Caucasians may result in unusually careful attention on the part of the underwriter to the design of plans for groups in certain areas and industries.

E. Location. While of less importance in group disability insurance than in medical expense coverage, the area in which insured persons are located can have an important effect on the rate of disability. Persons residing in areas in which the general level of health is poor may be expected to become disabled more often than their counterparts elsewhere. An unusually high incidence of disability is sometimes found among persons residing in rural areas who engage in part-time farming operations. Due to a general improvement in public health services and living conditions, location is not so frequently an important underwriting consideration as in the past.

F. Type of Industry. The nature of the employment in which a group of persons is engaged can have a significant effect on the frequency and duration of nonoccupational disability. This is true not only because of the living conditions associated with certain types of employment but also because persons who would be able to perform clerical duties or those required in light manufacturing operations during a minor illness may be entirely prevented from working in an industry such as mining or construction.

Working conditions in some industries may contribute to unusually high rates of disability due to respiratory infections and other conditions not so directly related to employment as to entitle employees to workmen's compensation benefits. Industries usually requiring extra rates include mining, quarrying, furrier, tanning, railroad, and lime, cement and gypsum manufacturing. The federal government, state governments and all political subdivisions usually require special underwriting consideration. Then, too, hospital employees necessitate more detailed study inasmuch as they must be fully recovered from even minor illnesses before returning to work. Where coverage is to be provided for occupational disabilities, complete information as to the type of activity in which all classes of employees, and employees at all locations, are engaged is necessary for accurate calculation of premium rates.

G. Previous Experience. As in underwriting other forms of group insurance, where disability income coverage has been in effect with another insurer, it is customary to require information as to the claim experience with that insurer. For groups of twenty-five to 100 lives, information must be submitted to indicate whether the previous insurer has requested an increase in premium rates and, if available, the reasons for this action. For groups of over 100 lives, premium and claim data must be submitted in order that the underwriter may determine whether claim rates can be expected to vary significantly from those assumed in the calculation of manual premiums. If previous experience indicates that substantial variation from normally expected claims is to be anticipated, higher or lower premiums may be charged.

Renewal Underwriting of Short-Term Disabilty Income Plans[3]

The underwriter does not have a major role in the retrospective experience rating process, which involves calculation of dividends or experience rating credits based on plan operations for completed policy periods.[4] However, in prospective experience rating, which involves calculation of renewal premium rates, the underwriter is responsible for evaluating circumstances or indicated trends which might cause future claim rates to vary from those experienced in the past.

The considerations discussed earlier in connection with initial underwriting, and particularly those factors which affect the frequency and duration of disability, may be taken into account in the calculation of expected claims at the time of renewal. The underwriter may also recommend changes in the arrangement of benefits or in administrative practices where necessary to correct abuses.

UNDERWRITING SINGLE EMPLOYER GROUPS OF TWENTY-FIVE OR MORE LIVES FOR LONG-TERM DISABILITY INCOME COVERAGE

Since long-term disability income plans differ from short-term plans in that individual claims involve much more substantial amounts, true loss ratios are slow to emerge and the right to increase premium rates may not afford the same protection, some considerations which are relatively minor in relation to short-term plans assume great importance in connection with long-term plans. Many life insurance companies suffered disastrous experience with disability income riders in connection with individual life insurance policies during the great depression of the 1930's. This has resulted generally in a cautious approach to the underwriting of plans which provide benefits payable over long periods of time in amounts sufficient to support a reasonable standard of living.

The factors that determine acceptability and influence plan design and rating in underwriting short-term disability income coverage also relate to

---

[3] See also the discussion of renewal underwriting in Chapter 19.

[4] Chapter 22 discusses experience rating procedures utilized in group health insurance.

long-term coverage. Some, however, assume particular importance because of the high benefit amounts and durations. Also, special emphasis is given to the careful selection of risks and arrangement of benefits under long-term plans since insurers are aware of (1) the aforementioned difficulties experienced in administration of disability income benefits under individual life insurance policies in times of economic stress; (2) the still somewhat experimental nature of group long-term coverage and the lack of a really reliable basis for estimating claim costs; and (3) the possibility that losses may be incurred in a single year which can well be impossible to recover through renewal action in subsequent years.

Acceptability and Plan Design

Where employment of a large number of employees is terminated due to cessation of all or a part of an employer's operation, or due to fluctuations in the level of business activity, many of the employees involved may turn to disability income plans for financial support. This is particularly likely in the case of older employees insured for substantial benefit amounts who find it difficult to obtain suitable new employment. Accordingly, insurance companies prefer to write long-term disability income coverage only for established employers in stable industrial or commercial activity. For similar reasons, plans covering groups of government workers or employees in high turnover industries are underwritten with unusual care.

Eligibility.   While the need for income during extended periods of disability is not limited to higher paid employees or those compensated by salary, there has been a greater awareness of this need among employees in the salaried, supervisory and executive categories because it has been customary for their salaries to be continued for indefinite periods during disability. Furthermore, benefits payable under the OASDI program during permanent disabilities are reasonably adequate in relation to the earnings of lower paid employees. As a result, most plans cover only limited classes of higher paid employees.

Where the group is of reasonable size, confining the coverage to a specified class of employees usually will not involve selection against the insurance company. In some cases, however, adoption of the plan may be influenced by the desire to provide substantial benefits for a single higher paid employee or owner who is in poor health, and the underwriter must give particular attention to the acceptability of the group if the eligible class is to comprise a small segment of the total employment.

Long-term disability income benefits cannot be successfully underwritten for persons whose incomes will not be reduced in the event they become disabled. Therefore, special care is exercised to be certain that only regular full-time employees will be insured.

A reasonable period of employment is virtually always a prerequisite for eligibility. Special actively-at-work provisions, which require that an employee not have been absent from work because of illness or injury for a specified number of days or weeks prior to the date his insurance becomes effective, are often used.

Insuring married women for long-term disability benefits is considered exceptionally hazardous because often they are not dependent on their own earnings and the existence of disability is difficult to establish. Where females account for a significant percentage of an employee group, the eligible class may be defined in such a way as to exclude as many female employees as possible.

Benefit Amounts. As explained in Chapter 20, it is essential that the insured benefit be limited insofar as is reasonably possible in order that the disabled person's combined total income from insurance benefits and other sources will not exceed 60 to 65 per cent of after tax earnings. Under some plans, monthly income from sources other than the insurance plan is applied to reduce the insured benefit. Under others, such income is integrated with benefits under the long-term plan only to the extent that the combined total exceeds a specified percentage of the employee's earnings prior to disability.[5] In recognition of the relatively greater need for income on the part of employees with family responsibilities, the integration percentage may be higher for employees with dependents than for other employees.

A maximum monthly benefit of $1,000 or more is common, and benefit amounts may exceed $2,000 under plans for larger employers. However, in order to place a reasonable limitation on the liability for an individual claim, some insurers may limit the maximum monthly benefit to perhaps $500 under plans covering twenty-five to fifty lives and $750 under plans

---

[5] Under a plan of this type providing benefits at the rate of 50 per cent of earnings, subject to a total disability income limitation equal to 65 per cent of earnings, two employees earning $500 and $1,000 per month, respectively, but each entitled to monthly disability benefits of $240 under the social security system would receive benefits under the insured plan determined as follows:

	Employee Earning	
	$500 Per Month	$1,000 Per Month
Benefits for which eligible:		
OASDI monthly benefit........................	$240	$240
Insurance benefit before reduction to reflect other income....................................	250	500
Total....................................	$490	$740
Maximum monthly income during disability permitted by plan................................	325	650
Excess over 65 per cent of earnings (applied to reduce insured benefit)........................	165	90
Insured benefit payable............................	85	410

covering fifty to 100 lives. Where substantial benefit amounts are provided for the smaller groups, evidence of individual insurability may be required with respect to that portion of the benefit in excess of a specified amount.

Benefit Duration. As the age of a disabled person increases, it becomes more difficult to determine whether an illness or injury, or the cumulative effects of more than one illness or injury, actually prevent him from engaging in gainful employment. Accordingly, long-term plans seldom provide sickness benefits beyond age sixty-five, although some insurers have successfully underwritten and administered plans which provide lifetime benefits for disability due to injuries. For smaller groups, duration of benefit payments may be limited to ten, five or even two years, particularly in the case of disability due to sickness, for the same reasons that benefit amounts are limited for these groups.

At least one major company has attempted to limit continuation of benefit payments to one year after termination of the group policy under which the employees were insured in order to control the underwriting loss which would otherwise be sustained in the event the policy is discontinued. Most insurers, however, continue benefits even though the group contract has been terminated.

Initial and Experience Rating. Procedures for calculating premiums for long-term plans are more complicated than for short-term plans, primarily because they relate more precisely to the ages of the employees insured and must be adjusted to reflect the reduction in liability resulting from integration with other benefits. Complete data, therefore, are essential for proper underwriting.

Since the estimated liability for benefits which may be payable under a single claim can be an amount equal to several times the total annual premium for an entire group, and because of the low frequency of long-term disability, relatively little credibility is assigned to individual case experience in either retrospective calculation of dividends or experience rating credits, or in prospective calculation of renewal premiums, except for very large groups. Thus, experience rating techniques used in connection with long-term disability income plans contemplate a considerable element of experience pooling even among large groups. Experience rating plans used by some insurers provide for pooling only of claims in excess of specified amounts and durations.

UNDERWRITING OF OTHER GROUPS

Single Employer Groups under Twenty-five Lives

Group short-term disability income coverage often is made available to groups under twenty-five lives only as a feature of the special package plans, and subject to the special underwriting and administrative procedures described in Chapter 19. The coverage is written separately, however, even for very small groups to provide benefits in accordance with the disability benefit laws of certain states, as explained in Chapter 20.

Since a great many businesses having fewer than twenty-five employees are individual proprietorships or partnerships, and are owner managed, the underwriter of a plan including disability income benefits must be particularly careful that coverage is provided only for persons who can properly be considered employees by virtue of devoting a major portion of their time to the conduct of the employer-policyholder's business.

Long-term disability income coverage often is written separately for groups under twenty-five lives comprising limited classes of employees of larger employers or for all employees of stable, well-established smaller employers. Benefits are limited in both amount and duration, and evidence of individual insurability may be required for all persons to be insured.

Trusteed Welfare Fund Groups Formed under the Taft-Hartley Law[6]

Where eligibility for group insurance is based on full-time employment with employers contributing to a Taft-Hartley Welfare fund, no special underwriting problems generally arise with respect to disability income coverage. However, where coverage is provided for building trades employees, or employees in other industries in which change from one employer to another is frequent and employees may be inactive for extended periods, administration of disability income coverage may involve special problems.

As has been noted, under regular employer-employee plans it is customary to require that an employee be actively at work on the date his insurance is to become effective, and disability coverage is seldom continued during extended periods of layoff or leave of absence. Under welfare fund plans, on the other hand, a participant may qualify for coverage for a period of three to six months or longer on the basis of his work history during some previous work period, and it may not be possible to require that he be actively at work on the date his insurance is to become effective. The underwriter must, therefore, give particular care to the drafting of eligibility provisions and to the arrangements for administration of claims in order to avoid covering pre-existing disabilities and to control to the maximum possible extent any use of the insurance benefits as unemployment compensation. As yet, there has been no great pressure from unions for long-term disability insurance to supplement disability benefits available under OASDI or private pension plans, and relatively little long-term coverage has been written for welfare fund groups.

---

[6] Taft-Hartley Welfare funds are discussed in detail in Chapter 33.

Voluntary Employer Association Groups

Group disability income coverage can be written legally in all states for employees of employers who are members of trade associations or other associations of employers, or for employees of two or more employers in the same industry who establish a trust to act as the group policyholder. While similar in general structure, employer association groups differ from Taft-Hartley Welfare fund groups in that participation in the former is voluntary on the part of employers who are members of the association (and where the insurance is contributory, on the part of the employees). Normally, interest in participating in these plans will be greatest among smaller employers. Therefore, the underwriting considerations with respect to groups with under twenty-five lives apply also to most of the employers eligible for a voluntary employer association plan. Small employers often are in a position to exercise adverse selection against the insurer. In order to minimize the effect of this selection, it is customary to be as conservative as possible in arranging benefits, to require use of the special actively-at-work provision (described in an earlier section) with respect to long-term disability insurance and to permit employers to enter the plan after the original enrollment only at specified times and subject to minimum requirements as to the number who must elect to enroll.

As in the case of group life and medical expense insurance, the ability of the administrator—whether it be the association sponsoring the plan or an organization performing the services for a fee—to maintain records properly, collect premiums and process claims, and to otherwise conduct the administration in an efficient manner, is essential to the success of these plans. As a result of the element of selection inherent in voluntary employer association plans, relatively little long-term disability insurance has been written.

Associations of Individuals

Many short-term disability income plans have been written for members of associations of individuals who have joined together for purposes other than that of obtaining insurance.[7] Plans for members of "employee benefit associations," formed for the specific purpose of providing or securing disability income insurance, were common some years ago, and a few remain in effect.

Where the association membership is comprised of employees of a single employer or of a limited number of named employers, as in the case of the employee benefit associations and some trade-union groups, the group will have many of the underwriting characteristics of single em-

---

[7] Group policies can be issued to these associations in all states except North Carolina.

ployer groups. Group disability income plans usually will be successful where eligibility can be determined on the basis of employment with named employers, provided adequate arrangements can be made for collection of premiums—preferably by payroll deduction—and for other administrative activities. With virtually all employers now contributing toward the cost of group insurance, many plans sponsored directly by unions and by other employee groups have been discontinued.

Until recent years, relatively few school systems were authorized by law to contribute toward the cost of group insurance, and teachers' salaries were seldom continued during disability. Plans for members of teachers' organizations, therefore, were quite common. In many cases, payroll deduction was not possible and premiums were collected directly from the teachers. Special coverages with a selection of benefit amounts and limited coverage during vacation periods were offered, often subject to a considerable degree of individual underwriting.

Group disability income coverage has long been of particular interest to members of professional associations and societies. Physicians, dentists and attorneys, and to a lesser extent accountants and other professional people, have been keenly aware of the need for disability income insurance because continuation of their incomes is so directly related to ability to engage in professional activity. Plans written for these professional groups generally have involved relatively higher benefit levels, often with a selection of benefit amounts by the individual and longer durations than are customary under short-term single employer plans. Benefits to age sixty-five are common, and at least one plan for a large group provides lifetime benefits for disabilities arising out of both injury and sickness.

At one time, it was not difficult to enroll a sufficient percentage of the members of a professional group to justify group underwriting. Since many professional people are now eligible to participate in several plans, however, and obtaining applications from an acceptable percentage of the eligible persons has become increasingly difficult, insurers normally reserve the right to reject the applications of individuals within the association or to limit benefit amounts for impaired lives.

In designing any plan for members of an association of individuals, the underwriter must be aware that the group policyholder will be interested only in securing maximum protection for the members at the lowest possible cost. In addition, the insurance company ordinarily must handle claims directly with the insured individuals and cannot look to the association for help in the administration of claims.

State Statutory Disability Income Plans

Disability income plans written to provide benefits required by laws in four states have the same general underwriting characteristics as other single or multiple employer short-term disability income plans.[8] However, the laws permit little flexibility in plan design, and provisions which would be considered undesirable from an underwriting standpoint, particularly with regard to continuation of insurance during periods of inactivity, are required by statute. Competition from plans administered by the states places arbitrary limitations on the premiums which can be charged. The compulsory nature of the coverage would generally be advantageous to insurers, but, as was noted in the previous chapter, the laws require coverage of persons who would not normally be considered eligible as full-time employees.

REINSURANCE OF GROUP DISABILITY INCOME COVERAGE

The two types of reinsurance described in Chapter 19, i.e., proportional and nonproportional, are also used in connection with group disability income insurance. One of these involves simply the sharing of larger risks between insurance companies and has no characteristics peculiar to disability income insurance. The other, which has the purpose of protecting the primary insurer against losses greater than it may wish to assume, may have a special usefulness in connection with long-term disability income coverage.

As a result of the possibility of substantial underwriting loss under long-term disability income plans—which has been referred to frequently in this chapter—considerable interest has been created in reinsurance of long-term disability income coverage. Some arrangements have been negotiated following a pro rata approach under which the reinsurer assumes liability for a specified percentage of every claim in order to limit the primary carrier's aggregate liability. Although the characteristics of long-term disability income insurance are such that an important reinsurance market may develop, little reinsurance has actually been placed because a majority of the plans in effect have been written by large, well-established insurers which are financially able to assume the risks involved. Few group writing companies have found it necessary to reinsure any portion of the liability under short-term plans.

SELECTED REFERENCES

HEALTH INSURANCE ASSOCIATION OF AMERICA. *Students' Guide for Principles of Health Insurance* (1962).

SOCIETY OF ACTUARIES. *Part 8 Study Notes* (1956).

---

[8] See Chapter 20 for a description of the state statutory disability income plans.

Chapter 22

MANUAL AND EXPERIENCE RATING FOR GROUP HEALTH COVERAGES

BY EDWARD A. GREEN

BASIC PRINCIPLES FOR PREMIUM DETERMINATION

The basic principles which insurance companies follow in establishing premium rates for group health coverages are the same as those applicable to other group insurance rate making and to pricing generally. Rates must be adequate to support claims, expenses and risk requirements. They must be competitive in the marketplace. They must be equitable for all classes of policyholders. They must be coordinated with underwriting standards, policy provisions and claim practices. Finally, the rate structure must be simple to understand and administer, especially for small cases that agents are expected to handle without much assistance from an insurer's group insurance department.

The major item needed to set a rate structure for policies providing group health insurance is an evaluation of expected claims. In general, these claims will be a function of the coverage components, coverage details and benefit levels included in the policy, and the risk characteristics of the case.

The coverage components which may be included in a group health insurance contract fall into two broad categories—those covering loss of income due to disability and those covering medical expenses. The first category is usually subdivided into short-term disability coverage, whose benefits are payable for one year or less, and long-term disability coverage, whose benefits are payable for a longer period. The second category includes hospital, surgical and medical insurance; the various forms of major medical and comprehensive medical expense insurance; and such supplemental coverages as laboratory and X-ray, supplemental accident, poliomyelitis and dental expense insurance. Expected claims are determined separately for each of these components.

The claims for each component will vary with the coverage details of that component. For example, the expected claims for a short-term disability income plan which provides benefits for a maximum of twenty-six weeks obviously will be greater than for a thirteen-week plan, and the expected claims for a comprehensive medical expense plan with a $50 deductible will be greater than for one with a $100 deductible. Coverage details of a component can differ from insurer to insurer according to the pattern of benefit design used, as referred to later in connection with the intricacies of medical expense coverages. For instance, anesthetists' fees may be covered under a basic hospital expense policy, a surgical expense rider or a separate anesthesia expense rider. Other examples include paying for radiation therapy under a surgical expense rider as compared to a separate radiation therapy rider and paying, under a comprehensive medical policy, the full daily cost of semiprivate room and board accommodations as compared to paying the daily cost of semiprivate room and board up to a prescribed dollar limit.

Certain characteristics of the group to be covered affect the level of expected claims, including the age, sex, geographic location, and income level of the covered individuals and the industry in which they are employed.[1] The extent of variation in cost associated with these and other risk characteristics and the way in which it is reflected in rates will be considered later.

Expenses and risk margins, the items in premium determination in addition to expected claims, are a function of the size of group, the coverage components and details and the administrative characteristics of a case. In general, expenses and risk margins are provided for in manual rates by loading expected net claim costs by a percentage or by a percentage plus a constant. In practice, basic manual rates are established which are considered adequate for the smaller size groups, excluding groups of under twenty-five lives inasmuch as the latter are usually subject to a separate rate structure. For larger groups a percentage discount is allowed which increases as the amount of premium for the policy increases. Sometimes the volume discount will be greater for noncontributory cases or for those which are administered on a self-accounting or employer draft basis.[2] Other expense characteristics are usually recognized in the experience rating process described later.

Adequacy

It is fundamental to satisfactory operations that the price of a product must be sufficient to cover the cost of raw material, manufacture and

---

[1] Variations by industry are tending to decline in importance for reasons outlined later.

[2] Under the employer draft method of claim administration the proof of claim is submitted by the claimant to the employer who prepares a draft on the insurer in conformity with instructions in a manual prepared for his use by the insurer. Difficult or unusual claims are reviewed in advance by the insurer and others at the time the draft is presented for payment.

distribution, and to provide for return on invested capital commensurate with the risk involved. If the test of adequacy in its broad sense, recognizing a degree of latitude for new or experimental coverages and additional income such as interest earnings on reserves, cannot be met because of competitive considerations, the sound decision is to withdraw the product from the market. In insurance, claim payments represent the cost of raw materials; the insurer's expenses, the cost of manufacture and distribution; and the risk margin, the provision for contingencies and return for use of capital. In a mutual company the risk margin is needed to maintain an appropriate contingency reserve or surplus account. In a stock company the risk margin is used partially to augment the contingency reserve or surplus account and partially to pay dividends to stockholders as a reimbursement for providing capital and sharing in the risk-taking function.

State laws deal to some extent with the adequacy of group health insurance rates. Section 221 of the New York law provides that no insurer doing business in that state shall issue, within or without the state, any policy of group health insurance which shall not appear to be self-supporting on reasonable assumptions as to morbidity or other appropriate claim rate, interest and expense. Five states have established a minimum initial rate basis for group life coverages by law, but none have done so for group health insurance. Although the New York law states that the "Superintendent may determine, after notice to all Insurers, . . . minimum premium rates," as yet it has not been found necessary to exercise this right.

Competitive Level

It is self-evident that a company's manual rate structure cannot depart radically from the rate pattern or level in general use by other companies. The bulk of group health insurance arises from the employer-employee relationship, with the employer paying a substantial part or all of the premium. His portion of the premium is a direct cost of doing business and enters into the end price of his product. Therefore, the force of competition in the employer's business pushes him toward a keen analysis of price and product when he buys group insurance. This does not necessarily mean purchasing from the company quoting the lowest rate, since other aspects are also pertinent, including quality of product and service. This is reflected in such things as assistance in designing a plan and keeping it up to date, claims handling, claim cost control activities, administrative services and flexibility in plan design and administration. Nevertheless, an insurance company must consider the prices of its competitors along with adequacy of its own proposed rates in establishing a rate level. In this connection it should be recognized that the supply of "raw material" in group health insurance, i.e., insuring capacity, is readily available to all insurers who meet legal requirements. Moreover the market, i.e., the over-all demand for group health insurance, is limited in aggregate. These two factors—generally unlimited supply and limited demand—are conducive to a highly competitive market.

The volume of group insurance in force has grown dramatically when compared to that of individually purchased insurance during the last two decades. During this period, it has become evident that the mass buyer of health coverages tends to use different criteria than the personal buyer. The group insurance buyer is spending a large sum of money in a pattern more akin to a business expenditure than a personal one. In his business expenditures he is accustomed to following economic cycles and business trends, rather than individual family circumstances, and he takes calculated business risks. It is not surprising, therefore, that the group insurance buyer tends to place more emphasis on net cost year by year and factors which affect it and less emphasis on future guarantees. This attitude of the buyer presents a real challenge in the establishment of group health insurance rates which will be reasonable and acceptable to the buyer while at the same time meeting the standard of adequacy.

Equity

A third basic principle of rate making is that rates must be equitable for all purchasers. Practically every state has a law against unfair discrimination in insurance transactions. In the New York insurance law, for example, Section 209 stipulates that no insurer doing the business of health insurance in that state shall make or permit any unfair discrimination between individuals of the same class in the amount of premiums, policy fees, or rates charged for any policy or contract of health insurance, or in the benefits payable thereunder, or in any of the terms or conditions of such contract, or in any other manner whatsoever. Section 221 of the New York insurance code provides that an insurer must file its schedules of premium rates, rules and classifications of risks, which may be revised from time to time, with the Superintendent, and no policy shall be issued with premium rates for the first policy year less than those determined by the schedule of the insurer as then on file. In permitting readjustment of the rate based on the experience under the policy at the end of the first or any subsequent year of insurance, the New York law states that any such readjustment shall be computed on a basis equitable to all group health insurance policies.

Even if equity were not required by law, it would be necessitated by practical considerations. The force of competition acts something like Gresham's law. For instance, if an insurer underpriced a particular plan of benefits for one industry and overpriced it for another, he would likely, in time, find that his business was coming largely from the buyers who were getting an unwarranted bargain, thus threatening the solvency of his operation. The combined need for adequacy and competitiveness motivates the establishment of rates which are in reasonable balance for all purchasers.

The concept of equity in insurance may seem to be in conflict with the sharing of risk principle. As at least one writer has pointed out,[3] if complete recognition were given to the risk-sharing or pooling of experience principle, there would be absolute uniformity of costs for all classes of policyholders. If, on the other hand, complete recognition were given to the individual accounting or equity principle, the operation would degenerate into an individual trust operation and could no longer be called insurance. As a practical matter, a position intermediate between the two extremes of complete pooling and complete individual accounting is needed. In general, equity requires that any recognition given to the experience of a particular class of policyholders should be in proportion to the contribution of that class to the item being allocated, be it claims or expenses. In addition, the classification system should be subdivided sufficiently to reflect any major differences in characteristics which affect financial results. Variations in rating practices from company to company can be an outgrowth of varying interpretations of the relative importance of risk-sharing, class equity and individual case equity.

Coordination with Operations

Rates cannot be set in a vacuum. They must be coordinated with the underwriting standards, policy provisions and claim practices of the insurer. A tight set of underwriting standards, whereby only the most select risks were accepted at standard rates, would reduce expected claims and warrant a lower standard rate level. This would give a competitive edge on select cases but would require a more extensive use of substandard loadings, thus making for a more complicated and higher rate structure for substandard risks that might well impair sales efforts.

Likewise, the regular use of tight policy provisions, such as those providing for reduced benefits in event of duplication of coverage, excluding benefits for pre-existing conditions, or using a severe definition of disability, can produce lower rates. However, sales activities might also be influenced adversely if policy provisions were too severe. The rate schedule might provide for an additional premium for the waiving of such policy provisions when desired by a prospective policyholder—again at the cost of a more complicated rate structure and increased administrative expenses.

Claim practices can have an effect on rate levels in at least two respects, namely through the levels of benefit payments and expenses. Claim ad-

---

[3] J. Edwin Matz, discussion regarding the article, "The Case for Refinement in Methods of Allocating Investment Income," *Transactions of the Society of Actuaries,* Vol. XIII (1961), p. 320.

ministration which involves extensive claim cost control activity as a regular procedure could reduce the amount needed for expected claims, but could also be expected to increase the amount needed for expenses. Even within the same level of claim cost control activity there can be a difference in the philosophy of claim handling. In most instances the validity of a claim and the amount of benefit will be clear-cut. There will also be some instances where the claim is obviously not valid. In between there will be a grey area where either the validity of claim or the amount of benefit, or both, will be questionable. The extremes of philosophy would be to pay as much as possible or as little as possible. Neither is necessarily the right approach, since an employee benefit plan is involved with personnel policy and employer-employee relationships. Nevertheless, the philosophy used will affect the level of claims to be expected under a coverage.

Simplicity

Finally, in addition to being adequate, competitive, equitable and consistent with underwriting standards, policy provisions and claim practice, a rate structure must be simple to understand and administer. Quotations are frequently made by representatives in the field from a rate manual which should not be unwieldy or difficult to use. As a practical matter, quotations need to be readily determinable from an employer's personnel or payroll records. Furthermore, once a group plan is sold and installed, the aggregate premium payable from time to time is usually determined as a by-product of such records.

There can be conflict between a desire for a sophisticated rate base, with its ability to sharpen quotations on selected cases, and a desire for a simple rate base, with its ease of use and lower chance of error or misunderstanding. As competition has increased, there has been a tendency towards greater sophistication in both manual and experience rating.

GREATER INTRICACY OF MEDICAL EXPENSE COVERAGES

In the rate section of a typical group insurance manual, rates for medical expense coverages will occupy 80 to 90 per cent of the space, with group life, accidental death and dismemberment and disability income rates comprising the remainder. Before considering in detail the determination of manual and experience rates for group health coverages, it should be noted that there are a number of reasons why rate making for group medical expense coverages is more intricate than for disability income and other group insurance coverages. First, the medical expense coverages are written in a wide variety of continually changing patterns. Moreover, there has been a lack of availability and use of standard morbidity tables in rate making. Then, too, claim costs are influenced by

GROUP INSURANCE HANDBOOK [Ch. 22

the level of medical expense charges as well as by frequency and duration of claim, and such costs are subject to a degree of control by the insured. In addition, the types of competition have been more numerous and varied than those encountered in connection with other group insurance coverages.

Variety of Patterns

Medical expenses include a wide range of types of services and of individuals who render them. There are doctors' fees for home, office and hospital visits, for consultation, anesthesia and surgery. There are the charges for X-ray, laboratory, several types of therapy services, drugs, medicines, prosthetic devices and ambulance services. In addition, there are the charges for care by both registered and practical nurses both in the home and in the hospital, and there are the charges for room and board and the many ancillary services and supplies provided by the hospital. This limited list emphasizes the multiplicity of components, one or more of which may be included in a particular medical expense coverage. Furthermore, the medical expenses covered may be limited to those connected with a particular cause such as in supplemental accident or poliomyelitis expense insurance.

The various components of medical expense insurance may be written on either a scheduled or blanket basis. For instance, the room-and-board benefit under hospital insurance and the benefits under surgical and medical insurance are usually scheduled to provide a maximum reimbursement of a certain number of dollars for each day hospitalized, for each surgical procedure and for each home or office visit, respectively. On the other hand, the benefits for ancillary services under hospital insurance and for benefits under supplemental accident and poliomyelitis expense insurance usually provide for the blanket payment of all covered charges up to a specified over-all dollar limit.

Under comprehensive or major medical expense insurance, many of the categories of medical expense may be covered under a single blanket provision, as was noted in Chapter 18. In this case there is usually a deductible amount and a percentage participation payable by the covered individual as well as a maximum amount payable by the insurer. The deductible and maximum may be related to a period of time, a period of disability or a cause of disability. The insurer's rate structure usually makes provision for a variety of deductibles, degrees of percentage participation and maximums. It should be noted that there is not a direct mathematical relationship in the effect of these items on expected claims, since a $50 deductible will eliminate more than half of the claims eliminated by a $100 deductible, and a $10,000 maximum will cover relatively few more claims than a $5,000 maximum. Even with the same deductible and maximum, a 75 per cent benefit may cost less than its proportionate part of an 80 per cent benefit because of the deterrent effect of the higher percentage participation on the utilization of services.

The establishment of a rate structure for group medical expense insurance is complicated not only by the wide variety of components that may be included and by the patterns in which it may be written but also by the fact that coverage is usually provided for dependents as well as employees. Expected claims differ according to the type and number of dependents and whether maternity benefits are included.

As a result primarily of the many possible combinations of medical expense insurance and the changing patterns in medical care and costs, there has been a lack of standard morbidity tables in rate making. As will be mentioned later, there have been tabulations of intercompany experience on certain basic plans and tables developed therefrom. However, it has been difficult to secure a sufficient volume of up-to-date homogeneous data from which to develop experience tables which will measure the effect on expected claims of all the variations in coverage components and patterns. Many of these variations have had to be measured by judgment.

Influences on Claim Costs

Benefits under group life, accidental death and dismemberment, short-term disability income and long-term disability income insurance are set forth in specific dollar amounts payable upon the happening or continuation of a contingency. However, in group medical expense insurance, the benefit is related, even to some extent with scheduled benefits, to charges incurred by the covered individual. Therefore, claim costs under group medical expense insurance are influenced by the level of medical expense charges as well as by the frequency and duration of claims. The sharp upward trend of the medical expense component of the cost-of-living index has affected this level. The philosophy of charging in accordance with ability to pay continues to have some effect on the cost of medical expense coverage, although not nearly to the extent it has in the past.

Also, expected claims are subject to change with the constantly changing pattern of medical care. For instance, there has been a trend toward greater frequency of hospitalization and shorter average confinements. Claims under poliomyelitis expense insurance dropped dramatically with the discovery of the polio vaccines. Patterns of medical care even vary with the availability of facilities. The frequency of hospitalization and length of stay tend to be higher in communities where the ratio of hospital beds to population is greater.

Claims under group medical expense insurance are subject to a degree of claim cost control as will be discussed in Chapters 23 and 24. For example, the quantity and type of medical care sought by an individual is flexible and may be influenced by his working and living conditions and attitude toward insurance. Frequently, the development of a cooperative program among insurers, policyholders, covered individuals and purveyors of medical services can reduce claims without lowering the quality of medical care. The effect of educational efforts among covered individuals, cooperative programs and other claim cost control activities on expected claims is an important element in rate determination.

Alternate Coverage

Rate making for group medical expense insurance must recognize that the coverage is subject to competition from sources other than insurance companies. Blue Cross and Blue Shield organizations with their flexible use of both community rating and experience rating methods and their contracts with hospitals and doctors often provide considerable competition. In addition, there are various types of health service organizations, including group practice prepayment associations where the subscription price is based on a salary or per capita remuneration of the doctor.

Medical expense coverages with a high claim frequency and low-average claim value approach that end of the insuring spectrum which lies nearest to the budgeting process and, hence, are more subject to the competition of an uninsured plan than are other forms of group insurance with lower claim frequencies and higher average claim values. In fact, a few arrangements, sometimes called minimum premium plans, have been worked out whereby an insurer handles the claim and administrative functions for an uninsured basic layer of benefits along with coverage for benefits above that layer. These arrangements, which have been designed to save premium tax on the presumption that the uninsured layer of benefits will not be subject to tax, are discussed further in Chapters 29 and 41.

In a broad sense, all of the private enterprise organizations insuring or prepaying the costs of medical care are in competition with proposed extensions of tax supported, government operated plans. The several State-65 plans provide an illustration of cooperative coverage design, pricing, marketing and claim cost control activity undertaken to fill in a coverage gap with a group-type arrangement. These organizations will be discussed in detail in Chapter 37.

MANUAL RATING

It is customary for an insurer to have a manual of rates which is used in setting the initial premium on a policy at the time of issue, with separate rates for each of the coverage components to be included in the policy. The rate level for each component is designed to be self-supporting, although it may recognize that other components contribute their share of policy expenses and contribute to the stability of loss experience. Thus, the use of a volume discount that increases with the size of the total premium under the policy has the effect of recognizing in advance some of the expense savings and greater stability of loss experience when several components are included in a single policy.

In general, manual rates are established only for broad classes of risk and are designed to apply to a wide range of cases for which no credible individual experience data are available. The rates reflect only the most important characteristics of the group which affect morbidity and expense experience. Experience rating, retrospectively through dividends or premium refunds, and prospectively through adjustment in renewal premiums, is relied upon to reflect other variations in risk and administrative cost from group to group.

The usual procedure of using the manual of rates in setting the initial premium on a policy at the time of issue is not followed when a case with a history of poor experience is transferring from one insurer to another. In this circumstance, the procedure follows the renewal rating pattern in recognizing the past experience of the case. Similarly, some recent rate structures have included a provision for recognizing properly documented prior experience of large groups with another insurer if the experience is more favorable than that contemplated in the manual rates.

Manual rates are usually filed with supervisory authorities and published for a network of standard plans of coverage. Adjustments in these rates may be calculated as needed using interpolation, extrapolation or judgment, whichever is appropriate, to reflect deviations from the standard plans in coverage details necessary for flexibility in employee benefit plan design.

Sources of Data

Intercompany Studies. There are a number of sources of morbidity data available for use in establishing manual rates. The Committee on Experience under Group Health Insurance of the Society of Actuaries regularly collects and processes experience data contributed by the large writers of group health coverages. The statistics of the contributing companies are combined and, with appropriate interpretation of the results, are published yearly in the separate "Annual Reports" volumes of the *Transactions of the Society of Actuaries.* These reports have covered experience under short-term disability income insurance and hospital and surgical insurance for both employees and dependents. Currently the experience under major medical expense insurance is being added, and it is anticipated that long-term disability income insurance experience will be included in the future.

In the Society of Actuaries' reports, experience is shown for a number of standard plans of coverage. Until recently the results of the studies have been presented in the form of annual claim costs. However, the latest reports set forth the experience in the form of ratios of actual to tabular claims. It is expected that this method will permit more meaningful analysis of certain cost relationships and qualify a wider variety of plans for inclusion in the studies. The intercompany reports have provided a limited breakdown of experience by sex, industry, size and geographical location, as well as by plan and year. The results necessarily reflect the composite experience of variations in insurance company administrative and claim practices.

Special Studies. Periodically, individuals have made special studies from the data submitted for the intercompany studies supplemented by additional intercompany and intracompany experience. There have been two such studies of experience under each of the following areas: group short-term disability income, hospital, surgical and major medical expense insurance. These studies are listed in items 1–8 of the Selected References at the end of this chapter. These special studies, which have been published as papers in the *Transactions of the Society of Actuaries*, examine in greater detail the many independent variables affecting group morbidity experience. They have provided the basis for the development of the tabular claims to which actual claims are compared in the latest intercompany studies and are of considerable value as a base point in rate making.

By way of illustration, Morton D. Miller's study of short-term disability income insurance[4] used individual claim data submitted by seven large insurers to develop continuation tables showing the number of those becoming disabled who continue disabled for various periods of time. The number is set forth by day for the first few weeks of disability and by week thereafter. This study also analyzes the variations in incidence of claims in such categories as age and sex of the claimant, season of the year in which claims were incurred and plan characteristics concerning both the day of disability on which benefits first become payable and the maximum duration for which benefits are payable. It examines the proportion of claims arising from accident and that arising from sickness and the variation in duration between accident and sickness claims. Finally, the results of the continuation study are combined with data from the regular reports of the Committee on Experience under Group Health Insurance in forming a basic morbidity table which shows both the monthly and annual tabular costs per unit of weekly indemnity cumulatively according to duration of disability.

The special studies on hospital, surgical and major medical expense insurance examine the effects of some of the same variables as the short-term disability income study. In addition, they consider the effect of such things as geographical location, policy benefit levels and the level of

---

[4] Morton D. Miller, "Group Weekly Indemnity Continuation Table Study," *Transactions of the Society of Actuaries,* Vol. III (1951), p. 31.

charges by hospitals and doctors. The studies cover both employee and dependent benefits.

Stanley W. Gingery's latest study of hospital insurance[5] developed a hospital continuation table, as well as tables dealing with frequency of hospitalization and average values of ancillary service benefits. The study considers claims by cause of disability in broad classes and the differences in claims between in-patient and out-patient care. The factors used for determining tabular claims in the regular intercompany studies were developed from this special study and are published in the 1960 and 1961 "Reports" volumes of the *Transactions of the Society of Actuaries*.

Morton D. Miller's study of surgical insurance[6] developed a table of annual frequencies of surgical claims and analyzed the relative frequencies by type of operation, including multiple procedures. It showed the average amount of reimbursement for hospital bed-patient, hospital out-patient and out-of-hospital claims and the relative importance of each by number of claims and amount of reimbursement. A schedule of relative values of the different surgical procedures was developed from the data concerning doctors' charges. The factors used for determining tabular claims in the regular intercompany studies were developed from this special study and are published in the 1961 "Reports" volume of the *Transactions of the Society of Actuaries*.

Burton E. Burton and Daniel W. Pettengill's study of comprehensive medical expense benefits[7] developed tabular expected claim costs for this type of coverage, utilizing data from an earlier study by Stanley W. Gingery and Richard J. Mellman[8] and supplemented by the experience of the authors' own company. The tabular cost for any given comprehensive medical coverage is determined by means of a ten-step formula which takes into account such things as amount of deductible and the type of expenses to which it applies, percentage participation, age, sex, geographical area and private room limit. The factors developed in this special study are used for determining tabular claims in the regular intercompany studies.

Since long-term disability income insurance is a comparatively new coverage in the group insurance field, there is little existing group experi-

---

[5] Stanley W. Gingery, "A Reinvestigation of Group Hospital Expense Insurance Experience," *Transactions of the Society of Actuaries*, Vol. XII (1960), p. 564.

[6] Morton D. Miller, "1957 Study of Group Surgical Expense Insurance Claims," *Transactions of the Society of Actuaries*, Vol. X (1958), p. 359.

[7] Burton E. Burton and Daniel W. Pettengill, "Development of Expected Claim Costs for Comprehensive Medical Expense Benefits and Ratios of 1959 and 1960 Actual Experience Thereto," *Transactions of the Society of Actuaries*, Vol. XV (1963), p. 10.

[8] Stanley W. Gingery and Richard J. Mellman, "An Investigation of Group Major Medical Expense Insurance Experience," *Transactions of the Society of Actuaries*, Vol. XIII (1961), p. 513.

ence data. As a consequence, experience under disability provisions of individually issued life and health policies, modified to reflect differences in risk and methods of underwriting group insurance, have been used in determining group long-term disability income insurance rates. Pertinent material is contained in the reports of two committees and a special study based on one of them.[9] It is interesting to note that one insurer gathered data for the establishment of rates for a new coverage with no prior experience available by sending questionnaires to its own employees.[10]

Intracompany Studies. In addition to the intercompany and special studies there are other sources of data useful in rate making. Many of the larger companies make annual analyses of their own group health insurance experience. These analyses are, of course, more up to date than intercompany studies and reflect the effect on claim costs of the sales, underwriting, administrative and claims procedures of the particular company. Some of these intracompany analyses are presented in part from time to time in the "Informal Discussions" reported in the *Transactions of the Society of Actuaries.* When calculated into rates, the results of these studies are on file with state insurance authorities.

Supplementary Materials. A wide variety of corroborative material is available. For instance, the American Hospital Association publishes an annual report, *Daily Service Charges in Hospitals,* which surveys current hospital charges by geographic location. The medical expense component of the Bureau of Labor Statistics' Consumer Price Index is helpful in following trends. Other government publications deal with such things as hazards characteristic to a particular industry. From time to time statistics of Blue Cross, Blue Shield and health service organizations have become available. Also, there are studies by private research organizations such as the *Prolonged Illness Absenteeism Report* prepared by the Research Council for Economic Security.[11]

Use of Data

While the mechanics of rate making differ materially from company to company, a normal procedure is to start with the basic tables in the special studies and bring them up to date with the trends shown in the intercom-

---

[9] "Experience under Certain Ordinary Disability Benefits between the 1930 and 1950 Anniversaries," *1952 Reports—Transactions of the Society of Actuaries,* p. 70; "Experience under Individual Loss-of-Time Policies, 1955–59," *1961 Reports— Transactions of the Society of Actuaries,* p. 101; and Manuel R. Cueto, "Monetary Values for Ordinary Disability Benefits, Based on Period 2 of the 1952 Inter-Company Study of the Society's Committee with $2\frac{1}{2}\%$ Interest," *Transactions of the Society of Actuaries,* Vol. VI (1954), p. 108.

[10] Alan M. Thaler, "Group Major-Medical Expense Insurance," *Transactions of the Society of Actuaries,* Vol. III (1951), p. 429.

[11] Published in book form by the Council (Chicago, 1957).

pany reports. These are then adjusted in accordance with the company's own experience data to reflect the effect on claim costs of the difference in its sales, underwriting, administrative and claim procedures from the composite entering the intercompany studies. These results are loaded for expenses and risk margin and checked for reasonableness with outside corroborative data and other existing rate schedules. Rates for the types of medical expense coverage not included in the intercompany and special studies are generally determined from intracompany experience with checks for reasonableness. Rates for an entirely new coverage or coverage detail may be based on a judgment evaluation of relevant data from fields other than insurance, such as public health publications or the employee

TABLE 22–1

TYPICAL VOLUME DISCOUNT SCHEDULE FOR
GROUP HEALTH INSURANCE

Monthly Premium before Reduction	Percentage Reduction
$ 300 but less than $ 500	2
500 " " " 750	3
750 " " " 1,000	4
1,000 " " " 1,500	5
1,500 " " " 2,000	6
2,000 " " " 3,000	7
3,000 " " " 4,000	8
4,000 " " " 5,000	9
5,000 " " " 7,500	10
7,500 " " " 10,000	11
10,000 " " " 15,000	12
15,000 " " " 20,000	13
20,000 " " " 25,000	14
25,000 and over	15

questionnaires mentioned earlier in connection with the introduction of major medical expense insurance, until experience data become available.

Expense and risk margin loadings generally are based on intracompany studies. In general, manual premiums are designed to produce loss ratios of approximately 70 to 75 per cent before volume discount. The discount may bring the anticipated loss ratios to between 85 and 90 per cent for the largest case. Table 22–1 shows a typical volume discount schedule applicable to group health insurance. The premium used in entering the table usually includes that for all coverages which are combined for commission calculation and experience rating.

In order to illustrate how a company might go about determining a manual rate for a short-term disability income benefit, a portion of the

TABLE 22–2

PORTIONS OF THE MILLER 1947–49 BASIC MORBIDITY TABLE—MALES

Duration t	Tabular Cost for Duration of Disability t or Less		Duration t	Tabular Cost for Duration of Disability t or Less	
	Annual C_t	Monthly C_t		Annual C_t	Monthly C_t
1 day	.0279	.0023	20 weeks	.7402	.0617
2 days	.0553	.0046	21 "	.7515	.0626
3 "	.0820	.0068	22 "	.7623	.0635
4 "	.1078	.0090	23 "	.7726	.0644
5 "	.1326	.0110	24 "	.7825	.0652
6 "	.1564	.0130	25 "	.7920	.0660
7 "	.1790	.0149	26 "	.8011	.0668
8 "	.1999	.0167	26 " , 3 days	.8049	.0671
9 "	.2191	.0183	27 "	.8099	.0675
10 "	.2365	.0197	28 "	.8184	.0682
. . . . .			. . . . .		
31 "	.4375	.0365	49 "	.9502	.0792
32 "	.4439	.0370	50 "	.9550	.0796
33 "	.4501	.0375	51 "	.9598	.0800
34 "	.4561	.0380	52 "	.9645	.0804
35 "	.4619	.0385	52 " , 3 days	.9665	.0805
6 weeks	.4977	.0415	53 "	.9691	.0808
7 "	.5265	.0439	54 "	.9736	.0811
8 "	.5505	.0459	55 "	.9780	.0815
9 "	.5718	.0476	56 "	.9824	.0819
10 "	.5914	.0493	57 "	.9867	.0822
11 "	.6099	.0508	58 "	.9909	.0826
12 "	.6274	.0523	59 "	.9950	.0829
13 "	.6440	.0537	60 "	.9991	.0833
13 " , 3 days	.6508	.0542			
14 "	.6598	.0550			
15 "	.6749	.0562			
16 "	.6893	.0574			
17 "	.7030	.0586			
18 "	.7160	.0597			
19 "	.7284	.0607			

Source: Morton D. Miller, "Group Weekly Indemnity Continuation Study," *Transactions of the Society of Actuaries*, Vol. X (1958), pp. 359–63.

basic morbidity table developed in Mr. Miller's special study is reproduced as Table 22–2. The tabular cost (C_t) designates the cost per dollar of weekly indemnity for disability from the first day up to and including the last day (designated "t"). The number of days in the elimination period is designated as "n" days. Consequently, $C_{t+n} - C_n$ gives the cost of disability for the period from duration n to $t + n$. Thus, the tabular monthly cost of a $10 weekly benefit for a plan with benefits beginning on the fourth day of disability and continuing during disability for a period of twenty-six weeks would be $10(.0671 − .0068), or $.603. That is, $10 is multiplied by the difference between the rate for 26 weeks, 3 days and the rate for 3 days. If the 1947–49 Basic Morbidity Table is to be used without adjustment, this figure would then be loaded for expenses and contingencies to get the standard rate for an all male group.

A review of the regular intercompany studies and experience within the company shows that no adjustment for trend is necessary. However, the 1947–49 table shows a substantially lower amount of disability during the first few days of disability than did the 1931–35 table developed in Gilbert W. Fitzhugh's earlier special study.[12] An analysis of the company's own experience or independent studies of absenteeism might show some modification of the 1947–49 table, such as that set forth below, to be desirable.

t	C_t
1 day	.0047
2 days	.0090
3 "	.0129
4 "	.0164
5 "	.0195
6 "	.0222
7 "	.0245
8 " and over	tabular figure (shown in Table 22–2) + .0096

The addition to figures for the eighth and subsequent days brings in the total additional disability for the first seven days, since C_t is cumulative from the first day. It can be noted that any plan with benefits beginning after the seventh day of disability would show the same cost under the modified table as under the basic table.

If the modified table is used, the cost for the plan previously calculated would be $10(.0767 − .0129)$, or $.638$. Adjustment in this cost is needed if the plan provides benefits beginning with the first day of disability in case of accident. According to the modified table, a first-day benefit would cost $10(.0764 − 0)$, or $.764$. Where the elimination period is not the same for disability resulting from sickness and that resulting from accident, the proportionate frequencies of both types of disabilities must be considered in the cost determination. If analysis of company experience shows that the relationship of one accident claim for each eight sickness claims developed in the special study is valid for use under the company's type of operation, the cost for a first-day accident—fourth-day sickness—twenty-six-week plan would be $\frac{1}{9}(.764) + \frac{8}{9}(.638)$, or $.652$. This figure would be the expected net claim cost.

An intracompany study would be conducted to determine the amount needed for expenses and contingencies. It might show, for instance, that a loading of $.03 per $10 of benefit plus 20 per cent of gross premium would be adequate for this purpose and produce a satisfactory rate consistent with the principles previously outlined. Then the gross premium would be

---

[12] Gilbert W. Fitzhugh, "Recent Morbidity upon Lives Insured under Group Accident and Health Policies and Premiums Based Thereon," *Transactions of the Actuarial Society of America*, Vol. XXXVIII (1937), p. 354.

(.652 + .030)/.80, or $.853. That is, the basic rate of $.652 plus $.03 equals 80 per cent of the gross premium, so dividing .682 by .80 yields .853. This rate would be subject to adjustments for the various characteristics of a group recognized in initial rating, such as female content, unusual age distributions, type of industry and size.

The same general principles of utilizing data from intercompany, special, intracompany and supplementary studies are used in calculating rates for hospital, surgical and major medical expense coverages. However, the calculation is more complex because of the greater intricacies previously described, such as trend, geographical variation, coverage detail differences and nonscheduled or blanket-type benefits. The continuation table technique can be used only with coverages which provide a dollar benefit related to a period of time such as a period of disability or a period of hospitalization. Basically, the net claim costs of other coverages are determined by multiplying the probability of claim by the average claim value.

RISK AND EXPENSE CHARACTERISTICS

There are characteristics surrounding any particular case which can result in its having a different level of claim and expense experience than another case with identical coverage components, details and levels. These characteristics can be divided broadly into those arising from (1) personal characteristics of the covered individuals in the group, (2) environment of the group, (3) secular trend, (4) statistical deviation and (5) size and administrative pattern.

Personal Characteristics

Age. The net claim costs for disability income and medical expense coverages increase with age, but the rate of increase varies by coverage. The net claim cost in the 61–65 age bracket is roughly two times that in the 26–30 age bracket for typical short-term disability income coverage, four times for long-term disability income coverage, and three times for hospital-surgical coverage. Limited statistics in connection with major medical coverages indicate that the increase in cost by age is greater than for the hospital-surgical coverage. When maternity benefits are included, they tend to level out the age differential in claim cost for the medical expense coverages on married women. Incidentally, the increase in claim cost of group health insurance by age is less steep than that of group life insurance, where the cost in the 61–65 age bracket is twenty times that in the 26–30 bracket.

Current manual rating practices use separate rates for each age or quinquennial group of ages for long-term disability income and major medical expense coverages. Recently revised manual rate structures have generally extended quinquennial age rates to hospital-surgical coverages and in some instances to other medical expense and short-term disability income coverages. In determining the rate for maternity benefits in these structures, separate quinquennial age factors, decreasing as age increases, have been used. For coverages where individual or quinquennial age rates are not used, an adjustment is usually made when an unusually large proportion of the coverage in a case is at the younger or older ages. Frequently, individual age rates are used for all coverages in connection with groups of less than twenty-five lives since the average age may fluctuate widely from case to case and from year to year within a case. The age factor is of special importance in the rating of the many group plans which now continue some or all of the medical expense coverage on individuals after they retire since, typically, the average age for such a group will increase for many years.[13] Sometimes separate rates for retired lives are set forth in the policy. Provision is being made in a few cases for pre-funding at least part of the cost of continuing medical expense coverages for retired lives through a special fund built up in the experience rating process.

Sex. Health coverages, with the exception of some minor categories such as supplemental accident and poliomyelitis expense insurance, show a higher cost for females than for males even when maternity benefits are excluded. In general, nonmaternity claim costs for short-term disability income insurance are 50 to 75 per cent higher for females than for males, with the higher percentages applying to the plans with shorter and earlier benefit periods. The claim costs for long-term disability income insurance are about 50 per cent higher for females than for males. The claim costs for nonmaternity medical expense coverage are in the general neighborhood of 35 per cent higher for females than for males, with the differential being somewhat greater in surgical coverage and less in hospital and medical coverage.

According to current manual rating practices, it is customary to add a loading to the basic male rate graded up by brackets according to the percentage of coverage on female lives for short-term disability income and some medical expense coverages. For instance, a base rate might be used when the proportion of females is less than 11 per cent, with successively higher rates applicable when the percentage is at least 11 but less than 21, at least 21 but less than 31, etc., continuing up to the last bracket when the proportion of females is at least 91 per cent. In determining the premium for a particular group, the rate for the appropriate

---

[13] A retired individual is covered as long as he lives, and the forms of turnover which tend to stabilize the average age of the active employees in the group are not present in connection with the retired lives. Also, it takes many years for the rate of retirement to level off in a young or growing organization.

bracket is applied to the coverage on both male and female lives. Major medical insurance rates are usually adjusted for the exact proportion of coverage on female lives, rather than by brackets. Recently revised manual rate structures also generally use the exact proportion of coverage on female lives for hospital-surgical coverages and in some instances for other medical expense and short-term disability income coverages. Long-term disability income insurance rates, and frequently all rates for groups of less than twenty-five lives, are determined separately for male and female lives and applied separately to the units of coverage for each.

Dependents.   Claim costs under dependent medical expense coverages will vary with the number and type of dependents. In the interests of simplicity, relatively little recognition is given to this variable in manual rates. Under the single rate approach, the rate is based upon a broad average of the number and type of dependents under all insured groups as a unit and is applied to the number of dependent units insured under the policy. Under the three-rate basis, the dependent units are categorized as to those involving a wife only, those involving a child or children only, and those involving both; and a separate rate is applied to each category. Under the two-rate basis, dependent units are broken down into those involving one dependent, either wife or child, and those involving two or more dependents.

Environment

Location.   There is a marked difference in the level and pattern of charges for health care by geographical location. This does not have as great an effect on claim costs when the coverages are written on a scheduled basis, such as in basic hospital-surgical insurance, but even then the ancillary service benefit is usually on a blanket basis.

Geographical variation is usually recognized in manual rates for hospital and major medical expense insurance. This is accomplished by establishing from seven to thirteen area classes with every city, metropolitan area or state being assigned to an area. Each area class has its own table of rates. The application of area class rating to hospital insurance is sometimes limited to that portion of the premium which is for the blanket ancillary services and sometimes applied to the entire premium to reflect the effect of geographical differences in frequency and duration of claim on the scheduled room and board benefit. If an overwhelming majority of the members of a group are in the same area class, the rate for that class is commonly used even though there may be members scattered through other area classes. Otherwise if members are in more than one area class a composite average is determined, according to the number of members in each area class. Major medical insurance rates are as much as 70 per cent higher for large cities on the West Coast than for some southern cities.

Industry. There is a variation in claim cost from industry to industry which is greater in the case of disability income coverage than in medical expense coverage. Analysis of the data in a recent intercompany study shows that the average deviation by industry, either upward or downward, from the average experience of all industries combined was 9.0 per cent for short-term disability income insurance and 5.7 per cent for hospital expense insurance. The opportunity to offset these deviations by combining coverages can be illustrated by noting from the intercompany study data that out of thirty-eight industry classes in which there was sufficient exposure to attach significance to the results in all of the four fields of life, accidental death and dismemberment, short-term disability income and hospital-surgical expense insurance, only twelve showed experience for all four either better or worse than the average. The other twenty-six classes showed experience better than average in one or more fields of coverage and worse than average in the others. Obviously, the combination of a coverage showing better than average experience with one showing worse than average experience tends to bring the aggregate experience closer to the average.

Manual rates for group health coverages are set at a level sufficient to cover the experience of industries which are not far above average, so that relatively few industries require an initial loading. With the reduction of dust, heat and other similar hazards through mechanization and plant improvement, and with the marked decline in the number of substandard wage scales, the number of industries requiring loading has become fewer and fewer.[14]

Income and Other Factors. The use of—and charges for—health care service tend to increase with income level, and major medical expense statistics show claim costs substantially above the average for persons with large incomes. Rating procedures for this coverage generally include a charge about two and one-half times as great for individuals with annual incomes over $25,000 as for those with incomes under $5,000. Conversely, there is evidence that the claim cost for short-term disability income coverage is greater for the lower paid than for the higher paid individual. However, this latter differential has not been of sufficient magnitude to be considered in initial rate structures other than as it may be inherent in an industry loading for an industry with a substandard wage scale.

Other intrinsic forces affecting the underlying level of morbidity of a particular case include such things as the extent of enrollment among those eligible for coverage, the extent of claim cost control activity of the employer and his employees, working conditions and employment stand-

---

[14] Examples of industries that still may require a loading of rates for nonoccupational health coverages include foundries, refractories, railroads, stone yards, furriers, tanneries, distilleries and breweries.

ards. The effect of these characteristics is, as a rule, reflected in experience rating rather than in manual rates, although it may be considered by the underwriter in determining whether a case qualifies initially for manual rates.

Secular Trend

The secular trend of claim costs is another important factor in rating. The cost of short-term disability income coverage seems to run in cycles, more or less paralleling economic conditions in a fairly constant long-term manner. As a result, changes in manual rate levels for this coverage have been infrequent. On the other hand, the cost of hospital-surgical expense coverage has shown a continual increase. The fact that approximately two thirds of the benefits in the hospital-surgical coverages are scheduled rather than blanket has dampened the effect of the increasing cost of health care on claim costs. However, it has been necessary to include a trend factor in establishing manual rates for hospital and major medical expense insurance and to revise the rates upward about once in every two years.

Statistical Deviation and Credibility

Another important risk characteristic is the frequency of claims. In a large number of typical groups, about 250 hospital expense claims and about the same number of short-term disability income claims for first-day accident and fourth-day sickness benefits can be expected for each 2,000 male life years of exposure. This compares with about one accidental death and dismemberment claim and ten to fifteen life claims, depending upon age composition. Since credibility is mathematically related to number of claims, considerably greater credibility can be given in experience rating for the same number of life years of exposure in connection with group health coverages than with group life coverages. The application of statistical methods for measuring variation shows that at the 100-life exposure level the probable deviation for health coverages is about 25 per cent of the probability of claim. In other words, it is equally likely that a single 100-life case in a single year will have actual claims within the 75 to 100 per cent range or the 100 to 125 per cent range of the expected claims. At the 1,000-life exposure level the probable deviation is about 7 per cent of the probability of claims, and at the 10,000-life exposure level it is about 2 per cent.

Size and Administrative Pattern

While certain characteristics result in a variation in claim costs from case to case, others result in variation in expenses incurred. These include such things as size of case, coverage components included and administrative patterns.

The expense level becomes relatively lower as the size of the case increases. Some expenses do not vary proportionately with the size of the group; claim settlement and billing procedures can be handled more efficiently in volume, and commission scales are graded downward as the premium increases.[15] Likewise, the introduction of additional coverages into the policy, whether they are health insurance coverages or not, does not increase the expense level proportionately. For instance, it costs comparatively little more to enroll a case, maintain enrollment records and prepare bills if life insurance and surgical insurance are included in a package along with hospital insurance than if the hospital insurance is written alone.

The costs of enrollment and maintenance of a case are lower under noncontributory plans than contributory ones since no individual solicitation or late enrollment procedures are involved. Cases which utilize the self-accounting procedure, whereby the employer maintains the records of the covered individuals, or the employer-draft method of claim settlement, or both, involve lower expenses to the insurer than those that do not, since they transfer functions from the insurer to the policyholder. The expenses of handling a multiple employer or association case are higher than for one covering the employees of a single employer because of the more complex enrollment, accounting, administrative and claim settlement procedures involved.

Premiums are normally payable monthly under group policies, but occasionally they are paid less frequently. Expense savings resulting from less frequent billings are offset by the cost of making later adjustment for new and terminating employees. Annual, semiannual or quarterly premium rates are usually the equivalent of monthly rates except for the interest factor.

As mentioned earlier, a volume discount in manual rates recognizes the effect of size on expense levels. It may also recognize the effect on expense levels of such factors as the type of accounting, claims administration or contributory status. Other than this, variations in expense from case to case are usually reflected in experience rating.

EXPERIENCE RATING

Experience rating is the means by which variations in claim and expense levels not taken into account in manual rates are incorporated into the cost of insurance to the policyholder. Experience rating takes two forms. Applied retrospectively, it produces dividends in mutual companies or premium refunds in stock companies for cases with experience that is better than that anticipated in the rates, and, in instances where the policy permits a retroactive upward adjustment of premium at the end of

---

[15] Compensation systems used in marketing group insurance are described in Chapter 27.

the policy year,[16] it calls for additional premiums when experience is worse than anticipated. Applied prospectively, experience rating results in adjustments of renewal premiums for cases with either better or worse than average experience. The prospective approach is made possible by the fact that most group health insurance is written on the yearly renewable term basis with rates guaranteed for a year at a time.[17] A prospective rate adjustment is usually delayed until there has been sufficient exposure to attach statistical reliability to the experience, that is, to assume it reflects the true risk characteristics of the case instead of random fluctuation. Thus, all other things being equal, a renewal rate adjustment will be made earlier on a large case than on a small one.

A prospective rate adjustment, since it is designed to reflect the basic long-term risk characteristics of the case, is usually set at a level which is expected to permit continuing dividends or premium refunds of a reasonable magnitude. While the formula for determining dividends or premium refunds is completely objective, that for determining prospective renewal rate adjustments generally has leeway for the underwriter's judgment in anticipating future claim levels based upon past experience and current status of the case.

Experience rating goes far in reconciling the sometimes conflicting principles of equity, simplicity and competitiveness. The multiplicity of manual rates is reduced by ignoring many of the variations in risk characteristics which do not have a major effect on claim costs and recognizing them in an equitable experience rating formula. Similarly, minor variations in coverage details to meet a policyholder's need in personnel relations can be made without change in manual rates. The substantial credibility given to case experience in experience rating a large case reduces the likelihood that a policyholder with better than average experience will transfer to another insurer or to an uninsured plan.

Experience rating of group health insurance is similar in principle to that of group life insurance. Basically, a dividend or premium refund is determined for a policy by subtracting from its premium the charges for claims, expenses and risk margin. Interest on claim and special contingency reserves may be credited directly in the formula or may be used as an offset to produce lower expense or risk charges. Experience rating charges may include factors to level out year-to-year fluctuations in experience on the case. For instance, if there is a deficiency in a particular year,

---

[16] This provision is included in only a small proportion of group health insurance policies. Where it has been included some supervisory authorities have required assurance that its use will be equitable and nondiscriminatory and that it is not a substitute for an adequate initial rate structure.

[17] A few group insurers guarantee rates for as long as three years for groups of a specified size class, such as those with 25 to 100 members. The rates for this class of business recognize the effect of expected trends during the guarantee period and defer experience rating until the end of such period.

when premiums are measured against total charges, this deficiency may be charged in whole or in part, either with or without interest, against the experience of subsequent years. The method of carrying forward a deficit, the portion carried forward and the period of time over which it is spread vary from company to company. Some experience rating formulas recognize the possibility of adverse fluctuation in advance by including a charge to create a claim stabilization reserve under the policy against which any future deficits are charged. In such a case, the formula usually makes provision for crediting interest on the stabilization reserve in the calculation of the dividend or premium refund.

Claim Charges and Credibility

In determining claim charges to be made in experience rating a case, the concept of credibility based on the theories of statistical reliability is utilized. Under this concept, the larger cases are given practically complete credibility, and their claim charges represent the claims incurred under the policy. The smallest cases are given little or no credibility, and their claim charges represent their share of the pooled experience of the class of business of which they are a part. Partial credibility is given to cases whose size is between that qualifying for full credibility and no credibility by using a weighted average of case and class experience. The relative weights assigned to each depend upon where a case falls on the credibility scale. Where credibility is given to individual case experience, a maximum may be set on the claim charge at a level designed to exclude from the charge nonrecurring catastrophic losses, which then would be spread over all cases through the charge for risk margin.

Some credibility factors use number of lives, and others the amount of premium, to measure the volume of exposure. An example of the latter type of formula would be one which assigned no credibility if the annual premium under the case for the coverage involved were less than $5,000 and full credibility if it were at least $10,000. Such a formula might read:

1. If the earned premium for the policy year is less than $5,000, the credibility factor shall be 0;
2. If such premium is at least $5,000 but less than $10,000, the credibility factor shall be determined by dividing the excess of such premium over $5,000 by $5,000; or
3. If such premium is at least $10,000, the credibility factor shall be 1.

Thus, if the coverage involved produced an annual premium of $6,500 the credibility factor would be .3 [i.e., $(6,500 - 5,000)/5,000$], and the claim charge would be based 30 per cent on case experience and 70 per cent on class experience.

A formula of the first-mentioned type might give no credibility if less than 100 lives were covered, graded up in the same general way to full credibility if 500 lives were covered. Usually minor components of medical expense coverages are combined with the major component in determining credibility and claims charges.

Credibility factors differ by coverages. Since group health insurance coverages other than long-term disability income involve a higher frequency of claim and lower average claim than group life and accidental death and dismemberment insurance, they have smaller indices of relative chance variation and, hence, require less exposure for full credibility. The establishment of credibility factors involves practical considerations, such as the need to meet the competition of other insuring organizations and uninsured plans, as well as statistical theory. In general, full credibility is given in retrospective experience rating at a lower volume of exposure than a mathematical calculation would indicate.[18] A typical formula might require about one third as much exposure for full credibility to short-term disability income or hospital coverage as for life insurance. On the other hand, long-term disability income coverage with its high claim value and low claim frequency generally involves more pooling of experience, that is, less credibility, than life coverage. In fact, some rate structures for long-term disability income coverage anticipate little or no experience rating.

The same general relationship is used in attaching significance to individual case experience for prospective renewal rate adjustments as for dividend or rate refunds, but usually with considerably more exposure required.[19] It should be noted that the normal operation of the prospective experience rating procedure has been obscured in the case of medical expense coverages by the secular trend in claim costs. Normally, prospective experience rating would produce both upward and downward adjustments in renewal rates. However, because of the rising cost of medical care, most adjustments for medical expense coverages have been upward.

Expense Charges

Expense charges used in calculating dividends or premium refunds are usually determined from a formula developed by cost accounting techniques. Charges for commissions are often expressed as a percentage of the premium, decreasing as the premium increases, parallel to the commission scale used. Charges for premium taxes are commonly expressed as a percentage of premium or a percentage of premium less dividend. Some companies apportion premium taxes among groups depending upon the

---

[18] While the volume of exposure required for full credibility would typically be much nearer to that shown in the previously cited example, some experience rating formulas may even give full credibility to all groups with at least twenty-five lives.

[19] Some insurers may give more credence to individual case experience for prospective rate adjustments than for dividends and hold dividends constant by class.

distribution of covered individuals in the various states, while others use a nation-wide average charge.

Charges for expenses of running the group insurance operation and related overhead are usually divided functionally into a flat charge per policy, a charge per life insured, a charge per transaction and a charge computed as a percentage of premium. The per policy and per life charges may be graded by the number and type of coverages provided under the policy. The percentage of premium charges may be established partially on a flat scale and partially on a decremental scale, with the percentage decreasing as the amount of premium increases. The cost of handling claims is sometimes expressed as a charge per transaction or as a percentage of incurred claims. Any of the forms of charges may be subdivided, with some being set at a lower level for cases with less expensive administrative patterns such as self-accounting or employer draft claim settlement. Frequently the excess of first-year expenses over renewal-year expenses is amortized over the early policy years.

Risk Margin

The charge for risk margin is designed to provide a contribution to the company surplus as a protection against future contingencies, to reimburse the company for its risk taking function and to offset losses on cases with unfavorable experience. As a result largely of the sharp upward trend in the cost of medical care and strong competitive pressures, the margin has been very small in recent years. The aggregate operating gain in all group health insurance over the last five years has been well under 1 per cent of net premium income.

Theoretically, the risk charge should be proportionate to the risk undertaken by the insurer and, hence, should be concerned with the relation between rate levels and expected claims, underwriting policy, volume of exposure, coverage combinations and the extent to which individual case losses are subsequently charged to the case. One pattern of risk charges would express the charge as a percentage of premium, or premium less dividend, decreasing as the cumulative life years of exposure under the policy increased. Thus, the risk charge percentage would decrease as either the size or duration increased. There is considerable justification for having the slope of the charges parallel that of the statistical standard deviation of the expected claims. Under this approach a case whose experience is largely pooled, with little or no credibility given to individual case experience, would carry a risk charge related largely to the size of the pool rather than of the case.

The frequently used pattern of risk charges decreasing by duration recognizes the effect on earnings of prior contributions by the case to the insurer's contingency reserve or surplus account and the greater degree of accuracy with which the risk can be evaluated for renewal rating. Alternatively, a risk charge that does not decrease by duration is justified by some people on the ground that risk does not change materially from year to year.

A schedule of risk charges might include a lower charge for cases having an expectation of greater loss stability as a result of combining more than one type of coverage in a single policy or cases that have evidenced a continuing satisfactory margin between premiums and claims. In this case, it would be logical to have a higher than average level of charges for cases under which a wide fluctuation in experience is expected.

There is a wide variety of credibility factors and expense and risk charges, and it is probable that in no two companies are they exactly alike. However, they follow the same general principles and produce results which stand up in a competitive market.

Frequently retention, either year by year or averaged over a period of years, is used as a measure of comparative performance between insurers by both the buyers and sellers of group insurance. While there is no standard definition of the word "retention" in this context, it is generally considered to be the excess of premium over claim payments and dividends under a particular contract. Since retention is influenced by such things as the quality and quantity of service rendered by the insurer and the insurer's practices in holding reserves and amortizing initial expenses and prior losses, its use as a measure of comparative performance is justified only if differences in these items are taken into account. Retention is not a valid measure of the cost of insurance to the buyer since it ignores claims. For instance, a sound claim cost control program might require an increase in retention which would be much smaller than the amount by which it would reduce claim payments. That is, a higher retention may result in a lower over-all cost of insurance.

SELECTED REFERENCES

Burton, Burton E., and Pettengill, Daniel W. "Development of Expected Claim Costs for Comprehensive Medical Expense Benefits and Ratios of 1959 and 1960 Actual Experience Thereto," *Transactions of the Society of Actuaries*, Vol. XV (1963), pp. 10–48.

Cueto, Manuel R. "Monetary Values for Ordinary Disability Benefits, Based on Period 2 of the 1952 Inter-Company Study of the Society's Committee with 2½% Interest," *Transactions of the Society of Actuaries*, Vol. VI (1954), pp. 108–77.

"Experience under Certain Ordinary Disability Benefits between the 1930 and 1950 Anniversaries," *Transactions of the Society of Actuaries, 1952 Reports*, pp. 70–180.

"Experience under Individual Loss-of-Time Policies, 1955–59," *Transactions of the Society of Actuaries, 1961 Reports*, pp. 101–25.

FITZHUGH, GILBERT W. "Recent Morbidity upon Lives Insured under Group Accident and Health Policies and Premiums Based Thereon," *Transactions of the Actuarial Society of America*, Vol. XXXVIII (1937), pp. 354–83.

GINGERY, STANLEY W. "A Reinvestigation of Group Hospital Expense Insurance Experience," *Transactions of the Society of Actuaries*, Vol. XII (1960), pp. 564–687.

——. "Special Investigation of Group Hospital Expense Insurance Experience," *Transactions of the Society of Actuaries*, Vol. IV (1952), pp. 44–112.

——, AND MELLMAN, RICHARD J. "An Investigation of Group Major Medical Expense Insurance Experience," *Transactions of the Society of Actuaries*, Vol. XIII (1961), pp. 513–75.

GREEN, EDWARD A. "Initial and Experience Rating of Combined Coverage Group Policies," *Transactions of the XVIth International Congress of Actuaries*, Vol. I, p. 112.

——. "Group Surgical Claims Study," *Transactions of the Actuarial Society of America*, Vol. XLIX (1948), pp. 142–202.

JACKSON, PAUL H. "Experience Rating," *Transactions of the Society of Actuaries*, Vol. V. (1953), pp. 239–55.

LARSON, ROBERT E. "A Method of Calculating Group Term Dividends," *Transactions of the Society of Actuaries*, Vol. IV (1952), pp. 308–16.

MILLER, MORTON D. "Group Weekly Indemnity Continuation Table Study," *Transactions of the Society of Actuaries*, Vol. III (1951), pp. 31–67.

——. "1957 Study of Group Surgical Expense Insurance Claims," *Transactions of the Society of Actuaries*, Vol. X (1958), pp. 359–487.

PIKE, BERTRAM N. "Gain and Loss Analysis and Related Concepts for Group Insurance, *Transactions of the Society of Actuaries*, Vol. XIII (1961), pp. 412–24.

THALER, ALAN M. "Group Major-Medical Expense Insurance," *Transactions of the Society of Actuaries*, Vol. III (1951), pp. 429–66.

Chapter 23

COST CONTROL THROUGH COOPERATION WITH PURVEYORS OF MEDICAL CARE

BY L. M. BRANSON

THE NEED FOR COST CONTROL

Disability and its cost to individuals and society are not a new problem. Such has been a complexing part of life since the earliest record of humanity. Yet, social and medical progress, particularly in the last half century, have brought this problem into such clear focus that today those who hope to contribute to the betterment of mankind are exploring all methods of eliminating disability and controlling its cost. Group health insurers have a substantial duty in this developmental pattern.

Nature and Extent of the Health Risk

W. Scott Allan has indicated that chronic disease is a major cause of disability. It is estimated that about 88 per cent of all disabilities fall into this category. Principal causes are mental and emotional disorders, diseases of the heart, and circulatory, arthritic or rheumatic disease.[1]

According to the Health Insurance Institute, chronic illness and bodily impairments affect four out of every ten Americans. In the recent United States National Health Survey, 81.5 million persons in the United States were found to have one or more chronic conditions, including asthma, diabetes, blood pressure difficulties, ulcers, and others. Also included are impairments such as hearing defects, paralysis, birth defects and similar problems. The National Health Survey Study, which covered the period from July, 1962, to June, 1963, indicated that of the 81.5 million persons, 58.8 million, or over 72 per cent, were able to carry on their major activity.

---

[1] W. Scott Allan, "The Need for Rehabilitation in Industry," an address presented to the annual conference of the American Physical Therapy Association, Pittsburgh, June, 1960. Published in the *Physical Therapy Review,* Vol. XXXX, No. 11 (November, 1960), p. 810.

However, the remaining 22.7 million persons were unable to carry on normal activity.[2]

Disability to the individual is a personal, economic and emotional event. As disabilities multiply, they become a social problem, and for the community such a problem can develop into a significant and practical economic situation involving doctors, hospitals and other parties, as well as the disabled individuals.

Today's costs of disability are a substantial liability on the balance sheet of the gross annual product (even though these same costs result in income and assets for the purveyors of medical care). As far back as 1960, the cost of disabilities was estimated to exceed $70 billion.[3] With expansion of our economy and increased cost of medical care, this figure mounts yearly. Statistics compiled by the Health Insurance Institute indicate that in 1963 the American public spent $23.7 billion for medical care, an increase of $8.2 billion over similar expenditures in 1957.[4] Much of this amount was spent for essential medical care, most of which is insurable, but some was spent for nonprescribed eyeglasses, minor drugs, band-aids and similar items. Also included in the total figure are charges for luxury services and facilities which depend on the individual desires of the patient (and the collective desires of our affluent society). Luxury services usually are not essential, and they tend to increase greatly the cost of illness. As such they, and the minor items of the types mentioned, generally are not insurable.

It is worthy of note, however, that the dollars that change hands between the purveyors of medical care and the patient are probably not the major part of the economic problem occasioned by the health risk. The loss of income due to disability is undoubtedly even larger than the extra expenses incurred by those who are attempting to regain normal health. For example, over 83 million days of work are lost each year from injuries to workers.[5] Then, too, one should also add the loss of productive days from work which results from illness. Finally, the over-all figure can also be increased by the productive days lost by dependents of many disabled members of the labor force. The magnitude of the aggregate loss resulting from disabilities is reflected further in studies of the Health Insurance Institute, which estimates that, in 1963, 260.4 million workdays were lost because of all types of disability.[6]

The economic and social losses arising from disabilities exceed the

---

[2] Health Insurance Institute, *Health Insurance News* (October, 1964), p. 1.

[3] Allan, *op. cit.*, p. 811.

[4] Health Insurance Institute, *Health Insurance Data* (New York, 1964), p. 7.

[5] U.S. Department of Health, Education and Welfare, Public Health Service, *Health Statistics from the United States National Health Survey* (Publication No. 584-B 40) (Washington, D.C., February, 1963), p. 3.

[6] *Health Insurance Data*, 1964, p. 69.

losses to individuals and families. The cost of producing a product, for instance, is influenced by the presence or absence of the person who has a hand in the production. If he is not at work, the cost to the employer may be much more than is reflected in the cost of a workmen's compensation or group disability income insurance premium. The disabled person generally will have produced more than his own wage cost for each day he was at work. His efforts will have contributed to a productivity that will cover overhead costs that are constant, and it is this type of loss that is difficult to measure.

Insurance Benefits Arising from Disabilities

Health insurance pays a substantial part of these losses. In 1963, $21.3 million was paid each day in health insurance benefits, or a yearly total of $7.8 billion, by all insuring organizations according to the Health Insurance Institute.[7] In addition, more than $800 million is paid annually in workmen's compensation benefits as a result of injury and disease that arise out of and in the course of employment.

The National Safety Council has stated that in 1963 there were 2 million disabling injuries from work accidents, 1.6 million disabling injuries from motor vehicle accidents (included in this figure are 100,000 work accidents), 4.4 million disabling injuries from home accidents and 2.2 million disabling injuries from general public accidents.[8]

With the prevalence today of general liability insurance, automobile liability insurance and medical payments coverage connected with both of these coverages, it is not difficult to envision the substantial payment in addition to health insurance and workmen's compensation benefits that is made by property and liability insurance companies because of disabilities. And when the payments made to the purveyors of medical care for terminal illness from the proceeds of life insurance are also considered, the magnitude of insurance payments for disability grows even greater.

Thus, it may be seen that insuring organizations have a stake—along with individuals, families, purveyors of care and society—in the economic losses occasioned by disabilities. In fact, the extent of these losses affects both insurance premiums and the reputation of the insurance industry. Some observers even feel that part, or all, of the role of private insuring organizations in this field should be taken over by governmental agencies. It is little wonder, then, that responsible individuals in the insurance business are highly concerned with cost control concepts and activities.

PURPOSE OF INSURANCE IN COST CONTROL

The primary function of insurance is to protect the insured from financial loss. This is not to say that insurance will necessarily prevent all

---

[7] Health Insurance Institute, *Health Insurance News* (January, 1964), p. 1.

[8] National Safety Council, *Accident Facts* (Chicago, 1964 ed.), p. 3.

risks, such as disabilities, from occurring, but rather that it will prevent or reduce the economic losses that result from such risks. The end product of insurance, i.e., protection, arises from public need and demand. Insurance did not create either the need or the demand.[9] Each person hopes to preserve his life, health and property, and through insurance each helps the other in reaching this goal.

Protection against financial loss due to disability has several facets. First, it concerns the prevention of sicknesses and accidents where possible. Secondly, it involves the minimization of lost wages and the control of medical expense costs which cannot be prevented. The third element is the maintenance of financial strength through risk spread and sound management to pay for losses that occur in spite of prevention and reduction activities. Conservation of the loss dollar, i.e., the optimum use of prevention and protection dollars, is intertwined in all three aspects. This broad concept of protection has been the heart of the insurance business in the United States since the time that Benjamin Franklin combined fire fighting with fire insurance. In the modern society the prevention concept has a natural application to the risk of disability, and members of society are coming more and more to recognize the existence of a mutual financial interest in each other's health and in the costs of ill health.

The costs of medical care are increasing annually, as is well documented not only by national statistics but also by those who have been unfortunate enough to suffer disabilities. Much of the increase in cost is the result of progress in medical techniques, skills, equipment and additional professionally trained people to use them successfully. The insurer, the public and the purveyors of medical care must not be so overwhelmed by this obvious progress that common sense is lost in evaluating charges that result. As expensive equipment is being purchased for the treatment of unusual and difficult to treat—but infrequent—disabilities, patients, the public, purveyors and payers of medical care should all be heard in the determination of how heavy a capital outlay should be made. This is desirable because the cost eventually is paid by members of the community. The American Medical Association agrees with others when its House of Delegates states, "It should be remembered that insurance does not create any new wealth. It merely assists in conservation."[10] Insurance is a pooling of existing funds. Each individual insured under a group contract contributes his share, or his employer pays part or all of the share in his behalf, for his coverage and for that of his dependents.

---

[9] S. Bruce Black, "Control of Loss in Accident and Health Insurance," an address presented at the annual meeting of the Health Insurance Association of America, Dallas, Texas, May 17, 1960.

[10] American Medical Association, *Voluntary Prepayment Medical Benefits Plans* (Chicago, 1963), p. 27.

When money is pooled, such as in the insurance arrangement, to pay the cost of medical care, the phrase "third party" comes into the economics of financing medical care. Since prepayment and insurance have been involved in the financing to an increasing degree in the last twenty-five years, early antagonism against third parties is being forgotten, although formerly they were looked upon by many observers as unnecessary intruders in the field of medical care. The relative future importance of various types of third parties will be determined by the purchasers of health insurance and the subscribers of other prepayment plans. In this regard, insuring organizations have a duty to others to spend money wisely, indeed, to spend it as though it were their own. It is natural, therefore, that cost control is a vital consideration for third parties.

The question has been asked whether or not cost control in group health insurance may involve lay interference in the practice of medicine. Many individuals feel it does not.[11] Rather, it concerns cooperation with physicians and hospitals who provide care for disabilities. The long-honored relationship between the physician and the patient or the relationship between the hospital and the patient is in no sense abrogated. To control cost resulting from disability is only to determine a reasonable charge for the work that was done and the time that was spent in doing it. There are, of course, many detailed and minute differences between physicians or hospitals and insuring organizations. Their basic function, however, is the same, namely to serve the people. As was stated at the 1960 Health Insurance Council annual meeting, service includes protection from loss as well as the care provided to alleviate and end disability which causes loss.[12]

ORIGIN OF COST PROBLEMS

Blue Cross, and later hospital insurance written by life and casualty insurance companies, removed the financial barrier to needed medical care for many individuals. At the same time, the increased sophistication in the practice of medicine tended to concentrate a great deal of medical treatment in the hospitals. The physician was not a bulwark of defense against over-use of hospital facilities. Few observers at that time foresaw the long-run effect of this change on the cost of medical care.

The growing problem of patients being hospitalized in order to make their prepayment coverage effective increased the cost. This pattern has been difficult to erase in spite of the fact that hospital out-patient coverage, medical coverage and diagnostic X-ray and laboratory coverage have been added to the basic insurance portfolio. Major medical coverage also should have obviated the thinking that the patient has to be hospitalized

---

[11] Black, *op. cit.*

[12] Health Insurance Council Annual Meeting, Hospital Relations Panel Discussion (Chicago, 1960).

to be covered. These developments in coverage, however, have not been well understood by either physicians or the public, and this understanding is necessary if health insurance is to fulfill properly its purpose. Obviously, cooperation between physicians and insurers is necessary to bring about understanding. Each must be aware of and comprehend the other's problems and philosophy.

Numerous examples also demonstrate the insurer's lack of understanding of the physician's problems. On the other hand, the physician's difficulty in clearly understanding the economics of financing medical care as it relates to an individual patient is magnified by his interest in the welfare of that patient and his family. The following statement by a physician reflects the over-all problem facing both insurers and insureds: "These same studies and fulguration of polyps could have been done with this patient as an out-patient. Instead of this the insurance required that the man be hospitalized to get his benefits."

The explosive growth of group health insurance was accompanied by a heavy emphasis on retentions with too little emphasis on the cost saving available through the use of good preventive and curative medicine.[13] With the rise in the cost of medical care, the amount of the premium dollar that goes for retentions is in reality insignificant when compared to the amount that is paid in losses. Authorities in many fields, employers and the public at large are becoming progressively more aware of the need to control the extent and cost of disability.[14] It is becoming apparent that dollars spent to control the extent and cost of disability are generally more than offset by the resulting reduction of losses.

Very few of those currently covered by group health insurance pay the entire cost of health care protection. A survey conducted by the Health Insurance Institute in 1963 indicated that only 1.2 per cent of the employees paid the entire cost, while 45.6 per cent had the full cost of protection paid by the employer. This latter percentage may be contrasted to 41.2 per cent found in 1962 in a similar survey.[15] Since the frequency of full payment by the employer is increasing, the control of loss becomes progressively more important to the employer as a cost of production. Thus, employers need to be shown that the retention is really less significant in the over-all cost of group health insurance than is commonly thought.

Average hospital costs have increased from $9.39 per patient day in 1946 to $38.91 per patient day in 1963, and there are strong indications that this rise will continue. The average length of stay, however, has decreased from 9.1 days in 1946 to 7.7 days in 1963.[16]

---

[13] Black, *op. cit.*
[14] Allan, *op. cit.*, p. 11.
[15] Health Insurance Institute, *Health Insurance News* (February, 1964), p. 1.
[16] *Health Insurance Data,* 1964, p. 67.

Patient care, however, has been improving over this period. In one very progressive and well-run hospital which now has a successful specialized "intensive care unit," the cost is more than $120 per day. Officials of this hospital believe that lives have been saved as a result of this type of care. An "intensive care unit" is designed to care for critically and seriously ill patients requiring highly skilled nursing care and close and frequent, if not constant, nursing observation. Such patients include, for example, major surgical cases following release from the recovery room, multiple injury or burn cases, and patients suffering from gastrointestinal hemorrhage, acute coronary occlusion, acute pneumonia, acute thrombophlebitis with danger of pulmonary embolus and critically ill traumatic patients. Patients receiving such care are assigned to intensive care based on nursing needs and not necessarily on the diagnosis. Patients requiring continuous gastric, intestinal or pulmonary drainage, and those requiring frequent recording of vital signs and intake and output of fluids are also intensive care candidates. Therefore, highly trained nurses and special equipment are required to be used in such a unit.[17]

As was suggested earlier, the public payment for medical expenses has increased markedly; in fact, the payment more than doubled between 1953 and 1963. During this same period, the percentage of the American public's disposable income devoted to medical care increased from 4.4 to 5.9 per cent.[18] And this is a warning of the problems ahead in cost control.

Much has been written concerning the increase of medical expenditure as compared to the other personal expenditures, but this is a questionable comparison. Some problems associated with hospital costs have been presented succinctly by Ray E. Brown, who has related some basic reasons and motivations for wanting or demanding care for illness that may not be necessary.[19] Mr. Brown points out, for example, the emotional family reasons for urging that a patient be hospitalized, particularly the fact that the family may have a feeling of guilt if the ill person is not furnished with the ultimate in medical care. Since medical care is prepaid at the time it is furnished, there is only a small outlay of personal dollars when illness occurs. This is a problem for the physician who not only has to determine the clinical situation, but also has to deal with the family emotional makeup as it may relate to the cost of medical care. The physician needs help from those who finance medical care costs in this complex situation. Thus, it may be seen that personal expenditures other

[17] U.S. Department of Health, Education and Welfare, Public Health Service, *Elements of Progressive Patient Care* (Publication No. 930-C-1) (Washington, D.C., September, 1962).

[18] *Health Insurance Data*, 1964, p. 60.

[19] Ray E. Brown, "To the Public a Hospital Is a Hospital," the Wilinsky Lecture delivered at the Harvard School of Public Health, Boston, April 16, 1963, published in the *New England Journal of Medicine*, Vol. CCLXIX, No. 12 (September 19, 1963), p. 610.

than for medical care are not influenced by the types of pressures which accompany prepayment.

COOPERATION AS A SOLUTION

Misunderstandings are often the result of semantics, and an increase in the face-to-face spoken word will help the purveyors and the payers understand each other. Only by free exchange of information can the philosophical chasm be bridged. Each party today is dependent upon the other. The service provided by physicians is unique in that it preserves health, reduces disability and saves lives. Yet, the best of medical care is of no value if no one can afford to pay for it and, therefore, does not seek it. Medical care is bought more frequently as the ease of payment increases, and group health insurance contributes to this ease of payment. This is not to say that medical care is never sought in the absence of ability to pay.

Providing health care involves the humanities, the sciences and economics. The physician is dominant in connection with the first two. The insurer has become dominant in the latter. The patient should have the care that the physician determines that he needs. He should not necessarily have the care that he wants, particularly if he is not directly paying all of the associated expenses. In this regard, there is significant evidence that the physician, the hospital and the insurer are learning to cooperate in solving the problems relating to furnishing and financing medical care.

Cooperation of the Medical Profession

Meetings of certain councils of the American Medical Association have emphasized that a medical evolution is taking place. The profession of medicine is learning that it, by itself, cannot continue to meet the challenge of informing the public about vital aspects of medical care and medical care financing. Other segments of our economy have realized the same fact. All have found that each party has to work with the other to bring about the conquest of disability and at the same time maintain our private enterprise system.[20]

The American Medical Association, through its Committee on Insurance and Prepayment Plans of the Council on Medical Services, adopted as far back as 1958 the following statement regarding the problem of financing medical care. The statement was reiterated in its 1963 publication:

1. The individual physician should advise hospitalization only when definitely indicated for the best care of the patient's condition and should

---

[20] This philosophy was developed in a symposium sponsored by Liberty Mutual Insurance Company with participation by medicine, business, law, labor, education, government and insurers on "The Growing Challenge of Disability Control in an Era of Comprehensive Medical Care," Boston, October 15, 1959.

return each patient to his home environment as soon as efficient professional care permits.

Many hospital staffs have found that an Admission Review Committee has assisted materially in assuring a more efficient utilization of hospital facilities.

2. The subscriber should expect hospitalization only when warranted, thereby avoiding the inevitable rise in premium rates resulting from excessive utilization.

3. The insurance company or prepayment plan should clearly delineate, in the policy, the risks assumed. In the selling of these policies the subscriber should receive a complete explanation of the nature and extent of the coverage provided.

Prepayment plans, insurance companies, and, in the case of group plans, management and union officials should improve educational procedures to inform subscribers of the advantages of health insurance and dangers of increased cost by unnecessary utilization.

Efforts should be made to revise coverage so that hospitalization is not the sole requisite for obtaining some types of benefits.

4. The hospital administrators should accelerate their studies and seek to improve management practices designed to stabilize hospital costs.

The key to an ever-increasing number of Americans protected by voluntary health insurance and to continued improvement in this protection is efficient utilization consistent with good health care. To accomplish this we must all "use" not "abuse" our insurance and prepayment plan contracts.[21]

At least one publication of the medical profession has suggested that medical abuses differ in severity, and there seems to be general agreement on this conclusion.[22] Medical people themselves disagree on the extent of abuses, but they concur that existing abuses should be eliminated by the means available to physicians in policing themselves by their own committees set up for that purpose. A later issue of the same publication stressed the point that insurance and Blue Cross arrangements do not produce a great group of rich people, i.e., physicians, hospital personnel, etc., merged in the health insurance pool.[23] It is commonly recognized, moreover, that submission to patient pressures is not in the best interest of the doctor, the hospital or the patient in the long run, and it is certainly not in the best interest of the American public.

Physicians have been more cooperative recently in the formation of committees to review the amount of charges for surgical service or other types of medical care. These committees will be discussed in some detail later in this chapter.

In another effort a number of medical organizations have adopted relative value studies as a guide to identifying proper fee relativities for medical or surgical services. Relative value refers to the unit value as-

---

[21] American Medical Association, *op. cit.*, p. 28.

[22] Editorial, *New York State Journal of Medicine,* January 15, 1964, p. 210.

[23] Editorial, *New York State Journal of Medicine,* February 1, 1964, p. 356.

signed to a particular procedure. Such unit value can be compared to a unit value for some other procedure. When a conversion factor is used, the unit value becomes a dollar value or fee. For example, if an appendectomy is assigned a unit value of 35 in such a study, and the physician's conversion factor is 5, his fee would be $175. If in the same relative value study a hysterectomy was assigned a unit value of 50, with the same conversion factor of 5 the fee would be $250. Relative value studies have tended to bring about uniform nomenclature for procedures and a standardized coding system, among other advantages. This effort has been of substantial help to insurers and to physicians in determining the range within which a "reasonable charge" should fall and in relating the charge for various procedures. According to the Health Insurance Council, twenty medical societies and eight society groups have adopted such studies.[24]

In addition to the aforementioned cost control factors, medical publications in various areas of the country have announced ranges for fees that seem to be "reasonable and customary" in the community. Moreover, when addressing medical groups many authoritative physicians have asked for the cooperation of the medical profession in helping solve the cost problem as it relates to utilization.

Many physicians are well aware that their attitude and influence can have a pronounced effect on the cost problems that exist. Unfortunately (or perhaps fortunately because the number is so small), a few physicians do not have such an awareness. It must be admitted that a few insurers also are not in tune with the effort to solve peaceably the cost problem between the purveyors and those that pay the bill. It seems, however, that a point of understanding is being reached, generally, which will encourage a closer relationship between medical care expenditures and an appropriate level of medical service.

Hospital Cooperation

Tissue and Audit Committees. Hospitals in many areas are becoming aware of a continuing need to evaluate the need for various health care services performed within the hospital. Thus, as part of hospital accreditation, or otherwise, Tissue Committees have been created to determine whether surgery that has been performed was necessary. Since the removal of tissue that is nonpathologic adds to both surgical cost and overall medical cost, discouraging unnecessary surgery has an obvious benefit financially as well as personally. Physicians and hospitals, along with insurers, are interested in this cost-reducing technique.

Hospitals are also developing Audit Committees to determine the need for hospitalization at the outset. Should the patient have been admitted in

---

[24] Health Insurance Institute, *Health Insurance Council Guides to Medical Relations* (March, 1964).

the first place? If so, how long should the hospital stay be? At what point should the patient be released to his home? These questions have been considered for many years, and hospitals are trying to answer them. Internal hospital audits by physicians connected with the hospital may produce a change that will be manifest in cost. Hospital utilization has also become a part of the deliberations of some Physicians' Review Committees.

Hospital Cooperation with Insurers. Most hospitals are willing to accept a certification of coverage by an employer-policyholder as credit against the hospital bill. This certification guarantees the charges of the hospital provided they are reasonable and medically necessary, and it is in this regard that insuring organizations become vitally interested parties in controlling abuses regarding medical care.

Hospitals have shown a cooperative attitude on a local level by sponsoring joint meetings with insurance groups in an effort to explore common problems relating to hospital costs or the financing of such costs. Since every hospital is interested in the money that is received daily to help make up the dollars that are spent daily to pay operating costs, a better cooperative understanding is being reached as insurers improve their promptness of payment. The more the individual hospital can feel a sense of payment security from the individual insurer, the better the relationship will be. This has been demonstrated over the past fifty years in insurance-hospital relationships resulting from the payment of hospital bills that arise in workmen's compensation claims.

Variations in Type of Care. As was mentioned earlier, certain hospitals have been experimenting with the use of different levels of care. This is an obvious attempt on the part of the hospitals to give each patient exactly the type of care that he needs. While this is for the benefit of the patient medically, it will also follow that a proper implementation of the approach will reduce the cost of over-all medical care. For example, hospitals are initiating the concept of "progressive care." According to the United States Department of Health, Education and Welfare, this idea embraces "the tailoring of hospital services to meet the patient's needs," and to state it even more clearly, "the right patient in the right bed with the right services at the right time."[25] The aspects associated with progressive care are as follows:

1. Intensive care is provided the critically ill who need around-the-clock or immediate lifesaving service.

2. Intermediate care is provided those who need a moderate amount of nursing care and who at intervals can care for themselves. Most patients are getting this type of care at the present time in general hospitals. Some need it and some do not.

---

[25] U.S. Department of Health, Education and Welfare, Public Health Service, *Elements of Progressive Patient Care*, p. 13.

3. Self-care is used for convalescent patients who require some therapeutic service but who are ambulatory and are able to care adequately for their own needs.

4. Long-term care is provided those not acutely ill who have need for long-term care, such as occupational and physical therapy, and who need to learn to live with their disability and to develop the ability and skills that remain.

5. Home care is provided those who can be maintained adequately in their own home with a minimum of hospital service. The hospital continues to assume responsibility for the patient and also assumes responsibility for the coordination of the services that the patient requires.

6. Out-patient care is provided those who can be cared for adequately without in-home help from outsiders but who still need coordination from medical sources to regain self-sufficiency and the ability to work. This is rehabilitation in one sense, but as will be mentioned later, rehabilitation starts immediately after the initial medical care following either an illness or injury.

Uniform Hospital Accounting. There is a growing interest among hospitals in developing a uniform system of accounting. This should result in a better patient and insurer comprehension of the costs associated with hospitalization. The Southern California Hospital Group, for example, has produced "Guiding Principles" for hospital charges. These principles include a consideration of the costs to the insurer, but they are not a final determinant in setting insured costs. When a form of accounting can be developed that does not differ to any great extent from one hospital to another, the public and the insurer will be better able to understand and accept the hospital bill.

As prepayment and insurance coverages have developed, a single insurer may receive many bills from the same hospital each day for many patients. This is in contrast to the single patient receiving one bill for his own illness. Hospitals have cooperated in attempting to produce bills that are generally understandable, uniform and consistent with charge levels that conform to community practices.

Combined Billing. The concept of combined billing for each insurer has been suggested on numerous occasions. The combination of bills each day for patients of a given insurer can also be broadened if a hospital would use one billing per month for each insurer. This bill would cover all insureds of the particular company who received treatment during that month. There has been some experimentation with this approach, and it works best where there is a policyholder with a large firm in a small community with a limited number of hospitals. The success under these conditions is obviously accounted for by the fact that a hospital has a considerable number of bills for a particular insurer. However, one insurer is known to have found that the procedure provides cost savings for hospitals, as well as itself, even under conditions where there are many hospitals and many large groups of insureds covered by group health plans of different insurance companies.

Hospital Planning. Area-wide planning as it relates to the construction of new hospitals and to the purchase of new and expensive equipment is receiving the attention of hospital personnel, with interest and cooperation from other groups. Centralized purchasing of materials and supplies is also part of this study. In the light of the intensity of medical care development, questions are being raised regarding the necessity for each individual hospital in a community to purchase the identical expensive item of equipment. The search is for a program that will allow such expensive items to be purchased by only one hospital but to be utilized by the entire community. Also a part of this philosophy is a survey to determine the extent of efficient utilization of existing hospital beds in a community before additional funds are spent to increase the bed census. Hospitals and hospital councils are the leaders in this undertaking. If it is properly and sincerely implemented and supported by medicine, insurance and the community at large, hospital planning could undoubtedly lead to a leveling off of the present hospital cost spiral.

Cooperation by Insurance Companies

Health Insurance Council. Health insurance companies are continually trying to move forward in the area of cooperation with the purveyors of medical care. This cooperative effort had its beginning in 1946, when the Health Insurance Council was formed. The purpose of the Health Insurance Council is to act as an insurance industry spokesman in providing an informational program to broaden the knowledge of and to be of technical assistance to the purveyors of medical care and to the public that insurers serve. The Health Insurance Council represents—and is financed by—eight constituent organizations, each of which in turn represents various sectors and interests of the health insurance industry. These organizations are: The American Life Convention, The American Mutual Insurance Alliance, The American Insurance Association, The Association of Life Insurance Medical Directors, The Health Insurance Association of America, The International Claim Association, The Life Insurance Association of America and The Life Insurers Conference. The constituent groups mentioned above represent 95 per cent of the group health insurance premiums written. While the Council in its early days was staffed by the constituent organizations, it now has its own staff. It is felt that this development will more adequately bring into focus the part that the insurance industry wishes to play in cooperating with hospitals, physicians and other purveyors of medical care.

The Health Insurance Council does not engage in legislative activity.

Rather, it aims to promote a mutual understanding of the problems that all participants involved in furnishing and paying for medical care have or feel that they have.

In the past few years the Health Insurance Council has fostered local, rather than national, meetings of individuals from the insurance field and the hospital and medical profession, as it is felt that the parties involved can understand each other more fully when their mutual problems are discussed on a local, rather than a national, level. As a result, state committees of the Health Insurance Council have been formed, and even these committees have been broken into regional and local groups. More than 900 individuals from many insurance companies are now involved in this state committee activity. This is felt to be the proper manner for the insurance industry to lend resources in attempting to educate interested parties about medical care financing and for the industry to learn the other side of the picture in the process.

At recent annual meetings of the Health Insurance Council, held in conjunction with regional meetings of state committees, several responsible hospital authorities have discussed their difficulties associated with medical care costs. Particular attention has been directed at problems of area planning. At one meeting, seven responsible physicians, each one a chairman of a state or local medical society review committee, served on a panel which discussed the activities of these committees in their relation to cost. The point was made that health insurance and its financing has progressed to the degree that the physician cannot stand alone in this cost area.[26] It is apparent that cooperation between health insurers and the physician is more important today than the founders of the Health Insurance Council anticipated in 1946. The furnishing and financing of medical care has become a dual mechanism in which divorce may be fatal.

The Health Insurance Council is guided by its Central Committee and its officers who have established standing committees for the purpose of understanding and working with the purveyors of medical care. These committees are concerned with medical relations, hospital relations, allied health services, uniform forms and technical advice.

Insurers' Activities in Medical Relations. The Health Insurance Council at its national level, and more particularly through its state committees, has been active in working with medical groups to establish Review Committees to determine the reasonableness of charges and the necessity for various medical services. Physicians' groups have been most cooperative in setting up this mechanism. Some individual physicians have been unhappy with this system of attempting to stabilize medical costs, but in general, it is working toward the end of reaching a common ground of

---

[26] Health Insurance Council Annual Meeting, Hospital Relations Panel Discussions (Philadelphia, 1964).

understanding. More than twenty-five such formal committees are operative throughout the nation according to the Health Insurance Council.[27] Some are on a state level, some are on a Councillor District level,[28] and some are on a county level. The action of the committees in evaluating the propriety of the charge in an individual case is interesting, but more important is the effect of the committee's influence on the general cost climate in the community. These committees are perhaps the most outstanding example of the effort to control cost through the cooperation of insurers and the purveyors of medical care.

One of the early successful Review Committees, organized in 1959, was that of the Tenth Councillor District of the Pennsylvania Medical Society serving the Pittsburgh area. This committee, which has a rotating membership of physicians, received cases from either physician or insurer involving the amount of the fee or the type or frequency of service. Another such successful committee, organized in August of 1961, is located in the First Councillor District of the Pennsylvania Medical Society serving Philadelphia. Representatives of medicine and the insurance industry meet jointly on this committee. It also receives cases either from physicians or insurers. Its considerations include the amount of the fee which the insurance company should pay and, in addition, the type and frequency of service. A third example is The Joint Medical Charges and Health Insurance Advisory Committee established in May, 1960, to serve the entire Commonwealth of Massachusetts as differentiated from the above two committees which each serve a particular area. The source and type of case submission is similar to the two committees previously mentioned. Certainly the work of such committees has tended to help insurers understand physicians and physicians understand insurers.

The antagonism that the third party has brought into this over-all picture seems to be disappearing as the work of these committees progresses. As was stated earlier, the third party has become and will continue to be a partner in proper cost control because the public's concern for its economic welfare in connection with the cost of illness and injury has made it so.

The Health Insurance Council, both nationally and on the state level, has sponsored talks to medical groups at all medical levels. Such a program is of considerable educational value to both the payer and the provider. A desired by-product is the resultant free exchange of information between the physician and the insurer which is necessary in order for the contractual control cost provisions to be able to work. Such contractual provisions are the subject of the next chapter.

Insurers, through various industry committees, have also endeavored to

---

[27] Health Insurance Council, *Review Committee Guide* (1962).

[28] A medical designation.

standardize claim reporting forms to be used by physicians. Physician groups have approved these forms. This standardization makes the necessary paper work a less substantial task for physicians, since the format and the questions on the form do not vary from company to company. This approach, of course, improves the image of the industry with physicians.

Insurers' Activities in Hospital Relations. The splendid cooperation of hospitals in sponsoring joint meetings was mentioned earlier. The insurers themselves have likewise been extremely active in such joint endeavors. With the advent of progressive care, health insurers are working experimentally with hospitals in paying claims where various types of care are given. If the patient is moved from one type of care to another in a timely fashion and as the need dictates with resultant charge reduction, it is currently felt that the progressive care idea will produce its intended cost control.

It is interesting to observe that insurance commissioners in several states are taking an active interest in audit and review committees. Several commissioners have refused to grant rate increases requested by Blue Cross plans until such audit and review committees are operative in hospitals cooperating with a plan. A few insurance commissioners have also indicated an intention to supervise more closely the rates insurance companies charge for medical expense coverage unless the companies take firm steps to "encourage" the establishment and proper functioning of review committees. The attitudes of insurance commissioners are noteworthy, because they support the contention that insuring organizations are going to have to take a more active role in cost control.

Insurers' Activities in Rehabilitation. It is being learned that rehabilitation can have an impact on claims in health insurance and, therefore, is a developing cost control tool. The National Council on Rehabilitation has defined rehabilitation as "restoration of the handicapped to the fullest physical, mental, social, vocational and economic usefulness of which they are capable."[29] Rehabilitation has not been well understood by health insurers, and its possibilities have not been discussed to any great extent until recent years.[30] Great strides have been made in rehabilitation in connection with workmen's compensation, and it is also moving ahead in the liability insurance area. It is now becoming a subject of interest to health insurance companies individually and to the industry groups such as the Health Insurance Council, the Health Insurance Association of America and the International Claim Association. Contacts are being made between the Health Insurance Council and the Association of

---

[29] National Council of Rehabilitation, Symposium on the *Processes of Rehabilitation* (Cleveland, 1944).

[30] W. Scott Allan, *Rehabilitation a Community Challenge* (New York: John Wiley & Sons, Inc., 1958), chap. xvii.

Rehabilitation Centers, Inc. This is being done in a spirit of cooperation with the hope of erasing any suspicion that may exist between insurers and the centers. Previously, many health insurers did not understand the function of such centers, and the centers did not realize that insurance may work to cover rehabilitation—which is an element of complete patient care. There are some who feel that rehabilitation cannot be of value in health insurance, particularly in connection with major medical coverage. Much has been done to prove this is not a fact. The following are two actual examples of cost control through rehabilitation:

Major medical—$5,000.00 maximum—Initial estimated cost $5,000.00. A twenty-six-year-old male sustained a fracture of the spine at Thoracic-12 with severe cord damage and complete paraplegia. Through cooperation among the physicians, the hospitals, Rehabilitation Center, community rehabilitation facilities and the insurer, the patient learned self-care and ambulation with braces and Canadian Crutches. There was return to employment. Total paid by major medical, $3,321.16.

Major medical—$10,000.00 maximum—Initial estimated cost $10,000.00. A fourteen-year-old male sustained a spinal lesion at Dorsal-4 with complete paraplegia from a bullet wound. There was complete inability to care for self. Through cooperation among physicians, hospitals, the community and the insurer, self-care was achieved to a degree. The patient had been moved to a specialized hospital and then to his home. Total paid by major medical, $7,404.86.

The idea of rehabilitation, and the research that goes with it in an attempt to learn how to do things better, have produced a dramatic example of cooperation among physicians, hospitals, universities, electronic engineers and insurers in attempting to develop an electronically controlled upper extremity prosthesis receiving its impulses or signals from the nerves and/or muscles at the point of amputation. If this can be accomplished and the theories applied to spinal cord injuries, the future of paraplegia and its cost may be vastly different.

Coverage of Skilled Nursing Home Charges. The skilled nursing home is coming to prominence as a substitute for hospitalization in the non-acute stage of illness. Under proper patient control by the physician, the hospital and the skilled nursing home, such medical care facilities may in the future be a means of controlling hospital cost. The insurance industry is currently studying this development in that light. One of the major problems relative to skilled nursing home coverage is to assure that benefits are not being paid for custodial care in which there is no particular medical problem.

The same thoughtful care must be given to the movement of the patient from the hospital to the skilled nursing home on a timely basis as must be given to the movement of the patient from segment to segment in the hospital progressive care arrangement. If this is not the case, there will be no control of cost—in fact there may be an increase. In one large metropolitan area, an experimental study is being made to determine whether or not the movement of the patient at the right time from acute hospital care to skilled nursing home care will demonstrate an over-all reduction in cost. Some insurers are cooperating in this study.

Loss Prevention Activities. Recently, the Health Insurance Association of America, through its committees, has been developing an interest in the prevention of loss as an element of cost control. Then, too, many individual companies have been active in this area by urging periodic physical examinations with cooperative communications to the attending physician. Keeping people healthy is a broad aim in cost control.

Although insurers' loss prevention activities in the health insurance field bear some resemblance to loss prevention in workmen's compensation coverage, the former is different in a number of respects, including the fact that dependents covered by health insurance outnumber the employees by two and one-half to one. Attempts are being made to reach the family of the insured employee through health education in the desire of lessening disability and medical costs. Cooperation between the insurers and the physician-hospital combination is being strengthened through research in the area of the aging processes and in other areas which are the causes of disability and cost mentioned earlier.

Use of Statistics. Some insurers and employers feel that broad statistics covering great numbers of individual claims, such as those derived by categorizing the length of disability or length of hospital stay by diagnosis, are of value in cost control. Some physicians also have indicated an interest in such comparisons. Since there undoubtedly are proper variances between averages, much is yet to be learned as to the value of this tool, but the growth of the computer and electronic systems has whetted the imagination of those who believe there is value in this idea. Many hospitals are considering computer systems not only for their own patient records but also for maintaining widespread community health statistics. Cooperation among the various segments of the socioeconomic-medical spectrum undoubtedly will be necessary before any real conclusion can be reached regarding the cost control value of such a program.

A subcommittee of the Health Insurance Council is studying the subject of hospital record keeping, and this group is concerned with the amount and type of information that may be made available through an electronic system. Members of the Health Insurance Council have been conferring with appropriate representatives of the American Hospital Association on this subject.

SELECTED REFERENCES

ALLAN, W. SCOTT. *Rehabilitation a Community Challenge,* chap. xvii. New York: John Wiley & Sons, Inc., 1958.

———. "The Need for Rehabilitation in Industry," *Physical Therapy Review,* Vol. XXXX, No. 11 (November, 1960).

AMERICAN MEDICAL ASSOCIATION. *Voluntary Prepayment Medical Benefits Plans,* pp. 27–28. Chicago, 1963.

BLACK, S. BRUCE. "Control of Loss in Accident and Health Insurance," an address presented at the annual meeting of the Health Insurance Association of America, Dallas, Texas, May 17, 1960.

BROWN, RAY E. "To the Public a Hospital Is a Hospital," *New England Journal of Medicine,* Vol. CCLXIX, No. 12 (September 19, 1963), p. 610.

HEALTH INSURANCE COUNCIL. *Review Committee Guide.* New York, 1962.

————. Health Insurance Council Annual Meeting, Hospital Relations Panel Discussion, Chicago, 1960, and Philadelphia, 1964.

HEALTH INSURANCE INSTITUTE. *Health Insurance Council Guides to Medical Relations.* March, 1964.

————. *Health Insurance Data,* pp. 58, 67, 70. New York, 1963.

NATIONAL COUNCIL OF REHABILITATION. Symposium on the *Processes of Rehabilitation.* Cleveland, 1944.

NATIONAL SAFETY COUNCIL. *Accident Facts,* p. 3. 1964 ed. Chicago.

New York State Journal of Medicine, editorial (January 15, 1964), p. 210.

New York State Journal of Medicine, editorial (February 1, 1964), p. 356.

U.S. DEPARTMENT OF HEALTH, EDUCATION AND WELFARE, PUBLIC HEALTH SERVICE. *Elements of Progressive Patient Care.* Publication No. 930-C-1. Washington, D.C., September, 1962.

————. *Health Statistics from the United States National Health Survey.* Publication No. 584-B 40. Washington, D.C., 1963.

Chapter 24

COST CONTROL THROUGH CONTRACTUAL PROVISIONS

BY DANIEL W. PETTENGILL

NATURE OF THE COST CONTROL PROBLEM

To control the cost of a group health insurance plan, one must either control the factors which affect cost or design the plan so as to minimize the impact of changes in the various cost factors. It is this latter approach of plan design which is the special province of the insurance company and the subject of this chapter.

The cost controls described in this chapter are valid for all size groups. They are of particular significance to the insurance company underwriting small groups, such as those with fewer than twenty-five employees. This is true partly because of the small employer's greater opportunity to select against the insurer through a more intimate knowledge of his personnel, and partly because a small group cannot be experience rated by itself. The large group, such as one with 500 or more employees, usually affords a sufficient spread of risk so that the premiums for the group can be based entirely on its own experience. Furthermore, it is· sometimes possible to estimate the dollar value of a given cost control with sufficient accuracy to permit waiver of that control if the large group is willing to pay the extra cost.

It should be realized that the group contract itself is usually written after the group plan has been made effective. It is difficult, if not impossible, for the policy to take away a benefit that a poorly worded announcement has implied would be available. Thus, the first step in cost control is to use announcement literature, as well as contract provisions, that clearly state who is eligible, when and for what benefits.

ELIGIBILITY PROVISION

Employees

In the early days of group insurance, the eligibility provision was often used to control variations in claim cost due to age. Since such control tends to leave the employee who needs the protection most without any coverage, the eligibility provision is seldom used today to eliminate active employees because of their old age. However, the eligibility provision is generally used to exclude retired employees under accidental death and dismemberment and disability income benefits. In the case of accidental death and dismemberment benefits, the retiree has relatively little need for the coverage since the risk is small in comparison with the risk of death due to disease. Disability income benefits are really loss of income benefits and hence have no meaning with respect to the retiree who no longer has a job and, hence, no income to lose. The retiree does need income, but this is the function of a pension plan, not a disability income benefit. At one time, retirees were also excluded from medical expense benefits, but the trend today is to include retirees and their dependents in the eligibility provision for such coverage. Where cost variations due to age are not controlled through the eligibility provision, they are controlled by the use of special limits on benefits or else are recognized by appropriate variations in the premium structure.

The principal control function of the eligibility provision today is to limit coverage to bona fide employees. The group plan must be protected against the sick friend or relative who is made an "employee" primarily for insurance purposes. The most effective provision in this respect is one that requires a person to be working regularly for the employer some minimum number of hours each week, such as thirty, in order to be considered an employee. This approach also eliminates the outside consultant and the strictly part-time employee. An employer with a significant number of temporary full-time employees may exclude such employees by requiring that a probationary period, such as three months of full-time employment, be served before an individual is eligible to be enrolled in the group plan.

Dependents

The vast majority of group medical expense plans cover certain dependents of the employee as well as the employee himself. The eligibility provision must, of course, define who will be a dependent in terms which will correspond to the premium assumptions which have been made. Thus, if a single extra premium is to be charged for all dependents of a given employee, regardless of their number, it is essential to realize that broadening the definition of a dependent will probably increase the average number of dependents per family unit and thus increase the cost.

The routine medical expenses of a healthy newborn child are of sufficient size that the eligibility provision has been used to exclude this cost by requiring that the child not be covered until after a certain period, such as fourteen days. The morbidity curve starts its upward swing at approximately age fifteen. This means that, if children continue to be eligible beyond their nineteenth birthday, a common group insurance termination date, an extra claim cost is involved per child as well as per family unit.

The principal control function of the dependents eligibility provision is to prevent the employee from selecting which dependents will be covered. Since most employees with dependents have a spouse and children, the definition of a dependent is usually limited to these two categories. The definition of a child may be broad, provided all children within that category must be covered. In other words, a group plan may suffer anti-selection if it regularly terminates a child's coverage at age nineteen, but permits employees who desire to do so to pay an extra premium to continue coverage of a child beyond this age. The group insurance plan faces similar anti-selection if dependent parents or other types of relatives may be covered at the option of the employee. For the large case, it may be possible to determine an extra premium which will permit coverage of additional classes of dependents.

There have been occasional attempts to use the eligibility provision as a means of controlling the over-insurance hazard. Generally, it is unwise to use the eligibility provision for this purpose. Either the provision is too general, such as exclusion of all husbands as dependents, in which event certain dependents who do not have other coverage are left completely unprotected, or the provision is so detailed as to be impractical to administer. For example, in this latter category would be the eligibility provision which requires that a dependent would not be eligible if working and insured elsewhere. Under this approach, a dependent might be eligible on the effective date but become ineligible soon thereafter, and if the employee forgets to report this change he may make contributions for that dependent beyond the time that he should. Conversely, the dependent who is denied coverage initially may become unemployed or may change to another job which does not provide insurance coverage. Will the employee report this change in time to secure coverage before the dependent has a claim? It is apparent that such an eligibility provision can lead to considerable employee dissatisfaction with the group insurance plan as well as consuming an undue portion of the employer's time in its administration. It would appear, therefore, that the over-insurance hazard is best controlled by an anti-duplication provision, as is discussed later in this chapter.

The eligibility provision is, however, the proper vehicle to guard the plan against duplicate coverage within itself. This is best accomplished by having the eligibility provision require that a person may not be insured (1) both as an employee and as a dependent, and (2) as the dependent of more than one employee.

PROVISIONS RELATING TO PRE-EXISTING CONDITIONS

The coverage of pre-existing conditions is one of the social objectives of group insurance. On the other hand, the extent to which pre-existing conditions are covered has a significant bearing on the cost of the plan and, hence, the handling of pre-existing conditions is a major consideration in plan design. From the point of view of claim administration, the simplest approach is to establish some criteria which, if met on the date the individual's insurance would normally become effective, allow that individual to become covered on that date for pre-existing as well as newly arising conditions. If the criteria are not met on that date, under this simple approach the individual's coverage for all conditions is deferred until they are met. For employees, this effective date provision typically requires that the employee be actively at work. For dependents, the provision usually requires that the dependent be free of hospital confinement on the effective date of his coverage and have been free of such confinement for at least the preceding thirty-one days.

While the effective date provision has provided a reasonable degree of control for most group health insurance benefits, it has not provided adequate control for major medical and comprehensive medical benefits by reason of the very broad scope of these coverages. Small group insurance cases providing these benefits particularly require not only an effective date provision but an actual exclusion or deferment of benefits for pre-existing conditions.

The typical pre-existing conditions provision included in major medical and comprehensive medical plans provides that no benefits (or some limited amount of benefits, such as $500 or $1,000) will be payable for expenses resulting from a pre-existing condition and incurred during the first so many months of coverage. Six, nine and twelve months are commonly used for this purpose. Longer periods of deferment generally do not provide sufficient additional cost control to warrant the probable employee dissatisfaction which would attend such a provision. While a fixed deferment period is most common, variable periods are also used. For example, the provision might specify that benefits will not be payable for expenses due to a pre-existing condition until the individual has been free of treatment for a period of ninety consecutive days ending after the effective date of his coverage. This provision allows more liberal treatment for minor pre-existing conditions but obviously provides for a lifetime exclusion with respect to any incurable condition that the individual may have and for which he will need continuing medical treatment. It has the disadvantage of tempting the individual to forego needed care in order to secure coverage.

Regardless of the type of provision used, it will be necessary to define what is meant by a pre-existing condition, since the term has no precise meaning of its own. A common definition which has been found to provide a reasonable combination of effective cost control with practical claim administration is one which considers a pre-existing condition to be any condition for which the individual received medical treatment, diagnosis, consultation or prescribed drugs during the ninety days preceding the effective date of his coverage. In this connection, it should be noted that the mere use of the word "treatment" would not be sufficient, since the employee will naturally construe the word "treatment" in a very narrow sense when it would be in his favor to do so. It is also well to note that any attempt to trace medical treatments more than one year prior to the effective date of coverage is usually not worth the expense involved. With respect to pregnancies, it is quite common to require that the pregnancy commence after the individual became covered or that the individual must have been covered for at least nine or ten months when the pregnancy terminates.

Whenever a new medical expense coverage is developed, careful consideration should be given to the probable effects of pre-existing conditions. Thus, at the present time, considerable study is being given to the nature of the pre-existing condition provision needed in dental expense coverage. As a minimum, the provision should exclude benefits with respect to the replacement of teeth which were extracted prior to the effective date of the individual's coverage. Such a provision, coupled with a deductible, may be the only controls needed on dental pre-existing conditions. On the other hand, where no deductible is used, it may be necessary to limit or reduce the benefits during the first year in order to control what might otherwise be a very high first-year cost, due to the repair of many years of accumulated neglect.

PROVISIONS EXTENDING COVERAGE AFTER CESSATION OF ACTIVE WORK

Two basic principles of group insurance underwriting are that the group to be insured shall have been formed for purposes other than obtaining insurance and that the plan of benefits shall preclude individual selection by the members of the group. Thus, any continuation of coverage after cessation of membership in the group seems contrary to these principles. On the other hand, there is growing public pressure for continuation of coverage; therefore, the insurance company must determine what types of continuation are feasible at a reasonable cost.

Disability Absences

Many employers do not have a standard practice with respect to the period of time that they will keep an employee in their employment when the employee is absent from work due to illness or injury. While it is socially desirable to continue coverage for a disabled employee, the group plan must protect itself against undue discrimination by the employer as to which employees will have their coverage continued during disability and which will not. Thus, it is customary to include a statement which provides specifically that the policyholder may continue coverage during a disability absence for some specified period of time. Cost considerations would indicate that this period of time might well be limited to one year.

The amount of control afforded by such a provision depends on both the liberality of the benefits provided and the length of time the individual is allowed to continue to be covered during his disability absence. As a further cost control, it is advisable to require that, once an employee has collected the maximum benefit during a period of disability, he shall not again be eligible for benefits until he has returned to active work for some specified period of time. The periods of time used for this purpose vary by coverage and are discussed in more detail later in this chapter.

Layoffs and Strikes

When a person is not working, he may be more prone to disability or at least to claim disability for an ailment that would otherwise be ignored. Furthermore, he may take advantage of a layoff or strike to have elective surgery or treatments performed which would not be done were he actively at work. Whatever the reasons, continuation of coverage during layoffs and strikes of more than a few weeks' duration has involved a significant additional claim cost even when the continuation was on a noncontributory basis. When the continuation of coverage is subject to employee contributions, anti-selection is particularly likely and higher claim costs have been experienced under dependents', as well as employees', coverage. Thus, extra premiums of 10 to 50 per cent may be required during the work stoppage for the various medical expense benefits, while for disability income benefits the extra premium required is so high as to be virtually unmeasurable for all but the largest groups. Indeed, the experience (shown in Appendix 8) during the 1959 steel industry strike was such that most major steel companies amended their labor agreements to discontinue disability income coverage immediately in the event of a work stoppage.

Retirement

As was discussed earlier in this chapter, it is not appropriate to continue either accidental death and dismemberment coverage or disability income coverage beyond the date of retirement. It is appropriate to continue medical expense benefits, provided due consideration is given to the extra claim costs involved. Retirees have higher rates of morbidity, longer periods of illness and higher average medical expenses. In the past, claim costs have often been reduced by severely limiting the amount of benefits payable for any given illness of a retiree or by limiting the total amount of benefits payable with respect to the balance of his lifetime. However, such cost savings are currently viewed as being socially undesirable since adequate health insurance is now recognized as a primary need of the aged.[1]

Other Terminations of Employment

From a cost control standpoint, there is no question but that coverage should cease as soon as an employee quits work or is fired. However, in order to protect the employee whose employment is terminated just when he or one of his dependents becomes sick, it is customary for most group medical expense plans to provide that benefits will continue to be payable with respect to the expenses of any disability existing on the date insurance is terminated, during the continuance of the disability up to some specified period of time. This period of extended insurance benefits is usually ninety days for hospital and surgical benefits and twelve months for comprehensive medical and major medical benefits. In addition, many of these same plans permit the terminated employee to purchase an individual or family policy providing hospital and surgical benefits without evidence of insurability provided he makes the purchase within thirty-one days of the date his group insurance ceased. An extra morbidity cost is experienced under these individual and family policies but this is generally absorbed by the insurer rather than being charged back to the group plan.

Termination of the Group Contract

Prior to pricing any of the foregoing provisions for continuing coverage after cessation of active work or benefits after cessation of insurance, the insurer must decide whether or not the terms of the provision will apply in the event the group contract itself is terminated and premiums are no longer available from which to pay such benefits. If this socially desirable course is followed, the reserves that must be set up are another cost that must be borne. Hence, some group plans specify that no benefits will be payable with respect to expenses incurred, or days of disability suffered, on and after the date the group contract is terminated. If another insurer acquires a plan of this latter type and is required to pick up where the prior insurer left off, the subsequent insurer has an added cost to take into account.

PROVISIONS RELATING TO OVER-INSURANCE

The coverage of an individual under more than one plan is not improper per se. If the benefits provided by a group plan are very modest, multiple coverage may be the only way that individual can secure the

---

[1] The predicted enactment of pending legislation for medical care coverage for the aged makes it appear likely that at least a portion of this coverage will be provided in the public sector.

degree of protection he desires. There is a possibility, though, that the aggregate of the benefits payable under the several plans will be greater than the individual's needs. When this situation exists, the individual is said to be over-insured, and there is a temptation to abuse the various plans. It is highly desirable that the group health insurance plan contain a provision coordinating its benefits with at least those of any other group plans that may exist.

Disability Income Benefits

The percentage of an individual's income which may be safely insured against loss as a result of disability is not readily determinable. This depends on both the level of the individual's income and his interest in his work. It is generally agreed, however, that this maximum percentage should be something less than the individual's net take-home pay in order that there may be an incentive for the individual to recover from his disability and return to work. This is especially true when part or all of the disability income benefit is exempt from income tax. The group insurance plan should be designed so that it is integrated with any program which the employer may have for continuing salaries during a disability absence. Also, its benefits should be self-adjusting to any material decrease in an individual's earnings. Aside from these two commonsense provisions, most temporary disability benefit plans do not attempt the difficult task of coordinating their benefits with those of any other plans.

Since a plan of long-term disability income benefits involves sufficiently greater risks, it cannot afford to ignore all of the many potential sources of over-insurance, such as the OASDI disability benefit, the various disability benefit provisions under group life insurance and pension plans and the disability income insurance provided under individual policies. There are two common types of provisions in long-term disability income contracts that attempt to coordinate the benefits with those payable under other plans. One provides that the benefits of the group plan will be reduced directly by the amount of any disability income benefits payable under certain other specified types of plans. The other provides that the benefits of the group plan will be reduced only to the extent necessary to keep the aggregate of the benefits under all of certain specified types of plans limited to some percentage of the individual's earnings, such as 60 per cent. While the amount of the OASDI disability benefit varies by the number of dependents which the disabled individual may have, some group plans ignore the variation and for ease of administration take only the primary benefit into account.

Medical Expense Benefits

When the aggregate of the benefits payable under two or more medical expense benefit plans would materially exceed an individual's necessary medical expenses, two temptations arise. One is for the insured to incur more expenses than necessary, and the other is for the provider of medical care to increase his fees. If either of these temptations is yielded to, the cost of the medical expense insurance is unnecessarily increased. In the 1930's and 1940's, it was customary to ignore the over-insurance problem on the grounds that few people had multiple coverage and that even those who had two hospital policies usually didn't make a real profit because they had many uninsured expenses, including nurses' fees and drugs. With the advent of collectively bargained plans, more husbands and wives jointly in the labor market and the very broad coverage provided by major medical benefits, the over-insurance problem can no longer be ignored.

In theory, the simplest method of controlling this problem would be to limit eligibility to only those persons who have no other insurance. As was pointed out earlier in this chapter, this method is quite unpopular and, in the case of dependents, rather impractical. A more equitable and practical approach is the use of an anti-duplication provision, which is also referred to as a "Coordination with Other Benefits" provision. Such a provision stipulates that the benefits of the group health insurance plan may be reduced when similar benefits are payable under certain other specified types of plans. The provision could specify that the benefits of the other plan or plans would be subtracted from the benefits of the group plan, and only the balance, if any, would be paid. While this approach provides the greatest degree of cost control, it causes considerable employee dissatisfaction when the total of his benefits is reduced below the total of his expenses, especially if the employee has paid part of the cost of any of the plans. This dissatisfaction can lead the employee to attempt to conceal the existence of his other coverage. Such concealment is a serious matter since many forms of other coverage are very difficult to detect without the employee's assistance. Hence, a different approach is needed which will encourage, rather than discourage, employee cooperation in reporting any other coverage.

A representative committee of the insurance industry has designed what may be the desired approach. This is the Model Group Anti-duplication Provision which was announced by the Health Insurance Association of America in late 1962. Under this model provision, a copy of which is contained in Appendix 9, the benefits of the group plan are reduced only to the extent necessary to limit the claimant's total benefits from all plans (usually limited to all group plans) to the aggregate of his "allowable expenses." An "allowable expense" is any necessary, reasonable and customary item of expense, at least a portion of which is covered under one of the specified plans insuring the person for whom claim is made. For example, an employee's wife might incur $1,000 of expenses, including a $700 hospital bill and a $300 surgeon's fee. Assume the wife worked and that her employer's plan paid $450 of hospital benefits and $200 of surgical benefits. Assume, also, that the employee's own employer's group plan would, in the absence of other coverage, pay $600 of hospital benefits but no surgical benefits. In the absence of an anti-duplication provision, the employee would collect $1,250 for bills of only $1,000. However, if his employer's plan has the Model Provision, it will count $1,000 as "allowable expenses"; it will deduct the $650 of benefits paid by the other plan and pay the balance of $350 as its reduced benefit.

This nonprofit approach makes sense to the fair-minded employee. Some of the group plans which have replaced more stringent anti-duplication provisions with the liberal Model Provision are already finding an improvement in employee reporting of other coverage.

The savings afforded by this or any other anti-duplication provision will depend on a number of factors,[2] the most important of which is the definition of a "plan" or what constitutes other coverage. One large insurer is currently experiencing claim savings of 1 to 3 per cent under the Model Provision when only other group insurance plans are taken into account. These savings have been considerably larger when individual Blue Cross–Blue Shield certificates have also been taken into account.

While these claim savings are important, the real value of the Model Group Anti-duplication Provision is a psychological one that cannot be measured in money. If the group health insurance benefits are reasonably adequate and the Model Provision is used, many employees will drop their other insurance, or at least they will not acquire any additional insurance. Much of the over-insurance hazard is completely removed in this manner, and the balance is under control.

BENEFIT PROVISIONS APPLICABLE TO MANY GROUP HEALTH COVERAGES

The very existence of most forms of health insurance increases the cost of that insurance. This is best seen in the case of medical expense benefits which, by their existence, may cause an insured to secure medical care that he otherwise might have felt he could not afford. This attribute of insurance is both desirable and undesirable. It is desirable to the extent that the additional medical care, which the individual seeks by reason of being insured, is necessary care. It is undesirable to the extent that this care represents luxurious or unnecessary services. Thus, an important cost control principle is that the group health plan should leave some area of the risk for the individual to bear himself.

---

[2] See *Health Insurance Association of America Group Insurance Bulletin 3–61*, dated November 30, 1961, for a detailed discussion of over-insurance and anti-duplication provisions.

Percentage Participation

One method of obtaining the insured's participation in the risk-sharing is to require that his participation in the payment of expenses be on a continuous basis. The term "percentage participation" (or "coinsurance") is used to describe this approach whether the insured's participation is a uniform percentage or a variable one.

Disability Income Benefits. With respect to disability income benefits, it is fairly evident that any plan which would provide an individual with more income by reason of being sick than by reason of working encourages abuse. Thus, it is essential for a plan to assure that an individual will not receive a benefit in excess of his net take-home pay after OASDI, state and federal income taxes. Since many plans provide a specified dollar benefit, it is desirable to include a provision whereby the benefit may not exceed a specified proportion, such as 70 per cent, of the individual's income at the time he becomes disabled. Such a provision applies not only to occasional employees who may be hired at an unusually low salary, but also to the employee whose salary warrants the dollar benefit currently but not five years from now.

Medical Expense Benefits. Many types of medical expense benefits do not require a specific percentage participation by the insured. However, an element of risk-sharing by the insured is often secured indirectly by setting the schedule of benefits at a level which is below that of the prevailing charges. Thus, the surgical schedule may provide benefits which, on the average, approximate 80 per cent of the customary charges in the area. The hospital daily room and board benefit may be that dollar amount which represents about 75 per cent of the most common semiprivate room charge in the area. A direct percentage participation is sometimes used in connection with benefits for hospital ancillary services. For example, the hospital plan may pay 100 per cent of the first $200 of hospital ancillary service charges and 75 per cent of the balance. Direct percentage participation after a deductible is generally used for comprehensive and major medical benefits.

It is difficult to say just how large the insured's participation in the risk should be in order to secure adequate cost control. As with disability income benefits, the answer probably depends to a considerable degree on the income status of the individual; the wealthier the individual, the greater the degree of participation required. Education and environment are also factors. The important point is that there appears to be a tendency on the part of most people to utilize more medical care as their share of the cost of this medical care decreases. The most recent statistical evidence of this tendency is the fact that group comprehensive medical plans providing an 80 per cent rate of reimbursement cost significantly more than 80/75ths of the cost of similar plans providing a 75 per cent rate of reimbursement.[3]

Deductibles

The use of a deductible is another method by which the insured's participation in the risk can be obtained. However, the principal purpose of the deductible, from a cost control viewpoint, is the elimination of small claims where the expense of investigating and paying the claim would be very high in proportion to the benefits actually payable. Thus, deductibles are generally used in conjunction with, rather than as a substitute for, percentage participation.

While the deductible is normally thought of as a dollar amount, it has many other equally effective forms. For example, there are numerous illnesses which last only two or three days; to attempt to pay disability income benefits for such brief illnesses would be uneconomical. The typical disability income plan, therefore, eliminates benefits for such illnesses by using a deductible in the form of a waiting period during which no benefit is payable. With respect to short-term disability income benefits, this waiting period is typically three or seven days, while for long-term disability benefits it is typically six months or more. A medical expense plan which covers physicians' fees for office calls often uses a deductible in the form of an exclusion of benefits for the first few visits, such as three, with respect to each illness.

Dollar deductibles may be expressed in terms of dollars of benefits payable or dollars of covered expenses incurred. The former type is generally used when the deductible applies to one specific type of expense, such as hospital expenses, while the latter is generally used when the deductible applies to a variety of expenses as is the case with comprehensive and major medical plans.

The value of a deductible depends on the frequency of occurrence of the event being insured against, the magnitude of the deductible and the frequency with which the deductible will be reapplied in the event of a long illness or a series of illnesses. Obviously, a large deductible provides a greater savings than a small one; however, the savings are not directly proportional to the deductible amounts because the frequency of a large claim is normally substantially less than the frequency of a small claim. Where a very large deductible is used or the deductible is frequently reapplied, it is generally for the purpose of reducing the price of the plan rather than for the purpose of discouraging abuse by the insured. A desirable, but not too common, practice is to increase the size of the deductible as the income of the insured increases because of the

---

[3] See Report of the Committee on Experience under Group Health Insurance, *Transactions of the Society of Actuaries, 1963 Reports Number,* Table 9, p. 224.

significant effect which income generally has on an individual's medical care expenditures.

Scheduled versus Unscheduled Benefits

The claim cost of any given benefit is the product of the frequency of occurrence of the event insured against and the average benefit that will be payable when the event does occur. Most of the cost controls described thus far have dealt with protecting the plan against variations in frequency. Variations in the average benefit could be controlled fairly well by scheduling the amount of benefit that will be payable under each and every circumstance. For disability income benefits this would mean providing the same dollar amount of benefit for all employees that would be appropriate for the lowest paid employee. A schedule of benefit amounts based on salary, or a benefit which is a specified percentage of salary, will produce an increasing average benefit amount as salaries rise. The flat benefit is seldom popular with employees, and the increasing cost of the graded schedule is sufficiently modest and predictable that most plans are written on this latter basis.

To control the average benefit under medical expense coverage, not only must there be a scheduled amount of benefit for each item of expense, but this amount must be at or below the prevailing level of charges for the expense concerned. Under such control, the scheduled amount of benefit is paid in virtually every instance. If the scheduled amount is set above the level of prevailing charges, the average benefit payment will increase as the level of charges rises toward the scheduled amount. The rapidity of this rise generally depends on the size of the margin between the scheduled benefit and the level of charges. Thus, a schedule of benefits substantially in excess of prevailing charges can be worse than no schedule at all, since there will be a temptation for the provider of services to charge the full scheduled amount, whereas he presumably would charge less than this amount if there were no schedule.

For many years, hospital charges have been rising at the rate of 6 to 8 per cent per year and most other medical care costs at the rate of 2 to 3 per cent per year. Since it is socially desirable for a group medical expense plan to provide a reasonably adequate degree of protection against medical care costs, these rising costs force the purchaser of medical expense insurance to make what, in baseball, would be called a fielder's choice. He can purchase either a scheduled benefit or an unscheduled one. If he purchases the scheduled benefit, then the average benefit payment should stay constant but will represent an ever-decreasing percentage of the individual's bill. Hence, if he wishes to maintain a constant level of protection, he must periodically purchase additional insurance. On the other hand, if he purchases an unscheduled plan, he should not have to purchase additional insurance (for the types of expenses covered by the plan), but the average benefit payment will continually increase and so will the premiums for the plan.

It is obvious that greater benefits involve a greater cost. What is not obvious, but is nevertheless true, is that a given benefit costs more when it is part of a liberal plan than when it is a part of a modest plan. For example, if an employer improves his group hospital insurance plan by increasing the maximum number of days for which benefits are paid from thirty-one to seventy, he will generally find that more of his employees will be confined at least thirty-one days under the seventy-day plan than were so confined under the thirty-one-day plan. The same phenomenon can be observed when a temporary disability income benefit plan has its maximum increased from thirteen weeks to twenty-six weeks, that is, more employees will still be disabled at the end of the thirteenth week than was previously the case. This phenomenon has particular significance in connection with evaluating the so-called retroactive waiting period type of deductible for disability income plans. For example, a fourteen-day retroactive waiting period means that individuals whose disability lasts less than fourteen days will not receive any benefits whereas those whose disability lasts at least the full fourteen days will receive benefits for the first two weeks of disability as well as for any subsequent weeks of disability. The phenomenon under discussion warns the underwriter that more people will still be disabled at the end of the fourteenth day of disability under such a retroactive waiting period plan than would still be disabled under a plan which provides no retroactive benefit.

MISCELLANEOUS BENEFIT PROVISIONS APPLICABLE TO SPECIFIC COVERAGES

Disability Income Benefits

There are a number of miscellaneous cost control devices for use with disability income benefits. Under short-term disability income benefits it is customary to consider an employee disabled if he is prevented from performing the duties of his own occupation even though he might be able to perform those of some other occupation. With such a definition of disability, an employee who is unfit to return to his former job could take a different job and still collect the disability benefit unless a provision is included to deny benefits for any day when the individual actually receives remuneration for work performed. For long-term disability income benefits, the definition of disability should be more strict, at least after the first few months, and should require inability to perform any gainful employment, except in accordance with a rehabilitation program approved by the insurance company.

It is desirable to require also that the existence of the disability be certified by a physician and that no disability be determined to have commenced until the individual has come under the care of his physician. Except for the unfortunate individual who is so disabled as to be beyond the help of a doctor, benefits should cease when the patient has ceased to be under the care of his physician.

Since the plan will have a waiting period, at least for disabilities due to diseases, the plan should contain a provision defining what constitutes a single period of disability and how successive periods of disability due to the same or similar causes are to be related to one another.

The employee who becomes disabled and never returns to work naturally expects to serve only one waiting period and to collect only one maximum benefit. The same is not true of the employee who recovers, goes back to work, and shortly thereafter becomes disabled again. He will not want to serve another waiting period; yet he will want a new maximum benefit. Both of his desires can be costly to the plan. If the subsequent disability is due to a cause that is entirely unrelated to the cause of the previous disability, it is both sound and equitable for the plan to provide a new maximum benefit and require a new waiting period after the employee has returned to full-time active work for one day. On the other hand, if a subsequent disability is related to a prior one, a longer period of return to work should be required. For short-term disability income plans, this longer period is usually two weeks, while for long-term plans, it is three to six months.

If the amount of weekly benefit varies with the employee's rate of earnings, the plan should be protected against incurring a retroactive liability by reason of a retroactive pay increase. In other words, the change in benefit should be effective on the date notification is given, not on the date the pay raise is effective, if the latter would be earlier.

Hospital Benefits

Inasmuch as different jurisdictions have different licensing requirements for hospitals, some of which are extremely liberal, a strict definition of a hospital is a desirable cost control provision. Homes for the aged and institutions which provide essentially custodial care should be excluded by the definition. In addition, since some hospitals act as collection agencies for nurses and other professional personnel, it is well to have a hospital expense benefit cover just the actual charges made by a hospital on its own behalf.

Frequently a plan covers the hospital's daily board-and-room charge only up to a specified dollar amount, and in such a case it is important to define exactly what hospital charges will be considered as board-and-room charges. One common definition includes not only the hospital's charge for board and room but also any charge which the hospital makes at a daily or weekly rate or which the hospital makes as a condition of occupancy. The use of such a definition protects against the possibility that a hospital will redesign its system of charging in order to take advantage of the plan that provides a modest board-and-room benefit but a liberal allowance for ancillary service charges. For example, some hospitals have separated their charges for general nursing care from their charges for board and room. Without a definition of the term "board-and-room charge" that encompasses general nursing care charges, the plan might be forced to consider general nursing as an ancillary service instead of board and room, and this would add materially to the cost of the plan if it were not contemplated by the premium structure.

Benefits for hospital ancillary services are usually provided on an unscheduled basis, subject to some dollar maximum. When this maximum is more than some modest amount, such as $100, it is desirable to limit coverage to those expenses which are incurred during the period for which the plan pays a room-and-board benefit. The plan may otherwise be liable for ancillary fee benefits long after board-and-room benefits have been exhausted.

A hospital plan must also define what constitutes one period of hospital confinement. For active employees, it is customary to provide that two periods of hospital confinement separated by at least one day of active full-time work constitute two different periods of confinement for benefit purposes. For retired employees and all dependents, it is customary to require that a period of ninety days free of hospital confinement have existed in order for two confinements to be considered as separate confinements for benefit purposes. A separation of substantially more than ninety days would provide only slightly greater cost savings except in the case of very old people.

Once an individual has successfully passed the acute stage of an illness, he seldom needs the complete and necessarily expensive facilities of a hospital for his convalescence. There is some current thought that much convalescence takes place in hospitals and that hospital stays might be shortened, particularly among the aged, if hospital insurance plans provided coverage for care in a skilled nursing home directly following a hospital confinement. Some experiments are being made with skilled nursing home coverage. They are too new to evaluate the cost or effectiveness of this coverage but should warrant careful study in the near future.

Surgical Benefits

Next to the schedule itself, the principal cost control provision required in a surgical benefit is the definition of what constitutes a surgical procedure. In addition to cutting operations and the treatment of dislocations and fractures, which are traditionally recognized as surgery, most work which a physician does with his hands can technically be called surgery, and hence surgical benefits may be claimed unless the work is excluded by such a definition. In particular, it is important to decide whether surgical benefits will be payable for medical procedures performed in lieu of cutting surgery, such as the removal of a tumor by radiation therapy. Such a decision will have a significant effect on the cost of the surgical benefit. Many of the newer surgical plans do not cover any X-ray and radium therapy; the basic group package either provides a separate benefit for such treatment or none at all. Oral surgery is another area involving a significant cost for which surgical plans usually provide little or no coverage.

Because of the widespread existence of surgical benefits, there is a trend among hospitals to make charges for surgery performed by a resident or intern whenever the patient has a surgical benefit. Thus, it is desirable that the plan specify whether such charges will be covered or not.

Successive disability rules similar to those used to define what constitutes one period of hospital confinement are used to determine when two or more operations will be considered as one operation for benefit purposes. However, special consideration must be given to the fact that certain surgical procedures are done in stages. Any limit on the amount of benefit payable for all such stages combined should clearly override the successive disability rule. This is particularly important under employee coverage, since the employee may have returned to active work for at least one day in between each stage of the operation.

In designing a surgical schedule, it is customary to provide an allowance for each procedure performed. It should be realized, however, that certain procedures are commonly performed in conjunction with each other. A special allowance should be established for such a combination if surgeons generally do likewise in setting their fee.

Physician's Fee Benefit

The high frequency of physicians' visits and the low-average claim payment involved make the use of some form of a deductible desirable, if not essential. Indeed, in many areas of the United States it is customary to exclude home and office visits and to pay benefits only for physicians' visits made while the patient is confined in a hospital. Another important cost control provision required in a physician's fee benefit is the list of services for which no benefits will be payable. As a minimum, this list of excluded services should include those for which some other benefit in the group plan has made complete or partial reimbursement, such as a surgeon's postoperative care which is normally covered under the surgical benefit. If the group plan provides a separate diagnostic X-ray and laboratory benefit or a separate radiation therapy benefit, the examination or treatment which would be covered under such benefits should not also be covered under the physician's fee benefit. Other areas to be considered are dental work, eye examinations and charges for drugs and medicines.

Occasionally there will be more than one physician's visit on a given day. Therefore, the plan should specify whether or not it will pay for more than one visit per day. In general, a maximum benefit is provided for all visits made in one day. Successive disability rules are needed. These are usually similar to those for hospital and surgical benefits.

Comprehensive and Major Medical Expense Benefits

The principal cost control provisions for comprehensive and major medical benefits are the deductible and percentage participation discussed earlier. In addition, it is essential that there be precise statements as to the expenses covered and not covered. The more elective a service is, the more difficult it is to control the rate of utilization of that service. Examples of highly elective services are travel for health and the use of a nurse at home to take care of a mother and her newborn child following discharge from the hospital.

Some plans specify dollar limits on the amount of each covered expense that will be recognized, the California Relative Value Study often being used for this purpose as far as physicians' fees are concerned. Many plans, however, specify that the full amount of each expense will be a covered expense and seek to control overcharging by requiring that the service be a necessary one and the charge be reasonable. Some plans use the term "usual and customary" rather than necessary and reasonable. It is important to realize that these terms do not have precise meanings and that this can complicate cost control. For example, "the usual and customary fee of the doctors in the community" may be different from "the usual and customary fee of the attending physician." Furthermore, usual and customary fees may well vary by income, type of hospital accommodations used and other characteristics. If strict cost control is desired, these variations should be taken into account in defining the level of charges covered by the plan.

Mental illness is the coverage area with which many comprehensive and major medical plans, particularly those covering higher paid employees, have had the greatest difficulty from a cost control standpoint. There is no clear dividing line between mental illness and simple behavioral problems, nor is there any real agreement as to what constitutes necessary treatment for many mental conditions. Furthermore, one study[4] indicates that 33 per cent of all psychiatric patients need treatment for longer than a year, and 27 per cent need treatment indefinitely. So far, the only effective cost control for comprehensive or major medical coverage in

---

[4] Helen Hershfield Avnet, *Psychiatric Insurance* (New York: Group Health Insurance, Inc., 1962), p. 197.

this area has been a severe restriction on the number of office visits covered. This can be accomplished directly by the use of a specific limit, such as twenty visits, or indirectly by the use of a dollar limit, such as $250, on the amount of benefits payable per year for expenses incurred in connection with a mental illness while not confined in a hospital. A higher percentage participation, such as 50 per cent instead of 20 per cent, is another useful control on the cost of ambulatory psychiatric care. It is believed to be particularly effective when combined with a limit on the number of office visits.

Dental Benefits

To the extent that dental benefits are completely scheduled, most of the control features discussed in connection with surgical benefits are applicable. Correspondingly, comprehensive dental plans need cost controls similar to comprehensive medical plans. There are many elective items, such as gold fillings, inlays, crowns and bridges, for which a higher percentage participation by the insured is believed to be necessary to control overutilization. Orthodontia is probably the most elective of all dental services and hence is frequently not covered. If orthodontia is to be covered, both a high percentage participation and a modest limit on the amount of benefit payable are desirable.

When the dental coverage is to be contributory, there is a special problem in minimizing anti-selection. The individual with healthy teeth feels he has little need for protection, and the individual who has lost all his teeth feels he has no need at all. Thus, a reasonable spread of risk can generally be obtained only by packaging contributory dental coverage with the other group benefits, that is, requiring the individual to subscribe to all the benefits or none.

SELECTED REFERENCES

PETTENGILL, DANIEL W., AND BURTON, BURTON E. "Development of Expected Claim Costs for Comprehensive Medical Expense Benefits and Ratios of 1959 and 1960 Actual Experience Thereto," *Transactions of the Society of Actuaries*, Vol. XV (1963), pp. 10–78.

REPORT OF THE COMMITTEE ON EXPERIENCE UNDER GROUP HEALTH INSURANCE. *1963 Reports Number, Transactions of the Society of Actuaries*, pp. 207–30.

Second Report of the Joint ALC-HIAA-LIAA Study Group on Non-Duplication of Accident and Health Insurance Benefits.

NATIONAL ASSOCIATION OF INSURANCE COMMISSIONERS. *Seventh Status Report on Overinsurance for the Subcommittee on Overinsurance of the Accident and Health Committee.*

PART V

Common Aspects of Group Insurance Coverages

Chapter 25

MASTER CONTRACTS AND CERTIFICATES

BY JOHN M. HILL, II

Group insurance policies are specifically authorized by the insurance laws of most states. In states having no group insurance laws, there is legal authority that a policy insuring any bona fide class of persons is valid.[1] Moreover, no problem of insurable interest is normally present where the benefits are payable to the insured lives, their estates or their beneficiaries.[2]

STANDARDIZATION OF GROUP CONTRACT PROVISIONS

The enactment of the model NAIC group life insurance bill, the model HIAA group health insurance bill and the model NAIC credit insurance bill has resulted in extensive regulation of both the types of groups which may be insured and the principal terms and conditions of the group contract.[3] These model laws have served to make the more important nonbenefit provisions in the contract standard thoughout most of the group insurance industry. The model bills and most standard provision laws permit policy provisions more favorable to insured lives than required by statute, or at least as favorable to insured persons and more favorable to the policyholder. This flexibility has served to develop standard policies which comply with the variations in the required provision laws of most of the states. The principal exceptions relate to such matters as (1) a life insurance conversion right upon policy termination or amendment for persons insured for five years; (2) a health insurance conversion right under policies delivered in New York for employees terminating employment and for union members terminating union membership; (3)

---

[1] *Mutual Bank and Trust Company* v. *Schaffner,* 248 S.W. (2d) 858 (Mo., 1952); *Freeport Sulphur Co.* v *Aetna Life Ins. Co.* (CA 5 La), 206 F. (2d), 41 ALR (2d) 762—group policy is not void for lack of mutuality.

[2] *Fomby* v. *World Insurance Company of Omaha,* 115 F. Supp. 913 (Ark., 1952) —the reasons for voiding wagering contracts are not present in group insurance.

[3] *Board of Ins. Com'rs.* v. *Great Southern Life Insurance Co.,* 239 S.W. (2d) 803 (Texas, 1951)—policy must conform with group statute if group underwriting is used.

the inclusion of podiatrist services in policies delivered in some states; (4) the continuation of insurance (other than the disability income benefits) during a strike under California policies covering collectively bargained insurance plans, subject to a maximum period of six months;[4] (5) a requirement that the policyholder apply any dividends or retroactive rate reduction credits which are in excess of his costs for the benefit of the lives insured under the policy; and (6) a required two-year incontestable clause with respect to individuals insured under health insurance policies delivered in Wisconsin.

It is a general legal rule that policy provisions required by a state will be read into the policy whether or not contained therein. Pursuant to this rule, the courts have held that designation of an employer or other policyholder as beneficiary of group life insurance is void because it is contrary to the usual statutory requirement that insurance be "for the benefit of persons other than the employer."[5] The courts also have held that the estate of an employee who was excluded under the policy because of age may recover the life insurance benefit, because such an exclusion is contrary to the usual statutory requirement in group life insurance that insurance be provided or offered to all employees or all of any class "determined by conditions pertaining to employment." It has thus been felt that age is a condition pertaining to the person, rather than to employment.[6]

Generally, the form of the group insurance policy and of the certificates issued under the policy must be filed with and approved by the insurance department of the state in which the policy is delivered.[7] The laws of Florida, Arkansas, Idaho and West Virginia require, in addition, that group certificates under out-of-state policies be filed with the insurance department for information purposes if requested by the department. No departments have made any general requests for such filings, but, of

---

[4] Continuation of insurance is contingent on 75 per cent of the insured persons electing to continue their insurance and making payment of the full policy premium. The policy may require that the premium be collected by the policyholder if a trustee, otherwise by the union. Insurance terminates with respect to any employee who accepts full-time employment elsewhere.

[5] *Tulipano* v. *U.S. Life Ins. Co.*, 154 A. (2d) 645 (Sup. Ct. App. Div., N.J., 1959).

[6] *Dudrey* v. *Equitable Life Assurance Society*, 10 N.Y.S. (2d) 639. Ohio law permits exclusions because of age, and many creditor group insurance statutes permit exclusion of debtors because of age. The departments of a number of states have ruled debtors may not be excluded under creditor insurance policies because of age where the law requires the insuring of all debtors or all of any class determined by conditions pertaining to indebtedness.

[7] The filing and approval of group health insurance contracts is not required in Alabama, Delaware, District of Columbia, Hawaii, Massachusetts (unless insured "in conjunction with and supplementary to" a group life insurance policy), Tennessee and Wyoming; the filing of group life insurance contracts is not required in Alabama, Hawaii and Vermont.

course, they may do so. The laws of several other states make reference to the filing and approval of certificates issued in the state but appear to relate only to certificates of group insurance policies delivered in the state.[8] It is a general legal rule that policies not conforming with filing requirements or standard provision requirements are valid and enforceable against the insurance company in accordance with standard provision requirements.[9]

POWER OF POLICYHOLDER TO PURCHASE GROUP INSURANCE

It is now well settled that the purchase of group insurance for its employees by a private corporation is included in its corporate authority to employ and compensate its employees. The authority of a governmental body to purchase group insurance is usually set forth in specific enabling statutes and in some cases has been inferred by the courts from statutory grants of general powers. In several cases the courts based the right on the ground that premiums constitute compensation and, hence, may be paid by a public body under its general powers to fix compensation of its employees.[10] However, this right on the part of a public body has been denied[11] or limited by other courts[12] and frequently involves a difficult legal question in the absence of a specific enabling act.[13]

While most private corporations and governmental employers may legally purchase group insurance for their employees, the courts also recognize group insurance benefits as a proper subject for collective bargaining between a union and an employer.[14] Under Section 302 of the Labor Management Relations Act of 1947, the Taft-Hartley Law, an employer is forbidden to make any payments to a union representative

---

[8] See Illinois Smith-Hurd Anno. Stats. Ch. 73, Sec. 755; Code of Iowa 509.6; N.C. General Statutes 58–54.

[9] Under N.Y. Ins. Law Sec. 143, Sub-Sec. 1 and the statutes of several other states, nonconforming insurance contracts are enforceable against the insurance company in accordance with standard provision and other requirements.

[10] *State* v. *City of Memphis,* 147 Tenn. 658, 251 S.W. 46 (1923); *Nohl* v. *Board of Education,* 27 N.Y. 232, 199 P. 373 (1921); *Bowers* v. *City of Albuquerque,* 27 N.M. 291, 200 P. 421 (1921).

[11] *People ex rel Terbush and Powell* v. *Dibble,* 189 N.Y. Supp. 29, affmd. without Op. 196 App. Div. 913, 186 N.Y. Supp. 951 (1921); in re Op. of Justices 249 Ala. 88, 30 So. (2nd) 14 (1947) in which the court held an act authorizing state bodies to purchase group insurance was "vague and unenforceable."

[12] *Lewis* v. *Independent School District City of Austin,* 132 Texas 65, 1615 W (2d) 450 (1942); *Public Housing Adm.* v. *Hsng. Auth. of City of Bogolusa,* 242 LA 519, 137 So. (2d) 315 (1962) holding the state constitutions prohibit purchase of insurance from mutual companies.

[13] Arthur M. Browning, "The Status of Group Insurance for Public Employees," *Proceedings of the Association of Life Insurance Counsel* (1956), pp. 53–95.

[14] *Inland Steel Co.* v. *NLRB* (CA7th), 170 F (2d) 247, 12 ALR (2d) 240, affmd. 339 U.S. 382, 94 L. Ed. 925, 70 S. Ct. 674 reh. den. 70 S. Ct. 1017; *Potlach Forest Inc.* v. *IWA* (D.C., Idaho) 108 F. Supp. 906 affmd. (CA9th) 200 F. (2d) 700.

under a collectively bargained health and welfare insurance program unless payments are made to the trustees of a prescribed insurance trust fund.[15] The trust fund must be used for the exclusive benefit of the members of the collective bargaining unit for whom the payments are made.[16] This law,[17] together with the requirements of the model group life insurance laws, has resulted in the extensive use of insurance trust agreements under which the trustees are authorized to purchase, hold and administer group insurance policies. Such trust agreements are required where the group life insurance policy insures the employees of two or more employers in the same industry, or the insurance plan is negotiated by a collective bargaining agreement and the policy is not to be issued to the employer. These agreements are described fully in Chapter 33.

Where members of unincorporated associations, such as unions, are to be insured it is often advisable to create an insurance trust and to issue the policy to the trustees of the trust rather than to the association. This is because of the legal rule that, in the absence of a permissive statute, an unincorporated association cannot sue or be sued in the association name, and enforcement of association contracts requires personal service of legal process on all its members. The trust device also may be used to issue single policies to insure several creditors in a number of states. An alternative arrangement consists of the appointment of an agent by two or more creditors or employers, as the case may be, to purchase, administer and hold a single group policy for the creditors or employers.[18]

MULTI-STATE GROUP COVERAGES

Most group insurance policies insure persons residing in several states having different laws and legal requirements. The laws of some of the states may not recognize or permit insuring the type of group desired. Alternatively, such laws may have different requirements concerning such matters as minimum enrollments, premium contribution requirements, maximum amounts of group life insurance, required extended benefits

---

[15] The Taft-Hartley Law requires that (1) payments be placed in trust to purchase insurance, (2) the detailed basis of the payments be contained in a written agreement entered into by the employer and the union, (3) the employer and the union be equally represented in the administration of the trust fund, (4) the trust fund be audited annually, and (5) payments intended to be used to purchase annuities be placed in a separate account under a trust which prohibits the diversion of such payments.

[16] *Kroger Company* v. *Blassie,* 225 F. Supp. 300 (1964), held officers of a union could not be beneficiaries of a welfare trust. Also see *U.S.D.CE. Mo.; Teamsters Local 688* v. *Townsend,* 5–18–64, 32 L.W. 2644.

[17] The Florida Attorney General has ruled the Taft-Hartley Law supersedes the Florida group definition requirements on the ground that it specifically relates to the business of insurance and hence is not subject to state law, by virtue of the federal McCarran-Ferguson Insurance Relations Act. Op. A.G. No. 055–145, June 27, 1955.

[18] Typical copies of such trust and agency agreements may be found in Appendix 10.

and required conversion rights. Contractual rights and obligations also vary among the several states.

The importance of a uniform plan of insurance for all members of a group, regardless of residence, is obvious. Without this uniformity, not only is the underwriting basis of the group seriously disturbed, but the desire of the policyholder to have uniform personnel practices or to have uniform benefits for members of associations, such as unions, cannot be fulfilled. These considerations raise such questions as the following: In which state may the policy be delivered and the group contract be made? Do the laws of the other states prohibit the insuring of their residents under the group policy? Which laws govern the rights and obligations under the group policy?

Situs of Group Contract

The group insurance policy must be filed with and approved by the insurance department of the state in which it is issued and delivered. The laws of the state of delivery determine the legal requirements for policy issue as well as the laws which govern the group contract. Therefore, determination of the appropriate situs of the policy should take into account the contacts of that state with the insurance transactions and the purposes of the group.

In a 1960 report on multi-state group policies made by the Joint Group Insurance Committee of the ALC–LIAA, the following situs criteria were recommended: (1) where the group policyholder (or, in the case of a trustee, where the union, association or one of the employers which established the fund) has its principal place of business or excutive offices, or is incorporated; (2) where the group policyholder performs its principal function in connection with the administration of the group policy; or (3) where the largest number of insured persons is located. It may be argued that any state possessing one of the criteria has sufficient connection with the insurance transaction and the purposes of the group to qualify as an appropriate situs for delivery of the group policy. In many cases, it may be preferable to issue the policy where at least two of these criteria are present and thereby avoid any substantial question as to the appropriate situs for the delivery of the policy or as to the law which governs the rights and obligations under the policy.

Extra-territorial Legal Requirements

The group insurance statutes of all the states, with the exception of the life insurance laws of Texas, Ohio and Maryland, either are limited to policies delivered in the state or otherwise indicate they are not intended to prohibit coverage of residents of the state under policies lawfully delivered in an appropriate situs outside the state. The reports of the 1945 and 1954 subcommittees of the NAIC Group Life Committee recognize that diversity of group regulations among the states requires that laws of a single state govern in order to make group insurance available to the public. As a result of these reports, the NAIC model group life insurance definition and standard provision bill specifies its requirements apply only to "policies delivered in the state."[19] The model creditor insurance bill, applicable to insurance on indebtedness of no more than five years' duration, constitutes an exception to this general rule, based on the premise that such insurance is part of an arm's-length transaction, the most essential features of which are local in character. Because of this consideration, this model bill requires the filing of group certificates and notices of proposed insurance together with the premium rate schedule in the state in which the insured loan is made and requires that these documents and the premium rate meet certain requirements.

The regulatory authorities have construed their group statutes not to prohibit the insuring of residents under out-of-state group policies,[20] with the following exceptions. The Attorney General of Wisconsin has ruled insurance companies licensed in Wisconsin are prohibited from insuring Wisconsin residents unless they are members of a group that complies with the Wisconsin group life definition law, on the assumption that this is prohibited under other provisions of the insurance code.[21] The New Jersey Insurance Department has ruled on similar grounds that insurance companies licensed in New Jersey may not insure New Jersey residents under out-of-state policies unless the general nature of the group is recognized by the New Jersey group life insurance definition law.[22] The Florida Attorney General has ruled that its group life insurance definition law is applicable to Florida residents who are required to furnish evidence of insurability to the insurance company as a condition to coverage. The theory is that the taking of evidence of insurability constitutes an application for insurance in Florida, which must be solicited by a Florida licensed agent and must comply with the Florida group life insurance

---

[19] *Proceedings of the National Association of Insurance Commissioners,* 1955, Vol. I, p. 127, reporting December, 1954, meeting: "After serious consideration, it is the opinion of your subcommittee that it would be unwise and inconsistent to recommend that such group contracts be made subject to the laws of each individual state at this time. The principal reason, as has been argued by the industry, is that the differences existing in the laws of the various states with respect to group life insurance are so extensive that it would be impractical and tend to discourage companies from offering this important coverage if such legislation were enacted . . . it would appear to be inconsistent to recommend this type of coverage be subjected to regulation by the state of residence."

[20] Op. A.G. Florida No. 654–76 dated Mar. 26, 1959; Op. A.G. of Mass. dated Sept. 7, 1951; Op. A.G. Hawaii No. 61–82 dated Aug. 10, 1961; Op. A.G. Colo., Nov. 23, 1943; Op. A.G. Ky., Aug. 20, 1962.

[21] Op. A.G. Wisc., July 28, 1958.

[22] New Jersey Ins. Dept. Ruling, Aug. 25, 1952.

requirements.[23] These three rulings have not been tested by the courts. The Texas and Ohio group life insurance definition laws contain special provisions prohibiting the insuring of residents unless the group qualifies as such under their laws. The Maryland law prohibits solicitation of group life coverage in the state unless the type of group conforms substantially with permissible Maryland law or unless approved by the Insurance Commissioner.[24]

Law Governing Rights and Obligations under Group Contracts

The courts have not yet determined finally whether the laws of the state in which the policy is delivered or those in which the insureds reside govern rights and obligations under multi-state coverage group policies. The leading case on this matter is the 1937 decision of the United States Supreme Court in *Boseman* v. *Connecticut General Life Insurance Company*.[25] In this case, the court stated: "The conclusion that Pennsylvania law [the law of delivery of the policy] governs the policy provision requiring notice of claim is supported not only by the making and delivery of the contract of insurance in that state, the declaration in the policy that Pennsylvania law shall govern the petitioner's acceptance of the insurance according to the terms of the policy, but also by the purpose of the parties to the contract that everywhere it shall have the same meaning and give the same protection, and that inequalities and confusion liable to result from applications of diverse state laws shall be avoided."

A review of court decisions indicates that, with the possible exception of Texas, the laws of the state of residence of lives insured under an out-of-state group insurance policy have no application to the rights and obligations under the group policy. Hence, in accordance with the *Boseman* ruling, such rights and obligations are governed by the laws of the state in which the group insurance policy is delivered. This assumes that the group insurance contract stipulates that the law of the state in which it is delivered shall govern and, further, that the wording of the certificate issued to residents does not vary in any material way from the wording of

---

[23] Op. A.G. Fla., Nov. 24, 1954.

[24] Anno. Code of Maryland, Art. 48A, Sec. 417(c) added June 1, 1965; letter March 12, 1965, from Maryland Ins. Dept. to Chairman of Committee on Banking, Insurance and Social Security, House of Delegates, Maryland—clarifying intent of proposed law; Op. of Ohio Attorney General dated June 19, 1950, and Texas Department rulings dated June 2, 1950, and June 22, 1948; *State of Texas* v. *State Mutual Life Assurance Company*, (Texas Supreme Court, 1962), 353 S.W. (2d) 412. The Georgia Insurance Department ruled in 1958 that the maximum insurance amount requirements of its group life law applied to its residents where a majority of the lives insured under an out-of-state group life policy are located in Georgia. However, since this ruling Georgia has enacted the NAIC Group Life Definition Model Bill which is limited to policies delivered in Georgia.

[25] 301 U.S. 196, 81 L. Ed. 1036, 57 S. Ct. 686.

the group insurance policy.[26] Although Texas court decisions have held Texas laws apply to rights of residents insured under out-of-state group policies,[27] it has been suggested that the 1947 decision of the United States Supreme Court in *Wolfe* v. *Order of United Commercial Travellers of America*[28] casts doubt on the validity of the Texas decisions under the federal constitution. The Supreme Court held that the law of the state of incorporation of a fraternal benefit association, permitting the association to limit the time within which suits must be brought against the association by its members, governs the rights of a member residing in South Dakota, whose laws prohibit such a limitation. The public policy of South Dakota was held not equal to the policy of the incorporating state requiring members of fraternal benefit associations to have the same rights regardless of residence. This case demonstrates that there are constitutional limits upon the right of one state to apply to its residents laws which are contrary to the laws of the state in which a contract is made. A group insurance contract issued in an appropriate situs may be said to involve the same considerations which were present in the *Wolfe* decision and recognized in the *Boseman* case.

NATURE OF THE GROUP CONTRACT[29]

The terms and conditions of the group contract are determined by negotiation between the insurance company and the master policyholder. Except for benefit provisions, they are largely determined by the model

---

[26] *Thieme* v. *Union Labor Life Insurance Company, Inc.*, 12 Ill. App. (2d), 110, 138 N.E. (2d), 857 (1956); and *Coleman* v. *Aetna Life Insurance Company*, 261 F. (2d), 296, 7th Cir. Ct. of Appeals (1958), held Illinois law governed rights under out-of-state group policies where the group policy was silent as to which law was to control. The *Thieme* case and *John Hancock Mutual Life Insurance Company* v. *Dorman*, 108 F. (2d), 220 (9th Cir. 1939), and *Azanich* v. *Metropolitan Life Insurance Company*, 180A 67, 180A 576, *Adair* v. *General American Life Insurance Company*, 124 S.W. (2d) 657, held the laws of residence of the certificate holder governed out-of-state group policies where the certificate varied substantially from the group policy. Cases holding the law of the place of delivery of the group policy governs include: *Fisher* v. *United Life Insurance Company*, 249 (2d) 879 (4th Cir.); *Vandenberg* v. *John Hancock Mutual Life Insurance Company*, 48 N.J.S. 1, 136A (2d) 661 (1957); *Extrum* v. *Union Casualty and Life Insurance Company*, 165 Neb. 554, 86 N.W. (2d) 568; *Protective Life Insurance Company* v. *Lamarque*, 177 So. 15. The cases giving contractual validity to a certificate which varies from the group policy are additional authority that the laws of residence do not apply where there is no conflict between the certificate and the policy.

[27] *Metropolitan* v. *Wann*, 130 Tex. 400, 109 S.W. (2d) 470; and *Brotherhood of Boilermakers, Iron Shipbuilders and Helpers of America* v. *Huval*, 140 Tex. 21, 166 S.W. (2d) 107 (1942), held Texas laws applied to the rights of Texas citizens under out-of-state group policies. Minnesota, North Carolina and South Carolina have statutes comparable to the statute relied upon in these cases. No decisions have been found making these statutes applicable to group insurance, and a similar Mississippi statute was held unconstitutional as applied to group in the case of *Hartford Accident and Indemnity Company* v. *Delta and Pine Land Co.*, U.S. 143, 54 S. Ct. 634.

[28] 67 S. Ct. 1355.

[29] Appendixes 11 and 12 contain a specimen group insurance master contract and certificate.

life and health insurance standard provisions, which have become generally accepted throughout the industry.

The group policy is an agreement between the insurance company and the policyholder to insure the lives or health of the members of a defined group of persons and to pay the insurance benefits to the insured persons or to their beneficiaries or other payees. The group policyholder is prohibited from becoming a beneficiary, except in the case of creditor insurance. Creditor policies differ in the sense that proceeds are payable to the creditor-policyholder to apply against the indebtedness of the insured debtor to the creditor.

The group contract is issued in consideration of the application of the group policyholder and the payment by the policyholder of the stipulated premiums. The "entire contract" provision states that the master policy, the application of the policyholder which is attached to the policy, and the individual applications, if any, of the insured lives shall constitute the entire contract. Such individual applications are taken and made a part of the contract for the purposes of contesting individual insurance where evidence of insurability is required because of late enrollment or other underwriting requirements. The policy provides that the insurance company shall issue an individual certificate to the policyholder for delivery to each insured person. Further, this certificate shall set forth the benefits to which such person is entitled under the policy, the beneficiary or payee of the benefits, and the rights to which such person is entitled in case of termination of employment or other eligibility or termination of the policy or of any coverage under the policy. The policy stipulates, however, that the certificate shall not constitute a part of the policy, and certificates recite that benefits are governed by and subject in every respect to the provisions of the group policy. The usual policy also states that the policyholder shall in no event be considered as the agent of the insurance company for any purposes under the policy.

Under these circumstances, the prevailing legal view is that the group contract is one between the insurance company and the policyholder for the benefit of the insured persons and their beneficiaries, who are not parties to the contract,[30] although they may enforce it according to its terms.[31] The majority rule is that the policyholder does not act as the agent of the insurance company, but acts for itself or as the agent for the insured persons in the procurement and the administration of the policy.[32] Admin-

[30] *Magee* v. *Equitable Life Assur. Soc.*, 62 N.D. 614, 44 N.W. 518, 85 A.L.R. 1457; *Alsup* v. *Travelers Ins. Co.*, 196 Tenn. 346, 268 S.W. (2d) 90; *Rivers* v. *State Capital L. Ins. Co.*, 245 N.W. 461, 96 S.W. (2d) 431, 68 A.L.R. (2d) 205.

[31] *Shea* v. *Aetna L. Ins. Co.*, 292 Mass. 575, 198 N.W. 909; *Carruth* v. *Aetna L. Ins. Co.*, 157 Ga. 608, 122 S.W. 226; *Johnson* v. *Inter Ocean Casualty Co.*, 112 W. Va. 396, 164 S.W. 411; *Mutual Benefit Health and Accident Asso.* v. *Bullard*, 270 Ala. 558, 120 So. (2d) 714.

[32] *Boseman* v. *Connecticut General L. Ins. Co.*, 301 U.S. 196, 81 L. Ed. 1036, 57 S. Ct. 686, 110 A.L.R. 732; *Duval* v. *Metropolitan L. Ins. Co.*, 82 N.H. 543, 136A 400, 50 A.L.R. 1276.

istrative functions include enrolling the insured lives under the contract, reporting to the insurance company additions and terminations of insured lives and amounts of insurance from time to time, collecting premium contributions by payroll deduction or otherwise and processing beneficiary nominations and changes. The insured is not a party to the contract and takes or rejects the terms and conditions negotiated by the policyholder. The certificate evidences rights under the contract and puts the insured on notice that the policy governs; it is not a part of the policy.[33]

The fact, however, that the group policy contemplates that the policyholder shall be the intermediary between the insurance company and the insured persons for insurance purposes has resulted in decisions by some courts that the insurance company is liable for forfeiture of insurance or insured rights caused by the negligence of the policyholder in performing these administrative functions. This responsibility has been predicated in some cases on the theory that the policyholder is in fact the agent of the insurance company for these purposes[34] and in other cases on general equitable principles.[35] Other cases have held that the policyholder owes the insured the duty of good faith and due care in administering the policy and must make clear to an insured person anything required of him to keep the policy in effect or to exercise rights under the policy upon termination of his coverage.[36] These cases demonstrate the importance of the administration of the policy, and most companies furnish policyholders with brochures that outline the steps which should be taken under various circumstances.

Although booklets and certificates are not a part of the contract, they may have a legal significance. Many courts have held the certificate evidences a separate contract if its provisions vary materially from the master contract. Moreover, booklets and certificates may have legal significance if they contain a representation which may be enforced under the legal doctrine of promissory estoppel.[37] Where they constitute an offer as distinct from an invitation to inquire, they must conform with certain requirements set forth under the NAIC model advertising code pertaining to health insurance. These considerations are especially important in light

---

[33] *Boseman* v. *Connecticut General L. Ins. Co.,* supra; *All States L. Ins. Co.* v. *Tillman,* 226 Ala. 245, 146 So. 393; *Metropolitan L. Ins. Co.* v. *Lewis* (La. App.), 142 So. 721; *Nick* v. *Travelers Ins. Co.,* 238 Mo. App. 1181, 185 S.W. (2d) 326, Affd. 354 Mo. 376, 189 S.W. (2d) 532; *Thull* v. *Equitable Life Assur. Soc.,* 40 Ohio App. 486, 178 N.E. 850.

[34] *Neider* v. *Continental Life Assur. Co.,* 213 La. 621, 35 So. (2d) 237, 2 A.L.R. (2d) 846.

[35] 1 Harv. L. Rev. 317.

[36] *Neider* v. *Continental Life Assur. Co.,* supra; *Quinten* v. *United States Steel,* 142A (2d) 370, 68 A.L.R. 2d 1.

[37] This legal principle precludes a promissor from denying a promise which the promisee has reasonably relied upon to his detriment. It rests largely upon the facts and circumstances of a particular case.

of the recent trend of offering a combined booklet-certificate for the purpose of enrolling the persons eligible for coverage under the contract.

Policyholder Contractual Provisions

Effective Date of Contract and Policyholder's Application. The date the contract becomes effective usually is set forth in the application for the group policy. It is required that the application be approved by the insurance company at its home office, an approximate monthly premium be paid, a specified percentage—usually 75 per cent—of eligible lives be enrolled under contributory plans, and the policy be filed and approved by the insurance department of the state of issue. The policy effective date may be a prior date, but it is subject to the fulfillment of these requirements.[38]

The typical application also contains the information concerning the policyholder and the insured lives, together with the plan of benefits desired. Space is provided for the policyholder to designate the writing agent to receive commissions on the sale of the group policy, and a detachable, conditional premium receipt is included.

Although the application contains much of the information upon which the policy is underwritten and is made a part of the policy, all pertinent provisions are inserted in the policy. For this reason it is the practice of many companies to substitute a brief application form on delivery of the policy containing the name and address of the applicant and a signed statement that the group policy is approved and the terms accepted. This procedure avoids the retyping of the long form application to include changes agreed to after its submission.

Policyholder Reports and Audit. In "regular accounting" insurance plans, the insurance company maintains a record of each insured life

---

[38] Many collectively bargained plans, changes in plans and plans transferred to a different insurer must be placed in force before the policy can be drafted and approved by the insurance department. This problem has been recognized by the N.Y. Insurance Department in adopting the "Murphy Rule" authorizing coverages before approval when there is "reasonable expectation of department acceptance and approval" of the plan. A written agreement between the insurance company and the policyholder is required setting forth (1) the nature and extent of the benefits or change in benefits; (2) the fact that the policy, certificate and other contractual forms may not be executed or delivered until filed and approved; and (3) if approval is denied, the parties be returned to the status quo insofar as possible or the coverage be modified retroactively to meet department requirements—N.Y. Ins. Dept. Letter dated January 9, 1964. The California insurance laws specifically provide for this contingency by permitting coverages to be placed in force under an agreement by the insurance company with the policyholder that coverages will terminate in 120 days unless the policy is filed, approved and delivered within ninety days. The agreement must specify in summary form: (1) the class or classes of employees eligible; (2) the benefits to be provided; and (3) the exceptions and restrictions to such benefits. This procedure is permissible only if the group is eligible under the California group insurance law. Provision is made for extension of the agreement where the insurance company cannot complete the policy form within a specified time limit.

showing the name, age, sex, amount and effective date of insurance, and the date insurance is terminated with the reason for such termination. Under the policy, the policyholder is required to furnish this information to the insurance company. The information serves as the basis for issuance of certificates to insured lives, for the monthly billing of total premiums due from the policyholder and for the payment of claims. Beneficiary changes are forwarded to the insurance company and, after acknowledgment and recording, are transmitted to the policyholder for delivery to the insured lives. Policies stipulate that failure of the policyholder to report the insurance of an individual does not deprive such person of his insurance. Similarly, failure of the policyholder to report the termination of insurance on an employee does not continue his insurance contrary to the provisions of the policy.

Under "policyholder administered" plans, the policyholder is required to keep the insurance records, to issue certificates to the insured lives, to acknowledge and record beneficiary changes and deliver a copy of the change to the insured life and to transmit the beneficiary records to the insurance company in case of claim. The policy requires the policyholder to furnish the information necessary for the insurance company to determine the premiums due, to make payment of claims and to perform similar policy functions.

Because the successful operation of the group insurance plan depends on the accuracy and completeness of the insurance records, group policies require all records bearing on the insurance, including payroll records, be open to inspection by the company. Periodic audits of policyholder records are made by the insurance company pursuant to this provision.

Premiums and Grace Period. Under the terms of the group contract, the payment of premiums is made the obligation of the policyholder and is a condition precedent to the continuance of the group policy. A thirty-one-day grace period is provided, and if premiums are not paid within that time, the policy automatically terminates at the end of the period of grace. The policyholder may terminate the policy on any premium due date or within the grace period by advance written notice. The policyholder is made liable for premiums for insurance continued during the grace period, and, in this respect, the group policy is clearly different from individual insurance contracts.

Premiums are based upon a table of rates contained in the policy[39] and usually are payable monthly in advance but, by agreement with the

---

[39] The laws of Maine, Michigan, New York, Ohio and Pennsylvania provide for a minimum group life insurance premium rate which must be charged for the first policy year and permit readjustment of the rate based on experience at the end of each year, which readjustment may be made retroactive only for one year. The New York and Ohio laws apply to policies issued within or without the state by insurers licensed in the state; the other state laws are limited to policies issued in the state. See Chapter 11 for a complete discussion of these minimum premium laws.

company, may be paid annually, semiannually or quarterly. The right is reserved by the insurance company to change the premium rate on the first anniversary of the policy and on any premium due date thereafter, but not more frequently than once every twelve months. However, a new premium rate may be required by the insurer at any time the contract is amended.

Modification or Termination of the Policy. Policies stipulate they may be terminated or amended at any time by written agreement between the policyholder and the insurer. Also as stated, the policyholder may discontinue the policy as of any premium due date by advance written notice and may discontinue the policy during the grace period as of the date the written notice is received by the insurer.

Policy amendments or termination may not deprive insured persons of rights which already have attached under the policy or which are intended to survive the policy, unless consent of the insured persons is secured. The majority legal rule is that, with this exception, consent of the insured persons is not necessary to a valid termination or amendment of the master contract and of the individual coverages thereunder, and most policies so stipulate. The courts are split on the question of whether advance notice of any change in the rights of a certificate holder by policy termination or amendment is required. The majority rule is that notice is necessary, especially where the insured person reasonably would believe that his coverages were being continued. One court has reasoned that this requirement is necessary to enable the certificate holder to exercise any conversion privilege that may be available on termination or reduction of his coverage or, where no such privilege is granted under the policy, to enable him to obtain similar insurance protection on his account elsewhere.[40]

Dividends and Retroactive Rate Credits. Most state laws require mutual life insurance companies annually to apportion and distribute divisible surplus to life insurance policyholders on the policy contribution to surplus plan. The New York Law makes this requirement with respect to both life and health insurance policies of such companies. Stock insurance companies may provide similar payments, which generally are referred to as retroactive premium rate reductions or experience rating refunds. A typical mutual company dividend provision states, "On each policy anniversary to which premiums have been paid, there shall be distributed hereon such share of a divisible surplus as may be apportioned

---

[40] *Poch* v. *Equitable Life Assurance Society* (1941), 22A (2d) 590; 142 A.L.R. 1279, 68 A.L.R. (2d) 249. Cf. *Quinten* v. *U.S. Steel*, 142A (2d) 370, which held that the employer was liable for the death benefit where insurance was continued during his disability by employer premium payments and subsequently terminated by notice to the insurance company without notice to the certificate holder. Liability was predicated on the loss of the certificate holder's right to convert the group life insurance within thirty-one days of termination of employment for insurance purposes.

hereto by the company." Under such a provision, the policy must complete the policy year to qualify for a dividend for such year.

Under applicable law, the dividends must be paid to the policyholder unless the policyholder elects that they be applied in abatement of premium payments. With respect to contributory policies, a number of states have enacted laws modeled after the New York law requiring "any dividend . . . apportioned on any such participating group insurance policy, or any rate reduction . . . on any non-participating group insurance policy for the first or any subsequent year of insurance under any such policy . . . issued to an employer, may be applied to reduce the employer's part of the cost of such policy, except that the excess, if any, of the employee's aggregate contribution under the policy over the net cost of the insurance shall be applied by the employer for the sole benefit of the employee."[41] These statutes have been interpreted to limit distribution of the excess dividends or premium rate credits or reductions for the benefit of employees who are participating in the plan at the time of the payment of the dividends or the granting of the rate reduction.[42] Upon payment of the dividend to the policyholder, the insurance company is fully discharged from any legal obligations with respect thereto.[43] Customarily, the policyholder applies any excess dividends or rate reductions in one of three ways: (1) by reducing the employee's contribution, either by eliminating it in one or more months or by making a smaller reduction throughout the year; (2) by increasing the benefits through amendments

---

[41] The 83rd Annual Report of the N.Y. Superintendent of Insurance for the year ended December 31, 1941, at page 27a, Vol. I, 1942, states: "Another and necessarily related matter is whether under a single policy, such as a group life policy, the excess of dividends or rate credits over the employer's contributions in a particular year may be applied to offset the employer's costs in previous years. If this principle were applicable without limit, it would permit an employer to recoup his entire cost through such application of the excess mentioned. On the other hand, it would be unduly severe to restrict the application of the excess to the experience of a single year only. Dividends and rate credits are dependent upon mortality and other losses and fluctuations can be expected. It is difficult to fix on a hard and fast rule but we feel that the accounting as to the employer's costs should be limited to some reasonably brief period, such as two or three years."

[42] This practice is, of course, no different from the treatment of retiring policyholders in a mutual life insurance company, who leave to their successors any accumulations made by the insurance company while the policies were in force—*Huber* v. *Martin*, 105 N.W. 1031; *Andrews* v. *Equitable Life Assur. Soc. of U.S.*, 124 F. (2d) 788.

[43] The fact that, in accordance with the general legal rule and a specific provision in the policy, the employer is not the agent of the insurance company makes this conclusion clear. Even if the employer were the agent of the insurance company, the insurance company would have no legal authority or obligation with respect to the distributions by the employer, since it is the general rule that in the absence of notice of intended misapplication of funds by a fiduciary, the rights and obligations of the principal are limited to payment to the agent. Austin W. Scott, *The Law of Trusts* (Albany, N.Y.: Matthew Bender & Co., Inc.; and Boston: Little, Brown & Co.), Secs. 321 and 321.1.

to the group policy; or (3) by using the fund for some kind of general welfare program. In the absence of a contrary provision in the policy or in the statutes of the state in which the policy is delivered, it has been held uniformly by the courts that an employee has no right against the employer to group policy dividends, even through they may exceed the employer's cost.[44]

Certificate Holder Contractual Provisions

Eligibility and Effective Date of Individual Insurance. The group insurance policy also describes the requirements the members of the group must satisfy to become insured. Generally, the group life insurance statutes require the policy to insure all the employees of an employer or all the members of an association or "all of any class or classes thereof determined by conditions pertaining to employment or membership in the association," subject to any premium contribution or insurability requirements contained in the policy.[45] As mentioned earlier, these eligibility requirements have been held to prohibit the exclusion of employees or members by reason of age, on the grounds that age is a condition pertaining to the person and not to his employment or membership in the association, and such illegal policy exclusions have been held unenforceable. For the most part, group health insurance statutes do not require the class of insured persons to be determined by employment or membership.

If the plan is noncontributory, persons in the eligible group on the effective date of the policy are insured automatically on that date, if they are then actively at work or then meet some similar requirement. If not, they are insured upon return to active work. In addition, under contributory plans, eligible persons must apply for the coverage and make the required contribution to the policyholder, usually by payroll deduction authorization. If an eligible person does not enroll within the period specified in the policy, or if he terminates his insurance voluntarily and later re-enrolls, the insurance company may require satisfactory evidence of insurability as a condition to being covered. Evidence of insurability also may be required for amounts of insurance in excess of the normal maximum determined by the total volume of insurance under the policy

---

[44] *Spuhler* v. *Industrial Rayon Corporation,* 25 Ohio Ops. 155, decided in 1942 by the Court of Common Pleas, Cuyahoga Ct. Ohio, Affmd. by the Court of Appeals of such County without opinion, review denied by the Supreme Court of Ohio; *Pelelas* v. *Caterpillar Tractor Co.,* 133 Fed. (2d) 629, Cert. denied 311, U.S. 700, 61 S. Ct. 138; *Slattery* v. *Pullman Co.,* 153A (2d) 575.

[45] N.Y. Ins. Law, Sec. 204, permits policies covering employees of a single employer to limit eligibility to all the employees or "all of any class or classes thereof determined by conditions pertaining to the employment, or by a combination of such conditions and conditions pertaining to the family status of the employee."

and the average amount of insurance per individual. When additional amounts of life insurance or additional benefits are added to the policy by amendment, the policy normally provides that the insured persons will become insured for the additional amount or benefit if actively at work on the date of the amendment, otherwise on the date such person returns to active work.

Beneficiaries of Group Life Insurance Benefits. The NAIC model group life insurance law and the laws of all states having group life insurance definitions require that insurance be carried for the benefit of someone other than the employer, union or other policyholder. With this exception, there is no legal prohibition against the designation of any beneficiary, as is conventional under individual insurance contracts.

Beneficiary designations are usually revocable and may be changed by filing written notice through the group policyholder. Acknowledgments of changes in the beneficiary are forwarded to the employee for filing with his certificate. The policy provides that the change is effective on the date the notice is signed, whether or not the employee is living at the date it is received by the insurer, but without prejudice to the insurer on account of any payment made by it before receipt of such change.

Successive Beneficiary Clauses. The laws of most states and the model life insurance standard provision laws permit successive beneficiary clauses governing the payment of death benefits. The successive beneficiary clause avoids the expense and delay of payment to the estate of the insured where he dies with no living designated beneficiary but leaves surviving close relatives. The typical clause is worded as follows: "In the event of the death of the beneficiary . . . last named by the employee prior to that of the employee, or if no beneficiary shall have been named, the . . . insurance . . . shall be paid to the executors or administrators of the employee, except that the company may in such case, at its option, pay such insurance to any one or more of the following surviving relatives: wife, husband, mother, father, child or children, brother or sister."

Facility of Payment Clauses. The facility of payment clause permits the insurance company to pay part of the death benefit for last illness and funeral expenses. Payments may be made even though a designated beneficiary is alive and competent. The model group life insurance law permits payment of such sum "not exceeding $500 to any person appearing to the insurer to be equitably entitled thereto by reason of having incurred funeral or other expenses incident to the last illness or death of the person insured." These provisions furnish equitable distribution of the proceeds in accordance with the insured's intent and avoid undue delay or expense.

Most companies also provide for the payment of death benefits to a relative or custodian of a beneficiary who is a minor or incompetent. The typical clause provides "the company may, at its option and until claim is made by the duly appointed guardian or committee of such beneficiary, make payment of the amount of life insurance payable to such beneficiary, at a rate not exceeding $50 per month, to any relative by blood or connection by marriage of such beneficiary, or to any other person or institution appearing to it to have assumed custody and principal support of such beneficiary, for the sole benefit of the beneficiary. Such payment shall constitute a full discharge of the liability of the company to the extent thereof."

Payees of Group Health Insurance Benefits. Accidental death benefits often are made subject to life insurance beneficiary provisions. Other health insurance benefits are payable to the insured person in most cases. Under the model group health insurance law and the health insurance statutes of many states, the contract may provide for the payment of benefits at the insurance company's option directly to the doctor or hospital or other organization furnishing the services or supplies insured, but the contract may not require that services be rendered by a particular hospital or person. Where policies do not contain the right of direct payment, most companies make use of an assignment form signed by the insured person directing the insurance company to pay hospital, surgical and medical benefits directly to the hospital or doctor and relieving the insurance company of liability to the extent of payments made under the assignment. Policy provisions or assignments authorizing direct payment to the hospital or doctor facilitate hospital admissions and medical care without advance payment by the employee.

Assignment of Death Benefits. Life insurance and accidental death and dismemberment benefits are not assignable under most group contracts. Some policies provide for assignment of death benefit rights with the consent of the insurance company, which does not assume responsibility for the validity of the assignment. Where large death benefits are provided, assignments made usually are designed to remove the proceeds from the insured's estate for federal estate tax purposes. Such assignments include all incidents of ownership of the insured, which consist of the right to receive the proceeds, the right to name the beneficiary, the right to make any required premium contribution and the right to convert group coverage to individual coverage. The tax consequences of such assignments are uncertain, since they have not been ruled upon by the Internal Revenue Service or the courts.

Settlement Options. Group life insurance and accidental death benefits may be made payable in a lump sum or in accordance with a settlement option which may be elected by the insured person or, in the absence of such an election, by his beneficiary at the insured's death. The two usual options are the fixed period installment option, providing for payments in equal installments, monthly, annually or otherwise, including both principal and interest, for a fixed period of years; and the fixed amount installment option, providing for payments of installments of a designated amount until the principal sum is exhausted, with interest credited periodically on the unpaid balance of the proceeds of life insurance. The life income option is available under some policies and provides for guaranteed equal installments for the lifetime of the beneficiary, as well as a guaranteed total payment in the event of death prior to a designated period. "Life annuity options" and "interest deposit options" also may be offered. Under the former, the beneficiary may elect to purchase a life annuity at less than the regular rates then in effect, and under the latter, proceeds are left with the company with interest payable periodically to the beneficiary for his life or for a specified period, with the right to withdraw a part of the principal from time to time and with any balance payable on the death of the beneficiary. Option terms and the effective rate of interest are determined by those in effect on the death of the insured person and are not set forth in the policy or certificate.

Discontinuance of a Member's Insurance. Subject to extended benefit provisions, the insurance of an individual ceases automatically (1) on the termination of his employment or membership in the insured classes; (2) on the expiration of the period for which his last required premium contribution, if any, was made by him; and (3) on the termination of the master policy or of his insurance by amendment to the policy. Where several coverages are provided under the same policy, the insurance terminates with respect to any coverage for which the required premium contribution is not made or which is terminated by reason of amendment or termination of such coverage.

The insurance of dependents ceases when the dependent no longer meets the policy definition of an eligible dependent; when the certificate holder's insurance ceases; or on the expiration of the period for which the last premium contribution for dependent coverage was made by the certificate holder. It also ceases upon termination of the policy or on amendment of the policy to terminate dependent coverages. Usually a dependent child is disqualified by attainment of twenty-three (or eighteen) years of age, marriage, full-time regular employment or when no longer dependent on the certificate holder for support. The dependency status of a wife is deemed to terminate on divorce or legal separation.

Termination of Employment. Termination of employment is often defined in the contract as the date the employee ceases active work, except that where cessation of work is due to sickness, injury, temporary layoff or leave of absence, employment is deemed to continue for insurance purposes until terminated by the employer by written notice to the company or by any other means. Policies specify that in exercising this election, the employer must act in accordance with rules which preclude individual selection, and in the case of layoffs and leaves, insurance is automatically terminated upon the lapse of a specified period. Employment is also defined to terminate upon entry into active duty in the armed forces of any country. If insurance is to be provided upon retirement, special provision is made for continuance in accordance with the employer's retirement plan.

Under these election clauses the employer determines whether to consider interruption of work as temporary or as a permanent discharge. Frequently, the question of whether coverage has terminated will depend upon the employer's intent in this regard. Intent to continue coverage has been inferred by the courts from such acts as continued premium payments or wage deductions, failure of the branch office to notify the employer's main office of the termination, failure to give timely notice of termination to the insurance company or failure to notify the employee of his discharge. Actions such as re-employment offers, occasional subsequent work or the granting of a leave of absence have been held to manifest an intent to continue coverage. Contrariwise affirmative notice to the employee of his termination or the lapse of the period during which the employer may elect to continue coverage manifest intent to terminate coverage.

It is a general rule that where the employee terminates employment by voluntarily resigning or quitting, no notice of termination is necessary to discontinue coverage. Under these circumstances, the employee is charged with knowledge of the group policy discontinuance provisions outlined in his certificate. Where the employee is fired or discharged, he should be given notice to avoid any misunderstanding and consequent loss of his conversion privilege, which must be exercised within thirty-one days of termination of employment. Where insurance is terminated by employer election during illness, leave or layoff, it is especially important to give notice in light of these considerations.[46] Under these circumstances, notice is necessary to effect a termination of employment within the meaning of the group policy.

The question of whether participation in a strike constitutes termination of employment may be a troublesome problem. Where the policy defines termination of employment as the date of cessation of active work or cessation of active employment and the policy does not give the employer an election to continue insurance during a strike, the courts have held participation in the strike constitutes a termination of employment.[47] In the absence of a policy definition of termination of employment, the courts are not in agreement on the effect of a strike. In the case of *Degnan v. Metropolitan Life Insurance Company*,[48] the court held a strike was a

---

[46] *Quinten* v. *United States Steel*, 142A (2d), 370; 68 A.L.R. 2d 1.

[47] *Chrosniak* v. *Metropolitan Life Insurance Company* (1923), 201 N.Y.S. 211, Affmd. without Op. 204 N.Y.S. 898.

[48] *Degnan* v. *Metropolitan Life Insurance Company* (1942), 34 N.Y.S., (2d) 238.

temporary interruption in work and not a change in the status of the employee necessary to effect a termination of employment.[49] A similar conflict of court opinion is present where an employee ceases work because of layoff and the policy contains no definition of employment and no specific provision regarding layoffs.

Conversion Rights. In the field of group life insurance, the laws of most states require a policy provision granting to the certificate holder the right to convert insurance terminating by reason of termination of employment or termination of membership in the eligible group, to an individual policy of permanent life insurance issued without evidence of insurability. The conversion right must be exercised within thirty-one days of the termination of group coverage, and an extended death benefit is provided under the group contract during the thirty-one-day conversion period. The individual policy may be in any of the forms then customarily issued by the insurance company at the age and for the amount applied for, except term insurance.[50] The policy is issued at a premium determined by the class of risk to which the certificate holder belongs[51] and his then attained age and may be equal to or, at his option, less than the amount of insurance which terminates under the group policy.[52] The certificate holder may elect an individual policy with not more than one year of preliminary term insurance under policies delivered in New York and West Virginia. Amounts of group insurance which have matured as endowments under permanent group life insurance plans are excluded in determining the amount that may be converted.

The laws of several states permit coverage of the dependent spouse and

---

[49] In this case the employer notified the insurance company to cancel insurance on the basis that the employee had quit work, and the insurance company canceled the insurance by reason of this notice and by reason of the failure of the employer to pay premiums. The court held the employer was liable for damages for wrongfully terminating the insurance coverage of the employee.

[50] The laws of New York, Ohio, Michigan and Minnesota retain the 1917 NAIC model bill language, which requires conversion to "any one of the forms customarily issued by the insurer, except term" and does not provide for limitation of convertible policies to those issued at the age and amount applied for.

[51] The specific wording of the conversion requirements of all states being modeled on either the 1917 or current NAIC group life insurance standard provision bill refer to "the class of risk" to which the insured person belongs after he has terminated employment or membership in the eligible group. This wording indicates the intent to require issue of a conversion policy regardless of the insurability of the applicant and to permit the insurer to base the premium for the conversion policy on occupational and other risk classifications unrelated to health and applicable to buyers of individual policies. However, the Wisconsin Insurance Department has ruled that such premium risk classification may be based on the excess mortality of all conversion policies as a class.

[52] The laws of New York, Michigan and Minnesota appear to permit the group policy to prohibit conversions in amounts less than the amount which terminates under the group policy. The laws of a number of states reduce the convertible amount by amounts of group life insurance for which the insured becomes eligible within the thirty-one-day conversion period under any other group life insurance policy.

minor children of the certificate holder for reduced amounts of group life insurance. Under these laws, a conversion right and extension of death benefits similar to that granted the certificate holder must be provided for the spouse with respect to the insurance on her life. This conversion right arises under the same circumstances that give rise to the rights of the certificate holder to convert his insurance. In some cases, the insurance on the minor children also is subject to a conversion right.

Under the model NAIC group life insurance bill and the laws of many states, a similar conversion right and extension of death benefit limited to $2,000[53] is required where the certificate holder has been continuously insured for at least five years and his group life insurance is terminated by reason of the amendment or termination of the group policy. This conversion privilege is not applicable with respect to amounts of group life insurance for which he becomes eligible within the thirty-one-day conversion period under any other group life insurance policy.

Under the laws of nineteen states, the certificate holder must be notified of the conversion privilege and its duration within fifteen days after termination of his insurance. If such notice is given after fifteen days have elapsed, the certificate holder is permitted to convert fifteen days after notice. Whether or not notice is given, the conversion right expires under these laws on the expiration of ninety-one days from the termination of insurance. Written notice to the certificate holder at his last known address furnished the insurance company satisfies the requirements of such laws. With the exception of New York,[54] these laws do not extend coverages under the group policy beyond the thirty-one-day conversion period.

Group health insurance contracts may provide for the right of the certificate holder to convert certain coverages to an individual policy without evidence of insurability upon termination of employment or termination of membership in the eligible group. Conversions on retirement are usually permitted where benefits continuing after retirement are not substantially equivalent to the benefits which may be converted on normal termination of employment. If the certificate holder elects to convert on retirement, the group insurance benefits are terminated.

Usually the certificate holder must have been insured continuously for at least three months prior to termination of group coverages, and permissible conversions are limited to hospital and surgical expense coverages. Dependent coverages also may be converted at the option of the certificate holder. However, because dependents often include adult children attending college, mentally retarded or physically impaired children

---

[53] $3,000 in Nebraska.

[54] *DeVille* v. *Continental Assurance Co.* (1960), 199 N.Y. Supp. (2d) 876, 170 N.E. (2d) 457, followed in *Payne* v. *Equitable Life Assurance Society of the U.S.* (1961), 220 N.Y. Supp. (2d) 493.

and dependent parents, many policies reserve to the insurance company the right to require separate conversion policies for each dependent in lieu of a single family conversion policy.

The conversion privilege also is made available to a child upon attaining the limiting age of coverage as a dependent under the group health insurance contract. The spouse also is given the right to convert dependent coverages, including any coverages on minor children, on the death of the certificate holder and consequent termination of dependent coverages.

The premium for the conversion is that applicable to the class of risk to which the covered persons belong and to the ages of such persons and the form and amount of insurance provided. Conversions are not permitted where similar benefits are provided under other policies which, together with the conversion, will result in overinsurance according to the insurance company standards. Convertible benefits are limited in amount, generally exclude maternity benefits, and also contain the exclusions or conditions customarily used in the insurer's individual health insurance policies. Provision is made for the nonduplication of other benefits under other policies in the conversion policy. For this purpose, the insurance company is given the right to require information regarding similar coverages under other policies.

Under the New York Russo Act,[55] hospital and surgical expense policies delivered in New York must provide for conversions for certificate holders who have been insured for three months and whose insurance ceases because of termination of employment or termination of membership in a union. The law prescribes minimum conversion plans and requires that written notice of the conversion privilege and its duration be given within fifteen days of termination of insurance. If such notice is not given, the conversion privilege is extended to fifteen days after written notice is given, subject to a maximum extension to ninety-one days after termination of insurance.

General Claim Provisions

Incontestable Clause. The period for contesting the validity of group life insurance is limited by state law.[56] The usual policy provision reads, "Except for non-payment of premium by the policyholder, this policy shall be incontestable after two years from the date of issue, and the life insurance of any insured person shall be incontestable after such insurance has been in force for two years during such person's lifetime." It

---

[55] N.Y. Ins. Law, Sec. 162, Sub-Sec. 5.

[56] Wisconsin law also requires that a group health insurance policy make the insured person's insurance incontestable for nonfraudulent misstatements after his insurance has been in force for two years during his lifetime: Wisc. Stat. 1953, Sec. 204.321 (2)(a).

should be noted that two separate incontestable periods are provided; one being the period to contest the master policy, and the other the period to contest the individual insurance of persons who were required to submit evidence of insurability.[57] Both group life and group health insurance policies also must provide that "all statements made by the policyholder or by the persons insured shall be deemed representations and not warranties, and no statement made by a person insured shall be used in any contest unless a copy of the instrument containing the statement is or has been furnished to such person or to his beneficiary." Under this provision, to contest coverage, the statement must be false and concern a fact which is material to the underwriting decision to assume the risk, and it must be relied upon by the insurance company. Under most laws, intent to deceive is not required.

Notice of Loss. Written notice of loss is not required to be given the insurance company within any prescribed period under group life insurance and many group health insurance policies. Some group health insurance policies require that written notice be given to the insurer within twenty days of the compensable event, such as the first day of absence from work, the first day of confinement in a hospital or the date covered medical expenses are first incurred. Such policies provide that failure to give notice within the prescribed period shall not invalidate or reduce the claim if the claimant can show that notice was given as soon as reasonably possible.

Proof of Loss. Many policies require that written proof of loss be furnished to the insurance company within a specified period in the case of waiver of premium death claims, accidental death and dismemberment claims and certain health insurance claims. Except for group life insurance, policy benefits are payable upon receipt of written proof on the insurance company's forms or, if such forms are not furnished by the company within fifteen days after demand, then upon receipt of written proof covering the occurrence, character and extent of the event for which claim is made. The requirement that claims be submitted on a prescribed form is necessary for the efficient and economical administration of most group health insurance claims.

Payment of Claims. Group life insurance and accidental death benefits are paid in a lump sum or pursuant to any settlement option. Dismemberment benefits are paid in a lump sum. Other group health

---

[57] Incontestable clause does not bar defense on ground deceased was not an eligible employee as defined in the policy—*Fisher* v. *U.S. Life Insurance Company in the City of New York* (1957), U.S. Dist. Ct. of Maryland, 145 F., Supp. 646, Affmd. 249F (2d) 879; *Rasmussen* v. *Equitable Life Assurance Society of the United States,* 293 Mich. 482, 292 N.W. 377; Contra where insurer accepted premium with knowledge of ineligibility—*John Hancock Mutual Life Insurance Company* v. *Dorman,* 9 Cir. 108 F (2d) 220; *Eagan* v. *Ulman Labor Life Insurance Company* (1957), 2 App. Div. (2d) 843; 156 NYS (2d) 57, Affmd. 3 N.Y. (2d) 758, 143 N.E. (2d) 793.

insurance benefits, such as disability income benefits and hospital benefits, usually are paid weekly, with any balance due upon termination of disability payable immediately on receipt of due proof.

Nonduplication of Group Health Insurance Benefits. The purpose of a nonduplication of benefit provision is to prevent an insured person from making a profit on his hospital, surgical and medical expense insurance by reason of duplicate coverages under several policies and benefit plans. Double coverage is sometimes justified as necessary to protect against the high cost of present-day health care. However, the use of insurance to secure profit increases premium charges to the general public and retards the expansion and development of new types of health coverage. The belief that an uncontrolled excess profit potential also creates the problems of both overutilization of health care facilities and the increased costs of such facilities has resulted in the growing acceptance of anti-duplication provisions. A joint life and health insurance industry committee has recently developed a model group anti-duplication policy provision.[58] The provision has three general functions: (1) to limit total insurance payments under all policies and plans to actual out-of-pocket hospital, surgical and medical expense;[59] (2) to permit the insured to benefit by multiple coverage to the extent of actual out-of-pocket expense; and (3) to limit payments by each insurer to the amount of its policy benefit. This is accomplished by a formula for apportionment of the benefits and savings among the insurers. The details of nonduplication provisions are discussed in Chapter 24.

Examination. Group insurance policies provide that, except for group life insurance, the insurance company shall have the right and opportunity to examine the insured person when and so often as it may reasonably require during the pendency of any claim and also shall have the right and opportunity to make an autopsy in the case of death where this is not forbidden by law. Examinations and autopsies are made at the expense of the insurance company. The right of examination is often necessary to determine the validity of a claim, and an autopsy is sometimes the only means of determining the cause of death.

Limitation of Action. Group insurance contracts also provide that, except for group life insurance, no suit at law or in equity shall be brought in connection with the contract prior to sixty days after proof of loss is filed, nor shall such suit be brought at all unless brought within two years and ninety days after the date of loss upon which the suit is based. Most contracts are required to provide that if the time limit for bringing suit under the policy is less than that permitted by the law in the state in

---

[58] *Group Health Insurance Viewpoints on Over-Insurance*, Bulletin of ALC–HIAA–LIAA Committee on Non-Duplication of Health Insurance Benefits, 1962.

[59] Individual health insurance policies purchased and owned by the insured are excluded.

which the employee resides at the time the policy is issued, the limitation for bringing suit is extended to the minimum period permitted by such law.

CREDITOR GROUP INSURANCE CONTRACTS

Regulation of Group Contract

Creditor group insurance is regulated by the state group insurance definition and standard provision laws applicable to other forms of group insurance. Such laws generally exclude creditor group life insurance from the conversion requirement. An exception is the New Jersey law, which requires a conversion privilege in the event insurance terminates on an absolute assignment of an indebtedness repayable over a period of more than ten years.[60] As is the case in other forms of group insurance, the law of the place of delivery of the master policy governs the rights and obligations under policies insuring lives residing in several states, but policies may not insure lives residing in Texas, Ohio, Wisconsin, New Jersey and, under certain circumstances, Maryland, unless the policy complies with the group life insurance definition requirements of these states. In New York, creditor group insurance laws require that insurance in connection with a New York credit transaction comply with maximum premium rates, certificate and similar New York regulations, regardless of the place of delivery of the master policy.[61]

Additional extensive regulation of creditor group health and life insurance is contained in the NAIC model credit insurance bill applicable to debts of not more than five years' duration. This bill has been enacted in twenty-nine states, the District of Columbia and Puerto Rico. Three other states, New York, West Virginia and Wisconsin, have enacted similar laws.

The model bill establishes maximum policy premium rates, prohibits insurance charges to debtors in excess of the premium rate and requires delivery of a certificate of insurance to the debtor at the time of debt or within thirty days. The certificate must disclose the charge separately for life and health insurance, describe the coverages and state that the benefits will be paid to the creditor to apply toward the debt. If a certificate is not delivered at the date of the debt, a notice of proposed insurance setting forth the charges to the debtor and describing the coverage must be signed by the debtor and a copy must be furnished to him. The term of insurance may not extend more than fifteen days beyond the scheduled maturity date of the debt unless extended without cost to the debtor. Where the debt is discharged prior to its scheduled maturity

---

[60] N.J. Rev. Stat., 1937, as amd., Sec. 17: 34–32.
[61] N.Y. Ins. Law, Sec. 154, Sub-Sec. 7; N.Y. Ins. Dept. Reg. 27A, Sept. 27, 1963.

date, insurance is terminated and unearned premium charges are refunded. Generally, the amount of insurance may not exceed the debt,
except in those states whose group life insurance definition laws permit
insurance on agricultural credit transaction commitments on a level term
insurance plan, or unless the state permits insurance on educational credit
transaction commitments in the amount of the commitment which has not
been advanced.[62]

The amount of periodic indemnity payable for disability may not
exceed the aggregate of the periodic unpaid debt installments. The
amount of each periodic payment may not exceed the original debt
divided by the total number of periodic installments.

The creditor is prohibited from settling or adjusting claims but may
draw drafts or checks on the insurance company in payment of claims due
the creditor, subject to audit and review by the insurance company. On
large cases, it is customary to permit the policyholder to credit such claims
against the premium becoming due to the company.

Policy Provisions

Generally, creditor insurance policies contain the same provisions
found in other types of group insurance contracts. They differ in the
following respects: (1) proceeds are payable to the creditor to apply
toward extinguishment of the insured indebtedness and not to a named
beneficiary unless level term agricultural loan commitments are insured;[63]
(2) insurance eligibility is determined by conditions pertaining to the
insured indebtedness and sometimes by age; (3) insurance may not
become effective with respect to existing indebtedness without evidence
of insurability unless 75 per cent of such eligible indebtedness is insured;
(4) insurance discontinues on the discharge of the debt or on default in
payments due on the debt; (5) special premium calculation and determination provisions are necessary; (6) if less than 100 new debtors or 75 per
cent of those eligible become insured in any year, the insurance company
reserves the right either to exclude new debtors or to require them to
submit satisfactory evidence of insurability.

Eligibility. The eligible class of debtors is usually determined by
conditions pertaining to the indebtedness and, if permissible, by the age
of the debtor. Eligible debtors are insured subject to any policy requirements as to premium contribution or submission of satisfactory evidence

---

[62] Mass. Gen. Laws, Ch. 175, Sec. 133C; N.Y. Ins. Law, Sec. 204, Sub-Sec. (1)
(C); Pa. Ann. Stat. tit. 40, Sec. 532.3(c).

[63] Under New York law, amounts in excess of the indebtedness under level term
agricultural loan commitment coverages are payable by the creditor to a beneficiary named by the debtor or, if none, then either to the estate of a debtor or under
the provision of a facility of payment clause. See Massachusetts and New York laws
referred to in previous footnote. Other states authorizing such insurance have similar
provisions or require payment by the insurance company directly to the debtor's beneficiary or his estate.

of insurability. Normally, the indebtedness must be either of the installment type or, in accordance with the NAIC group life insurance bill,
single payment indebtedness which is payable in one sum within eighteen
months or less from the initial date of the debt. Long-term indebtedness,
such as residential mortgages[64] and other types of indebtedness, usually
are insured under individual contracts. In either case, the indebtedness
must be that of a natural person and not of a partnership, association or
corporation. Generally only one person may be insured under each loan.
Where two people co-sign a note, the policy limits insurance to the
principal debtor or to the person on whose financial responsibility the
creditor made the loan.

Termination of Insurance. Insurance with respect to a debt terminates
upon discharge of the debt or upon one month's default in the scheduled
repayment of the debt. Provision usually is made, however, for an option
in the creditor to continue insurance for all defaulting debtors on a
uniform basis during a specified period, varying from one to six months
after default. Where the creditor assigns the debt to a creditor not
included in the policy, insurance usually terminates unless the assigning
creditor continues to service the debt and retain a sufficient equity to
justify his continuing as beneficiary of the insurance. Provision also is
made for the termination of insurance on secured loans if the security is
repossessed by the creditor or if it becomes subject to a court judgment.
Some policies insure short-term indebtedness on a single premium basis.
Except for these policies, insurance terminates upon termination of the
master policy.

Premiums. The policy premium under plans insuring long-term indebtedness, and sometimes short-term, is determined by applying the
premium rate to the monthly outstanding balance of the total insured
loans. A typical policy provision reads as follows:

The premium due on the Policy Effective Date shall be an estimated premium
determined by the Company by applying the initial Premium Rate to the anticipated monthly average amount of insurance. At the end of the first policy
month the actual premium for said first month shall be determined by applying
the initial monthly premium rate to the average amount of insurance in force
during the first policy month, which average amount shall, for the purpose
of insurance hereunder, be considered as 50 per cent of the amount of insurance
in force on the last day of said policy month. The excess, if any, of the actual
premium over the estimated premium shall be payable by the Policyholder
to the Company on the date it is determined, and the excess, if any, of the
estimated premium over the actual premium shall be credited by the Company to the account of the Policyholder. The premium due on any due date
after the Policy Effective Date shall be determined by applying the premium
rate then in effect to the amount of insurance then in force.

---

[64] Residential mortgage insurance may be written on a group basis in most states.
Five jurisdictions limit the insured loan to $5,000, twenty-three to $10,000, two to
$15,000, two to $20,000, two to $25,000, one to $35,000 (on mortgages), and sixteen
have no limit on the amount which may be insured

Where ages of insured debtors are required, appropriate changes are made in this provision.

Under short-term indebtedness insurance plans, the policy premium frequently is charged for the duration of the loan and made payable in full in the month during which the loan becomes insured. A typical policy provision reads as follows:

If indebtedness incurred prior to the Policy Effective Date is not included as Qualifying Indebtedness under the Policy Specifications, the premium due on the Policy Effective Date shall be an estimated premium and shall be credited to the account of the Policyholder against premium due on the last day of the first policy month. If indebtedness incurred prior to the Policy Effective Date is included as Qualifying Indebtedness, the premium due on the Policy Effective Date shall be determined by applying the appropriate single premium, from the Schedule of Single Premiums shown in the Policy Specifications, to the amount of insurance becoming effective on said date for each indebtedness incurred prior to said date, and such premium shall be based on the number of months in the period from the date the Debtor becomes insured to the scheduled maturity date of each such indebtedness. The premium due on the last day of each policy month shall be the sum of the individual premiums determined for each indebtedness in connection with which a Debtor becomes insured in such policy month. Such individual premium shall be determined by applying to the amount of insurance in force for the Debtor on the effective date of his insurance, the appropriate single premium based on the Schedule of Single Premiums in effect on said date and the number of months in the period from the date the Debtor becomes insured to the scheduled maturity date of the indebtedness.

When the single premium plan is used, insurance normally does not terminate on termination of the policy but continues for the duration of the insured loan, subject to the other policy requirements.

SELECTED REFERENCES

American Law Reports Annotated:

Conflict of laws as to group insurance, 72 A.L.R. 2d 695.

Group life insurance policy for benefit of union members, 17 A.L.R. 2d 927.

Effective date of group life insurance, as to individual policies of employees, 35 A.L.R. 2d 798.

Termination of coverage under group policy with regard to termination of employment, 68 A.L.R. 2d 8.

Time of disability or death with regard to termination of coverage under group policy, 68 A.L.R. 2d 150.

Nonpayment of premiums as termination of individual coverage under group policy, 68 A.L.R. 2d 215.

Cancellation or modification of master policy as termination of coverage under group policy, 68 A.L.R. 2d 249.

Group insurance; failure of employer or insurer to notify employee dropped from payroll of necessity for and time of contribution to premium, 2 A.L.R. 2d 852.

Scope of provision in group health and accident insurance policy excluding from coverage sickness or accidents arising out of, or in the course of, employment, 47 A.L.R. 2d 1240.

BAKER, HORACE R. "Employee Rights under Collectively Bargained Group Plans." Paper read before Association of Life Insurance Counsel, New York City, December 8, 1958.

BROOKE, DWIGHT. "Some Phases of Group Life Insurance Law," *Proceedings, Legal Section of American Life Convention,* October, 1948.

COLLIER, ABRAM T. "Termination of Employment under Group Policies." Paper read before Association of Life Insurance Counsel, New York City, December 11, 1946.

GOSE, GEORGE B. "The Doing Business Rule and Group Insurance." Paper read before Association of Life Insurance Counsel, White Sulphur Springs, West Virginia, May 15, 1950.

HALLETT, JAMES B. "Extra-territorial Effect of State Regulatory Laws: Some 1955 Comments." Paper read before Association of Life Insurance Counsel, White Sulphur Springs, West Virginia, May 9, 1955.

HILL, JOHN M., II. "Life Insurance and Consumer Installment Credit." Paper read before Association of Life Insurance Counsel, White Sulphur Springs, West Virginia, May 7, 1957.

JETER, WILLIAM H. "State Insurance Statutes Having Extra-territorial Effect," *Proceedings, Legal Section of American Life Convention,* October, 1941.

KING, CECIL G. "Proper Situs of Multi-State Group Policies." Paper read before Association of Life Insurance Counsel, White Sulphur Springs, West Virginia, May 9, 1961.

LESSER, SAUL. " 'Let the Employer Beware'—Potential Tort Liability under Employee Benefit Plans," *Proceedings, Legal Section of American Life Convention,* October, 1962.

MEYER, WILLIAM F. "Recent Developments in Group Life Insurance Law," *Proceedings, Legal Section of American Life Convention,* October, 1959.

National Association of Insurance Commissioners, Proceedings of the, 1955, Vol. 1, p. 127.

REEVES, GORDON C. "Some Recent Legal Developments Resulting from Extension of Group Coverage to Union Members and Related Groups," *Proceedings, Legal Section of the American Life Convention,* October, 1951.

————. "Recent Developments in the Field of Group Insurance." Paper read before Association of Life Insurance Counsel, New York City, December 12, 1955.

SMITH, THOMAS H. "The 'Actively at Work' Requirement in Group Insurance," *Proceedings, Legal Section of American Life Convention,* October, 1962.

Chapter 26

GROUP INSURANCE MARKETING

BY KENNETH C. FOSTER

In his preface to the only comprehensive history of life insurance marketing, written in 1941, J. Owen Stalson stated, " . . . the submergence of marketing is related to its unfavored position in the organization of the business and to a commonplace quality in its nature. Marketing . . . has not seemed to demand the services of experts; it does not lend itself readily to treatment by formula; and it has been slow to assume scientific and professional ways. These humble qualities have put life insurance marketing at a disadvantage in its own household. . . ."[1]

Although the nature of the marketing process, especially its selling aspects, may not lend itself readily to a scientific approach, significant changes have become evident since the quoted statement was made. These changes are especially obvious in the process of marketing group life and group health insurance, where the team play of many experts is a continuous and essential part of marketing and where scientific and professional ways are common.

Group insurance today is highly technical and complex. Its growth pattern is an explosive one. Its pattern of change is dramatic. The influences of employers, unions, specialized brokers and consultants, as well as state and federal laws and regulations are strong, frequently divergent and usually complicated. Competition is relentless. Group insurance marketing is challenging, often frustrating, usually rewarding and ever fluid. It demands of its successful practitioners a high degree of intelligence, continuous training in both technical and sales areas, ingenuity, integrity and industry.

NATURE OF THE GROUP MARKET

Differences between Mass and Individual Insurance Marketing

One way to describe the nature of group insurance marketing is to

---

[1] J. Owen Stalson, *Marketing Life Insurance* (Cambridge, Mass.: Harvard University Press, 1942), p. xxix.

make comparisons with the marketing of individual insurance in a number of specific areas.

Nature of the Buyer.   The group insurance buyer may have from ten to thousands of employees. Typically, he is more sophisticated and buys less on emotion and more on price and service than the individual buyer. The group buyer is usually under influences or pressures to provide group insurance coverage, so he is going to buy from someone in any event. The individual buyer, on the other hand, frequently buys only because of a motivating sales presentation.

Type of Selling Medium.   Both group and individual insurance are marketed through commissioned agents and brokers.[2] In group marketing, however, the broker plays a much more important role. Although the majority of group cases is sold through agents and smaller brokers, who tend to be more successful in the smaller case field, by far the largest percentage of total group premium is produced by brokers who specialize in or who have specialized departments for group insurance. In addition, because of the technical and specialized nature of the field, group marketing involves insurance company group specialists (both home office and field) who assist brokers and agents in group selling and servicing.

Compensation.[3]   Agents and brokers are compensated by means of commissions for both group and individual sales. Unlike individual commissions, however, group commissions generally grade downward as the size of the annual premium increases. Furthermore, in the group field some specialized brokers and consultants charge their clients on a fee basis and either do not accept commissions or request nominal commissions.

Marketing Area.   The individual market has almost no geographic limitations. It exists wherever there is a sufficient number of individuals to support a full or part-time agent or broker. The group market, on the other hand, is limited more to urban areas where a sufficient number of eligible groups exists. The market for large national group cases tends to be concentrated in a relatively few major cities, since only the headquarters offices of national organizations generally have the authority to buy.

Point of Sale.   Individual selling is done most often in the buyer's home and frequently in the evening (exceptions to this are in the area of sales to business and professional men). In most instances, group selling is done during business hours at the buyer's place of business, although some union and union-management cases frequently require evening meetings.

---

[2] Group marketing by hospital and medical service associations, however, usually is done directly through association "enrollment representatives," who are on a salaried or an incentive basis.

[3] See Chapter 27 for a detailed discussion of compensation systems used in group insurance marketing.

Competition. At the point of sale, group marketing usually is more competitive than individual marketing, particularly in the area of cost. With the exception of the buyer in a business insurance case or the buyer of a large amount of insurance, the individual insurance buyer is not apt to make cost comparisons among several insurance companies. With his limited knowledge of insurance, he more often buys from the company of the agent who motivates him to buy. In contrast, the group buyer, who may have considerable knowledge of the employee benefit field, usually reviews proposals from a number of insurance companies before buying and places heavy emphasis on comparative costs in selecting an insurance company. The established buying pattern of competitive bidding in the group field greatly intensifies competition.

Product Design. There is more flexibility in product design in group marketing since the insurance company is able and willing on all but the smaller cases to hand-tailor contracts to meet the specifications of informed buyers and the influences of competition. Larger group buyers often influence and may even decide basic product design for a particular case, whereas the individual buyer selects one or a combination of plans from an existing portfolio.

Product Pricing. Group insurance generally is based on the concept of one-year term insurance, so rates are usually guaranteed for only one year. Since most individual policies are for more than one year's duration, individual rates are set for a much longer period, often for life. Both group and individual insurance determine the premium rate from such characteristics of the group or individual as age, sex and occupation, but group insurance also uses such characteristics as income level and geographical location as well as the principle of experience rating. With some exceptions for smaller cases, the previous claim experience, if any, of the group is considered in establishing initial premium rates and experience rating is generally applied to the policy in establishing renewal premium rates.

Group rate calculation is often complicated and when done at the point of sale may be tentative, whereas individual policy rate calculations in the field are relatively simple and are usually final. Many agents consider this a handicap and because of it often fail to follow group sales opportunities.

Advertising and Sales Promotion. Because of the differences in the degree of sophistication and the influences that motivate the group buyer compared with the individual buyer, advertising and sales promotion play a less significant role in group marketing. Since emotion plays a small role in the purchase of group insurance and the buyer usually secures competitive bids, he is less influenced by the usual advertising and sales promotion approaches.

Servicing. Although important in both fields, servicing is essential in group insurance cases of all sizes. The greater administrative duties required of the group buyer necessitate more servicing than for the individual buyer. Also, frequent benefit plan changes occur on a group case which require service, whereas the plan of insurance sold on an individual policy seldom changes. Furthermore, the term nature of group coverage and the intense competition result in much more frequent transferring of coverage among insurers than in individual insurance, necessitating more intensive servicing as a defensive measure.

Similarities between Mass and Individual Insurance Marketing

While the marketing process for a typical group insurance case differs considerably from that for a typical single need individual policy, there are many situations where individual insurance marketing is quite similar to the marketing of group insurance. Examples of such marketing similarity are found in the sale of individual policies in a large business insurance case or in an individual policy pension trust case. In such instances the nature of the buyer, point of sale, degree of competition, emphasis on comparative costs and product design more closely approximate the conditions found in group marketing. The more complicated problems frequently involved in large individual insurance cases or in group insurance require a similar degree of expert knowledge, and the agent or broker often requires the assistance of a specialist. Examples of marketing similarities also are found in the small group case area (under twenty-five lives). Such cases are often handled by an experienced agent or broker with little or no assistance, and the conditions in the foregoing comparative areas more closely approximate those for individual insurance marketing.

Growth of the Group Insurance Market

The dynamic growth of the group insurance market continues each year. Group life insurance in force and group health insurance annual premiums in the United States more than tripled during the ten-year period ending in 1963. At the close of 1963, group life insurance in force in the United States (including creditor group life insurance) totaled over $265 billion under 255,000 master contracts and over ninety-seven million individual certificates.[4] Insurance company group health insurance premiums in the United States for 1963 were in excess of $4 billion.[5]

The remarkable growth of group insurance is attributable not only to more intensive cultivation of the group market, but to the growth of the group market itself. Many factors, several of which have been discussed in detail in earlier chapters, have contributed to this growth. The social

---

[4] Institute of Life Insurance, *Life Insurance Fact Book* (New York, 1964), pp. 27, 32. Figures exclude reinsurance acquired.

[5] *Health Insurance Review, 1964 Sales and Survey Number,* No. 5 (April, 1964), p. 53.

desirability of group insurance has assumed major significance with the industrialization of the economy, the change to a more urban population and the decreasing role of the family as a self-sufficient agrarian unit. Expansion of population and of the economy has increased the number of eligible groups. The long-range increase in wages and prices has generated a need for continuously increased amounts of life and health insurance coverage. As wages and living standards have increased, more attention has been focused on employee benefits rather than on wages alone (additional emphasis on employee benefits was provided by the federal wage freeze during World War II).

Public acceptance of group insurance has become widespread because of many factors. Among them are the fact that the economies of mass handling—marketing, underwriting, issue, billing and others—make for lower cost. In addition, employer contributions receive favorable tax treatment. A third major reason is the ease of satisfying insurability requirements.

The attitudes of management, labor and government also have contributed to the expansion of the group market. The use of group insurance as a prime fringe benefit by many *employers* to attract and hold highly qualified employees is well known. This has been true particularly in many rapidly developing industries where the demand for skilled and professional employees greatly exceeds the supply. The active interest of *organized labor* in negotiating health and welfare benefits has had a significant effect upon the expansion of the group market, particularly for group health coverages.

The recognition by *government* at both the state and federal level of the social desirability of group insurance has had both an expanding and limiting influence on the group market. The favorable income tax treatment of employer contributions for group insurance and group life proceeds has aided the expansion. Conversely, state statutory disability coverage in certain states[6] has had an adverse effect on the group disability market in these states. There are some indications that state premium taxes may have a limiting effect on certain areas of the group market. At the federal level certain restrictions on the group market have recently resulted from the inclusion of disability coverage under Social Security. Any federally sponsored health care plan for the aged through Social Security or otherwise has a further limiting effect.

The attitudes of insurance company *agency forces* also have had an influence on the growth of the group market. Recognition by agents of group selling as a source of additional income, prestige and service, both directly and through by-product sales of individual insurance, has been a favorable influence. A limiting influence has been the opposition of some

---

[6] California and Rhode Island. See Chapter 20 for a detailed analysis of the influence of these plans.

agents on the grounds that group coverages invade the agents' market for individual insurance.

Segments of the Group Insurance Market

The market for group insurance can be divided into various segments, such as by type of coverage or size of group, but the most meaningful division is in terms of the relationship of the people insured.

Individual Employers. Individual employers providing coverage for their employees form the primary segment of the group market. This division is by far the largest in terms of total annual premiums, number of policies and number of individuals covered. Although the employers are the policyholders, a large part of this market is strongly influenced by union attitudes and activities. A typical insurance company's group field force will concentrate most of its time in the individual employer market. It is in this segment also that insurance company agency forces enjoy nearly all of their success in group marketing, principally in the area of employers with less than 100 employees.

Associations of Employers. In most states a market exists for multiple-employer groups where the employers have a common interest by being members either of a trade association or in the same industry. Although this segment is much smaller than that for individual employers, it represents an important part of the group market.

Jointly Administered Labor-Management Trusts. Trusts covering one or more unions and one or more employers are also permitted by most state statutes. This group market, which arises out of collective bargaining, has become increasingly important during the past decade, and ranks as a major segment. Brokers and consultants play a dominant role in marketing coverage to groups of this type, and some work only in this market.[7]

Labor Unions. While most state statutes permit the issuance of group policies to cover members of labor unions, this segment is not nearly as large as those already discussed. Since federal law prohibits an employer in interstate commerce from making payments directly to a union for the purpose of providing group insurance, group benefits resulting from collective bargaining are provided under a jointly administered trust or are administered unilaterally by the employer.

Creditors. Group life and disability income coverages for installment debtors of a creditor represent an important segment of the group market. At the end of 1963, the volume of creditor group life insurance in force in the United States on the various types of financial institutions and retail vendors was over $37 billion under 52,000 master contracts and over forty-six million individual certificates.[8] The tremendous post–World War II

---

[7] Labor-management welfare funds, also called Taft-Hartley Welfare funds, are the subject of Chapter 33.

[8] Institute of Life Insurance, *op. cit.*, p. 32.

expansion in consumer credit has made this one of the fastest growing segments of the group market.

Miscellaneous Groups. Another segment of the group insurance market is made up of a variety of groups permitted by some but not all state statutes, and is not significant from the standpoint of relative premium volume. Examples of such groups are professional associations, such as medical societies and bar associations, associations of public and private

TABLE 26–1

RELATIVE SIZE OF VARIOUS SEGMENTS OF THE GROUP LIFE INSURANCE MARKET, 1956

Type of Group	Distribution of Policies (%)	Distribution of Certificates (%)	Distribution of Amount (%)
Individual employer groups............	93.8	79.5	87.4
Multiple-employer groups.............	1.8	3.9	3.2
Individual and multiple labor union groups.........................	2.0	6.6	2.1
Multiple: employers and labor unions...	1.2	6.4	4.9
Association of persons in same employment or profession, and non-employment groups................	1.2	3.6	2.4
	100.0	100.0	100.0

SOURCE: Institute of Life Insurance, "Analysis of Group Life Insurance in Force—1956," *The Tally of Life Insurance Statistics*, March, 1958. This survey excludes dependents' coverage, creditor group life, federal employees' group life, reinsurance assumed and insurance outside the United States.

employees, fraternal groups and national guard units. These groups frequently lend themselves better to wholesale or franchise insurance because of restricting state laws affecting group insurance, as will be discussed in Chapter 34.

Comparative Size. It is difficult to secure up-to-date statistics which measure accurately the size of each of these market segments. The most recent survey of group life insurance made by the Institute of Life Insurance, covering over 60 per cent of master contracts and certificates and 75 per cent of amount of insurance, is shown in Table 26–1.

Market Penetration

For many years, an uneasy feeling that the group market is saturated has existed in some quarters, and even the persistent, rapid growth of group insurance does not seem to dispel this feeling. While it is true that practically all employers with fifty or more employees have some form of group life and health coverage, there are sufficient areas of potential group business and sufficient influencing factors to assure the continued expansion of the group market. For example, additional amounts of group insurance will be necessitated by the modernization of existing health insurance plans to meet the continuously increasing cost of medical care, by rising wage levels and by the long-term increase in the cost of living. In addition, the development of new group coverages, such as long-term disability insurance and dental insurance, will continue as important new insurance needs of the public arise and are recognized. More intensive marketing of existing coverages which have relatively lower penetrations in the group market, e.g., various forms of permanent group life insurance, will also contribute to the further growth of the group insurance market. In addition, a number of American and Canadian insurance companies probably will begin operating in new foreign markets.

Other factors likely to contribute to the future growth of the market for group insurance are (1) new group insurance programs necessitated by mergers of corporations with different group plans and insurance carriers; (2) the continued increase in the number of firms eligible for group insurance in accordance with the general growth in our population and economy; (3) changes in state laws to permit coverage of groups now ineligible; and (4) more intensive cultivation of the small case market. In addition, there will always be a market among existing group cases for those insurance companies which can demonstrate superior performance in coverage, cost or service.

THE HOME OFFICE ORGANIZATION

General Considerations

The structure and size of the home office organization for group insurance marketing is influenced by a number of considerations. The major ones are discussed below.

Company Policy and Objectives. The insurance company's over-all objectives will influence the form and size of the home office group organization. The group organization may be assigned only the function of making an additional product available to the company's own agents. Or the objective may be extended to attract brokerage and aggressively seek new client relations through all available sources. Perhaps small employer-employee cases are to be the principal market, or plans may be made to specialize in union business, associations or creditor situations.

Company Organization. The nature and size of the agency force of the company and its brokerage relations will affect the structure of the group organization. A large established group insurance organization, administering thousands of cases of varying sizes and complexity, obviously will be organized differently from a newly formed department or one specializing in one segment of the market. The size, location and experience of the group field staff will also affect the home office organization.

Marketing Functions

The broad definition of marketing functions includes all home office and field policies and procedures that have a significant effect on the sale and service of group insurance. Group functions are usually divided into three main areas: (1) sales and service, (2) administration and (3) actuarial and technical services. Some of these functions may be properly assigned to either one or another of the areas, and some must be performed in more than one area. Some functions may be assigned to departments not exclusively concerned with group insurance, e.g., the claim department and the law department. The functions may be illustrated by Figure 26–1.

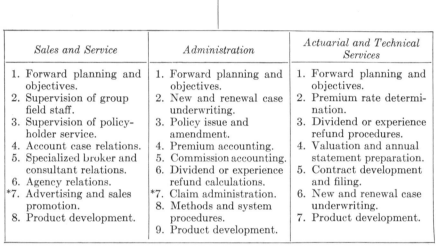

Sales and Service	Administration	Actuarial and Technical Services
1. Forward planning and objectives.	1. Forward planning and objectives.	1. Forward planning and objectives.
2. Supervision of group field staff.	2. New and renewal case underwriting.	2. Premium rate determination.
3. Supervision of policyholder service.	3. Policy issue and amendment.	3. Dividend or experience refund procedures.
4. Account case relations.	4. Premium accounting.	4. Valuation and annual statement preparation.
5. Specialized broker and consultant relations.	5. Commission accounting.	5. Contract development and filing.
6. Agency relations.	6. Dividend or experience refund calculations.	6. New and renewal case underwriting.
*7. Advertising and sales promotion.	*7. Claim administration.	7. Product development.
8. Product development.	8. Methods and system procedures.	
	9. Product development.	

* Frequently these functions may be assigned to a separate department as part of a company-wide function.

FIG. 26–1. Group insurance marketing functions.

The organization illustrated is quite fully integrated. Any one of the three major areas can be organized separately from each other and integrated or not with similar individual insurance functions. It will be noted that some functions may be given equal emphasis in more than one area, e.g., product development. Another example is case underwriting, where smaller and more routine cases may be handled in the administrative area following procedures developed by actuarial and technical services. On the other hand, larger or more complicated cases may be underwritten in the actuarial and technical services area.

Whatever the form of organization, it is essential that a high degree of integration and a spirit of team play exist. The varying points of view of many specialists must be reconciled to the needs of the policyholder as well as to the detailed requirements of law and regulation. As a consequence, a high degree of integration of the various functions is more common in group insurance marketing than in individual marketing.

THE FIELD ORGANIZATION

The company policy and marketing objectives previously discussed as influencing the nature of the home office organization are equally important considerations in determining the structure and size of the field organization for group marketing.

The Group Office

The local group field office is the basic organizational unit in the marketing of group insurance. The group office houses one or more company group representatives and is responsible for the sale and service of group insurance within a definite geographical area. The major group writing companies have group offices in most principal cities of the country. In charge of the office is a group manager who usually reports directly to a regional manager of sales and service located either in the field or home office. Group claim representatives may be located in the same office, in separate local offices or in the home office. The major functions of the typical group office are the sale of group insurance through brokers, consultants and agency field forces and the service of in-force group insurance cases.

The Group Representative

The typical group representative is a college graduate, carefully recruited and trained for his assignment, who has good sales ability plus a high degree of technical aptitude and communicative skill. Most of the larger group companies provide their new men with a substantial amount of specialized group training in both the classroom and the field. It is also customary for such companies to provide continuous education for their group field force through field supervision, continuous communication and periodic conferences and workshops to keep it abreast of current developments. Although some companies have separate staffs for sales and for service, many company group representatives handle both functions. Most group representatives are compensated by a base salary plus productivity bonus, while some receive a salary only.

The group representative's more important sales functions are working with brokers and agents in developing group prospects; preparing field group proposals; securing data and submitting it to the home office with recommendations for a proposal; presenting group proposals to prospects or their representatives and assisting in the closing of group cases; assisting in the enrollment of employees under new group cases; and keeping the home office informed of competitive developments in the group field.

In addition, the group representative performs many functions relating to the servicing of existing group insurance. These include setting up administrative procedures for new group policyholders; making regular service calls on in-force group cases to assist in their administration and plan modernization; placing necessary rate increases on in-force group cases; and conserving in-force business.

Agency Representatives

Insurance company agents play an important role in group insurance marketing, particularly with employer-employee cases of less than 100 lives. Where he is involved in a group case, the agent usually locates the prospect and then calls on his company's group representative for technical sales assistance in selling and installing the group program. In the segment of the group market in which he operates most successfully, the agent is able to provide a high degree of valuable personal service to his clients. The agent is compensated on a commission basis for the sale of the case. One of the outstanding advantages to an agent in writing a group case is the excellent source of prospects it provides for the writing of individual insurance, including business insurance. Some agents emphasize group insurance and become specialists in one or more segments of the market and, of course, require less assistance from the group representative.

Brokers, Consultants and Administrators

As previously indicated, the *broker* fills a dominant position in the larger case (over 100 lives) group insurance market. Although the smaller broker accounts for some portion of the market, the vast bulk of the market from a premium standpoint is controlled by specialized group brokers or consultants and by the larger brokerage firms with specialized group departments. The high level contacts developed in handling the general insurance lines give them a decided edge in handling the larger group accounts. Their specialized technical knowledge and knowledge of the clients' operations make them well qualified in this area. A number of the largest brokerage and consulting firms have nation-wide organizations with offices in principal cities throughout the country. Such firms are particularly adapted to serving the needs of large clients with widespread geographic organizations. The group broker assists his client in designing a benefit plan, secures proposals from insurance companies, analyzes these proposals and assists his client in the selection of the insurance company. Like agents, brokers are compensated on a commission basis by insurance companies for the sale of group insurance.

Consultants may perform the same services as the larger brokers and be compensated by commissions. However, some consultants do not accept commissions but work only on a fee arrangement with the client. Various combinations of services and differing compensation plans are available, and the definition of consultant or broker in the benefit field is quite fluid.

Another type of group specialist who has assumed increasing importance in group insurance marketing in recent years is the *administrator*. The professional group administrator handles the administration of one or more trust funds (usually association or labor-management negotiated) on a contract fee basis with the fund. There are also many administrators who work as salaried employees of the trust fund. While normally they do not perform the usual functions of the broker during the securing of group coverage by the fund but are concerned with the administration of whichever group plan is adopted, some professional administrators are also licensed as brokers and perform both functions.

THE SALES PROCESS

Prospecting

Although group representatives of some insurance companies prospect for buyers directly, most group representatives prospect for new clients almost entirely through agents and brokers. The group representative typically finds that among most agents and small brokers only a relatively small proportion have the necessary aptitude and contacts for successful group selling, and the majority of his training efforts is usually spent with these individuals. In working with such persons, the group representative attempts to establish a close working relationship, train them to be able to prospect for group insurance effectively and motivate them to prospect.

The group representative's approach must be different in prospecting through larger brokers. Here, training as such is not needed and the group representative seeks to establish as close a personal working relationship as possible. He demonstrates his own ability to the broker and explains the advantages of the group facilities of his particular company. An essential element of prospecting is securing the information necessary for plan design and proposal preparation.

Preparing the Proposal

Proposal preparation involves designing the plan of benefits, evaluating the prospect and calculating the applicable rates. On cases of all sizes from larger brokers, it is customary for the broker to request insurance company quotations on the basis of fairly rigid plan specifications which he has worked out in consultation with his client, and the group representative has little influence on plan design unless he is able to work with the broker at a very early stage. On cases from agents and smaller brokers, final plan design is a blend of the client's desires, the recommendations of the agent or broker and group representative and insurance industry practices. The group representative's influence is stronger in these latter situations, although for cases of less than twenty-five lives less plan flexibility is available. Where collective bargaining is involved, the employer and union negotiate either an employer monthly insurance contribution per employee (which affects the general level of benefits) or a specific benefit plan. Proper benefit plan design seeks to provide within the scope of the premium available reasonably balanced coverage that will be attractive and understandable to the employees, provide maximum coverage for nonbudgetable risks, minimize adverse selection against the plan and provide for maximum cost control and, finally, fit the over-all personnel objectives of the buyer.

Proposal underwriting is normally performed in the insurance company home office, although some companies use field underwriting on the smaller cases. The underwriter evaluates the data and recommendations from the group representative, approves or modifies the benefit plan, sets the rate level and specifies any special conditions pertaining to the case. One of the most important considerations in setting the rate level is any previous group claim history of the prospect, which is referred to as "transferred business information." Final rates are calculated either in the home office or group office, depending on the complexity of the plan and the practice of the insurance company.

Presenting the Proposal

Whereas the group representative naturally prefers to present his proposal directly to the client or at least to appear before the client with the agent or broker to close the sale for his company, the disposition of the proposal depends on the desires of the client and broker. The larger brokers want proposals submitted directly to them for analysis and recommendation to the client. This is also true of some smaller brokers. Smaller brokers and agents in particular encourage direct participation by the group representative in presenting the proposal to the client.

The final evaluation of the proposal will depend upon both general and specific considerations. In the general area, the insurer's facilities, experience and reputation will be considered. In the specific area, the insurer's constructive plan design, suggestions and degree of compliance with plan specifications will be considered, and special weight usually is given to the relative position of the insurer's rate quotation and retention projection. Projected retention illustrations are not customarily made for smaller cases because their size precludes the credibility of any long-range assumptions of claim experience. Even on retention projections for large cases, the illustrations depend upon the long-term credibility of the assumptions and are only as good as the experience and reliability of the insurance company preparing them. They may not illustrate the variations in quality of service from one insurer to another, which can be considerable.

Post-Sales Activity

Employee Enrollment. The first step following the selection of the insurance company is the presentation of the plan to the employees.

Where the employees are contributing toward the cost of the plan, it is most important that the enrollment be properly planned and executed if the customary 75 per cent minimum enrollment requirement is to be achieved easily. The most essential element is the active support of the employer and the use of his key personnel in securing the signed employee enrollment cards. After the insurance company prepares an announcement letter or booklet for use in explaining the plan to the employees, employee presentation meetings are held with follow-up by the key employees for the signed enrollment cards.

Even where the employer is paying for the entire cost of the plan, it is important for the plan to be presented properly to secure maximum employee understanding and appreciation. The group representative and agent or broker play an important part in this area.

Installation.[9] Upon completion of the enrollment, the group representative forwards the enrollment cards to the insurance company home office for final assumption of risk, final rate calculation based on the actual enrollment and issuance of the master policy, individual certificates and administrative material. When this work is completed, it is sent to the group representative for installation of the program. The group representative, usually accompanied by the agent or broker, delivers the material to the client and thoroughly reviews all aspects of the plan's administration. For smaller cases, the installation may be made by the agent alone, especially for cases of less than twenty-five lives. Proper installation is most important to the future success of the group plan and to the relationship among the insurance company, client and broker or agent.

Service and Conservation. The group representative makes periodic service calls on the policyholder to assist in the proper administration of the plan. It is customary for him to use a checkoff type form to guide him in making a thorough review of all administrative practices and to check on the status of various aspects of the case. This form generally is then used as a service report to his home office.

Good service contributes greatly to increased policyholder satisfaction and lessens future conservation problems. Poorly serviced cases are prime targets for sales efforts by other insurance companies and brokers. Persuading the policyholder (and often the broker) to accept rate increases on in-force cases is an important part of the service function. The conservation problems caused by frequent group health insurance rate increases of the past decade have been met best by frequent service and proper education of and close contact with the client. One very important advantage to the group representative who gives regular and efficient service is the opportunity he secures to sell expanded or additional group coverages to his client. Good service also helps maintain good broker relationships.

---

[9] See Chapter 28 for a detailed discussion of installation and servicing.

ENTERING THE GROUP MARKET

Motives

While only seven of the fifty largest (by assets) life insurance companies operating in the United States had not entered the group market as of the end of 1963, the consideration of whether or not to enter the group field will be of importance to many insurance companies. The general motives for entering this market might be summarized as follows:

1. To provide additional earnings and prestige for the company's agency force through direct group commissions and by-product sales of individual insurance;
2. To provide group facilities for the company's agents so they will not take group prospects to other insurance companies;
3. To maintain or increase the growth and prestige of the company and its position in the industry;
4. To contribute further to the profit or surplus of the company, thereby benefiting stockholders and/or policyholders;
5. To fulfill further the insurance industry's social responsibility to the insuring public.

A secondary motive for some insurance company executives might be the stimulation and challenge offered by the opportunity to deal more closely with business executives in other fields so as to take advantage of natural contacts and develop new ones.

Considerations

General Problems. A company considering whether to enter the group market will want to study several basic problems, including expected expenses and financial results, organization and agent relations. Substantial initial expenses will be involved, particularly if the group market is to be entered aggressively, so the initial and long-term effect on earnings will have to be carefully projected. A specialized group field and home office staff will be required. Coverages, rates, experience rating procedures and administrative practices must be established. Policy and certificate forms must be prepared and filed.

If the group market is going to be entered aggressively, it is probable that specially trained group personnel will have to be recruited largely from outside the company and integrated into its organizational structure. The decision to establish a separate group department or to integrate it into existing departments will depend largely on how extensively the group market is to be entered and on the general organization policy of the company.

A company with a full-time agency force must consider the reaction of its agents. In spite of the increased earnings potential made available to them, some agents will view their company's entry into the group market as an invasion of their individual market. The dominant position of brokers in the group market also will cause some agency morale problems.

Basic Marketing Problems. A company considering entry into the group market also faces a number of basic marketing problems. First, it must determine in which segments and in which geographical areas of the market it can compete most successfully. Second, because of the competition and its lack of established group reputation, the newly entering company often finds it difficult to secure group business. One solution is for it to use inadequate rates which will be substantially lower than those of its competitors, but at best this can be only a temporary solution. Third, if the company decides to enter the group market aggressively but previously has had little relations with brokers, new broker contacts will have to be made. Fourth, it is important to the newly entering company that its agency force enthusiastically markets group insurance, particularly in the small case area. This can create a conflict, however, between agency demands on the group field force and the available facilities of the latter, particularly during the early stages of entry into the group market when the group field force may be relatively small. The success in the group market of the newly entering company will depend largely on how it solves these problems.

TRENDS AND PROBLEMS

Many chapters in this text contain material that has a bearing on group insurance marketing in general, and some cover trends and problems in detail. Some major trends and current basic problems, however, affect marketing so directly they should be briefly mentioned here. Although a discussion of some of these subjects may appear negative, it should be remembered that the group insurance business has grown and prospered in the face of many unfavorable influences and difficult problems.

The basic trend of continued interest by so many influential segments of the population in those types of financial security that can best be provided by group insurance serves as a favorable climate in which unfavorable trends can be mitigated and problems lessened or solved. Although separate headings are used for each subject, this tends to oversimplify since so many of the influences are closely interrelated.

Increasing Costs

There is a continuing upward trend in both claim and administrative costs in group health insurance. Health claim costs are estimated to be increasing at the rate of 6 per cent to 7 per cent per year due to improvements in medical services and an increase in the utilization of health care facilities, as well as the general rise in wage levels. This latter factor adversely affects insurance company administrative costs as well.

There is also a trend toward higher administrative costs because of various state and federal regulatory requirements. Examples of this are federal and state disclosure acts, state credit insurance control regulations and federal income tax changes affecting group life and health insurance.

Because of the intense price competition in the group market, insurance companies explore every possible method of meeting rising costs other than by increasing rates. The influence of increasing costs is manifested in several areas in addition to the areas of competition and conservation.

Combined Coverages

To offset increasing costs, there has been a tendency for insurance companies to combine diverse group coverages such as life, disability income and medical expense coverage under one group master contract, rather than to issue a separate group contract for each coverage.[10] This not only reduces the cost of issuing and administering the coverages, but reduces commissions as well. It also provides for more stabilized claim costs and reduces risk charges.

Changes in Insurance Company Services

Over the years, there has been a tendency for insurance companies to permit or encourage group policyholders to do work in the accounting and claim areas that could be performed by the insurance companies. This reduces insurance company costs, of course, and often work can be done more efficiently and at less cost to the policyholder than if the insurance company performed the same functions because duplicate records and double handling are avoided or minimized. This has led to other problems, however, since some policyholders conclude that the insurance company is not doing enough for them for what it does charge.

In seeking more efficient ways to reduce administrative and claim costs and to improve services, insurance companies are increasing their use of electronic data processing equipment in the performance of such services as contract and certificate issue and changes, premium billing and claim payment. New equipment and procedures have enabled some companies to provide, at lower costs, periodic detailed claim information for use in more effective claim control.

Claim Control Activities

The merging of specified dollar claim limits under each of several group health coverages, such as basic hospital and surgical coverages, into one general over-all dollar claim limit, as in group major medical insurance, has resulted in a higher degree of correlation between claim pay-

---

[10] This trend does not apply to the hospital and medical service associations, of course, which do not provide life and disability income insurance.

ments and the cost of medical services. As a result, although a group policyholder wants the broad coverage afforded by major medical insurance, he finds himself faced with rising claim costs and consequent rate increases as hospital costs, doctors' fees and other medical costs continue to rise. Insurance companies have established claim control procedures designed to detect abuses of any kind and thus enable them to take corrective action. Claim control includes such measures as proper benefit plan design, general employee education, specific education of the employer's employee benefit personnel, special claim investigations and cooperative activities with providers of hospital and medical services.[11]

New Products

A continuing trend in group insurance marketing is the development of new products. Major medical insurance became generally accepted only a few years ago. More recent group product developments are long-term disability, personal accident and dental insurance. Future new product developments may be expected in such areas as home nursing care, coverage of periodic health examinations and vision care.

Increased Buyer Knowledge

Another noticeable trend is the better understanding of group insurance fundamentals by the average group buyer. There are indications among the larger buyers of increased knowledge of the details and technical aspects of group insurance. This often results in less transferring from one insurer to another as the result of rate increases. There is a tendency among large employers to expand their insurance departments to include employee benefit specialists. More buyers are adopting a better working relationship with the insurance company and broker in the administration of their group plans. The net result of this increasing understanding should be of benefit to the group market as a whole.

This increase in buyer knowledge occasionally results in a large buyer desiring to deal directly with an insurance company and to eliminate broker service and commission expense. These instances are not common, and such practice generally is discouraged by insurance companies.

Increased Specialization

The increased complexity in group coverages, occasioned by competition, technological improvements and increased statutory regulation, is causing a trend toward the development of insurance company specialists within the over-all group staff framework. Group specialists are emerging in such group fields as creditor insurance, group paid-up, long-term disability, Taft-Hartley Welfare funds, trade and professional associations

---

[11] For a detailed discussion of these and other claim control activities, see Chapters 23 and 24.

and electronic systems programing. Similar specialization also is increasing within the larger brokerage firms.

Problems of Agency Relations

Many insurance companies write individual maximum amounts of group life insurance considerably in excess of the more modest earlier amounts which were limited by law or the practices of the insurers. This has caused some anti-group feeling among a segment of the life insurance agency force. While the total amount so written represents an insignificant portion of the total amount of group life insurance in force, it is a sensitive point in the group insurance industry's agency relations. The 1964 change in the federal income tax law, which limits the amount of employer contribution that may be made without imputing taxable income to the employee, could minimize this problem. The so-called lateral extension of group insurance to other than employer-employee relationships, especially group insurance for members of associations, is also of concern to agents who work primarily in the individual policy market.

Agency relations are also impaired by group commission practices, which do not follow the pattern used for individual insurance. Almost all group insurance cases are placed through agents or brokers with payment of regular commissions on a decremental scale. However, an occasional case is placed directly with minimum commissions charged or is placed through a consultant who prefers to be compensated by the client on a fee basis.

Governmental Plans

Pressure will continue at both the state and federal level for increased governmental participation in coverage of the health risk. The continued future growth of the voluntary insurance system depends in large measure on a better public and political understanding of the ability of private enterprise to provide adequately for the health insurance needs of the public.

Self-insured Plans

Group insurance premiums are subject to state taxes which on major cases amount to a significant proportion of the insurance company's total retention. Self-insured plans are not subject to such taxes, and most states do not impose such taxes on service type plans. This results in a competitive inequity as employers seek ways to reduce costs. Currently, many comparisons are being advocated or made for possible tax savings in health coverage as against the value of insurance company services.

The situation is very fluid at this writing. It may be anticipated that if states lose substantial premium tax revenues, substitute taxation will result. Since self-insured plans are not currently regulated, it may also be assumed that state authorities will become concerned if many regulated insured plans change to a self-insured, nonregulated basis.[12] The National Association of Insurance Commissioners has already expressed its concern.

Problems of Marketing Creditor Group Insurance

Perhaps no other group insurance coverage in recent years has been faced with the plethora of problems associated with the marketing of creditor group insurance. The marketing of this coverage, both under the group and individual approach, has been subject to various abuses: lack of disclosure of coverage to the debtor, overcharging of the debtor by the creditor, excessive amounts of coverage for the debtor and failure of the creditor to refund unearned insurance charges to the debtor if the loan is prepaid. The NAIC Model Credit Insurance Bill of 1957, which was revised in 1960, sought to correct these abuses, and its principles have been enacted into law in about thirty states. With a few exceptions, however, the administration of the state laws patterned after it has not dealt effectively with the problem of overcharging the debtor. The problem manifests itself in the creditor group insurance field in "reverse competition"—the marketing of coverage on the basis of the highest instead of the lowest premium to permit the creditor to make a higher profit at the expense of its debtors. (The excess premium usually is returned to the creditor by the insurance company as a dividend, experience refund, expense allowance or in commissions.) While much progress has been made in solving the problems in this area, much more work remains to be done.

SELECTED REFERENCES

GREGG, DAVIS W. *Group Life Insurance.* 3d ed. Homewood, Ill.: Richard D. Irwin, Inc., 1962.

"Health Insurance Premiums and Benefits for 1963," *Health Insurance Review, 1964 Sales and Survey Number,* No. 5 (April, 1964), p. 53.

KAUF, DAVID K. "Marketing Group Health Insurance," paper presented at the Eighth Annual Group Insurance Forum, Health Insurance Association of America, February 11, 1964.

McDONALD, EDWIN C. "Group Insurance—The Concept, Market, and Sales Process," *Life and Health Insurance Handbook* (ed. DAVIS W. GREGG), chap. 22. Homewood, Ill.: Richard D. Irwin, Inc., 1959.

MILLIMAN, WENDELL. *Is Group Insurance for You.* New York: North American Reassurance Co., 1958.

PICKRELL, JESSE F. *Group Health Insurance.* Rev. ed. Homewood, Ill.: Richard D. Irwin, Inc., 1961.

STALSON, J. OWEN. *Marketing Life Insurance.* Cambridge, Mass.: Harvard University Press, 1942.

---

[12] Some state insurance departments may be expected to contend that a self-insured employer is doing an unauthorized insurance business.

Chapter 27

COMPENSATION SYSTEMS USED IN MARKETING GROUP INSURANCE

BY CHE LIN

The subject of compensation is of critical importance to all concerned with the group insurance field. To the field forces, compensation represents income and livelihood; to the companies and the policyholders, it represents costs. Although direct buying by policyholders from insurers is sometimes permitted in group insurance, it is not the standard procedure. Direct buying is particularly rare in group health insurance, and the fact remains that group insurance sold by agents and brokers still accounts for about 90 per cent of the total new group business written. Moreover, even business written directly by insurance companies without assistance from agents and brokers often entails some sort of compensation, as will be mentioned subsequently. Thus, group insurance is rarely bought without some compensation being involved.

NATURE OF GROUP INSURANCE COMPENSATION

Compensation Defined

The phrase "group insurance compensation" usually is defined as the total remuneration, in money or services, by insurance companies to agents and brokers in connection with group insurance sales or services. The term generally does not include the payment of salaries or other benefits to home office or branch office employees and personnel, nor does it include the fees paid by the policyholders to their consultants for special accounting, actuarial or legal services. Home office personnel, such as group representatives, nevertheless play a vital part in group insurance marketing, and a subsequent section will be devoted to the compensation of these individuals, even though the term "group insurance compensation" does not refer customarily to such payments.

In studies of compensation, commissions have always been emphasized because they constitute the most important single item of compensation. Commissions are payments to the agents for business which they personally sell or which is credited to them. Usually the purchase of a plan submitted by an insurance man implies that he will receive the commissions.

Conditions for the Payment of Commissions

The prevailing philosophy among most insurers that accept business from any licensed agent or broker is that the client has considerable latitude in dictating who is to receive the commission. Sometimes this is resolved by the client giving a so-called "agent of record letter" in advance to a broker or agent who may request quotations from more than one insurer. When there is no definite commitment to one agent or brokerage firm until the sale becomes definite, the question of who will receive the commissions may remain in doubt. The man who obtains the signed master application is recognized by a large majority of insurers if he is currently licensed in that state to write life and health insurance. The licensing with a specific company can usually take place after the business has been committed. Under this system, it is possible but infrequent for a prospect to buy a group plan from one insurer but name an agent who represents a competing company to receive the commissions.

In some instances an employer is not aware that he is naming an agent or broker when he buys a group insurance program, even though he realizes that the individual will be compensated. The consent of the policyholder is assumed, and his signing of the master application or another form showing the name of the agent or broker is considered proof of his consent.

Some insurers include group commission schedules in the contracts of their own agents but require single-case agreements for groups written by all other insurance men. Many insurance companies make a single-case agreement for every group, even those written by their own agents.

The power of a policyholder to decide, within limits, how much and to whom commissions should be paid is brought about by two factors. First, the purchaser often is aware of the identities of the persons receiving the commissions, and the amount of such commissions, because of the disclosures required by the Federal Welfare and Pension Plans Disclosure Act (Public Law 85–836). The second factor is that stiff competition in the group insurance business enables policyholders to transfer their coverage almost at will. The fear of losing business is undoubtedly a major reason that insurance companies give up their prerogative of determining the recipient of commissions.

Types of Commission Schedules

Two basic types of commission schedules are in general use by companies writing group life insurance: the standard commission schedule and the level commission schedule. The standard commission schedule provides higher commissions in the first year and lower commissions for renewal years. The level commission schedule provides the same commission rates, disregarding interest, over the first ten (or in some instances, twenty) years as those produced by the standard or higher first-year commission schedule. That is, after ten years a ten-year level schedule will have provided the same number of dollars as would have been available under a standard schedule during the same period for the same size group. If a group is likely to grow in size, the use of the level schedule will produce a larger aggregate amount of commissions in the long run than will the higher first-year schedule. This follows since the commission rate is higher under the level schedule than under the standard schedule during the renewal years.

Normally, the agent or broker has the choice of either the higher first-year commission schedule or the level schedule. However, the level commission schedule normally is required by the companies in the following instances: (1) business transferred from another insurance company; (2) reinstated cases; (3) labor union, trade association and similar cases where the employees or participants pay all the premiums; and (4) all other groups which, in the judgment of the company, may have a high chance of lapse.

Where the use of a level schedule is elected by the agent, a few companies provide for a special payment in case of death, retirement or separation of the agent for good cause. This amount is usually the difference between the amount payable under the higher first-year schedule and the amount actually paid under the level schedule, ignoring interest. On the other hand many insurers incorporate specific provisions in the agent's agreement whereby commissions are handled on a vested basis in the event of death,[1] particularly since this may be the very time that there is the greatest danger of the case being transferred to another insurer.[2]

Rationale of Group Insurance Commission Levels

Commissions paid for group insurance business are much lower percentagewise than for individual insurance. One of the major reasons for this is the larger premiums involved in group insurance cases as compared to individual insurance sales. Moreover, the agent or broker does relatively less work for each dollar of premium received on a group case than is true for individual coverage. It should not be implied that it takes less time or work to sell a group case; rather, for the time and work expended by agents and brokers in group sales, a much larger premium volume may be expected than would be generated in individual sales with the same amount of effort. Then, too, it must be recognized that salaried group

---

[1] Many companies provide for the payment of renewal commissions to the agents' designated beneficiaries in the event of death of the agents. This payment of renewal commissions is usually for a limited period, such as three or five years.

[2] Since level commissions generally are required on transferred cases, the death of the agent would not involve a refiguring of commissions on such cases.

representatives often do a great deal of technical and selling work to assist agents and brokers. Thus, the commission scale is understandably lower in group coverage.

Then, too, the intense competition in the group insurance field encourages the use of low commission scales. Since increased commissions would add to the cost of the plans, it is probably correct to conclude that fewer prospective purchasers would be willing to buy from a company with higher commission scales. Agents and brokers might spend more time soliciting group insurance business if commission schedules were higher, but insurers doubt whether this would bring in enough new business to make up for the premiums lost to competitors as a result of higher costs.

The theory of mass marketing of insurance assumes that group insurance commissions will be scaled down not only in recognition of the aforementioned factors; low expenses, including low commissions, are themselves goals of group marketing, since low cost encourages a more extensive use of goup insurance.

COMMISSIONS FOR REGULAR GROUPS

So-called "regular groups" are generally considered to be those covering a minimum of twenty-five persons. The commission rates for regular groups are "graded" according to the size of the premium volume; that is, the commission rates decrease as the premium volume increases. The schedules for group term life and group health insurance usually are identical, but they may differ somewhat from those of group permanent insurance, as will be discussed in the following sections.

Group Term Life and Group Health Insurance Commissions

The commission rates for group term life insurance generally are the same as those for group health insurance, and when both types of coverage are placed with the same insurer, it is now common to combine the premiums when calculating the commissions. Until the early 1950's, however, the premiums for group term life, disability income and medical expense benefits were each graded separately. Since commission rates are graded downward as the size of premiums increases, the combination of premiums has the effect of producing smaller commissions than if they were calculated separately.

Types of Commissions. Commissions for regular groups are sometimes further divided into selling or soliciting commissions and service fees, although the practice of splitting commissions into two parts is of relatively recent origin. The procedure was adopted by most companies after the National Association of Insurance Commissioners approved a "Code of Ethical Practices" in December, 1957. The division of commissions was also encouraged by the Federal Welfare and Pension Plans Disclosure Act passed in 1958. Since then there has been a distinct trend for all the companies to follow this practice. A major result of this change has been a shift by many insurers that formerly vested commissions for ten years to nonvested contracts.

Soliciting commissions can be a controversial type of compensation. Such commissions are paid to an agent or broker for introducing the business to the company. To be entitled to soliciting commissions, an agent must notify the company of the prospect's intent to consider a group insurance plan, and the agent may sometimes help arrange for a company representative to have an interview with the prospect. There is no specific requirement that the notification be in writing or that it should precede any formal negotiation between the company and the prospect; in fact, the notice can be given any time. The use of soliciting commissions precludes problems that might arise under regulations against the payment of so-called "phantom" commissions, that is, commissions to persons who have performed no service at all in connection with the case.

Soliciting commissions are generally set at a very low level. Often this fee equals the minimum commissions required to be charged in the experience rating formulas. It is primarily because of the small amounts involved that the occasional payment of soliciting commissions after meager effort by an agent or broker has occurred without much protest. It is important to note, however, that many, if not most, of the major group insurers view soliciting commissions as being unethical if paid to an individual who has had no real part in soliciting the business.

Service fees, the other component of commissions, are sometimes subdivided into consultation fees and regular service fees for the first year or for the first few policy years. When they are divided, the payment of consultation fees to the agent is contingent on the performance of consultation functions, such as helping the prospect develop his benefit structure, presenting a quotation to the prospect and securing the application and initial premium deposit.

The breakdown of commissions as described is more theoretical than actual with many companies. All of the segments are usually paid to the writing agent as long as he helps retain the business.

Commission Levels. The commission schedules used by the various companies differ with respect to the rates, the grading of premium volumes and the allocation of the commissions into soliciting commissions and service fees. A schedule of commissions currently in use by one large group insurer is presented in Table 27–1.

Because of the different ways in which premium volumes are graded, it is difficult to make direct comparisons of the commissions from the schedules used by different companies. In order to show the relative magnitude of the commissions, it is necessary to calculate the actual commissions for different amounts of premiums. For this purpose, a comparison of total commissions of six leading companies is presented in Tables 27–2 and 27–3. Table 27–2 gives the comparison of the total first-year commissions using the higher first-year schedule, and Table 27–3 sets

TABLE 27–1

ILLUSTRATIVE COMMISSION SCHEDULES FOR GROUP TERM LIFE AND
HEALTH INSURANCE

HIGHER FIRST-YEAR SCHEDULE:

First-Year Commission Rates

Annual Premium Volume		Soliciting Comm.	Consul- tation Fees	Service Fees	Total Comm.
From	To				
$ 0	$ 5,000	20.0%	0.0%	0.0%	20.0%
5,001	10,000	15.0	0.0	0.0	15.0
10,001	20,000	0.0	12.5	0.0	12.5
20,001	30,000	0.0	10.0	0.0	10.0
30,001	50,000	0.0	5.0	0.0	5.0
50,001	250,000	0.0	2.5	0.0	2.5
250,001	500,000	0.0	0.0	1.0	1.0
500,001	2,500,000	0.0	0.0	0.5	0.5
Over $2,500,000		0.0	0.0	0.1	0.1

Renewals, Two–Ten Years

Annual Premium Volume		Solic- iting Comm.	Service Fees	Total Comm.	Serv. Fees Eleventh and Later Years
From	To				
$ 0	$ 1,000	5.0%	0.00%	5.00%	5.00%
1,001	5,000	3.0	0.00	3.00	3.00
5,001	10,000	1.5	0.00	1.50	1.50
10,001	50,000	0.0	1.50	1.50	1.50
50,001	250,000	0.0	1.00	1.00	1.00
250,001	500,000	0.0	0.50	0.50	0.50
500,001	2,500,000	0.0	0.25	0.25	0.25
Over $2,500,000		0.0	0.10	0.10	0.10

LEVEL TEN-YEAR SCHEDULE:

First-Year Commission Rates

Annual Premium Volume		Solic- iting Comm.	Consul- tation Fees	Service Fees	Total Comm.	Serv. Fees Two–Ten Years*
From	To					
$ 0	$ 1,000	6.50%	0.00%	0.000%	6.500%	6.500%
1,001	5,000	4.70	0.00	0.000	4.700	4.700
5,001	10,000	2.85	0.00	0.000	2.850	2.850
10,001	20,000	0.00	2.60	0.000	2.600	2.600
20,001	30,000	0.00	2.35	0.000	2.350	2.350
30,001	50,000	0.00	1.85	0.000	1.850	1.850
50,001	250,000	0.00	1.15	0.000	1.150	1.150
250,001	500,000	0.00	0.00	0.550	0.550	0.550
500,001	2,500,000	0.00	0.00	0.275	0.275	0.275
Over $2,500,000		0.00	0.00	0.100	0.100	0.100

* Services fees for eleventh and later years are the same as those of the higher first-year schedule.

TABLE 27–2

COMPARISON OF TOTAL FIRST-YEAR COMMISSIONS ON GROUP TERM LIFE AND
HEALTH INSURANCE

Amount of Annual Premium	Company A	Company B	Company C	Company D	Company E	Company F
			Amount of Commissions			
$ 5,000	$ 750	$ 1,250	$ 1,000	$ 500	$ 1,000	$ 1,000
10,000	1,250	1,875	1,750	875	1,750	1,750
20,000	2,050	3,000	3,000	1,500	3,000	3,000
30,000	2,650	4,000	4,000	2,000	4,000	4,000
50,000	3,250	5,000	5,000	2,500	5,000	5,000
100,000	3,750	6,250	6,250	3,125	6,250	6,250
250,000	3,975	7,750	10,000	5,000	10,000	9,250
500,000	4,225	9,000	13,125	6,750	12,500	11,750
1,000,000	4,475	10,250	15,625	8,000	15,000	14,250
2,000,000	4,975	11,500	20,625	10,250	20,000	16,750
5,000,000	6,475	*	35,625	11,750	25,000	24,250
10,000,000	6,975	*	60,625	14,250	30,000	36,750
			Effective Rates			
$ 5,000	15.00%	25.00%	20.00%	10.00%	20.00%	20.00%
10,000	12.50	18.75	17.50	8.75	17.50	17.50
20,000	10.25	15.00	15.00	7.50	15.00	15.00
30,000	8.83	13.33	13.33	6.67	13.33	13.33
50,000	6.50	10.00	10.00	5.00	10.00	10.00
100,000	3.75	6.25	6.25	3.12	6.25	6.25
250,000	1.59	3.10	4.00	2.00	4.00	3.70
500,000	0.84	1.80	2.62	1.35	2.50	2.35
1,000,000	0.45	1.02	1.56	0.80	1.50	1.42
2,000,000	0.25	0.58	1.03	0.51	1.00	0.84
5,000,000	0.13	*	0.71	0.23	0.50	0.48
10,000,000	0.07	*	0.61	0.14	0.30	0.37
			Ratio to Company "A"			
$ 5,000	100%	167%	133%	67%	133%	133%
10,000	100	150	140	70	140	140
20,000	100	146	146	73	146	146
30,000	100	151	151	75	151	151
50,000	100	154	154	77	154	154
100,000	100	167	167	83	167	167
250,000	100	195	252	126	252	233
500,000	100	213	311	160	296	278
1,000,000	100	229	349	179	335	318
2,000,000	100	231	415	206	402	337
5,000,000	100	*	550	181	386	375
10,000,000	100	*	869	204	430	527

* Commissions for premium volume in excess of $4,000,000 are to be determined by the company.

forth the comparison of the total aggregate commissions payable in the
first ten years, assuming a constant premium volume for this ten-year
period.[3]

---

[3] The assumption of a constant premium volume has the effect of reducing the differences. If the premium volumes increase, as is often the case, the companies paying
higher aggregate commissions under a constant premium assumption will pay even
larger aggregate commissions.

TABLE 27-3

COMPARISON OF AGGREGATE TOTAL COMMISSIONS FOR FIRST TEN YEARS
GROUP TERM LIFE AND HEALTH INSURANCE

Amount of Annual Premium	Company A	Company B	Company C	Company D	Company E	Company F
			Amount of Aggregate Total Commissions			
$ 5,000	$ 1,875	$ 3,500	$ 2,530	$ 2,404	$ 2,530	$ 2,530
10,000	3,500	4,800	3,955	3,758	3,955	3,950
20,000	6,100	7,275	6,555	6,228	6,555	6,550
30,000	8,500	9,625	8,905	8,460	8,905	8,900
50,000	10,900	13,325	12,605	11,976	12,605	12,600
100,000	13,650	19,075	18,355	17,436	18,355	18,350
250,000	15,900	27,325	35,605	33,816	35,605	32,600
500,000	18,400	34,200	50,105	47,826	49,355	46,350
1,000,000	20,900	41,100	64,105	66,226	63,105	60,100
2,000,000	25,900	48,000	92,105	92,326	90,605	73,900
5,000,000	40,900	*	176,105	120,826	129,355	115,300
10,000,000	45,900	*	316,105	168,326	179,355	184,300
			Effective Level Rate per Year			
$ 5,000	3.75%	7.00%	5.06%	4.81%	5.06%	5.06%
10,000	3.50	4.80	3.96	3.76	3.96	3.95
20,000	3.05	3.64	3.28	3.11	3.28	3.28
30,000	2.83	3.21	2.97	2.82	2.97	2.97
50,000	2.18	2.67	2.52	2.40	2.52	2.52
100,000	1.37	1.91	1.84	1.74	1.84	1.84
250,000	0.64	1.09	1.42	1.35	1.42	1.30
500,000	0.37	0.68	1.00	0.96	0.99	0.93
1,000,000	0.21	0.41	0.64	0.66	0.63	0.60
2,000,000	0.13	0.24	0.46	0.46	0.45	0.37
5,000,000	0.08	*	0.35	0.24	0.26	0.23
10,000,000	0.05	*	0.32	0.17	0.18	0.18
			Ratio to Company "A"			
$ 5,000	100%	187%	135%	128%	135%	135%
10,000	100	137	113	107	113	113
20,000	100	119	107	102	107	107
30,000	100	113	105	100	105	105
50,000	100	122	116	110	116	116
100,000	100	140	134	128	134	134
250,000	100	172	224	213	224	205
500,000	100	186	272	260	268	252
1,000,000	100	197	307	317	302	288
2,000,000	100	185	356	356	350	285
5,000,000	100	*	431	295	316	282
10,000,000	100	*	689	367	391	402

* Commissions for premium volume in excess of $4,000,000 are to be determined by the company.

From Tables 27–2 and 27–3, it can be seen that commissions on group term life and health insurance are not uniform. Actually, there is a wide range among major companies, as can be seen in Table 27–4. It should be pointed out, however, that companies "A" and "D" deviate somewhat from the scales that generally prevail.

Further variations in commissions can develop among companies or even among policyholders of the same company when commission scales are applied to new premiums resulting from new or revised benefits or the addition of employees in branches or affiliates which were not previously included. When level commissions are being paid on a group, any additional premium is usually lumped with the existing premium, and the commission is calculated on the total new and old premium together. If an

TABLE 27–4

RANGE OF COMMISSION PAYMENTS ON GROUP TERM LIFE AND HEALTH INSURANCE FOR SIX INSURERS

Amount of Annual Premium	Low Amount	High	
		Amount	% of Low
First-Year Commissions Only			
$ 5,000	$ 500	$ 1,250	250
10,000	875	1,875	214
20,000	1,500	3,000	200
30,000	2,000	4,000	200
50,000	2,500	5,000	200
100,000	3,125	6,250	200
250,000	3,975	10,000	252
500,000	4,225	13,125	311
1,000,000	4,475	15,625	349
2,000,000	4,975	20,625	415
5,000,000	6,475	35,625	550
10,000,000	6,975	60,625	869
Aggregate for First Ten Years			
$ 5,000	$ 1,875	$ 3,500	187
10,000	3,500	4,800	137
20,000	6,100	7,275	119
30,000	8,460	9,625	114
50,000	10,900	13,325	122
100,000	13,650	19,075	140
250,000	15,900	35,605	224
500,000	18,400	50,105	272
1,000,000	20,900	66,226	317
2,000,000	25,900	92,326	356
5,000,000	40,900	176,105	431
10,000,000	45,900	316,105	689

agent has an active role in making a substantial addition to a group on which he is being paid renewals or service fees, he may receive first-year commissions on the new premium from the top of the scale or from the point on the scale previously reached.

Group Permanent Insurance Commissions

Less attention often is given to the commission structures of group permanent insurance because of the smaller volume of group permanent business in relation to that of group term life and health insurance. When group permanent insurance was first introduced, it was thought of as a true group product, and there was general sentiment that its commission structure should be similar to those of group term life and health insurance. On the other hand, it was designed to compete in a market where many individual contracts were sold. It was felt, therefore, that some of the commission practices of individual insurance to which agents were accustomed would have to be incorporated into this new product; agents otherwise would not be interested in selling group permanent insurance. The result was that group permanent commissions reflect a combination of group and individual insurance practices.

Commissions on Group Paid-Up Contracts. For commission purposes, group permanent insurance is divided into two groups: group paid-up contracts and group level premium plans. The commission schedules are relatively simple for group paid-up contracts. There is no separation of the commissions into soliciting commissions and service fees, and no commission payment is made after the tenth year. Although group paid-up insurance consists of a series of single premium payments, the premiums for additional paid-up amounts after the first policy year are considered as renewal year premiums.

Two types of commission schedules are used for the group paid-up contracts: one with first-year and renewal commissions and the other a cumulative type schedule. Table 27–5 shows illustrative first-year and renewal commission rates, while Table 27–6 indicates illustrative cumulative commissions. The first type is similar to that of group term life insurance, except that the rates are much lower. The cumulative type has even lower rates, and the premiums of one year are added to those of the previous years to further reduce the rates. These two types of schedules, however, are used by different companies, and thus the comparison is again between the companies rather than between types of schedules.

Commissions on Level Premium Group Permanent Contracts. There are also two different methods of establishing commission schedules for level premium group permanent plans. The first method involves the adjustment of the group permanent premiums, after which the group term rates are applied to the adjusted premiums. The other method is to adopt entirely new schedules for this type of insurance with rates somewhat higher than those of group term insurance.

When group term rate schedules are used, the most common practice is to multiply the level premium group permanent premiums by 150 per cent and then apply the group term commission rates to arrive at the amount of group permanent commissions. This method has the advantage of simplicity, but due to the grading down by size of premiums, the increase in commissions over that of group term is usually less than 50 per cent. Under this method, commissions may be split into soliciting commissions and service fees similar to the procedure previously described as being used sometimes in connection with group term life insurance.

If separate level premium group permanent commission schedules are used, adjustments usually are made for the number of annual premiums required. A plan might consider 100 per cent of the gross premiums with

TABLE 27-5

ILLUSTRATIVE COMMISSION SCHEDULE FOR GROUP PAID-UP AND
OTHER SINGLE PREMIUM PLANS
First-Year and Renewal Schedule

Annual Premium Volume	First Year	Renewals Two–Ten Years
First $ 250,000................	1.000%	2.00%
Next 250,000................	0.500	1.00
Next 1,750,000................	0.050	0.10
Next 5,250,000................	0.025	0.05
Over 7,500,000................	0.000	0.00

TABLE 27-6

ILLUSTRATIVE COMMISSION SCHEDULE FOR GROUP PAID-UP AND
OTHER SINGLE PREMIUM PLANS
Cumulative Type Schedule

Ten-Year Cumulative Single Premiums	Rate
First $ 50,000........................	0.75%
Next 450,000........................	0.10
Over 500,000........................	0.05

respect to coverage calling for ten or more annual premiums; 90 per cent of the gross premiums with respect to coverage calling for nine annual premiums; 80 per cent for eight annual premiums; and so on to 10 per cent for one annual premium. This adjustment reduces the amount of commissions payable with shorter durations of premium payments. Since level premium group permanent insurance requires individual or class determination of rates, this adjustment of premiums for commission purposes does not impose too much additional clerical work, as the adjustment can be made easily from the premium statements.

Two illustrative level premium group permanent commission schedules are presented in Table 27-7. One is for level premium group permanent whole life insurance, and the other is for level premium group permanent endowment and annuity income plans. For these particular schedules, the commissions are divided into 75 per cent soliciting commissions and 25 per cent service fees for the first ten years; thereafter all compensation is considered as service fees. For premiums paid from the eleventh to the twentieth years, inclusive, service fees are paid at the rate of one half the rate under the higher first-year scale for the second to tenth years. For premiums paid after the twentieth year, service fees usually are paid at the rate of one quarter of the second-to-tenth-year commission rates under the same scale.

Companies generally use only one type of level premium group permanent commission schedule, with the adjusted group term schedule being

TABLE 27–7

COMMISSION SCHEDULES FOR LEVEL PREMIUM GROUP PERMANENT INSURANCE

Net Adjusted Annual Premium		Higher First-Year Scale		Level Scale
From	To	First Year	Years Two–Ten*	Years One–Ten*
Group Permanent Whole Life				
$ 0	$ 5,000	40%	4.25%	9.25%
5,000	10,000	30	3.50	7.25
10,000	25,000	20	3.50	6.00
25,000	75,000	20	2.75	5.25
75,000	150,000	15	2.25	4.00
150,000	250,000	10	1.75	3.00
Over $250,000		To be determined by the company		
Group Permanent Endowment and Annuity Income				
$ 0	$ 5,000	20%	4.25%	6.75%
5,000	25,000	16	3.50	5.50
25,000	75,000	12	2.75	4.25
75,000	150,000	9	2.25	3.25
150,000	250,000	6	1.75	2.50
Over $250,000		To be determined by the company		

* Service fees at one half the rates for years two to ten under the higher first-year schedule will be paid for premiums paid for the eleventh to twentieth years, inclusive. In addition, a service fee of one quarter of the rates for years two to ten under the higher first-year scale will be paid for premiums after the twentieth year.

most common. The few companies which have both types of schedules usually require that the adjusted group term schedule be used for package policies, that is, policies which combine the benefits of level premium group permanent insurance with either group term life or group health insurance, or both. This has the advantage of administrative simplicity and also produces lower combined commissions for the companies.

COMMISSIONS FOR SMALL GROUPS

Small group contracts are designed to meet the needs of employers with few employees, usually those with less than twenty-five. In order to minimize underwriting and administrative costs, certain benefits are packaged in definite proportions, sometimes combining the coverages of group term, group permanent and group health insurance in a single policy. The packaging of the benefits has simplified agents' selling function, and this accounts for the active solicitation of small group cases by many agents.

TABLE 27-8

ILLUSTRATIVE COMMISSION SCHEDULES FOR SMALL GROUP CONTRACTS

Company	Annual Premium	Annual Volume	First Year	Renewals Two–Ten Years	Service Fees Eleventh Year and After
R	First	$ 1,000	20.0%	5.0%	5.00%
	Next	4,000	20.0	3.0	3.00
	Next	5,000	15.0	1.5	1.50
S	First	$ 2,000	25.0	10.0	10.00
	Next	3,000	20.0	1.5	1.50
	Next	5,000	18.0	1.5	1.50
T	First	$ 3,000	10.0	10.0	0.00
	Next	22,000	2.0	2.0	0.00
U	First	$ 3,500	25.0	7.0	1.00
	Next	6,500	20.0	2.0	1.00
V	First	$ 1,000	25.0	6.5	0.00
	Next	4,000	20.0	4.0	0.00
	Next	5,000	15.0	2.5	0.00
W	First	$ 5,000	25.0	5.0	5.00
	Next	10,000	12.5	1.5	1.50
X	First	$ 1,000	20.0	5.0	To be deter-
	Next	4,000	20.0	3.0	mined by
	Next	5,000	15.0	1.5	the com-
					pany
Y	First	$ 2,000	25.0	6.0	3.00
	Next	3,000	25.0	3.0	1.50
	Next	5,000	15.0	1.5	0.75
Z	First	$ 1,500	30.0	6.0	3.00
	Next	1,000	25.0	3.5	1.75
	Next	2,500	20.0	3.5	1.75
	Next	5,000	15.0	3.5	1.75

Commissions for small group policies are not separated into soliciting commissions and service fees, although the term "service fee" is used for commission payments made after the tenth policy year. This is because the agent usually receives the total commission, since theoretically he is expected to do much of the work connected with selling and installing the case. Insurers are coming to recognize, however, that salaried group men often spend considerable time working with agents on small group cases in many instances. Moreover, some companies actually want their group men to work on small cases where major medical or higher amounts of group life insurance are involved.[4] Another reason for not separating the commission into two categories is that groups covering less than twenty-

[4] Some insurers set minimum annual premium limits, such as $2,000 or $2,500, and they will not accept most cases with premiums under these amounts. If it appears that additional benefits may be added subsequently, a case below the minimum may be written by such companies.

five employees were originally exempted from complying with the Federal Welfare and Pension Plans Disclosure Act requirements.[5]

Like regular group commissions, small group commissions are generally graded downward as premiums increase, but the grading is often simpler than on so-called "regular groups" because of the smaller amount of premiums which can be expected from small cases. Level schedules also are available, but they are used primarily for transferred cases. Although level schedules can also be elected by the agents, there is little to be gained because the premium volume is not likely to increase by any appreciable amount.

A study of the commission practices of twenty-one leading group companies revealed that, like the commission schedules applicable to regular groups, small group commission schedules differ with respect to the manner in which the premiums are graded, the rates of commissions used and the amount of service fees payable after the tenth policy year. Two companies use uniform commission rates, one at $7\frac{1}{2}$ per cent and the other at $12\frac{1}{2}$ per cent, for all size premiums and for all policy years. Others use the higher first-year schedule and the level ten-year or level twenty-year schedules. Sixteen out of the twenty-one companies have commission rates which are higher than those for regular groups, presumably because the small group contracts usually include some element of group permanent insurance and also because less home office assistance is given to the agents. Illustrative small group commission rate schedules are presented in Table 27–8.

COMPENSATION OF GROUP REPRESENTATIVES

Insurers who entered the group field early soon learned that making group insurance available for their own agents or others to sell did not result in high production of this type of business. For most agents the group business was too technical and involved a type of market with which they were not familiar. By the 1940's, when the volume of group insurance began to skyrocket, a type of home office employee called group representatives, group managers or similar titles had developed. These men were specialists in group insurance and represented their company in major cities around the country. To this day, the group representative has maintained an important position in the sale of most large group cases, as well as in the sale of many small group cases.

Generally, group representatives are employed initially on a salary basis and undergo an extensive period of training and development within the company. Even after they are assigned to field positions, group representatives and managers are compensated largely or entirely by salary, although a few insurers use a commission basis for compensation.

---

[5] Plans covering less than 100 employees are also exempted under amended rules, unless a report is specifically asked for.

Intermediate approaches are taken regarding compensation by some insurers who, for example, pay commissions to salaried fieldmen on groups which they write through personal contacts developed outside of business hours. Since the intended role of most group managers or representatives is to promote the sale of their company's group product through agents and brokers, it would be detrimental to have them particularly interested in certain groups where they have commission interests.

Insurers frequently use a combination of salary and bonus to motivate their experienced men and better relate their incomes to their productivity. Bonuses may range from a small fraction of salary to more than the base pay. The commissions which most insurers pay to the selling agent usually are not affected by the compensation of the group representatives or managers. Many direct writing insurers also employ group representatives to work with their salesmen.

The rapid expansion of group insurance since World War II has resulted in a large majority of the group representatives and managers being under fifty years of age with a high percentage of them still in their thirties. The total compensation of these men ranges widely because their effectiveness can be measured rather directly by their sales and service results once they are established. During the decade after World War II, when many group departments were being formed or expanded, the competition for good experienced men pushed salaries higher and higher. Comparatively high incomes at an early age and challenging work have attracted bright young men to the position of group representative.

SELECTED REFERENCES

ASHMAN, C. R. "Discussions on Employee Benefit Plans," *Transactions of the Society of Actuaries*, Vol. XI, 1959.

DUNKLEY, H. C. "Agency Problems," *Transactions of the Society of Actuaries,* Vol. XI, 1959.

GREGG, DAVIS W. *Group Life Insurance,* pp. 151–57, Appendix K. 3d ed. Homewood, Ill.: Richard D. Irwin, Inc., 1962.

LIFE INSURANCE AGENCY MANAGEMENT ASSOCIATION. *Agents' Financing: Some Thoughts on the Purposes and Construction of Plans.* Hartford, Connecticut: The Association, 1961.

LIN, CHE. "The Compensation Structure in the Marketing of Group Insurance." Unpublished dissertation, University of Pennsylvania, 1963.

MENGE, WALTER O. "Life Insurance Growth," *Best's Insurance News,* Life Edition (March, 1963).

PAUMGARTTEN, PAUL VON. "Direct Writing," *Best's Insurance News,* Life Edition (July, 1962).

PICKRELL, JESSE F. *Group Health Insurance,* pp. 88–89. Rev. ed. Homewood, Ill.: Richard D. Irwin, Inc., 1961.

WOLFSON, I. S. Discussion on "Group Field Operations," *Transactions of the Society of Actuaries*, Vol. XIV, Part I, 1962.

Chapter 28

INSTALLATION AND GENERAL ADMINISTRATION OF GROUP PLANS[1]

BY A. B. HALVERSON

The title of this chapter may imply that there is a separation of installation and subsequent field administration (as opposed to the general administration at home office), but this should not obscure the fact that each area must be aware of what is happening in its counterpart. Commitments made in one area do not build good policyholder relations unless they are followed through in the other area.

The communications between the field and home office must be prompt and clear to ensure completion of commitments. If the policyholder is told by the fieldman that a certain thing will be done, the fieldman must see that the promised action is completed correctly and on time. To do otherwise might not only be embarrassing to the fieldman, but also serves to damage the standing of the entire company in the eyes of the policyholder.

Although many more persons are insured under labor-management trusteed plans, the largest number of group insurance contracts is written to cover employer-employee groups, with an individual proprietor, partnership or corporation being the policyholder. This chapter will deal primarily with the employer-employee type of group with some mention of the other types of group policyholders.

INSTALLATION

The installation of a group insurance plan involves two distinct aspects. The first is the enrolling of the eligible employees for the group plan; this

---

[1] Since so little formal information is available in articles or other sources regarding the subject matter of this chapter, most of the material dealt with comes from the general operations of group writing companies. The group administration manuals of the Equitable Life Assurance Society of the United States, the Metropolitan Life Insurance Company and the Occidental Life Insurance Company of California were used extensively through the kind cooperation of these companies.

is called the "solicitation." The second aspect involves explaining to the policyholder the administrative details regarding paper work which he is expected to process. The proper handling of both areas is a definite prerequisite to the success of any group.

During the installation of a group insurance plan, the insurer's group service representative goes through what is probably the most critical period in the relationship between the group and the insurance company (except for times when rates are increased). The representative's responsibilities include: (1) having a clear understanding of the particular plan the group policyholder has purchased and imparting enough of this knowledge to the group to prevent future misunderstandings; (2) making certain that enough employees enroll in the plan to qualify it; (3) knowing every detail regarding the administration of the plan and teaching the policyholder's administrator enough so that he can do his part correctly; and (4) keeping the agent, the group sales office and the home office fully informed as to the progress of the installation and problems that have developed.

While doing this, the insurance company representative must remember that he *is* the company in the eyes of the group, and his opinions often may legally be called facts or promises at some later date. An ounce of preventative instruction with regard to the operations of the plan is worth many pounds of subsequent effort to cure a problem situation arising from misunderstanding or misinformation.

As a result of differences in the field and home office organizations of the insurance companies and service organizations providing group insurance coverage today, the person or persons in contact with the policyholder during the various stages of installation and administration may be any of the following: a group sales representative, a group service representative, the agent or broker, or a person from the home office. In this chapter, the term group service representative will be used when discussing a person performing the group service functions outside the home office of the insurance company.

Solicitation of Eligible Employees

The first and most important task of the insurance company after the application has been signed is the solicitation of the eligible employees. Some groups do not require contributions from insured employees for their coverage or that of their dependents, and in such cases there is no solicitation in the usual sense. However, except for labor-management negotiated trust plans, completely noncontributory plans are a small percentage of the group insurance business written.

Reviewing Benefits and Solicitation Material. The group service representative has, or should have, a thorough knowledge of the standard policy language and benefits provided by his company. However, before he makes any arrangements regarding the solicitation of a group he must review its particular plan. This review has two facets. First, the abstract of the master policy must be read, particularly the text which is typed or has been prepared especially for that group and the description of the benefits and the amounts of each. If this is not available for review, a copy of the proposal may be used. Then, too, it is necessary to peruse the solicitation material, which includes a printed description of the benefits and amounts to be provided under the policy. This reading is to compare the solicitation material with the abstract to make certain there are no errors or omissions.

In the solicitation material describing the plan there may or may not be a letter from the policyholder recommending the plan to the employees. Such a letter is desirable to show the employer's interest. The language describing the plan in the solicitation piece can be one of two principal types: (1) that taken directly from the master policy pages applicable to the employee (this is usually reserved for booklet certificates); or, (2) a shortened, layman's language description of the policy terms and benefits.

A great variety of solicitation forms exists, but most are one of the following types. *Pamphlets* are mimeographed or multigraphed material, and they generally are used for smaller premium groups or for any size group when solicitation material is needed on short notice. *Folders* incorporate printed material and customarily are used when describing only one or two group coverages, such as life and disability income, or when an insurance company has developed very brief language to describe the policy. *Booklets* incorporate printed material and are bound with a heavy stock cover.

The folder and booklet may be prepared to be used also as the certificate. The certificate is the employee's evidence of coverage under the contract after he has enrolled in the plan and frequently uses language taken from, or very similar to, the master contract. If the folder or booklet is to serve as a certificate, a lined box is placed on the cover or first page. Inside the box is a statement to the effect that when the insurance for the employee becomes effective, this area will be personalized with a typed or printed sticker. This sticker will show the employee's name and his effective date of coverage under the plan. It may also indicate the amount of the employee's life insurance under the plan and the certificate number assigned to him. In some states on fully noncontributory cases, issuance of a no-name certificate is permitted by statute.

The cost of printing is one of the principal considerations in selecting the forms to be used for a particular case. The expense should bear a direct relationship to the number to be insured and the anticipated premium. Currently, the trend is toward greater usage of a combination solicitation piece and certificate, printed on paper of good quality and written in as simple language as can be used without misleading the employee by leaving too much unsaid.

Meeting Principals and Arranging for Solicitation. After the group service representative is completely familiar with the plan for the group, his next step is to meet the principals or key employees of the policy-holder. This may be accomplished in one meeting or may require several, depending on the size and possible multiple locations of the group. The purposes of these meetings are to strengthen the interest of the top management of the policyholder in the plan, to make arrangements for the actual solicitation and, at the same time, to explain fully the plan to the key people.

In both this type of meeting and during the actual solicitation, it is advisable for the group service representative to stay in the background as much as possible and let the policyholder's people explain the plan. The group service representative acts primarily as an expert advisor. This approach is advantageous from two points of view. First, the management of the company gets a better understanding of the plan and feels that it is really its plan. Also, the employees will receive the plan more favorably if they understand that management is completely behind it.

Although the company management may not be willing to take the spotlight, there are certain conditions which are almost mandatory if a successful solicitation is to be accomplished. First, management and labor must be enjoying harmonious relations; if problems exist, employees may believe they can retaliate against the boss by not signing up for the group insurance, thus causing poor participation. If a union is involved, it should be in favor of the plan, or at least not against it.

Second, management should provide the time and, if possible, a place for the employee, his manager or supervisor and the group service representative to meet for the explanation of the plan to employees and for the actual enrollment. The time *must* be during regular working hours; if solicitation is attempted before or after working hours or during the lunch hour there is little chance for success since the employee will be anxious to be about his own business. Similarly, if solicitation is carried on at the employee's work station, rather than an area set aside for this specific purpose, the employee's attention is likely to be diverted.

Third, the solicitation material should be provided to the policyholder a few days in advance of the solicitation so that it may be distributed and reviewed by the employees. The policyholder should also provide the group service representative with a list of those to be solicited including as much information as possible to permit the enrollment cards to be prepared prior to the actual enrollment. This is helpful because enroll-ment proceeds more smoothly when the employee has less information to provide, the partially completed card tends to make the employee feel he is important and encourages enrollment, and there is less chance of mistakes in the insurance records or on the employee's certificate as a result of errors in filling out the enrollment card or difficulty in reading the handwriting.

Enrolling the Employees. If all or most of the arrangements and conditions described above have been accomplished, the group service representative should have a highly successful enrollment. As mentioned before, the manager of the department should be present at the actual meeting with the employee. The manager may explain the management's reason for making the plan available, their wish for its success and the general nature of the benefits to be provided under the plan. For the last item, the group service representative is present to answer any questions regarding the details of the plan and to give examples. He should also help convince the hesitant or negative individual on the merits of the plan and the cost advantage to be realized if he enrolls.

The enrollment card (see Figure 28–1) has spaces provided for all the information necessary to the general administration of the employee's insurance. Where life insurance is provided, it is important that the beneficiary designation be completed and that the enrollment card be signed. The employee's signature is also necessary to authorize the deduction from his pay if the plan is contributory.

The policyholder retains the lower portion of the enrollment card (Figure 28–1), or he is given a carbon copy of the enrollment form (Figure 28–2) as his authority for making the payroll deductions. Several companies use another copy of the carbon copy enrollment card, with unnecessary information omitted, to personalize the employee's certificate by attaching the copy to the face of the certificate.

Any employees refusing to enroll in the plan should be asked to sign refusal cards stating they have been offered the plan but do not wish to enroll. Such action usually reduces the number of refusals and increases enrollment because it requires a definite decision, and the employee does not like to sign away something of potential value. It should also be explained to those signing refusal cards that if they change their mind, and later decide to enroll, they will have to furnish evidence of insurability which is acceptable to the insurance company.

As was explained in earlier chapters, underwriting restrictions or the state insurance code, or both, usually require that at least 75 per cent of the eligible employees be enrolled before the plan can be made effective. This 75 per cent requirement also applies to dependent coverage. However, the closer enrollment approaches 100 per cent, the greater the chance of success for the plan.

The enrollment or solicitation of other type groups, such as unions or associations, may be handled at meetings of the membership and through mail or advertisements in the group's literature. Solicitations of the latter types (i.e., mail or advertisements) are comparatively unsuccessful.

CERT. NO.	**ENROLLMENT CARD FOR GROUP INSURANCE**	CODE	POL. NO.
	Please Print All Answers	SUB-GROUP CLASS	

Your Full Name_____Date of Birth_____
              LAST   FIRST   MIDDLE   MO.   DAY   YEAR

Your Residence Address_____
            NO. & STREET   CITY & ZONE   STATE

YOUR OCCUPATION_____WEEKLY WAGES $_____ MALE ☐   FEMALE ☐

Name of Your Employer_____Date Employed_____
            COMPANY'S NAME   MO.   DAY   YEAR

Name of Union_____Local No._____

Full Name of
Your Beneficiary_____
         FOR EXAMPLE: WRITE "HELEN LOUISE JONES" NOT "MRS. H. A. JONES"

Relationship of
Beneficiary to you_____
        IF BENEFICIARY IS NOT A RELATIVE — ADDRESS IS NECESSARY

Your Contribution $_____per_____   Date this card signed_____

YOUR SIGNATURE_____

FOR INSURANCE COMPANY'S USE ONLY

OCCIDENTAL LIFE INSURANCE COMPANY OF CALIFORNIA	EFF. DATE OF INS.	INS. CLASS
GMA-274 ED. 5-60		

ORDER FOR PAYROLL DEDUCTION

Please Print Your
Full Name_____

I hereby authorize_____, my Employer,

to deduct from my salary (or wages) such amounts as may now or hereafter be payable by me under the Group
Insurance Plan purchased through

OCCIDENTAL LIFE INSURANCE COMPANY OF CALIFORNIA

The initial deduction for this coverage is $_____per month.

Date_____, 19_____

_____
Your Signature

GMA-274 ED. 5-60   PRINTED IN U.S.A.

FIG. 28–1.   Enrollment card (noncarbon) for group insurance.

Explanation of Policyholder Administration

With the solicitation of the employees completed, the next task for the group service representative is the explanation of administrative details to the proper persons in the policyholder's office. Arrangements should be made immediately for the payroll deductions, if the plan is contributory,

SEND ORIGINAL WITH PREMIUM REPORT TO OCCIDENTAL LIFE INSURANCE COMPANY OF CALIF. — KEEP DUPLICATE

UARCO BUSINESS FORMS OAKLAND, CALIF.

E-Z OUT ®

CERT. NO.

ENROLLMENT CARD FOR GROUP INSURANCE

POLICY NO.

LAST NAME OF APPLICANT FIRST NAME (IN FULL) MIDDLE INITIAL | SEX M | F | DATE OF BIRTH MO. | DAY | YEAR

HOME ADDRESS • NO. AND • STREET CITY STATE

EMPLOYER: | DATE EMPLOYED MO. | DAY | YEAR

OCCUPATION BASIC SALARY $ PER

BENEFICIARY DESIGNATION (WRITE "HELEN LOUISE JONES - WIFE" NOT "MRS. H. L. JONES") (IF NOT A RELATIVE, ALSO GIVE COMPLETE ADDRESS) (IF NO DESIGNATED BENEFICIARY SURVIVES THE APPLICANT, ANY BENEFITS FOR LOSS OF LIFE SHALL BE PAYABLE UNDER THE BENEFICIARY PROVISION OF THE POLICY)

NAME RELATIONSHIP

CHECK COVERAGE	LIFE	A.D. & D.	A. & S.	HOSP.	DEP. LIFE	DEP. HOSP.	MAJ. MED.	
LEAVE BLANK								

DO NOT USE	
EFF.	
P.S.	
H.E.	
C.I.	
CLASS	
CODE	

IF DEPENDENT COVERAGE IS PROVIDED: If any dependents are insured, all eligible dependents must be insured.

NO YES
☐ ☐ Do you want to insure your eligible dependents?
☐ Your wife (or husband if permitted under the plan)?
☐ Your children? How many children have you? ________

I HEREBY (1) ENROLL FOR GROUP INSURANCE, (2) AUTHORIZE MY EMPLOYER TO MAKE THE NECESSARY DEDUCTION FROM MY WAGES OR SALARY FOR THE CONTRIBUTIONS, IF ANY, REQUIRED OF ME FOR THE INSURANCE, AND (3) CERTIFY THAT THE BENEFICIARY DESIGNATION IS TRUE AND CORRECT.

OCCIDENTAL LIFE · MORE PEACE OF MIND PER PREMIUM DOLLAR

INITIAL DEDUCTION $________ PAYROLL OR IDENTIFICATION NO.________

MO. | DAY | YEAR

Ⓤ 252865 DATE SIGNED SIGNATURE OF APPLICANT

GMA 200 ED. 9-64 OCCIDENTAL LIFE INSURANCE COMPANY OF CALIFORNIA 11 PRINTED IN U.S.A.

FIG. 28–2. Enrollment card (carbon) for group insurance.

but discussion of other procedures should be postponed from one to three weeks. This delay is necessitated to give the insurance company's home office time to set up its records, issue the master policy and employee certificates, prepare the billing and assemble the various items which are included in the kit of initial supplies furnished to the policyholder. The personnel or salary administration unit or department handles the group insurance administration for the policyholder in most firms. Larger groups may have an insurance unit whose primary function is insurance administration.

As with the solicitation, it is important that the group service representative review the master policy for accuracy and the supplies for adequacy prior to his meeting with those who will be responsible for administering the plan. He must be certain that he will receive the undivided attention of the persons with whom he will be meeting, since lack of understanding may affect the entire plan rather than just a single employee.

Reviewing the Policy. One of the most difficult, if not practically impossible, things to accomplish in the insurance field is getting the policyholder to read his policy. The insured or beneficiary may read it when a claim arises but, too often, not before. It is especially important that those responsible for administration be familiar with the terms of the plan because when a certificate holder has an insurance problem or question, the overwhelming probability is that he will go to them for the solution or answer. For this reason, as well as for the general administration, the policyholder's administrator *must* be informed.[2]

The group service representative must keep the administrator informed. The aspects discussed below require particular emphasis when the contract is discussed initially with the administrator.

A. *Benefits.* The actual coverages provided under the policy and what is payable under each type obviously need to be made clear. The more detail and meaning the administrator can absorb from the policy, the better. This does not mean that he can become a policy contract technician or an expert claims adjuster with a few hours' instruction. It does mean that he can be made aware of the fact that most of the questions regarding the policy do not require home office interpretation, merely a careful reading of the proper policy provisions. If the administrator is a capable person and the group service representative can encourage him to understand the policy benefits, everyone will enjoy faster handling of problems or questions.

B. *Provisions and Limitations.* Almost as important as knowing the nature of policy benefits is understanding the conditions that must be satisfied before benefits are payable and the areas that are not covered. The conditions to be satisfied are called "provisions," while "limitations" or "exclusions" set forth areas or situations not covered.

Unfortunately, provisions and limitations are generally restrictive aspects of a contract which often are neither explained fully nor understood clearly. However, the sooner these aspects are clearly understood, the better. If the administrator tells an individual that his dependent is not eligible for a particular benefit when the claim form is requested, it is obviously better that this fact become known before the individual completes the claim form, takes it to the doctor's office for completion of his part, sends it and the bills to the insurance company and then receives a letter from the claims adjustor saying that nothing is payable. The following—all of which have been discussed in earlier chapters—must be discussed with the administrator: effective date, waiting period, definition of full-time employee, extension of coverage, pre-existing conditions and effects of other insurance.

Reviewing the Billing and Other Forms. One can well imagine the feelings an administrator might have when first exposed to the many forms furnished in the kit of supplies. To aid him in his job and provide

---

[2] For simplicity the term "administrator" is used to denote the person or persons handling the policyholder functions with regard to the group insurance policy. Although most of the following statements could apply equally to an independent, third party administrator, the term is intended to apply only to an employee of the policyholder who is acting as administrator.

continuously available information regarding the forms, most insurers supply an administration manual which explains when and how to use each of the forms provided.

A. *Billings*. The most important form from the company's viewpoint is the monthly billing. Since it is used so often, reflects practically all of the changes under the policy as well as all of the changes in personnel, and must be completely accurate, problems and actions arising out of the use of a billing are estimated to cause 50 per cent or more of an insurance company's group correspondence. Thus, the better the group service representative can instruct the policyholder's administrator as to the proper completion of the billing, the less it will cost all parties to administer the plan.

The group service representative should explain how the administrator is to handle the monthly billings with regard to the following situations: (1) It must be understood that additions must be approved by the insurer before an individual can be added to the billing. Removals or deletions from the billing should be made immediately. (2) Changes in classifications must be kept up to date. Marriage and birth dates, for example, must be checked to determine the eligibility of dependents. (3) A warning should be given against the practice of using the grace period to delay premium payments, as this causes unnecessary cancellations.

B. *Claim Forms*. The proper completion of the claim form will greatly facilitate the administration of a group case, and these forms should be thoroughly familiar to the administrator.

C. *Hospital Admission Forms*. They are used as a hospital claim form and, in areas where the Health Insurance Council's Hospital Admissions Plan has been instituted and accepted, as promise of payment by the insurance company of the benefits shown on the form.[3] The form also provides for assignment of the benefits to the hospital.

D. *Conversion Forms*. Conversion forms, as their name implies, are used by insured persons who terminate their group coverage to apply for individual policies as provided by the terms of the group policy.

E. *Other Forms*. The following are also among the items included in the kit that the insurer provides the policyholder's administrator: identification cards (by which insureds may substantiate their coverage), solicitation material to be distributed to future employees, enrollment cards to be used in enrolling future employees and submitted with the monthly billing, request form for duplicate certificates, change of name or beneficiary and envelopes addressed to the insurer's home office.

Whether this kit of supplies is used as intended or just put on a shelf to gather dust depends on how responsible the policyholder's administrator

---

[3] The details of this procedure are discussed in Chapter 23.

is and how well the group service representative explains its importance and use.

CONSERVATION

There are many reasons why policyholders cancel their coverage with a particular insurance company, but many if not most of the reasons can be traced to poor conservation practices. A great deal of time, effort and money are expended in selling, installing and setting up records on a group policy—only to lose the group subsequently in some cases, as a result of inadequate service and lack of attention. Good policyholder relations are not accidental. Careful attention to detail, accuracy and regularity is needed to conserve the hard-won business.

Follow-up Visit. The group service representative should visit the policyholder within three months following the installation of the group to check for problem areas and to make certain everything is understood and going smoothly. Any correspondence with the home office should be reviewed to be certain that this communication channel is satisfactory.

To be of maximum benefit to the administrator, the visit should be scheduled to suit his convenience and as much time as is needed allowed for the interview. After the administrator has had some time to work with the administration of the plan, he will understand the procedures and information more clearly. However, he probably will be receptive to a short review, particularly regarding the handling of additions and deletions to the group.

Service Calls. In addition to being on call at any time during the year, the group service representative should schedule visits to the policyholder at least every six months or year, depending on the size of the group, its accessibility and the wishes of those administering the insurance program. Being on call means not only visiting the policyholder to solve problems at his request, but also being able to anticipate these requests by reviewing copies of correspondence sent to the group service representative.

Many insurers utilize a group service report which serves as a guide to potential problem areas, and the group service representative is expected to complete this report during his regular service call. Besides the common problems that may arise with regard to billing and claims, the group service representative checks the enrollment procedure (its effectiveness and an audit to be certain only eligible persons are enrolled), present participation and the stock of supplies for the policyholder. If supplies are low, the group service representative orders replacements. If participation in the group is low, two things usually need to be done. First, the policyholder's key people and administrator may need to be resold on the importance of participation in the plan and the need for enrolling new individuals as they are hired. Second, it may be necessary to make arrangements for a resolicitation of those not participating in the plan. The latter action sometimes requires prior home office clearance.

As a result of transfers or turnover, the group service representative may find a new person handling the policyholder administration. If this person's instruction on administration has not been handled during a special call, the service call is the ideal time to make certain that the new administrator has received correct and complete instructions. Of course, depending on the need, this is also a good time for re-education of the administrator even if there has been no turnover.

Other Calls. Certain developments regarding the group plan may be discussed during service calls, but they will tend to receive the attention deserved if presented during a separate visit. The situations being referred to include new or revised benefits, dividends or rating refunds and rate increases. Calls of this nature are held with a higher level of management than the administrator. The person contacted should be one who can make the decision.

A. *New or Revised Benefits.* The group service representative must make certain that the policyholder's plan is kept up to date with regard to other similar industries and local conditions. If a bargaining agreement must be complied with, the service representative is not in a position to suggest benefit changes, beyond quoting the cost of possible changes. Under other circumstances, he should make the policyholder aware of new coverages and alterations that are needed to keep the group plan up to date.

B. *Dividends or Rating Refunds.* Groups of sufficient size which have favorable experience receive a portion of their premiums back in the form of cash dividends or rating refunds. The delivery of these dividends or refunds provides the opportunity to cement relationships with the policyholder (unless they are less than the policyholder anticipates). At the same time, it is important to emphasize that while the dividend or refund is the result of good claims experience, poor experience may necessitate a rate increase. The occasion also offers a chance to explain how a contingency fund or a reserve operates.

C. *Rate Increases.* Probably the most vulnerable time in the life of a group insurance plan is when a rate increase is required. If the increase is based on the experience of the group itself and the policyholder has had the warning signs pointed out to him ahead of time, chances for acceptance of the increase are fair. However, all too often other insurance companies are willing to quote lower rates and, consequently, the group case may be transferred. If the increase is the result of over-all poor experience of a pool of smaller groups, the resale effort will require particular expertise.

The underwriter and claims adjuster should be consulted to obtain detailed information concerning claim problems in a given case, and this provides the best groundwork for a rate increase visit. Nearly every month an article on rising medical costs appears in some national magazine. The policyholder is faced with higher costs in other areas of his operation. To put these factors together in a presentation that will persuade the policy-holder to accept the increase, rather than seek another insurance company, is one of the more difficult tasks given to the group service representative.

GENERAL ADMINISTRATION

The proper administration of a group plan requires that the efforts of the field force be supplemented by the continuous cooperation of the home office personnel. Insurers differ as to how they allocate various group insurance functions among the home office departments and the field, and plans differ regarding the administrative details that are handled by the policyholder. However, certain basic administrative functions must be performed by one party or the other.

Records of Insurance

An up-to-date record of each employee's insurance is essential in order that benefits may be paid to the persons entitled to them, in the proper amounts, and so that the policyholder will be billed for the correct amount of premium. This record will usually be maintained by the insurance company but may be retained by the policyholder or a third party administrator for a large group. The original information will be obtained from the enrollment card or, for a noncontributory plan not using cards, the enrollment list prepared by the policyholder. When an employee first enters the plan, the date of employment is compared with the date of enrollment to check the employee's eligibility, to determine when the insurance is to become effective and to ascertain whether evidence of insurability is required because of late enrollment.

A card is made up, showing all details required to determine the benefits, the effective date and the premium rate pertaining to the employee's coverage. The benefits or rates may vary by the employee's earnings, age, sex, number of dependents or some factor pertaining to his occupation. A schedule of classes appropriate to the case will be designed and the employee's class noted on the record of his insurance.

Changes are made in this record whenever changes occur in the employee's status, such as when he becomes entitled to larger amounts of insurance after a salary increase or after acquiring new dependents. Similarly, changes are necessitated when benefits are reduced as a result of age or termination of employment.

These records usually will be maintained on punched cards or tapes which may be processed by high-speed electronic machines. The one essential fact which often is not included on this record is the beneficiary designated for group life insurance. This is obtained directly from the enrollment card, to which any requests for beneficiary change will be attached after they have been processed.

Issuance of Certificates

The fill-in material on the employee's certificate either will be obtained from the record of his insurance or made up simultaneously from the enrollment data.

Billings

The most common form for billings is a machine listing of the employees who were insured on the previous premium due date. This is prepared electronically from punched cards or tape. It may be categorized by coverage or combine all coverages, but in either case, usually will show the class and the premium for each employee and the total premium due. The policyholder will notify the insurer of terminations, classification changes and new enrollees. Additions and changes are reviewed to verify eligibility and to be certain that enrollment took place within the eligibility period.

From the reported changes as received, the punched card file or tape is updated for preparation of the next month's billing by removing the data for those deleted from the billing by the policyholder, adding the new individuals and changing the classes as indicated.

Other types of billing include the short form (or Mancount), the per capita and special letter forms. The short form, which is used primarily for self-administered groups or large groups, does not list the names of insureds, but merely shows the number insured in each class. The names of persons who are additions, deletions and changes in the billings are shown for record keeping and auditing purposes. The per capita report is used for union groups and reports the number of members of the union (assuming all union members are insured). Special letter forms are used for very large groups, trustee negotiated groups and plans administered by professional administrators. These forms vary by plan and will contain the minimal information needed by the insurance company to calculate the premium.

Commissions and Other Credits

When the premium payment is entered into the insurance company's ledger, any commissions must be calculated and credited to the agents, brokers or managers entitled to them. Flat commission rates applying to all premiums for a particular class of business may be calculated and recorded by the electronic computers. Some insurers will also use their electronic data processing equipment for their most common commission schedules, e.g., those graded by the size of the premium. Adjustments to apply a first-year rate to a portion of the premium and a renewal rate for the balance may require a special calculation on a basic calculator to obtain input data for the electronic computer. Convention and club credits, bonuses not directly related to the premium for each policy and similar items will be handled in the way best suited to the formula adopted for each item.

The actual payment of the commission may be handled by the group accounting department, or the entries may be made to be added to the agent's individual insurance production and paid at the end of the month. Any administration fees payable as a percentage of the premium may be paid at the same time. The fees may be for general administration, such as preparation of the billing and issuing certificates, for claim administration, for enrollment cards obtained by the agent or for some other administrative function normally performed by the insurer which is being performed by someone else. These fees may be payable to the agent, the policyholder or an independent administrator.

Policy Records

The insurance company must, of course, maintain a file containing a copy of the master contract, any amendments and all correspondence relating to the case. Experience records will also be maintained showing all premiums received and all payments made, including claims, commissions and other expenses pertaining specifically to the contract. Summaries usually will be maintained by policy year for each coverage, with the employees' insurance shown separately from the dependents coverage. These policy experience records will be used for auditing, renewal underwriting or experience rating and in the preparation of the federal disclosure reports.

Federal Disclosure Reports. Under the Federal Disclosure Act, the policyholder of a contract covering twenty-six or more insureds must file with the Labor Department an initial description of the plan as well as names and addresses of the administrator and any trustees. The description and other information required can best be furnished by completion of a D-1 report accompanied by a copy of the group contract. A copy of the D-1 report is shown in Appendix 13. Copies of amendments to the group policy must also be filed with the Labor Department.

Each year, the policyholder must file a report (D-2)[4] showing the type of coverage, number of persons (including dependents) insured, and the total premiums, claim payments, experience rating refunds or dividends paid during the reporting year. In addition, he must show the name and address of each person who received a commission or fee and the amount

---

[4] See Appendix 14.

paid to each recipient. A shortened (D-3)[5] form is all that is required for a plan covering between twenty-six and 100 persons. The D-3 requires only the reporting of the number of insureds under the plan. Although the policyholder, not the insurance company, is responsible for the filing of the reports, the insurer must provide the policyholder with this information.

Statistical Analyses

The policy experience figures and the amount of claim payments made on account of each insured employee or dependent, with a great variety of identifying information, will usually be transferred to punched cards or tape. Thus, they will be available for the many statistical analyses required for the intelligent conduct of the group insurance business.

Insurers' management decisions are based on the facts available, and many questions arise. How effective are personnel in certain territories in their production and underwriting as opposed to their operations costs? What loss ratios are being produced by the rates being charged for the various coverages? How effective is home office underwriting? Are all expenses in line? How profitable are the various sizes of group cases? Such questions can be answered only through a thorough study of the area in question. This could be accomplished by hand calculation, but it would require a large staff and a long period of time. Moreover, decisions would be based on information that was many months old when it was produced. Through the use of electronic data processing equipment, however, decisions can be made to correct a problem situation much more quickly than once was possible.

Correspondence

One aspect of group administration which cannot be handled more rapidly by electronic devices is the day-to-day correspondence between the insurer and the policyholder, insureds and other parties, e.g., physicians and hospitals. In order to keep the administrative costs as low as possible, form letters are used commonly in situations which arise with great frequency. Reminder and warning letters to policyholders regarding overdue premiums, notices of general rate increases and requests for evidence of insurability for late enrollees will frequently be made on a pre-printed form. This is a regrettable necessity, and it is important that these form letters be carefully designed so as to retain a personal approach to the greatest possible extent.

---

[5] See Appendix 15.

Chapter 29

CLAIMS HANDLING IN GROUP INSURANCE

BY LA RUE S. WAGENSELLER

NATURE OF THE CLAIMS HANDLING FUNCTION

In the period since World War II there has been an astounding expansion in the variety of group insurance and health care prepayment coverages and in the number of United States and Canadian employees and their families covered by them. Both of these factors have greatly broadened the fields of knowledge and the techniques, skills and ingenuity required for claims administration. The group claim function is not simple and routine with all the answers spelled out in the policy. As with many other forms of insurance, it is utterly impossible to detail in a contract all the specifics of group coverage, including those which will come out of advancing technology in the health care field, for example. Thus, claims with new and different facets must be measured against various bench marks outside the contract, such as court decisions, insurance department rulings, opinions of the insurer's legal or medical staff and precedents from somewhat similar cases. Coupled with this fluidity of the claim function, itself, has been experimentation with new organizational structures and systems of claim administration. On all fronts change will undoubtedly continue for the foreseeable future.

The group claims administrator's activities and decisions touch the interests of an unusually broad cross section of the population. Parties affected either directly or indirectly can include the insured certificate holders and their beneficiaries and covered dependents; the employer, association, union, welfare fund trustees, creditor or other entity to whom the group contract was issued; union officials representing employees covered under collectively bargained plans; and a host of institutions and individuals involved in furnishing health care, such as hospitals, clinics, physicians, nurses, pharmacists and others. Inevitably, there are times when the divergence of interests among such parties presents the claims administrator with serious problems in striving to operate within the framework of the contract involved.

The rapid advance of medical technology sometimes requires seeking the underlying intent of specific health insurance contract language when a claim presents a situation which was neither existent nor foreseeable when the documents were issued. In these and other circumstances, the claims administrator will turn for technical advice and opinions to members of other departments of his company, particularly the law and medical departments. He will consult his group administration department when he needs background information on agreements with a policyholder as to how his plan should be administered or how a particular provision will be interpreted. At other times he will discuss a claim situation with his actuarial department to learn whether it comes within the boundaries of the risk intended to be underwritten when the rates were established.

In turn, the claims administrator should be a giver as well as a seeker of counsel. Out of his daily experiences he can make helpful suggestions to the actuary, the lawyer and other executives of his company, especially when new coverages or policies are being designed either for general marketing or for use in a special situation. It would be a mistake for a company to overlook the contribution which can be made by the claims administrator to the development of sound, competitive products.

Objectives of Claims Administration

While the insurance company or prepayment plan furnishes its group policyholders with a variety of services, surely one of the most important is its claim service. This service should pursue several key objectives. Foremost among these is *dealing fairly with the claimant* and any other parties at interest. This means *denying the improper claim* as well as paying the just one. It also means investigating and developing the facts further if initially they do not place the claim squarely in one category or the other.

A second objective of quality service is *prompt and accurate payment,* yet not so prompt that any unclear aspects of a claim go unnoticed or undeveloped for the sake of speed. That would be inconsonant with the primary objective of fair dealing. On the other hand, a balance must be struck between accuracy and speed of payment since excessive checking and rechecking of the various steps in claim processing can cause undue delay and expense.

Thirdly, claim decisions should be as *consistent* as practicable. In group coverage it is highly important that all certificate holders under a given policy be treated alike. But when interpreting the benefit clauses of different contracts, the claims administrator must take account of such things as any pertinent collective bargaining commitments made by an individual policyholder or variations in health care facilities or practices from one community to another.

Finally, good claims service should be as *economical* as is compatible with observance of the other objectives. This calls for finding the elusive points of optimum value in such matters as investigation of unclear aspects of a claim, functionalization of the review and calculation processes, referrals to higher levels of authority, checking and the like. Generally, the expenditure for investigating a given case will be related somewhat to the amount of potential claim liability. But with the relatively high claim frequencies that characterize some health insurance coverages, the possible effect on future claims of a similar nature must also be considered.

Performance of the Claims Function

The claims function is usually performed by the insurer itself, although for some of its cases an insurer may consent to delegate parts of the function either to the group policyholder or to a third party administrator. Such delegation rarely involves group life or accidental death and dismemberment insurance claims, both of which tend toward much larger average amounts and sometimes either involve legal questions as to whom may receive the proceeds or call for payment in installments over potentially long periods. Insurance companies generally are better equipped to deal with these and other special situations.

Types of Insurer Claims Organizations. The insurer's claims department may operate exclusively out of its home office and multifunctional regional or head offices, if any. On the other hand, the department may function with the aid of a few or many local claims offices which deal directly with group policyholders in their territory and issue benefit drafts in payment of claims received from them or from the providers of service.

A. Organization of the Insurer's Claims Department. Many variations or combinations of responsibilities for claims are possible. All claims work—life and health, individual and group—may function under one executive or department head. Or there may be separate departments for life and health, for example. Even in the comprehensive department, i.e., where all claims work is concentrated in one department, specialization of work below the managerial level is most likely since evaluation of death and health claims involves quite dissimilar considerations. An insurance company paying claims from the home office but having many distant policyholders usually will have a corps of field claim specialists who either operate from the home office or reside in the detached territory for which they have primary responsibility. They investigate specific or general claim problems and visit policyholders, claimants, hospitals, physicians and other providers of health care who figure in claims.

B. Local Claim Offices. Large multiple line insurance companies that settled their liability and other casualty claims from a network of local claim offices found it convenient to use the same offices for group health insurance claims, especially where an office was already dealing with the group policyholder on workmen's compensation claims. During the group health insurance explosion of the 1950's, some of the large life and health insurers set up claim offices in selected cities to receive and to process group health claims. In some instances group death claims also have been handled by these same offices, but this is likely to be limited to the smaller and routine claims not involving an optional mode of settlement or a complex beneficiary problem. Other cases might require authorization from, or complete processing in, the home office. In addition to its inside personnel, a claim office will usually have at least one field representative for investigations and visits to policyholders, claimants, attorneys, hospitals and doctors in the territory.

The operations of individual Blue Cross and Blue Shield plans are more localized than those of most group health insurers since the former have been incorporated to do business in restricted areas, usually a state or certain specified counties. However, many of these plans are affiliated with a national association through which, if permitted by the state laws under which they are incorporated, they may participate in providing coverage under a contract insuring lives residing within the territories of two or more local plans. Each local plan then administers claims of persons insured under such a contract who live in its territory.

C. Comparison of Centralized and Localized Operations. As in many things, the pros and cons of each method of operation are not always absolute and much depends upon circumstances peculiar to the company viewing the problem. An insurer which does not have a sizable amount of group health insurance and has no prospects of expanding substantially in this line within a very few years cannot afford to establish local claim offices. But for the insurer which does have a choice, the following are some of the more important advantages of a home office operation:

1. Economy, due to volume operations and the need for relatively few supervisory and managerial personnel;
2. Ease and speed of communications between executives and working force, keeping the former aware of developing trends and the latter uniformly current on management's wishes;
3. Ease of controlling consistency of decisions, especially for the policyholder with two or more plants at scattered locations;
4. Ready access of claims administrators to the company's legal and medical officers for discussion of individual case problems;
5. Potential for development of electronic programing or other mechanization of some of the routine processes involved.

A local office operation, on the other hand, can produce these significant advantages, among others:

1. Prompter service to those policyholders located nearer to the claims office—in terms of mailing time—than to the insurer's home office;

2. Concentration of attention on the patterns of medical practice, fee levels, individuals and institutions providing health care in just one area. If this area is not too large, there is opportunity for periodic personal contact with the providers of services;

3. Ability to draw on several or many employment markets for claim administration personnel;

4. Close, continuous and personalized contacts with policyholders or branches served. This tends to make the latter more aware of the service being rendered by the distant insurer.

Performance of the Claim Function by Policyholder or Third Party. While the insurer rarely delegates to others any of the responsibility for group life and accidental death claims computations and payment, there is rather extensive delegation—generally to the policyholder—for the more routine claims under group health insurance. Starting with disability income contracts of employers who had some experience administering the early mutual benefit association plans or salary continuance arrangements for their employees, delegation of the claim payment function spread to other group health coverages as they developed. Initially, policyholder payment arrangements were available only to larger groups, e.g., 1,000 or more employees, but these limits have been lowered radically by most companies, down to 100 employees or less. Some insurers do not delegate authority to deny claims, since they must defend any legal action brought under their contracts. Blue Cross and Blue Shield plans seldom, if ever, delegate any authority regarding claims.

Many policyholders do not want to assume responsibility for claim decisions but like to share in the payment process by having the insurer forward benefit checks to them for delivery to the claimants. They view this as a useful feature of their over-all employee relations program which helps to identify them with the group program in the minds of claimants. It also gives the policyholder an opportunity to verify the correctness of the payment and to accumulate benefit totals for subsequent comparison with the amounts reported by the insurer. The review by the policyholder of disability income benefit checks is especially useful since it helps to avoid making payments for a period running beyond the date the insured returned to work. The following paragraphs outline ways in which some policyholders participate more directly in the claim processing function.

A. *Policyholder Payment by Draft on Insurer.* The most frequently used technique for delegation of claims payment to a policyholder is called the "draft book system." Under this technique, the insurer not only instructs the policyholder on the handling of the more routine claims under his plan but also supplies sets of pre-numbered blank drafts on one of the insurer's bank accounts. Usually, a carbon of each draft issued by the policyholder is sent the insurer at once, so that validating advice can be given its bank, i.e., the bank is told to honor (or dishonor) the draft. The policyholder accounts carefully for every draft, whether issued or spoiled. Doubtful claims are sent the insurer for evaluation, possible investigation and eventual decision to pay or decline. The policyholder is instructed initially by the insurer's field claim personnel who also revisit the policyholder periodically to audit the operation, answer questions and help train new personnel. This system is not commonly used by Blue Cross, Blue Shield or the group practice prepayment plans.

The draft issued by a policyholder may be delivered to the claimant anywhere from several days to a week sooner than if the claim papers had been sent to the insurer's nearest claims office for processing. Another reason sometimes given in favor of the draft book system is that, after helping a claimant complete and assemble the necessary claim papers and explaining how much he should receive in benefits, the policyholder might as well draw the actual draft. But this involves additional competent staff in the policyholder's office who must be trained and supervised on work foreign to his regular operations. Moreover, the policyholder becomes accountable for their accuracy and honesty in drawing upon the insurer's funds. Except under the very largest groups, the exposure to varying claim situations obviously cannot match that experienced by claim-paying personnel of an insurance company under all their cases. There is no substitute for breadth and depth of experience as a means of developing the "sixth sense" which is so valuable in the appraisal of even seemingly routine claims.

B. Policyholder Payment by Own Funds. A small number of policyholders have an arrangement differing from the draft book system only in that benefits are paid with their own company checks. Then once or twice a month a list of the amounts paid, with sufficient details for accounting purposes, is sent the insurer which reimburses the policyholder in bulk.[1] Such settlements may represent the cumulative benefits on only those claims terminated in the period, or may be for current benefits paid in the latest period on all claims. The insurer's home office and field claim representatives render similar services to both reimbursement and draft book policyholders.

As compared with normal insurer payment of claims, the reimbursement system has the same advantages and disadvantages mentioned under "A" above. On the other hand, by contrast with the draft book

---

[1] Under so-called "minimum premium plan" contracts, of which there are no more than half a dozen at this writing, the insurer has no liability for claim payments unless and until the total amount disbursed by the policyholder in a contract year exceeds a predetermined figure. Hence, the policyholder would request reimbursement only for such excess, if any, and only during the remainder of that year. In the following year, no reimbursement would be available unless benefits aggregated more than the figure which had been set for that year.

system, the policyholder is temporarily withdrawing funds from his normal business uses for the payment of group claims, subject to later reimbursement by the insurer. This may occasion some sort of interest allowance by the insurer to the policyholder on the funds "advanced."

C. *Third Party Claim Administration.* Under some group plans neither the insurer nor the policyholder performs the claim function. Usually these contracts are issued to joint trustees of a bargained welfare fund set up under the Taft-Hartley Act. The trustees may contract with an insurance broker or consultant to bill and to collect premiums from the employers who finance the plan, to maintain the records of covered employees and dependents, and sometimes to administer claims. The draft book system is commonly used. The insurance company, being relieved of several of its normal functions, may pay the third party some form of service fee or compensation, at the request of the fund trustees. Third party claims administration, in cases of this nature, facilitates the checking of claims against in-force records to determine the status and extent of each claimant's coverage. The policyholder trustees adopting such an arrangement must form some judgment on the technical resources—in the form of experienced claims, actuarial, medical and legal specialists—available to the third party administrator in relation to those which would be provided under insurer administration.

FILING A CLAIM: REQUIREMENTS OF INSURANCE COMPANIES

Written proof of certain facts is needed to establish a claimant's entitlement to plan benefits. The insurer furnishes claim forms through the group policyholder for completion by the claimant and other parties involved in a loss. Supplemental statements and bills may be attached to prove the extent of the loss.

The major proof of claim requirements which are common to all group lines are:

1. Identification of the insured—name, age, sex, marital status, etc. This is furnished by the person completing the claim form and is cross-checked with similar data furnished by others to assure that all the proofs relate to the insured.

2. Proof that the person reported to have suffered a loss—death, illness, hospitalization or whatever—was then insured under the group policy against the broad category of loss. Such certification and the amount of the insured's protection usually comes from the policyholder who, under most group insurance plans covering more than from 50 to 100 workers, maintains the detailed in-force records. The insurance company maintains these records for the smaller groups.

3. Proof that the particular loss suffered was an insured risk, as defined by the specific conditions and exclusions of the policy. For group life insurance, which has practically no limiting conditions or exclusions, a

physician's certification or copy of the death certificate suffices. This may, although not often, suffice to substantiate death by accidental means, if that coverage is involved. Under other coverages, the claimant's proof consists of his own answers to pertinent claim form questions plus any necessary answers, statements or bills from third parties such as physicians, hospitals, nurses or druggists. Since most group health plans provide only nonoccupational coverage, claim forms generally ask both the employer and the employee to state whether or not the claimant's illness or injury arose from gainful employment.

There was concern about the confusion spreading among the health care professions from the endless variety of claim forms and questions used by different insuring organizations for the many kinds of group health plans. Consequently, the Health Insurance Council[2] appointed a Uniform Forms Committee to work with comparable committees set up by the American Medical Association and the American Hospital Association. These committees were asked to develop approved wording for the questions addressed to physicians and hospitals, respectively, on insurance claim forms. Copies of the basic group insurance forms and questions recommended by the Health Insurance Council for use by all insurers are reproduced in Appendixes 16 through 18.

Under the Health Insurance Council approach, an insurer may design a form containing the approved questions most appropriate to the combination of coverages provided by a particular group contract. So long as the approved wording and sequence of questions is adhered to, the claim form can bear the distinctive HIC symbol signifying its acceptability to the medical or hospital profession, as the case may be.[3] Doctors and hospitals thus recognize such a form at a glance and realize that their interests were considered in drafting the questions.

CLAIMS HANDLING FOR SPECIFIC GROUP INSURANCE LINES

Group Life Insurance

Since death from any cause while insured is covered under most group life insurance arrangements, the principal claims questions pertain to payment: how much, to whom and when. The amount of claim depends on the deceased's insurance class and, for some retired people, age at death. Payment is made normally to beneficiaries of record. If the amount payable to a minor exceeds the limit under statute or company rule, letters of guardianship are secured and payment is made to the guardian. Where

---

[2] See Chapter 23 for an explanation of the nature and functions of the Council.

[3]

there is no named, surviving beneficiary for all or part of the proceeds, payment may be made to one or more of the deceased's relatives specified in the policy's facility of payment clause.[4] Otherwise, payment is made to the deceased's estate, through the administrator or executor designated in the appointment papers furnished the insurer. Most companies permit the insured or the beneficiary, at the insured's death, to elect an optional mode of settlement. The variety of options available may approach that offered the company's individual policyholders. If an optional mode has been elected, a supplementary contract is issued evidencing its terms, and payment is made thereunder.

The installment total and permanent disability benefits[5] provided under some group life policies are payable to the insured employee who can prove disability meeting all the conditions stipulated in the policy. Usually, total disability is considered as inability to perform any reasonably comparable gainful work, not just his own occupation.[6] The claimant submits statements from his own physician, and the company may either require more information from him or appoint another doctor to examine the claimant independently. Other items taken into consideration include the employer's report on the claimant's most recent work history and whether investigation—if one was made—confirms restriction of the claimant's physical activities. The permanency of disability often cannot be proven (or disproven) in advance. As a practical matter, therefore, the claims administrator must base the decision regarding claim approval on his judgment that the medical statements portray a health condition which is most likely to persist indefinitely or to result in death. After approving a claim, he will generally use the contractual prerogative of calling for periodic proof of continued disability, to learn whether the insured has significantly improved to a point where benefits may be terminated.

Premium waiver claims resulting from total and permanent disability involve the same proof requirements discussed above, but these claims require less long-range forecasting by the claims administrator than installment benefit claims. He need only be assured that total disability has existed throughout the specified waiting period and is likely to persist until the next annual proof is due.

Group Accidental Death and Dismemberment Insurance

As court decisions on so-called "double indemnity" clauses have tended to minimize the distinction between accidental means (or cause) and

---

[4] See Chapter 25 for a discussion of the nature and purpose of this clause.

[5] This feature permits payment of the face amount of life insurance over a series of months (usually sixty), while the insured is disabled, rather than deferring payment until his death. For further details see Chapter 7.

[6] The range in variation of contractual definition of total disability can extend all the way from inability to perform any major duty of the insured's own occupation to the much more stringent test of incapacity to fulfill the duties of any occupation.

accidental results,[7] the claims administrator must make more use of specific contractual exclusions in separating the allowable claims from those which are not. A large proportion of the claims require extensive investigation to rule out the possibility that any of the excluded perils contributed to the loss to some extent or in some way.[8] In some instances clear proof of the complete circumstances of the deceased's death cannot be obtained. Depending upon the amount and import of available evidence, the claims administrator might offer a compromise settlement rather than deny liability completely. Dismemberment claims for the loss of hands, feet, arms or legs by accidental means are comparatively rare and present almost no unusual problems.

Where indemnity is available for total and irrecoverable loss of eyesight, the claims administrator must evaluate the permanency of the claimant's visual impairment. If in doubt, he can defer decision for a period, e.g., six months, and request another medical statement and prognosis at that time.

Group Short-Term Disability Income Insurance

The usual, but not universal, working definition of total disability in group short-term disability income insurance is inability to continue at one's normal work, and benefits are payable only while a claimant is under a physician's care. On the claim form, the attending physician describes the claimant's sickness or injury, states whether it was job-related, and gives the date disability started, dates of treatment and probable date by which the patient can return to work. If the initial prognosis is for an extended absence of several months or seems unduly long in relation to the ailment reported by the physician, the claims administrator may request supplementary reports at reasonable intervals to see that disability and treatment continue. When a claim has been approved, steps are set up to pay the appropriate amount of weekly benefits—subject to such additional proofs as may be requested periodically—until the claimant returns to work. Benefit checks or drafts may be sent to the employer for

---

[7] Accidental means may be described as a set of circumstances over which the person suffering a loss had virtually no control except, perhaps, by being in a particular place at a given moment. For instance, he may have been struck by a piece of loose stone falling from a building he was passing. This definition would not include the situation where the person initiated or voluntarily participated in activities resulting in his suffering a loss, however unforeseen or accidental that result may have been. Thus, he may have started or taken part in an argument which progressed from angry words to extreme physical violence. For a discussion of the distinction between means and results and a listing of some pertinent New York court decisions, the reader may consult J. Edwin Dowling and Richard E. Erway, *The Life Insurance Law of New York* (The Association of Life Insurance Counsel, 1962), Part Two, Sec. 1, subdivision II J, pp. 506–17.

[8] Among risks which are often specifically excluded are (a) contributory disease and bodily or mental infirmity, and medical or surgical treatment or diagnosis thereof, (b) hernia, (c) insurrection or war and (d) intentional self-destruction or intentionally self-inflicted injury.

review and delivery to the employees. If an employee has returned to work in midweek, his check or draft can then be sent back to the insurer for adjustment to the actual period of absence.

Recurrence of a particular disability following brief apparent recovery is treated as a continuance of the original claim. Thus, no new waiting period is invoked and a single maximum duration of benefits is applied to the two attacks. The longer the period between two sickness absences, the harder it often is to determine whether both were really due solely to the same cause. For this reason, most insurers either contractually or administratively treat any relapse as a new and unrelated claim if it occurs after the employee had returned to work for several weeks or months.

The uptrend in benefit levels under short-term disability income coverage in recent years and the favorable income tax status of the benefits have enabled many employees to be almost as well off financially when sick as when working. Unfortunately, some yield to temptation and either report nonexistent or deceptive symptoms to their physicians or pressure them for written statements exaggerating the severity or duration of their ailment. The claims administrator knows from experience those conditions, categories of claimants and other factors requiring close scrutiny and selection of the more dubious claims for investigation. On those culled out, he can request further facts from the attending physician or request the claimant to undergo examination by one of the insurer's medical examiners in his neighborhood. Or he may have an insurance company investigator or mercantile inspection agency make local inquiries to see whether the claimant's activities are consistent with those of a disabled person. Even a claim not calling initially for these precautions may arouse suspicion later by continuing beyond a reasonable duration for the ailment or injury involved. At any point the claims administrator can notify a claimant that weekly payments will be suspended as of a near-future date unless new satisfactory medical evidence is furnished.

Disability income insurance is free from the major source of over-insurance to which group hospital and medical expense coverages are exposed because the latter frequently include both the employee and certain members of his family. Then when two or more family members are employed by different firms, each having their own group plans, there is often duplicate coverage on each eligible member. However, even though most insurers observe fairly conservative underwriting rules for relating disability income weekly benefits to normal wages or salary when working, an occasional claim will involve over-insurance and warrant careful consideration of the genuineness of the full period of disability claimed. This sometimes occurs where a disabled employee is entitled to group disability income benefits and also to full or partial pay from his employer under a salary continuance arrangement which it was not expedient to terminate when the group program was adopted. Over-insurance also could occur when group disability income coverage is maintained in full effect for employees enjoying an extended vacation with pay e.g., under labor agreements that provide thirteen weeks' vacation every five years.

The group policyholder can help the claims administrator by seeing that his employees file claims promptly after the end of the waiting period. If a claim is submitted after the insured has gone back to work, the opportunity for effective investigation is minimal. If notice of a claim is submitted extremely late, the claim may properly be denied.

Group Long-Term Disability Income Insurance

In most aspects the claims processing of long-term disability income claims follows that already described for installment total and permanent disability claims under group life policies. One extra step that is required is observing the policy terms regarding the adjustment of benefits in recognition of income from other sources such as salary continuance, workmen's compensation awards or OASDI disability benefits. Such adjustment provisions are, of course, aimed at the control of the over-insurance problem which would otherwise prevail and jeopardize the claim experience.

Since long-term benefits are written primarily for salaried employees and in amounts up to and exceeding $1,000 per month, problems arise which do not exist in short-term coverage. The will to work is exceedingly important to the effectiveness of management personnel, and this sometimes disappears consciously or unconsciously after apparent recovery from a prolonged illness by a man who is only a few years from retirement. When a position disappears or is downgraded, a man sometimes becomes disabled from infirmities which have existed for years without interfering with day-to-day functions. Long-term disability insurance opens a new category of delicate claims problems which may be particularly frequent whenever there is a drop in the economy.

Group Hospitalization Insurance

In the settlement of group hospitalization claims primary reliance is placed upon hospital reports. In addition to identifying the patient, the hospital submits information regarding dates and hours of admission and discharge, type of accommodations used (ward, semiprivate or private), admitting diagnosis, nature and date of any surgery performed during the confinement and full details of charges. The latter may be itemized on the claim form or a copy of the bill to the patient may be supplied. Most claim forms also ask the hospital's most common semiprivate daily room-and-board rate.

After verifying that confinement was due to a nonoccupational illness or injury, the claims administrator considers the reasonableness of the length of stay and types and costs of ancillary services rendered, all in relation to the diagnosis and age and sex of the patient. He also notes any charges for excluded items such as telephone calls, TV rental and guest's meal trays. If the institution's name or other circumstances cause doubt about satisfaction of the policy definition of a hospital, the claims administrator will consult reference listings or obtain a report on the facility from a field representative or mercantile agency. A second confinement for the same ailment would be treated as a continuation of the previous claim unless a policy clause or administrative rule has the effect of deeming resumption of normal activities for a stated period to be equivalent to recovery from the ailment.

Benefits are computed under the policy formulas, observing the separate criteria governing benefits for room-and-board expenses and those for ancillary services. Administrative practices will have been developed to deal with any all-inclusive daily rates charged by a hospital which declines to subdivide them into the desired two categories. For example, a fixed proportion such as 60 per cent may be assumed to be the daily charge for room and board. Or, where the all-inclusive daily rate declines as the duration of confinement lengthens, the ultimate or minimum rate may be assumed to be the constant charge for room and board, with any excess during the early days representing ancillary service charges.

Space is provided on claim forms for the certificate holder to authorize payment of his benefits directly to the hospital, if he so elects. This is fairly common practice since many certificate holders obtain credit from hospitals on the strength of their group insurance. Realizing the value of hospital credit to the institution of insurance, the Health Insurance Council, working with regional hospital associations, has developed and sponsors two hospital admission programs which individual hospitals can use, if they wish. However, a great many hospitals extend credit to group claimants entirely outside the framework of these programs.

The two most common admission programs are a card index system and a certification of coverage system. Under the card index system, which is used principally in northern California, Chicago and New York City and environs, each hospital is furnished with cards showing brief details of all group plans in effect in the community. Names and addresses of policyholder representatives who can be contacted for further information, if needed, are also supplied. When a covered employee or dependent seeks admission, the hospital can call the policyholder and verify that such person is insured. Also, since the benefit provisions of the plan are known, the hospital can collect any remainder of its bill from the patient at discharge. Under the certification of coverage system, which has wider usage, the employee obtains a special form from his employer and submits it to the hospital upon admission or before discharge. The form's upper section is imprinted with pertinent details about the group plan, and the employer inserts the patient's and insurer's names and certifies that coverage is in force. This certification is valid for seven days after the employer has signed and dated it. The form's lower section, which is, in essence, a claim form, is completed by the hospital when the patient's account has been made up. There is also a space in which the claimant can authorize payment of benefits to the hospital. A copy of this form (HAP-4) is contained in Appendix 19.

Group Surgical Insurance

In connection with surgical claims, the surgeon's report on the claim form identifies the patient, describes the surgery and states the fee charged. So long as the surgery occurred because of a nonoccupational illness or injury, or a pregnancy, was performed by a type of practitioner specified in the contract and was among the categories of surgical procedures covered, the claim is acceptable. The contract terms may define the maximum benefit payable for two or more operations performed at the same time, through the same incision or during the same period of disability.

The amount paid is the lesser of the surgeon's fee and the maximum allowance for that operation as listed in the contract schedule. New or infrequent operations which are not listed are considered individually, and a maximum allowance is established consistent with the balance of the particular schedule. The benefits are due the claimant, but if he has signed an authorization to pay the surgeon directly, this will be done.

Other Medical Expense Coverages of Limited Scope

Other group coverages for specified categories of medical expenses include insurance against the expense of physicians' nonsurgical care (either in a hospital only or elsewhere), diagnostic X-rays and laboratory examinations and radiation therapy. Supplemental accident, polio and other "dread diseases" benefits cover the cost of services in excess of, or in addition to, those provided elsewhere in the plan. The physician or technician who rendered the services describes on the claim form their nature and extent, when and where rendered, the physician's diagnosis of the patient's condition and the fee charged. If the expense was incurred for diagnosis or treatment of a nonoccupational sickness or injury rather than for a general health checkup, for example, and met all the other conditions in the contract clause, the claim will be approved. Should the nature or duration of any of the services or examinations seem inconsistent with the diagnosis reported, the claimant may be asked to procure a clarifying report from the attending physician. Benefits are payable in the amount of the expenses charged, up to the limits of the benefit formula or schedule contained in the contract. As these expenses are usually rather moderate and the bills have already been paid in many cases, benefits are almost always drawn to the order of the certificate holder.

Group Major Medical Coverage

Whether of the supplementary or comprehensive variety, group major medical coverage combines all the claims administration requirements and processes of the different basic medical care coverages and adds several of its own. Because it provides benefits for such widely varied additional expenses as the cost of drugs and medicines, professional nursing, prostheses and durable medical equipment and supplies, bills are received from many different sources and suppliers, and each charge must be evaluated in relation to the patient's ailment and condition as reported by the attending physician. In the first place, the bills should identify the patient and adequately describe the services or supplies. For example, family drug bills should separate the charges by patient name and describe each item purchased so that the cost of prescription medicines can be separated from those for cosmetics and other merchandise. Since the contracts cannot contain an all-inclusive listing of specific expenses which are either covered or excluded, claimants sometimes submit bills for nonmedical expenses or purchases, such as an air conditioner, which were suggested or approved by their physician. Thus, firm guidelines as to the boundaries of the coverage must be developed by the claim department, usually in consultation with the actuarial and medical departments. These require modification at intervals to keep pace with changes in medical technology.

Reasonable, Necessary and Customary Expenses. Under the terms of major medical plans, the claims administrator must also consider the necessity for the services or supplies and—because there are almost no scheduled allowances for different items—the reasonableness of the charges for them. This naturally brings the administrator more frequently in contact with his medical department than in the case of any of the basic coverages. The type of expense coming under question most often is the surgical fee, and yet this happens in only a very small percentage of all claims. Factors taken into account in judging the reasonableness of a surgeon's fee include the time and place of the operation; the patient's economic status and that of his family, if known; the patient's age and medical history; any complications which arose during surgery, such as excessive hemorrhaging; the surgeon's experience and professional attainments; and many other factors learned from experience with claims. If the claim papers do not contain sufficient justification for the fee charged, a copy of the operative report may be secured from the hospital or the surgeon may be contacted directly for a discussion of the case and his fee. In most instances additional facts will be brought to light which, if originally reported on the claim form, would have permitted payment without question. In some other cases, discussion of the claim with the surgeon will result in a mutually satisfactory adjustment of his fee.

Deductible and Percentage Participation Provisions. Claims administration under major medical coverage differs in benefit calculation, too, because of the deductible and percentage participation (or "coinsurance") clauses. The dates of incurral of expenses must be watched so that the deductible is applied when a new benefit period is reached. Also, part or all of a deductible may be waived if the plan limits the number of deductibles or amount chargeable in a family within a year or as the result of a common accident.

Different percentage participation factors often apply to different types of expenses, and many comprehensive plans have no percentage participation for a specified amount of hospital or surgical expenses. Because of the deductible and percentage participation features, some insurers discourage or even refuse to let claimants authorize direct payment of supplementary major medical benefits to providers of services and supplies. The basic hospital and surgical benefits, if assigned, may cover a substantial part of those expenses. Under comprehensive plans it is customary to honor authorizations to pay hospital and physicians' bills directly instead of to the claimant. This may require allocation of the deductible and percentage participation amounts among different kinds of expenses.

Nonduplication or Coordination of Benefits. Until recently, major medical was the only form of group health insurance containing nonduplication provisions, and not all insurers originally used them even for this coverage. The model provision developed by a study group representing the American Life Convention, the Life Insurance Association of America, and the Health Insurance Association of America and recommended to all insurers by those associations late in 1962, is adaptable to basic health care coverages as well as major medical. It is probable that this provision—with minor variations—will be used increasingly in new and revised group contracts, for all the health care coverages they contain.

Administration of the provision requires information about the existence and amount of other coverage relating to the claim under review. This includes Blue Cross, Blue Shield and various service type plans, but usually does not include individual insurance contracts unless they are written on a franchise basis. The claimant must also answer and certify regarding other coverages on the claim form. Since a claimant may misunderstand the question or decline to acknowledge that other coverage exists, insurers may check independently those claims where there seems to be possibility of duplicate coverage which was not admitted. This can be checked either by the insurer's own representatives or through services of a mercantile inspection agency.

If there is duplicate coverage but the claims administrator does not know whether his contract or the other insurer's has priority of liability, or if he needs facts as to benefits available from the other insurer before computing the reduction in his own benefits, he can use a standardized duplicate coverage inquiry form, a copy of which is shown in Appendix 20. The latter was recently sponsored by the Health Insurance Council for the orderly exchange of needed information among insurers having an interest in the same claim. When all facts are at hand, the claim can either be paid in full or adjusted downward in recognition of other benefits also available, according to the provisions of the contract.

Very few Blue Cross and Blue Shield plans have adopted nonduplication clauses in their contracts as yet. It is likely, however, that many will soon incorporate similar provisions.

The new model coordination of benefits provision for group plans assumes that over-insurance does not exist until benefits from two or more plans exceed what are described as the "allowable" expenses involved in a claim. Allowable expenses are defined as those for kinds of services and supplies which are covered by at least one of the claimant's plans. Up to the point where aggregate benefits do not exceed allowable expenses, the nonduplication provision will not become operative even though those benefits may have offset part or all of the deductible and percentage participation. But beyond that point the clause comes into effect and causes benefits to be limited so that the claimant will not receive more than his allowable expenses in total benefits from all sources.

When two contracts with nonduplication clauses have a liability for the same claim, it is desirable that there be no undue delay in settlement pending a decision on how to share that liability. Thus, the model provision specifies an automatic order of priority of benefit determination based on the principle that one of the contracts has primary responsibility and should pay its full, regular benefits whereas the other has secondary liability and may adjust its normal benefits in the contemplated manner. Of course, a contract which has no coordination of benefits clause is always primary to one which does.

By the rules specified in the model provision, a contract which insures a patient as an employee (active or retired) is primary to one insuring that same patient as a dependent spouse. When a dependent child is the patient, the contract covering the father is primary to that which insures the mother. Where these rules do not establish an order of priority—as in the example of a person working for two firms and insured as an employee of each—the contract which has covered the patient for the longer period is the primary one.

The model provision also contemplates measuring over-insurance over a "claim determination period" of twelve consecutive months—preferably a calendar year. This can be more advantageous for an insured with several claims within the period than if each claim submission were computed independently of any other. For example, an individual may be covered by a basic Blue Cross contract as well as a group major medical plan, of which only the latter provides against duplication. If his first claim involves a $300 hospital bill which is fully taken care of by Blue Cross, the other plan would withhold its regular benefit of, let us say, $200. However, several months later the individual might become seriously ill and be treated at home, with the bills for physician's services, nursing care and medications running to $500. If the major medical plan would normally provide benefits of $400 for those expenses, there would be added $100 out of the $200 the plan had temporarily "saved" on the first claim. Considered together, the two claims involved $800 of allowable expenses and the combined benefits from the two plans would have equaled that sum. There would also remain a potential credit of another $100 for possible addition to subsequent normal major medical benefits for any claims incurred later in the same year. If the $100 is not used up within the claim determination period, it cannot be carried forward to any other period.

The model clause contractually gives the insurer several administrative rights of importance. First, it may receive from, or disclose to, others such information about a claim as may be needed for benefit computations. Also, it is entitled to recover excess benefits paid beyond those payable had all the facts concerning other coverage been known. Finally, the insurer may pay part or all of its benefits to another insuring organization which had unknowingly assumed some of the former's liability.

Medical Society Review Committees. A recent development, fostered by the state committees of the Health Insurance Council working with local medical societies, has been the establishment of Review Committees by many medical societies in different parts of the country. These committees are prepared to review problems submitted by insurers, physicians or patients and render informal advisory opinions. They function quite differently, therefore, from medical society Grievance Committees which conduct hearings on formal complaints filed against their members and decide whether censure or other disciplinary action is appropriate. Most Review Committee activities have concerned claims submitted by insurance companies seeking professional assurance that there has been no overtreatment, overcharging or other abnormal practice. Review Committees prefer to have a medical officer of the insurance company select claims submitted to them. The existence and spread of Review Committees have been helpful to the medical profession and the insurance industry in reaching better understanding of each other's problems. Chapter 23 discusses the operation of these committees in detail.

CLAIMS PROCESSING ASPECTS PECULIAR TO BLUE CROSS AND BLUE SHIELD PLANS

Instead of monetary benefits, most Blue Cross and Blue Shield plans arrange for their subscribers to be furnished with specified hospital or physician services for which those rendering the services make no charge to the patient if certain conditions are met. First, the provider of service must be a participating hospital or physician—one under contract to the plan to serve its subscribers. Second, as to Blue Shield plans, the patient's income—or that of his family—must often be within the limits stated in his contract for entitlement to services by a participating physician without a supplementary charge by the latter. The subscriber who meets these conditions is eligible for full service benefits and technically does not figure in the claim transaction which is between the plan and the provider of service.

However, when a subscriber under a Blue Cross or Blue Shield plan obtains services from other than a participating hospital or doctor, he may file a claim with his plan for the cash allowance his certificate guarantees. From whatever source the plan receives a claim, it verifies from its own records that coverage was in force for the patient and ascertains that the services qualified for benefit consideration. When a Blue Cross subscriber receives treatment outside the area serviced by the particular Blue Cross plan to which he belongs, his eligibility for benefits is often checked through the Blue Cross Private Wire Communications System.

Some Blue Cross plans pay their member hospitals the amount of the bill prepared for the insured patient, or some major percentage thereof as set by contract. Many others negotiate with each member hospital for an average payment per patient day, which average is related to the hospital's actual average per diem expenses[9] rather than its charges. Generally, the rate of daily payment is adjusted yearly to reflect any changes in hospital expenses. This is the payment method recommended by the American Hospital Association.

Blue Shield plans base their benefits on fee schedules, some having different schedules for each of several income-limit contracts sold by the plan. Hence, claim administration in this instance also involves confirming the level of coverage for the patient and the scheduled allowance payable for the specific services rendered. A few Blue Shield plans operate on a straight indemnity basis whereby a doctor may charge a patient any excess of his normal fee over the plan's allowance to him for his service, irrespective of the patient's (or family's) income level. Such plans, therefore, do not have participating physicians as that term applies to other service type plans.

---

[9] Usually, a hospital's losses from bad debts, the care of the medically indigent and underpayments by governmental units for services rendered welfare patients are not deemed "expenses" for this purpose, leaving such items to be covered from non-Blue Cross sources of income to the hospital.

Chapter 30

GROUP INSURANCE RESERVES

BY MILTON F. CHAUNER

Group insurance reserves are liabilities of an insurance company or, in some instances, earmarked portions of its surplus. In fact, the bulk of the liabilities of most insurance companies is composed of various types of reserves. Their importance in the operation of a particular company depends primarily upon the types of coverage that it issues. An explanation of the nature and extent of group insurance reserves is simplified if one first understands the origin of reserves created in connection with individual insurance contracts.

NATURE OF RESERVES

Nature of Premium Reserves in Individual Insurance Contracts

In individual life insurance policies providing permanent insurance, a large part of the premium in the early years is set aside for reserve purposes. This is because a *level* premium, determined for the age at issue, is paid during a specified period, while the life insurance benefit granted has a cost which increases year by year as the insured gets older. In essence, the individual policyholder with a level premium contract pays more in each of the early years than is necessary to cover his share of the claims and expenses. However, in later years his level premium is insufficient to cover his share of claims and expenses. Thus, in simplified terms, the overpayment in the early years is invested by the insurance company, and the accumulated amount is identified as a reserve.[1]

It is important at this point to recognize that "reserves," as such, are bookkeeping entries to identify financial obligations. As the payment of premiums brings cash to an insurance company, this money provides investment funds for the insurer. Because of the overpayment of premiums in the early policy years, as has been mentioned, a bookkeeping entry is then made on the liability side of an insurance company's financial

---

[1] Actually, reserves are calculated on the basis of assumed rates of interest, as will be seen, rather than using actual interest earnings.

records to indicate that a part of the assets is needed to meet future obligations (that is, in later policy years when the premiums on a contract are insufficient to meet the contract's share of claims and expenses).

The significance of reserves in individual health insurance contracts depends, in part, upon whether or not the premiums can be increased by the insurer. In a noncancelable health insurance contract the premiums cannot be changed by the insurance company during a specified period, such as prior to the policyholder's age sixty-five, in which case the contract is similar premiumwise to level premium life insurance. However, for health insurance contracts under which premiums can be increased if and when the claims increase, or if a particular contract can be canceled by the insurance company, there is less need for premium reserves.

Nature of Group Insurance Reserves

The foregoing discussion analyzed in some detail the significance of premium reserves in connection with individual insurance contracts because the relative importance of certain reserves in group insurance is dependent to a considerable extent upon the same factors. For example, most of the group life insurance now in force is group *term* protection, and, as a consequence, group insurance reserves have less relative significance than is the case for most individual life insurance coverage. This is not because of any difference in death benefits, but rather because term coverage permits premiums to be increased or decreased and the need for reserves which would assist in paying increased claims is therefore diminished. Practical and statutory reserve requirements under these circumstances are, consequently, very different from those applicable for level premium life insurance. Conversely, the reserve situation for certain special permanent forms of group life insurance bears closer resemblance to the individual level premium forms.[2] The premium basis for most group coverage, however, permits frequent adjustment of rates, and this has the effect of requiring less of the premium for the future (i.e., for reserves) than if longer period—such as lifetime—guarantees were to be given.

As a basic principle, then, for any group insurance coverage, the obligations of the insurance company must be determined so that its actual and potential liabilities can be adequately recorded in its financial statements. The amounts of such obligations, many of which are called reserves, appear in specified liability accounts. They are in a sense commitments (to be met in the future) against premiums already received.

From what has been said thus far, reserves may appear to be of concern

---

[2] One such product is group permanent life insurance, a combination of one-year term protection and permanent life insurance each with appropriate reserves. See Chapter 8.

only to the insurance company in determining its financial position and, hence, more of an internal accounting consideration than being of interest to the salesman or the buyer of group insurance. However, an understanding of reserves is highly important to each of these because of the obvious tendency to compare premiums paid with claims paid, particularly when premium techniques seem to apply to a one-year period. Thus, an understanding of both the philosophy and practices with respect to determining reserves is vital to an analysis of the cost of insurance.

Then, too, it is important to recognize the extent to which the obligations of an insurance company, and hence the types and amounts of reserves required, are affected by the basic characteristics of group insurance benefits provided. These basic characteristics may be summarized according to whether the company's obligation is for large infrequent claims, small current payments, or continuing benefits over a long period of time:

Type of Group Insurance Risk	*Principal Insurance Characteristics Affecting Reserves*
Life (normal or accidental death).	Single sum payment of relatively large amount compared to premium; occurrence varies widely.
Health: Basic coverages such as hospital and surgical.	Continuing, relatively small claims, the amount subject to charges by third parties (e.g., hospitals, doctors); settlement subject to delays in reporting claims or processing payments.
Health: Major medical coverage.	Longer duration of benefit payments; high limits of coverage; incorporates the characteristics of basic health coverages to extent benefits are similar or are combined.
Disability income.	Amounts related to salary to some extent; payments may be for long duration and dependent upon continued disability as evidenced by being unable to work.

Group insurers differ in the manner and extent to which they acknowledge the above characteristics in their reserves. However, considerable uniformity results because of instructions for completing the standard annual statement required by the insurance commissioner of each state in which a company is authorized to do business.

Irrespective of how reserve accounts are labeled and whether established for special commitments or required by regulating authorities, they are important for the protection of the policyholder. For purposes of description, the usual types of reserves may be classified as (1) premium reserves, (2) loss reserves, (3) contingency reserves and (4) special reserves. In the following sections a few examples of each type of reserve will be discussed to illustrate the calculations as well as the elements of judgment that enter into the determination of a company's reserves in aggregate. Then consideration will be given to the manner in which reserves affect particular policyholders.

TYPES OF GROUP INSURANCE RESERVES

Premium Reserves

The calculation of group insurance premium reserves is simplified considerably because group insurance is usually on a term basis with rates normally guaranteed for only one year. The form of the annual statement recognizes that a group company's obligations with respect to premium items as of any particular accounting date consist of premiums already collected for insurance after the date of the financial statement, i.e., for the unexpired portion of the current premium paying period; premiums paid in advance for periods later than the current premium paying period; and some part of earlier paid premiums that may be considered to be dividends or retroactive rate credits already earned (or provisionally earned) because of recent, favorable experience.

Unearned Premium Reserves. For all types of group life and health insurance issued for a one-year term, companies determine an unearned premium reserve using as the basis the pro rata part of premiums received which applies to coverage not yet provided. For example, as of December 31, the unearned premium for a group contract payable monthly on the fifteenth of each month would be one half the December premium; correspondingly, the semiannual premium payable as of December 1 would be five-sixths unearned as of December 31. There would be no unearned premium at the end of the month when premiums are payable monthly on the first day of the month. Thus, the combination of the mode of payment and the premium due date determine the amount of premiums to be allocated for obligations prior to the accounting date and the amount which must be designated as unearned. In any event, the aggregate liability for unearned premiums that appears in the financial statement as of December 31 must be suitable for the company's contractual commitments on its group policies until their next respective premium due dates.

The standard valuation law of individual states sets mortality and interest bases for minimum life insurance reserves. Group life insurance is subject either to these standards or to special regulations of the state insurance commissioner. Either the Commissioners Standard Ordinary (CSO) or the CSG (Commissioners Standard Group) Mortality Table and 3 per cent interest assumptions are usually specified. There is no comparable requirement for group health insurance, since morbidity is not conducive to forecast like mortality and the use of morbidity data varies widely by type of group health insurance.

The unearned premium reserve is quite similar for all types of group insurance. For special coverages which may involve a single premium for a considerable protection period or extra amounts collected to "pre-fund" future benefits, special reserve calculations are required. Such amounts may or may not be included in the unearned premium reserve, but if not, they must appear elsewhere among the liability items.

Reserves for Premiums Paid in Advance. Premiums paid in advance of regular premium due dates must be set aside for the future period to which they pertain. An exact tabulation of actual amounts paid in advance for each of its policyholders is usually made, even in the largest companies, rather than relying on estimates.

Reserves for Dividends. In the financial statement as of December 31, a retroactive rate credit or dividend reserve reflects the fact that a company's experience rating system will refund, or in some other manner credit, to policyholders premiums already collected where such experience credit has been earned. Experience rating is usually applied each year, and a company's reserve can reflect credits due for prior policy years and/or the current year. In the case of participating contracts where annual dividends are payable out of divisible surplus, the estimated accrued portion of those payable in the following calendar year must be established as a year-end reserve. Thus, earned experience rating credits or dividends (declared or undeclared) are properly assignable to the period of time when earned because they arise from premiums received by the company in that period of time.

Claim Reserves

A group insurer's financial position as of an accounting date, often December 31, must reflect various practical considerations with respect to claims or losses. For example, when a new group case is written, the claims paid in the first policy year are normally less than in subsequent years because in the first year no payments are generally made for claims incurred prior to the effective date of the policy. In the group's second policy year, claims will reach a normal level because the insurer pays claims incurred in the first year as well as claims incurred in the second year. To obtain a true picture of a policyholder's normal future claims level, as well as to portray a proper financial evaluation for the insurer, it is necessary to establish claims reserves with subsequent adjustments year by year resulting primarily from changes in the size of the group or in the benefits. A graphic example is shown in Figure 30–1.

As is shown in Figure 30–1, the $2,500 shown as claims paid early in the second year arises because some claims are being processed within the company, having been clearly determined as due but not as yet paid; others may have been only partially investigated or only partly paid. Still others are not yet reported to the company but the physical occurrence of death or disability has already taken place. In addition, many companies pay claims by checks which are actually bank drafts. Each of these is recorded by the insurance company as a paid claim only after being cashed by the person to whom the check was written and then returned to the company by the bank. This introduces a lag in reporting, since checks are not cashed immediately. Another example is "deferred maternity," where specified expenses are reimbursable for existing pregnancies but for which actual claims may occur up to nine months after the arbitrary accounting date.[3]

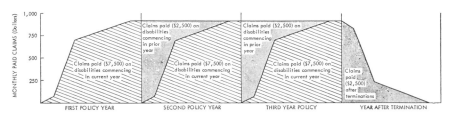

FIG. 30–1. Group health insurance claim reserves in operation.

In order to set up the reserves as required, i.e., determining a figure corresponding to $2,500 in the example, amounts for various types of loss liabilities must be arrived at by actuarial and accounting methods acceptable to state insurance departments. The descriptive wording of categories designated as parts of this reserve are specified as follows: (1) due and unpaid claims; (2) claims in course of settlement; (3) incurred but unreported claims; (4) deferred maternity and other extended benefit

TABLE 30–1

GROUP CLAIM RESERVES EXPRESSED AS PERCENTAGES OF
ANNUAL PREMIUMS IN FORCE

Type of Group Coverage	Percentage of Annual Premium in Force
Life insurance	10 %
Accidental death and dismemberment insurance	17.5
Disability income (without other health benefits)	17.5
Basic medical coverage exclusive of maternity	14
Maternity coverage	75
Supplemental major medical:	
First year	35
Second and subsequent years, an additional	15
Comprehensive medical expense	30

reserves; (5) present value of amounts not yet due; and (6) approved disability claims under group life insurance. Each item applies to one or more of the types of group insurance risk mentioned earlier. As an illustration of the combined total items (1) through (5) above, one insurance

---

[3] A substantial portion of the group health insurance in force reimburses for maternity expenses after a nine months' waiting period but extending for a similar period beyond actual remittance of premiums for the maternity coverage.

company, which is probably typical, has found a suitable relationship of reserves to annual premium as set forth in Table 30–1.

Thus it may be seen, for example, that this insurer would establish a reserve equal to 10 per cent of the in-force annual life insurance premium on each group to account for the unknown liability arising from death claims which have not been paid. This could be represented by one or more of items (1), (2) or (3) enumerated above. Another example would be an employee with group life insurance, including waiver of premium, who became disabled. In this instance insurers often charge the policy-holder, as a claim, 75 per cent of the employee's life insurance coverage and establish an equivalent reserve. If death occurs during continuation of the waiver of premium coverage, the remaining 25 per cent is also charged.[4] If the person ceases to qualify for the extension of his life insurance (e.g., he recovers), the policyholder is credited with the amount of the reserve. This accounting would be an illustration of category (6) above and would not be included in the percentages shown in Table 30–1.

To arrive initially at percentages such as those in Table 30–1 and to verify them from year to year, the insurer would have kept records of the payment date as well as the date of death, time of accident or inception date of the disability giving rise to claim payments. Past ratios of unpaid amounts, as of any given date, to total ultimate payments for different types of benefits indicate the factors to apply to current year payments to give an estimate of what remains to be paid as of the current date. Another technique is to develop from past records an average size open claim to estimate what currently remains to be paid.

Contingency Reserves

A separate category of reserves is designed to allow for unusual occur-rences or catastrophes. Contingency reserves differ from premium and loss reserves in that the former are largely voluntary allocations of surplus rather than actual liabilities. In the case of group life insurance, excess mortality fluctuations may arise from epidemics, earthquakes, explosions or other mass accidents. In group health insurance particularly, there are frequently upward trends in claim costs not anticipated in current pre-miums; an unexpected decline in premiums without a corresponding drop in claims has the same effect. To the extent that contingency reserves are not used for such occurrences, there is a drain on unassigned surplus.

The type and amount of each company's group insurance business is the guide to contingency reserve accumulation, where it is optional. There

---

[4] The continuation of this benefit is not dependent upon the master contract re-maining in effect. In the event of termination of the master contract, the remaining 25 per cent is charged at the time of death to the unreported life claim reserve built from all policyholders.

are numerous examples of widely fluctuating health insurance claims as well as several well-known instances of catastropic loss of life.[5]

The significance of the catastrophe aspect of group insurance is indicated by a suggestion of the New York Insurance Department that insurance companies accumulate a special "contingency reserve for group life insurance." Since 1935, companies have voluntarily accumulated reserve funds toward a goal of 50 per cent of one year's excess of group life premiums over dividends. The usual annual rate of accumulation is 2 per cent. Because of the rapid growth of group life insurance, the 50 per cent objective has not been achieved by most companies.

Particular significance is usually attached to the risk aspects of new coverages. Extension of group insurance to high limits or long periods of coverage (such as in long-term disability or mortgage life insurance) and dental insurance are examples. Specific contingency funds may be specified in advance or accumulated from early years' premiums if not required for claims and expenses. These could be considered as special reserves (see below) since, in some instances, amounts reserved may be attributable to particular policyholders.

The loss potential of group health insurance and the desirability of having contingency funds for those coverages are clearly recognized in the 1959 Federal Life Insurance Company Income Tax Law. A deduction from taxable income is allowed for this purpose in the amount of 2 per cent of premiums received during the year.

Special Reserves

Special reserves are often necessary to provide properly and adequately for particular commitments. There is considerable latitude in how they may be designated and in what amounts, but methods used in calculating or estimating must be appropriate to both the nature of the commitment and the available statistical or accounting data. Examples of special reserve situations are: extra mortality under group life conversions, assessments under state disability plans, reinsurance arrangements and special experience rating funds. (The special reserves for extra mortality under group life conversions are actually held as an individual ordinary life reserve. Funds to offset the reserve are obtained by a charge—often $65 per thousand of group insurance converted without evidence of insurability.) Also, special arrangements which involve joint insuring with other companies, as well as unusual accounting or coverage agreements with particular groups, often require reserves.

Special reserves are reviewed during the triennial examination con-

---

[5] For additional examples see Davis W. Gregg, *Group Life Insurance* (3d ed.; Homewood, Ill.: Richard D. Irwin, Inc., 1962), p. 234.

ducted by representatives of insurance departments of states in which an insurance company operates. These items are carefully inspected and compared with figures for corresponding items in prior years.

RESERVES FROM THE POLICYHOLDER'S STANDPOINT

Many of the business and financial reasons that dictate reserve methods to insurers do not concern the policyholder. However, even though his primary expectation may be the payment of claims when they occur, the reports of the transactions of his group insurance plan usually make him at least aware of the loss reserves. This is because "incurred" claims may exceed cash claim payments up to the accounting date. A particular year's true or incurred claims are the actual payments made during the year plus (or minus) any increase (or decrease) in loss reserves since the beginning of the year. If loss reserves at the end of the year are greater than those at the beginning of that year, the difference must be added to cash claim payments to obtain the amount of incurred claims.

Loss reserves are, in part, estimates and necessarily involve insurance concepts not entirely parallel to transactions by other businesses. They may be particularly confusing unless the lag in the payment of claims is understood. It is a common fallacy to consider that payment next year of claims arising this year should be made from next year's premiums even though the insurance contract specifies otherwise.

The large policyholder may also express an opinion on his contribution to contingency or risk reserves. Even though a large group of people may be less subject to unpredictable claims—particularly where each individual claim may be small and occur rather frequently—the risk element should not be judged entirely by hindsight. Some firms feel the risk involved in their employees' group insurance is small enough or predictable enough to be assumed by the company itself, rather than "averaged out" by an insurance company. Even if this were to be done, the need for adequate reserves is not eliminated; in fact, the need may be greater because the firm that handles its own coverage can easily misjudge the elements of insurance in which it may not be experienced.

A group insurer constantly studies the adequacy and reasonableness of reserve levels on its group business in the aggregate and also separately on many larger cases. In some instances these studies are required by state insurance departments for inclusion in annual statements.

Insurers are frequently asked to quote premiums for large prospects on the basis that will return any unused portion of the group's claim reserve upon termination of the master contract. Many group insurance companies will make a quotation on this basis only for very large groups which they expect to have as policyholders for many years. If the reserves were to be tallied on all terminating contracts and any existing balances refunded, it would be necessary to increase retentions over-all, thus making up for terminating groups whose reserves would prove to be inadequate.

Very large policyholders also occasionally ask an insurer to pay interest on their claim reserves. Insurers normally use this interest to pay part of their expenses; thus they must retain more of the premium if they credit such interest to the policyholder's account.

SELECTED REFERENCES

BRAGG, JOHN M. "Health Insurance Claim Reserves and Liabilities," *Transactions of the Society of Actuaries*, Vol. XVI (1964), pp. 17–54.

FAULKNER, EDWIN J. *Health Insurance*, chap. 12. New York: McGraw-Hill Book Co., Inc., 1960.

GREGG, DAVIS W. *Group Life Insurance*, chap. 9. 3d ed. Homewood, Ill.: Richard D. Irwin, Inc., 1962.

PART VI

Extensions of the Group Concept

Chapter 31

LIBERALIZATION OF BENEFIT AMOUNTS

BY ROBERT N. STABLER

GROUP LIFE INSURANCE BENEFIT AMOUNTS

Growth of Group Life Insurance Benefit Amounts

In recent years, average benefit amounts per certificate have increased significantly in both group life and group health insurance. It will be the task of this chapter to examine the nature and implications of this "vertical" extension of group insurance.

During its initial years, group life insurance generally was considered simply as a substitute for "passing the hat" when a fellow employee died. The early group life insurance policies were often written to provide a modest funeral benefit followed by installment payments for six months or a year, a form of salary continuance.

In addition, considerable fear existed that this new technique for providing life insurance might prove to be a financially disastrous venture because of the absence of individual underwriting and the consequent risk of a great deal of selection against the insurance company. Furthermore, it was feared that even if group life insurance proved to be economically practical, it would weaken the position of legal reserve life insurance because of its term insurance base and weaken the position of the career agent because of the drying up of the market for individual insurance as a result of the large number of people insured by a single sale of group insurance.

Early practices with respect to group life insurance reflected all of these factors, so that benefits for individual employees usually were limited. Even though the amount of insurance might equal as much as one year's salary of the employee, nevertheless the average amount of group life insurance per employee was less than $1,000 due to the low pay scales prevalent at that time.

As time went on, however, many of the fears concerning group insurance gradually were eased. Moreover, as experience with the group method was acquired by the insurance companies, new methods and controls were developed for minimizing adverse selection. As a consequence, it became possible for larger benefit amounts to be provided to individual employees through the group mechanism. Within a few years after the inception of group life insurance, many insurers were willing to issue benefit amounts as high as $5,000 on individual employees, and by the mid-1920's benefit amounts as high as $10,000 were being issued. Thereafter, the maximum for the larger groups gradually was increased, but it was not until about 1950, with the surge of life insurance companies entering the group insurance field, that large amounts became a competitive tool and not necessarily related to the number of employees insured or the volume of insurance produced under a particular group policy.

Today these group benefits constitute a major segment of the average American worker's total life insurance protection. Table 31–1 traces the

TABLE 31–1

GROUP LIFE INSURANCE PER CERTIFICATE IN THE UNITED STATES, 1911–63

Year	Amount	Year	Amount	Year	Amount	Year	Amount	Year	Amount
1911	$ 944	1921	$1,091	1932	$1,859	1943	$1,724	1954	$2,979
1912	1,083	1922	1,122	1933	1,772	1944	1,840	1955	3,166
1913	912	1923	1,197	1934	1,722	1945	1,848	1956	3,352
1914	970	1924	1,303	1935	1,595	1946	2,093	1957	3,616
1915	833	1925	1,327	1936	1,660	1947	2,002	1958	3,708
1916	775	1926	1,411	1937	1,708	1948	2,317	1959	3,898
1917	776	1927	1,439	1938	1,894	1949	2,365	1960	3,987
1918	840	1928	1,578	1939	1,795	1950	2,515	1961	4,178
1919	927	1929	1,578	1940	1,696	1951	2,590	1962	4,358
1920	981	1930	1,690	1941	1,736	1952	2,621	1963	4,481
		1931	1,739	1942	1,756	1953	2,804		

SOURCE: Institute of Life Insurance. Figures exclude creditor group life insurance.

growth that has taken place in group life insurance benefit amounts per certificate in the United States. It will be noted that it was not until 1921, a full ten years after the origin of group life insurance, that average benefit amounts began consistently to exceed $1,000. Furthermore, not until the end of World War II did these benefit amounts rise above $2,000. At the end of 1963, however, the average group life insurance benefit amount, $4,481, exceeded the average sized individual life insurance contract amount, $4,147.

Methods of Controlling Adverse Selection

When group life insurance benefits were confined to a few hundred dollars per covered worker and when amounts considerably larger than this were rare, the problem of adverse selection was relatively minor. In recent years, however, with the average certificate providing several thousand dollars in benefits and with increasing numbers of individual employees being furnished "jumbo" amounts of group life insurance, the problem has been magnified considerably.[1] As a consequence, insurance companies have been forced to modify many of their original group underwriting techniques and to introduce a variety of additional controls to minimize adverse selection.

Although these control devices have been dealt with in detail elsewhere in this volume,[2] it would be well to reiterate briefly at this point some of the major features directly relating to large benefit amounts on individual employees. One of the most fundamental of these is that, regardless of the type of benefit schedule utilized, insurers require that the benefit amounts provided to each class of employees bear a reasonable relationship to the annual earnings within that class. Typically, insurers attempt to limit group life insurance amounts to some multiple, such as two or three times, of the employee's annual wages.

Another safeguard commonly employed by insurers is the requirement that the maximum amount of group life insurance applicable to any employee in the top benefit classification must bear some relationship to the total volume of insurance on the group. For example, if the total amount of insurance on the entire group is less than $1,000,000, the maximum benefit for any employee might be $15,000, whereas if the total were between $1,000,000 and $2,000,000, the maximum might be $20,000. Many insurers vary the maximum not only according to the total amount of insurance on the group but according to other factors as well, such as the number of employees in the group and the amount of group life insurance covering employees outside the highest classification. With respect to the latter, for example, it might be stipulated that the maximum may not exceed two and one-half times the average benefit amount for all employees in the lower classifications.

Furthermore, insurers generally utilize additional underwriting precautions in cases where highly compensated employees are entitled, according to the benefit schedule, to life insurance amounts in excess of some normal maximum, such as $15,000. In such cases it is common to provide that the excess amounts will take effect only if the employee furnishes satisfactory evidence of insurability. This evidence may take the form of a simple health questionnaire or a complete medical examination.

Finally, some insurers employ a more stringent version of the actively-at-work rule in cases where individual members of the group are to be covered for large benefit amounts. Frequently it is provided that these

---

[1] Many of the same problems of "jumbo" benefit amounts also exist in groups other than employer-employee groups. Since these other types are discussed separately elsewhere in this book, however, the present discussion will emphasize employer-employee groups.

[2] See especially Chapter 10.

benefits, or that portion in excess of some stated amount, will not become effective until the employee involved has been actively at work for some period, such as one month.

Statutory Limits on Group Life Insurance Benefit Amounts

As mentioned previously, in the early stages of its development, there was substantial concern that group life insurance would adversely affect the market for individual life insurance. This fear has persisted up to the present because of the trend whereby larger and larger amounts of life insurance have been provided to individuals through the mechanism of group insurance. As a result, those who oppose this "vertical" extension of group life insurance have consistently taken the position that statutory controls should be established to limit the amount of group life insurance that may be written on the life of one individual. Despite this opposition, however, and despite the enactment of a variety of statutes designed to limit the vertical extension of group life insurance, this method of providing insurance has continued to grow dramatically,[3] both in total amount in force and in average amount per certificate.

As a consequence of this growth, increased attention was paid to group life insurance benefit amounts. In recognition of the financial dangers large benefit amounts might create for insurers and the possible infringement by group insurance on the individual life insurance market, the 1946 group life insurance model bill of the National Association of Insurance Commissioners contained the first direct statutory control over group life insurance benefit amounts. This model bill contained the following provision: ". . . No policy may be issued which provides insurance on any employee which together with any other insurance under any group life insurance policies issued to the employer or to the trustees of a fund established by the employer exceeds $20,000."[4]

The same basic rule also was established for members of a labor union and for employees insured under a policy issued to the trustee of a welfare fund. A different concept was established in limiting the individual maximum under a creditor group life insurance contract. Maxima under creditor group life insurance contracts seldom have been questioned because the amount of insurance usually is small, since normally it is used in connection with small loans granted by consumer finance companies or banks and for covering the unpaid indebtedness of individual purchasers of automobiles, refrigerators and other such equipment.

The State of New York in 1947 adopted the $20,000 maximum. Several other states adopted restrictions in the next few years, but many states still

---

[3] A full discussion of the growth of group life insurance is contained in Chapter 4.

[4] "Group Life Insurance Definition, Adopted at Portland, Oregon, June 12, 1946, by the National Association of Insurance Commissioners," p. 4.

had none. To further complicate the situation, the New York Insurance Department took the view that the $20,000 maximum applied to any group insured by a New York domiciled life insurance company, regardless of where the master contract was delivered, a position that the New York companies could not accept. As a result the New York group writing companies generated enough pressure to have the $20,000 maximum removed in 1952. In the meantime, work on the model law by the National Association of Insurance Commissioners continued.

Those who have sought to limit the spread of group life insurance have used the argument that, in addition to impairing the market for individual life insurance, group insurance has caused excessive emphasis to be placed on term life insurance, so that many insureds have been led to overlook the important values of permanent life insurance. This argument was turned to the advantage of the group insurers, who pointed out that the various forms of permanent group life insurance should be exempt from the $20,000 limitation imposed by the 1946 model bill. Consequently, in 1948 the model bill was amended in such a way that the $20,000 limitation on the amount of coverage issued to one individual was made applicable only to group term life insurance.

As a result of excluding group permanent insurance from the statutory maximum on group life insurance, supplemental group permanent insurance (level premium term insurance to age sixty-five, or double protection to age sixty-five) has been used on occasion to provide amounts in excess of the statutory limits. Since the cash value rights are vested in the group policyholder, usually the employer, the permanent insurance for federal income tax purposes has been treated in the same manner as has group term life insurance. While this technique has furnished the means whereby the high benefit amounts desired can be provided, it has proved to be a slightly more expensive way of providing large amounts of death benefit.[5]

In 1953, the so-called "20/40 rule" was adopted as a further revision to the model bill. Under this rule, the maximum permissible amount of group term life insurance covering an individual is $20,000 unless 150 per cent of the annual compensation of the individual from his employer exceeds $20,000. If such is the case, the amount may not exceed the lesser of (1) $40,000 or (2) 150 per cent of such annual compensation. This modification in the model bill was the result of a suggestion of the National Association of Life Underwriters.[6]

The 20/40 rule remains an important limitation on group term life insurance benefit amounts at the present time. It should be remembered, however, that not all states have adopted this rule. The current status of

---

[5] This subject is discussed in detail in Chapter 8.

[6] *Association of Life Insurance Council Proceedings*, Vol. XII (1954–55), p. 451.

state regulation of these benefit amounts may be summarized as follows:

1. The above described 20/40 rule has been enacted into law in twenty-two states[7] and the District of Columbia.
2. In six states[8] variations of the 20/40 rule have been enacted, with the principle of permitting benefit amounts in excess of a stated maximum only for more highly compensated employees being retained.
3. In two states[9] a fixed benefit maximum has been established, either by statute or by insurance department ruling, regardless of the level of the employee's compensation.
4. The remaining twenty states,[10] including many of the more populous and highly industrialized states, have established no maximum.

In addition to the foregoing regulation at the state level, recent federal legislation has, at least indirectly, imposed a "limit" on group term life insurance benefit amounts. The 1964 revisions in the Internal Revenue Code[11] include a provision that the cost of benefit amounts provided by an employer in excess of $50,000, less any contributions made by the employee himself, constitutes taxable income to the employee.[12] Group life insurance provided to retired employees has remained exempt from taxation regardless of face amount. Hence in a noncontributory plan, the federal income tax advantages usually accorded group term life insurance are lost beyond the $50,000 level. In a contributory plan, on the other hand, the effective ceiling is higher because of the fact that no taxable income results until the employer's share of the cost of the excess benefits exceeds the total contribution of the employee.

At the present time it is not clear as to what effect this change in the Internal Revenue Code will have on the amounts of group term life insurance issued by group writing companies. Several of the large group writing companies reported late in 1964 that almost no group policyholder has reduced its maximum benefit amounts to $50,000 or less, but requests for increases in existing benefits to an amount in excess of $50,000 also have been rare. Thus early indications are that this legislation will tend to lessen the demand for high benefit amounts, even though in most in-

---

[7] Arizona, Arkansas, Illinois, Indiana, Iowa, Kansas, Louisiana, Maine, Maryland, Montana, Nebraska, Nevada, New Jersey, Ohio, Oklahoma, Pennsylvania, South Carolina, Texas, Vermont, Washington, West Virginia and Wisconsin.

[8] Colorado—21/40 rule; Florida—20/100 rule, and substitution of 200 per cent for 150 per cent; Hawaii—30/50 rule; Kentucky—25/50 rule, and substitution of 200 per cent for 150 per cent; New Hampshire—20/60 rule; Tennessee—25/50 rule.

[9] Connecticut—$100,000 by ruling; North Carolina—$40,000 by statute.

[10] Alabama, Alaska, California, Delaware, Georgia, Idaho, Massachusetts, Michigan, Minnesota, Mississippi, Missouri, New Mexico, New York, North Dakota, Oregon, Rhode Island, South Dakota, Utah, Virginia and Wyoming.

[11] Public Law 88–272: Sec. 204.

[12] See Chapter 8 for a complete discussion of the federal income taxation of group life insurance.

stances group term life insurance remains an attractive coverage for individuals because of its relatively low cost.

Proposals to Limit Group Insurance Benefit Amounts

As mentioned earlier, the question of whether group life insurance benefit amounts should be limited and, if so, by what means, continues to be an important source of controversy within the life insurance business. The most comprehensive study of the problem to date was undertaken in 1957 by a joint committee of the American Life Convention (ALC) and the Life Insurance Association of America (LIAA). By mid-1960, this committee, the Joint Committee on Reexamination of Group Policy, had prepared its report, which was presented to the Executive Committee of the ALC and the Board of Directors of the LIAA.[13]

The portion of the report which dealt with benefit amounts recognized that the problem involved two separate issues, the first of which concerned "jumbo" benefit amounts, i.e., those in excess of $50,000 or $100,000. The second aspect of the problem is closely related to the first and involves the practice whereby group life insurance is issued in amounts which, although not necessarily large, might be unduly high for a particular individual in relation to his personal income and probable holdings of permanent life insurance.

In its report the Committee recognized that in many states where a large amount of group life insurance is sold no limits are placed on group life insurance benefit amounts. In addition, there appeared to the Committee to be no reasonable prospect of future enactments of this type in these states. In fact, there was evidence that some states currently imposing statutory limitations might follow the lead of New York and repeal existing limits. As a result, it seemed to the Committee that only four possibilities existed which were reasonably practical solutions to the problem.

A first possibility was to recommend continued support of the 20/40 rule. This solution was dismissed by the Committee as undesirable, since it would meet with substantial opposition from many buyers of group life insurance, from many group writing companies and from the legislatures of most states currently without limits.

A second solution, which also was rejected, was to develop more liberal limits than those provided by the 20/40 rule. The Committee considered the possibility of a maximum of, for example, two or three times annual salary. It decided, however, that any such limitation it might suggest probably would meet with proposals for such a multiplicity of exceptions for special forms of group life insurance as to be unacceptable.

Third, the possibility of recommending federal tax legislation to dis-

---

[13] For the full text of the Committee's report, see Appendix 21.

courage the issuance of large amounts of group term life insurance on individual lives was discussed. This solution was considered unacceptable for two reasons: reluctance to seek a solution to the problem at the federal level, and fear that such a control would be ineffective in that many highly compensated employees, particularly those who are uninsurable for individual life insurance or who are insurable only at substandard rates, would want large amounts of group life insurance despite the absence of federal tax advantages. (As mentioned earlier, a solution of this type has been enacted, nevertheless, as one of the 1964 revisions of the Internal Revenue Code.)

Fourth, the Committee discussed the possibility of recommending no specific limitation on group life insurance benefit amounts and the substitution of a nondiscrimination rule for the 20/40 rule. The purpose of the nondiscrimination rule was to assure that higher salaried employees would not be furnished larger amounts of group life insurance in relation to their salaries than lower salaried employees in the same group. This approach was the one recommended by the Committee in its report, partly because it felt some limitation was necessary and partly because it believed this type of limit would solve at least the most flagrant cases wherein group life insurance was provided to particular individuals in amounts completely out of line with their compensation. This solution, however, has not been adopted as yet by any state as a means of limiting group life insurance benefit amounts.

Arguments regarding Statutory Limits on Group Life Insurance Amounts

It is important to recognize the salient arguments that have been advanced on each side of the question regarding limitations on group term life insurance amounts. Each of these arguments was summarized in the report of the joint ALC–LIAA Committee referred to above.

Arguments Advanced in Favor of Statutory Maxima. Those who have taken the position that group life insurance benefit amounts should be limited argue first that the long-term future of the individual life underwriter and the insurance company which does not sell group insurance is being jeopardized by the vertical extension of group insurance. The growth of group insurance, including death benefits provided under private pension plans, together with the expansion of death benefits provided by the federal government, threaten to destroy the entire system of marketing individual life insurance through commissioned salesmen, they claim.

Second, it is alleged that group life insurance has an unfair competitive advantage over individual life insurance and, hence, its sale should be limited. This advantage arises out of the differing federal income tax treatment of the two types of life insurance. Individual insurance is, of course, purchased with after tax dollars, whereas most group insurance benefits purchased by an employer for his employees are bought by means of dollars which are tax-free.

A related argument that has been advanced is that widespread tax avoidance by highly compensated employees who accept large amounts of group insurance in lieu of salary may lead to loss of the favorable federal income tax treatment of group term life insurance. The 1964 revisions in the Internal Revenue Code indicate that this argument has at least some validity.

A fourth argument stems from the fact that most employees need a substantial amount of permanent life insurance protection which usually is not provided by group life insurance except in group permanent plans and plans where sizable amounts of insurance are continued beyond retirement date. Hence it is argued that group insurance gives the employee the impression that he is adequately protected when in fact this is not the case.

Allied to this is the fact that group life insurance benefits normally are not tailored to meet the individual insurance needs of the employee. Hence the insured loses the benefit of a carefully programed life insurance portfolio.

Finally, some have argued for limits on group life insurance benefit amounts on philosophical grounds. They point out that the individual's sense of self-reliance is injured when larger and larger amounts of economic security are provided by his employer, rather than by himself.

Arguments Advanced in Opposition to Statutory Maxima. On the other hand, those who oppose the establishment of statutory limits on group life insurance benefit amounts have advanced a number of arguments to support their position. They argue first that there is no evidence to support the contention that the growth of group life insurance has impaired the market for individual coverage. They point to the fact that only a negligible proportion of the population is eligible for extremely large benefit amounts under group plans. Moreover, group life insurance may serve even to promote the sale of individual life insurance by making individuals more "life insurance conscious."

Second, it is argued that the removal of the federal income tax advantages applicable to group term life insurance will not necessarily inure to the benefit of individual life insurance. Rather, it may result simply in greater sales of group permanent life insurance.

Third, the assumption that removal of these tax advantages will discourage the sale of large group term insurance amounts is open to some question. It may be that extremely large benefit amounts still will be sold to many highly compensated employees despite the taxability of employer contributions.

In answer to the contention that group insurance places too much emphasis on term insurance, opponents of statutory maxima point to the rapidly growing practice of extending group term coverage into the retirement years. Furthermore, group term life insurance usually is only one portion of an employee benefit plan. Often it is accompanied by a pension plan, stock purchase plan or other program for the accumulation of savings.

A fifth argument against statutory limits is the contention that employers demand that large amounts of group term life insurance be made available to their employees. They recognize group life insurance as an important means of attracting and retaining quality personnel. It is argued that statutory maxima may place insurers in a position where they are unable to fill this need and, hence, may lead to retaliation of various types by employers. For example, if group term life insurance benefit amounts were limited, death benefits under insured pension plans should be limited also. The effect of such limitations might be to lead employers to seek an alternative method, such as self-insurance, of providing these benefits.[14]

Lastly, it is argued that state laws limiting group insurance benefit amounts never can be more than partially effective. Unless a uniform limitation were established in every state, which is unlikely, there would be little to prevent selection of one of the most liberal states as the situs for group life insurance master contracts. Hence only federal legislation could effectively limit these benefit amounts, and few members of the life insurance industry would favor such a solution.

GROUP HEALTH INSURANCE BENEFIT AMOUNTS

Growth of Group Health Insurance Benefit Amounts

The trend toward higher benefit amounts in group life insurance has been accompanied in recent years by a similar trend in group health insurance. One important difference between the two, however, is the fact that in group health insurance there are no direct limitations on benefit amounts imposed by state statutes. As a consequence, insurers for the most part have been limited only by what they consider to be sound underwriting practice in meeting the demands of group policyholders for large benefit amounts and by the influence of federal income taxes on certain group health insurance benefits.

The historical trend toward higher benefit amounts of health insurance cannot be readily illustrated as directly as the trend in group life insurance. Nevertheless, it can be analyzed indirectly because of the correlation which exists between the level of benefits provided and the cost of services for which insurance is provided. This correlation exists

---

[14] In the past, most employers have been reluctant to self-insure basic death benefits for their employees. It appears that they would be even more reluctant to self-insure "jumbo" amounts for selected employees.

because of the constant demand by employers, employees or labor unions that coverage be reasonably adequate to offset financial losses and because of competition within the industry for new business. In the case of disability income insurance, this trend toward higher benefit amounts should reasonably follow the average hourly wage of employees, which can be illustrated by the data given in Table 31–2.

TABLE 31–2

HOURLY AND WEEKLY EARNINGS of PRODUCTION WORKERS IN MANUFACTURING INDUSTRIES

Year	Gross Average Weekly Earnings
1940	$24.96
1945	44.20
1950	58.32
1955	75.70
1956	78.78
1957	81.59
1958	82.71
1959	88.26
1960	89.72
1961	92.34
1962, March (preliminary)	95.91

SOURCE: *Statistical Abstract of the United States*, 1962, p. 230.

In the case of hospital insurance, the trend toward higher benefit amounts should reasonably follow the cost per patient stay, which is illustrated by the data given in Table 31–3.

The trend toward higher benefit amounts in group hospital-surgical-medical benefits in recent years is illustrated by the data given in Table 31–4 compiled by the Health Insurance Institute and American Hospital Association.

The accelerated trend of higher amounts of group health insurance benefits is a process attributable to many factors. Certainly, the aspect of competition among companies underwriting such coverage is such that public demand for not only higher amounts of benefits but for different types of protection leads to an automatic reaction on the part of the insurers in the design and dollar amount of benefit of the coverages available. Major medical insurance is an excellent example of such a coverage.

During the last fifteen years there was a further expansion, in addition to higher benefit amounts and the new coverages which were marketed. This expansion occurred in the duration for which benefits were payable. While this extension in the benefit period occurred for most coverages, it was especially noticeable under the newer forms of group health insur-

TABLE 31–3

AVERAGE COST PER PATIENT DAY, AVERAGE LENGTH OF STAY AND AVERAGE
COST PER PATIENT STAY IN NONFEDERAL SHORT-TERM GENERAL AND
OTHER SPECIAL HOSPITALS IN THE UNITED STATES, 1946–63

Year	Average Cost per Patient Day	Average Length of Stay (Days)	Average Cost per Patient Stay
1946	$ 9.39	9.1	$ 85.45
1947	11.09	8.0	88.72
1948	13.09	8.7	113.88
1949	14.33	8.3	118.94
1950	15.62	8.1	126.52
1951	16.77	8.3	139.19
1952	18.35	8.1	148.64
1953	19.95	7.9	157.61
1954	21.76	7.8	169.73
1955	23.12	7.8	180.34
1956	24.15	7.7	185.96
1957	26.02	7.6	197.75
1958	28.27	7.6	214.85
1959	30.19	7.8	235.48
1960	32.23	7.6	244.95
1961	34.98	7.6	265.85
1962	36.83	7.6	279.91
1963	38.91	7.7	299.61

SOURCE: *Source Book of Health Insurance Data*, 1964, p. 67.

ance, such as major medical insurance and long-term disability income coverage. Higher benefit payments also were reflected in the removal of many of the limitations and age restrictions found in some of the earlier group contracts.

TABLE 31–4

AVERAGE BENEFITS PROVIDED IN NEW INSURANCE COMPANY GROUP HEALTH
INSURANCE COVERAGES BY REGION IN THE UNITED STATES, 1961, 1962, 1963

Region	Average Daily Room-and-Board Benefits			Average Maximum Surgical Benefits		
	1961	1962	1963	1961	1962	1963
New England	$16.00	$17.00	$18.00	$280.00	$300.00	$310.00
Middle Atlantic	16.00	18.00	18.00	270.00	310.00	315.00
East North Central	16.00	17.00	17.00	275.00	290.00	300.00
West North Central	14.00	15.00	16.00	275.00	265.00	285.00
South Atlantic	13.00	13.00	13.00	255.00	265.00	270.00
East South Central	13.00	14.00	13.00	255.00	265.00	265.00
West South Central	12.00	12.00	13.00	290.00	305.00	300.00
Mountain	15.00	17.00	17.00	325.00	355.00	375.00
Pacific	18.00	19.00	20.00	355.00	365.00	395.00

SOURCE: *Source Book of Health Insurance Data*, 1962, 1963 and 1964, pp. 31, 30 and 30, respectively.

Liberalizations of Benefit Amounts in Specific Group Health Coverages

Perhaps the most fundamental principle of sound group health insurance underwritng, applicable to all lines except accidental death and dismemberment insurance, is that the insured himself should be required in some way to bear a portion of each loss. Unless benefit payments are by some means restricted to an amount which is less than the total loss arising out of each disability, the resulting moral hazard is likely to reach a prohibitive level. This requirement, then, establishes an important limitation on benefit amounts that may be issued to individual group members in most types of group health coverage.

Accidental Death and Dismemberment Coverage. It is difficult to measure accurately the economic loss arising out of death or dismemberment, and, hence, the underwriting rule discussed in the preceding paragraph cannot be applied readily to group accidental death and dismemberment insurance. On the other hand, the degree of moral hazard is minimal in this type of coverage, so that the requirement is not as important as in other types of group health insurance. Nevertheless, insurance companies normally establish underwriting limits on the amount of group accidental death and dismemberment benefits they will issue.

As has been pointed out earlier in this book,[15] this coverage normally is written in conjunction with other group coverages, most commonly group life insurance. When this is done, the amount of the principal sum available to each employee often is the same as his group life insurance benefit. In the case of small groups, the principal sum may be limited further, e.g., to $20,000 or the amount of group life insurance, whichever is less. In recent years, however, it has become increasingly common for group insurers to issue to large and medium sized groups accidental death and dismemberment benefits far in excess of group life insurance amounts. A few insurers make these large benefits available to group members on a purely voluntary, employee-pay-all basis. Some observers regard this as a practice which probably will become more common in the future. This would indicate that group accidental death and dismemberment benefit amounts may be liberalized substantially in the years ahead, with the principal limiting factor being the demand for such benefit amounts, rather than the supply.

Disability Income Coverage. In most types of group insurance, it is essential that benefit amounts be determined by a schedule which precludes individual selection. The most commonly used schedule is that which relates benefit amounts to earnings of the individual. This type of schedule is felt to be the most effective in minimizing moral hazard. Hence the extent to which group disability income benefit amounts can be

---

[15] See Chapter 9.

liberalized is limited by three principal factors: (1) the weekly or monthly earnings of group members; (2) the length of time for which group insurers are willing to continue the earnings of a disabled worker; and (3) the proportion of those earnings which group insurers deem it safe to cover.

The first factor is, of course, largely beyond the control of the insurer. Nevertheless, significant liberalizations in group disability income benefit amounts have taken place in the past, and they probably will continue in the future, as increases in the earnings of group members take place.[16]

A number of important liberalizations also have taken place with respect to the second factor, the length of the benefit period. For many years the most commonly used maximum benefit period in group disability income insurance was thirteen weeks. In the past decade, however, the trend in short-term coverage has been toward providing benefits for up to twenty-six weeks for each disability. In several cases benefit periods are as long as fifty-two or 104 weeks.

Another major liberalization has been the development of group long-term disability income insurance. At present, the benefit periods most commonly used under this coverage are two years, five years, ten years and to age sixty-five. Benefit periods are sometimes longer for disabilities due to accident than for those due to sickness. Athough its development has been hampered by a variety of factors, among them the absence of reliable statistical data, many group insurance experts consider long-term coverage to hold enormous future potential. If this potential is realized, substantial liberalizations in group disability income benefit amounts will result.

As to the third factor, the proportion of a group member's earnings which can be protected by group disability income insurance, substantial liberalizations have occurred here also. Due primarily to the pressure of competition, underwriting rules of group insurers concerning this proportion gradually have been loosened. It is now common for benefit amounts in short-term disability income coverage to equal two thirds of gross wages excluding overtime pay, but benefits rarely exceed $100 per week. This low maximum is due primarily to the fact that many employers carry this insurance only for their hourly wage employees. Benefits for salaried employees usually are provided under an uninsured plan of full salary continuance. Rules applicable to group long-term disability income insurance generally are more stringent than for short-term coverage. The percentage generally is low, usually between 33⅓ per cent and 50 per cent of gross salary. Insurers sometimes use a graduated percentage scale such as the following: 50 per cent of the first $1,000 of monthly salary and 30

---

[16] It should be remembered that, from an underwriting standpoint, it is the group member's net take-home pay, rather than his gross earnings, which ultimately must control benefit amounts.

per cent of the excess. An over-all maximum, which may be as high as $1,000 per month, frequently is used, but this varies with the size of the group.

Medical Expense Coverage. In the field of the various group medical expense coverages, a number of significant liberalizations of benefit amounts have occurred in recent years. These liberalizations have resulted in part from greater recognition of the need to cover the cost of several additional types of medical care.

For example, at one time it was generally believed that fees for physicians' visits outside a hospital were not proper subject matter for group health coverage. At present, however, a significant amount of such coverage is in existence. The development and growth of major medical insurance in recent years, whereby medical expense coverage was extended outside the hospital and to many types of medical expenses not covered previously, is an outstanding illustration of this type of liberalization. The near future may contain further expansion in over-all medical expense benefit amounts as coverage is developed to meet the costs of vision care, prescription drugs and psychiatric care.

A second cause of liberalization in group medical expense insurance benefit amounts has been the rapidly rising cost of adequate medical care. This inflation has been particularly pronounced in the field of hospital costs in recent years, with the result that maximum benefit amounts payable under group hospitalization contracts have been increased substantially by insurers. Whereas only a few years ago hospital room-and-board benefits of $10 per day were common, today such benefits are grossly inadequate, and group master contracts providing benefits as high as $30 per day are not unusual. Benefit maxima for hospital "extras" have, of course, been liberalized correspondingly, since these usually are expressed as a multiple of the daily room-and-board benefit. Similar liberalizations have occurred with respect to all medical care coverages, including major medical, where a maximum benefit of $10,000 is quite common today.

Attitudes toward Limitations on Group Health Insurance Benefit Amounts

Unlike the field of group life insurance, there has been little controversy or pressure to limit group health insurance benefit amounts. Perhaps this is due to the important role initially played by group health insurance when public demand for such coverage required mass marketing techniques. Then, too, it may reflect the fact that many giant life insurance companies were not active in the individual health insurance field until the late 1940's. Individual agents and their organizations eventually may become more outspoken in their opposition to high group health insurance benefits as the two marketing systems, individual and group, continue to compete to provide the same protection.

SELECTED REFERENCES

BRONSON, D. C. "Actuarial Note: One Year's Experience of Large Amounts on Employees under Group Life Policies," *Transactions of the Actuarial Society of America*, Vol. XXXVI (1935), p. 36. See also Discussion, p. 389, by J. B. Crimmins, E. C. Henderson and E. W. Crowe.

FERGUSON, LEONARD W. "Group Coverage and Its Relation to Life Insurance Purchased Privately," *The Journal of the American Society of Chartered Life Underwriters*, Vol. XII (Fall, 1958), pp. 368–74.

FOLLMANN, J. F., JR. *Medical Care and Health Insurance.* Homewood, Ill.: Richard D. Irwin, Inc., 1963.

Society of Actuaries, Transactions of the. "Small Employer Groups; Larger Maximum Amounts on Group Life Insurance," Vol. VII (1955), informal discussion, pp. 496–503, by A. G. Weaver, P. A. Alexander, J. W. Moran, N. H. Fischer, R. J. Mellman, G. W. Fitzhugh, J. B. Walker, J. H. Smith, G. L. Hogeman, J. P. Stanley, E. B. Whittaker, W. A. Halvorson, S. W. Gingery and G. C. Streeter.

TRABER, RALPH E. "High Maximum Amounts of Group Life Insurance," *Proceedings of the Insurance Accounting and Statistical Association* (1957), pp. 142–45.

Chapter 32

ELIGIBILITY OF ASSOCIATIONS

BY CLARENCE H. TOOKEY AND ROBERT C. TOOKEY

From the standpoint of the insurance company, there are two tests as to whether a particular type of group is eligible for group life and health insurance. The first test is whether the particular group qualifies for group insurance under the laws of the state in which the master contract is to be written. The wide differences in the statutory definitions of eligible groups in the various states were discussed in Chapter 6. The second test is whether the group is such that it can be underwritten in such a way that adverse selection can be held to a minimum, thus granting insureds lower rates than they would pay for individual insurance contracts providing comparable coverage.

The first test is purely legal so that no discretion or judgment factor exists to create an underwriting problem. If, however, the group passes the legal test, the underwriting insurance company must apply the second test. Whether the association will meet the second test will depend primarily on the type of association involved and secondarily on the underwriting techniques employed by the underwriting company. The two basic types are trade associations and associations of individuals.

TRADE ASSOCIATIONS

The typical trade association is an association of employers which has been formed for purposes other than obtaining insurance. In most trade associations there are many small employers who do not have a sufficient number of employees to qualify for group coverage, or, if they do have enough, the numbers are too few to qualify for the high amounts of coverage available to larger groups with which they must compete for employees. In many cases these employers are businesses which, prior to the rise of collectively bargained welfare plans, had their own group master contracts. Now, however, they have only a few office and supervisory employees in need of group coverage, because the union employees are covered under collectively bargained welfare plans. Members of trade associations which have a substantial number of employees usually carry their own plans of group insurance. This is due to the fact that normally the more employees a firm has, the lower will be the average age of the employee group. Hence the firm with 100 employees usually can obtain larger benefits for a given premium outlay than can a firm with five employees.

The following section of the California Insurance Code is a fairly typical example of a state law covering group life insurance on employees of members of a trade association. It should be recognized, however, that a considerable amount of variation exists from state to state in the legal requirements applicable to trade association group insurance.

A group life policy conforming to all of the following conditions may be issued to the trustee of a fund established by employer members of a trade association or by a trade association and maintained by contributions of such members for the sole benefit of their employees:

(a) The trade association (1) must have been formed and continuously maintained for purposes other than obtaining insurance and have been in existence for five years or longer prior to issuance of the policy or (2) must be a statewide association having over 500 members, which has been in existence for 10 years or longer and consists of employer members engaged in any one or more of the manufacturing, fabricating, or processing industries.

(b) The policy must cover at date of issue not less than 75 per cent of the eligible employees of at least 50 per cent of the total employer members of the trade association unless the total number of lives covered at date of issue exceeds 600, in which event the policy must cover when issued 75 per cent of the eligible employees of at least 25 per cent of the employer members of the trade association; provided, however, that in determining the total of the employer members of the trade association there shall be excluded any member whose employees are already covered by group life insurance.

The policy may provide that the term "employees" shall include retired employees and the individual proprietor or partners if an employer is an individual proprietor or a partnership.

(c) The group life policy must be issued pursuant to Section 10202 and the trustee shall be deemed to be the employer for purposes of administration.

(d) The group policy must cover when issued at least 100 lives.[1]

The California law originally was passed in 1945, and it represented a compromise between the insurance companies and trade associations on the one hand, both of whom wanted the legislation, and the Life Underwriters Association on the other, which was opposed to this type of broadening of the statute. Since it is a compromise, it does not necessarily conform in all respects to completely logical principles. For example, the differing participation requirements applicable to groups of 600 or fewer members, as opposed to those with more than 600 members, have no

---

[1] California Insurance Code, Sec. 10202.7 (added by Stats. 1945, CH. 436; amended by Stats. 1947, CH. 1510, by Stats. 1957, CH. 2247 and CH. 2248, by Stats. 1959, CH. 440, and by Stats. 1961, CH. 698).

particular underwriting significance in and of themselves. Moreover, the 600-member figure was included in order to qualify the State Association of Savings and Loan Companies for group life insurance. Nevertheless, because the California statute was one of the earliest to be enacted, it was rather widely copied in other states. It is rather amusing that the 600-member figure was retained in some of the states which copied the California definition.

In addition to legal requirements such as the foregoing,[2] a number of important underwriting controls limit the availability of group coverage for trade associations. For example, insurance companies often require that the association be contained within a rather small geographical area and have a full-time executive secretary who is willing and able to devote a substantial part of his time to the development of the plan and solicitation of new members. In addition, it is usually considered preferable for administrative purposes that only a small percentage of the covered employers have fewer than three employees and that a large percentage of them have between five and fifteen or twenty employees. Further, often the employers must contribute at least 50 per cent of the premium cost of the plan in order to improve the possibility of enrolling a large proportion of the employees both initially and in the future.

The danger of abuse of group insurance where there are many small units which may or may not subscribe to the plan usually arises from acts of the employer. The master policy must be so written that eligibility definitions are very strict. Normally, employees in the association's business office are eligible only if they work at least thirty hours a week. Once a trade association group has been written, any firms asking to come in after they have originally declined to participate should be looked upon with suspicion. Sometimes evidence of insurability is required of employees of latecomers.

Many of the group plans of trade associations are administered by the agent who wrote the case originally. He is often in a good position to know the members of the association and to remain in fairly close touch with the individual firms. Quite often he collects the premiums and pays the claims in the case of health insurance. It is to his benefit to see that the claim costs are not artificially inflated by abuse, since this might lead to termination of the coverage or appointment of another broker. In one case where a small firm had belatedly joined the insurance plan to obtain $30,000 of group life insurance on one of the partners who had cancer, the agent was able to convince the association to put such pressure on the firm that the claim was withdrawn.

In the case of medical expense insurance, the benefits for the employer

---

[2] The last section of this chapter provides further information on the types of association groups that may be covered in various states at the present time.

are usually the same as for the employees. In the case of life and disability income insurance, they are usually higher for the employer. The scale of benefits which can be provided safely depends largely on how many employers are covered. If there are several hundred firms, the amounts on the employers can be quite high, whereas if there are only a dozen firms, the amounts of insurance on employers should not be much greater than two and one-half times the average amount on the employees.

ASSOCIATIONS OF INDIVIDUALS

There are four types of associations of individuals which will be discussed in this chapter. The first two are unions and public employee associations. These are recognized as legal groups for group insurance purposes in most states, and there has been little public controversy as to the desirability of granting all forms of group coverage to members of these associations. The other two types of associations of individuals are the ones which have been responsible for very heated controversy during the past twenty years. These last types are professional associations and a variety of miscellaneous associations. In many states the laws are such that members of these last two types of associations cannot be covered under group contracts.

Union Groups

The test of eligibility of union groups is primarily one of underwriting. If the insurance premium is paid out of union dues, and 100 per cent of the active members are covered, the cost of group insurance will be similar to that for a regular employer-employee group. If the union is in a growing industry, the average age will not increase and may even decrease if the industry is growing rapidly. However, in some of the craft unions, particularly those which are declining due to the growth of automation, the average age will tend to increase quite rapidly due to the seniority rules under union contracts.

If the average age increases rapidly, substantial premium increases will be needed from time to time. This means increased union dues and possible dissatisfaction of members with the group insurance plan and with the officers of the union. Since one of the purposes of insurance paid by dues is to make union membership attractive and thus maintain it at a high level, group coverage which results in regular annual increases in union dues defeats this important purpose.

As a consequence, almost all group life insurance contracts issued to unions provide small benefit amounts, such as $1,000 or $1,500, on each active member. The premium is limited to approximately $1.00 per month. The premium for any larger benefit amount is difficult to provide out of union dues without increasing them sharply. A further result of this factor is that it is rare to include substantial group health insurance benefits on these plans, since the cost of such coverage normally is greater than can be included in union dues.

Prior to passage of the Taft-Hartley Act there were a few cases where the union had bargained with employers for a contribution based either on a cents per hour or a percentage of the wages basis. The union then purchased from an insurer the disability income and hospital insurance benefits under a policy issued to the union. Since the employers were paying the entire cost of the coverage, 100 per cent of members were insured, and no increase in dues was required.

Prior to the general adoption of collective bargaining for group insurance with the cost paid by employers, there was some experimentation with the issuance of group life and health insurance to unions under which the union member paid the cost by adding it voluntarily to the regular dues. Most of these experiments were unsuccessful due to the difficulty of maintaining high participation, which is generally necessary if claim costs are to be kept at a low level.

An insurance company writing a union group policy should take the future growth of the union into account as one of the underwriting factors. It should also take into account the feeling of the particular union regarding its retired members. Continuation of coverage to retired members will increase the cost substantially. On the other hand, making a retired member ineligible to carry insurance in the union may have an adverse effect on the satisfacton of the active members. The solution to this often is to reduce the amount of group life insurance on retired members to some percentage, e.g., 25 per cent, of the amount on active members, so that the coverage provided after retirement is limited to a modest funeral benefit.

Associations of Public Employees

Group insurance written on associations of public employees is recognized by nearly all states. As a result, the principal test of eligibility will be, as in the case of unions, the underwriting factors involved, rather than the legal question.

At this point a bit of history is interesting. It will be noted from other chapters in this book that the technique of writing group life insurance on employer-employee groups was quite advanced by 1930. Among the underwriting safety factors were the percentage requirement for participation and the requirement that the employer contribute to the cost so that the employee's share of the cost would remain level. However, in the early years of group life insurance many public employee associations had been covered by group life insurance plans under which the entire premium was paid by members of the association at a flat rate per $1,000, regardless of age. The experience on these contracts was unfavorable. There was no mechanism for bringing in new lives. Depression times came on, and the scarcity of jobs was particularly hard on young people, who represented a disproportionately high percentage of the total unemployed. With fewer eligible young people available, the average age of the insured group rose, and rates were increased, making the cost for young employees greater than the premium for an individual life insurance policy. The result was such a spiral in costs that by the middle thirties most of the large group writing companies would no longer write group life insurance covering public employee associations.

However, there still existed a demand by these associations for group insurance coverage. Consequently, some of the smaller insurance companies have developed new plans wherein premium rates are graded by attained age or benefits are reduced at the older ages. In addition, extensive servicing of the group plan is employed to maintain the flow of new, young lives into the plan. These techniques have largely solved the problem of increasing costs, so that today almost every state has a group insurance plan for its employees which is administered by the state employees association. Nearly all large counties and cities, as well as many smaller political subdivisions, have such plans.

In the case of group disability income insurance, grading of premium rates usually can be accomplished in much broader age groups than in the case of group life insurance. Often it is not necessary to grade premium rates for group medical expense insurance. Hence the problem of spiraling cost due to inadequate flow of young lives into the plan has not been as severe as in group life insurance.

An interesting problem has developed as a result of the gradual transition from employee-pay-all group coverage for public employees to participation in the cost by the employer. When a city or county starts to contribute to group insurance costs, it is common to find the employee associations, which have carried the entire cost burden for many years, in a controversy with the employer as to who will control the group insurance plan. Since unionism among public employees is frowned on by the general public, there is no way that the employees can get a hearing as to their insurance benefits other than through their association. In a union this would be done through collective bargaining. The association wishes to continue its control over the group insurance plan through its insurance committees.

The actual techniques of writing group insurance on associations of public employees are rather simple. One of the most important requirements for a sound plan of this type is that the rates for group life insurance must depend on the employee's attained age. Usually there are four or five age groups for life coverage, with rates ranging from $.30 per $1,000 in the youngest group to over $1.00 per $1,000 in the oldest group. Normally only two or three age groups are used under group disability income coverage. The rates for group medical expense coverage are normally not graded by age.

In an earlier chapter it was pointed out that an important fundamental requirement in group insurance is that there be a mechanism which provides for automatic payment of the monthly premiums, preferably by the payroll deduction method. Otherwise persistency may be poor, and participation may drop. Thus it is customary in the case of employee associations to pay premiums by salary allotment.

Moreover, arrangements must be made for the regular solicitation of all new employees. If possible this should be done on the job, or the cost of enrollment will be prohibitive.

Until recently, retired public employees lost their coverage at retirement. In some groups currently being written, special additional premiums are charged active employees. These premiums go into a retired life pool which is used to reduce the cost of the higher mortality and morbidity of retired members. It is customary to reduce group insurance benefit amounts on public employees at retirement so that the cost load on active employees is not excessive.

From the foregoing it will be observed that group insurance on associations of public employees has gone through an interesting period of development. These associations are now readily underwritten by most insurance companies that write group insurance. Eventually most public employees will be covered by regular employer-employee group contracts, but the political resistance to increased taxes probably will postpone a complete changeover far into the future. Therefore, association group insurance for public employees is likely to be of considerable importance for several more decades.

Professional Associations

The next two types of associations of individuals have been the source of much controversy for nearly twenty years. The professional association, which will be discussed first, is similar to a union group in one sense, viz., it is an association of persons in the same type of occupation. From an insurance standpoint, however, there is very little resemblance between the two. In union groups, the amount of insurance on each member typically is small. Professional associations, on the other hand, are made up of individuals with the need for substantial amounts of insurance. Hence the members of these associations represent the most lucrative markets for the professional insurance agent who is skilled in providing the insurance program which best meets the needs of his client within the client's capacity to pay. It is not surprising, therefore, that organizations of individual life and health insurance agents generally oppose the issuance of group life and health insurance to members of professional associations. Agents' organizations also believe that extending group coverages to members of professional associations is a perversion of the original purpose of group insurance, which they feel was to provide a moderate amount of coverage to employees of a common employer, where part of the cost was paid by the employer and employees were covered regardless of physical condition.

A common benefit formula for a professional association today is to provide $10,000 of group life insurance without any evidence of insurability, plus another $40,000 subject to evidence of insurability. The association member normally pays the entire cost. The agency organizations argue that a man with $50,000 of coverage needs professional advice. They also claim that the saving in expense through the group approach is nominal in professional associations, and that the professional man is better off with an individual policy. As a matter of fact, term insurance rates for individual life insurance contracts are very little higher than the rates charged for association group coverage. One of the arguments the agency organizations use against group insurance for professional associations is that the natural aging of the group will result in the same spiral of cost which was experienced by the old assessment associations. Professional association groups have not been in existence long enough to determine whether the dire predictions of the agency organizations will be realized.

There are two schools of thought as to the controversy regarding group life insurance for professional groups. There is no doubt that adequate life insurance is exceedingly important to the higher income group, and they need professional insurance advice. On the other hand, it is equally true that all of our population is woefully underinsured, and more life insurance coverage would be carried if its cost were less. Thus, the second school of thought is that physicians, lawyers and other professional men will continue to purchase approximately the same amount of individual coverage even though they also buy group coverage.

Thus far, the discussion of professional groups has been limited to group life insurance. These associations are also eligible for group disability income and medical expense coverage in many states. Unlike the situation with respect to group life insurance, there have been comparatively few serious objections to group health insurance for members of professional associations. The reason for this is probably that life insurance agents often are not particularly interested in writing health insurance, and there are few major organizations to represent the interests of those who do write a large volume of health insurance.

Disability income coverage on professional associations can assume many forms. Protection can be provided against short-term disability under a plan that will pay for up to twenty-six weeks of disability, or the long-term disability peril may be covered, with benefits being paid for five years, ten years or even until age sixty-five.

One of the great dangers in this type of coverage is the possibility of over-insurance. For example, a doctor can buy an individual disability income policy providing a benefit of as much as $1,000 per month. He may even have additional disability income coverage provided to secure the mortgage on his home. It is then possible to obtain further protection from the group contract issued to the American Medical Association, and in several states through another group contract issued to the particular state medical association.

Group medical expense insurance is a less commonly issued coverage in the case of a professional association. The constantly rising medical claim costs make it difficult to maintain one premium rate for any great length of time. Acceptance of a rate increase often is much more difficult to obtain from a professional association's membership than is true of other groups. Despite these difficulties many professional associations make such coverage available to their members.

To some extent the success of professional groups is influenced by the amount of support given the plan by the association. This support can be given in a number of ways. If the association has a publication, the plan can be given continual advertising. At meetings and conventions a certain amount of time can be allotted to discussion of the insurance plan. At local meetings some solicitation may be done by having the insurance representative distribute application blanks.

Usually the original enrollment without evidence of insurability is open only for a limited length of time, such as sixty or ninety days. Subsequent to the open enrollment period, evidence of insurability must be furnished by the member making application for insurance, unless he is becoming eligible for the first time. Usually about sixty days from date of membership is given to a new member for enrollment without evidence of insurability. After that the member must furnish such evidence. Normally evidence of insurability is limited to a simple health statement.

There is great variation in the method of obtaining high participation in the insurance plan by members of professional groups. In some cases, practically all solicitation is by mail. In other cases, there is a very active solicitation of each individual member. One company which is quite active in writing insurance on bar associations gives out the names of members to its regular agents so that every member is solicited. If this can be done at reasonable cost, the percentage of participation will be much higher than if mail solicitation only is used.

Usually there are no serious problems of administration in professional association group plans. Premiums are usually payable quarterly, semiannually or annually. They may be paid through the association, through the broker or directly to the insurance company. As in the case of trade associations, there is some advantage in having the broker or agent handle the administration, since usually he can be a little closer to the particular associations and their members than can the insurance company itself.

It will be remembered that member-pay-all group insurance on union members generally has not been successful. The reason may have been that at the time these plans were attempted union members did not have enough income to make it easy to pay the added cost. A substantial number of union members were on a rather tight monthly budget, and few were financially able to pay other than monthly. Consequently, persistency was often poor.

However, in the case of professional groups an annual premium of several hundred dollars is not a severe burden. As a result, the cost of group life and health insurance interferes to a lesser degree with the persistency of the business. There is, however, a danger of substantial premium increases in the future unless the number of young lives entering the group is sufficient to offset the gradual aging of the original insured members. It must be remembered that there is no forced retirement in the professions, most of whose members are self-employed.

There may, however, be a special favorable factor involved in professional groups, and that is the increase in financial security which usually accompanies increasing age. Many professional men become quite secure from an income standpoint after, e.g., age fifty and can afford the cost of continuing the coverage.

Miscellaneous Associations

In the case of each type of association discussed thus far, the members constituting the association have in common some purpose other than simply to purchase group insurance. In addition to these associations, there are a variety of miscellaneous associations whose members may be covered by group insurance under the laws of various states. The practice of furnishing group coverage to the members of such associations, which often are condemned as "fictitious groups" by individual insurance underwriters and others, has also been the source of considerable controversy in the life and health insurance business. For example, one of the agency leaders of the national organization said some years ago, "Anyone living in block 11 on Street X will be eligible for group insurance."

Normally insurance companies will not consider providing group insurance to any organization formed for the purpose of obtaining insurance. There are, however, many organizations formed for other purposes whose membership rosters may constitute preferred prospect lists. In order to make the offer of insurance interesting to the prospective insured member, some special incentive must be provided by the insurance company. Most states have discrimination laws, the effect of which is that an agent cannot offer to the member a lower rate than is offered to other individual insureds of the same class. As a result, group insurance has been used as a vehicle to pass along to the buyer the lower sales costs of insuring the association's members. The associations themselves generally are favorably disposed toward such an arrangement, in that they are interested in providing to prospective members an added incentive to join the association. Quite often group insurance written on members of a miscellaneous association involve the furnishing of evidence of insurability by means of a short form health statement in lieu of the normal 75 per cent participation requirement.

Miscellaneous associations of individuals are ineligible for group life insurance in most states. Some states, however, have no restrictions on types of eligible groups. The vast majority of states have no such restrictions on types of eligible groups for group health insurance.

The insurance company may, therefore, issue a master contract in a state which has no restrictions and insure under this contract members in many other states which have strict laws regarding group life insurance. The insurance commissioners of these latter states may feel the insurance company is doing indirectly in their state what it cannot do directly. This, in turn, raises the question of whether the company is violating the law, although the group master contract was written legally. As a result, very few miscellaneous type group cases have been written by major insurance companies.[3]

A recent exception which has caused a considerable amount of controversy is the so-called "Olympic Association" case written by the John Hancock Mutual Life Insurance Company. Under this plan, college students may obtain $10,000 of group life insurance at normal group rates, which are quite low at the young average age of students. The dividends on the group master contract are payable to the United States Olympic Committee. The group coverage is written for a relatively short period. The insurance terminates when the student ceases to be a student, or when he reaches age thirty, whichever occurs first, at which time he is permitted to convert to permanent individual insurance without submitting evidence of insurability. The plan contemplates that, as each student's group insurance terminates, he will be contacted by an agent of the insurance company, who will encourage conversion and receive the full commission on all insurance that is converted. Thus, in essence, the plan results in the creation of a list of preferred prospects for the company's agents as students graduate. In other words, it was a plan to provide low cost insurance protection to this segment of the market and at the same time give the company's agents an advantage over agents of other companies in writing permanent insurance on the students who will graduate in the next four years.

Another advantage of this plan is that the payment of dividends to the Olympic Committee, which constitutes only a very small contribution per student, in total probably will be of real financial assistance to a worthy cause. Moreover, the proportion of impaired lives during the college years is so small that neither group underwriting nor subsequent conversions represent a serious risk to the insurance company.

Another plan which was written some years ago was the Equitable's

---

[3] The subject of multi-state groups is discussed in detail in Chapter 25.

group coverage for members of the National Association for Retarded Children. The idea was that members of the Association had a greater financial obligation because of being parents of a retarded child. For a specified quarterly premium a parent was insured for an amount decreasing by age at death. The booklet explained that this was extra coverage for a specific purpose. Again, this was a way to furnish insurance very cheaply to individuals with special needs.

A number of group insurance plans covering members of miscellaneous groups also exist in fields other than group term life insurance. For example, recently a group insurance master contract was prepared to cover the cost of prescription drugs incurred by the members of an association of persons buying into a retired citizens real estate development. Similarly, some associations have been issued group insurance master contracts which provide substantial amounts of coverage for death while traveling in aircraft. Group policies providing accidental death and medical expense coverage on school children and school and college athletic teams have been written for many years. Such policies are legal in most states.

These miscellaneous association groups appear to be one aspect of mass selling as applied to insurance. Unless it can be proven that the public is injured by the use of the group mechanism as the vehicle by which to provide more insurance for less money, and so long as the wage earners of the United States are so underinsured in comparison with their economic value, it would appear that more experiments should be made with respect to furnishing group insurance to miscellaneous groups.

REGULATION OF ASSOCIATION GROUP INSURANCE

The legal definition of group insurance was discussed at some length in Chapter 6. Any company planning to write a group policy on an association group in a particular state should check the insurance law and regulations of that state, as well as any special rulings that might have been made in individual cases. This concluding section will attempt to provide a brief summary of the kinds of associations which may be issued group insurance in each state. Since the laws are amended from time to time, the reader's attention is called to the fact that the summary that follows relates to the state laws as of June, 1964.

Group Life Insurance

There are at present twelve states[4] whose statutes contain no definition of group life insurance. Here, then, an insurance company may issue any

---

[4] Alabama, Alaska, Connecticut, Delaware, Minnesota, Mississippi, Missouri, North Dakota, Rhode Island, South Dakota, Tennessee and Wyoming. In the case of Connecticut, when an inquiry concerning eligible types of groups is answered, reference is made to the NAIC model bill.

type of group plan which, in its underwriting judgment, it deems advisable. In addition, there are five states[5] which permit issuance of group life insurance to any type of association, the only restriction being that it constitute a bona fide association. In the remainder of the states and in the District of Columbia only specified types of association groups are eligible for group life insurance. The types that are eligible in these jurisdictions are as shown in Table 32–1.

TABLE 32–1

TYPES OF ASSOCIATIONS ELIGIBLE FOR GROUP LIFE INSURANCE
AS OF JUNE, 1964

Jurisdiction	Eligible Types
Arizona	Trade association
Arkansas	Trade association
	Public employees association
California	Trade association
	Public employees association
	Association of private employees of common employer
Colorado	Public employees association
Dist. of Columbia	Professional association
	Trade association
	Association of federal employees
	National veterans association
Florida	Trade association
Georgia	Trade association
	Employee association
	Public employees association
	Professional association
Hawaii	Professional association
	Occupation, industry or trade association
Idaho	Trade association
	Public employees association
Indiana	Trade association
	Voluntary industry association, but only for executive, supervisory, sales and professional employees of members
Iowa	Nonprofit industrial association
	Teachers, lawyers, voluntary firemen, fraternal society and similar groups
	Association of school or college teachers and students
Kentucky	Trade association
	Public employees association
Maine	Trade association
	Municipal employees association
Maryland	Trade association
	Professional association
	Public employees association
Massachusetts	Charitable or religious association
	Public employees association
Michigan	Nonprofit incorporated industrial association covering executives only
	State teachers association
	Postal clerks association

---

[5] Illinois, Kansas, Louisiana, Nevada and Oregon.

TABLE 32–1 *(Continued)*

Jurisdiction	Eligible Types
Montana	Trade association
	Public employees association
Nebraska	Trade association
	Public employees association
	Professional association
New Hampshire	Nonprofit industrial association
	Public employees association
New Jersey	Trade association
	State police benevolent association
New Mexico	Trade association
	Professional or business association
New York	Trade association
	Association of civil service employees or teachers
	State police, policemen's or firemen's association, municipal corporation, public housing authority, association of lawyers and similar professions, but not medical societies
North Carolina	Professional or business association
	Public employees association
Ohio	Professional association
	National Guard, state police, World War veterans association
	Agricultural or horticultural cooperatives
Oklahoma	Nonprofit industrial association covering executives only
	Professional association
Pennsylvania	Trade association
	Police and firemen's fraternal
	Teachers association
	Government unit or agency
South Carolina	Trade association
Texas	Public employees association
Utah	Public employees of state, counties, cities, incorporated towns, school districts, institutions of higher learning
Vermont	Trade association
	Public employees association
	Association of employees
Virginia	Trade association
	Association of public employees
	Professional association
	Employee association
Washington	Trade association
	Public employees association
	State Patrol
West Virginia	Trade association
Wisconsin	Trade association
	Public employees association
	Cooperatives

Group Health Insurance

The majority of states are more liberal in their attitude toward association group health insurance than toward association group life insurance.

Fifteen states[6] and the District of Columbia have no group health insurance law, while twenty-nine others[7] that do define eligible groups allow almost any bona fide association to be insured under a group health insurance master contract. Of the remaining six states, five[8] appear to be a little more exacting in their requirements applicable to association group health insurance. The sixth, North Carolina, makes no provision in its statute for group health insurance on a trade association or, for that matter, a union.

SELECTED REFERENCES

BROWNING, ARTHUR M. "The Status of Group Insurance for Public Employees," *Proceedings of the Association of Life Insurance Counsel* (1956–1957), p. 53.

McDOWELL, GEORGE L. "Professional Association Groups," *Proceedings of the Sixth Annual Group Meeting*, pp. 26–30. Chicago: Health and Accident Underwriters Conference, 1954.

SARASON, HARRY M. "Association Insurance," *The Journal of Insurance*, Vol. XXVIII, No. 4 (December, 1961), pp. 79–84.

Society of Actuaries, Transactions of the. "Group Insurance for Professional Associations and Similar Groups," Vol. XI (1959), informal discussion by R. C. Tookey, R. J. Learson and J. W. Moran, pp. 1008, 1012.

---

[6] Alabama, Alaska, Connecticut, Delaware, Mississippi, Missouri, New Hampshire, North Dakota, Oregon, Rhode Island, South Dakota, Tennessee, Texas, Virginia and Wyoming.

[7] Arizona, Arkansas, California, Colorado, Florida, Georgia, Idaho, Illinois, Indiana, Kansas, Kentucky, Louisiana, Maryland, Michigan, Minnesota, Montana, Nebraska, Nevada, New Jersey, New Mexico, Ohio, Oklahoma, Pennsylvania, South Carolina, Utah, Vermont, Washington, West Virginia and Wisconsin.

[8] Hawaii, Iowa, Maine, Massachusetts and New York.

Chapter 33

TAFT-HARTLEY WELFARE FUNDS

BY LAWRENCE M. CATHLES, JR.

INTRODUCTION

As has been mentioned earlier, during World War II wages and salaries were frozen and the excess profits tax took ninety cents of the corporate profit dollar. Since there were no similar restrictions on employer contributions to group insurance, this became an attractive way to provide additional incentives to workers in a competitive labor market.

Just after World War II, federal courts ruled that pensions,[1] and later group insurance,[2] were conditions affecting employment and, hence, proper subjects for collective bargaining. Almost immediately the subject of group insurance appeared at thousands of collective bargaining tables. The result was a dramatic expansion of group insurance coverage.

Nature of Welfare Funds

Up to this time group insurance had been generally available only to employers with twenty-five or more employees. When it became a collective bargaining issue, however, coverage had to be available for all union members. Therefore, when unions bargained on an industry-wide or multi-employer basis, which frequently occurred when large numbers of small employers were involved, it was necessary to develop a multi-employer policy; and it was at this time that the negotiated Taft-Hartley Welfare fund was born.

A welfare fund can be defined as a trust, usually formally established, for the purpose of providing benefits to employees and their dependents in the event of death, disability, incurrence of medical expenses or retirement. The collective bargaining agreement and the trust agreement define the broad classes of employees to be covered. The individual employee's eligibility for benefits is determined in accordance with rules established by the trustees and is usually based upon work performed for contributing

---

[1] *Inland Steel Co.* v. *N.L.R.B.* [170 F2d 247; 12 ALR 2d 240 (1948)].

[2] *W. W. Cross & Co.* v. *N.L.R.B.* [174 F2d 875 (1949)].

employers. Generally the fund is financed solely by employer contributions required by the terms of a labor agreement. The contribution usually is stated in cents per hour worked or as a percentage of payroll.

Among the first welfare funds were those established by the Amalgamated Clothing Workers, the Fur and Leather Workers, the International Ladies Garment Workers and the United Furniture Workers. As a rule, these early plans were not formally established trust funds. All were administered solely by the unions, with employer participation limited to the payment of the negotiated contribution. Most of these funds provided benefits through group insurance contracts issued to the unions. However, at least one, the Security Fund of Local 65 Department and Drug Store Workers, paid benefits directly out of the fund.

Influence of the Taft-Hartley Act

The Labor Management Relations Act, 1947, or "Taft-Hartley Act," prohibited the payment of money or other items of value by an employer to a representative of his employees if they were employed in an industry affecting interstate commerce. It further prohibited the receipt of such money by any representative of the employees. The Act provided, however, that this prohibition would not apply to money paid to a trust fund, where the payments were held for the sole purpose of providing welfare benefits to the employees and their families under a specific plan which had been agreed to by the union and the employer. It was also provided that if pension benefits were to be included, a separate fund was to be established solely for this purpose. Excerpts from the Act are set forth in Appendix 22. While the programs which commenced prior to January 1, 1946, were specifically exempted from the requirements of the Act, for the most part these early funds have voluntarily complied.

It would be difficult to justify the contention that the subsequent rapid development of welfare funds was due solely to the passage of the Taft-Hartley Act and the requirements it imposed. Although without the Act there might have been more employer resistance, it seems rather clear that other forces, independently set in motion, would have in any event forced a considerable expansion in this area. It can be established, however, that the participation of employers on the trustee boards, as required by the Taft-Hartley Act, has made a significant contribution to the successful development of these funds. The employer-trustees brought with them a slightly different point of view, a knowledge of business and finance and a balance which has been of great significance. Whereas some employer representatives have undoubtedly viewed the requirements of joint administration as an unwarranted imposition, generally speaking, they have joined with the union trustees as they would with partners in the operation of a business. The result has usually been a well-managed, well-run business enterprise.

Shortly after the passage of the Taft-Hartley Act funds began to be negotiated in the construction industry. It is here and in the transportation industry that the largest number and the most sizable welfare funds have been established.

THE TRUSTEES AND THEIR RESPONSIBILITY

When a labor agreement requiring an employer contribution to a welfare fund has been concluded, a board of trustees must be created to implement the benefits which the negotiators intended. The legal document formally establishing the trust is known as a "trust indenture" or "trust agreement." It is executed by the parties to the labor agreement—normally the union and the association representing the participating employers. If there is to be a corporate trustee, the trustee is also a party to the agreement. The trust agreement should, among other things, provide for trustees and successor trustees; define their liability; empower them to (1) establish and maintain an administrative office, (2) purchase insurance contracts or otherwise determine and provide welfare benefits, (3) establish a fund reserve and manage the reserve monies to accomplish the purposes of the trust, (4) require information from participating employers necessary to maintain records of eligibility, (5) provide for the inclusion of new participating employers and termination of employers no longer subject to the terms of the labor agreement, (6) collect employer contributions, (7) provide for annual audits, (8) determine eligibility of participants, and (9) provide for the disposition of fund monies in the event of the termination of the fund. The trustees are designated by the parties creating the trust. The trust agreement may provide for one or more neutral trustees, as in the case of the United Mine Workers Funds, but this is exceedingly rare. Most trusts provide instead for the appointment of an impartial umpire, either by the trustees or the court, in the event of a dispute between the labor and management trustees.

The circumstances of the particular situation will generally determine the number of trustees which will make up the board. Where many union locals are included, as in the case of a state-wide or national fund, it may be necessary to have a large board of up to twenty trustees or more. However, it is desirable generally to keep the size of the board smaller in order to facilitate efficient fund management. Since boards of less than six usually experience difficulty maintaining continuity and meeting quorum requirements, trustee boards of six and eight have become quite general. Where there are very large boards, executive or working committees of six or eight trustees usually make the major decisions, subject to the ratification of the full board.

The welfare fund trustee holds a very responsible position. Although the trust agreement will invariably limit his personal liability as much as possible, the fiduciary nature of the situation imposes certain inherent obligations. The test most frequently applied by the courts as a measure of this fiduciary responsibility is referred to as the "prudent man" rule. In essence, this rule provides that a trustee shall administer the affairs of the trust as a prudent man would administer his personal affairs. It is not expected that the trustee will be a paragon of knowledge or that he will be infallible. While it is expected that he will necessarily rely upon the advice of others, he must take every prudent precaution to protect himself against the results of poor advice.

ESTABLISHING THE BENEFIT PROGRAM

In establishing the benefit program, there are four main areas in which the trustees must take action: (1) they must define the rules of eligibility; (2) they must arrange for the establishment of the necessary administrative facilities; (3) they must determine the reserves necessary for the security of the fund and provide for their accumulation; and (4) they must determine the benefits and the manner in which they will be provided. All of this must be conducted, of course, within the scope and limitations of the trust agreement.

Eligibility

A welfare fund does not create—it can only distribute. The money paid out in benefits must first be earned for the fund by work performed for participating employers by members of the bargaining unit. Therefore, eligibility rules merely define the conditions which must be met by an individual to be eligible for benefits.

Since the pre–Taft-Hartley welfare funds were administered solely by the unions, it was natural that they should have restricted eligibility to union members, sometimes without regard to work performed or contributions earned. Soon after the passage of the Taft-Hartley Act, however, National Labor Relations Board decisions made it clear that welfare benefits, like wages and working conditions, were negotiated for all members of the bargaining unit, not only for members of the union.[3] Eligibility rules then began to require generally a certain number of hours, days or some attachment to the industry in order to be eligible for benefits.

Eligibility Philosophies. There are two basic philosophies of eligibility. Some argue that, since the employer's contribution is in fact wages, every member is entitled to at least what he has earned, and benefits should be available to all members of the bargaining unit irrespective of work performed. Others maintain that benefits should be available only to those

---

[3] Rockaway News Supply Co., Inc. [94 N.L.R.B. 1056 (1951)]; and Jandel Furs [100 N.L.R.B. 1390 (1952)].

regularly working within the industry and that qualification for benefits should be based upon meeting some minimum work requirement. Regardless of which philosophy is accepted, the amount of money available for benefits will be the same. Therefore, unless all members of the bargaining unit are steadily employed, the first approach will produce lower benefits for the bulk of the employees. As a result, while rules of this type are quite reasonable from the standpoint of logic and quite possible from an administrative point of view, they are not widely used. Although eligibility rules based on a minimum work requirement introduce problems of continuity of coverage during periods of reduced employment and require more extensive record keeping, they permit higher benefits for the "regular" employee. Therefore, in spite of the minor drawbacks, minimum work rules are chosen by most trustee boards.

Eligibility Formulas. Although various formulas are used to express eligibility requirements, the differences reflect for the most part the particular work characteristics of the industry involved. Generally speaking, there are three basic types of formulas. The first type requires a given number of days, weeks or months of employment, either with a participating employer or within the industry. It is comparable to the definition of "full-time employee" under single-employer plans and is appropriate for multi-employer funds where employment conditions of the participating employers are fairly stable and there is limited shifting of employees from one employer to another.

The second and third types of formulas are particularly applicable to industries, such as the construction industry, where employees are hired for a particular project and have no permanent relationship with any employer. Both of these formulas are based upon the accumulation of credited hours of employment. One of these formulas determines eligibility by considering the credited hours of work during a prior period, called an "accumulation period." For example, the formula might provide eligibility during January, February and March if sufficient work was performed during October, November and December. A variation would introduce a "lag" month between the accumulation period and the coverage period so that the employer report forms may be processed and an eligibility list prepared by the first day of the coverage period. The formula may also provide alternate tests so that if the required number of hours is not earned during the three-month accumulation period, the employee will be eligible nonetheless if he has worked a larger specified number of hours during the preceding six- or twelve-month period. These alternate tests are particularly appropriate in those industries which are subject to seasonal fluctuations in employment because of weather or other conditions.

The second credited hour formula is the so-called reserve bank arrangement under which all hours reported for an individual are credited to his "hour bank." Each month that the individual is provided coverage, a specified number of hours is withdrawn from his bank. When there are no longer sufficient hours in the bank to provide for the month's draw, coverage is terminated. To facilitate financial planning, it usually is necessary to limit the size of any individual's bank accumulation to the number of hours required to provide coverage for three or six months.

The choice between the two credited hour formulas is largely one of preference. The reserve bank is easier to explain to the employee and gives him greater recognition for the contributions which he personally has earned. The other formula is more difficult to explain to the employee. Furthermore, it tends to emphasize average results rather than the individual contribution of an employee. On the other hand, it is less complex and less costly from an administrative standpoint.

Eligibility Rules. The following principles have been found useful for formulating eligibility rules:

1. An initial waiting period of four or five months between the date employer contributions are to commence and the effective date of benefits is desirable in order to provide operating funds for the trustees, permit accumulation of employment data to determine initial eligibility and to provide time for the establishment of the necessary administrative facilities.
2. Eligibility should be based upon work which has already been performed and income which has already been produced for the fund.
3. To be insured, each worker should earn by his hours of credited work sufficient employer contributions to pay his approximate share of benefit costs.
4. Workers who fail to meet eligibility requirements but who earn some employer contribution and workers who work more than the minimum required for eligibility will both produce surplus income to the fund. While this surplus can be predicted, it is usually advisable, at least initially, to allocate this extra income to reserve accumulation rather than benefits.
5. Eligibility should cease when the worker fails to earn sufficient employer contributions to cover his share of fund expenses. However, the eligibility rules should be so drawn that, within the capacity of the fund, the individual who is "regularly" employed has sufficient continuation of coverage to tide him over normal employment fluctuations without coverage interruptions.
6. Since money spent to cover the costs of administration is unproductive in the sense that it does not contribute to benefits, eligibility rules should be considered in the light of the administrative procedures which they will entail.
7. Rules should be conservatively drawn initially. They can always be liberalized in the future as conditions permit. Moreover, when employment slackens, the trustees should be in a position to extend protection to unemployed workers or to reduce eligibility requirements if such action seems prudent in consideration of the business outlook, the reserve position of the fund and the effect of possible abuses of benefits by unemployed workers.
8. Eligibility rules should, in general, provide for credits during periods of

disability so that the employee may maintain his eligibility while disabled.

9. Usually the rules should provide for reinstatement of insurance following completion of service in the Armed Forces. Generally, coverage should be reinstated on the day the employee recommences work with one of the participating employers, provided this is within ninety days of the date of his discharge from the Armed Forces; otherwise, the employee should be treated as any other new worker.

Some trustees may want to provide coverage for self-employed individuals who agree to pay the premium cost directly to the fund, or they may want to permit an employee who fails to maintain eligibility to continue his coverage by contributing the premium cost of his insurance directly to the fund. These seemingly reasonable desires are actually quite unsound and should be discouraged. If acceded to, they would frequently permit the coverage of workers no longer active in the labor force and would invite a very substantial selection against the fund. Where separate statistics have been kept, benefit payments to direct contributors have been found to be ten to fourteen times those for the regular employee. When employment is high, the fund may be able to stand costs of this magnitude; but during periods of increasing unemployment, this adverse selection could have a very serious effect upon the fund's solvency.

Reciprocal Agreements. A problem which confronts most welfare fund trustees, although with varying degrees of urgency, is that workers customarily employed within the jurisdiction of the union locals participating in the fund sometimes are employed outside this jurisdiction. This situation arises when a contractor obtains work outside his regular area and takes a skeleton crew of key personnel with him out of one local's jurisdiction to work in another. It also arises when work is slack in one area. Both contractors and unions in the construction industry are generally in favor of this freedom of movement. In the structural steel business it is essential. It does cause problems insofar as welfare benefits are concerned, however, because employee contributions for welfare and pensions are governed by the labor agreements applicable to the area where the work is performed—not those of the area where the contractor's office or headquarters is located. If the job is a big one and the worker is away from his home territory very long, his eligibility in his home welfare fund is soon impaired or terminated; and he may or may not have qualified in the fund serving the area in which he is currently employed. Actually, the major damage to eligibility occurs when the jobs are small but the frequency of movement out of area is high. There is also a serious problem when pension benefits or post-retirement insurance coverage is predicated upon a number of years of continuous coverage under a single fund.

This problem has been solved by the funds' entering into reciprocal agreements. These agreements usually provide for the transfer of credits from one fund to another and spell out the rules that determine which fund will pay benefits if the worker has earned enough credits through all funds that are parties to the agreement to satisfy the eligibility rules of his "home" fund. Money is transferred sometimes from one fund to another, depending upon the equality of employer contribution rates negotiated in the several areas and the balance of the flow between the several funds. In other words, if a reasonable balance between the funds will usually be attained within a reasonable period of time, most trustees would not agree to the transfer of money. If, however, there were a marked bias in favor of one fund, the only workable solution would be an agreement which provides for the transfer of money.

Prior to making reciprocal arrangements, the fund attorney must determine that the trust agreement gives the trustees the power to enter into reciprocal agreements and that there is no conflict with the collective bargaining agreements. Reasonably typical examples of two types of reciprocal agreements are included in Appendix 23.

Administration

Administrative Functions. There are several ways in which a fund can be administered but, irrespective of the facility chosen, the administrative agency performs the following services:

1. Receives employer reports and contributions and keeps accurate records of hours reported and contributions received;
2. Identifies delinquent employers and reports them to the trustees;
3. Posts employee ledger cards recording hours of work performed each month;
4. Determines and reports periodically the total number of workers eligible for benefits;
5. Determines eligibility of claimants, processes claim forms either for submission to the local insurance claim office or for direct payment from the fund, and forwards claim drafts to employee-claimants;
6. Maintains claim control records as to type of claimant (employee or dependent), type of claim, amount paid and other pertinent information;
7. Maintains a file of worker information cards containing pertinent worker statistics such as date of birth, number of dependents, beneficiary designation and claim record;
8. Issues certificates to workers becoming eligible for benefits, and may be responsible for employee benefit plan handbooks that are distributed to employees;
9. Determines annually the age and dependency status of eligible workers and reports this information to the insurance company;
10. Furnishes the trustees with periodic reports of the fund's operation for use in making decisions regarding fund management;
11. Prepares the reports required by the applicable state and federal laws; and
12. Handles complaints and grievances.

Methods of Administration. The administration of a Taft-Hartley plan is under the direction of the trustees. However, it is not necessary or desirable that the trustees be burdened with routine administrative detail. The day-to-day record keeping can be handled in various ways. There are professional administrators in the business of providing the services required for welfare fund administration. In addition, certain banks provide welfare fund administrative services through their trust departments, and some insurance companies offer administrative services. Then, too, the trustees can establish their own administrative office and hire the personnel required to perform the necessary services.

All of these types of administration fund have been successful, and the selection of one must be based largely on subjective factors. The corporation (bank or insurance company) has the advantage of offering a continuity and a permanence which usually cannot be achieved through an office established by the trustees, unless the trust fund is exceptionally large, or by a professional administrator. The insurance company appears ideally suited to the job, because many of the required functions are regularly performed in the conduct of its insurance business.

To avoid delay in the implementation of the plan, it is important that the method of administration be decided promptly after the welfare fund has been negotiated. For example, employee data should be collected immediately so that benefit costs may be estimated. Furthermore, time is required to prepare the necessary administrative forms. Employer report forms should be distributed to employers promptly so that payments may be started as they first become due. Not only will this encourage good payment habits at the outset, but it may avoid the loss of some payments by contractors from outside the area who are completing jobs within the fund's jurisdiction. Since the employer report forms are usually the basis for initial eligibility, they should start flowing to, and being processed by, the administrator almost immediately following the effective date of the labor agreement. Moreover, if unprocessed employer reports are allowed to accumulate, catching up is a time consuming and expensive job.

Reserve

It is difficult to predict accurately annual income, actual administrative expenses and the cost of benefits for a Taft-Hartley fund. Furthermore, it is desirable that the fund be in a position to extend the normal period of protection provided under the eligibility rules in the event that business conditions should become depressed or substantial unemployment should develop. In addition, the cost and use of medical care has shown a marked tendency to increase, and there appears to be no probability that this trend will change for a number of years to come. Therefore, in a relatively short period, even the present level of certain benefits will increase the insurance costs of a fund that provides medical expense coverage.

To meet these needs and other contingencies, it is generally considered advisable to allocate part of estimated fund income to the accumulation of a reserve. This will be augmented by the initial reserve developed prior to the commencement of benefit payments and by any refunds which may be received from the insurance company because of favorable claim experience. If the plan has been based on reasonable estimates and assumptions and contributions have been accumulated for at least three months prior to commencement of benefits, the initial allocation of 10 per cent of fund income to a reserve will usually prove adequate.

The trustees should determine the maximum reserve they consider reasonable and the length of time in which it will be accumulated. In determining the maximum reserve, consideration should be given to the fund's terminal liability under the eligibility rules. For example, most trustee boards in the construction industry have considered one year's average fund income to be an adequate reserve plateau. In the printing industry generally half that amount has been considered reasonable.

The trustees should not attempt to attain the maximum reserve all at once, since the primary purpose of a fund is to provide benefits for the employees. Probably a goal of reaching the maximum in about five years is reasonable. Once the desired reserve has been attained, the trustees may periodically overspend the current income of the fund for benefits and expenses if a year-end experience refund is anticipated. Most insurance companies will set their premium rates so that they will produce a year-end surplus in most years. This is returned to the trustees in the form of a dividend or experience rating refund. Unless trustees consider these refunds as a part of anticipated income, reserves will continue to increase.

Benefits

General Structuring of Benefits. To develop the benefit plan, information must be available concerning the sex, date of birth and dependency status of the employees. Arrangements for the accumulation of this information should be one of the first items of business when the trustees are appointed. In addition, any statistics available regarding the average number of hours worked each year by the regular employees and the general range of fluctuation will be extremely helpful. The plan of benefits should be designed so that the employee who works the normal number of hours per year earns enough employer contributions to finance the plan. For example, if it is determined that the regular employee works 1,000 hours per year and if the employer contribution is negotiated at $.15 per hour, there will be $150 available to the fund for this regular worker. If 10 per cent of the contribution is allocated to the fund reserve and administrative expenses are estimated at $6 per employee per year, there will be $129 available for benefits. Assuming that the eligibility rules require 1,000 hours per year to qualify for coverage, the trustees are assured that the fund will not be in a deficit position since each eligible member will produce a minimum of $150 income to the fund annually.

Obviously, there will be extra income to the fund because of those employees who work consistently more than the average and also because of those who perform some work but attain eligibility intermittently, if at all. This excess income should not be anticipated in designing benefits, but rather allocated to reserve at least for the first year or so of the fund's existence.

From this point on there is no significant difference between designing a benefit plan for a welfare fund and designing a plan for a single-employer group. It should, however, be recognized that there will be a tendency for employees to use the temporary disability benefits under the welfare fund as unemployment compensation if the benefits provided are very much higher than the state benefit, and there will not be the controls which are usually present in single-employer plans.

Retirement Benefits.[4] Benefits for retired employees are sometimes provided under Taft-Hartley plans, but there are a few special problems which should be considered in this regard. One problem concerns administration, since retired employees tend to be quite mobile, and it is sometimes difficult to keep in touch with them. If a pension plan covers the same general group and deductions can be made from the monthly pension checks, insurance benefits for retired employees can be provided on a contributory basis. If there is no pension plan, insurance benefits for retired employees should be on a noncontributory basis since difficulty in obtaining and handling the employee contributions can be administratively complex and costly. Even under the most favorable conditions the administration will be difficult.

Another very real problem, particularly in the construction industry, is that it is not always easy to tell when the employee has in fact retired. Frequently an employee retires because there is no work available and he is eligible for OASDI benefits. When employment again becomes available, he may return to work but will try to keep his earnings below the point at which he would lose his OASDI income. Under these conditions it is quite possible for a retired employee again to earn eligibility under the fund rules unless special provision has been made. Therefore, eligibility rules for retirees should require: (1) that the employee have attained a certain age (presumably age sixty-five), (2) that he be drawing OASDI benefits (or has made application therefor) and (3) that he complete a request for retired employees coverage in which he agrees to relinquish all rights to eligibility as an active employee, irrespective of work he may perform in the future.

In addition to these requirements, trustees usually require that the

---

[4] While a United States District Court in the case *Kroger Company* v. *Blassie* (225 F. Supp. 300) concluded that the trustees' expenditure of trust funds for the benefit of retired employees was contrary to the provisions of the Taft-Hartley Act, the conclusions reached by the Court are disputable and the case is under appeal.

employee either have been eligible for active benefits for a period of years preceding the date he retires, or that he have been actively employed in the area for a specified period prior to retirement. Unless there is such a requirement, the trustees will find that union members from other areas tend to seek work within the territory covered by their fund when they contemplate retirement.

LEGAL AND TAX ASPECTS

Provisions of State Laws

The insurance laws of most states allow the issuance of both group life and group health insurance policies to the trustees of a fund established by one or more employers and one or more labor unions. Usually, these laws require that a minimum of 100 employees be covered initially, that the plan of insurance be written on a basis whereby its full cost is obtained from employer contributions and that there be an average of five or more employees per employer unit to be covered. These requirements are included in the model definition of group life insurance adopted by the National Association of Insurance Commissioners in 1956.[5] Although there has been no change in the model bill, recent amendments to some state laws have reduced the minimum number of lives to be covered at issue to fifty; employee contributions are often permitted; and the requirement regarding the average number of employees per employer unit has in some instances been eliminated, or reduced to three employees.

Taxation

Employer contributions to welfare funds established for group insurance purposes have been construed as a reasonable and necessary business expense and, therefore, are tax deductible. Moreover, these employer contributions have not been construed as taxable income to the employees. Presumably, this is partly due to the fact that employer contributions for group life and group health insurance have not generally been considered taxable income to the employee. Furthermore, the trust agreements of most funds specifically provide that the employee has no right, title or interest in the contributions made by the employer except as he may qualify for benefits provided by the trust.

There is no specific reference to Taft-Hartley Welfare funds in the Internal Revenue Code of 1954. However, the Internal Revenue Service has ruled that Section 501 (c)(9) is applicable. This section provides that voluntary employee beneficiary associations providing for the payment of life, disability or other benefits to the members of such associations or their dependents are wholly exempt if (a) no part of their net earnings

---

[5] See Appendix 2.

inures (other than through such payments) to the benefit of any private shareholder or individual, and (*b*) 85 per cent or more of the income consists of amounts collected from members and amounts contributed to the association by the employers of the members for the sole purpose of making such payments and meeting such expenses. In subsequent interpretations of the Code, the Internal Revenue Service has made it clear that a trust fund which includes sole proprietors, partners or trustees as beneficiaries cannot qualify as a "voluntary employee beneficiary association" and, therefore, is not entitled to tax exempt status under Section 501 (c) (9).[6]

EXPERIENCE RATING

Most welfare funds provide sufficient spread of risk so that an annual accounting of premiums and claims is justified and, therefore, the funds are handled on a "retention" basis; that is, any excess of billed premium over and above incurred claims plus the retention, or expense, charge is refunded to the welfare fund. There is no basic difference between the experience rating of a welfare fund and the experience rating of a single employer case. However, since there may be a difference between the reaction of a group of labor and management representatives on one hand and one or more corporation executives on the other hand, there may be differences in the psychology of handling the different groups. While executives today are cost conscious whether they are serving as trustees on a welfare fund board or representing a corporation, trustees of a fund are aware of their fiduciary responsibility and, therefore, sometimes do things which they would not do if motivated solely by sound business judgment. For example, they are sometimes inclined to make decisions based upon the short-term rather than long-term considerations; whereas, most corporate executives will be more inclined to act on the long range implications.

Most trustees feel an obligation to utilize fund income completely for benefits. During the early years of the fund, when it is desirable to add to the fund reserve, most trustees do not object to a year-end refund or dividend from the insurance company. Once the maximum desired reserve has been accumulated, however, the year-end refund becomes a source of irritation since it is a problem to convert the additional income into benefits. Either it is necessary for the trustees to overspend during the year in anticipation of a year-end refund or for the insurance company to use rates which contain no margin over expected claims.

The lack of a margin in the rating structure is incompatible with retention experience rating. Nevertheless, because most trustees dislike over-

---

[6] Rev. Rul. 59–28, C. B. 1959 1, 120; and *Kroger Company* v. *Blassie* (225 F. Supp. 300).

spending in anticipation of year-end refunds, severe pressure is exerted on insurance companies to use rates which contain little or no margin for claim fluctuation. To answer this problem some companies have developed a special contingency reserve into which refunds and dividends can be paid in years when favorable fluctuations occur and which can be used to absorb deficits caused by unfavorable fluctuations. If the special contingency reserve is maintained at the appropriate level and rates are set at the level of expected claims plus retention with reasonable accuracy, it is possible for the plan to be administered on a very tight cash flow basis, and the interests of both the trustees and the insurance company are well served.

APPROPRIATE USE OF FUND TECHNIQUE

The welfare fund is of great value in extending employee benefit plans to industries such as the garment and upholstering industries where the employees are highly organized but the employer units are traditionally small and unstable. It is also valuable in the construction and shipping industries where employees tend to work for the industry rather than for a particular employer. Unions, whose members are for the most part employed by large corporations, have from time to time tried to negotiate welfare funds without success. The welfare fund is not appropriate for such groups because it introduces additional administrative expense but cannot contribute the compensating economies due to size since the individual groups are already very large. Furthermore, the "level of benefit"[7] approach to employee benefit bargaining is traditional with these large corporations. Since administrative costs are seldom valued realistically by employers in "level of benefit" bargaining, the unions have not been anxious to negotiate these costs into the price of labor, and this would be the inevitable result of a labor contract providing for a "cents-per-hour" employer contribution to a welfare fund.

PRESENT SCOPE AND FUTURE POTENTIAL

Welfare funds currently represent about 10 per cent of the group insurance market in terms of premium volume and a higher proportion in terms of employees covered. By number of cases the percentage is much smaller.

The early development and growth occurred in the Northeast, Far West and Middle West, substantially in that order. In these areas, the extensiveness of current coverage limits future potential except for small-

---

[7] When the collective bargaining agreement stipulates that the employer will provide a specified plan of benefits, this is called a "level of benefit" agreement. When the employer agrees to contribute a certain number of cents per hour to a fund to be used to provide welfare benefits as determined by the trustees, it is referred to as a "cents-per-hour" agreement.

sized groups. There is still significant potential in the South and Southwest. Since the welfare fund is by definition a creature of collective bargaining, its potential in a particular area is determined by the extent to which unions are effectively organized.

SELECTED REFERENCES

BLAKEY, G. R. *Welfare and Pension Plan Disclosure Act Amendments of 1962,* 38 Notre Dame Lawyer, 1963, pp. 263–87.

BUREAU OF NATIONAL AFFAIRS, INC. *Federal-State Regulation of Welfare Funds.* Washington, D.C., 1958.

FOUNDATION ON EMPLOYEE HEALTH, MEDICAL CARE, AND WELFARE, INC. *Health Plan Administration.* New York, 1961.

ISAACSON, W. J. *Employee Welfare and Pension Plans: Regulation and Protection of Employee Rights,* 59 Colum. L. Rev., 1959, pp. 96–124.

McCOLLOCH, MURRAY. *Group Insurance Trusts.* Occidental Life Insurance Company of California, 1962.

MILLIMAN, W. A. "Group Insurance for Employee Welfare Trust Funds," *The Journal of the American Society of Chartered Life Underwriters,* Vol. XI (Spring, 1957), pp. 156–72.

NATIONAL FOUNDATION OF HEALTH, WELFARE, AND PENSION PLANS, INC. *Textbook for Welfare, Pension Trustees and Administrators,* Vols. I–VI. Elm Grove, Wis.

"The Taft-Hartley Welfare and Pension Trust—An Emerging Legal Entity," 35 N.Y. Univ. Law Rev., 1960, pp. 1181–89.

Chapter 34

WHOLESALE AND FRANCHISE INSURANCE

BY JAMES W. ROSE AND CARROLL J. McBRIDE

The terms "wholesale" and "franchise" have been used interchangeably at times, but more commonly wholesale denotes a plan of life insurance, and franchise denotes a plan of health insurance. These meanings will apply to wholesale and franchise plans which will be discussed separately in this chapter.

WHOLESALE LIFE INSURANCE

Employer-Employee Plans

The development of group life insurance and the social and economic benefits which resulted from it soon prompted a demand for a similar simple and economical plan of insurance for companies with too few employees to qualify for group insurance. As a result, a few years after group insurance became available there was created a plan called wholesale life insurance. This is a plan under which a number of individual life insurance policies are issued at special rates to certain types of groups not eligible for group insurance. Wholesale insurance plans usually utilize special policies and constitute a separate class of business for the insurer.

Wholesale insurance is intended to be similar to group insurance but sufficiently different so as not to fall within the scope of statutory restrictions applicable to group insurance. Thus, wholesale insurance is similar to group insurance in benefits provided, plan design, premium payment requirements and collection procedures, but it is dissimilar in its individual underwriting aspects and the use of individual insurance policies. As the terms "group" and "wholesale" commonly are used, the principal distinction between them is that group insurance is a plan insuring a number of persons under one master policy, whereas wholesale insurance is a plan insuring a number of persons under individual policies.

Basic Characteristics. When wholesale insurance is used to insure an employer-employee group, the coverage generally is yearly renewable term insurance, and each insured receives an individual policy which includes the standard policy provisions. Usually premium waiver and double indemnity benefits are provided.

The insurer may reserve the right to decline to renew the insurance in states so permitting by giving each insured at least thirty-one days' notice of its intention not to renew. Such right might be exercised if the number insured under the plan drops below either a specified number, for example, two or four, or a specified percentage of the eligible employees, for example, 75 or 85 per cent. More commonly, the insurance is noncancellable by the designated employer during the active employment of the insured, except for nonpayment of premiums. In some plans the insurance may be renewable either for the original amount or for a reduced amount during retirement, provided the retired employee receives retirement income from the employer or continues to be compensated as a result of service with the employer. Whether the insurance is canceled by action of the insurer or as a result of termination of employment, it is convertible to a level premium policy under essentially the same conditions as are applicable to group life insurance.

Generally, premium rates for wholesale insurance are somewhat lower than those for similar individual insurance but are somewhat higher than those for group insurance. Increases in premiums due to increasing age may be made annually but more commonly are on a step-rate basis by quinquennial age groupings. Sometimes premiums are level at the younger ages, for example, through age thirty-four or thirty-nine, and increase at age thirty-five or forty and each five years thereafter. Premium schedules may be guaranteed during the continuance of the policy, or the insurer may reserve the right in states so permitting to increase or decrease the premium schedule as experience warrants. Such adjustments, however, would apply to the class of business as a whole, rather than on an individual case basis.

The employer is expected to pay the entire premium for each insured employee or the amount of the premium in excess of a nominal employee contribution, for example, $.70 per $1,000 of insurance per month (except in Texas where the maximum permissible employee contribution is $.40 per $1,000 of insurance per month).[1] The employee contribution usually remains level regardless of the age of the insured. If employee contributions are required, a specified percentage, usually at least 75 per cent of all eligible employees, must participate. In noncontributory plans, 100 per cent participation normally is required. A minimum premium of $25 per month usually is required for each plan.

---

[1] A discussion of the particular regulations applicable in Texas appears later in this chapter.

The amount of insurance may be the same for all employees or may be graded by occupational or salary groups or by service, similar to group insurance, and may range from a minimum of $2,000 or $4,000 to a maximum of $20,000 or $30,000 for each employee. Larger amounts may be available subject to more stringent underwriting.

Underwriting. Some of the factors which are important in the underwriting of group and individual life insurance also are important considerations in the underwriting of wholesale insurance plans. As in the case of group insurance, the underwriter is concerned with the type and total number of employees, the number eligible for insurance, stability of employment, possible occupational hazards, and the plan of insurance, or formula, requested by the employer. The formula is very important because it specifies the classes of eligible employees and the amount of insurance available for each class.

To minimize selection against the insurer, each proposed insured must apply for the amount of insurance for which he is eligible under the formula applicable to the plan. Furthermore, each proposed insured must sign an application which includes health questions and is subject to individual underwriting. The type of application required for wholesale insurance, however, usually is much less comprehensive than that required for individual insurance, and the underwriting rules applicable to wholesale insurance are much more liberal than those applicable to individual.

It is the objective to accept all who apply for insurance under a wholesale insurance plan on the basis of the health information in the application, but in almost all plans the insurer reserves the right to request further evidence of insurability, including a medical examination, and to reduce the amount of insurance for, or to decline to insure, any proposed insured. Generally, there are no substandard ratings for physical impairments, but substandard extra premiums may be required for occupational hazards. An individual who has an impairment may be accepted at standard premium rates so far as physical condition is concerned either for the amount of insurance requested or for a reduced amount, or he may be declined altogether. Furthermore, the entire plan may be declined because there is a disproportionate number of employees in the higher age range, or because the medical evidence for a disproportionate number of employees is unsatisfactory. The basis of acceptance depends upon the total number to be insured, the number of physically impaired risks and the nature and severity of the impairments. Where very few people are to be insured, the underwriting obviously must be less lenient than for larger groups.

Employer-Employee Market for Wholesale Insurance. Wholesale insurance was available originally where ten to forty-nine employees of a single employer were to be insured at date of issue, and reduction in the number of lives required for group insurance from fifty to ten, or even fewer lives in some states, has greatly narrowed the market for wholesale insurance among employer-employee groups. Nevertheless, wholesale insurance still is important, and there is a growing demand for it for smaller groups, usually where four to nine lives (subject to a statutory minimum of ten lives in Arizona and five lives in Arkansas, Montana, Oklahoma, Nebraska, Iowa and Texas)[2] are to be insured on the effective date of the plan. Furthermore, some plans insuring as many as twenty-four lives are written by companies which will not write group insurance for fewer than twenty-five lives. Health insurance for employees and their wives and dependent children commonly may be provided in conjunction with life insurance under wholesale plans today, so it is possible to provide a package of protection for these small employer-employee groups.

Some insurers have found wholesale insurance plans for small groups to be good "feeders" for group insurance, because the number insured under many of these small plans will increase to a level where the plan may be changed to group insurance. Another, but less common, use for wholesale insurance is to supplement group insurance in states where group insurance benefit amounts are subject to statutory maxima. In such cases, wholesale insurance can be an effective means of providing larger amounts of insurance for certain classes of employees. The issuance of superimposed wholesale insurance apparently has not as yet been challenged as a violation of the group insurance statutes, but such superimposed insurance is not available in Nebraska and New York, where wholesale insurance may not be written as a supplement to group insurance, and is restricted in Texas, where wholesale insurance may not be issued in conjunction with group insurance so as to exceed the group insurance statutory maximum. In any event, the tax consequences of wholesale insurance serve as a deterrent to a more widespread development of this type of coverage, particularly for large amounts of insurance.

Tax Aspects of Employer-Employee Wholesale Insurance. It would seem equitable to treat premiums paid for wholesale and group term life insurance the same for federal income tax purposes, but the tax consequences to employees seem to be less favorable under wholesale plans. In general, premiums paid by an employer for group term insurance on employees are deductible as a business expense;[3] and the employer's contributions for the first $50,000 of such insurance payable to employees' personal beneficiaries are not taxable income to the employees.[4]

Premiums paid by an employer for wholesale insurance likewise are deductible for federal income tax purposes as additional compensation if

---

[2] The statutory minima in these and other states are discussed in a later section of this chapter.

[3] IRC Sec. 162(a)(1); L.O. 1014, 2 CB 88; Rev. Rul. 56–400, 1956–2 CB 116.

[4] IRC Sec. 79(a); Reg. Sec. 1.61–2(d)(2); L.O. 1014, 2 CB 88; Rev. Rul. 54–165, 1954–1 CB 17.

the employee owns the contract, the employer has no interest in the contract, directly or indirectly, and the premium payments constitute reasonable additional compensation for services rendered.[5] But there seems to be no doubt that the employer's contribution for the insurance constitutes taxable income to the insured if the insured can name the beneficiary (or if the proceeds are payable to his estate or named beneficiary) and the employer has no substantial ownership rights in the contract.[6]

There have been reports of local Internal Revenue Service rulings on individual wholesale insurance plans which would allow them to be treated the same as a group term insurance plan for federal income tax purposes. There has been no general ruling from the Treasury Department, however, authorizing such treatment, and it seems doubtful that the Treasury Department ever will rule that an employer's contributions for wholesale insurance are nontaxable to the insured employees.

Association Plans

Association insurance is not a new idea. Many of the old guilds had some form of association insurance, and fraternal insurance itself was a type of association insurance. As far back as the 1920's, wholesale insurance plans similar to those written today were available for associations, but in recent years there has been a tremendous growth in association wholesale insurance. This has been due to two principal reasons. First, the great popularity of group life insurance focused the attention of associations on the value of such insurance both as a device to increase membership and as an opportunity to provide members with insurance not available to them individually, or available only at a higher cost. Second, the popularity and remarkable growth of mass marketing has prompted some insurance companies to cultivate new markets for wholesale insurance. However, in the absence of an employer-employee or creditor-debtor relationship, conventional group life insurance cannot be written in some states, and there are some companies which will not write group insurance for associations even in the absence of statutory restrictions. As a result, various association wholesale plans have been created.

Basic Characteristics. Coverage under association wholesale plans may be very similar to group life insurance or may more closely resemble individual term insurance, and there is a wide variation in benefits provided by these plans. Furthermore, plans may be altered or new plans devised to meet competitive situations or unusual insurance needs. There are, however, certain points of similarity in the plans more commonly written by the companies active in this market.

---

[5] IRC Secs. 162(a)(1) and 264(a)(1); G.C.M. 8432, IX–2 CB 114.

[6] Reg. Sec. 1.61–2(d)(2); G.C.M. 8432, IX–2 CB 114.

Customarily, the form of insurance is yearly renewable term insurance expiring at a specified age, usually age seventy but in some plans as high as age eighty. Each insured receives an individual policy which includes the regular standard provisions. Usually a premium waiver benefit is included, and in some plans there also is a double indemnity benefit.

The insurer may reserve the privilege of nonrenewal for specified reasons, such as adoption by the association of another similar plan or failure to maintain insurance on a specified number or percentage of the eligible members, but in most plans the insurance is renewable at the option of the insured. The term insurance is convertible upon termination of membership or termination of insurance and in some plans is convertible without evidence of insurability during membership. Conversion during membership may be available at any time, after a specified period of time, for example, five years, or after attainment of a specified age. In some plans, conversion during membership is encouraged by payment of full first-year and renewal commissions on converted policies; in an occasional plan, the term insurance automatically converts at the end of a specified period, usually ten years, and commissions are payable on such conversions. Conversion may be permitted to any permanent form of individual insurance issued by the insurer at time of conversion or may be restricted to a specified form.

In addition to coverage for the association members, insurance on spouses and dependent children, likewise on the yearly renewable term form, is provided on an optional basis under many plans. The insurance for children may be available for those between the ages of fourteen days and twenty-one years, or between the ages of six months and twenty-one years, or six months and twenty-three years. Term insurance on the lives of the spouses and children usually is convertible if insurance terminates due to the death of the insured member, or if the insured becomes eligible for and is converting his own basic insurance, or in the case of children if insurance terminates because of attainment of the maximum age limit or for any other reason.

Premium rates are shown in each policy and usually are guaranteed for the duration of the policy, although some plans provide for increases or decreases in states so permitting at the option of the insurer. Where the insurer reserves the right to increase or decrease premiums, any such changes ordinarily would apply to the class of business as a whole and not on a case basis. However, large cases may be experience rated if all wholesale insurance plans of the same class are so rated by the insurer. Premiums may be paid solely by the association or jointly by the insured members and the association, but more commonly they are paid solely by the insured members. It is not economically feasible for the insurer to bill and collect premiums individually. Hence, the collection of premiums, which customarily are payable annually or semiannually because more frequent payments are not practical, usually is the responsibility of the association. Some large insurance agencies and brokers who specialize in the sale of association wholesale insurance plans, however, have facilities to handle premium collections.

Premiums may vary by age or age groupings. Usually, premiums are level at the younger ages, for example, through age twenty-nine, and thereafter are on a step-rate basis by quinquennial age groupings. However, in such plans the premium increases at the higher ages are substantial and might prompt quinquennial re-evaluation of the insurance by the insureds with a consequent probable increase in the lapse rate. Therefore, as a variation, the plan may provide for reducing insurance with level premiums or a combination of both plans may be utilized, with level insurance and increasing premiums to a specified age, for example, age fifty-five or sixty, and with decreasing insurance and level or decreasing premiums thereafter.

As an illustration, a plan commonly written provides level basic insurance in the amount of $10,000 or $20,000 with level premiums through age twenty-nine and with an increase in premiums at age thirty and each five years thereafter. As a variation of this plan, the basic insurance might be in the amount of $10,000 through age twenty-nine with such amount reducing at age thirty and every five years thereafter. Level premiums would be maintained through such reductions in insurance. A third plan which is commonly written provides level basic insurance for $25,000 through age fifty-four, reducing to $20,000 at age fifty-five, $15,000 at age sixty and $10,000 at age sixty-five. Through such reductions, substantial variations in premiums at the higher ages are avoided. In the last plan, the insured member has the option of maintaining his original amount of insurance in force by payment of the proportionately higher premium.

Where insurance is available for spouses, the maximum amount usually is $5,000. For dependent children, the maximum amount usually is $2,500, except that for children between the ages of two weeks and six months the maximum amount usually is $500, automatically increasing to the higher amount at age six months.

Under many plans, members below a specified age, for example, age sixty, who apply for the basic insurance also may apply on an optional basis for additional supplemental insurance on the same form and at the same premium rates. Supplemental insurance, which usually is not available for amounts in excess of $40,000, generally is issued under one or more separate contracts.

Despite an expected higher mortality, premium rates under association wholesale insurance plans are lower, and sometimes substantially lower, than would be charged for comparable individual insurance purchased outside the plan. This results from an expected savings in acquisition and administrative expenses. Part of the savings is passed on to the members in the form of lower premiums, and part is passed on in the form of more liberal underwriting treatment.

Market for Association Wholesale Insurance. Prospects for association wholesale insurance plans include professional associations (for example, associations of doctors, lawyers, engineers, teachers, accountants, architects, dentists, pharmacists and others), trade and farm associations, fraternal organizations, civil service and other employee associations, service organizations and unions. In more recent years, there has been considerable activity in promoting the sale of association wholesale plans to various associations of military personnel, veterans' associations and college fraternities. The preferred prospects are professional associations, organizations which will contribute a portion of the premium, and employee associations where there will be no contribution by the organization but where arrangements can be made for deduction of premiums from pay.

Installation. For successful development, the association should have a high degree of solidarity, that is, a concentration of members within a small geographical area, a strong central administrative staff which will vigorously promote enrollment, and facilities for the efficient collection of premiums. Results with any plan will depend upon these factors and on the method of solicitation. Solicitation by mail generally is agreed to be ineffective, although a vigorous follow-up campaign by letter and telephone will improve results. Personal solicitation is much more satisfactory. Participation substantially exceeding 50 per cent of the members has been reported in occasional cases, but there have been many plans where participation fell substantially below 50 per cent, sometimes down to as low as 10 per cent. Obviously, without adequate participation a high degree of adverse selection may result.

Underwriting. The underwriting of association wholesale insurance plans involves some of the considerations which are of importance in the underwriting of wholesale insurance plans for employer-employee groups, but there are several important points of dissimilarity. First, in association plans there usually are many more persons eligible for insurance. Second, in association plans there usually is no third party, as in the case of an employer-employee plan, to pay all or a substantial portion of the cost of the insurance, and hence there is a much greater chance for selection against the insurer. Third, in an employer-employee group those to be insured usually can be solicited in one location, whereas members of associations may be spread over a wide geographical area, perhaps over the entire country.

As in the case of employer-employee groups, the underwriter is concerned with the type and total number of members and the plan, or formula, requested by the association which specifies the amount of basic insurance to be available for members in the various age groupings. Other important considerations are the type of association and length of time it has been in existence, the willingness and capability of the administrative staff of the association to assist in promoting enrollment and to handle administrative functions, the extent of the geographical area over which the members are scattered and the experience and facilities of the agency promoting the sale of the plan. The importance of these factors cannot be overestimated since they have a significant bearing on the successful enrollment, underwriting and administration of a plan. Some underwriters feel that in order for a plan to be successful the membership should be confined within the borders of a single state.

The insurer must guard against organizations which were formed, or whose membership has been expanded, primarily for the purpose of securing insurance. It also must guard against associations which have maintained a self-insured benefit plan and are seeking to turn such plan over to an insurance company. Frequently in such situations there has been little or no recent enrollment of new members, with the result that the average age of members may be high and the death rate correspondingly high.

To be attractive, association wholesale insurance plans must involve a minimum amount of individual underwriting. Usually new plans involve a guaranteed issue offer which provides that if a specified number or percentage of the eligible members through age sixty (sometimes age sixty-five) apply within a specified enrollment period, for example, thirty, sixty or ninety days, or even six months, all will be accepted regardless of physical condition. Depending upon the number of members, the required percentage of participation may range from a low of 20 per cent to a high of 75 per cent. In some companies, the percentage varies by age groupings, for example, 30 per cent for members age forty and under, 40 per cent for members ages forty-one to fifty, inclusive, and 50 per cent for members ages fifty-one to sixty, inclusive. Or all may be accepted if a specified number, for example, 500 members age sixty or under, or 750 members age sixty-five or under, apply.

To minimize selection against the insurer, each proposed insured must apply for the amount of basic insurance for which he is eligible under the formula applicable to the plan, and each proposed insured also must sign a simple nonmedical application which includes several health questions. If insurance for the spouse and dependent children is involved, several health questions pertaining to such dependents also must be answered.

As in the case of wholesale insurance for employer-employee groups, the underwriting of association wholesale insurance is liberal, and while it is the objective to underwrite all who apply on the basis of the health information in the application, the insurer reserves the right, except in plans which meet specified guaranteed issue requirements, to request further evidence of insurability, including a medical examination, and to decline to insure any proposed insured. Generally, no substandard extra premiums are required for physical impairments, and in the preliminary underwriting review an individual who is physically impaired may be accepted at standard premium rates or may be declined. Cases involving physical impairments are resolved on the basis of the total number to be insured, the number of physically impaired risks and the nature and severity of the impairments. Obviously, where many people are to be insured the underwriting can be more liberal than for smaller groups.

If the percentage or number required under the guaranteed issue offer apply initially, individual underwriting will be waived, and the entire group will be accepted. If the required percentage or number do not apply initially, the applications will be subject to preliminary individual underwriting as outlined above, but if the guaranteed issue requirements subsequently are met within the specified enrollment period, any who were rejected on preliminary review will then be accepted. Where a guaranteed issue program is in effect, members who become eligible after the plan is placed in force usually are accepted without individual underwriting provided they submit application within a specified enrollment period.

Guaranteed issue treatment does not apply to any supplemental insurance which may be available on an optional basis. Generally, the underwriting of supplemental insurance is considerably more restrictive than for the basic insurance.

Marketing. Association wholesale insurance is written principally by insurance agencies and brokers who are specialists in the field of mass-produced business. They have had experience in selecting prospects, designing plans, soliciting members and servicing the business thereafter. Some of these agencies and brokerage organizations have elaborate facilities for premium collection and payment of claims. Insurance companies active in this field usually will not engage in the extensive and expensive work involved in the development of a large association wholesale insurance plan unless the agent or broker has the experience and facilities necessary for successful handling and a reasonably strong control of the business.

Special Problems in Connection with Association Wholesale Insurance. To an insurance company, association wholesale insurance presents many problems. Underwriting is difficult, the business is highly competitive, and competition may result in pressure for lower rates, more liberal benefits and greater leniency in underwriting. Expenses of acquisition and administration are greater than for employer-employee groups of the same size, and plans for very large associations involve much work and many problems to write and are likely to be expensive and time consuming to administer. Mortality may be expected to be higher than on business subject to regular individual underwriting but may stay within reasonable limits if participation is maintained at a satisfactory level. This may be difficult, however, particularly where there are overlapping plans as, for example, where similar benefits are available through membership in national, state and county associations. With the best of results, profit margins are likely to be thin, but volume may be very large. If a case is profitable, the business may be switched to another insurer which offers lower premiums or other advantages.

Controversial Aspects. There is general agreement that wholesale insurance for small employer-employee groups has served a useful purpose. Association wholesale insurance, however, has been the subject of considerable controversy within the insurance industry.

One advantage of association wholesale insurance is that the coverage is available with a minimum of individual underwriting, and thus members may receive insurance otherwise unobtainable. There also is a price advantage as compared with individual life insurance. One disadvantage of association wholesale insurance is that the members do not have the personal services of an agent to the same extent as in the purchase of insurance outside the plan, and their beneficiaries may not have any personal service in the event of a claim. Other important disadvantages are that periodic substantial increases in premiums or decreases in the amount of insurance may be required at the higher ages, and term insurance may involve a substantially higher premium outlay over a period of years than individual permanent insurance. In addition, some insurers reserve the right to cancel the term insurance if a sufficient number of members do not maintain their insurance in force.

The following comments from a report by the National Association of Life Underwriters summarize the problems that organization feels are inherent in association group and wholesale coverage.

Association Group insurance is, for the most part, the same as regular Group Life insurance on the annual renewable term plan. The essential difference is that premiums are paid by the insureds alone, without any contribution by an employer. This introduces the inherent problems of assessment insurance. These problems are attempted to be met by decreasing the insurance by age, using premium rates that vary by age rather than an average rate for all ages and by terminating the insurance at some advanced age. . . . Association Group life insurance—whether it be provided under a master Group policy or under individual policies issued on the basis of Group underwriting—deserves very serious and cautious treatment so long as the member-pay-all principle is incorporated in such plans.[7]

Proponents of association wholesale insurance contend (1) that members of associations adopting insurance plans, in general, are inadequately insured, and point to the rapid growth of association wholesale insurance

---

[7] "An Interpretive Analysis—NALU's Comments on the Study of Association Group Term and Wholesale Life Insurance," *Life Association News,* Vol. LVIII, No. 9 (September, 1963), pp. 23–34.

as evidence of this fact; (2) that in today's economy, much term insurance is being sold individually to meet insurance needs. Consequently, they feel that association wholesale insurance serves a useful purpose.

Due to both the problematical and controversial aspects of association wholesale insurance, many insurance companies will not write such business. Some companies have experimented with association wholesale insurance and have withdrawn from the field; other companies have curtailed their wholesale activities. Most of the association wholesale insurance business written today is placed in a few companies which seem to have found the answer to successful marketing and underwriting.

Regardless of differences of opinion as to the merits of association wholesale insurance, it undoubtedly will continue to be sold by many companies. There is a demand for such insurance, and the demand is being met, but there appears to be no disposition on the part of the majority of companies to enter this field. It is doubtful that this trend will change in view of the increasing opposition of agents' organizations to association wholesale insurance.

Legal Restrictions on Wholesale Insurance

By the early 1920's, wholesale insurance was being widely issued, but, presumably because such plans utilized individual contracts and the volume written was small as compared with individual and group insurance, there were few restrictions placed upon it then by insurance regulatory authorities. More recently, however, wholesale insurance has been given greater official attention in some states.

Because wholesale insurance is not generally regarded as group insurance, it would seem logical that it need not comply with the group insurance laws. The question then arises, however, as to whether it violates the anti-discriminatory laws applicable to individual insurance. Actually, wholesale insurance has been challenged on both grounds but more frequently on the grounds of discrimination. While any such questions could have been disposed of easily by the enactment of laws treating wholesale insurance as a separate class of insurance, only a few states have done so.

At the present time, fourteen states have imposed significant restrictions on wholesale insurance. It will be noted that the restrictions usually take the form of limitations on the type and size of the group for which wholesale insurance may be issued, on the amounts of insurance which may be provided and on the method by which the plan may be financed.

North Carolina. The law relating to wholesale insurance in North Carolina was passed in 1947 and now reads as follows:

Employee life insurance is hereby declared to be that plan of life insurance other than salary savings life insurance under which individual policies are issued to the employees of any employer where such policies are issued on the life of more than one employee at date of issue. Premiums for such policies shall be paid by the employer or the trustee of a fund established by the employer either wholly from the employer's funds, or funds contributed by him, or partly from such funds and partly from funds contributed by the insured employees.[8]

Arizona, Arkansas, Idaho, Montana and Oklahoma.[9] Laws enacted since 1947 in the states of Arizona, Arkansas, Idaho, Montana and Oklahoma use language similar to the North Carolina law, but differ on the number of employees who may be insured at date of issue. The present requirements are as follows: Arizona, ten to forty-nine, inclusive; Idaho, four or more; Arkansas, Montana and Oklahoma, five or more. Of the foregoing states, only Oklahoma permits payment of premiums wholly from funds contributed by the insureds.

Nebraska.[10] Individual life insurance policies may be issued on a wholesale basis in the state of Nebraska to the employees of a common employer where five to forty lives are to be insured at date of issue. Inclusion of individual proprietors or partners and directors of corporate employers, if devoting substantial time to the business, is expressly authorized. Employee-pay-all plans are expressly forbidden. Wholesale insurance may not be used to supplement group insurance nor group insurance to supplement wholesale insurance. The maximum amount of term life insurance which may be issued under a wholesale policy or policies is $20,000.

Iowa.[11] In the state of Iowa, individual life insurance policies may be issued at reduced rates to employees of a common employer covering five or more lives, and premiums may be paid wholly or in part by the employer. In addition, life insurance policies under a wholesale plan also may be issued at reduced rates covering members of an association. An "association" includes a labor union, trade association, association of employees, industrial association or professional association organized and operating more than two years for purposes other than procuring insurance. An association plan must cover at least 50 per cent of the insurable members, but not less than ten. Premiums may be paid entirely from funds of the association, entirely from funds of the members or partly from funds of each.

A term policy renewable only during the continuation of employment or membership must provide for conversion after termination of employment or membership. If written on any basis other than term insurance, it

---

[8] *Gen. Stat. of North Carolina*, Sec. 58–211.2 (1960 Repl.).

[9] *Arizona Rev. Stat. 1956 Ann.*, Sec. 20–1276; *Arkansas Stat. Ann.*, Sec. 66–3520 (1963 Supp.); *Idaho Code Ann.*, Sec. 41–2024; *Rev. Codes of Montana, 1947 Ann.*, Sec. 40–3922; *Oklahoma Stat. Ann.*, Title 36, Sec. 4111.

[10] *Rev. Stat. of Nebraska*, 1960, Secs. 44–1607.01 and 44–1607.02.

[11] *Iowa Code 1963 Ann.*, Secs. 509.4 and 509.14.

must give the policyholder the right to continue his policy upon termination of membership by paying renewal premiums which may be increased to the normal individual life insurance rate.

California.[12] The California law, effective September 15, 1961, defines wholesale insurance as a life insurance plan under which a number of individual life insurance policies are issued at special rates to a selected group. A special rate is any rate lower than that shown in the issuing insurance company's manual for individually issued policies of the same type and to insureds of the same class.

The law prohibits issuance of wholesale insurance in California unless the individuals to be insured are members of a professional association, employees of a common employer or affiliated employers, or unless the insurance is made available in connection with an indebtedness or a contract of sale. "Employees" include individual proprietors or partners. A professional association is one whose membership is restricted to one or more of the licensed professions, such as medicine, dentistry, pharmacy, law and accountancy. Any individual plan or policy existing before the effective date of the law need not be changed, but no individual may thereafter become insured for more than $25,000 under any such plan unless written in connection with a professional association, an indebtedness, a contract of sale or a pension plan.

Texas.[13] Under a law enacted in Texas in 1961, no policy of wholesale life insurance may be issued or delivered in the state unless it conforms to the requirements of the law. Wholesale life insurance is defined as a term life insurance plan under which a number of individual policies are issued at special rates to a selected group. A special rate is any rate lower than that in the issuing insurance company's manual for individually issued policies of the same type and available to insureds of the same class. Wholesale life insurance may be issued to the employees of a common employer or employers, members of a labor union or unions, or members of a credit union or credit unions, covering in each case at date of issue not less than five employees or members. An insured person may not contribute more than $.40 per $1,000 of insurance per month. No term insurance may be issued on a wholesale basis which, together with any other term life insurance issued on the same basis or on a group basis, exceeds the $20,000/$40,000 limit as that limit is defined for group life insurance. An individual application must be taken for each policy, and the insurer may rely upon the applicant's statements as to any similar coverage on his life.

Each policy may contain a provision to the effect that the policy is renewable at the option of the insurer only, that insurance terminates

---

[12] *West's Ann. California Insurance Code,* Secs. 10200 and 10200.5.

[13] *Vernon's Civ. Stat. of Texas, Ann.,* Insurance Code, Art. 3.50, Sec. 1(6).

upon termination of employment and that a person eligible for insurance must furnish evidence of individual insurability satisfactory to the insurer as a condition to coverage. If the insurance ceases on termination of employment or membership, each insured must have the right to convert similar to that required for group insurance. The law does not alter, impair or invalidate any policy or wholesale plan issued prior to the effective date of the law provided such policy or plan was legal and valid when issued.

Wisconsin.[14]   Under a Wisconsin law which became effective January 8, 1964, wholesale life insurance is defined as that form of insurance covering three or more members of any "franchise unit" under individual policies. Premiums are to be paid to the insurer periodically by the franchise unit, with or without payroll deductions, or by some designated person acting for the franchise unit or members. A franchise unit includes any governmental corporation, unit, agency or department thereof; any employer, whether a corporation, partnership or individual; any association, including a labor unit, having a constitution or bylaws and having existed for at least two years and having been formed in good faith for purposes other than to obtain insurance; and a processing plant to which raw materials are supplied by individuals. "Member" means an employee, officer, manager, partner or proprietor, a member of an association or labor unit or a supplier to a processing plant.

The amount of insurance issued under a wholesale insurance plan must not exceed the $20,000/$40,000 limit as that limit is defined for group life insurance. Insurers may file rates for wholesale life insurance which reflect a differential from the rates charged for identical policies issued on the individual basis provided there is no discrimination between the groups to which wholesale insurance is issued. Term life insurance renewable only during employment or membership must provide for conversion similar to the requirement for group life insurance. No policy of wholesale life insurance may be delivered in Wisconsin after the effective date of the law unless it conforms to the requirements of the law.

Florida.   The anti-discrimination law of the state of Florida expressly authorizes the issuance of wholesale insurance with reduced rates.[15] In 1930, the Attorney General reached the conclusion that the law prohibiting discrimination between individuals of the same class and equal expectation of life, excepting group life insurance, did not preclude issuance of wholesale insurance provided there is no discrimination within the class. There was no restriction as to number of lives.[16] In 1956, the Attorney

---

[14] *West's Wisconsin Statutes Ann.*, Sec. 206.64.

[15] *Florida Stat. Ann.*, Sec. 626.0612(4).

[16] Florida A.G.O., May 10, 1930, *The Weekly Underwriter Insurance Department Service* (Florida, 1930), p. 13.

General expressed the opinion that, within certain limits, wholesale insurance may be issued in Florida but concluded that, since the policy form then under consideration was dependent for renewal upon a stated level of participation of an employer's employees, it "reasonably offends the intent" of the group life insurance laws and should not be approved.[17]

Bulletin 201, "Wholesale Life Insurance—Filings with Department," included the following:

> This Department is of the opinion that the intent of the legislature of the State of Florida as contained in the Group Life laws is being circumvented by certain types of mass coverages which we designate as Quasi-Group coverages. The general characteristic of these plans is to keep most of the qualities of Group Insurance but to eliminate the master policies and certificates for an individual Term policy. This change supposedly makes the Group law inapplicable to the plan even though it operates like Group Insurance.[18]

In 1961, the Florida Insurance Department issued a bulletin, "Submission and Approval of Group Life Forms," which included the following statement in Item B(e): "No Quasi-Groups using individual renewable yearly term policies for associations or for any group which does not fit the group life law will be accepted (Bulletin 201)."[19] The insurance department later issued a letter reading as follows:

> Life Insurers desiring to file individual life forms offered on an employer-employee basis will do so in accordance with the following instructions:
> 1. No such form may be filed, referred to or sold as Group, Baby Group, Wholesale, Franchise, or other similar title which would denote that this term coverage to be anything other than an individual policy.
> 2. Since this is an individual term policy, a separate application, signed by each insured, must be taken by a licensed agent, the sale being individually underwritten by the insurer, and the form containing a conversion privilege.
> 3. Bulletin 201 of this Department dated March 11, 1957, must be satisfactorily answered.
> 4. It can be issued only to unaffiliated individuals or on an employer-employee relationship basis.
> 5. There must be no differential treatment of premiums between an unaffiliated individual insured and an insured who is a member of an employer-employee situation.
> 6. The renewal of the policy cannot be based upon any requirement as to minimum number of employees or minimum percentage of participation.
> 7. Group forms cannot be substituted for this individual coverage.
> 8. In cases of employer participation in payment of premiums, the insurer will furnish the insured employee within 31 days notice that the employer has

---

[17] Florida A.G.O., No. 056–16, January 18, 1956, *The Weekly Underwriter Insurance Department Service* (Florida, 1956), p. 10; and *LIAA Group Insurance and Group Annuity Manual*, Vol. II, Florida, Sec. 10:619.

[18] Florida Ins. Dept. Bulletin No. 201, March 11, 1957, *LIAA Group Insurance and Group Annuity Manual*, Vol. II, Florida, Sec. 10:618.

[19] Florida Ins. Dept. Bulletin No. 314, August 8, 1961, *LIAA Group Insurance and Group Annuity Manual*, Vol. II, Florida, Sec. 10:616.

ceased contributing toward the coverage in order that the insured may pay entire premium and continue for the balance of term period.

9. In a contributory case the policy cannot terminate the coverage because of cancellation of employer-insurer agreement. They must provide for conversion of the coverage or for new individual rates (like salary saving).

10. Policy cannot terminate the coverage because of termination of employment in contributory cases. They must provide for the employee to take the coverage with him at a possible new rate (like salary savings) or conversion to another policy.[20]

New York. Standards for wholesale life insurance in New York State, effective January 27, 1965, were forwarded with a letter dated January 25, 1965.[21] The effective date later was changed to March 27, 1965.[22] These standards are very comprehensive, and the following description is merely a general statement of the principal provisions.

Under the standards, wholesale life insurance means that form of term life insurance provided, with or without evidence of insurability, by (1) individual policies which are made available under a plan sponsored by (a) an employer, (b) an association consisting of persons having the same or similar occupation or profession, (c) a union, (d) two or more employers under common control, or (e) an association of civil service employees; or (2) individual policies which are made available to individuals supplying or delivering material to a central point of collection; under which the insured's right to renew his policy, with or without other permissible renewal conditions, is contingent upon a specified employment, membership or supplier status. Premium collection by payroll deduction does not, in and of itself, cause a policy to be classified as wholesale life insurance.

The amount of insurance provided must be based upon a plan which will preclude selection of disproportionate amounts of insurance by certain individuals. The classes of persons who may be insured consist of (1) for employer-employee plans: (a) not less than two nor more than twenty-five employees of an employer, except that in contributory cases 75 per cent of the number of employees may not exceed twenty-five ("employees" is defined to include directors, officers, proprietors, partners and retired employees), (b) two or more employees of a governmental corporation, unit, department or agency, including elected or appointed officials, (c) two or more employees of a "nonprofit" college, university or other institution engaged primarily in education or research; or (2) for association plans: (a) twenty-five or more members of an incorporated or unincorporated association having a constitution or bylaws where such

---

[20] Letter from Florida Insurance Department dated August 29, 1963, to all admitted life insurance companies, "Filing Instructions for Employee Protection Plans."

[21] New York Insurance Department Circular Letter 1 (1965).

[22] Letter of January 28, 1965, from Superintendent of Insurance to insurers licensed to write life or accident and health insurance.

association was formed and is maintained in good faith for purposes other than obtaining insurance, has been in active existence for at least two years and consists of persons having the same or similar occupation or profession, (b) not less than four nor more than twenty-five members of a labor union, (c) an association of civil service employees, (d) groups of individuals, such as dairy farmers, who supply or deliver materials to a central point of collection.

In employer-employee plans, all of the employees, or all of any class or classes determined by employment, employment and age or family status, or both, must participate except those whose evidence of insurability is not satisfactory to the insurer, and except that under a contributory plan insurance may be provided if not less than 75 per cent of all eligible employees participate. For association plans, including plans for associations of civil service employees, and suppliers, unless the insurer individually underwrites each applicant on the basis of either medical examination or a questionnaire concerning his present health and medical history, the participation requirements are: not less than 500 members, or 30 per cent of the first 500 eligible members plus 10 per cent of all eligible members in excess of 500, whichever is less, and for suppliers, not less than 30 per cent of the first 500 eligible suppliers, plus 10 per cent of the next 3,500 eligible suppliers; but not less than twenty-five insured persons in any event.

The insurer may reserve the right to terminate or nonrenew the insurance after sixty days' written notice, but if a policy is terminated or nonrenewed by the insurer or employer for any reason other than nonpayment of premium, it must provide for conversion in accordance with the New York requirements for conversion of group life insurance. In lieu of termination of insurance, the policy may provide for its continuance on an individual basis. Whenever a conversion privilege is available, the insured must be given written notice of the right to convert not more than fifteen days after termination of insurance. If such notice is given more than fifteen days but less than ninety days after termination of insurance, the time allowed for conversion must be extended for fifteen days after giving notice. If notice is not given within ninety days after termination of insurance, the time allowed for conversion expires at the end of such ninety days in an employer-employee case, or at the end of one year from date of termination of insurance under an association plan.

Premium rates must be self-supporting on reasonable assumptions as to mortality, morbidity, interest and expense and must not unfairly discriminate between any class or classes of persons. In an employer-employee wholesale plan, premium rates at least equal to the minimum rates prescribed for group life insurance[23] shall be deemed, a priori, to be self-

---

[23] New Regulation 32, September 26, 1961, Minimum Premiums for Group Life Insurance, *The Weekly Underwriter Insurance Department Service* (New York, 1961), p. 52.

supporting. In an association wholesale plan, if premium rates to be charged for the first year of insurance differ from premium rates otherwise charged for individual life insurance policies on the same or comparable plan, the insurer must file such premium rates, showing to the satisfaction of the Superintendent of Insurance that such differences result from demonstrable savings not solely in commissions or service fees but also from underwriting, issue costs and administrative expenses. Such savings are to be adjusted by any fees paid by the insurer for administration or collection of premiums and the anticipated increase in mortality or morbidity resulting from more liberal underwriting practices. In the event the insurer does not have the same or comparable plan, premium rates at least equal to those prescribed for group life insurance shall be deemed, a priori, to be self-supporting if commissions or service fees, underwriting or issue costs, administrative costs and mortality or morbidity will not exceed those for group insurance.

In an employer-employee wholesale plan, premiums shall be paid by the employer or jointly by the employer and employee. In an association wholesale plan, premiums may be paid solely by the association or union, by its members, or jointly by the members and the association or union. In the case of suppliers, premiums are to be deducted at the central point of collection from the payments for the materials or supplies delivered.

Premiums may vary by age or age groups, and for ages through forty may be the same for all ages or may be computed by quinquennial or decennial ages. For ages beyond forty they may be computed by not more than quinquennial ages. The insurer may reserve the right to change the schedule of premium rates and may experience rate a plan if all plans of the same class are so rated by the insurer on an equitable basis.

No wholesale life insurance policy will be approved for delivery in New York unless it contains the usual standard provisions, and all such policies must be filed with the Insurance Department. No separate agreement may be entered into which would change the terms and conditions of such policies.

Except as provided in the standards with respect to classes of persons who may be insured, wholesale insurance policies may not be issued in lieu of a group policy when such policy would be legally issuable. Moreover, wholesale insurance may not be issued to supplement group insurance on the same lives. Finally, the insurer's underwriting rules with respect to wholesale insurance must be filed in duplicate with the Superintendent of Insurance.

Colorado. Under a law effective April 9, 1965, in the state of Colorado, wholesale insurance is defined as a plan under which four or more employees of any corporation, co-partnership, or individual employer, or of any governmental corporation, unit, agency, or department; or ten or more members, employees, or employees of members of any labor union, or of any trade, business, industrial, or professional association, which has had an active existence for at least two years, are initially insured, and under which such persons, with or without dependents, are issued the same basic form of individual policy, varying only in respect to amounts and benefits applied for.

Premiums shall be paid to the insurer periodically by or on behalf of the employer or association from funds of the employer or association, or from funds contributed by the employees or members specifically for their insurance, or from both. Premium rates may reflect a differential from rates otherwise charged for identical policies on an individual basis, provided that the rates charged do not unfairly discriminate between groups to which wholesale insurance is issued.

The term "employee" includes officers, managers, partners and proprietors provided each such "employee" is actively engaged in, and devotes a substantial part of his time to, the conduct of the business of the corporation, partnership or proprietorship.

Term life insurance renewable only during employment or membership must provide for conversion similar to the requirement for group life insurance. If written on any basis other than term insurance, the policy may provide that any premiums becoming due after the date of termination of employment or membership shall be in amounts determined in accordance with the insurer's published rates for such policy.

It appears that, except for the restrictions outlined on the preceding pages, wholesale insurance is not likely to be otherwise seriously challenged, but it may be impossible to secure approval of a uniform policy to be used in all states for wholesale plans. Such variations as may be required, however, are likely to be minor. There is, of course, the possibility that the recent issuance by the New York Insurance Department of standards for wholesale life insurance and the new Colorado law may prompt other states to take similar action.

FRANCHISE HEALTH INSURANCE

By the early 1930's, group health insurance had developed sufficiently to demonstrate its tremendous potentiality, and foresighted health insurance underwriters began thinking of ways to apply some of the more favorable group insurance principles to health insurance programs using individual policies. Members of professional associations, who previously had found it necessary to obtain individually whatever health insurance they might need, were prime prospects for experimentation in the newly conceived franchise field and quickly adopted its advantageous features. The idea soon spread to small employer-employee groups, where the number of employees was too small to qualify for group insurance, and also to larger groups when circumstances rendered it difficult or impossible to fulfill the group insurance enrollment requirements. These circumstances frequently appeared when group insurance statutes required the insuring of a high percentage of the eligible employees and there was no arrangement for the employer to share in the premium payment.

Regulation of Franchise Insurance

In the beginning, franchise insurance grew without plan or design and without clear nomenclature or definition.[24] Then, on June 12, 1946, the National Association of Insurance Commissioners, at its annual meeting in Portland, Oregon, adopted a definition of franchise insurance as follows:

Accident and health insurance on a franchise plan is hereby declared to be that form of accident and health insurance issued to
- (1) Five or more employees of any corporation, copartnership, or individual employer or any governmental corporation, agency or department thereof; or
- (2) Ten or more members of any trade or professional association or of a labor union or of any other association having had an active existence for at least two years where such association or union has a constitution or by-laws and is formed in good faith for purposes other than that of obtaining insurance;

where such persons, with or without their dependents, are issued the same form of an individual policy varying only as to amounts and kinds of coverage applied for by such persons, under an arrangement whereby the premiums on such policies may be paid to the insurer periodically by the employer, with or without payroll deductions, or by the association for its members, or by some designated person acting on behalf of such employer or association.

The Commissioners specified that if a state has a health insurance anti-discriminatory law, the following should be added as an additional paragraph to the above section:

Notwithstanding the provisions of section _____ (insert section number of anti-discrimination statute), such section shall not prohibit different rates charged, or benefits payable, or different underwriting procedure for individuals insured under a franchise plan provided rates charged, benefits payable, or underwriting procedure used do not discriminate between franchise plans.

They further suggested that to the foregoing should be added appropriate language to incorporate the above definition into a bill for enactment according to the legislative requirements of each individual state.[25]

Within two years following the National Association of Insurance Commissioners' adoption of the definition of franchise insurance, fourteen states had legally accepted it, a few in slightly modified form, and a

---

[24] J. F. Follmann, Jr., "Regulation of Accident and Sickness Insurance," David McCahan (ed.), *Accident and Sickness Insurance* (Philadelphia: University of Pennsylvania Press, 1954), p. 245.

[25] *Proceedings of the Seventy-seventh Annual Session of the National Association of Insurance Commissioners* (Portland, Oregon, June 9–13, 1946), p. 271.

substantial number of states recognized franchise insurance without having formulated any decision pertaining to it. There was considerable variance among states in interpretations of similar definitions and in rulings regarding principles, such as use of the same policy for individuals within and outside of a franchise case, at reduced rates within the franchise; issuance of special policies under a franchise plan without also making them available to individuals outside of the plan; continuance of insurance for the remaining members of a group, on the same basis, after the group has decreased to less than five insured persons; and continuance of insurance on the same basis for a person after he has left the group.[26]

Franchise health insurance developed rapidly in the next fifteen years. A survey conducted by the Health Insurance Association of America in February, 1961, indicated the writing of franchise health insurance by 101 insurers out of 220 that responded to the questionnaire, and that approximately 7 per cent of the health insurance of the eighty-nine insurers that reported their premium volume was written on a franchise basis.[27]

Industry practices and insurance department rulings gradually became more uniform. In 1957, a definition of franchise health insurance, very similar to the NAIC definition, was adopted by the Health Insurance Association of America,[28] and it has been subsequently furnished to legislators desiring a model bill. A study of insurance laws, published rulings and the results of filings with insurance departments of franchise insurance policies in 1962 and 1963 indicates that the current regulatory status of franchise insurance[29] is as follows: twenty-four states[30] and Puerto Rico have laws adopting the NAIC, HIAA or a substantially similar definition of franchise health insurance; in addition, there are twenty states[31] and the District of Columbia having no law or published regulation pertaining to franchise health insurance, but their insurance departments have been approving franchise health insurance policies under laws regulating individual health insurance.[32]

---

[26] Harry L. Graham, "Study of Franchise Insurance," presented at Educational Seminar of Bureau of Accident and Health Underwriters, February 1, 1949.

[27] Health Insurance Association of America, Survey on Health Insurance Written on a Franchise Basis, February 1, 1961 (unpublished).

[28] The HIAA definition is shown in Appendix 26.

[29] Insurance law references are shown in Appendix 27.

[30] Arizona, Arkansas, California, Florida, Georgia, Hawaii, Idaho, Indiana, Kentucky, Louisiana, Maine, Maryland, Montana, Nebraska, New Hampshire, North Carolina, Ohio, Oklahoma, Pennsylvania, South Carolina, Vermont, Washington, West Virginia and Wisconsin.

[31] Alabama, Alaska, Connecticut, Delaware, Massachusetts, Minnesota, Mississippi, Missouri, Nevada, New Jersey, New Mexico, North Dakota, Oregon, Rhode Island, South Dakota, Tennessee, Texas, Utah, Virginia and Wyoming.

[32] Confirmed through approvals by respective insurance departments of franchise health insurance policies submitted in 1962 and 1963.

Colorado. Colorado's attitude is unique in that it classifies franchise health insurance as a form of group insurance and finds a policy unacceptable if it does not conform to the group Sickness and Accident Insurance section of the insurance laws.[33] This prevents use of the renewal conditions customarily found in franchise health insurance. However, a program of individual insurance can be made available to employees of an employer or members of an association provided it does not effect unfair discrimination in premiums, benefits or other provisions between individuals of the same class.[34]

Georgia. Georgia is included in the list of states that have adopted the NAIC, HIAA or similar definition of franchise health insurance by legislation. Nevertheless, Georgia laws and regulations otherwise deal sufficiently with franchise health insurance to justify separate comment. The chapter of the Georgia Code pertaining to individual health insurance[35] provides, among other things, for ten-day right of examination of policy,[36] anniversary nonrenewal conditions for policies other than accident insurance only policies,[37] outline of coverage,[38] and refund of a portion of the premiums in case of nonrenewal or cancellation under certain circumstances.[39] It does not apply to "any blanket or group policy of insurance."[40] Franchise health insurance has been relieved of these requirements by regulation of the insurance commissioner which construes the term "blanket or group policy of insurance," as used in the statute, to include the type of individual insurance commonly known as "franchise group insurance" when such individual policies are written under specified circumstances and contain specified renewal conditions.[41] The circumstances stated in the regulation conform to the statutory definition of franchise health insurance,[42] and the renewal conditions are those customarily found in franchise health insurance policies.

Iowa. Iowa insurance laws authorize a franchise plan of health insurance at reduced rates for an association, as defined in the statute, on either a group or individual policy basis. The plan must cover at least 50

---

[33] *Colorado Revised Statutes,* 1953, Sec. 72–11–16.

[34] Colorado Bill H–1177, enacted April 9, 1965, provides an individual franchise health insurance law similar to the NAIC definition.

[35] *Code of Georgia Annotated,* Chap. 56–30.

[36] *Ibid.,* Sec. 56–3007.

[37] *Ibid.,* Sec. 56–3006.

[38] *Ibid.,* Sec. 56–3008.

[39] *Ibid.,* Sec. 56–3009.

[40] *Ibid.,* Sec. 56–3001(3).

[41] Georgia Insurance Commissioner's Regulation of May 24, 1956, interpreting Senate Bill 14 of 1956, Sec. 10.

[42] *Code of Georgia Annotated,* Sec. 56–3018.

per cent[43] of the insurable members of the association, but in no case less than ten members.[44] The laws also authorize the issuance of individual health insurance policies at reduced rates to employees of a common employer, subject to the requirement that the number of employees to be insured must be more than four.[45]

Kansas, Michigan and Illinois. Kansas[46] and Michigan[47] have defined franchise insurance by ruling in a manner consistent with the NAIC definition. Illinois, in its rulings and regulations pertaining to construction and filing of health insurance forms, sets out rules of construction for franchise health insurance policies as follows:

Requirements for the so-called franchise insurance are different from those for individual contracts in the following respects: termination either by cancellation or refusal to renew any individual contracts of the group is prohibited, unless all like contracts of the group are terminated at the expiration of the contracts and upon at least ten days' notice in advance. The only other termination conditions which may be included in such contracts are those which terminate coverage because of nonpayment of premiums, discontinuance of employment of the insured by the named employer or the discontinuance of membership in the designated organization or association, and in addition, coverage may be automatically terminated at a designated attained age.[48]

New York. Prior to 1965, New York had repeatedly recognized franchise insurance[49] and had indicated that, in the absence of regulation of franchise insurance in the insurance law, any health insurance policy written on a franchise basis would be governed by the laws applicable to individual health insurance. It had further indicated that to avoid any unfair discrimination between individual and franchise policies, any rate or policy fee differential should be based on demonstrable savings in expense, such as lower commissions and savings in administrative expense.[50]

In August, 1964, the New York Insurance Department mailed to insurers a draft of its proposed standards for franchise insurance and invited

---

[43] Iowa Bill H–237 of 1965, if enacted, would amend Sec. 509.14 by deleting the 50 per cent participation requirement.

[44] *Iowa Code Annotated*, Sec. 509.14.

[45] *Ibid.*, Sec. 509.4.

[46] Kansas Insurance Department Regulation 48–12–14 of January 1, 1963.

[47] Michigan Insurance Department Ruling of July 29, 1946.

[48] Illinois Insurance Department Executive Bulletin XB–563 of March 20, 1952, Part 1, Paragraph 22.

[49] Francis T. Curran, "Fundamentals of Accident and Health Insurance," *Examination of Insurance Companies*, prepared under the direction of Deputy Superintendent Adelbert G. Straub, Jr. (New York City: New York State Insurance Department, 1955), Vol. I, p. 454.

[50] Max J. Schwartz, "Accident and Health Insurance Rates, Rating Plans, and Commissions," *Examination of Insurance Companies*, prepared under the direction of Deputy Superintendent Adelbert G. Straub, Jr. (New York City: New York State Insurance Department, 1955), Vol. VI, p. 454.

comments from the insurance industry. An industry committee[51] studied the proposed standards and at a meeting with the Insurance Department in October, 1964, suggested certain changes. The Insurance Department indicated that the need for franchise health insurance standards had grown out of the Department's concern that franchise health insurance is sometimes used in a manner which (1) creates rate discrimination among individual policyholders and (2) avoids participation and other requirements of the New York group insurance laws. In finalizing the franchise insurance standards, the Insurance Department adopted many of the insurance industry committee's suggestions. These standards, with an effective date of March 27, 1965, were included with the wholesale life insurance standards in the publication enclosed with the Insurance Department's January 25, 1965, letter referred to previously in this chapter.[52]

The standards for health insurance and for life insurance appear in separate sections of the publication. However, they are similar in so many respects that only the additional information needed to emphasize a few important features of the health insurance standards and to point out their differences from the wholesale insurance requirements is included in this section.

The definition of franchise insurance is substantially similar to that for wholesale life insurance. The explanation that premium collection by payroll deduction shall not, in and of itself, cause a policy to be classified as franchise insurance makes it clear that plans generally referred to as payroll budget or salary allotment can be written in such a manner that they will not be classified as franchise insurance, in which case it will not be necessary that they conform to the franchise standards. It also arouses speculation regarding what circumstances are needed, in addition to payroll deduction, to cause a plan to be classified as franchise insurance. It appears that (1) sponsorship of the plan by the employer, association or union, and (2) a policy provision showing that the insured's right to renew his policy, with or without other permissible renewal conditions, is contingent upon the continuing of employment, membership or supplier participation, are both essential conditions to the classification of an insurance plan as franchise insurance.

The franchise rules with respect to minimum and maximum number of persons are the same as those for wholesale life insurance, except that an employer-employee franchise health insurance plan may consist of groups of twenty-five or more employees where it has been demonstrated to the satisfaction of the Superintendent of Insurance that the franchise insur-

---

[51] New York Steering Committee.

[52] New York Insurance Department franchise insurance standards are shown in Appendix 28.

ance supplements and does not substitute for group insurance. For an association health insurance franchise, there is no participation requirement other than the minimum number of insureds, except in civil service employee association and supplier cases, for which the requirements are the same as those for wholesale life insurance.

The insurer's right to terminate or nonrenew a franchise policy is limited to specified reasons similar to those for wholesale life insurance. However, a conversion privilege is required only when one third or more of the premium for the policy is allocable to hospital, surgical or medical benefits and the policy terminates (1) in an employer-employee franchise case, because the insured has attained the age limit prescribed in the policy or the insured's employment in the eligible classes has terminated, or (2) in an association franchise case, because the insured has attained the age limit prescribed in the policy, or the insured has retired, or the insured has ceased to be (a) engaged in a profession or occupation with respect to which the franchise policies were issued, or (b) a member of the association or union, or (c) a supplier. The conversion privilege must be at least equal to that required for group hospital and surgical expense insurance.[53] When a conversion privilege is available the notice requirements are the same as those for wholesale life insurance. Also, after a policy in which one third or more of the premium is allocable to hospital, surgical or medical benefits has been in force two years, the insurer's right to terminate or nonrenew the policy in connection with the termination or nonrenewal of all policies of a case shall be subject to approval by the Superintendent of Insurance when the reason for the termination or nonrenewal is not one of those specified in the statute.[54]

Premium rates for an employer-employee franchise plan, in addition to being self-supporting, must be on a basis reasonably related to the mortality and morbidity assumptions used by the insurer for group health insurance. For an association franchise plan, they must be on a basis reasonably related to the mortality and morbidity assumptions used by the insurer for individual health insurance. Provision is made for use of some other basis in either case if such use is demonstrated to the satisfaction of the Superintendent of Insurance to be appropriate.

North Carolina. North Carolina is another state that has adopted the NAIC definition of franchise health insurance by legislation and has other laws and regulations of sufficient impact upon franchise health insurance to justify separate comment. It has a law requiring notice on a graduated scale ranging from thirty days to two years, depending upon the length of time the policy has been in force, for nonrenewal of individual or family

---

[53] *Insurance Law of New York,* Sec. 162.5 (group hospital and surgical expense requirements).

[54] *Ibid.,* Sec. 164.6.

health insurance policies other than noncancellable or nonrenewable policies, but including group, blanket and franchise policies covering less than ten persons.[55] This law has been interpreted by the Insurance Department of North Carolina as not applying to individual franchise health insurance policies if the number of persons covered under the plan is ten or more even though the number in the plan should subsequently fall below ten.[56]

Employer-Employee Plans

In the early years of group insurance, insurers generally felt that the group must include at least fifty persons to permit sound underwriting. Time passed, experience was accumulated, and soon it was found practicable to insure groups with twenty-five and, later, ten employees. In recent years the trend has been toward group contracts with as few as four employees where state laws permit. The laws of some states allow group health insurance for two persons, and in a few states there is no minimum number by law or regulation.[57]

During the time that the minimum number of persons for group health insurance was fifty, or even as low as twenty-five, there was a substantial market for franchise health insurance with small employee groups; but with the lowering of the minimum number and extensive activity on the part of group insurers in recent years in the "four or more" employee field, there has been a change in the pattern of employer-employee franchise health insurance. Occasionally, franchise health insurance is used as a means of providing additional health insurance for certain employees, with or without employer participation in premium payment. The franchise plan is also used to make health insurance available to all employees of an employer under a voluntary enrollment program. Some companies write the "four or more" employee groups on a franchise basis in the states where the number of employees is too few for group insurance, and a few insurers for purposes of standardization make country-wide use of the franchise procedure for writing cases with four to nine or four to twenty-five employees. Benefits may be prescribed in accordance with an established plan or, when the employees are paying the entire premium, each employee may have an opportunity of selecting his coverages and

---

[55] *General Statutes of North Carolina*, 1960, Sec. 58–251.2.

[56] HIAA Insurance Department Bulletin, N.C. No. 3–57, October 4, 1957.

[57] A minimum of ten persons is required for group health insurance in California, Colorado, Florida, Hawaii, Illinois, Indiana, Iowa, Louisiana, Maine, New Mexico, Ohio, Oklahoma, Pennsylvania, South Carolina, West Virginia and Wisconsin; five in Arizona, Georgia, Kansas, Michigan, Nebraska, Nevada and Vermont; two in Arkansas, Idaho, Kentucky, Maryland, Massachusetts, Minnesota, Montana, New Jersey, New York, North Carolina, Utah and Washington; and there is no minimum requirement in Alabama, Alaska, Connecticut, Delaware, District of Columbia, Mississippi, Missouri, New Hampshire, North Dakota, Oregon, Rhode Island, South Dakota, Tennessee, Texas, Virginia and Wyoming. In this last group of states there is no statutory definition of group health insurance.

amounts, subject to the insurer's underwriting rules. In the typical case, arrangements are made with the employer for the agent to solicit the employees for insurance, take applications, and obtain payroll deduction authorizations, and for the employer to deduct premiums from pay and report the premiums periodically (generally monthly) to the insurer.

Types of Benefits. The primary coverage in the employer-employee case is weekly or monthly indemnity for loss of business time. Elimination periods vary from zero days for accident and seven days for sickness to ninety days for both accident and sickness, or even to as long as 360 days for accident and sickness when the longer elimination periods are needed to coordinate the insurance with other components of the employee benefit program. The indemnity period may be one year, two years, five years or lifetime for total disability from accident, and may be one year, two years, five years, ten years or to age sixty-five for total disability from sickness. Frequently, accidental death and dismemberment, accident medical expense, hospital and surgical and major medical expense coverages also are available at the employee's option, or any of them may be the primary coverage.

Underwriting. The kind and amount of underwriting in employer-employee franchise insurance depends upon the size of the case and the percentage of the eligible persons that can be enrolled. When the circumstances are similar to those generally found with group insurance, the underwriting will likewise be consistent with group practices. On a case where it is expected that a high percentage of the eligible employees will apply, the insurer may agree to issue a policy to every applicant but may reserve the right to issue minimum amounts or to rate up the premiums for impaired risks. The magnitude of the benefits will also influence the amount and kind of underwriting needed. Generally, there will be no renewal underwriting while the insured continues in active employment with the employer, unless it becomes necessary to reunderwrite the entire case.

Renewability. The policy may give the insurer the right to refuse renewal only when the insured reaches some stated age, such as age seventy, or when he ceases to be in active full-time employment with the employer, or when the insurer gives to the insured advance written notice of at least thirty days that the insurer will decline renewal of all policies issued under the franchise. Alternatively, it may provide that every renewal is subject to the consent of the insurer. In any event, it is extremely important for the insurer's renewal practices to be acceptable to the employer since the successful operation of the franchise is dependent upon the employer's cooperation.

Association Plans

One of the early association franchise health insurance plans was written in 1936 for the Civil Service Employees Association of the State of

New York. The membership of this association consists of employees of the state and its political subdivisions. The case was written under a franchise arrangement because the employer was not paying any part of the premiums and the participation requirements for group insurance could not be satisfied. Individual policies have been issued and, except for brief open enrollment periods in the early years of the program, applications have been subject to underwriting approval. The plan was developed under the supervision of the New York Insurance Department. Regular enrollment has accounted for steady growth over the years, and benefits have been liberalized whenever experience has permitted. The plan continues to operate as a successful franchise health insurance program.

The members of professional associations are excellent prospects for franchise health insurance, and programs have been developed for associations of accountants, architects, automobile dealers, bankers, dentists, engineers, funeral directors, lawyers, optometrists, osteopaths, physicians, pharmacists, physiotherapists, veterinarians and others. Franchises have been written at the city, county, state, national and even international level. Many labor unions also have availed themselves of association franchise health insurance programs for their members.

Types of Benefits. Originally, weekly or monthly indemnity for total disability was the primary coverage, and the early offerings were conservative. Aggressive competition in this new field of insurance soon dispelled the conservatism, and the professional groups were offered excellent plans providing monthly indemnity benefits as high as $1,000, with lifetime indemnity for total disability from accidents, and an indemnity period of as long as five or even ten years (limited to two years after the insured's seventieth birthday) for total disability from sickness. Several elimination periods were available, popular choices being zero days for accident and seven days for sickness, thirty days for both accident and sickness, and six months for both accident and sickness. Accidental death and dismemberment coverage was included as a part of the program or on an optional basis, and hospital benefits generally were optional.

In recent years, associations have been offered comprehensive medical, major medical and high limit accidental death and dismemberment coverages; and when there is already a disability income program in effect, the insurer may offer to supplement it with business overhead expense insurance.[58]

---

[58] Business overhead expense insurance is a form of health insurance issued on an individual or franchise type policy basis providing reimbursement up to a stated maximum monthly benefit for specified business expenses incurred by the insured during total disability from sickness or injuries. The elimination period is generally thirty days or less, and the indemnity period limit is twelve months or more. The specified expenses include items such as rent, electricity, heat, water, laundry, telephone, employees' salaries, membership fees, dues, depreciation of office equipment and other fixed expenses normal and customary in the operation of the insured's business. Any

Underwriting. For a new association franchise plan involving a substantial number of eligible persons, the insurer may establish an enrollment period of about ninety days, at the end of which policies are to be made effective, and may offer in advance to insure all persons applying within the enrollment period if acceptable applications are received within that time from a specified percentage (generally 50 per cent) of the eligible members of the association. Some companies use an additional or alternative requirement, viz., a minimum number of lives. If the number of acceptable applications is insufficient to satisfy the percentage or minimum number requirement but is adequate for putting the case into effect on an underwritten basis, policies will be issued to the applicants satisfying the underwriting standards, and applications subsequently received will also be given underwriting consideration.

One of the most significant underwriting problems in this type of insurance is the problem of over-insurance. In the development of franchise health insurance the practice has been to provide benefits irrespective of other insurance, and, since benefits are not proratable on account of improper relationship to earnings, there is the possibility of over-insurance when persons are eligible for the same kind of benefits through membership in more than one association or when they have obtained similar benefits under other forms of insurance. This is particularly true among professional people who are frequently members of several associations through which health insurance is available.

Renewability. As is the general case with employer-employee franchise insurance, the insurer has the right to decline renewal of an association franchise insurance policy only under a limited number of circumstances. Typically, it may refuse to renew when the insured becomes seventy years of age, ceases to be actively engaged in the duties of his profession or ceases to be an active member of the association, or when the insurer gives to the insured advance written notice of at least thirty days that the insurer will decline renewal of all policies issued under the franchise.

Installation. Installation of an association franchise case should not be undertaken until there is complete accord among officials of the association, the insurer and the agent or broker regarding benefits to be offered, premiums to be charged, underwriting practices, procedures of solicitation, collection of premiums and handling of renewals. A letter of sponsorship of the program by an authorized official of the association is very important.

Enrollment by personal solicitation with the help of social gatherings, meetings and other arrangements for personal contact on a mass basis has

---

premiums paid on this type of policy constitute business expenses and are deductible from gross income under Section 162 of the 1954 Internal Revenue Code. Rev. Rul. 55–264, Internal Revenue Bulletin, 1955.

been very successful. Enrollment of a satisfactory percentage of eligible persons by mail solicitation is often difficult. In one of the most successful mail solicitations, there was first an invitation by the governing board of the association for its members to participate in the program. This was followed by a brochure describing the plan and containing a letter of endorsement by the director of the association and an application card. Next, there was a question and answer leaflet with a letter from the agent who was the administrator of the program. Then came another letter from the administrator enclosing a specimen policy. Lastly, there was a final letter from the director of the association. It informed members that the enrollment had exceeded the percentage requirement for waiver of underwriting and that the enrollment period had been extended for an additional month to give members who had not enrolled a final opportunity to obtain the insurance without being required to furnish evidence of insurability.

Administration.   Premiums for an association plan of franchise insurance generally are payable annually or semiannually, and are collected by the administrator of the plan and remitted to the insurer. They may be on a step-rate basis by age brackets, level for all ages or level but based on age at issue.

After a case has been established, frequent solicitations of members for additions to the insurance plan are necessary in order to avoid undue increases in average age of insureds and to enroll new, young members as soon as possible after they become eligible to participate in the plan. Some insurers encourage enrollment of young people by regular open enrollment periods for persons in the young age bracket.

Reserves in Franchise Insurance Plans

In 1962, the National Association of Insurance Commissioners Subcommittee to Study Active Life Reserves for Noncancellable Accident and Health Policies selected an industry advisory committee from persons recommended by the Joint Steering Committee on Health Insurance Morbidity Studies.[59] Within the next two years, this advisory committee developed a comprehensive report containing recommendations covering reserve requirements for all classes of individual health insurance policies. The report was submitted to and adopted by the National Association of Insurance Commissioners at its December, 1964, meeting.

The reserve requirement for a franchise health insurance policy is the same as that for an individual health insurance policy for which each renewal is subject to the consent of the company, i.e., the gross pro rata unearned premium, provided (1) the insurer has the right to refuse renewal of the franchise policy in connection with taking nonrenewal

---

[59] The Joint Steering Committee consists of representatives of the Health Insurance Association of America and the Society of Actuaries.

action on all policies in the case, and (2) the premiums for the franchise policy are not based on the level premium principle. Additional reserve requirements are specified in the report for (1) a policy which is guaranteed renewable during the insured's lifetime or to a specified age, (2) a policy which limits the insurer's right to refuse renewal to specified reasons not including deterioration of health and does not give the insurer the right to refuse renewal in connection with taking nonrenewal action on all policies of a case, and (3) a policy for which the premium is based on the level premium principle. A franchise policy in one of these latter categories should be so classified for reserve purposes.

Tax Aspects of Franchise Insurance

Premiums paid by an employer on health insurance policies for disability income, medical expense reimbursement, dismemberment and sight loss and accidental death benefit coverage for his employees are deductible as a business expense, whether paid on individual policies or on a group policy.[60] Furthermore, premiums paid by an employer on health insurance for his employees to provide health insurance benefits are not taxable to the employees, whether paid on individual policies or on a group policy, except possibly that portion of the premiums allocable to an accidental death benefit under individual insurance.[61] There has been no final determination regarding the tax status of this latter benefit. Medical expense benefits, dismemberment and loss of sight benefits are tax exempt to the employee. Disability income benefits provided by an employer for his employee also are tax exempt to the employee, subject to the sick pay exclusion rules discussed in Chapter 20.[62]

Significance of Franchise Insurance

A successful franchise health insurance program will not result automatically from use of franchise type policies for groups of persons having an employer-employee or association or union-member relationship. The group must be cohesive and properly managed, and the insurance plan must be adequately sponsored. Otherwise, marketing and underwriting techniques similar to those for individual policies will be required, and there will be little or no savings in either production or administration expenses. Under appropriate circumstances, the mass solicitation and enrollment methods and simplified administration procedures used with franchise health insurance result in substantial savings in expenses that can be reflected in the premiums, and participation in the program by a high percentage of eligible persons offsets adverse selection and reduces the need for policy restrictions. The resultant favorable benefits afford the

---

[60] IRC Sec. 162(a).

[61] IRC Sec. 106; Reg. 1.106–1; Rev. Rul. 58–90.

[62] IRC Sec. 105(b), (c), (d).

agent or broker the opportunity for large premium production and, consequently, substantial income from commissions, even though the rate of commissions may be lower than for individual insurance. Other advantageous features of a franchise health insurance plan are the lack of restriction with respect to pre-existing conditions, the opportunity of obtaining a policy during an initial enrollment period at an age as high as sixty-nine years, and the right of an insured to renew his policy until a specified age such as seventy, except for stated reasons, unless all policies under the franchise are terminated.

A few years ago, the term franchise health insurance indicated to many people little more than a method for the mass selling of individual and family policies. The promulgation of rules by insurance departments and the gradual development in the health insurance industry of franchise practices have given this term new stature.

SELECTED REFERENCES

"Aetna Life Lawyer Discusses Legal Problems of Wholesale," *The National Underwriter,* February 2, 1963, p. 4.

"Analysis That Unsold Medical Unit on Association Group Is Released," *The National Underwriter,* March 5, 1960, p. 1.

"An Interpretive Analysis—NALU's Comments on the Study of Association Group Term and Wholesale Life Insurance," *Life Association News,* Vol. LVIII, No. 9 (September, 1963), pp. 23–24.

"Association Group Seen as One Way to Close Gap between Total Need and Actual In-Force Figure," *The National Underwriter,* November 21, 1964, p. 1.

BOWLES, ANDREWS AND TOWNE. "Report on Study of Association Group Business," *Life Association News,* Vol. LVIII, No. 9 (September, 1963), pp. 37–46.

"California Bars Coverage on Dependent Lives in Franchise Plans," *The National Underwriter,* February 2, 1963, p. 1.

"Ethics, Morality Stir Serious Discussion at N.Y. State Meet," *The National Underwriter,* February 22, 1964, p. 1.

"Franchise Life: Definition and Description; A Variety of Opinion: Legal and Legislative; 'Indiscriminate and Unsound,' Says the Opposition," *Western Underwriter, Life Edition,* November, 1959, pp. 8–13.

GORDON, GEORGE L. "Group and Wholesale Insurance," *Proceedings of the American Life Convention, Legal Section,* October 12, 13, 1959, pp. 457–60.

HOWARD, ALVIN D. "Mass Merchandising Is Here to Stay in Life Insurance," *Insurance,* Vol. LXV, No. 6 (February 8, 1964), p. 29.

KALLAS, AADU. "Wholesale Life Insurance." Paper presented to Association of Life Insurance Counsel, December 11, 1962.

McFARLANE, WILLIAM. "N.Y.C. Agents Open Campaign against Association Group," *The National Underwriter,* January 18, 1964, p. 1.

Memorandum for the Joint ALC-LIAA Committee on Re-examination of Group Policy—ALC-LIAA Joint General Bulletin, No. 901 (August 26, 1960), pp. 21–23, 27–29.

MEYER, WILLIAM F. "Wholesale and Franchise Insurance," *Proceedings of the American Life Convention, Legal Section,* October 12, 13, 1959, pp. 396–401.

"NALU Trustee Urges All-Out Drive against Association Group Plans," *The National Underwriter,* February 13, 1960, p. 1.

"Pru. V-P Comments on Wood's Letter against Association Group," *The National Underwriter,* February 27, 1960, p. 2.

SARASON, HARRY M. "Association Insurance," *The Journal of Insurance,* Vol. XXVIII, No. 4 (December, 1961), pp. 79–84.

"Wholesale and Franchise Insurance," *Report of Joint Committee on Re-examination of Group Policy—ALC-LIAA Joint General Bulletin,* No. 901 (August 26, 1960), pp. 16–18.

Chapter 35

EXTENSIONS OF CREDITOR GROUP COVERAGES

BY STANLEY W. GINGERY

NATURE AND EXTENT OF CREDITOR GROUP INSURANCE

Basic Characteristics

The field of creditor group insurance consists of two types of coverage—creditor group life insurance and creditor group health insurance. Both are designed to perform the same basic function, viz., to assure the repayment of a loan in the event of an interruption or cessation of a debtor's earning power.

Creditor group life insurance, which was described in some detail in Chapter 7, is a special form of group term insurance. The master contract is issued to a creditor and covers the lives of his debtors on a group basis. The creditor is the policyholder and the beneficiary. The contract provides that, in the event of the death of the debtor, the insurer will pay to the creditor the unpaid balance of the indebtedness. The creditor is obligated to apply benefits paid toward discharge of the insured indebtedness. Creditor group life insurance normally is written to cover installment debt, in which the indebtedness is repaid in periodic installments (usually monthly) and the coverage provided is decreasing term insurance. The maximum amount of creditor group life insurance on an individual debtor usually is restricted both by law and insurance company practice. Where the unpaid amount of indebtedness exceeds the maximum amount of insurance provided in the master contract, the debtor typically is insured for that maximum until the point at which the unpaid balance equals the maximum. Thereafter, the insurance reduces as the outstanding balance declines.

Creditor group health insurance is issued on a similar basis. It is a special type of group disability income insurance which provides that, in the event the debtor becomes totally disabled as defined in the contract,[1]

---

[1] Total disability usually is defined as inability of the debtor, due to sickness or accident, to engage in any occupation for wage or profit.

the insurer will pay to the creditor the amount of the debtor's monthly installments. Benefit payments continue for the duration of the disability, but not beyond the point the indebtedness is extinguished or its maturity date is reached. A disabled debtor must complete a waiting period before benefits commence. Typically the waiting period is fourteen or thirty days. Some creditor group health insurance plans provide that benefits are paid retroactive to the first day of disability if the waiting period requirement is satisfied.

The cost of creditor group insurance usually is borne by the debtor through a specific identifiable charge included in the credit transaction by the creditor. The creditor, in turn, usually pays premiums monthly to the insurance company. Commonly, the amount of monthly premium due the insurance company is determined by applying a monthly premium rate to the amount of outstanding insured indebtedness on the premium due date. Another premium payment method frequently employed is one in which the creditor each month pays a single premium for each new indebtedness which became insured during the month just elapsed. Usually, premium rates charged in renewal years for both creditor group life and creditor group health insurance are subject to adjustment to reflect the actual experience under the plan. Depending upon the experience, dividends or retrospective rate credits, if any, are paid to the creditor by the insurance company. The creditor usually retains these as compensation for his expenses incurred in administering the plan.

Origin of Creditor Insurance

Life insurance on a debtor as part of the debt service had its inception in 1910 through the pioneering efforts of Arthur J. Morris, an attorney of Norfolk, Virginia. He founded the first Morris Plan Bank and based his lending operation on the premise that people were inherently honest and entered debt in good faith. Although credit was predicated on the individual's ability and intention to repay, in line with the loan philosophy of the day, full collateral was required, usually in the form of a co-signer (relative or friend) who also pledged his character and earning power as security for the loan along with the borrower. Because the untimely death of the debtor could place the co-signer and creditor in a difficult position, Mr. Morris sought to protect against this contingency. He contacted many insurance companies to interest them in the idea of providing short-term life insurance of small amounts on borrowers. However, because no mortality experience on borrowers existed, and because short-term small amount policies would involve a high expense rate, the idea had little appeal for the insurance industry at the time.

Mr. Morris then decided to provide such protection through his own efforts, and, as a consequence, the Morris Plan Insurance Society was formed in 1917. In the first year of operation, about 1,500 individual term life insurance policies were sold, amounting to about $170,000 of insurance, and each policy covered the debt for its amount and term. The Morris Plan Insurance Society became the Bankers Security Life Insurance Society in July of 1946. In addition to creditor insurance, its operation now encompasses the usual forms of individual and group coverages.

Creditor health insurance is of more recent origin, beginning sometime during the 1930's when health insurance generally appeared on the scene. The circumstances under which it was first employed as a debt service are unknown.

Development of Creditor Insurance on a Group Basis

Although creditor life insurance originated in the form of individual contracts, it also has been provided through the group insurance vehicle since an early point in its history. The Prudential Insurance Company of America issued the first creditor group life insurance master contract in 1928 for the then National City Bank in New York[2] to protect its unsecured personal loan borrowers. The contract provided that the Prudential would pay the amount of insurance to the bank as the creditor-beneficiary and that the bank, in turn, would use the insurance proceeds to reduce or extinguish the debt.

Extent of Creditor Group Insurance Coverages

From these small beginnings, creditor life insurance has grown to be an essential part of debt service to the American public. Today, about 76 per cent of all installment debt is protected by creditor life insurance, and the group form accounts for approximately 85 per cent, or $37 billion, of the total amount of creditor life insurance in force in the United States.[3]

Group health insurance is a relatively new coverage in the portfolios of many creditor insurance writers, particularly those companies which write on the group basis. For this reason, statistics concerning its growth and extent are meager. However, during a recent five-year period, written creditor health insurance premiums increased from $32.4 million to $50 million, an increase of about 65 per cent. About 65 per cent of creditor health insurance premiums is written under group policies.

Legal Requirements

Creditor group insurance is governed by two types of statutory requirements, viz., certain provisions of the general insurance laws and additional legislation enacted specifically to control creditor insurance.[4] The objec-

---

[2] Now the First National City Bank of New York.

[3] Institute of Life Insurance, *1964 Life Insurance Fact Book* (New York, 1964), pp. 31–32.

[4] Legislation (other than insurance legislation) dealing with the operations of creditors, such as banking laws, small loan laws, retail installment sales laws, etc., may also impose some limitation on the use of creditor group insurance.

tive of the first type is to regulate creditor group insurance so that coverage may be provided on a sound underwriting basis. Such statutes generally provide that—

1. Coverage is available only to creditors to insure their debtors.
2. To be eligible for insurance, the indebtedness must be repayable in installments.
3. A minimum number, usually 100, of new debtors must enter the insured group each year.
4. The insurer must reserve the right to obtain evidence of insurability if the number of new debtors becoming insured in a year is less than 75 per cent of the eligible debtors.
5. The amount of insurance may not exceed the indebtedness. For creditor group life insurance, the amount of insurance on a debtor may not exceed a stipulated statutory maximum, such as $10,000, regardless of the amount of indebtedness.

The need for the second type, legislation to control creditor insurance specifically, arose because of abuses which existed in the creditor insurance field. The abuses were (1) overcharging debtors by requiring them to pay higher insurance charges than warranted by the benefits provided; (2) lack of disclosure—failure to inform debtors of their insurance coverage and its cost; (3) excessive amounts of insurance, that is, insurance greater than the indebtedness; and (4) failure to refund unearned insurance charges to debtors when their coverage terminated. These abuses resulted from the inferior bargaining position of debtors in the credit transaction so that they comprised a captive market for insurance. This enabled some creditors to make unconscionably high profits through commissions or dividends from creditor insurance policies which some insurance companies were willing to sell at excessively high premiums.

The National Association of Insurance Commissioners, through appointed committees, examined these creditor insurance practices and, in 1957, composed a model bill to serve as a uniform standard to guide insurance supervisory authorities and the insurance industry in governing and conducting the business of creditor insurance. The bill, known as the NAIC Model Bill to Provide for the Regulation of Credit Life and Credit Accident and Health Insurance (see Appendix 24), if enacted, provides the means to control the abuses. Specifically, the principal features of the model bill as they affect creditor group insurance are, first, that a certificate evidencing the existence and nature of the group coverage must be furnished to the insured debtor on the date of the indebtedness. The certificate also must inform the debtor of the charge, if any, for the insurance. Second, if the certificate is not furnished the debtor on the date of the indebtedness, a notice of proposed insurance must be furnished the debtor. The notice contains essentially the same information as would be shown in the certificate. It is used in instances where the credit transaction originates with a creditor other than the creditor group insurance policyholder. Third, all policies, certificates and other insurance forms, as well as the schedule of premium rates, must be filed with and approved by the insurance commissioner. Fourth, if the creditor group insurance on a debtor terminates prior to the scheduled maturity date of the indebtedness, the debtor must receive a refund or credit of the unused portion of the insurance charge made to him. Fifth, if insurance is required as a condition to granting the credit, the debtor must be given the option of furnishing the required amount of insurance through existing policies he owns or controls or of furnishing the required coverage through any insurer authorized to do business in the state in which the credit is granted. Sixth, the insurance commissioner may disapprove insurance forms (policies, certificates, etc.) if the benefits are not reasonable in relation to the premium. Finally, the charge to the debtor for insurance may not exceed the premium to be paid by the creditor to the insurer.

To date, thirty jurisdictions have enacted specific credit insurance legislation patterned substantially after the NAIC model bill. The insurance departments of twenty-one of these jurisdictions have promulgated creditor insurance regulations to implement the intent of the law. The insurance departments of nine additional states have promulgated regulations under authority granted them by regular insurance laws other than specific creditor insurance laws. Thus, as of 1964, there are thirty-nine jurisdictions with laws and/or regulations controlling creditor life and/or health insurance. These control measures apply equally to group and individual creditor insurance. (See Appendix 25.)

To give meaning to the model bill provision relating to the reasonableness of benefits to premiums and to further guide insurance departments, the NAIC adopted the following resolution in 1959: "The Committee in executive session recommends to all insurance supervisors that a rate for Credit Life or Credit Accident and Health producing a loss ratio of under 50% should be considered to be excessive." The meaning of this resolution is that a rate producing premiums which are more than twice the claims is excessive.

The charge to the debtor for insurance probably is the most important aspect of creditor insurance control. To implement the model bill's intent on this aspect, fourteen states have promulgated the NAIC 50 per cent loss ratio criterion in their regulations. Additionally, ten of these states have promulgated premium rate standards which can be considered to satisfy the 50 per cent criterion. One state has adopted a minimum loss ratio of less than 50 per cent and promulgated rate standards accordingly, and four states have adopted premium rate standards without a loss ratio criterion.

As may be noted from Appendix 25, only sixteen states now have promulgated premium rate standards. However, it is to be expected that more states will adopt standards based on credible statistics of creditor life and creditor health insurance mortality and morbidity experience, respectively. In 1964, a subcommittee of the NAIC completed a study of creditor life and health insurance experience. This study was designed to provide further guidance to insurance departments in properly assessing the reasonableness of benefits in relation to premiums and in implementing the NAIC's minimum 50 per cent loss ratio principle. While a credible volume of creditor life insurance experience was collected and analyzed, the creditor health insurance portion of this study was inconclusive, but the NAIC subcommittee now is attempting to devise a study to be made over the next two or three years to produce statistics upon which appropriate rate standards may be based.

Underwriting

In addition to the above statutory and regulatory controls, creditor group life and health insurance are subject to underwriting rules of the insurance company. Eligible creditors generally include all institutions which lend money, finance companies which purchase installment sales contracts from dealers, and vendors selling and financing goods on an installment basis. The usual types of creditors are banks, finance companies, small-loan companies, credit unions, department stores, and furniture, appliance and automobile dealers. Most types of installment financing normally transacted by these creditors are eligible for creditor group insurance coverage, although some insurance companies will not insure collateralized loans, because the creditor may be less concerned with the debtor's ability to repay than he would be in the absence of collateral. Only indebtedness made by natural persons is eligible for coverage, so that partnership, corporation or association indebtednesses usually are ineligible. Most insurers restrict the duration of eligible indebtednesses to five years, and many will cover only installment type loans, even where loans repayable in one sum are permitted to be covered by law. In addition, most insurers require that the group must meet certain minimum size requirements, such as a minimum number of new debtors per year and/or a minimum volume of indebtedness to be covered. The purposes of these requirements are to minimize the effect of individual selection against the plan and to assure that the premium will be sufficient to cover the risk and expenses. Typically, a maximum is imposed on the amount of life or health insurance that may be issued on any one debtor. This frequently depends on the total volume of insurance on the group. Finally, additional underwriting safeguards may be applied to individual debtors. For example, age limitations may be used to exclude from coverage debtors who are over age sixty-five at the time the credit is granted or who will be age sixty-six or more when the indebtedness is scheduled to mature. Similarly, evidence of insurability ranging from a simple test of employment status to a medical examination may be required of certain debtors.

NEW AREAS FOR CREDITOR GROUP COVERAGES

For many years, creditor group life and health insurance have been available in connection with personal loan transactions and time purchases of consumer durables, such as automobiles and home appliances. Now, however, financial institutions have broadened their operations to provide credit in many other areas of public need. Quite naturally, creditor group insurance also has been extended into these areas in recent years. The purpose of the remaining sections of this chapter is to examine the nature of these types of credit transactions and the ways in which creditor group life and health insurance have been extended to them.

Revolving Credit

Many retail merchants provide debt service to their customers by allowing a line of credit so that customers may freely purchase goods and services on credit, up to a stipulated maximum amount. The maximum is determined by the customer's ability to repay, as measured primarily by his earning power. From the merchant's standpoint, this approach, called revolving credit, minimizes expenses because each purchase or service to be financed on the installment basis need not be separately handled, but permits an open account within the line of credit based on a simple agreement initially entered into by the customer and merchant. For example, if a customer establishes a line of credit for $300 with a retail merchant, the customer may purchase goods and services on credit as his needs arise as long as the total amount for which he is indebted and which he has not repaid does not exceed $300.

The customer becomes indebted to the merchant when he, the customer, uses his line of credit in whole or part by making time purchases. To the extent a customer is indebted, he is billed periodically, usually monthly, by the merchant for a proportionate amount of his outstanding debt, plus a service charge thereon of 1 or 1½ per cent. As the purchaser gradually pays for the article, the amount of further credit available to him gradually is restored.

The laws of many states permit creditor group life and health insurance only in connection with indebtedness which is repayable in installments. Revolving credit meets this test, so extension of the coverage took place early in the development of this type of debt service.

When creditor group life insurance is provided, the face amount payable to the merchant in the event of the customer's death is the amount of outstanding indebtedness unpaid at time of death. The insurance discharges or reduces the deceased customer's obligation, thereby also relieving his estate. Because the maximum line of credit normally is set conservatively, for example, $500, the insurance usually completely extinguishes the debt.

The cost of group life insurance on revolving credit in many instances is borne by the merchant, who absorbs it within the service charge. In cases where the customer pays for the insurance, the periodic billing includes a separately disclosed insurance charge which is usually added to the customer's balance. In either instance, the merchant pays monthly premiums to the insurer, which are based on the total outstanding insured indebtedness of all of his customers.

Two unusual underwriting aspects connected with revolving credit are that the amount of indebtedness and, therefore, the insurance may remain level or even increase and that the term during which a debtor is insured is indefinite. Underwriting control is achieved in covering revolving credit through modest maximum amounts of line of credit granted by the merchant and through use of age limitations and conservative maximum amounts of insurance by the insurer.

Mobile Home and Shell Home Financing

A significant development of the post–World War II period was the large-scale production, sale and financing of mobile homes (house trailers) and shell homes (prefabricated house exteriors). Since creditor insurance had been available in connection with the financing of motor vehicles for some years, financing of these new products resulted in a natural extension of creditor group life and health insurance to protect both the vendor and purchaser.

Insuring debtors who financed mobile or shell homes presented insurers with certain new problems which had to be overcome in order to provide coverage on a sound underwriting basis. First, the duration of indebtedness and, consequently, of insurance previously had been limited generally to thirty-six months. However, because mobile and shell homes involve considerably higher initial prices than automobiles, they are financed over a longer period. Initially five years, today the period averages approximately seven years for mobile homes and ten years for shell homes.

An additional underwriting problem is the fact that the users of this type of credit as a group often have characteristics that may be unfavorable from the standpoint of the insurance company. For example, both mobile and shell homes appeal to retired people desiring less expensive quarters than they previously required. On the other hand, mobile homes often are purchased by skilled workers in the oil, construction and similar heavy industries who migrate to where the work is located. These people, of course, tend to be relatively young and quite robust. Shell homes also have appeal to younger people interested in a relatively inexpensive house for vacation purposes or even as a permanent home in which they will complete the interior.

Insurers have satisfactorily underwritten creditor group life and health insurance on mobile and shell home transactions by (1) carefully screening the creditor's area of operations and assessing his potential clientele for such transactions, (2) using age limitations and/or higher than normal premium rates and (3) employing underwriting safeguards in the form of evidence of insurability.

Education Loans

As a result of the great increase in the number of students attending college and the substantial cost of a college education, credit is being used more and more to finance the cost. Financial institutions, particularly banks, have formalized lending plans tailored to meet the tuition payments and other normal expenses of a college education as these costs arise. They are for relatively large amounts, as much as $10,000, and are repayable in installments over long terms, up to ten years.

The nature of an education loan transaction differs materially from the usual type of installment debt to which creditor insurance has been applied. In the latter type, the credit extended is required and utilized by the debtor immediately. For educational purposes, on the other hand, funds are needed periodically over a period of years, e.g., once each semester during a four-year college period. To accommodate this need, the total funds required to finance an education are disbursed periodically by the creditor so as to be available as needed, and the debtor obligates himself by a commitment to repay the total funds on an installment basis over a given period. The repayment period may be the same as, or longer than, the disbursement period; for example, the creditor disburses funds once each semester during four years, while the debtor repays monthly during six years.

The objective of providing creditor insurance in this instance is to assure continuance or completion of the student's education in the event of the untimely disability or death of the student's parent, guardian or sponsor. For this reason, insurance is provided on the amount the debtor (the student's parent, guardian or sponsor) is committed to repay.

In relation to the funds actually advanced periodically by the creditor, the commitment itself is not a true indebtedness as is usually required by statute if creditor group insurance is to be provided. However, recognizing the social desirability of education loan programs, the NAIC model bill provides that a commitment is an indebtedness for the purpose of creditor insurance.

Because education loan programs normally entail large amounts, long terms and a high average age of the debtor (parent, guardian or sponsor), creditor group life and health insurance coverages written in conjunction with education loans usually are underwritten with age limitations or evidence of insurability requirements.

Corporation and Partnership Indebtedness

For many years, creditor group insurance was limited to the indebtedness of borrowers who were natural persons, rather than corporations or partnerships, because creditors tended to provide installment debt of modest amounts to individual borrowers. As creditors expanded installment debt facilities to provide larger loans and to finance higher priced commodity purchases, corporations and partnerships began to use installment credit, often called term loans, instead of the demand or single payment, short-term note. As a result, creditor group coverages soon were extended to this new type of loan.

When a bank makes an installment loan to a corporation, it is not uncommon, particularly in the case of smaller corporations, to require that an officer of the company be made personally liable for the indebtedness. Similarly, in the case of installment loans to small firms organized as partnerships, the partners are jointly and severally liable for the indebtedness. The duration of these loans varies somewhat, depending upon the size of the loan and the credit standing of the borrower, but most frequently is approximately five years. Only in rare cases does the duration extend beyond ten years.

There are two approaches in providing creditor insurance on these transactions. One is to provide coverage of the full amount of the indebtedness (subject to the policy maximum) on one officer of the corporation or one partner of the partnership. Alternatively, the insurance may be prorated equally among all of the officers or partners. To be eligible for insurance under either approach, the individual must be actively engaged in the productive activities of the corporation or partnership. In the case of corporation indebtedness, the officer or officers to be eligible for the insurance must be co-debtors with the corporation, because the insured must be a natural person. In the case of partnership indebtedness, because the partners are jointly and severally liable for the indebtedness, each partner is a debtor and so is eligible for insurance.

Under the first approach, there is an inherent element of adverse selection in covering corporation and partnership indebtedness in that the choice as to who is to be insured may rest solely with the entity incurring the debt. For this reason, underwriting safeguards consisting of age limitations and/or some form of evidence of insurability may be employed by the insurance company.

Commercial Loans

The term "commercial loan" for the purposes of this section refers to a loan repayable in a single amount at the end of a stipulated time period. As mentioned earlier, the laws of the various jurisdictions governing creditor group life and health insurance generally permit coverage of installment loans only, i.e., those repayable in other than a single payment. However, some jurisdictions permit creditor group life insurance on single payment loans of not more than eighteen months' duration and allow up to six months of additional coverage if the debtor defaults. When provided, availability of coverage is normally subject to the requirements described for corporation and partnership indebtedness.

Leases

A type of financial arrangement frequently used in modern business operations is a lease transaction. Under the arrangement, an individual, as the lessee, contracts for and employs the services of some tangible property for a stated period of time, up to twenty-four months, at a specific cost. The lessee pays the cost periodically, usually monthly. An example of this type of service is the leasing of equipment, such as motor vehicles or other mechanical devices essential to a particular operation, in instances where outright purchase would involve a prohibitive outlay of capital funds. Another example is a lease transaction for the use of a dwelling, such as an apartment.

Creditor group insurance is sometimes provided on lease transactions to ensure continued use of the tangible property during the lease period in the event of the lessee's death or disability without further lease payments to the lessor. Some recent impetus has been given to providing creditor group insurance on leases by the laws of certain jurisdictions, notably New York, recognizing a lease as an indebtedness and a lessor as a creditor. Under most states' laws, the amount of insurance cannot exceed the amount of indebtedness. Under a lease agreement, the actual indebtedness generally is not sufficient to allow insurance to the extent usually desired. For these reasons, only a relatively small amount of lease agreement coverage has been written.

From an insurance underwriting standpoint, an element of abnormal exposure exists in covering this type of financial arrangement. It arises because lessees tend to continue to use the service on a renewal lease basis for a number of years. Thus, unless there is infusion of a significant number of new accounts under the group contract, the steady aging of the group will have an adverse effect on mortality or morbidity experience. To minimize this effect, underwriting safeguards, consisting of age limitations and/or evidence of insurability requirements of some form—such as a simple questionnaire consisting of questions concerning health—normally are employed when creditor group insurance is provided on lease transactions.

Residential Mortgages

As a type of debt service to which creditor group insurance can be applied, residential mortgage financing undoubtedly involves the highest degree of social desirability and insurable interest. By its nature, this type of credit represents the largest amounts and longest terms of individual indebtedness to which creditor group insurance has been applied.

Because of the long initial terms (as much as thirty-five years) and large initial amounts (as much as $30,000 or more) of mortgage credit, underwriting creditor group insurance on it is usually more involved than underwriting applied to other types of credit. Customarily, the eligibility of a mortgagor for coverage depends upon his age and the term of the mortgage, a typical rule being that the mortgage maturity date must occur prior to attainment by the mortgagor of a stipulated age, such as age seventy. Premium rates are set according to the mortgagor's age at the time of his entry into the insurance program. Underwriting safeguards normally consist of some form of evidence of insurability, varying from a relatively simple test of employment status for young mortgagors to a medical examination for older mortgagors. Although creditor group insurance on residential mortgages involves a greater degree of individual debtor underwriting than generally exists for other types of credit transactions, the underwriting process is applied so as not to disrupt or impede the credit process, that is, in an uncomplicated manner which does not delay or otherwise postpone the consummation of the mortgage transaction.

There are two popular forms of creditor group life insurance covering residential mortgages. Under one form, the amount of insurance is the unpaid mortgage principal existing from time to time during the mortgage term. Thus, if the mortgagor dies during the term of the mortgage, the amount of insurance is sufficient to reduce or extinguish the mortgage, depending upon the maximum amount of insurance provided under the master group policy.

The objective of this form is to provide full coverage to the extent possible. Insurers generally permit liberal maximum amounts of insurance because of the greater degree of individual underwriting. However, it is not always possible to accomplish the full coverage objective because the statutes of many states permit only $10,000 ($5,000 in some states) of creditor group life insurance on a mortgagor, and the mortgage amount may be considerably more than the statutory maximum. There are two typical methods of covering mortgages which are greater than the statutory maximum. Under the first, the group policy provides that the amount of insurance is level at the maximum until the remaining mortgage principal reduces to the maximum. From that point to the mortgage maturity date the amount of insurance equals the remaining mortgage principal. The second method provides that the amount of insurance from time to time is the remaining mortgage principal multiplied by the ratio of the policy maximum to the initial amount of mortgage. Thus, the amount of insurance is always a proportionate part of the remaining debt. The method chosen for covering mortgage amounts greater than the permissible maximum insurance depends upon which one the creditor's (mortgagee's) administrative system can best accommodate.

An alternative form of benefit provides for payment of a specified number of monthly mortgage payments, such as twenty-four or forty-eight, if the mortgagor dies. If death occurs when the number of remaining mortgage payments is fewer than the number specified as a death benefit, the benefit payable is the number of remaining mortgage payments.

Although it is acknowledged that the plan covering the full mortgage may be more desirable, its cost is an important consideration to the mortgagor at the time he obtains the mortgage. Therefore, the alternate plan, with its relatively limited benefit and lower cost, has appeal because it provides substantial relief to the mortgagor himself in the event of his disability and to his survivors in the event of his death, since they are provided with the means to continue to occupy the dwelling during the critical adjustment period following the mortgagor's death.

This alternative form of mortgage coverage may also provide, as an adjunct to the life insurance, a disability income benefit which is payable after the mortgagor has been disabled for a stipulated period, usually fourteen or thirty days. Total disability usually is defined as the inability of the debtor, due to sickness or accident, to engage in any occupation for wage or profit. Monthly disability benefits in the amount of the monthly mortgage payment are payable during the mortgagor's continued disability, with the number of disability payments limited in the same way as the death benefit.

Land Development Financing

In recent years, land developers have subdivided large tracts of unimproved land into small parcels of a size suitable for individual purchase and marketed the parcels at a relatively low purchase price. As an alternative to an outright cash purchase, they have permitted purchases to be financed over a period as long as ten years, requiring minimal down payments and monthly payments of as little as $10. The market for this type of financing exists among people who finance such purchases for investment purposes, to erect a second home for vacation needs or to have a homesite available at retirement.

The credit instrument used in connection with such financing usually is much like that used for retail installment purchases of automobiles and home appliances, so creditor group life and health insurance normally can be provided readily. To the extent that the credit instrument establishes a true debt, the land developer meets the legal definition of a creditor, and the group comprised of the prospective debtors can be soundly underwritten. In this case, creditor group insurance can be, and to a limited degree has been, extended to land development financing.

Installment Purchases of Mutual Fund Shares

A mutual fund, or open-end investment company, is a fund which provides the means for an investor to realize the benefits of owning a widely diversified list of investment securities. By pooling the money of a number of investors, funds are available to provide the costs of professional management.

An investor may purchase shares in such funds on an installment basis and finance the purchase of such shares. This is accomplished by the investor entering into an agreement with the sponsor or distributor of the mutual fund. The agreement establishes a goal of a stipulated amount, e.g., $10,000, to be built up over a specified period of time, such as five or ten years. The agreement further provides for periodic payments, usually monthly, to be made by the investor to the sponsor or its agent to build up to the predetermined goal. Shares of the fund are purchased by the sponsor for the investor from time to time as the investor's periodic payments accrue.

Creditor insurance provided in connection with mutual fund purchases has the objective of permitting the investor's goal to be realized despite his disability or premature death. Creditor group health insurance pays the investor's periodic installment while he is disabled during the investment period. Creditor group life insurance provides for payment to the mutual fund of the difference between the investor's goal and the accumulated amount of his periodic payment in the event the investor dies; thus monies are available to the sponsor to purchase mutual fund shares for the investor's estate.

Creditor insurance has been employed to a limited degree to insure the lives of investors who are financing the purchase of such shares. In view of the fact that the investor may voluntarily withdraw from such plans and limit his obligation to the extent of the shares available for purchase based on the total amount of his payments at the time of withdrawal, some states have not permitted the use of creditor group insurance in connection with mutual fund programs, inasmuch as the purchase agreement does not provide for a true debt. However, provision may be made in the agreement that in the event of the investor's death the balance remaining unpaid at the time automatically becomes an obligation of his estate, in which event an indebtedness exists, and the insurance proceeds are applied to relieve the obligation of the estate. In view of the relatively high amount, long term and sophisticated market represented by this type of transaction, creditor insurance almost always is provided subject to age limitations and evidence of insurability.

SELECTED REFERENCES

CADE, A. J. "Fundamental Issues of Consumer Credit Insurance," *Insurance Law Journal*, No. 385 (February, 1955), pp. 76–93.

DOWNEY, F. R. "Insurance in Installment Credit Transactions," *Insurance Law Journal*, No. 423 (April, 1958), pp. 256–63.

———. *Report on Insurance Charges in Consumer Credit Transaction to Leffert Holz, Superintendent of Insurance.* Albany: State of New York, 1957.

DUNBAR, E. A. "Credit Insurance—Use by Licensed Lenders," *Insurance Law Journal*, No. 402 (July, 1956), pp. 443–58.

FOSTER, KENNETH C. "Credit Life and Health Insurance," *Life and Health Insurance Handbook* (ed. DAVIS W. GREGG), chap. 31. 2d ed. Homewood, Ill.: Richard D. Irwin, Inc., 1964.

JACOBSON, J. B. *An Analysis of Group Creditors Insurance.* Newark: Prudential Insurance Co., 1955.

KEDZIE, D. P. *Consumer Credit Insurance.* Homewood, Ill.: Richard D. Irwin, Inc., 1957.

MORS, W. P. "Consumer Installment Credit Insurance," *Insurance Law Journal,* No. 400 (May, 1956), pp. 299–318.

NATIONAL ASSOCIATION OF INSURANCE COMMISSIONERS. *Study on Credit Life and Credit Accident and Health Insurance.* New York, 1957.

———. *Subcommittee to Study Credit Life Insurance and Credit Accident and Health Insurance Experience.* June, 1964.

UNITED STATES CONGRESS (SENATE). *The Tie-in Sale of Credit Insurance in Connection with Small Loans and Other Transactions. Report of the Sub-committee on Antitrust and Monopoly Legislation of the Committee on the Judiciary, 83d Congress, 2d Session.* Washington, D.C.: U.S. Government Printing Office, 1955.

WHITTAKER, E. B. "Group Creditors Life Insurance," *Journal of the American Society of Chartered Life Underwriters,* Vol. VII (June, 1953), pp. 219–24, 254.

Chapter 36[1]

CONTINUATION OF MEDICAL EXPENSE
COVERAGE FOR RETIRED INDIVIDUALS

BY RAYMOND G. McCULLOUGH

Gradually over the years there has been a diminishing of the sharp line of demarcation that separated the approaches for insuring active and retired employees under group medical insurance plans. The practice of terminating all coverage at retirement was first modified to permit the continuance of very limited benefits for pensioners, while in recent years the types and scope of retirees' coverage have been expanded until currently many plans provide virtually the same benefits before and following retirement. This changing pattern of medical expense coverage for pensioners has been influenced by marked changes in the senior citizen group itself as well as by broad social, political and economic developments in our society.

HEALTH INSURANCE NEEDS OF PENSIONERS

Aging Nature of the American Population

Since the turn of the century, modern medicine has made tremendous advances in reducing deaths caused by infectious and nutritional diseases, particularly in the younger age groups. The result has been that a larger proportion of the population is living to the advanced ages. As illustrated in Table 36–1, there has been an absolute and relative increase in the number of citizens over age sixty-five, and it is expected that this trend will continue through 1980.

This growth in the aged portion of the population has been paralleled by the transition of America into an industrialized, urban society in which most older people are dependent largely upon pensions or savings accumulated from earnings during years of active employment to finance

---

[1] The enactment of pending (May, 1965) federal legislation to provide medical care coverage to persons age sixty-five and older would profoundly influence the coverages and approaches discussed in this chapter.

TABLE 36–1

NUMBER AND PERCENTAGE OF CITIZENS OVER AGE SIXTY-FIVE

Year	Citizens over 65	Citizens over 65 as a % of Total Population
1900	3,100,000	4.1
1910	3,985,000	4.3
1920	4,929,000	4.6
1930	6,706,000	5.4
1940	9,031,000	6.8
1950	12,287,000	8.1
1960	16,658,000	9.2
1970	20,035,000*	9.6*
1980	24,458,000*	10.0*

* Estimates.
Source: U.S. Department of Commerce, Bureau of Census, *Historical Statistics of the U.S., Colonial Times to 1957* (a statistical abstract supplement) (Washington, D.C.: U.S. Government Printing Office, 1960), p. 8; and U.S. Department of Commerce, Bureau of Census, *Statistical Abstract of U.S., 1963* (Washington, D.C.: U.S. Government Printing Office, 1963), p. 6.

their post-retirement needs, including the cost of medical care. This reliance upon the employment relationship has focused attention upon the employer's group insurance program as a most suitable vehicle for providing pensioners and their dependents with medical expense insurance.

Health of the Aged

The health problems of the senior citizens point to the importance of adequate insurance in the years following retirement. With advancing age the degenerative diseases have a greater impact and diseases that can be readily coped with in the younger, more vigorous years attain greater seriousness as the body's recuperative powers decline. Table 36–2 shows the increase in chronic illnesses and the greater severity of such illnesses with advancing age.

The increase in disabilities among the aged is reflected in the extent to which older people receive doctors' care and utilize medical facilities. As illustrated by Table 36–3, with advancing age, hospital confinements become more frequent and the hospital stays are of longer duration. Similarly, the need for doctors' care becomes greater at the older ages. The figures set forth in Table 36–4 show the advancing utilization trend with age. Expressed in terms of personal expenditures for various types of medical care, the figures in Table 36–5 illustrate the generally higher health care costs incurred by the aged.

Methods of Insuring Medical Expenses of the Aged

Many of our senior citizens are confronted with this increased need for medical treatment for themselves and their dependents at a time when a

TABLE 36–2

Per Cent of the Population with One or More Chronic
Conditions, United States, July, 1962–June, 1963

	Per Cent of Population		
Age	Without Limitation of Activity	With Limitation of Activity	Total
All ages	32.1	12.4	44.5
Under 15	17.5	2.0	19.5
15–44	37.9	8.0	45.9
45–64	43.6	20.7	64.3
65 and over	32.3	48.9	81.2

Source: U.S. Department of Health, Education and Welfare, "Medical Care,
Health Status, and Family Income, U.S.," *National Center for Health Statistics*,
Series 10, No. 9 (May, 1964), p. 55.

reduced income limits their ability to pay for such care. Realistically, this
problem is not confined to the aged's medical care requirements, but
rather should be viewed as part of retirees' much broader problem of
needing financial resources to meet all of their living costs. To some extent
this situation is mitigated by the older person's generally reduced economic obligations for such items as food, clothing and transportation, and
the fact that he no longer has responsibilities for the care and education of
children. Also, in recent years improvements in private pension plans and
OASDI, increased savings, home ownership and other equities of pensioners, and the much wider availability of medical expense insurance for
retirees have improved their ability to manage these problems.

TABLE 36–3

Hospital Confinements and Length of Stay
Average Annual Number of Patients Discharged per 1,000
Insured per Year and Average Length of Stay*

Ages	Patients per 1,000 Population	Average Length of Stay in Days — 120-Day Plan
18–24	87	6.8
25–34	88	7.7
35–44	104	9.0
45–54	120	10.9
55–64	143	13.9
65–74	166	17.7
75–84	208	22.8
Average	107	9.5

* Figures are for all causes except maternity.
Source: State of New York Insurance Department, *Voluntary Health Insurance and the Senior Citizen: A Report on the Problem of Continuation of
Medical Care Benefits for the Aged in New York State.* Figures are based on
1957 study, pp. 140–11.

TABLE 36–4

NUMBER OF DOCTORS' VISITS FOR VARIOUS AGE GROUPS
Average Annual Number of Doctors' Visits per Person per
Year, July, 1957–June, 1959

Age	Number of Visits
All ages	5.0
0–4	6.2
5–14	3.7
15–24	4.5
25–44	4.9
45–64	5.4
65 and over	6.8

Source: U.S. Department of Health, Education and Welfare, "Volume of Physicians Visits, U.S., July 1957–June 1959," *Health Statistics from U.S. National Health Survey.*

The greater availability of medical expense insurance for pensioners is in part a reflection of employers' willingness to help pensioners handle their economic problems. Although earlier emphasis was on pensions and continuing group life insurance beyond the cessation of active employment, in recent years there has been a growing employer concern with the medical expense insurance needs of retirees and their dependents. The terms of recently negotiated health and welfare plans also attest to the greater concern of unions in post-retirement medical benefits for their membership.

TABLE 36–5

ANNUAL EXPENDITURES PER PERSON (DOLLARS),
JULY–DECEMBER, 1962

	All Ages	65 and Over
All services	$129	$208
Hospital	30	53
Doctor	43	62
Medicine	26	54
Dental	19	15
Other	11	24

Source: U.S. Department of Health, Education and Welfare, "Medical Care, Health Status and Family Income, U.S.," *National Center for Health Statistics*, Series 10, No. 9 (May, 1964), p. 48.

This subject has been before Congress for many years. The Kerr-Mills Act enacted in 1960 provides liberal federal grants to states that will undertake a program to help older people with very limited or no financial resources pay their medical bills. A much broader governmental approach is advocated by those who favor a federal health care program for senior citizens financed through an increase in OASDI taxes. The debate[2] over

[2] See *Medical Care for the Aged, Hearing before the Committee on Ways and Means, House of Representatives, Eighty-eighth Congress on HR 3920, November 18, 1963 to January 24, 1964.*

such proposals has attained the proportions of a national issue with the lines sharply drawn between the advocates and opponents of a governmental plan. Those in favor contend that many of our senior citizens will be able to enjoy adequate protection only through such a program. The opponents are convinced that it would be the first step toward an eventual compulsory program for the entire population which would destroy voluntary health insurance and impair the quality of medical care. They point to the marked progress being made by private insurers in continually extending voluntary coverage to a larger portion of the retired population.

The figures in Table 36–6, based on the 1963 Survey of the Aged made by the Social Security Administration can be contrasted with the fact that in 1952 only 26 per cent of the population aged sixty-five and over were insured under voluntary health insurance plans.[3]

TABLE 36–6

HEALTH INSURANCE COVERAGE OF AGED, 1962

Age	Per Cent with Health Insurance
62 to 64 years	68
65 to 72 years	59
73 years and over	44

Source: Dorothy P. Rice, "Health Insurance Coverage of the Aged and Their Hospital Utilization in 1962: Findings of the 1963 Survey of the Aged," *Social Security Bulletin*, July, 1964, p. 14.

Wider availability of coverage and the improved economic status of recent pensioners account for the larger percentage of employees with coverage under age seventy-two than beyond that age. Barring further involvement of the government, officials of the Health Insurance Association of America predict that by 1969 at least 80 per cent of the aged requiring and wanting health insurance will have it.[4]

The ability of private plans to meet the needs of the great majority of the aged is related to the adequacy of coverage as well as the number of lives insured. Recognition of this fact by the insurance industry has resulted in substantial broadening of the scope of coverages available for pensioners. This trend in benefit liberalizations is discussed in a subsequent section of this chapter.

The versatility of the vehicles used by private plans to extend coverage to senior citizens accounts in large part for the success being achieved in increasing the number insured and improving the quality of coverage. At the same time the retiree has considerable choice in deciding upon the type of coverage that best meets his needs and pocketbook.

---

[3] Health Insurance Council, "The Aged and Private Health Insurance," *Health Insurance Viewpoints*, January, 1964.

[4] *Ibid.*

Continuance under the employer's group plan following retirement and conversion to an individual policy are two of the most important means of providing health insurance for pensioners. Chapter 37 discusses the senior citizens, mass enrollment programs conducted by several insurance companies, the joint efforts of many insurers to provide such protection through State-65 plans, and the issuance of group policies to insure older aged groups exclusively, such as the members of retirement communities. In addition to these group arrangements, many insurance companies also issue individual policies either specifically designed for older people or written so that coverage can be maintained in force at the advanced ages.

CONVERSION OF GROUP HEALTH COVERAGES TO INDIVIDUAL POLICIES

The conversion right permits the insured to obtain coverage under an individual contract when his participation in a group plan ceases. As under group life policies where this concept originated, those converting to individual health insurance contracts are not required to furnish medical evidence of insurability, but the right must be exercised within a limited period, such as thirty-one days, following termination of the group coverage. Once the converted policy is issued, the administration follows that of other forms of individual insurance with premiums paid directly to the insurer by the insured.

Eligibility for Conversion

Typically, the conversion right is available in the following circumstances: (1) to the employee upon termination of his employment in the classes eligible to participate in the group plan whether this occurs during years of active employment or at retirement; (2) to the surviving spouse upon the death of the employee if the family was insured under the group plan; (3) to a dependent child upon attaining the limiting age of coverage as a dependent or upon marriage. Usually this conversion right is available to the employee who has been insured under the group policy for at least three months and makes application for the individual policy within thirty-one days following termination of his group coverage.

Although the conversion right affords valuable protection to the person whose group benefits are terminated for the above reasons, converted coverage is usually only temporary coverage if obtained during an employee's working years. When the individual is re-employed and again becomes eligible to participate in a group plan, he usually discontinues premium payments for the converted policy and joins the typically less expensive group plan.

Where group benefits are not continued beyond retirement, the conversion right is an important source of long-term medical expense insurance for pensioners.

Cost of Converted Policies

The cost of insurance under converted policies is higher than under group plans because of the anti-selection and the greater administration expense. It is usually the less healthy risks, conscious of the greater likelihood that they will need medical treatment, who are more prone to exercise the conversion right. However, the anti-selection factor may be mitigated in the case of pensioners when the converted policies constitute the employer's way of making coverage available following retirement and broad use is made of this arrangement. The higher administrative expense reflects the fact that individual records and premium collection accounts must be maintained for the converted policies as contrasted with the economies inherent in the administration of group contracts. Furthermore, the high termination rate under these policies, which are often purchased as temporary protection, adds to the administrative expense. The extent to which this higher cost is reflected in the premium charge made to the insured differs widely between the insurance companies' and Blue Cross and Blue Shield plans, depending upon whether the premiums are established on an experience or community rating basis.

Blue Cross and Blue Shield Conversions

The conversion coverage, or "left employ benefits" as it is commonly called, is available under all Blue Cross and Blue Shield plans and has been the most important means of covering pensioners and their dependents under these programs. It has been estimated that ". . . some 25 per cent or more of all Blue Cross subscribers are persons who have left employment where they were covered on a group basis, or who have enrolled as individuals; a large segment of this group are persons sixty-five and over."[5]

The benefits provided usually follow the same pattern as those available under the group plan except in some programs the number of days for which hospitalization benefits are available is curtailed, while in others where both a comprehensive and deductible plan are available, only the latter is permitted upon conversion. A study made in 1958 showed that fifty-seven of the seventy-nine Blue Cross plans did not reduce benefits under the converted contracts except ". . . where the member had formerly been enrolled in one of the more comprehensive or special group contracts rather than in the standard or most-widely-held-group contracts."[6]

---

[5] Blue Cross Association and American Hospital Association, *Financing Health Care of the Aged; Part 1, A Study of the Dimensions of the Problem* (Chicago, Ill., 1962), p. 128.

[6] Agnes W. Brewster and Ruth Bloodgood, *Blue Cross Provisions for Persons Aged 65 and Over, Late 1958* (U.S. Department of Health, Education and Welfare, Research and Statistics Note No. 5). (Washington, D.C., 1959), p. 4.

Although the cost differences between group and conversion coverage vary from one Blue Cross–Blue Shield plan to another, the median cost for a family contract in 1959 was about 15 per cent higher for conversion contracts than for the group plan.[7] This relatively small increase in cost is largely a reflection of the community rating concept followed by most of the Blue Cross and Blue Shield plans, whereby all or part of the extra administrative and claim cost incurred under these individual policies is absorbed by the active participants.

Converted Policies Issued by Insurance Companies

Since insurance companies have generally emphasized continued participation in the group plan as the most suitable means of insuring pensioners and their dependents, they make the conversion right available to their group policyholders, but have not placed the same stress on it as have the Blue Cross and Blue Shield programs.

The broader use of the conversion right was given impetus by the "Metcalf Legislation" passed in New York State. Effective July 1, 1959, insurance companies were required to make a conversion right available upon request of a New York group policyholder. New York went one step further with the passage of the Russo Act which required the automatic inclusion of the conversion right in all group policies providing hospital, surgical, medical, specific diseases or accident only benefits issued or renewed in New York on and after January 1, 1963.

In addition to making the conversion right mandatory rather than optional as under the Metcalf Legislation, the Russo Act provided that an employee insured under a New York group policy must be given a choice of three plans to which he may convert.[8] Other important changes included assigning to the New York Insurance Department responsibility for promulgating maximum individual policy premium rates applicable to converted policies for employees age sixty and over and a requirement

---

[7] Based on figures furnished by Blue Cross Commission and Blue Shield Plans, Inc., and cited by Herman Miles Somers and Anne Ramsay Sommers, *Doctors, Patients and Health Insurance* (Washington, D.C.: The Brookings Institution, 1961), pp. 312 and 336.

[8] The following plan choices are available under the Russo legislation:

	Plan 1	Plan 2	Plan 3
Hospital room and board per day up to	$ 10	$ 15	$ 15
Maximum days per period of confinement	21	30	70
Additional hospital charges during a period of confinement are reimbursed up to a maximum of ten times the daily room and board benefit under the plan selected.			
Surgical schedule maximum	$200	$250	$300

that terminating employees must be issued a notice of the conversion right.

Typically, the individual who decides to convert upon termination of his group coverage can select from among several levels of hospital, surgical and medical benefits. Consistent with the insurance companies' approach of rating each class of policies on a self-supporting basis, the premium rates are usually graded by age and reflect the higher morbidity and administrative expenses under these contracts. Insurance companies generally have not adopted the practice of assessing part of the higher cost of these individual converted policies back to the group policyholder in the form of a conversion charge as is the practice with group life insurance, but some companies have indicated the possibility of utilizing this procedure in the future.

The right to convert to an individual policy at retirement has been an important source of medical expense insurance for pensioners. As the number of senior citizens insured for these benefits has rapidly grown, though, it has come to be recognized that because of their inherently greater cost, the converted policies are not usually the ideal way to insure retired lives. Covering pensioners under the group policies which insured them as active employees is generally the most efficient way of providing this protection, and thus there is reason to expect a continued decline in the use of converted policies for this purpose.

CONTINUANCE OF EMPLOYEES UNDER GROUP HEALTH COVERAGES

Rationale for Group Continuance

The various forms of group coverage dominate the spectrum of techniques used to meet the health insurance needs of the American people. Of the 88 million individuals with insured hospitalization benefits at the end of 1963, 60 million had this coverage under group contracts, while 61 of the 84 million with insured surgical coverage had group benefits. Also at the end of 1963 there were 62 million individuals covered by Blue Cross and 52 million by Blue Shield, and it is estimated that about three fourths of these lives were in group plans.[9] A still larger portion of the population can be expected to be brought within the scope of group plans as more small employer groups are reached through contracts written to insure employer members of trade associations and their employees and as standardized programs are used to make group insurance available to small employers at a low net cost.

This vast volume of coverage for employees during their years of active

---

[9] *The Extent of Voluntary Health Insurance Coverage in the U.S., 1963*, Survey conducted by the Health Insurance Council.

employment is the logical base from which to extend coverage to these same individuals after they retire. Including pensioners under the group plan brings this coverage within the framework of the low administrative expense structure of group insurance. The costs of issuing individual policies are avoided, as is accounting for premiums on an individual life basis and the necessity of dealing directly with the retiree on all matters affecting his coverage.

Furthermore, group continuance promotes a higher level of participation. This higher participation results from the lower cost of the group benefits, the fact that belonging to the plan involves the continuance of benefits enjoyed for many years as an active employee and, most importantly, the employer's willingness to play an important role in assuring the plan's success. The employer arranges to have these benefits provided under his group contract, helps administer the program and often pays all or a part of the cost of the coverage. Since the employee is continuing his participation in the group plan there is no exclusion of individuals because of their health status.

An important additional advantage of group continuance under insured plans is the extensive flexibility in plan design that is usually available. Just as benefits can be tailor-made to satisfy the needs of active employee groups, so too are group insurance plans for pensioners constructed in accordance with the benefit requirements and financial resources of the particular group.

Aside from the economic reasons favoring group continuance, there also may be a psychological benefit from having the employee belong to the group he was associated with while an active employee. At a time when many adjustments must be made in his way of living, he can enjoy the continuity of having his medical expense insurance needs taken care of by the group plan.

Group Continuance under Insurance Company Plans

In the past decade a marked shift has occurred in the approach of insurance companies toward insuring pensioners under group plans as the companies have responded to the challenge of meeting the health insurance needs of senior citizens. In addition to making coverage available under their plans, insurance companies are now encouraging their policyholders to provide these benefits and suggesting the most suitable plans for this purpose. The earlier practice of curtailing benefits at retirement is being replaced by a general willingness to provide the same benefits for active and retired employees.

Eligible Groups. Today, group continuance is usually available to all except the very small groups, such as those with less than twenty-five lives. The adverse selection problem, in terms of controlling who might be insured under the pensioners' plan, is greater in small, often family owned, firms. Also, these small groups frequently do not have the facilities for maintaining the contact with the pensioners required to administer the plan. While the advantages of group continuance in terms of cost and flexibility are not as pronounced in the small case area and the problems of anti-selection are greater, recently some insurers have announced programs for permitting even these cases to continue benefits following retirement on a group basis. In some instances these programs take the form of uniform plans for retirees of all small cases, while in others the pensioners are permitted to continue virtually the same benefits they had as active employees.

Eligible Employees and Dependents. Individuals eligible to participate in the pensioners' plan usually include all employees retiring under a company's pension plan. Where an employee does not qualify for such benefits or a pension plan is not in effect, insurers generally consider retirement under OASDI as qualifying an individual for eligibility in the medical expense insurance plan. In many instances, employees need to have worked for the employer for a stated period of time, such as five years, prior to retirement to be eligible.

When a pensioner's plan is initially installed, many insurance companies will cover the existing pensioners as well as those retiring in the future, if the employer so desires. To avoid adverse selection against the plan by individuals who would defer purchasing coverage until the likelihood of claim was greater, it is common to require that an employee have participated in the plan while he was an active employee if he wants to be insured following retirement. Where pensioners pay part or all of the cost of their insurance, they are usually given thirty-one days immediately following retirement in which to elect to participate. If existing pensioners are eligible, they are given a somewhat longer period, such as three months, in which to subscribe because of the time required to contact these individuals.

Eligible dependents of pensioners are normally defined in the same manner as for active employees—spouse (or wife) and unmarried children to age nineteen (or to a higher age in the case of full-time, unmarried students). Some plans, however, include only the spouse as an eligible dependent because not many employees at the advanced ages will have dependent children. It is becoming quite common to continue the dependent benefits in force under the group plan following the death of the pensioner, except that this insurance ceases if the spouse remarries. Although this continuance of coverage on the spouse can impose additional administrative burdens on the employer in terms of collecting contributions and assisting in processing claims, employers seem to be willing to assume this task in view of the spouse's reliance upon the benefits and the broad social need for this coverage.

Plan Design

In designing a group plan for pensioners, a key consideration is the economic resources available to purchase the insurance. This will vary widely from group to group and will depend upon the extent to which the employer will share the cost and also on the general level of income being received by the particular pensioner group. Once having established the approximate amount that can be expended for this coverage, the next step is to direct these premium dollars into the area of the greatest insurance need for the particular group. In developing the features of the plan, stress should be placed on simplicity of plan design. It must be kept in mind that in many instances the retiree no longer resides in the community where the group is located and reliance must be placed on the written description of the plan and correspondence to explain the program to pensioners and answer questions that arise in its administration.

Briefly, the range of benefits available for designing a plan of medical expense insurance for pensioners runs the gamut of active employee benefits. Included among the basic benefits are hospitalization, surgical and medical coverage, plus plans reimbursing for the expenses of diagnostic X-ray and laboratory services, X-ray therapy benefits, supplemental accident and other special coverages. The major medical expense benefits may be written either to supplement basic coverages or on a comprehensive basis.

Although still in the experimental state, the development of coverage for confinement in nursing homes has particular importance for older citizens because of the generally longer duration of their hospital confinements. The objective of this coverage is to shorten the period of hospital stay by encouraging the use of nursing homes when the patient still requires institutional care but no longer needs the intensive treatment furnished by general hospitals. The intent is to reimburse the insured for expenses for rehabilitory but not custodial care in nursing homes. This can be a difficult distinction to make among older patients. As a consequence, the inclusion of nursing home benefits in a plan is usually accompanied by the requirement that nursing home care must have been preceded by a period of hospital confinement of at least five days in order to be eligible for reimbursement.

One other type of service that will likely come within the scope of pensioners' plans in the future is the home care facilities operated by some hospitals. There has been very limited experimentation with this type of coverage, although it will undoubtedly increase as more hospitals adopt the practice of extending services into the homes of patients following their discharge from the hospital.

The cost considerations, which are reviewed subsequently in this chapter, and the limited ability of pensioners to pay for this coverage, commonly lead to the following modifications in the plans for retired employees:

1. Where funds are limited, emphasis should be placed on the greater insurance needs. For example, a group with a base plan plus major medical expense for active employees might want to continue just the major medical expense with a $100 or $200 deductible for pensioners.
2. The major medical expense maximum usually does not exceed $5,000. Where the maximum is on a per cause basis for active employees, it is often changed to an all cause, lifetime basis for pensioners because of the difficulty in separating medical expenses by cause at the older ages.
3. Frequently, where home and office medical expense benefits are applicable to active employees, they are eliminated from the pensioners' plans since a significant portion of the premium for these benefits is used for administrative expenses and it is desirable to direct the available dollars for pensioners insurance to more critical areas of coverage.
4. So-called "frill benefits," such as supplemental accident coverage, are often eliminated from a retiree's plan.
5. The test of return to active work used for active employee coverage to separate successive disabilities for the same or related causes is not appropriate for retired lives. For pensioners, therefore, successive disabilities for the same or related cause are usually considered as the same disability unless separated by a period of three months or more.

The desire to make maximum use of the premium dollar available for pensioners' insurance encourages the inclusion of the insurance industry's nonprofit, nonduplication provision in these contracts.[10] This helps assure that the premiums will be used to purchase necessary protection and not to produce a profit for a small portion of the insured lives.

Cost of Pensioners' Insurance

In an earlier section of this chapter, reference was made to the greater utilization of medical services by retired employees and their dependents, and this must be reflected in the premium rates for pensioners. The rates should be based on the age distribution of the pensioners which, in turn, will depend upon their retirement age and the relative maturity of the retiree group. That is, in the years immediately following the initiation of a retiree insurance program the number of insured pensioners will be relatively small and their ages will be close to sixty-five (if that is the normal retirement age), unless existing pensioners are brought into the new plan. With the passage of time the pensioners' group will grow to the point where pensioners will ultimately become about 18 per cent of the number of active employees and their average age will be about seventy-four.[11]

---

[10] Nonduplication provisions were discussed in detail in Chapter 24.

[11] The percentage of people over age sixty-five is based on a modification of the mortality table in E. E. Cammack's paper "Group Life Insurance—Recent Mortality, Insurance of Pensioners, and Cost of Conversions," *Actuarial Society of America Transactions,* 1940, Vol. XLI, Nos. 103, 104. The table was modified to allow for mortality improvement since 1941.

In practice a much simpler system of rating is generally used; the rate for retirees is determined as a multiple of the rate for active male employees. At the older ages women no longer experience greater medical expenses than men, and thus the same rates are used for male and female pensioners and for spouses.

The factors used as multiples for retirees' coverage differ somewhat from company to company, based upon their experience studies. The following factors presently in use by one large group writing company are believed to be representative:

Coverage	Retiree Rates as a Multiple of the Active Male Employee Rate
Hospital expense:	
31 days	2.50
70 days	2.75
120 days	2.90
180 days or more	3.00
Surgical expense	1.75
Medical expense:	
In-hospital	3.00
Home and office calls	2.50
X-ray and laboratory	1.75
Supplemental major medical expense	5.00
Comprehensive major medical expense	3.00

For example, the active male employee rates and the corresponding pensioners' rates might be as follows for a seventy-day hospitalization plan, surgical and in-hospital medical expense benefits:

	Active Male Employee Rate	Multiple	Pensioners' Rate	Rate for Pensioner and Spouse
Hospitalization	$3.02	2.75	$ 8.30	$16.60
Surgical	.70	1.75	1.22	2.44
In-hospital medical	.21	3.00	.63	1.26
			$10.15	$20.30

In contrast, to insure a typical group of active employees and dependents for the same plan the cost would be as follows, including the charge for maternity benefits and the cost of insuring female employees, spouse and children:

Employee	$ 4.55
Dependents	10.25
	$14.80

The scheme outlined above of applying multiples to the active male employee rates is merely a means of calculating premium rates for pensioners. The multiples used do not express the relative cost of pensioners and active employee protection. The following considerations tend to reduce sharply the cost differential between employee and pensioners' coverage in the typical group: (1) The rates for active employees and their dependents contain a loading for the higher morbidity among female employees and wives for nonmaternity disabilities during the childbearing and middle age years. At the advanced ages this difference in morbidity between the sexes tends to disappear. (2) The usual plan for active lives contains a substantial charge for the maternity risk which is absent in pensioners' coverage. In the typical basic hospital-surgical-medical plan the maternity charge may represent about 20 per cent of the total cost of employee and dependent benefits. (3) Since about two thirds of the active employees with dependents have dependent children, the premium rates for their coverage must include a charge for the children's benefits. On the other hand, pensioners rarely have dependent children.

When these offsetting factors are taken into account and the cost of insuring pensioners and their dependents is compared with the cost of coverage for active employees and their dependents, the cost is much more nearly equal. For basic benefits, pensioner costs on this basis are only approximately 35 to 45 per cent greater than for active employees and dependents, and not two or three times more as the multiples used in calculating the retirees' rates suggest. Even when major medical expense benefits are also included in the program, the cost for retirees on this basis becomes only about 60 to 70 per cent greater than for active lives. In given cases these relationships will, of course, depend upon the particular plan, the ages of the retired lives and the make-up of the active group.

Various procedures are followed in collecting premiums for pensioners' coverage. Separate rates may be established for the retirees, as explained above. Alternatively, the cost of active and retired employees' insurance may be combined and an average premium rate arrived at for both, to be redetermined periodically as the proportion of pensioners in the group increases. For some groups with adequate dividend margins the lower active employee rates may be charged for pensioners as well; in such cases the extra retiree cost reduces future dividends.

In any event, it is essential that a policyholder have a thorough appreciation of the underlying cost factors which, over an extended period, will determine his real cost. Such an understanding will help him decide upon the benefits he can afford and the level of retiree contributions if pensioners are to share the cost.

Group Continuance under Blue Cross and Blue Shield Plans

Although Blue Cross and Blue Shield plans have relied heavily upon the conversion right to meet the needs of pensioners, in recent years these plans have been placing greater stress on group continuance. It was reported in 1962 that "some 24 per cent of all Blue Cross active group subscribers . . . are now covered by programs which make this opportunity available to retirees." This report went on to comment that "this is a significant development, for job-connected group coverage is the most effective and economical arrangement for expanding coverage to all population groups."[12]

Typically, group coverage provided by Blue Cross and Blue Shield plans for pensioners and their dependents is the same as that for active lives, with the emphasis being placed on service type benefits. Eligibility is defined in the same manner as for active employees and dependents.

While the underlying cost factors are similar to those mentioned in the previous section on insured plans, the Blue Cross and Blue Shield organizations generally have wholly or partially community rated the cost of this coverage so that the incidence of the higher expense does not fall directly upon the retired employees.

Financing Arrangements for Continuation of Group Coverages

Pay-as-You-Go. To date almost all of the insured medical plans for pensioners are financed on a pay-as-you-go basis. To the extent that an average rate is adopted for active and retired lives or a community rating approach is used by Blue Cross and Blue Shield plans, the additional cost is spread among the active lives. Nevertheless, the actual over-all cost of the group coverage will increase as the insured pensioners become a larger portion of the total group.

Funding. Many companies are accumulating a substantial liability for pensioners' group life insurance, and they are also accruing a liability of large proportions for pensioners' medical expense insurance. It is only recently, however, that employers have begun to show concern about this problem.

Unfortunately, it is more difficult to project the cost of future medical expense insurance for pensioners than life insurance. In an era of changing patterns of medical care and a general upward trend in cost, predicting the price of pensioners' medical benefits ten or twenty years in the future is a complex task. Even without precise cost estimates, employers must realize that a substantial and growing liability exists, and they are well advised to begin taking steps to fund this cost. That is, thought should be given to setting aside money on a systematic basis prior to employees' retirement to pay for pensioners' medical expense protection. The rate of funding can be adjusted as periodic future studies re-evaluate the liability the group is accruing.

Provision for accomplishing this funding can be made in several ways. A separate fund can be established as an addition to the group medical

---

[12] *Financing Health Care of the Aged*, p. 127.

expense insurance plan. Based on cost studies by the insurer, deposits are made into this fund during the employees' years of active employment, and withdrawals are made from the fund to pay the cost of insurance for pensioners who continue to be insured under the group plan.

Some groups may want to accumulate these funds in other ways. Provision can now be made under P.L. 87–863, the so-called Curtis Bill, enacted by the 87th Congress, to fund the cost of pensioners' insurance under a qualified pension plan. The importance of this legislation is that it helps focus attention on the need to fund this liability and gives employers a vehicle for doing this that has a clearly defined favorable tax status. Under this arrangement coverage must be limited to persons eligible for retirement benefits, for age or disability, or their spouses and dependents; the plan may not discriminate in favor of highly paid employees; and the benefits may be paid for on a contributory or noncontributory basis. Aggregate contributions for medical payments, together with any life insurance protection under the pension plan, are limited so as not to exceed 25 per cent of the aggregate contributions for all benefits under the plan.

Employee Contributions. The reduced income of pensioners usually limits their ability to contribute toward the cost of group insurance. If satisfactory participation is to be maintained, and this is an important aspect of plan soundness, the pensioners' contributions should be kept at a reasonable level. Generally, insurance companies feel that pensioners should not contribute more than they did while active, and a more modest contribution is strongly recommended. If an employer wants to make group coverage available for pensioners but presently is not able to pay any portion of the cost, it may be practical to design a modest plan that can be continued on an employee-pay-all basis.

SELECTED REFERENCES

BLUE CROSS ASSOCIATION AND AMERICAN HOSPITAL ASSOCIATION. *Financing Health Care of the Aged.* Chicago, Ill., 1962.

BREWSTER, AGNES W., AND BLOODGOOD, RUTH. *Blue Cross Provisions for Persons Aged 65 and Over, Late 1958,* U.S. Department of Health, Education and Welfare, Research and Statistics Note No. 5. Washington, D.C., 1959.

EILERS, ROBERT D. *Regulation of Blue Cross and Blue Shield Plans,* chaps. iii, ix, xi, xiv and xv. Homewood, Ill.: Richard D. Irwin, Inc., 1963.

FOLLMANN, J. F., JR. *Medical Care and Health Insurance,* chaps. vii and xxii. Homewood, Ill.: Richard D. Irwin, Inc., 1963.

GROTH, ALAN A. "Prefunding of Post-Retirement Medical, Hospital, and Death Benefits," *Conference of Actuaries in Public Practice,* the Proceedings, Vol. XII, 1962–63.

HEALTH INFORMATION FOUNDATION. "Our Increased Spending for Health," *Progress in Health Services,* February, 1960.

HEALTH INSURANCE COUNCIL. "The Aged and Private Health Insurance," *Health Insurance Viewpoints,* January, 1964.

SOMERS, HERMAN MILES, AND SOMERS, ANNE RAMSAY. *Doctors, Patients and Health Insurance,* chap. 21. Washington, D.C.: The Brookings Institution, 1961.

SPIEGELMAN, MORTIMER. *Ensuring Medical Care for the Aged.* Homewood, Ill.: Richard D. Irwin, Inc., 1960.

U.S. DEPARTMENT OF HEALTH, EDUCATION AND WELFARE. *The Health Care of the Aged.* Washington, D.C.: U.S. Government Printing Office, 1962.
———. "Volume of Physicians Visits, U.S., July 1957–June 1959," *Health Statistics from U.S. National Health Survey.* Series B, No. 19 (August, 1960).

Voluntary Health Insurance and the Senior Citizen: A Report on the Problem of Continuation of Medical Care Benefits for the Aged of New York State, State of New York Insurance Department.

WHITE HOUSE CONFERENCE ON AGING, JANUARY 9–12, 1961. *Background Paper on Health and Medical Care.*

Chapter 37

STATE-65 AND OTHER MEDICAL EXPENSE PLANS FOR PERSONS AGE 65 AND OVER

BY GEORGE E. LIGHT

Mass enrollment programs, including the various State-65 plans and other similar group health programs for the elderly, are recent developments in the group health insurance field. These efforts date back only to late 1955 and on a nation-wide basis only to 1959. Nevertheless, they now provide the vehicle by which a significant proportion of the elderly persons in the United States obtain medical expense coverage. It should be noted, however, that the enactment of a federal program to provide medical care for the aged, such as through the legislation currently (May, 1965) pending in the Congress, would exert a significant influence on at least the number of the elderly who now have basic hospital-surgical coverage through insurers in the private sector.

The mass enrollment technique was developed to solve specific problems in the marketing and underwriting of health insurance for older persons. Generally, when a group of employees is to be insured, it may be assumed for underwriting purposes that the preponderance of those to be insured are in good health. However, the preponderance is on the other side when it comes to insuring elderly persons. The proportion of both males and females with chronic health impairments increases with increasing age to more than 75 per cent at age 65 and over.[1] It is not surprising, therefore, that persons age 65 and over use, on the average, more than twice the number of days of general hospitalization required by those of younger ages.[2]

---

[1] *Metropolitan Life Insurance Company Statistical Bulletin*, September, 1963. (It should be noted that the term "chronic" refers to the duration of disability, rather than to the severity of disability. Thus, many chronic conditions have virtually no disabling effect.)

[2] Agnes W. Brewster, "Meeting the Health Needs of the Aged," *The Annals of the American Academy of Political and Social Science*, Vol. CCCXXXVII (September, 1961), p. 116.

Furthermore, acknowledgment of individual susceptibility to loss is common among the elderly. Where younger people might feel, "It won't happen to me," older persons recognize that even the healthiest may be only a few steps or a few moments from an accident or an illness. Thus, regular underwriting procedures become difficult to apply. Then, too, underwriting individual lives is relatively ineffective at advanced ages because even those in apparently good health for their age—including those whose physical history makes them acceptable—can become ill quite easily or sustain an accident. The distinction between those in poor health and those in good health becomes so obscure at the older ages that examinations are rarely used.

Not only do the elderly have a greater incidence (frequency) of hospitalization and medical treatment, but in many instances they have limited financial ability to meet the hospital and physicians' costs that are incurred or to pay for insurance protection against these costs. As one observer has noted, "It is readily apparent . . . that no single private program is likely to solve all of the dilemmas associated with providing medical care protection for the aged, namely to (1) cover all of the aged, (2) with a program of *adequate* benefits, and (3) at rates which all of the elderly can afford. The financial condition of these individuals complicates the problem since not all of the aged can afford to pay the premiums even if the rate is determined by averaging the loss experience of those under age 65, not to mention the much higher premiums which result if they are based solely on the loss experience of the aged."[3]

Insuring organizations have used several approaches to attack the problem of providing medical care protection for the aged.[4] Chapter 36 discussed the various means by which retired individuals can continue the group medical expense protection they had while employed. Not all elderly persons, however, are members of groups that offer group insurance protection during their working years. Still others may be unable to retain their protection after retirement, as was discussed in the previous chapter. Thus, two additional group methods have been employed by insuring organizations in order to facilitate the issuance of medical expense coverage to persons who will be enrolling for the first time after reaching age sixty-five: (1) the guaranteed issue of such coverage by an individual insurance company or Blue Cross–Blue Shield association, and (2) the guaranteed issuance of such coverage within a particular state by an association of insurance companies, such an association being called a

---

[3] Robert D. Eilers, "Inter-Insurer Arrangements to Provide Over-65 Medical Care Coverage," *Journal of Insurance,* Vol. XXX, No. 4 (December, 1963), p. 484.

[4] The widespread development both of individual guaranteed renewable lifetime policies purchasable during the active working ages and continuable into retirement and of specially designed individual senior citizen policies is outside the scope of this volume.

"State-65 plan." This chapter will discuss the nature, use and problems of these two approaches.

GROUP COVERAGE ISSUED BY INDIVIDUAL INSURING ORGANIZATIONS FOR THE ELDERLY

Any plan for providing adequate medical expense coverage for a substantial portion of the older population must meet the following requirements if it is to be successful: individual underwriting must be liberalized drastically or even abandoned; premiums must be reduced to a level compatible with the financial resources of the aged; and marketing efforts must be intensified to reach the greatest possible number of prospective insureds. To satisfy these requirements three different types of issue have been developed by certain insurance companies and Blue Cross–Blue Shield plans that offer coverage to persons over age sixty-five: (1) group contracts covering associations of retired persons; (2) group contracts issued to business firms to cover their retired employees; and (3) mass enrollment programs using group underwriting but individual policies. The latter basis has received particularly widespread attention in insurance and public circles.

Group Coverage of Associations of Retired Persons

Group underwriting offered a possible means of circumventing the problems associated with the individual underwriting of medical expense coverage for the aged. Moreover, group underwriting offered the possibility of substantial expense savings. Thus, in 1955 the Continental Casualty Company pioneered a new type of coverage when it issued a group medical expense contract to the New York State Retired Teachers Association. The venture was successful in part because the group enjoyed a very high participation (even though on a voluntary basis). Similar coverage was subsequently issued by the same insurer to the American Association of Retired Persons, the National Association of Retired Civil Employees and the National Retired Teachers Association.

In general, the coverage of associations of retired persons under a group medical expense contract entails no individual underwriting. That is, no health questions are asked of the association members who choose to enroll. In addition, it is customary to cover all health conditions of insureds, including, after six months of coverage, health impairments that had their origin prior to the effective date of the contract.

The benefit structures initially were modest, e.g., hospital room-and-board benefits of $10 to $15 for thirty-one days and up to ten times the daily room-and-board allowance for other hospital charges, plus a schedule of surgical allowances. As experience was gained, benefits were gradually liberalized. Hospital coverage for 120 days per confinement, home and office physicians' visits, out-of-hospital drugs and even nursing home benefits now are included in some of the basic coverage plans. Major medical contracts with $5,000 and $10,000 maximum benefits and few internal limits also are available in many instances.

Group Coverage of a Firm's Retired Employees

The previous chapter described in detail the widespread practice of current issuance of group health insurance of formerly active employees as they reach retirement. In some instances a separate group contract is issued for the coverage of existing pensioners. The coverages for retired federal employees and retired railroad nonoperating employees are among the most prominent examples of group contracts of this sort. The group insurers that participated in issuing the federal employees coverage selected the Aetna Life Insurance Company to be the primary insurer, with the coverage being reinsured with a large number of insurance companies. The Travelers Insurance Company covered the retired railroad employees, with reinsurance being obtained from a few other companies.[5] The underwriting principles utilized in connection with coverage of this type are similar to the principles underlying group coverage of associations of retired persons.

The plan for retired federal employees became effective July 1, 1961. Some 400,000 eligible individuals were given the opportunity to join the uniform plan sponsored by the government and administered by the Aetna offering basic coverage or major medical expense coverage, or both. The basic benefits consisted of $15 a day toward hospital room and board for thirty-one days, plus up to $150 for other hospital charges and a schedule of surgical fee allowances with a maximum of $240.

The major medical benefits provided: (1) up to $12 a day for hospital room and board from the thirty-second through the 121st day in a calendar year, and up to $6 a day for thirty-one days following hospitalization of five days or more for convalescent hospital care; and (2) 75 per cent of (a) other hospital charges in excess of $150 (the amount allowable under the basic coverage), (b) surgical charges in excess of those payable under the basic schedule, (c) charges for doctors' home, office and in-hospital visits for nonsurgical treatment, (d) charges for private duty nursing up to $16 per day for thirty-one days, and (e) charges for drugs and medicines, for diagnostic X-rays and laboratory examinations, for blood, anesthetics and oxygen and for rental of hospital bed or wheelchair. The

---

[5] Group coverage of retired employees of particular firms is now being issued by at least one State-65 plan (New York-65), as well as by individual insurers. As will be noted in the latter part of this chapter, State-65 plans require special legislation before they can commence operation, and in New York further legislation was necessary to allow the plan to issue group coverage to a firm's active employees age sixty-five or over or retired employees who worked in New York or formerly worked in New York at time of retirement.

major medical benefits are subject to a $5,000 lifetime maximum for each covered person.

The government contributed $3.00 monthly toward individual enrollment and $6.00 monthly toward family enrollment (later increased to $3.50 and $7.00 respectively). The premiums originally were $6.50 a month for the basic and $6.00 a month for the major medical coverage for individual enrollment (later increased to $7.50 and $7.00 respectively) and twice as much for family enrollment. The annuitant's portion of the cost was deducted from his annuity checks. About 135,000 annuitants elected the uniform plan. Those not electing to come under the uniform plan were nevertheless eligible to receive the government's contribution toward any other qualified private plan the individual might have.

Mass Enrollment

Underwriting Philosophy of Mass Enrollment. By the late 1950's, underwriting experience with associations of retired persons suggested that the aged population had certain general characteristics which might make possible the broader application of group underwriting methods. It was evident that the over-age market for medical expense insurance was far from saturated; little more than one third had any coverage at all. Moreover, awareness of the need for health insurance was very high among elderly insureds; many were deterred from purchasing coverage only by the cost or by a belief that they were uninsurable due to physical impairment or advanced age. When offered coverage at a reasonable premium level, it was thought that a good portion of the healthier lives would enroll without too much anti-selection.

The association experience had shown that individual underwriting could be abandoned where the association's endorsement was effective enough to produce high participation among members. The next step was to attempt mass marketing and mass underwriting without endorsement, relying on the existing coverage void and high level of awareness of need to produce a substantial and comparatively unbiased response.

The first mass enrollment of elderly persons occurred in Iowa as a pilot program of one insurance company[6] in the fall of 1957. The insurer resolved the underwriting problem in issuing coverage for the aged by adapting the group insurance approach to its individual policies. That is, the policies (1) guaranteed issue regardless of the applicants' health, (2) guaranteed renewal with minor limitations, (3) provided a substantial measure of coverage for pre-existing conditions and (4) required the minimum possible premium (which could be paid on a monthly basis). The problems of participation and anti-selection were attacked by substituting an intensive advertising and public relations campaign for the usual

---

[6] The Continental Casualty Company.

association or employer endorsement, and by substituting a limited enroll-ment period for the usual requirement of group membership. The expense problems were met by planning a high-volume, completely electronic system of administering a standardized package of benefits, and by cen-tral handling with very limited agent effort and nominal commissions. These principles have since been followed in the bulk of the medical expense coverage that has been issued to elderly persons through the mass enrollment technique.

The success of the mass enrollment approach was evident not only from the rapid growth in the number of persons who obtained coverage through the technique, but also from the fact that benefit structures were broadened after the approach had been used for some time. The success of the mass enrollment technique relies upon the special circumstances which made this unusual underwriting procedure necessary in the first place: (1) Individual risk appraisal had been found less satisfactory as an underwriting tool for elderly persons because, for example, health ques-tionnaires provide much less definitive evidence of a person's condition at advanced ages. (2) There was a sufficient unfilled need for coverage among the elderly to produce a widespread response to advertising with-out excessive adverse selection against the insurer. (3) The potential market was large enough to support the advertising and administrative costs with a small fraction of the gross premium per unit of coverage. (4) Usual methods of production in the over-age field had been slow in developing so that neither the insurer nor its agents would normally suffer a loss of customary business to this low expense margin, semi-directly written program. On the contrary, favorable public reaction proved beneficial to both.

Expansion of Mass Enrollment.   Several insurance companies now issue mass enrollment coverage for the aged, and among the leading insurers that utilize this approach are the Continental Casualty Company, the Fireman's Fund Insurance Company and the Mutual of Omaha Insur-ance Company. Blue Cross and Blue Shield plans began to issue mass enrollment coverage for the elderly in 1962. Most insuring organizations have limited periods of a month or longer every year or so during which persons age sixty-five and older may enroll. One insurance company executive has noted in this regard, "By signing up as many as 100,000 people during limited periods, we are able to balance the good and poor risks in a single group, which makes such enrollments actuarially sound."[7]

---

[7] Lee R. Farmer, quoted in the *Wall Street Journal*, July 16, 1962, p. 11. (Some observers now question the future ability of periodic enrollment periods to reduce adverse selection to any great extent. They reason that as more plans become available for the elderly, a point may be reached whereby at least one plan is always open. Unless the plans use parallel enrollment periods, it is felt that all may be subject to adverse selection.)

Some of the major insurers that utilize the mass enrollment approach now offer major medical coverage, with limits of $5,000 or $10,000, as well as basic hospital coverage with several daily room-and-board limits from which to select. Medical and surgical coverage is also included in most instances. By late 1964, a million or more persons were covered under the mass enrollment approach.

The Future of Mass Enrollment. The mass enrollment technique was developed to meet the needs of a specific market—the over-age population—and was made possible by certain characteristics of that market in the late 1950's. The future of this technique will be determined by the changing character of the market it serves and, of course, by the possible enactment of a federal program to provide medical expense coverage for the elderly. Leading mass enrollment underwriters tend to regard the special market conditions that have existed as temporary. Within about one generation they anticipate that the aged generally will have medical expense coverage through other sources, such as continuation of retired employees coverage under group policies, group conversions, individual policies guaranteed renewable for life and possibly commercial policies more liberally underwritten than in the past.

STATE-65 PLANS

In 1961, a new dimension was added to the various approaches which have sought collectively to provide medical expense coverage for the aged. The new approach was totally unique; it involved a group of insurance companies that had agreed to form an association whose sole purpose would be to provide guaranteed issue coverage for the aged. Since the initial association, and several that were formed subsequently, covered only persons age sixty-five and over in a given state, plans of this sort became known as "State-65 plans." The plans are also referred to as "Over-65 plans" and "inter-insurer associations."

Development of State-65 Plans

The pioneering State-65 plan was established in Connecticut in 1961. It has been followed by similar plans in Massachusetts and New York, both of which began operation in 1962, in Texas in 1963, and in California, North Carolina–Virginia and Ohio. The plans in the latter states all commenced operations in 1964.

The concept of the State-65 plan in Connecticut, also known as "Connecticut-65," developed after the passage of the Kerr-Mills bill,[8] which provided federal funds to be matched with state funds under certain conditions in order to provide medical care to elderly persons with limited resources but who nevertheless were not eligible for benefits under the Old-Age Assistance program. Thus, a segment of the aged

[8] Kerr-Mills Medical Care Act, passed by the Congress in 1960.

remained who were not eligible for Kerr-Mills or Old-Age Assistance benefits and who presumably were able to finance their own medical needs through insurance or other methods. An ad hoc committee of representatives from certain Connecticut health insurance companies recognized that this latter group of elderly persons generally had a need for, and an interest in obtaining, insurance protection.

The ad hoc committee proposed a method for providing medical expense insurance which would be available to every resident of the state age sixty-five and over, and the dependents of such persons, at a low cost relative to the benefits to be provided. It was decided that the coverage would be issued without requiring a medical examination, and there would be as few limitations as practicable, particularly with respect to pre-existing health conditions of the applicants.

When the benefit structure for Connecticut-65 was being designed, the committee felt there was a particular void in the availability of major medical coverage for the aged, i.e., benefits for a wide range of medical expenses up to high amounts. Since the objective of the association was to fill an existing void rather than merely to provide another program to compete with coverage already available, it was decided that major medical protection should be the principal offering. However, a decision was also made to offer base plan benefits that would complement the major medical protection as an optional coverage for those who did not have basic benefits.

Another broad decision of the ad hoc committee was that the program should be so operated that the excess of premiums, if any, over losses, expenses and a small risk charge would be used for the benefit of the people insured rather than inuring to the benefit of the member companies.[9] Finally, the ad hoc committee decided that the product to be offered should follow generally the concepts of group insurance coverage as presenting the best and most economical approach in terms of underwriting, accounting and administrative consideration.

In the fall of 1960, a working committee was instructed to develop a program of coverage for the elderly following the broad concepts established by the ad hoc committee. Initially, an association of the ten Connecticut insurance companies was formed, with membership in the association being opened later to other companies writing health insurance in the state. The association was given the name "Associated Connecticut Health Insurance Companies."

The basic considerations underlying the decision to follow the association approach included (1) recognition of the lack of experience on which to found competitive programs and the need to pool resources, ability and experience in the development of a sound program; (2) a deep-seated

---

[9] See statement of William N. Seery to the Insurance Committee of the Connecticut General Assembly, March 7, 1961, in support of Senate Bill 815 and House Bill 3640.

feeling that extensive competition in this area would lead to disastrous results for individual companies or to more limited coverage for those to be insured than could be provided through the contemplated association approach; (3) a belief that the genuine interest of the companies in resolving the problems of the insurance needs of the elderly citizens could best be presented through an association; (4) a conclusion that the association approach would give companies with a real interest but perhaps small underwriting capacity an effective means of participating in this field of providing insurance for the older citizens; and (5) a hope that the association would be a positive force to work against the need and demand for governmental action in this area of coverage.

The working committee realized that many expenditures for medical care are subject to personal control or desire as much as to need, and in the interest of keeping claim costs within limits contemplated by the premiums, it was decided to include certain "inside limits" on the amounts to be paid for hospital expense and medical expense. Such limits are imposed in the Connecticut-65 plan with respect to coverage for hospital, convalescent hospital, surgical, medical and nursing charges. (Specific limitations are indicated in Table 37–1.)

A basic consideration with respect to the Connecticut-65 program was that the premium rates should be adequate to cover the benefits and expenses with the expenses being restrained in every way practicable. As a result, expenses were anticipated to be in the order of 10 to 12 per cent of premiums. It was realized, of course, that while dollars can be saved for future expenditures, hospital and medical services must be paid for at the time utilized and on the basis of prices effective at that time. Furthermore, improvements in medical care and the facilities for medical care frequently entail greater costs. Consequently, the right to adjust premiums for all insureds in the association was necessarily reserved, subject, of course, to review of the insurance commissioner of the state.

Authorizing Legislation

As was indicated in Chapter 6, the legal environment in which group insurance is marketed—in fact in which all insurance is marketed—has been influenced markedly by the passage of the McCarran Act (Public Law 15) by the United States Congress in 1945. This act provides that the Sherman Anti-Trust Act, the Clayton Act and the Federal Trade Commission Act shall not apply to the business of insurance, even when such business constitutes interstate commerce, to the extent that the states regulate the business adequately. In this connection it was felt that if the Connecticut insurance companies did not obtain authorization from the General Assembly of the State, their proposal to join together in offering a common policy and common premiums might be held to constitute a violation of the federal laws. For example, thirty-two companies participated in the initial organization of the Connecticut-65 plan, and more than forty insurers were involved in the Massachusetts and New York organizations. The act in Connecticut[10] and the acts in other states require that policies, applications, certificates and premium rates be filed with the insurance department of the state, and all these aspects are subject to the review of the insurance commissioner. The acts in the various states differ in the detail as to the prescribed regulations, but the provisions indicated are common to all.[11]

The Connecticut and Massachusetts plans do not offer basic benefits without major medical benefits. Unless the legislation is changed, it is doubtful whether Connecticut-65 could offer basic benefits without major medical benefits. On the other hand, the New York statute does not allow New York-65 to require the purchase of major medical before a basic benefit contract can be obtained.

The statute in New York stipulates that the program must be nonprofit. Moreover, New York exempts the premiums for the New York-65 insurance from premium taxes. The program in each of the other states provides that any excess of premiums over claims, expenses and a small risk charge shall be used for the benefit of the persons insured. The premiums paid to all State-65 plans except New York-65 and Texas-65 are subject to taxation.

In addition to those areas where State-65 plans are currently operative, legislation has been passed in several other states to permit the establishment of a State-65 organization. Included are Maine, Michigan, Mississippi, New Hampshire, Nevada, New Mexico and Washington. "It is interesting to note that legislators in several states have been encouraged by insurance company executives and regulatory officials not to back permissive legislation unless there is assurance that adequate insurer support is available for the success of a cooperative organization in their state. Industry officials suspect that a failure of insurance companies to implement an over-65 plan after the enactment of appropriate legislation would allow supporters of federal programs for medical care to claim that insurers lack interest in covering the aged. A potential situation of this sort has arisen in Mississippi, where no over-65 program has been established even though a permissive statute was passed [in 1962]. . . . (No insurers of any significant size are domiciled in Mississippi.)"[12] Thus, a report of the Health Insurance Association of America states, ". . . the staff should

---

[10] Public Act No. 95, State of Connecticut, *An Act Authorizing Insurance Companies to Join Together to Offer Senior Citizens of Connecticut Health Insurance Against Major Financial Loss.*

[11] Unlike the permissive legislation in other states, the New York statute requires that benefits and premiums receive the *prior* approval of the superintendent of insurance before they may be used.

[12] Eilers, *op. cit.*, p. 489.

TABLE 37-1
Benefits Offered by Three State-65 Plans

Types of Benefits and Size of Premium	Connecticut-65		Massachusetts-65	New York-65	
	Higher Limit	Lower Limit		Higher Limit	Lower Limit
Major Medical					
Monthly premiums	$10.00	$7.50	$9.00	$9.00	
Maximum benefits:					
Lifetime	$10,000	$5,000	$10,000	$100.00 for other medical expenses	
Yearly	$5,000	$2,500	$5,000	$3,600 of hospital and convalescent home charges per confinement	
Deductible (calendar year)	$100 plus the amount of benefits payable under Conn.-65 basic coverage whether insured thereby or not.		$100 plus the amount of benefits payable under the Mass.-65 basic coverage whether insured is covered thereunder or not.	31 days of hospitalization; and $150 for hospital charges and $75 for other medical expenses.	
Percentage participation	80% (Except that after the deductible all hospital expenses are paid up to $250)	80%	100% of hospital and convalescent home room-and-board charges, as well as surgical expenses (subject to maximum below), 80% of other allowable charges.	80%	
Internal limits (in addition to yearly maximum)					

Hospital:				
Daily charges	$18.00	$15.00	$18.00	$18.00
Convalescent home:	(After 5 days of hospitalization)		(After 5 days of hospitalization)	(After 5 days of hospitalization)
Daily charges	$10.00	$8.00	$8/day first 21 days; $6.43 thereafter.	$7.50
Number of days per year	90 days	90 days	16 weeks	60 days
Surgical expenses	$600 schedule	$600 schedule	$500 schedule	Blue Shield ($6,000 income) schedule used
Other expenses:				
Doctors' visits (in hospital, home and office)	$6.00	$5.00	$6.00	Blue Shield ($6,000 income) schedule used
Private nurses	$18/day	$15/day	$18/day	$1,000/year

Basic Hospital-Surgical				
	May be purchased only in combination with major medical. Basic benefits are identical under either combination policy.	May be purchased only in combination with major medical		
Monthly premiums	(Combination) $17.00 / (Combination) $14.50	(Combination) $17.50	(Combination) $19.00	$8.00 (Combination $17.00)
Hospital:				
Daily room and board charges	$12.00	$15.00	$18.00	$12.00
Maximum no. of days (per year)	31	31	31	31
Other hospital service charges (per year)	$125.00	$150.00	$150.00	$150.00
Convalescent home			(If entered within 7 days after having been in a hospital for at least 5 days)	(If entered within 7 days after having been in a hospital for at least 5 days)
Daily charges			$7.50	$7.50
Maximum no. of days (per confinement)			31	31
Surgical schedule maximum	$360.00	$300.00	$250.00	$250.00
In-hospital medical			Up to $6 for each of the first 7 days, $5 for each of the next 7 days, and $4 for each of the next 17 days.	Up to $6 for each of the first 7 days, $5 for each of the next 7 days, and $4 for each of the next 17 days.

Source: Robert D. Eilers, "Inter-Insurer Agreements to Provide Over-65 Medical Care Coverage," *Journal of Insurance*, Vol. XXX, No. 4 (December, 1963), pp. 496–97.

attempt to discourage the introduction of legislation until it can be determined whether companies are prepared to implement such legislation."[13]

Provisions in the Articles of Association

The eligibility of insurance companies to participate in State-65 plans must be defined in each plan's Articles of Association. Generally, any commercial insurance company licensed to write health insurance in the state is eligible, although those who do not normally write health insurance, or who write only a small volume of health insurance, may not desire to participate. The Articles specify how the participation of the various companies is determined, and usually a minimum participation, e.g., one half of 1 per cent or 1 per cent of the premiums written, will be specified.[14] It is customary for each participating company to be severally liable for its pro rata share of the coverage issued. The pro rata determination is based generally on the arithmetic mean of an insurer's percentage of health insurance premiums written within the state by member insurers and its percentage of health insurance premiums written in the United States by member insurers.[15]

When a participating insurer wishes to terminate its relationship with a State-65 plan, it may do so at the end of a calendar year after six months prior written notice. Then, too, the membership of a company may be terminated involuntarily if a majority of an association's governing board vote in favor of such action. A terminated insurer is still liable for its share of the risks underwritten during its membership, unless released from this obligation by a vote—usually of two thirds or three fourths—of the plan's member companies.

Other necessary items in the Articles of Association are the name, the purposes of the organization, the definitions of special terms, provisions establishing a governing body, provisions providing for association meetings as well as meetings of the governing body, provisions with respect to voting and provisions for operating expense funds and assessments. Other provisions relate to advertising, publicity and adding new member companies, together with provisions for amendments and termination.

Administration and Management

In each of the states that has inaugurated a State-65 program, it has been found desirable to have one company—generally one domiciled

---

[13] Report of the Health Insurance Association of America, Special Committee to Study Policy Statement on Connecticut-65 Type Programs, Draft of September 24, 1962.

[14] New York limits the share of any member to 30 per cent.

[15] New York applies weights to the state and national premiums by size.

within the state—administer the program, that is, collect the premiums, issue the certificates and pay the claims on behalf of the association. The administration, of course, also includes the furnishing and supervising of personnel and the keeping of records with provision for such statistics and statistical processing as may be found necessary or desirable. A manager is, of course, a necessary element for the purposes of the administration. General management, i.e., determination of policy, subject to vote of the association itself, is vested in a governing board with delegation of some responsibility to a smaller committee for practical functioning between board meetings. In general, the members of the governing board are selected by the member insurers, although in some of the plans an insurer which bears more than a certain percentage, such as 10 per cent, of the risks is permitted to name a board member.

In addition, special committees composed of executives from member companies are delegated various responsibilities. For example, each State-65 organization has a committee dealing with public relations and the presentation of the program to the public, with the same or another committee dealing with the presentation of the program to and through agents licensed in the state. Another committee will be concerned with relations with hospitals and the medical profession. An actuarial committee and a claims committee are also established. In these management arrangements, there is a continual contribution of up-to-date information by the companies. It is apparent that the extensive use of donated executive talent from member companies is one of the factors which facilitates low expenses for the plans.

Benefit Structures and Premiums

Both the benefits that are offered and the premiums vary somewhat among the various State-65 plans. As has been noted, for example, some of the plans offer basic benefits only if major medical coverage is purchased, while in other plans either type of benefits may be purchased separately. Likewise, the maximum benefits afforded under the major medical coverages and the deductibles and participation percentages that are used differ to some extent among the plans. Table 37–1 indicates the benefit structures and premiums that the Connecticut, Massachusetts and New York State-65 plans used when the coverage was first made available. Some minor modifications have occurred since that time in the benefits offered by these plans, and premium inadequacies have necessitated rate increases in some of the plans.

Most of the State-65 plans exclude benefits temporarily for any condition that was treated within ninety days prior to the effective date of the coverage if such a condition reoccurs within the initial six or nine months of protection under the State-65 plan. When a condition does reoccur during the specified period, benefits will be granted for the condition after the expiration of the period. In addition, it is common for the plans to include nonduplication of benefit provisions in their contracts.

Enrollment

Each State-65 program has been inaugurated with an open enrollment period and with further open enrollment periods being contemplated from time to time. The necessity for maintaining enrollment is constantly in the minds of those responsible for the success of the program; there is no unanimity of thought, however, as to how this can best be accomplished. Connecticut-65, for example, permits enrollments at any time, but the effective date of coverage is deferred for three months. With this program Connecticut has been successful in maintaining its enrollment. In Massachusetts, on the other hand, enrollment is permitted quarterly.

In the states where State-65 plans are operative, any broker or agent licensed to sell health insurance within the state may sell coverage for the State-65 plan. Commissions are minimal, averaging about two thirds of a month's premiums with no provision for renewal commissions.

In their first enrollment campaigns the State-65 plans have generally enrolled somewhat less than 10 per cent of the elderly citizens of their respective states. The average age of enrollees has been approximately seventy-three to seventy-five years, with about two thirds of the enrollees being females. It is estimated that more than 30 per cent of those enrolled have had their coverage purchased by their children.

Persistence after enrollment in the State-65 plans generally has been excellent. In a statement to the Subcommittee on Health of the Elderly, Special Committee on Aging, United States Senate, on April 28, 1964, Chairman Seery of the Connecticut Executive Committee stated, for example, "At the time of our initial enrollment period in 1961 we insured 21,849 people. On March 1, 1964, we insured 25,479 people. These included 15,619 of those who became insured in October, 1961. This persistence is notwithstanding the lapse rate contributed to by the high death rate in this age group, which is a major problem facing any health insurance plan to cover the aged. We estimate that at least 35 per cent of the drop-outs in Connecticut-65 have been the result of deaths."

The Future of State-65 Plans

The State-65 plans are going to be influenced importantly, of course, if a federal program of medical care coverage for the aged is enacted. The fact that several State-65 plans concentrate their efforts in providing major medical coverage suggests that the plans will have a continuing function, however, even if a social insurance program is instituted. This follows because it is probable that any federal program that might be passed would concentrate on basic coverage rather than on major medical protection.

It is conceivable that the present type of State-65 organization may be changed in some or all states from an association to some other form. It is also possible that the state plans may give way to regional or even to a national plan. The major impediment to multi-state operation is the lack of consistency in the statutes of the various states. However, one plan already covers two states (North Carolina and Virginia). Moreover, consideration has been given to the extension of existing plans into a New England-65 plan, a Gulf-65 plan and a Western-65 plan. In fact, the California plan currently uses the name "Western-65" and contemplates expansion to include thirteen states.

The expansion of the inter-insurer approach, i.e., State-65 or Regional-65, for providing medical expense coverage for the aged is likely to be influenced significantly and positively by a "Liaison Committee of State-65 Plans" that has been formed. Existing plans have been extremely cooperative in providing advice and assistance to those interested in forming Over-65 plans in additional states. However, the existence of one organization to act as a central source of information and help regarding the problems and procedures involved in these plans will undoubtedly be of even greater value in the extension of the technique.

As indicated earlier in this chapter, many leading underwriters feel the mass enrollment programs for the aged are only a temporary necessity. Many of the individuals actively engaged in the operation of State-65 plans feel, on the other hand, that these organizations will continue to make a contribution to medical expense coverage for the aged. They reason that there will be in the future, as there have been in the past, employers and unions who will not continue group insurance on retired employees either because of a policy on this point or because of financial inability to do so. Then, too, among small employers particularly there is a continual turnover, and for this and other reasons many individuals probably will not be eligible for retirement coverage even if it is available. Finally, it is possible that some employers and unions will find it less expensive to procure medical expense protection for retired persons from State-65 plans rather than retaining such individuals in the regular group coverage. Thus, it appears that the functions the State-65 plans set out to perform will be needed in a large measure in the future, barring the adoption of a comprehensive federal program, and so long as these needs exist the plans can be expected to persist in some form.

SELECTED REFERENCES

Actuarial Study Implementing the Provisions of Section 162 (6) of the New York Insurance Law. New York: State of New York Insurance Department, 1960.

BLUE CROSS ASSOCIATION AND AMERICAN HOSPITAL ASSOCIATION. *Financing Health Care of the Aged.* Parts I and II. Chicago, 1962.

EILERS, ROBERT D. "Inter-Insurer Arrangements to Provide Over-65 Medical Care Coverage," *Journal of Insurance,* Vol. XXX, No. 4 (December, 1963), pp. 483–504.

FARQUHAR, GORDON N. "Major Medical for the Aged—A Connecticut Story," *Journal of the American Society of Chartered Life Underwriters,* Vol. XVI (Spring, 1962), pp. 174–85.

FOODY, WALTER M., JR. *Statement before Subcommittee on Problems of the Aging and Aged, Committee on Labor and Public Welfare, United States Senate, April 11, 1960.*

HOUGHTON, ANTHONY J. "Continuance Study of Hospital Claims on Individually Underwritten Lives Age 65 and Over," *Transactions of the Society of Actuaries,* Part I (1963), pp. 530–47.

MILLER, MORTON D. "Experience of State-65 Plans Reviewed," *Employee Benefit Plan Review,* December, 1963, pp. 14–18.

Report of the Health Insurance Association of America Special Committee to Study Policy Statement on Connecticut-65 Type Programs, Draft of September 24, 1962.

SEERY, WILLIAM N. *Statement before Subcommittee on Health of the Elderly, Special Committee on Aging, United States Senate, April 28, 1964.*

U.S. DEPARTMENT OF HEALTH, EDUCATION AND WELFARE. *Chart Book of Basic Health Economics Data.* Public Health Service Publication No. 947–3. Washington, D.C., 1964.

WEAVER, ARTHUR G. "Progress of State-65 Plans Reviewed by Weaver," *Employee Benefit Plan Review,* June, 1963, pp. 16–17.

Chapter 38

DENTAL EXPENSE COVERAGE

BY HERBERT C. LASSITER

RATIONALE OF DENTAL EXPENSE COVERAGE

The national dental bill is about $2.4 billion dollars annually.[1] This sum is spent by somewhat less than 50 per cent of America's citizens. Almost all of it is paid directly and personally by individuals out of their current resources. Too frequently, dental expenses have not been planned for in the family budget, and accordingly, such expenses often present financial problems. In many instances those needing dental care forego treatment for financial and other reasons—including a fear of pain—to the possible future detriment of their health.

The evolution, advancement and final success of group insurance coverage of hospital, medical and surgical expenses included, almost without notice, acknowledgment that certain surgical procedures in the dental field also deserved coverage. This acknowledgment did not come quickly, for it was well recognized within the industry that the diseases which led ultimately to the most common of such surgical procedures—extractions—were the most prevalent of all of the diseases that afflict mankind: dental caries and periodontal (gum) infections. How, reasoned the actuaries, the underwriters and the claims men, could these almost universally experienced afflictions be covered? The basic principles of insurability simply did not seem to apply to an affliction and a service as universally experienced as dental disease and its treatment.

Joseph F. Follmann, Jr., said, as recently as 1961, that—

It might well be that the answer (to prepayment of dental expenses) will be found in the inclusion of certain dental care protection as part of major medical expense insurance, rather than as a separate entity. Possibilities present themselves in this direction since by such a plan the more serious and costly forms of dental care, being those which present hardships to many individuals, and hence which become a fit subject for insurance, could be included with a medical care program, leaving the more routine, less costly, anticipatory, con-

---

[1] U.S. Department of Commerce, *Survey of Current Business,* July, 1964, p. 16.

trollable, unnecessary, and luxury forms of care to be borne by the individual as the least costly, most expeditious manner of handling such costs. Such a plan would have the added virtue of not segmenting dental care costs from other costs of medical care, since to the individual pocketbook they become one total cost.[2]

Mr. Follmann was reflecting an opinion of the insurance industry at that time. Yet today, about 1,500,000 people have group dental expense coverage[3] that is separate from major medical protection.

There is no question that dental disease *is* the most prevalent of all of the diseases by which mankind is afflicted. Neither is there serious question that most people, if "sold" on the importance of dental health care, would be able to maintain their oral health for an annual dollar expenditure that would be far less than an average smoker spends on his cigarettes in the course of a year. For these very reasons, the bulk of the insurance industry until very recent years maintained that dental expenses should be budgetable; that the incidence of dental disease, in some form, was so widespread as to be virtually predictable for every individual; that the very fact of its universality, plus the built-in electiveness of the type of treatment sought by patients, made dental expenses uninsurable. It was felt that selection was bound to be adverse, initial loss experience was sure to be catastrophic and policyholder persistency was just as certain to be minimal. One of the major proponents of dental expense coverage, Lee R. Farmer, remarked in this regard:

It . . . [is] immediately apparent that dental care does not lend itself to a full application of the classic principles of insurability. The principles of insurance work best when applied to a risk which is infrequent in occurrence and unpredictable for the individual with reference either to frequency or to time of occurrence, but is predictable for the group with reference to both of these factors. . . .

Dental disease . . . attacks most people, and to a degree is predictable for the individual with respect to both time of occurrence and to extent of damage. On the basis of past experience, the individual may have some notion as to his own susceptibility. If everyone were to receive regular and complete dental care, the time of occurrence of dental defects could be predicted with a degree of accuracy even for the individual.[4]

The American Dental Association and several other organizations—including some insurers—eventually took issue with the contention that dental expenses were uninsurable. These organizations based their posi-

---

[2] Joseph F. Follmann, Jr., *A Current Picture of Insurance Programs for Dental Care,* Seventh Annual Workshop, National Conference of Health, Welfare and Pension Plans, Philadelphia, October, 1961.

[3] Donald J. Galagan, Assistant Surgeon General and Chief, Division of Dental Public Health and Resources, U.S. Public Health Service, Department of Health, Education and Welfare, departmental news release *HEW-D93,* February 5, 1965.

[4] Lee R. Farmer, "First Year's Experience with Dental Insurance: Dental Care Coverage Issued by an Insurance Company," *The Journal of the American Dental Association,* Vol. LXII, No. 2 (February, 1961), p. 200.

tion on the fact that only about 40 per cent of the American public seek dental care in any one year and, of that number, less than 25 per cent seek more than emergency care. On the basis of such statistics, it was felt unrealistic to assume that the introduction of a third party financing mechanism would precipitate a sudden reversal of habit by the public. It was admitted, however, that one of the reasons more people do not seek dental treatment when it is needed is that they feel they cannot afford it. Nevertheless, the percentage of the population to which this factor legitimately applied was not felt to be overwhelming; the real obstacle was a lack of understanding on the part of the public that good dental health was important to total well-being. This fact—however regrettable—was one upon which the insurance industry could count to confine claim losses to a manageable degree: "Since so few people do receive regular and complete care, their very neglect introduces a measure of insurability into the field of dental care."[5]

APPROACHES FOR PROVIDING DENTAL EXPENSE COVERAGE

Insurance Companies' Dental Expense Coverage

Development of Insurance Company Coverage. In the late 1950's, a combination of stimuli brought together an insurer that was not averse to experimentation and an employer, the Dentists' Supply Company of New York, headquartered in York, Pennsylvania, that wanted to expand the scope of its firm's employee benefit program. With the statistical advice of the American Dental Association and a reasonable guaranty against underwriting losses by the customer firm, the Continental Casualty Company agreed to write a group dental expense contract covering all employees of the firm, and their dependents, for a three-year period. The policy was constructed generally along the lines of traditional major medical expense coverage, using individual and family deductibles and percentage participation principles.[6] It also included annual ceilings on the covered expenses of a member of the family and the family as a whole. No fee schedule was employed. The policy committed the insurer instead to pay a percentage of "usual and customary fees" for the services provided up to an annual maximum amount after satisfaction of the deductible. The entire premium for the coverage was paid by the employer, and all employees and their dependents were covered.

This pioneer plan went into effect on August 1, 1959. It covered approximately 2,500 persons. Shortly thereafter a similar plan was negotiated for employees of Astra Pharmaceutical Products, Inc., with the Union Mutual Life Insurance Company as the insurer. Soon other insur-

---

[5] *Ibid.*

[6] In order to encourage insureds to maintain a good level of oral health, the plan did not apply the deductible to oral examination benefits.

ance companies entered the field, initially on an experimental basis, and the ice was effectively broken. Five years after the first case was instituted, seventeen insurers were actively writing group dental insurance business, and approximately 250,000 persons were covered.

Nature of Insurance Company Coverage. Structurally, most group dental policies have been designed to cover all forms of dental treatment, although varying inside limits have been used to reduce the underwriters' liability on certain high cost items, such as orthodontic treatment.[7] The design of the case can be influenced considerably by the characteristics of the group to be covered, particularly with respect to sex and age factors. If children are not to be eligible, for instance, the coverage of orthodontic services becomes almost an academic consideration. If, on the other hand, the program is to cover only children, orthodontics becomes an important consideration, while major prosthetic services, such as the construction or replacement of complete dentures, fade into insignificance.

The nature and extent of benefits available under one insurance company plan is shown in Table 38–1, which outlines the coverage of the Dentists' Supply Company of New York.

The cost of dental insurance coverage will vary greatly with the types of services covered and the degree of participation by the insured in the cost of care. The use of indemnity schedules has been adopted by some companies as an additional tool for estimating claims costs. The major factor that influences claims experience, however, is utilization. Generally, the pattern of experience has not indicated injuriously high utilization in the first year of coverage, contrary to the expectations of many of the early architects of dental insurance. While there have been exceptions, the utilization levels have not usually exceeded by more than a small margin the national utilization rates found in the uninsured population. To protect against the exceptional case, some insurers have found it desirable to market their policies on a three-year contract basis, with experience rating applied at the end of the contract term. This method has been used successfully as a means for effecting a leveling of losses during the contract period, with some resultant recovery of any heavy first-year losses occasioned by the elimination of accumulated dental neglect. All of the control factors mentioned have been considered necessary in order to permit the marketing of a sound product at a salable price. In the group field, with high participation assured, dental insurance has been shown to be a welcome addition to the health insurance spectrum. Individual insurance, however, because of the high risk of anti-selection, may never successfully evolve.

Operational Aspects of Insurance Company Coverage. The marketing practices used by the insurance companies active in the field to date have

---

[7] Generally, the straightening of malposed teeth.

TABLE 38-1. THE DENTISTS' SUPPLY COMPANY OF NEW YORK—Comprehensive Dental Care Plan

	Classification of Benefits			
	Routine Oral Examination	Basic Dental	Orthodontic	Full Denture Replacement
Services Included:	1. All or any combination of the following: a) Oral examination. b) Diagnosis. c) X-rays if prescribed. d) Prophylaxis (cleaning).	1. Treatment of any dental disease, defect or injury recommended on Form "A" submitted at time of Routine Oral Examination, or as a direct result of an examination other than a Routine Oral Examination. 2. Dental Services included: a) Fillings and Crowns. b) Extractions and all other types of oral surgery. c) Periodontal treatment. d) Initial installation of prosthetic appliances, including bridges and full and partial dentures. e) Replacement of existing bridges and partial dentures if qualitative or quantitative changes are prescribed. f) Repair of a denture.	1. Installation of orthodontic appliances and treatments as prescribed on the Treatment Plan of Form "A."	1. Replacement of existing full denture as recommended on the Treatment Plan of Form "A."
Limitations:	1. Form "A" must be returned to the Personnel Office not later than ten (10) days after the examination. 2. Not more than one Routine Oral Examination in any six-month period for each Insured Person. 3. Examination must have been given while insurance is in force.	1. Form "A" must be returned to the Personnel Office not later than ten (10) days after the examination. 2. Treatment must have begun and been rendered while insurance is in force. 3. No services rendered solely for cosmetic purposes. 4. No treatment of dental disease, defect or injury arising out of or in course of any occupation or employment.	1. Form "A" must be returned to the Personnel Office not later than ten (10) days after the examination. 2. Treatment must commence within 90 days following submission of Form "A." 3. Treatment must have begun and been rendered while insurance is in force. 4. No services rendered solely for cosmetic purposes. 5. Successive periods of treatment must be separated by at least five (5) years.	1. Form "A" must be returned to the Personnel Office not later than ten (10) days after the examination. 2. No replacement during first year of Insured Person's coverage except if made necessary by reason of initial placement of an opposing full denture. 3. Five (5) year wait after first replacement. 4. No replacement because of loss or theft of denture. 5. No replacement solely for cosmetic purposes. 6. Treatment must have begun and been rendered while insurance is in force.
Deductible Amounts:	None	1. $25.00 for each Insured Person in first Policy Year in which Insured Person receives a dental service. 2. $10.00 for each Insured Person after first Policy Year in which dental service or a Routine Oral Examination has been received by any insured member of family. 3. A maximum of three (3) Deductible Amounts for any one family will be applied in any Policy Year.		
Payment of Reasonable Expenses Incurred:	80% Insurance Company 20% Insured Person	After the Deductible Amount has been satisfied, payment is as follows: 80% Insurance Company 20% Insured Person	After the Deductible Amount has been satisfied, payment is as follows: 60% Insurance Company 40% Insured Person	After the Deductible Amount has been satisfied, payment is as follows: 60% Insurance Company 40% Insured Person
Maximum Annual Reasonable Expenses Payable by Insurance Company:		*Individual Maximum For All Services* Policy Year First $200 Second 300 Third and Subsequent 400		*Family Maximum for All Services* $ 500 750 1,000

A Maximum Aggregate Benefit of $400.00 for each Insured Person for each period of Orthodontic treatment regardless of the number of Policy Years through which such treatment may extend.

followed the pattern developed for the marketing of other forms of group health coverage. Generally, the plans are experience rated. Companies with large agency forces have educated their agency personnel in the new line and conducted their marketing through established channels. Companies with extensive brokerage business have similarly conducted informational seminars and mail campaigns in order to familiarize their major producers with the details of their dental product. In most instances, dental insurance has been marketed as a separate and distinct line of coverage, although its integration into a comprehensive health benefits package for a particular consumer group certainly has been encouraged where the resources of the group are adequate to support the costs. Generally, commission practices traditionally followed with respect to the older forms of group health insurance have been used in the marketing of group dental insurance.

Dental Service Corporations

Development of Dental Service Corporations. A dental service corporation is the dental counterpart to the medical society sponsored service corporation, known commonly as Blue Shield. It is a nonprofit organization, usually incorporated under a special enabling statute, and founded under the sponsorship of the state dental society in the state in which it operates. Its purpose is to permit the marketing of dental service plans under which dentists practicing in its area of operation agree to provide the services covered in the contracts between the corporation and its group customers.

Dental service corporations originated on the West Coast as the result of demands placed upon the dental profession by representatives of the Health and Welfare Fund maintained by the International Longshoremen's and Warehousemen's Union and the Pacific Maritime Association. The demands, exerted almost simultaneously in the states of Washington and California, occurred early in the 1950's and were aimed at the development of professionally controlled and administered plans whereby the children of union members could obtain essential dental services with the Fund supporting the costs of the plans. The initial planning negotiations resulted in the founding of the Washington Dental Service Corporation, in 1954, and California Dental Service, in 1955. The ILWU–PMA plans that were then placed in effect proved successful, after experiencing early growing pains, but the evolution of other contracts was slow. Much of the activity of these early corporations was related to contracts with state and county public welfare agencies. Slowly, however, other organizations, particularly in the field of negotiated health and welfare trusts, began to show interest in dental care as an area for inclusion in the collective bargaining process, and the pace of interest in dental service corporations accelerated, both within the profession and externally. Today, that interest has produced the passage of enabling statutes in twenty-nine states, the formation of twenty-two corporations and the activation of nine. Corporations currently operating are located in California, Colorado, Connecticut, Hawaii, Michigan, New York, Ohio, Oregon and Washington. Others are expected to begin functioning soon. This increase in activity has expanded the number of persons covered under group service plans to more than 500,000 persons.

The evolution of dental service corporations has been slow because of a variety of factors. The demand for group coverage of dental expenses, through any type of third party financing mechanism, was not strong until recently because priority was given by labor groups and the public to the purchase of coverage for other more catastrophic health care expenses. At the same time, the dental profession was reluctant to enter a field foreign to its normal scope of function. The practicality of attempting to prepay dental expenses was severely questioned. The need, in most states, for the passage of special enabling legislation, in order to create an exception to certain prohibitions in state insurance codes,[8] was felt to be an expensive and difficult obstacle to overcome. Time has eroded the strength of these negative considerations. However, in some states where dental service corporations have been formed, no business has been written or operations have ceased in order that the profession might further evaluate the attitude it should have toward the service corporation.

Nature of Dental Service Coverage. The structure of dental service benefits has varied considerably. A few "open-end" contracts have been marketed, i.e., contracts under which the group purchaser agrees to pay a stipulated gross sum to the corporation and the corporation agrees to provide dental services, through its participating dentists, to the members of the group until the sum has been exhausted. This type of arrangement, while ideal in some respects, has not sold well since some members of the covered group may not "reach the well until the water has run dry."

A much more common plan is one by which the group agrees to pay a sum analogous to an insurance premium and the corporation agrees to satisfy the full demand of the group for covered services during the period of the contract. This type of plan, of necessity, requires the application of actuarial factors based on the experience of similar groups. Initially, such experience was not available, and its absence, which contributed greatly to the slow progress of all dental prepayment mechanisms, had a marked depressive influence on the development of dental service plans. The accumulation of valid statistics is now a continuing endeavor of dental service corporations, however, and the increasing availability and reliability of such statistics is loosening some of the bonds of conservatism that have restricted the spread of service corporation activity.

Table 38–2 indicates the nature and extent of coverage in a dental service plan written by the California Dental Service.

---

[8] Such as, high initial capitalization, various license, tax and fee liabilities, heavy claim reserve requirements and annual insurance department audits.

TABLE 38–2

THE BAY AREA PAINTERS WELFARE FUND DENTAL CARE PLAN

General Features		Standard Benefits	Limitations
Fee Basis:	Usual, customary and reasonable	Recall services each six months (including oral prophylaxis)	*a) Prosthodontia:* (1) No replacement will be made of an existing denture which is satisfactory or can be made satisfactory. Services which are necessary to make such appliance satisfactory will be provided in accordance with the given contract. Prosthetic appliances will be provided once only in every five-year period.
Benefits:	Standard (excluding prosthetics)	Palliative treatment as needed by the patient	
Percentage Participation:	80–20 per cent	Endodontic treatment	
Deductibles	$50 lifetime deductible per patient	Periodontal care	*b) Optional:* In all cases in which there are optional plans of treatment carrying different fees, CDS will pay 75 per cent of the lesser fee. The patient must pay the entire remainder of the dentist's fee.
Maximums:	$500 per patient per calendar year	Space maintainers	
		X-rays as required	
Persons Covered:	Employee only	Surgical preparation of alveolar ridges for prosthetic restorations	(1) Inlays, crowns, and jackets. If tooth can be restored with amalgam, silicate or plastic, CDS will allow the cost of such procedures toward any other type of restoration that patient and dentist choose to use.
		Removal of teeth	
		Silver amalgam, synthetic porcelain and plastic restorations	(2) Partial dentures. If a cast chrome or acrylic partial denture will restore the case, CDS will allow the cost of such procedure toward a more complicated precision case that patient may choose to use.
		Inlays and Crowns	
		Prosthesis:	(3) Full dentures. If in the construction of a denture the patient and dentist decide on personalized restoration or employ specialized techniques as opposed to usual procedures, CDS will allow the amount as shown in the schedule toward such treatment and the patient must bear the difference in cost.
		Bridges	
		Partial dentures	
		Complete dentures	
		Denture adjustment and repair	(4) Complete reconstruction. CDS will allow the cost of procedures necessary to eliminate oral disease and for restorations required to replace missing teeth. Appliances or restorations necessary to increase vertical dimension or restore the occlusion are considered optional and the cost is the responsibility of the patient.
			In all cases in which there are optional plans of treatment carrying different fees, CDS will pay the appropriate percentage (as stated in a given contract) for the lesser fee. The patient must pay the remainder.

TABLE 38–2 (Continued)

Exclusions	Fee Basis and Definitions
Services for injuries or conditions which are compensable under Workmen's Compensation or Employer's Liability Laws; services which are provided the member by any federal or state government agency, or are provided, without cost to the member, by any municipality, county or other political subdivision.	Usual: "Usual" fees are those fees usually charged for a given service by an individual dentist to all his private patients—i.e., his own usual fee.
	Customary: A fee is "customary" when it is within the range of usual fees charged by dentists of similar training and experience for the same service within that same specific and limited geographic area.
Charges for which benefits or services are provided for a covered person under any group, franchise, Blue Cross, Blue Shield or other insurance or prepayment plan arranged through an employer, union, trustee or association.	
	Reasonable: A fee is "reasonable" when it meets the above two criteria and, in the opinion of the responsible dental society's review committee, is justifiable considering the special circumstances of the particular case in question.
Services with respect to congenital malformations, the results of such, cosmetic surgery or dentistry for purely cosmetic reasons.	
	Table of Allowance: A usual, customary and reasonable fee program. The dentist charges his normal fee and California Dental Service makes an allowance toward that fee. The patient will pay the difference, if the fee exceeds the allowance.
Orthodontic services (including tooth guidance procedures).	
Hospitalized cases—charges for hospital care other than benefits covered by this plan are the responsibility of the patient.	Schedule of Maximum Fees: A dentist charges his usual fee but may not exceed that listed in the schedule.
Charges for services of anesthetists or anesthesiologists.	
Prescription drugs.	

The scope of benefits available through dental service plans has been determined by an intermixture of professional opinion as to the relative importance of various services to the health of the individual and considerations related to the financial resources of the purchasing group. As mentioned earlier, the plans initially developed on the West Coast covered only children. That is one way to spread limited resources. The other way is to limit the scope of benefits. This has been done frequently since it has enabled the purchase of at least an austere plan, under which dental disease could be arrested, while permitting the group to negotiate for, or otherwise obtain, additional resources to be applied in the future to the broadening of the benefit structure.

Operational Aspects of Dental Service Corporations. The nonprofit status of a dental corporation enables it to enjoy freedom from taxation. It usually is permitted to operate on a low capitalization basis and is not required to maintain a high level of claim reserves. It is a *quasi*-public organization, often having substantial lay representation on its governing body. Its principal strength lies in the support of the dental profession. Usually each participating dentist, through written agreement, agrees to accept a reduction in the fee payments due him from the corporation for services provided subscribers if the corporation should find its resources inadequate to meet its commitments. While the implementation of this provision has seldom been necessary, its availability is a foundation upon which the safety and integrity of the service corporation's contracts may rest. The effect of this protective requirement is to transfer the risk of adverse loss experience to the participating dentists. This fact has precluded the support of some dentists, while others have not been deterred. Dentists who support dental service corporations feel the profession should offer a type of prepayment vehicle that provides health services rather than financial indemnity. In areas where dental service corporations are operative, generally 70 to 85 per cent of the licensed dentists participate in the arrangement.

The bases for reimbursement of the providers of service have varied considerably. Some service plans have used a rigid fee schedule and required that the dentist accept the scheduled fee as his full payment. Far more common has been a provision whereby the corporation agrees to pay the dentist a stipulated percentage of his usual and customary fee, with the dentist entitled to obtain reimbursement from the patient for the balance. This method permits the dentist to retain control of his own fee practices. Some service corporations require dentists to file their usual and customary fees with the corporation. The usual and customary fee approach requires the corporation to develop and utilize a method for reviewing claims in order to be sure that the fees charged are reasonable. In this activity, the corporations lean heavily on their sponsoring dental societies.

The marketing philosophies of the functioning dental service corporations are divisible into two categories: active and passive. This division is a direct reflection of the attitudes of the sponsoring dental societies. Some societies do not believe that active, aggressive sales promotion is consistent with the dignity of the profession. They believe that the service plan should be made available but sold only to groups that request it. Other societies do not share this attitude and believe that, since the operation of the service corporation clearly is in the public interest, it should be free to compete in the marketplace, leaving the public to determine which prepayment vehicle it prefers.

As in the case of dental insurance developed by insurance companies, and for the same reasons, dental service plans have been designed only for the group market. Again, most plans are experience rated. While it is far too early to deny the eventual evolution of community rated plans that would permit some type of individual marketing, the likelihood is remote.

Group Practice and Clinic Prepayment Dental Plans

Nature and Development of Group Practice and Prepayment Programs. A group practice may be defined, in the dental field, as a dental practice conducted by two or more dentists who share the business costs of the practice, such as those related to the rental or ownership of the physical plant and equipment, the employment of auxiliary personnel and the purchase of supplies and services. The number of group practices in dentistry is small, but it has increased significantly in the last few years and appears destined to grow at an even greater pace in the future. This growth has been responsive to many stimuli, most of which are related to professional and business considerations not germane to this volume. One stimulus, however, has been the rising demand for mechanisms through which dental care expenses can be prepaid by the public. Dentists practicing in a group arrangement can contract with unions or other groups to provide services for their members on a prepaid basis. Such contracts have not been prevalent, in part because they are not looked upon with favor by organized dentistry and also because most dentists still prefer to practice alone. They can work, however, as has been demonstrated particularly in California and New York. The range of variance in the specifications of such contracts is virtually limitless, since each can be tailored to suit the preferences and abilities of both the dentists concerned and the group customer. Benefits can be either comprehensive or severely limited. Compensation can be entirely on a service basis, on a per capita basis, on an indemnity schedule with varying percentage participation, or can combine the service and indemnity approaches. It is well known that some consumer interests, notably in labor circles, are advocating the rapid acceleration of group practice prepayment plans. The weight of that advocacy is respected, but its impact cannot yet be measured.

Nature and Development of Clinic Prepayment Programs. A "clinic" may be defined as an arrangement under which an employer, union or other responsible group agency either employs directly one or more dentists to practice in facilities provided by the group agency and to provide dental services to members of the group, or contracts with a limited number of private, independent practitioners for the provision of such services in their own offices. In the first instance, compensation to the dentist is usually on a salaried basis; in the second, it may be on a fixed fee, per capita or hourly rate basis. Such mechanisms are not uncommon, nor are they newcomers on the scene of dental prepayment. A few existing clinic plans originated in the late nineteenth century. Many more can trace their origins back for forty years or more. The oldest, founded in 1890,[9] covers only a minimal amount of care, with an estimated 2 per cent of the total health plan budget allocated for dental services. Such services as are covered, however, are available to approximately 6,300 members of the sponsoring organization through the offices of selected private practitioners. (In some respects, the plan might better be characterized as a self-insured plan.) A classical example of an "in-house" clinic is that maintained by the St. Louis Labor Health Institute. The program, which was instituted in 1945, offers virtually all services except orthodontics on a

---

[9] Colorado and Southern Railways Employees Hospital Association, Denver, Colorado.

service benefit basis at the Labor Health Institute Dental Clinic. The patient pays only for the laboratory costs associated with gold inlays and the fabrication of certain prosthetic appliances. At last report, some 18,000 persons were participating in the plan.

Present Status and Future Potential of Group Practice and Clinic Prepayment Plans. Despite anticipated opposition from organized dentistry, it is likely that group practice and clinic prepayment dental plans will continue to show some growth. As recently as June, 1964, according to a report published by the United States Public Health Service,[10] there were eighty-five group practice and clinic plans in operation. These plans covered 596,000 people, more than the combined number then reported to be covered by dental service corporations and the insurance company programs. Since insurance company coverage and dental service plans are recent entries on the prepayment scene, however, and in view of the great strides made in the past thirty years by medical service plans and the insurance industry in covering other types of health services, it is conceivable that these mechanisms will outstrip group practice plans and clinic plans quickly.

GENERAL PROBLEMS IN ISSUING DENTAL EXPENSE COVERAGE

Marketing Problems

The marketing of group dental expense coverage has been impeded by several factors. Some of these are essentially rate making problems which have already been mentioned, including the absence until comparatively recent times of reliable statistics concerning utilization, frequency of occurrence, the relationship between dental health appreciation and the economic and educational level of the group. Lack of understanding that comprehensive dental coverage cannot be obtained cheaply is another impediment which, like public apathy toward the importance of good dental health, cannot be removed merely by the introduction of a prepayment vehicle. Disagreements within the dental profession regarding the need for dental service corporations and within some segments of the insurance industry on the question of the insurability of dental expenses are yet to be resolved, and their existence certainly has not made marketing any easier. However, at least twenty-six major insurance companies have at least one dental coverage case in force. Then, too, many group writing insurers, including many Blue Cross–Blue Shield plans, are coming to feel they should write dental coverage to protect against the loss of existing group coverage.

Marketing has also been complicated for insurance companies and

---

[10] U.S. Public Health Service, *Digest of Prepaid Dental Care Plans—1963* (Washington, D.C.: U.S. Government Printing Office, 1964).

service corporations by the fact that unions seem to be leaning toward group practice plans or toward the construction and staffing of clinics. Temporarily, at least, many such unions have removed themselves from the marketplace. Many other groups, on the other hand, while reacting with enthusiasm to the potentials of prepaid dental coverage, have been unable to marshall sufficient resources to meet the costs of this new benefit. The funds are accumulating, but more time is needed.

Underwriting Problems

The underwriting of dental expense coverage probably has caused more than one actuary to pinch himself in hope that the nightmare would end. The near universality of dental disease, mentioned earlier, along with the anticipated avalanche of grievously deteriorated mouths, initially made the idea of dental insurance seem ridiculous, particularly in light of the comparatively modest cost of keeping a healthy mouth healthy. When dental expense coverage became a reality, however, these problems had to be overcome. Methods for reducing the exposure to heavy losses at least to a reasonably manageable level had to be discovered. To the credit of all parties concerned, they were discovered.

The initial requirement for 100 per cent participation by the group constituted a solid defense against anti-selection. The imposition of annual maxima on the insurer's responsibility for expenses incurred by both individual members and family groups provided protection against inordinately high claims. The utilization of deductibles and percentage participation requirements served the dual purpose of reducing the insuring organization's liability on small claims while assuring that the patient would retain a strong personal interest in the cost of the dental services he obtained.

The elimination, or separate handling, of certain types of more expensive services has been a tool used by some underwriters. Many early restrictions have been discarded as experience has shown them to have been unnecessary. Others, however, such as the assignment of waiting periods to certain services or the incorporation of schedules of allowances have subsequently been adopted. Deductibles are being reduced, percentage participation requirements adjusted more favorably to the customer and annual maxima elevated.

Cost Control Problems

As mentioned earlier, the dental service corporations, in most instances, have found it necessary to establish review mechanisms through which a reasonable degree of cost and quality evaluation could be assured. Insurance companies also need the use of professional review facilities to check upon the propriety of utilization and costs in certain instances. This evaluation usually is applied through the employment of professional review committees staffed by dentists who serve voluntarily and without compensation. The utilization of such committees not only permits identification of the occasional effort to abuse the program; in the case of dental service corporations it also permits effective eligibility checks to be carried out. This enables both the patient and the dentist who will provide the service to know exactly what types of services are covered under the patient's contract, what percentage of the dentist's charges will be paid by the insurer and how much will remain for payment by the patient. Some dentists resent the control element of this system of preauthorization and claims review. Others feel, however, that the proper administration of such a system by the dental profession should foster improved patient relations without interfering in any way with the professional judgment and prerogatives of the dentist.

It has also been suggested that claims review procedures under dental society sponsorship should likewise be available to commercial insurance companies. The recommended organizations would be similar in nature to the medical care foundations formed in California under the auspices of local medical societies.[11] It is felt that the utilization of comparable organizations in the administration of dental expense coverage purveyed by insurance companies would give the dental profession a more effective voice in the development and marketing of such plans while simultaneously enabling the underwriting companies to assure their prospective customers that cost and quality control will be exercised in the administration of their plans. This suggestion is of fairly recent origin and has not been formally considered for adoption by the American Dental Association. Two state dental societies (Maryland and Nebraska) have acted favorably upon it, however, and experimentation is already being carried forward. Should the foundation type organization become widely used, its effect on the advancement of dental service and insurance company coverage could be pronounced.

SELECTED REFERENCES

CONTINENTAL CASUALTY COMPANY. *Health Insurance Plans—A Statistical Analysis*. Chicago, 1964.

DENENBERG, HERBERT S. "Prepayment Dentistry and Commercial Insurance," *The Journal of the American Dental Association*, Vol. LXVII, No. 6 (December, 1963), pp. 830–41.

"Dental Care Programs," *Textbook for Welfare and Pension Trustees and Administrators*, Vol. IV (1962), chaps. 6–10.

EILERS, ROBERT D. "An Independent National Agency for Dental Service Corporations?" *The Journal of the American Dental Association*, Vol. LXIX, No. 2 (August, 1964), pp. 158–67.

---

[11] See Chapter 23.

———. "Organization and Growth of a Dental Service Association," *The Journal of the American Dental Association,* Vol. LXVII, No. 6 (December, 1963), pp. 842–54.

FARMER, LEE R. "First Year's Experience with Dental Insurance: Dental Care Coverage Issued by an Insurance Company," *The Journal of the American Dental Association,* Vol. LXII, No. 2 (February, 1961), pp. 200–204.

———. Unpublished paper, "Dental Health Insurance—Projections for Its Future," presented at the Fall Employee Benefits and Pension Conference, American Management Association, Chicago, November 9, 1964.

MELONE, JOSEPH J. "Prepaid Care and Employee Benefit Programs," *The Journal of the American Dental Association,* Vol. LXVII, No. 6 (December, 1963), pp. 855–61.

Chapter 39

GROUP PROPERTY AND LIABILITY INSURANCE

BY JAMES J. CHASTAIN

During this century the volume of group life and health insurance has grown to the point where more than 30 per cent of all life insurance in force in the United States is provided through group insurance, and more than 75 per cent of all health insurance (measured in terms of benefit payments) is under the group form. No parallel development has occurred in property and liability insurance. Although there are at the present time no completely reliable statistics on the matter, it is probable that less than 10 per cent (and possibly even less than 5 per cent) of property and liability insurance is written on a group basis.

An examination of group property and liability insurance is more important than its present position in the marketplace would indicate, however, because strong pressures exist which could cause it to become more significant in the future. Moreover, many of the technical problems involved in writing group property and liability insurance are identical to problems encountered in writing nonemployee groups in life and health insurance.

DEFINITION AND PRINCIPAL CHARACTERISTICS

Group property and liability insurance is defined here as that type of coverage which is marketed simultaneously to two or more different persons or businesses and which provides some rate, coverage, underwriting or service advantage not available in the same company on a nongroup basis. Such a general definition is necessary because the term has not been defined in state insurance statutes as have the terms group life insurance and group health insurance. If applied to life and health insurance, the concept of group insurance used here would include wholesale, franchise and blanket insurance, as well as group insurance.

Group property and liability insurance may be further defined by identifying the methods used to achieve rate, coverage, underwriting or service advantages for group members. The inclusion of one or more of the following features in an insurance contract covering members of a group is strong indication that the plan is a group plan.

Group Rating

In group rating, the premium charged the group is less than the sum of the premiums which would be charged to all insureds for comparable individual insurance. The amount of premium reduction may be based upon (1) the loss experience of the group, (2) favorable physical characteristics of exposure units included in the group, (3) administrative and acquisition expense savings resulting from grouping and (4) some combination of these factors.

Uniform Coverage

Uniform coverage for all insured group members is another feature of group plans. Uniform coverage may be achieved by means of a master policy issued in the name of the organization with certificates of insurance issued to group members or simply by issuing identical policies to group members. The amount of coverage may be different for different members of the group.

Group Underwriting

In group underwriting, the standards to be applied with regard to insuring or canceling insurance of individual group members are established before the group is insured and are a part (sometimes implicit) of the group agreement. The amount of coverage to be made available to individuals within the group also is agreed upon in advance. The essential element of group underwriting is that there is no underwriting discretion regarding individuals within the group after the group agreement goes into effect. Group underwriting standards are a factor in establishing the group rate.

Special Methods of Distribution of Cost among Group Members

Through group rating, a premium may be developed for the group as a whole. Distribution of the total premium among group members may then be made on the basis of an estimated contribution of individual group members to the total exposure. Such an estimate may be based upon the rating system used for rating individual risks which are similar to those included in the group. A more common practice, however, is for equal sharing of the total cost or for establishment of a few broad premium classes. For example, in a group package policy covering individually owned stores in a chain of franchise hamburger stands, it would be possible to charge each stand a portion of the premium the stand would have to pay if insured individually. It would also be possible to establish a flat premium for each stand or to establish the individual stand premium based upon certain broad classes of sales volume per stand.

Exclusive Agent Distribution

Most property-liability insurers are represented by many agents. Some group property and liability policies provide that any of the insurer's agents may provide coverage to individual group members under a group policy which is already in force. Other group policies provide that all the members of a given group will be insured through one agent.[1] For example, if a liability insurer wrote an errors and omissions policy on a voluntary participation basis for members of a state association of life underwriters, the insurer might provide that the coverage could be obtained by individual life underwriters through any agent of the liability insurer selected by the life underwriter. On the other hand, the insurer might designate one agent in the state to write all policies for association members. A variation of the exclusive agent distribution plan provides that all group business obtained by individual agents will be brokered through a designated agent.

Where an exclusive agent distribution plan has official support from a group organization, there is a strong indication that some rate, coverage, underwriting or service advantage is being made to group members which would not be available to them as individuals. In most cases, the exclusive agent receives a reduced commission. The saving in acquisition cost may be reflected to insureds through lower premiums, broader coverage or more favorable underwriting rules.

Combinations of Group Features

Group features may be combined in many ways in writing group insurance. One plan, for example, may provide for nonuniform and individually underwritten policies to be written through the American agency system and with group rating practiced. Another plan may involve individual rating and underwriting but special coverage advantages in contracts sold only to group members through an exclusive agent. For example, a group of electrical contractors may be able to obtain through an exclusive agent a liability policy which would be individually rated and underwritten but which would not include the usual care, custody and control exclusion.

DIFFERENCES BETWEEN GROUP PROPERTY AND LIABILITY INSURANCE AND GROUP LIFE AND HEALTH INSURANCE

The question often is asked whether the success of the group concept in life and health insurance indicates that group property and liability

---

[1] For a discussion of the types of marketing systems used in group property and liability insurance see Richard M. Heins, *Extension of Group Marketing Principles to Property and Casualty Insurance* (Philadelphia: Society of Chartered Property and Casualty Underwriters, 1957), p. 14.

insurance would be equally successful. Any attempt to draw such an analogy is dangerous because of several crucial differences between life and health insurance on the one hand and property and liability insurance on the other. An examination of some of these differences can help to explain why the group concept has not yet developed in property and liability insurance as it has in life and health insurance and may provide some indication of possible future developments in group property and liability insurance.

Differing Social Environment

Social pressure on employers to maintain at least minimal coverage for the benefit of employees generally has been greater in life and health insurance than in property and liability insurance. A possible explanation of this differing social environment lies in the fact that the employer is more directly concerned with continuation of the family's income which the employer is already providing in case of the death or disability of an employee than with replacement of a destroyed car or home which was purchased by the employee.

As early as 1912, there was serious consideration of social life insurance to be financed through employer contributions, and beginning in 1932 and continuing up to the present, there have been many proposals for social health insurance to be financed at least partially through employer contributions. These social and political pressures on employers to provide workers with greater financial security through social legislation have given rise to corresponding pressures to provide this security through voluntary group insurance as a means of warding off further governmental intervention into the insurance business. Many persons feel that the development of group life insurance in 1911 was an important factor in delaying the development of governmentally provided life insurance.[2] Similarly, the remarkable growth of employee group health insurance in the past thirty years has helped to weaken the case of those who advocate socialized health insurance.

The forces which led to the development of employee group life insurance in 1911 and to employee group medical expense insurance in 1932 did not exist at those times for property and liability insurance. The two major economic uncertainties related to property and liability insurance to which individual workers may be exposed are: (1) destruction of an owned dwelling or personal property by fire or other peril and (2) the possibility of being held legally liable for committing a negligent act. The most important source of negligence claims arises out of the ownership of automobiles.

---

[2] Davis W. Gregg, *Group Life Insurance* (3d ed.; Homewood, Ill.: Richard D. Irwin, Inc., 1962), p. 22.

In 1910, 61.6 per cent of nonfarm homes were occupied by renters,[3] and automobile, bus and truck registrations in the United States totaled only 468,500.[4] It seems safe to assume that most workers were neither automobile owners nor homeowners at that time. Negligence lawsuits for personal acts were rare and were of little concern to workers. Although there was a possibility of destruction of personal property by fire or other peril, the risk was minor compared to the perils of death and disability then facing workers.

During the past fifty years, as workers have accumulated property they also have accumulated property insurance. Where credit has been involved in the purchase of property, lenders generally have required the purchaser to have the property insured. Beginning in 1927, states began to encourage the purchase of automobile liability insurance through compulsory automobile liability insurance laws or through financial responsibility laws. These laws were a reflection of social pressure not upon employers but upon individual automobile owners. Property insurers have developed and modified policies as necessary to meet the changing needs for property insurance. Thus, it appears that the factors which may account for the greater social pressure on employers to provide life and health insurance than property and liability insurance are that (1) life and health insurance are income continuation plans closely associated with the employer as the source of the income, and (2) the original small and gradually increasing demand for property and liability insurance has never produced a major vacuum of coverage which would result in social pressure.

Differing Sales Efforts Required

The need for greater sales effort in the sale of individual life and health insurance than in the sale of individual property and liability insurance may have caused life and health insurers to be more interested than property and liability insurers in an alternative marketing channel. This difference in sales effort required in the insurance fields results partly from differences in the nature of needs for the coverages and partly from differences in the products themselves.

For example, the need for individual life insurance is greatest at a time of life when income is low. The need for property insurance, on the other hand, varies directly with the value of the property owned and, hence, with the ability to pay for the insurance. The frequency of claims is higher and the average size of claim is lower in property insurance than in life insurance. Individual insurance buyers usually tend to overemphasize the frequency factor and underemphasize the severity factor in insurance purchases. Through the purchase of property and liability insurance the

---

[3] U.S. Bureau of the Census, *Historical Statistics of the United States, Colonial Times to 1957* (Washington, D.C.: Government Printing Office, 1960), p. 395.

[4] *Ibid.*, p. 761.

insured protects primarily himself. The purchase of life insurance is usually for the protection primarily of others. Well over half of all property insurance is purchased by businessmen for business reasons. Only a small portion of life insurance is sold for business reasons. In addition to these inherent differences between life and property insurance, the near-compulsory nature of automobile insurance and dwelling fire insurance on mortgaged property makes these coverages easier to sell than coverages which are discretionary for buyers.

Any generalization concerning the difficulty of sale of health insurance is dangerous because of the wide variety of coverages available. Low limit medical expense policies have many sales characteristics in common with property insurance. Major medical insurance and long-term disability income policies with long waiting periods have many sales characteristics in common with life insurance. Other health insurance policies have sales characteristics which fall between these two extremes. With the present intense competition in marketing property and liability insurance, insurers are showing increased interest in the group concept.

Differing Degrees of Market Saturation

A precise comparison of the degree of market saturation in life and health insurance as compared to property and liability insurance is impossible because of the fact that the amount of personal life insurance needed depends upon a subjective decision of the insured, whereas the amount of property and liability insurance may be determined more objectively. However, based upon available facts, the present market for property and liability insurance appears to be more nearly saturated than the market for life and health insurance. According to a recent survey by the Opinion Research Corporation, "Virtually all homeowners have fire insurance on their houses and approximately nine in ten of all automobile owning families have one or more kinds of automobile coverage."[5] These are the two most important premium volume lines in personal property and liability insurance. The survey did not measure the extent of insurance to value on the property or the adequacy of limits of liability insurance. The effects of lenders requiring insurance to value and state financial responsibility laws requiring at least moderate liability limits increase the degree of market saturation in property and liability insurance.

The total amount of life insurance, including business life insurance and policies on the lives of children, women and retired persons, covers less than two times disposable income. As recently as 1961, health insurance covered only 28.3 per cent of medical care costs and 29.4 per cent of income lost through short-term disability.[6]

The high degree of saturation of the property and liability insurance

---

[5] *The National Underwriter*, Fire and Casualty Edition, April 20, 1962, p. 1.

[6] O. D. Dickerson, *Health Insurance* (rev. ed.; Homewood, Ill.: Richard D. Irwin, Inc., 1963), pp. 108–11.

market reduces the pressure by society and companies for a new marketing channel. Further, it is at least partly responsible for the militant opposition of property and liability agents' associations to extension of the group concept.

Differing Amounts of Post-Sales Service Required

The amount of necessary post-sales service is generally greater in property and liability insurance than in life insurance. Life insurance losses are total and occur only once, and the policy is a valued one. Property and liability losses usually are partial and may occur more than once, and the policy is one of indemnity. Thus, property and liability losses must be evaluated, and some type of field force is usually necessary to perform this function. Also, typical families change automobiles and homes far more often than family composition changes. Each change requires some post-sales service in property and liability insurance. With respect to post-sales service necessary, health insurance is more like life insurance than like property insurance. Although claims typically are partial in health insurance, the evaluation is usually performed by physicians and hospitals. There is no necessity to change health insurance coverage as property or health changes, although some change may be desirable as income rises. Where the need for insurance varies widely among group members and changes often, as in property-liability insurance, the demand for group insurance is weakened, and the technical problems of providing group insurance are increased.

Differing Regulatory Status

Rate regulation has been the custom in property-liability insurance, whereas there is little direct regulation of rates in life and health insurance. The reason advanced is that solvency regulation is more difficult in property and liability insurance than in life insurance. This is due in part to the availability in life insurance of a reasonably equitable, universal risk classification system—the mortality table. Statistics in life insurance are more reliable and operating results are more predictable than in property and liability insurance. The interest income on policy reserves provides a source of financial strength in life insurance which makes solvency regulation in life insurance somewhat less critical than property and liability insurance solvency regulation. Moreover, fire insurance has been more subject to catastrophe hazard than life insurance.

The attitude of insurers and insurance regulators toward rate regulation has been changing during the past few years in the direction of allowing greater rating flexibility. However, insurance regulators see in group property and liability insurance a means for insurers completely to avoid present rate regulatory laws. Effective regulation of group rates separately from individual rates would require radical changes in state insurance departments. For these reasons insurance regulators generally have opposed extension of the group concept to property and liability insurance.

Differing Federal Income Tax Treatment

A favorable federal income tax environment has been an important factor in the rapid growth of employee group life and health insurance during the past twenty years. The federal income tax laws and rulings providing favorable treatment of employee group life and health insurance premiums paid by the employer are not applicable to group property insurance premiums. The present trend is toward further restrictions in the income tax law, rather than extensions of the law. These crucial differences between life and health insurance as compared with property and liability insurance discourage the extension of the group technique to property and liability coverages.

NEEDS FOR GROUP PROPERTY AND LIABILITY INSURANCE

Insurance buyers have been interested in purchasing property and liability insurance on a group basis since the 1920's.[7] This interest in group insurance has grown especially rapidly during the past ten years. Since 1953, the National Association of Insurance Agents (hereafter NAIA) has maintained a file of group property and liability insurance proposals which have been made to various interstate organizations. The vigilance of many of the 35,000 members of the NAIA in informing the national office of new group proposals makes a list of organizations included in the file a reasonably representative sample of interstate organizations interested in group insurance. A list of organizations included in the file in 1960 shows forty-two trade associations, seventeen professional associations, seventeen franchise dealer groups, four employee groups, three eleemosynary groups and three miscellaneous groups, for a total of eighty-six groups.

Thus, based on this rather small sample it appears that the major demand for group property and liability insurance is coming not from employee groups, as in life and health insurance, but from associations. Furthermore, it seems that the demand is not for insurance to satisfy personal needs but to satisfy business needs, as will become apparent in the following pages. The major needs which the associations are attempting to meet through group insurance are coverage needs, cost needs and underwriting and service needs.

---

[7] In a 1953 speech on group insurance to the National Board of State Directors of the National Association of Insurance Agents, Robert E. Battles, a California agent, said: "The development of group buying, of group writing, depending on the point of view, of insurance, is not a new one. . . . We have been fighting developments of this type in California for over twenty-five years."

Coverage Needs

Some associations have sought broader insurance coverage for their members through group insurance. For example, Butler Brothers, which has granted franchises to more than 2,500 independently owned Ben Franklin Stores, has sought to aid store owners in obtaining otherwise unavailable flood insurance for merchandise through a group plan. The American Hotel Association has sought to help members obtain adequate limits of public liability insurance through a group policy because of the difficulty association members faced in obtaining adequate limits under individual contracts. The Boys' Clubs of America negotiated a group fidelity bond in 1958 which provided not only for bonding full-time and part-time employees of individual clubs but volunteer workers and members of boards of directors as well. Boys' Clubs Camp Operations were also included in the policy. In each of these examples such broad coverage was not generally available on an individual basis.

Thus, special insurance coverage needs have led groups of buyers to joint action. Individual insurers have been able to respond to these needs through group policies because the risk of insuring the group is not as great as the risk of insuring a few individual buyers.[8]

In some situations, two or more parties have a loss exposure in the same property or business operation. For example, organizations which grant franchises to dealers have a loss exposure in the property of the franchise dealers, even though title to the inventory, equipment or building involved rests with the franchise dealer. The loss exposure to the company granting the franchise may result from its position as creditor of the franchise dealer or from developmental costs in establishing the relationship. Likewise, employers have a loss exposure in employee automobiles which are used in the business of the employer, both because of the liability exposure and because loss to the automobile could impair the employee's usefulness. In addition, builders have a loss exposure in the activities of general contractors and subcontractors. In the first place, the builder may be held liable for activities of the prime or subcontractors. In the second place, the builder could suffer through a loss to contractors which delayed completion of the project. Still another illustration of this overlapping loss exposure is the insurable interest which lenders have in pledged property. Insurers have solved some of the problems involving multiple interests in loss exposures through issuance of certifications of insurance, loss payable and mortgage clauses, excess coverage and in other ways, but it is almost impossible to eliminate all overlapping coverage and coverage loopholes through individual insurance in situations of this kind.

---

[8] This is an application of the law of large numbers. As the number of exposure units increases, the probable percentage variation of actual results from predicted results decreases.

Coordination of insurance covering two or more interests in one loss exposure can sometimes be handled through application of the group concept. For example, for many years an insurance company-owned service organization covered under a group contract employee-owned cars which were used in business. Uniform coverage was provided for all employees, and the company protected itself further with an excess policy written through the group insurer.

Cost Needs

Reduction of operating expenses is an important goal in any business. Expense reductions may benefit consumers through lower prices and/or business owners through increased profits. Competitive business conditions make control over operating expenses essential in maintaining or improving a firm's market position.

The possibility of reduction in insurance costs has been an important consideration in many group plan proposals. The reduction in insurance costs may result from a refinement of rate classifications, improved loss control activity among group members or through expense reduction by the insurer.

Underwriting and Service Needs

In a previous section the question involved was one of whether more favorable contract provisions could be made available through group insurance. This section is concerned with whether standard contracts may be available through group insurance to some persons who might not be able to obtain individual insurance.

An advantage of group life and health insurance is that some persons otherwise uninsurable are able to obtain insurance under a group plan. Similarly, group property-liability insurance provides a means of insuring some otherwise uninsurable persons. For example, one of the important reasons why a group automobile insurance plan was developed for all employees of the Singer Sewing Machine Company was to enable salesmen of the company in the New York area to obtain insurance on their individually owned automobiles. Under the Singer plan, coverage is not uniform; employees may select from a wide variety of coverages, limits of coverage and deductibles. Similarly many of the workmen's compensation groups in the New York State Insurance Fund were formed because some members had great trouble finding an insurance market, and many medical association groups have been formed because of the difficulty of members in obtaining malpractice insurance on an individual basis.

A 1961 Supreme Court decision in New Jersey made the procurement of liquor liability insurance essential for tavern owners in the state. Although liquor liability insurance is available on an indivdual basis for "good" risks, it is difficult to find a market for "bad" risks. In order to provide a market for all association members, as well as for other reasons described in this chapter, the United Tavern Owners Association of New Jersey negotiated a group policy to cover the liquor liability exposure of members. Through use of cooperative buying the individual group members assured themselves of a present and continuing insurance market.

Providing a market for poor risks is both an individual problem for the risks to be insured and a social problem. Group insurance is one means of solving the problem for the individuals and for society.

In addition to the fact that coverage unavailable elsewhere may become available to applicants through the group mechanism, the purchase of group insurance may be considerably more convenient than the purchase of individual coverage. Buyers seek convenience in purchasing insurance just as they do in purchasing other things. No purchase is more convenient for employees than the purchase of group insurance, which may be effected on company time and paid for through payroll deduction. Similarly, the purchase of insurance by mail through a professional or trade association or through a franchise granter may be considerably more convenient than searching the market for correct coverage or for an agent competent to obtain the specialized coverage needed.

REGULATION OF GROUP PROPERTY AND LIABILITY INSURANCE

Insurance regulators have been hostile to most attempts to extend the group concept to property and liability insurance. In opposing group property insurance, regulators have cited violations of surplus lines laws,[9] agents' and brokers' licensing laws, countersignature laws, form and rate filings laws and premium tax laws. Where group plans have been written in compliance with these laws, insurance regulators have disapproved the plans on the basis of rate approval laws or authorized insurer laws.

Between 1956 and 1959, group property and liability insurance was the subject of departmental rulings in nineteen states[10] and of special statutes in eleven states.[11] These rulings and statutes are named "fictitious group" rulings or statutes in most states.[12]

---

[9] Surplus lines laws provide that agents licensed in a state must place insurance in insurers admitted to do business in the state if the admitted insurers are willing to write the insurance. Agents or brokers who place insurance with nonadmitted insurers must obtain surplus lines licenses.

[10] Alabama, Alaska, Colorado, Florida, Georgia, Illinois, Iowa, Kentucky, Maine, Maryland, Missouri, Nevada, New York, North Dakota, Ohio, Oregon, Rhode Island, Washington and West Virginia.

[11] Arkansas, Florida, Hawaii, Mississippi, Montana, North Carolina, Oklahoma, Oregon, South Dakota, Utah and Washington.

[12] In a speech to the 62nd Annual National Association of Insurance Agents' Convention in 1958, Insurance Director of Illinois Joseph S. Gerber pointed out that use of the word "fictitious" in this sense is incorrect. The employee, franchise, association and professional groups are almost invariably "real." Other writers and speakers have made the same point, but the name persists and is included in many state insurance statutes.

The insurance commissioner of the state of Washington issued the first fictitious group ruling on February 24, 1956, but a ruling issued by the Florida Insurance Department in 1957 served as a model for fictitious group rulings and statutes in most other states. The important element of the Florida ruling is the following sentence:

Therefore, no insurer, admitted or non-admitted, shall make available through any rating plan or form, fire, casualty or surety insurance to any firm, corporation, or association of individuals, any preferred rate or premium based upon any fictitious grouping of such firm, corporation, or association of individuals, which fictitious grouping is hereby defined and declared to be any grouping by way of membership, license, franchise, contract, agreement, or any other method or means; provided, however, that the foregoing shall not apply to accident and health insurance.[13]

A "clarification" of this bulletin issued three weeks later includes the following sentence:

Therefore, no master policy, or series of policies, or certificates of insurance of fire, casualty, or surety insurance which are issued to any fictitious grouping at any preferred rate or form shall include any Florida resident, or group of residents, in such coverage, and Florida residents or groups of residents shall be specifically excluded from solicitation for such fire, casualty or surety insurance issued to any fictitious grouping, at a preferred rate or form.[14]

The sentence quoted from the original bulletin was later incorporated into the Florida insurance statute entitled "Section 643.04 Unfair Methods of Competition and Unfair or Deceptive Acts or Practices." The two sentences quoted from the bulletin and letter of clarification were used verbatim for rulings or statutes in a number of other states. Portions of the wording in the sentences were incorporated into most other fictitious group rulings and statutes.

Between 1958 and 1960, a "Subcommittee on Fictitious Groupings of Fire and Casualty Insurance" of the National Association of Insurance Commissioners investigated the subject of group property and liability insurance. The final report of the subcommittee was written by a representative of the National Association of Insurance Agents, an association which had testified in opposition to group property and liability insurance before all six meetings of the subcommittee. The subcommittee report, which was approved by the NAIC in June, 1960, recommended no changes in state insurance laws but recommended standard procedures for handling complaints regarding fictitious groups and recommended that several other NAIC committees continue to study the problem.

No significant changes have occurred in the regulation of group property and liability insurance since 1960. The situation is essentially one in

---

[13] J. Edwin Larson, Insurance Commissioner of Florida, *Bulletin No. 211*, July 11, 1957.

[14] J. Edwin Larson, Insurance Commissioner of Florida, letter to Companies and Agents, August 5, 1957.

which all state insurance departments prohibit group property and liability insurance wherever possible, relying on fictitious group laws, rate regulatory laws or other general regulatory laws to justify the prohibition.

Among the reasons for opposition by insurance regulators are the beliefs that group property and liability insurance (1) unfairly discriminates against nongroup members and against the better exposure units in the group; (2) creates a chaotic rating situation; (3) threatens the effectiveness of state regulation of insurance by circumventing countersignature, surplus line, premium tax and other state statutes; (4) threatens destruction of the present marketing system with damage to the public interest; (5) threatens the caliber of service; (6) affects the incentive for individual loss prevention and (7) threatens insolvency for some insurers because of the increased competition of group insurance. Many of these arguments were presented to insurance regulators during the developmental period of group life insurance. Some proved to be groundless, and others were overcome through changes in state laws.[15] Some of the arguments are still being raised in opposition to further extensions of group life and health insurance. It appears that the feared harmful effects of group property and liability insurance could be eliminated or minimized through carefully designed permissive group property and liability insurance statutes.[16]

AVAILABLE METHODS OF PROVIDING GROUP PROPERTY AND LIABILITY INSURANCE

Despite the general opposition to group property and liability insurance by insurance regulators, this coverage is presently being provided by a number of circuitous but legal means. A discussion of several of these means follows.

Insuring through a Nonadmitted Alien Insurer

The United States Supreme Court has consistently upheld the right of insurance buyers to contract with nonadmitted insurers by direct negotiation with the insurer.[17] A state law attempting to void policies with

---

[15] J. Pierson Hammond, Actuary of the Connecticut Insurance Department, through research studies and speeches in the 1912–15 period, played an important role in acceptance of the group concept in life insurance by insurance regulators. No comparable champion for the cause of group property-liability insurance has emerged.

[16] For a discussion of the possible economic costs and benefits to society of group property and liability insurance, see James J. Chastain, "An Evaluation of Group Property Insurance" unpublished doctoral dissertation, University of Illinois, 1962.

[17] A nonadmitted insurer is an insurer which has not been authorized by the insurance commissioner of a state to transact insurance business within that state.

nonadmitted insurers has been held unconstitutional.[18] State laws fining[19] or taxing[20] persons who purchase insurance from nonadmitted insurers have been held unconstitutional.

Insurers are classified as domestic, foreign and alien. An insurer is (1) a domestic insurer in its home state, (2) a foreign insurer in states other than its home state and (3) an alien insurer in countries other than its home country. Some degree of control may be maintained over nonadmitted foreign insurers through the cooperation of state insurance commissioners.

By dealing directly[21] with a nonadmitted alien insurer, it is possible for insurance buyers to avoid all state insurance regulation. This approach has been used by a number of organizations for procurement of group property and liability insurance. For example, any of the Ben Franklin Stores (franchised by Butler Brothers) may participate in a group policy covering store contents on an all-risk (including flood) basis. The coverage is written in a Bermuda insurer through a Canadian agency.

Insuring through a Captive Insurer

A captive insurer may be defined as an insurer controlled by interests owning the risks insured therein.[22] Thus, one method of obtaining group insurance is for the group to form or obtain a captive insurer. The insurer usually needs to be admitted in only one state. Insurance regulators interpret insurance statutes liberally for captive insurers.[23]

Many of the captive insurers cover only the exposures of one business interest, but many others were formed by associations to insure association members. Examples include the Dealers National Insurance Company, formed in 1948 to insure members of the Texas Butane Dealers Association; the Florida Insurance Exchange, formed by the Florida Lumber and Millwork Association; the Hercules Casualty Company, formed by the Oklahoma Liquified Petroleum Gas Association; Kemba Mutual Insurance Company (Kemba stands for Kroger Employee Mutual Benefit Association), formed in 1939; and the National Mutual Church

---

[18] *Hammond* v. *International Railway Co.*, 116 N.Y. Supp. 854 (1909).

[19] *Allegeyer* v. *Louisiana*, 165 U.S. 578 (1897).

[20] *St. Louis Cotton Compress Co.* v. *Arkansas*, 260 U.S. 346 (1922). This decision was reaffirmed in the *Texas Board of Insurance* v. *Todd Shipyards Corporation* case decided in June, 1962.

[21] The question of whether conduct of business by mail subjects the insured to laws of the state to which the mail is sent was answered in the affirmative in the *Travelers' Health Association* v. *Commonwealth of Virginia*, 339 U.S. 643 (1950). The case dealt with direct-mail sale of health insurance to individual insurance buyers. Whether the decision applies in a broader context is still unknown.

[22] H. Wayne Snider (ed.), *Risk Management* (Homewood, Ill.: Richard D. Irwin, Inc., 1964), pp. 81–85.

[23] By forming an alien captive insurer all state regulation may be avoided and some income tax advantages gained.

Insurance Company of Illinois, formed by the General Conference of the
Methodist Episcopal Church in 1896.

Basing Dividends upon Group Loss Experience

The distribution of surplus to policyholders is usually considered by
regulators to be a matter entirely apart from rates. In commenting upon
the difference between rates and dividends, Commissioner F. Britton
McConnell of California has stated:

> If an Insurance Commissioner were given any authority to determine the amount
> and manner of distribution of dividends to either policyholders or stockholders
> he could by either intention or ignorance ruin one insurer or type of insurer or
> bestow a valuable competitive benefit upon a particular insurer or type of in-
> surer. And a Commissioner could justify such an order by pseudo-logic suffi-
> cient to make his orders invulnerable to reversal by the courts. I do not know
> that anyone has ever explicitly argued that the Insurance Commissioner should
> have authority to control the amount or manner of distribution of dividends of
> insurers to their policyholders.[24]

Seventeen states have statutes which prohibit unfair discrimination in
payment of dividends. Five other state statutes provide only that insurers
shall pay dividends according to a reasonable classification of policyholders.[25]

By insuring group members on an individual basis but then placing
them in a special class for dividend computation purposes, group rating
may be achieved. Whether or not group dividend plans are truly group
insurance depends upon whether nongroup insureds are included in the
plan. Although insuring nongroup buyers on a different basis from group
buyers may raise the question of rate discrimination, refusing to insure
nongroup buyers on any basis is an underwriting matter which cannot be
effectively regulated.

Issuing Specialized Package Policies to Groups

Insurance policies may be tailored to fit the needs of specific groups.
Although the plan may not be advertised as being exclusively for group
members, nongroup members are not likely to apply for coverage if they
are not solicited. If they do apply, they may be rejected for underwriting
reasons. In discussing the matter of insuring only association members in a
malpractice policy developed in cooperation with the National Hair-
dressers Association, Edmund O'Brien said:

> Strictly as a matter of underwriting judgment we will insure, as a general rule,
> only beauty parlor operators who are members of a recognized professional
> association, so that we may have the advantage of the operating standards re-

---

[24] California Department of Insurance, Ruling 96, July 26, 1957.

[25] For a discussion of these and other state laws relating to payment of dividends,
see C. Arthur Williams, Jr., *Price Discrimination in Property and Liability Insurance*
(Minneapolis: University of Minnesota Press, 1959), pp. 61–64.

quired by the association and the professional experience of the association in evaluating the risks. . . . I don't think anyone would be anxious to insure the malpractice liability of doctors who were not members of their medical associations or lawyers who were not members of their bar associations.[26]

Specialized package policies have been designed for United Quality Courts, Boys' Clubs of America, American Motor Hotel Association, Mobilgas Dealers and many other organizations. The question of legality of specialized package policies hinges upon (1) the method by which the plans are marketed and (2) justification of the rate charged. For example, if advertisements to group members state that only group members are eligible for coverage, or if rates are far below individual rates, the policy will likely face insurance regulator opposition. On the other hand, the policy will likely be approved if the rate reduction can be justified by the insurer and if the coverage is advertised as a package policy designed for all who face the types of risk faced by group members.

Soliciting Only Group Members

Another method of writing group property and liability insurance may be illustrated by an advertisement which appeared in an insurance periodical:

Wanted—Florida-licensed deviating auto liability and physical damage carrier of A:BBB+ min. for insuring school teachers. Class rate filing may be available. Potential of 40,000 teachers. Interested companies indicate by April 1, 1962, per cent deviation from standard rates. Inquiries or rates to Florida Education Association, 208 W. Pensacola Street, Tallahasse, Fla.[27]

The Florida Education Association plan has not yet been developed, but other plans involving group solicitation of organization members have been used by a number of insurers. The characteristic necessary to make group solicitation legal is that the company involved must write insurance for only one group in a given state. If the company issues policies to individual buyers with identical coverage, service, underwriting rules and rates, the plan ceases to be a group plan. If the insurer attempts to issue policies with different coverage, service, underwriting rules or rates to two or more groups in a state, the plan will likely be held illegally discriminatory. This has been the case even where it has been shown that insurer expense factors differ for the two groups.

Insuring in Traditional Group Plans

Some types of property and liability insurance have developed from the outset as group insurance. The Furriers Customer's Policy provides for

---

[26] Edmund J. O'Brien, Assistant General Counsel, American Motorists Insurance Company, Chicago, Letter to NAIC Subcommittee on Group Fire and Casualty Insurance, December 4, 1958.

[27] *National Underwriter,* Fire and Casualty Edition, March 16, 1962, p. 32.

insuring a coat while out of storage by means of a certificate issued by the furrier. The rate is less than that for a policy issued on an individual basis. Musical instruments policies are sold to cover not only the instruments owned by the organizations sponsoring bands or orchestras but also instruments owned by individual band or orchestra members. Policies sold to manufacturers of deepfreeze equipment which allow sale of certificates of insurance to individual buyers and certificates of insurance sold by moving companies are essentially group insurance. Each of these traditional group plans involves cost savings, exclusive agency distribution, uniform coverage and group underwriting to persons insured under the plans.

SELECTED REFERENCES

BATTLES, ROBERT E. "Group Writing of Insurance," Address to the National Board of State Directors of the National Association of Insurance Agents, Hollywood Beach, Florida, April 30, 1953.

CHASTAIN, JAMES J. "An Evaluation of Group Property Insurance," unpublished doctoral dissertation, University of Illinois, 1962.

GERBER, JOSEPH S. "Fictitious Groups," Speech to the 62nd Annual Convention, NAIA, New Orleans, Louisiana, December, 1958.

HEINS, RICHARD M. "Extension of Group Marketing Principles to Property and Casualty Insurance," *The Annals,* Society of Chartered Property and Casualty Underwriters, Vol. X (January, 1958), pp. 14–44.

SNOWDEN, H. N. "Group Automobile Insurance: Its Possibilities and Problems," Address to the Insurance Conference of the Cooperative League, Evanston, Illinois, September 19, 1956.

WHITFORD, GEORGE. "Unique Applications of Group Insurance Ideas," *The Annals,* Society of Chartered Property and Casualty Underwriters, Vol. X (January, 1958), pp. 45–51.

WILLIAMS, C. ARTHUR, JR. *Price Discrimination in Property and Liability Insurance.* Minneapolis: University of Minnesota Press, 1959.

PART VII

Self-Insurance

Chapter 40

MOTIVATIONS FOR SELF-INSURANCE

BY ROBERT C. GOSHAY

The controversy over self-insurance versus insurance has emerged as a major issue for consideration by the large business firm. This emergence has been caused by a number of factors. The basic factor, however, has been the increasing concern by management with the rising costs of the so-called "insurable" risks. Concern has extended not only to the costs of employee benefit programs, but also to the costs of the fire, liability and workmen's compensation coverages. This chapter presents a resume of this emergence, including the nature of self-insurance, the extent and significance of its practice, and the major motivations and issues which have induced firms to undertake the technique, especially with regard to employee benefit programs.

NATURE OF SELF-INSURANCE

The Semantic Problem

The term "self-insurance" involves certain problems in semantics. If one considers the concept of *transfer* of risk as being the essence of insurance, for example, then the term "self-insurance" is an incorrect one, since no element of risk transfer is apparent in the technique. Similarly, if one views the element of insurance as a two-party contract, or as an almost complete guarantee against the financial consequences of an unexpected loss, or as a particular method of financing risk costs, then the term "self-insurance" is likewise an inappropriate one, since inclusion of the word "insurance" is an implicit assumption that these elements are present in self-insurance.[1]

It is clear, however, that there are certain similarities between insurance and self-insurance. In theory, the individual or the business firm must have a large number of homogeneous exposure units in order for the

---

[1] For those wishing to pursue the semantic problems at greater length, the major issues are presented in the author's *Corporate Self-insurance and Risk Retention Plans* (Homewood, Ill.: Richard D. Irwin, Inc., 1964), pp. 19–21.

law of large numbers to operate in connection with whatever risks are self-insured. Likewise, in theory there should be independence of exposure units and fortuitous events causing losses, or practically, a reasonable system of loss control. All these theoretical requirements for insurance are requirements for self-insurance, although practical compromises of them often must be made.

Definition of Self-insurance

The commonly used definitions of self-insurance, once the semantic issues are whisked away, are quite similar. In one form or another, they consider the self-insurance technique as one of retaining recurring benefit cost, or retaining risk, or as a method of internal funding for benefits. These concepts are, of course, interlinked.

Retention of Recurring Losses or Expenses. Many firms find that the losses and expenses of their employee benefit plans are fairly stable and recurring in nature. These costs *tend* to fluctuate around a certain level or tend to fluctuate around a certain known variable in a reasonably stable pattern, only infrequently varying widely. Thus the belief develops among some that the insurance mechanisms involved in these costs are uneconomic, since they merely transfer monies from the business firm to the insurer, and back again in the form of benefit payments, somewhat reduced due to the insurer's expenses. The decision to retain these costs, perhaps with the purchase of insurance protection for fluctuations in costs above this level of normally expected and recurring losses, is considered to result in self-insurance.

Definitionally, this implies that self-insurance is the known retention of losses which emanate from exposures which permit reasonable predictions as to future losses. The protection against wide fluctuations in losses, being analogous to the insurer's practice of reinsuring, would appear to be a necessary ingredient in a self-insurance program.

Retention of Risk. Others consider self-insurance to be simply the assumption of whatever losses occur from exposures which could be insured commercially, whether such losses occur frequently or rarely. The rationale of such a view is that the technique is simply one of avoiding expenditures for insurance.

Definitionally, this type of view of self-insurance involves few notions of pooling, averaging or other actuarial concepts. It stresses the idea of internal absorption of risk, rather than the absorption of financial costs.

Method of Internal Funding. A third view of self-insurance is implicit when one speaks of a firm computing the costs of employee benefits and establishing a reserve for such costs against which claims are charged or setting up a trust to which such costs are contributed and out of which claims can be paid. This method is thus in contrast with simply paying costs from the working capital of the firm as they arise. This view implies that self-insurance is a method of internal funding. Of course, the concept of retention of risk and recurring losses is somewhat implicit as well.

The semantic problems of defining self-insurance can be dismissed at this point. It is clear, however,that the term self-insurance is used to cover a great variety of methods of treating risks and risk costs, which range from simple retention to application of the most advanced and sophisticated management techniques available. It should be noted, nevertheless, that the self-insurance definition problem has far-reaching legal significance. The self-insurance practice is extensive, as will be seen. It carries with it a host of social responsibilities and, thus, is viewed by some as a legitimate object of insurance-type regulation and taxation by governmental bodies.

EXTENT OF SELF-INSURANCE

Definitions and Statistical Measures

It is difficult to ascertain the extent of the self-insurance practice in the employee benefit field for two principal reasons. The first is the problem of defining the scope of employee benefit plans. As was indicated in Chapter 1, the term "employee benefit plan" is defined in different ways by different writers. According to a narrow definition, it includes only group life insurance, group health insurance and pensions. In a broader view, however, the term also includes workmen's compensation, supplementary workmen's compensation and unemployment agreements, compulsory and voluntary nonoccupational disability benefits and other benefit programs. Thus, any statistics are difficult to compare. Our concern here, of course, is the extent of self-insurance of group life and health insurance only.

The second problem is a more serious one, that of measurement of the technique, once identified. Statistics of self-insurers are not compiled in general. In those few places where they are compiled, they are incomparable. (Certain governmental bodies publish limited data, however, as will be noted.) Thus, there is the distressing fact that there are no direct measures of the extent of self-insurance, such as there are for insurance premiums.

Indicative Measures

Despite the lack of direct measures of the extent of self-insurance in general, there are some measures of the extent of self-insurance of particular risks. Self-insurance of workmen's compensation, disability income benefits required by law and pension programs give a good indication of the significance of self-insurance of group health (although not perhaps group life) benefits. For one reason, firms that self-insure often do so as a basic policy, rightly or wrongly, and this policy often extends to all of the so-called "insurable" risks. Firms practicing self-insurance on one particular risk become accustomed to finding internal financial and administrative solutions to risk and risk-related problems. Even if there is no policy established within the firm, extension of the practice to other risks quite often occurs naturally. Also, there is believed to be some complementarity in self-insuring more than one risk in a firm. For example, some of the administrative mechanisms required for the self-insurance of disability income benefits required by law are adaptable to the self-insurance of group health programs (or thought to be), as are those required for the self-insurance of workmen's compensation. Thus, what appears as the trend and extent, or both, of self-insurance of one risk can be presumed to be indicative of other closely related risks such as employee benefit programs.

Self-insurance of Workmen's Compensation. Self-insured workmen's compensation benefits have declined steadily from 18.8 per cent to 11.7 per cent of the total benefits paid in the United States over the 1939–59 period, but a slight upturn was noted in the practice in 1960 by the Department of Health, Education and Welfare.[2] At present, approximately 12.0 per cent of workmen's compensation benefits are paid by self-insurers.[3]

Self-insurance of Disability Income Benefits Required by Law and Voluntary Benefits against Income Loss. A second indication of the extent of self-insurance in the employee benefit field is suggested from self-insurance of disability income benefits in California,[4] New York, New Jersey and Rhode Island. Data indicate that self-insurers pay about $78.2 million in equivalent insurance premiums, or about 42 per cent as much as insurers. This relatively high percentage, however, is not an indication of employer preference for self-insurance as much as it is an indication that there is some employer preference for self-insurance rather than insuring through a state agency. Insurers are practically excluded from the market in California and Rhode Island. More significant in Table 40–1 are the data which suggest that voluntary (nonstatutory) agreements covering

---

[2] A. M. Skolnik, "New Benchmarks in Workmen's Compensation," *Social Security Bulletin,* Vol. XXV, No. 6 (June, 1962), p. 7.

[3] These data are the only estimates of the extent of self-insurance in workmen's compensation. The estimating technique is presented by M. M. Libman, in "Workmen's Compensation Benefits in the U.S.—1939–40," *Social Security Bulletin,* Vol. V, No. 1 (January, 1942), pp. 6–14.

[4] A California ruling effective in 1963 has practically excluded commercial insurers in this field and, apparently, has motivated a large number of formerly insured firms to self-insure or go to the state fund. Insurers covered approximately 1.4 million employees in California in 1958; by the end of 1963, they covered only 43,000 employees. During the same period of time, however, self-insurer coverage of employees increased markedly, from 83,200 to 265,000. Letter to the author, Department of Employment, State of California, October 21, 1964.

income loss are handled predominantly through insurance, rather than
self-insurance.

Pension and Welfare Benefits. A third indication of the extent of self-
insurance is derived from data of the U.S. Department of Labor. Data
filed in compliance with the Welfare and Pension Plans Disclosure Act as
of October, 1962, indicate that premiums and benefits of "self-insured and
unfunded" welfare benefit plans were 20.9 and 21.2 per cent of premiums
and benefits of "insured" welfare benefits plans, respectively, in 1960. (See

TABLE 40–1

RELATIONSHIP BETWEEN SELF-INSURANCE AND GROUP INSURANCE,
PREMIUMS AND BENEFIT PAYMENTS FOR DISABILITY INCOME
1948–62

Year	Voluntary*			Required†		
	(a) Group Insurance	(b) Self-insurance	(c) (b)/(a)	(a) Group Insurance	(b) Self-insurance	(c) (b)/(a)
	Premiums					
1948............	$162.2	$33.6	20.7%	$ 12.7	$ 0.4	0.3%
1955............	386.2	21.1	5.5	128.3	50.5	39.4
1960............	532.2	23.7	4.5	170.7	71.7	42.0
1961............	534.2	23.7	4.4	181.9	77.3	42.5
1962............	579.2	23.8	4.1	186.1	78.2	42.0
	Benefits					
1948............	$115.0	$21.5	18.7%	$ 9.0	$ 0.3	0.3%
1955............	292.0	15.2	5.2	97.0	38.2	39.4
1960............	430.9	18.2	4.2	138.1	58.0	42.0
1961............	414.7	17.5	4.2	141.3	60.1	42.5
1962............	454.9	17.8	3.9	146.1	61.4	42.0

* Basically all premiums and benefits provided through the employment relationship, other than those
required by law.

† California, Rhode Island, New York and New Jersey require employers to furnish certain nonoccupational disability insurance to employees. Employers can satisfy this obligation by insuring through a state
agency, through their own group insurances or by self-insuring. In California and Rhode Island, however,
insurers are practically excluded from the market, leaving the employer with the choices of self-insurance
and state insurance.

Source: *Social Security Bulletin*, Vol. XXVII, No. 1 (January, 1964), p. 7.

Table 40–2.) These premiums and benefits represent the great bulk of
trusteed employee welfare benefit plans[5] in the United States.

From these three measures, it can be seen that self-insurance is fairly
significant as a risk treatment technique, but it by no means represents a

---

[5] The term employee "welfare benefit plan" used by the U.S. Department of Labor
appears to cover somewhat more than group life and health insurances, so data defined
under this term as being self-insured include an element which is not usually insured,
unemployment. See definitions in Table 40–2.

TABLE 40-2

PREMIUMS AND BENEFITS OF WELFARE PLANS, 1959-60: RELATION-
SHIP BETWEEN INSURED AND SELF-INSURED PLANS
(Data Filed in Compliance with the Welfare and Pension Plans Dis-
closure Act as of October 2, 1962)

		(b)	
	(a)	(000,000)	(c)
	(000,000)	Self-insured and	
Year	Insured	Unfunded†	(b)/(a)
		Premiums‡	
1959...............	$3,648.8	$800.6	21.9%
1960...............	4,097.7	854.5	20.9
		Benefits	
1959...............	$2,891.5	$671.8	23.5%
1960...............	3,434.7	728.7	21.2

* A welfare benefit plan is defined as "a plan that provides for its participants or their beneficiaries, medical, surgical or hospital care or benefits, or benefits in the event of sickness, accident, disability, death or unemployment."

† Data are compiled on the basis of self-insured and unfunded, the distinction being trustee or separately maintained funds versus benefits paid from general assets or funds.

‡ In the case of self-insurance, this refers to contributions by employees and employers.

Source: Data are taken from Welfare and Pension Plans Statistics, 1960, Office of Welfare and Pension Plans, U.S. Department of Labor, February, 1963. To generalize, practically all administrators of employee benefit plans having more than 100 employees must file data with the Secretary of Labor.

large proportion of premiums or benefits paid. To that extent, one can assume from the closeness of these risks to employee benefit plans that self-insurance is also significant as a risk treatment technique for group health benefits, and perhaps to a lesser extent, group life benefits.

MOTIVATIONS AND DETERRENTS

The ultimate motivation to self-insure must be the financial benefit which is presumed will occur when the technique is undertaken, relative to other means of financing employee benefit programs. This must be the ultimate motivation, regardless of the explicit argument which is offered to justify self-insurance actions, because no other motivation is economically rational. Lest it be thought that there are only motivations to self-insure employee benefit programs, certain deterrents to self-insure them should be explicitly noted. These deterrents are difficult to measure, as are the motivations.

For the most part, individual risk circumstance determines the magnitude of these motivations and deterrents, although there is some indeterminancy. For example, it is very difficult to superimpose self-insurance conditions on an insured risk for comparative purposes, unless one assumes all risk conditions are static. This may not be the case. For such reasons, the discussion of the motivations and deterrents which follows is in terms of general principles and concepts, rather than in terms of specific identification and contrast of the details of insured and self-insured employee benefit plans.

The Concept of Opportunity Costs

As indicated, the most obvious motivation to self-insure is the assumption that the firm enjoys some gain financially. Specifically, the firm must consider the opportunities provided by alternative uses of funds as so advantageous that the "cost" of the insurance mechanism is too great to ignore. Use of funds to pay insurance premiums means foregoing using them for other purposes, such as reinvestment within the firm. For some firms, the investment return is sufficiently great to offset the advantages of insuring. The economic concept which is involved here is one of opportunity costs.

An example may make the importance of this concept clearer. Many firms in the United States earn, say, 20 per cent before taxes on capital. If such firms are able to retain any funds which might be expended on insurance, then they take advantage of this return. The extent of the advantage is the extent that employee benefit costs are not prepaid under self-insurance but are prepaid through insurance. (For example, reserves normally held by the insurer need not be prepaid by the self-insurer.) Even if benefit costs under self-insurance are greater than under insurance, it is possible that they might be offset in some firms through earnings on funds retained.

From a financial point of view, the self-insurance mechanism allows the firm to budget employee costs over periods of time which are shorter than those required by the insurer (and which are inherent in the rate making process of the insurer). For firms in financial difficulty, the motivation to self-insure and the opportunity costs of self-insuring may be so great that only through use of the self-insurance technique can the firm stay in business.

There are, however, offsets to the opportunity cost concept and, hence, factors which reduce this motivation to self-insure. Obviously, the entire amount which is not expended on premiums is not available for reinvestment in the firm. The extent of the advantage is limited to the difference between what would have been paid as premiums, had the program been insured, and actual self-insured claims paid at any one point in time. Provisions in insurance mechanisms which allow premium payments to be staggered or delayed over the policy period effectively lessen the working capital commitment of the insured firm over the insured period. Similarly, interest earnings allowances on reserves held by the insurer on behalf of the insured firm effectively reduce opportunity costs as well. (Seldom, however, do such allowances equal the internal earnings on capital of the insured firm.) Finally, the opportunity costs concept becomes greatly offset through various insurance programs, such as minimum premium plans,[6] which may provide for the firm to pay its own employee benefit costs. Under such plans, the insurer's obligation is limited, practically, to rendering claims services and providing insurance (in the indemnity sense) only for major fluctuations in costs. Such programs, which go under a variety of names, are becoming more and more popular.

The opportunity costs concept is the basis of the most obvious motivation to self-insure, financial gain to the firm. In fact, all other arguments for or against self-insurance resolve into the question of opportunity. The more specific sources from which these financial gains are said to emanate are investment control, loss control and administrative expense control.

The Investment Control over Funds

Related to the opportunity costs motivation is the control over funds which the self-insurance technique provides. That is, through self-insurance, the firm has control, wholly or in part, over the investment of self-insurance funds. The advantage is allegedly one of investment return greater than that which is enjoyed by the insurer. The insurer, of course, is somewhat restricted legally as to types of investments it can make. In addition, the insurer is basically conservative in its investment philosophy.[7]

The importance of investment control as a motivation to self-insure is often overstated for employee benefit plans, however. The insurer's investment philosophy has been developed to weather a variety of market conditions, as well as risk conditions; it does not depend on market vogues, nor does it need to contend with, for example, liquidity problems which the self-insurer may face. In other words, there is a good reason for the nature of the insurer's investment philosophy, despite the fact that it may yield an over-all rate of return which is less than the self-insured firm believes it could earn. Even more to the point, the magnitude of this motivation is not very large because the amount of funds which can be invested even semi-permanently is relatively small in group life and health insurance. Group life benefits, which are seldom self-insured, are usually term-type insurances which do not involve the accumulation of reserves. Moreover, the flow of funds is not large, relative to, say, pensions or

---

[6] Minimum premium plans are discussed in Chapter 41.

[7] In some types of pension plans the insurer may be able to establish segregated asset-investment accounts on behalf of insured funds, thereby providing some investment flexibility. Nevertheless, its investment portfolio objectives still may not coincide with those envisioned by the self-insurer.

individual life insurance. Frequency of claims is low. On the other hand, health benefits, while involving generally a greater flow of funds, also involve a high frequency of claims. In neither case is there a particularly large residual which is available for long-term investment. In other words, group life and health benefits involve a high "turnover" of funds which does not usually justify the time and administrative expense of separate investment management. To the extent that such investment is linked with a self-insured pension plan, however, some advantage may be obtained.

Except for this latter qualification, the investment control over funds under self-insurance of employee benefits is relatively limited. Those who champion the control of investment concept in this field are, for all practical purposes, addressing their remarks to the over-all control of funds in the firm. This latter type of control concept, of course, harks back to the opportunity costs concept and hinges for its advantage on what the firm is earning internally.

But clearly, the self-insured program—to the extent there is investment involved—does allow investment flexibility to a greater degree than insured programs. This tends to be true even in the case where the self-insured program is trusteed with a significant amount of investment discretion left with the trustee.

Loss Control

One of the most controversial of the motivations to self-insure concerns the control over benefit costs under insurance versus self-insurance. It is alleged that the firm self-insuring an employee benefit plan can exercise control over the conditions under which benefits are paid to employees, as well as the amounts that actually are paid, to a greater degree than can the insurer. The positions of the self-insurer and the insurer are almost irreconcilable on this point. The self-insured firm maintains that a variety of circumstances result in greater control over benefit costs: (1) it is familiar with employee conditions; (2) it has a natural interest in maintaining amicable employee relations; (3) it is able to maintain direct contact with employees and is able to scrutinize continually the various claimants and be alert to moral hazard propensities; and (4) it is the ultimate bearer of the cost of employee benefits.

The self-insurer, implicitly, considers the insurer's control over losses as the sum of the insured's control plus the insurer's, but maintains the presence of insurance always pushes loss costs up. This is because other than bona fide claims are attracted to the third party nature of insurance. Additionally, some claims are paid by the insurer which would not be paid by the administrators of a self-insured program because their knowledge of claims conditions is more intimate. In many cases, what the self-insurer really is saying is that the basic risk which would be insured in an employee benefit plan differs from that actually being self-insured. The self-insurer, for example, may pursue a benefit payment philosophy which may not be as consistent as one pursued by the insurer. Thus, the risk—or more specifically, the terms and conditions under which the insurer prices its service—has been altered.

The insurer, on the other hand, has some equally convincing arguments. The insurer may acknowledge the importance of the self-insurer's intimate knowledge of claims conditions, but would argue that such knowledge of claims conditions is not necessarily indicative of ability to settle claims. The insurer would point out (1) that the ability of the self-insured firm to deal directly with employees may result in harassment of employees or in union interference which the insurer, as a third party to the benefit program, might easily fend off; (2) that the advantage of flexibility in benefit payment philosophy may be dangerous insofar as it establishes precedent or leads to charges of employee favoritism in particular cases; and (3) that regardless of the fact that the self-insurer may be the ultimate bearer of employee benefit costs, the insurer has equal incentive to reduce costs, since the difference between actual and expected benefit cost represents a profit or an amount which can be returned to the insured firm. The insurer also maintains (4) that its long experience in claims matters gives it an advantage over the self-insurer and (5) with but few exceptions, the geographic breadth of its loss control is more extensive than the self-insurer's and is, thus, more adapted to widespread business activities and their attendant administrative problems.

What the insurer is alleging, then, is that it is a specialist in matters of loss control, that under self-insurance, unintended benefits are often paid with or without management's knowledge, that management does not realize the accumulative costs of making minor exceptions to the prescribed benefits of the program and, finally, that it has the breadth and depth of experience necessary to control these costs effectively. The difficulty in reconciling the allegations of the insurer and the self-insurer should be apparent.

Another motivation to self-insure which impinges on the concept of loss control and opportunity costs arises from the practice of insurance companies to accumulate reserves for incurred and unreported claims from the insured's premiums. These reserves are used to "run off" claims of the firm in the event it switches to another insurer or to self-insurance. The insurer then uses the reserves to pay claims incurred prior to the termination date of the insured program but not reported until after the termination date. After the insurer uses the reserve to pay out claims, it normally returns the unused portion to the firm, less an allowance for certain expenses. Occasionally, firms switching to self-insurance (or another insurance company) choose to recover the entire reserve *and thereby incur the liability of the insurer for claim payment.* In this situation, of course, there is the risk to the newly self-insured firm that the recaptured reserves are insufficient to run off the outstanding liabilities.[8]

The magnitude of this motivation or deterrent to self-insure is no easier to evaluate than the others. Obviously, the degree to which any advantage results will depend upon the presence of a differential between actual and expected claims, the degree with which the firm prizes the liquidity which is provided by release of the reserve, its ability to analyze the value of the reserve relative to the risk and, finally, its administrative ability to practice self-insurance. If part of the reserve, once recovered, is not paid out in claims, the firm has capitalized on whatever investment opportunities were possible with the reserve funds. All that has occurred, of course, is an "unfunding" of a future liability which, as far as the self-insurer is concerned, need not have been funded.

No generalizations can be made about the magnitude of incurred but unreported reserves. The amount of the reserves varies by company as well as according to the provisions of the employee benefits plan. Reserves which amount to 25 per cent of annual employee benefits costs are not unusual, however.

Although incurred and unreported claims reserves can amount to 25 per cent of annual benefit costs in an insured benefits program, switching to self-insurance or even to another insurer, while nominally releasing this amount, results in something less. The insured firm, for example, makes liberal use of thirty-day grace periods extended by insurers. Further, the insurer charges claims to reserves on the basis of drafts-presented rather than drafts-issued. In both cases, the advantage of float is lost to the newly self-insured firm, which reduces the opportunity costs value of these reserves. Finally, the advantage of funding these reserves on an after-tax basis may be lost to the firm, depending on the terms of the self-insurance plan. (See Chapter 41.) Some group insurers maintain that the combination of these and other factors reduces the effective reserves held by the insurer to one fourth or less of the nominal reserve held.

Administrative Expense

Another form of motivation to self-insure arises when the expenses of the insurer are considered to be greater than those which would be incurred under self-insurance. Of course, determining when this is the case is difficult. Typically, the firm considering self-insurance is likely to determine what the expense of self-administration would be. Most firms,

---

[8] The risk involved is not considered very important by many firms. This is because any such inadequacy is reflected only in a gradual rise in employee benefit costs which, even if insured, would still have to be paid through increased premium rates. Thus the idea of insufficiency relates more to a time period than it does on any loss to the firm switching to self-insurance or another insurance company. It is possible, nevertheless, particularly in smaller plans, for the newly self-insured firm to be left "holding the bag" in connection with some claims which the insurer would have been required to absorb.

having done so, agree that some of the expenses which become part of the rate charged by the insurer are not incurred or are incurred only in part by the self-insurer. Likewise, the self-insurer usually incurs some expenses which are not incurred or are incurred only in part by the insurer. This section will examine these expenses.

Premium Taxes and Acquisition Expenses. Two of the expenses charged by the insurer provoke little controversy in the self-insurance versus insurance question. The state premium tax which the insurer must pay, which ranges from virtually no charge to a charge as high as 4.0 per cent, is not paid by the self-insurer. To the extent that the state premium tax is a substitute for a state income tax, which seems to be the case in most states,[9] then the self-insurer avoids the premium tax only in a partial sense. The self-insuring firm, of course, must pay state income tax.[10] The equality of the two types of taxes seems to be the only controversy.

Acquisition expense, another major expense charged by the insurer in its rate, also is avoided by the self-insurer. Self-insurance involves no insurance acquisition expense, unless catastrophe insurance of some type is purchased to protect the self-insurer from wide fluctuations in losses.

Loss Adjustment Expense. The major controversy in the eyes of many over the expense of insured versus self-insured plans relates to three other expenses charged by the insurer through the insurance rate. The first of these is loss adjustment expense.

The insurer identifies certain expenses as being connected with the payment of benefits and so charges in the rate. The insurer's retention, in fact, usually is expressed in such a way to reflect the amount and incidence of loss adjustment expense, which in nontechnical terms is the administrative cost of getting the benefit to the employee. For the self-insurer, this administrative cost should include the salaries and wages of those charged with administering the claims function in the employee benefit program, such as executives, legal counsel, benefit counsellors and clerks, as well as indirect costs, such as heat, light and power. These types of expenses will be incurred by the self-insurer just as they are incurred by the insurer. The charges should reflect the degree to which costs are incurred for the benefit program.

The self-insurer typically alleges that these types of expenses are not of

---

[9] The diversity in premium tax structures in the various states is very wide. For the interested reader, data are compiled in J. Cowee, F. Morrissey and R. Goshay, *Taxation of the Life Insurance Industry in California* (Oakland, Calif.: Association of California Life Insurance Companies, 1964).

[10] Whether the self-insurer will continue to avoid the premium tax directly is of some current question. There is strong feeling that self-insurers, since they perform many of the same functions performed by insurers, should be subjected to insurance-type regulation, including taxation. The National Association of Insurance Commissioners has drafted model legislation to bring self-insurers under insurance regulation, particularly in the employee benefits area.

major importance to it, since benefit programs encompass a host of other activities among which health benefits, for example, are merely one part. Thus, the self-insurer believes the administrative cost of paying benefits is marginal in nature to the firm. In other words, the self-insurer believes only the *increased* cost of administering the health program, for example, is of comparative importance.

While this viewpoint of the self-insurer is solid from a theoretical standpoint,[11] the implication is that the insurer is charging the insured not for the *increased* cost of the claims function which arises from a particular benefit program but an *average* cost of all of its claims administration costs. If the difference between the two is considerable, and the self-insurer believes the former is the most pertinent to the decision to self-insure, then the decision to self-insure often follows, since the former is usually viewed as less than the latter for any additional program. The insurer, however, may not be charging on an average cost basis (see below). In any event, one can make no generalizations with respect to savings through self-insurance in this area. It is clear, however, that (1) self-insurers must establish, basically, the same types of mechanisms for the administration of the claims function and thereby incur costs as do insurers, and that (2) both insurers and self-insurers are capable of attaining economies in operations. Certain qualitative factors, such as whether or not there is better or worse control over benefit costs, complicate the analysis, but careful accounting under insurance or self-insurance conditions can produce indications of relative advantage.

General Expense. The general expense factor charged by the insurer through the premium is for the insurer's general overhead costs, as the term suggests. Broadly, all administrative expenses other than those mentioned previously fall into this category; the expenses associated with establishing, administering (other than claims administration) and terminating a particular benefit program fall into this category. Thus, the category includes actuarial expenses (identifying and pricing the risk), legal expenses (which can vary from plan to plan, but are basically for creating and maintaining the legal relationships among the employer, employees and insurer), and general corporate overhead of the insurer (which includes basically all of the expenses of the insurer, other than loss adjustment).

In general, the self-insurer can assume, as does the insurer, that the expenses of the employee benefit program will pervade throughout the firm. The insurer assumes through the rate making structure that certain expenses are best spread across a large number of insureds, for example, investment expense, policy printing costs or advertising to maintain the

---

[11] That is, marginal costs are the pertinent factor in decisions of this sort, up to the point where the firm no longer has any idle resources employed.

corporate image of the insurer. Likewise, the self-insurer should assume, for example, that its program will increase the responsibilities of the financial manager in the firm (by adding to his cash-flow maintenance responsibilities), increase the costs of the printing department (employee brochures, etc.), and so on. Thus it is logical to conclude, as before, that the self-insurance program is an activity which involves, basically, (1) the establishment and maintenance of general administrative facilities and thereby involves costs, and (2) the possibility for both parties to attain economies.

For the larger insured employee benefit plans, the principle of graded expenses is used in determining what the general expense factor is to be, although competition plays such an important role in determining the insurer's actual retention that it is difficult to make any generalizations here as well. Two factors should be explicitly noted, however. First, the insurer is conscious of the average versus marginal nature of costs. The former is generally what the insurer wishes to charge, while the latter is generally what the insured firm thinks it should pay. Moreover, the insured firm generally believes the latter is the only basis on which it will incur costs for comparative purposes, if it self-insures. The insurer, of course, makes every attempt to apportion such expenses as equitably as possible, and its rate making structure permits it to do so. Second, many of the general expenses of the insurer may not appear in the specific rate charge to one insured in the proportion which that insured may have enjoyed the services of the insurer over some particular period. Thus, there is an averaging of expense factors implicit in the insurance rate, in much the same fashion as there is an averaging of loss experience among a number of insureds.

Profit and Contingency. Finally, the profit and contingency factor is an "expense" which the insurer charges in its retention. This factor is for the accumulation of nonreturnable reserves as well as for profit. Insured employee benefit plans, however, appear as though they are charged little, if any, for this factor. Insurers maintain that profits are minimal with self-insurance competition, and they seem to have data to prove it. Firms considering self-insurance, however, often use only the formula of premiums expended less benefits paid to employees as the criterion for the self-insurance decision, considering, implicitly, that any residual is unwarranted. Of all the expenses which may appear in the self-insurer's guidepost, this would appear to be the least significant as a motivation to self-insure.

The contingency factor, however, is basic to the concept of insurance and should be basic to the understanding of the insured firm of what it is purchasing. If the firm is convinced it does not need any indemnification in connection with benefit program costs, then its self-insurance decision is based largely on the evaluation of the cost of the claims administration service. The firm recognizing the need for indemnification, in most cases, has little reason for questioning the presence of the contingency factor. Seldom, for that matter, has it a need to question the amount in present market conditions.

SIGNIFICANCE OF SELF-INSURANCE

This summary of motivations and deterrents indicates that the self-insurance technique has many imponderables connected with it. It would appear, however, that despite this aspect the technique has economic potential to those primarily affected with employee benefit costs. And while the extent of self-insurance in the benefits field is not clear, it would appear that the technique has significance to many parties, and for differing reasons.

The Employer-Firm

To the employer-firm, the self-insurance technique represents on one hand a means of attempting to reduce costs of employee benefits. On the other hand, it carries with it certain social and administrative responsibilities. The technique clearly imposes quasi-fiduciary obligations on the employer. To the extent the technique is practiced or believed to be practiced, self-insurance represents a constant reminder to the insured firm that others have chosen a means of allocating financial resources which differs markedly from its own. Likewise, the technique's actual or perceived extent would indicate that extensive economic analysis of the costs of employee benefits has been made and, perhaps, that rational conduct proceeded from this analysis.

The State Governments

To state governments, the self-insurance technique also has significance. Fiscally, the technique represents an erosion of one tax base, insurance premiums, with no offset, since self-insurance "premiums" are not taxed. Thus, to the extent such programs might have been insured, the state does not receive tax revenues. On the other hand, the technique represents a potential object of regulation and taxation. This is because it is not presently regulated or taxed, because it involves a sensitive area (security of benefits, claims administration and employee relations) and because its counterpart, the *insured* program, is taxed.

The Employee

Not to be forgotten is the employee's stake in self-insurance. To the employee, the self-insurance technique can represent a change in the security of benefits or an increase or decrease in the costs of the benefit program, or both. The technique may provide an opportunity for some control over the nature and direction of the claims and other administration of the program which might not be obtained through an insured program. As a result of this control or of any savings through self-insurance, or both, advantages may accrue to employees.

The Insurer

The significance of self-insurance to the insurer is far-reaching. The technique has had great competitive impact. It has forced insurers to give greater attention to loss control, expense control, reserves control and virtually all other control points in the insurance mechanism. It has forced insurers to examine critically the pricing mechanisms in insurance coverages. Self-insurance also has placed insurers in the perplexing position of trying to demonstrate that employee benefit plan costs are *insurance* expenditures, rather than merely another expenditure by firms which can be financed by alternative means. The position is perplexing because experience rating practices in employee benefit plans, especially as they apply to large employers, have had the obvious tendency to minimize the value of the risk-bearing and cost-stabilization functions of insurance to these same large employers.

Self-insurance will continue to have far-reaching influence to all concerned with the costs of employee benefits. The cost issues, the claims administration issues, the legal status issues and the employee relations issues, coupled with the dubious statistics which purport to evaluate them, will continue to plague those in the decision-making arena.

SELECTED REFERENCES

FOUNDATION OF EMPLOYEE HEALTH, MEDICAL CARE AND WELFARE. *The Advantages and Disadvantages of Self-insurance in Health and Welfare Plans.* New York, 1958.

GOSHAY, ROBERT C. *Corporate Self-insurance and Risk Retention Plans.* Homewood, Ill.: Richard D. Irwin, Inc., 1964.

NATIONAL INDUSTRIAL CONFERENCE BOARD, INC. *Company Medical and Health Programs.* Studies in Personnel Policy Number 146. New York, 1959.

———. *Computing the Cost of Fringe Benefits.* Studies in Personnel Policy Number 128. New York, 1952.

SEGAL, M. E. *The Employee Welfare Benefit Programs—Insured or Self-insured.* American Management Association Insurance Series Number 27. New York, 1959.

Chapter 41

METHODS OF SELF-INSURING GROUP COVERAGES

BY JAMES C. HIGGINS

As has been indicated in the preceding chapter, the decision to self-insure is one that is not easily made. The discussion of self-insurance in this chapter deals primarily with the various methods of self-insuring.[1] No attempt is made to endorse self-insurance or any of the methods enumerated but simply to outline some of the more popular techniques.

While there has been increasing interest in various forms of self-insurance, relatively few companies actually have changed from an insured to a self-insured basis as yet. The interest in partial or complete self-insurance stems from many sources, as was explained in Chapter 40. Among the factors that have led to this interest are the growing profit squeeze, resulting in critical analyses by employers of any and all business costs; the development of so-called "minimum premium" plans; the introduction of "no claim reserve" plans; the growing use of captive insurance companies; the claims of major cost savings by purveyors of services required by self-insured plans; the advantageous tax treatment which may be available to self-insurers; and the successful operation of noninsured trusteed pension plans.

The principal motivation leading to self-insurance of group benefits is to save money. It is hoped that this can be accomplished primarily by reduction or elimination of premium taxes, claim reserves, commissions and various insurance company overhead charges. The self-insurance methods described herein are designed generally to meet these objectives.

Complete self-insurance is relatively rare in the group insurance field. In a totally self-insured plan the employer would assume all the risks of

---

[1] It would, perhaps, be more precise to refer to such plans as "partial insurance" methods, since these plans usually involve the purchase of some outside insurance, as will be explained later in this chapter. Nevertheless, these plans commonly are referred to as self-insurance arrangements.

the various coverages provided and would undertake to provide, either directly or by subcontract, all of the necessary actuarial, legal, claims and general administrative facilities. Practically all corporations which have studied the question have concluded that it is not within the realm of economic prudence to assume the entire burden of risk.[2] However, the decision may be to self-insure some of the coverages and partially insure others.

The factors that usually are present when such a decision is reached are as follows: (1) large numbers of employees to provide the necessary spread of risk; (2) high claim frequency and low claim severity, as, for example, in group short-term disability income coverages or in basic hospital-surgical-medical plans; (3) concentration of employees in a few locations, preferably in smaller communities; (4) effective claim paying and claim control mechanism; (5) competent over-all administration; (6) union agreement and compatibility; and (7) stop-loss insurance where required.

While the significance of most of the factors listed above is largely self-evident, further comment may be helpful with respect to the second, fourth and fifth items. Group life and accidental death and dismemberment coverages present the most striking examples of coverages which do not lend themselves to self-insurance because of the very substantial liability involved as compared with the relatively modest premium. The premium is low because the incidence of life and accidental death and dismemberment claims is infrequent.

Effective claim paying and claim control procedures are found most frequently in companies where the "draft book" method of settling group claims has been used. Under this method of claim payment, the insurer furnishes the employer with a book of checks on the insurance company with which the employer can pay directly claims covered by the insured plan of benefits. The alternative to this system is to have the insurance company pay all claims either from the local claims office or from its home office. An employer utilizing the draft book method has had an opportunity to gain experience in the preparation and payment of claims that would not be the case if all claims were handled by the insurance company.

Large employers frequently do most of the premium accounting, issue employee certificates and perform other routine administrative functions under an insured plan and receive a so-called "self accounting" allowance from the insurance company, which is relieved of providing these services.

---

[2] Examples of the type of company currently self-insuring parts of its group insurance program include some of the major companies in the rubber industry. Even these very sizable corporations insure some of the coverages (notably, life insurance) comprising their group insurance programs.

This background of administrative experience is helpful in facilitating a change to self-insurance.

It should be remembered that, from the employees' standpoint, there are degrees of self-insurance in most well-designed group insurance programs. For instance, a comprehensive medical plan brings deductibles into play. Moreover, percentage participation provisions make the employee a self-insurer in a sense, in that the insurance plan rarely pays the entire amount of hospital charges and surgeon's fees, but involves a payment on the part of the insured employee as well as on the part of the insurance company.

Similarly, the employer frequently assumes a claims burden under his group insurance plan. For example, under a group short-term disability income insurance plan, the employer may pay the first week of salary continuation, and under a long-term plan the employer may continue the disabled employee's salary during the first three months or six months of disability. With this prologue, the discussion turns to some of the methods that may be considered by an employer who feels that self-insurance may reduce his employee benefit costs.

COMPLETELY SELF-INSURED BENEFITS

It will be assumed that the "ABC" Manufacturing Company has approval from its legal counsel to self-insure certain of its employee benefits, and its Industrial Relations Department has the necessary clearance from the unions involved. For all practical purposes, it is now ready to proceed. The determination has been to self-insure the group hospital-surgical-medical coverage and short-term disability income benefits and to continue the group life insurance program and major medical plan on an insured basis.

Training of Personnel for Claims Handling

A further assumption, and an important one, is that "ABC" Manufacturing has utilized the draft book system of claim payment under its insured plan. This implies experience in the handling of claims, although at the smaller locations, where the number of claims is small, additional training of the responsible individual may be necessary. At the larger locations it is assumed those individuals previously responsible for the draft book are sufficiently trained to continue payment of claims on a self-insured basis. In all instances, however, it will be necessary that one individual be responsible for making decisions on questionable claims and on all claims exceeding a certain amount. "ABC" Manufacturing Company must remember that reliance on an insurance company has been severed, and that it is solely responsible for the continuity of claim payments on an effective and efficient basis.

Development and Communication of Plan Provisions

Initially, "ABC" Manufacturing Company duplicated its previous insurer's booklet, certificate and policy language, which was psychologically beneficial to the employees. Claim forms also were duplicated, as were identification cards. The hospital and physicians most frequently utilized by the employees were contacted and advised of the change to a self-insured basis. The claim forms (including the assignment section) were discussed and approved by these medical care providers.

The necessary contractual language for future changes or for new coverages is easily obtained, since booklets and certificates of insurance companies are readily available. However, "ABC" Manufacturing Company must exercise caution in negotiating new benefits (such as convalescent nursing home care) where appropriate contractual language might not be readily available to meet the exact situation.

To summarize at this point, legal clearance has been obtained and the union has consented to the change from an insured to a self-insured basis. Claim facilities and procedures have been established, and the employees have been notified, as well as the hospital administrators and physicians. The company is now prepared to process its first claim—not a routine claim but a problem one.

Settlement of Claims

A vacationing employee had an operation performed in a city hundreds of miles from any of "ABC" Manufacturing Company's locations. Since it was an emergency, the hospital admitted the employee with a small deposit, and the physician was assured by the employee's wife that insurance was in force. The surgeon's bill appears to be excessive. It is at this point that a new area must be explored by the plan administrator; namely, he must establish a set of criteria for determining excess charges by physicians. Fortunately, the company has a medical director on its staff, so the administrator is able to discuss the situation with him. A formula must be devised for defining the necessary and reasonable charges as a guide not only for the claim adjustor at each plant, but for the administrator and the medical director as well. Through phone calls and correspondence it must be determined if the surgeon's charge is reasonable. This determination will be based on the surgical procedure, the employee's salary, the surgeon's normal charge, his reputation in the community and the average charge for the procedure in the area. Finally, based on the administrator's decision, payment is made to the satisfaction of all concerned.

The next claim may involve duplicate claim coverage, and another problem must be resolved. Duplicate coverage results from "ABC" Manufacturing Company covering its employees and their dependents under the company's hospital-surgical-medical plan. A dependent wife also may have family medical coverage at the company where she works. Thus, when either the employee or his wife has medical bills they may be eligible for double reimbursement. For example, if a dependent wife is hospitalized and undergoes a surgical operation, total expenses of $500 may be involved. She would be eligible for reimbursement of $400 from her company plan and $450 from the "ABC" Manufacturing Company plan as a dependent. Thus, she would be eligible for a total payment of $850 for a $500 expense.

The insurance industry has developed a model provision, called the "coordination of benefits" provision, whereby such duplication or profit is eliminated. This provision permits the insurance company to consider the payments from other group insurance plans before determining its payment to an insured employee or his dependent. In this connection, a serious question would arise in the administration of a self-insured plan for "ABC" Manufacturing Company as to whether it would be able to utilize the coordination of benefits provision. In any event, a substantial administrative problem would arise in determining benefits payable from other plans to avoid unnecessary duplication of benefits.

Within a short period of time other questions may arise regarding, e.g., the recognition of a hospital, dental surgery charges, prolonged absences under the disability income benefits plan and many other similar problems. These will result in a review of the manpower requirements to ascertain whether the addition of a claim investigator or assistance from the legal department is necessary.

To afford standardization in the processing of claims, the company may wish to change from decentralized to centralized claim handling. It must recognize, however, that by so doing it may incur certain disadvantages, such as loss of ease of administration, inability to continue to pay claims within a twenty-four-hour period and, perhaps more important, loss of processing previously familiar to the employee.

Of course, some of these same problems may exist under a fully insured plan also. The difference between an insured plan and a self-insured arrangement lies in the way in which they are resolved. In an insured plan they are brought to the attention of the employee benefit plan administrator by the insurance company, or the administrator brings them to the attention of the insurer. In either case, the solution emerges from the manpower pool of the insurance company—legal, underwriting, medical and claim—facilities and manpower which now must be supplied by the self-insurer.

In addition to the processing, investigating and payment of claims, the self-insurer must determine what statistics should be accumulated and interpreted. The annual financial experience must be filed under federal disclosure legislation. Some determination must be made of the company's liability for incurred but unreported claims or those claims reported but not paid due to lack of information. Existing accounting procedures in the company will dictate whether or not such liability is to be recognized formally.

The self-insurer will recognize his need of a consultant, either on a job-by-job basis or full-time. It is likely that a full-time consultant will be needed, since the employer can pass on many of his problems to the consultant for advice and information as to the practices of other employers, industry trends and objective evaluation of the basic plan costs.

As mentioned earlier in this chapter, the decision to self-insure is one that is not easily made and for which the principal motivation is to save money. The administrator of "ABC" Manufacturing Company's plan might rest a little easier if he secured stop-loss insurance. While the possibility of a catastrophe is not great under a plan providing basic hospital-surgical-medical benefits for nonoccupational accident or sickness, the fact that the employees are concentrated in a small geographic area creates at least some catastrophe potential.

Administration of the Plan

"ABC" Manufacturing Company's competitor, "XYZ" Corporation, also decided to self-insure and, like "ABC," obtained clearance from its legal department, labor union and others. The main difference between the two has been the claim payment method. Whereas "ABC" utilized the draft book system, "XYZ" Corporation used its insurer's claim offices for payment of claims.

"XYZ" Corporation decided that the clerical force previously used for routine claims handling work, such as checking claim forms to be certain all items were completed, would not be competent to pay claims under a self-insured program. It considered hiring and training new personnel to handle this function but decided that it would be more efficient to retain a third party, and, therefore, sought the services of a professional administrator.

After discussions and meetings with representatives of the leading professional administrators, one was chosen based on its experience in the employee benefit field, personnel locations and, of course, the cost. "XYZ" Corporation's studies indicated that the costs would not be substantially greater than its costs if it were to pay claims, and it felt that better claim control and more efficient handling would result.

The professional administrator's contract provided for supplying the following services: (1) processing and payment of all claims; (2) providing periodic analyses of claims paid; (3) providing assistance in designing a claim control program; and (4) providing professional advice and recommendations on all problems arising from claims. At first glance, it appears that "XYZ" Corporation has met most of its manpower needs by the employment of the professional administrator. It is important to realize, however, that the administrator's facilities for claims investigation, statistical analysis and modern industry liaison often are far more limited than those of an insurance company. The performance of the professional administrator will be successful only if the facilities which he has available match the needs of the employer.

MINIMUM PREMIUM PLANS[3]

In a desire to keep insurance company retention costs at the lowest possible level, it is quite natural for policyholders to concern themselves with the several distinct components that comprise an insurance company's retention. The principal components are premium taxes, commissions, administrative expenses (including claim expenses) and contingency reserves, which often include the profit margin.

In the case of a large company, which is in the best position to consider seriously the adoption of self-insured programs, the largest single component is the premium tax item, which can represent as much as 50 per cent of the total retention. Generally, state premium taxes are paid to the respective states in which the insured risks are located. Such taxes vary by state. The premium tax charge in a given retention usually amounts to approximately 2 per cent of net cost. Net cost, in turn, can be defined as claims plus retention (or premium less dividends or retroactive rate credits).

Since premium taxes represent such a large proportion of total retention in the case of large employers, a plan has been devised whereby the employer undertakes the payment of claims up to a specified percentage of the premium developed by the insurance company. This method results in a "minimum premium" being paid to the insurance company, with a considerable reduction in the usual retention charges for premium taxes.

In substance, the employer self-insures claims up to, e.g., 90 per cent of the total premium formerly paid to the insurance company, or to some specified dollar level. If claims exceed the specified proportion or figure, the employer continues claim payments, but reimbursement is obtained for the excess from the insurance company. Thus, an employer who chooses to assume full responsibility for the payment of claims up to 90 per cent of the premium (as determined by the insurance company) is not required to pay state premium taxes on the most substantial part of the program cost.

---

[3] This type of plan has on occasion been referred to as the "Illinois Plan" as well as the "Met-Cat Plan." This was prompted by the fact that the approach was initiated by some employers in the state of Illinois. One of the first plans devised involved Metropolitan Life Insurance Company and Caterpillar Tractor Company, thus "Met-Cat."

The insurance company continues to maintain claim reserves under this type of program, a combined self-insurance and insurance approach. The insurance company assumes full liability for claims that survive the term of the group insurance contract. In all other respects, the functions normally performed by the insurance company remain unchanged. The insurance company continues to assist in claims administration, field investigation, settling contested claims, physician and hospital liaison and other such services.

Conversion to a minimum premium plan generally is more feasible in those instances where the policyholder currently is utilizing the draft book method of paying claims. The change involves merely a substitution of employer checks for insurance company checks. As in the case of any self-insured program, it cannot be overemphasized that caution must be exercised in the payment of claims by the employer, as any claim payment error or undue liberality would defeat the purpose of entering into self-insurance at the outset.

As mentioned in the preceding chapter, there still is considerable question as to the approvability by most state insurance departments of the minimum premium plans. State governments are concerned with the loss of revenues and also the possible inadequacy of protection of the insured employee.

An example of what could happen if minimum premium plans and other forms of self-insurance become widespread occurred in Missouri in April, 1964. The Superintendent of Insurance brought suit against two large employers, one of whom has a minimum premium plan and the other a self-insured program. The suit, which was still pending in mid-1965, sought to enjoin both employers from engaging in the insurance business without a license.[4]

METHODS OF MEETING PAYMENTS UNDER SELF-INSURED PLANS

Pay-as-You-Go

The financial officers of the self-insuring company have several available methods for meeting the payments necessitated by self-insurance. One technique is simply to pay claims as they arise. Liability is thus recognized

---

[4] The Superintendent of Insurance of Missouri has brought two court actions to recover money penalties and to enjoin the two companies from carrying out such self-insured plans. The petition invokes Section 375:310 of Revised Statutes, Missouri, 1949, which in part provides, "Any association of individuals and any corporation transacting in this State any insurance business, without being authorized by the Superintendent of the Insurance Division of this State . . . shall be liable to a penalty. . . ." *The State of Missouri ex rel. Superintendent of Insurance* v. *Monsanto Chemical Corporation,* No. 259774, Circuit Court, St. Louis, Missouri, filed 4/23/64. *The State of Missouri ex rel. Superintendent of Insurance* v. *Joseph Schlitz Brewing Company,* No. 659765, Circuit Court of Jackson County, at Kansas City, Missouri.

only on payment of the claim. This pay-as-you-go approach does not fall within the scope of funding of self-insured benefits, since funding involves the accumulation of resources to pay for possible liabilities arising in the future. Some refer to this pay-as-you-go approach as noninsurance, rather than true self-insurance. Nevertheless, it is the most commonly used method of financing these plans. For example, many corporations have a formal salary continuation plan—in most cases an insured plan. The usual plan includes a waiting period, before benefits are payable, of from one day to six months. If the corporation continues any salary during such waiting period, it is, in effect, self-insuring these payments. Furthermore, it is the usual practice to meet such payments on a pay-as-you-go basis. There generally is no need for more complicated methods, since such self-insurance plans provide benefits which are rather easily predictable within narrow limits. As mentioned earlier, the benefits which are most commonly self-insured are short-term disability income benefits and basic hospital-surgical-medical benefits. In some cases death benefits of up to $5,000 per employee also are self-insured. Employers seldom self-insure large death benefits, major medical benefits or long-term disability income benefits.

Establishment of Trust under Internal Revenue Code Section 501(c)(9)

The typical self-insurer has substantial liabilities accruing each year under its group hospital-surgical-medical benefits program. In addition, the short-term disability income benefits program could develop unusually high claims in a short period of time because of disease, epidemics or economic recessions.[5] For these reasons, the employer's financial manager may urge the establishment of adequate reserves.

If the loss ratio under a plan has proven extremely unstable or could be in the future, a substantial reserve (more than one year's anticipated claims), in addition to day-to-day claim payment requirements, should be considered. The extent of the needed reserve depends, of course, on a great many factors, including the plan of benefits, annual claims, and age, number and location of employees.

The financial manager may decide that funding of the plan's benefits can best be achieved by a trust qualified under Section 501(c)(9) of the Internal Revenue Code. Such a trust is exempt from federal income taxation, since no private shareholder or individual benefits from net earnings of the trust other than through claim payment. Moreover, contributions by the employer are deductible for federal income tax purposes in the year in which they are made. The trust qualifies only if income from investments (inclusive of realized capital gains) does not exceed 15 per

---

[5] The moral hazard present in group disability income plans has been noted elsewhere in this volume. See Chapter 21.

cent of the total income from investments, employer contributions and employee contributions.

Establishment of Trust under Internal Revenue Code Section 401(a)

It may be impractical to fund self-insured benefits under a 501(c)(9) trust if the plan requires liabilities to accrue for medical benefits to retired employees. Proper reserves for post-retirement medical benefits most likely would result in investment income to such an extent that the trust would lose its tax-exempt status. Such benefits might better be funded under a pension trust, qualified under Section 401(a) of the Internal Revenue Code. Contributions to such a trust are deductible for federal income tax purposes, and the earnings which accumulate are free of current federal income taxation.

While the qualified pension trust arrangement avoids the restriction on interest earnings relative to contributions present in the 501(c)(9) trust, provision of medical benefits for retired employees must be subordinate to the primary purposes of the plan, viz., to provide pension benefits. The following definition is used to determine whether this requirement is met.

The medical benefits described in section 401(h) are considered subordinate to the retirement benefits if at all times the aggregate of contributions (made after the date on which the plan first includes such medical benefits) to provide such medical benefits and any life insurance protection does not exceed 25 per cent of the aggregate contributions (made after such date) other than contributions to fund past service credits.[6]

Disability income benefits for those forced to retire because of disability also may be funded under this qualified pension arrangement.

While the establishment of a trust might seem to be a complication to the average corporate employee benefit administrator who is considering self-insurance, it might in the long run be the simplest method. The trust is a separate legal entity. Therefore, under a contributory plan there is no opportunity of combining employee funds with those of the employer.

Establishment of Bookkeeping Reserve

In many self-insurance plans, formal funding through a trust arrangement may be unnecessary. Large reserves may not be required, and more flexibility may be desired. Moreover, a trust requires additional fees and legal work. The employer might, therefore, decide to fund his liability under a self-insured plan through a simple bookkeeping reserve. The employer would not enjoy a tax deduction solely by reason of setting aside funds in a special account or establishing a paper account through a book entry, but tax deductions may be taken at the time of claim payment.[7]

---

[6] Internal Revenue Regulation Section 1.401–14(c)(1)(i).

[7] A few corporations have established captive insurance companies in order to obtain supposed advantages in self-insurance, yet retain the tax deductibility of premiums (which normally is accorded only insurance company premiums).

Therefore, the company may establish a reserve equal to only about one half of the amount of its estimated liability, in recognition of the net, after-tax cost (assuming a 50 per cent tax bracket) of providing the benefits. It is recommended that at least one year's estimated benefit payments should be used as the basis for deciding on the proper size of the reserve. Favorable tax treatment on earnings can be achieved if bookkeeping reserves are invested in capital stock of other corporations.[8]

Stop-Loss Coverage

A great many conditions will affect the answer regarding a corporation's method of meeting its liability under a self-insured plan. Each company must weigh its own benefit plan and its own financial structure before deciding on (1) a pay-as-you-go option with no reserves, (2) a 501(c)(9) trust, (3) a qualified pension trust, or (4) a bookkeeping reserve. Regardless of the answer, the employer and his financial officers would be well advised to consider one more aspect of the problem of meeting the company's liability under a self-insured plan. As mentioned earlier, the self-insurer should consider stop-loss insurance.

In essence, this type of insurance is included in insured plans also. A risk charge is included in the retention of an insurance company. This is a small charge by the insurance company to all its group policyholders so that the catastrophic loss of one may be shared by all. Although catastrophes rarely occur with respect to group hospital-surgical-medical or short-term disability income coverage, every self-insurer should, nevertheless, be cognizant of the fact that it lacks the wide risk sharing that is present in most group insurers.

SELECTED REFERENCES

CLEVELAND, H. VAN B. "Self-insured Employee Benefit Plans," *Journal of Insurance*, Vol. XXVII, No. 2 (June, 1960).

GOSHAY, ROBERT C. *Corporate Self-insurance and Risk Retention Plans.* Homewood, Ill.: Richard D. Irwin, Inc., 1964.

JACKSON, PAUL H. "Self-insurance and Group Insurance," *Journal of the American Society of Chartered Life Underwriters*, Vol. XVI, No. 4 (Fall, 1962).

---

[8] Such treatment has to do with a special deduction for dividends received by a corporation. Internal Revenue Code, Secs. 244, 247.

Appendixes

Appendix 1

NATIONAL ASSOCIATION OF INSURANCE COMMISSIONERS
MODEL BILL:
GROUP LIFE INSURANCE DEFINITION
AND
GROUP LIFE INSURANCE STANDARD PROVISIONS
AS OF DECEMBER, 1956

GROUP LIFE INSURANCE DEFINITION

I. No policy of group life insurance shall be delivered in this state unless it conforms to one of the following descriptions:

(1) A policy issued to an employer, or to the trustees of a fund established by an employer, which employer or trustees shall be deemed the policyholder, to insure employees of the employer for the benefit of persons other than the employer, subject to the following requirements:

(a) The employees eligible for insurance under the policy shall be all of the employees of the employer, or all of any class or classes thereof determined by conditions pertaining to their employment. The policy may provide that the term "employees" shall include the employees of one or more subsidiary corporations, and the employees, individual proprietors, and partners of one or more affiliated corporations, proprietors or partnerships if the business of the employer and of such affiliated corporations, proprietors or partnerships is under common control through stock ownership or contract. The policy may provide that the term "employees" shall include the individual proprietor or partners if the employer is an individual proprietor or a partnership. The policy may provide that the term "employees" shall include retired employees. No director of a corporate employer shall be eligible for insurance under the policy unless such person is otherwise eligible as a bona fide employee of the corporation by performing services other than the usual duties of a director. No individual proprietor or partner shall be eligible for insurance under the policy unless he is actively engaged in and devotes a substantial part of his time to the conduct of the business of the proprietor or partnership.

(b) The premium for the policy shall be paid by the policyholder, either wholly from the employer's funds or funds contributed by him, or partly from such funds and partly from funds contributed by the insured employees. No policy may be issued on which the entire premium is to be derived from funds contributed by the insured employees. A policy on which part of the premium is to be derived from funds contributed by the insured employees may be placed in force only if at least 75% of the then eligible employees, excluding any as to whom evidence of individual insurability is not satisfactory to the insurer, elect to make the required contributions. A policy on which no part of the premium is to be derived from funds contributed by the insured employees must insure all eligible employees, or all except any as to whom evidence of individual insurability is not satisfactory to the insurer.

(c) The policy must cover at least 10 employees at date of issue.

(d) The amounts of insurance under the policy must be based upon some plan precluding individual selection either by the employees or by the employer or trustees.

(2) A policy issued to a creditor, who shall be deemed the policyholder, to insure debtors of the creditor, subject to the following requirements:

(a) The debtors eligible for insurance under the policy shall be all of the debtors of the creditor whose indebtedness is repayable either (i) in installments or (ii) in one sum at the end of a period not in excess of eighteen months from the initial date of debt, or all of any class or classes thereof determined by conditions pertaining to the indebtedness or to the purchase giving rise to the indebtedness. The policy may provide that the term "debtors" shall include the debtors of one or more subsidiary corporations; and the debtors of one or more affiliated corporations, proprietors or partnerships if the business of the policyholder and of such affiliated corporations, proprietors or partnerships is under common control through stock ownership, contract or otherwise. No debtor shall be eligible unless the indebtedness constitutes an irrevocable obligation to repay which is binding upon him during his lifetime, at and from the date the insurance becomes effective upon his life.

(b) The premium for the policy shall be paid by the policyholder, either from the creditor's funds, or from charges collected from the insured debtors, or from both. A policy on which part or all of the premium is to be derived from the collection from the insured debtors of identifiable charges not required of uninsured debtors shall not include, in the class or classes of debtors eligible for insurance, debtors under obligations outstanding at its date of issue without evidence of individual insurability unless at least 75% of the then eligible debtors elect to pay the required charges. A policy on which no part of the premium is to be derived from the collection of such identifiable charges must insure all eligible debtors, or all except any as to whom evidence of individual insurability is not satisfactory to the insurer.

(c) The policy may be issued only if the group of eligible debtors is then receiving new entrants at the rate of at least 100 persons yearly, or may reasonably be expected to receive at least 100 new entrants during the first policy year, and only if the policy reserves to the insurer the right to require evidence of individual insurability if less than 75% of the new entrants become insured. The policy may exclude from the classes eligible for insurance classes of debtors determined by age.

(d) The amount of insurance on the life of any debtor shall at no time exceed the amount owed by him which is repayable in installments to the creditor, or $10,000, whichever is less. Where the indebtedness is repayable in one sum to the creditor, the insurance on the life of any debtor shall in no instance be in effect for a period in excess of eighteen months except that such insurance may be continued for an additional period not exceeding six months in the case of default, extension or recasting of the loan. The amount of the insurance on the life of any debtor shall at no time exceed the amount of the unpaid indebtedness, or $10,000, whichever is less.

(e) The insurance shall be payable to the policyholder. Such payment shall reduce or extinguish the unpaid indebtedness of the debtor to the extent of such payment.

(3) A policy issued to a labor union, which shall be deemed the policyholder, to insure members of such union for the benefit of persons other than the union or any of its officials, representatives or agents, subject to the following requirements:

(a) The members eligible for insurance under the policy shall be all of the members of the union, or all of any class or classes thereof determined by conditions pertaining to their employment, or to membership in the union, or both.

(b) The premium for the policy shall be paid by the policyholder, either wholly from the union's funds, or partly from such funds and partly from funds contributed by the insured members specifically for their insurance. No policy may be issued on which the entire premium is to be derived from funds contributed by the insured members specifically for their insurance. A policy on which part of the premium is to be derived from funds contributed by the insured members specifically for their insurance may be placed in force only if at least 75% of the then eligible members, excluding any as to whom evidence of individual insurability is not satisfactory to the insurer, elect to make the required contributions. A policy on which no part of the premium is to be derived from funds contributed by the insured members specifically for their insurance must insure all eligible members, or all except any as to whom evidence of individual insurability is not satisfactory to the insurer.

(c) The policy must cover at least 25 members at date of issue.

(d) The amounts of insurance under the policy must be based upon some plan precluding individual selection either by the members or by the union.

(4) A policy issued to the trustees of a fund established by two or more employers in the same industry or by one or more labor unions, or by one or more employers and one or more labor unions, which trustees shall be deemed the policyholder, to insure employees of the employers or members of the unions for the benefit of persons other than the employers or the unions, subject to the following requirements:

(a) The persons eligible for insurance shall be all of the employees of the employers or all of the members of the unions, or all of any class or classes thereof determined by conditions pertaining to their employment, or to membership in the unions, or to both. The policy may provide that the term "employees" shall include retired employees, and the individual proprietor or partners if an employer is an individual proprietor or a partnership. No director of a corporate employer shall be eligible for insurance under the policy unless such person is otherwise eligible as a bona fide employee of the corporation by performing services other than the usual duties of a director. No individual proprietor or partner shall be eligible for insurance under the policy unless he is actively engaged in and devotes a substantial part of his time to the conduct of the business of the proprietor or partnership. The policy may provide that the term "employees" shall include the trustees or their employees, or both, if their duties are principally connected with such trusteeship.

(b) The premium for the policy shall be paid by the trustees wholly from funds contributed by the employer or employers of the insured persons, or by the union or unions, or by both. No policy may be issued on which any part of the premium is to be derived from funds contributed by the insured persons specifically for their insurance. The policy must insure all eligible persons, or all except any as to whom evidence of individual insurability is not satisfactory to the insurer.

(c) The policy must cover at date of issue at least 100 persons and not less than an average of five persons per employer unit; and if the fund is established by the members of an association of employers the policy may be issued only if (i) either (a) the participating employers constitute at date of issue at least 60% of those employer members whose employees are not already covered for group life insurance or (b) the total number of persons covered at date of issue exceeds 600; and (ii) the policy shall not require that, if a participating employer discontinues membership in the association, the insurance of his employees shall cease solely by reason of such discontinuance.

(d) The amounts of insurance under the policy must be based upon some plan precluding individual selection either by the insured persons or by the policyholder, employers, or unions.

II. No such policy of group life insurance may be issued to an employer, or labor union or to the trustees of a fund established in whole or in part by an employer or a labor union, which provides term insurance on any person which, together with any other term insurance under any group life insurance policy or policies issued to the employer or employers of such person or to a labor union or labor unions of which such person is a member or to the trustees of a fund or funds established in whole or in part by such employer or employers or such labor union or labor unions, exceeds $20,000, unless 150% of the annual compensation of such person from his employer or employers exceeds $20,000, in which event all such term insurance shall not exceed $40,000 or 150% of such annual compensation, whichever is the lesser.

GROUP LIFE INSURANCE STANDARD PROVISIONS

No policy of group life insurance shall be delivered in this state unless it contains in substance the following provisions, or provisions which in the opinion of the Commissioner are more favorable to the persons insured, or at least as favorable to the persons insured and more favorable to the policyholder, provided, however, (a) that provisions (6) to (10) inclusive shall not apply to policies issued to a creditor to insure debtors of such creditor; (b) that the standard provisions required for individual life insurance policies shall not apply to group life insurance policies; and (c) that if the group life insurance policy is on a plan of insurance other than the term plan, it shall contain a non-forfeiture provision or provisions which in the opinion of the Commissioner is or are equitable to the insured persons and to the policyholder, but nothing herein shall be construed to require that group life insurance policies contain the same nonforfeiture provisions as are required for individual life insurance policies:

(1) A provision that the policyholder is entitled to a grace period of thirty-one days for the payment of any premium due except the first, during which grace period the death benefit coverage shall continue in force, unless the policyholder shall have given the insurer written notice of discontinuance in advance of the date of discontinuance and in accordance with the terms of the policy. The policy may provide that the policyholder shall be liable

to the insurer for the payment of a pro rata premium for the time the policy was in force during such grace period.

(2) A provision that the validity of the policy shall not be contested, except for nonpayment of premiums, after it has been in force for two years from its date of issue; and that no statement made by any person insured under the policy relating to his insurability shall be used in contesting the validity of the insurance with respect to which such statement was made after such insurance has been in force prior to the contest for a period of two years during such person's lifetime nor unless it is contained in a written instrument signed by him.

(3) A provision that a copy of the application, if any, of the policyholder shall be attached to the policy when issued, that all statements made by the policyholder or by the persons insured shall be deemed representations and not warranties, and that no statement made by any person insured shall be used in any contest unless a copy of the instrument containing the statement is or has been furnished to such person or to his beneficiary.

(4) A provision setting forth the conditions, if any, under which the insurer reserves the right to require a person eligible for insurance to furnish evidence of individual insurability satisfactory to the insurer as a condition to part or all of his coverage.

(5) A provision specifying an equitable adjustment of premiums or of benefits or of both to be made in the event the age of a person insured has been misstated, such provision to contain a clear statement of the method of adjustment to be used.

(6) A provision that any sum becoming due by reason of the death of the person insured shall be payable to the beneficiary designated by the person insured, subject to the provisions of the policy in the event there is no designated beneficiary, as to all or any part of such sum, living at the death of the person insured, and subject to any right reserved by the insurer in the policy and set forth in the certificate to pay at its option a part of such sum not exceeding $500 to any person appearing to the insurer to be equitably entitled thereto by reason of having incurred funeral or other expenses incident to the last illness or death of the person insured.

(7) A provision that the insurer will issue to the policyholder for delivery to each person insured an individual certificate setting forth a statement as to the insurance protection to which he is entitled, to whom the insurance benefits are payable, and the rights and conditions set forth in (8), (9) and (10) following.

(8) A provision that if the insurance, or any portion of it, on a person covered under the policy ceases because of termination of employment or of membership in the class or classes eligible for coverage under the policy, such person shall be entitled to have issued to him by the insurer, without evidence of insurability, an individual policy of life insurance without disability or other supplementary benefits, provided application for the individual policy shall be made, and the first premium paid to the insurer, within thirty-one days after such termination, and provided further that,

(a) The individual policy shall, at the option of such person be on any one of the forms, except term insurance, then customarily issued by the insurer at the age and for the amount applied for;

(b) the individual policy shall be in an amount not in excess of the amount of life insurance which ceases because of such termination, provided that any amount of insurance which shall have matured on or before the date of such termination as an endowment payable to the person insured, whether in one sum or in installments or in the form of an annuity, shall not, for the purposes of this provision, be included in the amount which is considered to cease because of such termination; and

(c) the premium on the individual policy shall be at the insurer's then customary rate applicable to the form and amount of the individual policy, to the class of risk to which such person then belongs, and to his age attained on the effective date of the individual policy.

(9) A provision that if the group policy terminates or is amended so as to terminate the insurance of any class of insured persons, every person insured thereunder at the date of such termination whose insurance terminates and who has been so insured for at least five years prior to such termination date shall be entitled to have issued to him by the insurer an individual policy of life insurance, subject to the same conditions and limitations as are provided by (8) above, except that the group policy may provide that the amount of such individual policy shall not exceed the smaller of (a) the amount of the person's life insurance protection ceasing because of the termination or amendment of the group policy, less the amount of any life insurance for which he is or becomes eligible under any group policy issued or reinstated by the same or another insurer within thirty-one days after such termination, and (b) $2,000.

(10) A provision that if a person insured under the group policy dies during the period within which he would have been entitled to have an individual policy issued to him in accordance with (8) or (9) above and before such an individual policy shall have become effective, the amount of life insurance which he would have been entitled to have issued to him under such individual policy shall be payable as a claim under the group policy, whether or not application for the individual policy or the payment of the first premium therefor has been made.

(11) In the case of a policy issued to a creditor to insure debtors of such creditor, a provision that the insurer will furnish to the policyholder for delivery to each debtor insured under the policy a form which will contain a statement that the life of the debtor is insured under the policy and that any death benefit paid thereunder by reason of his death shall be applied to reduce or extinguish the indebtedness.

NATIONAL ASSOCIATION OF INSURANCE COMMISSIONERS SUPPLEMENTARY BILL RELATING TO CONVERSION PRIVILEGES

If any individual insured under a group life insurance policy hereafter delivered in this state becomes entitled under the terms of such policy to have an individual policy of life insurance issued to him without evidence of insurability, subject to making of application and payment of the first premium within the period specified in such policy, and if such individual is not given notice of the existence of such right at least 15 days prior to the expiration date of such period, then in such event the individual shall have an additional period within which to exercise such right, but nothing herein contained shall be construed to continue any insurance beyond the period provided in such policy. This additional period shall expire 15 days next after the individual is given such notice but in no event shall such additional period extend beyond 60 days next after the expiration date of the period provided in such policy. Written notice presented to the individual or mailed by the policyholder to the last known address of the individual or mailed by the insurer to the last known address of the individual as furnished by the policyholder shall constitute notice for the purpose of this paragraph.

Appendix 2

MODEL GROUP ACCIDENT AND SICKNESS INSURANCE BILL AS RECOMMENDED BY THE HEALTH INSURANCE ASSOCIATION OF AMERICA

SECTION (−) GROUP ACCIDENT AND SICKNESS INSURANCE

(a) Group accident and sickness insurance is hereby declared to be that form of accident and sickness insurance covering groups of persons as defined below, with or without one or more members of their families or one or more of their dependents, or covering one or more members of the families or one or more dependents of such groups of persons, and issued upon the following basis:

(1) Under a policy issued to an employer or trustees of a fund established by an employer, who shall be deemed the policyholder, insuring employees of such employer for the benefit of persons other than the employer. The term "employees" as used herein shall be deemed to include the officers, managers, and employees of the employer, the individual proprietor or partner if the employer is an individual proprietor or partnership, the officers, managers, and employees of subsidiary or affiliated corporations, the individual proprietors, partners and employees of individuals and firms, if the business of the employer and such individual or firm is under common control through stock ownership, contract, or otherwise. The term "employees" as used herein may include retired employees. A policy issued to insure employees of a public body may provide that the term "employees" shall include elected or appointed officials. The policy may provide that the term "employees" shall include the trustees or their employees, or both, if their duties are principally connected with such trusteeship.

(2) Under a policy issued to an association, including a labor union, which shall have a constitution and by-laws and which has been organized and is maintained in good faith for purposes other than that of obtaining insurance, insuring members, employees, or employees of members of the association for the benefit of persons other than the association or its officers or trustees. The term "employees" as used herein may include retired employees.

(3) Under a policy issued to the trustees of a fund established by two or more employers in the same or related industry or by one or more labor unions or by one or more employers and one or more labor unions or by an association as defined in (a) (2) which trustees shall be deemed the policyholder, to insure employees of the employers or members of the unions or of such association, or employees of members of such association for the benefit of persons other than the employers or the unions or such association. The term "employees" as used herein may include the officers, managers and employees of the employer, and the individual proprietor or partners if the employer is an individual proprietor or partnership. The term "employees" as used herein may include retired employees. The policy may provide that the term "employees" shall include the trustees or their employees, or both, if their duties are principally connected with such trusteeship.

(4) Under a policy issued to any person or organization to which a policy of group life insurance may be issued or delivered in this (state) to insure any class or classes of individuals that could be insured under such group life policy.

(5) Under a policy issued to cover any other substantially similar group which, in the discretion of the Commissioner, may be subject to the issuance of a group accident and sickness policy or contract.

(b) Each such policy shall contain in substance the following provisions:

(1) A provision that, in the absence of fraud, all statements made by applicants or the policyholder or by an insured person shall be deemed representations and not warranties, and that no statement made for the purpose of effecting insurance shall avoid such insurance or reduce benefits unless contained in a written instrument signed by the policyholder or the insured person, a copy of which has been furnished to such policyholder or to such person or his beneficiary.

(2) A provision that the insurer will furnish to the policyholder for delivery to each employee or member of the insured group, a statement in summary form of the essential features of the insurance coverage of such employee or member and to whom benefits thereunder are payable. If dependents are included in the coverage, only one statement need be issued for each family unit.

(3) A provision that to the group originally insured may be added from time to time eligible new employees or members or dependents, as the case may be, in accordance with the terms of the policy.

(c) Any group accident and sickness policy may on request by the group policyholder provide that all or any portion of any indemnities provided by any such policy on account of hospital, nursing, medical or surgical services may, at the insurer's option, be paid directly to the hospital or person rendering such services; but the policy may not require that the service be rendered by a particular hospital or person. Payment so made shall discharge the insurer's obligation with respect to the amount of insurance so paid.

Appendix 3

NATIONAL ASSOCIATION OF INSURANCE COMMISSIONERS CODE OF ETHICAL PRACTICES WITH RESPECT TO THE INSURING OF THE BENEFITS OF UNION OR UNION-MANAGEMENT WELFARE AND PENSION FUNDS

PREAMBLE

The business of life insurance, annuities, and sickness and accident insurance is an important factor in the provision of economic security for millions of Americans and their families. It is an example of accomplishment on a voluntary basis. It could not have attained its present degree of public acceptance if ethical standards of conduct had not generally been followed, and if it had not been motivated by a sense of public responsibility.

One of the most effective ways of providing this economic security has long been through group plans providing death, sickness, accident and pension benefits. While these benefits have been traditionally purchased by employers directly from insurers, in recent years an important new method for extending such benefits has been developed. This is the trusteed union-management welfare or pension fund, established by collective bargaining between labor unions and employers. Many of these trust funds provide their benefits through group insurance policies or group annuity contracts issued by insurance companies.

This new method of providing employee and dependent benefits has raised a number of problems. In most instances fund trustees have scrupulously respected their fiduciary responsibilities, and insurance companies, agents and brokers dealing with them have likewise generally conducted themselves in the best traditions of the insurance business in observing in both letter and spirit the laws of the several states. However, such has not been true in every case. With the rapid growth of these union-management trust funds, public interest points to the desirability of expressing, in the form of a Code of Ethical Practices, a statement of accepted good practices in the insuring of the benefits of trusteed union-management welfare and pension funds.

In adopting any such Code, it should be emphasized that only a part of the abuses which have occurred in the field of union-management welfare and pension funds has related to insurance associated with those funds. Accordingly, in adopting this Code the National Association of Insurance Commissioners stresses its belief that parallel action should be taken to correct abuses other than those relating to insurance. Because in general our responsibility relates only to insurance, this Code is confined to that area.

Furthermore, it must be realized that the cases of abuse which have occurred in the insurance area have, with very few exceptions, come about through the activities of persons whose primary business interests are outside the insurance business, and who have wrongfully twisted the traditional insurance mechanisms to their own purposes. The basic purpose of this Code is to prevent a recurrence of these insurance abuses, fortunately infrequent, through means which do not impair the normal operations of the insurance business as developed over many years.

The following Code of Ethical Practices, adopted by the National Association of

Insurance Commissioners, is intended to serve as a declaration of applicable principles in the proper conduct of insuring welfare and pension funds, and will serve to complement such existing state insurance laws as require that insurance benefits be reasonable in relation to the premiums charged, and which prohibit unfair discrimination, rebates, misrepresentation, misleading or deceptive acts, and other unfair trade practices or unfair methods of competition, as being prejudicial to the interests of beneficiaries of insured welfare and pension funds.

Section 1. Payment of Benefits

It is the responsibility of the insurer to pay benefits under its policies promptly, fairly and without discrimination, in accordance with policy terms. Insurers should make periodic audits of benefit payments made on their behalf by fund administrators or others. The results of such audits should be available to the trustees of the fund.

Section 2. Commissions, Fees and Other Allowances

It is recognized that the growth of insurance has been due in large measure to the insurance agency system, and that insurance agents and brokers ought to be fairly compensated for their services. However, excessive commissions, fees and other allowances tend to reduce the level of benefits payable to beneficiaries of welfare and pension funds. Consequently, it is in the best interests of the public and of the beneficiaries of such funds that commissions, fees and other allowances be reasonable and not excessive.

A. *Definitions*

"Commissions" for the purpose of this Code shall include all compensation of whatever nature, and by whatever name, payable by an insurer to an insurance agent or broker, compensated primarily on a commission basis.

"Fees and other allowances" for the purpose of this Code shall include administration fees, service fees, or any other payment of a similar character payable by an insurer to an insurance agent or broker, or to any other person, firm or corporation.

"Insurer" for the purpose of this Code shall include any insurance company, non-profit hospital and/or medical and/or dental indemnity or service corporation, and any other organization licensed by any state to provide insurance benefits.

"Welfare fund" for the purpose of this Code shall mean any program providing life insurance, accidental death or dismemberment, cash disability, hospital, surgical, medical or dental benefits to the members (and/or their dependents) of a collective bargaining unit under a policy or policies issued to the trustees of a union or a union-management welfare fund, or to a union as policyholder as a direct result of a collective bargaining agreement.

"Pension fund" for the purpose of this Code shall mean any corresponding program providing pension benefits to such persons.

B. *Commission Scales*

(1) One of the fundamental characteristics of group insurance policies is the economy of operation inherent in providing insurance and pension benefits to large numbers of persons under a master contract. The decremental commission scale, widely accepted and used in the group business from its inception, recognizes this characteristic of economy because of size by providing for decreases in the rates of commission as the size of the premium increases. Renewal commission rates, which are considerably lower than first-year rates, also decrease with increase in premium volume.

The table following illustrates on the basis of the effective rates for the indicated premium volume a generally accepted range of commission rates, first-year and renewal averaged over a ten-year commission-paying period, to insurance agents and brokers, derived from schedules currently in use on group life and group accident and sickness policies, which are considered to be reasonable and not excessive.

Annual Premium Volume	Average of First-Year and Renewal Commissions Over the Ten Years*	
	Effective Rates for Indicated Premium Volume	
	From	To
$ 20,000	3.2%	4.1%
30,000	3.0	3.7
50,000	2.6	3.2
100,000	1.7	2.3
150,000	1.3	2.0
250,000	.8	1.8
500,000	.5	1.2
1,000,000	.3	.8
2,500,000	.2	.5
5,000,000	.1	.4

* On an annual premium volume of less than $20,000, the range of effective commission rates would be somewhat higher than the largest indicated above and, on an annual premium volume of more than $5,000,000, the range of effective commission rates should be somewhat less than the lowest indicated above.

NOTE: The particular commission scale paid should not be taken as the sole indication of the ultimate net cost of insurance to the buyer, since such cost is affected by many factors, only one of which is the insurer's acquisition expense. Acquisition expense itself includes factors in addition to the commission scales set forth above.

(2) Any commission rate schedule used by an insurer for welfare funds is considered unreasonable and excessive if (a) it provides for the payment of commission in excess of the range shown in the preceding table, or more than would have been paid under the insurer's commission schedule applicable to a similar group policy of like premium volume issued to an employer whichever is less, or if (b) the schedule is not uniformly used as the maximum for all welfare funds. An insurer may provide in such commission schedule that a portion of its total commissions, in accordance with a predetermined scale established for the purpose is to be considered as the basic selling commissions, with the balance available for compensation for other services of the insurance agent or broker, such as assistance in designing, installing or servicing the welfare and pension program. Any commission rate schedule used by an insurer for group annuities issued in connection with pension funds should be appreciably lower than the commission rate schedule used by that insurer for welfare funds.

(3) Where two or more forms of group insurance are issued, concurrently or within six months from the issuance of any one such forms of coverage, by an insurer to a welfare fund, the premiums for all the insurance coverages, whether under one or more policies, should be combined in determining the total commissions payable; and where two or more welfare funds are combined through a master or administrative trust or otherwise, they should be similarly considered as one fund for commission purposes.

(4) Any increase in premium resulting at any time from normal additions to the group of insured persons (e.g., from additions resulting from the insuring of new employees of participating employers, from a reduction in the eligibility requirements of the plan, from the inclusion of employees of a new participating employer in the plan unless under the collective bargaining agree-

ment participation in the plan is optional with the employer, from salary increases, etc.) should be treated for commission purposes as part of the existing premium and not as a separate new premium.

(5) Where an existing policy is extended to insure a new classification of employees (e.g., where the plan is expanded beyond its original scope to include members of an additional union local, or employees of the employer members of an additional trade association, or additional classes of members within locals already participating, or additional classes of employees of employers already participating), or where the existing policy is revised to increase the schedule of insurance on those already insured, or where a new form of insurance is added, commissions payable with respect to the resulting additional premium should be not more than the amount determined by applying the insurer's commission scale to the additional premium as if there had been no previous insurance; provided that if such extension of policy takes place within 6 months after the original effective date of the policy or of another previous extension for which the additional premium was treated separately, under this rule, the additional premium for the current extension should not be treated separately for commission purposes but should be treated as a part of the previous new or additional premium.

(6) In lieu of its normal decremental commission schedule, providing for higher first-year commissions and lower renewal commissions, an insurer may use averaged decremental commission rates, applicable to the first policy year and nine renewal policy years, if such rates are the approximate mathematical equivalent of its normal schedule when applied to a uniform amount of premium over a ten-year period.

(7) Under no circumstances should the scale of commissions be contingent on the claim rate under the group policy.

(8) While in some circumstances the transfer of group insurance from one insurer may be of advantage to a welfare or pension fund, it results in duplicate acquisition costs. Accordingly, in cases of proposed transfer, the new insurer should so advise the prospective policyholder. Commission rates for the first and subsequent policy years should in all cases of transfer be payable only on a basis which averages the rates over the entire commission-paying period, and the total commissions payable over such commission-paying period should not be more than those which would be payable by the new insurer were there no prior insurance.

(9) Commissions should not be paid to any person, firm, or corporation who or which is not actually in the business of selling insurance, or is not a licensed agent or broker at the same time the sale was negotiated. Nor should commissions be paid, directly or indirectly, to any trustee, contributing employer, or labor union, or to an officer or employee of any such trustee, employer or labor union.

C. *Fees and Other Allowances*

(1) An insurer should not make any payment of fees or allowances of whatever nature, and by whatever name, to any person, firm, or corporation in connection with the sale, service or administration of a group policy issued to a welfare or pension fund, other than commissions to an insurance agent or broker as heretofore described, except in reimbursement for the reasonable value of one or more of the following services performed on behalf of the insurer.

(a) Issuing certificates.
(b) Maintaining employee records.
(c) Billing premiums.
(d) Processing claims.

In no event should any payment for such services (a) exceed the amount that would have been credited to the policyholder in the insurer's dividend, experience-rating, or premium-rate formula for the performance of the same services, or (b) be made to any person, firm, or corporation which does not maintain an organization equipped to furnish such services, or which does not in fact furnish such services.

(2) An insurer should not make any payment of fees or allowances of whatever nature, and by whatever name, to a policyholder, whether for doing work sometimes performed by an insurer or otherwise, except as part of a refund or dividend under the operation of the insurer's regular dividend or experience-rating formula.

(3) Where other administrative work involving normal policyholder functions is paid for by the insurer, an identifiable charge in addition to the premium, properly labelled, for the reasonable value of the services performed should be made to the fund for such work. If the insurer engages a third party to perform such work, it should maintain control and responsibility for its proper performance, and the amount of the fee or allowance paid therefor shall be reasonable in relation to the services rendered and should be consistent with the charge made by the insurer to the fund.

D. *Filings*

Whenever there may be particular circumstances under which an insurer believes that payments of commissions, fees or other allowances on a group policy, other than those conforming with the Code, are justifiable and should be paid, it should promptly furnish a complete explanation of the reasons therefor to the insurance supervisory official of the state in which the group insurance policy is delivered, and such explanation also should be available on request to the insurance supervisory official of any state in which certificates under such policy are outstanding. This subsection is not applicable in the case of any state which by law, regulation, or ruling requires filing of all schedules of commissions, fees or other allowances on group policies.

E. *Disclosure to Policyholder*

An insurer should upon request, disclose to a policyholder or prospective policyholder the commissions, fees, or other allowances paid or to be paid.

F. *General Agents and Other Representatives*

The common practice among insurers of paying salaries, providing other benefits, and making payments in the nature of an overriding commission to general agents and full-time home office representatives of the insurer who regularly design, install or service the welfare and pension plan, or who regularly assist insurance agents and brokers in selling, is a recognized and proper method of meeting overhead sales and service expense of the insurer and, therefore, is not intended to be affected by the preceding subsections B and E; provided, however, that any such overriding commissions should be determined on scales not higher than those applicable to group policies issued to employers, and provided further that the payment of any overriding commission is not used as a device for evading the intent of this Code.

Section 3. Relationship between the Trustees and the Insurer

An insurer should undertake to avoid any action which constitutes a condonation of conduct on the part of a trustee or any other person occupying a fiduciary position with respect to a welfare or pension fund which would constitute an evident breach of trust, or an evident failure to discharge faithfully the obligations which his fiduciary position imposes upon him.

Section 4. Improper Inducements

In the acquisition of new business and in efforts to keep such business in force, insurers, insurance agents and brokers, and their representatives should adhere to those practices in their dealings with the persons connected with or exercising responsibility for the affairs of any welfare or pension fund (e.g., trustees, unions, employers or employees, or representatives of any of them) as will avoid undue or improper inducement, and should refrain from offering or making any inducements in the form of gifts, loans, or payments, directly or indirectly, and all lavish entertainment.

Section 5. Cost Presentations

It is in the best interests of the beneficiaries of welfare and pension plans and contributing employers and participating union locals, as well as in the best interests of the insurance business, that incomplete or misleading comparisons and projections of costs should not be made. Undue emphasis on low cost may prejudice the proper consideration of those features which can be more lasting and meaningful, such as the responsibility and stability of the insurer and its ability to provide services affecting the successful operation of the plan. In fact, relative costs tend to vary from year to year. Projections which presume to predict costs over a long period of years may have no real significance, and may instead create misleading impressions as to guarantees.

Since the cost of a proposed plan is affected by dividends or experience-rating credits as well as by the initial gross premium rate, an estimated net-cost presentation is often made. Such presentations should be clearly stated, and unless based upon a rating formula contractually guaranteed by the insurer, should set forth the limitations inherent therein and the assumptions upon which the presentation is based.

Section 6. Equal Treatment of Policyholders

An insurer should not unfairly discriminate between group insurance or group annuity policyholders, in the establishment of premium rates or in the payment or crediting of dividend or experience rating refunds.

Section 7. Benefit Descriptions

Employee booklets or other literature intended to be explanatory of an insured welfare or pension plan should fairly and clearly describe the benefits and principal provisions and limitations of the plan.

Section 8. Accounting

An insurer insuring a welfare or pension fund should at the end of each policy year furnish an accounting statement to the policyholder. Such statement should include at least the following items, shown separately:

1. Premiums received.
2. Benefit payments.

3. Commissions, fees and other allowances paid.
4. Dividends, experience-rating refunds, or contractual returns of premium paid to the plan.
5. Resulting balance.

Insurers should encourage the trustees of each welfare or pension fund also to render a summary report of the operations of the fund, not less frequently than annually, to persons having a bona fide interest in the plan, and should to the fullest extent practicable cooperate with the trustees in the preparation of such a report.

Appendix 4

FEDERAL EMPLOYEES GROUP LIFE INSURANCE ACT OF 1954

5 U.S.C.A. §§ 2091–2103 (Supp. Pamphl. 1961),
as amended, 5 U.S.C.A. § 2093 (Supp. 1963)

§2091. Eligible employees

(a) Except as provided in subsection (b) of this section, each appointive or elective officer or employee (hereinafter called employee) in or under the executive, judicial, or legislative branch of the United States Government, including a Government owned or controlled corporation (including Gallaudet College but not including any corporation under the supervision of the Farm Credit Administration of which corporation any member of the board of directors is elected or appointed by private interests), and of the municipal government of the District of Columbia shall, at such time and under such conditions of eligibility as the Civil Service Commission (hereinafter called the Commission) may by regulation prescribe, come within the purview of this chapter. Such regulations may provide for the exclusion of employees on the basis of the nature and type of employment or conditions pertaining thereto such as, but not limited to, short term appointments, seasonal or intermittent employment, part-time employment, and employment of like nature, and shall be issued only after consultation with the head of the department, establishment, agency, or other employing authority concerned: *Provided,* That no employee or group of employees shall be excluded solely on the basis of the hazardous nature of employment.

(b) This chapter shall not apply to noncitizen employees whose permanent duty station is located outside a State of the United States or the District of Columbia.

(c) No person shall acquire insurance coverage under this chapter by virtue of his status as a member of a uniformed service. The insurance granted to any employee under this chapter (1) shall cease (except for a thirty-one day extension of life insurance coverage) on the day immediately prior to his entry on active duty or active duty for training, unless the period of such duty is covered by military leave with pay from a civilian position, and (2) shall not cease during any period of inactive duty training. The terms used in this subsection shall have the meanings assigned to them by section 1101 of Title 38.

(d) Persons employed by the county committees established pursuant to section 590h(b) of Title 16 shall, under such conditions of eligibility as the Commission by regulation may prescribe, come within the purview of this chapter. The Secretary of Agriculture is authorized and directed to prescribe and issue such regulations as may be necessary to provide a means of effecting the application and operation of the provisions of this subsection with respect to such persons.

§2092. Group insurance—Amount of life and accident insurance available

(a) Each employee to whom this chapter applies shall be eligible to be insured for an amount of group life insurance approximating his annual compensation not exceeding $20,000 plus an equal amount of group accidental death and dismemberment insurance, in accordance with the following schedule:

797

| If annual compensation is— | | The amount of group life insurance shall be— | The amount of group accidental death and dismemberment insurance shall be— |
Greater than	But not greater than		
0	$ 1,000	$ 1,000	$ 1,000
$ 1,000	2,000	2,000	2,000
2,000	3,000	3,000	3,000
3,000	4,000	4,000	4,000
4,000	5,000	5,000	5,000
5,000	6,000	6,000	6,000
6,000	7,000	7,000	7,000
7,000	8,000	8,000	8,000
8,000	9,000	9,000	9,000
9,000	10,000	10,000	10,000
10,000	11,000	11,000	11,000
11,000	12,000	12,000	12,000
12,000	13,000	13,000	13,000
13,000	14,000	14,000	14,000
14,000	15,000	15,000	15,000
15,000	16,000	16,000	16,000
16,000	17,000	17,000	17,000
17,000	18,000	18,000	18,000
18,000	19,000	19,000	19,000
19,000	. . . . . .	20,000	20,000

Schedule of Payments

(b) Subject to the conditions and limitations of the policy or policies purchased by the Commission under this chapter, as may be approved by the Commission, the group accidental death and dismemberment insurance shall provide payments as follows:

Loss	*Amount payable*
For loss of life.	Full amount shown in the schedule in (a) of this section.
Loss of one hand or of one foot or loss of sight of one eye.	One-half the amount shown in the schedule in (a) of this section.
Loss of two or more such members.	Full amount shown in the schedule in (a) of this section.

For any one accident the aggregate amount of group accidental death and dismemberment insurance that may be paid shall not exceed the amount shown in the schedule in subsection (a) of this section.

Conversion to Annual Rates

(c) The Commission shall by regulation provide for the conversion of other than annual rates of compensation to an annual basis, and shall further specify the types of compensation to be included in annual compensation.

§2093. Death claims; order of payment; claimants outside of order of precedence; escheat of amount to fund

Any amount of group life insurance and group accidental death insurance in force on any employee at the date of his death shall be paid, upon the establishment of a valid claim therefor, to the person or persons surviving at the date of his death, in the following order of precedence:

First, to the beneficiary or beneficiaries as the employee may have designated by a writing received in the employing office prior to death;

Second, if there be no such beneficiary, to the widow or widower of such employee;

Third, if none of the above, to the child or children of such employee and descendants of deceased children by representation;

Fourth, if none of the above, to the parents of such employee or the survivor of them;

Fifth, if none of the above, to the duly appointed executor or administrator of the estate of such employee;

Sixth, if none of the above, to other next of kin of such employee entitled under the laws of domicile of such employee at the time of his death.

If any person otherwise entitled to payment under this section does not make claim therefor within one year after the death of the employee, or if payment to such person within that period is prohibited by Federal statute or regulation, payment may be made in the order of precedence as if such person had predeceased the employee, and any such payment shall be a bar to recovery by any other person.

If, within two years after the death of the employee, no claim for payment has been filed by any person entitled under the order of precedence set forth in this section, and neither the Commission nor the Administrative office established by the insurance company or companies pursuant to subsection (b) of section 2096 of this title has received any notice that any such claim will be made, payment may be made to a claimant as may in the judgment of the Commission be equitably entitled thereto, and such payment shall be a bar to recovery by any other person. If, within four years after the death of the employee, payment has not been made pursuant to this section and no claim for payment by any person entitled under this section is pending, the amount payable shall escheat to the credit of the fund created pursuant to subsection (c) of section 2094 of this title.

§2094. Premiums—Withholding from salary; automatic coverage; notice of desire not to be insured

(a) During any period in which an employee is insured under a policy of insurance purchased by the Commission as authorized in section 2096 of this title, there shall be withheld from each salary payment of such employee, as his share of the cost of his group life and accidental death and dismemberment insurance, an amount determined by the Commission, but not to exceed the rate of 25 cents biweekly for each $1,000 of his group life insurance; *Provided*, That an employee who is paid on other than a biweekly basis shall have an amount so withheld, determined at a proportionate rate, which rate shall be adjusted to the nearest cent.

Any policy of insurance purchased by the Commission as authorized in section 2096 of this title shall provide that all employees eligible under the terms of this chapter will be automatically insured thereunder commencing on the date they first become so eligible: *Provided*, That any employee desiring not to be so insured shall, on an appropriate form to be prescribed by the Commission, give written notice to his employing office that he desires not to be insured. If such notice is received before the employee shall have become insured under such policy, he shall not be so insured; if it is received after he shall have become insured, his insurance under the policy will cease effective with the end of the pay period during which the notice is received by the employing office.

Contributions by Government

(b) For each period in which an employee is insured under a policy of insurance purchased by the Commission as authorized in section 2096 of this title, there shall be contributed from the respective appropriation or fund which is used for payment of his salary, wage, or other compensation (or, in the case of an elected official, from such appropriation or fund as may be available for payment of other salaries of the same office or establishment) a sum computed at a rate determined by the Commission, but not to exceed one-half the amount withheld from the employee under this section.

Insurance Fund; Deposits; Availability of Fund for Expenses, Dividends, and Rate Adjustments

(c) The sums withheld from employees under subsection (a) of this section and the sums contributed from appropriations and funds under subsection (b) of this section shall be deposited in the Treasury of the United States to the credit of a fund which is created. Said fund is made available without fiscal year limitation for premium payments under any insurance policy or policies purchased as authorized in sections 2096 and 2099 of this title, for the payment of any obligations under agreements assumed pursuant to section 2099 of this title, and for any expenses incurred by the Commission in the administration of this chapter within such limitations as may be specified annually in appropriation acts except that such fund shall be available, without regard to any such limitations, for payment of any such expenses incurred in assuming and maintaining the assets and liabilities of associations referred to in section 2099 of this title: *Provided,* That appropriations available to the Commission for salaries and expenses for the fiscal year 1955 shall be available on a reimbursable basis for necessary administrative expenses of carrying out the purposes of this chapter until said fund shall be sufficient to provide therefor. The income derived from any dividends or premium rate adjustments received from insurers shall constitute a part of said fund.

Investment of Insurance Fund

(d) The Secretary of the Treasury is authorized to invest and reinvest the moneys in the fund created by subsection (c) of this section, or any part thereof, in interest-bearing obligations of the United States and to sell such obligations of the United States for the purposes of the fund. The interest on and the proceeds from the sale of any such obligations shall become a part of the fund.

§ 2095. Termination of insurance—Policy provisions; temporary extension of coverage; conversion

(a) Each policy purchased under this chapter shall contain a provision, in terms approved by the Commission, to the effect that any insurance thereunder on any employee shall cease upon his separation from the service or twelve months after discontinuance of his salary payments, whichever first occurs, subject to a provision which shall be contained in the policy for temporary extension of coverage and for conversion to an individual policy of life insurance under conditions approved by the Commission.

Continuation of Life Insurance; Service Credit

(b) If upon such date as the insurance would otherwise cease the employee retires on an immediate annuity and (1) his retirement is for disability or (2) he has completed twelve years of creditable service, as determined by the Commission, his life insurance only may, under conditions determined by the Commission, be continued without cost to him, but the amount of such insurance shall be reduced by 2 per centum thereof at the end of each full calendar month following the date the employee attains age sixty-five or retires, whichever is later, s ubject to minimum amounts prescribed by the Commission, but not less than 25 per centum of the insurance in force preceding the first such reduction. Periods of honorable active service in the Army, Navy, Air Force, Marine Corps, or Coast Guard of the United

States shall be credited toward the required twelve years provided the employee has completed at least five years of civilian service.

Continuation of Insurance during Period Employee Is Receiving Benefits under the Federal Employees' Compensation Act

(c) If upon such date as the insurance would otherwise cease the employee is receiving benefits under the Federal Employees' Compensation Act because of disease or injury to himself, his life insurance may, as provided in subsection (b) of this section, be continued during the period he is in receipt of such benefits and held by the United States Department of Labor to be unable to return to duty.

§2096. Policies—Purchase from private companies; requirements

(a) The Commission is authorized, without regard to section 5 of Title 41, to purchase from one or more life insurance companies, as determined by it, a policy or policies of group life and accidental death and dismemberment insurance to provide the benefits specified in this chapter: *Provided,* That any such company must meet the following requirements: (1) Be licensed under the laws of forty-eight of the States of the United States and the District of Columbia to transact life and accidental death and dismemberment insurance, and (2) the amount of its employee group life insurance on the most recent December 31 for which information is available to the Commission shall on that date equal at least 1 per centum of the total amount of employee group life insurance in the United States in all life insurance companies.

Establishment of Administrative Office by Selling Company

(b) The life insurance company or companies issuing such policy or policies shall establish an administrative office under a name to be approved by the Commission.

Reinsurance

(c) The Commission shall arrange with the life insurance company or companies issuing any policy or policies purchased under this chapter to reinsure, under conditions approved by it, portions of the total amount of insurance under the policy or policies, determined as provided in subsection (d) of this section, with such other life insurance companies as may elect to participate in such reinsurance.

Formula for Apportioning Reinsurance; Fraternal Benefit Associations as Reinsurers

(d) The Commission shall determine a formula so that the amount of insurance in force to be retained by each issuing company after ceding reinsurance and the total amount of reinsurance ceded to each reinsuring company shall be in proportion to the total amount of each such company's group life insurance in force in the United States on December 31, 1953: *Provided,* That in determining such proportions, that portion of any company's group life insurance in force on December 31, 1953, which is in excess of $100,000,000 shall be reduced by 25 per centum of the first $100,000,000 of such excess, 50 per centum of the second $100,000,000 of such excess, 75 per centum of the third $100,000,000 of such excess, and 95 per centum of any excess thereafter: *Provided further,* That the amount retained by or ceded to any company shall not exceed 25 per centum of the amount of that company's total life insurance in force in the United States on December 31, 1953: *And provided further,* That any fraternal benefit association which is licensed under the laws of a State of the United States or the District of Columbia to transact life insurance and is engaged in issuing insurance certificates on the lives of employees of the Federal Government exclusively shall be eligible to act as a reinsuring company and may be allocated an amount of reinsurance equal to 25 per centum of its total life insurance in force on employees of the Federal Government on December 31, 1953.

Redetermination of Eligibility of Reinsurers; Reallocation of Reinsurance

(e) The companies eligible to participate as reinsurers, and the amount of insurance under the policy or policies to be allocated to each issuing company or reinsurer, may be redetermined by the Commission for and in advance of any policy year after the first, on a basis consistent with subsections (c) and (d) of this section, with any modifications thereof it deems appropriate to carry out the intent of such subsections, and based on each participating company's group life insurance in force in the United States on the most recent December 31 for which information is available to it, excluding that under any policy or policies purchased under this chapter, and shall be so redetermined in a similar manner not less often than every three years or at any time that any participating company withdraws from participation: *Provided,* That if, upon any such redetermination, in the case of any issuing company or reinsurer which insured employees of the Federal Government on December 31, 1953, under policies issued to an association of Federal employees, the amount which results from the application of the formula referred to in subsection (d) of this section is less than the total decrease, if any, since December 31, 1953, in the amount of such company's insurance under such policies, the amount allocated to such company shall be increased to the amount of such decrease: *Provided further,* That any increase in the amount allocated to such company by application of the preceding proviso shall be reduced by the amount or amounts of any policy or policies purchased from such company under the authorization of section 2094(c) of this title, and in force on the date of such redetermination.

Discontinuance of Policies

(f) The Commission may at any time discontinue any policy or policies it has purchased from any insurance company.

§2097. Basic tables of premium rates—Life insurance; accident insurance; readjustment of rates

(a) Each policy or policies purchased under this chapter shall include, for the first policy year, basic tables of premium rates as follows:

(1) For group life insurance, a schedule of basic premium rates by age which the Commission shall have determined on a basis consistent with the lowest schedule of basic premium rates generally charged for new group life insurance policies issued to large employers, this schedule of basic premium rates by age to be applied, except as otherwise provided in this section, to the distribution by age of the amounts of group life insurance under the policy at its date of issue to determine an average basic premium rate per $1,000 of life insurance, and,

(2) For group accidental death and dismemberment insurance, a basic premium rate which the Commission shall have determined on a basis consistent with the lowest rate generally charged for new group accidental death and dismemberment insurance policies issued to large employers.

Each policy so purchased shall also include provisions whereby the basic rates of premium determined for the first policy year shall be continued for subsequent policy years, except that they may be readjusted for any subsequent year, based on the experience under the policy, such readjustment to be made by the insurance company or companies issuing the policy on a basis determined by the Commission in advance of such year to be consistent with the general practice of life insurance companies under policies of group life and group accidental death and dismemberment insurance issued to large employers.

Tentative Average Premium Rate; Redetermination

(b) Each policy so purchased shall include a provision that, in the event the Commission determines that ascertaining the actual age distribution of the amounts of group life insurance in force at the date of issue of the policy or at the end of the first or any subsequent year of insurance thereunder would not be possible except at a disproportionately high expense, it may approve the determination of a tentative average group life premium rate, for the first or any subsequent policy year, in lieu of using the actual age distribution. Such tentative average premium rate shall be redetermined by the Commission during any policy year upon request by the insurance company or companies issuing the policy, if experience indicates that the assumptions made in determining the tentative average premium rate for that policy year were incorrect.

Maximum Expense and Risk Charges

(c) Each policy so purchased shall contain a provision stipulating the maximum expense and risk charges for the first policy year, which charges shall have been determined by the Commission on a basis consistent with the general level of such charges made by life insurance companies under policies of group life and accidental death and dismemberment insurance issued to large employers. Such maximum charges shall be continued from year to year, except that the Commission may redetermine such maximum charges for any year either by agreement with the insurance company or companies issuing the policy or upon written notice given by it to such companies at least one year in advance of the beginning of the year for which such redetermined maximum charges will be effective.

Annual Accounting; Contents; Creation of Special Contingency Reserve; Deposit of Excess

(d) Each such policy shall provide for an accounting to the Commission not later than ninety days after the end of each policy year, which shall set forth, in a form approved by the Commission, (1) the amounts of premiums actually accrued under the policy from its date of issue to the end of such policy year, (2) the total of all mortality and other claim charges incurred for that period, and (3) the amounts of the insurers' expense and risk charge for that period. Any excess of the total of item (1) over the sum of items (2) and (3) shall be held by the insurance company or companies issuing the policy as a special contingency reserve to be used by such insurance company or companies for charges under such policy only, such reserve to bear interest at a rate to be determined in advance of each policy year by the insurance company or companies issuing the policy, which rate shall be approved by the Commission as being consistent with the rates generally used by such company or companies for similar funds held under other group life insurance policies: *Provided*, That, if and when the Commission determines that such special contingency reserve has attained an amount estimated by it to make satisfactory provision for adverse fluctuations in future charges under the policy, any further such excess shall be deposited in the Treasury of the United States to the credit of the fund. If and when such policy is discontinued, and if after all charges have been made, there is any positive balance remaining in such special contingency reserve, such balance shall be deposited in the Treasury of the United States to the credit of the fund, subject to the right of the insurance company or companies issuing the policy to make such deposit in equal monthly installments over a period of not more than two years.

§2098. Benefit certificates; contents; issuance

The Commission shall arrange to have each employee insured under such policy receive a certificate setting forth the benefits to which the employee is entitled thereunder, to whom such benefits shall be payable, to whom claims should be submitted, and summarizing the provisions of the policy principally affecting the employee. Such certificate shall be in lieu of the certificate which the insurance company or companies would otherwise be required to issue.

§2099. Retired employees insurance agreements—Assumption by fund

(a) The Commission is authorized to arrange with any nonprofit association of Federal or District of Columbia employees for the assumption by the fund created by section 2094(c) of this title of all life insurance agreements, including all benefits contained therein, obtained or provided by such association for its members.

Purchase of Policies to Insure Agreements Assumed

(b) The Commission is authorized, without regard to other sections of this chapter and without regard to section 5 of Title 41, to purchase from one or more life insurance companies, as determined by the Commission, a policy or policies of group life insurance to insure all or any portion of the life insurance agreements obtained or provided by an association for its members and assumed under this section: *Provided*, That any such company must be either (1) the company then insuring such members under a policy or policies issued to such association; or (2) a company which is an insurer or a reinsurer under section 2096 of this title. The Commission may at any time discontinue any policy or policies it has purchased from any insurance company.

Premium for Purchase of Insurance Agreement

(c) Any association accepting such arrangement shall, in consideration therefor, pay over and transfer to the Commission (1) an amount equal to the actuarial value, as determined by the Commission, of the insurance obligations assumed by the fund created by section 2094(c) of this title, or (2) the total assets of the life insurance fund of such association, whichever is the lesser. Such payment and transfer shall be a premium for the purchase of the Government insurance arrangement, shall be deposited in the fund created by section 2094(c) of this title, and shall be accomplished in accordance with the procedures and conditions prescribed by the Commission, and in accordance with the requirements of applicable law.

Restrictions

(d) The arrangements authorized by this section shall be made not later than three months following April 11, 1958. Such arrangements shall apply only to life insurance agreements existing on August 11, 1955, and on the date of the respective arrangement.

Premium Payments for Continuation of Insurance Coverage

(e) Any such arrangement shall provide that the continuation of the insurance coverage of such members shall be conditioned upon their payment to the fund created by section 2094(c) of this title, in such manner and under such conditions as the Commission may prescribe, of premium payments equal to the premiums or dues previously payable by them for such insurance coverages.

Disqualification from Other Benefits

(f) The members of such associations shall not by reason of any such arrangements be disqualified from any other insurance benefits provided by this chapter if otherwise eligible therefor.

§2100. Regulations

Except as otherwise provided herein, the Commission is authorized to promulgate such regulations as may be necessary and proper to give effect to the intent, purposes, and provisions of this chapter.

§2101. Advisory Council on Group Insurance; composition; meetings; duty; employees' committee

(a) There is established an Advisory Council on Group Insurance consisting of the Secretary of the Treasury as Chairman, the Secretary of Labor, and the Director of the Bureau of the Budget, who shall serve without additional compensation. The Council shall meet once a year, or oftener at the call of the Commission, and shall review the operations of this chapter and advise the Commission on matters of policy relating to its activities thereunder.

(b) The Chairman of the Commission shall appoint a committee composed of five employees insured under this chapter, who shall serve without compensation, to advise the Commission regarding matters of concern to employees under this chapter.

§2102. Reports to Congress

The Commission shall report annually to Congress upon the operation of this chapter.

§2103. Jurisdiction of courts

The district courts of the United States shall have original jurisdiction, concurrent with the Court of Claims, of any civil action or claim against the United States founded upon this chapter.

Appendix 5

CONVENTION BLANK (ADOPTED BY THE NATIONAL ASSOCIATION OF INSURANCE COMMISSIONERS)

SCHEDULE H

ACCIDENT AND HEALTH EXHIBIT

	(1)	(2)	(3)	(4)	(5)	(6)
				Individual Policies		
			Accident Only	_Accident and Health_	_Non-Cancellable Accident and Health_	_Hospital and Medical Expense_
*Gross Premiums (Less Return Premiums)	_Total_	_Group Accident and Health_				
1. Direct Premiums Received						
2. Reinsurance Assumed						
3. Reinsurance Ceded						
4. Net Premiums Received						
5. Premiums Due and Unpaid Dec. 31, current year						
6. Premiums Due and Unpaid Dec. 31, previous year						
7. Premiums Written or Renewed during year						
8. Premiums Paid in Adv. Dec. 31, previous year						
9. Premiums Paid in Adv. Dec. 31, current year						
10. Premiums of current year $(7 + 8 - 9)$						
11. Unearned Premiums and Additional Reserves Dec. 31, previous year						
12. Unearned Premiums and Additional Reserves Dec. 31, current year						
13. Premiums Earned during current year						

*Initial premiums written and unpaid ("unplaced premiums") are excluded from these items.

SCHEDULE H—(Continued)
ACCIDENT AND HEALTH EXHIBIT

	(1)	(2)		Individual Policies		
			(3)	(4)	(5)	(6)
Gross Premiums (Less Return Premiums)	Total	Group Accident and Health	Accident Only	Accident and Health	Non-Cancellable Accident and Health	Hospital and Medical Expense

LOSSES

14. Direct Losses Paid
15. Losses on Reinsurance Assumed
16. Recoveries on Reinsurance Ceded
17. Losses Paid
18. Reinsurance Recoverable, Dec. 31, current year
19. Unpaid Losses, Dec. 31, current year
20. Reinsurance Recoverable, Dec. 31 previous year
21. Unpaid Losses, Dec. 31, previous year
22. Losses of current year
23. Reserve for Amounts not yet due on Claims and for future Contingent Benefits, Dec. 31, current year
24. Reserve for Amounts not yet due on Claims and for future Contingent Benefits, Dec. 31, previous year
25. LOSSES INCURRED DURING CURRENT YEAR
25A. *Group Conversions*

EXPENSES INCURRED

26. Allocated Claim Expenses
27. Unallocated Claim Expenses
28. Commissions: a. Direct
            b. Reinsurance Assumed

SCHEDULE H—(Continued)
ACCIDENT AND HEALTH EXHIBIT

| | (1) | (2) | Individual Policies | | | |
| | | | (3) | (4) | (5) | (6) |
	Total	Group Accident and Health	Accident Only	Accident and Health	Non-Cancellable Accident and Health	Hospital and Medical Expense
Gross Premiums (Less Return Premiums)						
c. Reinsurance Ceded						
d. Net Commissions						
29. Acquisition and Field Supervision Expenses (other than Commissions)						
30. General Administration Expenses						
31. Inspection and Bureau Expenses						
32. Taxes, Licenses and Fees (excluding Federal Income, Excess Profits and Real Estate Taxes)						
33. TOTAL EXPENSES INCURRED						
34. GAIN FROM UNDERWRITING (13–25–33)						
35. DIVIDENDS TO POLICYHOLDERS						
EXHIBIT OF PREMIUMS						
36. In Force, Dec. 31, previous year						
37. Premiums Paid in advance, Dec. 31, previous year						
38. Written or Renewed during year						
39. Excess of Original Premiums over Reinsurance Assumed						
40. Expirations and Excess of Original Premiums over Return Premiums on Cancellations						
41. Premiums Paid in Advance, Dec. 31, current year						
42. In Force at end of year						
43. Deduct Reinsurance Premiums in Force						
44. Net Premiums in Force:						
a) on policies running one year or less						

SCHEDULE H—(Continued)

ACCIDENT AND HEALTH EXHIBIT

| | (1) | (2) | Individual Policies | | | |
| | | | (3) | (4) | (5) | (6) |
	Total	Group Accident and Health	Accident Only	Accident and Health	Non-Cancellable Accident and Health	Hospital and Medical Expense
Gross Premiums (Less Return Premiums)						
b) on policies running more than one year						
c) Total						
45. Unearned Premium Reserve:						
a. on policies running one year or less						
b. on policies running more than one year						
c. reserve for rate credits, etc.						
d. Total						
REINSURANCE						
46. Assumed—amount included in line 5						
47. Assumed—amount included in line 9						
48. Ceded—amount deducted from line 5						
49. Ceded—amount deducted from line 9						
50. Ceded—amount deducted from line 12:						
a. Applicable to line 1 of Exhibit 9, Part 1						
b. Applicable to line 2 of Exhibit 9, part 1						
c. Applicable to line 4 of Exhibit 9, Part 1						
51. Ceded—amount deducted from line 23:						
a. Applicable to line 3 of Exhibit 9, Part 1						
b. Applicable to line 4 of Exhibit 9, Part 1						

CONVENTION BLANK—(Continued)

ANALYSIS OF OPERATIONS BY LINES OF BUSINESS

(Gain and Loss Exhibit)

	Ordinary					Group			Accident and Health	
	Total (1)	Life Insurance (2)	Total and Permanent Disability (3)	Additional Accidental Death (4)	Individual Annuities (5)	Supplementary Contracts (6)	Life Insurance (7)	Annuities (8)	Group (9)	Individual (10)
1. Premiums and annuity considerations (Exhibit 1, Part 1)										
2. Considerations for supplementary contracts with life contingencies										
3. Considerations for supplementary contracts without life contingencies and dividend accumulations										
4. Net investment income (Exhibit 2)										
5. *Sundry receipts and adjustments*										
6. *Sale of equipment*										
7. TOTAL										
8. Death benefits										
9. Matured endowments										
10. Annuity benefits										
11. Disability benefits										
12. Surrender benefits										
12A Group conversions *and other transfers*										
12B Transfers on account of group package policies and contracts										
13. Benefits under accident and health policies										
14. Interest on policy or contract funds										
15. Payments on supplementary contracts with life contingencies										

ANALYSIS OF OPERATIONS BY LINES OF BUSINESS—*(Continued)*

(GAIN AND LOSS EXHIBIT)

		Ordinary				Group		Accident and Health	
Total (1)	Life Insurance (2)	Total and Permanent Disability (3)	Additional Accidental Death (4)	Individual Annuities (5)	Supplementary Contracts (6)	Life Insurance (7)	Annuities (8)	Group (9)	Individual (10)

16. Payments on supplementary contracts without life contingencies and of dividend accumulations

17. Increase in aggregate reserve for policies and contracts with life contingencies

18. Increase in reserves for supplementary contracts without life contingencies and for dividend accumulations

19. *Increase in other reserves*

20. SUBTOTAL (Items 8 to 19)

21. Commissions on premiums and annuity considerations

22. ....

23. General insurance expenses (Exhibit 5, Cols. 1 and 2, Line 13)

24. Insurance taxes, licenses and fees, excluding federal income taxes (Exhibit 6, Cols. 1 and 2, Line 10)

25. Increase in loading on and cost of collection in excess of loading on deferred and uncollected premiums

26. ....

27. TOTAL (Items 20 to 26)

28. Net gain from operations before dividends to policyholders and

ANALYSIS OF OPERATIONS BY LINES OF BUSINESS—(Continued)

(Gain and Loss Exhibit)

		Ordinary					Group		Accident and Health	
	Total (1)	Life Insurance (2)	Total and Permanent Disability (3)	Additional Accidental Death (4)	Individual Annuities (5)	Supplementary Contracts (6)	Life Insurance (7)	Annuities (8)	Group (9)	Individual (10)
federal income taxes and excluding capital gains and losses (Item 7 minus Item 27)										
29. Dividends to life policyholders (Exhibit 7)										
30. Dividends on accident and health policies (Exhibit 7)										
31. Increase in amounts provisionally held for deferred dividend policies										
32. TOTAL (Items 29 to 31)										
32A Net gain from operations after dividends to policyholders and before federal income taxes, excluding capital gains and losses (Item 28 minus Item 32)										
32B Federal income taxes incurred (excluding tax on capital gains)										
33. Net gain from operations after dividends to policyholders and federal income taxes (excluding tax on capital gains) and excluding capital gains and losses (Item 32A minus Item 32B)										

Appendix 6

APPLICATION FOR EMPLOYEE INSURANCE

APPLICATION TO ██████████████ INSURANCE COMPANY

FOR EMPLOYEE PROTECTION PLAN INSURANCE

(Please Print — Use Black Ink)

Section A. PERSONAL AND EMPLOYMENT INFORMATION

1. Name of Proposed Insured (Employee)?	2. Date of Birth? Mo. Day Year	3. Place of Birth?	4. Male? ☐ Female? ☐	5. Account Number? G S_____

6. Name of Employer?	7. Exact Job Title?	8. Are you an active full-time employee of the Employer, working at least 30 hours per week? Yes ☐ No ☐

9. Date Full-Time Employment Began? Mo. Day Year	10. Basic Weekly Earnings?	11. If Married, Give Age of Spouse?	12. Number of Eligible Children, if any?

13. Beneficiary (subject to change as provided in policy). Full Name & Relationship to you?	14. Term Insurance Amount? $_____ Accidental Death Benefit? Yes ☐ No ☐

15. IS THE POLICY APPLIED FOR intended to replace, in whole or in part, insurance in force in this or any other Company? ... Yes ☐ No ☐ (If "Yes", give name of Company, plan and policy number, if known)

Section B. UNDERWRITING INFORMATION (ANSWER TO THE BEST OF YOUR KNOWLEDGE AND BELIEF)

16. Have you engaged in any aviation activity (other than as passenger on a commercial aircraft) during the past year? Yes ☐ No ☐ (If "Yes", complete aviation blank, Form 5794, as part of this application.)	17. Height? _____ ft. _____ in. 18. Weight? _____ lbs.	19. a. Are you contemplating any medical attention or surgical treatment? Yes ☐ No ☐ b. If "Yes", for what condition? _____

20. Have you ever had:

	Yes	No		Yes	No		Yes	No
a. heart trouble?	☐	☐	d. tuberculosis?	☐	☐	h. ulcers?	☐	☐
b. high blood pressure?	☐	☐	e. cancer?	☐	☐	i. other illness, disease or injury? State which? _____	☐	☐
c. albumin or sugar in your urine?	☐	☐	f. diabetes?	☐	☐			
			g. nervous disorder?	☐	☐			

21. a. Have you during the past 5 years consulted any physician or been confined or treated in any hospital, sanitorium or similar institution?
b. If "Yes", for what condition? _____   Yes ☐ No ☐

22. If any question in 19, 20 or 21 is answered "Yes" give full details here and date and sign authorization below:

Question Number?	Number of Attacks?	Treatment? and Results?	Duration: (Give Dates)?	Names of Physicians and Hospitals?

IT IS MUTUALLY AGREED THAT: (A) The policy hereby applied for shall not go into force unless (i) the ████████ Insurance Company receives evidence satisfactory to it that the undersigned Proposed Insured is an acceptable risk for said policy, (ii) the first premium therefor is paid in full during the Proposed Insured's lifetime, and (iii) the ████████ Insurance Company is satisfied that all its requirements for the Employee Protection Plan are met. (B) Neither the soliciting agent nor the medical examiner, if any, is authorized to accept risks or to pass upon insurability. (C) So long as the Proposed Insured remains in the employ of the employer named in Item 6 above, the employer is hereby designated as the Proposed Insured's representative for purposes of receiving premium and other notices and of remitting premiums for this policy to the ████████ Insurance Company.

Dated at .... on .... 19 ...

Signature of Proposed Insured (Employee) ....

Countersigned by ....
Licensed Resident Agent where required by statute or regulation
EPP-50A-B 8-64   Printed in U.S.A.

Witnessed by ....

For ████ ████ Use Only	Account Number	Eff. Date	ID Number	Class		Due	Am't	DC Yes ☐ No ☐

AUTHORIZATION TO PHYSICIANS OR PRACTITIONERS, HOSPITALS OR OTHER INSTITUTIONS

You are hereby authorized to furnish the ████████ Insurance Company, in return for this authorization or a copy thereof, with any information that you may have regarding conditions for which I was under observation or treatment by you, prior to the date shown below, including the history, findings and diagnosis.

This is a personal request from me and your cooperation will be appreciated.

Dated _____ 19 _____   Signature of Proposed Insured (Employee) _____

Appendix 7

COMPARATIVE ANALYSIS OF STATE DISABILITY BENEFITS LAWS

	NEW YORK	NEW JERSEY	CALIFORNIA	RHODE ISLAND
Name of Program	Disability Benefits	Temporary Disability Benefits	Unemployment Compensation Disability Benefits	Temporary Disability Insurance
Type of Law	Competitive between state fund and private plans—employer must choose.	Competitive between state fund and private plans—former automatic if latter not elected by employer and majority of employees.	Competitive between state fund and private plans—former automatic if latter not elected by employer or with his consent, and by employee.	Monopolistic state fund—no private plans allowed in substitution.
Approach Used	Employer required to provide benefits—like Workmen's Compensation but employees share cost.	Tax supported state fund provides benefits—like Unemployment Compensation but private plans may be substituted.	Tax supported state fund provides benefits—like Unemployment Compensation but voluntary (private) plans may be substituted.	Tax supported state fund provides benefits—like Unemployment Compensation.
Types of Private Plans	Insured and self-insured plans equalling or exceeding statutory requirements, and continuation of certain other existing plans.	Insured and self-insured plans equalling or exceeding state fund standards, and continuation of certain other existing plans.	Insured and self-insured plans exceeding state fund standards.	None.
Limitations Upon Right to Establish Private Plans	None.	None if private plan does not exclude any class of employees, determined by age, sex, race, or wages.	Must not result in substantial "adverse selection" against state fund. Voluntary plans must meet each of three tests based upon distribution of employees by sex, age, and amount of wages received, to be approved under this provision, ac-	———

COMPARATIVE ANALYSIS OF STATE DISABILITY BENEFITS LAWS—(Continued)

	NEW YORK	NEW JERSEY	CALIFORNIA	RHODE ISLAND
Contributions Began	January 1, 1950.	June 2, 1948 for employees. January 1, 1949 for employers.	cording to regulation adopted pursuant to 1961 amendment and effective January 1, 1963 following court test of regulation. May 21, 1946.	June 1, 1942.
Benefit Payments Began	July 1, 1950.	January 1, 1949.	December 1, 1946.	April 1, 1943.
Federal Unemployment Trust Fund Monies Used	None available for disability benefits.	$50 million.	$70.2 million.	$29 million.
Employee Contributions	½% of first $60 of weekly wages.	½% of first $3,000 of annual wages.	1% of first $4,100 of annual wages for 1962, $4,-600 for 1963, $5,100 for 1964, $5,600 for 1965 and thereafter.	1% of first $4,800 of annual wages.
Employer Contributions Required	Balance of cost.	¼% of first $3,000 of annual wages if in state plan; balance of cost, if any, in private plan.	None.	None.
Experience Rating of Contributions to State Fund	The net effect of competitive premium rates will be substantially the same as the results of experience rating.	Yes, employer's share only (between ¾% and 1⁄10%).	No.	No.
Employers Covered	Employers of 1 or more (4 or more domestics) on each of 30 days in one calendar year.	Employers of 4 or more in 20 weeks in calendar year—same as Unemployment Compensation.	Employers of 1 or more with $100 payroll in any calendar quarter—same as Unemployment Compensation.	Employers of 1 or more on any day—same as Unemployment Compensation.
Employees Excluded	Farm laborers, day students, casual employees,	Farm laborers, domestic servants, students, em-	Domestic servants, certain casual employees,	Farm laborers, domestic servants, students, em-

COMPARATIVE ANALYSIS OF STATE DISABILITY BENEFITS LAWS—(Continued)

	NEW YORK	NEW JERSEY	CALIFORNIA	RHODE ISLAND
	railroad and government employees, and certain others.	ployees of certain non-profit organizations, railroad and government employees, and certain others.	employees of certain non-profit organizations, railroad and government employees, real estate salesmen and certain others.	ployees of certain non-profit organizations, railroad and government employees, and certain others.
Religious Exemptions	Christian Scientists, etc., may apply for exemption.	Christian Scientists, etc., may apply for exemption.	Christian Scientists, etc., may apply for exemption.	Christian Scientists, etc., may apply for exemption.
Statutory Eligibility Requirements	Generally four consecutive weeks of covered employment, not necessarily with current employer.	17 weeks of work in covered employment during base year. Week counted when wages from one employer were $15 or more.	Earnings in base year of $300 in covered employment.	20 weeks of work or $1,200 of wages in covered employment during base year. Week counted when wages were $20 or more.
How Benefits Are Computed	$\frac{1}{2}$ of average weekly wage in preceding 8 weeks, subject to maximum.	Same basis as unemployment compensation benefits.	Depends upon wages in highest quarter of base year. Benefits exceed those for Unemployment Compensation.	55% of average weekly wage in base year, subject to maximum. Same as Unemployment Compensation.
Minimum Weekly Benefits	$20, or average weekly wage, whichever is less.	$10.	$25.	$12.
Maximum Weekly Benefits in State Plan	$50.	$50.	Adjusted each Jan. 1 on basis of $\frac{2}{3}$ of average weekly wage paid in covered employment (excluding farm laborers) but not less than $70.* Plus $12 per day for first 20 days of hospital confinement.	Adjusted each July 1 on basis of 50% of average weekly wage paid in covered employment preceding calendar year plus $3 per dependent up to $12. The maximum for period beginning July 1, 1964 is $45.00.
Maximum Duration	26 weeks.	26 weeks.	26 weeks.	26 weeks.
Waiting Period	7 days for each disability.	7 days for each disability.	7 days for each disability. None if hospitalized.	7 days for each benefit year.
Maternity Benefits	No.	Yes. Eligibility limited to 4 weeks prior to and 4 weeks following birth.	No.	Yes, limited to 14 weeks.

* Maximum for 1964 is $77.

COMPARATIVE ANALYSIS OF STATE DISABILITY BENEFITS LAWS—(Continued)

	NEW YORK	NEW JERSEY	CALIFORNIA	RHODE ISLAND
Duplication of Benefits With Workmen's Compensation	Not eligible for any period for which Workmen's Compensation (other than benefits for a prior disability) is paid or payable.	Not eligible for any period for which Workmen's Compensation (other than benefits for a permanent partial disability, previously incurred) is paid or payable.	Not eligible for any period for which Workmen's Compensation (other than benefits for a permanent disability) is paid or payable unless Workmen's Compensation is less than disability; in that case, the difference is payable.	Eligible up to a combined benefit of 85% of average weekly wage but not more than $62 total per week exclusive of dependents' benefits.
Effect of Continued Pay from Employer During Disability	None if voluntarily provided by employer, otherwise generally disqualifies for benefits.	Reduces benefits if total of benefits and sick pay would otherwise exceed regular wages.	None on hospital benefits. Combined benefits and sick pay cannot exceed regular wages.	None—benefits and sick pay may be received simultaneously.
Benefits for Disabled Unemployed Financed By	Assessments on insurance companies, self-insurers, state insurance fund and existing plans, without limit. Revolving fund set up by tax of 1/10% of taxable wages both on employers and employees from 1/1/50 to 6/30/50.	State plan, which may assess private plans for pro rata share of excess of cost over interest on $50 million of initial fund. Assessment limited to .02% of taxable wages.	State plan, by means of separate account credited each year with .12% of taxable wages, such amounts being obtained from private plans by assessment.	State plan.
Administrative Assessments Against Private Plans	Administrative costs of program assessed against carriers in proportion to taxable wages; no limit.	Added administrative costs attributable to private plans assessed against plans in proportion to taxable wages; limit of .02% of taxable wages.	Added administrative costs attributable to private plans assessed against plans in proportion to taxable wages; no limit.	————
Administrative Agency	Workmen's Compensation Board.	Department of Labor and Industry, Division of Employment Security.	Department of Employment.	Department of Employment Security.
Citation	Workmen's Compensation Law, Art. 9 (§§200–242).	Title 43, Ch. 21, Art. 2 (§§43:21–25 to 43:21–56), RS 1937, as amended.	Unemployment Insurance Code, Div. 1, Part 2 (§§2601–3271).	Title 28, Chs. 39–41, General Laws 1956.

Compiled by the Life Insurance Association of America, October, 1964.

Appendix 8

DISABILITY INCOME EXPERIENCE DURING 1959 STEEL STRIKE

EFFECT OF CONTINUING COVERAGE DURING A WORK STOPPAGE
ON CLAIM COST OF TEMPORARY DISABILITY INCOME BENEFITS

Prior to 1960, most steel company labor agreements provided that temporary disability income benefits could be continued during a work stoppage. The steel industry strike which occurred from July 15, 1959 to November 7, 1959 was of sufficiently long duration to permit the accumulation of significant statistics with respect to the effect of such a continuation provision on the cost of the plan. The statistics for three large steel companies are shown in the following table. For each company, the average paid loss ratio (paid claims to paid premiums) for the five month period (February 1959 through June 1959) preceding the strike was determined. Then the paid loss ratio for each of the succeeding months of 1959 was expressed as a percentage of this five month pre-strike average. It is these percentages which are shown in the table below.

Period	Co. A	Co. B	Co. C
February–June	100%	100%	100%
July	134	132	176
August	169	173	232
September	230	197	204
October	230	194	198
November	177	147	178
December	105	100	110

Appendix 9

MODEL GROUP ANTI-DUPLICATION PROVISON

PROVISION FOR CO-ORDINATION BETWEEN THIS POLICY AND OTHER BENEFITS

Section A. Benefits Subject to This Provision

All of the benefits provided under this policy are subject to this provision.

(Note: When policy provides both integrated Major Medical Expense Benefits and the underlying Basic Benefits, but provision applies to Major Medical only, use the following alternate wording: Only the Major Medical Expense Benefits provided under this policy are subject to this provision.)

Section B. Definitions

(1) (Note: Include here the definition of a Plan, that is, the benefits, including those provided by this policy, that are to be co-ordinated. The following definition is illustrative only.)

"Plan" means any plan providing benefits or services for or by reason of medical or dental care or treatment, which benefits or services are provided by (i) group, blanket or franchise insurance coverage, (ii) individual and family-type insurance coverage, (iii) Blue Cross, Blue Shield, group practice, individual practice and other prepayment coverage, (iv) any coverage under labor-management trusteed plans, union welfare plans, employer organization plans, or employee benefit organization plans, and (v) any coverage under governmental programs, and any coverage required or provided by any statute.

The term "Plan" shall be construed separately with respect to each policy, contract, or other arrangement for benefits or services and separately with respect to that portion of any such policy, contract, or other arrangement which reserves the right to take the benefits or services of other Plans into consideration in determining its benefits and that portion which does not.

(2) "This Plan" means that portion of this policy which provides the benefits that are subject to this provision.

(Note: Any benefits provided under this policy that are not subject to this provision constitute another Plan.)

(3) "Allowable Expense" means any necessary, reasonable, and customary item of expense at least a portion of which is covered under at least one of the Plans covering the person for whom claim is made.

When a Plan provides benefits in the form of services rather than cash payments, the reasonable cash value of each service rendered shall be deemed to be both an Allowable Expense and a benefit paid.

(4) "Claim Determination Period" means _____.

(Note: Insert here an appropriate period of time such as, "calendar year" or "Benefit Period as defined elsewhere in this policy.")

Section C. Effect on Benefits

(1) This provision shall apply in determining the benefits as to a person covered under this Plan for any Claim Determination Period if, for the Allowable Expenses incurred as to such person during such period, the sum of

    (a) the benefits that would be payable under this Plan in the absence of this provision, and

    (b) the benefits that would be payable under all other Plans in the absence therein of provisions of similar purpose to this provision

would exceed such Allowable Expenses.

(2) As to any Claim Determination Period with respect to which this provision is applicable, the benefits that would be payable under this Plan in the absence of this provision for the Allowable Expenses incurred as to such person during such Claim Determination Period shall be reduced to the extent necessary so that the sum of such reduced benefits and all the benefits payable for such Allowable Expenses under all other Plans, except as provided in item (3) of this Section C, shall not exceed the total of such Allowable Expenses. Benefits payable under another Plan include the benefits that would have been payable had claim been duly made therefor.

(3) If

    (a) another Plan which is involved in item (2) of this Section C and which contains a provision co-ordinating its benefits with those of this Plan would, according to its rules, determine its benefits after the benefits of this Plan have been determined, and

    (b) the rules set forth in item (4) of this Section C would require this Plan to determine its benefits before such other Plan

then the benefits of such other Plan will be ignored for the purposes of determining the benefits under this Plan.

(4) For the purposes of item (3) of this Section C, the rules establishing the order of benefit determination are:

    (a) The benefits of a Plan which covers the person on whose expenses claim is based other than as a dependent shall be determined before the benefits of a Plan which covers such person as a dependent;

    (b) The benefits of a Plan which covers the person on whose expenses claim is based as a dependent of a male person shall be determined before the benefits of a Plan which covers such person as a dependent of a female person;

    (c) When rules (a) and (b) do not establish an order of benefit determination, the benefits of a Plan which has covered the person on whose expenses claim is based for the longer period of time shall be determined before the benefits of a Plan which has covered such person the shorter period of time.

(5) (Note: This item (5) may be omitted if the Plan provides only one benefit. The wording shown is illustrative.)

When this provision operates to reduce the total amount of benefits otherwise payable as to a person covered under this Plan during any Claim Determination Period, each benefit that would be payable in the absence of this provision shall be reduced proportionately, and such reduced amount shall be charged against any applicable benefit limit of this Plan.

Section D. Right to Receive and Release Necessary Information

For the purposes of determining the applicability of and implementing the terms of this provision of this Plan or any provision of similar purpose of any other Plan, the Insurance Company may, without the consent of or notice to any person, release to or obtain from any other insurance company or other organization or person any information, with respect to any person, which the Insurance Company deems to be necessary for such purposes. Any person claiming benefits under this Plan shall furnish to the Insurance Company such information as may be necessary to implement this provision.

Section E. Facility of Payment

Whenever payments which should have been made under this Plan in accordance with this provision have been made under any other Plans, the Insurance Company shall have the right, exercisable alone and in its sole discretion, to pay over to any organizations making such other payments any amounts it shall determine to be warranted in order to satisfy the intent of this provision, and amounts so paid shall be deemed to be benefits paid under this Plan and, to the extent of such payments, the Insurance Company shall be fully discharged from liability under this Plan.

Section F. Right of Recovery

Whenever payments have been made by the Insurance Company with respect to Allowable Expenses in a total amount, at any time, in excess of the maximum amount of payment necessary at that time to satisfy the intent of this provision, the Insurance Company shall have the right to recover such payments, to the extent of such excess, from among one or more of the following, as the Insurance Company shall determine: any persons to or for or with respect to whom such payments were made, any other insurance companies, any other organizations.

NOTES ON SUGGESTED
MODEL GROUP ANTI-DUPLICATION PROVISION

1. The terms provision, section, and item are not intended to be construed as model terms. They were simply the terms which were most convenient to use in drafting the suggested model provision. It is presumed that each company would vary these three terms to suit the format of its own policies.
2. The provision may be used for any Group Medical Expense Benefit or any combination of such benefits.

3. Some companies have written integrated Major Medical plans with only a cash deductible and have relied on the anti-duplication provision to provide the so-called "Basic Benefits" deductible. With the adoption of the suggested Model Group Anti-Duplication Provision, this approach will no longer be possible. Instead, the integrated Major Medical plan will have to use a two part deductible: one part a cash amount and the other part the policyholder's other benefits.

4. The provision has been designed to be included in the general limitations and exclusions section of the group policy and hence to apply to all benefits provided under the policy. If one or more of the benefits are to be exempt from the provision, then an appropriate change should be made in the wording of Section A. Sample alternate wording is included for the case where the Major Medical but not the Basic Benefits are subject to the provision.

5. The first paragraph of the definition of a Plan is intended to be completely variable. The illustrative definition shown is generally about as broad a definition as can be drafted consistent with sound public relations. (See Study Group's first report for reasons why liability payments should be ignored.) Some carriers may wish to limit the definition of a Plan to group and governmental plans.

6. The second paragraph of the definition of a Plan should always be included. This wording, which divides certain policies into two Plans, will be necessary as long as there are group policies that apply the anti-duplication provision to only part of their benefits.

7. The blank space at the end of the definition of Claim Determination Period will normally be filled by inserting "calendar year." This period of time is obviously appropriate for Comprehensive and Major Medical plans which apply their deductible on a calendar year basis. It is also well suited for Basic Benefit plans where the various benefits have different "successive disability" rules. "Benefit Period" would be used for those Comprehensive and Major Medical plans which apply their deductible on a Benefit Period basis and the Benefit Period is not a calendar year.

8. Attention is directed to the phrase toward the end of the third sentence of item 2 of Section C which reads ". . . and all the benefits payable for such Allowable Expenses under all other Plans. . . ." At first glance, it may seem that the phrase "in the absence therein of provisions of similar purpose" should be inserted after the word payable. This is not so, however, because it is intended that this Plan shall accept benefits actually paid as "benefits payable." For example, if the other Plan pays a prorata benefit, it is intended that this Plan shall pay the balance of Allowable Expenses up to the amount of its benefits payable in the absence of this provision.

9. Although item 5 of Section C is variable, the wording shown has been designed to fit all types of plans. However, when there is an integrated Major Medical plan and both it and the underlying Basic Benefits plan are subject to anti-duplication provisions, then it may be desirable to vary this wording so that any reduction is applied first to the Major Medical Benefit.

10. Companies using this anti-duplication provision are expected to make every effort to instruct claimants to assign only the benefits of the Plan which is first in order of benefit determination. Even so, there will be situations where an HIC Hospital Admissions Form is executed with respect to the benefits of a Plan that is not first in order of benefit determination. In such a circumstance,

the carrier of that Plan will honor the hospital assignment in full and will then look to the carrier of the primary Plan for reimbursement of any amount by which the payment to the hospital exceeds what would have been paid in accordance with the anti-duplication provision. Note that Section E permits the primary Plan to make such reimbursement.

Appendix 10

SPECIMEN GROUP INSURANCE AGREEMENT
AND DECLARATION OF TRUST

(This instrument must be drawn by the Trade Association's lawyers so that it coincides with the laws of the political sub-division in which the trust is domiciled and with the wishes of the particular Trade Association. This specimen is drawn for sample purposes only. Preparing Trust Agreements belongs to the lawyers and is not one of our services.)

AGREEMENT AND DECLARATION OF TRUST
Establishing "John Doe Trade Association"

MADE this _____ day of _____, 196_, in and under the law of the State of _____, by and between JOHN DOE COMPANY of _____, HARRY DOE COMPANY of _____ _____, WILLIAM DOE COMPANY of _____, and CHARLES DOE COMPANY of _____; hereinafter referred to as "Employers," and _____(1)_____ of _____, _____, _____(2)_____ of _____, _____, _____(3)_____ of _____, _____, ___(4)___ _____ of _____, _____, and ___(5)___ _____ of _____, _____, who with their successors designated as hereinafter provided, are hereinafter referred to as "Trustees."

WHEREAS Employers are employers of employees in the _____ industry and are also members of the John Doe Trade Association; and

WHEREAS Employers desire to purchase group insurance covering their employees and are informed that many other members of the John Doe Trade Association have indicated their desire to purchase group insurance covering their employees; and

WHEREAS Employers believe that such other members may desire to become Employers under and for purposes of this Agreement and Declaration of Trust,

NOW THEREFORE, THIS AGREEMENT AND DECLARATION OF TRUST WITNESSETH:

THAT, in consideration of the cash sum of _____ paid by each of the Employers to Trustees and for other good and valuable considerations each to the other flowing, the receipt of which is hereby acknowledged, Employers and Trustees mutually covenant and agree as follows:

ARTICLE I
FUND AND TRUST CREATED

Section 1. The foregoing cash and all other payments of cash received by Trustees as provided herein, will be held by them In Trust, in a fund to be known as "John Doe Trade Association Group Insurance Trust Fund" (hereinafter called "Fund"), for the uses and purposes solely of purchasing and maintaining in force a policy or policies of group insurance subject to the provisions of (cite statute or statutes giving the authority in the state of situs).

824

Section 2. Employers hereby authorize and direct Trustees to do all things necessary and proper and to use the Fund to purchase and to maintain in force such policy or policies of group insurance, as Trustees acting in their sole discretion shall determine and agree to be in the best interest of Employers.

ARTICLE II
PURPOSE OF THE TRUST AND APPLICATION OF THE FUND

Section 1. The Trust and the Fund are created for the sole purpose of enabling Employers to join together and act as a single employer in the purchase and maintenance of a policy or policies of group insurance as authorized by the (statute or statutes) cited in Section 1 of Article I. The policies shall be issued by a licensed insurance carrier or carriers (on the lives and for the benefit of Employees of Employers and/or with respect to accident and health insurance on the employees of and, dependents of the Employees of, Employers for the benefit of said employees), the term "employees" as provided in said (statute or statutes), to include the (give here definition of "employee" as provided in the state statute). "However, for the purposes of coverage under any policy or policies, the term 'employee' under no circumstances shall include any person (a) whose coverage under the policy or policies is prohibited by the insurance laws of the place wherein the policy is issued or delivered, or (b) whose coverage under any policy or policies is prohibited by the insurance laws of the place wherein he resides or is principally employed." For this purpose, the Trustees shall be deemed to be the Employer and the policyholder and the amounts of insurance and benefits shall be such as the Trustees may determine and agree upon with such insurance carrier. The Fund and Trustees, their employees or agents are not authorized to and shall not engage in solicitation of Employers to subscribe to this Agreement and Declaration of Trust or otherwise to participate in such purchase of insurance; provided, however, this shall not prevent the Trustees from receiving soliciting materials from insurance carriers and making the same available to members of the John Doe Trade Association for their information.

A person insured pursuant to the terms of this Agreement and Declaration of Trust as an employee of one contributing Employer shall not be eligible for insurance pursuant to the terms of this Agreement and Declaration of Trust as an employee of any other contributing Employer.

Section 2. The Trustees may apply for such policies of group insurance in their names as Employer and may use the Fund to pay for, and accept and hold as part of the Fund, the policy or policies issued to them in their names as Employer, for the purposes specified in Section 1 of this Article II, provided such policy or policies conform to the description and meet all of the requirements of the law of the State of _____ cited in Section 1 of Article I, hereinabove; and further provided that such policy or policies shall not cover employees located in any state contrary to the law of such state.

Section 3. The Trustees may agree with the insurance carrier of any policy or policies specified in Section 2 of this Article II upon waiting periods, definitions of full-time employment, and all other necessary or desirable provisions, including the eligibility of Employers and of Employees which are authorized and within the scope of the Law of the State of_____.

Section 4. The Trustees shall use and apply the Fund:

(a) To pay or provide for the payment of all reasonable and necessary expenses of collecting the Employer Contributions and administering the affairs of the Trust and Fund, including, but without limitation, all expenses which may be incurred in connection with the establishment of the Trust and Fund, the employment of such administrative, legal, expert, and clerical assistance, the leasing of such premises, and the purchase or lease of such materials, supplies and equipment as the Trustees, in their discretion, find necessary or appropriate in the performance of their duties.

(b) To pay or provide for the payment of premiums due from Employers on the policy or policies, when such premiums shall become due; provided, however, Trustees shall not use the Fund to maintain in force any insurance for the account of any Employer who is in default of payment of contributions to the Fund as hereinafter provided.

(c) To establish and accumulate as part of the Fund an adequate reserve which the Trustees shall deem advisable to carry out the purpose of the Trust. Such reserve shall at no time exceed a figure equal to six nor be less than a figure equal to two times the amount then currently required for payment of a monthly premium on all the policies, together with the estimated plan expense.

(d) To make refunds of contributions of Employers for whom insurance may not be purchased for any reason; provided, however, in case of withdrawal of an employer from this Agreement and Declaration of Trust for any reason, the fund and trustees shall be under no obligation to make any refund of contributions of such employer if insurance has been purchased on his account (it being agreed that his contributions shall be used to maintain his insurance in force and to pay his fair share of trust expenses, to the extent of his contributions held in the fund), or (until such employer's pro rata share of all premiums and trust expenses, to the date of termination of group insurance on his employees, has been paid in full but, after payment of such pro rata share, the trustees shall return to the withdrawing employer such employer's pro rata share of the net reserve determined as of the date of the termination of such insurance).

(e) In the event of termination of this Agreement and Trust, to make equitable distribution among Employers then participating, of the Fund remaining after payment of all obligations then outstanding, as the Trustees may determine.

Section 5. All moneys received by the Trustees hereunder as part of the Fund shall be deposited by them in such bank or banks as the Trustees may designate for that purpose, and all withdrawals of moneys from such bank or banks shall be made only by check signed by a person or persons authorized by the Trustees to sign and countersign (provided, however, no bank shall be selected as a depository of the funds of this plan which is not a member of the Federal Deposit Insurance Corporation or is not supervised and insured by an instrumentality of the United States Government).

Section 6. All trustees, officers and employees of the Trust who are authorized to sgin or countersign checks or who otherwise may handle monies or other property of the Trust shall be bonded as required by the Regulations issued by the U.S. Department of Labor under the provisions of the Welfare and Pension Plans Disclosure Act of 1958, and all amendments thereto. This bond shall be at the expense of the Trust, in an amount and type required by such Regulations and written by an authorized surety company approved by the U.S. Department of Labor.

Section 7. Anything contained in this Agreement and Declaration of Trust to the contrary notwithstanding, the Trustees may agree with the insurer or insurers for the combination of financial experiences, for dividend purposes, of policies issued to the Trustees pursuant to this Agreement and of policies not so issued which insure employees of Employers who (are members of the John Doe Association or are engaged in the _____ business) and/or said Employers. The Trustees may agree with the insurer(s) and/or any policyholder(s) to provide for centralized administration of all such policies in any manner deemed advisable by the Trustees.

ARTICLE III
EMPLOYER CONTRIBUTIONS TO THE FUND

Section 1. Upon subscribing to this Agreement and Declaration of Trust, and as consideration therefor, each Employer shall pay to the Fund a cash sum of _____; and as determined by the Trustees, each Employer shall pay in advance an initial contribution in an amount equal to one monthly premium to be held as a part of the reserve established pursuant to paragraph (c) of Article II hereinabove. In addition to the initial Employer Contribution, each Employer shall pay to the Fund on such day of each month as shall be decided upon by the Trustees uniformly for all the Employers, such monthly Employer Contributions as the Trustees shall deem necessary to pay the premium due, and fair share of trust expenses on account of the insurance purchased for such Employers (provided, however, that all Employer payments shall be credited against premiums and shares of expenses due from Employers).

Section 2. In addition to the Employer Contributions specified in Section 1 of this Article III, each Employer shall make to the Fund on such dates as shall be decided upon by the Trustees, which may coincide with the date of the monthly Employer Contributions, further Employer Contributions in such amounts as will be sufficient to maintain at all times a reserve, as defined in paragraph (c) of Section 4 of Article II of the Agreement and Declaration of Trust.

ARTICLE IV
PARTICIPATION OF EMPLOYERS IN THE TRUST

Section 1. Eligibility. Any Employer and any person, firm or organization certified by the _____ of the John Doe Trade Association to be a member in good standing in that Association who, on a form furnished by the Trustees, adopts and subscribes to this Agreement and Declaration of Trust and requests inclusion of his Employees for the insurance under the policy or policies, shall participate in the Trust for such insurance provided that he satisfies the requirements for participation in such insurance as established by the insurance carrier or carriers of the policy or policies under which such insurance is afforded. An Employer's participation in the Trust shall commence on the date set by the Trustees provided that it satisfied the requirements as established by the insurance carrier or carriers. The insurance carrier of the policy or policies shall at all times be kept informed by the Trustees of the names of the Employers who participate in the Trust, as well as the names of their Employees.

Section 2. Termination of Qualifications of an Employer for Participation in the Trust. An Employer shall cease to qualify for participation in the Trust for any insurance when he fails to make an Employer Contribution as provided in Article III of this Agreement and Declaration of Trust for the insurance on the date when due or within the period of time allowed by the Trustees for the payment thereof; or if an Employer shall cease to qualify under or by reason of any state or Federal law; or when the Employer fails to comply with the rules and regulations made by the Trustees from time to time with respect to the administration of the group insurance trust fund, including, but without limiting the generality of the foregoing, the method and accuracy of employer reports of the number of his employees, the effective dates of insurance of his employees, the discontinuance of insurance of his employees, premiums due, and all other facts which the Trustees deem advisable to assure a sound administration of the group insurance program in accordance with the provisions of the group policy; or when such employer ceases to be a member (of the John Doe Association) and refuses to pay a reasonable service charge for excess administrative expenses as liquidated damages and not as a penalty; or when he no longer satisfies the requirements set forth in Section 1 of this Article IV.

Section 3. Termination of Participation of an Employer in the Trust and Termination of Insurance. When in accordance with the provisions of this Article IV, an Employer ceases to qualify for participation in the Trust for the insurance provided under the policy or policies, the Trustees shall forthwith give notice thereof to the insurance carrier of the policy or policies under which such insurance is provided, and such insurance shall then terminate at the time specified by, and as provided by such policy or policies and the participation of the Employer in the Trust shall terminate to such extent and at such time as the insurance terminates. In such event the Trust and Fund shall have no further liability to such employer whose participation and insurance has terminated (except to return to such employer his pro rata share of the reserve as set out in Article II, Section 4, Paragraph (d)).

ARTICLE V
RETURN OF MONEYS RECEIVED FROM ANY PERSON, PARTNERSHIP, CORPORATION, OR ASSOCIATION NOT QUALIFYING AS AN EMPLOYER AS DEFINED IN THIS AGREEMENT AND DECLARATION OF TRUST

Should any moneys be received by the Trustees for the purpose specified in Section 1 of Article II of this Agreement and Declaration of Trust from any person, partnership, corporation, or association failing to satisfy the requirements for participation in the Trust, or from any Employer whose Employees do not become insured under the policy or policies, such moneys shall be returned, and there shall be no further obligations whatsoever in connection therewith.

ARTICLE VI
ADMINISTRATION OF THE FUND

*Appointment, Resignation, Removal, and
Replacement of Trustees*

Section 1. The Trust and Fund shall be administered by five Trustees, who shall serve for such terms and be succeeded in office as may be determined at any time by formal resolution of the Executive Committee of the John Doe Trade Association in session assembled; provided, however, that such appointive authority delegated to the said Committee shall not connote, imply or authorize any other responsibility or liability, financial or otherwise, on the part of the John Doe Trade Association, its Committees or its officers. The Trustees shall select from among their number a Chairman of the Fund, hereinafter called the "Chairman," and a secretary of the Fund, hereinafter called the "Secretary."

Section 2. JOHN DOE COMPANY, HARRY DOE COMPANY, WILLIAM DOE COMPANY and CHARLES DOE COMPANY, by their execution of this Agreement and Declaration of Trust, do hereby appoint, designate and select (show names of trustees), and their successors in office as specified in Section 1 of this Article VI, Trustees of the Fund, and the Employers who hereafter adopt and subscribe to this Agreement and Declaration of Trust thereby confirm such appointment of (show names of trustees), and their successors, provided, however, that if any or all of such named Trustees are not serving as Trustee or Trustees at the time of the adoption of this Agreement and Declaration of Trust by any Employer, then and in that event the Trustee or Trustees confirmed by such adopting Employer shall be such as will then be serving as Trustee or Trustees.

Section 3. The Trustees named in Section 2 of this Article VI, by their execution of this Agreement and Declaration of Trust, do hereby accept the trusteeship and declare that they will receive and hold the Fund as Trustees by virtue of this Agreement and Declaration of Trust for the uses, purposes, and trusts, and with the powers and duties, herein set forth and none other.

Section 4. It is the intention that the Fund shall at all times be administered by five trustees, and that in the event of a vacancy, a successor Trustee shall immediately be appointed in the manner provided in this Agreement and Declaration of Trust, but until such time as a successor Trustee has been appointed, the remaining Trustees shall have power to act in the manner specified in this Agreement and Declaration of Trust.

Section 5. A Trustee may resign and become and remain fully discharged from all further duty or responsibility hereunder upon giving thirty days' notice in writing to the remaining Trustees, or such shorter notice as the remaining Trustees may accept as sufficient, in which notice there shall be stated a date and such resignation shall take effect on the date specified in the notice, unless a successor Trustee shall have been appointed at an earlier date, in which event such resignation shall take effect immediately upon the appointment of such successor Trustee. Immediately upon such resignation a notice shall be sent by the remaining Trustees, or any one or more of them, to the insurance carrier of each policy, to the employers and to any other person, partnership, corporation, or association with whom the Trustees are dealing.

Section 6. If any vacancy in the Trusteeship occurs, said vacancy shall be filled as provided in Section 1 of Article VI, and the Trustee so appointed by them shall serve as Trustee during their pleasure and until his successor is duly qualified, as provided in Section 1 of Article VI.

Section 7. Any successor Trustee shall immediately, upon his appointment as a successor Trustee and his acceptance of the trusteeship in writing, become vested with all the property, rights, powers, and duties of a Trustee hereunder with like effect as if originally named as a Trustee, and all the Trustees then serving shall be immediately notified.

Section 8. The insurance carrier of the policy or policies and any person, partnership, corporation, or association with whom the Trustees are dealing, shall at all times be kept informed by the Trustees of the names of the Trustees who are serving, and of their designation as Chairman or Secretary, as the case may be, and in that respect any such insurance carrier may rely upon the report last received in writing from the Trustees at the Home Office of such insurance carrier; and any other person, partnership, corporation, or association may rely upon the report last received from the Trustees.

ARTICLE VII

CONCERNING THE TRUSTEES—POWERS, DUTIES, ETC.

Section 1. The Trustees may exercise all rights or privileges granted to them as policyholder by provisions of each policy or allowed by the insurance carrier of such policy, and may agree with such insurance carrier to any alteration, modification, or amendment of such policy, and may take any action respecting such policy or the insurance provided thereunder which may be necessary or advisable, and such insurance carrier shall not be required to inquire into the authority of the Trustees with regard to any dealings in connection with such policy.

Section 2. The Trustees shall have power to construe the provisions of this Agreement and Declaration of Trust and the terms used herein, and any construction adopted by the Trustees in good faith shall be binding upon the Employers and Employees.

Anything contained herein to the contrary notwithstanding, each Employer shall be liable to the Trustees for the premium for his insurance and the insurance of his employees under the policy or policies issued to the Trustees for any period during which such insurance is in force and the Trustees shall enforce such liability for such premiums to the extent necessary to pay premiums due under any such policy or policies. In the event any such policy or policies are terminated and the premium due thereunder is not paid by the Trustees to the insurance carrier issuing the policy on the date the premium is due thereunder, such insurance carrier, if it shall so elect, shall immediately be subrogated to the right of the Trustees to enforce the liability of any Employer under this Trust and may apply any sums collected first toward its expense of suit including costs and counsel fees and then toward the discharge of the premium obligation under the policy or policies. Any such election by the insurer may be exercised at any time and shall not constitute a waiver of its right to enforce the liability of any other Employer under the Trust Agreement or constitute a waiver of its right to collect any deficiencies in premium from the Trustees out of the Trust Fund.

Section 3. The Trustees, acting as a Board as provided in Section 1 of this Article, shall have the general management, control, and direction of all the business, activities and affairs of the Trust, with full power to transact all its business, including the making of deposits in and disbursements from the Fund; provided, however, it is not the business of this Trust to solicit, and Employers and Trustees, their employees and agents shall not solicit subscriptions to this Agreement and Declaration of Trust or the purchase of insurance pursuant thereto or by means thereof. The Trustees, their Employees and agents are authorized, however, to receive soliciting materials from insurance carriers and to make the same available to members of the John Doe Trade Association. The Trustees as a Board, and any particular individual Trustee, employee, or agent authorized by them thereto in each instance, are specifically authorized to execute, acknowledge, and deliver any instruments of whatever nature which may be necessary or convenient for the administration of the Trust or carrying out its purpose; to determine the employees of the Trust, prescribe their duties, and fix their compensation and require satisfactory bonds from any of them in their sole discretion.

Section 4. The Trustees shall not receive compensation for their duties, but shall be reimbursed for all reasonable and necessary expenses which they may incur in the performance of their duties. Provision may, however, be made to compensate one or more Trustees for special executive or administrative services performed in connection with the direction, administration or operation of the Trust, the Fund or the policies.

Section 5. The Trustees may promulgate such rules and regulations as may, in their discretion, be proper or necessary for the sound and efficient administration of the Trust; provided, however, that such rules shall not take effect until a copy or copies thereof have been mailed to the carrier of such policy or policies.

Section 6. The Trustees may delegate any of their ministerial powers or duties hereunder to any one of their number and/or to any agent and/or employee.

Section 7. The Trustees shall keep true and accurate books of account and records of all their transactions, which shall be audited annually or oftener by a public accountant, and furnish to the Employers from time to time reports respecting the status of the Fund, and the status of the policy or policies, and the benefits paid thereunder, but the Trustees shall not be required to furnish such reports more often than annually.

Section 8.   Any action by the Trustees pursuant to this Agreement and Declaration of Trust may be taken either at a meeting or in writing without a meeting. A meeting may be called at any time by the Chairman or any two of the Trustees, upon giving ten days' written notice to the other Trustees. Notice of any meeting may be dispensed with if all the Trustees waive the same in writing, and shall be dispensed with if all the Trustees are present, and participate in any meeting.

Section 9.   Any Action taken by the Trustees pursuant to this Agreement and Declaration of Trust shall be by the concurrence of a majority of all of the Trustees serving at that time if there be more than two Trustees then serving, or by the unanimous concurrence of all the Trustees serving at that time if there be only two Trustees then serving.

Section 10.   Except as provided by Section 3 of Article VIII and Section 3 of Article IX of this Agreement and Declaration of Trust, the Fund and the Trustees shall be bound by the signature of the Chairman and the Secretary to or in any instrument in writing; and any person, partnership, corporation or association may rely thereon that the execution of such instrument on behalf of the Fund has been duly authorized.

Section 11.   The Trustees shall not have any liability with respect to the non-payment of Employer Contributions. All suits and proceedings to enforce or protect any other right, demand, or claim on behalf of the Trustees, or of the Fund, may be instituted and prosecuted on behalf of the Fund and the Trustees by the Chairman in his capacity as such, or by any two Trustees thereunto authorized by the Trustees.

Section 12.   The Trustees personally and individually, whether severally or jointly, shall not be liable in any matter or transaction or for any omission relating to the conduct of the business of the Trust nor their respective activities and performance of their duties with respect thereto. No Trustee shall be liable for errors in judgment of himself or of his Co-Trustees, nor for any act, judgment, or exercise of discretion of the Trustees' agents or employees, in the conduct of the Trust, and each shall be liable only for his own willful misconduct or wrong doing in respect thereto.

ARTICLE VIII
AMENDMENTS

Section 1.   This Agreement and Declaration of Trust may be amended to any extent at any time or from time to time by the unanimous concurrence of all the Trustees serving at that time, except that no amendment shall divert the Fund as then constituted, or any part thereof, to a purpose other than that as set forth in Article II of this Agreement and Declaration of Trust, nor may there be any amendment of this Article VIII and of the Articles II, IV, IX, and X of this Agreement and Declaration of Trust without the consent of the insurance carrier of the policy or policies.

Section 2.   Any action taken by the Trustees pursuant to Section 1 of this Article VIII may be taken either at a meeting called or held in accordance with the provisions of Section 8 of Article VII of this Agreement and Declaration of Trust, or in writing without a meeting.

Section 3.   The Trustees shall forthwith notify the insurance carrier of the policy or policies of any amendment or amendments adopted pursuant to Section 1 of this Article VIII, and execute any instrument or instruments necessary in connection therewith. In any instrument or instruments executed by the Trustees pursuant to this Article VIII, the insurance carrier of each policy and any person, partnership, corporation or association may rely upon the signature of a majority of all the Trustees serving at that time, if there be more than two Trustees then serving, or upon the signature of two Trustees if there be only two Trustees then serving.

Section 4. The provisions of this Article VIII do not apply to any action by the Trustees in accordance with Section 1 of Article VII of this Agreement and Declaration of the Trust.

ARTICLE IX
TERMINATION OF THE TRUST

Section 1. The Trust may be terminated at any time by the unanimous concurrence of all the Trustees serving at that time, and such action may be taken either at a meeting called or held in accordance with the provisions of Section 8 of Article VII of this Agreement and Declaration of Trust, or in writing without a meeting. The Trust may also be terminated by an instrument or instruments in writing signed by a majority of the Employers at that time and delivered to all the Trustees serving at that time.

Section 2. In the event of termination of the Trust, the Trustees shall apply the Fund to pay any and all obligations of the Trust, and distribute and apply any money and other property forming part of the Fund and in such manner as will, in their opinion, best effectuate the purpose of the Trust.

Section 3. Upon termination of the Trust, the Trustee shall forthwith notify each Employer at that time and the insurance carrier of the policy or policies, and any other person, partnership, corporation and association with whom they are dealing, and shall continue as Trustees for the purpose of dissolution, and may take any action with regard to any policy or policies which may be appropriate or required by the insurance carrier of such policy or policies. In any instrument or instruments executed by the Trustees pursuant to this Article IX the insurance carrier of each policy and any person, partnership, corporation, or association may rely upon the signature of a majority of all the Trustees serving at that time if there be more than two Trustees then serving, or upon the signature of two Trustees if there be only two Trustees then serving.

Section 4. This Trust shall terminate in any event upon the death of the last survivor of such persons who are living at the time of the creation of this Trust, who are entitled to receive benefits hereunder; provided, however, that if, as and when this Trust without the benefit of this provision shall not violate the rule against perpetuity, then this provision shall be of no force or effect, this Trust shall continue in perpetuity unless otherwise terminated.

ARTICLE X
MISCELLANEOUS PROVISIONS

Section 1. Employers shall furnish to the Trustees such records and any other information as the Trustees or the insurance carrier of the policy or policies may require in connection with the administration of the Trust, the Fund, and policy or policies. The insurance carrier shall have the right to audit all records of the Trustees or Employers pertaining to the insurance.

Section 2. No Employer nor any other person, partnership, corporation or association shall have any right, title or interest in or to the Fund, or any part thereof, and no Employee nor any person claiming by or through such Employee by reason of having been named a beneficiary in a certificate or otherwise, shall have any claim against the moneys or properties of this Trust, and the interests of such Employees, beneficiaries and other persons claiming through them shall be limited to those specified in the policy or policies.

Section 3.   No person, partnership, corporation or association dealing with the Trustees shall be obliged to see to the application of any funds or property of the Trust, or to see that the terms of the Trust have been complied with, or be obliged to inquire into the necessity or expediency of any act of the Trustees, and every act and instrument effected by the Trustees shall be conclusive in favor of any person, partnership, corporation, or association relying thereon that

   (a)   At the time of such act or the delivery of such instrument, the Trust hereby created was in full force and effect; and

   (b)   Such act or instrument was accomplished or executed in accordance with the terms and conditions contained in this instrument; and

   (c)   The Trustees were duly authorized and empowered to execute such instrument or accomplish such act, and if the act were accomplished or the instrument executed by one or more of the Trustees acting on behalf of a majority of the Trustees, that such accomplishment or execution was authorized by the Trustees.

Section 4.   Anything in this Agreement and Declaration of Trust to the contrary notwithstanding, a majority of the Employers at any time may, by an instrument or instruments in writing delivered to all the Trustees serving at that time, direct the Trustees to take any action permitted to be taken by the Trustees pursuant to this Agreement and Declaration of Trust, except such actions as specified in paragraph (d) of Section 4 of Article II of this Agreement and Declaration of Trust, and the Trustees shall thereupon forthwith notify all the Employers at that time and the insurance carrier of the policy or policies, and execute any instrument or instruments necessary to give effect to such direction. Any such direction and the action taken thereunder by the Trustees to give effect to such direction, shall be binding upon all of the Employers and the Trustees, and shall remain in force until revoked by the direction of a majority of the Employers at the time of revocation; provided, however, that no such revocation shall be effective retroactively to the prejudice of any person not a Trustee, Employer, Employee or participant of, in or in relation to the Trust who has relied upon the existence of the Trust and the authority and actions of the Trustees thereunder. Such revocation shall be made by an instrument or instruments in writing delivered to all the Trustees serving at that time, who shall thereupon forthwith notify all the Employers at that time and the insurance carrier of the policy or policies, and execute any instrument or instruments necessary to give effect to such revocation.

ARTICLE XI
SITUS AND CONSTRUCTION OF TRUST

Section 1.   The Trust is accepted by the Trustees in the State of _____ and all questions pertaining to its validity, construction, and administration shall be determined in accordance with the laws of the State of _____.

Section 2.   Wherever any words are used in this Agreement and Declaration of Trust in the masculine gender, they shall be construed as though they were also used in the feminine or neuter gender in all situations where they would so apply, and wherever any words are used in this Agreement and Declaration of Trust in the singular form, they shall be construed as though they were also used in the plural form in all situations where they would so apply, and wherever any words are used in this Agreement and Declaration of Trust in the plural form, they shall be construed as though they were also used in the singular form in all situations where they would so apply.

IN WITNESS WHEREOF the undersigned do hereunto set their hands and seals as of the date first above written.

JOHN DOE COMPANY
By/s/ John Doe

HARRY DOE COMPANY
By /s/ Harry Doe

WILLIAM DOE COMPANY
By /s/ William Doe

CHARLES DOE COMPANY
By /s/ Charles Doe

Employers

Trustees

Appendix 11

SPECIMEN GROUP INSURANCE MASTER CONTRACT

X Y Z

MUTUAL LIFE INSURANCE COMPANY
BOSTON, MASSACHUSETTS

The X Y Z Mutual Life Insurance Company (herein called the Insurer) agrees with the Policyholder, subject to all the conditions and provisions of this policy, to pay the benefits and to provide the other rights and privileges which are set forth in this policy.

Policy Number: [00000-GTC]   Policy Effective Date: [January 1, 1964]

Policyholder: ⌈JOHN DOE COMPANY⌉
                              ⌊ Boston, Massachusetts ⌋

Jurisdiction of Issue: [Massachusetts]

Policy Anniversaries: [January 1, 1965],   and   [January 1st]   of each succeeding year.

Premium Due Dates: The Policy Effective Date, and the   [first]   day of [each succeeding calendar month.]

This policy is issued in consideration of the Policyholder's application and payment of premiums, and shall take effect on the Policy Effective Date.

This policy is delivered in the Jurisdiction of Issue and is governed by the laws of that jurisdiction. The Policy Specifications and the conditions and provisions in this and the following pages, including any amendments or riders included at issue or added thereafter, are part of this policy.

In Witness Whereof, the X Y Z Mutual Life Insurance Company has, by its President and Secretary, executed this policy as of the Policy Effective Date and caused it to be duly countersigned at Boston, Massachusetts.

Secretary   *President*

Countersigned_____ [John Smith]_____   _____
                            Registrar

G-101(C-1)
Ed. 1-64   **GROUP INSURANCE POLICY**
                                                              Printed in U.S.A.

835

INDEX

The following is a list of the principal provisions of this policy and of the policy pages in which they will be found. [Policy pages are treated here as consecutive sections, separated by rules, and policy page numbers are set bold face in brackets at the end of each section.]

Part 5

   Standard Provisions

$$\begin{bmatrix} \text{Part 1} \\ \text{Page 1–IND} \end{bmatrix}$$ INDEX

PART 1—POLICY SPECIFICATIONS

Participating Employers

As of the Policy Effective Date, [the Employers included as Participating Employers are the Policyholder and each of the following subsidiaries or affiliates of the Policyholder:]

$$\begin{bmatrix} \text{A Company} \\ \text{B Company} \end{bmatrix}$$

Employees Who May Be Insured

⌈The class of employees who may be insured under this policy shall consist only of⌉
those persons who are permanent, full-time employees of a Participating Em-
⌊ployer.

Date of Eligibility

⌈Each employee in the class of employees who may become insured shall become⌉
eligible on the latest of the following dates:
   (1) the Policy Effective Date;
   (2) the date he becomes a member of the class of employees who may become
       insured;
   (3) if he is required to complete a Waiting Period (see below) then the date
       following completion of the applicable waiting period.
The effective date of insurance shall be determined in accordance with the provision entitled "Date Insurance of Eligible Employee Becomes Effective" in Part 2
⌊of this policy.

Waiting Period

The length of continuous active service with his Participating Employer which an
employee must complete to become eligible is as follows:

For employee whose employment commenced on or prior to date his Employer is
included as a Participating Employer: _____ [None] _____

For employee whose employment commenced after the date his Employer is
included as a Participating Employer: _____ [3 Months] _____

If there is more than one Participating Employer under this policy, an employee who terminates employment with one Participating Employer and who, within 30 days thereafter, becomes employed by another Participating Employer shall receive credit toward his Waiting Period for his continuous active service with his former Participating Employer.

Inclusion of Participating Employers

An Employer may qualify for participation in the policy and become a Participating Employer only by being certified in writing by the Policyholder and approved in writing by the Insurer except that no Employer shall become a Participating Employer which does not have at least one employee who can become eligible for insurance, in addition to the proprietor or partners or officers, as the case may be, of the Employer.

An Employer which qualified for participation in the policy may become a Participating Employer only on an Entry Date specified below:

Entry Date for Participating Employers

In 1965, on the 15th of January, February, March, June, September and December. Thereafter, on the 15th day of March, June, September and December.

However, if an Employer ceases to be a Participating Employer, that Employer may, provided it again qualifies for participation in the policy, again become a Participating Employer but only on a policy anniversary, and only if evidence satisfactory to the Insurer of the insurability of all the eligible employees of that Employer is submitted to the Insurer without expense to it, prior to such policy anniversary.

If insurance is to be provided on a Contributory Basis for the employees of an Employer, that Employer cannot become a Participating Employer unless at least [75%] of the employees of that Employer who are eligible for insurance make the required written application therefor; except that if when an Employer applies to become a Participating Employer, it has less than [five] employees in the class of employees who could become insured under this policy, then in addition to any applicable requirements for evidence of insurability set forth in Part 2 under "Date Insurance of Eligible Employee Becomes Effective," the Insurer may require that satisfactory evidence of insurability be submitted to it, without expense to the Insurer, with respect to all such employees, before the Employer can become a Participating Employer.

If insurance is to be provided on a Noncontributory Basis for the employees of a Participating Employer, all the eligible employees of that Participating Employer who are acceptable to the Insurer for insurance must be insured.

If insurance for dependents of eligible employees of a Participating Employer is provided on a Contributory Basis, the dependents of at least [75%] of the eligible employees of that Participating Employer having dependents must be insured, except that if the Participating Employer has fewer than [five] eligible employees, then, in addition to any applicable requirements for evidence of insurability set forth in Part 2 under "Date Insurance of Eligible Dependent Becomes Effective," the Insurer may require that evidence of insurability be submitted, without expense to it, with respect to all the dependents of all such employees.

If insurance for dependents is provided on a Noncontributory Basis the dependents of all eligible employees of that Participating Employer having dependents must be insured.

If the Insurer determines at any time that a Participating Employer is not in compliance with all of the requirements for participation in the policy, the Insurer shall have the right to terminate the participation of that Employer in accordance with the provision entitled "Amendment, Renewal and Termination" set forth in Part 2 of the policy.

$$\begin{bmatrix} \text{Part 1} \\ \text{Page 1–PS} \end{bmatrix}$$ Policy Specifications

---

POLICY SPECIFICATIONS (Continued)

Insurance after Retirement

The amounts and plans of insurance available to retired employees described in the provision entitled "Employees Who May Become Insured" and their dependents after the employee's retirement date are described in the following pages.

Reduction in the employee's amount of Life Insurance shall be effective at midnight of the date immediately prior to his retirement date but if his Life Insurance becomes payable by reason of his death within the period of 31 days which begins with his retirement date, the maximum amount of insurance that shall be payable under this policy shall be the amount that was in force on his life on the date immediately prior to his retirement date. However, if an individual policy of life insurance is issued to the employee on the basis of his application therefor in accordance with the Conversion Privilege applicable to him under this policy, in an amount greater than the amount by which his Life Insurance was reduced as a result of his retirement, then he shall cease to be eligible for any insurance under this policy, and all insurance for him and for his dependents, if any, shall cease as of midnight of the date immediately prior to his retirement date.

Basis for Insurance

In accordance with the determination made by the Policyholder, insurance shall be provided on the __[Contributory]__ Basis for employees and on the __[Contributory]__ Basis for dependents.

Insurance Records

The records with respect to insurance under this policy shall be maintained by the __[Policyholder]_____.

Reduction of Benefits

The hospital board and room benefit payable under this policy for any day for which an employee is entitled to additional benefits during hospital confinement by virtue of the California Unemployment Insurance Act shall be the amount, if any, by which the board and room benefit otherwise payable under this policy for that day exceeds $[6.00].

$$\begin{bmatrix} \text{Part 1} \\ \text{Page 2–PS} \end{bmatrix}$$ Policy Specifications

POLICY SPECIFICATIONS (Continued)

Classification of Employees

For the purposes of insurance under this policy, employees are classified as follows:

Employees under age 65

Class I. Less than $5,000 of annual earnings

Class II. $5,000 and over of annual earnings

Retired employees

Class V. Retired prior to Policy Effective Date

Class VI. Retired on or after Policy Effective Date

Employees age 65 or over

Class III. Less than $5,000 of annual earnings

Class IV. $5,000 and over of annual earnings

If employees are classified by earnings, classification shall be based on earnings for a 40-hour week, or for the basic work-week established by the employee's Participating Employer, whichever is less, and shall not include bonus, overtime pay or incentive pay.

Change in class by reason of attainment of age 65 and by reason of retirement shall be effective on the employee's 65th birthday and on his retirement date, respectively.

Coverages Provided

The coverages becoming effective on the Policy Effective Date are only those for which amounts of insurance are shown in the Schedule of Insurance under "Amounts of Insurance" below. Any coverage for which no amount is shown in the Schedule of Insurance is not provided under this policy as of the Policy Effective Date.

Amounts of Insurance

The amount of insurance for each insured individual shall be determined from the following Schedule of Insurance. [Any change in amounts of an employee's insurance resulting from change in his classification under the following Schedule shall become effective on the Policy Anniversary coincident with or next following the date of change in his classification; provided, that an increase in the employee's amount of insurance shall become effective on that Policy Anniversary only if he is then actively at work with his Participating Employer on a regularly scheduled, full-time basis; otherwise the increase shall become effective on the first date thereafter on which he is actively at work with his Participating Employer.

Any change in amounts of a dependent's insurance resulting from change in his classification shall become effective on the Policy Anniversary coincident with or next following the date of change in his classification, except that if on that Policy Anniversary the dependent is disabled so as to be unable to carry on any substantial part of the regular and customary activities of a person in good health and of the same age and sex, an increase shall not become effective until the dependent recovers from that disability and resumes his usual activities.

$$\begin{bmatrix} \text{Part 1} \\ \text{Page 3–PS} \end{bmatrix}$$ Policy Specifications

POLICY SPECIFICATIONS (Continued)

SCHEDULE OF INSURANCE

Life: For Employees only

Amount of Insurance

Class I $20,000   Class IV $5,000
Class II $10,000   Class V $2,000
Class III $10,000   Class VI 50% of amount
on date prior to
retirement date

Accidental Death and Dis-
memberment: For Em-
ployees only

Full Amount of Insurance

Class I $20,000   Class IV $5,000
Class II $10,000   Class V None
Class III $10,000   Class VI None

Accident and Sickness:
For Employees only

*Weekly Benefit

Class I $30   Class IV $30
Class II $50   Class V   None
Class III $30   Class VI   None

Day of Disability When Benefits Begin: For disability due to
Injury [1st day]   Disease [8th day]   Pregnancy [no benefit]
Maximum Duration of Benefits: For disability due to
Injury or Disease [13 weeks]   Pregnancy [No benefit]

*The amount of weekly benefit shall in no event exceed two-thirds of basic weekly earnings, exclusive of bonus and overtime pay.

Hospital Expense For:	*Employees*	*Dependents*
For Injury or Disease		
Rate of Maximum Daily Benefit for Board and Room	$ 20	$ 20
Maximum Board and Room Benefit	1,040	1,040
Maximum Special Services Benefit	400	400
For Pregnancy		
Maximum Pregnancy Benefit	200	200

Surgical Operation Expense For:	*Employees*	*Dependents*
For Injury or Disease		
Maximum Surgical Benefit	[$ 300	$ 300]
For Pregnancy		

See "Obstetrical Procedures" in the Schedule of Surgical Operations and Benefits in the Surgical Operation Expense coverage.

Benefits for Pregnancy Existing on Individual's Effective Date: [Notwithstanding the Limitations of this policy, any benefits provided for pregnancy of a female employee or of the dependent wife of an employee, shall be provided for a pregnancy of the employee or dependent wife existing on her effective date, if that date is on or prior to January 31, 1965.]

Major Medical Expense

Benefit Specifications

(A) *Benefit Percentage*

For Employees:

> (1) 100% of the first $300 of "hospital charges," and 80% of the remainder of such charges, incurred during each continuous period of hospital confinement which commences during the Benefit Period; and
>
> (2) 80% of all "surgical charges" incurred during the Benefit Period; and
>
> (3) 80% of the amount by which the sum of the "medical charges" incurred during the Benefit Period exceeds the Deductible Amount, except that the Benefit Percentage for medical charges made by a psychiatrist or physician, and treatment of nervous or mental conditions of the employee while he is not hospital confined, shall be 50% and the maximum benefit payable for all such charges incurred in any period of twelve consecutive months shall not exceed $500.

For Dependents:

> 80% of the amount by which the sum of all hospital charges, surgical charges and medical charges incurred during the Benefit Period exceeds the Deductible Amount, except that the Benefit Percentage for medical charges made by a psychiatrist or physician, and treatment of nervous or mental conditions of the dependent while he is not hospital confined, shall be 50% and the maximum benefit payable for all such charges incurred in any period of twelve consecutive months shall not exceed $500.

(B) *Aggregate Maximum Benefit*

For Employees: [$10,000]   For Dependents: [$10,000]

(C) *Maximum Covered Expense for Daily Board and Room*

	For Employees	For Dependents
In Private Room: The daily charge most frequently made by the hospital for the best type of semi-private accommodations.		
In Other Accommodations:	$20	$20

(D) *Maximum Primary Pregnancy Benefit*

For Employees: [None]   For Dependents: [$200]

Note: See following for Deductible Amount.

Deductible Amount

The Deductible Amount applicable to each individual insured under this policy shall be [the sum of (1) and (2) below:]

	Employees	Dependents
(1) Cash Deductible	$100	$100

> (2) The total amount of benefits (including the value of all benefits furnished on a service basis) provided under a Base Plan with respect to Covered Expenses of the individual.
>
> The term "Base Plan" includes all other coverages furnishing benefits of a type included in this coverage and provided under this policy or under any other Group Policy issued by the Insurer, or under any law which af-

fords such benefits by reason of employment or place of residence, and under all other policies, plans or programs for which any Employer participating under this policy pays any part of the cost or makes deductions from employees' earnings.

If a person is not covered under all Base Plan coverages for which he is eligible, his amount under this subdivision (2) for Deductible Amount purposes shall be $300.

Accumulation Period   (for incurring Covered Expenses equal to Cash Deductible)

For Employees: [6 months]   For Dependents: [6 months]

Charges Subject to Cash Deductible

The Covered Expenses which are defined under the coverage as "hospital charges" and "surgical charges" shall not be subject to the Cash Deductible and are referred to as "non-subject" charges under this coverage. Only "medical charges" shall be subject to the Cash Deductible and are referred to under the coverage as "subject" charges.

Life Insurance for Dependents

The amount of Life Insurance on each dependent shall be

(a) fifty per cent of the amount of insurance on the life of the employee under this policy, or

(b) the amount determined in accordance with the following Table, whichever is less.

Classification of Dependents	Amount of Insurance
Wife or husband	$1,000
Children (by age)	
Under 15 days of age	None
15 days or over but under 6 months	100
6 months and over	500

Part 1
Page 4–PS   Policy Specifications

PART 2—GENERAL PROVISIONS, WORDS AND PHRASES

GENERAL PROVISIONS

Date Insurance of Eligible Employee Becomes Effective

An eligible employee for whom insurance is provided on a Contributory Basis, as shown under Policy Specifications, may become insured only by filing with his Participating Employer written application for insurance in a form furnished by or acceptable to the Insurer for that purpose and, if required by the Insurer, by furnishing evidence of his insurability satisfactory to the Insurer and without expense to it.

The Insurer may require satisfactory evidence of the employee's insurability, without expense to it,

(1) if the employee makes written application for insurance more than thirty-one days after his date of eligibility; or

(2) if the employee reapplies for insurance after his insurance had been discontinued at his request or because of his failure to make the required premium contribution to his Participating Employer; or

(3) if the employee makes written application for insurance when any individual policy of life insurance or accident and sickness insurance issued previously to him in accordance with a Conversion Privilege under the policy remains in force on his date of eligibility.

The insurance of such an employee shall become effective on the latest of the following dates:

(1) the date he becomes eligible;

(2) the date he makes written application for insurance;

(3) the date of approval by the Insurer at its Home Office of evidence of his insurability, if required by the Insurer;

[(4) if the latest of the dates described in (1), (2), and (3) above is not the first day of a Policy Month, then the first day of the Policy Month next following the latest of those dates;]

provided the employee is actively at work on the latest of said dates, otherwise on the first date thereafter on which he is actively at work.

Dependent Eligibility

Each person who is a dependent of an employee for whose dependents insurance is provided under the policy shall become eligible for insurance on the latest of the following dates:

[(1) the date the employee becomes eligible for Employee coverages;]
[(2) the date the person becomes a dependent.]

Date Insurance of Eligible Dependent Becomes Effective

Dependents for whom insurance is provided on a Contributory Basis, as shown under Policy Specifications, may become insured only if the employee files with his Participating Employer written application for insurance for his dependents in a form furnished by or acceptable to the Insurer for that purpose and, if required by the Insurer, by furnishing evidence of his dependents' insurability satisfactory to the Insurer and without expense to it.

The Insurer may require satisfactory evidence of the insurability of an employee's dependents, without expense to it,

(1) if the employee makes application to insure a dependent more than 31 days after the date the dependent becomes eligible; or

(2) if the employee reapplies for insurance for his dependents after the insurance of his dependents had been discontinued at the employee's request or because of his failure to make the required premium contribution to his Participating Employer; or

(3) if the employee makes written application to insure a dependent while an individual policy of life insurance or of accident and sickness insurance issued previously to or for the dependent in accordance with a Conversion Privilege under the policy remains in force.

[While an employee has one dependent insured under the policy he is not required to make application to insure additional dependents.]

The insurance of a dependent shall become effective on the latest of the following dates:

(1) the date he becomes eligible;

(2) the date the employee makes appropriate written application, if required for insurance for his dependents;

(3) the date the employee's insurance becomes effective;

(4) the date of approval by the Insurer at its Home Office of evidence of the dependent's insurability, if required by the Insurer;

⌈(5) if the latest of the dates described in (1) through (4) above is not the first⌉
    day of a Policy Month, then the first day of the Policy Month next follow-
⌊   ing the latest of those dates.   ⌋

Notwithstanding anything to the contrary set forth above, if on the date insurance would otherwise become effective a dependent is confined because of injury or disease in a hospital or other institution, or is confined at home or elsewhere so as to be unable to carry on any substantial part of the regular and customary activities of a person in good health and of the same age and sex, or if a dependent has been confined in a hospital within 31 days prior to the date insurance would otherwise become effective, the insurance of such dependent shall not become effective earlier than (a) the date following a period of 31 days during which the dependent has not been confined as set forth above, either in a hospital, at home or elsewhere, or (b) the date evidence of the dependent's complete recovery is received by the Insurer at its Home Office, whichever occurs first.

The foregoing shall not apply to postpone the effective date of the insurance of a child born while the employee's dependents are insured under the policy, but no Life Insurance for Dependents (if provided under the policy for the dependents of the employee) shall be in effect for such child while he is under 15 days of age.

⌈   Part 2   ⌉
⌊Page 1–GP(C)⌋   General Provisions

_____

_____

GENERAL PROVISIONS (Continued)

Discontinuance of Insurance of Employees

Part A—The insurance of an employee under a particular coverage shall be discontinued on the earliest of the following dates:

(1) the date his classification changes to a class of employees which is ineligible for insurance under that coverage;

(2) the date as of which the policy is amended making the class of employees of which he is a member ineligible for insurance under that coverage;

(3) the date of termination of that coverage for the class of employees of which he is a member.

Part B—The insurance of an employee under all coverages for which he is insured shall be discontinued on the earliest of the following dates:

(1) the date of termination of his employment (see paragraph below);

(2) if his insurance is provided on a Contributory Basis, the date of expiration of the period for which he last made the required premium contribution to his Participating Employer for his insurance;

(3) the date the participation of his Participating Employer in all insurance under the policy is discontinued;

(4) the date of termination of the policy.

Employment for insurance purposes terminates on the date the employee ceases active work with his Participating Employer, except that, in the circumstances specified below, employment shall be deemed to continue for insurance purposes, for the coverages specified, until the earlier of (a) the expiration of the period specified below, or (b) the date the employee's Participating Employer, acting in accordance with rules which preclude individual selection, terminates the employee's employment for insurance purposes, either by written notice to the Insurer or by any other means.

While Employee Is Absent from Work Due to	**Employment May Be Deemed to Continue for This Period*	*For These Coverages*
(i) Sickness or Injury	Indefinite	All coverages
(ii) Temporary layoff	Not beyond end of policy month next following policy month in which layoff begins	All coverages
(iii) Leave of absence	Not beyond end of policy month next following policy month in which leave of absence begins	Life Insurance and Accidental Death and Dismemberment Insurance
(iv) Retirement	Indefinite	All coverages except Accident and Sickness Insurance and Accidental Death and Dismemberment Insurance

* In no event will employment be deemed to continue beyond the date on which the employee commences active duty in the armed forces of any country or state or international organization.

Discontinuance of Insurance of Dependents

Part A—The insurance of a dependent under a particular coverage shall be discontinued on the earliest of the following dates:

(1) the date the employee's insurance classification is changed to one in which his dependents are ineligible for insurance under that coverage;

(2) the date as of which this policy is amended making the dependents of that class of employees of which the employee is a member ineligible for insurance under that particular coverage;

(3) the date of termination of that coverage for the dependents of that class of employees of which the employee is a member.

Part B—The insurance of a dependent under all coverages for which he is insured shall be discontinued on the earliest of the following dates:

(1) the date of discontinuance of the employee's insurance under all coverages for which he is insured;

(2) the date the dependent becomes eligible as an employee for insurance under this policy;

(3) the date he ceases to be included within the definition of the term "dependent";

(4) the date the dependent commences active duty in the armed forces of any country or state or international organization, or becomes a member of any civilian force auxiliary to any military force;

(5) if the dependent's insurance is provided on a Contributory Basis, the date of expiration of the period for which the employee last made the required premium contribution for the insurance of his dependents;

(6) the date of termination of this policy.

$$\left[\begin{array}{c} \text{Part 2} \\ \text{Page 2–GP} \end{array} \right]$$ **General Provisions**

GENERAL PROVISIONS (Continued)

Beneficiary of Employee

The employee's beneficiary shall be the person or persons designated by the employee in writing and entered in the insurance records maintained as provided under Policy Specifications.

If no beneficiary designation is in effect at the employee's death, or if there is no designated beneficiary then living, as to any part of the amount of insurance, the Insurer may, at its option, pay such part to the employee's estate or to any one or more of the following surviving relatives of the employee: wife, husband, child or children, mother, father, brothers or sisters.

If the beneficiary is a minor or is otherwise incapable of giving a valid release for any payment due, the Insurer may, at its option and until claim is made by the duly appointed guardian of such beneficiary, make payment of the amount of insurance payable to that beneficiary, at a rate not exceeding [$50] per month, to any relative by blood or connection by marriage of the beneficiary, or to any other person or institution appearing to it to have assumed custody and principal support of the beneficiary, for the sole benefit of the beneficiary. The liability of the Insurer shall be fully discharged to the extent that payments are made under this provision.

Change of Beneficiary

Changes in the employee's designation of beneficiary may be made by the employee by notice in writing given to his Participating Employer, but the new designation shall become effective only when it is entered in the insurance records maintained as provided under Policy Specifications, and then shall relate back to take effect as of the date the notice is signed, whether or not the employee is living when the new designation is entered in the insurance records, but without prejudice to the Insurer for any payment made or other action taken by the Insurer before the entry is made.

Optional Methods of Settlement

Any amount of insurance payable under this policy on account of the death of the employee shall be paid either in one amount or in accordance with the terms of a settlement option which has been agreed to and acknowledged by the Insurer.

A settlement option may be elected by the employee while he is insured, and may be changed or revoked by him at any time.

If no settlement option elected by the employee is in effect at his death, the beneficiary may elect a settlement option after the employee's death, subject to the Insurer's agreement to and acknowledgement of the option elected.

No settlement option shall be available as to any amount of insurance payable to an executor, administrator, trustee, corporation, partnership or association.

The rate of interest applicable to payments under an option shall be that determined by the Insurer to be applicable for the year in which death of the employee occurs but shall not be less than 2% per annum.

$$\begin{bmatrix} \text{Part 2} \\ \text{Page 3--GP} \end{bmatrix}$$ **General Provisions**

GENERAL PROVISIONS (Continued)

Dual Coverage Precluded

No person shall be insured or eligible for insurance under this policy simultaneously as an employee of more than one Participating Employer, or as both an employee and a dependent (if coverage for dependents is included in this policy) or as a dependent of more than one employee. If husband and wife are both eligible to have dependents insured, a dependent child or dependent children otherwise eligible for insurance may be insured only as dependents of the husband.

If a person's insurance under a particular coverage is discontinued and if he subsequently becomes insured again under a coverage which provides similar benefits to those provided under the prior coverage, any benefits becoming payable for death occurring or for charges incurred during the period that benefits for such death or charges are extended under the prior coverage, shall be those determined in accordance with his prior coverage or his subsequent coverage, whichever benefits are greater, but not both.

Data Required

The Policyholder shall furnish to the Insurer all information which the Insurer may require to enable it to administer the insurance and to determine the premiums therefor.

The insurance records maintained as provided under Policy Specifications must be sufficient to identify each Participating Employer having employees insured and to establish the insurance status of each person who is insured under any coverage provided by this policy.

All records of the Policyholder and of all Participating Employers which have a bearing on this policy or on any insurance under this policy shall be open to inspection by the Insurer at all reasonable times.

Clerical error shall not prejudice the rights of the Insurer or of any person having a beneficial interest in the insurance hereunder.

Assignment

Except for benefits that may become payable under this policy for hospital, surgical or medical expenses, neither this policy nor any rights or benefits thereunder may be assigned unless the Insurer consents in writing to such assignment.

$$\begin{bmatrix} \text{Part 2} \\ \text{Page 4--GP} \end{bmatrix}$$ **General Provisions**

GENERAL PROVISIONS (Continued)

Amendment, Renewal and Termination

This policy may be amended or terminated at any time by written agreement between the Insurer and the Policyholder.

The Policyholder may terminate this policy at any time by giving written notice of termination to the Insurer at its Home Office, but the date of termination shall not be less than [31 days] after the date the Insurer receives such notice unless an earlier date is mutually agreeable to the Insurer and to the Policyholder.

The Insurer may terminate
- (a) any coverage provided under this policy on a Contributory Basis, as of [the last day of any policy month] if less than [75%] of the employees who are eligible for that coverage on a Contributory Basis are then insured thereunder, or, with respect to a dependent coverage, if less than [75%] of the employees having dependents eligible for that coverage then have their dependents insured thereunder;
- (b) any coverage provided on a Noncontributory Basis, as of [the last day of any policy month] if less than [100%] of the employees who are eligible for that coverage on a Noncontributory Basis are then insured thereunder, or, with respect to a dependent coverage, if less than 100% of the employees having dependents eligible for that coverage then have their dependents insured thereunder;
- (c) this policy as of [the last day of any policy month] if the Insurer determines that fewer than [25] employees are then insured under this policy, or if the Policyholder does not duly perform in good faith its obligations pertaining to this policy.

by giving written notice of such termination to the Policyholder at least [31 days] prior to the date of termination.

This policy shall renew for a further term of one policy year, on each policy anniversary to which premiums have been paid in full, except that if either the Policyholder or the Insurer has given written notice to the other in accordance with the foregoing paragraphs of this provision that this policy is to terminate, this policy will not renew following its date of termination.

No amendment, renewal or termination of this policy shall require the consent of or notice to any employee or beneficiary or other person having a beneficial interest herein.

Only the President, a Vice President, the Secretary or an Assistant Secretary has power on behalf of the Insurer to make or change or terminate this Policy. No agent has authority to change this policy or to waive any of its provisions.

$$\left[\begin{array}{c} \text{Part 2} \\ \text{Page 5–GP} \end{array} \right]$$ **General Provisions**

GENERAL PROVISIONS (Continued)

Non-Waiver of Policy Provisions

Failure of the Insurer to insist upon compliance with any provision of this policy at any given time or under any given set of circumstances shall not operate to waive or modify such provision, or in any manner whatsoever to render it unenforceable, as to any other time or as to any other occurrence, whether the circumstances are, or are not, the same.

Policyholder Not Insurer's Agent

Neither the Policyholder nor any Participating Employer shall be considered the agent of the Insurer for any purpose under this policy.

Entire Contract

This policy, the application of the Policyholder, a copy of which is attached hereto and made a part hereof, and the individual applications, if any, of the employees insured shall constitute the entire contract.

All statements made by the Policyholder or by the individual employees shall, in the absence of fraud, be deemed representations and not warranties, and no statement made by the Policyholder or any employee or on their behalf shall be used in defense to a claim under this policy, unless it is contained in a written application signed by the employee and a copy of that application is or has been furnished to him or to his beneficiary.

$$\left[\begin{array}{c} \text{Part 2} \\ \text{Page 6–GP} \end{array} \right] \qquad \text{General Provisions}$$

POLICY WORDS AND PHRASES

Certain of the words and phrases used in this policy are listed below with the definition or explanation of the manner in which the term is used for the purposes of this policy.

(1) "coverage" means all of the terms and provisions appearing under the caption of that portion of this policy providing the particular kind of coverage.

(2) "full-time employee" means only an employee who customarily works a regularly scheduled work week with a Participating Employer of at least [30] hours per week [and shall include a proprietor or partner of a Participating Employer which is a proprietorship or partnership, provided he is actively engaged in and regularly devotes at least 30 hours per week to the conduct of the business of that Participating Employer].

(3) "actively at work"—an employee shall be considered "actively at work" for the purposes of insurance if he reports for work on the date in question at his usual place of employment with his Participating Employer and such usual place of employment is outside of his home, and if when he so reports he is able to perform all of the usual and customary duties of his occupation on a regular, full-time basis. If an employee does not so report, or if his usual place of employment with his Participating Employer is not outside of his home, he shall be considered "actively at work" if at any time on the date in question, he is neither (i) hospital confined, nor (ii) disabled to a degree that he could not

then have reported to a place of employment outside of his home and performed all of the usual and customary duties of his occupation on a regular,
full-time basis.

(4) "written notice" means notice in writing in a form supplied by or satisfactory
to the Insurer for that purpose.

(5) "policy month" means the period of one month beginning with that day in
each calendar month which corresponds to the day of the month on which
premiums are payable, whether payable monthly or otherwise.

(6) "policy year" means the period which begins, as to the first policy year, with
the Policy Effective Date, and as to each subsequent policy year, with a policy
anniversary, and ends with the date immediately prior to the next policy
anniversary.

(7) "injury" shall mean only a bodily injury sustained accidentally by external
means.

(8) "nonoccupational" means, with respect to injury, an injury which does not
arise out of and in the course of any employment for wage or profit; and
with respect to disease, means a disease in connection with which the person
is entitled to no benefits under any Workmen's Compensation law or similar
legislation.

(9) "wholly disabled" as used in the Accident and Health coverages for Employees
means disability to the extent that the employee is able to perform none of
the usual and customary duties of his occupation; and in Dependent coverages (if provided under the policy) means disability to the extent that the
dependent can perform none of the usual and customary duties or activities
of a person in good health and of the same age and sex.

(10) "physician" means only a person who is duly licensed (a) to prescribe and
administer any drugs, or (b) to perform surgical procedures.

(11) "hospital" means only an institution licensed as a hospital (if licensing is
required) and operated pursuant to law for the care and treatment of sick and
injured persons, which institution provides 24 hours nursing care and has
facilities both for diagnosis, and, except in the case of a hospital primarily
concerned with the treatment of chronic diseases, for major surgery. The term
"hospital" shall not be construed to include a hotel, rest home, nursing home,
convalescent home, place for custodial care, home for the aged, or a place used
primarily for the confinement or treatment of drug addicts or alcoholics.

(12) "hospital confinement"—a person shall be deemed to be confined in a hospital,
for the purposes of this policy, if his confinement continues for [18 consecutive
hours or longer]; or if a board and room charge is made in connection with his
confinement; or if the confinement results from a nonoccupational injury
requiring emergency care and commences [prior to midnight of the day following the date of the injury]; or if the confinement is required because of a surgical procedure.

(13) "reasonable and customary"—a charge shall be considered reasonable and
customary to the extent that it does not exceed the general level of charges
being made by others of similar standing in the locality where the charge is
incurred, when furnishing like or comparable treatment, services or supplies
to individuals of the same sex and of comparable age and income, for a similar
disease or injury. The term "locality" means a county or such greater area
as is necessary to establish a representative cross section of persons or other
entities regularly furnishing the type of treatment, services or supplies for
which the charge was made.

(14) "surgical procedure" means only the following:
    (a) a cutting operation; (b) suturing of a wound; (c) treatment of a fracture;
    (d) reduction of a dislocation; (e) radiotherapy (excluding radioactive

isotope therapy) if used in lieu of a cutting operation for removal of a tumor; (f) electrocautherization; (g) diagnostic and therapeutic endoscopic procedures; (h) injection treatment of hemorrhoids and varicose veins.

(15) "Accident and Health coverages" means all coverages under the policy except Life Insurance.

(16) "dependent" shall include only the following, provided they are not eligible to be insured under this policy as employees and, if previously insured as employees, are not eligible to receive any benefits under this policy as a result of a disability existing when insurance as an employee was discontinued:

    (i) the [wife or husband] of an employee, while not divorced or legally separated from the employee;

    (ii) each child of an employee, from the earlier of

        (a) the date he attains 15 days of age, or

        (b) the first date on which he is confined in a hospital and his mother is not confined in the same hospital,

    and while the child is unmarried, is not employed on a regular and full-time basis, is dependent on the employer for support, and

        (1) for purposes of Accident and Health Insurance for Dependents, is under 23 years of age;

        (2) for purposes of Life Insurance for Dependents, is under 21 years of age.

$$\begin{bmatrix} \text{Part 2} \\ \text{Page 1--DEF} \end{bmatrix}$$ Policy Words and Phrases

---

PART 3—COVERAGES, SPECIAL PROVISIONS

THIS COVERAGE PROVIDES LIFE INSURANCE FOR EMPLOYEES

Death Benefit

The Insurer will pay to an employee's beneficiary the amount of life insurance in force on the employee's life at the time of his death, as determined in accordance with the Schedule of Insurance shown for this coverage under Policy Specifications, upon receipt of due proof at its Home Office that the employee died while insured under this coverage.

Conversion Privilege

Part A. An employee whose entire amount of life insurance is discontinued because
    (a) his employment for insurance purposes is terminated, or
    (b) his classification changes to a class of employees which is ineligible for life insurance,
will be entitled to have an individual policy of life insurance issued to him by the Insurer, in an amount which shall not exceed the amount of his life insurance which discontinued for whichever of the reasons in (a) and (b) above is applicable.

Part B. An employee whose entire amount of life insurance is discontinued because
    (a) all life insurance under this policy is terminated, or

(b) this policy is amended making the class of employees of which he is a member ineligible for life insurance, or

(c) his Participating Employer's participation in all insurance under this policy is discontinued,

and who had then been continuously insured for life insurance under this policy for at least 5 years will be entitled to have an individual policy of life insurance issued to him by the Insurer, in an amount which shall not exceed

(i) the amount of life insurance which discontinued for whichever of the reasons in (a), (b) and (c) above is applicable, less any amount for which the employee is or becomes eligible under this or any other Group Policy within 31 days after the date his life insurance was discontinued, or

(ii) $2,000,

whichever is less.

Part C. Issue of the individual policy will be subject to all of the following conditions:

(1) No evidence of insurability shall be required.

(2) Written application for the individual policy and the first premium therefor must be delivered or mailed to the Insurer within 31 days after the date on which the employee's insurance under this coverage was discontinued.

(3) The individual policy will be in any one of the forms then customarily issued by the Insurer, except a policy of term insurance, and shall be without disability or other supplementary benefits.

(4) The premium for the individual policy will be determined by the Insurer from its then current rates, based upon the employee's attained age at his birthday nearest to the date of issue of the individual policy, upon the class of risk to which he then belongs, and upon the form and amount of the individual policy.

(5) Insurance under the individual policy will not become effective until the end of the 31-day period described in (2) above.

Benefit for Death during Conversion Period

Upon receipt of due proof at its Home Office of the death of the employee during the 31-day period within which he could have made application for an individual policy of life insurance under the provision entitled "Conversion Privilege," the Insurer will pay to the beneficiary as a death benefit the maximum amount for which an individual policy could have been issued to him under that provision, whether or not the employee had made application for an individual policy.

If he had made application for an individual policy, the designation in that application of a beneficiary different from the beneficiary under this Policy shall, notwithstanding any other provision of this Policy, effect a change of beneficiary under this Policy to the beneficiary designated in that application.

Waiver of Premium Benefit

The Insurer will waive the payment of premiums for the life insurance of an employee and will continue that insurance in force, upon receipt at its Home Office of due proof that the employee,

(1) while insured under this coverage and before his [60th] birthday, became

totally disabled (which as used in this provision shall mean totally disabled by injury or disease to the extent that he was able to perform no work for compensation or profit and was able to engage in no business or occupation), and

(2) has been continuously so disabled for at least [9 consecutive months] when the required proof is furnished.

The required proof may be furnished while the employee is insured but if not, then it must be furnished not more than [1 year] after the last date for which premium for his life insurance was paid by the Policyholder.

The initial period for which premium will be waived will commence with the date the required proof is received by the Insurer and will continue while the employee remains totally disabled, for up to 12 months from receipt of the required proof. Premium will be waived for succeeding periods of 12 months each while the employee continues to be totally disabled if due proof that his total disability continues is received by the Insurer at its Home Office during the last 3 months of the immediately preceding 12-month period.

The Insurer will have the right to require proof of the continuance of total disability of the employee from time to time during the first 2 years following receipt of due proof. After 2 years proof will be required not oftener than once a year. As part of any proof, the employee may be required to be examined at the Insurer's expense by a medical examiner designated by the Insurer.

The amount of life insurance on which premium will be waived under this provision shall be the amount which was in force on the life of the employee on the date he became totally disabled, or, if this provision applies to less than all of his life insurance under this policy, then the amount to which this provision applied on that date. In any event, his amount of life insurance on which premium is waived will be reduced if and when it would have been reduced under the Schedule of Insurance that would be applicable to him if he were insured under this coverage but not totally disabled.

If the employee dies within [1 year] after the last date for which premium was paid for his insurance under this coverage but before proof of his total disability was furnished to the Insurer, the amount of his life insurance for which premium was last paid will be paid by the Insurer to his beneficiary if due proof of his death, and that he was totally disabled from the date of cessation of premium payments to the date of his death, is received by the Insurer at its Home Office not more than [1 year] after his death.

If the employee ceases to be totally disabled, or if he fails to submit proof of continuance of his total disability when required, or if he fails to be examined medically when required, no further benefit will be provided for him under this provision in connection with that disability. If the employee does not return to active work in a class of employees eligible for life insurance under the policy, within 31 days after the date his benefits under this provision ceased, he may convert the life insurance that was subject to this provision, in accordance with the provision entitled "Conversion Privilege," as though his insurance had ceased on that date because of termination of employment.

If a benefit is payable under the provision entitled "Benefit for Death during Conversion Period" on account of the employee's death, the amount, if any, payable under this provision will be reduced by the amount of that benefit.

If an individual policy was issued on the employee's life in accordance with the provision entitled "Conversion Privilege" no payment will be made under this provision, if the individual policy is not surrendered to the Insurer without the payment of any claim on that policy except for refund of any premium paid thereon. The designation of a beneficiary under such an individual policy or in the application therefor (if the individual policy had not become effective) different from the beneficiary under this Policy shall, notwithstanding any other provision of this Policy to the contrary, effect a change of beneficiary under this Policy to the beneficiary so designated.

Termination of this policy will not affect the rights of any employee who is entitled to this benefit by reason of becoming totally disabled prior to termination of this policy. Benefits provided in accordance with this provision after the date of termination of this policy will not affect that termination or continue this policy in force after that date.

$$\begin{bmatrix} \text{Part 3} \\ \text{Page 1–EL} \end{bmatrix}$$ Coverages

THIS COVERAGE PROVIDES ACCIDENTAL DEATH AND DIS-MEMBERMENT INSURANCE FOR EMPLOYEES

Accidental Death and Dismemberment Indemnity

If an employee suffers any of the losses listed below as a result of a non-occupational injury, the Insurer will pay the amount of insurance specified for the loss in the Schedule of Indemnities below, upon receipt of due proof that
    (1) the injury occurred while the employee was insured under this coverage;
    (2) the loss occurred within 90 days after the injury;
    (3) the loss resulted directly and solely from the injury and independently of all other causes.

Schedule of Indemnities

Full Amount of Insurance for Loss of	One Half of the Full Amount of Insurance for Loss of
Life	Sight of One Eye
Both Hands	One Hand
Both Feet	One Foot
One Hand and One Foot	
Sight of Both Eyes	
One Hand and Sight of One Eye	
One Foot and Sight of One Eye	

Loss of hands or feet shall mean loss by severance at or above the wrist or ankle joint, and loss of sight shall mean total and irrecoverable loss of sight.

The total amount payable for all losses resulting from any one accident shall not exceed the employee's Full Amount of Insurance shown for this coverage under Policy Specifications.

Limitations

No benefit will be payable for any loss caused wholly or partly, directly or indirectly, by
    (a) disease, or bodily or mental infirmity, or medical or surgical treatment thereof; or

(b) ptomaines, or bacterial infections, except infection introduced through a visible wound accidentally sustained; or

(c) suicide while sane or insane, or intentionally self-inflicted injury; or

(d) war, or any act of war, whether declared or undeclared.

$$\begin{bmatrix} \text{Part 3} \\ \text{Page 1–ADD} \end{bmatrix}$$ Coverages

---

THIS COVERAGE PROVIDES ACCIDENT AND SICKNESS INSURANCE FOR EMPLOYEES

Benefit for Disability

If an employee, while insured under this coverage, becomes wholly disabled by a nonoccupational injury, or by a nonoccupational disease, or by a pregnancy (which term includes resulting childbirth or miscarriage) the Insurer will pay a weekly benefit at the rate applicable to the employee on the date the period of disability began, as determined in accordance with the Schedule of Insurance shown for this coverage under Policy Specifications.

Benefits will begin with that day in the period of disability which is shown under Policy Specifications as the Day of Disability When Benefits Begin for that disability, and will continue while the employee remains so disabled, but for not more than the number of weeks shown as Maximum Duration of Benefits during any one continuous period of disability, whether from one or more causes.

Not more than one benefit will be payable for any day of disability whether the employee is disabled by one or more causes on that day.

Continuous Period of Disability

Successive periods of disability which are due to injury or disease and which are separated by less than 2 weeks of active work on full time will be considered one continuous period of disability unless the Insurer receives evidence satisfactory to it that the subsequent disability is due to causes which are unrelated to the causes of the previous disability and commences after the employee has returned to work and has completed one full day of active service with his Participating Employer.

Successive periods of disability due to the same pregnancy shall be considered one continuous period of disability.

Limitations

No benefit shall be payable,

(a) for that portion of a period of disability during which the employee is not under treatment by a physician;

(b) for any day in a period of disability which occurs prior to the day shown under Policy Specifications as the Day of Disability When Benefits Begin;

(c) for any disability caused by or resulting from a pregnancy which existed on the date the employee became insured under this coverage unless so provided under Policy Specifications.

$$\begin{bmatrix} \text{Part 3} \\ \text{Page 1–AS(MB)} \end{bmatrix}$$ Coverages

THIS COVERAGE PROVIDES HOSPITAL EXPENSE INSURANCE FOR EMPLOYEES AND DEPENDENTS

Benefits for Expenses Due to Injury or Disease

The Insurer will pay the benefits described in (A) and (B) below for the charges described therein which are made to an employee or to a dependent in connection with his hospital confinement,

(1) which results directly from a nonoccupational injury or a nonoccupational disease of the employee or dependent, as the case may be, and

(2) which commences while he is insured under this coverage.

(A) Benefit for Board and Room

A benefit equal to the reasonable and customary charges made by the hospital for board and room of the employee or dependent, as the case may be, up to a maximum of

(i) the applicable Rate of Maximum Daily Benefit for Board and Room shown for this coverage under Policy Specifications, multiplied by

(ii) the number of days in the period of confinement for which the hospital charges for board and room of the employee or dependent,

but the total benefit that shall be payable for the charges made for board and room during all hospital confinements which are considered as occurring during a continuous period of disability shall not exceed the applicable Maximum Board and Room Benefit shown for this coverage under Policy Specifications.

(B) Benefit for Special Services

A benefit equal to the reasonable and customary charges made in connection with the confinement,

(i) by the hospital for services or supplies furnished to the employee or dependent, as the case may be, for his use during his hospital confinement, including charges for blood and blood plasma to the extent the charges are not reduced by blood donations (but not including charges for board and room, or for special nursing services, or for services of a physician),

(ii) for anesthetics and the administration thereof, and

(iii) for local use of an ambulance,

and which are incurred before the Maximum Board and Room Benefit provided in (A) above becomes payable, but the total benefit that shall be payable for the charges described in (i) through (iii) above made in connection with all hospital confinements which are considered as occurring during a continuous period of disability shall not exceed the applicable Maximum Special Services Benefit shown for this coverage under Policy Specifications.

Extension of Benefits

If an employee or dependent is wholly disabled as a result of a nonoccupational injury or a nonoccupational disease when his insurance under this coverage is discontinued and if he becomes confined in a hospital as a result of a nonoccupational injury or a nonoccupational disease, within 3 months thereafter and during the continuance of that disability, the same benefits shall be payable for the charges made in connection with that hospital confinement that would have been payable if the confinement commenced while he was insured.

Continuous Period of Disability

Successive periods of hospital confinement shall be considered as occurring during one continuous period of disability unless the Insurer receives evidence satisfactory to it that the causes of the later period of hospital confinement are unrelated to the causes of the previous period of hospital confinement, or that the later period of hospital confinement commenced after the employee or dependent, as the case may be, completely recovered from the causes of his previous period of hospital confinement, or, in the case of an employee, commenced after he had returned to work and completed one full day of active service with his Participating Employer.

Benefit for Expenses Due to Pregnancy

The Insurer will pay the benefits described in (A) and (B) above for charges described therein, if incurred by a female employee or by the dependent wife of an employee in connection with hospital confinement which results directly from pregnancy, if the confinement commenced while she was insured under this coverage, or after the date her insurance ceased if the pregnancy existed on that date.

The total benefit that shall be payable for all such charges resulting from any one pregnancy shall not exceed the applicable Maximum Pregnancy Benefit shown for this coverage under Policy Specifications, and shall be subject to the respective maximum benefits provided under (A) and (B) above (the benefits being those applicable on the date insurance ceased, if the confinement commenced after that date); provided, however, that no benefit shall be payable for any charge made in connection with pregnancy which existed on the date the female employee or the dependent wife, as the case may be became insured under this coverage, unless so provided under Policy Specifications.

Limitations

No benefit shall be payable for a charge,
   (a) which is incurred in connection with confinement for general health examination or confinement for a surgical procedure or treatment performed primarily for beautification;
   (b) which is incurred under any of the circumstances described in the provision entitled "General Exclusions" set forth in the Special Provisions section of this Part 3;
   (c) which is incurred in connection with confinement of a child prior to the date the child attains 15 days of age and while the mother is confined in the same hospital.

$$\begin{bmatrix} \text{Part 3} \\ \text{Page 1--EDH} \end{bmatrix}$$ Coverages

---

THIS COVERAGE PROVIDES SURGICAL OPERATION EXPENSE INSURANCE FOR EMPLOYEES AND DEPENDENTS

Benefits for Expense Due to Injury or Disease

The Insurer will pay a benefit for the charge made to an employee or to a dependent by a physician in connection with each surgical procedure performed on the employee or dependent, as the case may be, while he is insured under this coverage and as a result of a nonoccupational injury or a nonoccupational disease.

The benefit shall be equal to the amount of the charge made by a physician,
  (1) for performing the procedure, and
  (2) for necessary pre-operative treatment during hospital confinement, and customary post-operative treatment, furnished in connection with the procedure,

SCHEDULE OF SURGICAL PROCEDURES AND BENEFITS

	MAXIMUM PAYMENT
INTEGUMENTARY SYSTEM	
Incision and drainage of one or more sebaceous cysts, furuncles, carbuncles or any other superficial abscesses:	
requiring hospital confinement	$ 25.00
not requiring hospital confinement	10.00
Excision (including simple closure) of one or more benign lesions of skin, subcutaneous tissue or mucous membrane:	
requiring hospital confinement	25.00
not requiring hospital confinement	10.00
Excision of malignant tumors of face, lip or skin	50.00
Excision of pilonidal cyst or sinus	50.00
Suture of wound, simple	
1 inch or less (25 mm)	5.00
over 1 inch up to 2 inches (2.6-5.0 cm)	10.00
over 2 inches up to 3 inches (5.1-7.5 cm)	12.50
50% for each additional wound by size.	
Breast	
Partial mastectomy or excision of cyst or tumor requiring hospital confinement	50.00
Complete (simple) mastectomy	100.00
Radical mastectomy, including breast, pectoral muscles and axillary lymph nodes	150.00
MUSCULOSKELETAL SYSTEM	
Bones (alveolar processes excepted)	
Excision of bone cyst, chondroma or exostosis: humerus, femur, tibia or radius	50.00
Fracture, treatment of, simple	
Thigh, vertebra or vertebrae, pelvis (coccyx excepted)	75.00
Leg, kneecap, upper arm, ankle (Pott's)	50.00
Lower jaw, collar bone, shoulder blade, forearm, wrist (Colles'), skull	25.00
Hand, foot	15.00
Fingers or toes, each	10.00
Nose	10.00
Rib or ribs, three or more	25.00
fewer than three	10.00
Compound fractures — maximum will be one and one-half times the amount for corresponding simple fracture.	
Open operation — maximum will be twice the amount for corresponding simple fracture (bone grafting or bone splicing or metallic fixation at point of fracture considered as open operation).	
Joints	
Arthrotomy or capsulotomy with exploration or drainage (tapping excepted)	25.00
Tapping: paracentesis	15.00
Excision of intervertebral disc	150.00
Excision of semilunar cartilage, knee joint	100.00
Arthrectomy or Arthrodesis	
Hip joint	150.00
Knee or elbow joint	125.00
Shoulder, wrist or ankle joint	100.00
Dislocations, reduction	
Hip, ankle joint, elbow or knee joint (patella excepted)	35.00
Shoulder	25.00
Collar bone	20.00
Lower jaw, wrist or patella	15.00
Open operation — maximum will be twice the amount shown above.	
Ligaments and Tendons	
Cutting or transplant, single	50.00
multiple	75.00
Suturing of tendon, single	35.00
multiple	50.00
Extremities	
Amputations, complete procedure:	
Thigh, leg	125.00
Upper arm, forearm, entire hand or foot	100.00
Fingers or toes, each	15.00
RESPIRATORY SYSTEM	
Submucous resection, nasal septum	50.00
Sinus operation by cutting (antrum puncture excepted)	50.00
Laryngectomy	200.00
Tracheotomy	75.00
Bronchoscopy, diagnostic	40.00
Lobectomy, total or subtotal	200.00
Complete thoracoplasty	200.00
Pneumothorax: intrapleural injection of air, initial	25.00
subsequent, each (not more than 12)	10.00

	MAXIMUM PAYMENT
CARDIOVASCULAR SYSTEM	
Valvulotomy or commissurotomy, mitral	$200.00
Varicose Veins	
Injection treatment, complete procedure, one or both legs	40.00
Cutting operation, complete procedure, one leg	50.00
both legs	75.00
DIGESTIVE SYSTEM	
Tonsillectomy, adenoidectomy or both	30.00
Esophagotomy, transthoracic	200.00
Esophagoscopy, diagnostic	40.00
Gastroenterostomy	150.00
Gastrectomy, subtotal	200.00
Transthoracic approach to stomach or diaphragm	200.00
Bowel resection, small or large	200.00
Appendectomy	100.00
Proctectomy, complete, combined abdomino-perineal	200.00
Fistulotomy or fistulectomy, single	50.00
multiple	75.00
Fissurectomy	25.00
Hemorrhoidectomy, external	25.00
internal or internal and external	50.00
Enucleation or excision of external thrombosed hemorrhoids	15.00
Cholecystectomy or other operation on gall bladder	150.00
Exploratory laparotomy or lysis of abdominal adhesions	100.00
Herniotomy, single	100.00
more than one hernia	125.00
URINARY SYSTEM	
Nephrectomy or nephrotomy	200.00
Nephropexy	150.00
Removal of tumors or stones in ureter or bladder	
by cutting operation	100.00
by endoscopic means	35.00
Cystoscopy, diagnostic	25.00
MALE GENITAL SYSTEM	
Circumcision	15.00
Orchiectomy or excision of hydrocele, varicocele, epididymis,	
unilateral	50.00
bilateral	75.00
Prostatectomy, perineal or suprapubic	150.00
transurethral	100.00
FEMALE GENITAL SYSTEM	
Repair of cystocele, with or without urethrocele	75.00
Repair of rectocele	75.00
Repair of cystocele, rectocele and perineoplasty, with or without repair of urethrocele	100.00
Hysterectomy, total or subtotal	150.00
Trachelectomy: amputation of cervix	50.00
Dilatation and curettage of uterus (non puerperal), cervix cauterization or conization, polypectomy or any combination of these	25.00
Other cutting operations on uterus and its appendages by laparotomy	100.00
ENDOCRINE SYSTEM	
Excision of cyst or adenoma of thyroid	100.00
Thyroidectomy, subtotal	150.00
NERVOUS SYSTEM	
Craniotomy (other than burr holes)	200.00
Sympathectomy, thoracic	200.00
Trephination (burr holes), unilateral	25.00
Operation for lesion of spinal cord or meninges	200.00
Operation with removal of portion of vertebra or vertebrae (except coccyx, transverse or spinous process)	150.00
Removal of part or all of coccyx, or of transverse or spinous process	50.00
EYE	
Removal of eyeball	75.00
Reattachment of retina or corneal transplant	200.00
Cataract, extraction of lens, unilateral	150.00
Any other cutting operation into the eyeball (through the cornea or sclera) or operation for strabismus	100.00
EAR	
Mastoidectomy, unilateral or bilateral, simple	100.00
radical	150.00
Fenestration, unilateral or bilateral	200.00
OBSTETRICAL PROCEDURES	
Caesarean section	100.00
Removal of extrauterine embryo (ectopic pregnancy) by laparotomy	100.00
Delivery of child or children	50.00
Miscarriage, treatment	25.00

The Insurer shall determine a benefit for any surgical procedure not included in this Schedule consistent with the benefit for any listed procedure of comparable difficulty and complexity, unless payment of a benefit for the procedure is excepted by the Schedule or by the other terms of the Policy, but such benefit shall not exceed the largest benefit shown in this Schedule.

but shall not exceed the Maximum Payment determined for the procedure in accordance with the applicable Schedule of Surgical Operations and Benefits, except that

(a) the total benefit that shall be payable for two or more procedures performed through the same abdominal incision shall not exceed the amount determined in accordance with said Schedule for that one of such procedures for which the largest amount is payable;

(b) the total benefit that shall be payable for two or more procedures performed on the anus or rectum or both (except for cancer) at the same operative session shall not exceed one and one-half times the maximum payment determined in accordance with said Schedule for that one of such procedures for which the largest amount is payable;

(c) the total benefit that shall be payable for all procedures performed at the same operative session, or during one continuous period of disability, shall not exceed the applicable Maximum Surgical Benefit, shown for this coverage under Policy Specifications.

Continuous Period of Disability

Successive procedures which are performed at separate operative sessions shall be considered as having been performed during one continuous period of disability, unless the Insurer receives evidence satisfactory to it that the causes of the later procedure are unrelated to the causes of the previous procedure, or that the later procedure was performed after the employee or dependent, as the case may be, completely recovered from the causes of the previous procedure, or, in the case of an employee, was performed after he had returned to work and completed one full day of active service with his Participating Employer.

Extension of Benefits

If an employee or dependent is wholly disabled as a result of a nonoccupational injury or a nonoccupational disease when his insurance under this coverage is discontinued and if he undergoes a surgical procedure as a result of a nonoccupational injury or a nonoccupational disease, within 3 months thereafter and during the continuance of that disability, the same benefit shall be payable for that procedure that would have been payable if it had been performed while he was insured.

Benefits for Expenses Due to Pregnancy

The Insurer will pay a benefit, in an amount determined in accordance with the foregoing provisions, for the charge made to a female employee or to the dependent wife of an employee, in connection with a surgical procedure specified in the Schedule under the heading "Obstetrical Procedures" which is performed on the employee or dependent wife while she is insured under this coverage, or after the date her insurance ceased if the pregnancy existed on that date (the benefit being that applicable on the date insurance ceased, if the procedure is performed after that date); provided, however, that no benefit shall be payable for any charges made in connection with a pregnancy which existed on the date the female employee or the dependent wife, as the case may be, became insured under this coverage, unless so provided under Policy Specifications.

Limitations

No benefit shall be payable for any charge,

(a) in connection with a surgical procedure performed primarily for beautification;

(b) in connection with a surgical procedure performed by a dentist, other than the excision of impacted teeth or of a tumor or cyst;

(c) which is incurred under any of the circumstances described in the provision entitled "General Exclusions" set forth in the Special Provisions section of this Part 3;

(d) in connection with a surgical procedure for circumcision of a child prior to the date the child attains 15 days of age.

$$\begin{bmatrix} \text{Part 3} \\ \text{Page 1–EDS} \end{bmatrix}$$
Coverages

THIS COVERAGE PROVIDES MAJOR MEDICAL EXPENSE INSURANCE FOR EMPLOYEES AND DEPENDENTS

ON THE CALENDAR YEAR PLAN

Benefits for Expenses Due to Injury or Disease

The Insurer will pay a benefit for Covered Expenses (as defined below) incurred by an employee or by a dependent during a Calendar Year (as described below) following satisfaction of the Cash Deductible, while insured under this coverage and as a result of a nonoccupational injury or a nonoccupational disease.

The benefit payable for the covered expenses so incurred shall be equal to the amount determined in accordance with the provision entitled "Benefit Percentage" shown for this coverage under Policy Specifications but the total benefit that shall be payable for all covered expenses incurred during the lifetime of the employee or dependent, as the case may be (whether or not he is continuously insured), including any benefits payable for expenses incurred following discontinuance of his insurance under this coverage, shall not exceed the applicable Aggregate Maximum Benefit shown for this coverage under Policy Specifications, except to the extent that it has been reinstated in accordance with the provision below entitled "Reinstatement of Aggregate Maximum Benefit."

Extension of Benefits

If an employee or dependent is wholly disabled as a result of a nonoccupational injury or a nonoccupational disease when his insurance under this coverage is discontinued and if he incurs charges as a result of a nonoccupational injury or a nonoccupational disease, within 1 year after that date and during the continuance of that disability, the same benefit shall be payable for the charges so incurred that would have been payable if they had been incurred while he was insured.

Satisfying the Cash Deductible

(Under this provision, a "subject" charge is a charge which is subject to the Cash Deductible, as specified under Policy Specifications, and a "non-subject" charge is a charge which is not subject to the Cash Deductible.)

(1) When the provision entitled "Charges Subject to Cash Deductible" under Policy Specifications stipulates that all charges for covered expenses are "subject" charges, the employee or dependent, as the case may be, shall satisfy the Cash Deductible by incurring, while insured under this coverage and within a period equal to or less than the applicable Accumulation Period, covered expenses in an amount which exceeds the applicable Base Plan Deductible (if any) by the amount of the applicable Cash Deductible.

(2) When the provision entitled "Charges Subject to Cash Deductible" stipulates that covered expenses defined as (a) hospital charges, or (b) hospital charges and surgical charges, are "non-subject" charges, the employee or dependent, as the case may be, shall satisfy the Cash Deductible by incurring, while insured under this coverage and within a period equal to or less than the applicable Accumulation Period, "subject" charges in an amount which exceeds the applicable Base Plan Deductible (if any) by the amount of the applicable Cash Deductible.

(3) Only covered expenses incurred in a Calendar Year may be included in the total amount of covered expenses for that year, or applied to satisfy the Cash Deductible for that Calendar Year, except that if the Cash Deductible for a Calendar Year is satisfied in whole or in part by covered expenses incurred during the last three months of that year, the amount of covered expenses incurred in that three-month period and applied toward satisfaction of the Cash Deductible for that year shall be carried forward and applied toward satisfaction of the Cash Deductible for the next Calendar Year, but in that event the date of incurral of the first covered expense carried forward shall commence an Accumulation Period.

(4) A charge for a covered expense shall be deemed to be incurred on the date the employee or dependent receives or is furnished the item or service for which the charge is made.

Common Accident

If an employee and one or more of his dependents, or if two or more of his dependents, while insured under this coverage, sustain injuries in the same accident and incur covered expenses as a result of such injuries, the largest of the Deductible Amounts applicable to the persons sustaining injuries in that accident shall be applied, but only once with respect to those covered expenses which are received by such persons as a result of such injuries. However, if any of such persons had, prior to the date of the accident, satisfied the applicable Deductible Amount in that Calendar Year, the covered expenses incurred on his account as a result of the accident shall be included, for the purpose of determining benefits, with his covered expenses which are not incurred as a result of injuries sustained in that accident, but shall not be included for any purpose with the covered expenses incurred by the other persons sustaining injuries in that accident.

Definitions

For the purpose of this coverage, the following terms shall have the meanings set forth below:

(1) The term "hospital charges" shall mean only the following covered expenses:
   (a) charges made by a hospital for board and room, and charges made by the hospital for other hospital services and supplies furnished to the employee or dependent, as the case may be, for his use while he is confined therein (but not including charges for special nursing services or for services of physicians or surgeons);
   (b) charges for anesthetics and the administration thereof when incurred during hospital confinement;
   (c) charges for local use of an ambulance when incurred in connection with hospital confinement.

(2) The term "surgical charges" shall mean the covered expenses incurred for a surgical procedure and for necessary post-operative treatment in connection with the surgical procedure.

(3) The term "medical charges" shall mean the covered expenses incurred for radioactive isotope therapy, and for any other radiotherapy which does not qualify as a surgical procedure (as defined in Page 2–DEF), and those other covered expenses which are not hospital charges or surgical charges as defined above.

Covered Expenses

Charges made for any of the services or supplies in the following List of Covered Items shall be considered "covered expenses" to the extent that the charges are reasonable and customary, except that

(a) charges made by a hospital for board and room for each day shall be considered "covered expenses" only to the extent of the applicable Maximum Covered Expense for Daily Board and Room shown for this coverage under Policy Specifications; and

(b) charges made by a psychiatrist or physician for medical treatment of nervous or mental conditions of the employee or dependent, as the case may be, furnished to him while he is not hospital confined shall be considered "covered expenses" only up to a maximum of $20 for each treatment and for a maximum of 3 treatments in any one calendar week.

LIST OF COVERED ITEMS

(1) Board and room furnished by a hospital while the employee or dependent, as the case may be, is confined.

(2) Hospital services and supplies furnished by a hospital to the employee or dependent, as the case may be, for his use while he is confined (not including board and room, special nursing services, or services of a physician).

(3) Medical treatment by a physician.

(4) Surgical procedure performed by a physician.

(5) Private duty nursing service furnished in a hospital or elsewhere by a registered graduate nurse who is entitled to use the suffix "R.N." after his or her name [and private duty nursing service furnished by a registered or licensed practical nurse in a hospital (but not elsewhere) if the attending physician certifies in writing that a registered graduate nurse (R.N.) was not available], provided in any case that such nurse is one who does not ordinarily reside in the home of the employee and is not a member of the employee's immediate family (which, for purposes of this coverage, consists of the employee's wife or husband, and the children, brothers, sisters and parents of the employee and of the employee's wife or husband).

(6) Local use of an ambulance.

(7) The following services and supplies:

(i) Drugs and medicines obtainable only on a physician's prescription;

(ii) Anesthetics and oxygen and the administration thereof;

(iii) Rental (or, at the Insurer's option, purchase if the Insurer determines that cost of purchase is less than anticipated total rental charges) of iron lung, oxygen tent, hospital bed, wheel chair and similar durable medical equipment designed primarily for use in a hospital for therapeutic purposes;

(iv) Blood and blood plasma, and the administration thereof, to the extent the charges therefor are not reduced by blood donations;

(v) Braces, crutches and prostheses when necessitated by an injury which occurs, or by a disease which commences, while the employee or dependent, as the case may be, is insured under this coverage, including charges for replacement when required because of pathological change, but not including charges for repair or maintenance;

(vi) X-ray examinations and laboratory tests;

(vii) Physiotherapy.

Exclusions

The term "Covered Expenses" shall not include any charge,

(1) for or in connection with general health examinations;

(2) for eye examinations made for or in connection with diagnosis or treatment of astigmatism, myopia or hyperopia;

(3) for the fitting or cost of eye glasses or hearing aid, except when necessitated by damage to the natural eye or ear as a result of an injury which occurs while the employee or dependent, as the case may be, is insured under this coverage;

(4) for a surgical procedure performed by a dentist, other than the excision of impacted teeth or of a tumor or cyst, or for orthodontia or other dental work or treatment, except when necessitated by damage to sound natural teeth as a result of an injury which occurs while the employee or dependent, as the case may be, is insured under this coverage;

(5) for or in connection with a surgical procedure or treatment performed primarily for beautification, or for hospital confinement for such surgical procedure or treatment;

(6) for transportation or travel other than local use of an ambulance;

(7) for any item described in the provision entitled "Covered Expenses,"

(i) which is received in connection with an injury or disease resulting from war or any act of war, whether declared or undeclared, which war or act of war occurs while the employee or dependent, as the case may be, is insured under this coverage;

(ii) which is received in connection with an injury or disease which existed on the date the employee or dependent, as the case may be, became insured under this coverage, unless

(a) in the case of an employee, it is received after the employee completed a period of at least 90 consecutive days of employment with his Participating Employer, including the date on which he became insured under this coverage, or

(b) in the case of a dependent, it is received after the dependent completed a period of at least 90 consecutive days while the employee was continuously employed by his Participating Employer, including the date on which the dependent became insured under this coverage,

during which period the employee or dependent, as the case may be, neither received medical care or treatment, nor consulted a physician, for or in connection with that injury or disease; [provided, that this subdivision (ii) shall not apply to any employee or dependent who became insured under this coverage on the date this coverage first became effective under this policy, or within 31 days after that date, or within 31 days after return to active work of an employee who became eligible for this coverage on the date it first became effective under this policy but who was not actively at work on that date; nor shall this subdivision apply to a child who became insured under this coverage on or prior to the date he attained 15 days of age];

(iii) which is received as a result of pregnancy (which term includes resulting childbirth or miscarriage), except when received as a result of and in connection with a surgical procedure for extra-uterine pregnancy or complications of pregnancy (both of which conditions shall be considered "disease" for the purposes of this coverage) for which a medically-indicated intra-abdominal surgical procedure is performed, but in that event the charges for items received as a result of and in connection with such surgical procedure shall be included as "covered expense" only to the extent that the sum of the charges exceeds the amount of any Primary Pregnancy Expense Benefit that may be payable under this coverage for hospital and surgical charges incurred in connection with that pregnancy;

(iv) which is received after the applicable Aggregate Maximum Benefit becomes payable and before any reinstatement of that benefit;

(v) which is received under any of the circumstances described in the provision entitled "General Exclusions" set forth in the Special Provisions section of this Part 3.

Reinstatement of Aggregate Maximum Benefit

If benefits in an aggregate amount of $1,000 or more become payable for covered expenses incurred by an employee or dependent, as the case may be, the applicable Aggregate Maximum Benefit may be reinstated if evidence of his insurability satisfactory to the Insurer is submitted to it. The Aggregate Maximum Benefit applicable on the date of approval of such evidence by the Insurer at its Home Office shall be reinstated on that date if he is eligible under this coverage on that date, provided, (1) in the case of an employee, that he is then actively at work with his Participating Employer, otherwise reinstatement shall be effective on the first date thereafter on which he is actively at work with his Participating Employer in the class of employees eligible for insurance under this coverage; and (2) in the case of a dependent, that he is not then prevented by injury or disease from carrying on any substantial part of the regular and customary duties of a person of like age and sex, otherwise reinstatement shall be effective on the date he recovers and resumes substantially all of said duties, if he is then eligible for insurance under this coverage.

Primary Pregnancy Expense Benefits

If a female employee or the dependent wife of an employee, as a result of pregnancy
(1) becomes confined in a hospital and incurs hospital charges, or
(2) undergoes a surgical procedure specified below as an obstetrical procedure and incurs surgical charges for that procedure,
while insured under this coverage, or after the date her insurance ceased if the pregnancy existed on that date, a benefit shall be payable in an amount equal to the hospital charges and surgical charges incurred as a result of that pregnancy, but the total amount payable under this provision for all charges incurred in connection with any one pregnancy shall not exceed the Maximum Primary Pregnancy Benefit shown for this coverage under Policy Specifications (the benefit being that applicable on the date insurance ceased, if the confinement commences or the procedure is performed after that date); provided, however, that no benefit shall be payable for any charges made in connection with a pregnancy which existed on the date the female employee or the dependent wife, as the case may be, became insured under this coverage, unless so provided under Policy Specifications.

Any benefits paid or payable under this provision shall be included in calculating the aggregate benefits paid or payable to or on account of the employee or dependent wife, as the case may be, under Major Medical Expense Insurance, of which this provision is a part.

Obstetrical Procedures

For the purpose of this provision the term "obstetrical procedure" shall include only (1) delivery of child or children, (2) treatment of miscarriage, (3) non-elective, medically indicated Caesarean section, and (4) abdominal operation for extra-uterine pregnancy.

$$\left[\begin{array}{c} \text{Part 3} \\ \text{Page 1–EDMM(BP)} \end{array} \right]$$ Coverages

---

THIS COVERAGE PROVIDES LIFE INSURANCE FOR DEPENDENTS

(The term "spouse" as used in this coverage shall mean only the dependent wife of an employee, unless the term "dependent" as defined in Part 2, Page 3-DEF, of this policy includes the wife or husband, as the case may be, of an employee, in which case the term "spouse" shall mean wife or husband, who shall be referred to in this coverage in the feminine gender.)

Death Benefit

The Insurer will pay to a dependent's beneficiary the amount of life insurance in force on the dependent's life at the time of his death, as determined in accordance with the Schedule of Insurance shown for this coverage under Policy Specifications, upon receipt of due proof at its Home Office that the dependent died while insured under this coverage.

Conversion Privilege

Part A. A spouse whose entire amount of life insurance is discontinued because
    (a) the employee's employment for insurance purposes is terminated, or
    (b) the classification of the spouse is changed to a class of dependents in which she is ineligible for life insurance under this coverage,
will be entitled to have an individual policy of life insurance issued to her by the Insurer, in an amount which shall not exceed the amount of her life insurance which discontinued for whichever of the reasons in (a) and (b) above is applicable.

Part B. A spouse whose entire amount of life insurance is discontinued because
    (a) all life insurance for dependents under this policy is discontinued, or
    (b) the policy is amended making the class of dependents of which the spouse is a member ineligible for life insurance, or
    (c) the participation of the employee's Participating Employer in all insurance under this policy is discontinued,
and who had then been continuously insured under this coverage for at least 5 years will be entitled to have an individual policy of life insurance issued to her by the Insurer, in an amount which shall not exceed
    (i) the amount of her life insurance which discontinued for whichever of the reasons in (a), (b) and (c) above is applicable, less any amount for which she is eligible or becomes eligible under this or any other Group Policy within 31 days after the date her insurance was discontinued, or
    (ii) $2,000,
whichever is less.

Part C. Issue of the individual policy will be subject to all of the following conditions:

(1) No evidence of insurability shall be required.

(2) Written application for the individual policy and the first premium therefor must be delivered or mailed to the Insurer within 31 days after the date on which the spouse's insurance under this coverage was discontinued.

(3) The individual policy will be in any one of the forms then customarily issued by the Insurer, except a policy of term insurance, and shall be without disability or other supplementary benefits.

(4) The premium for the individual policy will be determined by the Insurer from its then current rates, based upon the attained age of the spouse at her birthday nearest to the date of issue of the individual policy, upon the class of risk to which she then belongs, and upon the form and amount of the individual policy.

(5) Insurance under the individual policy will not become effective until the end of the 31-day period described in (2) above.

Extension of Death Benefit

Upon receipt of due proof at its Home Office of the death of a spouse during the 31-day period within which she could have made application for an individual policy of life insurance under the provision entitled "Conversion Privilege," the Insurer will pay to the beneficiary as a death benefit the maximum amount for which an individual policy could have been issued to her under that provision, whether or not she had made application for an individual policy.

If the insurance of both the employee and his spouse was discontinued under conditions which give the employee but not the spouse the right to convert his own life insurance to an individual policy, then upon receipt of due proof at its Home Office that the spouse died within the 31-day period following the date her insurance was discontinued, the Insurer will pay to the beneficiary as a death benefit the amount of insurance that was in force under this coverage for the spouse on the date her insurance was discontinued.

If the insurance of both the employee and his dependent child was discontinued (1) after the child had been continuously insured under this coverage for 5 years or more, and (2) under conditions which give the employee the right to convert his own life insurance to an individual policy, then upon receipt of due proof at its Home Office that the child died within the 31-day period following the date his insurance was discontinued, the Insurer will pay to the beneficiary as a death benefit the amount of insurance that was in force under this coverage for the child on the date his insurance was discontinued.

Beneficiary

The employee shall be the beneficiary for all the insurance provided under this coverage for his dependents.

Insurance becoming payable as a result of the death of a dependent shall be paid to the employee if he survives the dependent, otherwise to the employee's estate, except that the Insurer may in such case, at its option, pay the insurance to any one or more of the following surviving relatives of the dependent: child or children, mother, father, brothers or sisters.

$$\left[\begin{array}{c} \textbf{Part 3} \\ \textbf{Page 1–DL} \end{array} \right]$$ Coverages

SPECIAL PROVISIONS

GENERAL EXCLUSIONS

The calculation of benefits payable under this policy shall not include or be based upon any charge made for or in connection with any hospital confinement, or any examination, or any surgical, medical or other treatment, or any service or supply,

(a) which was furnished before the date on which the individual on whose account the charge was made became insured under the particular coverage, or which was furnished in connection with or during a hospital confinement which commenced before that date; provided, that if a dependent child becomes insured on or prior to attaining 15 days of age, and while hospital confined, that confinement shall be deemed to have commenced after he became insured, and charges incurred during that hospital confinement and on or after the date he became insured may be included in the calculation of benefits, subject to the other conditions of this policy;

(b) which is furnished without the recommendation and approval of a physician acting within the scope of his license;

(c) which is not medically necessary to the care and treatment of any injury, disease or pregnancy of the insured individual on whose account the charge is made;

(d) which is furnished in connection with an injury which is not a nonoccupational injury or disease which is not a nonoccupational disease;

(e) which is furnished by or through any government or any subdivision or agency thereof, or the charge for which is paid or payable or reimbursable by or through any plan or program of any government or any subdivision or agency thereof, other than a plan or program established for the civilian employees of a government or of a subdivision or agency thereof;

(f) which charge would not have been made in the absence of insurance, or which none of the individuals insured under the policy is legally obligated to pay;

(g) to the extent that the Insurer is prohibited from providing benefits for such charge, by any law or regulation.

$$\begin{bmatrix} \text{Part 3} \\ \text{Page 1–GE} \end{bmatrix}$$ General Exclusions

---

COORDINATION OF BENEFITS

Benefits Subject to This Provision

All of the benefits provided under this policy [except Life Insurance, Accidental Death and Dismemberment Insurance and Accident and Sickness Insurance].

Definitions

(1) "Plan" means any plan providing benefits or services for or by reason of medical or dental care or treatment, which benefits or services are provided by (i) group, blanket or franchise insurance coverage, (ii) group Blue Cross, group Blue Shield, group practice, and other prepayment coverage on a group basis, (iii) any coverage under labor-management trusteed plans, union welfare plans,

employer organization plans, or employee benefit organization plans, and (iv) any coverage under governmental programs, and any coverage required or provided by any statute, which coverage is not otherwise excluded from the calculation of benefits under this Plan, but the term "Plan" shall not include any individual policies.

The term "Plan" shall be construed separately with respect to each policy, contract, or other arrangement for benefits or services and separately with respect to that portion of any such policy, contract, or other arrangement which reserves the right to take the benefits or services of other Plans into consideration in determining its benefits and that portion which does not.

(2) "This Plan" means those portions of this policy which provide the benefits that are subject to this provision.

(3) "Allowable Expense" means any necessary, reasonable, and customary item of expense at least a portion of which is covered under at least one of the Plans covering the person for whom claim is made.

When a Plan provides benefits in the form of services rather than cash payments, the reasonable cash value of each service rendered shall be deemed to be both an Allowable Expense and a benefit paid.

(4) "Claim Determination Period" means calendar year, except that if in any calendar year the person is not covered under this Plan for the full calendar year, the claim determination period for that year shall be that portion thereof during which he was covered under this Plan.

Effect on Benefits

(1) This provision shall apply in determining the benefits as to a person covered under this Plan for any Claim Determination Period if, for the Allowable Expenses incurred as to such a person during such Claim Determination Period, the sum of
  (a) the benefits that would be payable under this Plan in the absence of this provision, and
  (b) the benefits that would be payable under all other Plans in the absence therein of provisions of similar purposes to this provision,
  would exceed such Allowable Expenses.

(2) As to any Claim Determination Period with respect to which this provision is applicable, the benefits that would be payable under this Plan in the absence of this provision for the Allowable Expenses incurred as to such person during such Claim Determination Period shall be reduced to the extent necessary so that the sum of such reduced benefits and all the benefits payable for such Allowable Expenses under all other Plans, except as provided in item (3) immediately below, shall not exceed the total of such Allowable Expenses. Benefits payable under another Plan include the benefits that would have been payable had claim been duly made therefor.

(3) If
  (a) another Plan which is involved in item (2) immediately above and which contains a provision coordinating its benefits with those of this Plan would, according to its rules, determine its benefits after the benefits of this Plan have been determined, and
  (b) the rules set forth in item (4) immediately below would require this Plan to determine its benefits before such other Plan,
  then the benefits of such other Plan will be ignored for the purposes of determining the benefits under this Plan.

(4) For the purposes of item (3) immediately above, the rules establishing the order of benefit determination are:

    (a) The benefits of a Plan which covers the person on whose expenses claim is based other than as a dependent shall be determined before the benefits of a Plan which covers such person as a dependent;

    (b) The benefits of a Plan which covers the person on whose expenses claim is based as a dependent of a male person shall be determined before the benefits of a Plan which covers such person as a dependent of a female person;

    (c) When rules (a) and (b) do not establish an order of benefit determination, the benefits of a Plan which has covered the person on whose expenses claim is based for the longer period of time shall be determined before the benefits of a Plan which has covered such person the shorter period of time.

(5) When this provision operates to reduce the total amount of benefits otherwise payable as to a person covered under this Plan during any Claim Determination Period, each benefit that would be payable in the absence of this provision shall be reduced proportionately, and such reduced amount shall be charged against any applicable benefit limit of this Plan.

Right to Receive and Release Necessary Information

For the purpose of determining the applicability of and implementing the terms of this provision of this Plan or any provision of similar purpose of any other Plan, the Insurer may, without the consent of or notice to any person, release to or obtain from any other insurance company or other organization or person any information, with respect to any person, which the Insurer deems to be necessary for such purposes. Any person claiming benefits under this Plan shall furnish to the Insurer such information as may be necessary to implement this provision.

Facility of Payment

Whenever payments which should have been made under this Plan in accordance with this provision have been made under any other Plans, the Insurer shall have the right, exercisable alone and in its sole discretion, to pay over to any organizations making such other payments any amounts it shall determine to be warranted in order to satisfy the intent of this provision, and amounts so paid shall be deemed to be benefits paid under this Plan and, to the extent of such payments, the Insurer shall be fully discharged from liability under this Plan.

Right of Recovery

Whenever payments have been made by the Insurer with respect to Allowable Expenses in a total amount which is, at any time, in excess of the maximum amount of payment necessary at that time to satisfy the intent of this provision, the Insurer shall have the right to recover such payments, to the extent of such excess, from among one or more of the following, as the Insurer shall determine: any persons to or for or with respect to whom such payments were made, any other insurance companies, any other organizations.

$$\left[\begin{array}{c} \text{Part 3} \\ \text{Page 1–CB} \end{array}\right]$$ **Coordination of Benefits**

SPECIAL PROVISIONS
ACCIDENT AND HEALTH CONVERSION

The following provision is applicable to [all employees except salaried employees], provided, however, that no Personal Health Policy shall be issued to a person who is a resident of Canada or Puerto Rico:

Accident and Health Conversion Privilege

Part A. An employee whose insurance under all Accident and Health coverages for which he is insured under this policy (other than Accidental Death and Dismemberment Insurance and Accident and Sickness Insurance, if any) ceases solely because
  (a) his employment, for purposes of insurance, is terminated, or
  (b) his classification changes to a class of employees which is ineligible for insurance under such coverages,
will be entitled to have issued to him by the Insurer a Personal Health Policy—Group Conversion (herein referred to as Personal Health Policy) provided
  (1) the date his insurance ceases is not coincident with the date of termination of this policy, or of termination of said Accident and Health Insurance for all of the employees of a class of which he is a member, and
  (2) the employee is not otherwise eligible to be insured under this policy for any coverage providing benefits similar in kind to those for which the employee was insured under this policy when his insurance ceased.

Part B. The Personal Health Policy shall cover the employee himself, and, if coverage for dependents is shown below in the Schedule of Personal Health Policy Benefits, and if dependent coverage is elected by the employee in his application for the Personal Health Policy, shall also cover all those dependents whose insurance under this policy ceased solely by reason of cessation of the employee's insurance and who are not otherwise eligible to be insured under this policy for any coverage providing benefits similar in kind to those for which the dependent was insured under this policy when his insurance ceased.

Part C. Issue of the Personal Health Policy will be subject to all of the following conditions:
  (1) No evidence of insurability will be required.
  (2) Written application for the Personal Health Policy and the first premium therefor must be delivered or mailed to the Insurer within 31 days after the date on which the employee's Accident and Health Insurance ceased as set forth in (a) or (b) in Part A above.
  (3) The form of the Personal Health Policy, the benefits provided thereunder, the individuals covered, the amount of premium payable, and all other terms and conditions thereof shall be such as are provided by the rules of the Insurer pertaining to individual policies available for conversion purposes at the time application for the Personal Health Policy is received by the Insurer.
  (4) The Personal Health Policy shall include only those of the coverages

included in the Schedule of Personal Health Policy Benefits for which all of the persons to be covered under the Personal Health Policy ceased to be insured under this policy solely by reason of cessation of the employee's insurance.

(5) Insurance under the Personal Health Policy will become effective on the date following the date on which insurance under this policy ceases.

If the dependent spouse of an employee ceases to be insured under this policy solely by reason of the death of the employee, the privilege of obtaining a Personal Health Policy may be exercised by the spouse, subject to all of the applicable conditions for such conversion set forth herein. The Personal Health Policy shall cover the spouse, and, if dependent coverage is elected by the spouse in the application for the Personal Health Policy, shall also cover all other dependent children who are dependent on the spouse for support and whose insurance under this policy ceased solely by reason of the employee's death.

If any dependent child ceases to be insured under this policy solely for the reason that the child's attained age exceeds the maximum age specified in the definition of "dependent" in this policy, the privilege of obtaining a Personal Health Policy may be exercised by the child, subject to all of the applicable conditions for such conversion set forth herein, to cover only that child; provided, however, that the insurance of the employee under this policy need not have terminated.

Part D. The Daily Hospital Benefit under the Personal Health Policy shall be elected at the time of conversion, by the person converting, within the limits shown below. However, in no event shall the amount of Daily Hospital Benefit under the Personal Health Policy be greater than the smallest Rate of Maximum Daily Benefit for Board and Room for which any person to be covered under the Personal Health Policy was insured under this policy when insurance hereunder ceased.

SCHEDULE OF PERSONAL HEALTH POLICY BENEFITS

| | Hospital Expense Benefit | |
Daily Hospital Benefit	Maximum Hospital Expense Benefit Period	Maximum Hospital Services Benefit
Not less than $6 nor more than $15 (in full dollar units)	31 days for confinements commencing under attained age 65	10 times Daily Hospital Benefit for confinements commencing under attained age 65
	21 days for confinements commencing at attained age 65 or over except for residents of California	5 times Daily Hospital Benefit for confinements commencing at attained age 65 or over
	25 days for confinements commencing at attained age 65 or over for residents of California	

		Physicians' In-Hospital Medical Expense Benefit

Maximum Normal Maternity Benefit	Surgical Expense Benefit-Schedule Maximum	Daily Benefit	Maximum Medical Benefit
10 times Daily Hospital Benefit	$300	$3.00	$93 for confinements commencing under attained age 65
			$63 for confinements commencing at attained age 65 or over except for residents of California
			$75 for confinements commencing at attained age 65 or over for residents of California

Part 3 Page 1–CP	Accident and Health Conversion

PART 4—PREMIUMS

Premium Payment

Premiums are payable to the Insurer in advance on each Premium Due Date, at the Home Office of the Insurer unless otherwise specified by the Insurer in writing. The payment of any premium shall not maintain the insurance under this policy in force beyond the date when the next premium becomes payable, except as set forth in the provision below entitled "Grace Period."

Premium for Changes in Insurance

Premium for additional or increased insurance becoming effective during a policy month shall be charged from the first day of the policy month next following the date such insurance becomes effective, except that if insurance becomes effective on the first day of a policy month the premium charge shall commence on that day.

Premium charge for insurance discontinuing during a policy month shall cease at the end of the policy month in which the insurance discontinues.

Payment of any balance due or credited on account of the first premium or adjustments in premiums due to changes in insurance by reason of additions, increases and terminations will be due when determined.

If premiums are payable quarterly, semiannually, or annually, premium charges or credits for a fraction of a premium-paying period shall be made on a pro-rata basis for the number of policy months between the date premium charges commence or cease and the end of the period for which each premium is payable.

Grace Period

If any premium after the first premium is not paid in full by the Policyholder on or prior to the due date of such premium, and if the Policyholder has not given written notice to the Insurer on or prior to that due date that this policy is to terminate, a grace period shall be granted to the Policyholder for the payment of that premium without interest charge.

The grace period shall begin with the premium due date and shall continue for 31 days unless terminated on such earlier date as the Policyholder may specify in a written notice given to the Insurer at its Home Office during the grace period, but such earlier date shall in no event be prior to the date the notice is received by the Insurer; or unless the grace period is continued for more than 31 days by the Insurer by written notice to the Policyholder, but in no event shall the grace period continue for more than two policy months beginning with said premium due date.

The Policyholder shall be liable to the Insurer for all premium remaining unpaid on the date of termination of this policy, including pro-rata premium for the days of grace during which this policy remains in force.

$$\begin{bmatrix} \text{Part 4} \\ \text{Page 1–PR} \end{bmatrix}$$ Premiums

---

PREMIUMS (Continued)

Insurer's Right to Change Premium Rates

The Insurer reserves the right to fix new premium rates for any or all of the coverages provided under this policy, as of that date in each policy month which corresponds to the day of the month on which the first policy anniversary occurs, except that the Insurer shall not fix new rates to be effective on any date which is less than 12 months after the Policy Effective Date.

Notice of any new premium rates shall be given to the Policyholder before the date specified by the Insurer for the rates to become effective.

The Insurer shall not increase the premium rate for any one coverage less than 12 months after a rate was previously made effective for that coverage unless the Policyholder consents to the increase.

Annual Surplus Distribution

As of each policy anniversary to which premiums have been paid in full there shall be distributed hereon such share, if any, of a divisible surplus as may be apportioned hereto by the Insurer.

Any such divisible surplus shall be paid in cash to the Policyholder or, at the election of the Policyholder, may be applied in abatement of premium payments; provided, that in the event the employees contribute towards the cost of the insurance, any excess of such share of the divisible surplus over the aggregate premium contribution of the Participating Employers having employees insured under this policy shall be applied by the Policyholder for the sole benefit of the employees who are insured hereunder at the time such share of the divisible surplus is received by the Policyholder, but payment of such share by the Insurer to the Policyholder shall completely discharge the Insurer of all responsibility with respect to the amount so paid.

$$\begin{bmatrix} \text{Part 4} \\ \text{Page 2–PR} \end{bmatrix}$$ Premiums

PREMIUMS (Continued)

Accident and Health Premium Rates

The initial basis of premium calculations for the Accident and Health coverages provided under this policy as of the Policy Effective Date shall be as shown below. The absence of a premium rate for a given coverage means that the coverage is not applicable and is not provided under this policy.

MONTHLY PREMIUM RATES
FOR ACCIDENT AND HEALTH COVERAGES

For Employee Coverages:

Accidental Death and Dismemberment	Accident and Sickness	Health Insurance (Combined Hospital, Surgical, Medical)
$_____per $1000 of insurance	$_____per $10 of weekly indemnity	$_____per employee

The following rates are per insured employee:

Hospital Expense	Surgical Expense	Medical Expense	Major Medical Expense
$_____	$_____	$_____	$_____

Laboratory and X-Ray Examination	X-Ray Examination	Supplemental Accident Expense	Poliomyelitis Expense
$_____	$_____	$_____	$_____

For Dependent Coverages (per employee having dependents insured):

Hospital Expense	Surgical Expense	Major Medical Expense
$_____	$_____	$_____

Health Insurance (Combined Hospital, Surgical, Medical)	Medical Expense	Laboratory and X-ray Examination
$_____	$_____	$_____

X-Ray Examination	Supplemental Accident Expense	Poliomyelitis Expense
$_____	$_____	$_____

Premium Rate for Life Insurance for Dependents

The initial basis of premium calculations for this coverage shall be $_____ per dependent unit.

Average Premium Rate for Life Insurance

The premium due on each Premium Due Date for Life Insurance for Employees shall be calculated by the Insurer by applying an average premium rate to the amount of insurance on which premiums are due.

The premium depends upon the attained age of each insured employee at his birthday nearest to the Policy Effective Date and to each policy anniversary, and will increase with advancing ages.

An average premium rate for Life Insurance for Employees shall be determined by the Insurer as of the Policy Effective Date and as of each policy anniversary, by applying the premium rates for Life Insurance for Employees under the Schedule of Monthly Premium Rates then in effect to the amount of Life Insurance for Employees then in force at the respective ages at nearest birthday of the insured employees on such date, adding to the total thus obtained the appropriate Additional Charge, reducing the sum by the applicable Percentage Reduction, and dividing the remainder by the number of thousands of dollars of insurance then in force.

The average premium rate shall also be used in calculating adjustments of Life Insurance premiums due the Insurer for insurance of additional employees becoming covered hereunder and for increases, if any, in amounts of Life Insurance for Employees, and in calculating unearned premiums, if any, due the Policyholder on account of terminated Life Insurance for Employees.

Instead of using the age at nearest birthday in calculating an average premium the Insurer may, at its option, use the number of whole years between the calendar year as of the date of the calculation and the calendar year of birth of the insured employee, provided the premium thus obtained is adjusted for the date as of which the average premium rate is calculated.

If premiums are payable other than monthly, the average annual, semiannual or quarterly premium rate shall be determined by multiplying the average monthly premium rate by 11.82, 5.956, 2.985 respectively.

Maximum Employee Contribution

If any employees make contributions for Life Insurance for Employees, the maximum amount that any employee may contribute for that coverage shall be [$.60 per month] for each $1,000 of his life insurance.

Initial Schedule of Monthly Premium Rates (for each $1,000 of Insurance)

(1) *Tabular rates*

Age Nearest Birthday	Rates	Age Nearest Birthday	Rates	Age Nearest Birthday	Rates	Age Nearest Birthday	Rates
15	$.19	35	$ .32	55	$1.65	75	$ 8.56
16	.20	36	.34	56	1.80	76	9.24
17	.21	37	.36	57	1.97	77	10.00
18	.22	38	.38	58	2.14	78	10.86
19	.23	39	.41	59	2.32	79	11.81
20	.23	40	.45	60	2.51	80	12.83
21	.24	41	.49	61	2.72	81	13.93
22	.24	42	.53	62	2.96	82	15.07
23	.25	43	.58	63	3.21	83	16.26
24	.25	44	.63	64	3.48	84	17.50
25	.25	45	.68	65	3.78	85	18.80
26	.25	46	.74	66	4.11	86	20.16
27	.26	47	.81	67	4.48	87	21.60
28	.26	48	.89	68	4.89	88	23.13
29	.26	49	.97	69	5.34	89	24.79
30	.27	50	1.06	70	5.81	90	26.62
31	.27	51	1.16	71	6.32	91	28.68
32	.28	52	1.26	72	6.84	92	31.03
33	.29	53	1.38	73	7.38	93	33.75
34	.30	54	1.51	74	7.95	94	36.95

(2) Additional Charge. An additional charge of $.20 per $1,000 of the first $40,000 of insurance in force must be added to the total premium obtained by applying the tabular rates above at each attained age to the amount of insurance in force at that age

(3) Percentage Reduction. The sum of (1) and (2) above shall be reduced by the applicable percentage shown below:

Monthly Premium before Reduction	Percentage Reduction	Monthly Premium before Reduction	Percentage Reduction
$ Less than $ 200	0%	$ 1,000 but less than $ 1,500	11%
200 but less than 250	1	1,500 but less than 3,000	12
250 but less than 300	2	3,000 but less than 5,000	13
300 but less than 350	3	5,000 but less than 10,000	14
350 but less than 400	4	10,000 but less than 15,000	15
400 but less than 450	5	15,000 but less than 20,000	16
450 but less than 500	6	20,000 but less than 30,000	17
500 but less than 600	7	30,000 but less than 40,000	18
600 but less than 700	8	40,000 but less than 60,000	19
700 but less than 800	9	60,000 or greater	20
800 but less than 1,000	10		

$$\begin{bmatrix} \text{Part 4} \\ \text{Page 3–PR} \end{bmatrix}$$ Premiums

PART 5—STANDARD PROVISIONS

Employee's Certificate

The Insurer will issue to the Policyholder for delivery to each insured employee a certificate setting forth a summary of the essential features of the insurance and stating to whom the benefits are payable.

Misstatement of Age

If the age of any person insured under this policy has been misstated there shall be an equitable adjustment of premiums, and if his amount of insurance depends on his age, his amount of insurance shall also be adjusted to that determined by his correct age.

Incontestability

The policy shall not be contested, except for nonpayment of premium, after it has been in force for 2 years from the Policy Effective Date.

No statement made by any person insured under this policy relating to his insurability shall be used in contesting the validity of his insurance, or that coverage or portion of his insurance with respect to which the statement was made, after that insurance or coverage or portion, as the case may be, has been in force prior to the contest for a period of 2 years during his lifetime, and in no event unless the statement is contained in a written application signed by him and a copy of that application is or has been furnished to him or to his beneficiary.

Conformity with Applicable Law

Any provision of this policy which, on its Effective Date, is in conflict with the applicable law of the Jurisdiction of Issue is hereby amended to conform with the minimum requirements of that law.

If the Insurer determines that persons who are residents of a particular State or Province or other political subdivision are precluded by the laws or regulations of that jurisdiction from being insured for one or more of the coverages provided in this policy, such persons shall not be included in the class of persons eligible for such coverage or coverages.

$$\left[\begin{array}{c} \text{Part 5} \\ \text{Page 1--SP} \end{array}\right] \qquad \textbf{Standard Provisions}$$

STANDARD PROVISIONS (Continued)

(The following provisions apply only to Accident and Health coverages.)

Proof of Loss

Written proof covering the occurrence, character and extent of loss for which claim is made must be furnished to the Insurer, in case of claim for loss for which this policy provides any periodic payment contingent upon continuing loss, within 90 days after termination of the period for which the Insurer is liable, and in case of claim for any other loss, within 90 days after the date of such loss. (For charges which are applied to satisfy a Deductible Amount the date of loss shall mean the date when the sum of such charges equals the Deductible Amount. For other charges the date of loss shall mean the date the charge is incurred.)

Failure to furnish such proof within the time required shall not invalidate nor reduce any claim if it shall be shown not to have been reasonably possible to furnish such proof within the required time and that proof was given as soon as was reasonably possible.

Time of Payment of Claims

Claims made for indemnities provided under this policy shall be paid as follows, immediately upon receipt of due written proof of loss:

(1) If Accidental Death and Dismemberment Insurance indemnities are provided under this policy, indemnity for loss of life will be payable in accordance with the beneficiary designation and the provision of the policy entitled "Beneficiary of Employee," and the provisions respecting such payment which may be prescribed in this policy and effective at the time of payment.

All other indemnity will be payable to the employee.

(2) If this policy includes coverage providing indemnities for hospital or surgical or medical expenses, those benefits shall be payable to the employee, at his request, each week during any period for which the Insurer is liable.

(3) If this policy includes coverage providing weekly or monthly payments contingent upon continuing loss, the indemnities for such loss shall be payable to the employee each week or each month, as provided in the particular coverage; provided, however, that if such coverage provides such payments for loss due to pregnancy, the Insurer may, at its option, accelerate the payment of any or all of the indemnities that would otherwise become payable under the coverage in connection with any one pregnancy.

Any accrued indemnity unpaid and unassigned at the employee's death shall be paid in accordance with the beneficiary designation, or at the Insurer's option, to the employee's estate.

$$\left[\begin{array}{c} \text{Part 5} \\ \text{Page 2--SP} \end{array}\right]$$ Standard Provisions

---

STANDARD PROVISIONS (Continued)

(The following provisions apply only to Accident and Health coverages.)

Physical Examination and Autopsy

The Insurer at its own expense shall have the right and opportunity to have the person of any individual whose injury or sickness is the basis of claim examined by a physician designated by it, when and as often as it may reasonably require during the pendency of a claim under this policy and to make an autopsy in case of death, where it is not forbidden by law.

Legal Action

No action at law or in equity shall be brought to recover on this policy prior to the expiration of sixty days after written proof of loss has been furnished in accordance with the requirements of this policy. No such action shall be brought after the expiration of three years after the time written proof of loss is required to be furnished.

If any time limitation of this policy with respect to bringing an action at law or in equity to recover on this policy is less than that permitted by the law of the state in which the employee resides at the time the disability or other loss on which claim is based commences or is incurred, that limitation is hereby extended to agree with the minimum period permitted by that law.

Workmen's Compensation

This policy is not in lieu of and does not affect any requirement for coverage by Workmen's Compensation Insurance.

$$\left[\begin{array}{c} \text{Part 5} \\ \text{Page 3--SP} \end{array}\right]$$ Standard Provisions

Appendix 12

SPECIMEN GROUP INSURANCE CERTIFICATE

A B C

MUTUAL LIFE INSURANCE COMPANY
BOSTON, MASSACHUSETTS

Certifies that under and subject to the terms and conditions of the Group Policy(ies) listed below issued to

RICHARD ROE COMPANY

(herein called the Policyholder)

the Insured Person named below and his insured dependents, if any, are insured for those coverages listed in the following Schedule of Insurance for which amounts of insurance are shown, as of the effective date shown below, provided he is then actively at work, otherwise on the date he returns to active work.

This certificate describes in general terms the Insured Person's insurance under said Policy(ies), but does not constitute a waiver of any of the terms and conditions of said Policy(ies), all of which are controlling.

The Policy(ies) under which this certificate is issued may at any time be amended or discontinued by agreement between the Insurance Company and the Policyholder without the consent of or giving of notice to the Insured Person.

The Policy(ies) is (are) not in lieu of and does (do) not affect any requirement for coverage by Workmen's Compensation Insurance.

The provisions set forth on the following pages hereof are hereby made a part of this certificate.

Name of Insured Person	Effective Date	Certificate Number
Name of Policyholder **(See above)**		Control Number
Name and Relationship of Beneficiary		Policy Number(s)

SCHEDULE OF INSURANCE

	Life Insurance		Accidental Death and Dismemberment Insurance Full Amount	Accident and Sickness Insurance—Weekly Benefit	Hospital Expense Insurance Maximum Daily Benefit	Surgical Operation Expense Insurance Maximum Benefit	Medical Expense Insurance—Maximum Benefit			
Amounts of Insurance of Insured Persons →	$ 5,000	$	$ 5,000	$ 65	$ See Page 2	$ 450	$ 350	$	$	$
Amounts of Insurance of Dependents →					$	$	$	$	$	$

(Schedule continued on the following page)

Life Insurance, Accidental Death and Dismemberment Insurance and Accident and Sickness Insurance provided under the Policy(ies) are not assignable.

This certificate replaces and makes void any and all insurance certificates, for the coverage(s) contained herein, that may have been issued previously to the within-named Insured Person under the afore-mentioned Group Policy(ies) issued by the Insurance Company.

A B C   MUTUAL LIFE INSURANCE COMPANY

Form G-01C   Ed. 7-52
Series M
Printed in U.S.A.

President

GA-56911264

LIFE INSURANCE

Insuring Clause

On receipt of due proof at its Home Office of the death of the Insured Person, the Insurance Company shall pay to the beneficiary the amount of Life Insurance in force on the Insured Person at the date of death as determined in accordance with the Schedule of Insurance.

Waiver of Premium Benefit in the Event of Permanent and Total Disability

The Insurance Company will waive the payment of further premiums on the amount of Life Insurance in force on the Insured Person on the last day on which he is actively at work and will, upon the Insured Person's death, pay the amount of such insurance to the beneficiary, provided:

(a) the Insured Person ceases active work on account of permanent and total disability resulting from bodily injuries or disease which prevents the Insured Person from engaging in any business or occupation and from performing any work for compensation or profit;

(b) such disability is continuous until the death of the Insured Person;

(c) the Insured Person ceases active work before attaining age 60;

(d) the Insured Person furnishes the Insurance Company at its Home Office, after nine months following the date the Insured Person ceased active work but within twelve months following the date of termination of his employment, written proof on the Insurance Company's prescribed forms that he is permanently and totally disabled as defined in (a) of this provision, and has been so disabled continuously since the date he ceased active work. At the time the Insured Person furnishes such proof of disability the Insurance Company will endorse his certificate to indicate acknowledgment of receipt of said proof and the date upon which it was received, such date to be referred to as Original Date of Endorsement;

(e) the Insured Person furnishes the Insurance Company at its Home Office with written proof on the Insurance Company's prescribed forms of continued permanent and total disability within the three months immediately prior to each anniversary of the Original Date of Endorsement during the life of the Insured Person; the Insurance Company will endorse the Insured Person's certificate each year when such proof of continued permanent and total disability is furnished;

(f) written proof on the Insurance Company's prescribed forms of the Insured Person's death is furnished to the Insurance Company at its Home Office within one year of the death of the Insured Person. In the event of death of the Insured Person within one year from the date of termination of employment and before any such proof of disability has been submitted, written proof on the Insurance Company's prescribed forms that the Insured Person was continuously disabled from the date of termination of his employment to the date of death shall be furnished to the Insurance Company within one year after the death of such Insured Person;

(g) no death benefit is payable within thirty-one days following the date of termination of employment, or the date of termination of the Life Insurance under the Policy, or the date of termination of the Policy as provided in the provision entitled "Conversion Privilege".

The Insurance Company shall have the right to have any Insured Person who submits proof of disability in accordance with this provision examined at any time by physicians designated by it; provided, that after such disability shall have continued for two full years, such examination will not be required more often than once in each subsequent year. All rights of the Insured Person under this provision shall cease on the earliest of the following dates:

(1) the date of cessation of the Insured Person's permanent and total disability;

(2) the date the Insured Person engages in any business or occupation or performs any work for compensation or profit, whether or not the Insured Person continues to be permanently and totally disabled;

(3) the last day of any twelve-month period of continued insurance under this provision, if the proof of disability required by subsection (e) of this provision is not furnished within the three-month period specified therein;

(4) the date on which the Insured Person refuses to submit to examination, by physicians designated by the Insurance Company, upon its request.

No judicial proceeding shall be brought to enforce the endorsement of any Insured Person's certificate under this provision unless brought within two years after the Insurance Company refuses to make such endorsement. If any time limitation of the Policy with respect to the bringing of any judicial proceeding to enforce endorsement of any Insured Person's certificate under this provision is less than that permitted by the law of the state in which the Insured Person resides at the time the Policy is issued, such limitation is hereby extended to agree with the minimum period permitted by such law.

If an individual policy shall have been issued and become effective in accordance with the provision entitled "Conversion Privilege", no payment shall be made under the terms of this provision unless such individual policy shall be surrendered to the Insurance Company without claim thereunder, in which case the Insurance Company will refund to the beneficiary under such individual policy the premium paid thereon.

LIFE INSURANCE (*Continued*)

Conversion Privilege

A. The Insured Person, upon written application made to the Insurance Company within thirty-one days after the earlier of the following dates:

    (a) the date of termination of his employment, as herein defined, for any reason whatsoever, or

    (b) the date of termination of his membership in the class or classes of persons insured under the Policy, or within thirty-one days after:

    (c) the date of cessation of his rights under the provision entitled "Waiver of Premium Benefit in the Event of Permanent and Total Disability",

shall be entitled to have issued to him by the Insurance Company, without evidence of insurability, an individual policy of life insurance subject to the following conditions and provisions:

    (1) such individual policy shall be in any one of the forms then customarily issued by the Insurance Company, except term insurance;

    (2) the premium for such individual policy shall be the premium applicable to the class of risk to which the Insured Person belongs and to the form and amount of the policy at the Insured Person's attained age (nearest birthday) at the date of issue of such individual policy;

    (3) the amount of such individual policy shall be equal to (or at the option of the Insured Person, less than) the amount of the Insured Person's insurance under the Policy which was discontinued on whichever of the dates specified in paragraphs (a), (b), and (c) above is applicable;

    (4) the first premium payment on such individual policy of life insurance so issued shall be made to the Company within the thirty-one-day period during which application for such individual policy may be made.

B. The Insured Person, upon

    (a) termination of the insurance of the class of insured persons of which he is a member, or

    (b) termination of the Life Insurance under the Policy, or

    (c) termination of the Policy by either the Policyholder or the Insurance Company,

shall be entitled to the rights and benefits set forth in subdivision A of this provision, in accordance with its terms and conditions, provided his Life Insurance has been continuously in force for at least five years immediately preceding such termination, except that the amount of such individual policy shall not exceed the lesser of

    (i) the amount of the Insured Person's Life Insurance under the Policy at the date of such termination, less any amount of life insurance for which he may be or may become eligible under any Group Policy issued by the Insurance Company or by any other insurer within thirty-one days after such termination, and

    (ii) $2,000.

C. Insurance under any individual policy issued in accordance with this provision shall become effective at the end of the thirty-one-day period during which application for such individual policy may be made.

Extension of Death Benefit During Conversion Period

In the event of the death of the Insured Person during the thirty-one-day period within which the Insured Person may make application for an individual policy, as set forth in the foregoing provision, the Insurance Company shall pay to the beneficiary as a death benefit the maximum sum for which an individual policy could have been issued under the foregoing provision, whether or not the Insured Person shall have made written application for such individual policy.

LIFE INSURANCE (Continued)

Beneficiary

In the event of the death of the beneficiary or beneficiaries last named by the Insured Person prior to that of the Insured Person, or if no beneficiary shall have been named, the Life Insurance or the commuted value of any remaining instalments thereof payable as provided in the Policy, as the case may be, shall be paid to the executors or administrators of the Insured Person, except that the Insurance Company may in such case, at its option, pay such insurance to any one or more of the following surviving relatives: wife, husband, mother, father, child or children, brothers or sisters.

If the beneficiary is a minor or is otherwise incapable of giving a valid release for any payment due, the Insurance Company may, at its option and until claim is made by the duly appointed guardian or committee of such beneficiary, make payment of the amount of insurance payable to such beneficiary, at a rate not exceeding $50.00 per month, to any relative by blood or connection by marriage of such beneficiary, or to any other person or institution appearing to it to have assumed custody and principal support of such beneficiary, for the sole benefit of such beneficiary. Such payments shall constitute a full discharge of the liability of the Insurance Company to the extent thereof.

Modes of Settlement of Claims

Any valid claim under the Policy shall be paid either in one amount, or upon the written election of the Insured Person, in a fixed number of instalments which may be mutually agreed upon in writing by the Insured Person and the Insurance Company and which will provide for payment of the full amount due during the limited period specified in the Policy. Such instalment payments shall be computed upon the basis of the effective rate of interest applicable under this provision at the date of death of the Insured Person.

In the event that no such mode of settlement becomes effective upon the death of the Insured Person, the beneficiary or beneficiaries entitled to the insurance may elect such a mode of settlement.

ACCIDENTAL DEATH AND DISMEMBERMENT INSURANCE

Benefit in the Event of Accidental Death and Dismemberment

If the Insured Person suffers any of the losses described below, as a result of bodily injuries sustained solely through external, violent and accidental means, directly and independently of all other causes and within ninety days from the date of such injuries, the Insurance Company shall pay to the Insured Person, if living, otherwise to the beneficiary, the amount of insurance specified for such loss in the Schedule of Indemnities below determined in accordance with the Schedule of Insurance; provided, however, that no payment shall be made for any loss caused wholly or partly, directly or indirectly, by

(a) disease, or bodily or mental infirmity, or medical or surgical treatment thereof; or

(b) ptomaines, or bacterial infections, except infection introduced through a visible wound accidentally sustained; or

(c) suicide while sane or insane, or intentionally self-inflicted injury; or

(d) war, or any act of war, whether declared or undeclared.

SCHEDULE OF INDEMNITIES

Full Amount of Insurance for Loss of
    Life
    Both Hands
    Both Feet
    One Hand and One Foot
    Sight of Both Eyes
    One Hand and Sight of One Eye
    One Foot and Sight of One Eye

One Half of the Full Amount of
    Insurance for Loss of
    One Hand
    One Foot
    Sight of One Eye

Loss of hands or feet shall mean loss by severance at or above the wrist or ankle joint, and loss of sight shall mean total and irrecoverable loss of sight.

If the Insured Person shall suffer more than one of the losses described above as a result of any one accident no more than the full amount of insurance of the Insured Person shall be payable.

ACCIDENT AND SICKNESS INSURANCE

Benefit in the Event of Accident or Sickness

If the Insured Person becomes wholly and continuously disabled by

(1) an accidental bodily injury which does not arise out of and in the course of any employment for wage or profit, or

(2) disease for which the Insured Person is not entitled to a benefit under any Workmen's Compensation Law or Act,

and is thereby prevented from performing any and every duty of his occupation, the Weekly Benefit shown in the Schedule of Insurance is payable to the Insured Person for the period of such disability, but not exceeding during any one period of disability, whether from one or more causes, the applicable number of weeks specified as Duration of Benefits in said Schedule, and no benefit is payable for the days of the Waiting Period specified in said Schedule.

Successive periods of disability separated by less than two weeks of active work on full time shall be considered one period of disability unless the subsequent disability is due to an injury or disease entirely unrelated to the causes of the previous disability and commences after the Insured Person has returned to active work on full time.

Maternity Benefit

In the event of disability caused by a pregnancy, which term includes resulting childbirth or miscarriage, weekly benefits are payable for not more than the applicable number of weeks specified as Duration of Benefits in the Schedule of Insurance for all disability resulting from any one pregnancy; provided, however, that the payment of any such benefit is subject to the Maternity Limitation, if any, shown in said Schedule.

Limitation

No benefit is payable for any period of disability during which the Insured Person is not under treatment by a legally qualified physician.

HOSPITAL EXPENSE INSURANCE FOR INSURED PERSONS

Benefits in the Event of Accidental Bodily Injury or Disease

If the Insured Person is confined as hereinafter provided in a legally constituted hospital, other than a hospital or other facility owned or operated by the United States Government, or any other hospital where care is provided to the Insured Person at federal government expense, as a result of

(1) an accidental bodily injury which does not arise out of and in the course of employment, or

(2) disease for which the Insured Person is not entitled to a benefit under any Workmen's Compensation Law or Act,

the following benefits are payable to the Insured Person during any one continuous period of disability:

(a) a Benefit in an amount equal to the charges incurred during such confinement for board and room of the Insured Person, but not more than the amount obtained by multiplying the Maximum Daily Benefit shown in the Schedule of Insurance by the number of days of such confinement for which the hospital charges the Insured Person for board and room, and in no event shall the total amount payable for all such charges exceed the Maximum Board and Room Benefit for accident or disease shown in said Schedule; and

(b) a Supplementary Benefit for the charges which are made to the Insured Person, in connection with such confinement,

  (i) by the hospital (except charges for board and room, charges arising from special nursing services, and charges for physicians' or surgeons' services), and

  (ii) for anaesthetics and the administration thereof, and

  (iii) for necessary ambulance service,

  and which are incurred before the total amount set forth in subdivision (a) above for board and room of the Insured Person becomes payable, and the amount of said Benefit shall be determined in accordance with the Schedule of Insurance, but in no event shall the total amount payable under subdivision (b) hereof exceed the Maximum Supplementary Benefit for accident or disease shown in said Schedule.

If the Insured Person is wholly disabled on the date his Hospital Expense Insurance under the Policy ceases and is confined as herein provided as a result of an accidental bodily injury or disease hereinbefore described within three months after such date and during the continuance of such disability, the benefits shall be payable to the Insured Person which would have been payable if such confinement had commenced while the Insured Person was insured.

Successive periods of hospital confinement shall be considered as having occurred during one continuous period of disability if the later period of hospital confinement is due to an accidental bodily injury or disease which is not entirely unrelated to the accidental bodily injury or disease which caused the previous period of hospital confinement, unless the later period of hospital confinement commences after the Insured Person either completely recovers from the injuries or diseases which caused the previous period of hospital confinement, or returns to active work and completes one day of active service.

Maternity Benefit

If the Insured Person is confined as herein provided in a legally constituted hospital as a result of pregnancy (which term includes resulting childbirth or miscarriage) and if such confinement commences while the Insured Person is insured, or after the date her Hospital Expense Insurance ceased if the pregnancy existed on such date, a Benefit is payable to the Insured Person in an amount equal to the charges incurred during such confinement for board and room of the Insured Person, together with the benefit described in subdivision (b) above, but in no event shall the benefits payable as a result of any one pregnancy exceed the Hospital Expense Benefits for Pregnancy shown in the Schedule of Insurance; provided, however, that the payment of any such benefit is subject to the Maternity Limitation, if any, shown in said Schedule.

Period of Confinement

No minimum period of hospital confinement is required because of a surgical operation, or as a result of accidental bodily injury requiring emergency care, or if a board and room charge is made; otherwise, hospital confinement must be for eighteen consecutive hours or longer.

Limitation

No payment shall be made for any charges incurred for board and room, or for any charges made for services and supplies, in connection with hospital confinement unless such confinement and the services and supplies for which charges are made are recommended and approved by a legally qualified physician or surgeon.

SURGICAL OPERATION EXPENSE INSURANCE FOR INSURED PERSONS

Benefit for an Operation Resulting from Accidental Bodily Injury or Disease

If the Insured Person undergoes a surgical operation specified in the applicable Schedule of Surgical Operations and Benefits contained herein, as a result of

(1) an accidental bodily injury which does not arise out of and in the course of employment, or

(2) disease for which the Insured Person is not entitled to a benefit under any Workmen's Compensation Law or Act,

a benefit is payable to the Insured Person in an amount equal to the surgical fees actually charged to the Insured Person for the operation, but not in excess of the maximum payment specified for the operation in said Schedule of Surgical Operations and Benefits.

If more than one of the above described operations is performed while the Insured Person is insured for Surgical Operation Expense Insurance under the Policy, the aforesaid benefit shall be payable for each such operation, except that the total benefits payable for all operations which are not entirely unrelated to the bodily injuries sustained in any one accident or to the same disease and which are performed before the Insured Person either completely recovers from such injury or disease, or returns to active work and completes one day of active service, shall not exceed the Maximum Surgical Benefit shown in the Schedule of Insurance; provided, however, that if more than one operation is performed

(a) through the same abdominal incision, the total benefit payable for all such operations shall not exceed the maximum payment specified in said Schedule of Surgical Operations and Benefits for that one of such operations for which the largest amount is payable; or

(b) on the anus or rectum, or both (except for cancer) at any one time, the total benefit payable for all such operations shall not exceed one and one-half times the maximum payment specified in said Schedule of Surgical Operations and Benefits for that one of such operations for which the largest amount is payable.

If the Insured Person is wholly disabled by an injury or disease as hereinbefore described on the date his Surgical Operation Expense Insurance under the Policy ceases and undergoes a surgical operation specified in said Schedule of Surgical Operations and Benefits within three months after such date and during the continuance of such disability, a benefit which would have been payable if his insurance had not ceased shall be payable to the Insured Person.

Obstetrical Benefit

If the Insured Person undergoes a surgical operation specified in the Schedule of Surgical Operations and Benefits under the heading "Obstetrical Procedures", while insured, or after the date her Surgical Operation Expense Insurance ceased if pregnancy existed on such date, the aforesaid benefit is payable to the Insured Person; provided, however, that the payment of any such benefit is subject to the Maternity Limitation, if any, shown in the Schedule of Insurance.

Limitations

No payment shall be made for any operation

(a) not recommended, approved, and performed by a legally qualified physician or surgeon; or

(b) performed in a Marine or Veterans hospital, or elsewhere at federal government expense.

SCHEDULE OF SURGICAL OPERATIONS AND BENEFITS

DESCRIPTION OF OPERATION	MAXIMUM PAYMENT FOR EACH OPERATION (Maximum Benefit of $200)
ABDOMEN	
Appendectomy, freeing of adhesions or surgical exploration of the abdominal cavity	$100.00
Removal of, or other operation on gall bladder	150.00
Gastro-enterostomy	150.00
Resection of stomach, bowel or rectum	200.00
ABSCESSES (See Tumors)	
AMPUTATIONS	
Thigh, leg	125.00
Upper arm, forearm, entire hand or foot	100.00
Fingers or toes, each	15.00
BREAST	
Removal of benign tumor or cyst requiring hospital confinement	50.00
Simple amputation	100.00
Radical amputation	150.00
CHEST	
Complete thoracoplasty, transthoracic approach to stomach, diaphragm, or esophagus; sympathectomy or laryngectomy	200.00
Removal of lung or portion of lung	200.00
Bronchoscopy, esophagoscopy	40.00
Induction of artificial pneumothorax, initial	25.00
Refills each (not more than 12)	10.00
DISLOCATION, REDUCTION OF	
Hip, ankle joint, elbow or knee joint (patella excepted)	35.00
Shoulder	25.00
Collar bone	20.00
Lower jaw, wrist or patella	15.00
For a dislocation requiring an open operation, the maximum will be twice the amount shown above.	
EAR, NOSE OR THROAT	
Fenestration, one or both ears	200.00
Mastoidectomy, one or both sides, simple	100.00
radical	150.00
Tonsillectomy, adenoidectomy, or both	30.00
Sinus operation by cutting (puncture of antrum excepted)	50.00
Submucous resection of nasal septum	50.00
Tracheotomy	75.00
EXCISION OR FIXATION BY CUTTING	
Hip joint	150.00
Knee or elbow joint	125.00
Shoulder, semilunar cartilage, wrist or ankle joint	100.00
Removal of diseased portion of bone, including curettage (alveolar processes excepted)	50.00
EYE	
Operation for detached retina or corneal transplant	200.00
Cataract, removal of	150.00
Any other cutting operation into the eyeball (through the cornea or sclera) or cutting operation on eye muscles	100.00
Removal of eyeball	75.00
FRACTURE, TREATMENT OF	
Thigh, vertebra or vertebrae, pelvis (coccyx excepted)	75.00
Leg, kneecap, upper arm, ankle (Pott's)	50.00
Lower jaw (alveolar process excepted), collar bone, shoulder blade, forearm, wrist (Colles'), skull	25.00
Hand, foot	15.00
Fingers or toes, each	10.00
Nose	10.00
Rib or ribs, three or more	25.00
fewer than three	10.00

The amounts shown above are for simple fractures.

For a compound fracture, the maximum will be one and one-half times the amount for the corresponding simple fracture

For a fracture requiring an open operation, the maximum will be twice the amount for the corresponding simple fracture (bone grafting or bone splicing or metallic fixation at point of fracture considered as open operation).

DESCRIPTION OF OPERATION	MAXIMUM PAYMENT FOR EACH OPERATION (Maximum Benefit of $200)
GENITO-URINARY TRACT	
Removal of, or cutting into, kidney	$200.00
Fixation of kidney	150.00
Removal of tumors or stones in ureter or bladder	
By cutting operation	100.00
By endoscopic means	35.00
Cystoscopy	25.00
Removal of prostate by open operation	150.00
Removal of prostate by endoscopic means	100.00
Circumcision	15.00
Varicocele, hydrocele, orchidectomy or epididymectomy, single	50.00
bilateral	75.00
Hysterectomy	150.00
Other cutting operations on uterus and its appendages with abdominal approach	100.00
Cervix amputation	50.00
Dilatation and curettage (non-puerperal), cervix cauterization or conization, polypectomy, or any combination of these	25.00
Vaginal plastic operation for, cystocele or rectocele	75.00
Cystocele and rectocele	100.00
GOITRE	
Removal of thyroid, subtotal	150.00
Removal of adenoma or benign tumor of thyroid	100.00
HERNIA	
Single hernia	100.00
More than one hernia	125.00
JOINT	
Incision into, tapping excepted	25.00
LIGAMENTS AND TENDONS	
Cutting or transplant, single	50.00
multiple	75.00
Suturing of tendon, single	35.00
multiple	50.00
PARACENTESIS	
Tapping	15.00
PILONIDAL CYST OR SINUS	
Removal of	50.00
RECTUM	
Hemorrhoidectomy, external	25.00
Internal, or internal and external	50.00
Cutting operation for fissure	25.00
Cutting operation for thrombosed hemorrhoids	15.00
Cutting operation for fistula in anus, single	50.00
multiple	75.00
SKULL	
Cutting into cranial cavity (trephine excepted)	200.00
Trephine	25.00
SPINE OR SPINAL CORD	
Operation for spinal cord tumor	200.00
Operation with removal of portion of vertebra or vertebrae (except coccyx. transverse or spinous process)	150.00
Removal of part or all of coccyx, or of transverse or spinous process	50.00
TUMORS	
Cutting operation for removal of one or more benign or superficial tumors, cysts or abscesses:	
Requiring hospital confinement	25.00
Not requiring hospital confinement	10.00
Malignant tumors of face, lip or skin	50.00
VARICOSE VEINS	
Injection treatment, complete procedure, one or both legs	40.00
Cutting operation, complete procedure, one leg	50.00
both legs	75.00
OBSTETRICAL PROCEDURES	
Delivery of child or children	50.00
Caesarean section	100.00
Abdominal operation for extra-uterine pregnancy	100.00
Miscarriage	25.00

Except for operations expressly excepted in the Schedule, the Company shall, subject to the terms and conditions of the Policy, determine a payment for any cutting operation not listed in the Schedule consistent with the payment for any listed operation of comparable difficulty and complexity, but in no event shall such payment exceed the applicable Maximum Surgical Benefit.

MEDICAL EXPENSE INSURANCE FOR INSURED PERSONS

Medical Expense Benefits

If the Insured Person receives medical treatment by a legally qualified physician as a result of

(1) an accidental bodily injury which does not arise out of and in the course of employment, or

(2) disease for which the Insured Person is not entitled to a benefit under any Workmen's Compensation Law or Act,

a benefit is payable to the Insured Person in an amount equal to the fees charged by the physician for each such treatment if received while the Insured Person is insured, but not in excess of the applicable Maximum Payment per Treatment shown in the Schedule of Insurance; provided that no benefit shall be payable

(a) in excess of the Maximum Medical Benefit shown in said Schedule for all treatments received by the Insured Person in connection with any one accident or any one disease (the phrase "any one disease" shall include a recurrence of the disease unless complete recovery has intervened) ; or

(b) for more than one treatment on any day; or

(c) for any treatment caused by or resulting from pregnancy, which term includes resulting childbirth or miscarriage; or

(d) for dental work or treatment, or for eye examinations or the fitting of glasses, or for X rays, drugs, dressings, or medicine; or

(e) for any treatment received in connection with and on or after the date of an operation or procedure for which a Surgical Operation Expense Benefit is payable under the Policy; or

(f) for any treatment received in a Marine or Veterans hospital, or elsewhere at federal government expense; or

(g) for the applicable number of treatments specified as Waiting Period in said Schedule, received after commencement of disability.

If the Insured Person is wholly disabled as a result of an injury or disease as hereinbefore described on the date his Medical Expense Insurance under the Policy ceases, is thereby prevented from performing any and every duty of his occupation, and receives medical treatment by a legally qualified physician within three months after the date his insurance ceased and during the continuance of such disability, the benefit hereinbefore described shall be payable to the Insured Person for such treatment, provided such benefit would have been payable if his insurance had not ceased.

LABORATORY AND X RAY EXAMINATION EXPENSE INSURANCE
FOR INSURED PERSONS

Laboratory and X ray Examination Expense Benefits

If the Insured Person receives a laboratory examination or an X ray examination specified in the Schedule of Laboratory and X ray Examinations and Benefits below and if such examination is made or recommended by a legally qualified physician in connection with a diagnosis of

(1) an accidental bodily injury which does not arise out of and in the course of employment, or

(2) a disease for which the Insured Person is not entitled to a benefit under any Workmen's Compensation Law or Act,

a benefit is payable to the Insured Person in an amount equal to the fees actually charged to the Insured Person for each such examination if received while the Insured Person is insured, but not in excess of the maximum payment specified for such examination in said Schedule, except that if two or more of the examinations are received by the Insured Person in connection with any one accident or any one disease (the phrase "any one disease" shall include a recurrence of the disease unless complete recovery has intervened), the total amount payable shall not exceed the Maximum Benefit shown in the Schedule of Insurance; provided that no payment shall be made for

(a) any examination received by the Insured Person while confined in a hospital if the Insured Person is entitled to any hospital expense benefits under the Policy during such confinement; or

(b) any examination due to or resulting from pregnancy, which term includes resulting childbirth or miscarriage; or

(c) any dental X ray examination unless it is the result of an accidental bodily injury which does not arise out of and in the course of employment; or

(d) any examination received from or in facilities owned or operated by the United States Government, or elsewhere at federal government expense.

If the Insured Person is wholly disabled as a result of an injury or disease hereinbefore described on the date his Laboratory and X ray Examination Expense Insurance under the Policy ceases, is thereby prevented from performing any and every duty of his occupation, and receives an examination hereinbefore described, made or recommended by a legally qualified physician, within three months after the date his insurance ceased and during the continuance of such disability, the benefit hereinbefore described shall be payable to the Insured Person for such examination, provided such benefit would have been payable if his insurance had not ceased.

SCHEDULE OF LABORATORY AND X RAY EXAMINATIONS AND BENEFITS

Description of X ray Examination	Maximum Payment
Abdomen or organs therein (unless otherwise specified in this Schedule)	$10.00
Arm or leg	5.00
Chest (heart and lungs)	10.00
Gall bladder, kidney, ureter, or bladder — dye method	15.00
Gastrointestinal series — barium meal	25.00
Head (skull or sinuses)	10.00
Joints (shoulder, knee, elbow, ankle, wrist, hands, or feet)	5.00
Pelvis	10.00

Description of Laboratory Examination	Maximum Payment
Basal Metabolism Test	$ 5.00
Electrocardiogram	7.50
Hinton, Kahn, or Kline Test (one or more types at one time to be considered one examination)	3.00
Malaria smear	2.00
Sputum Test	2.00
Sugar Determinations, blood and urine (one of each)	5.00
Sugar Tolerance (three or more blood and urine determinations)	10.00
Wassermann Test	5.00

The Insurance Company shall determine a consistent payment for any laboratory or X ray examination not covered in this Schedule unless payment for the examination is expressly excepted by the other terms of the Policy; provided, however, that such payment may be less than the smallest maximum payment listed but such payment shall in no event exceed the largest maximum payment listed.

GENERAL PROVISIONS

Definition. The term "Insured Person" as used herein shall mean a person who is insured under the Policy(ies).

Discontinuance of Individual Insurance of Insured Persons. The insurance of the Insured Person shall cease automatically as determined in accordance with the following paragraphs:

A. All coverages shall cease on the earliest of the following dates:

    (1) the date of termination of employment of the Insured Person. Cessation of active work in the eligible class of insured persons shall be considered termination of employment except that while the Insured Person is absent from work due to sickness, injury or temporary layoff (or, with respect to any Life Insurance, retirement or leave of absence; or, with respect to any Accidental Death and Dismemberment Insurance, leave of absence), employment shall be deemed to continue thereafter, for the purposes of insurance under the Policy(ies), until terminated by the Policyholder, acting in accordance with rules which preclude individual selection, either by written notice to the Insurance Company or by any other means; provided further, that in the event of temporary layoff or leave of absence, employment shall in no case be deemed to continue beyond the limited period specified in the Policy(ies) for each coverage; and that, in any event, employment shall be deemed to terminate on the date the Insured Person commenced active duty in the military or naval or air forces of any country at war, whether such war be declared or undeclared;

    (2) the date of termination of the membership of the Insured Person in the class or classes insured under the Policy(ies);

    (3) the date of termination of the insurance of the class of persons insured under the Policy(ies) of which the Insured Person is a member;

    (4) the date of termination of the Policy(ies).

B. An individual coverage of the Insured Person shall cease on the earliest of the following dates in addition to the dates listed in paragraph A above:

    (1) with respect to any such coverage,

        (a) the date of expiration of the period for which the last premium payment for such coverage was made either by the Policyholder to the Insurance Company or, if required, by the Insured Person to his employer, or

        (b) the date of termination of such coverage under the Policy.

(Applicable only to any Life Insurance or Accidental Death and Dismemberment Insurance)

Change of Beneficiary. The Insured Person may change the beneficiary by filing written notice thereof with the Policyholder. After such written notice has been received, the change shall relate back to take effect as of the date the Insured Person signed said written notice of change, whether or not the Insured Person is living at the time of the receipt of such written notice, but without prejudice to the Insurance Company on account of any payment made by it before receipt of such written notice. Consent of the Insured Person's beneficiary shall not be requisite to any change of beneficiary, or to any changes in the Policy(ies).

(Applicable to all coverages except Life Insurance)

Proof of Claim. All benefits provided in the Policy(ies) shall be paid, as stated in the following provision, upon receipt of written proof on the Insurance Company's forms or, if such forms are not furnished by the Insurance Company within fifteen days after demand therefor, then upon receipt of written proof covering the occurrence, character, and extent of the event for which claim is made.

Payment of Claim. Any Accidental Death and Dismemberment Insurance indemnities provided in the Policy will be paid immediately after receipt of due proof. Indemnity for loss of life is payable to the beneficiary if surviving the Insured Person, otherwise to the estate of the Insured Person. Any other Accidental Death and Dismemberment Insurance indemnities provided in the Policy are payable to the Insured Person.

    Subject to due proof of loss, any accrued Accident and Sickness Benefits, and Hospital Expense Benefits if requested by the Insured Person, will be paid to the Insured Person each week during any period for which the Insurance Company is liable, and any balance remaining unpaid at the termination of such period will be paid to the Insured Person immediately upon receipt of due proof; any other benefits provided in the Policy(ies) will be paid to the Insured Person immediately after receipt of due proof.

Examination. The Insurance Company shall have the right and opportunity to examine the person of the Insured Person when and so often as it may reasonably require during the pendency of a claim under the Policy(ies) and also the right and opportunity to make an autopsy in case of death where it is not forbidden by law.

Limitation of Action. No action at law or in equity shall be brought to recover on the Policy(ies) prior to the expiration of sixty days after proof of loss has been filed in accordance with the requirements of the Policy(ies), nor shall such action be brought at all unless brought within two years and ninety days after the date of loss upon which the cause of action is based. If any time limitation of the Policy with respect to bringing an action at law or in equity to recover on the Policy is less than that permitted by the law of the state in which the insured resides at the time the Policy is issued, such limitation is hereby extended to agree with the minimum period permitted by such law.

PLEASE ATTACH TO YOUR CERTIFICATE

NOTICE

to all Employees of

RICHARD ROE COMPANY

who are insured under Group Policy No.

Effective as of   said Policy is amended by the addition of the following provision which shall supersede and replace all other provisions, if any, of similar purpose to this provision, with respect to the benefits subject to this provision:

COORDINATION OF BENEFITS
UNDER THE POLICY WITH OTHER BENEFITS

A. Benefits Subject to this Provision

All of the benefits provided under the Policy *except Life Insurance, Accidental Death and Dismemberment Insurance and Accident and Sickness Insurance.*

B. Definitions

(1) "Plan" means any plan providing benefits or services for or by reason of medical or dental care or treatment, which benefits or services are provided by (i) group, blanket or franchise insurance coverage, (ii) group Blue Cross, group Blue Shield, group practice, and other prepayment coverage on a group basis, (iii) any coverage under labor-management trusteed plans, union welfare plans, employer organization plans, or employee benefit organization plans, and (iv) any coverage under governmental programs, and any coverage required or provided by any statute, which coverage is not otherwise excluded from the calculation of benefits under this Plan, but the term "Plan" shall not include benefits under any individual policies.

The term "Plan" shall be construed separately with respect to each policy, contract, or other arrangement for benefits or services and separately with respect to that portion of any such policy, contract, or other arrangement which reserves the right to take the benefits or services of other Plans into consideration in determining its benefits and that portion which does not.

(2) "This Plan" means those portions of the Policy which provide the benefits that are subject to this provision.

(3) "Allowable Expense" means any necessary, reasonable, and customary item of expense at least a portion of which is covered under at least one of the Plans covering the person for whom claim is made.

When a Plan provides benefits in the form of services rather than cash payments, the reasonable cash value of each service rendered shall be deemed to be both an Allowable Expense and a benefit paid.

(4) "Claim Determination Period" means calendar year, except that if in any calendar year the person is not covered under this Plan for the full calendar year, the claim determination period for that year shall be that portion thereof during which he was covered under this Plan.

C. Effect on Benefits

(1) This provision shall apply in determining the benefits as to a person covered under this Plan for any Claim Determination Period if, for the Allowable Expenses incurred as to such person during such Claim Determination Period, the sum of

(a) the benefits that would be payable under this Plan in the absence of this provision, and

(b) the benefits that would be payable under all other Plans in the absence therein of provisions of similar purpose to this provision,

would exceed such Allowable Expenses.

(2) As to any Claim Determination Period with respect to which this provision is applicable, the benefits that would be payable under this Plan in the absence of this provision for the Allowable Expenses incurred as to such person during such Claim Determination Period shall be reduced to the extent necessary so that the sum of such reduced benefits and all the benefits payable for such Allowable Expenses under all other Plans, except as provided in item (3) of this Section C, shall not exceed the total of such Allowable Expenses. Benefits payable under another Plan include the benefits that would have been payable had claim been duly made therefor.

(See reverse side)

A B C   MUTUAL LIFE INSURANCE COMPANY

Form 2326(C)   (Cal.)
Series *2*
Ed. 12-68   *President*

COORDINATION OF BENEFITS
UNDER THE POLICY WITH OTHER BENEFITS (Continued)

C. Effect on Benefits (Continued)

(3) If

    (a) another Plan which is involved in item (2) of this section C and which contains a provision co-ordinating its benefits with those of this Plan would, according to its rules, determine its benefits after the benefits of this Plan have been determined, and

    (b) the rules set forth in item (4) of this section C would require this Plan to determine its benefits before such other Plan,

then the benefits of such other Plan will be ignored for the purposes of determining the benefits under this Plan.

(4) For the purposes of item (3) of this Section C, the rules establishing the order of benefit determination are:

    (a) The benefits of a Plan which covers the person on whose expenses claim is based other than as a dependent shall be determined before the benefits of a Plan which covers such person as a dependent;

    (b) The benefits of a Plan which covers the person on whose expenses claim is based as a dependent of a male person shall be determined before the benefits of a Plan which covers such person as a dependent of a female person;

    (c) When rules (a) and (b) do not establish an order of benefit determination, the benefits of a Plan which has covered the person on whose expenses claim is based for the longer period of time shall be determined before the benefits of a Plan which has covered such person the shorter period of time.

(5) When this provision operates to reduce the total amount of benefits otherwise payable as to a person covered under this Plan during any Claim Determination Period, each benefit that would be payable in the absence of this provision shall be reduced proportionately, and such reduced amount shall be charged against any applicable benefit limit of this Plan.

D. Right to Receive and Release Necessary Information

For the purposes of determining the applicability of and implementing the terms of this provision of this Plan or any provision of similar purpose of any other Plan, the Company may, without the consent of or notice to any person, release to or obtain from any other insurance company or other organization or person any information, with respect to any person, which the Company deems to be necessary for such purposes. Any person claiming benefits under this Plan shall furnish to the Company such information as may be necessary to implement this provision.

Appendix 13

DEPARTMENT OF LABOR FORM D-1 (DESCRIPTION OF EMPLOYEE WELFARE OR PENSION BENEFIT PLAN)

U. S. DEPARTMENT OF LABOR
Form D-1
DECEMBER 1958

EMPLOYEE WELFARE OR PENSION BENEFIT PLAN
DESCRIPTION FORM

Form approved.
Budget Bureau No. 44-R1114.

This form is made available by the U. S. Department of Labor as directed by the Welfare and Pension Plans Disclosure Act, Public Law 85-836, to assist administrators of welfare and pension plans in discharging their responsibilities under the act. Use a separate form for each separate employee welfare benefit plan and each separate employee pension benefit plan or combination thereof. Read Instructions carefully before completing the form.

Is this an original filing ☐ or an amended filing ☐ ?   File No. _____

1. NAME OF PLAN AND ADDRESS OF ITS PRINCIPAL OFFICE *(Include the name of the employer or employee organization with which plan is identified.)*	2. FINANCIAL RECORDS OF THE PLAN ARE MAINTAINED ON A CALENDAR, POLICY, OR FISCAL YEAR ENDING

2. FINANCIAL RECORDS OF THE PLAN ARE MAINTAINED ON A CALENDAR, POLICY, OR FISCAL YEAR ENDING

MONTH   DAY

3. INDICATE BY CHECKING THE APPROPRIATE BOX BELOW THE TYPE OF PLAN FOR WHICH THIS DESCRIPTION IS BEING SUBMITTED

A. WELFARE BENEFIT PLAN	B. PENSION BENEFIT PLAN	C. COMBINATION OF A. AND B.
☐	☐	☐

4. CHECK THE CATEGORY THAT BEST DESCRIBES THE GROUPS COVERED BY THE PLAN:

A. ALL EMPLOYEES	B. HOURLY RATE EMPLOYEES	C. SALARIED EMPLOYEES	D. OTHER (SPECIFY):
☐	☐	☐	

5. INDUSTRY IN WHICH MOST OF THE PARTICIPANTS ARE EMPLOYED: (CHECK ONE)

MANUFAC-TURING	MINING	CONSTRUC-TION	TRANS-PORTATION	COMMUNICATION AND UTILITIES	WHOLESALE AND RETAIL TRADE	FINANCE, INSURANCE, AND REAL ESTATE	SERVICES	OTHER (SPECIFY):
A.☐	B.☐	C.☐	D.☐	E.☐	F.☐	G.☐	H.☐	I. _____

6. IS THE PLAN MENTIONED IN A COLLECTIVE-BARGAINING AGREEMENT? YES ☐   NO ☐

7. PARTIES MAKING CONTRIBUTIONS TO THE PLAN: (CHECK ALL THAT APPLY)

A. EMPLOYER(S)	B. PLAN PARTICIPANTS	C. UNION (OUT OF GENERAL FUNDS)	D. OTHER (SPECIFY):
☐	☐	☐	

8. PROVIDE THE FOLLOWING INFORMATION:

A. OFFICIAL NAME (OR TITLE) AND ADDRESS OF PLAN ADMINISTRATOR*

B. ADMINISTRATOR OF THE PLAN IN 8A IS AN:

(1) EMPLOYER OR EMPLOYER ASSOCIATION	(2) JOINT EMPLOYER-EMPLOYEE BOARD OF TRUSTEES	(3) EMPLOYEE ORGANIZATION INCLUDING EMPLOYEE BENEFICIARY ASSOCIATION	(4) OTHER (SPECIFY):
☐	☐	☐	

C. INDIVIDUAL NAMES AND ADDRESSES OF PERSONS CONSTITUTING THE ADMINISTRATOR UNDER THE ACT, AS IDENTIFIED IN 8A ABOVE (1)	OFFICIAL POSITION WITH RESPECT TO THE PLAN (2)	RELATIONSHIP, IF ANY, TO EMPLOYER(S) OR TO EMPLOYEE ORGANIZATIONS (SEE INSTRUCTIONS) (3)	ANY OTHER OFFICES, POSITIONS, OR EMPLOYMENT HELD (4)

**The act defines the administrator of the plan as follows: "(1) the person or persons designated by the terms of the plan or the collective-bargaining agreement with responsibility for the ultimate control, disposition, or management of the money received or contributed; or (2) in the absence of such designation, the person or persons actually responsible for the control, disposition, or management of the money received or contributed, irrespective of whether such control, disposition, or management is exercised directly or through an agent or trustee designated by such person or persons." Under the act, the term "person" means "an individual, partnership, corporation, mutual company, joint-stock company, trust, unincorporated organization, association, or employee organization."*

894

9. DESCRIPTION OF TYPE OF ADMINISTRATION. OPPOSITE EACH OF THE FUNCTIONS LISTED IN COLUMN (1), INDICATE THE PARTY OR PARTIES WHO PERFORM SUCH FUNCTION, FOR EXAMPLE, EMPLOYER, UNION, TRUSTEE, CARRIER, AS SHOWN IN THE INSTRUCTIONS.   IN CASE DIFFERENT PARTIES PERFORM A PARTICULAR FUNCTION WITH RESPECT TO DIFFERENT BENEFITS, FOOTNOTE EACH PARTY AND SHOW IN FOOTNOTE SPACE THE BENEFIT OR BENEFITS FOR WHICH HE PERFORMS THE FUNCTION.

FUNCTION (IF APPLICABLE) (1)	PARTY PERFORMING FUNCTION (2)
A. MAINTAINS RECORDS OF PLAN PARTICIPANTS	
B. DETERMINES ELIGIBILITY OF INDIVIDUAL CLAIMANTS FOR RECEIPT OF BENEFITS	
C. PROCESSES CLAIMS FOR BENEFITS UNDER THE PLAN	
D. MAKES DETERMINATION ON APPEALS	
E. AUTHORIZES PAYMENT OF BENEFITS	
F. MAKES PAYMENTS TO BENEFICIARIES	
G. AUTHORIZES INCURRENCE OF EXPENSES	
H. SELECTS CARRIER OR SERVICE ORGANIZATION	
I. SELECTS CORPORATE TRUSTEE	
J. DETERMINES INVESTMENT POLICY	

FOOTNOTES:

10. IDENTIFY EACH PARTY THROUGH WHICH PLAN BENEFITS ARE PROVIDED, FOR EXAMPLE, INSURANCE COMPANY, CORPORATE TRUSTEE, TRUSTEES OTHER THAN CORPORATE, COMMUNITY HOSPITAL-SURGICAL ASSOCIATION, HEALTH CARE CONTRACTOR, AND INDICATE BENEFITS PROVIDED THROUGH EACH.

STATE NAME AND ADDRESS (If benefits are provided directly by the plan administrator enter term "plan administrator" in lieu of his name and address.) (1)	ENTER BELOW EACH BENEFIT PROVIDED THROUGH THE PARTY OR ORGANIZATION LISTED IN COLUMN (1) (2)

11. STATE THE NAMES, TITLES, AND ADDRESSES OF ANY TRUSTEE OR TRUSTEES NOT LISTED IN ITEMS 8C (1) OR 10 (1) ABOVE.

12. SUBMIT AS PART OF THIS DESCRIPTION:
    (A) COPIES OF THE PLAN OR BARGAINING AGREEMENT, TRUST AGREEMENT, CONTRACT, OR OTHER INSTRUMENT
        UNDER WHICH THE PLAN WAS ESTABLISHED AND IS OPERATED;
    (B) THE SCHEDULE OF PLAN BENEFITS;
    (C) THE PROCEDURES TO BE FOLLOWED UNDER THE PLAN IN PRESENTING CLAIMS FOR BENEFITS AND FOR
        APPEALING DENIAL OF CLAIMS.
    IDENTIFY BELOW EACH DOCUMENT OR OTHER MATERIAL BEING SUBMITTED.

NOTE: If schedule of benefits and procedures for appeals, required in (B) and (C) are part of one of the documents submitted and listed, specify on the list those documents containing this information.

LIST OF DOCUMENTS SUBMITTED

SIGNATURE AND VERIFICATION

    The plan description after its completion shall be signed by the plan administrator, in the presence of a Notary Public or other officer authorized to administer oaths, using (A) or (B) below, whichever is appropriate.

STATE OF ------------------------------------ \
                                 } ss.

COUNTY OF ---------------------------------- /

    (A) ---------------------------------------, being duly sworn, says that he is --- of
                                                      (Title of officer)

--, administrator of the plan and that the information in this plan description (including the
        (Name of company)
information contained in any accompanying documents described in Item 12) has been examined by him and is to the best of his knowledge and belief, true, correct, and complete.

    (B) --

--- the
administrator of the plan, being duly sworn, each for himself deposes and says that the information in this plan description (including the information contained in any accompanying documents described in Item 12) has been examined by him and is to the best of his knowledge and belief, true, correct, and complete.

Signed and Sworn To Before Me

This ------------------------------- Day of -------------------, 19------
                                 (Month)

                (Notary Public)

    Mail <u>two</u> copies of the form completed in accordance with the instructions and two copies of each accompanying document to the Office of Labor-Management and Welfare-Pension Reports, U. S. Department of Labor, Washington, D. C., 20210.

    This will constitute a receipt for documents submitted for filing with the Secretary of Labor as a description of a welfare or pension benefit plan under the provisions of the Welfare and Pension Plans Disclosure Act, when stamped opposite with the date and the file number with which such documents have been marked. Please self-address the receipt form below and enter the name of the plan as given in Item 1, page 1, of this form.

For official use by the U. S. Department of Labor
(DO NOT WRITE IN THIS SPACE)

NAME OF PLAN ---

      NAME ---

     ADDRESS ---

    CITY, ZONE,
    AND STATE ---

Appendix 14

DEPARTMENT OF LABOR FORM D-2 (ANNUAL REPORT FOR EMPLOYEE WELFARE OR PENSION BENEFIT PLAN)

U.S. DEPARTMENT OF LABOR
Form D–2
JANUARY 1959

EMPLOYEE WELFARE OR PENSION BENEFIT PLAN
ANNUAL REPORT FOR THE YEAR ENDING --

Form approved.
Budget Bureau No. 44–R1115

(Month, Day, Year)

This form is made available by the U.S. Department of Labor as directed by the Welfare and Pension Plans Disclosure Act, Public Law 85–836, to assist administrators of welfare and pension plans in discharging their responsibilities under the act. Use a separate form for each separate employee welfare benefit plan and each separate employee pension benefit plan or combination thereof. Read instructions carefully before completing the form.

PART I

This part is to be completed for all plans

Except as otherwise indicated, all items should be filled in or marked "none" or "NA" (not applicable), as appropriate.

1. NAME OF PLAN AND ADDRESS OF ITS PRINCIPAL OFFICE (*Include the name of the employer or employee organization with which plan is identified.*)

2. LABOR DEPARTMENT FILE NUMBER (*Enter the file number appearing on the Department's acknowledgment of the receipt of your description of this plan.*)

3. INDICATE BY CHECKING THE APPROPRIATE BOX BELOW THE TYPE OF PLAN FOR WHICH THIS REPORT IS BEING SUBMITTED

A. WELFARE BENEFIT PLAN ☐   B. PENSION BENEFIT PLAN ☐   C. COMBINATION OF A. AND B. ☐

4. OFFICIAL NAME (OR TITLE) AND ADDRESS OF PLAN ADMINISTRATOR*

SIGNATURE AND VERIFICATION

(Complete all parts of this annual report applicable to the plan before executing this)

This report shall be signed by the administrator* in the space provided and the information contained in it (including exhibits, schedules, and other documents attached) shall either be (1) sworn to by the administrator* before a Notary Public or other officer authorized to administer oaths, using (A) or (B), whichever is appropriate, or (2) certified to by an independent certified or licensed public accountant, based upon a comprehensive audit conducted in accordance with accepted standards of auditing. If method (2) is used, attach the accountant's certificate, which shall state facts indicating that the above requirements are met, and check this box: ☐ Certification described in (2) above is attached.

Signature(s) of administrator:* --

--   --

STATE OF ----------------------------------

COUNTY OF ------------------------------- } ss.

(A) ---, whose signature appears above, being duly sworn, says that he is -----------

-- of ---,

(Title of officer)   (Name of company)

administrator* of the plan to which this annual report pertains and that the information in PARTS ---------------------- and -------------------- which constitute this report, including all exhibits, schedules, and other documents referred to therein and attached hereto, has been examined by him and is to the best of his knowledge and belief, true, correct, and complete.

(B) ---

--,

whose signature(s) appear(s) above, the administrator* of the plan to which this annual report pertains, being duly sworn, each for himself

deposes and says that the information in PARTS ---------------- and ---------------- which constitute this report, including all exhibits, schedules, and other documents referred to therein and attached hereto, has been examined by him and is to the best of his knowledge and belief, true, correct, and complete.

SWORN TO BEFORE ME this ----------- day of -------------------------, 19------   ---

(Notary Public)

Mail *two* copies of the form completed in accordance with the instructions and two copies of each accompanying document to the Welfare and Pension Reports Division, Bureau of Labor Standards, U.S. Department of Labor, Liberty Loan Building, Washington 25, D.C.

* The act defines the administrator of the plan as follows: "(1) the person or persons designated by the terms of the plan or the collective-bargaining agreement with responsibility for the ultimate control, disposition, or management of the money received or contributed; or (2) in the absence of such designation, the person or persons actually responsible for the control, disposition, or management of the money received or contributed, irrespective of whether such control, disposition, or management is exercised directly or through an agent or trustee designated by such person or persons." Under the act, the term "person" means "an individual, partnership, corporation, mutual company, joint-stock company, trust, unincorporated organization, association, or employee organization."

[1]

o59—16—74778–1

5. PROVIDE THE FOLLOWING INFORMATION ON FUNDING PLAN BENEFITS:

A. ARE ANY OF THE PLAN BENEFITS PROVIDED OR FUNDED THROUGH AN INSURANCE CARRIER OR SERVICE OR OTHER ORGANIZATION?

☐ YES ☐ NO. IF YES, LIST SUCH CLASSES OF BENEFITS BELOW (SEE INSTRUCTIONS):

B. ARE ANY OF THE PLAN BENEFITS FUNDED OR PROVIDED THROUGH THE MEDIUM OF A TRUST OR OTHER SEPARATELY MAINTAINED FUND?

☐ YES ☐ NO. IF YES, LIST, ACCORDING TO THE INSTRUCTIONS, THE CLASSES OF BENEFITS PROVIDED DIRECTLY BY THE TRUST (EXCLUDE BENEFITS PROVIDED THROUGH AN INSURANCE CONTRACT PURCHASED BY THE FUND WHICH SHOULD BE ENTERED UNDER A):

C. ARE ANY OF THE PLAN BENEFITS COMPLETELY UNFUNDED? ☐ YES ☐ NO. IF YES, LIST THE CLASSES OF SUCH UNFUNDED BENEFITS BELOW (SEE INSTRUCTIONS):

| Completely unfunded plans do not answer ITEMS 6 and 7 but answer ITEM 8 instead |

6. IF IN ITEM 5 EITHER "A" OR "B" IS CHECKED "YES,"

A. ENTER THE AMOUNT CONTRIBUTED TO THE PLAN DURING THE PERIOD COVERED BY THIS REPORT BY:

1. EMPLOYERS $................... 2. EMPLOYEES $................... 3. OTHER (SPECIFY) .... $...................

B. STATE THE NUMBER OF EMPLOYEES COVERED BY THE PLAN DURING THE YEAR COVERED BY THIS REPORT ....

7. IF IN ITEM 5 EITHER "A" OR "B" IS CHECKED "YES," STATE AMOUNT OF BENEFITS PAID OR OTHERWISE FURNISHED BY THE PLAN EITHER DIRECTLY OR THROUGH INSURANCE, DURING THE YEAR COVERED BY THIS REPORT (SEE INSTRUCTIONS): $...................

8. FOR COMPLETELY UNFUNDED PLANS ONLY:

A. IF IN ITEM 5, "C" IS CHECKED "YES," AND "A" AND "B" ARE CHECKED "NO," SHOWING THAT THE PLAN IS COMPLETELY UNFUNDED, FILL IN THE FOLLOWING TABLE FOR THE YEAR COVERED BY THIS REPORT AND FOR EACH OF THE PRECEDING FOUR YEARS. ALL COMPLETELY UNFUNDED PLANS SHOULD COMPLETE THIS TABLE.

YEAR ENDING (MONTH, DAY, YEAR) (1)	WELFARE PLAN BENEFITS		PENSION PLAN BENEFITS		
	TOTAL BENEFITS PAID UNDER PLAN (2)	AVERAGE NUMBER OF EMPLOYEES ELIGIBLE FOR PARTICIPATION (3)	TOTAL BENEFITS PAID UNDER PLAN (4)	AVERAGE NUMBER OF EMPLOYEES ELIGIBLE FOR PARTICIPATION (5)	TOTAL BENEFITS PAID TO RETIRED EMPLOYEES[1] (6)
------------------	$----------	------------	$----------	------------	$----------
------------------					

------------------					

[1] *Enter total in this column only if it differs from amount shown in column 4.*

B. IF IN ITEM 5, "C" IS CHECKED "YES" AND "A" AND "B" ARE CHECKED "NO," SHOWING THAT THE PLAN IS COMPLETELY UNFUNDED, ARE THE ONLY ASSETS FROM WHICH CLAIMS AGAINST THE PLAN MAY BE PAID THE GENERAL ASSETS OF THE EMPLOYER? ☐ YES ☐ NO. IF NO, EXPLAIN:

INSTRUCTIONS TO ADMINISTRATOR OF <u>COMPLETELY UNFUNDED PLANS</u>

The completion of PART I provides all the information required by the Act for an annual report of a **completely unfunded plan.** The administrator of such a plan, after completing Items 1 through 5 and Item 8 of PART I, should execute the signature and verification on the face of the report in accordance with the instructions and mail **two** copies of the completed form to the Welfare and Pension Reports Division, Bureau of Labor Standards, U.S. Department of Labor, Liberty Loan Building, Washington 25, D.C.

[2]

c59—16—74778-1

U.S. DEPARTMENT OF LABOR
Form D-2
JANUARY 1959

(Name of plan)

PART II

Those who have checked "Yes" in "A" of Item 5, PART I, fill in PART II to the extent applicable. Plan administrators should complete this part only if some or all the benefits provided by the plan are underwritten by an insurance carrier or service or other organization. Such plans should also complete PART III to the extent applicable. PART III should also be completed, to the extent applicable by those who have checked "Yes" in "B" of Item 5.

If PART II is not applicable to your plan, check below and leave Items 9 and 10 blank.

☐ PART II not applicable to this plan.

9. ALL PLANS WITH BENEFITS PROVIDED BY AN INSURANCE CARRIER OR SERVICE OR OTHER ORGANIZATION WHICH MAINTAINS SEPARATE EXPERIENCE RECORDS FOR THE GROUPS IT SERVES SHOULD COMPLETE AND ATTACH EXHIBIT A-1.

ALL PLANS THAT PROVIDE INSURED PENSION BENEFITS SHOULD COMPLETE AND ATTACH EXHIBIT A-2.

ALL PLANS WITH BENEFITS PROVIDED BY AN INSURANCE CARRIER OR SERVICE OR OTHER ORGANIZATION WHICH DOES NOT MAINTAIN SEPARATE EXPERIENCE RECORDS FOR THE GROUPS IT SERVES SHOULD COMPLETE AND ATTACH EXHIBIT A-3.

SEPARATE EXHIBITS SHOULD BE COMPLETED AND ATTACHED FOR EACH SEPARATE INSURANCE CARRIER OR SERVICE OR OTHER ORGANIZATION PROVIDING BENEFITS UNDER THE PLAN.

A. COMPLETED EXHIBIT A-1 ATTACHED ☐ YES ☐ NO

B. COMPLETED EXHIBIT A-2 ATTACHED ☐ YES ☐ NO

C. COMPLETED EXHIBIT A-3 ATTACHED ☐ YES ☐ NO

10. PROVIDE THE FOLLOWING INFORMATION ON ANY INSURED WELFARE OR PENSION PLAN BENEFITS UNDERWRITTEN BY AN INSURANCE CARRIER OR SERVICE OR OTHER ORGANIZATION. INFORMATION IS TO BE PROVIDED FOR THE SAME CONTRACTS FOR WHICH DATA ARE SUBMITTED UNDER EXHIBITS A-1, A-2, OR A-3. A PENSION TRUST OR OTHER MASS PURCHASE OF INDIVIDUAL CONTRACTS MAY BE TREATED AS A UNIT. REPORT THE DATA FOR EACH CONTRACT IN A SEPARATE COLUMN.

1. NAME OF CARRIER OR SERVICE OR OTHER ORGANIZATION:

2. CONTRACT IDENTIFICATION[1]:

3. DATA FOR PERIOD: (FROM) (TO) (FROM) (TO)

4. PREMIUM RATE OR SUBSCRIPTION CHARGE: $ $

5. TOTAL PREMIUM OR SUBSCRIPTION CHARGE PAID (IN CASH OR BY APPLICATION OF DIVIDENDS OR OTHER CREDITS): $ $

	CLASS OF BENEFITS PROVIDED	APPROXIMATE NUMBER OF PERSONS COVERED	CLASS OF BENEFITS PROVIDED	APPROXIMATE NUMBER OF PERSONS COVERED
6. CLASS OF BENEFITS PROVIDED AND APPROXIMATE NUMBER OF PERSONS COVERED BY EACH CLASS OF BENEFITS:				

[1] The identification used here should agree with that used in each Exhibit A-1, A-2, or A-3, which is a part of this submission. Each contract should be identified by contract number or by some other appropriate identification.

o59—16—74778-1

[3]

PART III

> Those who have checked "Yes" in "B" of Item 5, PART I, fill in PART III. This part should be filled in for any plan that involves a trust or other separately maintained fund.
>
> Those who have checked "Yes" in "A" of Item 5, PART I, may also have to fill in PART III. PART III should be filled in to the extent applicable if the plan (1) has incurred expenses other than (a) payments for unfunded benefits or (b) insurance or annuity premiums or subscription charges paid to an insurance carrier or service or other organization or (2) has assets other than (a) insurance or annuity contracts or (b) contributions in the process of payment or collection.
>
> If PART III is not applicable to your plan, check below, leave Items 11, 12 and 13 blank, and see instruction following Item 13.

☐ PART III not applicable to this plan.

11. COMPLETE AND ATTACH, IF APPLICABLE:

A. EXHIBIT B-1, STATEMENT OF ASSETS AND LIABILITIES—

EXHIBIT B-1 COMPLETED AND ATTACHED .... ☐ YES ☐ NO

B. EXHIBIT B-2, SUMMARY OF RECEIPTS AND DISBURSEMENTS—

EXHIBIT B-2 COMPLETED AND ATTACHED .... ☐ YES ☐ NO

C. SCHEDULE 1, SALARIES PAID AND CHARGED TO PLAN—

SCHEDULE 1 COMPLETED AND ATTACHED .... ☐ YES ☐ NO

D. SCHEDULE 2, FEES AND COMMISSIONS PAID AND CHARGED TO PLAN—

SCHEDULE 2 COMPLETED AND ATTACHED .... ☐ YES ☐ NO

12. THIS ITEM IS TO BE COMPLETED ONLY FOR PENSION BENEFITS PROVIDED DIRECTLY FROM A TRUST FUND:

A. STATE THE TYPE AND BASIS OF FUNDING:

B. ATTACH A STATEMENT OF THE ACTUARIAL ASSUMPTIONS USED IN DETERMINING THE CONTRIBUTIONS TO THE PENSION TRUST FUND. A COPY OF THE LATEST ACTUARIAL REPORT, WHICH INCLUDES SUCH A STATEMENT OF THE ACTUARIAL ASSUMPTIONS, MAY BE SUBMITTED IN LIEU OF THE FOREGOING. ANY STATEMENTS OR SUCH REPORTS SUBMITTED AS ATTACHMENTS SHOULD BE CLEARLY MARKED WITH THE NAME OF THE PLAN INVOLVED.

(1) STATEMENT OF ACTUARIAL ASSUMPTIONS ATTACHED ☐ YES ☐ NO

(2) ACTUARIAL REPORT ATTACHED ☐ YES ☐ NO

C. THE AMOUNT OF CURRENT AND PAST SERVICE LIABILITIES WAS $................................ AS OF ....
(Date of determination)

D. STATE NUMBER OF EMPLOYEES COVERED BY THE FUND: RETIRED .... NONRETIRED ....

13. PARTY IN INTEREST TRANSACTIONS:

A. WERE ANY OF THE ASSETS OF THE FUND INVESTED IN SECURITIES OR PROPERTIES OF THE EMPLOYER OR EMPLOYEE ORGANIZATION, OR ANY OTHER PARTY IN INTEREST BY REASON OF BEING AN OFFICER, TRUSTEE, OR EMPLOYEE OF THE FUND? ☐ YES ☐ NO. IF YES, COMPLETE TABLE A AND TABLE C OF EXHIBIT C OR, IN THE ALTERNATIVE, COMPLETE TABLES B AND C OF EXHIBIT C AND FULFILL THE REQUIREMENTS OF COLUMN (3) OF EXHIBIT B-1.

(1) TABLE A OF EXHIBIT C COMPLETED AND ATTACHED ☐ YES ☐ NO

(2) TABLE B OF EXHIBIT C COMPLETED AND ATTACHED ☐ YES ☐ NO

(3) TABLE C OF EXHIBIT C COMPLETED AND ATTACHED ☐ YES ☐ NO

B. WERE ANY LOANS TO THE EMPLOYER, EMPLOYEE ORGANIZATION OR OTHER PARTY IN INTEREST BY REASON OF BEING AN OFFICER, TRUSTEE, OR EMPLOYEE OF THE FUND MADE DURING THE YEAR OR OTHERWISE OUTSTANDING AT END OF THE YEAR? ☐ YES ☐ NO. IF YES, FILL IN TABLE D OF EXHIBIT C.

TABLE D OF EXHIBIT C COMPLETED AND ATTACHED ☐ YES ☐ NO

INSTRUCTIONS TO ADMINISTRATORS

The administrator of a plan completing the Annual Report Form D-2, together with applicable exhibits, schedules and documents, should execute the signature and verification on the face of the annual report form in accordance with the instructions, and mail **two** copies of the completed form and **two** copies of each accompanying document to the Welfare and Pension Reports Division, Bureau of Labor Standards; U.S. Department of Labor, Liberty Loan Building, Washington 25, D.C.

U.S. Department of Labor
Form D-2
January 1959

EXHIBIT A-1
WELFARE AND PENSION INSURANCE DATA

(Name of plan)

(Address of plan's principal office)

The information should be obtained from the insurance carrier or service or other organization and should be for the period covered by the annual report. If the information is not available for such period, information for the latest completed policy year may be entered.

A. Provide the following information on any insured welfare or pension plan benefits underwritten by an insurance carrier or service or other organization which maintains separate experience records covering the specific groups it serves. Report the experience under each contract in a separate column. If the amount called for in any line in this exhibit is available only on a combined-contract basis, the amount for such line may be given on such combined-contract basis. In such case add a footnote identifying the contracts to which the figure is applicable. Where each individual in the group for which benefits are provided under the plan is the subject of a separate contract, the entire group of such contracts may be treated as a unit in making the report.

	(1)		(2)	
(1) Name of carrier or service or other organization:				
(2) Contract identification [1]:				
(3) Data for period:	(from) ____ (to) ____		(from) ____ (to) ____	
	CLASS OF BENEFITS PROVIDED	APPROXIMATE NUMBER OF PERSONS COVERED	CLASS OF BENEFITS PROVIDED	APPROXIMATE NUMBER OF PERSONS COVERED
(4) Class of benefits provided and approximate number of persons covered by each class of benefits:				
(5) Total premium received (in cash or by application of dividends or other credits):	$		$	
(6) Total claims paid:	$		$	
(7) Dividends or retroactive rate refunds (adjustments) paid:	$		$	
(8) Commissions paid [2]:	$		$	
(9) Administrative service or other fees paid [3]:	$		$	
(10) Other specific acquisition costs paid:	$		$	
(11) Any amounts held to provide benefits after retirement:	$		$	
(12) Remainder of premium:	$		$	

[1] Each contract should be identified by contract number or by some other appropriate identification.

[2] Include amounts paid to general agents, other agents, brokers, or other persons. Report details in "B" on the reverse side of this page.

[3] Fees include administrative fees, service fees, and payments (not including commissions reported in line (8)) for services, expenses or other reasons which are paid to a policyholder, agent, broker or other individual or firm. Report details in "B" on reverse side of this page.

o59—16—74778-1

B. Provide the following information on commissions and fees reported in lines 8 and 9 of "A" in Exhibit A–1. This information should be obtained from the insurance carrier or service or other organization.

CONTRACT IDENTIFICATION [1] (1)	NAME AND ADDRESS OF EACH RECIPIENT OF COMMISSIONS OR FEES (2)	AMOUNT OF COMMISSIONS PAID EACH RECIPIENT [2] (3)	AMOUNT OF FEES PAID EACH RECIPIENT [3] (4)	PURPOSE FOR WHICH PAID (5)
		$	$	

[1] *Use same identification as in line 2, of "A" of this exhibit.*

[2] *Include amounts paid to general agents, other agents, brokers, or other persons.*

[3] *Fees include administrative fees, service fees and payments (other than commissions reported in column (3)) for services, expenses or other reasons which are paid to a policyholder, agent, broker or other individual or firm.*

o59—16—74778-1

U.S. Department of Labor
Form D-2
January 1959

EXHIBIT A-2
INSURED PENSION DATA

_____ (Name of plan) _____   _____ (Address of plan's principal office) _____

Complete this exhibit for those pension plan benefits funded through the medium of a contract with an insurance carrier. A pension trust involving individual contracts may be treated as a unit.

A. Type and basis of funding: Indicate in column (1) the type of contract such as group deferred annuity, group permanent life insurance, individual policy pension trust, group deposit administration, under which plan benefits are provided and identify each contract. In column (2) state the type and basis of funding each contract listed in column (1).

TYPE AND IDENTIFICATION OF CONTRACT[1] (1)	TYPE AND BASIS OF FUNDING (2)

B. State the number of employees covered under each contract:

CONTRACT IDENTIFICATION[1] (1)	NUMBER OF EMPLOYEES (BOTH)—	
	RETIRED (2)	NONRETIRED (3)

C. Attach a statement of the actuarial assumptions used in determining the premium payments under each contract identified in A, above. A copy of the latest actuarial report which includes such a statement of the actuarial assumptions may be submitted in lieu of the foregoing. Relate any statements or reports submitted as attachments to the contract involved by marking such attachments with the contract identification.[1]

    (1) Statement of actuarial assumptions attached   ☐ Yes   ☐ No

    (2) Actuarial report attached   ☐ Yes   ☐ No

D. Except for the benefits which are completely guaranteed by the carrier, give the following information for each insurance contract listed in A, above.

CONTRACT IDENTIFICATION[1] (1)	AMOUNT OF CURRENT AND PAST SERVICE LIABILITIES, BASED ON ACTUARIAL ASSUMPTIONS DESCRIBED IN C, ABOVE (2)	AMOUNT OF ACCUMULATED RESERVES (3)	DATE OF DETERMINATION (4)
	$		
	$		

[1] Each contract should be identified by contract number or by some other appropriate identification.

o59—16—74778-1

Appendix 15

DEPARTMENT OF LABOR FORM D-3 (INFORMATION ON EMPLOYEE WELFARE OR PENSION PLAN COVERING LESS THAN 100 PARTICIPANTS)

Form D-3
September 196'

U.S. DEPARTMENT OF LABOR
Office of Welfare and Pension Plans
Washington 25, D.C.

Form Approved
Budget Bureau
Number 44-R1196

INFORMATION ON EMPLOYEE WELFARE OR PENSION BENEFIT PLAN COVERING LESS THAN 100 PARTICIPANTS

This form is prescribed by the U.S. Department of Labor pursuant to the Welfare and Pension Plans Disclosure Act as amended for use in notifying the Department that the employee welfare or pension benefit plan identified below, a description of which has been filed with the U.S. Department of Labor, covered less than 100 participants during the entire reporting year. Unless specifically required by the Secretary of Labor, Annual Report Form D-2 is not required to be filed for such plans.

(SEE EXPLANATORY NOTES ON REVERSE SIDE BEFORE COMPLETING THIS FORM)

1. LABOR DEPARTMENT FILE NUMBER *(Enter the file number assigned to this plan by the U.S. Department of Labor)* _____

2. NAME OF PLAN AND ADDRESS OF ITS PRINCIPAL OFFICE *(Include the name of the employer or employee organization with which plan is identified)*

   Employer, Employer Association or
   Employee Organization_____

   Name of Plan _____

   Address of Plan—
   Street and Number_____

   City, Zone and State _____

3. INFORMATION FOR PLAN YEAR ENDING _____
   (Enter the ending date of the calendar, policy, or other fiscal year upon which the records of the plan are maintained)

4. GREATEST NUMBER OF PARTICIPANTS COVERED BY PLAN AT ANY TIME DURING REPORTING YEAR INDICATED IN ITEM 3.
   Check one box

   A. ☐ 26-99

   B. ☐ Less than 26 *(See explanatory notes on reverse side)*

_____   _____
(Signature)   (Signature)

_____   _____
(Title)   (Title)

_____
(Date)

Two copies of this form shall be signed by the plan administrator or by the person(s) authorized to act for him and mailed to the Office of Welfare and Pension Plans, U.S. Department of Labor, Washington 25, D.C., within 150 days after the end of the plan year.

IMPORTANT: If, at any time during the reporting year, the plan covered 100 or more participants, plan administrators are required to submit 2 copies of an annual report on U.S. Department of Labor Form D-2 rather than this Form D-3.

TO ADMINISTRATORS OF PLANS COVERING
LESS THAN 100 PARTICIPANTS

The administrator of any employee welfare benefit plan or employee pension benefit plan, subject to the Act, which covers less than 100 participants at all times during the calendar, policy, or other fiscal year on which the records of the plan are maintained, is not required to file an annual report for such year unless specifically required to do so by the Secretary of Labor.

However, the administrator of any plan which is otherwise subject to the requirements of the Act, but exempt under Section 7(a) of the Act from filing an annual report by virtue of the plan covering less than 100 participants must, pursuant to Regulation 29 CFR Part 1304, submit two properly completed and signed copies of this Form (Form D-3) within 150 days after the end of each calendar, policy, or other fiscal year during which the plan, at all times, covers less than 100 participants.

It should be pointed out that Section 4(b)(4) of the Act exempts from its requirements plans which cover 25 or less participants for the entire plan year. However, the administrators of such plans, for which a description has been filed, are requested to submit this form to enable the Department to keep its records current, and thereby avoid unnecessary and burdensome correspondence with the administrators.

The term "participant" is defined in the Act as "any employee or former employee of an employer or any member of an employee organization who is or may become eligible to receive a benefit of any type from an employee welfare or pension benefit plan, or whose beneficiaries may be eligible to receive any such benefit."

Administrators exempt from filing annual reports on plans covering less than 100 participants, but otherwise subject to the provisions of the Act, are cautioned that they must comply with all other provisions of the Act, to the extent that they are applicable, including the bonding requirements, the retention of records, and the filing of plan descriptions and amendments thereto.

The law provides penalties for a willful failure to file a required report or for making any false statement or representation of a material fact, knowing it to be false, or for knowingly failing to disclose any fact required by the law or regulations promulgated thereunder. Penalties are also provided for willfully making any false entry in or concealing, withholding, or destroying any books, records, reports or statements required to be kept for any employee or pension benefit plan.

Mail completed forms to
Office of Welfare and Pension Plans
U.S. Department of Labor
Washington 25, D.C.

U.S. GOVERNMENT PRINTING OFFICE : 1962 OF—657567

Appendix 16

ATTENDING PHYSICIAN'S STATEMENT (HEALTH INSURANCE COUNCIL FORM GD-1)

(COMPANY NAME)

ATTENDING PHYSICIAN'S STATEMENT
(GROUP INSURANCE)

(This form should be completed immediately and returned to the patient or, employer, or company, as appropriate)

(1) Patient's name .... Age........................

(2) Nature of sickness or injury (Describe complications, if any)..
....

(3) Did this sickness or injury arise out of patient's employment? Yes............ No............
    If "Yes," explain ....
    ....

    *Is disability due to pregnancy? Yes............ No............
    If "Yes," what was approximate date of commencement of pregnancy?...19........

(4) Nature of surgical or obstetrical procedure, If any (Describe fully)...
    ....
    ....

(5) Date performed ....19........

    *Charge for this procedure $.......................................
    *Where performed ....If in hospital, in-patient............. out-patient.............

(6) Give dates of treatments: *Charge Per Call
        Office .... $.............................
        Home .... $.............................
        Hospital... $.............................
    or, *Give dates of treatments and fees charged:

Date Treated	Home	Treated at (✔) Hospital	Office	Fee Charged
....	....	....	....	....
....	....	....	....	....
....	....	....	....	....
....	....	....	....	....

(7) *What other services, if any, did you provide patient? (Itemize, giving dates and fees) ....
    ....
    ....

(8) The patient has been continuously disabled (unable to work) from.......................19...... through...................19........ ,
    If still disabled, when should patient be able to return to work?..19........

(9) Remarks:...
    ....

Date...19........   Signed .... *Degree
                                                                            *(Attending Physician)   *M.D.

                                                              Address ....
                                                              ....
*To be included at company's option.   *Phone ....
(GD-1)

906

Appendix 17

ATTENDING PHYSICIAN'S SUPPLEMENTARY STATEMENT (HEALTH INSURANCE COUNCIL FORM GDS-1)

(COMPANY NAME)

ATTENDING PHYSICIAN'S SUPPLEMENTARY STATEMENT
(GROUP INSURANCE)

(This form should be completed immediately and returned to the patient or, employer, or company, as appropriate)

(1) Patient's name..*Age.......................

(2) Nature of sickness or injury (Describe complications, if any) ....

....

....

(3) (a) Date of first treatment...19.....

    (b) Date of most recent treatment...19.....

    (c) Frequency of treatments...

(4) The patient has been continuously disabled (unable to work) from............................19...... through...................19......

    If still disabled, when should patient be able to return to work?...19......

(5) Remarks:...

....

....

....

                                                                                               *Degree

Date.., 19......   Signed ....*M.D.

                                                               *(Attending Physician)

                                     Address ....

                                              ....

                                     *Phone ....

*To be included at company's option.

(GDS-1)

Appendix 18

SURGEON'S STATEMENT (HEALTH INSURANCE COUNCIL FORM GS-1)

(COMPANY NAME)

SURGEON'S STATEMENT

(GROUP INSURANCE)

(This form should be completed immediately and returned to the patient or, employer, or company, as appropriate)

---

(1) Patient's Name..Age.....................

(2) Nature of surgical or obstetrical procedure (Describe fully)...

....

Charge for this procedure $...........................Date performed.. 19.......

Where performed...If in hospital, in-patient ☐ out-patient ☐

(3) *Was procedure due to pregnancy? Yes ☐ No ☐
If "Yes," what was approximate date of commencement of pregnancy?... 19.......

(4) *Is further operative procedure anticipated? Yes ☐ No ☐
If "Yes," explain...

(5) *Was surgery due to injury or sickness arising out of patient's employment? Yes ☐ No ☐
If "Yes," explain...

....

Remarks:...

....

....

....

Signed ....*M.D.

Address ....

....

Date.., 19......   *Phone ....

AUTHORIZATION TO PAY SURGEON

(To be completed by the insured employee if payment is to be made directly to the surgeon)

I hereby authorize payment directly to...
(PRINT—Name of Surgeon)

of the Group Surgical benefits otherwise payable to me but not to exceed the charge stated above. I understand I am financially responsible to the surgeon for charges not covered by this authorization.

Date.., 19......   Signed ....
(Insured Employer)

*To be included at company's option.

(GS-1)

908

Appendix 19

HOSPITAL INSURANCE FORM (HEALTH INSURANCE COUNCIL FORM HAP-4)

GROUP HOSPITAL INSURANCE FORM *TO BE PRESENTED TO THE HOSPITAL IN DUPLICATE*

Spaced for Typewriter — Marks for Tabulator Appear on this Line

To _____ Hospital. This certifies that _____ is insured for the following Group Hospital Benefits (in behalf of his dependent _____) By

(Name) (Relationship)

_____
(Name of Insurer)

BENEFITS FOR OTHER THAN MATERNITY CASES	BENEFITS FOR MATERNITY CASES
A. HOSPITAL ROOM AND BOARD (INCLUDING GENERAL NURSING SERVICES) ACTUAL HOSPITAL CHARGES UP TO $_____ FOR EACH DAY OF HOSPITALIZATION UP TO _____ DAYS.	HOSPITAL ROOM AND BOARD (INCLUDING GENERAL NURSING SERVICE) AND OTHER HOSPITAL SERVICES . . . ACTUAL CHARGES UP TO $_____ OR 1. HOSPITAL ROOM AND BOARD (INCLUDING GENERAL NURSING SERVICES) $_____ FOR EACH DAY OF HOSPITALIZATION UP TO _____ DAYS
B. OTHER HOSPITAL CHARGES FOR HOSPITAL CARE AND TREATMENT (EXCLUDING CHARGES FOR NURSES' AND PHYSICIANS' SERVICES AND TAKE HOME DRUGS) $_____	2. OTHER HOSPITAL CHARGES FOR HOSPITAL CARE AND TREATMENT (EXCLUDING CHARGES FOR NURSES' AND PHYSICIANS' SERVICES AND TAKE HOME DRUGS) $_____

THE MINIMUM HOUR HOSPITALIZATION REQUIREMENT WILL BE MET IF _____

GROUP POLICYHOLDER	ADDRESS	PHONE

BY (Name and Title)	ABOVE CERTIFICATION VALID FOR ONLY SEVEN DAYS FROM THIS DATE (Exception — Maternity Cases)	DATE

HOSPITAL COMPLETE FOLLOWING AND FURNISH COPY TO ADDRESS

NAME OF PATIENT	AGE	DATE ADMITTED	TIME ADMITTED AM PM	DATE DISCHARGED	TIME DISCHARGED AM PM
IF PATIENT HAD OTHER THAN SEMI-PRIVATE ROOM, INDICATE SEMI-PRIVATE DAILY RATE	$		OTHER INSURANCE INDICATED BY HOSPITAL RECORDS. IF YES, NAME OF COMPANY ☐ NO ☐ YES		

DIAGNOSIS FROM RECORDS (If Injury, Give Date and Place of Accident)

OPERATIONS OR OBSTETRICAL PROCEDURES PERFORMED (Nature and Date)

HOSPITAL CHARGES (Complete This Section or Attach Copy of Itemized Bill Showing Information Below).

ROOM AND BOARD						
☐ WARD	DAYS AT $	TOTAL	$		TOTAL CHARGES	$
☐ SEMI-PRIVATE	DAYS AT $	TOTAL	$			$
☐ PRIVATE	DAYS AT $	TOTAL	$			$
☐ OTHERS			$			$
	OPERATING OR DELIVERY ROOM					
	ANESTHESIA					
	X-RAY					
	LABORATORY					
	EKG BMR					
	PHYSICAL THERAPY					
	AMBULANCE			THIS FORM APPROVED BY THE HEALTH INSURANCE COUNCIL AND ACCEPTED BY THE AMERICAN HOSPITAL ASSOCIATION FOR USE BY HOSPITALS (see explanatory instructions).		
	MEDICAL AND SURGICAL SUPPLIES					
	PHARMACY (Except Take Home Drugs)					
	INHALATION THERAPY					
	INTRAVENOUS SOLUTIONS					
	TOTAL		$			

HOSPITAL	ADDRESS
TAKEN FROM RECORDS ON _____ 19	SIGNED BY

AUTHORIZATION TO RELEASE INFORMATION: I hereby authorize the above named hospital to release the information requested on this form.
Date _____, 19___ Signed _____

Patient (Parent if a Minor)

AUTHORIZATION TO PAY INSURANCE BENEFITS: I hereby authorize payment directly to the above named hospital of the Group Hospital Benefits herein specified and otherwise payable to me but not to exceed the hospital's regular charges for this period of hospitalization. I understand I am financially responsible to the hospital for charges not covered by this authorization.

Date _____, 19___ Signed _____

(Insured)

HAP-4 (1961)

PRINTED IN U.S.A.

909

Appendix 20

STANDARDIZED DUPLICATE COVERAGE INQUIRY FORM

MEDICAL EXPENSE INSURANCE DUPLICATE COVERAGE INQUIRY

Spaced for Typewriter-Marks for Tabulator Appear on this Line

□ Initial　□ Subsequent

Name of Patient	Relationship to Our Insured

TO:　⌐　　　　　　　　　　　　　　　 ¬

Name of Our Insured

Name of Our Group Policyholder or Individual Policy Number

Address of Our Policyholder

└　　　　　　　　　　　　　⌐ Name of Your Insured　　Relationship to Patient

Name of Your Group Policyholder or Individual Policy Number

Gentlemen:

We cover this patient under □ GROUP PLAN　□INDIVIDUAL POLICY　□ OTHER (Please explain)*

Effective date of our coverage is_____

Our policy contains a non-duplication provision in □ BASIC　□ MAJOR MEDICAL

Our Claim Determination Period is_____

We administer non-duplication by means of □ ORDER OF BENEFIT DETERMINATION　□ PRORATION

Please complete the remainder of this form if you have coverage on our claimant.

(1) Identify your coverage: □ BASIC　□ MAJOR MEDICAL and if □ GROUP　□ INDIVIDUAL

(2) Effective date of your coverage is_____

(3) Does your policy contain a limitation against duplicate benefits from our insurance? □ Yes　□ No

(4) If "Yes," does your non-duplication apply to your □ BASIC　□□ MAJOR MEDICAL?

(5) Has a claim been submitted under your policy? □ Yes　□ No　If "Yes," please complete remainder of this form.

We have received bills for the following medical expenses:

In the absence of duplicate coverage, payment would be computed as follows:

OUR PLAN

YOUR PLAN

Service	Dates (Inclusive)	Charges		Basic benefits	Covered under Major Medical		Basic benefits	Covered under Major Medical
(6) Hospital			(6)			(6)		
(a) R&B	_____	$_____	(a)	$_____	$_____	(a)	$_____	$_____
(b) Extras	_____	_____	(b)	_____	_____	(b)	_____	_____
(7) (a) Surgery	_____	_____	(7) (a)	_____	_____	(7) (a)	_____	_____
(b) Assist.	_____	_____	(b)	_____	_____	(b)	_____	_____
(c) Anest.	_____	_____	(c)	_____	_____	(c)	_____	_____
(8) (a) Dr. Home	_____	_____	(8) (a)	_____	_____	(8) (a)	_____	_____
(b) Dr. Off.	_____	_____	(b)	_____	_____	(b)	_____	_____
(c) Dr. Hosp.	_____	_____	(c)	_____	_____	(c)	_____	_____
(9) Other:			(9)			(9)		
(a)	_____	_____	(a)	_____	_____	(a)	_____	_____
(b)	_____	_____	(b)	_____	_____	(b)	_____	_____
(c)	_____	_____	(c)	_____	_____	(c)	_____	_____
Totals		$_____	Totals	$_____	$_____	Totals	$_____	$_____

(11) Assignments (Identify by line number and indicate if payment made):*

OUR PLAN	YOUR PLAN
_____	_____
_____	_____
_____	_____

(10) (a) Deductible　$_____
　　　　　　　　　　　$_____

(b) Coinsurance　_____%

(c) Payable　$_____

Total payment of $_____ has been made.

(10) (a) Deductible　$_____
　　　　　　　　　　　$_____

(b) Coinsurance　_____%

(c) Payable　$_____

Total payment of $_____ has been made.

From:_____　Tel. No._____

(Return to): ⌐　　　　　　　　　¬

└　　　　　　　　　　　┘

Date_____

(12) If answer to question 3 is yes, do you administer non-duplication by means of:

□ Order of Benefit Determination?　□ Proration?

(13) If proration, what will your payment be, considering our benefits? $_____

(14) What is your Claim Determination Period?

_____

Signed_____

Name

Address (if different from above)　Tel. No.

*COMMENTS: (Use reverse side and identify by line number.)
Retain copy and return original to the inquiring company.

11913 (7-63) PRINTED IN U.S.A.

INSTRUCTIONS FOR USE OF MEDICAL EXPENSE

INSURANCE DUPLICATE COVERAGE INQUIRY FORM

The Inquiring Company

The Inquiring Company will complete the following portions of the form in triplicate:

1. In the upper right corner of the form enter the identifying information for the Insureds and Policyholders.

2. Indicate by checking the appropriate box in the upper left corner if this is the Initial or Subsequent inquiry.

3. In the space provided in the upper left corner, insert the name and address of the insurance company to whom this form will be directed.

4. Identify your coverage in the top sentence of the first paragraph. Indicate by checking the appropriate box if your Non-duplication Provision pertains to Basic or Major Medical coverage. (Check both boxes if it pertains to Basic and Major Medical.) Describe your Claim Determination Period. Your Claim Determination Period may be a calendar year or some Benefit Period. If latter, please enter inclusive dates. Also, indicate if Non-duplication is administered by Order of Benefit Determination or Proration.

5. In the large boxed section at the left side of the form insert the medical expenses received. On a subsequent inquiry, only new expenses should be listed.

6. In the center of the form in the large box titled "Our Plan" insert the Basic Benefits and those benefits covered under Major Medical in the absence of Non-duplication.

7. In Section 11 include any assignments applicable to the claim.

8. In the lower left corner of the form, insert your name and telephone number. In the space provided, type in the address of your office where the form is to be returned.

Two copies of this form will be sent to the other carrier for their completion. The third copy will be retained for your file

The Responding Company

Upon receipt of the Inquiry Form, the Responding Company will provide the following information on both copies.

1. If you have no coverage on claimant, write NONE across the face of the form and return it to the Inquiring Company.

2. Answer Questions 1 through 5 if you have coverage on the claimant.

3. In the box titled "Your Plan," if a claim has been submitted, insert the amount of your Basic Benefits and those benefits covered under Major Medical in the absence of Non-duplication. If you have not received the claim, DO NOT complete this section, but DO return the form.

4. Complete the answers to Questions 11, 12, and 13.

5. In answer to Question 14, your Claim Determination Period may be a calendar year or some Benefit Period. If latter, please enter inclusive dates.

6. Insert your name and telephone number just below Question 14. Also, insert the address of your office if it differs from the address shown at the top of the form.

7. Return the original form promptly to the Inquiring Company and retain the duplicate for your file. If there will be a delay in answering, please so notify the Inquiring Company.

8. If any comments are to be made, use the reverse side of the form.

NOTE: Medical Comprehensive coverage should be considered as Major Medical. Full pay or "first dollar" Comprehensive benefits should be entered as Basic Benefits:

Appendix 21

REPORT OF THE JOINT COMMITTEE ON
REEXAMINATION OF GROUP POLICY
TO THE
EXECUTIVE COMMITTEE OF THE AMERICAN LIFE CONVENTION
AND THE
BOARD OF DIRECTORS OF THE LIFE INSURANCE
ASSOCIATION OF AMERICA

The following is the report of your Committee, as developed pursuant to its assignment to reexamine "the entire question of statutory underwriting restrictions on group life insurance."

This report is based on conclusions arrived at during a series of ten meetings extending over a period of somewhat more than three years, during which your Committee received and evaluated reports from three specially appointed subcommittees with membership drawn largely from other than the Committee's own roster. Representatives of the National Association of Life Underwriters have attended and participated in four of our meetings.

Background

State insurance laws have for a great many years limited the freedom of action of insurance companies in underwriting group life insurance plans. These laws have usually been looked upon as serving one of two broad classes of purposes. On the one hand, they have been regarded as a means of resolving conflicts between two different systems of life insurance marketing—that of individual policies sold through separate, direct, personal contacts with the insuring public by life insurance salesmen, and that of group insurance sold through mass marketing procedures. On the other hand, they have also been regarded as a means of achieving other results deemed to be even more directly in the public interest, such as the avoidance of those unstable group insurance arrangements which are not likely in the long run to provide life insurance protection on a basis satisfactory to the public.

Space does not permit an adequate discussion in this report as to the propriety or validity of these purposes inherent in restrictive state laws which govern group life insurance underwriting. The issues involved are not simple, and the answers are hard to come by because of deep philosophical differences both within and without the membership of your Committee. The following report, however, represents a consensus subscribed to by all members of the Committee, with the reservations noted.

Those interested in further background discussion may wish to read the attached research memorandum entitled "Background of Present and Proposed Statutory Controls Over Group Insurance Underwriting," prepared in 1957 by ALC–LIAA staff for the information of your Committee and now updated for the guidance of others. A brief history of group life insurance laws is set forth in this memorandum, together with an analysis of some of the implications of current controversies. This analysis makes it clear that, with the exception of a few side issues, the problems surrounding the issue of statutory controls over group life insurance underwriting divide themselves into two broad groups.

The first of these two groups concerns large amounts of group life insurance on the lives of individual persons ("vertical" extension of the principle of group insurance underwriting). The second concerns so-called "fictitious groups" and other special forms of group life insurance coverage ("lateral" extension of the principle of group insurance underwriting). Our recommendations similarly divide themselves. As to large amounts, our report reflects in large degree a predecessor report by the Subcommittee on Amount Limits, chaired by Willis H. Satterthwaite. As to "fictitious" or other special forms of group coverage, our report reflects in large degree a predecessor report by the Subcommittee on Lateral Extensions of Group Insurance Underwriting, chaired by Charles J. Zimmerman. The report of a third Subcommittee on Taxation, chaired by Charles G. Dougherty, is also referred to and reflected in our recommendations as to large amounts.

Large Amounts of Group Life Insurance on Employed Persons

The issue of large amounts of group life insurance on individual employed persons is itself divided into two parts—the matter of "jumbo" amounts above, say, $50,000 or $100,000 ($1 million certificates on individual lives are said to be not unknown), and the matter of smaller amounts which, for a particular individual in modest circumstances, may be unduly large in relation to his personal income and his probable holdings of permanent forms of life insurance. Jumbo amounts are the more spectacular issue, and have received more trade journal linage. However, smaller amounts of group life insurance, when out of line with the insured's income, may pose an even greater ordinary insurance market problem for the rank and file life underwriter, particularly the new life underwriter.

The so-called statutory $20,000/$40,000 amount limit, which is an integral part of the model group life insurance regulatory bill sponsored by the National Association of Insurance Commissioners, deals with both these divisions of the amount question. Spelled out, the $20,000/$40,000 amount limit provides that no employee may be insured for group term life insurance for more than one and one-half times his annual salary, subject to an overriding minimum of $20,000 and to an overriding maximum of $40,000. The limit does not apply to group creditor life insurance, where the NAIC bill stipulates a straight $10,000 limit instead.

The $20,000/$40,000 limit is now law in some 25 states and the District of Columbia—nine states more than had group life insurance laws of any sort when the predecessor $20,000 limit was originally adopted by the NAIC in 1946. Seven other states provide higher limits ranging upwards to a straight $100,000. But the following states still have no statutory limits on employer-employee coverage at all: Alabama, Alaska, California, Delaware, Massachusetts, Michigan, Minnesota, Mississippi, Missouri, New Mexico, New York, North Dakota, Oregon, Rhode Island, South Dakota, Utah, Virginia and Wyoming.

It is immediately evident from an examination of the foregoing list that many important life insurance producing states are among those imposing no statutory amount limits at all. Moreover, in your Committee's opinion there doesn't appear to be any reasonable prospect of future law enactments in most of these remaining states. On the contrary, there is even some possibility that a few states now with group life insurance amount limits on their statute books will follow the lead of New York in repealing its once existing limit.

Your Committee has therefore been faced with a number of alternatives, of which only four seemed to be within the realm of practicality.

First, there is the possibility of recommending continued support of the $20,000/$40,000 limit. After much discussion, we conclude that this would not be realistic. Too many buyers of group life insurance want larger amounts, and too many sellers want to provide these larger amounts. There is a strong likelihood that ALC–LIAA would be effectively opposed in the legislatures of most states now without limits—by member companies and by certain segments of the public such as employers—if they were to continue to support the $20,000/$40,000 limit. These practical considerations would not, however, necessarily be controlling upon your Committee were it not for the additional fact, as brought out below, that a substantial number of your Committee have doubts as to whether continued support of the $20,000/$40,000 limit is philosophically correct.

Second, there is the possibility of developing more liberal dollar amount limits than the $20,000/$40,000 limit. Your Committee has spent a great deal of time discussing this possibility. A major difficulty is that any alternative limit within reason is likely to meet with proposals for exceptions for special purpose forms of group life insurance, such as that designed to be an alternative to separate widows' annuities under pension plans. Exceptions for widows' and other types of survivor annuities would have the effect of changing a limit of, say, 2 or 3 times annual salary to one of 5 or 6 times salary or even more. Other apparently legitimate demands for group life insurance in large amounts can also result in quite high ratios of group life insurance to annual salary. To meet these demands would entail substituting a new limit so high as to be completely unacceptable to advocates of limits, and almost meaningless in terms of effective control. Accordingly, your Committee considered but rejected this solution.

Third, there is the possibility of our initiating and/or supporting federal legislation, especially federal legislation in the form of income tax deterrents to the placing of large amounts of group life insurance on individual lives. This alternative was also rejected by us. However serious the group life insurance limit question may be regarded, very few would go so far as to suggest that the situation requires either federal regulation or federal taxes. As to the latter, it would certainly be ironic if the life insurance business, fresh from a schism-making legislative battle over federal taxation of the companies themselves, were now to propose new federal taxes on some of its customers in order to resolve one of its internal problems. Especially is this true if, as many believe, income tax deterrents such as the attributing of income to employees with respect to employer-paid group life insurance premiums would not do very much to control the issuance of large amounts. Too many executives, especially those uninsurable for ordinary insurance at standard rates, would want the large amounts of group life insurance anyway.

Fourth, there is the possibility of recommending no amount limits at all. This would at least have the advantage of avoiding any distortion of the purpose, such as might occur if statutory limits on group life insurance amounts were turned into positive sales aids for large amounts. That this can happen is evident from the fact that the $20,000/$40,000 amount limits now on the statute books of so many states have sometimes been made into "targets" for the sale of new group business. Statutory limits then become not only ceilings on what buyers may purchase, but also floors below which lower amount schedules are subject to being characterized as subnormal by quotable legislative standards. Higher statutory limits than the $20,000/$40,000 limit would also be subject to the same sales use, so that it can be argued with considerable force that those who would severely control the underwriting of large amounts of group life insurance on individual lives would be better served by no statutory limits at all than by limits as high as or higher than the $20,000/$40,000 limit.

Your Committee feels that while it is not feasible to establish a specific dollar amount limit, another possibility of limitation exists which should be explored as outlined in the next paragraph.

This possibility is to substitute a simple non-discrimination rule for the $20,000/$40,000 limit, so as to provide that higher salaried employees may not be insured for more in relation to their salaries than lower salaried employees within the same group. From an examination of a number of group insurance cases involving very large amounts on individual lives, it is clear that the more flagrant instances of abuse of the group life insurance principle have occurred in some of the smaller and medium sized groups where the amounts of group insurance on the top executives, often substantial stockholders, are completely out of line with those provided for other employees. Usually these very large amounts are only made available by the insurance carrier subject to evidence of individual insurability, and under other circumstances which make it clear that ordinary life insurance would probably have served the purpose better were it not for federal tax considerations related to income tax treatment of group life insurance. The problem of very large amounts of group life insurance would in these instances be greatly diminished if owner-managers, and others controlling the placing of the group life insurance contract, were required to provide proportionate amounts for lower echelon employees.

Your Committee, therefore, recommends that no further support be given to the $20,000/$40,000 limit or other specific dollar amount limit. What we do recommend is that the Group and Legislative Committees be given the assignment of working out some statutory means of providing in effect that, with respect to the ratio of the amount of insurance to annual compensation, schedules of amounts of insurance shall not discriminate in favor of higher salaried employees as compared with lower salaried employees of the same group. To be effective and yet not produce burdensome administrative problems, such a non-discrimination rule should take into account a number of practical situations: for example, as in connection with part-time employees; temporary employees; over-time pay; executive or key-man bonuses; or cases in which schedules of amounts are desired which take into account age, sex, family status, family size, length of service, collective bargaining agreements, etc. Just how far the statute should go in being explicit can best be determined after a review of the various problems involved by the Group and Legislative Committees.

Special Forms of Group Life Insurance

The NAIC model bill now restricts group life insurance coverage to four types: (1) employer-employee groups of ten lives or more, (2) credit insurance groups, (3) labor union groups, and (4) certain multiple-employer groups arising out of Taft-Hartley collective bargaining situations or similar arrangements.

By thus enumerating the permissible types of group life insurance coverage, the model bill excludes all others. However, individual state enactments of the model bill have gone on to authorize various additional kinds of group life insurance, e.g., on dependents of employees, on the members of certain loosely-knit social and service organizations, on mutual fund shareholders and savings bank depositors, and on many others.

In general, your Committee agrees with the principle of confining group life insurance to enumerated types, and in broad outline with the basic approaches of the NAIC model bill. However, as detailed below we do believe that there are certain additional forms of group life insurance coverage which should properly be recognized in the model bill. These are rather limited in number. We reiterate the belief that on the whole the various marginal forms of group life insurance should be severely controlled or eliminated entirely, either out of considerations related to the orderly marketing of life insurance, or out of general public policy considerations related primarily to the expected instability of the proposed group plan, or both.

After a review of the detailed recommendations of its Subcommittee on Lateral Extensions of Group Insurance Underwriting, the Committee specifically comes to the conclusion that opposition should be continued to such proposed extensions of the group life insurance principle as the following:

(1) Group life insurance on employee groups of less than ten lives.
(2) Group life insurance on members of professional associations.
(3) Coverage on members of fraternal, social, service or similar organizations, and of local chambers of commerce or similar associations having a membership drawn from unrelated businesses and industries.
(4) Various group life insurance plans designed as an inducement to the purchase of goods or other services, such as the so-called double-dollar group life insurance plan in connection with savings bank deposits, group life insurance issued in connection with purchases of mutual fund shares on a periodic plan, and group life insurance made available in redemption of trading stamps.

Attached hereto is a copy of the NAIC model bill, showing modifications which up to now it has been ALC–LIAA policy to seek when the bill is proposed to enactment in a particular state. We recommend that support be continued to the model bill with these modifications, subject to the following changes (in addition to the proposed substitution, already mentioned, of a type of non-discrimination rule for the present $20,000/$40,000 limit on amounts of group life insurance on individual lives):

1. *Authorization of limited coverage on dependents of employees.*
    Group life insurance on wives and children of employees is now specifically authorized by statute in seventeen states and the District of Columbia, sanctioned by insurance commissioners in at least four more, and permitted in ten other states having no restrictions on group life insurance at all.
    Dependents of employees are freely insurable for group hospital, surgical and medical expense insurance, and your Committee supports also the principle of group life insurance on dependents, provided the coverage is limited to amounts suitable only for last illness and burial purposes, and provided a suitable conversion privilege is required for the spouse in the event of the employee's death or termination of employment.

2. *Elimination of the dollar limit on the amount of group credit life insurance.*
    In line with our recommendation that the $20,000/$40,000 limit for employee group insurance be replaced by a simple non-discrimination rule, we recommend that the present $10,000 limit for group credit insurance be eliminated. A non-discrimination rule to take the place of the $10,000 limit would have no application here.
    Elimination of the $10,000 limit in the group credit life insurance field will have little practical effect except where this form of coverage is used to insure unpaid balances under amortized real estate mortgage loans. Few personal loans or installment sales are for more than $10,000, so that they are now freely insurable for group credit insurance. Amortized real estate loans are also freely insurable, except for the $10,000 limit and except for the time limit (usually 5 or 10 years) still existing in the laws of a few states (but not in the NAIC model bill) on the repayment period of insurable loans.
    Suggestions have been made that the policy recommendation of your Committee include a 5 or 10 year limit on the repayment period of loans insurable for group credit life insurance, and retention or even reduction of the $10,000 limit, all in the interests of inhibiting the use of group credit life insurance policies for insuring amortized mortgages. A majority of your Committee, however, has on balance rejected these suggestions. However, we do believe that the model bill is defective in not requiring a conversion privilege to apply if and when the group credit insurance on the mortgage loan ceases because of sale of the mortgage by

the lender to another lender. Such a conversion privilege should be added in the interest of protecting the borrower from loss of insurance for reasons beyond his control.

3. *Amendment of the credit insurance section to preclude group life insurance supplements to mutual fund shares purchased on a periodic plan.*

In two separate sessions of the NAIC Convention in 1956, the NAIC, at the instance of the National Association of Life Underwriters, amended the credit section of the model group life insurance bill to provide:

"No debtor shall be eligible [for group credit life insurance] unless the indebtedness constitutes an irrevocable obligation to repay which is binding upon him during his lifetime, at and from the date the insurance becomes effective upon his life."

The purpose of this amendment was to preclude the use of the credit insurance section of the model group life bill so as to provide group life insurance supplements to mutual fund shares purchased on a periodic plan. Until this amendment was added to the model bill, it was possible to circumvent restrictions otherwise inherent in the limited enumeration of the types of insurable groups, and thereby provide group insurance supplements to mutual fund shares purchased on a periodic plan, by the simple but rather artificial device of having a prospective purchaser of mutual fund shares sign an agreement (revocable during the purchaser's lifetime but binding on his estate after death) to complete his announced target purchases. This would create a "debt" with respect to which group credit insurance could be provided. So far, ALC-LIAA have not gone along with this amendment.

Your Committee recommends that ALC-LIAA change its policy and accede to the substance of this change in the NAIC model bill,* or to any better plan which may be devised to preclude the insuring of mutual fund shares by the group insurance approach. Your Committee does not believe that this form of group life insurance is in the public interest, or in the best interest of the institution of life insurance.

4. *Revision of the multiple-employer group subdivision (4) of the model bill.*

Subdivision (4) of the NAIC model group life insurance bill now authorizes multiple-employer group life insurance plans of certain restricted types. The restrictions are primarily designed to confine single policy group coverage on multiple-employer plans to the so-called Taft-Hartley type of case, arising typically out of industry-wide collective bargaining, or to other multiple-employer plans which are residual to or complementary to a collective-bargained plan.

In the model bill this multiple-employer group authorization is further limited to non-contributory plans, and certain participation requirements and other restrictions are also stipulated to keep the authorization from being used for unintended purposes such as the insuring of groups of professional persons who happen also to act as employers in a very limited way. Current ALC–LIAA policy calls for a series of modifications, mostly but not entirely of a minor nature. One of these modifications would further restrict the types of multiple-employer plans eligible for coverage, by introducing certain "state-line" restrictions where a labor union is not a party to the trust fund out of which premiums are paid for the group coverage. Another would lift the requirement that the coverage be non-contributory in certain cases.

It is a difficult task to specify just which types of multiple-employer group

---

* In this connection, as in connection with all similar matters, the Joint Group and Legislative Committees should give consideration to the need for and form of a "grandfather" clause with respect to group plans already outstanding.

life insurance cases should be permitted because there is a legitimate business reason for their existence, and which types should be prohibited because they merely represent the aggregation, into what might be called a super-group, of a large number of separate group life insurance plans which might otherwise be separately underwritten. The test should be whether the group is sufficiently homogenous to permit adequate servicing of the risk through the entity chosen as policyholder, with practical and efficient administration. Unless this test is met, the grouping is an artificial one, designed perhaps for the primary purpose of channeling the whole insurance plan to a single insurance carrier through a single insurance agency outlet, and perhaps bypassing local insurance service facilities to the disadvantage of both the buyer of the group coverage and the life insurance institution as a whole.   [

We believe the line of demarcation between a properly insurable multiple-employer group and an improperly insurable one can be more accurately defined than by existing model law restrictions. In place of the model law restriction that the policy must cover not less than an average of 5 persons per employer unit, we think that such restriction need be required only for other than (a) "Taft-Hartley law" plans (multiple-employer collective bargaining plans), (b) "Taft-Hartley law residual" plans (multiple-employer plans covering non-unionized employees left out of collective bargaining arrangements), and (c) trust funds established by labor unions. In place of some of the other restrictions dealing primarily with the degree of relationship between the different employers insured under the one master group policy, we believe it desirable merely to exclude employer units where the relationship of one employer to another is that of commercial correspondent or business client or patron. Additionally, the state-line restrictions now constituting part of ALC–LIAA policy, while good in their intended purpose of breaking up what might otherwise be large aggregations of different group insurance plans under one roof, can well be relaxed so as not to place barriers in the way of Taft-Hartley law and Taft-Hartley law residual plans. Without going further into detail, we suggest that subdivision (4) of the "definition" of group life insurance of the NAIC model law be reworded along the lines shown in the attachment immediately following the conclusion of this report, subject to detailed review by the Group and Legislative Committees as to wording and as to any principle not directly at odds with the general recommendation above.

Group Accident and Health Insurance and Group Annuities

While the underwriting of group life insurance is now widely regulated by state statute, that of group accident and health insurance and that of group annuities are not. Only three states now have group accident and health insurance underwriting statues which in any way compare, as to restrictions, with the usual group life insurance underwriting statutes. Most group accident and health insurance underwriting statutes, where they exist, do little more than restrict the minimum number of lives which may be insured, typically ten. Similarly, in the group annuity field there are only three state statutes which even purport to regulate underwriting, and these do so only in an inconsequential way.

Your Committee sees no reason for further enactments of laws regulating the underwriting of either group accident and health insurance or group annuities. Whatever conflicts there may be between the marketing of these two forms of group coverage and their individual policy counterparts, the conflicts have not resulted in anywhere near the amount of controversy as in the life insurance field. Furthermore, it has long been recognized that statutory underwriting restrictions on group accident and health insurance accomplish little more than grant a competitive advantage to Blue Cross–Blue Shield and encourage self-insurance. Likewise, statutory underwriting restrictions on group annuities only grant competitive advantages to banks and trust companies in pursuit of their uninsured pension trust business.

Wholesale and Franchise Life Insurance

The sale of individual policies by group underwriting methods, but without the outward contract form of group insurance, has long been known in the small or "baby" group field. In life insurance, the coverage has usually been designated as "wholesale." In accident and health insurance, the coverage has usually been called "franchise" or "blanket" insurance.

The use of the individual policy approach is appropriate in that part of the small employee benefit plan field, say below ten lives, where group insurance underwriting tends to lose its identity as such and instead merges gradually into what amounts to individual policy underwriting. However, recent tendencies have been observed in the use of wholesale and franchise in what would be strictly the group insurance field, in order to avoid statutory group underwriting restrictions which would otherwise apply. Wholesale life insurance plans covering members of professional societies are a good example. Individual policies to provide "double-dollar" coverage on savings bank depositors where it is not permitted under the group insurance laws are another.

Basic policy issues surrounding the use of wholesale and franchise insurance in place of group insurance are many in number, and they deserve detailed analysis and treatment in a way that does not impose prohibitive restrictions on the bona fide writing of individual policies of insurance for payroll deduction plans, pension trust plans, etc. However, these issues are not solely of concern as a means of avoiding statutory group insurance controls. Your Committee has therefore not attempted to arrive at any specific recommendations with respect to them; in fact, we have regarded the matter as technically beyond our assignment although with the reservation that many of our recommendations may not be too effective unless something is done about the unrestrained recourse to wholesale and franchise insurance. We do note, however, that one likely means of control of wholesale and franchise insurance might be through a strengthening of state anti-discrimination statutes, particularly as to premium rates. State laws are well adapted to handle the various wholesale and franchise insurance problems, without the multiple-state jurisdiction complications so characteristic of many of the group insurance matters which have been before your Committee.

We suggest that the various fundamental issues concerning wholesale and franchise insurance be referred to the Joint Legislative Committee for its appraisal.

Direct Writing of Group Insurance Without Commissions

While the direct writing of group insurance plans without commissions, or at specially reduced commissions, is not an underwriting problem in the usual sense of the term, it is nevertheless a matter which causes wide concern to life insurance field forces. Your Committee likewise regards the issue quite seriously.

There is a good deal of misinformation within our business as to whether life insurance laws now permit or do not permit the sale of group insurance without commissions. Public statements are made from time to time to the effect that state antirebate laws prohibit the placing of such insurance without commissions. Actually, no state has such a prohibition on its statute books. What is prohibited is granting the buyer of an insurance policy a direct or indirect price concession because of the non-payment of some or all of the commissions for the sale of the business as provided for by the company's applicable commission rules. This has long been regarded as an indirect form of unlawful rebate, or a violation of the antidiscrimination laws with respect to premium rates.

Your Committee strongly believes in the wisdom of this interpretation of the antirebate laws, whether the price rebate be at the point of initial premium rates or in the form of group insurance dividends or experience-rated premium rate reductions. Group insurance dividends and rate reduction formulas customarily take into account the expenses incurred on each case, some expenses being determined by an expense formula, some from a record of actual disbursements. There is a good deal of divergence among companies as to internal methods. Whatever the method, whenever an exception is made in an individual case and less commission is paid than the amount provided for by the company's applicable commission rules, the latter amount must be charged if rebate is to be avoided. And if the company uses two or more scales of commission, care must be taken to see to it that the choice of scales is based upon objective criteria, and that the selling commission provided for by the company's rules is charged regardless of whether the commission is or is not paid.

The placing of group insurance wholly without commissions is a rather rare occurrence. Your Committee believes that the companies will find that good agency relations will require that this state of affairs continue. However, if it can not be established that any services are performed, either for selling or otherwise, then to pay an unearned commission will lay our business open to further and perhaps more successful attacks by those who already charge that "phantom" commissions are now being paid by life insurance companies where no services are provided. We do not believe a successful defense can be made of the payment of "phantom" commissions in the field of group insurance. From the recent report of the Special Committee on Group Insurance of the National Association of Life Underwriters, adopted by NALU National Council and Board of Trustees, it is apparent that the NALU agrees.

The assignment given your Committee has not been an easy one. Throughout this report an attempt has been made to sharpen up the various basic issues, but this has not always been possible in full degree. Perhaps as a result, compromise between conflicting opinions has been necessary on a number of our recommendations. To achieve this compromise has required a good deal of give and take by individual Committee members.

No doubt there will also be considerable differences of opinion on these issues outside the membership of your Committee. We do hope that our recommendations will be accepted in the spirit in which they are offered, that is, as compromise findings thought to be in the best interests of the life insurance business as a whole, rather than of individual segments of it, and in the best interests of the insuring public. On this score, it might be well to recall the words of Benjamin Franklin, in his address of September 17, 1787 to the Constitutional Convention, when he said:

"I confess that there are several parts of this Constitution which I do not at present approve, but I am not sure I shall never approve them. For having lived long, I have experienced many instances of being obliged by better information, or fuller consideration, to change opinions even on important subjects, which I once thought right, but found to be otherwise.* * * Thus I consent, sir, to this Constitution, because I expect no better, and because I am not sure that it is not the best. * * * On the whole, sir, I cannot help expressing a wish that every member of the Convention who may still have objections to it, would with me, on this occasion, doubt a little of his own infallibility, and to make manifest our unanimity, put his name to this instrument."

It would not be fitting to conclude without acknowledgment of the important help given us by our three subcommittees. Their memberships were as follows:

Subcommittee on Amount Limits: Willis H. Satterthwaite, Chairman, (Penn Mutual); Norman T. Fuhlrodt (Central Life Assurance); Roger Hull (Mutual of New York); E. M. Neumann (Prudential); William N. Seery (Travelers); J. Henry Smith (Equitable Society).

Subcommittee on Lateral Extensions of Group Insurance Underwriting: Charles J. Zimmerman, Chairman, (Connecticut Mutual); John Barker, Jr. (New England Life); Raymond H. Belknap (United States Life); Thomas A. Bradshaw (Provident Mutual); M. R. Dodson (Ohio National); Charles H. Schaaff (Massachusetts Mutual); Clarence H. Tookey (Occidental of California).

Subcommittee on Taxation: Charles G. Dougherty, Chairman, (Metropolitan); Frank P. Aschemeyer (General American); Henry E. Blagden (Prudential); John J. Magovern, Jr. (Mutual Benefit Life); Walter J. Rupert (Minnesota Mutual); Raymond W. Simpkin (Connecticut Mutual); Allen C. Steere (Lincoln National).

> Respectfully submitted,
> Charles G. Dougherty (Metropolitan)
> Robert E. Dineen (Northwestern Mutual)
> T. A. Sick (Security Mutual)
> J. Henry Smith (Equitable Society)
> Clarence H. Tookey (Occidental, California)
> James Ralph Wood (Southwestern Life)
> Charles J. Zimmerman (Connecticut Mutual)
> Henry S. Beers, *Chairman* (Aetna Life)

August 26, 1960

TENTATIVE SUGGESTED REWORDING OF SUBDIVISION (4) OF THE "DEFINITION" OF GROUP LIFE INSURANCE OF THE NAIC MODEL BILL

(Changes shown by underlining and strike-outs are with respect to official NAIC bill without those changes which up to now it is ALC–LIAA policy to propose.)

(4) A policy issued to the trustees of a fund established by two or more employers, in the same industry, or in related industries, or by one or more labor unions, or by one or more employers and one or more labor unions, which trustees shall be deemed the policyholder, to insure employees of the employers or members of the unions for the benefit of persons other than the employers or the unions, subject to the following requirements:

(a) No policy may be issued (i) to insure employees of any employer whose eligibility to participate in the fund as an employer arises out of considerations directly related to the employer being a commercial correspondent or business client or patron of another employer (regardless of whether such other employer is or is not participating in the fund), or (ii) to insure employees of any employer which is not located in this state, unless the majority of the employers whose employees are to be insured are located in this state, or unless the employer has assumed obligations through a collective bargaining agreement and is participating in the fund either pursuant to those obligations with regard to one or more classes of his employees which are encompassed in the collective bargaining agreement or as a method of providing insurance benefits for other classes of his employees, or unless the policy is issued to the trustees of a fund established by one or more labor unions.

(b) ~~(a)~~ The persons eligible for insurance shall be all of the employees of the employers or all of the members of the unions, or all of any class or classes thereof determined by conditions pertaining to their employment, or to membership in the unions, or to both. The policy may provide that the term "employees" shall include retired employees, and the individual proprietor or partners if an employer is an individual proprietor or a partnership. No director of a corporate employer shall be eligible for insurance under the policy unless such person is otherwise eligible as a bona fide employee of the corporation by performing services other than the usual duties of a director. No individual proprietor or partner shall be eligible for insurance under the policy unless he is actively engaged in and devotes a substantial part of his time to the conduct of the business of the proprietor or partnership. The policy may provide that the term "employees" shall include the trustees or their employees, or both, if their duties are principally connected with such trusteeship.

(c) ~~(b)~~ The premium for the policy shall be paid by the trustees wholly from funds contributed by the employer or employers of the insured persons, or by the union or unions, or by both, or partly from such funds and partly from funds contributed by the insured persons. ~~No policy may be issued on which any part of the premium is to be derived from funds contributed by the insured persons specifically for their insurance.~~ A policy on which part of the premium is to be derived from funds contributed by the insured persons specifically for their insurance may be placed in force only if at least 75% of the then eligible persons, excluding any as to whom evidence of insurability is not satisfactory to the insurer, elect to make the required contributions. A ~~The~~ policy on which no part of the premium is to be derived from funds contributed by the insured persons specifically for their insurance must insure all eligible persons, or all except any as to whom evidence of individual insurability is not satisfactory to the insurer.

(d) ~~(c)~~ The policy must cover at date of issue at least 100 persons; and it must cover an average of not less than five persons per employer unit unless the policy is issued to the trustees of a fund established by employers which have assumed obligations through a collective bargaining agreement and are participating in the fund either pursuant to those obligations with regard to one or more classes of their employees which are encompassed in the collective bargaining agreement or as a method of providing insurance benefits for other classes of their employees, or unless the policy is issued to the trustees of a fund established by one or more labor unions, ~~and not less than an average of five persons per employer unit; and if the fund is established by the members of an association of employers the policy may be issued only if (i) either (a) the participating employers constitute at date of issue at least 60% of those employer members whose employees are not already covered for group life insurance or (b) the total number of persons covered at date of issue exceeds 600; and (ii)~~ The policy shall not require that, if a participating employer discontinues membership in the association, the insurance of his employees shall cease solely by reason of such discontinuance.

(e) ~~(d)~~ The amounts of insurance under the policy must be based upon some plan precluding individual selection either by the insured persons or by the policyholder, employers, or unions.

It should be emphasized that the rewording suggested above is purely illustrative, and should not preclude refinements, or even material changes not at variance with our general recommendations, by the Joint Group and Legislative Committees.

8/26/60

Appendix 22

RESTRICTIONS ON PAYMENTS TO EMPLOYEE REPRESENTATIVES

(The Term "Employee Representative" Includes a Labor Union)

Sec. 302. (a) It shall be unlawful for any employer to pay or deliver or to agree to pay or deliver, any money or other thing of value to any representative of any of his employees who are employed in an industry affecting commerce.

(b) It shall be unlawful for any representative of any employees who are employed in an industry affecting commerce to receive or accept, or to agree to receive or accept, from the employer of such employees any money or other thing of value.

(c) The provisions of this section shall not be applicable. . . .

(5) with respect to money or other thing of value paid to a trust fund established by such representative, for the sole and exclusive benefit of the employees of such employer, and their families and dependents (or of such employees, families, and dependents jointly with the employees of other employers making similar payments, and their families and dependents): PROVIDED, That (A) such payments are held in trust for the purpose of paying, either from principal or income or both, for the benefit of employees, their families and dependents, for medical or hospital care, pensions on retirement or death of employees, compensation for injuries or illness resulting from occupational activity or insurance to provide any of the foregoing, or unemployment benefits or life insurance, disability and sickness insurance, or accident insurance: (B) the detailed basis on which such payments are to be made is specified in a written agreement with the employer, and employees and employers are equally represented in the administration of such fund, together with such neutral persons as the representatives of the employers and the representatives of the employees may agree upon and in the event the employer and employee groups deadlock on the administration of such fund and there are no neutral persons empowered to break such deadlock, such agreement provides that the two groups shall agree on an impartial umpire to decide such dispute, or in event of their failure to agree within a reasonable length of time, an impartial umpire to decide such dispute shall, on petition of either group, be appointed by the district court of the United States for the district where the trust fund has its principal office, and shall also contain provisions for an annual audit of the trust fund, a statement of the results of which shall be available for inspection by interested persons at the principal office of the trust fund and at such other places as may be designated in such written agreement: and (C) such payments as are intended to be used for the purpose of providing pensions or annuities for employees are made to a separate trust which provides that the funds held therein cannot be used for any purpose other than paying such pensions or annuities.

* * * * *

(f) This section shall not apply to any contract in force on the date of enactment of this Act, until the expiration of such contract, or until July 1, 1948, whichever first occurs.

Appendix 23

RECIPROCAL ELIGIBILITY AGREEMENTS

RECIPROCAL AGREEMENT—I

This Agreement is entered into by and between ——————————————————————, herein referred to as "Party A" and ——————————————————————, herein referred to as "Party B."

Witnesseth:

Whereas each of the parties are severally charged with the responsibility under the terms of their respective Trust Indentures, of administering a Health and Welfare Fund for the benefit of eligible employees of participating contractors and eligible members of the unions representing said employees, and,

Whereas it is the responsibility of the parties under their respective Trust Indentures to establish and administer certain rules pertaining to the eligibility of employees as beneficiaries of the Trust, and

Whereas it is recognized by the parties that a hardship to the employees resulting in loss of insurance coverage may exist under certain conditions when:

(a) An employee currently eligible under the rules of the Trust of Party A, is transferred by a contractor normally operating in area A, from a job location in the area of Party A to a job location under the jurisdiction of Party B; or vice versa, or

(b) An employee currently eligible under the rules of the Trust of Party A voluntarily obtains employment in the area of Party B; or vice versa, and

Whereas the Trustees of ———————————————————————— ———————————————————————— and the Trustees of ——————

———————, wish to conclude a reciprocal agreement to relieve such hardship as may result from such conditions,

Now therefore,

It is hereby resolved and agreed by the contracting parties as follows:

1. Any employer normally operating within the jurisdiction of and contributing to Party A who shall transfer men on a temporary basis to a job location coming within the jurisdiction of Party B, which men shall have secured Permit Cards authorizing them to work in the area of Party B, shall continue to contribute to Party A with respect to work performed by such Permittees, but shall contribute to Party B with respect to such men as are locally hired within the jurisdiction of Party B, and likewise

Any employer normally operating within the jurisdiction of and contributing to Party B who shall transfer men on a temporary basis to a job location coming within the jurisdiction of Party A, which men shall have secured Permit Cards authorizing them to work in the area of Party A, shall continue to contribute to Party B with respect to work performed by such Permittees, but shall contribute to Party A with respect to such men as are locally hired within the juridsiction of Party A.

2. Any employee currently eligible under the rules established by Party A who shall seek and receive a Permit Card to work under the jurisdiction of Party B, shall continue as eligible under the Trust of Party A so long as the aggregate total of his credited hours with both Party A and Party B satisfy the eligibility requirements of Party A; but in no event shall he continue as eligible under the Trust of Party A after the date on which he would, except for the above proviso, become eligible under the rule of Party B based upon his credited hours with Party B; and likewise

Any employee currently eligible under the rules established by Party B who shall seek and receive a Permit Card to work under the jurisdiction of Party A, shall continue as eligible under the Trust of Party B so long as the aggregate total of his credited hours with both Party B and Party A satisfy the eligibility requirements of Party B; but in no event shall he continue as eligible under the Trust of Party B after the date on which he would, except for the above proviso, become eligible under the rules of Party A based upon his credited hours with Party A.

In the implementation of the above provisions it shall be the responsibility of the local unions to advise their members of their rights under this agreement and it shall be the responsibility of the individual employee to present with his claim for benefits a statement of credited hours certified by the Administrative Agent of Party A or B as the case may require.

Nothing in the foregoing shall be construed to imply any transfer of monies from Party A to Party B or from Party B to Party A: rather it shall be construed that credits certified by Party A to Party B will, over a period of time, balance with credits certified by Party B to Party A.

RECIPROCAL AGREEMENT—II

This Agreement is entered into by and between _____

_____, herein referred to as "Party A" and _____

_____, herein referred to as "Party B."

Whereas each of the parties are severally charged with the responsibility under the terms of their respective Trust Indentures, of administering a Health and Welfare Fund for the benefit of eligible employees of participating contractors and eligible members of the unions representing said employees, and,

Whereas it is the responsibility of the parties under their respective Trust Indentures to establish and administer certain rules pertaining to the eligibility of employees as beneficiaries of the Trust, and

Whereas it is recognized by the parties that a hardship to the employees resulting in loss of insurance coverage may exist under certain conditions when:

(a) An employee customarily works in two or more classifications of employment, which are covered under separate labor agreements providing for an employer contribution to a health and welfare fund, and

Whereas the Trustees of _____

_____ _____, and the

Trustees of _____

_____, wish to conclude a reciprocal agreement to relieve such hardship as may result from such conditions,

Now therefore,

It is hereby resolved and agreed by the contracting parties as follows:

1. Any employee who customarily works in two employment classifications, the one under the jurisdiction of Party A, and the other under the jurisdiction of Party B, shall have his eligibility computed based upon the aggregate total of his credited hours both with respect to Party A and Party B.
The determination as to which Party shall be liable for payment of benefits shall be as follows:

    (a) If the hours credited with Party A satisfy the eligibility requirements of Party A, Party A shall be liable for any claim for benefits according to the Benefit Plan of Party A.
    (b) If the hours credited with Party B satisfy the eligibility requirements of Party B, Party B shall be liable for any claim for benefits according to the Benefit Plan of Party B.
    (c) If the hours credited with Party A fail to satisfy Party A's requirements and if the hours credited with Party B fail to satisfy Party B's requirements, but the aggregate total of credited hours with both A and B satisfy both A's requirements and B's requirements, then either Party A or Party B (but not both) shall be liable depending upon which party's requirements are most nearly satisfied by the hours reported separately to that Party.

    If the aggregate total of hours reported does not satisfy the eligibility requirements of both Parties, the employee will not be considered eligible by either Party.

    It shall be the responsibility of the Union Locals involved to certify to the Party liable, that the employee is customarily employed in two employment classifications and to furnish statement of credited hours certified by the Administrative Agent of the Party not liable.

Nothing in the foregoing shall be construed to imply any transfer of monies from Party A to Party B or from Party B to Party A; rather it shall be construed that credits certified by Party A to Party B will, over a period of time, balance with credits certified by Party B to Party A.

NOTE: Since it appears there is no practical way to compute premiums due by reason of eligibility established under Paragraph 1 of this Reciprocal Agreement, the Trustees agree to reimburse the insurance company for all claims paid together with the underwriting expenses incurred with respect to this provision.

Appendix 24

**NATIONAL ASSOCIATION OF INSURANCE COMMISSIONERS
REVISED RECOMMENDED BILL OF DECEMBER, 1960**

TO PROVIDE FOR THE REGULATION OF
CREDIT LIFE INSURANCE AND
CREDIT ACCIDENT AND HEALTH INSURANCE

*With Modifications Suggested by American Life Convention,
Health Insurance Association of America and
Life Insurance Association of America as of
February 10, 1961*

BE IT ENACTED

By the state of _____ _____

_____(adapt caption and
formal portions to local requirements and statutes)

1. PURPOSE:

The purpose of this Act is to promote the public welfare by regulating credit life insurance and credit accident and health insurance. Nothing in this Act is intended to prohibit or discourage reasonable competition. The provisions of this Act shall be liberally construed.

2. SCOPE AND DEFINITIONS:

A. CITATION AND SCOPE

(1) This Act may be cited as "The Model Act for the Regulation of Credit Life Insurance and Credit Accident and Health Insurance."

(2) All life insurance and all accident and health insurance in connection with loans or other credit transactions shall be subject to the provisions of this Act, except such insurance in connection with a loan or other credit transaction of more than five years duration; nor shall insurance be subject to the provisions of this Act where the issuance of such insurance is an isolated transaction on the part of the insurer not related to an agreement or a plan for insuring debtors of the creditor.

B. DEFINITIONS

For the purpose of this Act:

(1) "Credit life insurance" means insurance on the life of a debtor pursuant to or in connection with a specific loan or other credit transaction;

(2) "Credit accident and health insurance" means insurance on a debtor to provide indemnity for payments becoming due on a specific loan or other credit transaction while the debtor is disabled as defined in the policy;

(3) "Creditor" means the lender of money or vendor or lessor of goods, services, or property, rights or privileges, for which payment is arranged through a credit transaction, or any successor to the right, title or interest of any such lender, vendor, or lessor, and an affiliate, associate or sub-

928

sidiary of any of them or any director, officer or employee of any of them or any other person in any way associated with any of them;

(4) "Debtor" means a borrower of money or a purchaser or lessee of goods, services, property, rights or privileges for which payment is arranged through a credit transaction;

(5) "Indebtedness" means the total amount payable by a debtor to a creditor in connection with a loan or other credit transaction;

(6) "Commissioner" means . . . (Insurance Supervisory Authority of the State).

3. FORMS OF CREDIT LIFE INSURANCE AND CREDIT ACCIDENT AND HEALTH INSURANCE:

Credit life insurance and credit accident and health insurance shall be issued only in the following forms:

A. Individual policies of life insurance issued to debtors on the term plan;

B. Individual policies of accident and health insurance issued to debtors on a term plan or disability benefit provisions in individual policies of credit life insurance;

C. Group policies of life insurance issued to creditors providing insurance upon the lives of debtors on the term plan;

D. Group policies of accident and health insurance issued to creditors on a term plan insuring debtors or disability benefit provisions in group credit life insurance policies to provide such coverage.

4. AMOUNT OF CREDIT LIFE INSURANCE AND CREDIT ACCIDENT AND HEALTH INSURANCE:

A. Credit Life Insurance

(1) The initial amount of credit life insurance shall not exceed the total amount repayable under the contract of indebtedness and, where an indebtedness is repayable in substantially equal installments, the amount of insurance shall at no time exceed the scheduled or actual amount of unpaid indebtedness, whichever is greater.

[Note: If desired the following provisions may be added as subsections (2) and (3).]

(2) Nothwithstanding the provisions of the above paragraph, insurance on agricultural credit transaction commitments, not exceeding one year in duration may be written up to the amount of the loan commitment, on a non-decreasing or level term plan.

(3) Notwithstanding the provisions of Paragraph A (1) of this or any other subsection, insurance on educational credit transaction commitments may be written for the amount of the portion of such commitment that has not been advanced by the creditor.

B. Credit Accident and Health Insurance

The total amount of periodic indemnity payable by credit accident and health insurance in the event of disability, as defined in the policy, shall not exceed the aggregate of the periodic scheduled unpaid installments of the indebtedness; and the amount of each periodic indemnity payment shall not exceed the original indebtedness divided by the number of periodic installments.

5. TERM OF CREDIT LIFE INSURANCE AND CREDIT ACCIDENT AND HEALTH INSURANCE:

The term of any credit life insurance or credit accident and health insurance shall, subject to acceptance by the insurer, commence on the date when the debtor becomes obligated to the creditor, except that, where a group policy provides coverage with respect to existing obligations, the insurance on a debtor with respect to such indebtedness shall commence on the effective date of the policy.

Where evidence of insurability is required and such evidence is furnished more than thirty (30) days after the date when the debtor becomes obligated to the creditor, the term of the insurance may commence on the date on which the insurance company determines the evidence to be satisfactory, and in such event there shall be an appropriate refund or adjustment of any charge to the debtor for insurance. The term of such insurance shall not extend more than fifteen days beyond the scheduled maturity date of the indebtedness except when extended without additional cost to the debtor. If the indebtedness is discharged due to renewal or refinancing prior to the scheduled maturity date, the insurance in force shall be terminated before any new insurance may be issued in connection with the renewed or refinanced indebtedness. In all cases of termination prior to scheduled maturity, a refund shall be paid or credited as provided in Section 8.

6. PROVISIONS OF POLICIES AND CERTIFICATES OF INSURANCE: DISCLOSURE TO DEBTORS:

   A. All credit life insurance and credit accident and health insurance shall be evidenced by an individual policy, or in the case of group insurance by a certificate of insurance, which individual policy or group certificate of insurance shall be delivered to the debtor.

   B. Each individual policy or group certificate of credit life insurance, and/or credit accident and health insurance shall, in addition to other requirements of law, set forth the name and home office address of the insurer, the name or names of the debtor or in the case of a certificate under a group policy, the identity by name or otherwise of the debtor, the rate or amount of payment, if any, by the debtor separately for credit life insurance and credit accident and health insurance, a description of the amount, term and coverage including any exceptions, limitations and restrictions, and shall state that the benefits shall be paid to the creditor to reduce or extinguish the unpaid indebtedness and, wherever the amount of insurance may exceed the unpaid indebtedness, that any such excess shall be payable to a beneficiary, other than the creditor, named by the debtor or to his estate.

   C. Said individual policy or group certificate of insurance shall be delivered to the insured debtor at the time the indebtedness is incurred except as hereinafter provided.

   D. If said individual policy or group certificate of insurance is not delivered to the debtor at the time the indebtedness is incurred, a copy of the application for such policy or notice of proposed insurance, signed by the debtor and setting forth the name and home office address of the insurer, the name or names of the debtor, the premium or amount of payment by the debtor, if any, separately for credit life insurance and credit accident and health insurance, the amount, term and a brief description of the coverage provided, shall be delivered to the debtor at the time such indebtedness is incurred. The copy of the application for, or notice of proposed insurance, shall also refer exclusively to insurance coverage, and shall be separate and apart from the loan, sale or other credit statement of account, instrument or agreement, unless the information required by this subsection is prominently set forth therein. Upon acceptance of the insurance by the insurer and within thirty (30) days of the date upon which the indebtedness is incurred, the insurer shall cause the individual policy or group certificate of insurance to be delivered to the debtor. Said application or notice of proposed insurance shall state that upon acceptance by the insurer, the insurance shall become effective as provided in Section 5.

   E. If the insurer named in either the application or notice of proposed insurance does not accept the risk, then and in such event the debtor shall receive a policy or certificate of insurance setting forth the name and home office address of the substituted insurer and the amount of the premium to be charged, and if the amount of premium is less than that set forth in the application or notice of proposed insurance an appropriate refund shall be made.

7. FILING, APPROVAL AND WITHDRAWAL OF FORMS:

A. All policies, certificates of insurance, notices of proposed insurance, applications for insurance, endorsements and riders delivered or issued for delivery in this State and the schedules of premium rates pertaining thereto shall be filed with the Commissioner.

B. The Commissioner shall within thirty (30) days after the filing of any such policies, certificates of insurance, notices of proposed insurance, applications for insurance, endorsements and riders, disapprove any such form if the premium rates charged or to be charged are excessive in relation to benefits, or if it contains provisions which are unjust, unfair, inequitable, misleading, deceptive or encourage misrepresentation of the coverage, or are contrary to any provision of the Insurance Code or of any rule or regulation promulgated thereunder.

C. If the Commissioner notifies the insurer that the form is disapproved, it is unlawful thereafter for such insurer to issue or use such form. In such notice, the Commissioner shall specify the reason for his disapproval and state that a hearing will be granted within twenty (20) days after request in writing by the insurer. No such policy, certificate of insurance, notice of proposed insurance, nor any application, endorsement or rider, shall be issued or used until the expiration of thirty (30) days after it has been so filed, unless the Commissioner shall give his prior written approval thereto.

D. The Commissioner may, at any time after a hearing held not less than twenty (20) days after written notice to the insurer, withdraw his approval of any such form on any ground set forth in subsection B above. The written notice of such hearing shall state the reason for the proposed withdrawal.

E. It is not lawful for the insurer to issue such forms or use them after the effective date of such withdrawal.

F. If a group policy of credit life insurance or credit accident and health insurance

    (i) has been delivered in this State before the effective date of this Act, or

    (ii) has been or is delivered in another State before or after the effective date of this Act,

the insurer shall be required to file only the group certificate and notice of proposed insurance delivered or issued for delivery in this State as specified in subsections B and D of Section 6 of this Act and such forms shall be approved by the Commissioner if they conform with the requirements specified in said subsections and if the schedules of premium rates applicable to the insurance evidenced by such certificate or notice are not in excess of the insurer's schedules of premium rates filed with the Commissioner; provided, however, the premium rate in effect on existing group policies may be continued until the first policy anniversary date following the date this Act becomes operative as provided in Section 12.

G. Any order or final determination of the Commissioner under the provisions of this section shall be subject to judicial review.

8. PREMIUMS AND REFUNDS:

A. Any insurer may revise its schedules of premium rates from time to time, and shall file such revised schedules with the Commissioner. No insurer shall issue any credit life insurance policy or credit accident and health insurance policy for which the premium rate exceeds that determined by the schedules of such insurer as then on file with the Commissioner.

B. Each individual policy, or group certificate shall provide that in the event of termination of the insurance prior to the scheduled maturity date of the indebtedness, any refund of an amount paid by the debtor for insurance shall be paid or credited promptly to the person entitled thereto; provided, however, that the Commissioner shall prescribe a minimum refund and no refund which would be less than such minimum need be made. The formula to be used in computing such refund shall be filed with and approved by the Commissioner.

C. If a creditor requires a debtor to make any payment for credit life insurance or credit accident and health insurance and an individual policy or group certificate of insurance is not issued, the creditor shall immediately give written notice to such debtor and shall promptly make an appropriate credit to the account.

D. The amount charged to a debtor for any credit life or credit health and accident insurance shall not exceed the premiums charged by the insurer, as computed at the time the charge to the debtor is determined.

[Note: Where a state prohibits payments for insurance by the debtor in connection with credit transactions, the following paragraph may be included.]

E. Nothing in this Act shall be construed to authorize any payments for insurance now prohibited under any statute, or rule thereunder, governing credit transactions.

9. ISSUANCE OF POLICIES:

All policies of credit life insurance and credit accident and health insurance shall be delivered or issued for delivery in this state only by an insurer authorized to do an insurance business therein, and shall be issued only through holders of licenses or authorizations issued by the Commissioner.

10. CLAIMS:

A. All claims shall be promptly reported to the insurer or its designated claim representative, and the insurer shall maintain adequate claim files. All claims shall be settled as soon as possible and in accordance with the terms of the insurance contract.

B. All claims shall be paid either by draft drawn upon the insurer or by check of the insurer to the order of the claimant to whom payment of the claim is due pursuant to the policy provisions, or upon direction of such claimant to one specified.

C. No plan or arrangement shall be used whereby any person, firm or corporation other than the insurer or its designated claim representative shall be authorized to settle or adjust claims. The creditor shall not be designated as claim representative for the insurer in adjusting claims; provided, that a group policyholder may, by arrangement with the group insurer, draw drafts or checks in payment of claims due to the group policyholder subject to audit and review by the insurer.

11. EXISTING INSURANCE—CHOICE OF INSURER:

When credit life insurance or credit accident and health insurance is required as additional security for any indebtedness, the debtor shall, upon request to the creditor, have the option of furnishing the required amount of insurance through existing policies of insurance owned or controlled by him or of procuring and furnishing the required coverage through any insurer authorized to transact an insurance business within this state.

12. ENFORCEMENT:

The Commissioner may, after notice and hearing, issue such rules and regulations as he deems appropriate for the supervision of this Act. Whenever the

Commissioner finds that there has been a violation of this Act or any rules or regulations issued pursuant thereto, and after written notice thereof and hearing given to the insurer or other person authorized or licensed by the Commissioner, he shall set forth the details of his findings together with an order for compliance by a specified date. Such order shall be binding on the insurer and other person authorized or licensed by the Commissioner on the date specified unless sooner withdrawn by the Commissioner or a stay thereof has been ordered by a court of competent jurisdiction. The provisions of Sections 5, 6, 7 and 8 of this Act shall not be operative until ninety (90) days after the effective date of this Act, and the Commissioner in his discretion may extend by not more than an additional ninety (90) days the initial period within which the provisions of said sections shall not be operative.

13. JUDICIAL REVIEW:

Any party to the proceeding affected by an order of the Commissioner shall be entitled to judicial review by following the procedure set forth in _____ _____ .

14. PENALTIES:

In addition to any other penalty provided by law, any person, firm or corporation which violates an order of the Commissioner after it has become final, and while such order is in effect, shall, upon proof thereof to the satisfaction of the court, forfeit and pay to the state of _____ a sum not to exceed $250.00 which may be recovered in a civil action, except that if such violation is found to be willful, the amount of such penalty shall be a sum not to exceed $1,000.00. The Commissioner, in his discretion may revoke or suspend the license or certificate of authority of the person, firm or corporation guilty of such violation. Such order for suspension or revocation shall be upon notice and hearing, and shall be subject to judicial review as provided in Section 13 of this Act.

15. SEPARABILITY PROVISION:

If any provision of this Act, or the application of such provision to any person or circumstances, shall be held invalid, the remainder of the Act, and the application of such provision to any person or circumstances other than those as to which it is held invalid, shall not be affected thereby.

Appendix 25

STATES WHICH HAVE CREDITOR INSURANCE CONTROLS

State	Control Instrument*	Rate Regulation†
Alabama	3	1
Alaska	1	
Arizona	2	1
Arkansas	2	
California	2	3
Connecticut	2	3
District of Columbia	1	
Florida	2	
Georgia	1	
Idaho	1	
Illinois	2	3
Indiana	2	3
Iowa	3	
Kansas	3	
Kentucky	3	
Maine	2	3
Michigan	2	3
Montana	1	
Nebraska	2	3
Nevada	2	3
New Hampshire	2	3
New Jersey	2	2
New Mexico	2	3
New York	3	2
Ohio	2	2
Oregon	2	1
Pennsylvania	2	2
Rhode Island	2	2
South Carolina	3	
South Dakota	1	
Tennessee	3	
Texas	2	3
Utah	1	
Vermont	2	
Virginia	2	
Washington	1	
West Virginia	3	
Wisconsin	3	
Wyoming	1	

*Legend 1 = Law Only
2 = Law and Regulation
3 = Regulation Only

†Legend 1 = Loss Ratio Only
2 = Rates Only
3 = Loss Ratio and Rates

Appendix 26

HEALTH INSURANCE ASSOCIATION OF AMERICA DEFINITION, FRANCHISE ACCIDENT AND SICKNESS INSURANCE, APRIL 3, 1957

Accident and sickness insurance on a franchise plan is hereby declared to be that form of accident and sickness insurance issued to:

(1) Five or more employees of any corporation, co-partnership, or individual employer or any governmental corporation, agency or department thereof; or

(2) Ten or more members, employees, or employees of members of any trade or professional association or of a labor union or of any other association having had an active existence for at least two years where such association or union has a constitution or by-laws and is formed in good faith for purposes other than that of obtaining insurance;

where such persons, with or without their dependents, are issued the same form of an individual policy varying only as to amounts and kinds of coverage applied for by such persons under an arrangement whereby the premiums on such policies may be paid to the insurer periodically by the employer, with or without payroll deductions, or by the association or union for its members, or by some designated person acting on behalf of such employer or association or union. The term "employees" as used herein shall be deemed to include the officers, managers and employees and retired employees of the employer and the individual proprietor or partners if the employer is an individual proprietor or partnership.

Appendix 27

LEGAL STATUS OF FRANCHISE HEALTH INSURANCE
MARCH, 1965

Jurisdiction	Source-Law or Regulation	Minimum Participation Requirements with Respect to Employees of a Common Employer or Members of an Association or Labor Union	
		Employer-Employee Franchise	Association or Union Membership Franchise
Alabama	Law sil nt		
Alaska	Law silent		
Arizona	Law: Sec. 20–1375	5	10
Arkansas	Law: Sec. 418	5	10
California	"Selected Group" Law: Sec. 10270.97	5	10
Colorado	Law silent. Franchise insurance prohibited by interpretive ruling.		
Connecticut	Law silent		
Delaware	Law silent		
District of Columbia	Law silent		
Florida	Law: Chapter 22, Sec. 594	5	10
Georgia	Law: Sec. 56–3018	4	10
Hawaii	Law: Sec. 8467.39	5	10
Idaho	Law: Chapter 21, Sec. 526	4	10
Illinois	Insurance Department Bulletin XB–563 of 3–20–52, Part 1, Paragraph 22		
Indiana	Law: Title 59, Sec. 4261	5	10
Iowa	Law: Sec. 509.14, Sec. 509.3		50% of insurable members, but in no case less than 10.
Kansas	Insurance Dept. Reg. 48–12–14 of 1–1–63	5	10
Kentucky	Law: Sec. 304.746	5	10
Louisiana	Law: Part VI R.S. 22:125. (4)	5	10
Maine	Law: Chapter 60, Sec. 123	5	10
Maryland	Law: Art. 48A, Sec. 469	3	10
Massachusetts	Law silent		
Michigan	Insurance Dept. Ruling of 7–29–46	5	10
Minnesota	Law silent		
Mississippi	Law silent		
Missouri	Law silent		
Montana	Law: Chapter 286, Sec. 383	5	10
Nebraska	Law: Chapter 44, Article 7, Sec. 44–759	5	10
Nevada	Law silent		
New Hampshire	Law: 415:19 Sec. 15, pp. 149–150	5	10
New Jersey	Law silent		
New Mexico	Law silent		
New York	Ins. Dept. Circular Letter I (1965)		
North Carolina	Law: Sec. 58–254.6	5	10
North Dakota	Law silent		
Ohio	Law: Sec. 3923.11	5	10
Oklahoma	Law: Article 44, Sec. 4410	5	10
Oregon	Law silent		
Pennsylvania	Law: Title 40, Sec. 756.4	5	10
Puerto Rico	Law: Chapter 6, Sec. 16.340	5	10
Rhode Island	Law silent		
South Carolina	Law: Sec. 37–551	5	10
South Dakota	Law silent		
Tennessee	Law silent		
Texas	Law silent		
Utah	Law silent		

Vermont..............Law: Title 8, Chapter 107, Sec. 4078	5	10
Virginia..............Law silent		
Washington..........Law: Sec. 48.20.350	5	10
West Virginia.........Law: Article 15, Sec. 3472 (133) 10	5	5
Wisconsin............Law: Sec. 204.32 (1)	3	3
Wyoming.............Law silent		

Appendix 28

NEW YORK INSURANCE DEPARTMENT FRANCHISE INSURANCE STANDARDS

Franchise Accident and Health Insurance*

The expression "franchise accident, health or accident and health insurance" as used herein shall mean that form of accident and health insurance provided, with or without evidence of insurability, by (1) individual policies which are made available to persons under a plan sponsored by: (a) an employer, or (b) an association consisting of persons having the same or similar occupation or profession, or (c) a union, or (d) two or more employers under common control, or (e) an association of civil service employees, or (2) individual policies which are made available to individuals supplying or delivering materials to a central point of collection; and under which the insured's right to renew his policy, with or without other permissible renewal conditions, is contingent upon the continuing of such employment, membership, or supplier participation. Premium collection by payroll deduction shall not, in and of itself, cause a policy to be classified as franchise accident and health insurance. A plan may be administered by an agent or trustee.

No franchise accident, health or accident and health insurance policy shall be approved for delivery or for issuance for delivery in this State unless it conforms to the requirements listed below.

A. Employer-Employee Franchise

1. PERMISSIBLE CASES

Whether contributory or non-contributory, the following eligibility criteria shall be applicable at the effective date of the case. The insurer may require evidence of insurability.

    a. *Employees of an employer.* The class or classes of persons to be insured shall consist of:

        (1) Not less than two nor more than twenty-five employees of an employer except that in contributory cases 75% of the number of eligible employees may not exceed twenty-five. The term "employees" may include (a) directors and officers, if the employer is a corporation, (b) an individual proprietor or partners, if the employer is an individual proprietor or a partnership, and (c) retired employees.

        (2) Two or more employees of a governmental corporation, unit, department or agency, including elected or appointed officials.

        (3) Two or more employees of a "non-profit" college, university or other institution engaged primarily in education or research.

        (4) Groups of twenty-five or more employees where it has been demonstrated to the satisfaction of the Superintendent that the franchise insurance coverage actually supplements and does not substitute for group coverage (including self-insured coverage).

    b. *Participation Requirements.* All of the employees or all of any class or classes thereof determined by conditions pertaining to employment or such

---

*Effective January 27, 1965.

conditions, together with age or family status, or both, or except those employees as to whom the evidence of insurability submitted is not satisfactory to the insurer. If part or all of the premium is contributed by the insured employee pursuant to payroll deduction, such insurance may be provided if not less than seventy-five per cent of all eligible employees or not less than seventy-five per cent of all eligible employees in any class or classes are insured.

2. POLICY PROVISIONS

a. The right to terminate or non-renew is limited to the following reasons:
   (1) Non-payment of premium.
   (2) The insured has attained the age limit prescribed in the policy.
   (3) The employee's employment in the eligible classes terminates.
   (4) The insurer terminates or non-renews the insurance on all employees of the employer after sixty days written notice.
   (5) If the plan is terminated by the employer and the insurer terminates or non-renews all policies issued to all insured employees of the employer.
   (6) Participation falls below the minimum stated in the policy and the insurer terminates or non-renews all policies issued to all insured employees of the employer of the same class or classes.
   (7) Such other reasons as the Superintendent may approve.
b. The insurer's right to terminate or non-renew any policy of insurance subject to Section 164(6) of the Insurance Law, when terminated pursuant to either (4), (5) or (6) of paragraph a. hereof, shall be as prescribed in and limited by Section 164(6), including the requirement that the right to terminate shall be subject to the approval of the Superintendent of Insurance when reasons for non-renewal other than those specified therein are involved.
c. A policy of hospitalization or surgical or medical expense insurance or any other policy in which one-third or more of the total premium is allocable to hospital, surgical or medical expense benefits, or any combination thereof, must also contain a conversion privilege at least equal to that required under Section 162(5) of the Insurance Law should coverage be terminated pursuant to either (2) or (3) of paragraph a. hereof.
d. Where the insurer reserves the right to change the premium rate, a statement to that effect shall be made on page one of the policy, either as part of the brief description or elsewhere.
e. Where step-rate premiums are charged, the policy shall include a schedule of premiums.
f. The policy shall specify the ages, if any there be, to which the insurance provided shall be limited.

3. PREMIUMS

The premium rates shall be self-supporting and shall be on a basis reasonably related to the mortality and morbidity assumptions used by the insurer for group accident and health insurance, unless some other basis is demonstrated to the satisfaction of the Superintendent of Insurance to be appropriate.

4. NOTICE OF CONVERSION

Whenever a conversion privilege is available, the insured individual shall be given written notice of the right to convert not more than fifteen days after termination of insurance. If such notice is given more than fifteen days but less than ninety days after termination of insurance, the time allowed for the exercise of the privilege of conversion shall be extended for fifteen days after the giving of such notice. If such notice be not given within ninety days after the termination of insurance, the time allowed for the exercise of such conversion privilege shall expire at the end of such ninety days. Written notice given to the insured individual by the employer or written notice mailed either by such employer or the insurer, to the insured individual at his last known address shall be deemed full compliance with the above.

B. *Association Franchise*

1. PERMISSIBLE CASES

The following eligibility criteria shall be applicable on the effective date of the case. The insurer may require evidence of insurability:

a. The class or classes of persons to be insured shall consist of:
   (1) Twenty-five or more members of an incorporated or unincorporated association having a constitution or by-laws where such association (a) was formed and is maintained in good faith for purposes other than that of obtaining insurance for its members, (b) has been in active existence for at least two years prior to the inception of the insurance of its members, and (c) consists of persons, having the same or similar occupation or profession.
   (2) Not less than four nor more than twenty-five members of a labor union.
   (3) An association of civil service employees.
   (4) Groups of individuals, such as dairy farmers, who supply or deliver materials, e.g., milk, to a central point of collection.
b. *Participation Requirements.*
   (1) Eligible members shall be informed in writing of the sponsorship of the plan by the sponsoring organization or by its representative, agent, or trustee.
   (2) Not less than (a) five hundred members of an association of civil service employees, or (b) thirty per cent of the first five hundred eligible members thereof plus ten per cent of all eligible members in excess of five hundred, whichever is the lesser, unless the insurer individually underwrites all applicants on the basis of either medical examination or a questionnaire concerning the applicant's present health and medical history. However, in no event shall the number of persons insured be less than twenty-five.
   (3) Not less than 30% of the first 500 eligible suppliers plus 10% of the next 3500 eligible suppliers, unless the insurer individually underwrites all applicants on the basis of either medical examination or a questionnaire concerning the applicant's present health and medical history. However, in no event shall the number of persons insured be less than twenty-five.

2. POLICY PROVISIONS

a. The right to terminate or non-renew is limited to the following reasons:
   (1) Non-payment of premium.
   (2) The insured has attained the age limit prescribed in the policy.
   (3) (a) The insured retires, or (b) ceases to be (i) engaged in a profession or occupation with respect to which the franchise policies were issued, or (ii) a member of the association or union, or (iii) a supplier.
   (4) The insurer terminates or non-renews the insurance on all members of

the union or association or all suppliers after sixty days written notice.

(5) If the plan is terminated by the sponsor, and the insurer terminates or non-renews all policies issued to all insured members of the association, union or all suppliers.

(6) Participation falls below the minimum stated in the policy, and the insurer terminates or non-renews all policies issued to all insured members of the association or union or all suppliers.

(7) Such other reasons as the Superintendent may approve.

b. The insurer's right to terminate or non-renew any policy of insurance subject to Section 164(6) of the Insurance Law, when terminated pursuant to either (4), (5) or (6) of paragraph a. hereof, shall be as prescribed in and limited by Section 164(6), including the requirement that the right to terminate shall be subject to the approval of the Superintendent of Insurance when reasons for non-renewal other than those specified therein are involved.

c. A policy of hospitalization or surgical or medical expense insurance or any other policy in which one-third or more of the total premium is allocable to hospital, surgical or medical expense benefits, or any combination thereof, must also contain a conversion privilege at least equal to that required under Section 162(5) of the Insurance Law, should coverage be terminated pursuant to either (2) or (3)(b)(ii) or (iii) of paragraph a. thereof.

d. Where the insurer reserves the right to change the premium rate, a statement to that effect shall be made on page one of the policy, either as part of the brief description, or elsewhere.

e. Where step-rate premiums are charged, the policy shall include a schedule of premiums.

f. The policy may specify the ages, if any there be, to which the insurance provided shall be limited.

3. PREMIUMS

a. The premium rates shall be self-supporting and shall be on a basis reasonably related to the mortality and morbidity assumptions used by the insurer for individual accident and health insurance, unless some other basis is demonstrated to the satisfaction of the Superintendent of Insurance to be appropriate. Such premium rates may differ from the premium rates otherwise charged for the same or comparable individual accident and health policies, on showing to the satisfaction of the Superintendent that such differences result from demonstrable savings in expenses not only in commission or service fees paid to agents, but also savings in underwriting and issue costs and/or administrative expenses. If the insurer does not have the same or comparable plan, premiums at least equal to those used by the insurer for group accident and health insurance shall be deemed to be self-supporting if it can be shown to the satisfaction of the Superintendent that (1) commissions or service fees paid to agents, (2) underwriting or issue costs, (3) administrative costs and (4) mortality or morbidity will not exceed those for such group insurance.

b. The premium shall be paid either solely by the association or union, or its members or jointly by the members and the association or union. In the case of suppliers, the premiums are to be deducted by the central point of collection from the payments for the materials supplied or delivered.

4. NOTICE OF CONVERSION

Whenever a conversion privilege is available, the insured individual shall be given written notice of the right to convert not more than fifteen days after termination of insurance. If such notice is given more than fifteen days after termination of insurance, the time allowed for the exercise of the privilege of conversion shall be extended for fifteen days after the giving of such notice. If such notice be not given, the time allowed for the exercise of such conversion privilege shall expire at the end of one year from the date of termination. Written notice given to the insured individual by the sponsor of the plan, or written notice mailed, either by such sponsor or the insurer, to the insured individual at his last known address shall be deemed full compliance with the above. If application for the conversion policy is made to the insurer more than thirty-one days after termination, the effective date of the conversion policy will be the date the application is received by the insurer.

C. *General*

The following is applicable to both Employer-Employee and Association Franchise insurance:

1. The premium rates shall not unfairly discriminate between franchise cases of the same class. Rates may recognize age, sex, occupation, location, industry, marital status, family composition and other factors affecting utilization.

2. Where an insurer reserves the right to change the premium the filing of the premium rates shall include a commitment by it that:

   a. In the event the scale of premiums should be changed at some future date, the new rates, before becoming effective, will first be submitted to the Superintendent of Insurance with supporting data, and their acceptance obtained.

   b. Adequate records of experience will be maintained and any filing of a change in rates will be accompanied by the experience data and other pertinent information to support it.

3. In lieu of termination of insurance pursuant to either A.2.a.(6) or B.2.a.(6), provision may be made in the policy or by issuance of a rider to the policy for direct premium notice billing on an individual basis. The policy or rider shall set forth the additional premium, if any, required for such direct premium notice billing, which additional premium shall be reasonably related to the increase in the cost of collection and administration of the policy.

4. The insurer shall submit a statement as to its rule, if any, with respect to the minimum participation requirement for insuring all applicants without a statement of good health.

5. The insurer's underwriting rules with respect to franchise accident and health insurance shall be filed in duplicate with the Superintendent. Such rules shall not be open for public inspection.

6. No franchise accident and health insurance policy shall be approved for delivery or for issuance for delivery in this state unless it conforms in substance to the provisions of Section 164, or contains provisions which in the opinion of the Superintendent are more favorable to policyholders. Franchise accident and health insurance policies must be filed with the Department pursuant to Section 154.

7. The amount of benefits provided shall be based upon a plan which will preclude selection of disproportionate amounts of insurance by certain individuals.*

---

*See Insurance Department Circular Letter of July 19, 1962, for standards required to preclude individual selection.

Indexes

INDEX OF NAMES

INDEX OF SUBJECTS

A

Accidental death and dismemberment coverage; *see* Group accidental death and dismemberment insurance

Accidental means, 153–54

Actively-at-work requirement, 171–72, 589–90

Administration, Appendixes 13, 14, 15
association group insurance, 605, 611
billings, 548–50, 553
commission payments, 553–54
creditor group life insurance, 126
duties of group policyholder, 487–88
Federal Employees Group Life Insurance, 161–64
group paid-up plans, 148–49
need for simplicity and efficiency, 42
policy records, 554
statistical analyses, 555
Taft-Hartley welfare funds, 625–26
trends in insurance company practices, 522

Administrators, 517, 772–73

Aetna Life Insurance Co., 59

Aged
alternatives to group term life insurance, 132–34
Federal Employees Group Life Insurance, 161
group accidental death and dismemberment coverage, 155
group medical expense coverage
associations of retired persons, 702–3
continuation in group, 690–98
cost of, 694–96
mass enrollment, 704–6
retired employees, 703–4
group term life insurance, 121–22, 128–32, 176
medical expense coverage
approaches to, 701–2
nature of, 682
number covered, 78–79
proportion covered, 686
types of coverage, 78–79
number of, 682–83
proportion of, 682–83

Aged—*Cont.*
risk characteristics of, 424–25, 683–85, 700–701

Agent of record, 527; *see also* Commissions

Alcoholism exclusion, 334

All-lines groups of companies
definition, 230
writing group health insurance, 230

American Dental Association, 719

American Hospital Association, 60, 82, 249, 252, 310, 420
claims forms approval, 563
recommended hospital reimbursement procedures, 574
relations with Blue Cross Association, 263

American Life Convention, 95–96, 99, 571–73, 593–96, Appendix 21

American Medical Association, 60, 82, 310, 324, 439, 443
attitude toward group practice prepayment plans, 274–77
claims form approval, 563

Assignment, 117, 138–39, 493

Associations
franchise health insurance
administration, 663
installation, 662–63
renewability, 662
types of benefits, 661
underwriting, 662
group insurance
administration, 168–69, 605, 611
controversial aspects, 609–10
"fictitious" groups, 612–14
health insurance coverage, 79–81
member-pay-all groups, 607–8, 611–12
miscellaneous associations, 612–14
"Olympic Association," 613
professional associations, 609–12
public employee groups, 607–9
regulation, 614–17
trade associations, 603–6
underwriting, 605–7
union groups, 480, 606–7
retired persons, 702–3

This book has been set in 10 point Caledonia, leaded 2 points, and 9 point Caledonia, leaded 1 point. Part numbers are in 18 point Perpetua caps; part titles in 24 point Perpetua italics. Chapter numbers are in 18 point Perpetua italics; chapter titles in 18 point Perpetua caps. The size of the type page is 27 x 46 picas.